THE OKLAHOMA FOOTBALL ENCYCLOPEDIA

Ray Dozier

SP
SPORTS
PUBLISHING
L.L.C.

SportsPublishingLLC.com

ISBN-10: 1-58261-699-x
ISBN-13: 978-1-58261-669-5

Publishers: Peter L. Bannon and Joseph J. Bannon Sr.
Senior managing editor: Susan M. Moyer
Acquisitions editors: Mike Pearson and Joseph J. Bannon Jr.
Developmental editor: Erin Linden-Levy
Art director: K. Jeffrey Higgerson
Dust jacket design: Joseph Brumleve
Interior design and layout: Kathryn R. Holleman

Sports Publishing L.L.C.
804 North Neil Street
Champaign, IL 61820
Phone: 1-877-424-2665
Fax: 217-363-2073
SportsPublishingLLC.com

Printed in the United States of America

Library of Congress Cataloging-in-Publication Data

Dozier, Ray, 1955-
The Oklahoma football encyclopedia / Ray Dozier.
    p. cm.
  ISBN-13: 978-1-58261-699-5 (hard cover : alk. paper)
  ISBN-10: 1-58261-699-X (hard cover : alk. paper)
  1. Oklahoma Sooners (Football team)--History. 2. University of Oklahoma--Football--History. I. Title.
GV958.O4.D69 2006
796.332'630976638--dc22
                                        2006024104

This book is dedicated to my dad, who introduced me to Sooner football, and my mom, who was a great inspiration.

CONTENTS

INTRODUCTION

When my dad took me to my first Oklahoma football game, I was immediately captivated even at the age of five. Since then I have attended many Sooner games from Bud Wilkinson to Bob Stoops.

Sooner football fanaticism has run deep in my family's blood. My grandfather, Russell "Gluck" Dozier, started it in 1918 and he was a member of the Jazz Hounds.

The Oklahoma Football Encyclopedia takes you through a journey of the illustrious history of Oklahoma football from 1895 through 2005. You will read how the program emerged onto the national stage of college football—seven national championships, 39 conference championships, 24 bowl wins and 141 All-Americans. Although OU has had 19 head coaches, I emphasized only four, which I call the Four Bs—Bennie Owen, Bud Wilkinson, Barry Switzer and Bob Stoops.

Bud Wilkinson was a great teacher of the Split-T formation, who guided the Sooners to three national championships, 72 consecutive conference games without a loss and a 47-game winning streak, a major collegiate record that may never be broken. Barry Switzer was the mastermind behind the Wishbone-T. He was a master motivator and teacher who continued to feed the monster Wilkinson had created by adding three more national titles. After several downtrodden seasons, Stoops returned the program to national prominence with his teachings and a no-nonsense approach.

Wilkinson, Switzer, and Stoops are the only head coaches in Sooner history to direct the Sooners to college football's elite prize. But Bennie Owen had a vision that laid the foundation for his successors. He created the forward pass long before Knute Rockne, who received credit for it. Owen coached for 22 years, longer than any coach in Sooner history. He won 122 games and supervised the construction of a new stadium.

Many of the games in this book are defined as "Sooner Magic." The phrase, used to describe late-game heroics, did not enter into the vocabulary of OU fans until the 1980s, but Sooner Magic began in 1905 when the University of Oklahoma defeated the Haskell Indians. Was the magic sleight of hand? Smoke and mirrors? No, just pure talent and inspiration that helped push the Sooners to the overwhelming tradition the teams have displayed on the gridiron.

Sooner Magic is the incredible comebacks by the offense or the power of the defense to hold off the opponent from ripping the victory from the Sooners.

Recently, the NCAA added records from bowl games into season and career marks. The records you read about were what was reported at the time.

You will also read about the prominent play-by-play announcers and brief stories about a handful of fans, because without them, OU football would not be a successful program.

This book took numerous hours of research and interviews, and could not have been completed without the help of family and friends: Margaret Dozier (my mother), Bill Dozier (my father), Bill Dozier III (my brother), R.C. Cunningham (my uncle, who rescued me with a better computer and printing facilities), Ben Brewster, Lee Allan Smith, G.T. Blankenship, Jakie Sandefer, and Jack Clift. Richard Davis, Nathaniel McVay, Belinda Chambers and Raymond Glidewell were saviors when I needed my computer tweaked. It seems you can't write a book these days without a computer.

I express grateful appreciation to Erin Linden-Levy and Mike Pearson at Sports Publishing, Kenny Mossman, athletic director for media relations at the University of Oklahoma and Debra Bishop, administrative assistant of media relations at OU.

Thanks also to Margolyn Woods, my mentor who gave me terrific guidance on how to go about seeking publishers and how to get my work published. And of course, thank you to all who allowed me to interview them for this project.

I hope you will enjoy *The Oklahoma Football Encyclopedia* as much as I enjoyed writing it. It gave me such great pleasure to relive many of the great Sooner moments. Whether you are a Sooner fan or not, I know you will receive tremendous satisfaction in reading the history of OU football.

Boomer Sooner!

Sources of Reference: *The Daily Oklahoman, Norman Transcript, Tulsa World, Dallas Morning News, Oklahoma Kickoff* by Harold Keith, *Forty-Seven Straight: The Wilkinson Era at Oklahoma* by Harold Keith, *President's Can't Punt* by Dr. George Lynn Cross, *Bud Wilkinson: An Intimate Portrait of An American Legend* by Jay Wilkinson.

FOREWORDS

Being a part of a great football tradition at the University of Oklahoma was a great thrill for me. Bennie Owen laid the foundation, Bud Wilkinson created the "monster," and I continued to feed it, but I could not have accomplished it without the help of a tremendous staff and players. What we accomplished has helped Bob Stoops continue the great tradition today.

The rich legacy of OU's winning football program has spanned more than a century with seven national championships, 39 conference championships, 24 bowl victories, 141 All-Americans, and dozens of major award winners.

To me, winning three national championships, 12 Big Eight Conference championships, and 157 games was only a small part of why I enjoyed coaching at OU. The relationships with my players and staff were what made my 16-year tenure a pleasure as the Sooners' head football coach. And, of course, all of this success could not have been accomplished without the support of you, the fans.

Nothing is more valuable than helping build a future for so many of my players and the friendships that continued with them years after we conquered the college football world. That more than anything is what coaching is all about.

Ray Dozier has written a comprehensive history of the Sooners football program. This book will allow you to relive the rich heritage of this great football program from John Harts to Bob Stoops. Many of the stories include some great come-from-behind victories in the fourth quarter. Some call this Sooner Magic. It may have seemed like magic, but to me it was good Oklahoma players making great plays.

I hope you enjoy *The Oklahoma Football Encyclopedia*, an outstanding description of one of the greatest college football programs in the United States.

—Barry Switzer
Head Football Coach
1973-88

I have been very fortunate to announce Oklahoma football games for 27 years. It is a great thrill for me to be a part of the great Sooner tradition.

The Oklahoma Football Encyclopedia is a complete journey of one of the most illustrious and colorful college football programs in the nation. Ray Dozier has written one of the most comprehensive books about the Sooner football program with more information than any book that has been written about OU's football history.

The idea for the football team was born in a barbershop on Main Street in Norman. Bennie Owen, OU's sixth head coach, was an innovator who laid the groundwork for the football program and the construction of a new stadium, the site of where the Sooners still play today.

The program did not begin to thrive on the national scene until Bud Wilkinson took over the program in 1947. During the next 17 years, he produced a monster of a program with 129 victories, three national championships, 14 conference titles and a 47-game winning streak that may never be matched by any major college football program.

I was fortunate that Bud selected me over 13 other contestants to be OU's play-by-play announcer in 1961. I continued calling Sooner football and basketball games through the 1972 season. Due to contractual obligations, I announced games for the Sooners' rival, Oklahoma State, from 1973-1990. During that time, Barry Switzer continued to produce winning teams year after year for the Sooners and matched Coach Wilkinson with three national championships.

I returned behind the mike for OU games in 1991. From 1991 to 1998, Oklahoma struggled through a 46-43-3 record. Although the Sooners did not win championships, they still were a prominent figure on the national scene.

When Bob Stoops arrived in 1999, it did not take him long to return the football program to the summit. He won a national championship in his second year as head coach. Stoops exemplifies the same characteristics of discipline and determination to continue a winning program.

Each of those four coaches is featured in a chapter titled "The Four Bs."

The Oklahoma Football Encyclopedia is a must read for every Sooner fan. I know you will enjoy it. I am proud to have called the radio play-by-play for many Sooner teams; many of which established OU's proud heritage.

—Bob Barry
Announcer
1961-72, 1991-01

1895 - 1909

1895

After the dust had settled, stirred by horses hooves and wagon wheels racing westward across the territorial prairie on April 22, 1889, an estimated 11,000 agricultural homesteads were claimed. Tent cities sprung up across the barren land at Oklahoma City, Kingfisher, El Reno, Guthrie, Stillwater, and Norman.

The Oklahoma Land Run began at noon by the firing of a rifle or boom of a cannon. The 50,000 claimants of unassigned lands had established their property—160 acres each. Some had staked claim to their land before the land rush began. They were known as the "Sooners." Those who raced across the prairie at noon were known as "Boomers."

Nineteen years before that great land rush, the United States Land Office contracted with professional engineers to survey much of Oklahoma Territory. Abner Ernest Norman, a young engineer from Kentucky, was hired and later promoted as supervisor of a surveying unit to survey the land, which included present-day Cleveland County.

Norman's crew camped near a spring three-eighths of a mile south of what is now Classen Boulevard and East Lindsey. The party removed a large part of a huge elm tree and burned the words "Norman's Camp" into the tree.

The city got its name 16 years later when a railroad car was placed beside the tracks with the words "Norman Switch" painted on the side.

In addition to tents, log cabins and sod houses were constructed. Lumber was soon brought in by rail and sold to settlers.

While several towns contended to be the capital, Norman's mayor, T.R. Wagoner, directed a bill through the Territorial Legislature to become home of the state's first institution of higher learning. Twenty months after the land rush and settling of Norman, the town was selected as the location for the University of Oklahoma. The university was chartered on December 19, 1890, five months before Norman was incorporated on May 13, 1891.

The university officially opened in 1893 with an enrollment of 119 students, 82 of them were children of Norman residents. Its lone building was a two-story red brick structure, which stood about a half-mile southwest of town. This was the university's Administration Building.

Two years later down at Bud Risinger's barber shop on the north side of Main Street near the Santa Fe railroad tracks, several men discussed forming a football team. One of them was John A. Harts, who, at 20 years old, attended OU to teach a class in elocution. Harts had played football at Winfield College and at Harvard University.

Edwin Debarr, OU's first faculty member and professor of chemistry and physics, and several male students had pooled resources and purchased a football. Debarr, a former player at Michigan University, and the students formed two teams. It was not until Harts arrived that a formal team began to organize.

Harts, in barber shop conversation, spoke of forming a regular football team. "Let's get up a football team!" he said. The idea was popular, and he was selected as coach and captain. Harts recruited his friends to form the team. The first Oklahoma football team included Fred Bean, Jasper "Jap" Clapham, Bert Dunn, John P. Evans, Bert Long, Newt Medlock, Joe Merkle, Bernard Reuter, Will Short, and Horace Sommers.

Although some had seen a football, they weren't familiar with the game. The team laid out its gridiron northwest of present-day Holmberg Hall. They hauled in dirt to fill in the buffalo wallows. The players made their own uniforms—overalls cut off at the knees and padded in front. They nailed cleats on their shoes for traction. Most grew their hair long to protect their heads.

Meanwhile, a committee consisting of May Overstreet (the university's only female faculty member), Ray Hume, and Ruth House were given the task of choosing the team colors. They chose crimson and cream. Pieces of crimson material were sewn onto the players' jacket lapels.

On November 7, 1895, the team played its first and only football game that year against a team from Oklahoma City, which consisted of high school boys and some Methodist College students. Harts suffered a knee injury before the game, but he recruited Bud Risinger and Fred Perry the night before the game to round out the team of 11 players. Perry was a driver of the Norman street-sprinkling wagon. He had played some football at the University of Kansas six years earlier. Neither he nor Risinger were students at the university, but there were no eligibility rules back then.

Early-day American college football required only five yards in three downs to gain a first down and maintain possession of the ball. Captains, not quarterbacks, called the signals. Games were played in two halves, not four quarters. Touchdowns were worth four points, and games began with the firing of a pistol. The forward pass had not yet been created, so running was aplenty.

The ball was round, not oblong, made from a pig's bladder. Stadiums were years away, so spectators sat in horse-drawn buggies or stood around the gridiron's perimeter.

Since the quarterback was small, he and the center never ran with the ball. The quarterback would take the snap from center and feed it to the bigger backs, who mostly lunged into the line. When a ball carrier lunged into the middle of the line of scrimmage, which was taken from the game of rugby, it was legal then for teammates to push him from behind or pull him forward. Runs around the ends were rare.

The Oklahoma University team scored no points nor made a first down in the game. The longest play was Dunn's 50-yard return of the opening kickoff. As the game winded down, many university players were tired and dropped out. The Oklahoma City team loaned some of its players as substitutes.

The game was so rugged that even an experienced farm hand like Clapham went home to his farm and climbed into bed, too tired to do his chores.

The university lost 34-0 that day, but more important it was the birth of Oklahoma University football.

1895 Season Record: 0-1-0			
Date	**Opponent**	**Result**	**Score**
October 7	Oklahoma City	L	34-0

1896-1900

Shortly after the first game, John Harts left the university to prospect for gold in the Arctic. The following year, the university had no designated football coach. The team played two games against Norman High School, winning both—12-0 and 16-4.

Dr. David Ross Boyd, the university's first president, was searching for someone to head the English department. Boyd was discussing his desire to find an outstanding leader for the university's English department with Grace King, who at 16 years old was head of the university's music department. She suggested Vernon L. Parrington, whom she had known when she lived in Emporia, Kansas. The two traveled to Emporia to visit Parrington, who was hired almost immediately.

Harold Keith, in his book *Oklahoma Kickoff*, described Parrington as a "well-groomed, gentile young bachelor, a trifle eccentric but very likeable. He wore well-pressed tweeds with a cap to match, and his fingers were always stained from incessant rolling and smoking of brown-papered cigarettes." Keith also described Parrington as "square-jawed with a wide, prominent mouth, and dark, quizzical eyes."

Parrington also was hired as the first full-time football coach in 1897. He had played football at Emporia College and Harvard University where he was a backup quarterback. A committee of students from Harvard, Princeton, Yale, and Columbia had established a uniform code of rules in 1876. The rules adopted Harvard's combination of soccer and rugby, advancing the ball by picking it up and carrying it. This made Parrington the talk of the town, as many locals were excited to have a Harvard man lead the university football team.

He coached the "tackle back" style, a cross blocking technique he learned at Harvard. Not enthusiastic about the game after the initial season, Joe Merkle and Jap Clapham did not play in 1896, but returned in '97. Merkle and Clapham anchored the left side of the line at tackle and end respectively. They learned the new technique well, which opened holes in the lines for backs to spring through.

Oklahoma's 15 players included Fred Merkle (Joe's brother) at center. The '97 squad was a determined bunch and worked hard for Coach Parrington. Many performed their chores by lantern light late in the evening after a grueling afternoon of practice.

Oklahoma won the first game of the season on Thanksgiving with a 16-0 victory over the same Oklahoma City team, which embarrassed them two years earlier. Leading 4-0 in the first half, Oklahoma scored three touchdowns in the second half for the victory.

Foul weather cancelled two other scheduled games—a rematch against Oklahoma City was called off due to heavy sleet, and snow cancelled a match against Fort Reno.

The only other game of 1897 was against Kingfisher College on December 31 on the fairgrounds in Guthrie, capital of the territory's Republican commonwealth. This was Oklahoma's first game against another college team, and the players paid their own train fare and hotel expenses.

Although Oklahoma won 17-8 after trailing 8-6 at the half, the game had its memorable moments. Oklahoma lineman Bill McCutcheon complained that his collisions with a Kingfisher lineman were hurting him. Keith wrote that McCutcheon discovered the Kingfisher lineman was wearing armor:

"Beneath his jersey, he had concealed an elbow of stovepipe over each shoulder and arm, and at the varsity's insistence the game was stopped and the illegal protection removed."

In the second half, the Logan County sheriff, who had never seen a football game, arrived at the game. He thought he was witnessing a drunken brawl and, with his gun drawn, ran onto the field to stop the contest. President Boyd and officials convinced him that it was a football game, not a drunken brawl. The game was allowed to continue.

The following February, an athletic association was formed with Parrington chosen as its president. President Boyd served on the board with other faculty members.

University regents voted to purchase a shower bath for the players and had it installed in the basement of the Administration Building. Previously, players had to clean up using a bowl of water and a wash rag. But now water was fed into the building as the first municipal water supply replaced private wells.

More trees were added to the campus drives at Boyd's direction. The campus also was fenced on the east and south sides to prevent driving on the campus during games.

The following season, the Oklahoma squad traveled out of the territory for the first time. The team rode the Santa Fe rail north to Arkansas City, Kansas to meet that community's town team, made up of rail yard workers. Joe Merkle recovered a fumble at the Ark City one-yard line then scored the game's only touchdown on a tackle-around play. Oklahoma won 5-0. The value of touchdowns was raised to five points in 1898.

Back at the hotel, the Oklahoma players were astounded to see that the hotel was furnished with custom-built bathtubs. Players would climb into them two at a time to help clean each other from the gridiron grime before scurrying to the dining room for dinner.

Oklahoma hosted Fort Worth University on Thanksgiving Day. Oklahoma scored two and one-half minutes after the opening kickoff for the only score of the first half. Coach Parrington ordered Fred Merkle to kick the ball low into the cold, southeast wind. The ball caromed off a Fort Worth player and Oklahoma recovered. Five plays later, Merkle plowed across the goal line.

Oklahoma's halfback Henry McGraw hurtled over the line and raced 70 yards for a touchdown on the first play in the second half. Harv Short and Lum Roberts scored two more touchdowns, and Clapham succeeded on all four extra-point kicks for a 24-0 Oklahoma victory.

The 1898 season ended with a 2-0 record.

The next year, the Oklahoma team was nicknamed the "Rough Riders," after the regiment of Teddy Roosevelt's U.S. Cavalry volunteers who seized San Juan Hill in the Spanish-American War.

Like the volunteers at San Juan Hill, the Oklahoma Rough Riders were victorious, defeating Kingfisher College to the tune of 39-6. Next up was a powerful University of Arkansas team, played on a cold, drizzly afternoon in Shawnee, Oklahoma.

Oklahoma featured its own powerful player by the name of Fred Roberts, Lum's cousin. He was muscular and tan from working on his family's Kansas farm and had learned football from his cousin on the farm. He was so fast and powerful that he was described as a cat and a locomotive combined.

A controversial play spoiled the mettle of some Oklahoma players, coaches and fans. Arkansas had the ball at the Oklahoma 45-yard line when its captain and punter Chester Sloan called for a drop kick. He booted the ball 50 yards through the goal post

---

It's a Fact

C.C. "Lum" Roberts was captain for four years, longer than any other player in Oklahoma football history.

---

uprights. The referee signaled field goal to give Arkansas a 5-0 lead. Field goals also counted for five points then.

Oklahoma players and fans had protested to officials that Sloan had punted, not drop kicked. The field goal stood. Not pleased, Coach Parrington accepted the decision.

In the second half, Oklahoma drove 95 yards for a touchdown highlighted by Fred Merkle's 10-yard end-around run and Fred Roberts' 30-yard off-tackle scamper. Near the goal line, Roberts stiff-armed an opponent en route to crossing the goal line. He later scored on a slashing crossbuck.

Oklahoma threatened another score late in the game, but the contest ended at the three-yard line. The Rough Riders won, 11-5.

Joe Merkle broke his collarbone in the game and continued to play. Although he never saw a doctor about the injury, he never played football after the Arkansas game.

The Arkansas City town team came to Norman on Thanksgiving Day and rolled up a 17-5 lead in the first half. In the second half, Fred Roberts bolted 70 yards to the goal line, eluding one tackler and slipping from the grasp of another along the way. Clapham kicked the extra point, and the Rough Riders trailed, 17-11.

Late in the game, Oklahoma had marched toward the winning touchdown, but spectators had encroached onto the field. Harv Short carried the ball toward the goal line but slowed down to avoid colliding with spectators. He was tackled as the game ended, and Oklahoma suffered its first defeat in four years.

An early December game against mighty Kansas University in Oklahoma City was cancelled. University of Oklahoma officials had sent money for traveling expenses for the Kansas squad, but a Kansas University official wired that the game was cancelled without giving an explanation. At the time, Kansas was riding a 10-game winning streak and featured a great quarterback named Bennie Owen.

First Game Against Texas

The storied rivalry against Texas University began at the turn of the century. Texas had played football two years longer than Oklahoma, including 44 games for Texas to only 10 for Oklahoma.

Coach Parrington was without the services of four of his best players—Clapham, the Merkle brothers, and Fred Roberts. Clapham was unable to make the trip, Joe Merkle married and started farming, and Fred Merkle retired. Roberts was coaxed into playing at Washburn College in Topeka, Kansas. Washburn started a football team, and its first coach to persuade Roberts in playing there was Owen.

The 500-mile train ride to Austin, Texas, on October 9, 1900, was equally as rough as football. Players boarded the Santa Fe's "chair car," which provided little comfort to Coach Parrington and his charges. The train made 18 stops during the nearly 17-hour journey, which included changing trains in Milano, Texas, 70 miles northeast of Austin. Today one can drive a straight shot down Interstate 35 from Norman to Austin in about six and one-half hours, eight and one-half hours via Amtrak.

When the train arrived in Austin the next morning, the exhausted team checked into the Driskill Hotel to rest before the game that afternoon.

Right from the start, the Oklahoma team received no respect. The headline in the *Austin American-Statesman* read: "THE RED FOOTBALL WARRIORS ARRIVE IN THIS CITY TO PLAY THIS AFTERNOON."

The following day the *American-Statesman*'s headline screamed "PRACTICE GAME YESTERDAY—VARSITY FOOTBALL

Norman, Oklahoma, was becoming a busy town as evidenced by this view of Main Street looking west during the late summer cotton harvest. *(OU Athletics)*

TEAM HAVE A STIFF PRACTICE GAME WITH OKLAHOMA."

Texas handily defeated the Rough Riders, 28-2. Texas fullback John DeLesdernier scored an early touchdown for the Texans, and Walter Schriener booted the extra point to give Texas a 6-0 lead.

DeLesdernier was also the Texas punter, and soon after his touchdown, the snap sailed over his head and past the goal line. He was tackled when he tried to retrieve the ball.

Near the game's end, Oklahoma made a late drive. Lum Roberts took the ball from the Texas eight-yard line and headed for the goal line, but he fumbled and Texas recovered before he crossed the line.

The Rough Riders never yielded a point the rest of the season. A week after the Texas game, the Chilocco Indian School came to Norman and was sent away with a 27-0 defeat. Clapham kicked a field goal, scored a touchdown, and booted the extra point in the game's first 10 minutes. John Hefley and John McCartney also scored a touchdown.

The more experienced Oklahoma squad was rougher than the Indians. Keith wrote that some Oklahoma players remembered Hefley's opponent on the line wore a "broad-brimmed cowboy hat, and that the roguish Hefley handled him by the original method of

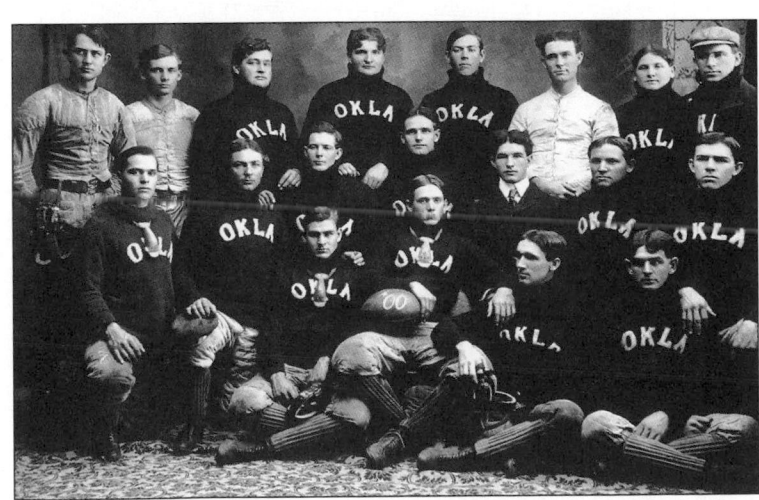

The 1900 Oklahoma football squad *(OU Athletics)*

grabbing the Stetson with both hands and jamming it down over the Indian's eyes and ears, after which he could maneuver his opponent about like a window dresser moving a waxed dummy."

A week later, a team of soldiers from Fort Reno arrived in Norman wearing blue army uniforms. Oklahoma won 79-0, and the longest run made by the soldiers in the game was to the sidelines to light a cigarette.

On November 17, Kingfisher College battled the Rough Riders to a scoreless tie in Norman. This was the first time since the first game against Oklahoma City that Oklahoma failed to score in a game.

The Rough Riders then traveled to Arkansas City, Kansas, to meet its town team on Thanksgiving. Roberts scored two touchdowns in the 10-0 victory, closing the 1900 season with a 3-1-1 record.

A new game arrived on campus that year though still seven years from becoming a varsity sport. Dr. Lawrence Northcote Upjohn, who was the new instructor of Anatomy and Physical Culture at the University of Oklahoma, organized basketball. Three football players—McCartney, Roberts, and Oscar Johnson—thought they'd give the new sport a try. All three would carry the round ball instead of bouncing it at Upjohn's insistence. All three quit.

1896 Season Record: 2-0-0

Date	Opponent	Result	Score
October 28	Norman High*	W	12-0
November 11	Norman High*	W	16-4

*Game played in Oklahoma City, OK

1897 Season Record: 2-0-0

Date	Opponent	Result	Score
November 25	OKLAHOMA CITY	W	16-0
December 31	Kingfisher College#	W	17-8

#Game played in Guthrie, OK

1898 Season Record: 2-0-0

Date	Opponent	Result	Score
November 17	at Arkansas City	W	5-0
November 24	FORT WORTH	W	24-0

1899 Season Record: 2-1-0

Date	Opponent	Result	Score
October 20	KINGFISHER COLLEGE	W	39-6
October 28	at Arkansas%	W	11-5
November 30	ARKANSAS CITY	L	17-11

%Game played in Shawnee, OK

1900 Season Record: 2-1-1

Date	Opponent	Result	Score
October 10	at Texas	L	28-2
October 19	CHILOCCO	W	27-0
October 26	FORT RENO	W	79-0
November 17	at Kingfisher College	T	0-0
November 22	at Arkansas City	W	10-0

1901

Vernon Parrington's academic responsibilities had increased, and he asked to be relieved of his coaching duties, which President Boyd granted. Parrington won nine games, lost two and tied one. Eight years later, he, President Boyd and several other faculty members were fired.

Parrington later taught at Washington University where he won a Pulitzer Prize for his book *Main Currents of Political Thought*. He died suddenly in 1929 in Gloucestershire, England, while taking the first vacation of his life.

Fred Roberts was brought back as a player/coach in 1901, and like his predecessors, he had no coaching experience. He was the first former player to coach at his alma mater.

Gone from the backfield were his cousin, Lum, Harv Short, and John McCartney. John Hefley had graduated but enrolled as a graduate student and played another year. Roberts returned in one halfback position, and Frank McCoy of Sawyer, Kansas, was the other halfback. McCoy was a speedster who set the university's dirt track record of 21 seconds in the 200-yard dash in the Territorial Intercollegiate meet in 1902.

Horse collars were used as shoulder pads, and the players wore shin guards.

The Rough Riders opened against Texas in Austin and rode to Austin this time in Pullman coaches. Ex-coach Parrington requested extra money to have the players ride in Pullman coaches with sheets on the beds. Although some players could not sleep because of the excitement, many were delighted with the added luxury. Those who slept bunked two per berth.

Texas' touchdown in the final 56 seconds of the game broke a 6-6 tie to win, 12-6. Tom Tribbey scored Oklahoma's only touchdown, and Roberts kicked the conversion.

Two days later, the team stopped in Waco, Texas, on its return to Oklahoma to play against Baylor University. This game helped defray the expenses of traveling to Austin.

Although weary from the Texas game and train ride, Oklahoma prevailed, 17-0. Roberts was unstoppable and scored two touchdowns. He also played linebacker on defense and was knocking Baylor players off the field. The referee ruled Roberts' tackling as "foul tactics" and twice penalized the Rough Riders.

Oklahoma captain Ray Crowe protested by removing his team from the field. The team, realizing it could forfeit the $150 guarantee if the game was not completed, returned.

The Rough Riders defeated Fairmont College of Wichita, Kansas, 42-0, in the home opener in Norman.

Kingfisher College came to Norman in a game that was advertised as for the territorial championship. Kingfisher College was undefeated and yielded no touchdowns.

The enemy scored first then McCoy raced 40 yards for an Oklahoma touchdown, but Roberts missed the conversion kick. Oklahoma trailed, 6-5, at the half.

1901 Season Record: 3-2-0

Date	Opponent	Result	Score
October 19	at Texas	L	12-6
October 21	at Baylor	W	17-0
November 8	FAIRMONT	W	42-0
November 16	KINGFISHER COLLEGE	W	28-6
November 28	TEXAS	L	11-0

McCoy scored three more touchdowns, and the Rough Riders won, 28-6.

For the first time, Texas played football in the territory on Thanksgiving Day. The game was well promoted by the Oklahoma student manager, and an estimated 1,200 spectators attended the game. Fans came from Oklahoma City, Guthrie, El Reno, Lexington, Shawnee, and Purcell. Not all of them rooted for the crimson and cream. Among them were many ex-Texans who made the Land Run of '89. They dressed in orange and rooted for the team from their home state.

The Umpire, University of Oklahoma's first student newspaper, thanked fans for coming out and supporting the event, which helped pull the athletic association out of debt.

Texas won, 11-0. Oklahoma had a good drive near the end of the first half aided by McCoy's 40-yard run and Roberts' 20-yard dash. Tom Tribbey chugged toward the Texas goal line carrying some Longhorns with him, but he was finally brought down at the Texas 10-yard line as the first half expired.

Oklahoma fumbled three times in the second half.

The Texans were given a reception after the game and before boarding the train back to Austin.

The Rough Riders finished 3-2 in 1901 and with increasing farm duties, Roberts declined to return the following year.

1902

Oklahoma was without a coach during the first three games of 1902. Captain Clyde Bogle and manager Tom Tribbey supervised practices. Thomas Matthews of Ardmore had played center at Kendall College of Muskogee. When word spread that he had experience at center, he was given the starting nod before the first practice.

The Rough Riders defeated Guthrie, 62-0, in Norman on September 29 to open the season, then lost to Texas, 22-6, three days later in Austin. Oklahoma played for the first time at the Texas State Fair in Dallas in the third game against the Dallas Athletic Club, a team of railroad workers.

Trick plays, an element of surprise, were growing among football teams, and DAC had one as well. On one play, after the ball was placed by officials at the line of scrimmage, the Dallas center, instead of crouching over the ball, walked over to it, snatched it from the ground and handed it to the quarterback. Dallas scored on a 75-yard touchdown run using this play and caught the Rough Riders off guard.

DAC won the game 11-6. Mark McMahon, a Dallas guard who also played tackle for Texas University in 1901, inquired about the open coaching spot at Oklahoma. He met with University of

Oklahoma officials at the hotel following the game. They said they'd hire him if he would teach the trick play to the team. He agreed and was hired for a $250 salary.

Many teams were adding trick plays to their play books, but Oklahoma lacked one. McMahon was energetic and modernized the game by introducing the first tackling dummy and added more games to the schedule.

The Rough Riders won five of their next six games. They defeated an unbeaten Arkansas team, 30-0, in Norman. Tribbey had knocked out three Arkansas players in the first half with his new tackling technique—wrapping his arm around the player's neck, shoving his hip into him, tossing him to the ground and falling on him. Arkansas had to forfeit the game after a fourth player was KO'd in the second half.

The next game was a first for Oklahoma to play in Oklahoma City. Colcord Park was a grand site to behold with a grandstand and reserved parking for carriages. A 25-cent admission was charged. Oklahoma was not a gracious guest, winning 30-0.

After defeating Kingfisher College, 15-0, three games had gone by without the use of the trick play Coach McMahon had promised. He wanted to wait for the right game.

The next week, players packed their lunch for the long train ride to Columbia, Missouri, to play the Missouri Tigers for the first time. Chester Reeds' mother did not allow him to make the trip. Needing an extra player, McMahon convinced Fred Roberts to go. Roberts had not played in a year, so he was held back as a reserve.

After Missouri's opening kickoff went out of bounds, the referee placed the ball at the 20-yard line. Thomas Matthews walked over to the ball, plucked it off the ground and handed it to quarterback Bryom McCreary. McCreary pitched it to Frank McCoy as the Missouri defense was setting up at the line of scrimmage. McCoy raced to the goal line outdistancing his blockers. He had one man to beat near the goal line—the Missouri safety. McCoy swiveled his hips, causing his opponent to lose his balance before crossing the goal line. Missouri's fullback scored three touchdowns en route to a 22-5 Tiger victory.

Two days later, the team stopped at Emporia, Kansas, to play Emporia College to help finance the trip to Columbia. The battered Rough Riders defeated Emporia, 6-5. Roberts scored the lone Oklahoma touchdown on a 40-yard run. The difference was Dan Short's foot, which successfully nailed the extra point.

Oklahoma again shut out Kingfisher College, 17-0, to close the season with a 6-3 record. The 11 varsity players each purchased red sweaters with white "Okla" lettering across the front.

Enrollment grew to 465 in 1902 and student life was prospering at the University of Oklahoma with fraternities, sororities, and a mandolin club being formed. The campus grew from 40 acres to 60.

At the end of 1902, the first Rose Bowl game was played in Pasadena, California, a rich tradition, which OU would not be a part of for another century.

1903

On January 6, 1903, the Administration Building burned down. Students tried to extinguish the blaze, but it continued to flourish. Classes were moved to other buildings in Norman, and by the fall, a new administration facility was being built. A new $10,000 gymnasium was also built and provided a locker room with showers for the football team.

The football team played only two of its 12 games in Norman, although three games were played at Oklahoma City's Colcord Park, 20 miles to the north. Oklahoma defeated the Chilocco Indians,

1902 Season Record: 6-3-0

Date	Opponent	Result	Score
September 29	GUTHRIE	W	62-0
October 2	at Texas	L	22-6
October 4	at Dallas Athletic Club	L	11-6
October 25	ARKANSAS	W	28-0
October 29	at Oklahoma City Athletic Club	W	30-0
November 5	KINGFISHER COLLEGE	W	15-0
November 12	at Missouri	L	22-5
November 14	at Emporia College	W	6-5
November 24	KINGFISHER COLLEGE	W	17-0

35-6, in the opener in Norman. Chester Reeds scored four touchdowns, and Hugh Carroll kicked three field goals.

The Rough Riders fought Kingfisher College to a scoreless tie in Kingfisher, the first time the crimson lads hadn't scored since losing to Texas in late 1901. Texas was next, and the university of orange and white now had an official nickname—Longhorns. Oklahoma and Texas battled to a 6-6 tie, the first game without a loss to the rivals south of the Red River. Two days later, the Rough Riders beat Texas A&M, 6-0, in Bryan, Texas.

When the team returned to Norman, they were given a hayride and paraded through the streets, a spontaneous celebration for not losing to Texas and the Texas A&M victory.

After defeating Fairmont College, 11-5, and tying Emporia College, 6-6, the Rough Riders made its first trip, 14 hours by train, to Lawrence, Kansas, to meet the Kansas Jayhawks. Coach McMahon's training regimen included no sweets or coffee, but two of his players begged him to allow them coffee with the dinner the night before the game. Everyone drank sweet milk at the Lawrence hotel. It was laced with a drug that caused the team to have diarrhea; everyone except the coffee drinkers.

The players tried to keep their composure during the game, but their stomachs were too painful. Kansas won, 17-5. Oklahoma's only score came on a play beyond the field. There was no out of bounds in those days, and when Reeds blocked a punt, the ball bounced over a fence behind the Kansas goal line. A spectator picked up the ball and tossed it over the fence to Claude Reeds, who was pursuing it. When he retrieved the ball, he immediately touched it on the ground for the score.

The Longhorns returned to Oklahoma for a rematch at Oklahoma City's Colcord Park. Texas won, 11-5. Oklahoma's lone score was a field goal by Dan Short, the first field goal by a university player. Texas also scored beyond the gridiron. UT's Don Robinson punted the ball past the goal line. He and OU's Bryom McCreary gave chase. The ball had settled under a horse hitched to a buggy. McCreary, went around the horse, but Robinson dove underneath it and smothered the ball.

Four days later, the team was to meet Arkansas University in Fayetteville, but Arkansas University had insufficient funds to guarantee Oklahoma's advance travel expenses. Tribbey asked local drug store proprietor, John Barbour, to lend $300 until the team returned. Barbour lent the money and the team made an unpleasant trip.

The train was rerouted and took longer than expected. The players had little sleep, and when they arrived, they were greeted with a muddy, frozen field with protruding rocks. Arkansas won, 12-0, on two second-half touchdowns. The game included holding and slugging by the Arkansas players, which officials failed to stop. Arkansas spectators tossed rocks at the Oklahoma players. To top that off, Arkansas University refused to pay the expenses.

Two days later, the beaten and weary Rough Riders stopped in Joplin, Missouri, to meet the Rolla Miners, another game to help pay for expenses. Oklahoma jumped to a 12-0 lead. Jim Monnett

John Barbour, a local drug store owner, loaned the Oklahoma football team $300 to cover traveling expenses for the team to play in Arkansas.
(OU Athletics)

broke his arm and was replaced by Robert Severin, the last reserve on the squad. Lee Arnold was also sidelined with a broken shoulder in the Arkansas game. Alex Clement left the Rolla game with a shoulder injury, leaving only 10 men for Oklahoma. Monnett tried to return to the game, but teammates led him back to the sideline.

Rolla closed the gap to 12-6 with a score.

Both coaches kept time of the game, and Coach McMahon's watch showed that time had expired, whereas Rolla's coach still showed some time left. McMahon agreed to split the difference between the two times. Rolla was driving closer to the Oklahoma goal line. Again McMahon's watch showed time had expired, but Rolla's coach disagreed. McMahon withdrew his players from the field.

Rolla continued and scored a touchdown unopposed. The Miners' kicker could tie the game, but he missed. To this day, the Oklahoma football media guide shows Oklahoma had won 12-6, but Rolla records report a 12-11 Oklahoma victory.

On Thanksgiving Day, Bethany College of Lindborg, Kansas, met the Rough Riders at Colcord Park. Bennie Owen, a protégé of Fielding Yost at Michigan, coached the Terrible Swedes. Down 12-0, Oklahoma fought back only to lose by two points.

The Swedes were the fastest, cleanest, most well behaved, and best-coached team the Rough Riders had seen. Not a single penalty was called in the game.

The team had had enough football for one season. Eleven games in two months, but the Lawton town team guaranteed $300 to meet them in Lawton. The ante was upped to $400, which was agreed on by Dr. Albert Van Vleet, member of Oklahoma's athletic association. The expenses would help pay the remainder of McMahon's salary.

McMahon let Lawton know he was two players short of a full squad and would have to call up some "ringers." They agreed. Once again, Fred Roberts was called from his farm. Bob Wingate, who played in '99 and '00 was called back. McMahon also practiced and played.

1903 Season Record: 5-4-3

Date	Opponent	Result	Score
October 2	CHILOCCO	W	38-5
October 9	at Kingfisher College	T	0-0
October 17	at Texas	T	6-6
October 19	at Texas A&M	W	6-0
October 23	Fairmont*	W	11-5
October 30	EMPORIA COLLEGE	T	6-6
November 6	at Kansas	L	17-5
November 13	Texas*	L	11-5
November 18	at Arkansas	L	12-0
November 20	at Rolla	W	12-6
November 26	Bethany*	L	12-10
December 4	at Lawton	W	27-5

*Game played in Oklahoma City, OK

Oklahoma won, 27-5. Roberts starred on offense and defense in his last game for Oklahoma.

McMahon returned to Durant, Oklahoma, to practice law.

1904

Fred "Buck" Ewing, from Knox College in Illinois was hired as the fifth University of Oklahoma football coach. At Knox he was considered the greatest tackle of all time. Although Ewing was coach for one season at OU, he implemented a system to tape players' ankles with adhesive tape. This allowed players with sore ankles to return to action much quicker.

Ewing utilized the Minnesota Shift, a formation created at Minnesota University. This formation called for one offensive tackle to line up behind the other tackle and carry the ball or block on most plays.

Roy Waggoner and Jim Monnett were the biggest players at Oklahoma in 1904. Waggoner would line up behind Monnett. Both players had padding put in the backs of their jackets. A halfback would leap upon Waggoner, then Monnett and swan dive into the air over the line of scrimmage.

Only four regulars returned for the 1904 season—Clarence Cook, Byrom McCreary, Chester Reeds, and Monnett. Monnett missed the first two games, still nursing the broken arm suffered against Rolla a year ago.

Rule changes allowed only five players behind the line of scrimmage and the quarterback replaced the captain as the signal caller. The quarterback also was allowed to carry the ball.

The first university band was formed in September 1904. The 19-member ensemble wore military style suits trimmed in crimson and cream. They played during football and baseball games and at track meets.

Oklahoma and Kingfisher College fought to a scoreless tie in the season opener in Norman. Oklahoma then defeated the Pauls Valley Town Team, 33-0, at Pauls Valley.

Pauls Valley's field was only 75 yards long, and Oklahoma players helped chalk lines and erect goal posts before the game, which began at 5 p.m. Due to the late start, the second half was shortened to 10 minutes (from 20) making it the shortest game in Oklahoma football history.

The next week, Kansas defeated the Rough Riders, 16-0, in Oklahoma City. Monnett returned to the team for the Kansas game.

Oklahoma rebounded with a 6-0 win over Lawton in Lawton, then met Oklahoma A&M for the first time on November 5.

The game was played on a blistering cold and windy day at Old Island Park in south Guthrie, about halfway between Norman and Stillwater. Cottonwood Creek surrounded the field and was nearly full with ice forming near the water's edge.

A&M's first possession was held in check by the Oklahoma defense. The Aggie punter kicked the ball, which blew over his head by the brisk northern wind.

"A loose ball!" the spectators cried.

A loose pigskin in those days belonged to the team that retrieved it. The ball carried back and hit the ground behind the A&M goal line. If Oklahoma recovered it: touchdown; if the Aggies recovered it: touchback.

Harold Keith, in his book *Oklahoma Kickoff*, described the pursuit of the ball: "With players of both teams in pursuit, it bounded down a foot path and into the murky waters of the creek where it bobbed and floated like a cork as the swift current swept it down stream."

An A&M player reached creekside first and stooped to retrieve it with a stick. Oklahoma tackle Becker Matthews struck the Aggie from behind and knocked him into the water. Matthews noticed that this put his opponent closer to rescuing the ball, so he jumped in. Both waded side-by-side trying to fetch the slippery ball, which kept squirting through their hands.

Many spectators crowded around the bank to watch as the Aggie gave up.

Oklahoma's Ed Cook and Frank Long and another A&M player also jumped in the water.

"Cook, who could swim like a bull frog, finally reached the ball, convoyed it to the bank and touched it down in the sand for the oddest touchdown a varsity man ever scored," Keith wrote. "While the crowd roared with laughter, the players waded out looking very wet and cold and bedraggled as the icy wind whipped drops of dirty water off their soaked quilted jackets and moleskin pants."

Matthews, Cook, and Long continued to play in the first half but were given drier uniforms from substitute players in the second half.

The Rough Riders won, 75-0. Every Oklahoma player scored in the game.

The following week, Oklahoma and Texas played for the first time at the Texas State Fair in Dallas. Texas held a slim lead of 17-10 at the half but ran away in the second half en route to a 50-10 victory.

Undefeated Bethany College came to Norman on Thanksgiving Day. Swede coach Bennie Owen used hurry-up offenses he learned at Michigan University. His offensive players would line up quickly and snap the ball before the defense could line up. Bethany won, 36-9.

The next day, Ewing returned to medical school at Chicago University.

Vernon Parrington discussed with President Boyd the possibility of hiring Owen. Boyd approved of Owen's clean style. Parrington wrote Owen, then met with him. Knowing that the job paid very little to start, Owen accepted immediately.

1905

Bennie Owen was given a one-year contract at Oklahoma with no guarantee for an extension. At the time, the university's athletic association was $712 in debt with salaries still to be owed to Mark McMahon, Fred Ewing, and John Barbour, the local druggist who financed the Arkansas trip in 1903. The association had to pool resources to pay for Owen's services.

Owen played quarterback at Kansas University while studying pharmacy and Latin. He also played quarterback and coached Washburn University of Topeka, Kansas. He coached for three years

1904 Season Record: 4-3-1			
Date	**Opponent**	**Result**	**Score**
October 8	KINGFISHER COLLEGE	T	0-0
October 14	at Pauls Valley Town Team	W	33-0
October 21	Kansas*	L	16-0
October 28	at Lawton	W	6-0
November 5	Oklahoma A&M#	W	75-0
November 12	Texas at Dallas	L	40-10
November 18	O.C. MILITARY	L	22-5
November 24	Bethany*	W	6-5
*Game played in Oklahoma City, OK			
#Game played in Guthrie, OK			

at Bethany College of Lindsborg, Kansas, where he won 22 games, lost two, and tied two.

He had gained a reputation as one of the finest college coaches in the nation. The University of Pittsburgh, then a powerhouse team, had invited Owen to coach its team in 1905. He turned them down.

Owen learned the hurry-up style of offense from Fielding Yost, his coach at Kansas.

College football was never more rugged than in the late 19th century and early 1900s. Players had very little to protect their bodies. There were no helmets to protect the head. No mouthpieces, face guards, no pads to shield their shoulders, and small padding in the pants were of little benefit to them. Their bodies were vulnerable to painful blows.

The flying wedge, a V-like formation, was a popular method of advancing the football. Hurdle plays, where teammates would launch another player over the line, were common. The result—serious injury or death. A total of 18 deaths resulted from playing football in 1905, and 149 players were seriously injured.

The game had no rules to govern the contests. There was no forward pass, no neutral zone and no limit to how many players could be on the line at the same time.

President Theodore Roosevelt, a fan of the game, believed changes were necessary for the game of football to thrive. He requested reforms to the game or football would be outlawed. At his request, a committee was formed in an attempt to reduce the violence in the game and to issue rules for play. In March 1906, the Intercollegiate Athletic Association of the United States was established. The organization became the National Collegiate Athletic Association (NCAA) in 1910, which continues to govern collegiate athletics today.

No deaths occurred on the 1905 Oklahoma football team, but injuries were aplenty—many from brawls.

Prior to the 1905 season, the Oklahoma football team name was changed to "Boomers." That same year, the team's fight song was born. Oklahoma student Arthur M. Alden, son of a Norman jeweler, penned the lyrics to "Boomer Sooner," a mix of Yale's "Boola Boola" and North Carolina's "I'm a Tar Heel Born."

"Sooner Magic" was coined about 70 years later, but actually began in 1905 in the season's second game. What is Sooner Magic? Incredible comebacks by the offense or power of the defense to hold off the opponent from ripping victory from the Sooners. Although the team wasn't named the "Sooners" for another three years, the magic was established.

Owen's team started the 1905 season with a 28-0 victory over Central Normal of Edmond, Oklahoma. Meanwhile, the Haskell Indians of Tulsa shut out a good Texas team before their matchup against Oklahoma in Norman.

Sooner Magic: Slugfest

The Indians were a burly bunch of boys led by two muscular brothers, Pete and Emil Hauser. The Haskell team was larger than the Oklahoma squad, which was considered light even by standards of the early 20th century.

Haskell scored the first touchdown of the game, which was marred by fumbles. Eleven minutes into the game, after a couple of fumbles by both teams, a Haskell player stole the ball from an Oklahoma player and ran 25 yards to the first score.

The Boomers had a couple of chances to score in the first half, but both efforts were thwarted by fumbles deep in Indians territory. Haskell held on to a 6-0 lead at halftime.

Oklahoma got on the board early in the second half when freshman halfback Owen Acton dashed 20 yards around end. Leonard Rumbeck tied the extra point, and the game was knotted at 6-6.

The Haskell team answered with a drive to the Oklahoma goal line. John Aiken scored the touchdown, and Pete Hauser kicked the extra point to give the Indians a 12-6 lead.

Four minutes later, Becker Matthews scored Oklahoma's second touchdown, and Rumbeck booted the tying conversion with eight minutes left in the game.

By this time, the Haskell players were growing weary of the Oklahoma team and began throwing punches at the Boomer players. On one play, Matthews flattened Emil Hauser with a powerful block, then stayed on top of the Haskell halfback for a moment. Hauser swung a right punch at Matthews and cut the Oklahoma tackle over his eye. Matthews then swung at Hauser. Officials saw this activity but allowed both players to stay in the game.

With a little more than three minutes remaining, Oklahoma began its offensive attack from its own 43-yard line. The Boomers marched down the field with precision runs, peeling chunks of yards at a time behind blocks and wearing down an opponent showing signs of fatigue.

The Boomers had marched to the Haskell 10-yard line with the help of Claude Reeds, who had never played before. He didn't even have a full uniform, just a sweater tucked into his football pants. Acton and a Haskell player were ejected for slugging, and Reeds substituted for his teammate.

Harry Hughes crashed through the line for five yards, then Matthews gained another four to the one-yard line. On the next play Reeds shoved through the line and across the goal line for the score.

"The game itself was not devoid of features, but was marred to some degree by the slugging, commenced by the visitors and frequently indulged thereafter by both teams," the *Daily Oklahoman* reported.

Many Oklahoma players had complained about the unnecessary roughness provided by the Indians. One player complained about a Haskell player trying to rip his ears off. The Oklahoma players did not back down as evident by Acton's and Matthews' retaliations.

Nevertheless, the new Oklahoma coach was not pleased with the roughness of either team. Owen was a coach who had a reputation of coaching with clean tactics—no profanity, fouling, kneeing, slugging, or dirty play by his players.

Owen's clean style of coaching turned into success on the field.

The Boomers lost to Kansas, 34-0, in the next game, then defeated the Kansas City Medics, 33-0, and lost to Washburn, 9-6. Texas was next, the fourth game in two weeks. In the previous seven meetings, Oklahoma was without a win against its rival from south of the Red River. A 6-6 tie in 1903 disallowed the Longhorns from having a perfect record in the young series.

Sooner Magic: First Victory Over Texas

Both teams entered the 1905 game with identical 3-2 records. The Horns were a heavy 2-1 favorite in posted pool room odds, according to the *Dallas Morning News*. The 1905 matchup was played in Oklahoma City before 2,500 frenzied fans.

Both offenses were sluggish in the first half, which was highlighted by fumbles, penalties, and no points.

Late in the second half, Texas marched from midfield to the Oklahoma goal line, but the Boomers held inside their one-yard line.

Oklahoma drove 105 yards (in 1905 the length of the field was 110 yards), highlighted by a crowd-pleasing play by halfback Harry

Hughes. Hughes, also a track hurdler, took the football and leaped over a charging Texas safety. The Texas player got into position to make a tackle, but Hughes amazed the crowd by jumping over the Texas defender then had a clean shot to the goal line. After gaining 55 yards on the run, Hughes was caught from behind by a Longhorn inside the UT 10. Oklahoma could get no closer than the five-yard line and had to give up possession on downs.

With about a minute left in the game, Texas' left halfback and team captain, Don Robinson, took the ball and proceeded around end. Before Robinson could get behind his wall of blockers, Oklahoma center Robert Severin smashed through the line and grabbed Robinson around the knees and carried him back across the goal line and slammed the Texas player to the turf for a safety.

Longhorn coach Ralph Hutchinson protested the safety to officials. He believed Severin was offside on the play. The play stood.

The Oklahoma fans tossed their hats, canes, ribbons, and chrysanthemums in the air celebrating Oklahoma's 2-0 lead. That's the way the final score stood.

"When the safety was made, the crowd rushed madly across the field and carried the Oklahoma players off on their shoulders, by way of celebration of the first victory over the University of Texas," the *Fort Worth Star-Telegram* reported.

The *Dallas Morning News* wrote "the Texas team did not finish the one minute of play, seeing that victory was out of the question."

Hutchinson said it was "useless" to try to continue the game because of the swarming crowd.

The *Daily Oklahoman* reported that the game was halted several times when the crowd had to be moved off the field.

The celebration by the Oklahoma fans "was kept up until midnight and after," the *Star-Telegram* wrote.

"Tonight, hundreds of Oklahoma students are parading in the streets celebrating their victory," the *News* wrote.

"The greatest football game ever played in the territory," the *Oklahoman* accounted.

The *Austin American-Statesman*, however, was bitter in its remarks about the Longhorns' first-ever loss to Oklahoma. "The result of the game may be that Texas will hereafter refuse to play these small colleges unless it be here [in Austin] or at some place where all the arrangements can be made beforehand to eradicate any such foolish performances as were tolerated in Oklahoma City."

Although the two teams met in Oklahoma City again in 1906, in Austin in 1907, 1909, 1910 and 1911, Norman in 1908 and Dallas in 1912, that prognostication of "someplace" else finally came true eight years later. The two teams met in Houston in 1913, then in Dallas the next five years. A game was played in Norman in 1922 and Austin in 1923. For five years after that both teams did not play each other. Oklahoma and Texas resumed their rivalry in 1929 in

Dallas. Since then, the game each year has been played in Dallas, which is about halfway between the two universities, at the Texas State Fair.

Coach Owen's first Boomer team finished the season 7-2 with three more shutouts—55-0 over Kingfisher College, 58-0 over Central Normal and 29-0 over Bethany College.

1906

The university's athletic association made a profit of $905.80 from the 1905 football season, which paid the debts owed to John Barbour, Fred Ewing, and Mark McMahon.

New rules to reduce the game's brutality were established in the spring of 1906 by the Intercollegiate Athletic Association of the United States. Tackling out of bounds, hurdling, and piling on after the referee ruled a play dead were prohibited. Defensive players were forbidden to strike a ball carrier in the face with the palm of the hand.

Other new rules included six men required on the line of scrimmage. A forward pass was permissible, but the ball had to be thrown at least five yards. This required the re-chalking of fields to include stripes every five yards.

Games were shortened from 45-minute halves to 30-minute halves. Ten yards were necessary to gain a first down in three plays to maintain possession of the ball. All players, except the kicker on the kicking team, were eligible to recover the punt once it touched the ground. Most coaches preferred this method to the forward pass.

Head coach Bennie Owen said in the *Umpire* that the new rules would be good for football, and he believed the forward pass would open the game "considerably."

Owen taught the forward pass to roll off the hand with a sidearm motion. It was a technique that would take his charges a few years to get used to.

The Oklahoma football gridiron was named Boyd Field in honor of its president. It included a grandstand with bleachers to seat 500 spectators.

The Boomers opened the '06 campaign on September 28 with a 12-0 victory over Central Normal, then defeated Kingfisher College, 11-6, both games in Norman. Halfback Owen Acton scored both touchdowns for OU on 25- and 50-yard runs against Kingfisher. Fred Allen of Tonkawa intercepted a Kingfisher pass, and he is credited with the first interception for Oklahoma.

Many OU players suffered injuries in the Kingfisher game. Owen's squad was reduced to 14 players as they traveled to Stillwater to meet Oklahoma A&M. Nevertheless, the Boomers prevailed, 23-0.

1905 Season Record: 7-2-0

Date	Opponent	Result	Score
September 29	at Central Normal	W	28-0
October 16	HASKELL	W	18-12
October 21	at Kansas	L	34-0
October 25	KANSAS CITY MEDICS	W	33-0
October 28	WASHBURN	L	9-6
November 3	Texas*	W	2-0
November 11	at Kingfisher College	W	55-0
November 17	CENTRAL NORMAL	W	58-0
November 30	Bethany College	W	29-0
*Game played in Oklahoma City, OK			

1906 Season Record: 5-2-2

Date	Opponent	Result	Score
September 28	CENTRAL NORMAL	W	12-0
October 5	KINGFISHER COLLEGE	W	11-6
October 12	at Oklahoma A&M	W	23-0
October 20	at Kansas	L	20-4
November 2	Texas*	L	10-9
November 10	at Central Normal	W	17-0
November 23	SULPHUR TOWN TEAM	W	48-0
November 29	at Washburn	T	0-0
December 7	at Pawhuska Town Team	T	0-0
*Game played in Oklahoma City, OK			

The Oklahoma team received another setback the next week before it traveled to Lawrence, Kansas, to face the Kansas Jayhawks. Guard Wyatt Burch was declared ineligible. A contract with Kansas University had a provision that required a list of players must be submitted 10 days prior to the game. At the time Burch was not enrolled at the University of Oklahoma.

Kansas won, 20-4. Harry Hughes, halfback and kicker for OU, booted a 35-yard field goal for the only Boomer points.

Two weeks later, Texas rolled into Oklahoma City. The Longhorns won, 10-9, in the closing minutes. OU had a return engagement with Central Normal in Edmond the following week. Central Normal scored first, but the touchdown was nullified.

Normal's center, Roy Campbell, was hurled over the line by two teammates into the OU backfield. He then ran 25 yards for the TD. The referee whistled the play dead. Normal fans stormed onto the field to toss Campbell into the air in appreciation for the team's first ever score against Oklahoma. They were disappointed when the referee stood by his decision of ruling the play dead; one of the effects of the new rules implemented before the season.

OU fullback George Truesdale scored all three touchdowns for his team. The Normal fans were so angry that Edmond police had to escort the Oklahoma team from its hotel to the train station.

Oklahoma defeated Sulphur Town Team, 48-0, in the snow at Boyd Field. Sulphur was unable to gain a single first down.

On Thanksgiving, OU and Washburn battled to a scoreless tie on a muddy field in Topeka, Kansas. A week later, OU and Pawhuska Town Team fought to a scoreless tie in Pawhuska. Owen played quarterback in the second half, his last game ever as a player.

Pawhuska, mostly a team of Indians, included Pete Hauser, who played at Haskell a year earlier. Pawhuska threatened to win the game, but the Boomers held them on downs at the two-yard line as the game expired.

Oklahoma finished the 1906 season with a 5-2-2 record. Although many of Owen's men suffered injuries, the number of injuries dropped significantly because of the new rules.

1907

The University of Oklahoma and its football team experienced one of its darkest years in 1907. The university president and faculty members were fired, the Administration Building burned again, head coach Bennie Owen lost his right arm in a hunting accident, a player was declared ineligible during the season, and another was kicked out of a game for fighting.

Owen had to find replacements for four key players who were no longer eligible to play. Gone were halfback George Truesdale, guard Wyatt Burch, and tackles Jim Monnett and Roy Waggoner. New players included Ralph Campbell, who played for Central Normal in 1906, Charley Wantland, Jimmy Nairn, and Earle Radcliffe.

Wantland showed up for practice with a helmet, but soon ditched it in bushes near Boyd Field when he discovered he was the only one with a helmet. Owen didn't believe the players needed extra protection, and he taught them conditioning and ways to reduce possible injuries such as blocking with the shoulder rather than a body block. None of his players suffered serious injury.

The Boomers opened the season with two shutouts—32-0 over Kingfisher College and 43-0 over the Chilocco Indians. In the Chilocco game, OU scored a touchdown for the first time with the forward pass. Records indicate Vernon Walling caught the ball, but no indication of who threw it, although Bill Cross was the quarterback that year.

Three days before the Kansas game, Owen and local drug store owner John Barbour, went quail hunting. They were returning home in the early afternoon in Barbour's buggy. Owen was riding passenger and when one of the hunting dogs nearly fell out of the buggy, Owen stuck out his right arm to keep the dog from falling. Holding his shotgun with his left hand, it fired. Pellets entered his arm four inches below the shoulder, severing an artery, and Owen was bleeding profusely.

Barbour helped him put on a tourniquet to stop the bleeding. An Oklahoma City specialist was called in, and he had to amputate the arm to save Owen's life.

Vernon Parrington substituted as Oklahoma's coach against the Jayhawks. Kansas won, 15-0, the team's first home loss under Owen's regime. OU would not lose another home game until 1910.

Cross, also the team captain, took charge of the team in the next game against Epworth College at Oklahoma City's Colcord Park. Harry Hughes scored three touchdowns as the Boomers prevailed, 29-0. The field and ball were covered with sand burrs, and not many backs wanted to carry the ball. "That was one game I had all the indirect passes I wanted," Cross said.

Owen returned to coach the team during the next three grueling games—all three played within seven days. The team suffered another blow when it was discovered Hughes was ineligible to play the rest of the season. He had not enrolled in the required 12 hours of classes.

Oklahoma A&M came to Norman and was soundly beaten, 67-0. Jimmy Nairn scored five TDs, and Earle Radcliffe scored another on a 70-yard punt return in the second half. Campbell and his brother, Roy, faced off on the field. Ralph played center at OU, and Roy was a center for the Aggies.

Two days later, Texas A&M defeated the Boomers, 19-0. Five days later, Texas beat OU, 29-10. Oklahoma guard Key Wolf was expelled from the Texas game for slugging.

The next day, with a swift stroke of a pen, President Theodore Roosevelt signed his name, proclaiming Oklahoma as the 46th state of the union.

On Thanksgiving Day, Washburn scored two second-half touchdowns to defeat the Boomers, 12-0.

Oklahoma won four games and lost four, which might have been considered a success, considering the misfortunes the team had to endure. Adversity spilled over throughout the university.

On December 20, the Administration Building again burned down. A gasoline stove, heating paint in the building's dome, exploded.

The state's first governor, Charles Haskell, in a political move, discharged OU president Boyd and replaced him with Rev. Grant Evans, who served as president at Kendall College in Muskogee. Republicans had controlled the Oklahoma Territory. Haskell, a Democrat, wanted Republican-appointed faculty members

1907 Season Record: 4-4-0

Date	Opponent	Result	Score
October 4	at Kingfisher College	W	32-0
October 11	at Chilocco	W	43-0
October 18	KANSAS	L	15-0
October 25	at Epworth	W	24-0
November 8	OKLAHOMA A&M	W	67-0
November 11	at Texas A&M	L	19-0
November 15	at Texas	L	29-0
November 28	WASHBURN	L	12-0

throughout the state fired including 22 at OU. One of them was Parrington, who had served as chairman of the English department and athletic director.

Owen was disconcerted with the firings and his team's lack of big victories over the past two years. Through all of this he still hadn't been paid all of his salary. Many coaches would have looked elsewhere for greener pastures. Yet the OU coach pressed forward to produce one of the finest teams of his 22-year tenure.

1908

Bennie Owen had designed two new plays for the 1908 season, and the team had a new nickname by mid-season.

The Oklahoma coach was delighted with his new team, which was quicker and heavier than in the past. The line, which included Ralph Campbell's brother Roy at center, averaged 195 pounds. Ralph Campbell was switched to right tackle, and Willard Douglas bolstered the left side at tackle.

Owen's concern was replacing Harry Hughes, Bill Cross, and Owen Acton in the backfield. Charley Wantland, Earle Radcliffe, and Charley Armstrong stepped in as replacements. Sixteen-year-old Fred Capshaw, an all-star at Norman High a year earlier, also saw action in the backfield.

Owen whipped his team into shape, which included two-mile runs accompanied by the coach. He taught his backs to depend on their speed, which provided more finesse than before.

He also taught them the cross buck, a play where the ball was tossed to a halfback who bucked the offensive tackle, then flipped the ball back toward the other halfback, who then charged over the opposite guard.

Douglas and Ralph Campbell were so quick for linemen that they were effective with the tackle-around play, scoring 15 to 20 touchdowns during the season. The quarterback would take the snap, turn his back away from the line of scrimmage and fake a hand off to one of his backs. All three backs swung toward the sideline, then the quarterback would pivot to the opposite direction and hand the ball to one of the tackles who pulled from the line of scrimmage. The tackle would run the same direction as the backs, then suddenly reverse his direction over the opposite offensive tackle.

Central Normal scored on the third play in the opening game at Edmond. A punt shot straight up in the air hit a Normal player then bounced into the arms of Earl Yeakel, who sped 70 yards for the touchdown. OU then scored nine touchdowns en route to a 51-5 decision.

Artie Reeds, brother of Chester and Clarence who played a few years earlier, would only play one game that year after having contracted typhoid.

Two more backs were unavailable in the next game against Oklahoma A&M at Stillwater. Radcliffe's mother was ill, and Wantland had a severely bruised leg suffered in practice.

OU scored three second-half touchdowns in an 18-0 win, which saw more backs sustain injuries. Capshaw broke his nose, and

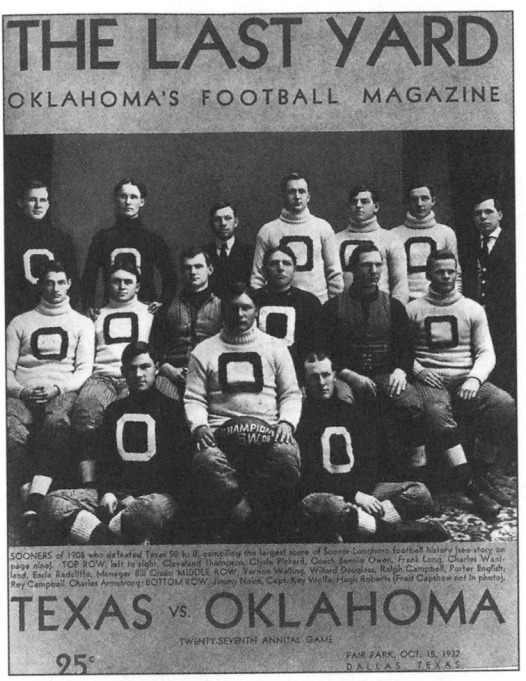

THE LAST YARD
OKLAHOMA'S FOOTBALL MAGAZINE

TEXAS vs. OKLAHOMA
TWENTY-SEVENTH ANNUAL GAME
FAIR PARK, OCT. 15, 1932
DALLAS, TEXAS.
25¢

The 1908 Sooners defeated Texas, 50-0. The team held the series record for most points scored and margin of victory for several decades.
(*Western History Collections, University of Oklahoma*)

Armstrong received a bad cut over one eye, but both still continued to play.

Capshaw scored four TDs in the first half of Oklahoma's 51-0 victory over Kingfisher College in Norman. Ralph Campbell also scored twice off the tackle-around play.

The Boomers traveled to Lawrence to meet the undefeated Kansas Jayhawks. The 11-0 loss to the Hawks was the closest margin yet for the Oklahoma team. OU threatened to score five times, but the KU defense held them off each time. Kansas went 8-0 that year, and the team is considered one of the all-time best KU teams.

Three days later, a battered OU team went to Manhattan, Kansas, for the first encounter against the Kansas Aggies (now Kansas State). The first OU touchdown began with the cross buck, but instead of running, Capshaw backed up and fired a short pass to Douglas who flew across the goal line. Wantland later scored on a 65-yard run from the cross buck.

Hugh Roberts scored from the cross buck in the second half, but the play was called back due to an Oklahoma penalty. Quarterback Jimmy Nairn called the same play, and Roberts scored again. This time the play was not negated by a penalty. OU won, 33-4.

OU hosted Arkansas in the second home game of the season. Students had organized a club called the "Sooner Rooters." A 10-cent membership fee was charged each student, and they elected Warren Hazeltine of Norman as their president and yell leader. The *Umpire* mentioned the club in a story about the Arkansas game, and from then on the Oklahoma football team was called "Sooners." The following spring, the name of the school's yearbook was changed from *Mistletoe* to *Sooner*.

After battling through a scoreless first half, OU won, 28-5. The last Sooner TD was a trick play devised by Coach Owen. It was a pass off the old wing shift play to one of the players entering the field from the sideline. Vernon Walling tossed the ball to Nairn who rifled a pass to Wantland, who sped 50 yards for the score.

The Sooners defeated Epworth University, 24-0, the following week.

1908 Season Record: 8-1-1			
Date	**Opponent**	**Result**	**Score**
September 25	at Central Oklahoma	W	51-5
October 5	at Oklahoma A&M	W	18-0
October 9	KINGFISHER COLLEGE	W	51-0
October 16	at Kansas	L	11-0
October 19	at Kansas Aggies	W	33-4
October 30	ARKANSAS	W	27-5
November 6	EPWORTH	W	24-0
November 13	TEXAS	W	50-0
November 20	at Fairmont	W	12-4
November 26	at Washburn	T	0-0

Friday the 13th proved unlucky for the Texas Longhorns but lucky for Oklahoma. The Horns came to Norman on November 13 and left with the biggest defeat in their 15-year history. The game was played in bitter cold aided by a stout north wind. Spectators got up at half time and performed a snake dance around the field just to keep warm, but the victory warmed their hearts.

Early in the game, Ralph Campbell caught a Longhorn from behind near the goal line to save a touchdown. OU soon scored its first TD on Wantland's 90-yard punt return.

Capshaw later scored on a 40-yard run. A Texas defender used his head to hit Capshaw in the side and to the ground. The Sooner got back up and finished his run to the goal line. Capshaw suffered four broken ribs from that blow, but he kept playing in the game. He scored again on a 30-yard run, dodging and weaving the enemy to the goal line. Douglas and Ralph Campbell each scored on the tackle-around play.

Capshaw left the game when Oklahoma had a 40-0 lead. He never played again that year and also became ill with typhoid.

As darkness loomed over Boyd Field, automobiles were moved closer to the gridiron to illuminate the field. With OU ahead, 50-0, the game was halted with seven minutes remaining. The 50-point margin stood as the widest margin in the Oklahoma-Texas series for 98 years.

The Sooners rushed for 778 yards in the game. Douglas accounted for 220 yards and Campbell 181. Combined they rushed for 36 carries averaging 11.1 yards a pop.

Students celebrated in the streets of Norman, which ended with a rally attended by players, coaches, faculty, and locals.

The Sooners beat Fairmont College, 12-4, in Wichita. Roberts scored a 25-yard run from the cross buck, and Armstrong added an 80-yard TD run with four minutes to go in the first half. Fairmont had two scoring threats turned away by the OU defense. A 20-yard drop kick by Fairmont was the only second-half scoring in the game.

Oklahoma and Washburn battled to a scoreless tie in the rain at Topeka. The muddy field was too slippery for either team to gain any kind of a charge.

The Sooners finished with an 8-1-1 record, the best so far in school history.

1909

With the addition of a law school and journalism department in 1909, the University of Oklahoma had established itself as one of the finest education institutions in the nation.

Improvements were also taking shape at Boyd Field. A water pipe was laid to the center of the field, allowing it to be watered before practices, and a ticket booth was added to the field's entrance. However, improvements were not the order for the football team, following an 8-1-1 record the year before, the Sooners went 6-4. Head coach Bennie Owen had to replenish his offensive line—the Campbell brothers, Ralph and Roy, Vernon Walling, and Charley Pickard were gone. Earle Radcliffe and Charley Wantland had to be replaced in the backfield. Wantland did not return for personal reasons.

Most of Owen's charges were young and inexperienced. Some of Oklahoma's opponents were larger institutions with greater enrollment. Those schools abided by a rule of not allowing first-year players to participate in varsity games. The Sooners were required to abide by the same rule and were at a disadvantage in those games. Still, the '09 Sooners fought through a respectable, but enduring schedule with four road games in 12 days.

Boyd Field is covered with a tarp protecting the field from a major snowstorm. The field was named in honor of Dr. David Ross Boyd, the first university president. It included a grandstand with bleachers to seat 500 people. (*OU Athletics*)

OU defeated Central Normal, 55-0, and Kingfisher College, 46-5, then dropped an 11-0 decision to Kansas. The Sooners rebounded with a 23-2 victory over Northwest Normal School of Alva, then lost to Arkansas, 21-5.

The undefeated Razorbacks retaliated for what they believed were unnecessary injuries their players suffered in Norman a year earlier. Harold Keith, in his book *Oklahoma Kickoff*, wrote that the Arkansas team gave the Sooners a choice of accepting two Arkansas alumni as officials or risk losing the expense money.

The Razorbacks also had rocks piled on the sidelines "and all through the game pegged them indiscriminately at the Sooners," Keith wrote. He added that Oklahoma was forced to make 11 or 12 yards for first downs to Arkansas' eight or nine yards. When the head linesman protested about this unfairness, "he was told to mind his own business."

Two Oklahoma touchdowns were also called back in the game. Owen was not happy about how his squad was treated.

Again the OU gridsters came back with a 42-8 win over Washburn before the grueling road swing that began in St. Louis and ended in Oklahoma City. OU defeated St. Louis University, 12-5, then lost to Texas A&M, 14-8, four days later. Texas walloped the Sooners, 30-0, two days after that in Austin.

Sooner Magic: Preserving a Winning Season

A victory in the final game of the 1909 season against the Epworth Methodists would save a winning season for the 5-4 Sooners. The Epworth contest, on Thanksgiving, came six days on the heels of the Texas loss.

The slightly favored Methodists had pointed to this game all season long and especially since the 24-0 blasting by the Sooners the year before, the only previous meeting between the two teams. A crowd of 4,000 turned out for the game at Oklahoma City's Colcord Park. About 3,000 packed the west side grandstand. Another 1,000 sat in the bleachers at the south end, lined the north fence, or watched from their automobiles.

The Sooners had to rely on a defense that was depleted by an injury to their star defensive center, Key Wolf, who suffered a dislocated shoulder in the Texas game. The Epworth game would have been his last as a Sooner, but he had to watch from the sidelines, arm in a sling. It was the first time in five years he did not start in a game for Oklahoma.

OU struck quickly, scoring a touchdown in the first 1:45 of the game. Fred Capshaw returned an Epworth punt to the Methodists' 24-yard line. On the first play from scrimmage, Capshaw gained five yards off left end. Artie Reeds smashed up the middle for 10 more. Captain Charley Armstrong and Capshaw each picked up four yards to the Epworth one. Reeds plowed over for the TD. Armstrong booted the extra point to give OU a 6-0 advantage.

Epworth scored near the end of the first half on a pass from Bob Martin to Lawrence Yeardley. Delbert Clancy kicked the extra point to tie the game at 6-6.

At halftime, Epworth coach P.S. St. Clair added an incentive bonus to his squad if they won the game. According to the Epworth yearbook, St. Clair "spoke to the team and promised them a hundred dollars to be divided between them if they won, and also promised each player a new hat." There was no rule then that said a player could not receive money or gifts.

OU moved to the Methodists' goal line three times in the second half, but the stout Epworth defense, led by center Dewitt Waller, stalled the Sooners' drives. Waller saved one touchdown by tackling an OU ball carrier short of the goal line.

The Methodists scored following a fumbled punt by the Sooners at the OU 20. On the first play Martin scooted around the end but was pushed back and tackled. As he lay on the ground, he managed to flip the ball to Diggs, who circled round the opposite end and raced to the goal line untouched. Yeardley's kick sailed wide by a foot, but the Methodists held an 11-6 lead with about seven minutes in the game.

OU took the ensuing kickoff and marched to the Epworth 20-yard line. In the huddle, quarterback Jimmy Nairn called for a pass to tackle Willard Douglas. To make this a legitimate play, left end Glenn Clark lined up behind the right end, which left Douglas eligible. Douglas caught Capshaw's pass in the far corner of the field for the TD. Armstrong nailed the extra point, and the Sooners led 12-11 with five minutes to go.

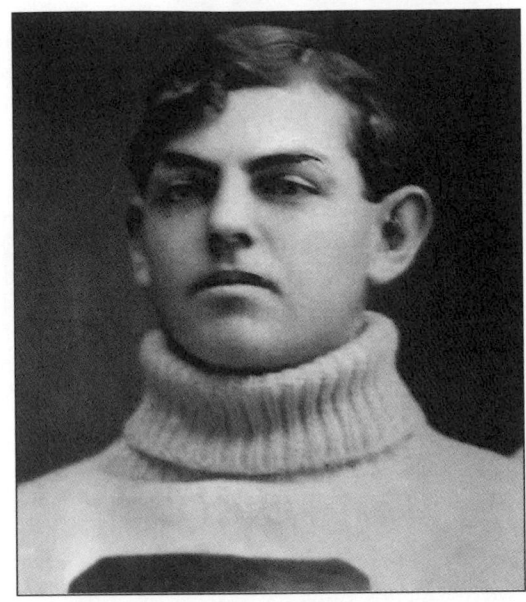

Charley Wantland played halfback for two years at OU and later had a stellar career as head coach at Central Normal (now the University of Central Oklahoma). UCO's stadium was named for him.
(*OU Athletics*)

OU held on to win by the slim margin and finished the season 6-4, the fifth non-losing season in Owen's five-year career. The only non-win season was 1907 when the Sooners finished 4-4.

Although the Sooners were still trying to establish themselves as one of the finest teams in the country, the team gained respect by capping off a strenuous end to the season with a victory.

1909 Season Record: 6-4-0

Date	Opponent	Result	Score
September 24	CENTRAL OKLAHOMA	W	55-0
October 1	KINGFISHER COLLEGE	W	46-5
October 9	at Kansas	L	11-0
October 15	NW NORMAL ALVA	W	23-2
October 30	at Arkansas	L	21-5
November 5	WASHBURN	W	42-8
November 13	at St. Louis	W	12-5
November 17	at Texas A&M	L	14-8
November 19	at Texas	L	30-0
November 25	at Epworth	W	12-11

THE FOUR Bs

Four of the University of Oklahoma's most prominent head coaches have one thing in common—the letter "B"—Bennie, Bud, Barry, and Bob. This is a biographical salute to those four men who have a combined record of 499-98-24 and 32 of the school's 39 conference championships. Three of these men won national championships and the other man built the stepping stones for their success.

Bennie Owen

No one is credited more with laying the foundation for the Oklahoma football program than Bennie Owen. When hearing talk about the Sooner tradition, people mention Bud Wilkinson, Barry Switzer, and Bob Stoops. Many do not speak often of Owen, perhaps because he coached so long ago and most who remember him have passed on. Perhaps it is because Bud, Barry, and Bob are the only coaches in Sooner history to win national championships.

Benjamin Gilbert Owen was born in Chicago on July 24, 1875. He was a fan of baseball, and his family moved to St. Louis when Bennie was 12 years old. After graduating from St. Louis' Clay High School in 1891, he moved with his family to a wheat farm in southern Kansas near Arkansas City. Arthur St. Leger Mosse, the town's iceman, was teaching a new, rugged sport to the town's youth—football. Owen made the town's team as a halfback.

Owen attended Hendershot Academy in Arkansas City and worked as boxing and wrestling instructor at the local Y.M.C.A.

Owen played quarterback at Kansas University while studying pharmacy and Latin. Owen learned from one of the greats in college coaching history while playing for Fielding Yost at Kansas in 1899 and as Yost's assistant at Michigan in 1901. Owen coached the quarterbacks and freshmen and reserves. Yost was famous for the hurry-up offense.

Owen also played quarterback and coached Washburn University of Topeka, Kansas. He coached for three years at Bethany College of Lindsborg, Kansas where he won 22 games, lost two and tied two.

Owen was a coach who had a reputation for clean tactics—no profanity, fouling, kneeing, slugging or dirty play by his players. "Gee, Cly!" was his most common expression. He never shouted, never cussed, nor ever abused a player. Owen's philosophy insisted that men on the first string would have to work to stay there—no loafing, no late shows to practice and no violating orders.

"They would have to report on time, keep training rules and continue to show up better than the second-string men," he said.

This reputation earned Owen respect around the nation as one of the finest coaching

prospects. After turning down an offer to coach at Pittsburgh, Owen became the sixth head coach at the University of Oklahoma. He taught his players the cross buck, a formation that helped him win games at Bethany. The cross buck was accomplished with speed as Owen used smaller and faster players in an age of big, brutal men. He also taught his charges the forward pass, long before Knute Rockne, who was credited with introducing the forward pass years later.

Owen was OU's head coach for 22 years, longer than any other head coach in OU history. He won 122 games, lost 54 and tied 16. In 1907, he was named OU's athletic director, a position he served for 27 years. The Sooners were undefeated in 1911, 1915, 1918, and 1920 under Owen. Three of his Sooner teams won conference championships: Southwest Conference in 1915 and 1918 and the Missouri Valley Conference in 1920. Oklahoma scored over 100 points eight times and 50 or more points 31 times during Owen's tenure.

He never won a national championship, because the eastern United States press rarely recognized any team from the Midwest.

During his tenure, he orchestrated the fund raising and building of a new stadium. The new 30,000-seat stadium was named Memorial Stadium to honor Oklahomans who died in World War I. The stadium still stands today at the northwest corner of Lindsey and Jenkins Streets. The gridiron, where a great tradition has burned for nearly all of the 20th Century, was named for him—Owen Field.

Bennie Owen coached the Sooners for 22 years, the longest tenure for an OU head coach. (© 1922, The Daily Oklahoman)

> **"There is one man who is doing more to teach the right living and right thinking to the youth of Oklahoma than any other one man. He is Bennie Owen."**
>
> —Dr. Stratton D. Brooks,
> OU president (1912-1923)

> **"For more than 20 years, Bennie Owen has stood for good sportsmanship and high ideals. No man identified with athletic activities in this country has contributed more than he has to the wholesomeness of athletic sports."**
>
> —Dr. William Bennett Bizzell,
> OU president (1925-1941)

Bud Wilkinson

Charles Burnham "Bud" Wilkinson was born April 23, 1916, on Easter Sunday in Minneapolis, Minnesota. He was the second son of Charles P. and Edith Wilkinson. Bud grew up in a middle-class neighborhood as his father provided for the family as a mortgage banker. His mother died when he was seven years old, and his father was his mentor.

At 13 years old, Bud and his brother attended Shattuck Military Academy in nearby Fairbault, Minnesota. Bud lettered in four sports (football, baseball, hockey and basketball) his senior year at the academy. He later enrolled at Minnesota University and played football for the Gophers, which won three straight national championships from 1934-1936.

Bud played guard the first two years, but coach Bernie Bierman moved him to quarterback in his senior year. Bud became a two-time All-American and was awarded the Big Ten medal as Minnesota's finest athlete. Following his senior year, Bud quarterbacked the college all-stars to a 7-0 upset over the Green Bay Packers of the professional league.

Wilkinson married Mary Shiflett in 1938 and later had two sons. Bud took a job as an assistant football coach at Syracuse University on a scholarship while earning a master's degree in English. His father wanted him to work in the family's mortgage business, but Bud opted for coaching, where he learned that physical conditioning and discipline were important in his life.

He later became an assistant at Iowa Pre-Flight, a naval service team during World War II. Wilkinson tutored the centers and quarterbacks under head coach Don Faurot. Jim Tatum also was one of Faurot's assistants. Tatum and Wilkinson learned the spilt-T formation under Faurot.

Tatum was hired as OU's head coach in 1946 with the stipulation that Wilkinson come with him as his assistant. University of Oklahoma regents were more impressed with Wilkinson and wanted to offer him the head coaching job, but OU president Dr. George Cross intervened by telling the regents they should honor their "word" and hire Tatum.

Together, Tatum and Wilkinson (the backfield coach) implemented the split-T formation in the Sooner offense. Tatum left the Sooner program after only one year, and Wilkinson was promoted to head coach in 1947 and athletic director in 1948.

Wilkinson devised a new defensive alignment, which dropped two defensive ends off the line of scrimmage to become linebackers. His defense would become known as the "Oklahoma 5-2," and is still used by many teams today.

Wilkinson lured Gomer Jones away from Nebraska as his line coach and assistant head coach. Bud knew Gomer when both served in the navy. Wilkinson's philosophy of discipline and preparation lifted him to success during his 17-year tenure at OU.

"The will to prepare is the key ingredient to success ... so the will to prepare is tantamount, really, to the ability to win," Wilkinson once said.

Wilkinson strolled the sidelines at every game sporting a gray flannel suit, white oxford button-down shirt, a red necktie and fedora. Rarely did he lose his cool during a game.

"He never got rattled or lost his presence of mind," said Frank "Pop" Ivy, Wilkinson's assistant coach from 1948-1954.

While confining OU's recruiting to a 150-mile radius of the Norman campus, Oklahoma's 13th football coach produced teams that were 6-2 in postseason play, won the National Championship in 1950, 1955 and 1956 and did not lose an astounding 74 straight conference games from 1946-1959 (72 wins, two ties). His Sooners still hold the modern record for wins by a Division I-A school with 47 straight victories from 1953-1957, a streak that ended when the Sooners lost to Notre Dame, 7-0. The Sooners won 12 straight conference championships. In 17 seasons at Oklahoma, Wilkinson fostered racial integration and graduated players at an 87.2 percentage rate while becoming the eighth winningest coach in Division I-A history.

The Bud Wilkinson Show, which began airing on television in 1953, was the first coach's show in the nation to be broadcast. Howard Neumann produced and hosted the show, which allowed viewers to hear Wilkinson's strategy. The Sooner skipper used magnets to represent players on a painted gridiron and teach his audience how plays would unfold.

In 1964, he resigned from OU and ran for the U.S. Senate as a Republican, but lost to Fred Harris. Wilkinson served as analyst for NBC's broadcast of college games in 1966 and was hired by ABC when that network won the contract to air college football beginning in 1967. Wilkinson was ABC's college analyst from 1967-1978. After a two-year stint as head coach of the St. Louis Cardinals, Bud returned to the broadcast booth as ESPN's analyst for three more years. He also served as a consultant to President Nixon and was a member of the White House staff from 1969-71. Wilkinson died in 1994 of congestive heart failure at age 77.

"Everybody held Bud in the highest esteem. We called him the 'Great White Father,' because we had so much respect for him. Bud represented everything good about college athletics. He was a disciplinarian ... very

Bud Wilkinson was named head coach in 1947 and served for 17 years. (© 1949, The Daily Oklahoman)

Bud Wilkinson Honors

- 1949: American Football Coaches Association's Coach of the Year
- 1969: Inducted into College Football Hall of Fame
- 1969: Helms & Citizens Athletic Coaches Hall of Fame

organized. Things that he represented were what every parent would like their son to be involved in."

—Leon Cross, offensive guard (1960-1962)
and graduate assistant (1963)

"He seldom if ever used emotional oratory to bring his team to a peak before kickoff or between halves. He always spoke briefly, quietly, and logically, with restrained emotion."

—George Lynn Cross, OU president (1946-1968)

"He was so much ahead of his time. Plus, no one prepared as well as Bud Wilkinson. If it took 20 times to run a play, that's what they did—run the same play. He had the ability to recognize what was happening and to counter it."

—Mike Treps, former OU play-by-play announcer, color analyst and sports information director

"Bud Wilkinson was a special human being. He was a very polished and dignified gentleman. He knew how to deal with people, and he was so organized in everything he did. I had total respect for him. It was a treat to play for him."

—Jakie Sandefer, halfback (1956-1958)

Barry Switzer

Barry Switzer was born on October 5, 1937, in Crossett, Arkansas. He was the son of a bootlegger and grew up in a rickety house with no electricity, no running water, no telephone. An outhouse in the back was the bathroom.

Barry began playing football in the sixth grade. He graduated from Crosset High with honors and was named outstanding lineman in the state of Arkansas his senior year. He played center and linebacker for the University of Arkansas. Before coming to Oklahoma as an offensive line coach in 1966, Switzer was a B team coach and scout for the Razorbacks. In 1967, he was named offensive coordinator for the Sooners.

In 1970, he convinced Chuck Fairbanks, then OU head coach, to make the most significant and gutsy move in OU's football history, a switch to the wishbone offense. The only vehicles for learning this novel offense were films of the 1968-69 OU/Texas games, since Texas was the only school that used the wishbone.

"Watching Texas have a track meet every game," Switzer recalled about why he was inspired by the offensive formation. "We watched it …we knew they had something special, we recognized how talented it was, how tough it was and the philosophy of it. We had to play against it."

Switzer said he would watch the films with the defensive coaches, and he realized the Sooners had just as good or better talent to run the offense.

"We had more speed with Greg Pruitt, Joe Wylie, and Jack Mildren," he said. "We had the talent to do it [and] we just made a decision to go with it."

This offense saved the career of Fairbanks and his seven assistants and made possible Oklahoma's second football dynasty. When Switzer was appointed OU's head coach in 1973, he continued to deploy the wishbone. This offensive weapon, plus a stout defense and kicking game, helped Switzer become Oklahoma's all-time winningest coach. He won nearly 84 percent of his games with a 157-

29-4 record. He also is rated as the fourth all-time winningest coach in college football history in winning percentage.

During his 16-year tenure, the Sooners won three national championships, 12 Big Eight Conference championships, and eight bowl wins in 13 appearances. Switzer led the Sooners on a 28-game win streak from 1973 (his first season as head coach) to 1975. When the Sooners won the national championship in 1975, it marked the first time in history a team had won back-to-back titles more than once.

Switzer resigned as Sooner coach in June of 1989, saying that, "coaching was no longer fun."

He stayed out of coaching, despite many offers, until Jerry Jones, the owner of the Dallas Cowboys, offered him the head coaching position in April of 1994. During the 1994 season, Switzer led the Cowboys to a 13-5 record and the NFC championship game. In 1995, he led Dallas to a Super Bowl win over Pittsburgh. He coached the Cowboys through the 1997 season.

Switzer currently lives in Norman with his wife, Becky.

Q&A With Barry Switzer

Q: Would it be an understatement to say you had fun coaching?

BS: Yeah. I enjoyed it, it was a great run. I was fortunate we won enough to make it enjoyable. But the key thing was it wasn't the championships or the wins. It was the relationships with the players; that's what coaching is about.

Q: Oklahoma was a great running team and we won some games with the pass. Did opponents underestimate OU?

BS: No, I think what happens is our playbook is to run the ball and we were a great rushing team, but when we did throw the ball, we had to throw it to make a play because our running game was so good. We were good enough on defense to know we're going to be in the ball game. OU's offense controlled the football. It was our philosophy to win that way. We were a percentage-consistent offense—control the ball, control the clock, rush for over 400 yards on average and control the ball 32 minutes of the game. Make the opponent's offense sit on the sideline, and we're going to keep the ball. That was our goal and we accomplished it many times.

Q: What did you enjoy most about recruiting?

BS: I had a great product to sell. Oklahoma was a great product to sell. It opened doors and they listened to what I was telling them was true, and they had seen it. We told them we were on national TV, winning championships, competing for national championships and we were going to the Orange Bowl; we were the team to beat. I enjoyed that and Bud Wilkinson made it easy because he created the monster, and our job was to feed it. And what I accomplished helped (Bob) Stoops with his job. The kids Stoops recruits today…their grandparents grew up with Bud and me. They knew what that tradition was. They talked to their kids and their grandkids about this tradition.

Q: Please comment about our closest rivals—Oklahoma State, Texas and Nebraska.

BS (about Oklahoma State): They always wanted it more than we did. They were more ready to play than we were and the reason why—they wanted to win for all the right reasons. I told our players that you had an opportunity to go to both schools and you chose Oklahoma. And most of those guys over there we didn't want, we didn't recruit, we didn't ask to come and be a part of this program

---

Barry Switzer Honors
- 1974: Walter Camp Foundation Coach of the Year
- 2001: Inducted into College Football Hall of Fame

and its tradition. I had to educate my team of that fact. It's a psychologically motivating factor to those guys. They (OSU) wanted it more, they had more to prove. With my players, Nebraska and Texas was where they proved their value. They didn't have to prove their value against Oklahoma State in my era.

BS (on Texas and Nebraska): We knew that was what proved our worth. That's what we built our tradition on—beating Texas and Nebraska. That proved our mettle. If we're good enough to beat those guys, then we're good enough to play anybody for the national championship.

Q: Who was the most underrated player during your head coaching career?

BS: Steve Bryan. He was a three-year starter, and he gave it his all down after down. He studied films on Sundays (the day after the game). Grade the players, grading against the competition, looked at the plays he made. Get to the ball, getting off blocks, chasing the ball. When you talk about a guy who didn't make All-Conference, didn't make All-American, didn't make any honors. Stevie Bryan to me was great football player, but no one knew that he was. He was an undersized, underappreciated guy who played every snap and played underneath everybody's pads. Get off the blocks, go make plays, just get to the ball. He was a special player. A very intelligent and sound football player.

Q: Does any one game stand out above the rest?

BS: 1978 in Lincoln, Nebraska. We were number one in the country, we were ranked number one all year, 9-0. We were leading every category in the nation offensively and defensively. We led the nation in rushing and Billy [Sims] was the leading individual rush-

er and he went on to win the Heisman. We were a great football team that year, but we fumbled nine times that day and lost six of them and only lost 17-14. That tells you how good you are.

Billy made a great run to the 3-yard line. We were going to win the game, we were going to be first and goal, but he fumbled the ball and that was the last fumble of the day and we lost the game. But that game cost us the national championship. The Orange Bowl had to take the highest ranked team, and we were the highest ranked team available. And we beat Nebraska, and that game wasn't even as close as the score indicated. We were ahead 31-10 after three quarters.

Q: Does any one play stand out above the rest?

BS: 1975, Missouri in Columbia. It's fourth and two and Joe [Washington] went 71 yards to win the game, then scored the two-point play. Those two plays helped us win the national championship. That's Sooner Magic…that's a great player making a great play in a tight ball game to make a difference.

Q: What do you want people to remember most when they think of Barry Switzer?

BS: My relationship with my players. I cared about my players; I was a team guy and always was for the players. And they respected me. That's what coach-player relationships mature to…friendships that expand a lifetime. When you recruit a player, you have him for life. You spend 365 days a year, 24/7 for four or five years, you get to know someone…their passion, you get to know their goals. It's relationship-based. We're trying to develop young men for the next 30, 40, 50, 60 years of living. That's our job, that's our goal, and yes, win football games along the way, but we're developing a quality product the rest of their lives.

"Barry was a players' coach. He was fun to play for. He had a lot of good assistants and he delegated authority, but he also really knew his Xs and Os."

—Uwe von Schamann, placekicker, 1976-1978

"He was such a great coach in evaluating talent. He's a great motivator in tapping that talent at just the right time. One thing that we never wanted to do was to look on the sideline … and disappoint the head man."

—Brian Bosworth, linebacker, 1094-1986*

"Barry had an open-door policy with his players. He was accessible to his players at all times and that earned their [players'] respect. He was, without a doubt, a players' coach."

—Mike Treps, former OU play-by-play announcer, color analyst and sports information director

"Of all the schools I visited, only one talked about family, and that was Oklahoma. Coach Switzer stayed in my corner and believed in me."

—Billy Sims, running back, 1975-1979*

Oklahoma Football Legends Reunion

The Sooners won three national championships during Barry Switzer's 16-year tenure. (© 1986, The Daily Oklahoman)

Bob Stoops

The Oklahoma football program had plummeted to mediocrity after Barry Switzer resigned. Gary Gibbs, a Switzer assistant, succeeded his former boss. During the next six years he led the Sooners to a respectable 44-23-2 record, but no conference championships. Gibbs only defeated Texas once (1983), Nebraska once

(1990), and never beat Colorado in his half-dozen years at the helm. His mediocre record forced him out in 1994.

Howard Schnellenberger succeeded him and could not back his claims of movie scripts and a national championship in his rookie year as coach. Schnellenberger was known for taking mediocre football programs to national prominence. He did it at the universities of Miami and Louisville. But he couldn't do it at Oklahoma. After leading the Sooners to a 5-5-1 record, he was fired and replaced by another Sooner football alum—John Blake. On the field, the team spiraled into darkness in his three years as head coach, winning only 12 of 34 games.

Blake was fired following the 1997, season and Joe Castiglione, hired as athletic director in April 1998, searched for a new wizard to return the Sooner football program to national prominence. In December 1998, he hired Bob Stoops, who at the time was defensive coordinator at Florida.

Upon his hiring, Stoops said no excuses would be allowed, and under his tenure he expected the Sooners to have a chance to win many games, if not all of them.

"We'll operate with no excuses," he said the day of his hiring. "There are no excuses; you succeed or you don't."

He brought in a new system—a spread offense that was dominated by the pass, not the run as Sooner fans were accustomed for more than a quarter-century. The Sooners in Stoops' first year went 7-5, an improvement that had the Crimson-clad faithful excited once again.

Stoops led the Sooners to the school's 37th conference championship (Big XII) and seventh national championship with a 13-0 record the next year. His 2001 squad went 11-2, including a win in the Cotton Bowl. Stoops guided the Sooners to another conference crown in 2002 and a Rose Bowl victory, the first appearance by an Oklahoma football team in Pasadena, California. The 2003 team went undefeated during the regular season (12-0) and lost the final two games—the Big XII championship game and the national championship game in the Sugar Bowl. The Sooners went undefeated again in 2004, won another conference crown, but stumbled against Southern California for the national championship in the Orange Bowl. His seven-year record is 79-16 as the Sooner skipper.

Bob Stoops was born on September 9, 1960, in Youngstown, Ohio. He played football at Cardinal Mooney High School, graduating in 1978.

Bob started at defensive back for four years (1979-1982) for the Iowa Hawkeyes under head coach Hayden Fry and was known as a punishing hitter on the field. Stoops made the All-Big 10 team his freshman and senior year and named honorable All-America and the Hawkeyes' most valuable player in 1982. Stoops' career total included 205 tackles and 10 interceptions.

After graduating at Iowa with a B.A. in marketing, Stoops joined Fry's staff as a graduate assistant from 1983-1984 and as a volunteer coach from 1985-1987. In 1988, Stoops was hired as defensive backs coach under Bill Snyder at Kansas State. Stoops was promoted to defensive coordinator at KSU, serving in the position for four years. He assisted KSU to its first 10-win season with a defense that allowed seven or fewer points in six games, including three shutouts.

Bob Stoops became OU's head coach in 1999.
(© 2004, The Daily Oklahoman)

In 1995, the Wildcats led the nation in total defense (250.8 yards per game) and four defensive backs were named All-Big Eight.

In 1996 he was hired by Steve Spurrier as defensive coordinator at Florida. The Gators' defense scored a school-record six touchdowns during a national championship year.

Stoops is the first OU head coach to lead his first five squads to bowl berths. His 43 victories in the first four seasons is more than any other Division I-A coach since 1900.

Stoops and his wife, Carol, have three children—daughter MacKenzie and twin sons Isaac and Drake.

"You go full speed and you can't hold anything back. And we know Coach isn't going to hold anything back. It works hand in hand."

—Kory Klein, defensive lineman, 2000-2003.

"We have the greatest coach in football. We know going into games that we have that advantage."

—Brandon Everage, defensive back, 2000-2003.

Bob Stoops Honors
- 2000: American Football Coaches Association's Coach of the Year
- 2000: FWAA/Eddie Robinson Coach of the Year
- 2003: Bobby Dodd Coach of the Year
- 2003: Walter Camp Foundation Coach of the Year

1910 - 1919

1910

More changes to the rules of American football were in order prior to the 1910 season. The game was divided into four 15-minute quarters, seven players were required to line up on the line of scrimmage, forward passes were limited to 20 yards, and the ball had to travel at least 20 yards on onside kicks. Pushing and pulling a ball carrier was also outlawed.

One new rule highly embraced by coach Bennie Owen was the direct pass. The ball could now be snapped to the ball carrier. This replaced the quarterback having to take the snap and feeding it to the ball carrier. The ball carrier could also penetrate the defense anywhere along the line of scrimmage. Owen saw this as an opportunity to add variety and deception to his running game.

The year began with a sad note as Porter English, who started at guard the prior two seasons, died from complications during an appendectomy. Owen and some of his players accompanied English's body to his hometown of Galena, Oklahoma, 175 miles northwest of Norman.

The NCAA also allowed spring practices for the first time. This extra time helped Owen to devise his new offensive game plan. Since his linemen were lighter than in the past, he devised a short, diagonal line of backs forming an acute angle with a balanced line. The quarterback was shifted to one yard behind the right end and became the primary blocker and was another receiver in the passing scheme. The backs were aligned where they could touch each other at arm's length. The right halfback was positioned two yards behind the line of scrimmage, the left halfback three yards behind the line, and the fullback three yards behind the line.

The left halfback's responsibility was to run off tackle or around the end. The right halfback's assignment blocked or reversed over the middle after retreating a step and taking a lateral with the left halfback leading. The fullback's task was bucking up the middle.

Although Glenn "Pop" Warner, who coached at Carlisle, Pittsburgh, and Stanford, was credited with inventing the direct pass in 1919, Owen's players contended he was the creator.

Bennie Owen was allowed to hire an assistant coach. Harry Hughes, who was his halfback for two years, was the choice. Hughes served only one year as Owen's deputy before moving on to coach Colorado Agricultural College for 31 years.

In addition to the loss of English, linemen Key Wolf and Willard Douglas used up their eligibility. Among the new players in 1910 were quarterback Herbert Armbrister, guard Roger Berry, center Ed McReynolds, and fullback Claude Reeds, the fourth of the Norman Reeds family to play at OU.

The 20-year-old Reeds stood six feet tall and weighed 168 pounds. He had attended the University of Oklahoma's prep school. Reeds

Fred Capshaw kicked the winning field goal in the third quarter to give OU a 3-0 win over Texas. *(Western History Collections, University of Oklahoma)*

played fullback in every game except against Kansas and Missouri. Both schools were members of the Missouri Valley Conference, which prohibited freshmen to play.

Among the returnees were Charley Armstrong, Cleve Thompson, Fred Capshaw, Earle Radcliffe, and Jimmy Nairn. Nairn was switched from quarterback to tackle when he showed up at 175 pounds, 15 pounds heavier than the year before.

The Sooners pitched three shutouts to begin the 1910 campaign—66-0 over Kingfisher College, 79-0 over Central Normal and 12-0 over Oklahoma A&M. OU fumbled seven times in the Aggie game. Sooner tackle Harry Price blocked an Aggie punt and recovered it in the end zone for the first touchdown. Radcliffe scored the second TD off an onside kick.

Fairmont College cancelled a game in Norman three days prior to the contest, which allowed extra rest and practice for Kansas. The Jayhawks won, 2-0, before 2,000 fans at Oklahoma City's Colcord Park. OU's Mort Woods intercepted a KU pass on the goal line but was tackled behind the line for a safety. The Kansas game marked the 100th game in Oklahoma football history.

The 3-2 Sooners were headed to Austin for a Thanksgiving showdown against the Longhorns.

Sooner Magic: Ricocheted Field Goal

Fans were treated to a defensive battle and a punting duel between UT's Arnold Kirkpatrick and Reeds. Kirkpatrick wowed the orange faithful with a 75-yarder, which was aided by a roll. Reeds did better by kicking the entire length of the 110-yard field.

The 4-1 Horns opened the game with a fierce drive to the OU one-yard line, but the Sooner defense held its ground and yielded no points. Texas had deceptive plays of its own, such as the double pass.

After the Texas defense held Oklahoma, Reeds shanked a punt four yards out of bounds. Again the OU defense held the Horns on downs.

In the second quarter, Reeds punted. As the ball descended toward Armstrong, Sabe Hott was streaking toward the Texas player. As soon as Kirpatrick hauled in the punt, Hott popped him, jarring the ball loose. Armbrister snatched the ball off the turf and raced to the goal line.

The play was nullified when officials penalized Hott for hitting Armstrong an instant before he caught the ball.

Shortly before halftime, Hott had retrieved Capshaw's onside kick and dashed to the goal line. Officials flagged the play because the ball had not traveled the necessary 20 yards. Officials penalized the Sooners again on another punt coverage. The half ended in a scoreless tie.

The officials did not have to whistle Jimmy Rogers' clean hit on punt coverage in the third quarter. Rogers smacked Texas safety Joe Russell and recovered the loose pigskin for the Sooners.

Texas held on downs, but Capshaw nailed a 37-yard field goal for a 3-0 lead. Field goals were reduced to three points in 1910.

Texas swiftly moved to the Oklahoma 10-yard line. The Sooners held the Horns inches short of the goal line. The Horns asked for a measurement and were credited with a first down six inches from the goal line. Charley Orr, a substitute quarterback for OU, was working the first-down chains and explained that since the ball was exactly at the ten-yard stripe, Texas had first and goal.

"I thought we held them for downs," he said. "They asked for a measurement. It showed they made a first down. I squawked to the referee that either the field was laid out wrong or the Texas boy on the front end of the chain had wound up part of his end on the stick, but Bennie came running out from our bench and kicked me on the shins."

Owen scolded him. "You keep still! Let the referee run the game."

"He was a good sport if there ever was one," Orr said about his coach.

The Sooner defense became more determined to keep the Texas players from making that one-half foot. Bob Wood tossed the Texas ball carrier for a slight loss. On the next play, Capshaw blasted through and slapped the ball from Kirkpatrick's hands. OU recovered at the one-yard line.

The Longhorns held, and Reeds was called to punt out of his end zone. With a slight wind behind his back, Reeds lifted the ball off his foot, and it descended to the turf 75 yards from the line of scrimmage. With Kirkpatrick in pursuit, the ball continued to roll toward the Texas goal line. It stopped at the UT two-yard line.

Overall, the punt had traveled about 113 yards from Reeds' foot. Kirkpatrick scooped it up and returned it to the Texas 30, dodging Oklahoma tacklers along the way.

Both defenses held their opponents through most of the second half, but the Horns had one last opportunity to win or tie the contest.

On the last play of the game, Kirkpatrick's field goal attempt hit the left crossbar and ricocheted onto the playing field.

Oklahoma escaped with a 3-0 victory, only its third in the 13-game series. Throngs of students met the players who departed the train the following afternoon in Norman.

The season was to have ended after the Texas game, but Epworth University pressed for a game to be played in Oklahoma City with an offer of $800. Owen left the decision to a vote of his players. Owen reminded his charges that it had been a long season, and if they were tired of football, "Say so and we'll turn it down."

He also reminded them that $800 would buy new equipment, which was needed. Most players wore tattered shirts that had been stitched up. The freshmen and reserves wore what varsity players tossed away.

The players loved to play football and approved another game.

1910 Season Record: 4-2-1

Date	Opponent	Result	Score
October 7	at Kingfisher College	W	66-0
October 17	CENTRAL NORMAL	W	79-0
October 21	OKLAHOMA A&M	W	12-0
October 28	Missouri*	L	26-0
November 12	Kansas#	L	2-0
November 24	at Texas	W	3-0
December 3	at Epworth	T	3-3

*Game played in Joplin, MO
#Game played in Oklahoma City, OK

The following week, OU tied the Methodists 3-3 at Colcord Park. Capshaw's 37-yard field goal in the fourth quarter tied the game.

The Sooners finished 1910 with a 4-2-1 record.

1911

For the first time, in a season of more than two games, the 1911 Oklahoma Sooners went undefeated, including three wins on the road against its mightiest opponents. Right halfback Fred Capshaw returned for his final season and made an impact in all three victories against Missouri, Kansas, and Texas.

Fullback Claude Reeds and quarterback Hubert Armbrister returned. Ray Courtright replaced the graduated Earle Radcliffe at left halfback. Jimmy Nairn and Sabe Hott returned to anchor the line, which was described as light but fast and aggressive. Bill Moss, Glenn Clark, Roger Berry, and Ed Meachem joined them. End Jimmy Rogers and center Cleve Thompson had graduated, the latter becoming coach Bennie Owen's assistant while doubling as Norman High's football coach.

Charley Wantland, Owen's halfback in 1907-08, also served as an assistant coach.

Owen created more deceptive plays for his swift backs to employ. The team would line up to one side of the field then run to the other side. Trickery also included one halfback taking the snap, run nine one way then handing off to the other halfback running in the opposite direction.

This helped the Sooners outscore their first four opponents, 225-0. They blasted Kingfisher College, 105-0, at Boyd Field in the season opener. The next week, OU defeated Oklahoma Christian of Enid, coached by former Sooner Earle Radcliffe, 62-0, in Norman. The game originally was scheduled for Friday, October 13, but Friday the 13th lived up to its billing when a train wreck delayed the Oklahoma Christian players until 10 p.m. About 1,000 Sooner fans were disappointed in the "no show" but returned to Boyd Field the next day.

The Sooners defeated Oklahoma A&M, 22-0, in Stillwater. The Aggies had a chance to score its first ever touchdown against OU in the second quarter when an A&M player picked up a Sooner fumble and sprinted 55 yards to the goal line. Reeds, who started out four yards behind the Aggie, caught him from behind at the OU four-yard line. The Big Red defense held off the Aggie threat.

A week later, the Sooners beat Washburn, 37-0, in Norman. October moved into November and the meat of the schedule with Missouri, Kansas, and Texas looming on the horizon.

The 1911 game against Missouri was described by Harold Keith in *Oklahoma Kickoff* as lifting the Sooners out of obscurity. "It was Oklahoma's Declaration of Independence," he wrote.

Early in the game at Columbia, Fred Capshaw scored on a 30-yard run and kicked the extra point for a 6-0 Oklahoma lead. Three minutes later he nailed a 30-yard field goal, but the field judge declared the kick no good, yet the referee and umpire disagreed. The three points stood, and Oklahoma led, 9-0.

Following a Tiger fumble, the Sooners moved to another score. OU lined up on the left side, then ran right with Ray Courtright sprinting 35 yards for the touchdown. The play left Missouri defenders tasting the turf in pursuit.

Oklahoma prevailed, 14-6, the first victory in three encounters with the Tigers. A multitude of students and Sooner fans had gathered outside Barbour's Drug Store to listen to a description of the game by telegraph received by a telegraph operator attained from

Fred Capshaw's first-quarter field goal sails through the uprights as the Sooners defeat Kansas for the first time, 3-0.
(Western History Collections, University of Oklahoma)

had their first win against the Jayhawks. The Norman crowd heard the game at Barbour's Drug Store.

The fans in Oklahoma City and Norman experienced a "Blue Norther," which swooped down from Kansas. To this day, the record high and low in the Oklahoma City area for November 11 was set on that day in 1911. The high of 83 degrees was reached at noon and the temperature plummeted to 17 degrees by midnight. Nevertheless, the victory warmed the Sooners' hearts.

A formal celebration was organized for Monday as students petitioned OU's acting president, Julien Monnet, to arrange a holiday. Monnet was elected by the regents to replace Grant Evans, who was not given a contract renewal by new Governor Lee Cruce.

The following week, OU defeated Alva Normal 34-6 in Norman. Courtright scored two touchdowns, and Reeds added another. Alva scored late on a fumble return.

Coach Owen arranged for his squad to arrive in Austin a few days before the Texas matchup to keep his charges from being fatigued.

Clark Field was packed with 4,000 fans. Texas marched to the Sooner goal, but the Oklahoma defense held and pushed the Horns 10 yards back. Arnold Kirkpatrick nailed a 27-yard field goal, and the Sooners trailed for the first time all year, 3-0.

OU began a drive from its own 15. A few plays later, Courtright tossed a pass to Clark, who raced 43 yards, but was tackled short of the Texas goal line. The Longhorn defense dug in, and Capshaw's field goal attempt sailed wide.

Following a Texas punt, the Sooners drove from their 40, culminated by Capshaw's five-yard TD run. He also booted the extra point for a 6-3 Oklahoma lead. Texas had a touchdown called back because a pass had gone past the 20-yard limit.

OU finished the season 8-0, and the Sooner football dynasty was just beginning.

1912

Prior to the 1912 campaign, touchdowns were increased to six points, the forward pass 20-yard limitation was nullified, and the field's length was reduced to 100 yards, with 10 additional yards at each end of the gridiron. This would be known as the "end zones."

In the spring, Bennie Owen married Nina Bessent, daughter of a Norman bank president. The two built a home on Elm Street but lived with her parents until it was finished.

Expectations were high for the 1912 season, especially with the return of all but three players from the year before. Fred Capshaw and Jimmy Nairn graduated, and Bill Moss did not attend school that year. Some new players were Capshaw's brother, Elmer, and Glenn Clark's brother, Bill.

Owen had to teach his players the skills of throwing and catching the longer passes. Players still wore very little equipment, because Owen thought it would impede their speed. They wore red cotton sweaters and stockings and reed ribs in their pants. Sabe Hott was the only player to wear a helmet because butting heads was causing headaches.

OU played three home games in 1912, hosting Central Normal, Missouri, and Oklahoma A&M. Three games were played on the enemy's turf—Kingfisher College, Kansas, and Nebraska. Three were played on neutral fields—Texas at Dallas, Texas A&M at Houston and Colorado at Denver.

The Sooners pitched two shutouts to begin the season—40-0 over Kingfisher College and 87-0 over Central Normal, coached by Charley Wantland, former Sooner player and assistant coach. Wantland would have a long, illustrious career in Edmond. The

Oklahoma City. A diagram of a football field was placed outside the second-story window over the store to show position of the ball.

Owen decided to keep his team in Columbia to save expenses and exhaustion from two consecutive train excursions. He took his charges on a 10-mile hike in the country to work out the stiffness from the game. They practiced on the fairway of a golf course and twice scrimmaged the Tigers during the week. The players also took along their books to maintain their studies. Six of his players attended classes at Missouri University.

The Sooners traveled to Kansas City and bunked in a hotel for the night before the short journey to Lawrence. About 3,000 fans turned out at McCook Field to cheer on the undefeated Jayhawks. In the first two minutes, Capshaw kicked a field goal to give Oklahoma the lead and eventual victory as no more points were tallied in the game.

The day grew colder and windier with sleet pelting the players. Before the game was over, the temperature had dropped to zero degrees with heavy snow falling.

Back in Oklahoma City, a crowd gathered outside the *Daily Oklahoman* building and listened to the game. The *Daily Oklahoman* received direct wire from Lawrence and the plays were barked by megaphone to the fans below on 4th Street. Celebration ensued on the streets of Oklahoma City and Norman as the Sooners

1911 Season Record: 8-0-0			
Date	**Opponent**	**Result**	**Score**
October 6	KINGFISHER COLLEGE	W	104-0
October 14	OKLAHOMA CHRISTIAN	W	62-0
October 20	at Oklahoma A&M	W	22-0
October 27	WASHBURN	W	37-0
November 4	at Missouri	W	14-0
November 11	at Kansas	W	3-0
November 20	ALVA NORMAL	W	34-6
November 30	at Texas	W	6-3

Edmond stadium is named in his honor. The OU-Normal game was called with seven minutes remaining so the Normal players could catch the train back to Edmond.

The game against Texas was played again in Dallas as an attraction for the Texas State Fair. The Sooners went 3-0 with a 21-6 victory over the Longhorns, the third straight win over the Steers. Hubert Armbrister scored two touchdowns, and Claude Reeds added another before 6,000 rabid fans at Gaston Field.

Ray Courtright, OU's starting halfback, safety and kicker, received a bruise to a boil on his right arm down to his fingers. The injury caused blood poisoning, so he wasn't even able to don a uniform and was told to rest in bed.

The injury kept Courtright sidelined against Missouri the following week, a 14-0 loss to the Tigers at Boyd Field. It was Missouri's first trip to Norman. Reeds left the first quarter with a hip injury, and OU lost some punch in its offense with two starting backs out of the game. He was allowed to watch the game from a wheelchair on the sideline. He was still listed as doubtful for the trip to Lawrence, Kansas, one week later.

The 1911 victory over Kansas was won on Fred Capshaw's field goal, but Capshaw had graduated, and Courtright earned the duty for 1912, although he never had any previous kicking experience.

Prior to the KU game, the swelling on Courtright's arm had subsided and he was available to suit up against the Jayhawks.

Sooner Magic:
Lame Kicker's Field Goals Boot Jayhawks

A soggy and slippery field held both offenses in check with neither team scoring in the first quarter. In the second stanza, KU punted to Courtright who fumbled, and the Hawks recovered at the OU 12-yard line. The Sooners' defense held their ground, and Bill Weidline booted a 15-yard field goal to give KU a 3-0 advantage.

Kansas threatened again by moving to the OU 10, but the Jayhawks fumbled, and the Sooners recovered. The rest of the quarter was a punting duel, and KU held the slim margin at halftime.

Fred Capshaw scores the winning touchdown on a five-yard run against Texas. He also kicked the conversion in OU's 6-3 triumph. *(Western History Collections, University of Oklahoma)*

Both defenses held off offensive charges through the third period. KU was pinned at its own five-yard line, and following a 25-yard punt, the Sooners drove to the Jayhawks' seven but were held for downs.

On the first play of the fourth quarter, Courtright dropped back to the 15-yard line and nailed a field goal to tie the game at 3-3.

Later in the quarter, the Jayhawks blocked a punt that sent the pigskin rolling behind the Sooner goal. Armbrister recovered the ball, but was downed behind the goal giving Kansas a safety and a 5-3 lead.

With the Jayhawks pinned deep in their own territory, center Charles Milton hiked the ball over H.E. Burnham's head in punt formation. Burnham recovered, but OU was given possession. KU's defense held, and Courtright booted a 30-yard field goal to give the Sooners a 6-5 advantage.

After Courtright missed another 30-yard attempt, KU took possession and drove to the Sooner 25-yard line as the game was coming to a close. Weidline attempted a field goal from there, but the ball sailed wide as the whistle blew to end the game.

After the 6-5 victory over Kansas, the Sooners lost 28-6 to Texas A&M, but rebounded with a 16-0 victory over Oklahoma A&M. OU ended the season at 5-4 with a pair of losses to Nebraska (13-9) in Lincoln and Colorado (14-12) in Denver.

The Colorado loss was controversial. The Sooners held a 12-0 lead on a touchdown in each of the first two quarters. In the third period, a Buffalo punt struck the goal post cross bar and bounced back onto the field. A Colorado player grabbed the ball and scored a touchdown. The referee ruled that Courtright had touched the ball before it hit the cross bar. Owen protested, and Colorado coaches admitted that the play was unfair, but the referee did not change his mind, and the score stood. The Buffs scored again in the fourth stanza to win the game.

Although the team suffered a dismal season on the field, its finances were $62.97 in the plus column. Gate receipts for football reached $6,945—more than double the year before. Football at Oklahoma was becoming a popular spectator sport. Winning will do that for a team.

1912 Season Record: 5-4-0

Date	Opponent	Result	Score
September 27	KINGFISHER COLLEGE	W	40-0
October 11	CENTRAL NORMAL	W	87-0
October 19	Texas at Dallas	W	21-6
October 25	MISSOURI	L	14-0
November 2	at Kansas	W	6-5
November 11	Texas A&M*	L	28-6
November 16	OKLAHOMA A&M	W	16-0
November 23	at Nebraska	L	13-9
November 28	Colorado#	L	14-12

*Game played in Houston, TX
#Game played in Denver, CO

1913

Tackle Sabe Hott lost an eye in the summer of 1913 when a spike nail he was hammering ricocheted. His parents were against him playing football that fall, but his love for the game could not keep him away. When he suited up, he would wrap his glass eye and place it on top of the locker. He covered the socket with a cotton bandage and wrapped gauze around his head to secure it.

He only played against Missouri, Kansas, and Texas, as his family was pressuring him not to continue as he might injure the other eye. His two brothers joined the varsity that year after a season as freshman substitutes. Oliver and Willis were rough competitors, and head coach Bennie Owen welcomed them, as he needed more linemen. The three brothers would be known as "The Terrible Hotts."

Also joining the team was Homer Montgomery, a transfer from Texas A&M. When the Sooners played the Aggies a year earlier, Montgomery liked OU's style of play. Following the 1912 game, he asked his coach for permission to meet Owen. From their meeting, Owen discovered Montgomery was from Muskogee. He asked the lad why he was playing at a Texas school when Oklahoma had fine schools. Montgomery enrolled at OU in 1913.

Neil Johnson replaced Hubert Armbrister at quarterback. Forest "Spot" Geyer, a passer with a strong arm, also joined the team. Chuck Rogers and Tom Lowery, a speedster on the track relay team, replaced the graduated Glenn Clark and Dortis Holland at ends. Elmer "Trim" Capshaw also returned. Owen had experimented Claude Reeds at end, but figured he was more valuable at fullback and switched him back.

Oklahoma thrashed its first three in-state opponents, 258-0. They downed Kingfisher College, 74-0, Central Normal, 83-0, and Northwestern of Alva (formerly Alva Normal), 101-0.

The Sooners were stunned when they arrived in Columbia, Missouri, to play the Tigers. Missouri officials declined to allow Reeds and Armbrister to play, claiming both had used up their eligibility in Missouri Valley Conference games, when in fact they had not. Either the Sooners played the game or they would lose their guarantee money. Owen deferred his decision to a vote of his players, who chose to play the game. Geyer replaced Reeds at fullback.

Missouri scored the first touchdown, then Geyer delivered a 40-yard field goal. Capshaw then scored following Geyer's 35-yard punt return. Ray Courtright booted the extra point and OU led, 10-6.

The Tigers added a couple of second-half TDs to claim a 20-10 lead. OU answered with a Geyer touchdown pass to Lowery. Geyer's conversion pulled the Sooners within three, 20-17. Oklahoma marched to the MU 16-yard line when time expired.

The Sooners had two weeks before their next contest against Kansas in Norman. Owen went to Lawrence to scout the Jayhawks who were playing Kansas A&M. The Hawks were using the Minnesota Shift, a potent running attack. Owen used the extra practice time to work on defending the Kansas running game. He boxed his defense with seven linemen and moved his linebackers closer to the line of scrimmage.

Although it was a Missouri Valley Conference game, Reeds was allowed to play against the Hawks. He scored two touchdowns in the first half on runs of 28 and 10 yards, and the Sooners led 14-0 at intermission.

Kansas scored early in the third quarter, but Capshaw soon after scored on a 46-yard TD run. Oklahoma won, 21-7, using no substitutes in the game.

Texas won the following week, 14-6, in the first and only contest held in Houston. The Horns led 14-0 at the half. A fourth-quarter pass from Courtright to Jess Fields was the only score for Oklahoma. Reeds, however, had a great day punting 10 times and averaging 49.1 yards per kick.

Reeds scored the only touchdown in OU's 7-0 win over Oklahoma A&M the next week on a muddy Stillwater field.

The last game of the season against Colorado on Thanksgiving was also played on a soggy field at Oklahoma City's fairgrounds. Two days of rain preceded a clear game day, but the field was so muddy both offenses could barely manage a drive. Reeds was the only player untamed by the boggy turf.

The Sooners had set up to punt, but instead of kicking the ball, Reeds took off to the right with it tucked under his arm. He zigzagged the field, dodging Colorado players and throwing stiff-arms as he headed toward the Colorado end zone. It appeared he run a total of 200 yards to attain the 70-yard touchdown. Courtright added a five-yard TD and kicked both extra points in the 14-0 victory over CU.

Outing magazine named its honor roll of football players following the '13 season. Reeds was named one of six best fullbacks that year.

The Sooners finished the year with a 6-2 mark.

1914

The forward pass was rapidly becoming a new offensive weapon for the Sooners in 1914 and going virtually unnoticed by the press in the Eastern United States. Walter Camp, the greatest sports writer of that day, wrote his review of the 1914 season *Spalding's Football Guide* stating that combining the forward pass with running, "no team has succeeded in combining both with proper skill."

Had Camp paid more attention to football outside of the east, he might have learned a thing or two—like the Oklahoma Sooners had hurled the pigskin the distance of one mile and scored 25 touchdowns, according to Harold Keith in *Oklahoma Kickoff*.

Bennie Owen's 1914 team was light, averaging about 145 pounds. Forest "Spot" Geyer was the biggest, who stood 6 foot, 2 inches and weighed 165 pounds. He earned the nickname by his teammates because he could complete a pass to one or two spots behind the defensive safety. He could throw while running toward either sideline and was adept at eluding defenders.

He also had good receivers with good hands to catch his aerials. Homer Montgomery and Montford "Hap" Johnson, Neil's brother, among them. The Sooners had three sets of brothers on the squad that year—the Johnsons, Billie and John Clark, and Oliver and Willis Hott. Guard Curry Bell and halfback Elmer "Trim" Capshaw also returned.

Owen's plan to open up the offense was evident from the start. In a 67-0 defeat of Central Normal, the Sooners totaled 300 yards and scored five of their 10 touchdowns through the air at Oklahoma City's Fair Park.

1913 Season Record: 6-2-0

Date	Opponent	Result	Score
September 26	KINGFISHER COLLEGE	W	74-0
October 3	CENTRAL NORMAL	W	101-0
October 10	NORTHWESTERN-ALVA	W	21-6
October 18	at Missouri	L	20-17
October 31	KANSAS	W	21-7
November 10	Texas*	L	14-6
November 21	at Oklahoma A&M	W	7-0
November 27	COLORADO#	W	14-6

*Game played in Houston, TX
#Game played in Oklahoma City, OK

OU repeated its opening game score against Kingfisher College, then blasted East Central Teachers of Ada, 95-6. Both games were scored mostly on passes, but Geyer injured his shoulder against the Ada team.

A new one-story building, built north of Boyd Field, served as locker room for players and included an office for Owen.

Missouri rolled into Norman October 17 in the first official homecoming game for the Sooners. Neil Johnson scored a touchdown, and brother Hap scored on a pass from Geyer in the 13-0 victory.

The Sooners were black and blue from the Tiger game. Geyer had a pulled muscle in his neck and suffered a bruised hip. Bell had a bruised tendon and Captain Billie Clark had a "Charley Horse" (cramped muscles). Not a good time for wounds with Texas looming on the horizon.

The Longhorns won, 32-7, at Dallas. Hap Johnson took the opening kickoff and scored on a 75-yard return. OU led, 7-6, at halftime, but Texas hailed a barrage of forward passes in the second half.

"The best team won," coach Owen was quoted in the *Dallas Morning News* after the game. "They got us going with their forward passes. We couldn't stop them."

Injures continued to rise on the Sooner squad. Hap Johnson tore two ribs on his left side and pulled a ligament in his right hip. Brother Neil suffered a sore shoulder.

The team traveled to Lawrence to meet the 4-0 Jayhawks on October 31. The two teams fought to a 16-16 tie. Kansas broke a 9-all deadlock midway through the fourth period, and the ensuing kickoff went through the end zone and the Sooners marched 80 yards for the tie.

Geyer was feeling better in this game as was evident in the final drive. He connected a 20-yard pass to Hap Johnson, then hit Jess Fields for 25 more and Hap again for another 15. Following a penalty, Geyer rifled to Fields, who caught the ball at the KU five.

Neil Johnson lobbed a pass over a KU safety to his brother for the touchdown. Capshaw kicked the extra point. OU had 240 yards passing completing 11 of 35 aerials.

In Norman the next week, the Sooners beat Oklahoma A&M, 28-6, scoring all four TDs through the air. The Aggies also scored against the Sooners for the first time in 10 meetings.

The following week in Manhattan, Montgomery caught four passes for 165 yards in a 52-10 victory over Kansas State. He scored two touchdowns, and the other two catches put OU in scoring position.

1914 Season Record: 9-1-1

Date	Opponent	Result	Score
September 26	Central Normal*	W	67-0
October 2	KINGFISHER COLLEGE	W	67-0
October 9	EAST CENTRAL	W	95-6
October 17	MISSOURI	W	13-0
October 24	Texas at Dallas	L	32-7
October 31	at Kansas	T	16-16
November 6	OKLAHOMA A&M	W	23-6
November 13	at Kansas State	W	52-10
November 20	Arkansas*	W	35-7
November 26	Haskell#	W	33-12
December 1	at Henry Kendall	W	26-7

*Game played in Oklahoma City, OK
#Game played in Kansas City, KS

The Sooners defeated Arkansas, 35-7, in Oklahoma City and Haskell, 33-12 in Kansas City. The Indians played dirty, clipping the Oklahoma players whenever possible. Geyer's passing skills improved as he connected 10 of 17 passes for 175 yards.

Five days later, the Sooners stopped off in Tulsa to meet Kendall College. The players were so sore from the Haskell game that Owen had his entire backfield soak in mineral baths in nearby Claremore.

Geyer sat out with a "Charley Horse," but his backup, Tom Boyd, scored a touchdown and passed for another in the 26-7 Oklahoma win.

The 1914 Sooners led the nation in scoring with 431 points. Still, no one outside of the central part of America sat up and took notice. The press in the heartland did, however.

The *State Journal* in Lincoln, Nebraska wrote: "… eastern writers are spinning yarns this year that their coaches sent to Canada for rugby experts, who drilled the eastern players on the tricks of the forward pass … Western coaches began experimenting with the forward pass the very moment the play was grafted into the rules of football eight years ago. No coach in the country has had more success with the pass than Bennie Owen of Oklahoma … the Sooners are probably more adept at handling the long pass than any other team in college football.

"It was not necessary that the East should import Canadian instructors. The eastern chaps might better have come west to consult with Oklahoma."

1915

The Southwest Intercollegiate Athletic Conference was officially formed in December 1914, and the following year was the conference's inaugural season. The University of Oklahoma joined the SIAC, along with Arkansas, Baylor, Oklahoma A&M, Rice, Southwestern, Texas, and Texas A&M.

A male pep squad was also formed at the University of Oklahoma. The men in that elite group were called "Rufneks," decked out in red flannel shirts and white trousers.

Bennie Owen had to find replacements at both halfback slots. Neil Johnson graduated, and Trim Capshaw was only eligible against non-Missouri Valley Conference teams. The MVC only allowed players three years of eligibility to compete against its teams.

Rayburn Foster and Frank McCain had previous playing experience from other schools. Foster at Connell School of Agriculture in Helena and McCain had played at East Central in Ada. Fullback Spot Geyer and Hap Johnson returned to round out the backfield. Oliver and Willis Hott returned to anchor the front line along with guard Curry Bell. Hap Johnson and Jess Fields were back to give the Sooners experience on the ends.

The Sooners were riding a four-game winning streak heading into the 1915 campaign and would extend it to 15 by season's end with a 10-0 record.

Oklahoma was scheduled to play Central Normal at Oklahoma City's Fair Park, but state fair officials cancelled the game due to a muddy field. One official said the gridiron was "a sea of mud."

The Sooner defense also surrendered no points in their first four games: 67-0 over Kingfisher College, 55-0 over Weatherford Normal, 102-0 over Northwestern of Alva and 24-0 over Missouri at Columbia. Several hundred fans stood outside Barbour's Drug Store to hear the play-by-play returns from Columbia, but a raging rainstorm forced many to take cover. Still, about 100 did not want to miss a play and were soaked listening to their beloved Sooners.

Classes were cancelled at OU the following Monday, and a dance was held at the Armory. A ten-cent admission was charged, and

$175 was raised to send 22 band members to Dallas for the Texas game.

Sooner Magic: A Victory Deserving of a Holiday

As members of the Southwest Intercollegiate Athletic Conference, the 18th meeting between Oklahoma and Texas had an extra incentive in addition to pride between the two schools and states. The Horns were the Sooners' first conference opponent. OU was second for Texas, which had demolished Rice, 59-0. The Burnt Orange troops also held other opponents scoreless—72-0 over Texas Christian and 92-0 over Daniel Baker. The 92 points scored against Daniel Baker remains as the highest score ever by a Longhorn team.

Would the stout defenses force a 0-0 tie in the Red River war in Dallas? Odds favored the Horns by 2-1 to extend their winning streak to three over the Big Red. Texas led the overall series 11-5-1, including two straight.

The 22 OU band members made the trek to Dallas to attend its first ever Texas game along with about 200 Sooner fans.

The largest crowd to witness a football game in the State of Texas—11,000 at Gaston Park—barely settled in their seats when the Longhorns struck paydirt first.

Geyer took the opening kickoff for the Sooners, but fumbled when two Steer defenders hammered him. UT's James Goodman smothered the ball at the OU 25-yard line. Paul Simmons gained 12 yards, then three more to the Sooner 10. On second-and-seven, Bert Walker carried to the end zone for the touchdown. J.A. Edmond kicked the extra point for a 7-0 Texas lead.

UT again threatened later in the quarter, but Charles Turner fumbled the pigskin at the OU 22, and Johnson recovered for the Sooners. The Steers threatened again when the defense blocked a punt and recovered at the OU 10. Texas managed only five yards from two runs, followed by an incomplete pass. Paul Simmons' field goal sailed wide, and the Sooners exhaled a sigh of relief.

Oklahoma took possession at its own 20-yard line. Geyer nailed a 25-yard pass to Homer Montgomery. Frank McCain smashed through the line for 10 yards on a crucial fourth-and-two play at the UT 47. The next play, OU lost 10 yards on Geyer's fumble, but maintained possession. Rayburn Foster then connected a 20-yard pass to Fields for a first down at the UT 27.

Foster gained one yard, and McCain slashed through for 15 yards to the Longhorns' 11. Foster was stopped at the line of scrimmage, and McCain lunged forward for two yards. On third-and-goal at the UT nine, McCain shot a pass to Johnson in the end zone. Geyer added the extra point, and the score was knotted at 7-7 in the opening quarter.

The Sooners drove to the UT 12 early in the second period, but stalled, and Geyer's field goal veered wide. Bell picked off a Texas pass, but again the Sooners stalled and again Geyer missed another field goal try.

Later in the second quarter, the Horns marched to the OU 12, but Turner lost possession, and George Anderson recovered for the Sooners.

Neither team threatened again in the first half or in the early moments of the second half. The third quarter witnessed a series of punts by both teams, then Texas got a break with a short Sooner

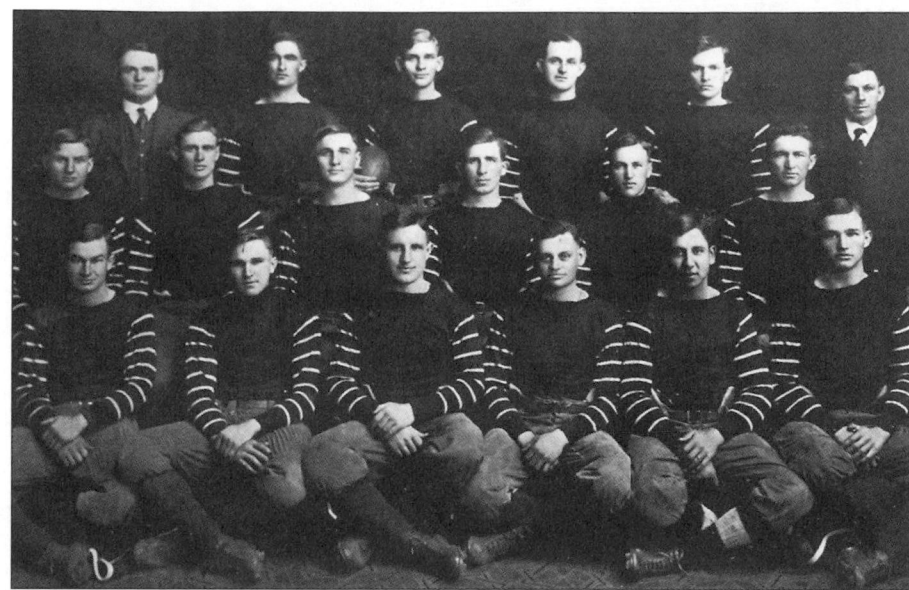

The 1915 Sooners captured the Southwest Conference title in the conference's inaugural season and gave OU its first league title. *(Western History Collections, University of Oklahoma)*

punt midway through the third quarter. OU stalled at its own 30-yard line, and Geyer's punt sailed only 23 yards into Bob Simmons' hands at the UT 47. Simmons returned the pigskin to the OU 35.

On fourth-and-goal from the five, Simmons scooted around end for the touchdown. Edmond missed the extra point, yet the Orange clad faithful were ecstatic about the 13-7 lead.

Midway through the fourth stanza, OU took possession at its 30-yard line following a UT punt. Geyer fired a 20-yard pass to Montgomery, who then raced another 25 yards to the UT 25. The Sooners got a break when Geyer's fourth-down incomplete pass from the 22 was overshadowed by a holding call against the Steers.

The Texas defense held the Sooners to only four yards on the next four plays, but the UT offense sputtered for no yards and punted to midfield. Geyer zipped a pass to Capshaw at the UT 35, then Capshaw flew to the end zone for the touchdown. Officials nullified the TD when one of them ruled Capshaw had stepped out of bounds at the 30. Texas took possession at its own 20-yard line—a touchback when Geyer's fourth-down pass was tipped away in the end zone.

The Longhorns managed only four yards, then Kelso's punt wobbled off the side of his foot and traveled only 16 yards to the UT 40.

Three minutes remained on the clock. Johnson connected a 20-yard pass to Montgomery. Capshaw slammed through the middle for only a yard, then Geyer fired a pass to Johnson who caught the ball at the two and dragged a couple of Texas defenders with him across the corner of the goal line. Oklahoma 13, Texas 13.

Rules of that day required the extra point to be kicked from where the TD was scored—this one a tough, almost impossible angle for Geyer from the sideline boundary. Amid the screaming fans, Geyer split the uprights to give OU a 14-13 lead.

The Longhorns returned the ensuing kickoff to their 30-yard line, then drove seven plays to the OU 28. Johnson intercepted Littlefield's pass at the 10. Owen didn't want to risk a turnover deep in his own territory, so on second down he ordered Geyer to punt the ball away, which landed at the Texas 40.

After Texas gained 10 yards, the Sooners picked off a Longhorn pass, then stalled and punted to the UT 15. Two plays later,

Capshaw intercepted another Texas pass, the Steers' ninth turnover and sixth interception of the game.

The Sooners killed the clock with two runs, and the Longhorns' hopes of a perfect season were dashed at Gaston Park.

The next day, the Sooner football team was cheered in each town when the team's train crossed north of the Red River. About 4,000 turned out at the Santa Fe station as the train pulled into Norman. The OU band and throngs of fans surrounded the train then marched through downtown Norman to the campus. University president Dr. Stratton Brooks declared Monday a holiday, and a victory barbecue was held for the team and fans at Boyd Field. A symbolic steer was cooked as the main entrée. The university and Norman businesses closed down for the celebration.

Oklahoma went on to defeat Kansas, 23-14, Henry Kendall, 14-13, Arkansas, 24-0, Kansas State, 21-7, and Oklahoma A&M, 26-7. The Kansas State victory marked the 100th win in OU football history.

The Sooners were tied at 3-0 with Baylor in the conference but neither met that year on the gridiron. Baylor voluntarily relinquished its share of the title when Baylor officials discovered one of its players was ruled ineligible.

The SIAC championship was the first title of any kind won by the University of Oklahoma. Sportswriters around the country were beginning to take notice of the football power on the prairie.

Spot Geyer became the Sooners' first official All-American when he was chosen by the Newspaper Enterprise Association, which represented about 100 newspapers. Brown Holmes, an NEA sportswriter who selected Geyer on the All-America team wrote, "Geyer of Oklahoma is touted as the passingest thing in football this year. His ability with the forward pass alone would make him a star wherever he might be dropped."

Parke H. Davis of the *New York Herald*, wrote that Geyer was "one of those wonderfully developed all-around players whose exceptional ability with the forward pass has been a factor in the Oklahoma team's success."

Capshaw was named to the honor roll by *St. Nicholas* magazine. *Outing* magazine selected Geyer and Montgomery to its honor roll team.

Six Sooners were named on the All-Southwest Conference team—Geyer, Capshaw, Johnson, Montgomery, Oliver Hott, and Willis Hott. Willis was chosen as the best guard in the southwest.

Although no national statistics were recorded in 1915, Geyer led the nation in extra-point kicks.

1916

Before the 1916 season, Kansas and Nebraska tried to hire Bennie Owen away from Norman. He declined their offer of a higher salary, stating that building and developing a team was as much fun as coaching.

Most of the 26 players who came out for football in 1916 were freshmen or sophomores. Claude "Tubby" Tyler was the biggest at 225 pounds, and Graham Johnson, brother of Neil and Hap, was the smallest at 5-3½ and 125 pounds. Still, Owen wasn't disappointed, for he had seasoned veterans returning in Jess Fields, Hap Johnson, Frank McCain, Homer Montgomery, and the Hott brothers. Montgomery was elected captain of the '16 squad. Willis Hott wasn't sure he wanted to play that season, but teammates coaxed him off his farm near Wakita.

After breezing through the first three opponents, hopes were high for another undefeated campaign, but injuries riddled the squad in the fourth contest. The Sooners beat Central Normal. 27-0, in Norman then blasted Catholic Normal of Shawnee, 107-0, and Weatherford Normal, 140-0.

Henry Kendall of Tulsa, who the Sooners edged 14-13 the year before, shut out Oklahoma, 16-0. The Sooners had blown two scoring drives with turnovers near the Presbyterians' goal line. The loss was the first to an in-state team in school history, the first shutout and loss in Norman since the fourth game of the 1912 season when OU lost to Missouri. It also ended an 18-game winning string, which extended back to the seventh game of 1914.

To top that off, Hap Johnson reinjured his hip and had to leave the game. Fields suffered a "Charley Horse," and Montgomery broke his left arm and was sidelined for the rest of the season. Everett Wilmoth, Spot Geyer's heir apparent at fullback, was out with an infected toe.

Not great news with the Texas Longhorns looming the next Saturday in Dallas. A Sooner scoring opportunity was lost on an interception at the UT 22 in the first quarter. Graham Johnson scored the only Sooner points with a 10-yard end run and converted the extra point to tie the game at 7-7 in the third quarter. Still in the third quarter, a Longhorn punt touched OU's Albert Briscoe at the Sooner five-yard line, and Maxey Hart scooped up the pigskin to score for Texas. The Horns won, 21-7.

1915 Season Record: 10-0-0				
Southwest Conference: 3-0-0 (Champions)				
Date	**Opponent**		**Result**	**Score**
October 2	KINGFISHER COLLEGE		W	67-0
October 6	at Weatherford Normal		W	55-0
October 9	NORTHWEST NORMAL		W	102-0
October 16	at Missouri		W	24-0
October 23	Texas at Dallas		W	14-13
October 30	KANSAS		W	23-14
November 6	at Henry Kendall		W	14-13
November 13	at Arkansas		W	24-0
November 19	at Kansas State		W	21-7
November 25	Oklahoma A&M*		W	26-7
*Game played in Oklahoma City, OK				

1916 Season Record: 6-5-0			
Southwest Conference: 2-1-0 (Third)			
Date	**Opponent**	**Result**	**Score**
September 23	CENTRAL NORMAL	W	27-0
Spetember 30	CATHOLIC NORMAL	W	107-0
October 7	WEATHERFORD NORMAL	W	52-9
October 14	HENRY KENDALL	L	16-0
October 21	Texas at Dallas	L	21-7
October 28	MISSOURI	L	23-14
November 4	at Kansas	L	21-13
November 11	at Kingfisher College	W	96-0
November 18	KANSAS STATE	L	14-13
November 25	Arkansas*	W	14-13
November 30	Oklahoma A&M#	W	41-7
*Game played in Fort Smith, AK			
#Game played in Oklahoma City, OK			

Both Hott brothers were ineligible to play the homecoming contest against Missouri the following week, leaving McCain as the only experienced veteran on the Oklahoma squad.

OU led, 14-13, at the half on Rudolph Von Tungeln's two touchdown runs. The Tigers scored a TD and a field goal in the fourth quarter to win, 23-14.

Reeling from three consecutive losses, Coach Owen put his charges through longer practices carrying into darkness with the headlights from his automobile illuminating Boyd Field.

Kansas defeated the Sooners, 21-13, the following week in Lawrence. The four straight losses were the first in OU history. Adrian Lindsay of Kingfisher quarterbacked and kicked for the Jayhawks. Lindsay would become Owen's successor 11 years later. In fact, nine of Kansas' players hailed from the State of Oklahoma, mostly the northern part of the state.

Von Tungeln's touchdown gave the Sooners a 7-0 lead. KU tied the game off an Oklahoma fumble and scored twice more for a 21-7 advantage. McCain intercepted a Jayhawk pass and returned it 80 yards for the other Sooner tally.

The Sooners annihilated Kingfisher College, 96-0, then hosted Kansas State the following week at Boyd Field, the first time the Wildcats played in Norman. Kansas State's nickname went through several changes before becoming the Wildcats in 1920. They were known as the Wildcats in 1915 and then the Farmers from 1916-19. Kansas State won, 14-13, with Graham Johnson's missed extra point being the difference. Johnson's kick ricocheted off the crossbar.

The next week the score was identical but favored the Sooners in a win against Arkansas at Fort Smith. Willis Hott played fullback and scored the first OU touchdown, and Tommy Graham added the second. Tackle James Tolbert took over the kicking duties and was successful on both conversion attempts. Wilmoth returned for the game but broke three ribs, and his season was over.

Oklahoma had one more game against Oklahoma A&M. A victory over the Aggies would save a winning season for the 5-5 Sooners. OU scored three touchdowns each in the first quarter and fourth quarter en route to a 41-7 victory. The Sooners took a 7-0 lead on Graham's crossbuck in the game's first four minutes. Willis Hott scored minutes later, and Graham added his second touchdown late in the first stanza.

The Sooners finished the season with a 6-5 record and tied for third in the Southwest Conference with a 2-1 record. Willis Hott was the only OU player named to the All-Southwest Conference team.

The world was about to change, which also altered the world of college football.

1917

The United States declared war against Germany on April 6, 1917. Germany had sunk American ships, forcing Congress to declare an act of war. Two months later over 175,000 American troops were training in France, then were deployed into action in World War I. The war depleted the rosters of every football team around the country. Prior to the 1917 season, 13 of 20 Sooners joined the military, and more players left the team as the season rolled on. Head coach Bennie Owen had to rely on younger and more inexperienced players to carry the load that year.

The Sooners opened the '17 season with huge victories—99-0 over Central Normal and 179-0 over Kingfisher College, the largest margin in the history of Oklahoma football. The Sooners led, 40-0, after the first quarter, 89-0 at halftime and 138-0 after three quar-

ters. Arlo "Skivey" Davis ran for two TDs, threw two more and returned an interception for a score. He also kicked 23 of 26 extra points that day, including 18 in a row.

OU spotted Phillips University of Enid nine points before rolling up 52 unanswered points to win, 52-9. Halfback Hugh McDermott dislocated his shoulder in the Phillips game, creating more worries for the war-depleted Sooners. The next week Oklahoma tasted its first defeat—44-0 to Illinois. Prior to the Illinois contest, end Lawrence "Jap" Haskell contracted typhoid and yellow jaundice and had to be hospitalized the rest of the season.

Freshman Wallace Abbott replaced McDermott against the Fighting Illini. Sooner turnovers thwarted a couple of nice drives in the first half and another in the third period.

The Sooners rebounded to shut out Texas, 14-0. Abbott accounted for both OU scores against the Longhorns. He threw for one TD and scored another on an intercepted pass. One day later, the United States first entered combat on October 21 when units from the U.S. Army's First Division were assigned to allied trenches in the Luneville sector near Nancy, France.

Sooner Magic:
Carrying the Load

The following week, the Sooners traveled to Columbia, Missouri, and Abbott was ineligible to play against the Tigers. Although Oklahoma was a member of the Southwest Conference and not the Missouri Valley Conference, the MVC (of which Missouri was a member) still disallowed freshmen to play in conference games.

Tiger fans had packed Rollins Field and were delighted when their home team scored a touchdown in the first seven minutes of the game, marching down field from the opening kickoff for a 7-0 lead. Ed Davis punched the ball across from the one-yard line, and Bill Collins converted. Missouri held the lead through the rest of the first half.

Prior to the end of the first half, OU quarterback and captain Everett Wilmoth broke his collarbone. The excruciating pain did not keep him out of the contest. Owen convinced him to play in the second half since Wilmoth was his only quarterback that day. The other quarterback, Graham Johnson, quit the team since his father believed he was too small to play football.

Owen told Wilmoth to call the signals, hand off and get out of the way. He insisted that Wilmoth not block or tackle. Wilmoth engineered the Sooners' 80-yard, 10-play TD march in the third period. The highlight of the drive was when end W.E. "Spot" Durant slipped past a Tiger end and gained 27 yards on a fake

Arlo "Skivey" Davis scored five touchdowns to lead the Sooners to a 179-0 victory over Kingfisher College. It was the largest victory in Oklahoma football history. *(OU Athletics)*

Wallace Abbott scored the only touchdowns in OU's 14-0 victory over Texas. (*OU Athletics*)

end play to the MU 41-yard line. From the Tiger seven, Wilmoth got open in the end zone, and Davis fired a pass to the injured quarterback for the touchdown. Davis toed the extra point, and the game was knotted at 7-7.

Midway through the final stanza, Davis punted 40 yards, but the ball touched Missouri's George Stevins as it descended, and Ross Johnston recovered for the Sooners at the Tiger 14. On the next play, Davis slammed through the line and into the end zone. He also booted the extra point to give OU a 14-7 advantage.

Two Tiger drives ended fruitlessly as the game was winding to a close. Wilmoth intercepted a pass to kill one drive. The other Missouri threat ended with an incomplete pass inside Sooner territory.

Kansas delivered an unpleasant homecoming loss to the Sooners the next week. Without a quarterback, Owen turned to Davis who had to learn his new duty the week leading up to the game. Earl Bechtold scored the lone Sooner touchdown on a one-yard plunge in the 13-6 loss.

OU and Arkansas battled to a scoreless tie in Fort Smith the following week. McDermott returned, and Abbott was eligible. Davis missed three field goals, and Abbott's apparent 50-yard touchdown run was called back because he stepped out of bounds at the Arkansas 30.

The Sooners got back in the win column the next week with an 80-0 blasting of Henry Kendall.

Oklahoma A&M won its first game against the Sooners the next week in Oklahoma City. The Aggies got a safety when Durant was tackled in the end zone after recovering Abbott's fumbled punt return.

A&M capitalized on another Sooner fumble at the OU 25. Two plays later Wib Ray scored a touchdown for the Aggies for a 9-0

lead. Oklahoma blew a scoring opportunity late in the game when Abbott fumbled on the A&M three after catching Davis' pass.

The Sooners concluded the 1917 season with a 21-7 loss to Camp Doniphan, a military team including former players from Kansas, Missouri, and Haskell. Benefits from the game, held in Oklahoma City, were used to purchase athletic equipment for American soldiers overseas.

The 1917 Sooners finished the season 6-4-1 and third in the Southwest Conference with a 1-1-1 mark. Abbott and Durant were selected to the All-Southwest Conference team.

1918

World War I was raging in 1918 and had depleted college football players from competing on the gridiron that year. Of the 18 players who lettered on OU's football team a year earlier, only Erl Deacon, Alfred Douglas, Dewey "Snorter" Luster, and Jap Haskell returned to the squad. As a result of the war, every college football program was allowed to field freshmen that year.

Luckily for the Sooners, all seven seniors from the state-champion Oklahoma City High School enrolled at the university that fall. The contingent of freshman players was said to be the best in the university's 24-year football history.

The Spanish Influenza swept from east to west across the United States in the fall, claiming 600,000 lives and forcing OU to cancel games against Missouri, Texas, and Northwest Normal of Alva. The Sooners only played six games in 1918.

OU opened the season September 28 at home with a 58-0 pounding of Post Field, an aviation base located at Fort Sill. Fumbles led to the first two Sooner touchdowns. Freshman halfback Harry Hill scored four TDs, and quarterback Phil White passed for one touchdown and returned a punt for another.

White dislocated his shoulder in practice the following week, which hampered him through the season, yet he continued to play. Ross Johnston joined the Navy and the killer virus had reached Oklahoma. No games were played for three weeks.

When the influenza subsided, the Sooners blasted Charley Wantland's Central Normal, 44-0. Military companies were ordered to sit in isolated areas of Boyd Field to keep from infecting each other.

The Sooners then defeated Kansas, 33-0. Paul Johnston, Buzz Bartlett, and Luster joined the Army after the Jayhawks game. Germany surrendered by signing the armistice as a prelude to peace negotiations two days after the Kansas game, but the trio was still kept in the Army until the end of the football season.

Oklahoma scored six TDs in the first quarter en route to a 103-0 pounding of Arkansas. Meanwhile, the Phillips Haymakers were overpowering their opponents, disallowing a single score as the Sooners had done.

Sooner Magic: Ankle Tackle Saves the Day

Phillips coach Johnny Maultbetsch was commissioned in the Navy before the OU game. He was relieved of his coaching duties by team captain and fullback Douglas Roby. Steve Owen, who later became a player-coach for the New York Giants, was a star for the Haymakers.

OU tackle Page Belcher, who later became an Oklahoma Congressman, had his suitcase stolen on the train ride to Enid, home of Phillips University. Belcher borrowed a Phillips uniform and shoes from teammate Bill McKinney.

1917 Season Record: 6-4-1
Southwest Conference: 1-1-1 (Third)

Date	Opponent	Result	Score
September 22	Central Oklahoma*	W	99-0
September 29	KINGFISHER COLLEGE	W	179-0
October 6	PHILLIPS	W	52-9
October 13	at Illinois	L	44-0
October 20	Texas at Dallas	W	14-0
November 3	at Missouri	W	14-7
November 10	KANSAS	L	13-6
November 17	Arkansas#	T	0-0
November 24	HENRY KENDALL	W	80-0
November 29	Oklahoma A&M*	L	9-0
December 15	Camp Doniphan*	L	21-7

*Game played in Oklahoma City, OK
#Game played in Fort Smith, AK

Erl Deacon's ankle tackle on a Phillips player ended the Haymakers' chance to defeat the Sooners. (*OU Athletics*)

Phillips was seeking revenge on November 23 for the 52-9 thrashing by the Sooners the year before, the only previous encounter between both teams.

A stingy Haymaker defense and later a soggy field stalled the Sooner running game at Allton Field.

Just before halftime, Roby raced 35 yards for the first score of the game and first all season against the Sooners' defense. He also kicked the extra point to give Phillips a 7-0 lead. OU trailed for the first time all season and yielded its first score.

The weather grew colder and wetter in the second half. Snow fell, softening the ground and making runs difficult. OU head coach Bennie Owen changed his game plan from run-dominated to pass oriented. In doing so, he replaced quarterback Phil White with Russell "Stub" Hardy, a decision that paid off for the Sooner skipper.

In the fourth quarter, Hardy led a march to the Haymakers' goal line. On the scoring play, Haskell blocked a Phillips defender, then cut toward the middle of the field. Hardy zipped a pass to his teammate. Haskell grasped the slippery ball and tumbled into the end zone. White booted the extra point and the score was tied, 7-7. It was the first score against Phillips' defense all season long.

OU again drove to the Phillips four-yard line, but a determined Haymaker defense stalled OU's scoring effort.

The crimson defense was just as stingy. Phillips was unable to gain any yards, and OU got the ball back at the Phillips 10-yard line after Franklin Coppan shanked a punt.

The Haymaker defense controlled the first three plays. On fourth-and-goal, Howard Marsh cut toward the sideline, hauled in Hardy's pass and tumbled across the goal line. White missed the extra point, but the Sooners held a 13-7 edge with three minutes left in the game.

Phillips moved the ball to the OU 10 following the kickoff. The Sooner defense stopped the Haymakers on the next three plays. Phillips quarterback Newt Weatherly took the fourth-down snap, but OU center Dow Hamm shoved the Phillips center back into Weatherly. This allowed lineman Deacon to grab Weatherly by the ankle to stop the Haymaker threat as the gun sounded.

The Sooners finished the season with a 27-0 victory over Oklahoma A&M in Oklahoma City on Thanksgiving. Major E.A. Pritchard, who coached the Aggies to its first victory over OU a year earlier, returned from the war two days before the game to coach his team. Haskell scored the first touchdown, capping a 75-yard Sooner march. Marsh caught two TD passes and Fred Martin scored another on a 70-yard fumble return.

OU finished the season with a 6-0 record (2-0 in limited conference play) and outscored its opponents, 278-7. No team was crowned conference champion since the war, and influenza cancelled games. Deacon was named to *Outing* magazine's All-American honor roll. World War I was over and football was back to normal for a while.

1919

As students returned from the war, enrollment at the University of Oklahoma reached over 2,600 in the fall of 1919, and the varsity football team swelled to 26 returning lettermen. A few more would also return during the season.

Bennie Owen was delighted to have so many experienced players on his squad, and he decided to scrimmage the 1918 returnees against the returning veterans to see who would step up for the starting roster, which consisted of a mixture of both.

Wallace Abott did not return, exercising his option to attend school back east.

The Sooners opened with a 40-0 victory over Central Normal, but Owen was unhappy with the sloppy tackling by his charges. So the following Monday he ordered extra tackling drills in which three players suffered injuries. Jap Haskell dislocated three vertebrae in his spine and was confined to a straitjacket the rest of the season. Ross Johnston and Henry Bass dislocated their shoulders.

Phil White returned before the Kingfisher College game, which OU won, 157-0. It was the final game against the Kingfisher team. In 22 meetings, Oklahoma won 19 and three ended in scoreless ties. The Sooners outscored KC 1,161-31, an average of 52.8-1.4, and won the final 14 in a row.

Frank McCain returned to the team before the game against Henry Kendall, replacing Haskell at end. The Presbyterians scored on a fumble return off an OU interception to take a 7-0 lead in the first quarter, which they held through halftime. A light rain turned heavier in the second half and so did the Presbys' scoring blitz. They

1918 Season Record: 6-0-0
Southwest Conference: 2-0-0 (N/A)

Date	Opponent	Result	Score
September 28	POST FIELD	W	58-0
October 19	CENTRAL NORMAL	W	44-0
November 9	at Kansas	W	33-0
November 16	ARKANSAS	W	103-0
November 23	at Phillips	W	13-7
November 28	Oklahoma A&M*	W	27-0
*Game played in Oklahoma City, OK			

Another pep club was formed in 1919. The jazz era was sweeping the nation, and the new club was called the Jazz Hounds, established to promote the football team during home and road games. They financed their travels through student minstrels and selling concessions during home games.

The group sported red bellhop caps, bow ties and flannel vests, with white tennis shoes, socks and pants. They later added red and white vertically striped jackets. They performed at halftime, and their yells were laced with profanity. Prior to the Texas game in Dallas, they paraded a real schooner through the Texas State Fair grounds carrying co-eds called "Jazzettes."

They also borrowed a cow from a Sooner alum in Dallas and hung a sign on the bovine, which read: "This ain't no bull. We're gonna beat Texas!" They led the cow through downtown Dallas and in the lobby of the Adolphus Hotel.

After the Sooners beat the Longhorns, they put a new sign on the cow, which read: "We beat Texas" and again paraded the cow through the streets of downtown Dallas.

Howard "Tarz" Marsh blocked three Texas punts, one resulting in an OU safety. A year earlier, he caught the winning touchdown pass to help the Sooners beat Phillips. Marsh was twice named to the All-Missouri Valley Conference first team. (OU Athletics)

scored three touchdowns all by pass en route to a 27-0 win.

Several players were unable to play against Texas the following week. McCain was called away on business, and Fred "Soupy" Smoot had a singing engagement in McAlester. The strapping tackle also had a passion for opera. White, who dislocated his shoulder early the previous season, injured it again.

The Sooners then defeated Texas 12-7 in Dallas. Howard "Tarz" Marsh blocked three Texas punts; the last resulted in a safety for the Sooners before halftime. Skivey Davis fired a 40-yard pass to Myron Tyler in the third period to cap a 60-yard drive with every play engineered on the right side of the Sooner line. The Longhorns scored off a blocked Davis punt and returned the pigskin 70 yards for a touchdown in the fourth quarter. Davis toed a 30-yard field goal with two minutes left.

Oklahoma met Nebraska the next week on a snowy and blustery day in Omaha. The game was the second bill of a doubleheader. The first contest was a scoreless tie between Creighton and Marquette.

The Cornhuskers scored off a 50-yard drive in the first quarter to take a 7-0 lead. Roy Smoot blocked a Husker punt at the NU 20, but a penalty on the following play moved the Sooners back 15 yards. Davis faked a pass and kept the ball to his right. Earl Bechtold provided a lead block down the right sideline and delivered another block to a Nebraska safety opening a free lane to the end zone for Davis. Davis kicked the extra point. Although the game ended in a 7-7 tie, OU outgained the Huskers, 336-155 yards. Oklahoma had 217 on the ground and 119 through the air. Nebraska's yards were all on the ground, as they did not complete a single pass.

The Sooners hosted Missouri in a homecoming contest that ended in a 6-6 tie. The Tigers kicked two field goals. Roy Swatek scored a touchdown for OU, but Davis missed the conversion. His

field goal attempt later struck the goalpost and bounced back to the playing field.

Oklahoma and Kansas fought to a scoreless tie the following week in Lawrence. The next week in Fayetteville, Arkansas, the Sooners scored first on Dutch Hill's interception return for a touchdown, but Davis missed the extra point. Arkansas scored on a fumble return, and the extra point was the difference in the contest, 7-6. OU marched to the Razorbacks' six-yard line as time expired.

Four straight games without a win makes a team hun-

Dewey "Snorter" Luster was the second Sooner alumnus to become head coach. (Western History Collections, University of Oklahoma)

gry for a victory. The Sooners got it the next week in Manhattan against Kansas State, 14-3. Dewey "Snorter" Luster scored on an end-around for the first touchdown. Owen gave Luster his nickname because he snorted when he returned punts. Dorsey Boyle's pass to Johnston accounted for the other Sooner score.

The final game of the season was on Thanksgiving against Oklahoma A&M. Sleet crusted the field at Western League Park in Oklahoma City. The Sooners routed the Aggies 33-6. Myron Tyler accounted for Oklahoma's first four TDs in the game. He also blocked three of Wib Ray's punts in the first 20 minutes and scored another on a pass.

The Sooners capitalized on all three blocked punts. Luster recovered the first in the end zone. Tyler smothered the second one, then Luster swept around end to the end zone on the next play. Tyler recovered the third one at the Aggie 10-yard line, then Boyle fired a pass to Davis in the end zone.

In the second half, Davis hurled a pass to Tyler for another TD. A&M's Walter Weaver took the ensuing kickoff and skated 65 yards for the Aggies' lone TD. Bechtold plowed through the line for the fifth OU touchdown.

The Sooners finished the season 5-2-3 and placed third in the Southwest Conference with a 2-1 mark. Swatek, Johnston, Claude Tyler, and Hugh McDermott were named to the All-Southwest Conference team.

1919 Season Record: 5-2-3
Southwest Conference: 2-1 (Third)

Date	Opponent	Result	Score
September 27	CENTRAL NORMAL	W	40-0
October 4	KINGFISHER COLLEGE	W	157-0
October 11	HENRY KENDALL	L	27-0
October 18	Texas at Dallas	W	12-7
October 25	Nebraska*	T	7-7
November 1	MISSOURI	T	6-6
November 8	at Kansas	T	0-0
November 15	at Arkansas	L	7-6
November 22	at Kansas State	W	14-13
November 27	Oklahoma State#	W	33-6

*Game played in Omaha, NE
#Game played in Oklahoma City, OK

1920 - 1929

1920

The University of Oklahoma withdrew from the Southwest Conference and joined with the more affluent Missouri Valley Conference. Higher attendance at games was one of the reasons for joining the MVC. The conference included Drake, Iowa State, Kansas, Kansas State, Missouri, and Nebraska.

One conference rule stipulated that schools play on their home turf, and since Texas insisted on meeting the Sooners in Dallas, the two would not meet again for two years. The Oklahoma A&M contest would no longer be held in Oklahoma City while OU was a member of the conference.

The return of the entire offensive line and others had enthusiasm running high in Norman in 1920. Returnees included Erl Deacon, Jap Haskell, Skivey Davis, Paul Johnston, Roy "Soupy" Smoot, Snorter Luster, Howard "Tarz" Marsh, Myron "Tub" Tyler, Phil White, Harry "Dutch" Hill, Roy "Sol" Swatek, and Big Bill McKinley. Luster was elected captain, and Smoot, a 215-pound tackle, was a proficient blocker who was occasionally deployed as a running guard because of his speed.

Bennie Owen also had the pleasure of adding two more assistants to the team. In addition to Ed Meacham, Grover Jacobsen and Sam Burton joined the staff.

Swatek scored two touchdowns and Davis booted a field goal in defeating Central, 16-7, in the season opener in Norman.

Two weeks later, the team traveled to St. Louis to meet Washington St. Louis in the first Missouri Valley Conference contest. The Pikers scored twice off the screen pass to take a 14-0 lead. Davis' field goal cut the Piker lead to 14-3 before halftime. Owen had used the break to adjust his defense to the screen. He instructed his ends to drop back and shadow the Piker ends and his halfbacks to move in to pressure the quarterback.

Rain soaked the field as the third quarter began, and Owen's strategy was beginning to pay off. Following an interception at the OU 20, the Sooners drove 80 yards with Clarence "Ram" Morrison scoring the touchdown. White kicked the conversion to pull OU closer, 14-10.

Soon after, Washington fumbled deep in its own territory, and Smoot recovered in the end zone. White's kick was good and OU led, 17-14.

The Sooner defense continued to stymie the Pikers. In the fourth period, White connected to Tyler for another touchdown, and White's kick gave OU a 24-14 victory.

Next up was Missouri, defending conference champi-

ons, in Columbia. The OU team received a huge sendoff with 2,000 fans cheering them at the Santa Fe station. The rally included fans, faculty, students, Jazz Hounds, Rufneks, the ROTC band, and Mex, the team mascot.

The Tigers took the opening kickoff, but the Sooner defense forced them to punt. OU swiftly drove 50 yards to score. Morrison's TD plunge capped the drive and Davis' toe gave Oklahoma a 7-0 lead, which remained through halftime.

Haskell scored on an end around in the third quarter, and Davis' kick gave the Sooners a 14-0 advantage. The Tigers scored when they blocked a punt and raced 85 yards to pay dirt. OU answered with a drive, capped by Swatek's leap over players and across the goal line. Johnston intercepted a Tiger pass and raced 35 yards for the next Sooner touchdown.

Oklahoma rolled up 500 total yards, 385 rushing. The 28-7 victory was the only defeat handed to Missouri that season.

Spirits were running high in Norman following the Tiger win. A crowd of 7,000 turned out for the homecoming clash against Kansas, sporting a 4-0 record. Two dollars was charged for general admission and $2.50 for reserved seats. Oklahoma Governor James Robertson also attended the game.

The Jayhawks took a 9-0 lead on a touchdown and a safety. OU drove 30 yards with Swatek scoring the touchdown before halftime. In the third quarter, the Sooners were on the move again. Hill fired a 27-yard pass to Tyler to the KU three-yard line. Hill's touchdown run and White's extra point vaulted the Sooners to a 14-9 lead.

The Sooners capitalized on White's interception in the fourth stanza. OU drove 30 yards in four plays capped by White's TD. He faked a pass and darted down the left side to the end zone. His kick

Harry "Dutch" Hill scored four touchdowns twice in this career. The first time as a freshman against Post Field in 1918 and the second time as a junior against Oklahoma A&M in 1920. *(OU Athletics)*

Phil White was the first OU halfback to earn All-America honors. *(OU Athletics)*

1920 Season Record: 6-0-1			
Missouri Valley Conference: 3-0-1			
(Champions)			
Date	**Opponent**	**Result**	**Score**
October 9	CENTRAL NORMAL	W	16-7
October 23	at Washington St. Louis	W	24-14
October 30	at Missouri	W	28-14
November 6	KANSAS	W	21-9
November 13	at Oklahoma A&M	W	36-0
November 20	KANSAS STATE	T	7-7
November 25	at Drake	W	44-7

All-American Roy "Soupy" Smoot not only blocked and tackled, he toured the nation as an opera singer. (*OU Athletics*)

put Oklahoma up, 21-9, which was the final tally. The Sooners gobbled up 425 yards on the ground.

The next week in Stillwater, Hill scored four touchdowns and rushed for nearly 200 yards as OU defeated Oklahoma A&M, 36-0.

Kansas State came to Norman the following week looking for its first conference win. The Wildcats took a 7-0 lead in the first quarter, but the Sooners answered with a 50-yard TD pass from White to Tyler. Davis' kick tied the game at 7-7. OU drove into Wildcat territory late in the first half but was held for downs at the 11.

The Sooners drove 70 yards in the third period, only to turn the ball over on downs at the K-State two-yard line. The Wildcats missed three field goals in the fourth quarter, and the game ended in a 7-7 stalemate.

If OU defeated Drake on Thanksgiving, it would claim the Missouri Valley Conference championship in its first year in the conference. Davis' field goal put the Sooners up, 3-0, in the first stanza. Hill scored on a 76-yard end sweep, and White connected to Johnston for a touchdown before halftime to give OU a 16-0 edge.

White, who completed 11 of 26 passes for 185 yards, completed a TD pass to Haskell in the third period. Morrison scored a TD in the fourth, then White fired a TD pass to Johnston to boost OU to a 37-0 lead.

After Drake scored a touchdown, White connected to Tyler for 50 yards to the Bulldog's one-yard line. White plowed over for the score, and his extra point gave Oklahoma a 44-7 decision.

Owen had negotiated for his squad to meet Ohio State in Columbus a few days later, but the Buckeyes backed out when they received an invitation to the Rose Bowl. OU-Ohio State would have to wait for another 57 years.

The Newspaper Enterprise Association named White to its All-American team and Smoot was selected to the Collegiate World All-American team. Ironically, White was not named to the All-Missouri Valley Conference team. Marsh, Smoot, McKinley, Hill and Swatek were named to the all-conference team.

1921

Not only was Jap Haskell elected captain for the 1921 season, he was in the best health of his career. After suffering typhoid and yellow jaundice one year and dislocating his spine in another year, he was free of illness and injury in 1921. His good health was attributed to working on the alfalfa crop on his farm near the Washita bottoms.

In a September interview in the *Daily Oklahoman*, Haskell said he believed the 1921 Sooners would be as good as the 1918 team that went undefeated and the 1920 team that won the Missouri Valley Conference championships.

"…We're going to have a razzum, jazzum gang and then some," he said.

Two All-Americans from the 1920 roster did not return. Halfback Phil White graduated, and tackle Soupy Smoot took some time off

to pursue an opera-singing career. However, the interior linemen were back for another year. All-Missouri Valley guard Big Bill McKinley and guard Charles Van Edmondson flanked Dow Hamm who was back at center. All-conference end Tarz Marsh and Haskell returned at end. Sol Swatek and Dutch Hill, both all-conference halfbacks, and Tub Tyler returned to the backfield.

A week prior to the opening game, the varsity scrimmaged against the freshmen, or Sooners vs. Boomers. The game at Boyd Field was billed as "Monty Day." At 50 cents per ticket, all gate receipts were turned over to Homer Montgomery, OU end from 1913-16, who suffered from tuberculosis.

Of course, the varsity manhandled the freshmen, 35-0.

Yeine Hendricks got the starting nod at quarterback prior to the October 8 opener against Central Normal. Hendricks battled Eddie Johnson for the starting quarterback position. Johnson was younger brother of Graham, Montford and Neil Johnson who starred earlier for the Sooners.

Coach Bennie Owen after the game said the 1921 Sooner squad "work with a better spirit than they have this year."

Many expected the Central Normal contest in Norman to be no more than a practice game for Oklahoma. Central Normal just hoped to make a good showing. The defense did make a good showing, stopping OU twice at the one-yard line in the second and third quarters, but the Sooners prevailed, 21-0.

The Sooners' aerial attack was sluggish in the first half, but got on track late in the third stanza when Tyler fired a 22-yard touchdown pass to Hill.

Tyler also ran for an eight-yard TD in the fourth period. C.E. "Ram" Morrison intercepted a pass on Normal's next possession to set up Tyler's TD. Moments later on third down, Tyler smashed across the goal line for the final blow. Hill was perfect on all three extra-point kicks.

Oklahoma totaled 324 yards to Normal's 22. Normal only gained four first downs, two by penalty.

Hill injured his foot in the game, and Marsh and Swatek both suffered sore shoulders, and all three were doubtful for a home contest against 2-1 Oklahoma A&M the next week.

Seven Aggie starters were declared ineligible by the Missouri Valley Conference four days prior to the OU game. They lacked a number of credit hours, below standard for scholastic standing. Captain and center Bill Williams did qualify later in the week. Oklahoma A&M was not a member of the conference, but since Oklahoma was a member and hosted the game, MVC rules prevailed.

The Sooners won, 6-0, on Hill's 30-yard touchdown run midway through the second period. He plunged through right tackle, lost his balance, but maintained his composure and shed a couple of tacklers during the run. He missed the extra point and a couple of field goal attempts in the game. OU totaled 219 yards while holding A&M to 82 total yards.

Prior to meeting 2-1 Washington University of St. Louis on October 22, Coach Owen promised he would produce a scoring team. His word rang true as the Sooners downed the Pikers, 28-13, in Norman.

The Big Red rolled up four touchdowns before the Pikers got on the board. Tyler had a four-yard TD run in the first quarter and added an 11-yard run in the second. Harold James also scored in the third stanza, and Hill scored the final touchdown in the fourth period.

Washington did not cross into Sooner territory until the fourth quarter. By that time, reserves were in the game. Two fumbles by the reserves in OU territory allowed the Pikers to score both times.

Oklahoma Sooners in action against Central Normal. The Sooners won, 21-0. (*OU Athletics*)

Oklahoma rolled up 324 total yards while holding Washington to 48.

About 500 OU students, alumni, and fans stood in drizzling rain outside Barbour's Drug Store to hear the results of the Nebraska game on October 29. They arrived at 2 p.m., and 30 minutes later had jammed Norman's Main Street.

Nebraska had more than drizzle. Heavy rains fell in Lincoln for 24 hours prior to kickoff, forcing both teams to play in ankle deep mud. The 2-1 Huskers won, 44-0, in the conference opener. They had specially designed conical mud spikes on their shoes to prevent them from sinking and giving them a firm hold in the mud. Oklahoma slipped all day long, and fumbles killed Sooner drives deep in Nebraska territory.

Husker quarterback Glen Preston and his backup, Dave Noble, each scored three touchdowns.

"We'll get a shot at them on our ground next year," Owen said, "and let us hope that we'll have Oklahoma sunshine and dryness."

The Sooners exploded for 21 first-half points en route to a 24-7 victory over 3-1 Kansas before a homecoming crowd of more than 10,000 in Norman on November 5. Many fans had to be turned away from the gate, and rumors were flying that a new stadium was needed.

Hill's 35-yard TD run gave OU a 7-0 lead in the first quarter. The Sooners moved rapidly downfield early in the second period on runs by Marsh, Morrison, Hill, and Tyler to the Jayhawk 15. On the next play, a KU defender deflected a pass to Morrison, but the pigskin fell into Hamm's hands in the end zone.

Moments later, OU recovered a fumble at the KU 20. Tyler zipped a 10-yard pass to Hill, who fumbled as he crashed to the ground. The ball bounded toward the goal line, and Hendricks recovered in the end zone.

1921 Season Record: 5-3-0

Missouri Valley Conference: 2-3-0 (Seventh)

Date	Opponent	Result	Score
October 8	CENTRAL NORMAL	W	21-0
October 15	OKLAHOMA A&M	W	28-13
October 22	WASHINGTON ST. LOUIS	W	28-13
October 29	at Nebraska	L	44-0
November 5	KANSAS	W	24-7
November 12	at Missouri	L	24-14
November 19	at Kansas State	L	14-7
November 24	at Rice	W	27-0

Hill added a 35-yard field goal in the third stanza.

Hun Griffin, a 1916 quarterback at OU, entertained the spectators with aerial stunts flying his plane at half time. He dropped red and white streamers over the field, then ended the stunt with a loop and landed at midfield. The Rufneks spelled R-U-F-N-E-K-S with white powder on the ground, then exploded two gallon cans.

More than 10,000 turned out for Missouri's homecoming the following week, and Tiger fans were treated to a 24-14 victory over the Sooners. The 5-1 Tigers were led by Chuck Lewis' brilliant punting that kept the Sooners pinned deep for most of the day. Two fumbles by Hendricks deep in Tiger territory thwarted any OU effort to make a comeback.

Missouri led 10-0 at the half then took a 17-0 edge in the third quarter. Hill took the ensuing kickoff and raced 70 yards to the MU 20. The Sooners scored to close the gap. Missouri took a 24-7 lead in the fourth period, and James scored a TD for the Sooners.

The Sooners' 200th game in history was the following week against Kansas State in Manhattan. The 4-2 Wildcats won, 14-7.

Kansas State took a 7-0 lead in the second quarter, but OU tied it early in the third when Hill shot an 18-yard TD pass to Hendricks down the middle and R.C. Bowles converted. The Wildcats scored a touchdown in the fourth period for the win.

The Sooners stepped outside conference play to meet 4-3-1 Rice in a warm Thanksgiving Day clash in Houston. Oklahoma aerial attacks did in the Owls, 27-0, with Hendricks twice on the receiving end.

The Sooners rapidly moved through the air for their first score in the opening quarter. Morrison zipped a 25-yard pass to Hendricks. Hendricks then hurled a 20-yarder to Tyler to the Rice eight. After being thrown for a loss on the next play, the Sooners went to the air again—Tyler to Hendricks—for the touchdown.

Bowles missed a 25-yard field-goal try in the second stanza, but the Sooners held a 7-0 lead at intermission.

Hill tossed a touchdown pass to Hendricks in the third quarter to put Oklahoma ahead, 13-0. James threw two touchdown passes (to Haskell and Hill) in the fourth quarter.

The Sooners ended the season a disappointing 5-3 record, 2-3 and seventh in the MVC conference. Marsh was the only Sooner selected to the all-conference team.

1922

A funding campaign was underway for a new stadium. The track and field fund was combined with the stadium fund since a cinder track would be built around the football field.

"The entire field is being tilted and prepared for a real gridiron as found in every stadium in the United States," the *Daily Oklahoman* reported.

Head coach Bennie Owen expected to raise enough money to begin building the stadium within one year, but plans to build it would begin as soon as the money was pledged for one section.

"Just as soon as enough money is available, one side of the bowl will be erected, and this process will be continued until the $500,000 structure is completed," he said.

Owen estimated the entire project would take five years to complete.

The Sooner head coach received bad news before the start of fall practices. All-Missouri Valley conference end "Tarz" Marsh was declared ineligible to compete on the team. Quarterback Yiene Hendricks announced he would not return to school, leaving OU with only one quarterback—Eddie Johnson.

Eight varsity lettermen graduated from the 1921 roster—among them halfbacks Dutch Hill, Tub Tyler, and Sol Swatek; end Jap Haskell; and guards Big Bill McKinley and Dow Hamm.

Ram Morrison and R.C. Bowles were among the returnees. New faces included fullback Gordon "Obie" Bristow and halfback Pete Hammert.

The Sooners opened the 1922 campaign on October 14 with a 19-0 victory over Central Teachers College (formerly Central Normal). Bowles scored on a six-yard run in the first quarter and he also toed the extra point.

Central did not penetrate OU territory until the third period, but never posed any scoring threat.

The Sooners got on the board again when Morrison intercepted a pass at the OU 20 then fired a 10-yard TD pass several plays later. Morrison missed the conversion kick. After exchanging punts, Morrison rocketed a 45-yard TD pass to Don Mathes for the final tally.

The Sooner defense held Central to 43 total yards, and the offense rolled up 370.

Guard James Thompson was carried off the field unconscious in the third quarter. He injured his spine during a Central line plunge. Bristow received a wound in the game and spent most of the next week in the hospital. However, both played against Kansas State.

Three days before the game against the favored Wildcats, Coach Owen surprised his team with a real bucking machine. He constructed a bucking apparatus on the rear of a worn-out 1904 automobile. The car had no bearings in the wheels and no tires, but was equipped with a high-powered brake. The linemen skidded the vehicle over the field with the rear wheels locked. The players named their new apparatus "Hearse," due to the man-killing work attached to pushing it.

The day before the game, Marsh was declared eligible for the rest of the season. That brought a smile to Owen's face and all he could say was, "Oh, boy."

The teams battled to a 7-7 tie at Boyd Field on October 21. The 2-0 Wildcats scored their touchdown in the first period. The Sooners had three advances to the Cats goal in the third stanza, but came away empty handed. Hammert scored on an 11-yard end run with four minutes remaining in the game. Bowles' kick notched the score. Oklahoma had a chance to win the game on Bowles' 42-yard field-goal try, but it failed with 30 seconds remaining.

Morrison played the game with the flu and high fever. Despite the illness, he punted 13 times, averaging 36 yards per kick. Doctors diagnosed him with the flu that night, and he would be doubtful for the upcoming Nebraska contest the following week.

The heavily favored Cornhuskers, defending MVC champs, wired Soonerland, claiming to be bringing the best football team in America to Norman. Boyd Field was sold out at 11,000.

The undefeated Huskers (2-0) lived up to their billing as they crushed OU, 39-7. A 50-yard pass from Morrison to Marsh to the NU seven set up the Sooners' lone score in the first quarter. After a no gain on the next play, Morrison flipped a pass to Johnson, but a Husker defender tipped the ball. The pigskin fell into center Herbert Schaefer's hands in the end zone.

After trailing, 7-6, in the first stanza, the Cornhuskers scored a touchdown in the second and third quarters and twice in the fourth.

Nebraska's defense held the Sooners to four first downs and 38 total yards.

Circulars were handed out before the game proclaiming "Oklahoma must have a new stadium." The push for a new stadium was further evident at the next Sooner home game two weeks later.

OU was not expected to lose another game the rest of the season, but after a sluggish offensive performance against the Huskers, Owen put his team through a vigorous offensive workout before the Kansas tilt on November 4.

The offense remained sluggish in a 19-3 loss to the 1-2-1 Jayhawks in Lawrence. Bowles' 23-yard field goal gave OU a 3-0 lead in the second period, but it was all Kansas after that. The Jayhawks scored a touchdown in the third quarter and added two more in the fourth.

The Sooners had six turnovers (five fumbles and one interception) and were held to five first downs and 71 total yards.

Marsh replaced Charles Van Edmondson as team captain prior to the homecoming matchup against 3-2 Missouri on November 11. Johnson scored two touchdowns to lead the Sooners to an 18-14 win over the Tigers. His first came on a 75-yard punt return early in the second quarter. Bristow tossed an 18-yard TD pass to him early in the third period.

Bristow added a three-yard TD plunge in the second quarter.

The Tigers scored twice in the fourth stanza. One Tiger scoring threat was thwarted when Allen Lincoln fumbled at the OU eight, and Schaefer recovered for the Sooners. Schaefer injured his shoulder in the game and was lost for the season, leaving inexperience at center. James Pennick shifted from tackle to center for the rest of the season.

Late in the game, Bristow's punt rolled out of bounds at the Missouri three-yard line for the Tigers' last possession. Bristow intercepted the Missouri pass two plays later to seal the victory.

The game was played before a crowd of 15,000, the largest crowd to see an OU football game to date. The reason for the large crowd was a specially constructed pavilion for the extra fans. The pavilion on the north side of the field collapsed, injuring seven persons. The *Daily Oklahoman* published pictures of the tragedy the following day with the headline, "Here's Why Oklahoma University Must Have Athletic Stadium!"

Oklahoma and Texas had a plethora of injuries leading up to their contest in Norman the following week. Hammert was the only back able to scrimmage for the Sooners that week, and although Morrison, Van Edmondson, Bowles, and Johnson did not practice, they did play against the Longhorns.

Both teams were tied 7-7 at halftime, but 6-1 Texas exploded for two touchdowns in each of the final two quarters and added a safety to down the Sooners, 32-7. Ivan Robertson and Joe Ward each

1922 Season Record: 2-3-3

Missouri Valley Conference: 1-2-2 (Sixth)

Date	Opponent	Result	Score
October 14	CENTRAL NORMAL	W	21-0
October 21	KANSAS STATE	T	7-7
October 28	NEBRASKA	L	39-7
November 4	at Kansas	L	19-3
November 11	MISSOURI	W	18-14
November 18	TEXAS	L	32-7
Novemebr 24	at Oklahoma A&M	T	3-3
November 30	at Washington St. Louis	T	0-0

scored two touchdowns for the Horns. Ward blocked Morrison's punt in the fourth period, which resulted in a safety for the Steers.

Hammert scored OU's only touchdown, a 41-yard run five minutes into the first period, and Bowles added the extra point. Poor passing and turnovers killed the Sooners. OU completed only one of 12 passes with three intercepted. The Sooners also lost five fumbles.

The score might have been worse, but the Big Red defense stopped four Texas drives to the Oklahoma goal line.

The Sooners practiced for two days in a secluded location three miles outside of Norman in preparation for the 3-4 Oklahoma Aggies. OU's poor showing against Texas gave the Aggies high hopes of defeating Oklahoma for only the second time in the 15-year rivalry.

Both teams battled to a 3-3 tie in Stillwater on November 24. Bowles nailed a 24-yard field goal in the first quarter, and A&M added one early in the second period. The Aggies advanced to the OU 10-yard line late in the third stanza and continuing early into the fourth, but were held to only six yards on the next three plays. Marsh blocked the field-goal try, and Clinton Steinberger recovered for the Sooners, returning the ball to midfield. Bowles' 30-yard field-goal attempt fell short of the target late in the game.

The Sooners outgained the Aggies in total yards with 204 to 195 and in first downs (11 to eight).

The Sooners ended the season with a scoreless tie with Washington St. Louis. The Thanksgiving Day game was played in St. Louis in a drizzling rain. The tie kept Oklahoma out of the conference cellar, yet the 2-3-3 record was the worst of Owen's 18-year tenure. OU finished sixth in the MVC with a 1-2-2 record.

Marsh was the only Sooner selected to the All-MVC team.

1923

As the new stadium was being built, Bennie Owen had to rebuild his football team with the return of only four lettermen—halfback Pete Hammert, quarterback Eddie Johnson, guard James Thompson, and tackle/kicker R.C. Bowles. Yiene Hendricks also returned to the squad after a year layoff and was switched to halfback. Though he was only a junior, Hammert was elected captain, the first junior to be voted the honor since Erl Deacon in 1919.

Center Herbert Schaefer quit school and returned home to Drumright, leaving a big gap in the line. Glen Hartford and L.B. Fleming battled to become Schaefer's replacement. Hartford got the nod as the season began.

Owen had to turn to an inexperienced but talented bunch from the 1922 freshman squad. The freshmen were touted as one of the best class of newcomers in Owen's regime as they outperformed the varsity squad in daily practices.

"The first-year men were so deadly that the coaches had to disband the squad a week before the season closed in order to have a varsity 11 at all to finish the season," the *Daily Oklahoman* reported.

The newcomers included fullbacks Roy "Goat" Lamb and William Wolfe and halfbacks Dale Arbuckle, Bernard Hunter, and Loyal Woodall.

Four steel bleachers were added to the 15 wooden ones brought over from Boyd Field. Reserved capacity grew from 3,000 to 4,000 seats and was expected to rise to 10,000 by homecoming against Kansas. A new locker room with showers also was being built.

Nebraska also was constructing a new stadium, and 15,000 turned out for the first game against Oklahoma. Illinois stunned the Huskers, 24-7, in the season opener in Champaign, Illinois.

Nebraska, the defending Missouri Valley Conference champs, returned to form by dropping the Sooners, 24-7 on October 13 in Lincoln. The Huskers rolled up 360 yards and 19 first downs behind the running attack of Dave Noble, brothers Rufus and Herb Dewitz, and Rolland Locke.

Hammert gift-wrapped two NU scores. His fumble led to a field goal in the second quarter, and the Huskers only led 3-0 at intermission. The Sooners marched to the NU 10-yard line late in the third stanza, but Hammert's fumble was returned 90 yards for a touchdown.

The Sooners hosted Washington St. Louis (1-1) the following week, and Owen expected "to win this game." Hendricks scored four touchdowns as the Sooners blasted the Pikers, 62-7.

OU opened the game with an impressive display of passes, line bucks and end sweeps. Hendricks scored off a 50-yard interception three minutes into the game, and the onslaught was on. He scored again later in the opening quarter.

The Sooners led 21-0 at halftime, and Coach Owen sent in the reserves in the second half. OU recovered a fumble at the Pikers' 15, and Hendricks drilled a TD pass to end King Price. Hammert added the fifth touchdown on an end run. Obie Bristow fired a 40-yard TD pass to Johnson late in the third quarter. Arbuckle scored a 74-yard touchdown run and added a 60-yard run, but was stopped short of the goal.

Oklahoma totaled 413 yards and 28 first downs while holding the Pikers to minus four total yards and six first downs.

The 1-3 Oklahoma Aggies were fresh off a 13-0 victory over Rice and were looking to upset the Sooners on October 27 in Norman. The Sooners spoiled the upset bid with a 12-0 shutout.

Oklahoma drove to the A&M 17 late in the first period. Hendricks, Hammert, and Bristow continued to hammer out line plunges to the A&M four. Hendricks then blasted off right tackle for the touchdown.

Both teams were forced into a punting duel in the third quarter and most of the fourth stanza. The Aggies drove to the OU 15 late in the game on a series of long passes. The next pass, a five-yarder intended for Nate Hasbrook, was intercepted. Johnson stepped in front of Hasbrook, leaped high in the air to snag the pass, and flew 90 yards down the sideline for the touchdown.

Kansas, 2-0-2 and fresh off two scoreless ties, arrived in Norman for homecoming on November 3 and won 7-3 on a soggy field. Lamb had started for an injured Bristow at fullback, and Fleming replaced Hartford at center. Owen said he wanted a bigger body up front with Fleming.

Bowles kicked a 45-yard field goal to put the Sooners on top in the second stanza, but KU scored the decisive touchdown on Charles Black's end run in the third.

OU twice moved to the KU goal, but the Jayhawks held.

The Sooners shut out Missouri, 13-0, on November 10 before a record crowd of 12,000 in Columbia. Bristow scored the first touchdown in the second quarter, but Bowles' conversion veered wide. Bristow also had a 38-yard TD run called back due to an offside penalty. Hammert added another touchdown in the third period. Johnson, holding for Hammert to kick the extra point, took an errant snap from Alfred McFadden and raced around end for the conversion.

The Tigers twice marched inside the OU 25, but one field goal sailed wide and the other was blocked. Missouri drove inside the Sooner 20 late in the game but surrendered the ball on downs.

The Missouri win had the Sooners feeling good about their chances against Texas in Austin the next week, especially when they learned six Longhorn stars were sidelined with injuries. The

Oklahoma squad rode the train to Austin, and when it stopped in Ardmore, Bristow's mother met the team. She gave her son a box of chocolate candy, and he declared every piece as a Sooner touchdown.

Owen and his assistants took advantage of the long ride by planning the 1924 schedule and talking strategy with the players for Texas.

The Steers jumped to a 26-0 lead through the first three quarters en route to a 26-14 victory. OU scored its only points in the fourth period. Following Johnson's interception, Bristow's TD pass to Don Mathes capped a five-play, 82-yard drive. The second Sooner touchdown came later on Bristow's line plunge.

The game against the 3-1-2 Kansas State in Manhattan was changed to a day earlier (November 23) in order for both teams to get in condition for their Thanksgiving Day finales. The game against the Wildcats was billed as an aerial attack by both teams.

The Sooner players dedicated the game to Johnson and Bowles with a victory, but it was not to be when Bowles missed an extra point to tie the game in the waning minutes. The Cats won, 21-20.

Lamb scored a touchdown for Oklahoma in the first five minutes. K-State's TD in the second stanza tied the game, then the Cats added two more touchdowns in the third quarter for a 21-7 advantage.

Bristow returned an interception 90 yards for a touchdown in the fourth period to cut the Cats' lead. Johnson later hooked up with Arbuckle for a 25-yard TD pass, but R.C. Bowles' missed kick dropped the Sooners' record to 3-4. The Wildcats also won the aerial battle, completing 18 of 28 passes for 161 yards and two touchdowns. OU managed to complete only eight of 16 for 104 yards.

Hendricks cut his left hand when he tried to "alight from a motor car," the *Daily Oklahoman* reported. The newspaper continued that Hendricks "grasped the glass in the door, was thrown away from the machine as it rounded a turn and the glass broke." Hendricks received seven stitches to his hand.

The injury list grew. Price broke a finger in the Kansas State game, and backup end C.E. Strouvelle wrenched his back and was out for the finale against 4-2 Drake in Norman.

Strouvelle and Hendricks were suspended from the team when OU's faculty revealed both had violated school rules. This news placed the entire team in an ugly, fighting mood. Hendricks' suspension took away any possible aerial threat. Lamb replaced Hendricks in the lineup, but he was not as good a ball catcher.

Drake quarterback Sam Orebaugh scored three touchdowns to lead the Bulldogs to a 26-20 victory. After Drake took a 7-0 lead in the opening quarter, Bristow's 15-yard pass to Price in the second period tied the game. The Bulldogs took the lead driving 50 yards for a touchdown following Lamb's fumble.

Orebaugh scored his second TD in the third stanza. Bristow scored a touchdown each in the third and fourth quarters. Bowles' extra-point kick after the second Bristow TD tied the game, but Orebaugh later added his third touchdown.

The Sooners' three-game skid to end the season was the worst since dropping four straight in 1916. Oklahoma ended the season 3-5 and in the conference cellar with a 2-4 mark. Price was the only Sooner selected to the all-conference team.

1924

All-America tackle Roy "Soupy" Smoot returned to the Sooners to complete his final year of eligibility after touring the country as an opera singer. Smoot's goal was to get into "trim" condition after the four-year layoff. At 190 pounds, he was 20 pounds lighter than when he last suited up.

Claude Reeds, a Sooner star from 1910-1913, also returned as assistant coach and the head man of the freshman squad. He whipped the newcomers into shape, and many times the freshmen outperformed the varsity. In fact, the freshmen Boomers defeated the varsity Sooners, 13-0, during a break in the third week of the season.

Still head coach Bennie Owen was optimistic with the return of many veterans. Yiene Hendricks, Obie Bristow, Roy "Goat" Lamb, and Dale Arbuckle returned to the backfield. Hendricks was switched from halfback to quarterback to replace the graduating Eddie Johnson.

James Thompson and Glen Hartford returned to bolster the line. Herbert Schaefer returned to the team after quitting a year ago, but he was sidelined most of the year with injuries. Ends King Price and Loyal Woodall also returned. Halfback Pete Hammert did not return for personal reasons, so the team elected Bristow as captain.

A new NCAA rule prohibited the use of kicking tees for place kicks. Owen had his kickers work on getting used to not having a tee.

Central Teachers College defeated OU for the first time in 18 years, 2-0, in Norman on October 4. Bristow attempted to punt from deep in Sooner territory in the third quarter. The Bronchos blocked the kick, and Bristow smothered the pigskin in the end zone to give Central a safety. Bristow was soon ejected from the game for slugging.

The Bronchos outplayed the lethargic Sooners during the entire game, which was mostly played in OU territory. The Sooners had a chance to score in the first stanza, but turned the ball over at the Bronchos' four. The uninspired performance had many Sooner faithful scratching their heads.

Owen moved Hendricks back to halfback to reinvigorate the backfield and installed Johnny Carroll as the starting quarterback.

With 0-1 Nebraska coming to Norman the next week, the freshmen used Nebraska plays and scored five touchdowns on the varsity during a mid-week scrimmage. The Cornhuskers, coming off a 9-6 setback to Illinois, was favored to beat OU by three touchdowns, although their star halfback Rolland Locke was out with an injury.

Owen asked Bristow if he had anything to say to the team in the locker room before the game.

"I'll say I have something to tell them," Bristow responded. "Fellows, we've been trying for years to beat Nebraska. We tied her once, but we have never beaten her.

"This is my last chance. Smoot, it's your last chance. Yes, Yiene, Pennick, and White and Price, you're taking your last crack at the Cornhuskers, too. Wouldn't you like to go out with the honor of being on the first Oklahoma team to beat Nebraska?"

1923 Season Record: 3-5-0
Missouri Valley Conference: 2-4-0 (Sixth)

Date	Opponent	Result	Score
October 13	at Nebraska	L	24-0
October 20	WASHINGTON ST. LOUIS	W	62-7
October 27	OKLAHOMA A&M	W	12-0
November 3	KANSAS	L	7-3
November 10	at Missouri	W	13-0
November 17	at Texas	L	26-14
November 23	at Kansas State	L	21-20
November 29	DRAKE	L	26-20

Roy "Goat" Lamb, scores the deciding touchdown in the second period in OU's 14-7 win over Nebraska. (*Western History Collections, University of Oklahoma*)

Bristow evidently inspired his teammates as the Sooners dropped Nebraska for the first time in six meetings, 14-7, in the conference opener. In the game's first minute, Nebraska punter Elbert Bloodgood attempted to punt from his own 15-yard line. The Sooners blocked the kick, and Woodall scored after scooping the ball up at the five.

Bloodgood had more trouble with the Sooner defenders on another punt attempt in the second period as he was smothered by crimson jerseys. OU gained possession at its own 47. After Bristow was tossed for a six-yard loss, Hendricks fired a pass to Woodall to the Husker 15. Bristow and Hendricks hammered to the one, and then Lamb plowed through for the score. Bristow made good on both extra-point kicks.

Halfback Monte Ledford experienced a cracked rib and was out for the year. Lamb suffered a shoulder injury and was doubtful for the rest of the year, but returned to the team following the scrimmage the next week against the freshmen.

The following week, the Sooners traveled to Des Moines, Iowa, to face Drake. The 3-0 Bulldogs had won 18 of their last 20 games. Drake quarterback Sam Orebaugh, who scored three touchdowns against the Sooners the year before, did it again as the Bulldogs shut down Oklahoma, 28-0 on October 25. He also successfully booted all four conversions.

The 1-2 Sooners were back on the road again on November 1, this time to Stillwater. The 4-1 Oklahoma A&M Aggies believed they might pull off the upset. They were right as Jim Lookabaugh's second-quarter touchdown was the only score of the 6-0 contest.

OU again was lethargic as most of the game was played in Sooner territory. A&M totaled 162 yards, with Lookabaugh rushing for 129. OU managed only 45 total yards and three first downs.

Hendricks, with two crushed ribs, was out for the Missouri game the next week. Woodall also was sidelined with a sprained ankle. Don Mathes replaced him at left end.

Missouri defeated the Sooners, 10-0, on November 8 before a homecoming crowd of 9,471 at Owen Field. Arthur Coglizer nailed a 20-yard field goal follow-

Obie Bristow, team captain, scored a six-yard touchdown to defeat the Washington Pikers, 7-0. He also sparked the winning TD drive with a 17-yard pass. (*OU Athletics*)

ing the Tigers' recovery of Bristow's fumble in the second stanza. H.R. Jackson scored a three-yard TD in the third period.

OU completed only four of 15 passes and had five intercepted. The Sooners also lost two of three fumbles.

Kansas scored a touchdown in each of the first three quarters to deal the Sooners their fourth straight shutout, 20-0, in Lawrence the following week. KU fullback Harold Burt scored two TDs for his team.

Sooner Magic: A Bright Moment in a Losing Season

Oklahoma had never lost to the Washington Pikers in five previous meetings. The Sooners held a 4-0-1 record against their conference rival, but the sixth meeting on November 23 was no guarantee. After all, this had been a year of firsts—the first time Central Teacher's College defeated OU and the first time Oklahoma beat Nebraska. OU and Washington were playing to avoid the Missouri Valley cellar.

In Washington's six games that season, the results ended in a shutout. The Pikers defeated Drury, 7-0, lost to Grinnell College, 14-0, defeated Missouri Rolla, 13-0, lost to Kansas, 48-0, defeated James Millikin, 10-0, and lost to Missouri, 35-0.

The Pikers were favorites against Oklahoma, because they were playing on their home field.

The Sooners' 7-0 victory over the Pikers could have been more decisive. Numerous blown scoring opportunities had frustrated Owen and his troops.

Early in the second quarter, Bristow's 47-yard field-goal attempt fell short of the target.

The Sooners marched 45 yards on their next possession to the Washington 10, but the Piker defense held. A few minutes later, the Sooners advanced the ball to the WU 36, and again Bristow was called on to attempt another 47-yard field goal. Just like the first kick, the ball never reached the goal posts.

James Pennick's recovery of a Piker fumble at the WU seven gave the Sooners another scoring chance. Bristow burst ahead for four yards. Halfback Bill Haller was thrown for a two-yard loss on the next play. An offside penalty pushed the Big Red back to the 10. On fourth down, Bristow connected a pass to Elmer Slough, but the Pikers stopped him at the two and took possession.

The first half ended scoreless.

The third quarter and nearly all of the fourth was a defensive struggle, as both teams were unable to gain huge chunks of yards and punted on each possession.

Late in the game, OU put together the winning drive. Lamb took a Piker punt eight yards to the OU 48. A Bristow-to-Lamb pass play

1924 Season Record: 2-5-1
Missouri Valley Conference: 2-3-1 (Sixth)

Date	Opponent	Result	Score
October 4	CENTRAL NORMAL	L	2-0
October 11	NEBRASKA	W	14-7
October 25	at Drake	L	28-0
November 1	at Oklahoma A&M	L	6-0
November 8	MISSOURI	L	10-0
November 15	at Kansas	L	20-0
November 23	at Washington St. Louis	W	7-0
November 27	KANSAS STATE	T	7-7

gained 17 yards to the WU 35. Bristow attempted another pass, but the Sooner line crumbled and Bristow was nailed for no gain. The Piker defense was called for offside, which moved the ball to the Washington 30.

Two plays later, Bristow hurled a pass to halfback Doc Ruppert in the open, and Ruppert bolted 20 yards to the WU 10. Ruppert ran for three yards on the next play, which was followed by his one-yard off-tackle plunge to the six.

Bristow crashed through the line and crossed the goal line for the touchdown. This time he was able to boot the ball through the uprights, and OU escaped St. Louis with a victory.

The Sooners and Kansas State fought to a 7-7 standoff on Thanksgiving Day in Norman.

Lamb picked off a Wildcat pass six minutes into the first period and flashed 40 yards down the right sideline for a touchdown. Bristow's toe gave OU a 7-0 lead. The Cats scored a tying touchdown in the fourth quarter and later threatened with another TD, a drive from their 20 to the OU four. On fourth down, Smoot stopped their halfback on an end run and nailed him for a 10-yard loss.

The Sooners ended the season with a 2-5-1 record, the worst in Owen's career. Oklahoma finished sixth in the conference with a 2-3-1 mark. Bristow and Smoot were the only Sooners selected to the all-conference team.

1925

Football tickets were sold via mail for the first time, and prior to each game, seats were also sold throughout the state's principal cities.

The university also had a new president—Dr. William Bennett Bizzell. He served 16 years as the university's top man and led a campaign to have a new library built. The library was completed in 1929 and dedicated in his honor a year later.

The 1925 Sooners had new faces in the backfield. Gone were Yiene Hendricks, Obie Bristow, and Roy "Goat" Lamb. Lamb decided to transfer to Stanford University. This left a huge vacancy at fullback and punter. Frank Potts fulfilled both duties, although his punting averages in practices were considerably shorter than Lamb's. Potts was nailing punts an average of 30 yards. Lamb averaged 45 to 50 yards. Lamb returned before the second game of the season. He said he did not like the appearance of Stanford. Ray LeCrone was the backup fullback and his brother, Roy, started at end.

Potts and Houston "Bus" Hill were fresh faces in the backfield, joining veterans Elmer Slough, Dale Arbuckle, and Bill Haller. The front line was a complete overhaul of newcomers, with Captain Ed Brockman moved to left tackle, and Roy Guffey and Granville "Granny" Norris battled for the right tackle spot. Zetta Wolfe and Bob Sumpter were the guards, and Leigh "Polly" Wallace took over Brockman's slot at center. Mart Brown and Abe Voth vied with Roy LeCrone for the end positions.

A sore shoulder kept Haller out of the season opener on October 3 against Kansas State in Manhattan. After a scoreless first half, the 1-0 Wildcats scored two touchdowns and a field goal in the final 20 minutes for a 16-0 win.

The Sooners outgained K-State in total yards (174-140) and first downs (10-6), but the Big Red was plagued with five turnovers (three fumbles and two interceptions) and nine penalties.

Bennie Owen was very unhappy with his team's performance, and following the Kansas State loss, he announced that all first-string positions were wide open. The Sooners had two weeks to find out who would step up before the next game against Drake on October 17 in Norman. Lamb had no trouble gaining his starting job at fullback and punter. The other starters held onto their positions by the time the Bulldogs came to town.

Two new sections, containing 7,500 seats, of the stadium were open for the Drake game. The entire west wing of the stadium would be open for the homecoming contest against Kansas.

Drake had shut out its first two opponents—5-0 over Washington St. Louis and 19-0 over the Kansas Aggies. The Sooners were looking to end their two-game skid against the Bulldogs.

Lamb's one-yard leap into the end zone in the game's first five minutes was the only score as the Sooners dropped the Bulldogs, 7-0. Lamb's touchdown capped a 59-yard drive and Brockman converted the extra point.

Lamb's poor punt to the OU 29 gave Drake an opportunity to tie the game later in the first period, but the Bulldogs fumbled, and Wolfe recovered at the 20. Another Drake drive was snuffed by Slough's interception. The Bulldogs had three more opportunities in the fourth quarter, but a fumble and two interceptions killed their efforts.

John "Firpo" Wilcox, a tackle for the 1923 Sooners, had returned to the Sooners and started at right tackle against Southern Methodist the next week in Dallas. But Haller, Voth, and umpter were sidelined with injuries.

Oklahoma shut down 3-0 SMU, 9-0, on October 24 in the first meeting between both schools. The Sooners intercepted 10 Mustang passes, and Arbuckle picked off half of them. SMU also lost two fumbles in the game.

Brockman booted a 32-yard field goal late in the second quarter for the only scoring of the first half. Hill's 27-yard TD pass to Slough in the fourth quarter increased the Sooner lead to 9-0, but Brockman's extra-point kick was wide. The Sooners had another scoring chance in the fourth quarter, but that stalled at the SMU three.

The Sooners were hampered with injuries prior to the big contest against Nebraska at Lincoln. Norris suffered a fractured ankle, Potts a sore shoulder, and Bob Sumpter a twisted knee. Lamb was banged and bruised but made the trip.

But the big story came from Cy Sherman, sports editor of the *Lincoln Star*. He wrote that Wilcox was threatened with ineligibility because the Sooner lineman had engaged in professional boxing in Tulsa in 1920. Wilcox contended that he fought only as an amateur as a student at Kendall College.

Wilcox would have been ineligible if he fought as an amateur on the same card with the pros, yet he received no money for his work. Dean S.W. Beyers of Iowa State University and chairman of the Missouri Valley eligibility committee believed such participation would make Wilcox ineligible. Dr. S.W. Reaves, George Wadsack, and Dr. Edgar Meacham, members of the OU eligibility committee, said his participation should not affect his eligibility.

Professor R.D. Scott of Nebraska University wrote members of the Oklahoma committee, whose findings deemed that Wilcox did nothing illegal. Wilcox not only made the trip to Lincoln, he started.

Nebraska defeated the Sooners, 12-0, on October 31. The 2-1-1 Huskers drove 69 yards following the opening kickoff for the first score and added a touchdown pass in the fourth stanza.

OU marched to the Nebraska 20-yard line late in the first half, but time expired. The Huskers also had two scoring threats in the third period, but fumbled away both opportunities.

Coach Owen unveiled new plays to his battered and bruised charges before Kansas came to town November 7 for homecoming.

Sumpter and Potts returned to the lineup. The 1-4 Jayhawks lost four straight after defeating Oklahoma A&M in the season opener.

The Sooners and Jayhawks battled to a scoreless tie on a soggy field under cloudy skies and a stinging north wind.

OU was unable to score off two penetrations inside the KU five and turned the ball over on downs. Lamb's 51-yard run to the KU seven sparked the first drive, but he slipped in a mud hole after outmaneuvering the Jayhawks. The Sooners moved to the Jayhawks' one following a blocked punt in the second quarter but could not score.

Another cold game on a muddy field greeted the Sooners on November 14 in Columbia. The Tigers won, 16-14, in the final game at Rollins Field. MU won five straight victories after tying Tulane in the season opener and was undefeated at 3-0 in the conference.

Potts hooked up with Roy LeCrone for a 30-yard touchdown in the game's first five minutes to give the Sooners a 7-0 lead after Brockman booted the conversion. Another drive into Tiger territory came up empty when Brockman's 27-yard field goal was blocked.

The Tigers blocked Lamb's punt in the second stanza but turned the ball over on downs at the one-yard line. Missouri held the Sooners deep, and Bert Clark returned Lamb's punt 28 yards for a touchdown.

Bill Coglizer later kicked a 34-yard field goal to put the Tigers ahead, 10-7. H.R. Jackson's touchdown put MU ahead, 16-7, in the fourth period. The extra-point attempt was blocked. Lamb scored on a one-yard run to cap a 69-yard Sooner drive following the kick-off. Brockman converted both Sooner extra points in the game.

The 2-3-1 Sooners returned home the following week to host the 1-4-1 Washington Pikers. Sumpter returned to the roster for the first time in weeks, but Owen suspended Wilcox and backup end Sonny Strouvelle for violating training rules on the Missouri trip.

A healthy Potts began to improve his passing. During practice the week of the Piker game, he sailed the pigskin 90 yards to Hill several times. He would give Hill a 60-yard lead, then sailed the ball to his teammate who caught the aerials.

Dale Arbuckle intercepted five passes against Southern Methodist to lead OU to a 9-0 victory. (*OU Athletics*)

Potts' improved passing proved fatal as the Sooners downed Washington, 28-0, before a crowd of 6,000. The Big Red only completed four of 14 passes, but for 145 yards.

OU scored twice in the first stanza and again in the fourth. The first touchdown was a 52-yard bomb from Potts to Roy LeCrone. Minutes later, a poor Piker punt set up the Sooners at the WU 15. Hill blasted through the line four plays later to up the Oklahoma lead to 14-0.

Midway through the fourth period, Lamb's one-yard TD run capped a 67-yard drive, which was highlighted by Potts' 36-yard run to the Piker 24. About five minutes later, Hill intercepted a Washington pass and returned it 25 yards to the WU four. Hill then blasted across the goal line for the final tally. Brockman was true on all conversions.

The Sooners ended the season with another shutout, 35-0, over Oklahoma A&M, the newest member of the Missouri Valley Conference, on Thanksgiving Day in Norman.

OU drove to the Aggie five in the first quarter, but Lamb fumbled the ball away. Moments later, Guffey recovered an Aggie fumble, and Lamb redeemed himself with a touchdown on the following play.

A&M rode an aerial attack to the OU 12, but had to settle for a field goal, which the Sooners blocked.

In the third period, Lamb picked off an Aggie pass and returned it 53 yards for a touchdown. The Sooners blocked an A&M punt at the end of the third stanza. Three plays later, Hill scored from the four to up the OU lead to 21-0.

The lead grew larger moments later when Potts fired a 53-yard TD pass to Roy LeCrone. Wallace's interception at midfield set up the final Sooner tally. OU drove to the Aggie three sparked by Arbuckle's 27-yard scamper to the A&M 14. Four plays later, Potts blasted through for a touchdown. Brockman converted all five extra points.

The victory assured the Sooners of a winning season with a 4-3-1 record and fifth in the conference 3-3-1 mark. Wilcox and Polly Wallace were named to the All-Missouri Valley first team.

1926

Bennie Owen and the Sooners laid their hopes on experience in 1926. Three-fifths of the front line returned—Captain Polly Wallace at center, Bob Sumpter, and Granny Norris. Sumpter was moved to tackle opposite Norris. Hal Muldrow and Howard "Doc" Martin were the new faces at guard. Roy LeCrone and Mort Brown returned at ends.

Changes were made to the backfield as Goat Lamb, Elmer Slough, and Bus Hill did not return. Dale Arbuckle stepped in at quarterback, Frank Potts was moved to halfback. Lynwood "Bus" Haskins, Prentiss Mooney (a transfer from Oklahoma Baptist), and Ben "Wildhorse" Taylor vied for the other halfback position. Ray LeCrone, Roy's brother, got the nod at fullback.

1925 Season Record: 4-3-1
Missouri Valley Conference: 3-3-1 (Fifth)

Date	Opponent	Result	Score
October 3	at Kansas State	L	16-0
October 17	DRAKE	W	7-0
October 24	at Southern Methodist	W	9-0
October 31	at Nebraska	L	12-0
November 7	KANSAS	T	0-0
November 14	at Missouri	L	16-14
November 21	WASHINGTON ST. LOUIS	W	28-0
November 26	OKLAHOMA A&M	W	35-0

Searching for a faster backfield, Owen started Potts and Taylor as halfbacks before the season opener against Arkansas in Norman on October 9. Sooner backs also wore lighter rubber moleskins to aid their speed.

The Razorbacks already had two games under their belts. They crushed Central Oklahoma, 60-0, and defeated Mississippi, 21-6. The Oklahoma-Arkansas matchup was the first since 1919. It would also be the last time the two teams would meet for another 49 years.

OU prevailed, 13-6, on a muddy Owen Field. After a scoreless first half, Norris' touchdown run gave Oklahoma a 6-0 lead in the third quarter. Potts missed the extra point.

The Sooners drove with inches of the Hogs' goal late in the third stanza but turned the ball over on downs. Potts tossed a touchdown pass to Ray LeCrone early in the fourth period, and Paul Ward booted the extra point. The Hogs scored later in the quarter, and Potts blocked the extra point.

The soggy field held both teams to low total yards. OU gained 85 and Arkansas only 22.

The Sooners traveled to Des Moines, Iowa, the following week to meet winless Drake. The Bulldogs had lost to Nebraska and Navy. OU shut down the Dogs, 11-0, in the final contest between the two.

Mooney nailed a 16-yard field goal in the second stanza, and Drake later took an intentional safety instead of punting. The Bulldogs later fumbled away an opportunity after marching to the OU 15.

The Big Red had an opportunity to score after Ray LeCrone returned an interception to the Drake 12, but fumbled. Martin later blocked a punt, and Norris scooped up the ball at the Drake 16 and scored.

Kansas State (3-0) rolled into Norman October 23, and the Wildcats stayed undefeated as Dewey Huston stunned the 15,000 fans with a 25-yard field goal late in the game.

The Sooners drove to pay dirt following the opening kickoff. Ray LeCrone capped the drive with his touchdown run followed by Haskins' extra point. Haskins added a field goal in the second period, and a safety in the same quarter gave OU a 12-0 halftime lead.

The Wildcats scored a touchdown early in the third stanza, but the conversion hit the crossbar. K-State drove for another score in the fourth period after blocking Haskins' field-goal attempt. The score was tied at 12-12 after the Cats' extra point bounced off the goal post, but Huston's field goal dropped the Sooners to 2-1 on the season.

Wallace wrenched his knee in the third period and was out of the lineup against the Washington Pikers on October 30.

The Sooners shutout the 1-3 Pikers, 21-0, in St. Louis. Haskins tossed a 17-yard TD pass to Brown early in the second period. Potts' 65-yard run to the Piker two sparked a drive early in the fourth period. Ray LeCrone carried the ball across on the next play.

Potts later sailed around right end for a 20-yard TD. Haskins was true on all extra-point conversions.

100th Home Game

Wallace was back at practice for the homecoming clash with the Missouri Tigers. The Sooners dropped the 3-0-2 Tigers, 10-7, before a record crowd of 16,235 in the 100th home game in Sooner football history on November 6.

Haskins' 40-yard field-goal attempt fell short in the first quarter, and minutes later, Mooney's 35-yard drop-kick try veered left of the goal post.

A 35-yard TD pass from George Flamank to Bert Clark put Mizzou on top, 7-0, midway through the second quarter.

OU had the ball at its 46 with 15 seconds remaining until half-time. Potts dropped back to pass then dashed through an opening on the left side and raced to the end zone. Potts stiff-armed a Tiger safety at the MU 10, sending him crashing to the turf. Potts crossed the goal line as the pistol cracked to signal the end of the first half. Haskins booted the extra point, and both teams were tied at intermission.

Norris blocked a Missouri punt early in the third quarter, and Roy LeCrone smothered the pigskin at the Tiger 27. The Sooners had to settle for Haskins' 32-yard field goal, which was the final tally of the game.

Mizzou drove to the OU eight early in the fourth stanza, but Haskins batted away a fourth-down pass in the end zone. Another Tiger drive stalled at the OU 20 late in the game.

The Big Red had little time to rest in preparation for the Kansas Jayhawks five days later. The game was scheduled for Armistice Day, and Dwight F. Davis, President Calvin Coolidge's secretary of war, attended. The Sooners took the rail to Kansas City where they lodged and practiced before heading to Lawrence. The 1-5 Jayhawks stunned the Sooners, 10-9, with a field goal in the final minute.

A poor Kansas punt in the first quarter set up Oklahoma at its 45-yard line. Arbuckle's 15-yard pass to Potts and Potts' 30-yard pass to Haskins sparked the drive to the KU five. From the two, Potts dropped back to pass, then handed off to Arbuckle, who scampered across the goal line. Haskins missed the conversion.

Harold Zuber scored on a one-yard run in the second period, and Charles Wall's conversion put the Jayhawks ahead, 7-6. After Wall missed a 34-yard field-goal try for Kansas early in the fourth quarter, the Sooners marched to the KU six. Mooney nailed a 15-yard field goal to lift OU to a 9-7 advantage.

Two ensuing Jayhawk drives were squelched by interceptions. Backup center Summie Kidd picked off the first, and Ward robbed the second. The third drive, late in the game, aided the Jayhawks to victory. A 40-yard pass set up George Mackie's 20-yard field goal.

Wallace injured his knee again and had to watch practices from the sidelines wearing a cast. Kidd was pegged the starting center nine days later when the Sooners hosted the St. Louis Billikens. Muldrow kept his spot as reserve center allowing Bob Cooke to start at right guard. Bus Haskins also was injured and did not play against St. Louis.

The Sooners blasted the Billikens, 47-0, on November 20 before a crowd of 5,000 shivering fans. Seven Sooners scored touchdowns in the onslaught. Roy LeCrone returned the opening kickoff 52 yards for the first score. After OU took a 21-0 first-quarter lead, many reserves played the rest of the game.

1926 Season Record: 5-2-1

Missouri Valley Conference: 3-2-1 (Fifth)

Date	Opponent	Result	Score
October 9	ARKANSAS	W	13-6
October 16	at Drake	W	11-0
October 23	KANSAS STATE	L	15-12
October 30	at Washington St. Louis	W	21-0
November 6	MISSOURI	W	10-7
November 11	at Kansas	L	10-9
November 20	ST. LOUIS	W	47-0
November 25	at Oklahoma A&M	T	14-14

The Sooners rolled up 313 total yards to only 20 for St. Louis. OU also led in first downs, 19-8.

Wallace and Haskins returned to practice in time for the Thanksgiving Day clash against Oklahoma A&M. The Aggie fans believed this was their year to beat the Sooners. "Hang it on OU," was the cry around Stillwater. If the Aggies beat the Sooners, they would win the Missouri Valley Conference crown.

The Sooners and Aggies battled to a 14-14 tie before 12,000 homecoming spectators at Lewis Field, including 1,000 crimson fans. The Aggies jumped ahead, 7-0, with a touchdown in the first quarter. Ray LeCrone's four-yard TD run and Ward's conversion knotted the game in the second period.

Ray LeCrone added another touchdown run to cap a 60-yard OU drive in the third stanza. Haskins kicked the extra point. A 20-yard pass from A&M's Gordon Peery to Claude Poole in the fourth quarter and Charlie Strack's kick tied the game.

The Big Red finished the season 5-2-1 and finished fifth in the conference with a 3-2-1 mark. Potts, Wallace, and Roy LeCrone were selected to the All-MVC first team.

On February 3, 1927, 80 days after the Oklahoma Aggie game, Owen resigned as the head coach of the Sooners to devote more time as the university's athletic director. Adrian "Ad" Lindsey was appointed seventh head coach. Like Owen, Lindsey played at Bethany College and at Kansas. A native of Kingfisher, Oklahoma, Lindsey was also an assistant at KU when he was chosen as the Sooners' new coach.

1927

A week before the first Sooner game at Chicago, six of the Missouri Valley Conference institutions organized a new conference to become effective in June 1928, the end of the 1927-28 academic year. In addition to the University of Oklahoma, the other schools were Iowa State, Kansas State, Kansas, Missouri, and Nebraska.

The schools wanted to break from the MVC, citing the conference was too "unwieldy" and was unfair in conference scheduling. Teams were not of equal caliber, the round-robin basketball schedule took too much of the students' time, there was too much difference in size and enrollment and in equality in athletic powers.

The name of the new conference had not yet been determined.

A major change to the college game moved goal posts back 10 yards from the goal line to prevent players from running into the unpadded uprights.

After Bennie Owen resigned as head coach in February, Frank Potts decided not to return for his final year at OU, stating he would "rather make a career than another letter." He was married in September and was hired by Colorado University as the freshman football coach and head coach for the Buffaloes' track team.

Claude Reeds was added to the Oklahoma varsity staff as line coach.

Ad Lindsey's first Sooner football team was one of the lightest rosters in years. At 185 pounds, right guard Hal Muldrow was the heaviest player on the squad. Veterans Ray LeCrone and Bus Haskins returned to the backfield. Tackle Granny Norris and ends Mort Brown and Roy LeCrone also were back. Summie Kidd got the starting nod at center, and Harry Berry started at left guard. Prentiss Mooney earned the starting slot at quarterback and sophomore Frank Crider at fullback.

Lindsey said he expected his "mighty" new material to be "in fine shape for all conference games."

Oklahoma's first opponent was the Chicago Maroons, coached by Amos Alonzo Stagg, who was in his 34th year as head coach. The Maroons debuted knit trousers, which were three pounds lighter than the traditional moleskins.

The Oklahoma contingent left by rail on Wednesday, four days before the game, and lodged and practiced in Kansas City. Ray LeCrone and Ben Taylor did not make the trip. LeCrone had battled the flu, and Taylor suffered broken ribs in a scrimmage.

That same day, Charles Lindbergh came to Oklahoma City. He was paraded through the city and later performed an aerial exhibit in the "Spirit of St. Louis" at the Oklahoma State Fair.

Haskins performed an aerial show of his own in the Windy City as the Sooners dropped the Maroons, 13-7, on October 1, impressing the crowd of 25,000.

Neither team generated much offense in the scoreless first quarter. Chicago had one first down, and the Sooners had none. Stagg inserted 10 new players into his lineup in the second period, and the Maroons drove 65 yards for a touchdown. Chicago held its 7-0 lead through the third quarter.

A poor Chicago punt in the fourth stanza gave OU possession at the Maroons' 36. The Sooners drove to the five, but faced fourth-and-goal. Haskins zipped a pass to backup end Tom Churchill in the end zone. Haskins missed the conversion.

Haskins later fired a 65-yard TD pass to Crider, who caught the aerial on the Maroons' 40 and flew to the end zone. Haskins nailed the extra point.

Haskins pulled a muscle in practice before Oklahoma hosted 2-0 Creighton two weeks later. Paul Ward replaced Haskins, who sat out three quarters before coming in to charge his teammates with a touchdown drive to tie the game, which ended at 13-13.

The Big Red drove 60 yards in 10 plays for a touchdown following the opening kickoff. Ray LeCrone's four-yard plunge up the middle capped the drive. Ward kicked the conversion.

The Sooners threatened again in the opening quarter, but Albert Mayhew's pass was intercepted near the goal line and returned to the Bluejays' 33. Creighton marched to a tying TD.

The Bluejays took a 13-7 lead with a touchdown late in the third period, but the extra point failed.

Mooney returned the ensuing kickoff and weaved 67 yards through traffic before being caught from behind at the Creighton 27 as the quarter ended. Coach Lindsey put Haskins in the lineup. Haskins tossed a pass to Crider to the Bluejay 11. Haskins scooted off right end on the next play and was tackled at the five, but he skidded across the goal line for the score. Haskins missed the extra point.

Creighton gained 293 total yards all on the ground. OU had only 96 total yards. The Bluejays also had more first downs, 18-9.

Both of the Sooners' starting tackles suffered injuries. Norris had a sore knee and would not play for several weeks. Bill Hamilton had a dislocated shoulder. Churchill was moved to Norris' slot, and Olin Clammer replaced Hamilton.

Oklahoma opened the conference slate on October 22 with a 20-14 loss to Kansas State in Manhattan.

The Wildcats scored off a blocked punt in the first quarter, but the Sooners answered with a Haskins-to-Roy LeCrone TD pass.

The Cats scored on a 40-yard fumble recovery in the third period and added another touchdown minutes later.

Backup fullback Gacicuis Short scored a touchdown in the fourth stanza to draw OU within six (20-14), but the Big Red never threatened again. K-State had more total yards than Oklahoma 356 to 243.

Frank Crider catches Bus Haskins' pass for Oklahoma's first score against Washington St. Louis.
(*Western History Collections, University of Oklahoma*)

OU hosted Central College on October 29 before a crowd of only 3,000. The teams fought to a 14-14 deadlock.

Central held a 7-0 lead at intermission. Ray LeCrone scored a touchdown early in the third stanza. Minutes later, Haskins, who rushed for 177 yards, added a 37-yard TD run.

The Bronchos marched 87 yards for the tying score by completing four of six passes in the drive.

Hamilton returned to practice the next week. The Sooners crushed the Washington Bears (formerly Pikers), 28-7, on November 5 before 6,000 shivering fans in Norman.

A poor Bears punt in the first quarter set up the Sooners at the WU 33. Six plays later Haskins fired a four-yard TD pass to Crider, who caught the ball on his fingertips as he crossed the goal line.

Moments later, Haskins returned a punt 40 yards to the WU 20. From the 16, Brown took the ball on a fake line smash and skirted to the end zone. He was tackled at the goal line but scrambled across for the score.

OU tried to score again with a march to the Bears' 21 as the first half ended.

Washington scored four plays following Ray LeCrone's fumble in the third period.

Roy LeCrone scored on a three-yard end around in the fourth stanza. Jack Carman, who subbed for Crider, raced 19 yards for the final Sooner tally. He was tackled at the line, squirmed free, stiff-armed a defender, eluded another, and zipped to the end zone. Churchill connected his fourth straight conversion.

Oklahoma led the Bears in total yards (251-77) and first downs (12-3).

Crider pulled a leg muscle and would not play the rest of the year. Haskins re-injured his pulled muscle and would not play against Kansas the following week. Scholastic deficiencies kept Mooney from playing against the Jayhawks. So Lindsey had to design a makeshift backfield. Churchill, who played halfback for the freshman team a year earlier, was moved to halfback. Bruce Drake also moved up to starting halfback.

Amid the bad news of injuries came some good news. Mayhew returned at quarterback and Norris to left tackle.

The Sooners thumped the 2-3-1 Jayhawks, 26-7, before a homecoming crowd of nearly 20,000 at Owen Field on November 12. Norris led the line's effort to open huge gaps for the improvised backfield.

Churchill intercepted a pass at the OU 45 late in the opening period. From the KU 38, Mayhew fired a 20-yard pass to Roy

LeCrone, who leaped high in the air to snare the aerial and then dashed to the Jayhawk seven. The Sooners pounded out four yards as the second quarter began. Ray LeCrone then dove over the goal line from the three. Churchill's conversion was wide.

OU later capitalized on another Kansas mistake. Howard Cooper fumbled Churchill's punt and Kidd smothered the pigskin at the KU 32. Ray LeCrone, Churchill and Drake hammered runs to the 20. Mayhew zipped a pass to Drake at the five, and Drake darted to the end zone. This time Churchill's kick was true, and the Sooners held a 13-0 lead through halftime.

The Big Red defense held the Jayhawks to minus-10 yards rushing in the first half.

Oklahoma marched for another score after taking the second-half kickoff. Mayhew's 29-yard TD pass to Roy LeCrone capped the drive, but Churchill missed the conversion.

The Hawks scored a touchdown in the third stanza to squelch a shutout.

The Sooners drove 56 yards for the final tally early in the fourth period. On fourth-and-goal inside the KU five, Norris opened a huge hole, and Churchill scooted through for the score and then nailed the extra point. The Jayhawks returned the kickoff to the OU six, but the crimson defense stiffened, and Kansas turned the ball over on downs.

The Sooners, at 3-2-1, appeared poised to give Lindsey a winning season in his inaugural year. A victory against Oklahoma A&M on November 19 and Missouri on November 24 would bring another Missouri Valley title to Norman.

The 2-4 Aggies came to Norman the next week and dropped the Sooners, 13-7, before 12,000 spectators. A&M returned Drake's fumble for a touchdown early in the second stanza. The Sooners answered with Ray LeCrone's touchdown run and Churchill's conversion.

The Aggies scored on a 50-yard TD pass in the third quarter.

Missouri (6-2) scored 20 unanswered points to defeat OU, 20-7, on Thanksgiving Day in Columbia. The Sooners scored early in the contest after recovering a fumble at the MU 19 in the first minute. Three plays later, Haskins tossed a pass to Mooney to the MU nine. A Tiger penalty moved the ball to the two, but OU was offside on the next play, moving the ball to the seven. Churchill took a pitch out and ran across the goal line. He also booted the extra point.

Missouri scored a TD in each of the final three quarters and claimed the MVC championship.

The Sooners ended 1927 with a dismal 3-3-2 record and seventh place with a 2-3 mark in the MVC.

Norris was selected All-American, but he was not named to the all-conference first team. Roy LeCrone was the only Sooner named to the All-MVC first unit.

1927 Season Record: 3-3-2
Missouri Valley Conference: 2-3-0 (Seventh)

Date	Opponent	Result	Score
October 1	at Chicago	W	13-7
October 15	CREIGHTON	T	13-13
October 22	at Kansas State	L	20-14
October 29	CENTRAL NORMAL	T	14-14
November 5	WASHINGTON ST. LOUIS	W	28-7
November 12	KANSAS	W	26-7
November 19	OKLAHOMA A&M	L	13-7
November 24	at Missouri	L	20-7

1928

Big Six was the name of the new conference. To compete in the conference, Oklahoma had to find new players to step up in the line.

Most of the line was inexperienced in 1928 with the graduation of All-America tackle Granny Norris, center Summie Kidd, guard Hal Muldrow, and ends Roy LeCrone and Mort Brown. The only veteran returnees up front were tackle Bill Hamilton and guard Curtis Berry.

Ad Lindsey still experimented with moving players in different positions to find out who would stand out in the lineup. Hamilton was elected captain for the '28 season.

Bob Sumpter, who started at tackle in 1926, returned to the squad, which helped provide more experience in the trenches. Tom Churchill returned to the right end slot. He also returned from the 1928 Summer Olympics in Amsterdam where he placed fifth in the decathlon.

Ray LeCrone and Prentiss Mooney were gone from the backfield, but Bus Haskins, Paul Ward, Frank Crider, Abe Kitchell, Bruce Drake, Al Mayhew, Jack Carmen, and Gacicuis Short provided plenty of depth in the backfield.

The Sooners opened the 1928 campaign with a 10-7 loss to Indiana on October 6 in Bloomington. Ed Hughes booted a 32-yard field goal to put the Hoosiers on top, 3-0, in the first quarter. OU was unable to penetrate the IU defense in the opening period.

The Sooners chewed up huge chunks of yards in their lone scoring effort midway through the second stanza. Churchill's seven-yard TD run capped a 57-yard drive in five plays. Churchill also nailed the conversion to give OU a 7-3 lead.

Kitchell intercepted a Hoosier pass to squelch their threat at the OU 15 late in the third period. Indiana capitalized on Kitchell's fumble at midfield late in the game. Eight plays later, George Reinhardt's one-yard TD plunge was the game's deciding tally.

Displeased with his starting line, Coach Lindsey shook up the roster before the second game at Creighton. Hamilton was moved to left end replacing Fenton Taylor. Guards Weldon Gentry and Curtis Berry were moved to the tackle slots. Harry Berry and Ellis Orr took over the guard positions. Bob Fields remained at center.

Churchill and Bus Mills suffered pulled muscles in practice a few days later. So when nothing seems to go right for your team, what's a coach to do? Send in the hobbled guys.

Sooner Magic:
Injured Players Aid Sooner Victory

That's exactly what Lindsey did against the Creighton Bluejays. Mills and Churchill sat on the bench through the first three quarters against the Bluejays.

The Sooners traveled to Omaha on October 13 to meet Creighton before 10,000 homecoming fans, the largest crowd to witness a football game in Nebraska. It was Creighton's 50th anniversary as a school, and the homecoming crowd celebrated the university's Golden Jubilee. The Sooners spoiled the party with a 7-0 victory.

The Jays were 0-1 after a 49-0 loss to Minnesota. One of the two OU ties in 1927 was a 13-all deadlock with Creighton in Norman, the only previous meeting between the two teams. They were headed for a deadlock again, except this time neither team was able to put any points on the scoreboard.

The game was marred by 12 fumbles—seven by the Bluejays and five by the Sooners.

Creighton marched deep into OU territory in the first stanza but fumbled the ball away. Still in the opening period, OU drove to the Bluejays' seven, but Ward bobbled the pigskin and Creighton recovered.

The Jays drove to the OU three but fumbled the ball, and Crider recovered for the Sooners. Crider was injured soon after and never returned to action.

Creighton marched to the OU four-yard line in the second period, but the Big Red defense kept the Jays from reaching the end zone. The Sooners then marched to the Creighton 10, but again Ward lost the ball and the Jays recovered.

If the teams did not fumble after driving deep into each other's territory, the defenses rose to the occasion. Another Creighton drive stalled at the OU 10, and a Sooner drive stalled at the Jays' eight. Both teams were scoreless at intermission.

The third quarter and most of the fourth were highlighted by tough defenses and a series of punts.

Late in the fourth period, Creighton's quarterback, Johnny Scott, fumbled, and Churchill recovered at the Jays' 39-yard line.

Kitchell's pass to Mills gained four yards. Mills carried up the middle but was stuffed for no gain. On third-and-six at the Creighton 35, Kitchell fired a pass to Churchill, who was tackled at the one.

Mills slammed through the middle but was stopped an inch from the goal line. Again Mills got the call, and this time he crossed the goal line for the touchdown. Haskins booted the extra point, and the Sooners led 7-0 with five minutes remaining in the game.

The victory boosted the Sooners' record to 1-1 for the season. Bus Haskins suffered a charley horse and was doubtful for the Sooners' home opener against Kansas State on October 27.

Memorial Stadium's east bleachers were finished in time for the first home game and raised the capacity to 30,000.

Oklahoma had not beaten the Wildcats since 1919 (0-5-3 including three straight losses) and was eager to eliminate the jinx. The 1928 Cats won three straight games before dropping a 7-0 decision to Kansas the week before the OU game.

Coach Lindsey went with the same lineup as previous except Haskins started for Drake at left half. The head coach challenged his charges to be more aggressive. They answered with a 33-21 victory before 18,000 spectators.

Haskins scored three touchdowns to lead the Sooner attack. Trailing 7-0, Kitchell tossed a 25-yard TD pass to Haskins in the first period to tie the game. Minutes later, the Big Red faced third down at its own four-yard line. Haskins gained 45 yards to the K-State 48. One play later, Kitchell fired a 43-yard TD bomb to Mills to give the Sooners a 14-7 advantage.

A Wildcat touchdown tied the game in the third quarter, then Drake bulled over from the one-yard line to cap a 67-yard Oklahoma march. Moments later, Haskins intercepted a pass and weaved to the end zone, stiff-arming several Cats along the way.

Kitchell, who completed five of six passes overall for 99 yards, later tossed a 40-yard TD aerial to Haskins in the fourth stanza.

Haskins rushed for 104 yards, punted three times for a 35-yard average and also returned a kickoff 55 yards in the game. But the linemen still caused Coach Lindsey to scratch his head as they were penalized 100 yards due to overcharging.

The Sooners traveled to Ames on November 3 to face winless (0-3-1) Iowa State College. The Cyclones stunned OU, 13-0, on a snow-covered field, which slowed the crimson backs. Three days of rain and snow soaked the field, and by game time snow banks were five feet high along the sidelines. I-State halfback Paul Trauger starred for his team by running for one touchdown and passing for another.

Herbert Hoover won the presidency three days later with a landslide victory over Al Smith. Four days later, Nebraska spoiled the Sooners' homecoming with a 44-6 rout before a record 18,346 fans. It was the worst OU defeat in seven years, a 44-0 loss to the Huskers in 1921.

A loudspeaker system was used to announce players' names and plays for the first time at OU's Memorial Stadium.

Oklahoma had eight turnovers (four fumbles and four interceptions). The lone Sooner touchdown was a 45-yard strike from Kitchell to Mills in the third period. Kitchell also tossed a 25-yard pass to Mills on the play before. The Sooners were the first conference foe to score on the Huskers.

Many of the Sooners received bumps and bruises from the Nebraska contest. Kansas also had players banged up in its previous game against Marquette. The 2-2-2 Jayhawks had not scored in the three prior games, and Oklahoma made it four straight with a 7-0 victory.

About four inches of rain fell in Lawrence a day before the game, making for a soggy field. Sooner fans did not arrive at the game until halftime as floods in southern Kansas slowed their train.

Kitchell returned the opening kickoff to the OU 37 and scored three plays later. Kitchell hurled a 39-yard pass to Mills to the KU 24. Mills gained three yards, then blasted up the middle for a 21-yard touchdown. Haskins nailed the extra point.

A punting duel ensued in the second period. Late in the third stanza, Fields picked off a KU pass and returned the ball to the Jayhawk 31, but the Sooners turned the ball over on downs at the 22 early in the fourth quarter.

The Hawks later drove to the OU 18 but had to turn the ball over on downs.

The Sooners outgained the Hawks in total yards (184-127) and first downs (6-5).

The 1-6 Oklahoma Aggies had two weeks to prepare for the Sooners. Extra bleachers had been erected, adding to the 8,500 permanent seats for the homecoming crowd in Stillwater.

The Aggies won their opening game, then dropped six straight. The extra preparations didn't help as OU hammered the Aggies, 46-0, on November 24. Haskins and Mills each scored two touchdowns to lead the Sooner touchdown barrage.

The Big Red defense held the Aggies to 70 total yards. The OU offense rolled up 314 total yards.

Missouri came to Norman five days later for a big Thanksgiving Day clash. A Sooner victory would share second place with the Tigers in the Big Six Conference. Oklahoma got its share of the runner-up spot by dropping 4-3 Missouri, 14-0.

Mills pounced on John Waldorf's fumble at the MU 29 in the first quarter. The Sooners marched to the MU one, then Kitchell plowed through for the score on fourth down. Mills kicked the conversion.

Midway through the fourth stanza, Churchill returned a fumble 20 yards for the second score. Ward kicked the extra point.

The Sooners' defense was more solid in their third straight shutout, as the Tigers never moved closer than the OU 32-yard line. The defense held Mizzou to 90 total yards and four first downs. Oklahoma gained 169 total yards and seven first downs.

The Big Red finished the 1928 campaign with a 5-3 record, 3-2 in the Big Six. Nebraska won the conference title with a 5-0 record. Churchill was the only Sooner selected to the all-conference first team.

1929

Sixteen loud speakers were installed before the first home game. Four sets of amplifiers were installed at each end of Memorial Stadium, allowing spectators to hear player identification and play calls. The speakers were purchased for $5,000 from the Western Electric Company in Kansas City.

Oklahoma also renewed its rivalry with the Texas Longhorns by signing a 10-year contract to play the game at the Texas State Fair in Dallas. The game has been played at the State Fair ever since.

Claude Reeds was hired as head coach at Central State Teacher's College in Edmond. Dewey "Snorter" Luster left his job as Norman High's head coach to tutor the Big Red linemen. Unlike last year, the line was more experienced yet suffered a setback in preseason practices. A doctor's X-ray revealed junior guard Alvan Muldrow had a fractured dorsal vertebra. The younger brother of Hal (who played the previous three years) had been a backup in 1928 and he had promise to start in '29, but the injury ended his football career.

Bruce Drake and Bus Haskins were gone from the backfield. Fullback Frank Crider returned and was elected captain. Bus Mills was back for another year at right half. Tom Churchill, all-conference end a year earlier, was moved to the left halfback position, but later returned to end before the first game. Earl Flint took over at left half, but "Silly" Guy Warren got the nod by the fourth game.

Al Mayhew beat out Abe Kitchell for the starting quarterback slot. Two brothers, Hilary (guard) and John Lee (tackle), anchored the front line.

The Sooners opened the season October 12 with a 26-0 pasting of 1-0 Creighton before 10,000 fans in Norman. Warren scored two touchdowns in backup duty, and the Bluejays did not gain a first down until the fourth quarter.

Crider's four-yard TD run capped a 31-yard drive in eight plays early in the first stanza.

A 55-yard TD pass from Mills to Warren sparked the Sooners in the third quarter. Warren also highlighted the next scoring drive with a 38-yard run to the Jays' 11. Clyde Kirk scored on the next play.

Warren added a 13-yard TD run in the fourth period.

Texas already had three games under its belt, surrendering nary a point. The Sooners were no exception as they dropped a 21-0 decision to the Longhorns on October 19. About 5,000 Sooner fans purchased tickets for the game, and many traveled to Dallas by automobile, buses, and special trains.

After a scoreless first half, Texas scored once in the third quarter and twice in the fourth. The Steers outgained OU in total yards (264-88) and first downs (16-7).

1928 Season Record: 5-3-0
Big Six Conference: 3-2-0 (Second)

Date	Opponent	Result	Score
October 6	at Indiana	L	10-7
October 13	at Creighton	W	7-0
October 27	KANSAS STATE	W	33-21
November 3	at Iowa State	L	13-0
November 10	NEBRASKA	L	44-6
November 17	at Kansas	W	7-0
November 24	at Oklahoma A&M	W	46-0
November 29	MISSOURI	W	14-0

Crider suffered a broken finger, and guard Weldon Gentry had a sore knee. Both would be out for the next game.

There was talk among Sooner fans and the media that the Sooners should add a game or two before taking on the Longhorns. Bus Ham, a writer for the *Daily Oklahoman*, suggested the Sooners drop the varsity-freshmen game, calling it "horseplay."

Five days after the Texas loss, the stock market crashed, and $30 billion disappeared, which eventually damaged the American economy and sent the nation spiraling into a depression.

A loss to 1-2 Kansas State on October 26 would have damaged the Sooners' chances for a run at the Big Six title. Oklahoma escaped with a 14-13 win in Manhattan thanks to a botched kick after the Wildcats' first touchdown in the opening quarter. Al Tucker missed the conversion, but the Cats had a 6-0 advantage.

Mills' five-yard TD run in the second period capped a 10-play, 64-yard drive. Mayhew's extra point gave the Sooners a 7-6 lead.

Churchill recovered a fumble at the K-State 13 in the third stanza. Three plays later, Kirk skirted around left end for a touchdown. Mayhew kicked the conversion. The Cats scored a touchdown in the fourth quarter, but the Sooners escaped with their first conference win.

Crider and Gentry returned to the lineup, but guard Ray Stanley and tackle Curtis Berry were unable to start the next week against 1-3 Iowa State. Darrell Ewing replaced Stanley, and Hilary Lee took over for Berry.

A year ago, the winless Cyclones embarrassed Oklahoma with a win. Another loss, this time in Norman, would be more humiliating. It didn't happen. OU defeated the Cyclones, 21-7, on November 2 before 10,000 in Norman. Trailing 7-0 in the first half, the Big Red exploded for three touchdowns in the final 30 minutes.

Warren, in his first start at left halfback, fired a 48-yard TD pass to Mills in the third stanza, then scored on a 65-yard run minutes later. Warren appeared to have a third TD in the fourth period, but he stepped out of bounds at the Cyclone three after a 27-yard run. Crider scored on the next play to cap a 52-yard drive in four plays.

Kansas coach Bill Hargiss threw out some trash talk before his Jayhawks came to Norman on November 9. Ad Lindsey (Bethany College) and Hargiss (Emporia College) both coached against each other in the Kansas collegiate conference. Lindsey's teams seldom beat Hargiss' squads.

"He couldn't beat me in the Kansas conference, and he can't beat me in the Big Six," Hargiss said the week of the OU-KU match up. He obviously had a short memory, because the Sooners defeated the Jayhawks, 7-0, in 1928.

Kansas (2-3) spoiled the Sooners' homecoming with a 7-0 victory before a crowd of 16,000 and on a muddy Owen Field.

Forrest Cox blocked Guy Warren's punt late in the first quarter, and Kirk recovered for the Sooners at the OU five, but the Hawks took possession. Cox gained a yard as the first stanza ended. On the first play of the second period, Cox ripped over the left side for the score. He also kicked the extra point.

The Big Red had a chance to tie the game minutes later. Warren returned a punt to the KU 33, then sailed a pass to Churchill to the Hawks' five. Crider was stopped for no gain, and Mills was tossed for a four-yard loss. Warren's third-down pass to Crider was incomplete, then Crider fumbled at the KU 12 and the Hawks recovered.

The rest of the game was a punting duel. The Sooners gained more yards (161-158), but Kansas had more first downs (12-6).

Oklahoma and Nebraska (2-1-2) struggled to a 13-13 tie the next week in Lincoln on yet another muddy field.

The Sooners drove 70 yards in four plays following the opening kickoff. Warren's 55-yard pass to Mills, on third down, took OU to the Huskers' one-yard line. Crider bulled ahead for the touchdown on the next play, and Mills kicked the extra point.

Nebraska scored two TDs in the second quarter, one following Crider's fumble at the OU 25. Oklahoma threatened with a drive later in the period, but surrendered the ball over on downs.

A blocked punt set up the Sooners at the Husker 49 late in the third period. Mayhew's four-yard TD run capped the drive in nine plays in the fourth stanza. Mayhew's conversion attempt veered off the mark.

The Sooners returned home November 24 to face 4-2-1 Oklahoma A&M before a crowd of 16,000. The game ended in a 7-all draw.

Warren's four-yard TD run in the second quarter capped a 68-yard march, which followed Bob Fields' interception late in the first stanza.

The Aggies tied the game with a touchdown midway through the second period. The Aggies had a chance to win the game with a field goal midway through the fourth quarter, but the kick was wide.

Oklahoma outgained A&M in total yards (180-156) but the Aggies had more first downs (10-8).

Injuries from the Aggie game depleted the Sooner lineup for their final game against Missouri. John Lee suffered an ankle injury, Kirk and Gentry had sore knees, and Ewing suffered a stiff neck when he was knocked unconscious in the Aggie game.

The Tigers defeated OU, 13-0, on a frozen, snow-covered field in Columbia on Thanksgiving. After a scoreless first half, MU quarterback Russell Dills delighted the 8,000 fans by returning the second-half kickoff 93 yards for a touchdown. Bernard Schaff missed the conversion.

Dills raced around left end for a six-yard score in the fourth quarter. Schaff made this extra point.

The Sooners tossed the pigskin 35 times, completed 12 for 238 yards but could not find the end zone. Oklahoma outgained the Tigers (318-230) in total yards and 17-13 in first downs.

The Big Red finished the season with a 3-3-2 record and fourth (2-2-2) in the Big Six. Nebraska repeated as the conference champions.

Churchill and Crider made the all-conference first team.

1929 Season Record: 3-3-2

Big Six Conference: 2-2-2 (Fourth)

Date	Opponent	Result	Score
October 12	CREIGHTON	W	26-0
Ocotber 19	Texas at Dallas	L	21-0
October 26	at Kansas State	W	14-13
November 2	IOWA STATE	W	21-7
November 9	KANSAS	L	7-0
November 16	at Nebraska	T	13-13
November 23	OKLAHOMA A&M	T	7-7
November 28	at Missouri	W	13-0

RIVALRIES

Texas

Oklahoma vs. Texas is one of the most respected and heated college football rivalries in the nation. The game has experienced a sellout every year since 1952.

Since 1929, the game has been played every year in Dallas at and during the Texas State Fair. Known as the Fair Park Stadium from 1929-1935, the facility was renamed the Cotton Bowl in 1936. Dallas is located approximately halfway between Norman and Austin. The city practically turns crimson and orange during "Big D" weekend, which begins a day or two before the two teams kick-off.

Fans of both teams plan months ahead to make this a holiday weekend. Many hotels are sold out months in advance. Most fans drive to Dallas on Friday, and Interstate 35 is flooded with traffic converging on Big D. Although 72,000 fans have tickets to the game, many just go to Dallas for the abundant parties in the Dallas Metroplex. An estimated 250,000 invade Dallas during Big D Weekend. The West End Marketplace and Deep Ellum are popular hangouts with bars, restaurants, and entertainment. Fans are nearly elbow to elbow.

From the mid-1930s to 1992, Commerce Street was ground zero for the weekend parties, which included numerous hotels such as the Adolphus, Baker, Fairmont, and Hilton. In the 1960s, fans spilled out onto the sidewalks lining Commerce, and some rowdy drunks smashed windows of the retail stores. An estimated 1,000 persons were arrested in 1968, mostly for public drunkenness.

In 1970, the Dallas City Council passed an ordinance proclaiming the sidewalks of Commerce Street one-way for six blocks. Fans could only walk in one direction to avoid clashing with each other. Barricades were placed along the curbs so fans would not step into the traffic. Two police officers would be positioned about every 20 feet to maintain some kind of order. If a fan went against the sidewalk flow, he would receive a warning. A second violation would usually mean jail time. Local law enforcement authorities from the Dallas metro area would not be allowed time off the night before the game.

Commerce Street also is one way, running from west to east. Fans would drive by with honking horns and gesturing team preference—a hook 'em sign with index and pinkie finger skyward for Longhorns and the opposite "to Hell with the Horns" for Sooner fans. Sometimes the middle finger would be flashed to the enemy.

The revelry would continue until about 2 a.m., when the city's water trucks would drive by, soaking the fans. The hoopla was reduced to 1 a.m. in the mid-1980s and midnight in the late-1980s. Arrests for public drunkenness were reduced to about 100-200 in the late 1970s and 1980s. The

Commerce Street revelry ended in 1992 when a carjacking occurred in front of the Sixth Floor Museum, formerly the Texas School Book Depository. One man was shot to death near where President John F. Kennedy was gunned down in 1963. The following January a riot nearly broke out during a parade honoring the Dallas Cowboys, who won the Super Bowl a few days earlier. Dallas had had enough and squelched the Commerce Street revelry.

The festivities resumed a few years later at West End and Deep Ellum entertainment districts.

On game day, fans drive their own vehicles, grab a taxi or ride a bus to the fairgrounds. At game time, the Cotton Bowl is full with one-half fans decked in crimson and the other half in burnt orange. The south "horseshoe," from the 50-yard line west to the 50-yard line east is predominantly filled with Sooner fans. The north horseshoe is filled with mostly Longhorn fans. A handful of the enemy can be seen in the opponents' sections.

The stadium is noisy. Fans are cheering or jeering on every play. Nearly every year the game has a national significance. Since the Associated Press began its football poll in 1936, 31 times both teams were ranked in the poll when they met. Both teams have been rated in the top 10 15 times, and nine times both have been rated in the top five.

The winning team's fans would pour out onto the fairgrounds whooping and hollering, and the losing fans try to sneak out without being noticed, but that's impossible. Saturday night is reserved for rehashing the game over a drink or two, maybe more. Winners drink to celebrate, and the losers drink to drown their sorrows. When the game ended in a tie, which it has five times, the fans don't know what to do, so they drink anyway.

History has a role in understanding all this craziness.

At the Cotton Bowl, an OU Rufnek chases a Texas Cowboy, a common pregame scene at at every OU-Texas showdown. *(OU Athletics)*

It's a Fact

• OU and Texas both have been undefeated (minimum of one game) 26 times before they met. Texas won 14 times, OU 11 times and once they tied.

The Longhorns' first loss of the season came at the hands of the Sooners 15 times (1912, 1915, 1917, 1939, 1949, 1950, 1971, 1972, 1975, 1978, 1982, 1985, 2001, 2002, and 2004).

• The Sooners' first loss of the season came at the hands of the Longhorns 22 times. (1900, 1901, 1902, 1914, 1929, 1930, 1932, 1934, 1935, 1936, 1940, 1941, 1943, 1947, 1958, 1963, 1967, 1969, 1977, 1979, 1990 and 1991).

• OU was the lone spoiler three times at Texas' chance for an undefeated season (1912, 1972, and 2004). Texas was the lone spoiler four times to the Sooners' chance at an undefeated season (1914, 1958, 1967 and 1979).

Texas is about four times larger than Oklahoma and has six times more people. Texans contend everything in their state is better.

The rivalry between Oklahoma and Texas extends beyond the gridiron, which began in 1900. The Red River separates the two states, and both states have disputed where the boundary of each state belongs. Texas claimed to own land along the river comprising 16,000 square miles; however, the United States Supreme Court contended the land belonged to the United States. In the compromise of 1850, Texas had ceded this land, which included the Red River.

Greer County was among that portion of land and became a territory of the United States in 1896. Ten years later, the 1.5 million-acre county became a part of Oklahoma.

In 1923, the Supreme Court ruled that Texas begins at the south bank of the river.

In 1931, a controversy began whether a bridge (built by both states across the river from Durant, Oklahoma to Denison, Texas) should be a toll bridge or toll-free.

The Red River Bridge Company, a private firm operating a toll bridge paralleling the new free bridge, filed a petition in United States district court in Houston asking for an injunction preventing the Texas Highway Commission from opening the bridge. A temporary injunction was issued on July 10, 1931, and Texas Governor Ross Sterling ordered barricades constructed across the Texas approach to the new bridge.

On July 16, 1931, Oklahoma Governor William "Alfalfa Bill" Murray opened the bridge by executive order, claiming that Oklahoma's "half" of the bridge ran lengthwise north and south across the river, and that Oklahoma held title to both sides of the river. Oklahoma highway crews crossed the bridge and destroyed the barricades.

Gov. Sterling dispatched three Texas Rangers, accompanied by the Texas Adjutant General to rebuild the barricades and protect the Texas Highway Department employees charged with enforcing the injunction. On July 17, Gov. Murray ordered Oklahoma highway crews to tear up the northern approaches to the bridge, thus halting traffic over the river.

Sixty-nine years later, the boundary dispute was settled when Texas Gov. George W. Bush and Oklahoma Gov. Frank Keating signed their respective state bills enacting into law the Red River Boundary Compact defining the boundary between the two states as the vegetation line along the south banks of the Red River. On October 10, 2000, Congress granted consent of the new law.

Nebraska
"Go Big Red!"

That cry can be heard from both sides in the Oklahoma-Nebraska rivalry. OU's dominant color is crimson, a deep purplish red color. Nebraska's dominant color is scarlet, a bright red color. The rivalry has been billed as the "Battle of the Big Reds."

Most Sooner fans will admit the Nebraska rivalry is more about respect between the two schools, whereas the Texas rivalry is based on hatred for the other institution.

Oklahoma and Nebraska first met as conference foes in 1922, but the rivalry did not receive national recognition until the 1971 battle of unbeatens. The game in Norman was billed as the "Game of the Century." The Huskers were 10-0 and sitting atop the Associated Press poll. Oklahoma was right behind at No. 2 with a 9-0 record. Nebraska won, 35-31, on a touchdown by Jeff Kinney with 1:38 remaining in the game.

The Huskers led, 7-0, and then extended it to 14-3. But OU countered with a couple of second-quarter touchdowns to lead 17-14 at the half.

NU regained the lead in the third. OU regained the lead, 31-28, midway through the fourth period.

The two Big Reds first met in 1912 in Lincoln and except for a 7-7 tie in 1919, the Sooners did not beat the Huskers until the sixth game of the series, a 14-7 decision in Norman.

NU dominated the next 17 meetings, winning 13 of 17. From 1943 to 1958, Oklahoma never lost to their northern rivals, a string of 16 consecutive victories.

Nearly every year since then, the Sooner-Cornhusker tilt was for the conference title, a major bowl bid and in the national championship hunt. In the 30 meetings between 1971 and 2001, both were nationally ranked 21 times. During that span, both teams were nationally ranked in the top 10 17 times, and eight times both were in the top five. Twice both met undefeated as the top two ranked teams in the nation. In addition to 1971, both teams sported perfect records in 1987.

Billed as "Game of the Century II," in 1987, No. 2 Oklahoma rolled into Lincoln with a 10-0 record. The Huskers sported a 9-0 mark as the nation's top-ranked team. Unlike the first "Game of the Century," this contest was a defensive battle.

The Huskers opened with a 7-0 lead and held it until intermission. A Sooner TD in the third quarter tied the game. Late in the period, Patrick Collins raced 65 yards to put the Sooners ahead 14-7. Tim Lashar's field goal iced the 17-7 Sooner victory in the fourth quarter.

The Oklahoma Sooners and Nebraska Cornhuskers have been members of the same conference since 1920, but did not meet as conference opponents until 1922. Both were members of the Missouri Valley Conference from 1921-1927, the Big Six from 1928-1947, Big Seven from 1948-1958, Big Eight from 1959-1995 and the Big 12 from 1996-today. In the 86 years both teams have been members of the same conference, one of the two teams has won or shared the conference championship 66 times. Oklahoma has won 37 conference titles and Nebraska has won 34 titles from 1921-2005.

Oklahoma State

Only recently has the rivalry with Oklahoma State intensified. Between 1995 and 2002, the Cowboys won five of eight times.

It's a Fact

• Both schools shared the Big Eight Conference title three times, 1975, 1978 and 1984.

• Twenty-nine contests have been decided by a touchdown (seven points) or less.

• Twice Nebraska dashed the Sooners' perfect season hopes—the 1971 game and again in 1978. Oklahoma was never the lone blemish on Nebraska's run for a perfect season, but 11 times the Sooners dealt the Huskers their only conference loss (1924, 1955, 1964, 1966, 1972, 1975, 1979, 1980, 1984, 1985 and 1987).

• Nebraska was OU's only conference loss eight times (1940, 1942, 1959, 1963, 1971, 1978, 1982 and 1988).

• Oklahoma and Nebraska have 12 national championships combined (OU 7, NU 5). Nebraska has won 46 conference championships and Oklahoma has been tops 38 times. OU boasts 141 All-Americans and Nebraska has had 98. The Sooners have four Heisman Trophy winners and the Huskers have three.

• Oklahoma owns the longest streak in the series with 16 straight wins from 1943-1958. Nebraska's greatest winning string was seven from 1991-1997. Oklahoma knocked the Huskers from atop the national rankings twice (17-7 in 1987 and 31-14 in 2000). Nebraska bumped OU from the No.1 ranking once (17-14 in 1978).

• Nebraska hosted the Sooners 11 times in the 1970s and 1980s. The Sooners won seven of those games in Lincoln.

• OU was never the only defeat in any Nebraska season, but the Sooners did hand the Cornhuskers their first loss of the season seven times (1930, 1964, 1966, 1975, 1979, 1987 and 2000). Nebraska was the only loss for the Sooners in 1971 and 1978. The Huskers were OU's first loss seven times (1921, 1922, 1923, 1931, 1971, 1978 and 2001).

• OU and Nebraska both have been undefeated (minimum of one game) six times before they met. OU won three of those contests and Nebraska had won four.

Before that, OSU had not defeated the Sooners in 19 years, save for a tie in 1992.

Some Sooner fans may not view Oklahoma State as a major rival, but when the two teams meet, state pride is on the line. Although OU fans outnumber OSU fans in the state, losing to the Cowboys allows their fans to gloat for a whole year. Some Sooner fans work with, are married to, or have friends who are Cowboy fans. So to say this isn't a rivalry is like saying OU doesn't have seven national championships.

The Sooners dominated the series from the outset in 1904, winning the first 11 games of the series and pitching shutouts in the first eight. OSU was then known as the Oklahoma A&M Aggies.

After the Aggies won their first game in 1917, OU won the next four. During the next 14 years, the Sooners only won only three games, lost five and tied four.

A 25-0 Oklahoma victory in 1935 began a string of eight victories. The Cowboys won two straight in the mid-1940s, then the Sooners won the next 19. Bud Wilkinson never lost to the orange and black in his 17 years as the Sooners' head coach.

The Cowboys won two straight in 1965 and 1966, each by one point. OU then put together a nine-game streak, which ended in 1976, Barry Switzer's only loss to OSU. Oklahoma followed that with a 15-game winning streak, which ended with a 15-all tie in 1992. Since then, OU owns an 8-5 edge.

The series has some terrific memories for Sooner fans, especially because OU came out on top. The oddest contest between OU and OSU was the first one, when Ed Cook swam for a touchdown at Guthrie's Cottonwood Creek.

In 1985, both teams met on an "ice rink" in Stillwater. Sleet had covered Lewis Field, and the wind chill plummeted below zero degrees. OU prevailed, 13-0, in the "Ice Bowl."

Switzer said it was the "worst conditions" he had ever seen for a game.

The 1984 contest was the only time both teams were ranked in the top five nationally. The 8-1-1 Sooners were No. 2 in the AP poll, and the 9-1 Cowboys were third. Both teams were flip-flopped in the UPI poll. OU and OSU had identical 5-1 conference records. The winner would be crowned Big Eight champions and receive an automatic bid to the Orange Bowl.

The Sooner defense held the Cowboys to minus four yards rushing, nine first downs and 198 total yards.

The 1988 contest came down to who had the ball last. Fortunately for Sooner fans, the Pokes came up short, 31-28. The Cowboys had a chance to ruin the Sooners' national championship hope in 2000, but OSU failed to score a late TD and the Big Red held on, 12-7.

OSU did spoil OU's national title hopes in 2001 and 2002 with 16-13 and 38-28 victories respectively.

A missed OSU field goal on the final play in 2004 allowed the Sooners to escape with a 38-35 win.

1930 - 1939

1930

For the third straight year, Adrian Lindsey experimented moving players to different positions. This drew criticism from the media, but Lindsey defended the shuffling of his players.

"The material is the poorest it has been since I have been here, and it has not always been so good in my other years, either," he said.

Although two-time all-conference end Tom Churchill graduated, Lindsey had a solid corps of returnees—Bob Fields, Curtis Berry and Hilary and John Lee—on the line. Yet, it was another light front wall, as the linemen averaged 174 pounds.

All-conference halfback Frank Crider graduated, but Bus Mills, Clyde Kirk, and Guy Warren returned. Sophomore Hardie Lewis won the quarterback slot, and Ernest "Iron Mike" Massad earned some playing time at fullback.

The 1930 Sooners started the season hot and had a chance at the Big Six title, but injuries plagued the squad late in the season, hindering chances for a conference crown.

The Sooners opened the season October 4 with a 47-0 shellacking of New Mexico in Norman. Warren and his backup, Dick Simms, each scored two touchdowns. The Lobos did not gain a single first down and had minus-15 total yards. New Mexico gained only nine yards passing and 19 yards from scrimmage. The Lobos were thrown for losses totaling 43 yards.

The Big Red gained 345 total yards and made 16 first downs.

OU stunned Nebraska, 20-7, the following week before 20,000 fans in Norman. The victory was only the second in 10 meetings for the Sooners and the Huskers' first conference loss since the Big Six began in 1928.

Mills flashed 53 yards down the west sideline for the first score in the opening quarter. End Fred Cherry threw a key block near the goal line. Mills also booted the conversion.

The 1-0 Huskers did not cross midfield in the first stanza.

Warren excited the crimson faithful with a 45-yard punt return for a touchdown late in the second period. The Sooner halfback sidestepped several Huskers en route to the end zone. Lewis missed the extra point. Nebraska returned the ensuing kickoff to the OU 15. A pass moved the Huskers to the five, but they could not score as the first half ended.

Backup quarterback Ab Walker intercepted a Husker pass at midfield. On the first play from scrimmage he fired a 15-yard pass to Cherry, then hurled a 35-yard TD pass to Cherry again. Mills kicked the conversion.

Ernest Snell scored the winning touchdown as OU dropped Iowa State, 19-13. (*Western History Collection, University of Oklahoma*)

Nebraska scored its only touchdown in the fourth period.

A 2-0 record had OU fans excited, and 8,000 tickets were quickly sold for the Texas game. The Longhorns calmed the Sooner excitement, 17-7, the next week in Dallas before a crowd of 25,000 at the state fair's new stadium. Construction of the new stadium began in May, five months before the contest. The stadium, later to be named the Cotton Bowl, seated 46,200.

The Sooners thrice had a chance to score first. After UT's Wilson Elkins, back to punt, fumbled the snap, Cherry recovered at the Steers' 28. OU turned the ball over on downs after Warren failed to notice Cherry wide open in the end zone on fourth down.

Center Paul Young's interception of Dexter Shelly's pass late in the first quarter gave the Sooners another opportunity at the UT 47. Oklahoma marched to the Horns' five in five plays, but failed to make any progress and fumbled the ball away three plays later.

The third time was a charm. Mills' interception of a Texas pass in the third period set up the lone Sooner score at the OU 34. After Mills gained 15 yards, he hurled a 55-yard TD bomb to Cherry and booted the extra point.

Texas drove to the OU one late in the third stanza. As the fourth quarter began, Ernest Koy slammed across for the touchdown to tie the game at 7-7. A field goal later in the period gave Texas a 10-7 advantage, and the Steers added a touchdown following an Oklahoma interception.

The defeat could have been worse. Mills had a touchdown-saving tackle at the OU five on the final play. Texas led in total yards (341-132) and first downs (12-4).

Warren and Berry suffered injuries and would not play the next game. Warren had two fractured ribs.

The Sooners got back on the winning track with a 7-0 homecoming victory over Kansas State in Norman. OU had a chance to score early after recovering a Wildcat fumble at the enemy 18, but had to turn the ball over on downs.

The Cats then stalled and punted. Mills took the punt at midfield, darted to the sideline, shifted back to midfield, and shot to the end zone. Mills also nailed the conversion.

Mills, who also punted, averaged 42 yards per kick, and several times his kicks pinned the Cats deep in their own territory. The Aggies had a chance to tie the game in the third period but stalled after driving to the OU 19.

Berry and Warren still were out of the lineup for the Iowa State game on November 1.

Sooner Magic: Lindsey's Premonition Paid Off

The Big Red would have been embarrassed if they lost to Iowa State, losers of 10 consecutive football games, including the first three of the year. The Cyclones were poised for the upset. The Sooners had to rely on a couple of substitute players to pull them through in Ames for the third encounter between both teams. The series was tied at 1-1.

The Cyclones threatened with a march of 64 yards to the OU two-yard line early in the first quarter, but fullback Robert Tegland fumbled the ball away. Neither team scored in the first period.

Early in the second, Cyclone head coach Noel Workman replaced his starting quarterback with sophomore Dick Grefe, who moved the team downfield for the game's first score. He fired a long pass to Franz Swoboda, who wrestled the pigskin from two Sooner defenders and scampered to the end zone. Swoboda also booted the conversion, and the Cyclones led, 7-0.

OU recovered an I-State fumble midway through the period at the 26 in enemy territory. OU lost five yards on a mix up of signals, then Mills sailed a 25-yard pass to Massad to the Cyclone one. On the next play, Massad bulled over the goal line, but Mills' extra point veered wide, and Iowa State held a 7-6 lead.

Late in the second stanza, Greefe sprinted 57 yards toward the end zone, but Young caught him from behind for the saving tackle at the OU 23. Greefe rocketed a pass to John Moen in the end zone. Moen also had to wrestle the ball from two Sooner defenders to give I-State a 13-6 lead. Swoboda's extra point failed, and the Cyclones held a one-touchdown lead heading into the locker room.

Late in the third period, Mills flew 84 yards down the sideline to the end zone, but the play was called back when officials noticed he stepped out of bounds at the OU 43. The Sooners were unable to score in the drive, and the Cyclones held a 13-6 lead after three quarters.

In the fourth, Tegland again fumbled, giving OU possession at the Cyclones' 36. Warren hooked up with Kirk on a 25-yard pass. Four plays later, Kirk crossed the goal line. Mills' kick was successful, and the score was knotted at 13-13.

Another Sooner score was squandered when a clipping penalty nullified Hilary Lee's interception for a touchdown.

With just a few minutes remaining, Greefe fumbled in his own territory, and OU recovered. Lindsey placed C.C. Buxton and Ernest Snell into the lineup. Buxton replaced Mills at right halfback, and Snell subbed for Cherry at right end.

Lindsey must have had some premonition as Buxton sailed a pass to Snell inside the Iowa State five-yard line. Snell just barely broke the plane of the goal line for the winning touchdown. Mills' kick was no good, but it didn't matter as the Sooners shed possible humility, 19-13.

Oklahoma was in the conference driver's seat with a 3-0 record. Kansas (4-2) knocked the Sooners off the perch with a 13-0 decision two weeks later in Lawrence. James Bausch and Elmer Schaake each scored a touchdown for KU in the second quarter. OU never threatened to score in the game.

Massad suffered severe bruises, and the Lee brothers had to return to Missouri due to an illness in the family. Kirk had a high fever, and Warren was still nursing a lingering injury.

Oklahoma A&M (4-2-1) defeated the Sooners, 7-0, in a late season non-conference matchup. Quarterback Hayden Trigg's 26-yard TD run in the first quarter was the game's only score. The Aggies also outplayed OU, gaining 200 total yards to 70 for the Sooners. They also had more first downs, 11-5.

Oklahoma and 2-5-1 Missouri battled to a scoreless tie before a Thanksgiving crowd of 12,000 in Norman. The Sooners blew a chance to score in the first quarter by driving to the Tigers' six, but had to turn the ball over on downs.

Sooner faithful exhaled a sigh of relief when John Van Dyne's 41-yard TD pass to Hubert Campbell in the second stanza was called back due to a backfield in motion penalty.

Oklahoma drove to the MU 20 later in the quarter but again turned the ball over on downs. Missouri marched into OU territory in the third period, but Massad's interception at the OU nine squelched the threat.

The Tigers picked off two Sooner passes inside their 35 in the fourth stanza. OU had 219 total yards to 103 for Mizzou. The Big Red also led the game in first downs, 10-5.

The Sooners finished the 1930 campaign with a 4-3-1 record and finished second in the Big Six with a 3-1-1 mark. The Kansas Jayhawks were crowned Big Six champs.

Mills and Hilary Lee were named to the all-conference first team.

1931

The 12-game regular-season schedule was the longest slate of games in 28 years and would be the lengthiest schedule for another 52 more seasons. The Sooners played 12 games in 1903 and did not play that many again until 1983.

An eight-game schedule had been the norm since 1921, so the players would have to stay fit for an extra four weeks. The schedule was extended to include Oklahoma City University, Tulsa, Honolulu Town Team, and Hawaii University. The final three games would be played on the road, and OU was the first team from the Midwest to ever play on the Pacific island.

University of Oklahoma officials finalized negotiations on November 17 to play two charity games with Oklahoma City and Tulsa universities. About $15,000 was raised during the OCU game at Owen Field to benefit the Oklahoma City Community Fund. The fund helped to relieve poverty stricken families in Oklahoma City.

Assistant coach Dewey Luster created line-blocking dummies made from seven bags filled with sand and swung by ropes on a steel crossbeam. The bags were bunched together to simulate an offensive or defensive line. Luster said it would help the linemen learn team position and skill in using wedge charging, high-low and rolling blocks. The backs also used the apparatus to learn three-point, roll, and shoulder-to-shoulder blocks.

The 1931 Sooner roster had a slew of talent although inexperienced. Halfback Guy Warren, fullback Ernest Massad, and center Paul Young were the only returnees on the squad. Massad was hard pressed by Marvin "Swede" Ellstrom to keep his starting slot. Ellstrom beat him out, but Massad was moved to right halfback. C.C. Buxton Jr., slated to start at quarterback, injured his back and was lost for the year. Bill Dunlap took over the role.

A pair of Charleys (Wilson and Teel) flanked Young at the guard slots, and Orville Corey and Gordon Graalman started at the tackle positions. Ernie Snell and Smith Watkins rounded out the lineup at ends.

The Sooners defeated 1-0 Rice, 19-6, in the season opener October 3 in Norman. Dunlap fired a 30-yard TD pass to Watkins early in the first quarter. Watkins grasped the ball between two defenders at the Rice five and lunged into the end zone. Warren mishandled a bad snap, and the extra-point attempt was blocked.

Ellstrom's five-yard TD run capped a 45-yard drive in seven plays early in the second stanza. He toed the conversion to increase

1930 Season Record: 4-3-1

Big Six Conference: 3-1-1 (Second)

Date	Opponent	Result	Score
October 4	NEW MEXICO	W	47-0
October 11	NEBRASKA	W	20-7
October 18	Texas at Dallas	L	17-7
October 25	KANSAS STATE	W	7-0
November 1	at Iowa State	W	19-13
November 15	at Kansas	L	13-0
November 22	at Oklahoma A&M	L	7-0
November 27	MISSOURI	T	0-0

Oklahoma's lead to 13-0. Reserve halfback Bill Pansze took a Rice punt early in the third quarter and weaved through traffic dodging tacklers for a 77-yard touchdown. Ellstrom's kick was blocked.

The Owls scored later in the third period. Both teams had equal total yards (156), but the Owls had one more first down (10-9).

Dunlap, who completed three of six passes for 73 yards, received praise for his aerial performance. Reserve end Edsel "Red" Northcutt earned a starting spot the next week for his outstanding blocking performance. He replaced Snell on the left side.

The Sooners traveled to Lincoln the following week for a conference showdown with 1-1 Nebraska. Husker halfback George Henry Sauer scored two touchdowns in the fourth quarter to lead his squad to a 13-0 victory. The first touchdown came on a 47-yard run and the second on a 65-yard interception of Dunlap's pass. Both scores came on a muddy field as rain and hail pelted the field during the third quarter.

OU never penetrated past the Huskers' 30-yard line in the game.

Fourteen thousand seats were allotted to Oklahoma for the Texas tilt on October 17. The 2-1 Longhorns lost to Rice the week before meeting the Sooners, making OU the favorite. Warren failed to pass a makeup exam earlier in the week and was declared ineligible for the contest.

The 26th edition of the rivalry, before 20,000 at Dallas' Fair Park Stadium, was a punting duel for most of the game. Both teams combined for 33 punts equaling 1,141 yards. Dunlap handled all of the Sooners' punting chores, kicking 15 times for a 36.9 average.

The Sooners marched into Texas territory twice in the first half but surrendered the ball on downs. The Steers drove 52 yards to the OU seven in the second stanza. Wilson Elkins scored on the next play, but a holding penalty wiped out the score. Both teams went to the dressing room scoreless for the third straight year.

Late in the fourth period, Texas drove 44 yards to the OU seven but stalled. Ernest Koy picked up four yards, then was stopped for no gain. Pansze dumped Albert Stafford for a seven-yard loss on the next play. Claude Blanton nailed a 26-yard field goal to give the Horns a 3-0 victory.

The statistics were not as close as the score. The Steers totaled 228 yards to only 73 for the Sooners. The Horns also had 12 first downs to OU's two.

The Sooners were back on the road the following week at Manhattan to face Kansas State. A sore shoulder sidelined Young, who had a tremendous game with numerous tackles against Texas. Grady Jackson replaced him in the lineup. Warren returned to the roster, and Pete Maloney got the starting nod over Massad at fullback.

The undefeated Wildcats (3-0) defeated Oklahoma, 14-0. Elden Auker tossed a 33-yard TD pass to Henry Cronkite in the first period, and Ralph Graham scored on a three-yard run in the third quarter. The Cats also dominated statistically with 205 total yards to 89 for the Sooners and 15-9 in first downs.

The Sooners hosted a game for the first time in four weeks and since entertaining Rice in the season opener. Reeling from three straight shutouts, Coach Lindsey changed his backfield to add more offensive punch for the Iowa State contest on October 31. Charles Stogner started at quarterback, Pansze at left half, Ellstrom at right half, and Massad returned to fullback.

The 3-1 Cyclones spoiled the homecoming of sorts with a 13-12 victory before 6,000 spectators. Fumbles and Ellstrom's foot hurt the Sooners' chances by missing an extra point and two field goals.

Pansze electrified the crowd with a 77-yard punt return for a TD in the opening period. Ellstrom's kick veered wide, and the Sooners held a 6-0 lead through intermission.

OU blew a couple scoring opportunities in the second stanza. Young picked off a Cyclone pass at the Iowa State 20, but Dunlap fumbled several plays later at the nine-yard line. The Sooners intercepted another I-State pass moments later at the Cyclone 42. The Big Red pushed to the four, where Massad spilled the pigskin and Iowa State recovered.

Dick Grefe scored twice for the Cyclones in the third quarter, catching a 56-yard pass for the first and ran eight yards for the second. I-State held a 13-6 lead into the fourth period. Massad intercepted a pass and hurdled three defenders for a 56-yard score. Massad also booted the extra point to pull OU within one, 13-12.

Ellstrom missed two field goals later in the quarter, which would have iced the game for Oklahoma.

The Sooners remained home the next week to entertain Kansas for a fight to climb out of the Big Six cellar. The 2-4 Jayhawks and OU shared the conference basement with identical 0-3 records.

Lindsey stayed with the same backfield and was determined to open up the offense with laterals, reverses, and double and triple passes. The real homecoming crowd of 15,000 was only entertained with one exciting play in the 10-0 Sooner victory. That came on Dunlap's long run in the fourth stanza.

The Sooners stopped a Jayhawk march to the OU 25 early in the opening quarter. Wilson led the charge of holding the Hawks at bay. The Sooners got a chance to score when Richard O'Neil touched a bounding ball off an OU punt. Reserve guard Ellis Bashara smothered it at the KU 25, but the Hawks' defense stiffened, and OU turned the ball over on downs.

Kansas blew two scoring opportunities in the third stanza. End Jay Plumley fumbled after catching Carnie Smith's pass at the OU 21, and Pansze recovered. The Hawks later drove 40 yards to the OU 15, but on fourth-and-five, Massad picked off Smith's pass inside the five and returned the ball 24 yards. The Sooners then gained their initial first down of the game as the quarter ended.

Midway through the fourth stanza, Dunlap took a direct pass off a semi-punt formation at midfield and sprinted around left end. A Kansas defender hemmed him in as he tried to get in the open, but reserve center Jackson's block set him free down the west sideline. Dunlap reversed to the middle of the field and scored in the east corner of the end zone. Massad toed the conversion to lift OU to a 7-0 advantage.

Moments later, Bashara intercepted Smith's pass at the KU 41 and returned the ball 17 yards to the 24. The Sooners gained little yards, and Warren booted a 33-yard field goal with three minutes to go. The Sooners had another chance to score following Warren's 55-yard interception return to the KU five, but lost possession on downs.

The Jayhawks had more total yards (108-104) and first downs (8-4). Both teams combined for 24 punts. Kansas kicked 13 times, averaging almost 31 yards per punt. The Big Red punted 11 times for a 37-yard average.

The Sooners traveled to Columbia to square off against Missouri without Warren and Young. Warren suffered a spinal injury against the Jayhawks, and Young was still hampered with a sore shoulder. The 1-5 Tigers won their season opener then lost the next five games, giving Sooner faithful hope for another victory. The Tigers won 7-0 without the services of their head coach Gwyn Henry, who was hospitalized and recovering from minor surgery. His assistants, Jack Crangle and Henry Lansing, filled in on the sideline.

OU's Ab Walker fumbled the opening kickoff at the Sooner 25. Missouri's George Stuber tossed a 15-yard TD strike to Frank Bittner seven plays later for the only tally two minutes into the game.

The Big Red had a chance to even the count late in the fourth period, but Massad fumbled on the Mizzou one-yard line.

The Sooners got 12 days to heal before hosting Oklahoma A&M on Thanksgiving. Dunlap would be the only Sooner who missed the game due to torn rib cartilage in the Missouri game. The 8-2 Aggies were riding a four-game winning streak. Both teams fought to a scoreless tie on a muddy Owen Field before 6,000 spectators.

The Aggies had two scoring opportunities, and both times the Sooners defense stiffened. They drove to the OU four in the first quarter. On fourth-and-goal, Gordon Graalman and end Edsel Curnutt nailed Merle Collins for a one-yard loss.

The Aggies marched to the OU 16 early in the fourth stanza, but Clarence Highfill's 35-yard field-goal try was short and wide. The Aggies made 10 first downs to two for the Sooners. The Aggies totaled 142 yards to only 23 for OU. Both teams combined for 29 punts. The Sooners kicked 17 times and A&M 12 times.

The OCU Goldbugs, formerly Epworth Methodists, were undefeated at 11-0. The Goldbugs outscored their opponents by a 24-4 average and shut out seven of them. The Sooners would be the eighth victim, dropping a 6-0 decision.

After three scoreless quarters, Warren fumbled a punt return in the fourth stanza, and OCU's Jim Smith recovered at the OU eight. Ted Hand scored three plays later, but the Sooners blocked the conversion. The Goldbugs later drove to the OU 10 but turned the ball over on downs.

Disappointed by the first losing season in seven years, OU students circulated a petition a few days later seeking the ouster of Lindsey, his staff, and Bennie Owen as athletic director. The students cited Lindsey's lack of leadership, offensive punch, and Owen's refusal to schedule "big-name" opponents.

Owen continued as athletic director for three more years, but Lindsey would not return as the Sooners' skipper in 1932.

The next charity game in Tulsa raised funds for the unemployed and for handicapped children under the care of the Tulsa Junior League. The Sooners showed a little more offensive firepower with a 20-7 victory over 8-2 Tulsa. They also displayed defensive muscle, intercepting eight Tulsa passes, recovering four fumbles and blocking a punt. Pansze picked off five passes.

As heavy rain fell in the second stanza, Pansze intercepted a pass and returned it 51 yards to the TU 31. Massad took a lateral from Stogner and scored five plays later. Stogner's toe gave the Sooners a 7-0 lead.

Oklahoma recovered a fumble in the third quarter and Massad scored two plays later. Stogner missed the extra point. The Golden Hurricane scored early in the fourth stanza. Young later picked up a fumble and returned it 15 yards for the third OU touchdown. Stogner was true on this kick. Tulsa led in total yards (243-130) and first downs (8-6), but the turnovers killed them.

Oklahoma traveled to Honolulu to meet the Honolulu Town Team, champions of the Honolulu senior football league, on Christmas. The Townies scored four times in the fourth quarter to win, 39-20.

The second period was all Sooners after the Townies scored first. OU answered with a Dunlap to Massad TD pass and Stogner's extra point. The Big Red added two more touchdowns in the final two minutes of the first half. Dunlap rocketed a 57-yard bomb to Massad. Seconds later, Dunlap recovered a Townies fumble in the end zone.

The Sooners ended the dreadful long season with a 7-0 victory over Hawaii University on New Year's Day.

Fred Cherry replaced Snell at left end for the Sooners in the third quarter. A couple of plays later, he hauled in Stogner's 26-yard pass and raced 34 more to the Hawaii one. Massad then plowed up the middle for the touchdown, and Stogner added the conversion. OU had another scoring chance by charging to the Hawaii 20, but had to give up possession on downs.

The Sooners ended the season with a 4-7-1 record and tied for last in the conference with a 1-4 mark. Teel was the only Sooner to make the all-conference team.

Lindsey resigned the following winter to accept an assistant position at Kansas University under his nemesis Bill Hargiss. Luster also resigned to accept a backfield coaching job at Colorado School of Mines in Golden. Lindsey's four-year record at OU was an even 19-19-6.

1932

Athletic director Bennie Owen hired Lewie Hardage, a backfield coach from Vanderbilt University, as the Sooners' eighth head coach. Hardage also played for the Commodores and earned third-team All-America honors in 1912. John "Bo" Rowland, formerly of Ouachita College, was tabbed as Hardage's line coach.

Hardage immediately went to work to design lighter uniforms for his Sooner charges. Pants ended three inches above the knees and were one and a half pounds lighter than the previous ones. He also added foamed rubber headgear, kneepads and shin guards, and cotton jerseys would keep his players a little cooler. Hardage believed the new uniforms, approximately eight and a half pounds lighter than the old ones, would add one second to his players' speed and still provide ample protection.

The new coach also built OU's fastest all-weather football field by adding loads of sand to the turf. This made for less sore feet.

Center Paul Young and guard Ellis Bashara returned to anchor the front wall. Young was elected captain. Graduation depleted the rest of the line. Smith Watkins and Edsel Curnutt provided experience at the ends. Graduation also depleted some of the backfield, but veterans like quarterback Bill Dunlap and left halfback Bill Pansze returned. Pansze's brother Art earned a starting slot at right halfback.

"[I] aim to give Oklahoma a team it can be proud of even in defeat," Hardage said before the season opener October 1 against Tulsa.

The Sooners defeated the Golden Hurricane, 7-0, in Norman before 10,000 fans.

1931 Season Record: 4-7-1
Big Six Conference: 1-4-0 (Fifth)

Date	Opponent	Result	Score
October 3	RICE	W	19-6
October 10	at Nebraska	L	13-0
October 17	Texas at Dallas	L	3-0
October 24	at Kansas State	L	14-0
October 31	IOWA STATE	L	13-12
November 7	KANSAS	W	10-0
November 14	at Missouri	L	6-0
November 26	OKLAHOMA A&M	T	0-0
December 5	OKLAHOMA CITY	L	6-0
December 12	at Tulsa	W	20-7
December 25	at Honolulu Town Team	L	39-20
January 1	at Hawaii	W	7-0

OU drove 52 yards to the TU eight late in the opening quarter, but surrendered possession on downs. A poor Hurricane punt on the next series set up the Big Red at the TU 41, and a roughing penalty gave the Sooners 15 more yards to the 26 as the period ended. Dunlap gained three yards, then the Sooners were flagged for offside. Tulsa was again guilty of roughness on the next play and the penalty placed the pigskin at the TU 18. Dunlap dropped back to pass on the next play, but found an opening up the middle and scampered to the four. He scored on the next play and converted the extra point.

The Hurricane did not penetrate past the OU 40 in the first half, but twice threatened to tie the game in the final 30 minutes.

TU's Roy "Skeet" Berry returned the second-half kickoff to the OU 45. The Hurricane then moved to the Sooner 17, but Art Pansze swatted down the fourth-down pass. A fourth-quarter Tulsa drive ended when the Hurricane failed to make a first down at the OU 22.

Oklahoma totaled 200 yards, 30 more than Tulsa.

The Sooners faced their former mentor Ad Lindsey the next week in the conference opener at Lawrence. Kansas escaped with a 13-12 victory over Denver University the week before. The Sooners defeated the Jayhawks, 21-6, before 7,000 fans.

The Hawks made the only scoring threat in the first stanza with a march to the OU 12 but gave up possession on downs. The Sooners capitalized on two Jayhawk fumbles in the next two quarters. The first came at the KU 45. Dunlap's one-yard plunge eight plays later and his conversion put the Sooners on top, 7-0.

Dunlap recovered the second gift at the KU 47, and Bill Pansze sailed to the end zone on the next play. Dunlap's conversion missed its mark.

The Big Red later stalled a KU drive at the OU 23, but the Jayhawks scored in the fourth stanza. The Sooners returned the ensuing kickoff to their own 35 and were on the KU nine two plays later. KU's defense stiffened, and Dunlap booted a 15-yard field goal to lift OU to a 15-6 edge. Dunlap scored the final tally later on a 13-yard run and again missed the extra point.

Bill Hargiss resigned as Kansas' head coach two days later, and Lindsey was named interim head coach.

The 2-0 Sooners were seeking to end Texas' five-year reign in the rivalry October 15 in Dallas. The 2-1 Longhorns extended their streak to six with a 17-10 victory before about 23,000 fans.

Dunlap's 20-yard field goal gave OU a 3-0 lead early in the second quarter. Texas answered with a 58-yard touchdown following the kickoff—a razzle-dazzle play that had four Steers touching the ball. Ernest Koy passed to Ed Price for 11 yards, and Price added four more yards before lateraling the ball to a trailing Albert Stafford. Stafford lateraled to Bohn Hillard at the OU 27, and Hilliard zipped to the end zone. Claude Blanton's conversion gave Texas a 7-3 lead.

Dunlap later picked off a pass at the UT 31, but the drive stalled as the first half expired with the Sooners at the 10.

Hilliard returned Dunlap's punt 94 yards for a touchdown in the third period and eclipsed the series record of 90 yards set by OU's Charles Wantland in 1908. Watkins smothered a Texas fumble late in the period, and Dunlap passed the Sooners to the Texas one. He scored on the next play and added the conversion to put OU back in the game, down 14-10.

The Horns marched 78 yards to the OU two after the kickoff. Hilliard then coughed up the pigskin, and Art Pansze recovered. The Sooners stalled and punted to midfield. The Steers moved to the OU 13 but had to settle for Blanton's 30-yard field goal for the final tally.

Texas led the game in first downs (18-12) and total yards (321-197). Hilliard touched the ball 27 times for 363 total yards—108 yards in 18 carries, returned seven punts for 202 more, ran back a kickoff for 26 and caught one pass for 27 yards.

Kansas State (3-1) rolled into Norman the next week minus its head coach, Bo McMillin, who was hospitalized from burns received the previous Sunday. The burns failed to heal sufficiently, and doctors advised him to stay in the hospital. The Sooners would be without Bill Pansze, who suffered a sprained knee in the Texas game. He would not return the rest of the season.

Oklahoma defeated the Wildcats, 20-13, before about 7,000 spectators. OU scored on the game's second play, a 35-yard TD pass from Dunlap to Art Pansze. Dunlap was true on his conversion kick.

Ralph Graham's touchdown in the second stanza got the Cats back in the game, but Young blocked Graham's extra-point kick, and the Sooners held a 7-6 lead. Douglass Russell later scored a touchdown for K-State to give the Cats a 13-7 advantage through halftime.

Dunlap fired another 35-yard TD pass, this time to Ab Walker, in the fourth period. Dunlap's toe gave the Sooners a 14-13 lead. Minutes later, Dunlap intercepted a pass (his third of the game) at the K-State 45 and flew to the end zone. His conversion gave OU a 21-13 lead, which was never relinquished.

The Sooners hadn't defeated Oklahoma A&M since 1928. A loss and two ties in the past three years had crimson fans itching for a win against their instate rivals. The 5-0-1 Aggies had a stout defense, yielding only 3.8 points per game. OU only threatened to score once but came up empty in the 7-0 loss before 14,000 at Stillwater.

The Sooners marched to the A&M 11 in the first quarter but turned the ball over on downs.

A&M quarterback Clarence Highfill directed the Aggies' only score in the second period. He completed two passes covering 48 yards to the Sooner one-yard line. From there he plowed through for the score.

The Aggies had three chances to turn the game into a rout in the fourth quarter. One drive to the OU 11 ended when Highfill's pass fell short. Walker slapped down a fourth-down pass to stall the next drive to the OU 20. Highfill's incomplete pass ended the third chance at the OU six.

The Aggies had more first downs (13-5) and total yards (272-101). Poor passing killed the Sooners. They completed only five of 20 passes for 78 yards and tossed three interceptions.

Oklahoma dropped to 3-2, but a 2-0 conference record still provided hopes of winning the Big Six conference crown.

Ticket prices were slashed to $1 each for the final two home games. Winless Missouri came to Norman on November 5 and stunned the Sooners, 14-6, before a homecoming throng of 12,000.

The Tigers took a 7-0 lead in the game's first five minutes. Carl Johanningmeier's one-yard TD run capped a 62-yard drive in four plays.

With the Tigers pinned deep late in the second stanza, a poor punt set up the Sooners at the MU 20, but the Big Red could not capitalize as the half ended.

Henry Haag recovered a Tiger fumble at the MU 19 in the third period. Three line plunges and an incomplete pass killed the Sooners' chance to again tie the game. The Tigers later upped their lead to 14-0 on Woodrow Hatfield's 20-yard TD run.

OU closed the gap to 14-7 in the fourth period. Dick Simms returned a Tiger punt 20 yards to the MU 35. Dunlap fired a pass to Jim Stacy, who replaced an injured Watkins, at the Mizzou 12.

Dunlap scored three plays later, but his conversion kick was blocked. The Sooners never threatened again.

The Tigers had 142 total yards, all on the ground. They passed only once, and that was incomplete. The Sooners had negative net rushing yards. They gained 60 yards but were thrown for losses totaling 78. The Sooners completed seven of 27 passes for 114 yards.

Stacy rapidly became a household word the following week, as he scored all three Sooner touchdowns in a 19-12 victory over Iowa State on a slippery field in Ames. Chilly temperatures held the crowd to only 1,500.

Dunlap rocketed a 40-yard TD bomb to Stacy in the opening quarter. Dunlap's conversion veered wide. The Cyclones scored a touchdown in the second period, but their extra point also sailed wide and the score was tied at 6-6.

OU later recovered a fumble at the I-State 35. The Sooners moved to the 14 in six plays, but the Cyclone defense held. A muffed I-State punt later gave OU possession at the Cyclones' 31. Four plays later, Stacy slammed through for a two-yard TD. Dunlap's kick split the uprights. The Sooners' 13-6 lead remained through the fourth quarter.

Oklahoma drove 54 yards in the fourth quarter for another touchdown. Simms carried 11 times in the drive and sparked it with a 26-yard run. Stacy then plowed over from the one. Dunlap missed the extra point.

The Cyclones added a touchdown in the final minute.

The Sooners held a 3-1 conference record and still had a chance to win the title with a win over Nebraska. The 4-1-1 Cornhuskers were 3-0 in the conference and had two more conference games remaining. Nebraska brought a stout defense to Norman on November 19, yielding 5.3 points per game.

The Huskers held the Sooners scoreless in a 5-0 victory before 15,000 fans.

Nebraska marched to the OU five in the second stanza. The Sooner defense stiffened, and Simms forced Chris Mathis out of bounds a foot short of the goal line on fourth down. The two teams went to the locker room knotted at zero.

Bennie Masterson's 15-yard field goal in the third quarter gave the Huskers a 3-0 lead. The Sooners' only threat of the game came up empty when Dunlap missed a 15-yard field goal in the fourth period.

Nebraska got a safety late in the game when an errant lateral to Fred Cherry rolled back 20 yards and into the end zone. Cherry was tackled when he retrieved the pigskin.

The Huskers had more first downs (12-5) and total yards (195-88).

1932 Season Record: 4-4-1
Big Six Conference: 3-2-0 (Second)

Date	Opponent	Result	Score
October 1	TULSA	W	7-0
October 8	at Kansas	W	21-6
October 15	Texas at Dallas	L	17-10
October 22	KANSAS STATE	W	20-13
October 29	at Oklahoma A&M	L	7-0
November 5	MISSOURI	L	14-6
November 12	at Iowa State	W	19-12
November 19	NEBRASKA	L	5-0
November 24	at George Washington	T	7-7

The Sooners' final game was a non-conference tilt with the George Washington Colonials in Washington, D.C. The Sooner team and band embarked for D.C. on Monday and arrived two days later for the Thanksgiving Day game.

The Sooners and Colonials battled to a 7-7 tie before 19,000 spectators. The Colonials scored in the second period. OU capitalized on a Colonial fumble when Dunlap tossed a TD pass to Cherry in the third quarter. Dunlap kicked the conversion.

Oklahoma finished the '32 campaign with a 4-4-1 record and tied Kansas for second place in the conference with a 3-2 mark.

Dunlap and Bashara were selected to the all-conference first team.

1933

In 1931, OU athletic director Bennie Owen was criticized for not scheduling a "big-name" opponent. He answered by scheduling Lewis Hardage's alma mater, Vanderbilt University, for the 1933 season opener in Norman.

The Commodores were the power of the south. Dan McGugin, brother-in-law of the legendary Fielding H. Yost, coached the team for 30 years and won 10 Southern Conference championships. When he retired in 1934, McGugin's teams had won 76 percent (197-55-19) of their games.

Quarterback Bill Dunlap and guard Ellis Bashara, both all-conference a year before, returned to the 1933 squad as did halfback brothers Bill and Art Pansze. Graduation had thinned the line, so Hardage moved Jim Stacy from end to guard. Sophomores Cassius "Cash" Gentry and Casey Cason, both able blockers and tacklers, stepped immediately into the tackle slots.

A fan would have to put down $5 for a season ticket to four Sooner home games. The cost of individual tickets ranged from $2.75 for the Vanderbilt game and $2.20 for the remaining three games, so purchasing a season ducat saved the fan $4.35.

The Commodores rolled into Norman for the September 30 clash with a 1-0 record. They pasted Cumberland, a non-Division I team, 50-0.

Although the two teams battled to a scoreless tie before 18,000 fans at Memorial Stadium, the Sooners clearly dominated the game statistically. Oklahoma gained eight first downs to only one for the Commodores. OU totaled 177 yards (123 rushing and 52 passing) and Vandy gained 36 total yards (36 rushing and zero passing).

Both teams combined for 30 punts. Dunlap kicked nine times for a 42-yard average, and Gentry booted the ball four times for a 40-yard average. Vanderbilt punted 17 times for a 41-yard average.

Neither team threatened in the first half. The 10-yard line was the closest either team had possession and that came in the final two quarters. OU fullback Leroy Robinson fumbled at the Sooner 20, but Vanderbilt recovered and gave the ball back moments later when Vernon Close was smacked hard and spilled the ball. Reserve quarterback Karey Fuqua smothered the pigskin at the 10 for the Sooners.

The Big Red drove to the Commodore 10 in the fourth stanza but fumbled. Dunlap also missed two 30-yard field goals in the final period.

The Sooners traveled upstate to meet Tulsa in the Golden Hurricane's season opener on October 7. Tulsa beat OU, 20-6, before 15,000 fans at Skelly Stadium with all points being scored in the second half.

The Sooners threatened with a drive to the TU 20 early in the second period but turned the ball over on downs. Roy "Skeet" Berry's touchdown run in the third quarter put Tulsa on top 6-0. Moments later, the Hurricane added another score when they recovered their own fumble in the end zone. Tulsa 13, Oklahoma 0.

Berry later had a 48-yard touchdown called back, and Tulsa had to punt.

Following a Tulsa punt in the fourth quarter to the TU 45, the Sooners went to work and needed only two plays to score, both passes from Dunlap to end Jack Harris. The first pass was for 23 yards and the second for 22 yards and the touchdown. Dunlap's conversion kick was blocked.

Tack Dennis later scored another Tulsa touchdown to put the game out of reach. Tulsa gained 13 first downs to only four for OU. The Hurricane totaled 273 yards to 105 for the Sooners.

Dunlap was switched to halfback, and Fuqua took over at quarterback the next week.

The Sooners had no time to think about their loss. Texas was on the horizon. Oklahoma had not defeated the Longhorns since 1919, six straight losses and crimson faithful were clamoring for a victory. They got it. OU dropped Texas, 9-0, in Dallas on October 14 before a Fairpark Stadium crowd of 18,000.

The story of the game found its way into *The Daily Oklahoman*'s front page, although other state and national stories could have buried it. But this was the Texas game. George "Machine Gun" Kelly and his wife were found guilty of kidnapping Oklahoma City millionaire Charles Urshcel in an Oklahoma City federal courtroom.

The other headline was that of German Chancellor Adolf Hitler's withdrawal from the League of Nations and the World Disarmament Conference. The withdrawal would eventually lead to World War II.

The 2-1 Steers were drubbed 26-0 by Nebraska the week before. Star halfback Bohn Hilliard, who almost single-handedly beat the Sooners a year before, was sidelined with an ankle injury he suffered in the Husker contest.

Although both teams had deep drives in the first half, (Texas to the OU 11 and OU to the UT eight) both came up empty. With less than two minutes remaining in the half, Texas fielded Dunlap's punt at midfield. The Steers were twice penalized, moving the ball back to the Texas 28. Harris, on the next play, crashed through and nailed Buster Baebel for a 16-yard loss.

The Horns decided to punt out, but center Carlos Bell's snap sailed over the head of punter Ron Fagan and back of the end zone. The safety gave the Sooners a 2-0 halftime lead.

In the third quarter, Dunlap punted to the Texas 12, but the Horns couldn't move and punted two plays later. Sooner end Jeff Coker charged through the line, and Texas punter James Hadlock tucked the ball to his chest, but Cason dropped him at the UT eight. Hadlock fumbled, and Cason recovered.

Dunlap returned to quarterback, and after two plays gained only one yard. He then called his own number and raced off the right side and dove into the end zone, inches inside the boundary. Halfback Beede Long kicked the extra point, and the Sooners held the 9-0 margin to the end.

Sophomore Melbourne Robertson showed potential at quarterback in the preseason practices, but an injury held him out of the first three games. He got the starting nod before Iowa State came to Norman the following week. Dunlap had suffered fractured ribs against the Longhorns but played against the Cyclones.

The Sooners scored two fourth-quarter touchdowns to propel them past I-State, 19-7, before 8,000 spectators.

Oklahoma marched to the Cyclones' 25 in the opening stanza but failed to complete four straight passes. Iowa State took a 7-0 lead in the second period following Bill Pansze's fumble of a punt return.

Coker later blocked a Cyclone punt, and Leroy Robison recovered for the Sooners at the IS 10. Dunlap sailed a TD pass to Harris, but the Sooners trailed 7-6 when Long's conversion failed.

The Cyclones held the one-point advantage through the third quarter. Gentry blocked an I-State punt in the fourth, and Stacy smothered the pigskin at the IS 34. Gentry had three blocked punts for the day.

Dunlap sailed a 14-yard pass to Robertson then Art Pansze ran for 16 to the Cyclone four. Robison crossed the goal line two plays later. Dunlap's kick was wide, but the Sooners had the lead, 12-7.

Dunlap scored on a three-yard run four plays following Art Pansze's interception at the IS 25. Fuqua toed the extra point.

The Big Red rolled up 228 total yards to 36 for Iowa State. Oklahoma also gained 13 first downs to only three for the Cyclones.

The Sooners went to Lincoln on October 28, hoping to break Nebraska's two-game winning streak over OU. It would be a tall order since the 3-0 Huskers had not been scored upon in the first three games. OU was the first team to score on the Huskers in a 16-7 loss. Only three teams scored on Nebraska all year.

The Sooners made a huge mistake at the kickoff. NU's Bernie Masterson's kickoff went into the end zone, but no Sooner player went to cover it. However, NU's Hubert Boswell did, and the Huskers had a touchdown before the ball was ever snapped.

Nebraska scored again in the second stanza and held a 14-0 lead through intermission. Several Sooners nailed Boswell in the third quarter, forcing him to fumble, and OU's Kenneth Little recovered at the NU 19. Dunlap fired a fourth-down pass to Bill Pansze to the Husker six. Four plays later, Dunlap hurdled two Nebraska tacklers into the end zone.

Lee Penny recovered a bad snap by backup OU center Morris McDannald at the Sooner five. The Oklahoma defense held the Huskers for three plays, but George Sauer kicked a field goal to put the game away.

After the game, Dunlap took the blame for failing to cover the opening kickoff. He and Robertson were the deep returnees for the kickoff. Dunlap said he thought the ball would roll out of the end zone. When he saw Robertson attempting to grab the ball, he told him, "Let it go!"

"It was my fault," Dunlap said. "I don't know what in the world I was thinking about. I'll make up for that in the remaining games of the season, no matter what I have to do.

"I'll give Kansas plenty [of] hell Saturday."

He did give Kansas (2-2-1) plenty of hell the next week before 9,000 homecoming fans in Norman. Dunlap completed six of nine passes, averaged 44 yards per punt and scored once himself in the Sooners' 20-0 victory. The game was highlighted by blocked kicks and missed conversions.

Oklahoma marched to the Jayhawks' eight-yard line early in the first period but had to surrender on downs.

J.W. "Dub" Wheeler blocked KU's punt early in the second stanza, and Gentry tackled KU punter Fred Harris trying to retrieve the ball in the end zone. The safety gave the Sooners a 2-0 lead. Dunlap later scored on a two-yard run, but the conversion was no good.

Robertson scored from three yards out in the third period to give the Big Red a 14-0 lead. Robertson also carried for 45 yards and passed for another 20 to set up the score. The extra point failed again.

John Miskovsky blocked Harris' punt, and Cason recovered in the end zone. The third conversion was missed, but the Sooners had a deciding lead, 20-0, which was never relinquished.

OU gained 10 first downs to only five for the Hawks. The Sooners totaled 220 yards and Kansas had a minus-11 total yards.

The Hawks had minus-19 net rushing yards and gained eight yards on one pass completion. The Jayhawks never moved past midfield all day.

The Sooners defeated 1-5 Missouri, 21-0, on November 11 before 7,000 homecoming fans in Columbia. Mizzou won its season opener, then lost its next five games.

Dunlap's three-yard TD run capped a drive that was set up by his two long passes to Harris in the opening stanza. Dunlap also converted. In the third quarter, Dunlap hurled a pass from midfield to Harris, who cut back toward the ball at the MU 23 then sped to the end zone. Long toed the extra point.

McDannald intercepted a Missouri pass at the Tiger 14 late in the fourth period. A roughing penalty by the Tigers moved the ball to the one. Robertson smashed through on the next play, and Long converted.

The Sooners gained 213 total yards and nine first downs in the contest. Missouri gained 114 total yards and three first downs and never penetrated past the OU 40-yard line.

Dunlap sprained his right wrist (on his throwing arm) three days before the Sooners traveled to Manhattan to meet 5-1-1 Kansas State. Fuqua replaced him. With a record of 3-1 in the Big Six, the Sooners could claim second place in the Big Six Conference with a victory. Nebraska had already wrapped up its third straight title.

Kansas State won, 14-0. Wildcat halfback Doug Russell scored once in the second quarter and again in the fourth. His first TD came on a 49-yard scamper and the second on a 38-yard run. Oklahoma had two drives into Cat territory, but had to turn the ball over on downs both times.

A victory over Oklahoma A&M would preserve Hardage's first winning season and the first for OU in three years. The Aggies defeated the Sooners, 13-0, before a Thanksgiving Day crowd of 18,000 in Norman.

A&M's Lester List scored a touchdown with 20 seconds remaining until halftime, which capped a 45-yard drive. Jess Rossett's five-yard TD run topped a 61-yard march early in the third quarter.

The Aggies dominated as they collected 15 first downs and 238 total yards. The Sooners managed to get only four first downs and 59 total yards.

OU finished the season with another 4-4-1 record and placed third in the Big Six with a 3-2 conference mark.

Dunlap, Gentry, Bashara, and Stacy were selected to the all-conference first team.

1933 Season Record: 4-4-1
Big Six Conference: 3-2-0 (Third)

Date	Opponent	Result	Score
September 30	VANDERBILT	T	0-0
October 7	at Tulsa	L	20-6
October 14	Texas at Dallas	W	9-0
October 21	IOWA STATE	W	19-7
October 28	at Nebraska	L	16-7
November 4	KANSAS	W	20-0
November 11	at Missouri	W	21-0
November 18	at Kansas State	L	14-0
November 30	OKLAHOMA A&M	L	13-0

1934

Seven starters, including two all-conference selections, from the previous year returned to the 1934 squad, which had the Sooners primed for claiming their first Big Six conference championship. Guard Jim Stacy and tackle Cash Gentry, all-conference in '33, were back to anchor the front line. Veteran returnees included center Morris McDannald, tackle Dub Wheeler, and ends Jack Harris and Jeff Coker.

Beede Long, Melbourne Robertson, and Ben Poynor returned to the backfield, but Bill Dunlap graduated, creating a big void at quarterback. No one appeared to be the favorite for his replacement, but Karey Fuqua got the starting nod before the season opener against the Centenary Gentlemen in Norman.

Centenary had already played three games and were undefeated by outscoring its opponents, 57-0. The Gentlemen were 19-0-5 dating back to 1931. The Sooners ended the visitors' unbeaten string with a 7-0 victory on October 6 before 10,000 fans at Owen Field.

Both teams threatened to score in the first three quarters, but each time came up empty. The Sooners marched to the Centenary 16 in the first period, following Gentry's fumble recovery at the Gentlemen 35, but had to turn the ball over on downs.

The Gentlemen moved to the OU four in the second period, but backup center Bill Conkright hammered a Centenary ball carrier for no gain on fourth down.

The Gentlemen drove to the OU 18 in the third quarter, but the Big Red defense stiffened.

Harris blocked a Centenary punt with 11 minutes remaining in the game, and Coker smothered the pigskin in the end zone. Long's extra point sailed true.

At 2-0, Texas was fresh off a 7-6 upset of Notre Dame, yet the Sooners were favored to defeat their southern rivals the next week in Dallas. Halfback Irvin Gilbreath scored three touchdowns to lead the Steers to a 19-0 victory before 21,000 fans.

Texas coach Jack Chevigny started his second string in the first quarter. His reserves once drove to the OU six-yard line in the first period, but the Sooner defense held.

The Longhorn starters entered the lineup in the second quarter and moved to the OU 20, but once again the Big Red defense was unyielding. UT's James Hadlock returned the ensuing Sooners punt to the OU 27. Two plays later, Bohn Hilliard fired a TD pass to Gilbreath to put the Steers ahead, 6-0. Hilliard missed the conversion.

Texas scored on its next possession, a 20-yard run by Gilbreath. Hilliard booted the extra point to put the Horns up, 13-0. Hilliard was sidelined with an injury early in the third quarter and did not return. Heavy rain soaked the field in the second half.

A 32-yard pass midway through the third quarter set up the Horns at the OU nine, but the crimson defense yielded zero yards on the next four downs. The Sooners later drove to the UT 37 but fumbled.

After a series of punts, Texas drove 34 yards for its final touchdown. Gilbreath carried three straight times and capped the drive with a nine-yard run. Hadlock's extra point failed, but Texas held on.

The Sooners had to turn their attention from one rival to another—Nebraska on October 20. Art Pansze started at quarterback and although the Sooners lost, 6-0, they had more offensive firepower than in the first two contests. In those first two games, the Sooners had only 112 total yards and five first downs. The Sooners gained 160 yards and 11 first downs against the Huskers.

The 15,000 spectators in Norman witnessed a scoreless first half. Oklahoma drove 47 yards in the second quarter, but reserve halfback Elmo "Bo" Hewes fumbled at the goal line to squelch the drive. The first half ended with a 0-0 deadlock, but the Sooners had eight first downs to Nebraska's zero.

NU's Sam Francis recovered a partially blocked Sooner punt in the third quarter, setting up his team at the OU 25. Lloyd Cardwell carried for 23 yards, then Francis scored from the two for the deciding tally.

Nebraska equaled OU in first downs (11-11) but had more total yards with 186.

Oklahoma and Kansas battled to a 7-7 draw the next week in Lawrence. Both teams were scoreless in the first half, then the Sooners struck first in the third stanza. OU got the ball following a punt to the OU 49, and backup fullback Leroy Robison gained nine yards on the next two carries. Facing third-and-one at the KU 40, Poyner blasted up the middle and shot to the end zone. Coker threw a key block near the goal line. Long booted the extra point to give the Sooners a 7-0 advantage.

KU's George Hapgood tossed a 50-yard TD pass to Mano Stukey early in the fourth quarter to tie the game. Both teams had five first downs, but Kansas had more total yards, 182-111. The Sooners tossed only three passes, completed none, and two were intercepted.

Unhappy with his lineup, Lewie Hardage shook it up before the Sooners hosted Missouri for homecoming on November 3. Robertson started at quarterback, Long and Hewes at halfback, and Poyner at fullback. Stacy remained at right guard, but Mickey Parks was moved to center, and Connie Ahrens replaced him at the left guard slot. Dewey Tennyson and Ferd Ellsworth got the starting nods at tackle, and Ralph Brown and John Miskovsky rounded out the lineup at the ends.

Hardage's reorganization was a gamble that paid off as the Sooners blasted the Tigers, 31-0, before 15,000 fans. OU president Dr. William Bizzell gave a pep talk to the team prior to kickoff. Hardage said the president's "words of encouragement were needed."

Poynor's two-yard TD run capped a 75-yard Sooner drive late in the opening stanza. Gentry's conversion was blocked. Moments later, Wheeler recovered a Tiger fumble at the MU 25. Robertson, who rushed 20 times for 113 yards, scored from the one five plays later early in the second quarter. Long's extra point was true, and suddenly OU had a 13-0 lead.

A poor Missouri punt later set up the Sooners at the MU 29. On the first play, backup halfback Harland Page fired a pass to Harris in the end zone. Two Tiger defenders tipped the ball in the end zone, but backup end R.A. Cox grabbed the ball for the score. Page's conversion was blocked, but the Sooners held a comfortable 19-0 lead.

Long added a one-yard TD run in the fourth quarter, then the Sooners scored again following Parks' interception at midfield. Parks returned the interception 25 yards, then Page tossed a touchdown pass to Miskovsky.

The Sooners also dominated in the stat department. OU rolled up 24 first downs and 376 total yards. Missouri gained only four first downs and 54 total yards all on the ground. The Tigers failed to complete a pass in six attempts.

The Sooners scored two touchdowns in the first 11 minutes to drop 4-1-1 Iowa State, 12-0, the following week in Norman. Poynor's one-yard run capped a 28-yard drive following a Cyclone fumble. Minutes later, Miskovsky grabbed the pigskin from a par-

tially blocked punt and ran eight yards for the score. Both extra-point attempts failed.

The Sooners had three scoring opportunities in the second half, but each time the Cyclone defense stiffened.

OU's defense also created havoc for Iowa State quarterback Bill Allender. The D sacked him six times and intercepted five of his six passing attempts. The Sooners gained nine first downs and 190 total yards, all on the ground. The Cyclones managed only two first downs and 10 total yards, also on the ground.

Gentry punted seven times and averaged 56.4 yards per kick.

A safety before halftime helped propel 4-2-1 Kansas State to an 8-7 victory before 7,300 fans on November 17 in Norman.

Backup quarterback Raleigh Francis' 18-yard TD pass to Harris and Long's extra point gave the Sooners a 7-0 lead in the second period.

Later, Gentry was setting up to punt from his end zone and was tackled trying to retrieve a bad snap. The Sooners held a 7-2 lead at intermission.

The Cats scored on a two-yard pass in the third quarter for the deciding tally. K-State outplayed the Sooners with more first downs (12-8) and total yards (206-193).

The Sooners were seeking their first win against 4-4 Oklahoma A&M for the first time since 1928. Three losses and two ties the past five years had crimson faithful itching for a victory.

The Sooners wasted four scoring chances in the scoreless tie on November 22 in Stillwater. After Robertson took the opening kick-off to the OU 42, the Sooners moved to the A&M 19, but the Aggies intercepted to squelch the drive.

A blocked punt later gave OU possession at the A&M 34, but the Sooners had to turn the ball over on downs.

The Sooners drove to the Aggie 11 in the second stanza on runs of 36 yards by Raleigh Francis and 13 by Robertson. Francis' fourth-down pass to Harris in the end zone was batted away by A&M's Beuford Barnum.

The Sooners later marched to the Aggie 10, but the Aggie defense stiffened again.

A&M's only chance came in the fourth quarter when it moved to the OU 26, but the threat ended on a missed field goal.

Both teams gained seven first downs apiece, but the Sooners had more total yards (148-113).

The Sooners traveled to Washington, D.C. to meet the George Washington Colonials on Thanksgiving. This was the second time in three years the Big Red had met the Colonials in the nation's capital. Both battled to a 7-7 standoff in 1932.

The Colonials won 3-0 on Harry Deming's 15-yard field goal in the second period, moments after Deming recovered a Sooner fumble at the OU 26.

1934 Season Record: 3-4-2
Big Six Conference: 2-2-1 (Third)

Date	Opponent	Result	Score
October 6	CENTENARY	W	7-0
Octber 13	Texas at Dallas	L	19-0
October 20	NEBRASKA	L	6-0
Ocotber 27	at Kansas	T	7-7
November 3	MISSOURI	W	31-0
November 10	IOWA STATE	W	12-0
November 17	KANSAS STATE	L	8-7
November 24	at Oklahoma A&M	T	0-0
November 29	at George Washington	L	3-0

Page blocked a Colonial punt late in the game, then Coker dashed 50 yards to the GWU nine. The Colonial defense stiffened, and Stacy's 25-yard field goal try was low.

The field, ankle deep in mud, kept the stats down as well. GWU had three first downs and 57 total yards in the game. The Sooners managed only one first down and minus-18 total yards.

Oklahoma ended the season with a 3-4-2 record and finished third in the Big Six with a 2-2-1 mark. Gentry was named All-America and Wheeler, Stacy, and Poynor joined him on the all-conference first team.

Hardage resigned, leaving OU with an 11-12-4 record. Bennie Owen also resigned as athletic director.

1935

Lawrence "Biff" Jones was hired as the Sooners' ninth head coach and athletic director. He had previously coached four years at Army and three years at Louisiana State. During those seven years he rolled up an incredible record of 53-17-7.

A captain in the army, Jones had the coaches' offices refurbished, cleaned, and reorganized. During his 19-month tenure at Oklahoma, Jones rebuilt the athletic training department with a new dressing room and added whirlpool baths and needle showers in the training room.

The players had new uniforms in 1935. The red jerseys had large white numbers and three white stripes on each arm. They wore khaki pants made from airline linen, red socks and black shoes with white laces. Jones regarded morale as 85 percent of playing football, and the new unis certainly provided that for his charges.

Jones hired Robert "Doc" Erskine and Tom Stidham as his assistants. Erskine, from Loyola University, coached the backs, and Stidham, from Northwestern University, tutored the linemen.

Jones installed the double wingback system, which was developed by Glenn "Pop" Warner at Stanford in the 1920s. The formation required a wingback to be positioned outside the end at each side of the line of scrimmage. It was designed to be a better passing formation, and to provide a better short side running game. The fullback was positioned directly behind the center and took most snaps. He could spin and hand off to either wingback.

The line was usually unbalanced, which also allowed for sweeps, reverses, and passes with both guards pulling out of the line to block for the ball carrier. The fullback was required to be a husky fellow, for he must block defensive linemen coming from the opposite side.

Jones implemented the system to strengthen the Sooners' running game. Halfback Melbourne Robertson and fullback Ben Poynor returned to the backfield, but Jones was searching for a quarterback to run his new formation. Sophomore J.R. Corbett, of Amarillo, Texas, stepped to the forefront.

Other veterans who returned in 1935 included tackle Dub Wheeler, centers Morris McDannald and Mickey Parks, guard Connie Ahrens, ends Jack Harris and R.A. Cox, and tackle Ferd Ellsworth. Poynor did not play in the first three games due to injury.

King Price, assistant athletic director and former Sooner star, announced that not all OU home games would be broadcast on the radio. The announcement was an attempt to boost season ticket sales, which reached 6,500 before the first kickoff. Tickets prices were $2.20 a game for the west side seats, $1.65 for the east side stands, and $1.10 for general admission.

The Sooners opened the 1935 campaign September 28 against Colorado, the first meeting between both schools since 1913. The Buffaloes came to Norman as the defending co-champs of the Rocky Mountain conference.

The Sooners won 3-0 on Raphael Boudreau's second-quarter field goal before 12,000 fans. OU drove to the Buffs' 14 in the opening period, but lost the opportunity to score when Corbett's handoff to halfback Woody Huddleston was fumbled on an attempted reverse, and Hank Simmons recovered for Colorado.

Jones inserted the second unit in the second stanza. The Sooners marched to the CU 27, but had to rely on Boudreau's 43-yard field goal. CU's Byron "Whizzer" White fumbled on the first play following the kickoff, and McDannald pounced on the ball at the Buffs' 25. Oklahoma moved to the 11, but Jack Baer fumbled it away.

Colorado made a late charge to the OU seven in the fourth quarter, but Ed Wagner's field goal sailed wide with three minutes remaining.

The Buffs had more first downs (8-5) and total yards (172-104) in a game dominated by punting. Both teams combined for 27 punts.

New Mexico came to Norman the following week boasting a strong passing game, but the Sooners shut down quarterback Abbie Paiz's aerial attack, limiting him to 77 yards (completing seven of 18 attempts and one interception). The Lobos shut out their first two opponents by a combined score of 66-0, but wound up with a goose egg. An improved Oklahoma offense helped the Sooners roll to a 25-0 decision before a crowd of 7,000.

The Sooners drove to the Lobos' 30 on their first series, but Huddleston fumbled.

Corbett later took a Lobo punt and returned it 28 yards to the NMU 48. Robertson then darted 37 yards around left end to the Lobos' 11. Three plays later, Corbett started around right end and was bottled up at the line of scrimmage, but he tossed a long lateral to end Pete Smith who sidestepped two defenders to the end zone.

As in the first game, Jones put in his second unit in the second stanza, and on the first play of the period, Boudreau fired a 30-yard pass to halfback Bo Hewes to the NMU 14. The Sooners fumbled three plays later at the Lobo three.

Baer's 23-yard punt return to the NMU 27 moments later set up a short scoring drive for the Sooners. Bill Breeden zipped a seven-yard pass to Dean Cutchall. Breeden carried to the Lobo one on the next four plays. He capped the drive with a one-yard plunge. Boudreau's conversion, the only good extra point all day, put the Sooners ahead, 13-0.

Corbett scored on a five-yard run from Huddleston's lateral in the third stanza to up the Sooner lead to 19-0. The Lobos marched to the OU five in the fourth period, but Ahrens sacked Paiz for a five-yard loss to end the threat. The Sooners then drove 90 yards for the final tally, a five-yard pass from Huddleston to Cutchall. A forward lateral from Huddleston to John Miskovsky to Corbett for 30 yards sparked the drive.

The Sooners rushed for 292 yards, totaled 402 yards and 20 first downs. The Big Red defense held the Lobos to seven first downs and 92 total yards.

The fired up 2-0 Sooners headed south to Dallas on October 12 to face Texas.

Construction of the Texas Centennial Exposition had cancelled the Texas State Fair and only 16,000 showed up for the 30th edition of the rivalry. Yet ticket sales in Oklahoma City and Norman were up 25 percent from the prior year. The 2-1 Longhorns defeated the Sooners, 12-7.

UT's Morris Sands returned the opening kickoff to the UT 49. Although the Horns scored, the Sooners made them work for every yard. Bill Pitzer's two-yard TD run capped a 51-yard, 12-play drive. Jay Arnald's conversion sailed under the crossbar.

Early in the second quarter, Cox recovered a Steer fumble at the Texas 19. The Sooners needed only two plays to score. After a run for no gain, Boudreau fired a pass to Hewes, who had slipped behind the Texas secondary in the end zone. Boudreau's extra point gave the Big Red a 7-6 advantage.

Boudreau's poor punt set up the Horns at the Texas 40 late in the first half. On third down from the OU 35, Judson Atchison tossed a pass to Irvin Gilbreath, who hauled in the ball at the OU 11 and scored. Oklahoma blocked the extra point and could not mount a charge the rest of the day.

Texas gained more first downs (18-7) and total yards (359-169).

Jones shook up his starting roster before Iowa State came to Norman for the Big Six opener the following week. Ahrens and tackle Ralph Brown were the only mainstays in the front line. Breeden and Hewes started at the halfback positions with Poynor at fullback. Corbett remained at quarterback.

Oklahoma got back on the winning track with a 16-0 victory over the 1-1-1 Cyclones before 12,000 at Memorial Stadium.

Boudreau's 15-yard field goal in the second stanza gave the Sooners a 3-0 lead, which they held through halftime. OU totaled 139 yards all on the ground in the first half while holding the Cyclones to 12 total yards.

The Sooners began to move the ball more effectively in the second half with blasts up the middle, off tackle spins, and end sweeps for 191 yards.

Breeden's one-yard TD run in the third quarter capped a 71-yard drive in six plays. The Sooners' only pass of the day came on Breeden's 26-yarder to Hewes on the drive's first play. Huddleston's extra point was blocked.

Karey Fuqua's 10-yard TD run topped an 80-yard drive late in the game, which was highlighted by Huddleston's 30-yard run on the drive's first play. Huddleston kicked the conversion.

Oklahoma dominated with 18 first downs to only three for I-State. The Sooners' 356 total yards was the best so far in the season. The defense held the Cyclones to 88 total yards.

The Sooners traveled to Lincoln on October 26 seeking to end Nebraska's four-game winning streak over OU. The 2-1-1 Huskers dominated Oklahoma, 19-0, on a blustery day and a slippery field.

Nebraska scored a touchdown in the game's first nine minutes, added another early in the second quarter and a third in the third period. Lloyd Cardwell scored twice for the Cornhuskers.

The Sooners lost many chances to make a game of it. Wheeler blocked a Nebraska punt in the first stanza, and OU took over at the NU 25. The Sooners lost four yards during the next three plays and turned the ball over on downs.

Two second-half OU drives were squelched by John Howell's interceptions. Oklahoma drove to the NU 16 in the third quarter, where Howell got his first pick off. OU then marched to the Husker seven, but Nebraska coach Dana X. Bible inserted his first unit to kill the drive, which ended with an incomplete fourth-down pass.

Howell's next interception ended a Sooner march to the NU 26 in the fourth quarter. OU later drove to the Husker 20 then Huddleston fired four incompletions.

Coach Jones again changed his backfield before 2-2 Kansas came to Norman the next week. Fuqua started at quarterback, replacing Corbett, who was injured in the Nebraska game. Huddleston started at left half, Robertson at right half, and Al Corrotto at fullback. The Jayhawks were seeking their first win over Oklahoma since 1930.

It looked as though the homecoming crowd of 12,000 would have to settle for a scoreless tie, but George Hapgood's 53-yard TD

pass to Rutherford Hayes in the final 30 seconds doomed the Sooners, 7-0.

Oklahoma blocked a Kansas punt in the first period, but stalled at the Hawks' 20, and KU blocked Brown's field-goal try.

Two Sooner drives deep into Hawk territory in the second half came up empty. The first drive to the four came on a mix of runs and short passes, but the KU defense held, and Edwin Phelps partially blocked Boudreau's field-goal attempt. Breeden was stopped short of the goal line on fourth down on the second threat.

The Sooners traveled to Columbia on November 9 and defeated Missouri, 20-6, before 8,000 homecoming fans.

Hewes intercepted a Tiger pass at midfield and returned it 10 yards in the opening period. Breeden and Hewes pounded out gains to the MU one, then Breeden's one-yard blast off tackle on the first play of the second quarter gave OU a 6-0 lead, but his conversion was blocked.

The Sooners capitalized on two Missouri turnovers with Robertson scoring the touchdown each time. Miskovsky forced a fumble late in the second stanza and recovered it at the Missouri 37. The Sooners moved to the 18, then Robertson shot to the end zone off a reverse, and Huddleston's foot gave OU a 13-0 advantage.

Robertson added a three-yard TD run in the third quarter, and Missouri's only tally came in the fourth against the Sooners' third unit.

Oklahoma outgained the Tigers in first downs (17-8) and total yards (221-149).

Breeden nailed a 13-yard field goal in the second quarter as the Sooners dropped 2-3-2 Kansas State, 3-0, the next week in Manhattan. The victory ended Oklahoma's two-game losing streak to the Wildcats.

Huddleston intercepted a K-State pass at the OU 29 to halt their threat in the first period. A poor punt in the second stanza gave OU possession at the Cats' 43. Breeden, Fuqua and Hewes carried to the K-State 20. After Breeden completed a 12-yard pass to Hewes, the Sooners stalled and settled for Breeden's field goal.

Oklahoma led the Wildcats in first downs (7-6) and total yards (160-67).

The Sooners also hoped to end a six-game non-winning streak against Oklahoma A&M. Oklahoma had not beaten the Aggies since a 46-0 decision in 1928. OU blasted the Aggies, 25-0, before 12,000 fans in Norman on Thanksgiving.

A&M marched to the OU 18 in the first quarter, but a stout Sooner defense forced a field goal. The kick was low and wide.

Miskovsky recovered an Aggie fumble at the A&M 24 in the second period, but Breeden's pass was intercepted soon after. A poor Aggie punt moments later into a stiff wind set up the Sooners at the

1935 Season Record: 6-3-0

Big Six Conference: 3-2-0 (Second)

Date	Opponent	Result	Score
September 28	COLORADO	W	3-0
October 5	NEW MEXICO	W	25-0
October 12	Texas at Dallas	L	12-7
October 19	IOWA STATE	W	16-0
October 26	at Nebraska	L	19-0
November 2	KANSAS	L	7-0
November 9	at Missouri	W	20-6
November 16	at Kansas State	W	3-0
November 28	OKLAHOMA A&M	W	25-0

A&M 27. Breeden gained 20 yards, and Hewes added four more. Breeden scored two plays later for a 6-0 lead, but his extra-point kick was blocked.

The Big Red stalled A&M deep in Aggie territory, and Ned Stuart's punt off the side of his foot gave OU possession at the A&M nine. Huddleston sailed a pass to Harris to the one, then Huddleston bulled ahead for the score, but his conversion was wide.

Neither team threatened to score in the third stanza.

Robertson's 59-yard TD run sparked the Sooners to a 18-0 lead in the fourth quarter. He swept around right end and was momentarily trapped by Aggie defenders near the sideline, but slipped through their grasps and followed Breeden's block to the end zone. Breeden's extra point veered wide.

Hewes later picked off A&M's pass at the Aggie 45 and returned it to the 16. Breeden carried on all three plays and scored from the five. He made true on his extra point.

OU had six first downs and 189 total yards. The Aggies gained five first downs and 79 total yards.

The Sooners ended the season with a 6-3 record, the first winning season in five years. OU finished second in the Big Six conference with a 3-2 mark. Nebraska won the conference crown. Wheeler was selected All-American and was joined on the all-conference team by Brown, Breeden, and Robertson.

1936

The Sooners opened practices at the tail end of one of the hottest summers in Oklahoma history. The temperature on the first day of practice was 100 degrees. The 44 players who went out for the team lost a total of 252 pounds during the opening day of practice. Coach Biff Jones welcomed the weight loss, because many of his players had gained weight during the off-season.

The heat wasn't the only thing that caused the weight loss. Assistant coach Tom Stidham, who weighed 248, stood on the charging sleds while linemen pushed him around the practice field.

Halfback Bill Breeden and tackle Ralph Brown, All-Big Six a year earlier, returned to the lineup. Guard Connie Ahrens and tackle Ferd Ellsworth also returned to bolster the front line. Pete Smith provided experience, returning to the right end slot. Sophomore Roland "Waddy" Young provided plenty of sparks at the left end position. In addition to Breeden, the backfield was solid with the return of Woody Huddleston, Bo Hewes, Ralphael Boudreau, and Al Corrotto.

For the second straight year, Jones searched for a quarterback since J.R. Corbett had a career-ending injury from a year ago, and Karey Fuqua had graduated. Sophomore Jack Baer, of Shawnee, got the nod before the season opener.

Jones was promoted to major during the off-season, yet the players who were in awe of his military orderliness and coaching record the year before, began to feel more at ease, especially when he started to call them by their first names.

Jones, a man who believed morale was 85 percent of the game, said, "Our morale is much higher than it was a year ago."

The temperatures began to cool by the end of the first week of practice and one inch of rain fell, forcing players to practice indoors. The rain was a welcome sight in Oklahoma, as only one inch fell between May 28 and September 17.

Legendary sportswriter Grantland Rice wrote that Oklahoma would "be on the map in larger letters" in 1936. His prognostication fell short as the Sooners finished the season with a .500 record, three wins, three losses and three ties.

OU and Tulsa dueled to a scoreless tie in the season opener September 26 in Norman on a soggy field and before 7,000 fans. Breeden missed two field goals in the opening quarter, and the Sooners also squelched two opportunities in the fourth stanza.

In the fourth quarter, Baer sailed a pass to end John Bridges, but the ball brushed his fingertips, and Young clutched it at the Hurricane 15. The play was nullified since rules stated that a defensive player must touch the ball first.

Huddleston fired a pass to Baer at the TU 25 with seconds left, but Breeden's field goal fell short.

Tulsa's only threat came early in the fourth period when halfback Morris White scampered 32 yards to the OU 28. Brown caught him from behind, and the crimson defense held Tulsa to minus-one yard on the next four plays.

Oklahoma led the game in first downs (9-6) and total yards (157-89).

The Sooners defeated Colorado, 8-0, in the Buffaloes' season opener the next week in Boulder in the first of three straight road games for OU. The 6,500 spectators enjoyed clear skies in the first half, then rain fell in the final 30 minutes.

The Buffs drove to the OU two in the first quarter, but the Sooners blocked the field-goal try. A second-quarter safety gave OU a 2-0 lead. Byron "Whizzer" White's punt was blocked, and several Sooners tackled him as he tried to retrieve the ball in the end zone. Breeden had a chance to add three more points, but his field-goal try veered wide.

Hewes' two-yard TD run late in the fourth stanza gave OU the deciding advantage, but Breeden missed the conversion.

Oklahoma had the edge in first downs (14-6) and total yards (268-90).

The Cotton Bowl, hosted in Dallas, was established as the fourth postseason bowl game. J. Curtis Sanford, an oil and business executive from Tyler, Texas, organized the new bowl game to begin on January 1, 1937. Cotton Bowl was also the new name of Fair Park Stadium, where Oklahoma and Texas had met each year since 1929.

Excitement ran high as Texas celebrated its 100th birthday and thousands of Oklahomans joined the celebration and hoped to end the two-year Texas jinx. For this one year only, Dallas renamed the fair the Texas Centennial Central Exposition, a six-month-long expo at the fair site. A record turnout was expected, and round-trip train fare to the OU-Texas game was $4.75. Sooner fans traveled by train, bus, or automobile. Admission to the game was $2.70, including 50 cents for admittance to the fairgrounds. Those who parked near the grounds had to shell out another half-dollar.

"Football-mad Oklahomans, thousands of them, stormed into Dallas Saturday and spent a year's pent-up fury in a vain effort to bulldog the Longhorn footballers," the *Daily Oklahoman* reported. "In downtown Dallas, it was a tough battle. To get into a hotel you had to call for a line plunge; to get into a café you needed a crowbar; to get a taxicab or a coco cola [sic] you had to get mad and knock somebody down."

The 0-0-1 Longhorns had tied Louisiana State (6-6) the prior week in Austin. An impressive mark for the Steers since LSU was the defending Southeastern Conference champs.

Six points was all that was needed as Texas defeated the Sooners, 6-0 before a record crowd of 30,000 on October 10.

The Sooners drove to the UT 20 early in the second quarter. The ball squirted from Webber Merrill's hands on an end sweep several plays later, and Othello Wolfe recovered for the Horns at the nine. Both teams waged a punting duel the rest of the first half. Texas had moved to the OU 22 when the gun sounded.

The Steers marched 47 yards to the Oklahoma nine late in the third stanza, but Baer grabbed his second interception in the end zone. Early in the fourth quarter, Texas quarterback Bill Pitzer lobbed a 50-yard TD pass to Homer Tippen. Baer and Hewes battled Tippen for the ball at the OU 20, but Tippen grabbed the ball and skirted to the end zone. The play surpassed the Guy Warren-to-Fred Cherry 45-yarder in 1930 as the series' longest pass play. The Sooners blocked the extra point.

The Sooners later drove to the Texas six, and the Cotton Bowl's decibel level swelled. After losing five yards, Oklahoma managed only one yard on the next three plays. OU soon got another chance after Merrill returned a Texas punt 12 yards to the UT 32. Merrill unleashed a pass to Pete Smith in the end zone. The pass was on target, but it bounced in and out of Smith's hands.

Texas had more first downs (9-4) and total yards (383-141) in the game.

The Sooners rebounded with a 14-0 victory over Kansas in the Big Six opener the next week in Lawrence. Six interceptions killed the Jayhawks. An interception stalled OU's first chance to score early after recovering a Kansas fumble at the KU 11. The Jayhawks stole the pass three plays later.

Center Bill Conkright intercepted George Hapgood's pass later in the first stanza and raced 40 yards to the end zone. Breeden toed the conversion.

The Sooners later recovered a Jayhawk fumble at the KU 42. Two plays later, Merrill bolted around end and was swamped by Jayhawks, so he cut back to the middle and into an open field for the 39-yard score. Nathan Anderson booted the extra point.

Kansas blocked Hewes' punt at the OU 24, but the second-unit defense held the Hawks at bay. Backup center Vernon Mullen later intercepted a Kansas pass at the OU 15 to squelch another Jayhawk threat.

Kansas advanced to the OU 12 late in the first half, but Merrill intercepted a pass to end Jayhawk hopes. Neither team threatened in the second half.

Kansas had more first downs (9-4) and total yards (187-179). Oklahoma's yards were all on the ground as they completed zero of three passing attempts.

The Sooners hosted 2-1 Nebraska on October 24. The Huskers were ranked 15th in the nation in the first year of the Associated Press poll. Oklahoma was seeking to end Nebraska's five-game streak in the series, but the Huskers proved why they were one of the country's elite college football teams with a 14-0 victory before 25,000 on a chilly, gray day.

Fullback Sam Francis hurled a 25-yard TD pass to halfback Lloyd Cardwell in the opening quarter. The Nebraska receiver had to reach over Merrill's head to grab the ball in the end zone.

The Sooners had one opportunity to tie the game early in the second period when reserve end Clay Casey forced NU halfback Harris Andrews to fumble. Guard Fred Ball recovered the free pigskin at the Husker 15. Three plays later, Nebraska intercepted Merrill's pass intended for Smith in the end zone.

Andrews later raced 66 yards and eluded the grasp of five Sooners en route to the end zone. Nebraska led the contest in first downs (9-6) and total yards (280-205).

Merrill got the starting nod at quarterback before the Sooners traveled to Ames for the Iowa State tilt. Both teams sported an identical 2-2-1 record. Oklahoma held a four-game win streak over the Cyclones, but No. 5 was not to be on October 31 as the teams fought to a 7-7 tie before a crowd of 7,000.

Everett Kischer's 41-yard TD pass to Tommy Neal put I-State up 7-0 in the first stanza. Neal caught the ball near the goal line and spun out from the grip of Sooner defenders.

Breeden busted up the middle and scampered 45 yards to put OU on the board in the third period. Several Cyclones had a chance to stop the high-stepping halfback. Young's block cut down the last Cyclone defender 10 yards from the goal line. Breeden nailed the extra point.

Baer later returned an Iowa State punt 40 yards to the Cyclone 13, but Merrill's pass was intercepted moments later.

Oklahoma dominated the game with more first downs (12-2) and total yards (201-49).

An extra point would have defeated 3-2-1 Kansas State the following week in Norman, but the two teams tied 6-6 before 6,000 fans.

The Cats struck first less than five minutes into the game. OU punted to the K-State 26, and Maurice Elder streaked down the left sideline on the first play from scrimmage. A missed conversion gave the Cats a 6-0 lead, which they held through the fourth period.

The Sooner line played better in the second half and blocked two Kansas State punts. Young came charging through the line and blocked the second punt. The ball rolled into the end zone where Conkright smothered it. Crimson faithful held their breath as Breeden set up for the go-ahead conversion, but K-State's Ralph Hemphill blocked it.

Smith later forced the Cats to fumble and recovered the ball at the KS 27. The Wildcat defense stiffened, and Breeden shanked a 30-yard field goal into the wind with four minutes left.

Kansas State had the statistical edge with 10 first downs and 244 total yards. Oklahoma had seven first downs and 149 total yards.

Missouri's late fourth-quarter touchdown dropped the Sooners to 2-3-3 for the season with a 21-14 victory on November 14 in

Halfback Bo Hewes scores on an eight-yard reverse to tie Missouri at 14-14 in the third period. (*OU Athletics*)

Columbia. The 3-2-1 Tigers ended Oklahoma's three-game win streak in the series.

Mizzou's Jack Kinnison blocked Breeden's punt midway through the first period, and teammate Godfried Rau recovered in the end zone. Jack Frye, the hero of the game, kicked the extra point.

Breeden's one-yard plunge midway through the second stanza capped a 69-yard, 17-play march midway through the second quarter. Merrill's 24-yard run to the Tiger 28 highlighted the drive. Breeden's toe tied the game at 7-7.

Frye's one-yard TD run and his extra point gave the Tigers a 14-7 advantage midway through the third period. Minutes later, Hewes' eight-yard TD scamper capped a 52-yard drive in eight plays to knot the game again.

Mizzou drove from its 40 to the OU 10 early in the fourth stanza, but fumbled, and Corrotto recovered. The Tigers later put together a 79-yard drive, which was topped by Frye's one-yard leap into the end zone and his conversion.

Both teams gained nine first downs apiece, but Missouri had more total yards (186-158).

Four days before the final game against Oklahoma A&M, Jones received orders from the war department in Washington, D.C. to the command and general staff school in Fort Leavenworth, Kansas. Jones was surprised by the announcement, because he said transfers usually occur in the spring.

"Here it is November 17 and right before our last game," he said.

The news stunned the players. "I hope it isn't true," Conkright said.

True it was, so his players gave Jones a nice going-away present—a 35-13 rout of the Aggies before 9,000 fans in Stillwater. For the first time in 18 years, the Sooners did not play on Thanksgiving.

OU took a 7-0 lead midway through the first quarter on Baer's 38-yard TD run. Baer began the play around right end, cut back toward the middle, and Breeden's block set him free to the end zone. Breeden toed the conversion.

The Sooners added a safety moments later when the Aggies fumbled a high snap and the ball rolled into the end zone. Several Sooners tackled the Aggie in the end zone as he tried to retrieve the ball.

Breeden later scored on a 10-yard scamper, carrying several Aggies with him to the end zone. His extra point gave the Sooners a 15-0 lead.

Merrill fumbled L.B. Asbury's punt early in the second stanza, and A&M recovered at the OU 20. Merrill redeemed himself by intercepting an Aggie pass in the end zone on the next play.

The Aggies scored minutes later, but the extra-point kick sailed under the crossbar.

A poor A&M punt early in the third period set up the Sooners at the Aggie 34. Baer gained 14 yards and on the next play bolted another 20 to the end zone. He stumbled but crashed over the goal line. Breeden's conversion upped the Sooners' lead to 22-6.

A 35-yard Aggie touchdown minutes later cut Oklahoma's lead to 22-13. Hewes recovered an A&M fumble at the Aggie 37 late in the third period to set up the next Sooner score. OU moved to the A&M two in three plays early in the fourth quarter. A&M stopped the Sooners on the next two plays, but backup fullback Earl Crowder's two-yard plunge put Oklahoma ahead, 28-13, as Crowder missed the extra point.

Crowder added another touchdown late in the game for the final tally following Smith's theft of an Aggie pass at the A&M 20. His six-yard run came three plays after the interception, and his kick sailed true.

The Sooners rolled up 273 total yards and 16 first downs. A&M gained 138 total yards and seven first downs.

The 1936 Sooners finished 3-3-3 and fourth in the Big Six with a 1-2-2 mark. Conkright and Brown were chosen to the all-conference team.

Three weeks after Jones received the official notice from Washington, University of Oklahoma regents appointed Stidham as the Sooners' 10th head coach. The regents believed that promoting from within would allow the team to move forward with Jones' system.

"I'll be mighty happy, if I can carry on, to the best of my ability, the great job Biff Jones has started at Oklahoma," Stidham said upon his hiring.

Jones resigned from the army the next spring after he received and accepted an offer to coach at Nebraska. He succeeded Dana X. Bible, who took the head coaching position at Texas.

1937

Tom Stidham, one-sixteenth Creek Indian, grew up in Checotah, Oklahoma. He played football at Haskell Indian Institute of Lawrence, Kansas, in 1925-26 under Coach Dick Hanley. A year later he went to Iowa University, but before gaining eligibility there, Hanley was hired at Northwestern and hired Stidham as his assistant. Stidham coached the Northwestern line from 1933-34 before joining Biff Jones as line coach at OU in 1935.

Stidham was a personable man who was close to his players.

"My door is always open to every kid on the squad," he said. "They bring me their problems. I want them to. They feel the same way toward me that I do toward them. They don't call me Coach . . . they call me Tom."

The 1937 Sooner squad was a mystery with so many new players. Twenty lettermen from the prior year returned. The starters who returned from the 1936 team were quarterback Jack Baer, center Mickey Parks, halfbacks Woody Huddleston and Al Corrotto, guard Fred Ball, and ends Pete Smith and Waddy Young.

The line was big, but the backs were small yet quick and agile. Only two of the backs weighed as much as 180 pounds.

The Football Annual tabloid reported on the 1937 Sooners as follows: "Nothing phenomenal expected of the Sooners, but they can always be depended upon to play real football."

A new play-by-play announcer made his debut in the 1937 season. His name: Walter Cronkite. He was the Sooners announcer for only one season.

The Sooners traveled to Tulsa to meet the Golden Hurricane in the season opener on September 25. Round-trip train fare from Norman to Tulsa cost $2.74, 33 cents less for those who boarded in

1936 Season Record: 3-3-0
Big Six Conference: 1-2-2 (Fourth)

Date	Opponent	Result	Score
September 26	TULSA	T	0-0
October 3	at Colorado	W	8-0
October 10	Texas at Dallas	L	6-0
October 17	at Kansas	W	14-0
October 24	NEBRASKA	L	14-0
October 31	at Iowa State	T	7-7
November 7	KANSAS STATE	T	6-6
November 14	MISSOURI	L	21-14
November 21	at Oklahoma A&M	W	35-13

Oklahoma City. However, a train ride to home games from Oklahoma City's 36th Street station to Norman cost 50 cents.

Young predicted before the game that OU would not lose to anyone by 12 points when he heard the Sooners were underdogs by two touchdowns.

The Hurricane beat Oklahoma by exactly 12 points, 19-7, before 16,000 fans at Skelly Stadium.

OU moved into Tulsa territory twice in the first quarter. The second drive ended in a missed field goal when Baer's kick was short and wide. The crimson defense held off Tulsa's threat at the OU 10 late in the second stanza, and both teams headed to the locker room knotted at 0-0.

Tulsa scored early in the third quarter but missed the extra point for a 6-0 lead. Midway through the period, Smith recovered a Hurricane fumble at the TU 21. Baer zipped an 11-yard pass to Huddleston, then Huddleston bolted 10 yards on the next play for the only Sooner tally. Raphael Boudreau toed the conversion to give the Sooners a 7-6 advantage.

Tulsa scored with a long pass on the first play following the kickoff. The Hurricane added another score off a punt return in the fourth quarter.

Tulsa also had the edge in first downs (8-4) and total yards (586-320).

The underdog Sooners defeated the Rice Owls, 6-0, the next week before 10,000 fans in Norman. The Owls punted to their 44 early in the first quarter then Baer's short passes moved the Sooners to the Rice 30. A roughing penalty on the Owls moved the ball to the 15. On the next play, Baer rifled a TD pass to Smith, who slipped behind the Rice secondary in the end zone. Baer's extra-point try sailed wide.

Parks had two interceptions that killed two Rice advances. His first came at the OU 22 late in the third period and the second at the Sooner 18 late in the game.

Baer completed 15 of 20 passes for 64 yards, and the Sooners totaled 116 yards in the game. Rice had more yards (149) mostly on the ground. The Owls completed only two of 13 passes for 31 yards. Rice led the game in first downs (9-5).

Baer suffered a broken jaw against Rice and would miss the next three games. The Sooners went 0-1-2 during his absence.

There was no Texas State Fair for the third straight year. The Greater Texas & Pan American Exposition, held on the fairgrounds from late June to late October, replaced the fair. Sooner fans were excited about their chance to beat the Longhorns on October 9, especially since Texas had one of its worst records in years (2-6-1) in 1936. The University of Texas lured Dana X. Bible from Nebraska to coach the Longhorns. Texas defeated Texas Tech, then lost to LSU before the Red River showdown.

Oklahoma and Texas battled to a 7-7 stalemate before 20,000 at the Cotton Bowl. The Sooners scored first in the second stanza, having to earn every yard for the touchdown. After Texas punted to its 41, OU gained six yards in two plays, then Huddleston busted a 28-yard run to the Steers' seven. From there it took the Sooners eight plays to cross the goal line.

Huddleston gained four yards, then Bob Seymour picked up one yard each on the next two carries. Texas was offside on the next play to give the Sooners a first down on the one. Huddleston was stopped for no gain, then Gene Corrotto, Al's brother, carried to the one-foot line. After Huddleston was stuffed for no gain, both teams were assessed a penalty, so they replayed the down. Seymour fumbled the next carry, and Huddleston recovered back at the four. On fourth-and-goal, Huddleston found an opening in the Texas line and scored.

Boudreau's extra point gave OU a 7-0 lead.

Texas answered with a 62-yard march in seven plays to even the score. Huddleston was flagged for interference in the drive, which put the Horns at the OU 18. Two plays later, quarterback Lewis Gray zipped a 12-yard TD pass to Judson Atchison, and Gray's toe tied the game.

Oklahoma marched to the Horns' 18 in the third stanza, but Al Corrotto dropped a pass in the end zone to stop the drive. Nether team threatened again.

The Sooners had more total yards (175-137), but Texas had one more first down (7-6).

A downpour in Lincoln the following week produced a muddy field and no scoring as the Sooners tied Nebraska, 0-0, before 15,000 spectators. Nebraska was undefeated at 2-0, including a victory over Minnesota, the defending national champions.

The soggy field forced a punting duel. OU punted 17 times, and the Huskers had 19.

The Sooners' deepest penetration was to the NU 28 in the first period, but they had to turn the ball over on downs. OU moved into Husker territory in the second quarter, but Hugh McCullough's 41-yard field-goal attempt fell short of the target.

Another drive later in the period ended when Marvin Plock intercepted McCullough's pass at the Nebraska 13. Neither team threatened in the second half, and Nebraska's deepest penetration in the game was to the Oklahoma 47.

Both teams gained five first downs each, but the Sooners had the yardage edge (69-48).

The tie was a moral victory for the Sooners, since they had not defeated their northern foe since 1930.

Kansas (2-1) was next in Norman on October 23, and the last time the Jayhawks came to town (1935) they stunned the Sooners with a touchdown bomb in the last 30 seconds. It happened again as Kansas won, 6-3, and shocked the 12,000 fans.

The Sooners had to settle for Raphael Boudreau's 20-yard field goal in the first quarter. OU had marched to the KU eight, but a five-yard penalty and Webber Merrill's fumble set them back.

With 10 seconds left in the game, KU quarterback Don Eberling hurled a 50-yard bomb to Dick Amerine. The ball struck OU's Earl Crowder's arm and bounced into Amerine's hands. The extra point was no good, but it didn't matter.

Jack Baer returned to the lineup the next week sporting a special iron mask to protect his fractured jaw. He helped guide the Sooners to a 19-0 blanking of 2-2 Kansas State in Manhattan on October 30.

Both teams battled to a scoreless tie in the first half, then lightning struck early in the second. OU halfback Otis Rogers returned the second-half kickoff 90 yards for a touchdown. His teammates cleared out Cat defenders along the way, and after eluding the last defender at midfield, Rogers shifted to his left and sailed to the end zone. Kansas State blocked the extra point.

Baer returned a punt 25 yards to the OU 48 in the fourth quarter, and a roughing penalty on the play gave the Sooners 15 more yards. Seven plays later, Baer scored from the one, but Hugh McCullough's conversion veered wide. Reserve halfback Howard McCarty later added a seven-yard TD run, and McCullough nailed the extra point.

The Sooners had a chance later for more points after driving from midfield to the Cats' three, but Huddleston lost a fumble, and Caesar Cardarelli recovered for K-State.

Otis Rogers got the starting nod at right halfback the following week against Iowa State. The Sooners pounded the Cyclones, 33-7, before 8,000 fans at Owen Field. The 1-5 Cyclones won their season opener and dropped five straight.

Both teams battled through a scoreless first quarter, which included a missed 43-yard field goal by Jack Baer. The ball caromed off the goalpost and bounced back onto the playing field.

Waddy Young recovered Hugh Vickerstaff's fumble as the quarter came to a close at the Cyclone 13. As the two teams changed ends of the field, the Sooners scored six plays later. On third and goal at the I-State one, Hugh McCullough plowed over, and Boudreau converted the extra point.

The Cyclones tied the game moments later when quarterback Everett Kischer took a lateral from Gordon Reupke and fired a 24-yard pass to George Bazik.

OU took the lead midway through the third stanza when Howard McCarty tipped a Cyclone pass, and Baer grabbed the ball and flew 65 yards to the end zone. Baer missed the extra point.

Minutes later, Baer intercepted a Cyclone pass at the OU 30. Gene Corrotto's seven-yard end reverse capped the 70-yard drive in eight plays. Baer completed two passes (15 yards to Smith and 16 to McCarty) to spark the drive. Baer's kick was blocked, but the Sooners held a 19-7 advantage.

The Sooners blocked Paul Morin's punt at the I-State 13 early in the fourth stanza. Bob Seymour scored from four yards out three plays later, and Jiggs Walker booted the extra point.

Earl Crowder intercepted a Cyclone pass late in the game and dashed 24 yards to the I-State one. He then plowed over for the final tally, and Walker toed the conversion.

Oklahoma gained 12 first downs and 228 total yards. Iowa State had six first downs and 124 total yards.

Freshmen Nathan Stufflebeam (left) and Orville Mathews are ready to ride the Oklahoma City-to-Normal special train and sell programs for the OU-Tulsa game. *(OU Athletics)*

Sooner Magic: A Sooner Legend Single-Handedly Beats the Tigers

Just like most college football players, Baer played two-platoon football—offense and defense. But Baer did even more for the Oklahoma Sooners. In addition to being the team's quarterback on the offense and halfback on defense, he kicked off and punted. Against Missouri in 1937, Baer also intercepted passes and scored the winning touchdown.

The 2-4 Tigers hosted the Sooners on November 13 before a homecoming crowd of 15,000 in Columbia. Oklahoma had four chances to score in the first three quarters, but came away empty. Early in the first period, OU drove from the MU 49 to the Tiger 19, but managed only three yards in four plays, and Missouri took possession on downs.

Early in the second quarter, OU began at its own 23-yard line. McCullough gained 17 yards. Three plays later, on third-and-five at the Sooner 45, Baer faked a handoff to McCullough and scooted off tackle for 15 yards. McCullough then fired a nine-yard pass to Crowder at the MU 31.

Rogers picked up the first down with a two-yard carry, then Baer zipped a pass to Smith, who then lateraled the ball to Parks. Parks rambled to the Tiger four-yard line. McCullough was thrown for a four-yard loss on the next play, then MU's Stan Mondala intercepted Baer's pass at the four.

As the first half was winding down, OU began another drive from its own 39. Huddleston carried for one and then eight yards. On third-and-one, Huddleston connected a pass to Rogers, who was shoved out of bounds at the Tiger 36. An offside flag then pushed the Sooners back five yards. Huddleston got the first down with an eight-yard gain. He again got the call and picked up 11 more yards

to the MU 22, but fumbled, and James Christensen recovered for the Tigers as the half ended.

Missouri was unable to make any scoring threat against the Sooners in the first half. The Tigers possessed the ball only once in OU territory, and that was because an unnecessary roughness penalty put them there. Baer's punt rolled out of bounds at the MU 36, but the infraction placed the ball at OU's 49. The Tigers gained only three yards before kicking the ball away.

But as OU's defense stalled every Missouri drive, the Tiger defense also rose to the occasion to stop the Sooners from scoring. The stout defenses continued in the third stanza.

Late in the period, Huddleston took Dale Everly's punt at the OU 40 and raced 36 yards to the Tiger 24. Rogers gained four, followed

1937 Season Record: 5-2-2
Big Six Conference: 3-1-1 (Second)

Date	Opponent	Result	Score
September 25	at Tulsa	L	19-7
October 2	RICE	W	6-0
October 9	Texas at Dallas	T	7-7
October 16	at Nebraska	T	0-0
October 23	KANSAS	L	6-3
October 30	at Kansas State	W	19-0
November 6	IOWA STATE	W	33-7
November 13	at Missouri	W	7-0
November 20	OKLAHOMA A&M	W	16-0

by Huddleston's five-yard carry. A fumble by Baer was recovered by a teammate, but the Sooners faced fourth-and-two at the 17. Huddleston picked up five yards. Later, on fourth-and-six at the eight, Huddleston swept off right end, but Christensen tossed him for a four-yard loss. Tigers' ball.

Missouri picked off two of Baer's passes in the fourth quarter, but Baer grabbed the important interception off MU's Vernon Ewing at the MU 49. Baer sprinted to the 24, where he was tossed out of bounds.

On third-and-eight, Baer shot a pass to McCullough who stumbled and dove to the 10. Baer then gained one yard. On the next play, Baer faded back and raised his arm to pass, but he could not find an open receiver, so he tucked the pigskin under his arm, circled around right end and gained six yards to the MU three. The Sooners only gained two yards in the next three snaps and faced fourth-and-goal at the one with 45 seconds remaining in the game.

Baer kept the ball and plunged across the goal line. He raised his hands as he trotted toward the OU bench. Boudreau booted the extra point and OU led, 7-0, with 40 seconds left.

The Tigers completed a pass to the midfield as time expired.

The Sooner defense held Missouri to only 70 total yards and five first downs. The OU offense picked up 15 first downs and 237 total yards.

OU shut out 4-4 Oklahoma A&M, 16-0, a week later in Norman before a crowd of 15,000 shivering fans. Baer kicked a 46-yard field goal midway through the first quarter. The kick broke the school record of 45 yards set by Cliff Bowles against Kansas in 1923.

Baer's one-yard TD leap late in the third period capped a 75-yard drive in 11 plays. Baer's conversion gave the Sooners a 10-0 lead.

Early in the fourth stanza, McCullough returned an Aggie punt 24 yards to the A&M 35. On the next play, he tossed a pass to Crowder, who stiff-armed an Aggie defender, spun around and raced to the goal line. McCullough kicked the extra point.

The Sooners gained 14 first downs and 256 total yards. The Aggies had 143 total yards and only three first downs.

OU finished the 1937 season with a 5-2-2 mark and second in the Big Six with a 3-1-1 record. Smith was selected to the All-America team, and Baer, Parks, and Young joined him on the all-conference first team.

But it was Baer who made his mark in Sooner history long after his football prowess was just a memory. Biff Jones said that Baer was always eager to display his football skills on the practice and playing field. "First one out," he said.

Harold Keith once wrote about Baer: "Spirit and courage. You can't get him down. Performs with enthusiasm."

Baer continued his association with the University of Oklahoma for the next half-century. He coached the OU baseball team for 23 years (1942-67). His enthusiasm helped the Sooners win six conference baseball championships. Baer's 1951 squad won the national championship and he was named the NCAA's national coach of the year.

In the early 1950s, then-OU head coach Bud Wilkinson named Baer equipment manager for the football team, a position he held until he retired in 1985.

Baer died on March 8, 2002 at the age of 87.

1938

Oklahoma's four-game win streak at the end of 1937 had Crimson faithful upbeat for a terrific season in 1938. The Sooners didn't disappoint, as they produced one of the best seasons in school history with a 10-1 record, a conference championship, and their first bowl appearance in history.

The Big Red defense surrendered only 12 points during the season, then ran into trouble against powerful Tennessee in the Orange Bowl.

All-America end Pete Smith graduated but returned to the squad as an assistant coach. He replaced Frank Moore to tutor the ends. Waddy Young returned and turned in an All-America performance.

The backfield was stacked with experienced veterans—quarterback Otis Rogers, fullback Hugh McCullough and halfbacks Earl Crowder, Bob Seymour, and Gene Corrotto. Tackle Gilford "Cactus Face" Duggan anchored the front line. Duggan was expected to start in 1937, but an injury kept him out of action during the previous year.

Raphael Boudreau also returned to provide the Sooners with one of the best placekicking performances in years.

Season tickets cost $8.40 for the five 1938 home games, but the Sooners would not host a contest until the fourth game of the season. Their first opponent, Rice, was touted as a favorite to go to the Rose Bowl at season's end. The Owls won their final three games in 1937, including the Cotton Bowl.

The Sooners traveled to Houston October 1 for the season opener and upset the favored Owls, 7-6, before 17,000 fans. The game was played in humid and hot conditions 110 degrees in the shade.

After a punting duel in the first quarter, the Owls scored first midway through the second. Late in the first half, McCarty took a lateral, swept around right end, shed three Rice defenders, and shot to the end zone. Boudreau's conversion gave the Sooners the deciding 7-6 advantage.

Rice moved to the OU 18 early in the fourth stanza, but had to settle for a field goal. Scheule's kick sailed wide. Young pressured Rice's highly touted quarterback, Ernie Lain, all day, including a 15-yard sack and an interception.

The Sooners returned to the Lone Star State to battle Texas the next week in Dallas.

The Longhorns were upset by Kansas in their opener. The 19-18 setback was the Steers' first season-opening loss in history. LSU defeated the Horns, 20-0, the following week.

Oklahoma defeated Texas, 13-0, before 20,000 on a sultry Dallas afternoon. The Sooners moved to the Steers' 11 late in the first quarter, but the Texas defense stiffened, and McCullough's 18-yard field-goal attempt sailed wide.

McCollough's 17-yard run gave OU a 7-0 lead to cap a 58-yard drive.

Rogers later recovered a Texas fumble at the UT 24. Two plays gained zero yards, then Bob West's 10-yard pass to Young was just enough for a first down. OU was penalized for an excessive time out, then Seymour lobbed a pass to Bill Jennings over the Texas secondary for the touchdown with five seconds until intermission. Johnny Martin's conversion was low.

The Longhorns had two chances to score in the fourth quarter, but OU's defense stiffened both times.

Oklahoma gained 11 first downs and 194 total yards. The crimson defense held the Horns to seven first downs, 11 rushing yards and 88 passing yards.

The Sooners had defeated Texas for the first time in five years. They next turned their attention to Kansas, who stunned the Big Red with a last-effort touchdown pass the year before. After beating Texas, the Jayhawks were blasted, 52-0, by Notre Dame, then bounced back with a 58-14 win over Washburn University.

The Sooners dropped Kansas, 19-0, on October 15 in Lawrence. McCullough's two-yard TD run late in the first stanza capped a 50-

Howard McCarty's second-quarter touchdown was the only Sooner TD, but it was enough to defeat Rice, 7-6. (*OU Athletics*)

He scored his first TD midway through the first quarter, and Boudreau's toe gave the Sooners a 7-0 lead. The score capped a 38-yard drive in eight plays after McCarty's 12-yard punt return. McCullough completed a 17-yard pass to Jennings to the NU 16 on third down to highlight the drive.

Nebraska's only threat of the game came early in the second period with a march to the OU two. On fourth-and-goal, Herman Rohrig caught Harry Hopp's pass, but Crowder dumped him short of the goal line.

McCarty's 21-yard punt return to the Husker 35 set up the Sooners' deciding tally early in the fourth quarter. After Jennings scooted around right end for a 20-yard run, Nebraska's defense tightened. OU took four plays to gain a first down. Three plays later at the two, McCullough plowed ahead for the score, carrying several Huskers with him into the end zone. Boudreau nailed the extra point.

McCullough's performance, which included a 72-yard punt, drew praise from head coach Tom Stidham.

"Hugh McCullough deserves special credit," he said. "He was in there for 60 minutes and his kicking was a dandy."

OU gained nine first downs and 188 total yards. The defense held the Huskers to seven first downs and 127 total yards.

The Sooners jumped to 10th in the AP poll, but not all news was pleasant. Duggan suffered a fractured cheekbone and would be lost for several weeks. Harold Edgeman replaced him at left tackle.

OU hosted Tulsa on October 29. The Sooners scored by all means possible—on the ground, through the air, by blocked punt, and by safety—in their 28-6 victory before 17,000 fans.

Otis Rogers' two-yard TD run early in the second quarter gave Oklahoma a 6-0 lead. Boudreau missed the extra point. Late in the half, Jerry Bolton hammered Tulsa quarterback Tommy Thompson, knocking the ball loose and rolling to the end zone. A host of Sooners smothered Thompson as he tried to retrieve it. The safety upped the lead to 8-0.

Three plays into the second half, OU end John Shirk blocked Mickey Ayers' punt, and Sooner tackle Justin Bowers recovered in the end zone. McCullough converted.

Tulsa punted to its own 40 late in the third stanza, and four plays later McCullough lobbed an eight-yard scoring strike to Corrotto. McCullough booted the extra point for a 22-0 Sooner advantage.

After the Golden Hurricane punted to the OU 36 as the third quarter ended, the reserves marched to another score early in the fourth. West's 17-yard TD pass to Crowder capped the drive, but Crowder's conversion was blocked. Tulsa later scored following an OU fumble at the Sooner 20.

The Sooners dominated in the statistics with 17 first downs and 283 total yards. The defense held the Hurricane to seven first downs and 83 total yards.

Even though they won, the Sooners slipped a notch (to 11) in the AP poll. Yet Oklahoma would receive national attention the next week. Grantland Rice praised OU in his weekly column. "This Oklahoma team is one of the best from coast to coast," he wrote. He also predicted the Sooners would win the remainder of their games.

The second half of the Kansas State game in Norman was broadcast on NBC's Red Network, the first time an OU game was aired nationally.

The Sooners trounced the 3-2 Wildcats, 26-0, on November 5 before 15,000 at Owen Field.

yard march in eight plays. Kansas blocked Boudreau's conversion, and it was the first time that Boudreau had failed to convert an extra point in three years.

Seymour intercepted a Jayhawk pass early in the third quarter and returned it 15 yards to the KU 47. The Sooners moved to the KU nine in seven plays then Seymour took a lateral and outran two KU defenders to the end zone. McCullough booted the extra point for a 13-0 lead.

McCarty's 14-yard TD run late in the game capped a 60-yard drive in seven plays, but Crowder's conversion bounced off the goal post. Rogers' 23-yard pass to Jennings to the KU 37 sparked the drive.

The Sooners gained 17 first downs and 288 total yards (211 rushing, 77 passing). The defense held the Jayhawks to 12 first downs and 114 total yards.

Oklahoma entered the Associated Press poll two days later for the first time. The Sooners were rated 14th with a 3-0 record.

OU met Nebraska for the home opener on October 22. The Huskers, defending Big Six champs, were winless (0-2-1) in their first three starts for the first time since 1919. The Sooners defeated Nebraska, 14-0, before a crowd of 30,000, thanks to a couple of two-yard TD runs by McCullough.

Kansas State's defense frustrated Oklahoma by squelching two Sooner drives in the first half.

Edgeman recovered a Kansas State fumble at the Cats' 31. Seven plays later, Rogers scored from two yards out. Boudreau's conversion put the Sooners on top, 7-0 in the second period.

McCarty's 73-yard punt return to the Wildcat nine early in the third period sparked the next Sooner score. McCarty carried for five yards, then bolted off right tackle into the end zone. Boudreau missed the extra point.

Kansas State punted on its next possession, and the Sooners set sail for another score. McCullough fired a 22-yard TD pass to Shirk, who slipped past the Wildcat secondary. The 55-yard, nine-play drive began with McCullough's 16-yard pass to Shirk. McCullough toed the conversion to lift OU to a 20-0 advantage.

The Sooners moved rapidly for their final score late in the third stanza. McCullough tossed an 18-yard pass to Shirk, then Jennings carried for nine yards. McCullough rocketed a 16-yard pass to Jennings to the K-State 22 on the final play of the third quarter. West carried to the 10, but fumbled, and Dick Favor picked up the pigskin and bowled into the end zone. Favor's conversion sailed wide.

OU gained 18 first downs and 385 total yards. The Big Red defense held Kansas State to three first downs and 125 total yards.

Oklahoma rose to 10th in the AP poll, and Duggan returned to practice the next week sporting a steel face guard on his helmet.

The Sooners dropped 4-2 Missouri, 21-0, on November 12 before 25,000 homecoming fans in Norman.

Crowder returned the opening kickoff 48 yards to the Tiger 42, then the Sooners scored 13 plays later on McCullough's one-yard run. McCullough gained a crucial first down on fourth-and-two at the MU 32 to keep the drive alive. Boudreau's conversion gave Oklahoma a 7-0 lead in the first five minutes.

Corrotto added a one-yard TD run early in the second period, capping a 77-yard march in 13 plays that began late in the first quarter.

McCullough missed a 27-yard field goal early in the fourth stanza, but the Sooners scored minutes later when McCullough hurled a 34-yard TD pass to Corrotto. Corotto leaped into the air to snag the ball, then dodged three Tigers to the end zone. McCullough highlighted the 80-yard, 11-play drive with a 10-yard pass to Corrotto, an 18-yard pass to McCarty and a 13-yard run.

Missouri's star quarterback, Paul Christman, who had passed for 800 yards in the first six games, completed only six of 22 passes for 70 yards. The Sooner defense intercepted six passes, four of Christman's. OU gained 382 yards and 21 first downs while holding the Tigers to 182 total yards and nine first downs.

No. 7 Oklahoma traveled to Ames the next week to meet Iowa State for the Big Six conference championship. The 7-0-1 Cyclones won their first seven games then tied Kansas State. Oklahoma sat in the conference driver's seat with a 4-0 record, and Iowa State followed with a 3-0-1 mark.

The Sooners won, 10-0, before 21,500 fans, the largest attendance for an Iowa State football game.

Young recovered a Cyclone fumble at the Iowa State 36 late in the first quarter. Facing third-and-six at the 32, McCullough fired a 30-yard pass to Jennings. Seymour scored on the next play, and Boudreau nailed the extra point.

A trick play early in the second quarter failed to increase the Sooner lead. McCullough intercepted a Cyclone pass and returned it 21 yards to the I-State 26. The Cyclone defense stiffened and held the Sooners to fourth-and-one at the seven. Boudreau came in to kick a field goal. He took a direct snap and tried to pass to Jennings open in the end zone, but I-State's Bill Blass deflected the ball.

McCullough booted a 31-yard field goal late in the third period. The Sooners were pinned deep early in the fourth quarter, and Everett Kischer returned McCullough's punt nine yards to the OU 31 for the deepest Cyclone possession of the game. Gordon Reupke fumbled Kischer's lateral on the next play, and Bowers recovered it at the 32.

Iowa State had more total yards (83-51) and first downs (9-7), but Oklahoma laid claim to its first conference championship in 18 years.

University of Oklahoma students pleaded to president William Bizzell the next day to cancel Monday classes. He denied their request but supported a school dance on Monday night. The students skipped classes anyway, and Bizzell backed out on his dance offer. The doors to the student union were locked, so students bor-

The 1938 Sooners—Big Six Conference champions—were the first in school history to play in a bowl game.
(*Western History Collections, University of Oklahoma*)

rowed a nickelodeon and danced in the streets on campus corner anyway, despite temperatures in the low 40s.

The football team climbed another step to sixth in the AP poll, but had little time to celebrate and turned its attention to Oklahoma A&M. The Sooners defeated the 2-7 Aggies, 19-0, before 9,000 spectators in Stillwater on November 26.

OU failed to score after marching to the A&M five in the first quarter when Jennings dropped McCullough's pass in the end zone. The Sooners did score on their next possession. Seymour's six-yard TD run capped a 47-yard drive in seven plays. McCullough's 17-yard pass to Jennings, on third-and-nine at the Aggie 46, kept the drive alive. McCullough's conversion was wide.

McCarty broke his hip while fielding a punt in the third period. He would be out the remainder of the season and would not return to action until 1939. The halfback was confined four months in an Oklahoma City hospital.

Minutes later, Seymour returned an Aggie punt 19 yards to the A&M 47. Rogers sailed a 29-yard pass to Corrotto two plays later to the A&M eight. Three plays later, Rogers bolted off right tackle for a two-yard touchdown. Boudreau toed the extra point to give the Sooners a 13-0 advantage.

A poor Aggie punt late in the third stanza gave OU possession at the A&M 22. The Sooners managed only five yards on the next three plays, then Rogers hurled a 17-yard TD strike to Jennings. McCullough's conversion again was wide.

OU gained 18 first downs and 324 total yards. The Aggies were held to three first downs and 82 total yards. The Aggies gained their initial first down in the third quarter and never drove past their own 45-yard line in the game.

Oklahoma moved to fifth in the AP poll three days following the Aggie tilt.

The Orange Bowl in Miami, Florida, wanted an Oklahoma-Tennessee match up. Ernie Seiler, an Orange Bowl representative, came to Norman and plastered the OU campus with posters of palm trees and Miami's women. He also gave a pep talk to the Sooners squad. It had quite an influence as the team accepted an invitation to play the Volunteers in Miami on January 2.

The buzz around campus was about the first postseason activity in school history and Tennessee, but OU still had one more game to play, and injuries began to mount. Center Norvel Wood suffered a leg injury, Jennings fractured his right ankle, and Bolton suffered a split knee cartilage. Jennings and Bolton were finished for the season, but Wood returned for the Orange Bowl.

The Sooners hosted 2-7 Washington State College on December 3 and were ungracious hosts, defeating the Cougars, 28-0, before 15,000 at Owen Field.

Both teams battled to a scoreless tie, but Oklahoma lit up the scoreboard in the final 30 minutes.

A poor Cougar punt set up Oklahoma at the WSC five early in the third stanza. Three plays later, the Sooners were inches short of the goal line, but McCullough blasted through on the next play, and Boudreau kicked the conversion.

Seymour returned a Cougar punt 14 yards to the WSC 45 moments later. McCullough then tossed a 32-yard pass to Shirk, and three plays later Seymour scored on a three-yard run. McCullough toed his extra point and OU led, 14-0.

Late in the third period, the Cougars gambled on fourth down deep in their own territory and lost. Oklahoma took over at the 16, then Crowder connected a 12-yard pass to Seymour to the four. Two plays later, McCullough scored from the three, and Crowder converted.

The reserves got in on the act late in the fourth stanza with a 28-yard TD pass from Beryl Clark to Bill Martin, and Boudreau toed the 28th point. The score topped a 60-yard march in four plays.

Oklahoma rolled up 17 first downs and 442 total yards. The defense held the Cougars to one first down and 62 total yards, including minus-three net rushing yards.

The University of Oklahoma band worked feverishly to raise $5,000 to make the trip to Miami for the Orange Bowl. Contributions slowly trickled in, but a performance by the band on WKY radio at Skirvin Towers studio helped it raise the final $2,500 on December 17.

The football team would depart for a 48-hour train ride to Miami on Christmas Day. That morning, Stidham dressed as Santa Claus and distributed presents to players before the final workout in Norman. He presented players with gold footballs awarded to them by the Sooner athletic council for winning the conference championship. He also distributed a variety of other presents under a huge Christmas tree in the university field house.

About 1,000 Sooner fans traveled to Miami via auto or train. Train fare cost $95.50 round trip. Tickets to the game ranged from $3.30 to $4.40. The team lodged at the Hotel Flamingo and practiced at Flamingo Park, seven miles east of the stadium by the beach.

Like the Sooners, Tennessee was undefeated at 10-0 and appearing in its first bowl game. The Volunteers were ranked fourth in the AP poll above the No. 5 Sooners. OU had outscored its opponents 185-12, including eight shutouts. The Vols outscored their foes 276-16, including three shutouts. Oklahoma would be the fourth shutout victim, 17-0, on a balmy 85-degree January afternoon before 32,191 fans.

A low-flying airplane clipped some wires in Jacksonville, Florida, knocking the Orange Bowl radio broadcast off the air for several minutes. Columbia broadcasting officials worked feverishly to reroute the circuit via New Orleans to Los Angeles to New York and back over the network.

Flaring tempers, which resulted in 220 yards in penalties, marred the game. The Volunteers were flagged 16 times for 130 yards and OU nine times for 90 yards.

Oklahoma looked ragged, and lack of offensive firepower proved it. The Sooners only had 94 total yards (25 rushing and 69 passing). Tennessee gained 16 first downs and 268 total yards.

Leading 7-0, the Vols kicked a field goal with a minute until intermission.

Tennessee marched 74 yards for the final tally.

1938 Season Record: 10-1-0
Big Six Conference: 5-0-0 (Champions)

Date	Opponent	Result	Score
October 1	at Rice	W	7-6
October 8	Texas at Dallas	W	13-0
October 15	at Kansas	W	19-0
October 22	NEBRASKA	W	14-0
October 29	TULSA	W	28-6
November 5	KANSAS STATE	W	26-0
November 12	MISSOURI	W	21-0
November 19	at Iowa State	W	10-0
November 26	at Oklahoma A&M	W	19-0
December 3	WASHINGTON STATE	W	28-0
January 2	Tennessee*	L	17-0

*Orange Bowl at Miami, FL

The loss snapped OU's 14-game winning streak but the Sooners owned the Big Six conference crown. The Sooner defense did not yield a single point in the final 20 quarters of the regular season and also shut out every conference foe.

Young was selected All-America and Duggan, McCullough, and Crowder joined him on the all-conference first unit.

1939

Television made its debut at the New York World's Fair in 1939. *Gone with the Wind* and the *Wizard of Oz* delighted movie audiences. But in September, the news was unpleasant when Germany invaded Poland. Warsaw succumbed to Hitler's Nazi regime by the end of the month.

The NCAA established a new rule prohibiting interior linemen (center, tackles and guards) from advancing beyond the line of scrimmage on pass plays. The rule was implemented to forbid the linemen from acting as decoys and hindering the secondary. A violation of this rule resulted in a 15-yard penalty.

The line was solid with the return of all-conference tackle Gilford "Cactus Face" Duggan. Center Norvel Wood also returned, along with end John Shirk. End Frank Ivy and tackle Justin Bowers established themselves as all-conference selections at year's end.

Veteran Dick Favor won the starting quarterback slot. Bob Seymour was switched to fullback to make room for Jack Jacobs at right half. Left halfback Bill Jennings also returned.

The Sooners were picked to repeat as Big Six conference champs in 1939 and one of the top teams in the Midlands. Notorious sports scribe Grantland Rice projected Oklahoma to be "one of the strong teams of the year . . . one of the strongest between two of our oceans."

Sloppy practices of bad blocking and poor timing had head coach Tom Stidham concerned that such praise swelled his players' egos.

"We're ripe for a licking . . . with everybody telling us how good we are," he said. "The boys' heads have swelled so much they haven't been able to get their helmets on. We ought to be in better shape."

The Sooners improved during the final days leading up to the home opener against Southern Methodist. The squad practiced after sundown, and coaches continued their planning after practice concluded. Stidham told team manager Boyd Montgomery to call his (Stidham's) wife and tell her he would be late coming home.

"Monty," he gruffed. "Go phone my wife and tell her I won't be home for supper. I'm scared to."

Advance ticket sales for the Southern Methodist tilt exceeded 20,000. Tickets went for $2.25 for the center sections on the west and east sides and $1.70 elsewhere. The crimson majority of the 25,000 in attendance were disappointed as the Sooners and Mustangs battled to a 7-7 tie on September 30.

Seymour's interception of an SMU pass late in the first quarter led to the only OU touchdown. He had to reach high above his head to come down with the pigskin at the Mustang 42. Jacobs fired a 21-yard pass on first down to Shirk to the Ponies' 18. The next three plays netted only eight yards, then Jacobs gained a crucial first down with a two-yard run to the SMU five. Seymour carried twice for four yards then was stuffed for no gain. On fourth-and-goal, he ripped off right tackle for the score. Favor toed the extra point.

The Mustangs twice threatened to score in the second quarter but came away empty. Sooner halfback Orv Mathews intercepted a pass at the OU five, then SMU had to turn the ball over on downs after marching to the OU nine.

The Ponies drove to the OU 19 midway in the third stanza, but again the crimson defense stiffened and gained possession on

downs. Jacobs fumbled on the next play, and the Mustangs recovered. They scored two plays later, and the conversion knotted the game.

The Sooners fumbled away two opportunities in the fourth period. A poor SMU punt early gave Oklahoma possession at the Mustangs' 37. Jacobs and Seymour hammered gains to the 11, but Jacobs fumbled, and SMU recovered at the eight. The Mustangs fumbled it back moments later, and reserve end Lyle Smith recovered for OU at the 23. Three plays later, Mathews spilled the ball at the 15, and SMU recovered.

The Ponies had more first downs (15-7) and total yards (284-112). OU lost three of four fumbles, but the Sooner defense intercepted five SMU passes.

The Sooners traveled to Evanston, Illinois, the next week to meet Northwestern. The OU ticket office had sold 1,700 tickets to the game weeks before the season opener against SMU. Rock Island offered a package of $25.95 round-trip train fare. The cost included double occupancy at a hotel, tickets to the game and transportation to and from the game and a dinner dance on the train.

Northwestern was tabbed as 14-point favorites, but Oklahoma capitalized on two fumbles to defeat the Wildcats, 23-0, before a crowd of 45,000 at Dyche Stadium.

OU marched to the NU 10 midway through the first quarter but surrendered on downs. The Wildcats' Oliver Hahnenstein fumbled it right back on the next play. Shirk grabbed the ball in the air and carried it to the six. Seymour plowed over from the one four plays later, but Favor's conversion veered wide.

Favor kicked a field goal late in the opening period to lift Oklahoma to a 9-0 advantage.

Hahnenstein fumbled again midway in the third period, and backup center Cliff Speegle recovered it at the Cats' five. Seymour's two-yard TD run two plays later and Favor's extra point put the Sooners up, 16-0.

The Wildcats threatened early in the fourth stanza on a 42-yard pass to the OU three but failed to score when the fourth-down pass fell incomplete.

Johnny Martin scored on a 54-yard pass interception late in the game, and he also booted the conversion.

Northwestern had one final chance to erase the goose egg on their side of the scoreboard, marching 68 yards to the OU five, but an incomplete pass ended the drive on the final play, and Sooner fans poured onto the field.

Although the Wildcats were shut out, they had more total yards (256-171) and first downs (14-10).

Crooner Bing Crosby saluted OU's victory on his Thursday night radio show by singing "Oklahoma Hail" dedicated "to the boys from the plains," he said.

Jacobs injured his leg in the game, and Beryl Clark replaced him in the second half and turned in a stellar performance against Texas on October 14 in Dallas.

The 2-0 Longhorns defeated Florida, 12-0, and Wisconsin, 17-7, before their annual clash against the Sooners. Clark scored two touchdowns to lead OU to a 24-12 victory before 30,000 at the Cotton Bowl.

Fans witnessed a punting duel in the first quarter, and then the Sooners got a break late in the period. Shirk blocked R.B. Patrick's punt, and reserve tackle Harold Lahar scooped up the pigskin at the UT 45. Eleven plays later, Favor toed a 25-yard field goal early in the second period for a 3-0 Oklahoma lead.

A poor Steer punt in the next series set up the Sooners at the UT 41. Clark sailed an 18-yard pass to Jennings on the first play. Seymour gained three yards, then a Texas penalty put the ball at the

15. Seymour carried for three yards and three more to the nine. Two plays later, OU faced fourth-and-two at the three. Seymour's two-yard run got the first down, then Clark plowed off left tackle for the touchdown. Favor kicked the conversion for a 10-0 Sooner lead.

Jennings intercepted the Steers' pass at the Texas 33 late in the third period to set up another OU score. Seymour tossed a screen pass to Jennings on the next play, but Jennings was about to be swarmed by Horn defenders, so he flipped a lateral to Clark, who raced down the sideline to the end zone. Reserve end Louis Sharpe threw a key block on the play. Favor's conversion put OU ahead, 17-0.

Jack Crain scored two TDs in the fourth period to put Texas back in the contest. He maintained his balance along the sideline on his first score, a 68-yard run. Al Coppage blocked the extra point.

The Sooners answered with what appeared to be an 11-yard Martin-to-Mathews TD pass, but Mathews fumbled as he stumbled across the goal line. The officials ruled a touchback and Texas' ball. Two plays later, Crain sailed 72 yards for a touchdown. Bowers blocked the conversion. Crain, who accounted for 140 of Texas' 209 total yards, scored both TDs on the Sooners' second unit.

Seymour's four-yard TD run minutes later and Favor's conversion capped a 63-yard drive to put the game away. Matthews' 21-yard run and halfback L.G. Friedrich's 28-yard pass to Ivy to the UT five sparked the drive.

Oklahoma dominated with 13 first downs to three for the Horns. The Sooners were well balanced in the total yards category—177 rushing and 173 passing.

OU debuted at No. 3 in the first AP poll of the season and hosted 2-1 Kansas the following week. The Jayhawks posted two straight shutouts after their opening season loss. The Sooners manhandled Kansas, 27-7, on a hot (88 degrees) October afternoon before 22,000 spectators. It was the Sooners' first home win against the Hawks in six years.

Clark scored a 14-yard TD run late in the first stanza to cap a 77-yard march. Clark began the drive with a 19-yard run and later added 22 yards to the KU nine. Favor booted the conversion, but a holding penalty set the ball back 15 yards, and his second try went wide.

Clark returned a Kansas punt 15 yards to the KU 37 late in the second period. Six plays later, Clark fired a 10-yard pass to Jennings, who caught it at the goal line and fell across with KU's Dick Amerine holding on to him. Favor converted, and OU led 13-0 at halftime.

A poor Jayhawk punt early in the third quarter set up the Sooners at the KU 32. Clark scored from two yards out five plays later. Favor's conversion veered wide, but Kansas was flagged for offside, and his second attempt sailed true.

Mathews returned a Hawk punt 13 yards to the KU 37 midway through the fourth stanza. Reserve fullback Byron Potter rambled 28 yards to the nine. Potter carried for four more, then Mathews added four yards and one more for the final Sooner tally. Paul Woodson toed the extra point for a 27-0 Oklahoma lead.

Potter entered the game for the first time in the fourth quarter and began to bowl over the Jayhawks with his 6-1, 205-pound physique. He gained 45 yards of a 92-yard scoreless drive early in the fourth period.

Kansas scored later in the game. OU gained 16 first downs to nine for the Hawks. The Sooners gained 523 total yards (283 rushing and 240 passing), while the defense held Kansas to 159 total yards. Although Oklahoma won big, it was penalized 14 times for 123 yards.

The Sooners dropped to sixth in the AP poll. The entire top ten was different from the week before.

OU hammered the Oklahoma Aggies, 41-0, before 25,000 at Owen Field on October 28. Several days before the game, the team invited former Sooner halfback Howard McCarty to sit on the bench. McCarty broke his hip against the Aggies a year earlier. He had been working in an oil field in Illinois when he received the invitation. He accepted.

Defense and turnovers allowed OU short field position in each touchdown drive. The Sooners averaged 38 yards in each scoring march.

The Big Red made a charge late in the scoreless first quarter and into the second. Seymour's one-yard TD run on fourth down capped a 39-yard march in 11 plays. Favor toed the extra point.

Beryl Clark added a one-yard score midway through the period, capping a 32-yard drive, and Favor converted. The Aggies later marched 41 yards to the OU 18, but reserve halfback J.S. Munsey intercepted Jack Wurtz's pass at the goal line four plays later.

Wurtz fumbled the second-half kickoff, and guard Ralph Stevenson recovered for OU at the A&M 21. Clark was sacked for a 14-yard loss, then sailed a 35-yard TD strike to Jennings, who shed several Aggies tacklers to the end zone. Favor nailed the extra point.

Aggie Ray Portillo intercepted Clark's pass moments later, but he fumbled at the A&M 48, and Jennings pounced on it. On first down, Clark connected a 17-yard pass to Favor, then Seymour and Clark hammered the ball to the two. Clark carried across for the score on the next play, and Favor toed the conversion.

With a 28-0 lead, Coach Stidham inserted the reserves, who scored twice more in the fourth stanza. Friedrichs scored on a three-yard run and later hurled a 28-yard scoring strike to Munsey.

The Sooners rolled up 20 first downs and 495 total yards. The defense held the Aggies to three first downs and 197 total yards.

Harold Lahar injured his knee in the second quarter and would not play against Iowa State the next week. Olin Keith replaced him in the Aggie game and against the Cyclones the next week.

No. 6 Oklahoma blasted Iowa State, 38-6, before 25,000 homecoming fans on the next week in Norman. The Sooners got a break early when Merle Osborne had trouble fielding Favor's opening kickoff. He tried to kick the ball, attempting to pick it up. Kicking a fumbled ball gives possession to the other team. The Big Red gained possession at the Cyclone 21. Seymour scored from one yard out six plays later, but Iowa State blocked Favor's conversion.

Seymour returned a punt 20 yards to the I-State 30 moments later. Jacobs scored on a six-yard run nine plays later, but Favor's conversion was wide.

Martin's three-yard TD run midway in the second stanza put the Sooners up, 18-0. Favor's kick again was off the mark.

Oklahoma needed only two plays to cover 54 yards to score again after fielding a punt late in the third quarter. Jacobs fired a 22-yard pass to Ivy, who shed several defenders. Jacobs then rifled a 32-yard TD pass to Jennings, and Ivy converted for a 25-0 advantage.

Coach Stidham let most of the reserves play in the fourth period. Sooner guard Norval Locke blocked Osborne's punt and immediately fell on the pigskin at the Cyclones' 34. The Sooners were flagged 15 yards for having an ineligible receiver on the next play, moving the ball back to the IS 49. Clark sailed an 18-yard pass to Gus Kitchens and a 16-yarder to Pete Smith. Potter carried for five, then scored from 10 yards out. Clark toed the extra point for a 32-0 Sooner lead.

Tackle Roger Eason intercepted a Cyclone pass minutes later and returned it seven yards to the OU 47. Clark tossed an eight-yard pass to Kitchens, then Clark galloped 39 yards untouched to the end zone. Woodson missed the extra point.

The Cyclones drove 60 yards to score on the next series.

The Sooners gained 20 first downs and 205 total yards. Clark was a perfect six for six, passing for 80 yards.

Friedrichs tore a knee cartilage and was done for the season. Shirk suffered a charley horse. Both would also miss the Kansas State tilt the next week in Manhattan.

A steady rain softened the field for two days and slowed the Sooner offense, which averaged nearly 31 points per game in the last five outings. No. 6 Oklahoma edged the Wildcats, 13-10, on a mushy field before 17,000, the largest crowd for a Kansas State football game.

Jacobs fumbled while fielding a punt, and Don Crumbaker recovered for the Wildcats at the OU 32. The Big Red defense stiffened, but Jim Brock nailed a 33-yard field goal for a 3-0 Kansas State lead, and Oklahoma trailed for the first time all season.

The Sooners moved to the Cats' 17 late in the first stanza but had to turn the ball over on downs. Clark scored on a 10-yard run midway through the second period to cap a 43-yard march, and Favor's conversion gave Oklahoma a 7-3 lead.

Minutes later, the Sooners moved from their 36 to the Cats' 21, but Kansas State intercepted Clark's pass as the first half ended.

Kansas State scored a touchdown early in the third quarter for a 10-7 lead.

OU answered with the deciding touchdown on the next series. Clark returned the kickoff 41 yards to the K-State 43. Eleven plays later, Seymour's one-yard plunge put the Sooners back on top, 13-10. Favor's kick was low.

The Wildcats marched 50 yards to the OU three early in the fourth period, but Kent Duwe fumbled, and the Sooners recovered. Neither team threatened the rest of the game.

OU gained 14 first downs to 10 for Kansas State. The Sooners rolled up 243 total yards, 224 on the ground. Kansas State gained 207 total yards.

The No. 5 Sooners traveled to Columbia to face No. 12 Missouri for the Big Six conference driver's seat. Both teams were 3-0 in the conference with two games remaining. Mizzou edged OU, 7-6, before 27,000 fans, the largest attendance at a Tiger game in 50 years.

Two days of steady rain presented a mushy field, and the first quarter was a punting duel. Oklahoma made a charge from its 46 to the MU four late in the first period and into the second but surrendered possession on downs.

Bill Cunningham's 59-yard reverse run minutes later put the Tigers at the OU 10. The Big Red defense stiffened, holding Mizzou to zero yards on the next four plays.

Neither team threatened the rest of the first half.

Late in the third stanza, Missouri's Charles Moser blocked Martin's punt at the OU six. Bob Orf fielded the ball at the goal line, and Ron King converted.

Jacobs hurled a 15-yard TD pass to J.S. Munsey midway through the fourth stanza to cap a 71-yard drive in 11 plays. Favor's conversion was low and wide.

Coppage recovered Paul Christman's fumble at the MU 42 with five minutes remaining. Facing fourth and a foot, Seymour blasted ahead for a first down at the Tigers' 28. OU managed only four yards in the next three plays. Favor came on to boot the winning field goal, but his 41-yard attempt failed.

Oklahoma gained 12 first downs and 254 yards. Missouri totaled 218 yards and seven first downs, but the Tigers held the reins to the conference title. The loss also snapped OU's 11-game conference winning string dating back to 1937.

Norvel Wood suffered a sprained knee, and Seymour and Favor had concussions in the Missouri game. All three would be sidelined for the final game against 6-1-1 Nebraska.

A victory against the Cornhuskers and a Missouri loss would give the Sooners a split of the conference crown. Missouri defeated Kansas, and Oklahoma finished third in the conference with a 13-7 loss to Nebraska on November 25 before 34,900 fans in Lincoln.

Nebraska scored two touchdowns early in the second quarter, both times on passes from Herman Rohrig to Roy Petsch.

The Sooners drove 52 yards to the NU 28 following the second-half kickoff, but Potter fumbled on the next play, and Nebraska recovered.

The Sooners' lone score came late in the game when Clark fired a 28-yard TD pass to Coppage and Clark toed the extra point.

Nebraska had more first downs (11-10), but the Sooners had more total yards (202-173).

Munsey broke his shoulder against the Huskers and would not return to action for another two years, in a limited role for the 1941 Sooners.

Oklahoma finished the season with a 6-2-1 record and 3-2 in the Big Six. Ivy and Duggan were named All-Americans. Bowers, Clark, and Seymour joined them on the all-conference first unit.

1939 Season Record: 6-2-1
Big Six Conference: 3-2-0 (Third)

Date	Opponent	Result	Score
September 30	SOUTHERN METHODIST	T	7-7
October 7	at Northwestern	W	23-0
October 14	Texas at Dallas	W	24-12
October 21	KANSAS	W	27-7
October 28	OKLAHOMA A&M	W	41-0
November 4	IOWA STATE	W	38-6
November 11	at Kansas State	W	13-10
November 18	at Missouri	L	7-6
November 25	at Nebraska	L	13-7

1940 - 1949

1940

World War II was underway as practices began for the 1940 Sooner season. Though determined to maintain its neutrality, the United States was gradually drawn closer to the war by the force of events. In 1940, the United States Congress adopted the nation's first peacetime military draft anticipating the escalation of the war. College football would not be affected for another year.

Sooner assistant Dewey Luster was hired as backfield coach for the New York Giants. Doc Erskine returned to OU as his replacement. Stanley Williamson was named line coach, and former Sooner Dale Arbuckle (1923-26) was added to the staff as an assistant.

Guard Harold Lahar was the only seasoned veteran who returned to the line, but Cliff Speegle provided ample experience at center, and junior Roger Eason would step forward to help anchor the front line at right tackle.

Marv Whited earned the starting nod at quarterback. Fullback Johnny Martin and halfbacks Jack Jacobs and Orv Mathews returned to the backfield. Jacobs' punting duties would place him in the school record book at season's end. Bill Jennings was moved from left halfback to left end. Howard McCarty also returned to the squad after a year and a half layoff, but a bone specialist advised him against playing football again. The physician told him the hip was fine, but McCarty could risk further damage if he continued his football career. McCarty left the squad during the second week of practices.

OU president William Bizzell asked him to stay with the squad to be an inspiration to the team, but McCarty returned to the oilfield in Illinois, where he had worked after suffering the injury.

Head coach Tom Stidham was not pleased with his squad's performances in the second week of practice. The second unit consisted of mostly sophomores, and Stidham said the team was "green as toad frogs and needs a world of seasoning before they make first-class ball players."

The Sooners opened the season against 1-0-1 Oklahoma A&M at home for the second straight year. University of Oklahoma officials had pushed for a plan to have the game played in Norman, citing more fans would attend the game since OU had a larger stadium.

Henry Iba, Oklahoma A&M's athletic director, requested the game be switched back to home-and-home the following year or risk canceling the series. The game returned to Norman in 1941, then returned to Stillwater in 1942. After two contests in Oklahoma City in 1943 and 1944, the series returned to home-and-home in 1945.

The Sooners won the 1940 contest, 29-27 on October 5. OU rolled to a 29-6 lead but nearly saw it slip away as the Aggies scored three fourth-quarter touchdowns before 25,000 spectators.

The Big Red marched 56 yards to pay dirt following the opening kickoff. Martin's one-yard TD run capped the six-play drive, which was highlighted by Mathews' 26-yard run to the A&M 16. Ralph Harris' conversion was wide.

The Aggies later scored on a 32-yard drive set up by a short OU punt.

The Sooners drove to the A&M three early in the second stanza but had to turn the ball over on downs. The Aggies stalled and punted out to the A&M 31. Four plays later, backup quarterback Jack Steele's five-yard TD run put the Sooners up, 12-6. It was Steele's first time to carry the football as a Sooner. Jacobs hurled a 20-yard pass to Jennings to the A&M nine two plays before the touchdown.

Stidham sent in Jack Haberline to kick the conversion. The sophomore had impressed coaches in practices, hardly missing a kick. Haberline missed only two conversions in high school and made his first attempt in a crimson uniform.

Martin scored again on a one-yard plunge midway through the third period. Jacobs hurled two long passes to trigger the 60-yard, five-play drive. His first was a screen to Jennings, who then lateraled to Mathews, and Mathews scampered 24 yards to the A&M 37. Two plays later, Jacobs connected a 19-yarder to Jennings to the Aggie one. Haberlein toed the extra point.

A heavy rush by OU end Louis Sharpe forced a poor Aggie punt to the A&M 17 early in the fourth quarter. Backup halfback Boyd Bibb scored four plays later, and Haberline's toe put the Sooners ahead, 27-6.

Martin's punt, minutes later, pinned the Aggies at their eight. A&M was forced to punt, and Harris blocked the kick. Sharpe fell on the ball in the end zone for two more Sooner points. The safety would be the deciding factor in the ball game.

The Aggies scored three touchdowns on the next three series, two of them from OU fumbles. The final A&M touchdown came with five seconds left in the game.

OU gained 11 first downs and 278 total yards. The defense held the Aggies to seven first downs and 204 total yards. Jacobs, who did most of the Sooner punting, averaged 47.8 in five kicks.

The Sooners traveled to Dallas the next week to face the 2-0 Longhorns before 33,000 fans. Texas won, 19-16. Two bad snaps from center allowed each team to score, but the final one by Oklahoma, with five minutes left, boosted Texas to victory.

OU rolled 82 yards in 15 plays after the opening kickoff for the game's first score. Martin (40) and Jacobs (22) combined for 62 rushing yards in the drive, which Martin capped with a one-yard TD run, the first opening-quarter touchdown against Texas since 1922. Haberlein's toe gave the Sooners a 7-0 advantage.

Mathews intercepted a Texas pass, late in the first period, and returned it 16 yards to the UT 45. Oklahoma advanced to the seven early in the second stanza, but the Steer defense stiffened. Texas sacked Bibb for eight and three yard losses on the next two plays and forced him to toss an incompletion on third down. Harris' 40-yard field-goal try was short of the mark.

Texas tied the game minutes later when R.L. Harkins took Orban Sanders' lateral and sped 60 yards for the score. Sanders' toe knotted the game at 7-7.

Jacobs recovered a Texas fumble at the UT 38 early in the third quarter. The Sooners faced fourth-and-two at the Texas nine, but James Sweeney hammered Jacobs for a five-yard loss. The Horns went nowhere, and Glen Jackson's snap to his punter sailed beyond the end zone for an Oklahoma safety.

Texas' free kick set up the Sooners at the OU 49. Jacobs completed an eight-yard pass to Martin to the UT 43, then sailed a pass to Jennings at the 25. Jennings grabbed the ball between two Texas defenders, followed Lyle Smith's block and raced to the end zone. Haberlein's conversion was partially blocked, but the ball made it over the crossbar.

Harkins returned the kickoff to the 35, then Crain bolted 63 yards before Mathews shoved him out of bounds at the OU two. Harkins bulled over for the score three plays later, but Crain missed the extra point. OU 16, Texas 13.

OU lost an opportunity to put the game away early in the fourth stanza by fumbling at the Steers' 30. Texas drove to the OU 39 with more than five minutes remaining, but Woodson tipped Harkins' pass, and Whited intercepted at the 36.

The Sooners set up to punt after gaining only three yards in two plays. Speegle sailed a high snap to Jacobs, but the quick-thinking Jacobs knocked the ball down and fell on it at the 27. Speegle's next snap skipped along the ground, but the Longhorns swarmed Jacobs as he tried to retrieve the ball at the 18.

Texas took over, and Crain scored from nine yards out two plays later. John Gill's conversion was wide, but with four minutes to go the Steers led, 19-16.

Aided by a pass interference penalty, Oklahoma moved to the UT 35, but Crain intercepted a 30-yard pass in the end zone four plays later.

OU had more first downs (12-9) and total yards (270-252).

The Sooners returned home October 19 and shut down 1-2 Kansas State, 14-0, in the conference opener. A crowd of 18,000 sat through intense heat of 87 degrees.

After a scoreless first quarter, the Sooners advanced 61 yards for their first touchdown early in the second. Jacobs' 19-yard TD pass to Sharpe completed the seven-play drive. Sharpe caught the ball at the Wildcat five and scooted across the goal line. Haberlein toed the conversion. Jacobs completed a 26-yard pass to reserve halfback Tom Rousey to highlight the drive.

Mathews returned an interception 70 yards for an apparent score, but officials whistled him for interference. The penalty gave Kansas State possession at the OU 30, the deepest possession for the Cats all day. The fans howled in disapproval, but the Sooner defense got them cheering again by forcing four straight incomplete passes.

Oklahoma marched 83 yards in 10 plays for its other score midway through the fourth period. Jacobs ran for 40 yards to the Cats' 43 on the first play of the drive. Two plays later, he hurled an 18-yard pass to Jennings to the 15. Jacobs and Martin took turns hammering to the one-foot line on the next six plays. Martin then banged ahead for the score, and Haberlein toed the conversion.

Oklahoma gained 14 first downs and 301 total yards. The defense held the Cats to three first downs, 74 total yards and forced them to punt 16 times. Jacobs averaged 52 yards in five punts for Oklahoma.

The 2-1 Sooners traveled to Ames to face 2-3 Iowa State on October 26. Martin scored two touchdowns as the Sooners dropped the Cyclones, 20-7.

Martin's one-yard TD run topped a 65-yard drive in 13 plays on the Sooners' second possession of the game. Haberlein toed the extra point.

Iowa State scored minutes later to tie the game. The Cyclones threatened to take the lead by advancing to the OU nine early in the second period, but the Big Red defense did not yield, and I-State surrendered on downs.

Jacobs' three-yard TD run late in the third stanza and Haberlein's conversion put Oklahoma ahead, 14-7. The score capped a 64-yard,

11-play drive. Jacobs accounted for all of the yards by rushing for 41 and passing for 23 more. He tossed a 23-yard pass to Martin to the Cyclones' 41 on the drive's second play. Two plays later, he carried for 14 yards to the 20. Jennings barely missed Jacobs' next pass in the end zone. Jacobs then carried three times to the three-yard line before scoring.

The Sooners faced third-and-five at the IS 48 with four minutes left in the game. Martin burst up the middle, cut to the west sideline, and sailed to the end zone. Jacobs ran alongside Martin to shield a Cyclone safety from catching him. Haberlein missed the conversion, but Oklahoma had the deciding 20-7 lead.

Iowa State gained more total yards (241-221), and both teams gained 12 first downs apiece.

Ticket sales reached 26,000 the following week for the Nebraska contest in Norman. Anticipating an overflow crowd, University of Oklahoma officials added 5,000 bleacher seats to the north and south portion of the cinder track. A new $5,000 tarpaulin was purchased to cover Owen Field in case of rain. It came in handy as nearly an inch of rain fell on Norman three days before the game, and the tarp kept the field dry.

The No. 12 Cornhuskers won three straight after losing to Minnesota in the season opener. Oklahoma and Nebraska sported 2-0 conference records and the winner would be in the driver's seat for the conference crown. The Huskers shut down the Sooners, 13-0, before a record crowd of 33,377—the largest crowd to see a football game in the State of Oklahoma.

Oklahoma lost an opportunity early in the first period after Mathews bolted 43 yards to the NU 23. Nebraska's defense stiffened, and OU surrendered possession when Roy Petsch swatted away Jacobs' fourth-down pass to Jennings.

Harry Hopp's 31-yard TD pass to Allen Zikmund put Nebraska on top, 6-0, with 20 seconds left until halftime. The conversion was wide.

The Sooners marched to the Huskers' 16 early in the third quarter. Facing fourth-and-six from the 12, Jacobs passed to a wide-open Mathews, but the ball went in and out of the halfback's hands.

Walter Luther returned a Sooner punt 53 yards to the OU 39 as the third quarter ended. Vike Francis plowed over for the score eight plays later, and Herman Rohrig converted.

The Sooners never threatened again. Nebraska gained 14 first downs and 409 total yards. The Sooners made six first downs and gained 162 total yards. Jacobs punted nine times for a 52.3 average, which included an 80-yard kick in the second quarter.

Oklahoma rebounded with a 13-0 victory over 1-4 Kansas on November 9 in Lawrence. A driving mist made for a sloppy field, yet the Sooners pounded out 223 rushing yards led by Martin's 138 yards.

Both teams battled through three scoreless quarters. The Big Red advanced from its 49 to the Jayhawk 20 midway through the first period, but lost nine yards on the next four plays. The Sooners got the ball at the KU 43 on their next possession and drove 42 yards, but the Jayhawks held them inches from the goal line on fourth down.

Kansas threatened with a 56-yard drive to the OU 25, but the Sooner defense forced a fumble and recovered.

The Sooners took the second-half kickoff and drove 78 yards only to have a fumble stop the drive. Jacobs recovered his own fumble on fourth down, and Kansas took over.

Early in the fourth quarter, Mathews took a shovel pass from backup halfback Huel Hamm and flew 41 yards around left end for a touchdown. Whited took out two Jayhawks with one block along the way. Haberlein converted for a 7-0 Sooner lead.

Oklahoma's defense stalled the Jayhawks after the kickoff, and Hamm returned the Kansas punt 16 yards to the OU 49. Ten plays later, Hamm crossed the goal line, but officials whistled the Sooners for offside. Martin scored two plays later from the KU four, but Ralph Harris' conversion was wide.

OU gained 16 first downs and 271 total yards. The defense held Kansas to five first downs and 81 total yards.

The Oklahoma-Missouri matchup the next week in Norman featured several of the top scorers in the Big Six conference. Martin was the league's leading scorer with 42 points on seven TDs. Four Missouri players were not far behind—Harry Ice was second with 36 points on six TDs, Bob Steuber was third with 32 points, Bill Cunningham was fourth with 25 points, and Jack Christman was eighth with 18 points.

The Sooners and Tigers (5-2) held identical 2-1 conference records. The winner would place second behind Nebraska in the Big Six.

Christman was the highly touted Tiger quarterback. He was mentioned as an All-America candidate with his cannon arm. Christman could throw the ball 50 to 60 yards downfield, but he had yet to toss a touchdown pass against the Sooners in the previous years. The Sooner defense intercepted four of his passes and held him to 64 passing yards in 1938 and 39 yards in 1939.

Christman nearly hurled a touchdown bomb in the final seconds, but Oklahoma held on for a 7-0 victory before 27,000 homecoming fans.

OU twice moved to the Missouri 20 in the second quarter and both times had to surrender on downs. The first advance came after a poor Tiger punt set up OU at the Missouri 30. The Sooners drove from their own 45 on the following series. Neither team threatened the rest of the half.

Oklahoma marched 68 yards in 10 plays for the only score of the game early in the third stanza. Martin's one-yard dive over the goal line capped the drive, and Haberlein converted. Hamm's 17-yard run and 15-yard pass to Pete Smith sparked the drive.

The Tigers took the ensuing kickoff and drove 62 yards to the OU 25, but Christman's fourth-down pass fell incomplete.

Missouri had the ball on its 34-yard line with 15 seconds remaining. Christman hurled a long pass to Harold Adams. The ball deflected off Jennings and into Adams' hands at the 20. The Tiger receiver slipped through Hamm's grasp, but Whited caught him from behind at the OU 14 as the game ended.

Missouri had more first downs (15-9) and total yards (235-133). The Big Red defense held Christman to 11 completions in 24 attempts for 103 yards. The Sooners also picked off two of his passes. If not for his long bomb at the end of the game, Christman would have had only 51 yards passing. Yet in three years, he had not thrown a touchdown against Oklahoma's defense.

With conference play out of the way, OU still had two more games. Temple (4-3-1) came to Norman the next week. The Sooners won, 9-6, before 7,000 fans, the lowest attendance in four years. A light rain and cold temperatures kept many fans at home. Those who attended were wrapped in blankets or donned slickers. It was the first wet game at Owen Field under Coach Stidham's tenure.

Temple's Sid Besunsky missed a 22-yard field goal into the wind in the first period.

The Owls' James Yeager intercepted Jacobs' pass at the Temple 15 to squelch an OU threat late in the second stanza. The Sooner defense dropped Temple for a six-yard loss on the next play and a delay of game moved the Owls back to the four. Andy Tomasic tried to sweep off right end but was met by Harold Lahar and Smith, who chased him behind the goal line. Jennings and Roger Eason smothered Tomasic for a safety.

Oklahoma held a 2-0 lead through halftime.

With three minutes gone in the third quarter, Mathews took a Temple punt at his 22. Yeager hit Mathews and knocked off his helmet. Mathews staggered, but kept going all the way for a touchdown. Martin delivered a block to Tomasic, the only player who had a chance to catch Mathews. Haberlein converted to give OU a 9-0 advantage.

The Owls scored a touchdown late in the game, but Oklahoma held on by milking the clock after the kickoff.

Temple had more first downs (10-7) and total yards (205-159). Jacobs sprained an ankle late in the game and would not make the trip to San Francisco for the final game against Santa Clara on November 30.

Oklahoma jumped to a 13-0 lead only to see it slip away as No. 15 Santa Clara (5-1-1) won, 33-13, at Kezar Stadium.

Mathews returned the opening kickoff 92 yards for a touchdown. Haberlein toed the extra point for a 7-0 Sooner lead. The Bronchos fumbled on the first play following the kickoff, and Smith recovered at the SC 26 for Oklahoma. The Big Red moved to the six, but failed to gain a first down at the four.

The Sooners drove to the one on their next possession, but Martin was stopped inches short of the goal line on fourth down. The third time was a charm.

Hamm returned a Broncho punt 10 yards to the SC 25. Hamm tossed an incomplete pass then fired a screen pass to Mathews, who followed Eason's key block and spun away from a Broncho defender for the score. Ralph Harris' conversion veered off the mark, but the OU held a 13-0 lead.

Broncho passing killed the Sooners the rest of the way. Santa Clara scored three times through the air and twice on the ground. After tying the game, 13-13, in the second period, the Bronchos added a touchdown in the third period and two more in the fourth. Santa Clara completed 11 of 19 passes for 229 yards. The Bronchos rolled up 16 first downs and had 206 rushing yards. The Sooners managed only five first downs and 149 total yards.

The Sooners ended the season with a 6-3 mark and 4-1 in the Big Six conference. Jennings, Eason, Lahar, and Martin were chosen to the conference's first team.

Fifty-four days later, Stidham accepted an offer to coach at Marquette University in Milwaukee, Wisconsin, and tendered his resignation at the University of Oklahoma. Although he had two more years on his contract at OU, university regents accepted his resignation and released him from his contract.

1940 Season Record: 6-3-0
Big Six Conference: 4-1-0 (Second)

Date	Opponent	Result	Score
October 5	OKLAHOMA A&M	W	29-27
October 12	Texas at Dallas	L	19-16
October 19	KANSAS STATE	W	14-0
October 26	at Iowa State	W	20-7
November 2	NEBRASKA	L	13-0
November 9	at Kansas	W	13-0
November 16	MISSOURI	W	7-0
November 23	TEMPLE	W	9-6
November 30	Santa Clara*	L	33-13

*Game played in San Francisco, CA

Stidham won 27, lost eight and tied three games during his four-year tenure at Oklahoma. He placed more Oklahoma players with professional teams than any other coach. In 1940, 17 Sooners started in pro football and 10 remained through the season.

1941

Dewey "Snorter" Luster was hired as the 11th Sooner head coach 11 days after Tom Stidham resigned. Luster was the second OU alum to coach at his alma mater. Luster lettered four years at OU. He started at end his last two years and was captain on the 1920 team, which won the Missouri Valley conference championship.

Lawrence "Jap" Haskell, a former Sooner player and teammate of Luster, was named athletic director at OU and line coach. Dale Arbuckle, a Sooner star from 1923-26, tutored the backfield.

Luster was coaching backs for the New York Giants and studying for a master's degree at Columbia when he took the Oklahoma job. He had coached the Sooner line from 1929-1931. The soft-spoken Luster had poor eyesight and while on the OU staff, he kept a player nearby to tell him what was happening on the field.

More nations fell to the Nazi regime, and the United States was drawing closer to the war. President Franklin Roosevelt froze German and Japanese assets during the summer. Relations with Germany became increasingly strained. The United States, through the Land Lease Act, provided military aid to Great Britain, thus bringing the United States one step closer to entering the war.

Back in Norman, eight Sooners joined the military—guard Olin Keith, tackle Tommy Tallchief, halfbacks Gus Kitchens and Bill Blancett and Harvey Stone, who was touted as one of the best new linemen to come out of the freshman ranks in years.

The draft board deferred tackle Roger Eason's draft status, since he had his nose broken several times, and kicker Jack Haberlein's status also was deferred since he was an engineer. Veteran halfbacks Orville Mathews and Jack Jacobs returned to the 1941 squad. Marv Whited was moved to fullback, and Sophomore Joe "Junior" Golding would round out the backfield. Guard Ralph Harris and ends Louis Sharpe and Lyle Smith also returned.

Despite a new rule allowing free substitution, Luster continued to employ the two-team system as his predecessor Stidham did. The free substitution rule allowed a coach to replace as many players after each down had concluded. Luster also devised the "A" formation, which was "productive of finesse, forward passing and surprising power… to bring gains of longer dashes rather than by shorter punching Sooner fans have been accustomed to," wrote Harold Keith in *The Daily Oklahoman*.

The Sooners opened the 1941 campaign on September 27 against a confident Oklahoma A&M team. The Aggies believed this was their year to beat OU. They were wrong as the Sooners dropped the Aggies, 19-0, before 28,000 fans.

The Oklahoma defense shut down the Aggies six times inside the OU five-yard line.

The Sooners first scored on a 48-yard pass late in the opening period. Jacobs lobbed a short pass to end Dub Lamb, who then shed an Aggies defender and sped to the end zone. Haberlein missed the conversion.

The Aggies recovered Jacobs' fumble moments later at the OU 19. The OU defense stuffed Marvin Salmon's fourth-down run short of a first down at the five-yard line and gained possession. A&M advanced to the OU five early in the second stanza, but Bill Mattox belted Jimmy Reynolds forcing a fumble, and Mathews recovered at the five.

The Aggies stalled at the Sooner two on their next possession and had to surrender on downs. The Aggies drove to the OU two on the following series, but the first-half clock expired.

Midway through the third quarter, A&M was on the move again to the OU five, but Jacobs knocked down Salmon's fourth-down pass in the end zone. The Aggies were knocking on the touchdown door again on their next series, but halfback Bill Campbell stopped Reynolds inches short of the goal line.

The Sooners put the game away late in the fourth quarter. Mathews took a punt at the OU 34, cut to the middle of the field and scored untouched. Sharpe and guard Mitch Shadid threw key blocks on the play. Haberlein booted the extra point for a 13-0 lead.

Golding intercepted Salmon's pass moments later and returned it 25 yards to the A&M 17. Huel Hamm connected a touchdown pass to Golding on the next play. Haberlein's kick was wide right.

The Aggies had more first downs (9-8), but the Sooners had more total yards (288-221).

Pat M. Greenwood of Dallas, and the Texas State Fair athletic committee came up with an idea for an annual trophy to be presented to the winner of the Oklahoma-Texas game each year.

Greenwood said: "It would be something symbolic of our section of the country, say a 10-gallon hat on bronze, to be passed along to the winning team each succeeding game with the score of each game inscribed."

Although made from bronze, the award would be known as the Golden Hat Trophy.

Texas got to keep the trophy as the Longhorns thrashed Oklahoma, 40-7, on October 11 before 45,000 at the Cotton Bowl. The Steers entered the Red River rivalry with a 2-0 record and were one of the favorites to go to the Rose Bowl at season's end.

Jack Crain scored the first two Texas touchdowns, and Pete Layden ran for another to put the Longhorns up 21-0 at halftime.

The Sooners' only score came early in the third quarter after Eason recovered R.L. Harkin's fumble at the UT 21. The Big Red made only six yards in three plays, but Texas was flagged for offside, giving OU a first down at the 11. Hamm then hurled the ball to Golding, who caught the ball with a leap in front of the goal line and carried it across. Haberlein toed the conversion.

Texas soon jumped to a 27-7 lead on a 19-yard pass from Harkins to Malcom Kutner. Harkins tossed another TD pass and ran for a score in the fourth period.

Texas gained 11 first downs and 441 total yards. The Sooners were held to eight first downs and 199 total yards.

The Sooners' two starting tackles were injured against Texas and would not play against Kansas State the following week. Roger Eason was out with a bruised hip, and Howard Teeter suffered a sore foot. Plato Andros replaced Eason, and Homer Simmons took over for Teeter.

Oklahoma shut out the 0-2-1 Wildcats, 16-0, before 6,500 fans in Manhattan. Golding scored two touchdowns for the Sooners. His first came on a 10-yard run early in the second stanza to cap a 40-yard drive in five plays, and Haberlein converted.

The Sooners advanced to the Cats' 23 late in the half but stalled on four failed pass attempts.

Kansas State marched deep into Sooner territory early in the third quarter. On fourth-and-five from the nine, Simmons nailed a Wildcat halfback for a seven-yard loss, and the Sooners took over.

Haberlein booted a 29-yard field goal late in the third period to put Oklahoma ahead, 10-0. Midway through the fourth quarter, Jacobs returned a punt 17 yards to the Cats' 37 and Coach Luster inserted the second unit. Five plays later, Golding swept around left end and followed Eddie Davis' key block for a six-yard touchdown.

Haberlein's kick sailed wide. Davis fired a 12-yard pass to Golding to the Cats' eight to keep the drive alive two plays before the score.

The Big Red had 16 first downs and 318 total yards. Kansas State totaled 11 first downs and 150 total yards.

No. 8 and undefeated Santa Clara came to Norman on October 25. The Bronchos' defense had allowed only 13 points in their first four victories. The Sooners stunned the Bronchos, 16-6, before a crowd of 21,000 and in a heavy downpour.

Eason returned to the Sooner lineup and made the first big play late in the opening quarter. He popped Broncho halfback Ken Casanaga, forcing a fumble, and Lyle Smith recovered for OU at the SC 31. Jacobs hurled an eight-yard TD pass to Mathews seven plays later, and Haberlein converted. Jacobs tossed a 14-yard pass to Sharpe and a 12-yard aerial to Mattox to keep the drive going.

Casanaga completed a 12-yard TD pass to Al Beal early in the second period, but Oklahoma held a 7-6 advantage when Shadid blocked the extra point.

The Sooners stalled at their own 18 early in the fourth quarter and Jacobs, standing on his nine, booted a punt that flew 70 yards in air and rolled 15 more yards to the Bronchos' six. The 85-yard kick was officially logged as a 76-yard punt. He also had a 60-yarder in the first stanza.

OU took a 10-6 lead minutes later when Haberlein toed a 30-yard field goal. Campbell recovered a Broncho fumble with about two minutes remaining. The Sooners then faced fourth-and-one at the five but Jacobs' three-yard carry gave OU new life at the two. Jacobs bulled ahead for the TD on the next play with 15 seconds to go. Haberlein's conversion was wide.

Oklahoma had more first downs (13-12) but Santa Clara gained more total yards (165-109).

The Sooners hammered 2-3 Kansas, 38-0, the following week in Norman. Jacobs scored the first two touchdowns and passed for another. His first, a three-yard run late in the first quarter, capped a 52-yard drive in 11 plays. His second score, a one-yard run early in the second period, came six plays after a Jayhawk fumble on the next series. Haberlein converted both times.

Kansas later advanced past midfield for the first time on a 25-yard pass to the OU 25. The Sooner defense held off the Jayhawks and took over at the OU 34. Jacobs hurled a 16-yard TD pass to Junior Golding seven plays later. The pass play was Jacobs' eighth straight completion in the game. Haberlein's toe made it 21-0.

Haberlein's 16-yard field goal upped the lead to 24-0 early in the third stanza. Backup halfback Jim Tyree added a touchdown later in the quarter, and Haberlein converted.

Kansas failed to gain a first down, moments later, and Oklahoma took over at the KU 20. Golding scored on the first play from scrimmage. He tried to find an open receiver, but instead found a huge gap in the line and scooted to the end zone. Haberlein added the extra point.

OU gained 17 first downs and 393 (276 rushing and 117 passing) total yards. The defense held the Hawks to three first downs and 98 (36 rushing and 62 passing) yards.

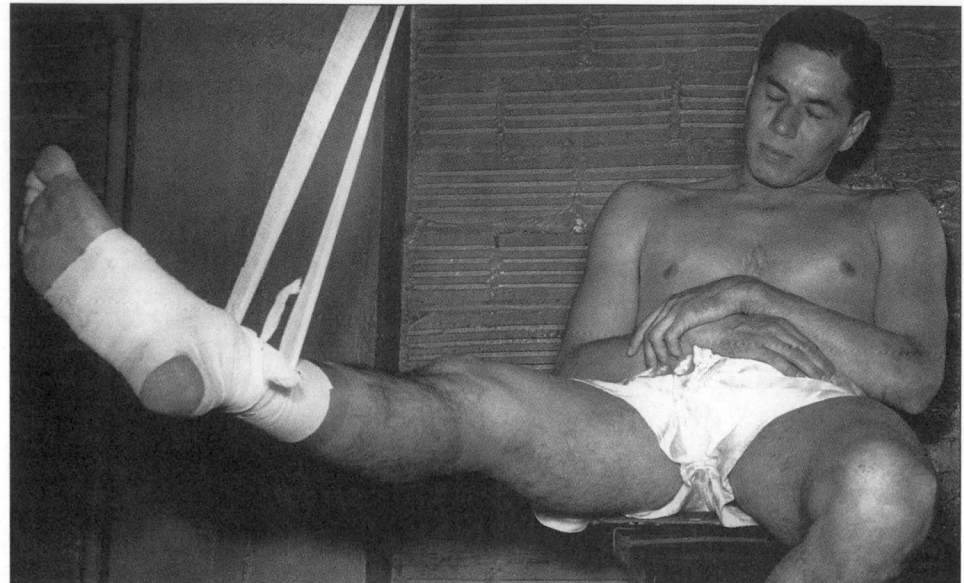

Jack Jacobs rests his foot in a sling after booting a 76-yard punt in the rain against Santa Clara. Jacobs set the school record for punting average in a season with 47.84 yards per kick. (*OU Athletics*)

The Sooners delighted 15,000 homecoming fans with a 55-0 win over 2-3 Iowa State on November 8 in Norman. It was the largest margin of victory since the Sooners whipped Washington St. Louis, 62-7, in 1922. The Sooners scored the most points in the conference's history, eclipsing Nebraska's 53 points in 1940.

The Sooners took a 7-0 lead in the first three and a half minutes. Campbell's two-yard TD run came five plays after Jacobs recovered a fumble at the Cyclone 30. Haberlein kicked the extra point. Luster inserted the sophomores in the second period, and it didn't take long for them to score. Eddie Davis rifled a 31-yard TD scoring strike to Lamb, and Haberlein converted.

Pete Cawthon intercepted the Cyclones' pass moments later and returned the ball 15 yards to the OU 40. Golding tossed a 31-yard pass to Davis, and Davis followed it with a 26-yard aerial to Lamb to the IS three. Two plays later, Jacobs scored from the one. Haberlein toed the 21st point.

Whited scored on a two-yard run early in the third quarter to cap a 50-yard drive in nine plays. Hamm hurled a 31-yard pass to Mattox to spark the drive. Haberlein toed his fourth straight kick for a 28-0 Sooner advantage.

Reserve halfback Carl Brewington's seven-yard TD run and Haberlein's toe made it 35-0 late in the third stanza. The Sooners scored three more times in the fourth quarter. Haberlein missed one conversion in the process.

The Big Red defense held the Cyclones to 88 (22 rushing and 66 passing) total yards and three first downs. Iowa State advanced once past midfield on a kickoff return after OU's first score. The Sooner offense piled up 21 first downs and 411 total yards.

OU traveled to Columbia the following week to face No. 16 Missouri (6-1) for first place in the Big Six conference. Missouri and Oklahoma each sported 3-0 conference records. The Tigers lost their opener then won the next six games, including four shutouts. Missouri's defense posted three straight shutouts before the Oklahoma contest. The Tiger offense boasted a powerful running game totaling 2,019 rushing yards in its first seven games. Missouri also enjoyed a 13-game home winning streak dating back to 1938.

The Tigers ran for 285 yards in the 28-0 victory over OU before 28,000 fans, a new Missouri football attendance record that included 1,700 Sooners.

Jacobs fumbled the ball away on OU's first series at the MU 36. The Tigers advanced to the Sooner seven, then Lyle Smith nailed Harry Ice for a six-yard loss. Missouri managed only three yards on the next three plays and surrendered on downs.

The Sooners punted out to the Tiger 36, and Missouri drove 64 yards for the first touchdown—a 23-yard run by Maurice Wade. The Tigers shot to a 14-0 lead on a 24-yard pass on their next series.

Oklahoma then drove to the MU 13 but could not capitalize. Mathews' forward lateral cost the Sooners a 15-yard penalty then Jacobs' pass to Golding in the end zone fell incomplete as the first half expired.

Wade's one-yard TD run, midway through the third period, increased the Tiger lead to 21-0. The Sooners lost another scoring opportunity when Campbell was stopped one foot short of the goal line early in the fourth quarter.

Wade, who rushed for 110 yards, scored his third touchdown on a 34 yard run late in the game.

The Tigers gained 16 first downs and 353 total yards. Oklahoma was held to 147 total yards. Jacobs punted six times for a 50.6-yard average for the only shining statistic for OU.

The Sooners returned home on November 22 to host Tom Stidham's Marquette Golden Avalanche. Oklahoma made Stidham's return unpleasant with a 61-14 victory before 8,000 shivering fans. Mathews and Jacobs each scored three touchdowns in the onslaught.

Mathews scored on a 56-yard run on the third play of the Sooners' first possession, but Haberlein's extra point was blocked. The Avalanche scored on their next two possessions for a 14-6 lead.

The Sooners scored on two straight possessions midway through the second period to regain the lead, 19-14. Jacobs tossed a 27-yard TD pass to Mathews, and Mathews followed it with a 56-yard TD run. Haberlein kicked the first conversion, but his second sailed wide.

Jacobs scored twice in the third quarter, the second TD on a 54-yard punt return. Campbell added a touchdown late in the third stanza when he recovered a fumble in mid-air and scooted 20 yards to the end zone.

The Sooners scored on three straight series in the fourth quarter—a 61-yard interception by reserve guard Clare Moreford, a two-yard run by Jacobs, and a two-yard run by Brewington.

OU totaled 14 first downs, 254 yards rushing and added 92 through the air. Golding gained 192 total yards. The defense held the Hilltoppers to 10 first downs and 185 total yards.

A missed extra point and three failed field goals doomed the Sooners as they dropped a 7-6 decision to 3-5 Nebraska on November 29 in Lincoln. A crowd of 22,000 turned out to see which team would be the Big Six conference runner up to Missouri.

Haberlein, who converted 16 of 22 extra points and made all three of his field goal attempts leading up to the game, missed all four kicks against the Huskers. The extra point would have tied the game, and any one of the field goals would have won the game.

The Sooners got on board first when Golding scored on a four-yard reverse on the last play of the first quarter. Haberlein's kick veered wide, but Oklahoma led 6-0.

Layne Blue intercepted Jacobs' pass for a touchdown late in the second stanza. Vic Schleich's conversion put the Huskers ahead, 7-6.

Mathews returned the ensuing kickoff 48 yards to the NU 45. The Sooners were at the Husker 19 two plays later. Jacobs hurled a 16-yard pass to Sharpe and a 13-yarder to Campbell. Six plays later, the Sooners were knocking on the touchdown door at the NU one. Jacobs misfired on a third-down pass, and Haberlein's 10-yard field goal was wide.

Eason blocked a Nebraska punt late in the third quarter, and Shadid recovered for OU at the Husker 30. The Sooners gained zero yards in the next three plays, and Haberlein's 47-yard field goal attempt was wide.

Nebraska marched 41 yards to the OU four midway through the fourth stanza but had to surrender on downs. Moments later, Mathews took Jacobs' shovel pass and flew 69 yards to the NU 21, but the Sooners were whistled for clipping. The penalty moved the ball back to the OU 37.

Jacobs tossed two incompletions, then connected a 12-yard pass to Mathews for a first down. Coach Luster stopped the clock to make a substitution, but the Sooners were penalized five yards for a delay of game, placing the ball back to the OU 44. Two plays later, Jacobs fired a 39-yard pass to Mattox to the Husker 17 with 15 seconds left in the game. Haberlein was sent in to boot the Sooners to victory, but his 37-yard attempt from an angle sailed wide right.

"We all thought it was in there," Haberlein said of the kick.

The Sooners finished Luster's first season with a 6-3 record and tied for second place in the Big Six with a 3-2 mark. Eason and Jacobs were named to the conference's first team.

On the same day of the OU-Nebraska tilt, President Roosevelt announced, "Our boys in military and naval academies may be fighting for the defense at American institutions" by the next Thanksgiving.

Eight days later, the Japanese bombed Pearl Harbor. The United States declared war on Japan one day after the bombing.

1941 Season Record: 6-3-0
Big Six Conference: 3-2 (Second)

Date	Opponent	Result	Score
September 27	OKLAHOMA A&M	W	19-0
October 11	Texas at Dallas	L	40-7
October 18	at Kansas State	W	16-0
October 25	SANTA CLARA	W	16-6
November 1	KANSAS	W	38-0
November 8	IOWA STATE	W	55-0
November 15	at Missouri	L	28-0
November 22	MARQUETTE	W	61-14
November 29	at Nebraska	L	7-6

1942

"Sport will have to get along with what it has left. There won't be any stars on the professional side. I don't think there will be many stars left on the amateur side for college football, either."

—Grantland Rice, September 1, 1942

The United States was immersed in World War II. A total of 22 Sooner players and assistants, including Junior Golding, Plato Andros, and Carl Brewington, volunteered for military duties. J.S. Munsey returned to the Sooners but was waiting a call from the air corps. He received his orders from the air corps after the Texas game.

Jap Haskell, OU's athletic director and coach Dewey Luster's line assistant, served as a lieutenant commander in the Navy. Orville Tuttle, who had just played five years for the New York Giants, replaced Haskell tutoring the Sooner linemen. Dale Arbuckle, assistant backfield coach, assumed the duties as acting athletic director.

Numerous military football teams also surfaced around the country, including Norman Naval Air Station, which would be on the Sooners' schedule the next two years. Luster built his team with students from the university's naval reserve training corps.

Forty-two players showed up for the first practice, the smallest turnout in years. Yet there were enough returnees to give OU hope for success in 1942. Halfbacks Bill Campbell, Eddie Davis, and fullback Huel Hamm returned to the backfield. Tackle Homer Simmons and guard Clare Morford and end Dub Lamb returned to the line.

The Sooners opened their schedule with four road games and would not play at home until October 24 against Nebraska. OU also had a difficult time punching the ball across the goal line in its first three games. The Sooners were shut out in all three contests.

Oklahoma A&M also did not score in the Sooners' season opener on September 26, a scoreless tie in Stillwater before a crowd of 13,000.

The Aggies, three-touchdown underdogs, again believed this was their year to beat OU. The Sooners recovered a bad snap from center at the A&M 18 late in the first period. Backup end Archie Bradley fumbled it right back on the next play.

A&M was set up at the OU 35 following a punt early in the second quarter. Al Scanland completed a 26-yard pass to Lee Cook, who outmuscled J.S. Munsey for the ball. Oscar Williams gained only one yard on the next two runs, then Scanland sneaked ahead for three yards to the five. Williams was stopped a foot short of the goal line by several Sooners.

OU's next punt set up the Aggies at the Sooner 27. A&M gained nine yards on the next three plays, but Jack Steele stopped Ralph Tate short of a first down at the 17.

A punting duel ensued in the second half. The Aggies outgained OU in first downs (8-4) and total yards (183-82).

Luster was disappointed with his squad's 47-yard rushing performance and shook up the backfield roster before traveling to Tulsa the next week. The entire second unit was promoted to first string—Pat Shanks at quarterback, Sonny Wright and Davis at halfbacks, and Steele at fullback. The new backfield would provide bigger and faster players.

Tulsa, 1-0, was fresh from an 84-0 thrashing of Waco Field, one of many military teams. The Golden Hurricane shut down Oklahoma, 23-0, before 11,000 at Skelly Stadium.

The Sooners drove 42 yards to the Tulsa 15 in the second stanza, but Lamb fumbled Hamm's four-yard pass there, and the Hurricane recovered.

Tulsa quarterback N.A. Keithly hurled a 10-yard TD pass to Sax Judd on the final play of the first half. After stopping Tulsa inside the OU one early in the third quarter, the Sooners stalled, and Davis fumbled the punt snap in the end zone and Tulsa was awarded a safety.

The Hurricane scored twice more in the fourth stanza. Tulsa gained 14 first downs in the game and 301 total yards. Oklahoma, which gained nine first downs, improved in the running department with 135 yards and added 42 more through the air. Keithly, who completed 11 of 18 passes for 186 yards, scored on a five-yard run for the final TU tally.

Coach Luster jumbled the backfield again before the Big Red traveled to Dallas to meet Texas the following week—Davis, Hamm, Campbell, and Steele.

The Texas State Fair was cancelled, and the grounds had been turned over to armed forces camps. The 2-1 Longhorns were heavily favored to defeat Oklahoma on October 10 but won only 7-0 with a third-quarter touchdown. A crowd of 20,000 turned out for the game, less than half of the prior year.

A short Texas punt in the second stanza gave OU possession at the UT 29. Several plays later, OU had to turn the ball over when Hamm's four-yard completion to Davis was inches short of a first down at the eight. Texas stalled deep in its own territory, and Roy Dale McKay boomed a punt to the OU 17 to get the Horns out of trouble.

The Steers advanced into OU territory following the second-half kickoff. The Big Red defense held them at the 31, but McKay's punt pinned the Sooners deep at the two. Oklahoma also stalled, and Hamm punted to Jackie Field who returned the ball to the OU 32. On the next play, McKay fired a touchdown pass to Kenneth Mathews. McKay missed the conversion, but OU was flagged for offside. McKay's second effort was good.

Texas marched to the OU 19 on its next series, but safety Boone Baker intercepted McKay's pass at the five and nearly got away for a touchdown. McKay was the only Longhorn chasing him, and Baker was stopped at midfield by numerous orange jerseys.

Oklahoma later gained possession at the UT 30 on a wild snap from center. The Sooners moved to the Texas 10, but Hamm's third- and fourth-down passes misfired. The Steers later intercepted Hamm's pass at the OU 17, but Jack Marsee picked off the Steers' pass three plays later at the 10.

Texas gained 276 yards, and the Sooners managed 130 total yards.

The Sooner backfield remained the same for the Kansas tilt the next week. OU found its offensive punch with a 25-0 victory on a drizzly day before 4,000 fans in Lawrence.

The offense, unable to get past the Jayhawks' 40 through the first 20 minutes, drove to the first touchdown of the year following Hamm's punt return to the KU 47. Hamm completed a 22-yard pass to Bill Mattox down the middle. Kansas was flagged for too much time on the next play, moving the ball to the 14. Four plays later, Davis scored from the one, but Hamm's conversion was wide.

OU scored again with slightly more than a minute gone in the third stanza. Davis returned the second-half kickoff to the OU 35 then gained 15 more on a carry to midfield. Hamm fired a pass over the middle to Mattox at the KU 23. Mattox nearly lost his balance after the catch then stiff-armed KU's Ray Evans and shot to the end zone. Hamm's conversion was low.

Davis returned a Kansas punt 17 yards to the KU 42 late in the third period. Two plays later, Hamm tossed a pass to reserve end Don McDonald to the Hawks' five. Davis gained four yards on the next play but was a foot short of the goal line. He plowed over for the score on the next play. Hamm's extra point was good, and the Sooners held a 19-0 advantage.

Oklahoma made it 25-0 early in the fourth quarter. Hamm's five-yard TD run capped a 61-yard drive in nine plays. Steele's conversion was wide.

The Sooners gained 16 first downs and 333 (201 rushing and 132 passing) total yards. The defense held the Jayhawks to eight first downs and 144 total yards. Kansas never moved past the OU 38 in the game.

Oklahoma's first home game was not pleasant. Nebraska (1-3) defeated the Sooners, 7-0, the next week before 20,000 fans.

NU's Vic Schleich blocked Davis' punt early in the second period, and Bill Bryant recovered for the Huskers at the OU 31. Dale Bradley carried on all six plays, capping the drive on a two-yard run. On second-and-eight at the 29, he looked for an open receiver to throw to, but found a huge gap in the line and scooted for 13 yards. Schleich toed the extra point.

The Sooners blew two scoring chances in the first and fourth quarters. After advancing to the Husker 18 in the first period, Davis gained a first down on a five-yard run, but OU was penalized for backfield in motion, erasing the play. Hamm's fourth-down pass to Sonny Wright was incomplete.

Early in the fourth quarter, the Sooners drove 74 yards to the NU six, but Hamm fumbled there, and the Huskers recovered.

"We've got a case of the goal-line jitters," Luster said about his offense.

Oklahoma gained 317 yards and 11 first downs. The Huskers had eight first downs and 170 total yards. Starting left tackle Sam Stephens broke his wrist and was lost for the remainder of the season. Stanley Green was moved from backup center to replace him. Bradley quit the team to be with his sick mother. Mattox did not play against Iowa State due to an injured leg.

The Sooners traveled to Ames on October 31 and edged the Cyclones, 14-7, before a crowd of 7,500. Oklahoma scored the first touchdown in the game's first six minutes.

Huel Hamm's punt rolled out at the three putting Iowa State in a hole. The Cyclones punted out to the IS 46. Davis picked up 11 yards to the 35 on the next three carries, then Hamm hurled a pass to Baker who pulled in the ball at the 15 and scored untouched. Hamm toed the conversion.

Marsee intercepted a Cyclone pass midway through the second stanza and returned it to the I-State 14. Five plays later, Davis plowed over from the two, and Hamm converted. Baker caught a seven-yard pass from Hamm for a crucial first down two plays before the score.

Late in the third period, Royal Lohry returned Hamm's punt 27 yards to the OU 23 then scored on a one-yard run four plays later.

Neither team threatened the rest of the way. Iowa State led the way with nine first downs to six for Oklahoma, but the Sooners had the edge in total yards (156-107).

OU broke its own Big Six scoring record the following week with a 76-0 rout of Kansas State before 8,000 fans in Norman. The Wildcats had lost six straight after winning their season opener. Lt. George Halas, Chicago Bears coach, attended the game. He was stationed at the Norman naval base at the time.

Eight Sooners combined for 11 touchdowns on a cloudy and overcast day. Wright scored three times and Shanks twice. Davis, Hamm, Don Fauble, Pete Cawthon, Myrle Greathouse, and Leroy Neher also crossed the goal line.

The Sooners scored twice in the first quarter and once in the second to lead 21-0 at halftime. None of the starters saw action after the first 13 minutes of action. The Big Red scored on seven straight possessions in the second half, and the third string played in the fourth period, adding five touchdowns.

The victory eclipsed OU's 55-0 record set a year earlier against Iowa State. The Sooners gained 28 first downs, rushed for 323 yards and passed for 172 more. The Cats were held to four first downs, 102 passing yards and minus-33 rushing yards.

Marsee injured his shoulder and was out for the vital Missouri tilt the next week. Green moved over from guard to replace him. Jack Jacobs returned to Norman after a stint with the professional league's Cleveland Rams. He stopped off in Norman before heading out to Air Force duty in California. While in Norman, he attended

by the Sooners' practice and threw passes simulating Missouri's T formation.

The Tigers (6-2 overall and 3-0 in the Big Six) rolled into Norman on November 14 fresh off a 26-6 win over Nebraska, the worst defeat Missouri had ever put on the Huskers.

Oklahoma spoiled the Tigers' perfect conference record with a 6-6 tie before 20,000 homecoming fans.

Missouri's Harold Adams took the opening kickoff at the 15, sped downfield and lateraled the ball to Bob Steuber, who raced the final 25 yards for a touchdown. The Tigers were penalized for being offside on the kickoff, which wiped out the score. Hamm kicked off again, but the ball rolled out of bounds, giving Mizzou the ball at the Tiger 35.

Adams fumbled on the next play, and Green recovered for Oklahoma. The Sooners advanced to the MU 14, but Davis fumbled and Missouri took over at the 16.

Campbell blocked Fred Bouldin's punt late in the first half, and Lamb scooped up the ball, returning it seven yards to the Tiger 10 with 30 seconds remaining. Hamm rifled an eight-yard pass to Lamb. Oklahoma called a timeout with 20 seconds until intermission.

Mizzou's Ralph Carter deflected Hamm's next pass to Boone Baker. Six ticks remained on the clock. Davis bulled through the middle, and officials signaled "touchdown" after unpiling the players with two seconds left. Hamm's conversion sailed wide, but OU held a 6-0 halftime lead, the first time Missouri trailed at halftime all year.

The Tigers whirled 80 yards in five plays to tie the game early in the fourth stanza. An unnecessary roughness penalty on the Sooners aided the drive, placing the ball at the MU 49. On the next play, Steuber faked a handoff and uncorked a high spiral to end Marshal Shanuas. Baker was shadowing the Tiger end on the play, and both leaped for the ball but Shaunas clutched it when he crashed to the turf at the OU nine. Ervin Pitts scored from the five two plays later. Steuber's conversion was wide right with 13:30 remaining.

Neither team threatened the rest of the way. The Sooners had 13 first downs and 219 total yards. Missouri gained 10 first downs and 196 total yards. The Tigers had 167 rushing yards, but the Big Red defense pushed them back for 32 yards, giving Mizzou 135 net rushing yards. The defense had forced opponents 318 yards behind the line of scrimmage through eight games.

The Sooners traveled to Philadelphia on November 21 to meet the Temple Owls. The 1-4-3 Owls won, 14-7, before 14,000 fans.

Oklahoma failed to tally a point on three scoring opportunities in the first three quarters. A first-quarter drive to the Temple 20 ended when Hamm misfired a fourth-down pass to Baker. The Sooners charged to the Owls' five moments later but had to surrender on downs. OU again advanced to the Temple five, midway through the third period. On fourth down, Hamm's 10-yard pass to Lamb was five yards short of a first down.

The Owls first scored with six minutes remaining until halftime. Joe Nejman connected an eight-yard pass to Bill Walitis on fourth down. Jim Woodside intercepted Hamm's pass and returned it 25 yards to give Temple a 14-0 lead with six minutes left in the game.

The Sooners got on board with two minutes to go after Don Fauble hammered Harry Sylvester, forcing a fumble. Don McDonald recovered for OU at the Owls' 44, but Fauble had to be carried off on a stretcher with a slight concussion. Two plays later, Mattox's reverse gained 13 yards, then Hamm hurled a 31-yard TD pass to Shanks. Hamm booted the extra point.

Temple gained 11 first downs and 245 total yards. OU picked up eight first downs and 202 total yards.

The Big Red hosted No. 19 William and Mary (8-1-1) in the final game without Luster, who was confined at home with influenza. Arbuckle and Tuttle took over the head coaching duties.

The Indians came to Norman on December 5 sporting an 8-1-1 record. They had outscored their opponents 231 to 48.

The game marked the 50th anniversary celebration of the University of Oklahoma's founding. William and Mary spoiled the festivities with a 14-7 victory, but the Sooners would not bow without a fight to the end before 4,500 shivering fans.

The Indians took a 7-0 lead midway through the second quarter on John Korczowski's eight-yard run. William and Mary upped the lead to 14-0 with a 47-yard march in three plays late in the third stanza. Bobby Hubard tossed a 32-yard pass to Glenn Knox to cap the drive.

The Sooners answered with a 69-yard scoring drive in three plays early in the fourth stanza. From the OU 33, Hamm faked a pass and gained 20 yards up the middle to the Indians' 47. The Sooners were flagged for offside on the next play, then Hamm shot a 13-yard pass to Davis to the WM 39. Davis took a handoff on the next play and scooted to the end zone. Hamm converted.

The Big Red threatened twice on the next two series but had to surrender on downs. Davis fumbled at the Indians' 25 to end the first threat, and Hamm's fourth-down pass misfired on the second charge.

The Sooners threatened late in the game, which had the crowd on its feet. OU took possession after Bob Longacre's punt rolled out of bounds at the Indians' 36. Jack Fauble replaced Hamm, who was slightly injured earlier in the game. Fauble tossed two passes to Mattox to the Indians' nine. Sooner guard George Gibbons was flagged for clipping on the second pass, placing the ball back at the 25.

Hamm replaced Fauble, but his third-down pass to Davis sailed over the end zone. Hamm directed a pass to Lamb, but the Indians' Nick Forkovitch knocked it down at the goal line with 15 seconds remaining.

OU gained 13 first downs, rushed for 165 yards and passed for 103 more. Davis rushed for 121 yards. William and Mary gained seven first downs and 165 total yards.

The Sooners finished the season with a disappointing 3-5-2 record and second (behind Missouri) in the conference with a 3-1-1 mark.

Six Sooners were named to the All-Big Six first team, the most Sooners named to an all-conference team to date. Those selected were: Campbell, Hamm, Lamb, Marsee, Morford, and Simmons.

1942 Season Record: 3-5-2
Big Six Conference: 3-1-1 (Second)

Date	Opponent	Result	Score
September 26	at Oklahoma A&M	T	0-0
October 3	at Tulsa	L	23-0
October 10	Texas at Dallas	L	7-0
October 17	at Kansas	W	25-0
October 24	NEBRASKA	L	7-0
October 31	at Iowa State	W	14-7
November 7	KANSAS STATE	W	76-0
November 14	MISSOURI	T	6-6
November 21	at Temple	L	14-7
November 29	WILLIAM & MARY	L	14-7

1943

College football rosters around the country were being depleted by the war. Young men were either drafted or volunteered for the military. Many college teams abandoned football altogether in 1943 and some did not return to field a team until after the war. The University of Oklahoma, however, was not one of them, yet only halfback Boone Baker and reserve tackle Lee Kennon were returnees from the 1942 lineup.

Forty-two of the Sooners' 44 lettermen and 45 of 50 freshmen in 1942 did not return to the squad. Head coach Snorter Luster's roster was built with military trainees and high school lads. His team was younger, lighter, and shorter.

The Sooners did receive good news at the start of training camp when Bob Brumley joined the team. The 26-year-old Brumley, a former Rice halfback from 1939-1941, was on the physical fitness staff of OU's naval trainee program. End Jim Desmond also joined the team bringing some experience to the lineup. Desmond came to OU from Santa Clara, one of the teams that canceled football that year.

W.G. "Dub" Wooten and Thurman Tigart also returned to the team. Wooten played sparingly at end in 1942, and Tigart was an upstart tackle from the freshman squad.

The Sooners held a closed practice scrimmage against Will Rogers Field, an Oklahoma City military team, in Norman a week before the home opener. No results were reported on the outcome.

OU won its first two games, lost the next two, and finished with a flurry of wins all against conference foes to claim the school's fifth conference championship.

The Sooners opened the '43 campaign against Norman Naval Air Station, another military team, which had a roster consisting of players from 12 major colleges and universities.

The Sooners defeated the Zoomers, 22-6, on September 25 before 10,000 fans. Soldiers and sailors filled most sections of Memorial Stadium. A Navy band and a squad of 275 preflight cadets entertained at halftime.

Brumley scored two touchdowns and passed for another for the Big Red, but a first-quarter gaffe nearly got the Zoomers on board first. Brumley fumbled a punt return, and John Svenson recovered for NAS. The Zoomers advanced to the Sooner five, but Derald Lebow nailed Dave Currie for a nine-yard loss, and Steve Andrejkos missed a 32-yard field-goal try.

Lewis Dunn later intercepted a Zoomer pass at the NAS 41 and returned it seven yards. Brumley slammed through right tackle three plays later and converted the extra point.

Brumley missed a field-goal attempt early in the second stanza when the ball bounced off the upright.

Oklahoma held a 7-0 lead through intermission but scored on the opening drive of the second half. Brumley's four-yard run capped a 65-yard drive in seven plays. Brumley's conversion was wide, but he did spark the drive with a 32-yard pass to Desmond to the Zoomers' 21.

The Zoomers later marched 70 yards for a touchdown but missed the extra point.

OU's lead increased to 15-6 when Desmond and John Harley later blocked George Clay's punt, and the ball rolled behind the end zone. Brumley returned the free kick 28 yards to the NAS 33. Halfback Charley Heard carried on a reverse to the five, but the Sooners could not punch it over in three plays. On fourth-and-goal at the six, Brumley zipped a TD pass to Baker. Brumley also converted.

Oklahoma City's Taft Stadium, site of the OU-Oklahoma A&M game, hosted the first night game in Sooner football history. (*OU Athletics*)

OU gained eight first downs and 333 total yards. The Zoomers had six first downs and 182 total yards.

The Sooners scored 22 points for the second straight game as they dropped Oklahoma A&M, 22-13, at Oklahoma City's Taft Stadium the next week. A crowd of 12,000 turned out for OU's first night contest.

The Sooners jumped to a 3-0 advantage late in the first period on Brumley's 16-yard field goal moments after Wooten recovered Bob Fenimore's fumble at the A&M 13.

Baker's two-yard touchdown off a reverse capped a 55-yard march in 11 plays late in the second quarter. Brumley's toe made it 10-0 for Oklahoma.

The Aggies then moved to the OU 21, but Fenimore was dropped for a three-yard loss on fourth down, and the Sooners took over.

For the second straight game, OU marched to a touchdown following the second-half kickoff. Brumley circled left end, followed Lebow's block and scooted seven yards to the end zone. Brumley carried seven times for 56 yards in the 65-yard, 11-play drive, which included runs of 17 and 18 yards. His conversion was low and wide, but the Sooners held a 16-0 lead.

The Aggies scored minutes later on Fenimore's 20-yard pass to Bob Askey, but Fenimore's extra point sailed wide.

Tigart recovered Fenimore's fumble at the A&M 21 to set up another Sooner score late in the third stanza. Four plays later, Brumley scored from the one, but Neil Armstrong blocked Brumley's conversion.

Fenimore hooked up with Askey again with a six-yard TD pass early in the fourth quarter.

Oklahoma advanced to the Aggies' 15 when the game ended.

The Big Red gained 14 first downs, 261 yard rushing and 38 passing. Brumley carried 39 times for 146 yards. He also completed two of five passes. The defense held the Aggies to eight first downs and 167 total yards.

Desmond was injured in the Aggie game, and Omer Burgert replaced him at right end. Desmond would not play again in a crimson uniform as he received orders to join the Navy three weeks later.

OU traveled south to Dallas on October 9 for the annual war against 1-1 Texas. But the war overseas was also having its effect back in America. The Texas State Fair was canceled for a second straight year, and the war effort called for rationing of gasoline and tires. The crowd of 18,500 was the lowest turnout ever for the rivalry played at the Cotton Bowl.

Texas won 13-7 on a "Hail Mary" pass at the end of the first half and defense in the final 30 minutes.

The Steers set sail for an early touchdown after Ralph Park returned Brumley's 45-yard quick kick 16 yards to the OU 38. UT's Ralph Ellsworth lost three yards on the first play, and Bobby Lee fumbled on the next play, but Texas kept the ball as officials ruled the ball dead before the fumble. Park took a lateral on the following play and raced to the end zone. Lee's conversion was blocked.

Oklahoma threatened with a drive to the Horns' one late in the first stanza. The Sooners faced fourth-and-goal at the start of the second quarter, but Brumley failed to get the necessary yard to tie the game. A short Texas punt on the next series set up the Sooners at the UT 22, but the Big Red went nowhere on four downs.

The Sooners threatened again minutes later, but Lee intercepted Lebow's pass at the goal line and returned it eight yards. Oklahoma's defense pinned Texas deep, and another short punt gave the Sooners possession at the Steers' 18 with three minutes left until intermission.

The Horns swatted down Lebow's pass, but Texas was penalized for offside. Lebow picked up three yards to the 10. Brumley took a screen pass, but the Horns dumped him for a three-yard loss. Lebow gained eight yards and a first down as the UT five. Lebow slammed off tackle for the touchdown on the next play. Brumley's conversion gave OU a 7-6 lead, which they were unable to hold through halftime.

Lee returned the ensuing kickoff to the UT 37. Lee dropped back and unleashed a bomb to Ellsworth near the sideline at the OU 30. Ellsworth clutched the pass, slipped through several Sooner defenders and shot to the end zone. Park converted, and Texas had a 13-7 lead heading into the locker room.

Texas advanced to the OU 22 following the second-half kickoff but surrendered on downs. The Sooners punted eight times and tossed two interceptions in the second half. One final drive ended at the UT 22 when time expired.

Bob Brumley starred at halfback and fullback for the Sooners in 1943. The 26-year-old Brumley played for Rice before joining the physical fitness staff at OU's naval trainee program. He ran for eight touchdowns during the year, passed for two more, and caught one for another score. He also punted, kicked conversions, returned punts, and played on defense. Brumley also was the team captain. (*OU Athletics*)

Bob Brumley scores the first touchdown of the season on a four-yard run against Norman Naval Air Station. (*OU Athletics*)

OU's Louis Dollarhide fired a nine-yard TD pass to Joe Breeden on the next Sooner possession to cap a 61-yard drive in 14 plays. Lloyd Meinert converted for a 30-0 lead.

Meinert scored on an eight-yard run early in the fourth quarter, three plays after Hillard Parsons intercepted a Kansas State pass and returned it to the Cats' 15.

OU gained 10 first downs and 330 total yards. The defense held the Wildcats to six first downs and 54 (21 rushing and 33 passing) total yards.

Iowa State invaded Norman the following week. Although the Cyclones were 2-2 for the season, they had won both conference games to date. The Sooners sent the Cyclones back to Ames with their first conference loss, 21-7.

Oklahoma capitalized on two Cyclone punting mistakes in the first quarter. Iowa State was forced to punt on its first possession. The ball sailed against a stiff breeze and out at the Cyclone 19. Brumley scored on a 10-yard run four plays later. Heard took out two Cyclones with one block to open a lane for Brumley. Lebow converted, and the Sooners held a 7-0 lead in the game's first three and a half minutes.

Dinkins later blocked Howard Tippee's punt, and Gale Fulghum recovered for the Sooners at the Cyclones' 32. Brumley carried for 17 yards on the next play, and an I-State penalty placed the ball at the 10. Four plays later, Lebow scored from the one, and he also converted.

Iowa State drove from its 40 to the OU 23 late in the second quarter, but the Sooner defense stiffened from there. The Cyclones recovered its own fumble two yards back. Brumley then swatted away a second-down pass at the five. Iowa State tossed an incompletion, and Dinkins sacked Tippee for an 18-yard loss on fourth down.

The Cyclones drove to the OU 15 following the second-half kick-off but had to surrender on downs. They did score on their next series, a 46-yard drive capped by Joe Noble's 16-yard TD run.

The Sooners scored their final tally late in the fourth stanza, when Lebow zipped a four-yard TD pass to Wooten, who leaped two feet in the air to snag the pass in the end zone. Lebow kicked the conversion. Lebow sparked the drive with a 26-yard run to the IS 30, then tossed a 21-yard pass to Brumley to the IS seven.

Iowa State had more first downs (12-8) and total yards (286-233) in the loss.

The Sooners returned home November 6 for a homecoming clash with 2-3-1 Kansas. The winner would have the overall series lead as they were tied at 18-18-4 in prior meetings. OU gained the series edge with a 26-13 victory before 6,000 homecoming fans.

The Big Red scored on its first possession, a seven-yard run by Lebow. Brumley highlighted the 42-yard drive with runs of 20 and 13 yards. Brumley's conversion veered wide.

The Sooners faced third-and-nine at the KU 41 on their next possession. Lebow tossed a six-yard pass to Burgert who flew 35 more down the sideline for a touchdown. The score capped a 43-yard drive in three plays, and Brumley converted for a 13-0 lead.

The Jayhawks advanced from their 31 to the OU six late in the first quarter and into the second. Brumley intercepted Bob George's pass at the two and returned the ball 15 yards. The Sooners then set sail for another touchdown. Brumley's 39-yard TD run gave the Sooners a 19-0 lead, but he missed the conversion.

The Sooners had more first downs (11-7) and rushing yards (143-115), but the Horns had more passing yards (120-74).

Undefeated Tulsa (3-0) handed the Sooners their second defeat of the season, 20-6, the next week before 15,000 in another night game at Oklahoma City's Taft Stadium. The Golden Hurricane won with depth and experience. Tulsa's first and second units had 16 players who had competed in intercollegiate football prior to 1943. The Sooners only had six men with prior collegiate experience.

Tulsa threatened with a march to the OU 13 early in the first quarter, but the Sooner defense stiffened. Bob Mayfield's interception late in the first period sparked the only Sooner touchdown. Mayfield returned the interception five yards to the OU 49.

Lebow's one-yard TD run capped the scoring march in which he carried for all but three yards in the drive. Brumley's conversion was wide, but OU held the 6-0 lead through halftime.

Tulsa tied the game early in the third quarter with a 29-yard pass from Clyde LeForce to Clyde Goodnight. LeForce, who completed only four of 13 first-half passes, completed all six in the scoring drive, and he converted the extra point for a 7-6 Hurricane advantage.

The Hurricane scored again early in the fourth period after blocking Brumley's punt. Jim Stegman scooped up the ball at the OU 20 and sped to the end zone. LeForce toed the conversion.

LeForce fired a 10-yard TD pass to Ed Shedlosky early in the fourth stanza for the final tally. The Sooners never threatened again.

The Hurricane gained 11 first downs and 247 total yards. OU picked up only five first downs and 197 total yards.

Lewis Dunn suffered a torn rib cartilage, which further diminished the OU roster. Coach Luster moved Brumley to fullback and Lebow to halfback for the conference opener against Kansas State on October 23 in Manhattan.

OU blasted the 1-2 Wildcats, 37-0, before 3,000 fans on a muddy field in Manhattan.

Lebow returned a Kansas State punt 22 yards to the Wildcats' 34 to set up the first score late in the first period. Brumley scored on a 10-yard run eight plays later and toed the extra point.

Lebow completed a 33-yard TD pass to Merle Dinkins early in the second stanza. Brumley's conversion gave the Sooners a 14-0 lead. OU added a safety on a wild snap to the K-State punter. The ball rolled into the end zone, and Dinkins tackled the punter there.

Lebow's 23-yard punt return to the Wildcat 46 set up the next Sooner score midway through the third period. Lebow shot to the end zone on the next play, and Brumley converted.

The Hawks then drove to the OU 16 on a 46-yard pass from Don Barrington to George. Brumley's tackle saved a touchdown, and the Hawks had to surrender on downs four plays later. Kansas scored midway through the second quarter on George's three-yard run. John Bergin's conversion bounced off the crossbar.

Late in the third period, Burgert returned a KU pass 61 yards for a touchdown. Brumley's extra point lifted the Sooners to a 26-6 advantage. The Jayhawks answered with a 60-yard George-to-Bergin TD pass, and George converted.

Kansas advanced from its 42 to the OU 27 early in the fourth stanza, but center Bob Stover picked off George's pass at the 12. Neither team threatened again.

The Jayhawks gained more first downs (13-9) and passing yards (234-48), but Oklahoma had more rushing yards (216-45). Lebow gained 105 yards on 25 carries.

Kennon suffered a sprained ankle against the Cyclones and would not return the rest of the season. John Harley replaced him at right tackle. Wooten also missed the next game, a Big Six showdown with Missouri.

The Big Six conference lead was on the line November 13 when the Sooners met Missouri in Columbia. OU and Missouri sat atop the conference standings with identical 3-0 records. The 3-3 Tigers won all their games against conference foes. Mizzou averaged 343.8 yards per game in total offense to rank eighth in the nation.

The Sooners ended the Tigers' 44-game home winning streak with a 20-13 victory before a crowd of 7,000.

The Tigers marched 60 yards in seven plays to score on their first possession. Fullback Don Reece's one-yard plunge capped the drive, but Jack Morton missed the conversion.

Burgert's recovery of a Tiger fumble at the MU 26 late in the first quarter led to a Sooner touchdown early in the second period.

Lebow then hurled a 22-yard pass to Brumley to the MU four. Four plays later, Lebow plowed ahead from the three, but Brumley's conversion missed the target.

The Sooners jumped to a 13-6 lead minutes later when Lebow fired a 46-yard TD pass to Brumley. Brumley caught the ball in the flat and raced in for the score. Brumley converted this extra point. The score capped a six-play, 75-yard drive.

John Harley recovered a fumble at the MU 15 on the next Tiger possession, but moments later the Sooners gave the ball back when Missouri picked off Lebow's pass.

Early in the fourth stanza, Fulghum blocked Ralph Watzig's punt, and Mayfield recovered at the Tiger 20. Lebow scored three plays later on a five-yard run. Brumley's conversion struck the crossbar, but the ball went through for a 20-6 Sooner lead.

A short Oklahoma punt minutes later set up the Tigers at the OU 37. Ten plays later, Paul Collins scored from the one, and Morton converted. The Sooners held on as the Tigers failed to threaten again.

Missouri gained more first downs (13-9) and total yards (313-231). The Big Red defense held the Tigers to 31 yards less than their average total.

The 6-2 Sooners took over first place in the Big Six with a 4-0 conference record. The team arrived in Norman two days later and was welcomed by 1,000 fans. The players received kisses from the coeds as they stepped off the train. The women also gave the players kisses as they departed before the game. Brumley was the only one who didn't get bussed since he was married. Coach Luster was impressed by the show of emotions after they arrived back home.

"This looks like it pays to win," he said. "I believe this kissing was a good idea. Maybe we should have started it earlier in the season."

The Sooners had two weeks to prepare for Nebraska on November 27 in Lincoln. Kansas upset Missouri the next week, which clinched the Big Six championship for Oklahoma. The Sun Bowl and Cotton Bowl were mentioned as a possible postseason games for the Sooners. Oklahoma defeated 2-5 Nebraska, 26-7, in sub-freezing temperatures and under a gray sky. The victory before 3,500 fans was the first ever for Oklahoma in Lincoln.

Bob Brumley fumbled the ball away on the first two Sooner series. The second gave the Huskers' possession at the OU 29. Nebraska's Ted Kenfield fumbled it back moments later.

OU took a 6-0 lead later in the first period after Dinkins recovered a Husker fumble on the NU 28. Lebow hurled a 16-yard pass to Brumley then followed it with a 12-yard TD pass to Wooten. Brumley's conversion sailed wide left.

A President and Avid Sports Fan

Joseph A. Brandt resigned as president of the University of Oklahoma in 1943. Dr. George Lynn Cross was named acting president and appointed to the position in 1944.

Cross, a graduate of South Dakota State College, came to OU in 1934 after serving four years as head of the department of botany at the University of South Dakota. Cross was assistant professor of botany and microbiology at OU and also served as head of the department. He later was acting dean of the university's graduate college.

Cross, who played at South Dakota State on a football scholarship, said he always enjoyed sports as a participant and spectator who believed intercollegiate athletics provided "wholesome and exciting extracurricular activities," he wrote in his biography, *Presidents Can't Punt.*

Cross once quoted, "I would like to build a university of which the football team would be proud."

Cross made the statement when he appeared before the joint House-Senate Appropriations committee of the Oklahoma State Legislature in February 1951 to explain the university's needs for increased appropriations. After Dr. Cross made his presentation, the committee's chairman asked if anyone had any questions.

One senator replied, "I'd like to ask the good doctor why he thinks he needs so much money to run the University of Oklahoma?" Cross responded with his famous quote, which was spread nationally through newspapers and the *Reader's Digest, Time* and *Life* magazines.

"Some readers missed the gentle irony," Cross wrote in *Presidents Can't Punt.* He added that he made the statement by concluding, "that nothing by the way of logic would impress my questioner."

Cross would serve a quarter-century as OU president, longer than any president in the school's history.

1943 Season Record: 7-2-0

Big Six Conference: 5-0 (Champions)

Date	Opponent	Result	Score
September 25	NORMAN NAS	W	22-6
October 2	Oklahoma A&M*	W	22-13
October 9	Texas at Dallas	L	13-7
October 16	Tulsa*	L	20-6
October 23	KANSAS STATE	W	37-0
October 30	IOWA STATE	W	21-7
November 6	KANSAS	W	26-13
November 13	at Missouri	W	20-13
November 27	at Nebraksa	W	26-7

*Game played in Oklahoma City, OK

Nebraska intercepted Lebow's pass at the Husker nine to squelch a Sooner threat early in the second stanza, but OU scored on its next possession. Brumley's six-yard TD run and conversion gave the Sooners a 13-0 advantage. The score capped a 65-yard drive in seven plays. Lebow's 23-yard pass, on second-and-six from the NU 46, sparked the drive. Lebow hooked up with Wooten, who then lateraled to Brumley, and Brumley raced to the Husker 23.

The Sooners threatened again minutes later, but the half ended with the ball at the Husker 27.

OU got another chance early in the third quarter when Don Tillman's block of a Nebraska punt rolled out of bounds at the NU 35. Two plays later, Brumley picked up 19 yards to the 16. Two more plays had the ball inches short of the goal line, then Brumley plowed ahead for the score. Brumley missed the extra point, but the Sooners held a commanding lead, 19-0.

OU took a 26-0 lead when Lloyd Meinert scored on a three-yard run early in the fourth period and Brumley's conversion. The touchdown came 11 plays after Brumley returned a Husker punt 37 yards to the NU 49 late in the third quarter. Brumley completed a 12-yard pass to Homer Sparkman to overcome a fourth-and-one situation at the Nebraska 24.

The Huskers answered with a 68-yard TD drive and OU had possession at the NU 18 when the final gun cracked.

The Sooners gained 14 first downs and 392 (300 rushing and 92 passing) total yards. Brumley led the ground attack with 121 yards on 22 carries. OU's defense held the Huskers to nine first downs and 154 total yards.

The Cotton Bowl contemplated inviting the Sooners to play in Dallas but had already invited Texas. Longhorn coach Dana X. Bible was in favor of an OU-Texas rematch but said his players vetoed the idea.

Oklahoma finished the season with a 7-2 record and 5-0 atop the Big Six conference. Players received ruby-studded gold footballs as gifts from the university's athletic council.

For the second straight year, six Sooners were chosen to the all-conference first team—Wooten, Kennon, Fulgham, Mayfield, Brumley, and Lebow.

1944

Head coach Snorter Luster and Dale Arbuckle, assistant coach and acting athletic director, lobbied to change a kickoff rule during the Big Six meeting in Kansas City in August. The two Sooner mentors requested to have kickoffs made from the middle of the 40-yard line instead of near the sideline on the 40. They contended that their non-conference opponents had adopted the rule. The league agreed.

Thirteen lettermen returned to the 1944 Sooner squad, including seven starters. Derald Lebow and Charley Heard returned to a backfield that had more depth than the prior year. Bob Brumley was commissioned in the Navy, but Homer Sparkman, Bobby Estep, and Louis Dollarhide were veteran returnees with some playing experience. Tackle Thurman Tigart, guard John Harley, and center Bob Mayfield returned to anchor the front line. Veterans Dub Wooten and Merle Dinkins returned to the end positions. Wooten took over the placekicking duties in 1944.

The war continued to rage overseas, but the Allies were overwhelmingly commanding the enemy.

Coach Luster had employed three offensive formations for the season. The Single-Wing T had a tailback positioned 10 yards behind the line of scrimmage. Luster explained that many teams used this formation on punts, passes, and fake kicks and runs. It was not designed as a power running formation.

The Single Wing has the wingback positioned behind and a little outside the right end. Luster said this was designed as a power running formation with plenty of "ball faking and spinning."

The T formation positions one or both ends wide out to spread the defense. One back goes in motion either "swinging wide for a pass or coming back and blocking the defensive end," Luster said. He added, in some cases, two backs would go in motion. Missouri head coach Don Faurot was a "disciple" of the T formation but did not put a man in motion. Faurot's formation would change the future of Oklahoma football in two years.

"The T formation is a tough one to stop," Luster said. "I haven't found a way to stop it yet."

The Sooners opened the season for the second straight year against Norman's Naval Air Station Zoomers. The Zoomers were 16 pounds heavier to the man and had many seasoned players, including back Len Eshmont and Emil Sitko. Eshmont formerly played for the New York Giants, and Sitko played one year for Notre Dame.

The Zoomers defeated OU, 28-14, before 15,000 spectators at Owen Field on September 30.

Lebow returned the opening kickoff 46 yards to the OU 49, and the Sooners set sail on a 10-play scoring march. Lebow capped the drive with a one-yard TD run, and Wooten converted. Lebow and freshman fullback Bobby Wright carried on all but one play in the drive, which was a pass from Lebow to Dinkins.

Minutes later, Eshmont raced 40 yards for a touchdown after the Sooners were flagged for a pass interference call, which moved the ball from the Zoomers' seven to the OU 40. Dick Miller's conversion tied the game at 7-7.

The Zoomers added a field goal midway through the second stanza after they had blocked Lebow's quick kick. OU missed an opportunity to take the lead when Archie Bradley recovered a Zoomer fumble at the NAS 25. Tommy Meason zipped a pass to Bradley on the next play, but the first half ended when Bradley was tackled at the Zoomers' nine. Bradley later injured a knee and was lost for the rest of the season. Heard, who alternated with Bradley, replaced him the rest of the season.

NAS took a 16-7 lead early in the third period, eight plays after intercepting Meason's pass at the OU 44. Minutes later, Eshmont intercepted Lebow's pass and sprinted 60 yards for a touchdown. The Zoomers led, 28-7, on a 55-yard pass play midway through the fourth quarter.

The Sooners scored again minutes later when Dollarhide swept around left end for an 18-yard run one play after Estep returned a Zoomer punt 39 yards to the NAS 18. Don Weir converted.

The Zoomers gained 12 first downs and 433 total yards. OU had nine first downs and 349 total yards. The Zoomers never lost another game, going 6-0 in 1944.

The Sooners rebounded with a 21-14 victory over Texas A&M the following week before 15,000 at Oklahoma City's Taft Stadium. The night game was the first of four OU contests during the year at Taft. The Aggies played the first of seven contests in Oklahoma due to contractual negotiations. OU and Texas A&M played in Norman the next six years.

The Sooners took a 14-0 lead in the game's first 23 minutes. Lebow scored all three OU touchdowns, and Wooten successfully converted all extra points. The first score came on fourth-and-goal at the A&M two, and Lebow ripped through the middle for the score. Lebow's next touchdown came midway through the second quarter, capping a 76-yard march in six plays. Heard ignited the drive with a 62-yard run while shedding four tacklers to the Aggie five.

A&M countered with a 34-yard TD pass from Jimmy Cashion to Gene Spires to cap a 67-yard march in four plays. The Aggies tied the game at 14-14 on Paul Yates' one-yard run late in the third stanza.

The Sooners answered with 69-yard drive, using a mix of runs and passes. Lebow scored from the three with 11 minutes left in the game. The Aggies then advanced from their 35 to the OU 27, but had to surrender on downs. A&M did not threaten the rest of the game.

The Aggies edged the Sooners in first downs (15-14) and rolled up 417 total yards. Oklahoma gained 324 total yards.

OU and Texas met October 14 in Dallas in a battle of conference champions. The Sooners won the Big Six crown in 1943, and the Longhorns were tops in the Southwest Conference. This year's Steers (1-1) also lost to a military team, dropping a 42-6 decision to Randolph Field.

The Texas State Fair was silenced for the third straight year except for the 25,000 noisy partisans in the Cotton Bowl that afternoon. Bobby Layne, a freshman quarterback from nearby Parkland High School, tossed two touchdowns and booted two conversions in the 20-0 Texas victory.

Oklahoma had a chance to score early when a UT punt rolled out of bounds at the Texas 38. The Sooners quickly moved to the six for a first down, but a penalty moved the ball five yards back. OU got six yards on two plays then Lebow fired a pass to Sparkman, who was stopped inside the one. On fourth down, Lebow plowed through the middle, but the Horns held him short of the goal line.

The Steers scored their first touchdown late in the first period when Layne hurled a 17-yard TD pass to Hubert Bechtold. Layne converted for a 7-0 advantage.

Texas held the one touchdown lead through the third quarter then scored twice in the fourth.

OU had more first downs (5-4), but Texas gained more yards (206-157).

The Sooners smacked 0-2-1 Kansas State, 68-0, on October 21 before a crowd of 6,500 in Norman. Sparkman, Basil Sharp, Meason, and Estep each scored two touchdowns in the onslaught. Johnny West returned an interception for an 82-yard score and also passed for another touchdown. Wooten converted eight of 10 conversions, missing after the sixth and seventh TDs.

Oklahoma's first touchdown came on Sparkman's three-yard run on the Sooners' second possession of the game. Sharp scored on a one-yard plunge on the next series, one play after he sprinted 35 yards to the Wildcat one. It was Oklahoma, 14-0.

Sparkman sneaked across for a one-yard score on the next series early in the second quarter. Bill Hallett recovered a Cat fumble moments later at the KS 35. Meason slashed around right end for 28 yards on the next play, and then scored from the seven, making it OU 28, Kansas State 0.

Moments later, Estep returned a Cat punt 26 yards to the KS 44 to set up the next Sooner touchdown. Estep zipped around left end for a 25-yard TD six plays later.

Lebow returned the second-half kickoff 46 yards to the OU 49. On the first play from scrimmage, Sparkman lateraled to Sharp, who sailed around left end to the end zone. Wooten missed the conversion.

Coach Luster sent in the second and third stringers, and the reserves got their first score late in the third quarter. OU tackle Ed Parker blocked a Wildcat punt and Bob Gambrell recovered on the K-State 27. Meason's 23-yard scamper two plays later put

the Sooners ahead, 47-0, but Wooten again missed the conversion. He didn't miss the next three.

Moments later, Meason intercepted a Wildcat pass and returned it 35 yards to the KS 13. He scored from the three-yard line three plays later.

Kansas State then made its deepest penetration of the day, 37 yards to the OU 26. West intercepted a pass at the OU 18 and sprinted down the sideline for a touchdown.

West tossed a five-yard TD pass to Johnny Austin minutes later for the final tally. The Sooners had advanced 31 yards to the K-State 10 when the game ended.

OU rolled up 744 total yards (404 rushing and 158 passing) and 17 first downs. The defense held the Wildcats to nine first downs, 52 rushing yards, and 50 passing yards.

The win was Oklahoma's fifth straight shutout over the Cats and eighth consecutive victory dating back to 1937.

The next game against Texas Christian October 28 in Oklahoma City would be the final game for four Sooner players who were commissioned to the Navy—Estep, Harley Smalley, Ed Parker, and Jim Marr.

The Horned Frogs were 3-0-1 and had yielded only 13 points in their first four games. OU more than doubled that figure with a 34-19 victory before 11,000 fans in a night contest at Oklahoma City's Taft Stadium.

Two blocked punts propelled the crimson boys to a 14-0 lead. Dinkins blocked Ransom Jackson's punt early in the opening period. The ball bounced back to the end zone where Dinkins smothered it for a touchdown. Wooten nailed the extra point.

Wooten partially blocked Albert Cragwell's punt early in the second stanza. The ball traveled forward less than 10 yards, and OU was awarded possession at the Frog 22. TCU coach Dutch Meyer came onto the field protesting to officials. His team received a 15-yard penalty for unsportsmanlike conduct. OU's ball at the TCU seven. Lebow gained three yards, then fired a TD pass to Heard.

The Frogs drove 78 yards for a score following the second-half kickoff. OU countered with a 37-yard scoring strike from Lebow to Wooten. The touchdown capped a 74-yard march in six plays, and Wooten converted.

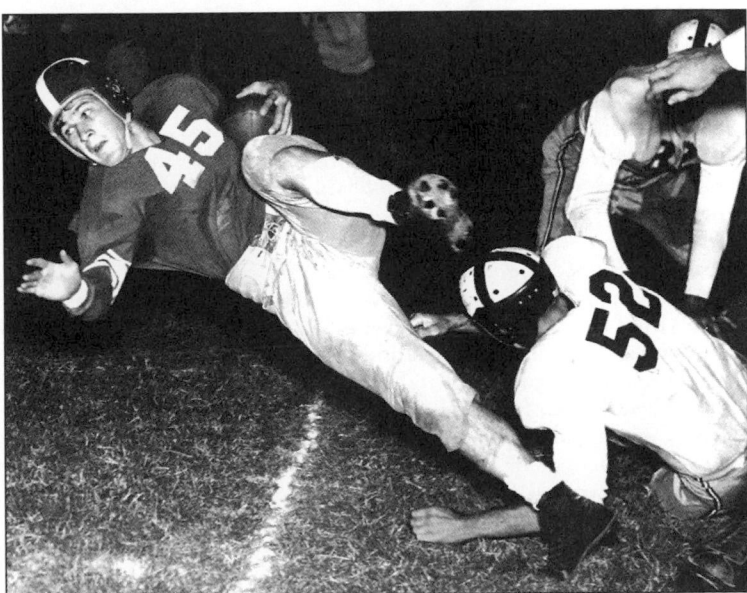

Halfback Charley Heard lunges for extra yards on a 12-yard run against Texas A&M. (*OU Athletics*)

TCU responded with another touchdown and blocked Lebow's punt moments later to set up another score.

Oklahoma held a 21-19 edge going into the fourth stanza. Mayfield intercepted Kucera's pass early in the period and returned it 18 yards to the TCU six. Two plays later, Lebow scored from the four, and Wooten converted for a 28-19 lead.

Elvin Jackson later intercepted a Frog pass at the TCU 44, and the Sooners scored three plays later. Estep scored his final touchdown as a Sooner on a 28-yard run. Wooten missed the extra point.

Tommy Meason scores on a nine-yard run for the Sooners' second touchdown against Nebraska at Oklahoma City's Taft Stadium. Thurman Tigart (dark uniform on the ground) blocks out two Huskers. (*OU Athletics*)

Oklahoma had more first downs (8-7), but the Horned Frogs had the most yards—162 to 158 rushing and 109-95 passing.

The Sooners returned to conference action November 4 and spoiled Iowa State's homecoming with a 12-7 victory before a crowd of 9,000.

Hallett set up the first Oklahoma score when he recovered a Cyclone fumble at the IS 25 on the final play of the first quarter. Four plays later, Derald Lebow slanted off tackle for an eight-yard touchdown. Don Tillman, Harley, and Dinkins flattened the left side of the Cyclone line to provide Lebow an alley to the end zone. Wooten missed the conversion. Lebow also bumped his head on the ground in the end zone and staggered back to the Sooner bench. He would not play the rest of the day.

West replaced Lebow and led the charge to another Sooner touchdown on the next series. Oklahoma advanced from its 35 to the IS 17, but a holding penalty moved the ball back 15 yards. Sparkman threw an incomplete pass, then West gained 14 yards on the next play. West completed the third-down pass to Sparkman to the seven, one yard shy of a first down. Sharp blasted through to the end zone on the next play. Wooten made the conversion, but the Sooners were guilty of holding again. Wooten's 35-yard extra-point kick missed the target.

Oklahoma led 12-0 with six minutes until halftime and Coach Luster put in the reserves. Moments later, I-State's Gene Phelps rambled 69 yards for a touchdown. Meredith Warner toed the conversion to trail the Sooners, 12-7.

The Cyclones had a chance to capture the lead late in the third period after James Riding recovered Sharp's fumble at the OU four-yard line. The Big Red defense rose up and successfully protected the lead.

Tillman stopped Joe Noble for no gain on first down. Tillman and Wooten stopped Noble after a two-yard gain. Noble tried a fake pass on third down and ran to the weak side. Harley met him there and dropped Noble for a two-yard loss. Noble lateraled to halfback Dick Howard on fourth down. West and Sparkman charged fast and knocked Howard out of bounds inside the one.

The Cyclones advanced to the OU 12 early in the fourth quarter but were again met by a stubborn Sooner defense. Neither team threatened to score again.

Oklahoma doubled the Cyclones in first downs (14-7) and gained more total yards (287-200).

Lebow saw limited duty against Missouri the next week, not due to the concussion suffered in the Cyclone game, but by a cold. Physicians limited the halfback to one play per half. Lebow scored a touchdown on each play. Heard also had a cold and was confined to the university's infirmary.

The Sooners and Tigers battled to a 21-21 standoff on November 11 before 12,000 homecoming fans in Norman.

The Tigers scored first, eight plays after recovering Max Culver's fumble at the OU 30. Paul Collins' four-yard TD run and Jim Kekeris' conversion put Mizzou up 7-0 late in the first period.

OU drove 65 yards to the MU one mostly on West's running and passing. Lebow entered the game with the ball at the Tiger one. He got the call on the next play and plowed off right tackle for the score. Wooten converted for the tie.

The Sooners drove to their second touchdown following the second-half kickoff. Dinkins returned the kickoff to the MU 45, but a 15-yard penalty moved the ball back to the OU 40. West fired an 18-yard pass to Wooten, and Culver then gained 22 yards to the Tigers' 10. West picked up four more yards, then Sharp slashed over left tackle for the score. Wooten converted, and the Sooners led, 14-7, with three minutes into the second half.

West returned a Tiger punt 23 yards to the MU 12 moments later. Culver gained 10 yards to the two, and Lebow reentered the game and scored on the next play. Wooten's conversion put the Sooners up, 21-7.

Missouri continued to capitalize on OU's mistakes. Early in the fourth stanza, Dan Robinson intercepted West's pass and returned it 40 yards to the OU 30. Collins scored on a three-yard run five plays later, and Kekeris converted.

West, who also punted for Oklahoma, later left the game with a twisted ankle. Sparkman replaced him and shanked a punt off the side of his foot late in the game. The ball sailed out of bounds at the OU 34. Collins scored on a two-yard run 12 plays later and Kekeris' foot tied the game with 30 seconds remaining.

OU gained more first downs (11-6) and total yards (367-259). Before West left the game with an injury, he had 245 total yards— 62 rushing, 84 passing and 89 on kick returns.

Kansas governor Andrew Schoeppel was in Oklahoma City for a meeting on Monday prior to the OU-Kansas matchup the following Saturday. He said the Jayhawks would defeat the Sooners. Schoeppel, a former Nebraska end in the early 1920s, said he would attend the game in Lawrence "to see the Jayhawkers win."

Lebow and Heard returned to the Oklahoma lineup, but starting tackle Millard Cummings (bruised knee) and West would not play against the Jayhawks. Hallett replaced Cummings, and Meason filled in for West.

OU defeated 3-4-1 Kansas, 20-0, on November 18 before a crowd of 4,500. The Sooners' first score came moments after Wooten blocked a Kansas punt late in the first quarter. Oklahoma took over at the KU 33, and moments later Lebow scored from the one. Wooten converted, and OU held a 7-0 lead with six minutes left in the opening stanza.

The Hawks advanced into Oklahoma territory late in the second period, but the Sooner defense stiffened and OU took over at the 15. The Sooners drove downfield, but Kansas took over at its one-yard line when officials said Sharp did not cross the goal line.

Oklahoma drove 78 yards in four plays for its second touchdown following the second-half kickoff. Lebow shot a 33-yard pass to Heard, then carried for 15 yards on the next play. Lebow hurled a 29-yard pass to Sharp to the KU one. Sparkman hammered through for the touchdown, and Wooten converted.

Tillman recovered a Kansas fumble on a poor punt snap at the Hawks' 19 late in the third quarter. Meason fired a pass on the next play, but KU's Ken Dannenberg intercepted in the end zone.

Kansas advanced into Oklahoma territory in the fourth quarter, but Bobby Wright intercepted Charles Moffett's pass at the 30. On the next play, Meason carried for 53 yards to the KU 17. Wright sprinted to the end zone on the following play, but Wooten missed the conversion.

The Sooners had one more first down (12-11), but clearly dominated in total yards (368 241).

Oklahoma A&M defeated the Sooners, 28-6, on November 25 before 18,000 at Oklahoma City's Taft Stadium. A&M, at 6-1, lost only to Norman Naval Station. The Aggies scored twice in the first quarter and twice more in the third period for their first win over OU since 1933.

Bob Fenimore scored on a one-yard run early in the first stanza, and Cecil Haskins scored on a 40-yard punt return minutes later.

The Sooners twice had a chance to make a game of it in the first half. They advanced 42 yards to the A&M 16 but had to surrender on downs. OU moved from its 42 to the A&M four in the second period, but Lebow was stopped short on a fourth-and-one play.

Jim Spavital's one-yard TD run gave the Aggies a 21-0 advantage in the third quarter, then John Gattis intercepted West's pass for another score.

The Sooners got on board early in the fourth period. Lebow returned Joe Thomas' punt 26 yards to the Aggie 39. Dollarhide took the ball from Sparkman and scored on the next play. The Aggies blocked Wooten's kick.

The Aggies had more first downs (9-7) and total yards (371-280).

The Sooners returned to Taft Stadium again on December 2 to host 2-5 Nebraska. Oklahoma clinched its second straight Big Six title with a 31-12 victory over the Cornhuskers, the most points ever scored on a Nebraska team to date.

Omer Burgert recovered a Nebraska fumble on the second play of the game at the Husker 40. Eleven plays later, Lebow scored from the one. He also sparked the drive with a 22-yard pass to Dollarhide. Lebow missed the conversion.

The Sooners jumped to a 12-0 lead on Meason's nine-yard TD run early in the second stanza to cap a 65-yard drive that began late in the first period. Meason missed the extra point.

A poor Nebraska punt a minute later gave OU the ball at the Husker 20. On the next play, Sparkman hit off right guard and cut back left to the end zone. Wooten converted the only extra point all day for a 19-0 advantage.

The Sooners later marched 47 yards in five plays for another score. Meason completed a 36-yard pass to Wooten on the fourth play of the drive to the NU 14. Wooten had to wrestle the ball from NU's Bill Betz for the completion. Meason then arched the ball to Wooten, who was all alone in the end zone. Wooten caught the pass just before stepping out of the end zone.

The Huskers scored twice in the second half, both times against the Sooner reserves.

Oklahoma's final touchdown came late in the third quarter when Lebow fired a 31-yard pass to Dinkins.

Oklahoma gained nine first downs and 269 total yards. The defense held the Huskers to eight first downs and 254 total yards.

The Sooners finished the season with a 6-3-1 record and their second straight Big Six Conference crown. Dinkins, Harley Mayfield, and Wooten were selected to the all-conference first unit.

1945

The war was over. Germany surrendered in May, and Japan surrendered in August. Servicemen would be coming home, and many of them still had football eligibility remaining. Tommy Tallchief and Harvey Stone, both freshmen in 1941, returned to the Oklahoma football squad in 1945. Tallchief and Stone were the first Sooner players to enlist in the service.

Guards Thurman Tigart and Don Tillman and end John Harley returned to anchor the line, but Harley suffered a knee injury in preseason practice and was lost for the year. Omer Burgert, a starter in 1943 and sub in '44, replaced Harley at right end. Aubrey McCall, a six-foot, five-inch Naval trainee from Maryland, started opposite at left end. Tallchief moved to the starting slot at left tackle, and freshman Bob Bodenhamer earned the nod at center.

Halfback Johnny West and fullback Basil Sharp were the only backfield returnees with playing time in 1944. New faces in the backfield included quarterback Clifford Stone, halfback Bill Irvin, and fullback Jack Venable. Sharp was held out of the first game due to scholastic ineligibility.

Reserve seats went for $2.50 each per game, but service personnel got into OU home games for $1.

The Sooners opened the season September 22 with a 21-6 victory over Hondo (Texas) Army Air Field before a crowd of 10,000 in Norman. Since the war was over, it would be the final game for a Sooner team to play a military installation squad.

After a scoreless first quarter, both teams scored in the second. Irvin's 63-yard TD run and Bodenhamer's conversion gave the Big Red a 7-0 lead.

The Comets scored minutes later following an intercepted pass, but the extra point failed, and OU held a 7-6 advantage through the third stanza.

1944 Season Record: 6-3-1			
Big Six Conference: 4-0-1 (Champions)			
Date	**Opponent**	**Result**	**Score**
September 30	NORMAN NAS	L	28-14
October 7	Texas A&M*	W	21-14
October 14	Texas at Dallas	L	20-0
October 21	KANSAS STATE	W	68-0
October 28	Texas Christian*	W	34-19
November 4	at Iowa	W	12-7
November 11	MISSOURI	T	21-21
November 18	at Kansas	W	20-0
December 2	Nebraska*	W	31-12
*Game played in Oklahoma City, OK			

Backup halfback Johnny Steward scored on a 45-yard run early in the fourth period to cap a 77-yard drive, and Bodenhamer converted. Venable scored the final Sooner tally late in the game on a three-yard run, and Bodenhamer kicked the extra point.

Forty-one Sooners got in on the act, with the second unit seeing most of the action in the second and fourth quarters. OU had seven first downs and 307 total yards, 251 on the ground.

The game produced bad news and good news for Coach Snorter Luster. The bad: Irvin suffered a fractured vertebra and was lost for the year. The good: Luster was more pleased with production in the T-formation compared to the single wing. The 'T' averaged 8.7 yards per play, while the single wing averaged only 1.7.

West was switched to left halfback, and Joe Richardson moved up to right half. Sharp returned to the squad in time for the Nebraska tilt on September 29.

Freshman halfback Howard Hawkins scored two touchdowns to lead the Sooners to a 20-0 win over the Huskers. A crowd of 18,000 turned out for Nebraska's season opener in Lincoln.

Both teams appeared to be heading to a scoreless deadlock at halftime, but late in the second period, Nebraska punted, and a Husker player was penalized for illegal use of hands. Officials awarded OU the ball at the NU 24. The Sooners rode four straight T-formation plays to the end zone. Sharp and Al Needs combined for nine yards on the next two carries, then Hawkins bolted for 15 more to the one. He carried the ball across on the next play, but the Huskers blocked Bodenhamer's kick.

Oklahoma advanced into Nebraska territory late in the third quarter, but Chick Story intercepted Steward's pass at the Husker 10. The Sooners got the ball back on the next play when Stone intercepted Mack Robinson's pass at the NU 14.

It took OU only one play for another score. Venable slammed through the line and dragged half a dozen Huskers into the end zone. Bodenhamer converted for a 13-0 lead.

Needs recovered a Husker fumble at the NU 40 with five minutes remaining in the game. Five plays later, Hawkins scored from the five, and Bodenhamer converted.

Four fumbles, two interceptions, and 12 penalties kept the Sooners from scoring more. OU gained 18 first downs to only four for the Huskers. The Sooners gained 514 total yards, 372 on the ground. The defense held Nebraska to 239 total yards, but only five rushing. For the second straight game, the Sooners were getting their greatest production from the T-formation. They ran it nearly three-fourths of the time against Nebraska and averaged 7.3 yards per play compared to 3.4 yards per play in the single wing.

"I'm going to start burning ethyl instead of standard if Snorter stays with the T," said West.

The undefeated Texas Aggies (2-0) used the T formation full time. The Aggies cashed in on three Sooner fumbles and defeated OU, 19-14, before 20,000 spectators the next week in Norman. Bob Goode scored all three A&M TDs.

Richardson fumbled on the first play of the game, and the Aggies recovered at the OU 21. Goode scored eight plays later on a 13-yard run, but the conversion was wide. Steward fumbled minutes later, and the Aggies pounced on it at the OU 37. Goode scored on a one-yard run, and the Aggies led 13-0 in the game's first five minutes.

Joe Harrell recovered an Aggie fumble at the A&M seven early in the second stanza. Hawkins scored on the next play and Bodenhamer converted.

The Sooners captured the lead with a 77-yard march following the second-half kickoff. Venable capped the drive with a one-yard TD run, and Bodenhamer converted to give OU a 14-13 edge.

Tallchief recovered an Aggie fumble on the OU 37 midway through the third quarter. Venable was about to be tackled for a loss on the next play, so he tried to lateral to Steward. The ball never made it to Steward's hands, and the Aggies recovered at the OU 46. The Aggies drove for the final tally in seven plays and converted a first down on fourth-and-16 to the Sooner eight. Goode scored on the next play, but the conversion failed.

The Sooners didn't wave the white flag. With eight minutes left in the game, OU took six minutes to advance to the Aggie 31. West gained two yards on the first play, then misfired two passes to Aubrey McCall. He tried to pass again on fourth down but ran instead and lost four yards. The Aggies took over with 90 seconds remaining.

Texas A&M had eight first downs and 371 total yards. OU was held to seven first downs and 212 total yards.

Hawkins came down with a case of the hives the day of the 40th edition of the Texas rivalry on October 13. The hives were caused by a reaction from a penicillin treatment for an infection. A late Texas touchdown allowed the 3-0 Longhorns to escape Dallas with a 12-7 victory before 43,381 at the Cotton Bowl.

Oklahoma took a 7-0 lead late in the opening quarter when West hurled a 21-yard TD pass to McCall. McCall caught the ball at the five and rolled into the end zone. West and McCall sparked the 80-yard drive with two other pass plays, one for 37 yards and another for 10 more.

The Steers answered with a 68-yard TD drive capped by Bryon Gillory's 13-yard scoring strike to Hubert Bechtol early in the second stanza. Richardson fell down in the end zone trying to defend the pass. Tom Harrell, brother of OU backup end Joe Harrell, missed the extra point, and the Sooners held a 7-6 lead through the third period.

Following a Texas punt, the Sooners advanced 36 yards to the Steers' three early in the third quarter. The next call was a West-to-McCall pass, but Maxie Bell intercepted for Texas in the end zone. Oklahoma later marched to the UT 31, but stalled. That's when the Horns went on their victory march.

Larry Graham scored the winning touchdown with about six minutes to go. Emory Bellard's conversion was wide, but the Longhorns won their sixth straight in the series.

OU had the statistical edge with 16 first downs to 13 for Texas. The Big Red rushed for 126 yards to 100 for the Steers. Oklahoma passed for 129 yards, three more than Texas. McCall caught seven passes to set a new OU record.

Two Sooner starters were sidelined with injuries the next week. Tackle Bill Hallett suffered a season-ending injury. Guard Don Tillman was out for a couple of games. Backup halfback Alan Greenberg also was sidelined for one game. Hawkins and Steward returned to the squad in time for the Jayhawk game on October 20.

Despite the injuries, the Sooners blasted the Hawks, 39-7, before 13,000 spectators in Norman. Sharp's nine-yard run capped a 61-yard

Al Needs intercepted a Kansas State pass and returned it 99 yards for a touchdown and a school record for the longest interception return.
(*OU Athletics*)

drive in the game's first four minutes, but Bodenhamer's conversion was wide.

Bodenhamer intercepted a Jayhawk pass late in the first quarter and returned it 25 yards to the KU 22. Seven plays later, West scored from the seven-yard line, and Bodenhamer converted.

Venable's 52-yard TD run upped the lead to 20-0 midway through the second period. Venable took West's lateral, swept wide to the left and flew down the east sideline to the KU 35 where he cut toward the middle to the end zone. Richardson threw a key block on the last Kansas player in pursuit. Bodenhamer converted.

The Sooners scored again on their next possession when Steward bolted 72 yards for the score. Bodenhamer's extra point was blocked, but OU held a 26-0 lead at halftime.

Burgert recovered a Jayhawk fumble at the KU 21 early in the third period to set up another Sooner score. Venable scored on a 10-yard run four plays later, bowling over KU's Chuck Conroy as he crossed the goal line. Bodenhamer missed the conversion.

OU's reserves played the rest of the way, and Kansas scored late in the third stanza. Fourth string halfback Gayl Pair scored on a three-yard run in the fourth quarter for the final Sooner tally. Bodenhamer converted for the 39th point.

The Big Red rushed for 375 yards and passed for 167 more. The Sooners gained 7.1 yards each time they ran the ball. Venable led all rushers with 108 yards on 11 carries, and Steward added 96 more yards on six carries. The Jayhawks totaled 325 yards. OU led with 14 first downs to eight for Kansas.

The Sooners hammered Kansas State, 41-13, on October 27 before 9,000 in Manhattan. The Wildcats led 13-0 and threatened to score again early in the second period from the OU five-yard line. Needs picked off the Wildcats' fourth-down pass at the one and returned it 99 yards for a touchdown. No Kansas State player was within 10 yards in pursuit of Needs. The interception set the school record for the longest interception return. Bodenhamer converted to cut the Cat lead to 13-7.

Oklahoma got the ball at the KS 41 with less than two minutes remaining until intermission. West gained two yards, then Sharp rolled around left end for 27 more to the Wildcat 11 with 20 seconds to go. The Sooners were penalized five yards for delay of game, then West hurled a TD pass to McCall. McCall ran his pattern to the outside, but West tossed the ball to the inside. McCall quickly pivoted toward the ball and caught it over his left shoulder. Bodenhamer toed the extra point, and OU led 14-13 at the half.

Early in the third quarter, Needs returned a Wildcat punt 22 yards to the KS 15. Six plays later, Venable scored from the two, and Bodenhamer converted.

Needs again set up the next score with an interception, which he returned to the K-State 36 early in the fourth stanza. Eight plays later, Hawkins swept off right end for a three-yard TD run. Bodenhamer missed the extra point, but OU led 27-13.

Hawkins intercepted a Wildcat pass a minute later and returned it 19 yards to the KS 25. Venable scored from the two moments later and Bodenhamer converted.

Leading 34-13 lead, Coach Luster put in the reserves, and Pair's 47-yard punt return to the Cat 20 set up the final touchdown. Greenberg gained 10 yards, and fullback Gerald Lovell picked up

Naval trainee Aubrey McCall caught the winning pass against Iowa State. McCall played only one season at OU. (*OU Athletics*)

seven more to the three-yard line. Pair scored on the next play, and Bodenhamer converted.

Oklahoma gained 447 total yards, 294 on the ground and made 16 first downs. Kansas State had eight first downs and 348 total yards.

Texas Christian defeated OU, 13-7, the next week before a crowd of 21,000 in Norman. TCU quarterback Leon Joslin tossed two first-quarter TD passes to lead the Horned Frogs to victory.

His first scoring strike, a 36-yarder to end Beekie Ezell, came midway through the opening period. Joslin connected a 12-yard TD pass to fullback Norman Cox late in the first stanza.

West tossed a 76-yard touchdown pass to Needs late in the second period, but a backfield in motion penalty wiped out the play, and the Sooners still trailed 13-0 at halftime.

OU got the crowd excited with a 71-yard TD drive following the second-half kickoff. West hurled a 27-yard pass to Needs on the fifth play of the drive to the Frogs' 16. Sharp bolted off tackle and scored on the next play. Bodenhamer kicked the extra point.

Neither team threatened the rest of the game. Oklahoma was plagued with poor tackling and blocking and was unable to overcome TCU's shifting defenses.

Frank Crider, who played for the Sooners from 1927-1929, was added to the squad as an assistant coach. OU did not have an end coach, and Crider was hired to tutor the ends. He had been serving 35 months in the navy.

On November 8, two days before Oklahoma's homecoming tilt against Iowa State, Luster announced his resignation as OU's head coach effective at the end of the season. He cited poor health as the reason for his resignation.

"I guess I've got football battle fatigue," Luster joked during his announcement. He would accept a position in the university's intramural athletics department.

Sooner Magic: Post-War Hero

The Iowa State Cyclones (3-2-1) carried a two-game win streak into Norman the following week. The Cyclones lost to Northwestern, beat Northern Iowa, tied Kansas, lost to Missouri, then walloped Nebraska and Kansas State. I-State threatened Oklahoma's Big Six title hopes and the Sooners' eight-game winning streak in the series and 16 straight conference game-winning string. OU led the overall series 14-2-1.

About 11,000 fans turned out for the Homecoming contest at Memorial Stadium to see if the Big Red could extend the conference streak. The only excitement in the first quarter was Sharp's long run. From the OU 37-yard line, he slammed through the line and bolted for 47 yards to the Cyclone 16, but fumbled when ISU defenders tackled him from behind.

The first stanza ended in a scoreless tie. Early in the second period, Cyclone halfback Gene Phelps tossed a screen pass to end Carl Paetz, who raced 46 yards down the sideline before finally being bumped out of bounds at the Sooner four. Phelps gained two yards up the middle, then overthrew Dick Howard in the end zone. On third-and-goal, Tallchief, Ernest Davis, and Joe Harrell smothered Phelps for no gain. Iowa State chose to go for the touchdown, where Phelps kept the ball again, and again Davis and Tallchief dumped him for a two-yard loss.

Two minutes later, the Sooners advanced 68 yards in eight plays. Pair sparked the drive with a couple of long runs and a pass. From the OU 34, he shot around left end for 24 yards to the Cyclone 42-yard line. On the next play, he fired a seven-yard pass to Joe Harrell. Venable powered through the middle for eight yards and a first down.

Pair raced around right end for 22 yards to the Cyclone five. Venable plowed through the middle again for the touchdown. Bodenhamer booted the extra point, and the Sooners held a 7-0 advantage.

Late in the third period and into the fourth, the Cyclones drove 59 yards to the OU 15, but the Sooner defense held. Moments later, Hawkins fumbled, and Jim Marks recovered for Iowa State at the OU 26-yard line.

OU linebacker Everett Harvel nailed Dick Howard for a three-yard loss, but halfback Ev Faunce swept around right end for 10 yards on the next play. The Cyclones were flagged for backfield motion, and on fourth-and-nine from the OU 29, Phelps flipped a pass to Paetz who was popped by Harvell. The play was ruled as interference and gave the Cyclones new life with a first down at the Sooner 23.

Faunce sailed around right end, followed a convoy of blockers and dodged a couple of OU defenders en route to the end zone. Marks added the extra point to tie the game at 7-7 with about 10 minutes left in the game.

Neither team made much progress over the next eight minutes. The Sooners got the ball at ISU's 49-yard line with 1:50 remaining. West took the snap, rolled right and pulled up to lob the ball to McCall. McCall clutched the ball on his fingertips at the ISU 12 and crossed the goal line untouched. Bodenhamer kicked the conversion to give the Sooners a 14-7 lead.

The Cyclones' comeback effort was thwarted when Phelps' desperation pass was intercepted by Venable at the ISU 46 and returned 20 yards.

As the final gun sounded, Naval trainees hoisted McCall on their shoulders and carried him off the field.

The Sooners traveled to Columbia on November 17 to meet 4-3 Missouri in a battle for the Big Six Conference championship. The Sooners and Tigers had identical 3-0 conference records. Missouri ended Oklahoma's two-year conference stronghold and 17-game conference win streak with a 14-6 victory before 22,000 fans.

Lloyd Brinkman's 30-yard TD run late in the first period capped a 77-yard drive to give the Tigers a 7-0 lead. The Tigers threatened to score three more times, but the Sooner defense stiffened on the first two efforts. The third time was a charm for Missouri. After

fielding Hawkins' punt at the MU 30, the Tigers moved to the OU 12 early in the second quarter, but faced fourth-and-six. Bob Hopkins completed a seven-yard pass to Leonard Brown for the first down. Hopkins scored on the next play.

The Sooner defense pinned the Tigers deep on the next Mizzou series, and the Tigers punted to their own 38. Stone was stopped for no gain then West fired a touchdown pass to Burgert, who slipped behind the Tiger secondary. Missouri blocked Bodenhamer's conversion.

The Tigers held the statistical edge with 12 first downs to eight for the Sooners. Missouri gained 295 yards to 190 for Oklahoma. The powerful Sooner running game was held to only 113 yards.

Oklahoma A&M handed the Sooners their worst defeat to date with a 47-0 win the next week before 34,000, a new attendance record, in Norman. Bob Fenimore, the Aggies' All-America halfback, tossed two TD passes and ran for another to lead the Aggie assault.

Leading 21-0 at halftime, the Aggies scored four more touchdowns in the final 30 minutes.

The Sooners finished the season with a 5-5 record and second in the Big Six with a 4-1 mark. Burgert, Tallchief, Lester Jensen, West, and Venable were named to the All-Big Six first team.

Luster ended his five-year career with a 27-18-3 record and two conference titles. He also organized the university's first wrestling team and boxing team when he was an undergraduate in 1920. He was an amateur boxer as a teenager, but gave up the sport at the age of 15 when he lost a 10-round bout to professional Mutt McGee. The boxing team was winless in two meets the first year, but 36 years later in 1956, Luster's boxing team placed sixth in the NCAA Championships.

Luster died at age 81 in his Norman home.

1946

The first full season following World War II in 1946 not only brought new talent to the Sooner gridiron, but also a new head coach—Jim Tatum, whom OU officials chose after reviewing a few choices ahead of him.

OU president George L. Cross and athletic director Jap Haskell discussed finding a replacement for Dewey "Snorter" Luster. Haskell recommended Tatum, a graduate of North Carolina University who also served as the Tar Heels' head coach in 1942. He also coached the Navy team in Jacksonville, Florida, during the war.

Tatum and Harold "Red" Drew, University of Alabama assistant coach, were the finalists for the head coaching position at OU. When Tatum interviewed for the head coaching position with the university's board of regents in January 1946, he requested bringing a friend he believed would be a good assistant—Charles "Bud" Wilkinson. The regents agreed, and after interviewing both men, some of the regents were more impressed with Wilkinson and wanted to hire him as head coach and Tatum as assistant coach. Cross intervened, stating that offering the position to Wilkinson may compromise institutional ethics. The board agreed and offered the job to Tatum as head coach, provided he brought Wilkinson with him as his assistant. Tatum and Wilkinson accepted the offer 10 days later.

Wilkinson tutored the backs, and Tatum hired Walter Driskell, former line coach at Colorado and Wyoming, as line assistant. The trio toured 23 Oklahoma cities getting acquainted with Sooner fans.

Although he was the football skipper for one year, Tatum left his mark on the Oklahoma football program in more than one way. He recruited many servicemen who had played at other colleges before

1945 Season Record: 5-5-0
Big Six Conference: 4-1-0 (Second)

Date	Opponent	Result	Score
September 22	HONDO TEXAS AAF	W	21-6
September 29	at Nebraska	W	20-0
October 6	TEXAS A&M	L	19-14
October 13	Texas at Dallas	L	12-7
October 20	KANSAS	W	39-7
October 27	at Kansas	W	41-13
November 3	TEXAS CHRISTIAN	L	13-7
November 10	IOWA STATE	W	14-7
November 17	at Missouri	L	14-6
November 24	OKLAHOMA A&M	L	47-0

the war and he also raided other rival campuses for players. Before the first game against mighty Army, Tatum spent the entire $125,000 of the athletic department's budget and left a $113,000 deficit after his resignation.

New Offensive Weapon

Tatum and Wilkinson introduced the Split-T formation they had learned as assistant coaches at Iowa Pre-Flight, a Naval Air Station team during World War II. Don Faurot, head coach at Iowa Pre-Flight, created the formation. Faurot later would be notorious for building the University of Missouri football team.

Quarterback Jack Mitchell, a transfer from the University of Texas, guided the Sooners' new offense, which was supported by three All-America linemen—guards Paul "Buddy" Burris, Plato Andros and center John Rapacz. Mitchell's leadership ability earned him the nickname "General Jack." Dave Wallace, also saw some action at quarterback as well as handling the placekicking chores.

"He was a great runner," recalled Claude Arnold, Mitchell's future teammate. "A crazy-legged runner ... very elusive. He could run and keep the ball when he should have pitched it and still picked up good yardage."

Mitchell's tremendous running ability was aided by his talent of cutting a 90-degree angle, not off of the front of his foot, but by planting the heel into the turf.

Halfbacks Joe Golding, Eddie Davis, and Jim Tyree were the only returnees from Luster's pre-war teams who returned to make a contribution for the 1946 Sooners. Tatum kicked off most of Luster's players from the previous year. Tackle Tommy Tallchief was the only returnee from the 1945 squad, but he broke his toe in preseason practice and was out for the season.

The Sooners also had a new play-by-play announcer—Curt Gowdy, who would later work as an announcer for the New York Yankees, Boston Red Sox and major networks.

The Sooners flew to New York City to meet Army in the season opener at Yankee Stadium on September 28. This was the first time a Sooner football team traveled to a game via air.

The Cadets were defending national champions and held a 19-game winning streak. Army featured the dynamic halfback duo of Glenn Davis and Felix "Doc" Blanchard, who was Tatum's cousin. Blanchard suffered a leg injury against Villanova a week earlier and would miss the Oklahoma game. President Harry S. Truman attended the game, the first time an Oklahoma football team played before a United States president. Army, favored by 38 points, won, 21-7.

Early in the second quarter, with the score tied 0-0, Davis punted out at the Army 13. The Big Red defense pushed the Cadets back toward the goal line on the next three plays. Norman McNabb blocked Army's punt on the goal line and fell on the ball for a touchdown. Wallace converted, and OU held a 7-0 advantage.

Army marched 30 yards to tie the game with 45 seconds until halftime.

Early in the third stanza, Army scored four plays after blocking Charles Sarratt's punt at the OU 15. The Sooners then drove 86 yards, but Tucker intercepted Mitchell's pass at the Cadet six.

Oklahoma had another chance to close the gap when Myrle Greathouse recovered an Army fumble minutes later at the Cadet 18. The Sooners moved to the nine in three plays as the third period came to a close. The Cadets were about to tackle Wallace on the fourth-down play. Wallace tried to lateral to halfback Darrell Royal, but Royal tipped the ball, and Tucker scooped it up at the 15 and raced 85 yards for a touchdown.

OU's defense held Army to 86 yards rushing. Andros led the defense in holding Glenn Davis to 19 yards on 12 carries (an all-time low) and no touchdowns. Army had more total yards (237-205), but the Sooners had the rushing edge (129-83).

Sooner Magic: A Chip Shot Win

The Sooners hosted Texas A&M the following week. The Aggies were 1-2 with a win over North Texas and a loss to Texas Tech. A&M also held a 4-2 edge over OU in previous meetings.

Cloudy skies, with a possible threat of showers, kept the homecoming crowd to around 28,000, but the sun broke through in the final quarter.

The Big Red made the only threat late in the scoreless first period by marching 84 yards to the Aggies' one-yard line. Wallace sparked the drive with a 42-yard pass to end Warren Giese to the A&M 22. On the next play, Golding bolted 16 yards to the six.

On fourth-and-goal at the Aggie one, Davis was nailed for no gain by Aggie guard Odell Stautenberger, and A&M took over at its 20-yard line.

Midway through the second stanza, OU drove to the A&M 19, but Marion Flanagan picked off Mitchell's pass in the end zone. From their 20, the Aggies did not gain a single yard against the Sooner defense. Punter Barney Welch took the punt snap, but McNabb charged through and blocked the kick. The pigskin rolled back to the six yard line where McNabb had a temporary grasp on it, but fumbled. OU tackle Jess Trotter was fortunate to smother the ball at the six.

Royal was stopped for no gain then Mitchell picked up three yards and Golding gained one more to the two-yard line. OU's fourth-down gamble paid off as Mitchell hit the hole off tackle and crossed the goal line. Wallace booted the extra point, and the Sooners led 7-0, which remained through halftime.

Early in the third quarter, the Aggies marched from their own 40 to the OU 18, but the Big Red defense held for downs. The Aggie defense then stalled the OU offense. Davis punted to Flanagan, who took the ball at the A&M 28 and sprinted down the sideline for the touchdown. John Ballentine's extra point was good, and A&M tied the game 7-7 with five minutes left in the third quarter.

The Aggies had another scoring chance early in the fourth stanza. Davis, back to punt for OU at his 10-yard line, fumbled the low snap from center and A&M recovered the ball at the nine.

Ralph Daniels whirled for four yards and Bobby Dew gained one more up the middle. Daniels fumbled the snap but recovered the ball at the five. Linebacker Myrle Greathouse blocked Ballentine's 13-yard field goal try into the wind.

The Sooners put together a drive late in the game, sparked by a 30-yard end sweep by Royal to the A&M seven. Golding picked up three yards on the next two carries. Wallace tried to sneak up the middle but was smothered for no gain.

The Sooners were then penalized for delay of game, which moved the ball back to the nine. Still, a good chip shot for Wallace with the wind behind his back. The ball split the uprights with 40 seconds remaining to give OU a 10-7 lead and victory.

Thousands of fans poured onto the track surrounding the field.

The Big Red defense held the Aggies to 87 total yards (79 passing, eight rushing) and three first downs.

John Rapacz pulled his rib muscles and was carried off on a stretcher. Pete Tillman replaced him against No. 1-ranked Texas.

The 3-0 Longhorns had no trouble against their first three opponents—a 42-0 win over Missouri, 76-0 over Colorado and 54-6 over Oklahoma A&M.

Backup QB Dave Wallace kicked the winning field goal to lift the Sooners to a 10-7 victory over Texas A&M. (*OU Athletics*)

two more in the fourth. Golding raced 81 yards for this second touchdown in the fourth stanza, one play after Royal picked off the Wildcats' pass.

OU rushed for 329 yards and passed for 50 more. The defense held the Wildcats to 46 rushing yards and 84 through the air.

Oklahoma dropped to 14th in the AP poll, but handed 1-4 Iowa State its worst defeat in school history with a 63-0 victory the following week in Ames. The rout not only ended the Cyclones' 36-game scoring streak, it also spoiled their homecoming.

OU scored four touchdowns in the fourth stanza, three times in the final five and a half minutes. Eight Sooners crossed the goal line with reserve Johnny Allsup leading the pack with two scores.

Oklahoma gained 15 first downs, rushed for 398 yards, passed for 130 more and returned kicks for 204 yards. The defense held the Cyclones to four first downs and 134 total yards (91 rushing and 43 passing). Iowa State never advanced past the Sooners' 30-yard line.

Sooner Magic:
Slugging It Out in the Sludge

The No. 14 Sooners were two-touchdown favorites against 1-4-1 Texas Christian the next week in Fort Worth. A driving rain and a sloppy field kept the contest close as the Sooners pulled out a 14-12 victory before a crowd of 6,000.

The clouds burst open just as the game kicked off. Oklahoma drove to the TCU nine in the game's first few minutes. From there, Royal lateraled to Davis, but the Frogs' Weldon Edwards batted the pigskin in the air. TCU's Harold Kilman hauled it down at the 15 and rambled to the 30 where he pitched the ball to Edwards, who then raced to the end zone. Tom Bishop missed the conversion, but the Horned Frogs held a 6-0 lead.

The rain continued in buckets.

Oklahoma advanced to the TCU 12 late in the first stanza, but fumbled the slippery ball and TCU recovered. The Frogs lost six yards in the next two plays and punted out to their own 28. OU hammered the ball up the middle on the next five plays for the score. Wallace maintained his balance for a nine-yard gain. Golding blasted ahead for four more and a first down at the 15. Davis picked up nine more. Wallace's four-yard run gave the Sooners a first down at the two. Mitchell scored on the next play, and Wallace converted.

The Sooners held the 7-6 edge through halftime, and the rain showed no signs of letting up.

Mitchell returned the second-half kickoff 80 yards to the Frogs' 11. Wallace then fumbled, and the Frogs recovered at the 11. TCU's Tom Stout fumbled it right back on the next play, and Davis recovered for the Sooners on the 12. Wallace lost the ball again three plays later, and Bill Hale recovered for TCU at the four.

The Big Red defense held and forced the Frogs to punt. Mitchell fielded the kick at the TCU 40. He slanted to his right, splashed through a couple of puddles but maintained his balance all the way to the end zone. TCU's Lindy Berry tackled Mitchell near the goal line, but Mitchell fell across for the score. Wallace converted for a 14-6 lead.

Gray skies turned darker and the rain kept pouring.

The Frogs blocked Royal's punt early in the fourth quarter. TCU's Doug Brightwell grabbed the ball at the OU 25 and splashed his way to the end zone. Bishop again missed the extra point.

The Longhorns defeated Oklahoma, 20-13, on October 12 at the Cotton Bowl before 50,000 fans, the largest crowd to see a football game in the State of Texas. About 5,000 fans had to be turned away from the gates. The Texas State Fair also set a new one-day attendance record with 205,469.

Trailing 14-0, Wallace intercepted Tom Landry's pass at the OU 44 in the second quarter. Wallace completed three passes to freshman end Jim Owens for 48 yards. Six plays after stealing Landry's pass, Wallace sailed an 11-yard TD pass to Owens. Wallace also hurled a 25-yarder to Owens one play before the score. Wallace missed the extra point.

Wallace got his second interception minutes later when he stole Bobby Layne's aerial at the UT 39. The Sooners advanced to the 15, but Royal tossed an interception in the end zone.

Texas appeared to drive the final nail in the Sooners' coffin by marching to the OU two early in the fourth period. Under a heavy rush by reserve Jess Trotter, Layne directed a pass to Hubert Bechtol for the score. Golding stepped in front of the Texas receiver at the one and away he went, all the way for a touchdown. The 99-yard interception return tied Al Needs' record return set against Kansas State the year before. Wallace converted to bring Oklahoma within one, 14-13.

The Horns did drive that final nail as they marched 75 yards in six plays for a touchdown.

Texas had more passing yards (240-87), but OU had the rushing advantage (142-83). Although the Longhorns won, they dropped to third in the AP poll. OU was ranked 13th.

Golding scored three touchdowns and rushed for 164 yards on seven carries to lead the Sooners to a 28-7 win over 0-3 Kansas State in the conference opener on October 19 in Norman.

Golding's first score came late in the first quarter, two plays after the Wildcats punted to the 50-yard line. Royal picked up seven yards, then Golding scooted off left tackle and dashed to the end zone. Wallace kicked the first of four conversions.

The Wildcats tied the game early in the second stanza, then the Sooners took command with a touchdown in the third period and

TCU marched to the OU 19 late in the game, but fumbled, and OU recovered at the 17. Royal set up to punt in the next play, but Edwards blocked it. Fortunately, the Sooners recovered it. Royal got the next one off his foot to the TCU 41.

Berry gained 26 yards to the OU 33. He carried again on the next play and neared the goal line, but Mitchell saved the day by bumping Berry out of bounds at the nine. Stout fumbled on the next play, and Burris recovered for the Sooners to save the day.

When the final gun cracked, the rain stopped and a rainbow appeared over the north Texas skies. Weather records indicated Fort Worth had received two and three-quarters inches of rain that day.

TCU had the edge in passing yards (62-4), but OU had more rushing yards (96-70).

The No. 16 Sooners would see no sunshine on November 9 in Lawrence, Kansas—not in the sky or on the scoreboard. Kansas upset the Sooners, 16-13, on a late field goal in another downpour.

KU took a 6-0 lead in the first quarter after recovering Royal's fumble at the OU 24.

Early in the second period, Golding shot the gap off right tackle and raced 65 yards for a touchdown, leaving Jayhawks sprawling in his wake. Wallace missed the extra point, and the score remained tied at 6-6.

Kansas recovered Mitchell's fumble and jumped to a 13-7 lead minutes later.

Golding, who rushed for 130 yards, scored his second touchdown on a 14-yard run in the third stanza. The score capped a 72-yard march in 13 plays. Wallace's toe tied the game.

With 75 seconds left in the game, KU kicker Paul Turner attempted his first collegiate field goal. He nailed the 31-yarder to lift the Hawks to victory.

Oklahoma had more rushing yards (193-75), but Kansas gained more through the air (35-2).

The Sooners dropped out of the AP poll. They hosted 5-2-1 Missouri on November 16 before 33,000 homecoming fans. The Tigers also were unbeaten in the Big Six Conference at 3-0. The Sooners capitalized on two Tiger fumbles, a blocked punt and a 75-yard pass interception en route to a 27-6 triumph.

Missouri's Bob Hopkins fumbled on the third play of the game, and Homer Paine recovered at the MU 37. Golding, Wallace and Mitchell carried to the 3 on the next seven plays. Golding scored on the next play and Wallace converted.

Minutes later, Tiger punter Leonard Brown attempted a punt from his 10-yard line. Burris slipped through the line and blocked the kick. Paine fell on it at the MU 12. On the next play, Mitchell pitched out to Wallace who swung to his right and hurled a TD pass to Giese, who was deep in the end zone. Wallace converted and OU held a 14-0 lead.

Missouri's Loyd Brinkman fumbled two plays after the ensuing kickoff, and Paine recovered at the Tiger 15. Three plays later, Golding scored from three yards out, but Wallace missed the conversion.

The Tigers advanced to the OU 22 early in the second period then Golding intercepted Bob Teel's pass at the eight and wheeled 75 yards to the MU 17. A penalty set the ball back to the 22. Allsup gained seven yards, then Davis scored on the next play. Wallace converted and OU led, 27-0.

The Tigers, who had minus five yards rushing in the first three quarters, drove 71 yards against the Sooner alternates to score.

Oklahoma rushed for 185 and passed for 36 more. Missouri rushed for 54 and passed for 36.

OU, Missouri, Kansas, and Nebraska all stood at 3-1 and tied for first place in the Big Six race. The Sooners climbed back into the AP poll at No. 18.

The Sooners hosted 3-4 Nebraska the following week and scored a touchdown in every quarter for another 27-6 victory.

Davis, Golding and Mitchell scored on runs and Royal sailed a TD pass to Bobby Goad. Nebraska tied the game at 6-6, but it was all OU after that.

The Sooners gained more rushing yards (257-60) and passing yards (119-60).

Kansas defeated Missouri, 20-19, on Thanksgiving, and the Sooners and Jayhawks shared the Big Six Conference title.

The Sooners celebrated the conference crown with a 73-12 annihilation of Oklahoma A&M (3-6-1) in Stillwater on November 30.

Bob Fenimore, the Aggies All-America halfback who accounted for three touchdowns against OU in 1944, was sidelined with an injury. Golding turned in an All-America performance by scoring three touchdowns—all in the second half of the crimson rout. Owens caught two touchdown strikes, one from Sarratt who also ran for a TD. Wallace nailed nine conversions in the 10-touchdown barrage and also added a 16-yard field goal. J.L. Martin booted the final conversion.

The Sooners only led 7-0 after the first quarter, 31-0 at the half and 52-0 after three periods.

Oklahoma not only crushed the Aggies on the scoreboard but in the statistics, too. OU gained 21 first downs, 415 rushing yards and 249 through the air. The defense held A&M to three first downs, seven yards on the ground and 174 passing.

The next week, Oklahoma accepted an invitation to play North Carolina State on January 2 in the second annual Gator Bowl in Jacksonville, Florida. The 18th-ranked Wolfpack defense yielded only 6.7 points per game en route to an 8-2 season.

Davis scored two touchdowns as the 14th-ranked Sooners pounded NC State, 34-14, before a crowd of 10,134.

OU marched 65 yards in eight plays from the opening kickoff to take a 7-0 lead. Davis topped the drive with a one-yard plunge, and Wallace converted. A 46-yard pass play off a fake end sweep highlighted the drive. Mitchell lateraled to Sarratt, who swung around end and stopped to fire a pass to Merle Dinkins. Dinkins grabbed the ball over his head, juggled the ball and clutched it when he crashed to the turf at the NCS six.

1946 Season Record: 8-3-0
Big Six Conference: 4-1-0 (Champions)

Date	Opponent	Result	Score
September 28	Army*	L	21-7
October 5	TEXAS A&M	W	10-7
October 12	Texas at Dallas	L	20-13
October 19	KANSAS STATE	W	28-7
October 26	at Iowa State	W	63-0
November 2	at Texas Christian	W	14-12
November 9	at Kansas	L	16-13
November 16	MISSOURI	W	27-6
November 23	NEBRASKA	W	27-6
November 30	at Oklahoma A&M	W	73-12
January 1	North Carolina State#	W	34-13

*Game played in New York, NY
#Gator Bowl at Jacksonville, FL

The Wolfpack answered with a 42-yard TD pass to tie the game at 7-7.

Golding returned the ensuing kickoff to the OU 35, and as he was about to be tackled, he lateraled to Sarratt, who flashed down the sideline for a touchdown. The play was called back when Wade Walker was flagged for clipping on the play.

The Sooners exploded for three touchdowns in the second quarter. Davis found a gaping hole up the middle and scooted seven yards to the end zone. Wallace's conversion made it 14-7.

The Big Red defense stalled NC State on the next series and took over at the Wolfpack 46. Sarratt weaved for 25 yards, and Golding added 18 more before being bumped out of bounds at the NCS five. Wallace ripped over left tackle for the score, but he missed the conversion.

With more than two minutes until halftime, the Wolfpack's Les Palmer faked a punt and tried to pass. Tackle Bill Morris intercepted at the NCS 30 and rambled to the five. Golding scored off right end and added the conversion for a 27-7 halftime lead.

NC State marched 67 yards for a touchdown following the second-half kickoff. Palmer redeemed himself for the earlier faux pas with an eight-yard run. Jim Byler missed the extra point.

The Wolfpack moved to the OU 36 early in the fourth quarter but surrendered on downs. Golding scooted around left end for 15 yards, then hauled in Sarratt's pass for 14 more to the NCS 35. Moments later at the Wolfpack 15, Mitchell handed off to Sarratt who swung around right end, pulled up and heaved a scoring strike to Owens.

The Sooners outrushed the Wolfpack (195-136), but the Wolfpack had more passing yards (103-74). Golding, who led the Sooners' ground attack with 91 yards on 12 carries, was named the game's most valuable player.

Oklahoma's front line was so powerful that three players—Rapacz, Burris and Andros—were named All-Americans. The entire front line was named to the All-Big Six first unit. Wade Walker and Homer Paine joined Rapacz, Burris, and Andros to round out the conference's front wall. Giese and Golding also were named to the All-Big Six first team. The seven players were the most Sooners chosen for an all-conference lineup to date.

After the Gator Bowl victory, the University of Maryland offered its head coaching position to Tatum. He accepted the offer, and OU promoted Wilkinson to head coach.

1947

Bud Wilkinson was hired as the Sooners' 13th head coach. He also was asked to replace Jap Haskell as the university's interim athletic director. Haskell was fired as AD for knowing about the athletic department's deficit. Wilkinson accepted the AD position with no further compensation.

Wilkinson added Gomer Jones to his staff as line coach. Jones, a former All-America center at Ohio State, had coached the Nebraska line and Wilkinson was impressed with the Cornhuskers' line performance. Dutch Fehring and Bill Jennings, a Sooner star end from 1938-1940, also were added to Wilkinson's staff.

Wilkinson emphasized discipline and preparation to his players, which helped the Sooners develop the Split-T into a masterpiece that would later project Oklahoma as the premier football team in the country. But Wilkinson's coaching debut was filled with question marks. Three of his stars from the previous year graduated—halfback Joe Golding, end Warren Giese and guard Andros. Golding had one more year of eligibility left and Plato Andros had two more years, but both opted to turn professional.

Wilkinson still had many veterans returning from the '46 squad, including four linemen who were named All-Big Six a year before—tackles Wade Walker and Homer Paine, center John Rapacz and guard Buddy Burris. Jim Tyree was a returning starter at end and Jim Owens and Bobby Goad had plenty of playing time at the other end slot. The backfield was loaded with the return of Jack Mitchell, Darrell Royal, Charley Sarratt, Dave Wallace, Laddie Harp, Eddie Davis, Ed Kreick, and Norman McNabb.

Davis did not play in the opener due to a pulled groin muscle.

Sooner Magic: The Creation of a Monster

Wilkinson was the creator of a monster of a football team that would win national championships and set many records in years to come. That monster coughed through a 2-2-1 record in the first half of the season but devoured its last five opponents in the second half.

Yet it wasn't going to be easy, as was evident in the season opener in Detroit.

The Detroit Mercy Titans became the Sooners' first course of nourishment, on September 26—a rare Friday night game. The referee of the game was Jay Berwanger, the first Heisman Trophy winner in 1935.

The Sooners marched 68 yards for a 7-0 lead on their first possession and nearly milked 10 minutes off the clock. Mitchell scored on a four-yard end sweep and Wallace nailed the conversion.

Detroit answered with a 66-yard drive to tie the game at 7-7 late in the opening quarter. Titan halfback John Kurkowski scored on a 56-yard run.

Wilkinson took the blame for his rookie mistake on Kurkowski's touchdown. Myrle Greathouse went to the sideline to replace his chin strap before the play, and the Sooners had only 10 men on defense.

Oklahoma blew a couple of scoring opportunities in the second stanza in an attempt to put the game out of reach.

Following an exchange of punts, Oklahoma got the ball back at the Titan 24. George "Junior" Thomas' 14-yard run gave the Big Red a first down at the 10, but the DU defense stiffened, and the Sooners could manage only eight yards to the two. A penalty moved the ball back to the seven. On trotted a maimed Wallace to kick a 23-yard field goal. Despite two sore knees, Wallace sailed the kick through the uprights, and Oklahoma was back on top, 10-7, with less than five minutes before halftime.

In addition to playing quarterback, Mitchell was a proficient punt returner and was the 1946 national leader in punt returns. After two penalties had pinned the Titans deep in their own territory, Mitchell took Wright's punt at the OU 40-yard line, crossed the field and faked a handoff to Sarratt before darting down field. He was swarmed by DU tacklers at midfield, but spun out and raced down the sideline for the touchdown. Wallace booted the extra point, and the Sooners held a comfortable 17-7 lead with less than a minute left in the second period.

Early in the third quarter, Mitchell was smacked by a couple of Titans when he tried to lateral to Royal. The ball dribbled on the turf, and DU defensive end Archie Kelly smothered the pigskin at the Sooner 41. On the first play from scrimmage, fullback Leon Rittof ripped up the middle to the end zone, shedding a couple of Sooner tacklers along the way. O'Leary cut the Sooner lead to 17-14 with a little more than 12 minutes left in the third stanza.

A few minutes later, the Sooners partially blocked a Titan punt, and the ball stopped cold on the DU 20-yard line. Five plays later, Sarratt blasted over from the one. Wallace toed the conversion, and the Sooners were back in the comfort zone with a 24-14 lead.

The Titans drove 62 yards for a touchdown midway through the fourth quarter. Owens blocked the extra point, and OU held a 24-20 advantage with 4:10 to go in the game.

The blocked kick was vital in case the Titans got the ball back. If the kick was successful, Detroit could possibly go for a tie with a field goal. DU did get the ball back with about a minute to play, but had to go all the way to try to win the game.

At the DU 27, a forward lateral picked up 25 yards to the Sooner 48. Royal broke up a long pass play at the OU 10-yard line, but there was still time for one more play. Thomas intercepted a long heave by DU quarterback Malinowski at the 15 with three seconds remaining. Thomas carried the ball back to the 32 as the gun sounded.

The Sooners returned home to beat 2-0 Texas A&M, 26-14 on October 4.

Mitchell rushed for 114 yards on 15 carries, completed six of six passes for 87 yards and accounted for each score. Rapacz intercepted two Aggie passes and recovered a fumble, all in the third quarter.

OU rushed for 257 yards, passed for 87 more. The defense held the Cadets to 131 rushing yards and 80 yards passing.

The AP poll had OU ranked 15th after the 2-0 start.

The Sooners traveled to Dallas on October 11 for a showdown with No. 3 Texas, undefeated at 3-0. The Longhorns outscored their first three opponents, 105-13, under new head coach Blair Cherry. Cherry was an assistant under Dana X. Bible, who resigned to take a position as athletic director at Texas.

The Steers handed Wilkinson his first defeat, 34-14. The game was laced with controversial calls and ended with angry Sooners fans hurling pop bottles and cushions toward the field.

A crowd of 46,000 witnessed the Texas rout, but the ones in the crimson colors would say the Sooners got robbed, or "Siscoed," a better word for getting screwed. The moniker derived from the name of the game's referee—Jack Sisco.

Trailing 7-0 in the first quarter, the Sooners advanced 61 yards to the UT nine in the second stanza, but two penalties stalled the drive.

OU forced Texas to punt then the Sooners set sail for the tying score. Mitchell's three-yard TD run and Royal's conversion came with 3:45 left in the first half.

Texas was not done. The Steers drove 57 yards to the OU three. With 20 seconds remaining, Texas halfback Randall Clay gained one yard. He carried on the next play but the Sooners stopped him for no gain. Sisco signaled "touchdown" for Texas, but changed it to a "time out" signal as he noticed the Horns had not scored.

The clock showed one second to play, but Oklahoma fans screamed that the half was over. Texas got one more play, and Jim Kennedy took Bobby Layne's handoff, but the ball squirted from Kennedy's hands. The ball then bounded off a Sooner player's arm, and Clay retrieved it at the three and scooted into the end zone. Guess converted and Texas held a 14-7 lead.

Wilkinson stormed onto the field to berate officials. The OU skipper and many Sooner fans contended that one of Clay's knees had touched the ground when he scooped up the ball and scored. He didn't change the officials' minds.

Midway through the third period, Royal returned a punt to the OU 25, but the Sooners were whistled for clipping, which placed the ball back to the one-yard line. The clip was called on Tyree's block at the OU 14 on the return. Sooner fans contended that it was a clean block and began to express their displeasure.

OU went nowhere, and Texas scored moments later for a 21-7 lead.

The Sooners needed only one play to score from their 20 early in the fourth quarter. Thomas slammed through the line for eight yards, then lateraled to Mitchell, who raced 72 more yards to the end zone. Royal converted, and OU was back in the game, down 21-14.

Texas advanced from their 16 to the OU 38, following the kickoff. Royal's interception appeared to squelch the Steers' threat, but Sisco penalized the Sooners for unnecessary roughness. Texas got the ball back at the OU 23. One Sooner fan hurled a pop bottle onto the field. Soon others joined in, some tossing cushions. Wilkinson and the OU cheerleaders waved their arms to get the fans to stop, but to no avail.

The game had to be stopped to clear the field of debris, then Texas scored in three plays to take a 28-14 lead. The Longhorns scored their final touchdown with about two minutes remaining. Texas recovered a fumble at the OU 44, and Layne completed a TD pass to George McCall on the next play.

Hundreds of Sooner fans poured out of the stands in pursuit of the officials. A Dallas police car was quickly rolled to midfield to whisk away Sisco and his crew.

"Enraged Sooner partisans were out for blood, and it required some stout slugging by the police to get the officials to their car," reported the *Daily Oklahoman*.

Some fistfights broke out, but the football players were shaking hands by the locker rooms for a game well played.

Wilkinson said he was disappointed with the fans for their behavior and added, "It's too bad it had to happen."

The following night, about one thousand OU students hung Sisco in effigy from an elm tree in front of the administration building. Fans would use the phrase "Siscoed" many years later when they thought the Sooners got a bad call in a game.

A win the next week would soothe the Sooner fans' boiling blood, but Oklahoma tied Kansas, 13-13, before 34,700 in Norman.

OU threatened with a march to the KU 20 late in the opening stanza, but Thomas was stopped inches short of a first down on a fourth-down play. The 3-0-1 Jayhawks then drove the length of the field to take a 6-0 lead.

Sarratt recovered a Kansas fumble at the KU 41 to set up the first Sooner score late in the first half. Eight plays later, Royal scored from the one, and Wallace converted for a 7-6 lead.

Ray Evans returned the ensuing kickoff 35 yards to midfield. The Jayhawks advanced to the OU four, but a bad snap lost 30 yards as the half ended.

The Sooners needed only three plays to score after Mitchell returned the second-half kickoff to the OU 30. George Brewer gained 21 yards to the KU 49 on the next two plays. Sarratt completed a 30-yard pass to Mitchell, who dashed to the end zone. Wallace missed the conversion, but OU held a 13-6 advantage.

Kansas marched 52 yards to tie the game late in the third period.

The Sooners drove to the KU 16 with 1:45 remaining in the game, but OU was twice penalized for delay of game, and Evans intercepted Royal's desperation pass on the goal line.

OU gained 227 rushing yards and passed for 109 more. Kansas' defense had yielded an average of 54 rushing yards in the first four games. The Hawks held Mitchell to 24 rushing yards, 91 yards below his average. Kansas rushed for 102 and passed for 82 more.

It's a Fact
The Sooners led the nation in rushing defense, yielding an average of 58 yards per game.

The Sooners suffered their first home loss since 1945 on October 25. Texas Christian defeated OU, 20-7. The game was played in a light rain in contrast to the heavy downpour the previous year in Fort Worth.

The 2-2-1 Horned Frogs intercepted four Oklahoma passes, turning two of them into touchdowns.

TCU drove 68 yards to score first late in the first stanza. Minutes later, Mitchell tossed a pass to Sarratt, but Morris Bailey intercepted and scampered 51 yards for a touchdown and a 14-0 Frog lead.

The Sooners marched 48 yards in 10 plays for their only score of the game. Sarratt scored on a one-yard run and J.L. Martin converted.

TCU scored again four minutes later after Bailey intercepted Royal's pass and returned it 21 yards to the OU eight. Fullback Pete Stout scored from the one, moments later.

Neither team threatened in the second half. Oklahoma had more rushing yards (169-93), but TCU held the passing edge (64-30).

Displeased with his squad's performance, Wilkinson shook up his backfield before hosting Iowa State the following week. Royal started at quarterback, Buddy Jones at left half, Johnny Allsup at right half and Greathouse at fullback.

The 1-5 Cyclones rolled into Norman riding a five-game losing streak after winning the season opener. The Sooners won, 27-9, on a cold and windy November afternoon before 23,000 homecoming spectators.

Iowa State took a 3-0 lead on a 37-yard field goal late in the first period.

Early in the second quarter, Royal clutched a fumble out of the air and dashed 13 yards for a touchdown. Wallace converted for a 7-3 Sooner lead.

Thomas intercepted Don Ferguson's pass and returned it 48 yards to the Cyclone 22. Ray Klootwyk tackled Thomas to save a touchdown then popped off to an official. Iowa State was penalized 15 yards for unsportsmanlike conduct, and officials moved the ball to the seven. Brewer smashed up the middle for four yards, then sliced off right guard for the touchdown. Wallace toed the conversion.

The Cyclones threatened with a drive to the OU six in the third period, but the Big Red defense stiffened.

OU fullback Ed Kreick carried the ball only once on an 85-yard touchdown play early in the fourth stanza. Thomas slammed through the line for 12 yards and was hemmed in by Cyclones, so he lateraled to Kreick, who followed a wall of blockers and galloped the final 73 yards down the east sideline. Wallace missed the conversion.

Iowa State answered with a 70-yard scoring drive in three plays.

OU had the ball at its own 41 with 1:25 left in the game. Mitchell faked a handoff then pitched out to Brewer on a reverse, and Brewer flashed down the west sideline for the score. Kreick threw a key block at the Iowa State 35, taking out the last Cyclone in pursuit. Wallace converted.

Iowa State had more passing yards (57-7), but OU gained more on the ground (270-231).

Injuries kept several Sooners from making the trip to Manhattan on November 8. Mitchell and Dee Andros, Plato's brother, were the only starters sidelined and both had ankle injuries. Several Sooners stayed home with the flu. Tyree and Paine were the only starters with the flu; however, Paine made the trip and played against 0-7 Kansas State, winless in their last 23 games. The Sooners escaped Manhattan with a 27-13 victory.

It was a good thing Paine felt well enough to play, because he recovered a K-State fumble at the Cats' 38 early in the first quarter. Brewer and Jones carried on the next seven plays, and Brewer's two-

yard scoot around end struck pay dirt. Wallace toed the seventh point.

The Wildcats answered with a TD, but the extra point was low, and the Big Red held a slim 7-6 margin. K-State threatened again after intercepting Royal's pass at the OU 22. The Cats moved to the three, but Rapacz intercepted a short pass and scampered to the OU 28.

The Sooners wheeled 72 yards for another Brewer touchdown, a four-yard run, and Wallace converted.

Oklahoma jumped to a 21-6 lead late in the third stanza on Royal's 44-yard TD pass to Owens. Royal connected to a streaking Owens who caught the pigskin over his head at the Cats' 10 and zoomed into the end zone. Wallace toed the extra point.

The Cats closed the gap with a 55-yard TD pass early in the fourth period.

The Sooners marched 73 yards for the final tally following the kickoff. Brewer and Jones again ripped off huge gains in the drive. Jones for 24, Brewer for 14 and Jones hammered for 10 more. Brewer gained two to the Cats' one-yard line, then Jones burst over left guard for the score. Wallace missed the conversion.

For the first time in Oklahoma football history, two backs rushed for more than 100 yards. Brewer gained 135 on 22 totes, and Jones added 115 on 19 carries.

The Sooners traveled to Columbia to face No. 17 Missouri the next week with the Big Six title on the line. OU, at 2-0-1 in the conference, was tied with Kansas for second place, and behind Missouri at 3-0. The No. 17 Tigers (6-2) were riding a five-game winning streak, yielding only 27 points during that stretch. The Big Red nearly matched it with a 21-12 victory.

Burris' fumble recovery at the MU 48 gave OU a chance to score first late in the opening quarter, but the Sooners had to surrender on downs at the 21.

Oklahoma did score first early in the second stanza when Brewer took a Tiger punt and jettisoned 69 yards to the end zone. Brewer crossed the field to fake a handoff to Mitchell then sailed down the sideline. Rapacz, Goad, Paine and Burris each mowed down a Tiger pursuer along the way. Wallace converted the first of three conversions for a 7-0 OU advantage.

An OU fumble minutes later set up Missouri's first touchdown. Mitchell fumbled the pigskin, and MU's Jim Dusenberry recovered at the OU 48. Bus Entsminger moments later completed a 14-yard TD pass to Mel Sheehan. Wade Walker blocked Bob Dawson's conversion.

The Tigers took a 12-7 lead late in the second period with a 47-yard drive.

The Sooners threatened with a 72-yard march to the MU 14, but the first half expired. OU again moved into scoring position after the second-half kickoff but stalled at the MU 20.

Royal, who punted five times for an average of 41.6 yards per kick, had three precision punts that pinned the Tigers deep, and two of them came in the second half. Entsminger fielded the first one in the first quarter, but the Tigers fumbled it out of bounds at the two, and Missouri had to punt it away.

Early in the fourth stanza, Royal angled a punt out at the Mizzou one. The Tigers punted back, but the Sooners stalled, and Royal angled another kick out at the 4. Howard Bonnett fumbled on the next play, and Greathouse pounced on it. Davis carried on the next two plays, one for three yards and the next just inches short of the goal line. Brewer sliced off tackle for the score and a 14-12 Oklahoma lead.

The Tigers drove 46 yards to the OU 20 after the kickoff, but Ed Quirk fumbled, and Walker recovered for the Sooners. The Big Red marched the distance in 11 plays, and Mitchell's one-yard run off left end capped the drive. Mitchell also sparked the drive with a 41-yard run to the MU six several plays before he scored.

OU gained 264 rushing yards and 46 passing yards. Missouri, which had 302 yards rushing the week before, was held to 81 yards on the ground.

The Sooners hit the road again on November 22 to face 2-5 Nebraska in Lincoln, and again the Big Six crown was on the line. An Oklahoma victory and Kansas loss would give OU the outright title. Both teams won that day to split the conference championship for the second straight year. OU defeated the Huskers, 14-13, and the Jayhawks defeated Missouri, 20-14.

A bundled-up crowd of 25,000 turned out on a cold and snowy day in Lincoln. The temperature at game time was 22 degrees, and several inches of snow banked the sidelines. Husker Cletus Fischer warmed up the fans when he intercepted Royal's pass 60 yards for a touchdown midway through the second quarter. Dick Hutton missed the extra point, which would come back to haunt the Huskers in the end.

The Sooners scored three and one-half minutes later on Thomas' 10-yard touchdown. Sarratt started the 63-yard drive with a 30-yard sprint off right end, and Thomas followed it with a 26-yard dash off left end to the NU 14. Thomas scored three plays later. Wallace booted the conversion to give OU a 7-6 edge, which remained through halftime.

The Cornhuskers were caught snoozing on the second-half kick-off. Burris' kick bounced around deep in Nebraska territory, but no Husker retrieved it. Thomas, racing downfield, pounced on it for the Sooners at the NU 28. Seven plays later, Thomas scooted off right tackle for a two-yard TD. Wallace's conversion barely cleared the cross bar.

The Huskers scored minutes later when Dick Thompson completed a 27-yard pass to Alex Cochrane. Hutton converted this time, but Nebraska still trailed, 14-13.

OU had a chance to put the game away late in the third period when Rapacz intercepted Thompson's pass at the NU 47. The Sooners advanced to the three, but the Huskers stopped Mitchell short on fourth-and-one. Neither team threatened again.

Oklahoma totaled 217 yards on the ground and 15 more passing. The defense held the Huskers to 109 rushing yards and 35 more through the air.

The Sooners hosted Oklahoma A&M the next week under sunny skies and 50 degrees. Thomas scored twice on long runs in the second half to lead OU to a 21-13 victory.

The Sooners trailed 13-7 after three quarters. Merle Dinkins recovered an Aggie fumble early in the fourth stanza at the A&M 38 after Burris clobbered A&M's Billy Grimes. Mitchell lateraled to Thomas on the first play, and the Sooner halfback darted down the sideline for the touchdown. Wallace converted and OU led, 14-13, with 10 minutes to go.

With two minutes remaining, Thomas took Mitchell's handoff, burst into the secondary, and dashed 59 yards to the end zone. Wallace converted for the 21st point. Royal, who already had two interceptions, stole his third Aggie pass moments later at the A&M 42. The Sooners drove to the A&M five as the gun sounded.

OU doubled the Aggies in rushing yards (324-160). Thomas led the Sooners with 106 yards on six carries. Oklahoma passed for only five yards, while the Aggies totaled 44 through the air.

The Sooners received bids from four bowl games—Alamo in San Antonio, Gator in Jacksonville, Sun in El Paso and Harbor in San Diego. Bud Wilkinson left it up to a vote of his players, who chose to decline a bowl.

The Sooners ended the year with a 7-2-1 record and a share of the Big Six championship with a 4-0-1 record. Burris was the only Sooner chosen to the All-America team. Burris, Tyree, Walker, Mitchell, and Rapacz were named to the All-Big Six first team.

1948

The 7-2-1 record in Bud Wilkinson's first year drew criticism from some Sooner supporters. Wilkinson went to Annapolis, Maryland, in January 1948 to interview for the Navy head coaching job. The press speculated that Wilkinson would take the Navy position. Navy did offer, but Wilkinson declined.

Wilkinson was given the official title of athletic director in the spring. Frank Ivy (OU star from 1937-39) replaced Dutch Fehring as end coach.

Colorado became the newest member of the conference, and the name of the league was changed to Big Seven. The Buffaloes would not be on Oklahoma's schedule for two more seasons.

The Sooners had a solid corps of returnees in 1948—All-America guard Buddy Burris, tackles Homer Paine and Wade Walker, and Jim Owens and Bobby Goad at the ends. Center John Rapacz signed a contract to play in the pros. Don Tillman would replace him in the middle of the line. Jack Mitchell, Darrell Royal, George Thomas, and George Brewer returned to the backfield. Royal and Mitchell shared quarterbacking duties in 1947 and both would share them again in '48. Royal got the nod as the starter, and Mitchell was moved to fullback to start the season.

Wilkinson said alternating Mitchell and Royal at quarterback gives the team "a better balance to the passing attack."

The balance worked, as the Sooners won 10 straight games following a loss in the season opener.

With so many returning veterans, Wilkinson was not pleased with practices the week before the season opener September 25 against Santa Clara in San Francisco. The Sooners' skipper said practices were the "worst since I've been here."

The offense was sluggish, and four defensive backs were sidelined with injuries—starters Bill Price and Calvin Steinberger and reserves Bill Lambeth and Lindell Pearson.

The lack of experience in the secondary doomed the Sooners in the second half of the Santa Clara game. The game was reminiscent of Santa Clara's come-from-behind victory over the Sooners in the second half of the 1940 match up. OU led that game, 13-0, and the Broncos went to the air to win, 33-13, in the final 30 minutes. After trailing 17-7 at halftime of the '48 tilt, 0-1 Santa Clara defeated

1947 Season Record: 7-2-1

Big Six Conference: 4-0-1 (Co-Champions)

Date	Opponent	Result	Score
September 26	at Detroit	W	24-20
October 4	TEXAS A&M	W	26-14
October 11	Texas at Dallas	L	34-14
October 18	KANSAS	T	13-13
October 25	TEXAS CHRISTIAN	L	20-7
November 1	IOWA STATE	W	27-9
November 8	at Kansas State	W	27-13
November 15	at Missouri	W	21-12
November 22	at Nebraska	W	14-13
November 29	OKLAHOMA A&M	W	21-13

Oklahoma, 20-17, before a crowd of only 7,000 at San Francisco's Kezar Stadium.

The Sooners outrushed the Broncos, 252-116. Thomas led the OU ground attack with 159 yards in nine carries. The Sooners added 62 yards through the air.

OU scored four TDs in the second half, three in the fourth quarter, to crush Texas A&M, 42-14, on October 2 in Norman.

The Big Red gained 304 yards rushing and 151 yards passing. The defense handcuffed the Aggies to 75 total yards (47 rushing and 28 passing).

Sooner Magic: Breaking the Drought

Just like the drought conditions of the 1930s, the Oklahoma Sooners suffered a drought beginning a decade later—eight miserable years of losing to the Texas Longhorns. It was the longest winning streak in the series, which raised Texas' series record to 29-11-2.

The Sooners snapped the Longhorns' streak with a 20-14 victory on October 9 before a Cotton Bowl crowd of 67,435, the largest crowd to see a football game in the Southwest. The stadium had a newly constructed upper deck on the west side and more seats were added to give the appearance of a bowl. The final work of numbering the seats was completed one hour before kickoff. WPAB in Fort Worth broadcast the game in the Dallas-Fort Worth area.

The Steers, ranked 16th and two-touchdown favorites, lost their season opener 34-6 to North Carolina, then defeated LSU, 33-0, and New Mexico, 47-0.

After a scoreless first quarter, the Sooners marched 73 yards for a touchdown midway through the second. Leon Heath scored on a one-yard run, and Les Ming converted. Pearson sparked the drive with two carries for 20 yards and two plays before the touchdown, and Mitchell picked up 10 yards to the Steers' two.

Texas threatened with a drive to the OU 25 but fumbled the ball away early in the third stanza. Minutes later, Frank Guess punted out on the OU 34, and the Sooners set sail for a 14-0 lead in 11 plays. Thomas capped the drive by slicing through right tackle from the one and Ming booted the conversion. Thomas and Heath carried for huge gains in the drive. Thomas picked up 23 yards off a Mitchell lateral, Heath gained 10, and Thomas gained 10 to the Horns' one before he scored.

Texas marched to the OU 11 early in the fourth period but surrendered on downs. Royal punted out to the OU 49 moments later, and the Steers scored in six plays. Paul Campbell sailed a 15-yard scoring strike to Randall Clay, and Clay toed the extra point. OU 14, Texas 7.

The Sooners answered with an 86-yard scoring drive in three plays. Mitchell gained six yards on the first play, then Heath ripped off right tackle for 68 more to the UT 13. Thomas burst over right tackle, cut back, and bowled over UT's Billy Pyle en route to the end zone. Ming missed his first extra point after making the first 11.

Perry Samuels returned the ensuing kickoff 65 yards to the OU 20. Royal caught him from behind for the TD-saving tackle. Three plays later, Tom Landry slipped through a huge gap for a five-yard touchdown. Clay converted, and Texas cut the Sooner lead to 20-14. The last three touchdowns came in a span of five and one-half minutes.

Texas kicked off and forced OU to three-and-out. Royal punted to the UT 37 with less than a minute remaining. Landry tossed an incomplete pass then was sacked by several Sooners. On the next play, Thomas intercepted Landry's pass at midfield with 15 seconds remaining.

With one play remaining, Mitchell cradled the ball as he dropped to the ground. The crimson-clad fans began chanting the clock's final seconds, "Five … four … three … two … one … zero!" They stormed the field and the wooden goal post, decorated with red and white ribbons, quickly came down. Sooner fans carried them the length of the field. The posts were later broken into pieces for souvenirs. Oklahoma fans celebrated in downtown Dallas late into the night. Enthusiastic Sooner fans greeted the team as they arrived at Oklahoma City's Will Rogers Airport that night.

The Sooners entered the AP poll for the first time all year at No. 20. Myrle Greathouse, Walker and Tillman sat out the next game with minor injuries. Royal scored two touchdowns and passed for two more as Oklahoma clobbered 1-2 Kansas State, 42-0, on October 16 on a windy (35 mph) day in Norman.

OU rushed for 230 yards and passed for 92 more. Thomas led the ground attack with 118 yards on 11 carries. Royal only completed two passes, both of them scoring strikes. The Big Red defense held the Cats to two first downs and 94 total yards.

The No. 18 Sooners traveled to Fort Worth the following week for a non-conference tilt with 4-1 Texas Christian. The Sooners won, 21-18, against the Frogs' surprise 4-4 defense. Wilkinson moved Heath from fullback to flanker, outside the end. This forced TCU coach Dutch Meyer to put a linebacker to key on Heath, but that maneuver opened up the Sooners' running game in the middle.

The Frogs got on board first and last with safeties. Oklahoma had trouble hanging on to the pigskin, losing it five times on seven fumbles. The first lost fumble came after Heath ran back the opening kickoff 21 yards to the OU 37. TCU then advanced to the OU one, but had to surrender on downs. The Sooners could not get uncorked and were forced to punt from the end zone. Bob Bodenhamer's snap skidded along the grass. Royal had trouble getting a handle on the ball and fumbled it in back of the end zone. TCU, 2-0.

The Sooners drove 90 yards for the lead early in the second quarter. Mitchell's 13-yard end sweep and Ming's conversion put OU ahead, 7-2.

Jack Archer scored on a 29-yard run minutes later, and Homer Ludiker converted to give TCU a 9-7 advantage.

Pearson, who led the Sooners with 145 yards rushing on 20 carries, scored on a one-yard plunge at the end of a 60-yard drive following the second-half kickoff. Mitchell returned the kickoff 37 yards to the OU 40. Pearson carried for most of the eight-play drive including a 25-yard run to the TCU 12. Ming converted to put the Sooners back on top, 14-9.

Berry raced 69 yards two plays after the ensuing kickoff, and Ludiker toed the extra point to give TCU a 16-14 lead.

Oklahoma moved to the TCU four following the Frogs' kickoff, but Mitchell fumbled. Minutes later, Mitchell returned a Frog punt 21 yards to the OU 48 to set up the next touchdown early in the fourth stanza. Pearson ripped through the line, stiff-armed a couple of defenders and sprinted to the end zone three plays later. Ming converted to lift the Big Red to a 21-16 lead.

A Frog punt pinned the Sooners deep at their own 10. Three plays gained only seven yards, and a delay penalty moved the ball back to the 12. On fourth-and-eight, Coach Wilkinson ordered an intentional safety. Mitchell took the snap, retreated, and spun his way back to the end zone where the Frogs tackled him. The second TCU safety drew the Frogs within three points, 21-18, with 20 seconds remaining. Royal punted on the free kick from his 20 to the TCU 44. Berry faded back and hurled a pass, which hit Archer on the arm at the OU 24, but the gun sounded.

The Big Red outgained TCU in rushing yards (360-189), but the Frogs had more passing yards (103-14). Jack Mitchell added 113 yards on 19 totes.

No. 16 Oklahoma hammered 3-3 Iowa State, 33-6, on October 30 before 10,000 in Ames. Burris recovered Pearson's fumble in the end zone. I-State answered with a TD, but missed the conversion.

Mitchell scored on a 55-yard punt return, Heath scored on a one-yard run, and Claude Arnold hurled a six-yard TD pass to Ed Lisak.

OU rushed for 198 yards and passed for 130 more. The Cyclones picked up 146 rushing yards and 74 more through the air.

The 15th-ranked Sooners returned home the next week for a showdown with No. 9 Missouri. The 5-1 Tigers lost their season opener, then won five straight. Oklahoma blasted Missouri, 41-7, for the largest margin in the 38-game series and before a home-

Jack Mitchell scores OU's first touchdown against North Carolina in the Sugar Bowl. *(OU Athletics)*

coming crowd of 38,500, a new attendance record. NBC radio broadcasted the game, and an impromptu addition was made to the press box to accommodate additional personnel. Steel pipes were added to support the expanded press box, which extended over the fans on the top rows.

Trailing 7-0, OU tied the game on Thomas' four-yard leap into the end zone and Ming's extra point early in the second stanza.

The Sooners jumped to a 14-7 lead in the first three minutes of the second period following a Missouri fumble. Mike Ghnouly returned Royal's punt to the MU 35, but Goad's hit forced him to fumble, and Goad pounced on the free ball. Ghnouly was taken from the field and to the OU infirmary, where it was discovered he had three broken ribs.

On the next play, Mitchell faked a handoff and accelerated through right tackle for a touchdown. The Tigers went nowhere on their next possession. Paine and Owens charged through the line and blocked Bob Robinson's punt, which rolled back 24 yards to the MU 16. Six plays later, Thomas sliced through right tackle for a two-yard score and a 21-7 Sooner lead.

Minutes later, Mitchell took Robinson's punt at the OU 30, crossed over to Royal, faked a handoff, eluded one defender at the 45 and raced to the end zone. Oklahoma made it 35-7 when Mitchell took another Missouri punt and this time he handed off to Royal on the crisscross. Royal gained 25 to the MU 35. Nine plays later, Heath took Mitchell's lateral at the three and scooted across the goal line.

Heath scored on a 25-yard run to cap a 60-yard drive early in the fourth quarter. The Tigers later advanced to the OU 24, but Buddy Jones picked off Bus Entsminger's pass at the 10.

OU rushed for 289 yards and passed for 44 more. The Tigers gained 114 yards on the ground and 111 passing.

Major bowl rumors began circulating through the newspapers, but Wilkinson maintained that such talk was premature with three games remaining.

The Sooners also handed Nebraska its worst defeat in the series with a 41-14 victory on November 13 before 28,000 in Norman. Like the Tigers a week earlier, Nebraska took a 7-0 lead, then the No. 9 Sooners took command.

However, errors plagued Oklahoma early on. A clipping penalty erased Mitchell's 70-yard punt return for a score. The Sooners marched 65 yards to the Husker 23 on their next series, but had to surrender on downs. The third Oklahoma possession ended with a fumble at the NU 15.

OU capitalized on Husker mistakes and scored three touchdowns in four and one-half minutes. Callopy's punt rolled out at the NU 36, and the Sooners scored eight plays later. Thomas ripped through the middle for a five-yard touchdown, and Ming converted for the 7-7 tie.

Callopy's punt on the next Husker possession rolled out at the NU 39. After a couple of penalties were assessed to each team, Royal hurled a 35-yard TD pass on the next play to Mitchell. Ming toed the extra point.

Seconds later, Heath recovered Callopy's fumble at the Nebraska 37. Royal then fired a TD pass to Frankie Anderson. Ming converted, and OU held a 21-7 advantage with six seconds until halftime.

The Sooners took the second-half kickoff and drove to the NU one, but Mitchell fumbled. Nebraska gained no yards and punted back. Callopy's kick rolled out on the NU 17. Two plays and a Husker penalty later, Royal slashed off left tackle for a nine-yard score.

Pearson and Brewer each scored on one-yard runs to put the game away.

Oklahoma thoroughly dominated the stat department with 27 first downs and 549 total yards (395 rushing and 154 passing). The

Lindell Pearson of Oklahoma City was touted to be one of the best sophomores to play for the Sooners in years. He announced he would enroll at OU in the fall of 1947, but he failed to register in September. Head coach Bud Wilkinson called Dr. C.B. McDonald, an Oklahoma City dentist, an ardent Sooner supporter and friend of Pearson's family.

McDonald went to the Pearson home to investigate Lindell's whereabouts. The parents did not know, but Lindell's mother said their son's girlfriend might. McDonald discovered, through the girlfriend, that Lindell had enrolled at the University of Arkansas. McDonald went to Fayetteville, but Razorback officials did not allow him to see Lindell.

McDonald returned to Oklahoma City to enlist the help of Eugene Jordan and Bob Bowers, two other OU supporters. The three men and a detective went to Little Rock and checked into a hotel. The detective, representing himself as an assistant coach at another school, called an Arkansas assistant coach and said he was in town and wanted to discuss football at their respective schools.

The detective and Razorback coach met in the hotel's coffee shop. Meanwhile, McDonald, Jordan and Bowers went to Lindell's room and convinced him to return to OU. They helped him pack his clothes and had him out of his room before the assistant returned. Lindell enrolled at OU the next day.

OU president Dr. George Lynn Cross wrote in his book, *Presidents Can't Punt*, that that event led to the forming of the Touchdown Club, an organization to support Sooner athletics, primarily football. The new organization was established on October 8, 1947, as a corporation for the sole purpose of receiving, holding and disbursing money for the support of athletics.

defense held the Huskers to four first downs and 82 total yards (22 rushing and 60 passing). Officials tossed penalty flags 29 times and stepped off 228 yards. OU was flagged 17 times for 153 yards and Nebraska 12 times for 75 yards.

OU and Kansas shared the conference championship the previous two years. Their showdown on November 20 in Lawrence was for all the marbles in the Big Seven Conference. The 7-1 Jayhawks won seven straight after losing their season opener. Both teams were tied at 4-0 atop the conference standings.

The No. 8 Sooners blasted the Hawks, 60-7, to win the outright conference crown.

Mitchell scored twice for the Sooners, including a 67-yard punt return. Royal also scored on a 73-yard punt return.

Oklahoma gained 493 total yards (346 rushing and 146 passing). Heath who scored once, led all runners with 70 yards. The defense held the Hawks to six first downs and 66 total yards.

The bowls were eagerly awaiting the Sooners' final game against Oklahoma A&M. The Orange, Sugar and Cotton Bowls were interested in inviting OU to play on New Year's Day.

No. 6 Oklahoma traveled up state for the season finale against 6-2 Oklahoma A&M. Despite a cold and drizzly day, a crowd of 30,000 turned out, the largest crowd to witness a game in Stillwater. The Big Red was looking to extend their streak to three straight in the 43rd edition of the instate rivalry. OU held a 28-8-6 lead in the overall series.

Sooner Magic: Safety Preserves Safe Victory

A penalty wiped out the Sooners' first scoring effort early in the first quarter. Royal fired a 40-yard bomb to Goad, but OU was flagged for backfield in motion. Mitchell, playing with a sore leg, fumbled at the A&M nine later in the drive, and Troy Ledbetter recovered for the Aggies. Moments later, Greathouse laid a jarring tackle on A&M's Jim Spavital who fumbled, and Ed Lisak smoth-

ered the ball at the Aggie six. Two plays later, Pearson scored from the four, but Ming missed the conversion.

The Sooners needed only three plays and an Aggie penalty to cover 64 yards for their next score. The drive began late in the first period and carried into the second. Thomas picked up 21 yards off right end. Pearson busted up the middle for 24 more. A delay-of-game penalty moved the ball to the A&M 14, then Mitchell scored on the next play. Ming missed the first conversion, but the Aggies were offside, and his second attempt was good. OU led, 13-0, with 40 seconds gone in the second stanza.

Pearson's fumble at the OU 10 late in the first half led to an Aggie touchdown to cut OU's lead to 10-7.

The Aggies punted out to the OU 37 on their first series of the second half. Heath juggled Mitchell's handoff, but held on to gain 13 yards to midfield. On the next play, Pearson cut through left tackle and sped to the end zone. Ming's conversion was wide, but the Sooners held a comfortable 19-7 advantage. Or was it comfy?

A&M scored lickety split on their next possession. Ledbetter returned the kickoff 22 yards to the A&M 44. Spavital scored on the next play, but Hartman missed the conversion. Sooners 19, Aggies 13. The Aggies later drove to the OU 27, but Royal squelched the threat by picking off Spavital's pass at the OU 15.

Mitchell fumbled on the first play of the fourth stanza, and Ledbetter pounced on it at the OU 33. The Big Red defense forced the Aggies to surrender on downs at the OU 20. Two plays later, Royal's lateral sailed wild and rolled back to the two-yard line where A&M's Don Von Pool recovered.

A delay-of-game penalty moved the ball back to the seven, then Owens sacked Hartman for a loss of six yards. Jones knocked down Hartman's second-down pass in the end zone. Hartman's next pass was dropped in the end zone.

The Sooners lost another fumble minutes later as Thomas swept around end and lateraled to Royal. John Gattis recovered for the Aggies at the OU 29. Hartman completed two passes to the Sooner 10, but an interference penalty on OU moved the ball to the six. Hartman overthrew his next pass. Bob Meinart gained three yards, and Spavital was held for no gain. Hartman's pass in the end zone was dropped.

OU got the ball back at its two with two minutes left in the game. Mitchell gained nothing, as he had to recover his own fumble. He gained zero on the next carry, then the Sooners were penalized back to the one for delay of game. Royal, back to punt, ran wide to his right to elude the rushing Aggies, who trapped him and tackled him in the end zone for a safety. The Aggies were whistled for offside on the play moving the ball to the six with six seconds to go.

Not risking an Aggie touchdown and victory, Royal took an intentional safety in the end zone as the gun sounded.

Oklahoma rushed for 247 yards, three more than the Aggies. A&M had the passing edge with 68 yards to only seven for OU.

The Sooners accepted an invitation to play in the 15th Sugar Bowl in New Orleans on New Year's Day against North Carolina.

The Sooners traveled on Christmas Day to Biloxi, Mississippi, 90 miles east of New Orleans. Wilkinson wanted his charges to practice in warmer climate. The team then moved to Algiers Naval Base, in New Orleans, on New Year's Eve.

The No. 3 Tar Heels had been ranked among the top five for most of the season in the AP poll and were No. 1 in the third week of the season. Texas was the only common opponent between both teams, and North Carolina easily handled the Horns, 34-7, in the season opener. The 9-0-1 Heels outscored their opponents, 255-80. A tie against William and Mary in the seventh week marred their perfect record.

Paul "Buddy" Burris, Oklahoma's left guard, was named All-America in 1946 and became the Sooners' first two-time All-American in 1947. He was again named All-America in 1948 to become the first three-time All-American.

Burris was born in Claremore, Oklahoma, and grew up in Muskogee. At Muskogee Central High School, he started at end his freshman season, but a new coach came in the following year and moved Burris to tackle, a position he played his final three years in high school.

He was a backup guard for Tulsa University in 1942, then served time in World War II. He served nearly three years with the Army engineers in the Pacific, Rhineland, and European theaters. He came to the University of Oklahoma, in 1946 and started at left guard for the next three years.

Burris was surprised to be named All-America for a third straight year. "You know, I don't see any difference in any of our six guards … they're all tough. I know because I have to scrimmage 'em every week," he told the Daily Oklahoman.

Gomer Jones, Burris' line coach at OU, said Burris was an exceptional lineman. "Fast for a big man. He plays each game with heart. He's a hard worker. He is easy to coach. He loves to play football."

(© 1948, The Daily Oklahoman)

Charlie "Choo Choo" Justice was the Heels' star left halfback, who finished second to SMU's Doak Walker in the Heisman Trophy race. Justice was a catalyst in the Tar Heels' single-wing attack. He not only carried the ball, he passed, returned kicks and punted. Justice scored eight touchdowns and passed for 13 more. He rushed for 766 yards and passed for 854 yards. Justice returned 19 punts for 332 yards, five kickoffs for 141 yards, and averaged 44 yards per punt.

The Sooners shut down the Tar Heels' single wing with a 14-6 upset before a record crowd of 80,383. Oklahoma employed an overshifting defense to stop Justice and contain star end Art Weiner from getting open.

North Carolina threatened to score on the opening drive of the game. Justice's 23-yard pass to Weiner moved the Tar Heels to the OU 15.

Greathouse intercepted Justice's next pass at the OU 18 and raced 69 yards to the NC 13. Mitchell carried five times to the two. His sneak on fourth and a foot gained a first down at the three. An off-side penalty moved the ball back to the seven, then Thomas carried for four and two yards respectively. Mitchell scored from the one, and Ming's conversion put Oklahoma ahead, 7-0.

The Tar Heels capitalized on an OU fumble moments later. Hosea Rodgers scored five plays later, but the conversion was wide and OU held a 7-6 advantage.

The Heels threatened to score late in the second stanza, wheeling from their 15 to the OU eight. Weiner dropped Justice's fourth-down pass in the end zone.

The Tar Heels punted out to the OU 47 in the third period. Royal faked a handoff, faded back, and unleashed a 43-yard bomb to Anderson to the NC 10. It was the Sooners' only completion of the day, and Anderson caught the ball in a traffic of Tar Heels. Thomas plowed up the middle for two yards, then Pearson smashed over left tackle for the score, dragging NC's Bill Macey with him into the end zone. Ming converted, and OU held a 14-6 lead with 5:15 remaining in the third quarter.

Neither team threatened the rest of the way. Wilkinson was carried off the field on the shoulders of his jubilant players.

Mitchell was awarded the William V. Miller Trophy as the game's outstanding player. Oklahoma gained 15 first downs to 12 for North Carolina. OU rushed for 185 yards and passed for 43 more. The Tar Heels rushed for 128 yards and passed for 78 yards. North Carolina gained 65 total yards in the second half.

Wilkinson said the win was a total team effort.

"Our lines were great," he said. "Jack Mitchell proved he is a great quarterback by the way he kept the team driving for that first touchdown."

The Sooners finished the 1948 campaign with a 10-1 record and a conference title. Burris was named All-America for the third straight year. He was also named to the All-Big Seven first team along with Owens, Walker, Paine, Mitchell, and Thomas.

1949

Sooner head coach Bud Wilkinson was beginning to receive national recognition after a 10-1 season in 1948. Other universities began to take notice and tried to lure him from OU. Rumors thrived that he would take a coaching job at Wisconsin or at his alma mater, Minnesota. Wilkinson did visit Madison, Wisconsin, in January 1949. He was not offered a coaching job there, but visited with Wisconsin's school president about its coaching problems.

When Wilkinson returned to Norman days later, he signed a new five-year contract with the University of Oklahoma.

Many veterans returned to the 1949 squad, bringing Sooner faithful hopes for extending their 10-game winning streak, which began with the second game of the previous year. OU did extend its streak to 21 games with a perfect 11-0 record, the first perfect season in 31 years. The 1918 Sooners had a perfect record of 6-0.

All-America guard Buddy Burris, Sugar Bowl MVP Jack Mitchell, and All-Big Seven tackle Homer Paine had graduated and left the biggest voids to fill, but not too difficult to fill. Dee Andros stepped into the left guard slot, and Darrell Royal had experience at quarterback. Leon Manley took over Paine's slot at left tackle. Stan West

1948 Season Record: 10-1-0

Big Seven Conference: 5-0-0 (Champions)

Date	Opponent	Result	Score
September 25	Santa Clara*	L	20-17
October 2	TEXAS A&M	W	42-14
October 9	Texas at Dallas	W	20-14
October 16	KANSAS STATE	W	42-0
October 23	at Texas Christian	W	21-18
October 30	at Iowa State	W	33-6
November 6	MISSOURI	W	41-7
November 13	NEBRASKA	W	41-14
November 20	at Kansas	W	60-7
November 27	at Oklahoma A&M	W	19-15
January 1	North Carolina#	W	14-6

*Game played in San Francisco, CA
#Sugar Bowl at New Orleans, LA

returned to the right guard position, and Jim Owens and Bobby Goad returned at the end positions with Frankie Anderson providing plenty of experience in a backup role. Wade Walker, two-time All-Conference tackle, returned to start at right tackle for the third straight year.

In addition to Royal, the backfield was solid. All-Big Seven halfback George Thomas returned along with halfback Lindell Pearson, fullback Leon Heath, and George Brewer was capable of taking a starting role at any time.

A season ticket for the Sooners' five home games cost $17.50. Individual game tickets sold for $3.50 in the reserved seats and $3 general admission. Children could get into a game for 50 cents. The Sooners hit the road to Boston, Massachusetts, for a first ever meeting with Boston College.

The Sooners were slated to play the Eagles on a Friday night in the season opener for both teams. The September 23 contest was postponed one day as heavy rains soaked Braves Field, also the home of baseball's Boston Braves. Braves officials declined to allow the football game to be played on Friday night, as they believed it would have damaged the field. The rain postponed the baseball game to the next afternoon, and OU and BC kicked off later that night.

So the Sooners and Eagles kicked off the next night in the first meeting between both teams. Actually, the Sooners kicked off more as they hammered BC, 46-0. The Eagles had not been shut out in four years.

Thomas led the Sooner scoring spree with three touchdowns, the first one on a 95-yard return of the opening kickoff. Ken Tipps booted the extra point, and OU had a 7-0 lead in the first 12 seconds.

Leading 27-0, Walker recovered an Eagle fumble at the BC 28 minutes later when Anderson hammered Eagle quarterback Ed Songlin. Seven plays later, Pearson scoored from the one, and Tipps converted for a 27-0 lead with five seconds remaining in the half.

The Big Red added three more touchdowns in the second half.

Oklahoma gained 358 rushing yards and passed for 48 more. Boston College picked up 35 rushing yards and 154 more through the air.

The Sooners extended their winning streak to 12 straight with a 33-13 victory over Texas A&M the next week in Norman. The game also was aired on WKY-TV, Oklahoma City's NBC affiliate. WKY contracted to broadcast all Sooner home games at a total cost of $3,000 to the University of Oklahoma.

Pearson and Thomas each scored twice in OU's fourth consecutive win over the 1-1 Aggies.

The Cadets' Yale Lary punted into a mild south wind late in the first period, but the ball wobbled five yards back to the A&M 19, where Stan West smothered it. Pearson swept off right end five plays later from the one-yard line, and Thomas converted.

The Aggies advanced to the OU 20 in the second quarter, but Goad nailed Don Nicholas for a five-yard loss on fourth down, and the Sooners took over. From there, the Big Red marched to another score in eight plays. Thomas, Pearson, and Heath picked up huge gains in the drive. Pearson scored on a 12-yard run off right end, and Thomas converted for a 14-0 lead midway through the second stanza.

A&M drove 54 yards late in the second quarter for its first score to trail, 14-6. Oklahoma took a 20-6 lead when Thomas scored on a one-yard plunge midway through the third period to cap an 86-yard march in 11 plays. Heath gained 23 yards, and Royal passed to Anderson for 37 yards to spark the drive. The Aggies blocked Thomas' extra point.

The Sooners marched 80 yards in eight plays on their next series. Pearson capped the drive with an eight-yard pass to Thomas. But Thomas' conversion veered wide. The big play of the drive came when the Cadets were whistled for a 38-yard pass interference penalty as Royal tried a pass to Thomas.

The Aggies scored off a 65-yard drive early in the fourth stanza.

The Sooners cruised 64 yards in nine plays for the final tally minutes later. Royal zipped a 10-yard pass to Goad, and Thomas converted.

OU gained 340 yards on the ground. Thomas led all Sooner carriers with 100 yards on 16 totes, and Pearson added 91 on 17 carries. The Aggies collected only 54 rushing yards and 156 passing yards, three more than OU in the air.

A record 75,504 fans turned out at the Cotton Bowl on October 8 for the 44th edition of the Red River rivalry. The Cotton Bowl was expanded in 1948 with the addition of an upper west deck. An upper deck was added to the east side before the 1949 OU-Texas tilt.

One Oklahoma travel agency offered a round-trip rail excursion to Dallas for a total of $23.50, and it didn't take long for the agency to sell out. The cost included lunch and round-trip transfers to the game and back to the train station.

The Sooners matched their score of a year ago with a 20-14 victory. But it wasn't easy in the first quarter as the Big Red bogged down and failed to cross midfield.

Royal had crimson hearts skip a beat when he fumbled at the OU 10 early in the first quarter returning a punt from out of the end zone. Charley Dowell intercepted the Horns' pass moments later.

Texas later drove to the OU 20, but the Big Red defense held and forced quarterback Paul Campbell to ground his fourth-down pass. The Steers then drove 46 yards for a 7-0 lead early in the second stanza.

The Sooners quickly moved 66 yards in six plays after the kickoff. From the Texas 40, Thomas burst up the middle and outran UT's Joe Arnold to the end zone. Tipps converted, and the score was even at 7-7. The clouds then burst open and showered on the rest of the game.

Thomas missed a 21-yard field goal late in the second period moments after Ed Lisak recovered Lewis Levine's fumble at the UT 30.

Pearson returned the second-half kickoff 40 yards to the OU 47, and Oklahoma rolled to the end zone in five plays. Pearson shot 11 yards up the middle for the score, carrying the Horns' Bobby Lee Cox on his back. Tipps converted for the 14-7 lead.

Early in the fourth stanza, Pearson took a Texas punt, crossed over and handed the ball to Thomas, who streaked 45 yards to the UT 25. The Sooners moved into scoring position, but on fourth and goal at the two, Thomas was stopped inches short of the goal line.

Texas stalled and punted out on the UT 37. Heath bulled ahead for 20 yards, then Royal hurled a 17-yard scoring strike to Owens, who sprinted laterally to catch the ball in the corner of the end zone.

Texas later marched 57 yard to the OU six, but fumbled it away there, and Jack Lockett recovered for the Sooners. The Horns marched 68 yards late in the game for their final score with 29 seconds to go.

The Steers gained more passing yards (139-35), but OU led in rushing with 216 yards to 118 for Texas. Royal punted seven times for a 45-yard average. Two of his boots sailed 71 yards (barely missing the coffin corner) and 51 yards.

The Sooners remained third in the AP poll and hosted Kansas the following week. Thomas delighted the 37,000 in attendance with a four-touchdown performance to lead OU to a 48-26 victory. Thomas' four scores set the school record and ran his season total to 10 TDs, equaling his entire touchdown total from the prior year.

Oklahoma rolled up 306 rushing yards and 91 passing yards. Thomas led all Sooner runners with 119 yards on 15 carries. He also had one pass reception for the first-quarter TD. The Jayhawks picked up 51 rushing yards and 189 yards in the air.

The Sooners dropped to fourth in the AP ranking and would travel to Lincoln the next week without the services of guard Stan West, who sat out with a minor knee injury. Clair Mayes filled in over the next two games.

Just a year before, Oklahoma handed Nebraska the worst defeat in the rivalry with a 27-point victory. The 1949 Sooners did much better with a 48-0 victory on October 22. Nebraska held a record of two wins and two losses.

Seven Sooners scored touchdowns, which came on long, sustained drives chewing up little chunks of yards in ferocious thrusts.

Wilkinson emptied the bench in the fourth quarter to let the reserves in on the action. Fourth-string halfback, Nolan Lang was the Sooners' leading rusher with 94 yards on five carries. OU hammered out 436 yards on the ground and 35 through the air. The defense held the Huskers to four rushing yards and 34 passing yards.

The Sooners did not score in the fourth quarter in the next three games. They didn't need to as they got the job done in the first 45 minutes.

200th Home Game

The No. 3 Oklahoma routed 4-1-1 Iowa State, 34-7, the next week, which marked the 200th home game in Sooner football history. The Sooners had to win it without Royal, who sat out with a leg bruise. Lisak also was sidelined with an injury, and West sat out his second straight game. A record crowd of 39,000 homecoming fans turned out at Oklahoma Memorial Stadium.

Bud Wilkinson and Gomer Jones created a new defensive alignment that became notorious as the "Oklahoma 5-2" defense. Instead of playing opposite the offensive ends, the linebackers were moved closer to the middle to counter the offensive guards, and the defensive tackles were moved to the outside shoulder of the offensive tackles and keyed on the offensive guards.

"The guard will pull or double-team, or do something to tell us what the play will be," Wilkinson said. "As soon as the offensive guard moved, we knew what to do."

Many teams continue to deploy the alignment today.

Gomer Jones (left) and Bud Wilkinson created the "Oklahoma 5-2" defense, an alignment used today by many colleges. *(OU Athletics)*

Iowa State featured Bill Weeks at quarterback, who completed 65 percent of his passes before the OU tilt. He completed 18 of 27 for 281 yards against the Big Red defense, but the defense yielded only one long pass play, which scored in the third quarter.

Claude Arnold played tremendously in Royal's stead. He completed four of four passes for 115 yards and ran for a touchdown. He completed a 35-yard pass to Pearson to the IS 35 on the first play of the game. The Sooners continued to the goal line in 10 plays, but Thomas fumbled at the goal line, and the Cyclones took over on a touchback.

The Cyclones marched to the Oklahoma 10, but Bill Chanucey's fourth-down pass fell incomplete. Iowa State continued to be a thorn in the crimson offense. John Tillo later intercepted Pearson's lateral on the OU 14. The Big Red defense held, and Dick Heatly punted 53 yards to get the Sooners out of danger.

Late in the second period, Don Ferguson returned Heatly's kick 13 yards to the OU 40. Leon Manley's tackle forced Ferguson to fumble, and Walker pounced on it. A delay penalty moved the Sooners five yards back, and Pearson lost 12 more on the next play. The crimson cog began spinning to the first score. The Sooners took nine plays to move from their 23, and Thomas scored from the two. Malcolm Schmidt blocked Tipps' conversion. Arnold sparked the drive with a couple of long passes to his ends—a 26-yarder to Goad and a 24-yarder to Owens.

Less than two minutes later, OU linebacker Ken Parker recovered Chauncey's fumble at the Cyclone seven. Heath scored on the next play, and Tipps converted.

Moments later, the Cyclones punted from their own 47. Buddy Jones fielded the kick at his 17 and raced 83 yards down the sideline for the score. Thomas threw a key block on the last Cyclone in pursuit near midfield. Tipps converted, and OU held a 20-0 lead with six seconds until intermission. The three touchdowns came in a span of six minutes.

Leon Heath, of Hollis, Oklahoma, received the nickname "Mule Train" for the way he ran with the football, dragging tacklers behind him. The moniker came from the song of the same name sung by Frankie Laine and was No. 1 on the charts for six weeks in 1949:
Mule train!! Clippety cloppin' over hill and plain
Seems as how they never stop, clippety clop, clippety clop.

The Sooners drove 80 yards in six plays for another score following the second-half kickoff. Pearson, who carried for 52 yards in the drive, scored on an eight-yard run. Tipps missed the conversion.

The OU defense pushed Iowa State back to the IS 13 on the next two plays following the kickoff. Cyclone quarterback Bill Weeks then caught the Sooner secondary napping. He tossed a pass to Jim Doran at the 30, and the Cyclone end outran David Lockett to the end zone.

A short punt set up the final Sooner touchdown five minutes later. Iowa State's Bob Angle punted to its 30. Five plays later, Arnold sneaked through the middle from the three.

Wilkinson emptied the bench again in the fourth stanza. Iowa State threatened with a march to the OU 15, but Weeks' pass to Doran was fumbled in the end zone, and the Sooners took over. Oklahoma later moved into position but stalled when Frank Silva's fourth-down pass to Gene Heape fell incomplete.

Oklahoma picked up 336 rushing yards. Pearson led all runners with 115 yards on 16 carries. Iowa State gained only 23 on the ground, but gained 281 in the air.

Royal still nursed his sore leg and saw limited action against Kansas State on November 5 in Manhattan. Arnold played most of the game at quarterback. The 2-4 Wildcats won their first two games of the season, then dropped four in a row.

No. 3 Oklahoma spoiled Kansas State's homecoming with a 39-0 victory.

Thomas and Heatly each scored twice—once via the run and again on a pass play.

Oklahoma gained 305 rushing yards. Pearson led the Big Red ground attack with 108 yards on six carries. Arnold and Royal combined to complete nine of 12 passes for 155 yards and three touchdowns. Kansas State was held to 48 rushing yards and 109 through the air.

Oklahoma and Missouri sat atop the Big Seven conference with identical 3-0 records. A record 37,152 fans, including 2,000 crimson rooters, turned out in Columbia for the Big Seven championship showdown. Missouri was only two points from an undefeated season, losing its first two games by one point each, and both losses were due to missed extra points.

No. 3 OU defeated the 5-2 Tigers, 27-7, to claim its third conference title in Wilkinson's third season. The victory also gave OU its fourth straight conference championship and six in the last seven years.

The Sooners had trouble getting into the end zone early. They moved 60 yards following the opening kickoff, but the Tigers took over at their own 13 when Royal failed to gain a first down.

OU advanced to the MU 27 on its next possession, but a hard hit by Missouri forced Heath to spill the pigskin. Walker recovered a Tiger fumble moments later at the MU 26, but the Sooners gave it right back when Thomas fumbled several plays later at the Tiger 11.

The Big Red finally got on board early in the second period. Pearson scored on a three-yard plunge, and Tipps converted. Pearson sparked the 41-yard drive with a 25-yard sprint moments earlier to the MU five.

Missouri drove 50 yards to tie the game five minutes later.

The Sooners answered with a 70-yard scoring drive in 14 plays. Pearson scored on another three-yard plunge, and Tipps converted. Short runs dominated the drive that included only one pass—a six-yard flip from Royal to Owens. Royal had the longest run of the drive with 13 yards.

Early in the third stanza, Ken Parker flopped on a Missouri fumble at the MU 27 to set up another Sooner score. Pearson fired a seven-yard scoring strike to Anderson wide open in the end zone. Tipps converted for a 21-7 lead.

Royal intercepted Dick Braznell's pass late in the third quarter to lead to the final Sooner tally. Royal stepped in front of John Glorioso and carried the ball back to the MU 16. Six plays later, Heath scored from the six, and Tipps missed the conversion.

Neither team threatened in the fourth period.

OU gained 257 rushing yards and only 12 through the air. The Tigers rushed for 45 yards and tossed for 118 more.

A record crowd of 60,145 jammed into Memorial Stadium on November 19 to witness the showdown between two top-rated teams—No. 2 Oklahoma vs. No. 19 Santa Clara. The fans expected to see a defensive duel on this warm (75 degrees) fall afternoon. The 7-1-1 Broncos yielded an average of 8.1 points per game, and Oklahoma allowed an average of 8.4 per game.

The fans were treated to a scoring bonanza of seven touchdowns, four in the second quarter.

Midway through the first stanza, the Broncos' Hall Haynes tried to get off a punt but fumbled instead and ran for 16 yards to the SC

Leon Heath (left) and Bud Wilkinson share a smile after OU's 35-0 victory over LSU in the Sugar Bowl. Heath holds the most valuable player trophy while Wilkinson clutches the game trophy. *(OU Athletics)*

28—not enough for a first down, and OU took over. Seven plays later, Thomas ripped over right guard for the one-yard touchdown. Tipps converted all extra points that day.

Santa Clara moved rapidly for a touchdown early in the second period, covering 67 yards in three plays. West blocked Joe Vargas' conversion, and the Sooners held a 7-6 edge.

Twenty-six seconds later, Oklahoma led, 14-6. Royal returned the kickoff to the OU 18. Pearson picked up one yard. Heath took the handoff on the next play, shot through the right side and flew untouched down the west sideline to the end zone. Owens threw the key block to spring Heath through the secondary.

Three minutes later, the Sooners held a 21-6 advantage. Jones returned the Broncos' punt 34 yards to the SC 44. Heath shot up the middle for 16 yards. Royal tossed an incomplete pass, then Thomas picked up six more to the 24. Thomas ripped off left tackle and dashed to the end zone.

The Big Red defense forced the Broncs to punt on the next series. Royal fielded the punt, and momentum carried him back into his end zone. He tried to run it out, but instead, thinking that he had a touchback, he scooted laterally where he was buried for a safety.

Santa Clara recovered Royal's fumble minutes later at the OU four. A goal-line stand by the OU defense yielded three yards in four plays. Walker and West stopped the Broncos short on fourth down.

Santa Clara scored minutes later, set up by a punt return to the OU 35. Oklahoma held a 21-14 lead at the half.

The Sooners stormed out of the gate to take a 28-14 lead before most fans settled back into their seats from intermission. SC's Abe Dung fumbled the kickoff, and Walker pounced on it at the SC 15. Thomas burst through the left side on the first play and OU scored with 23 seconds gone in the third stanza.

Pearson raced 65 yards to the end zone in the fourth quarter, but a penalty wiped out the score. Moments later, Santa Clara scored on a 59-yard run. Oklahoma 28, Santa Clara 21 with 11:21 remaining.

The Broncs recovered a fumble minutes later in their territory but could not gain a first down. OU milked the clock by picking up two crucial first downs in the waning minutes.

The Sooners rushed for 295 yards and passed for 75 more. Heath and Thomas each crossed the century rushing mark. Heath led the pack with 128 yards on 13 carries, and Thomas gained 115 on 19 carries. Santa Clara rushed for 122, the most allowed by the Oklahoma defense all year. The Broncs added 89 yards through the air.

The Sooners' 19th straight victory broke the school record of 18 set from late 1914 through early 1916.

The Sooners dropped to third in the AP rankings and hosted 4-3-2 Oklahoma A&M the next week. The 50,000 fans in attendance were treated to another warm (73 degrees) November day and a 41-0 thrashing over the Aggies.

OU scored twice in each of the first three quarters. The Aggies stacked nine men on the line most of the game to stop the powerful Oklahoma split-T formation. It did not work, as the Sooners went to the air many times to pick up huge gains, and other times the Aggies just could not stop the run.

Thomas scored two touchdowns, one on a 90-yard run that broke Bob Cook's 80-yard run record set in 1904. Royal and Pearson

---

On December 30, three days before the Sooners and LSU kicked off, Bud Wilkinson received a message from a man who identified himself as Clarence Johnson, a Biloxi resident. Johnson's message revealed that three men had been watching Sooner practices from the roof of a garage near the practice field.

The "spies" were shielded by a tarpaulin and were working with cameras and binoculars. Wilkinson enlisted Dr. C.B. McDonald's services to investigate the spies. McDonald, an Oklahoma City dentist, helped get Lindell Pearson to return to the Sooner squad after enrolling at Arkansas a year earlier.

McDonald rounded up some helpers to investigate the spies—Ned Hockman, an OU employee and motion picture photographer; John Askin Jr., a Biloxi policeman; Bill Dennis, a Biloxi photographer; and John Scafidi, a former Tulane football player. McDonald and his crew found a man atop the garage during practice the next day.

The man saw them approach with cameras and quickly tried to make an escape from the top of the garage and threatened to smash the camera if anyone tried to photograph him. Scafidi grabbed the man by the collar. The victim shielded his face with a handkerchief, but McDonald grabbed it as Dennis photographed him. The victim then broke free and ran into a nearby house.

Dennis quickly had the film developed, and the print was displayed at the Roosevelt Hotel lobby in New Orleans, where the OU alumni association was lodging. Some New Orleans residents identified him as Piggy Barnes, a former LSU football player. Darrell Royal also recognized him as he had met Barnes several years earlier.

After the story circulated through the press, LSU officials denied that anyone from their institution had spied on Sooner practices, claiming it to be a hoax.

Dr. George L. Cross, in his book *Presidents Can't Punt*, wrote that Wilkinson issued a statement the day of the game describing in detail the events and invited Barnes and his accomplice, Elbert Manuel, to present themselves for identification.

Cross wrote: "Neither Barnes or Manuel presented himself for identification. Their failure to appear was duly noted in the papers, and the football fans were free to draw their own conclusions."

OU completed only two passes in the victory, both by Pearson, who first took laterals from quarterback Darrell Royal. Royal drew his own conclusion: "There was no doubt but that we were scouted," Royal said after the game. "Our drop-back passes were completely useless, because they knew exactly what was coming. The passes we did complete were a set of plays that we didn't practice."

---

delighted the crowd with 58-yard TDs. Royal scored on a punt return and Pearson scored from the line of scrimmage.

Oklahoma rushed for 363 yards and passed for 181. A&M rushed for 35 and passed for 199.

The Sooners were invited back to the Sugar Bowl, this time against No. 9 Louisiana State on January 2. OU moved back to the second spot in the AP poll. Notre Dame, which rode the No. 1 spot from the second week of the season, was declared national champion with an early December win over Southern Methodist.

Some hoped OU and the Fighting Irish would meet in a bowl, but the Irish had a policy of not competing in postseason bowl games.

Just as they did the year before, the Sooners lodged and practiced in Biloxi, Mississippi.

Louisiana State won eight of 10 games prior to the Sugar Bowl tilt. The Tigers won six straight to end the season and had defeated three conference champions (Rice of the Southwest Conference, Tulane of the Southeast Conference and North Carolina of the Southern Conference). The Tigers' defense yielded an average of 7.4 points per game.

It's a Fact

The 1949 Sooners led the nation in rushing defense, yeilding an average of 55.6 yards per game and ranked sixth in total defense. The offense ranked second in rushing offense and third in total offense.

The Sooner defense allowed an average of 8.8 points per game and only 53.5 rushing yards per game. A defensive battle was expected in the 16th Sugar Bowl before 82,000 at Tulane Stadium. Oklahoma's defense did its job, and OU's line on both sides of the ball played superbly. OU hammered LSU, 35-0, the most points scored by one team and the largest margin of victory in the bowl's 16-year history.

After a scoreless first quarter, the Sooner offense got uncorked in the second stanza. The Tigers surprised Oklahoma with passes in the first quarter and rode a mix of runs and passes to the OU 10-yard line. Royal swatted away the fourth-down pass, and the Sooners took over.

The Tigers stacked seven to nine men on the front line, trying to stop the OU ground attack. It worked in the first period, as the Sooners did not penetrate LSU territory. Splendid blocking up front helped OU score twice in the second stanza.

OU scored early in the second quarter three plays after Jones returned a Tiger punt to the LSU 37. Heath picked up three yards, and OU was penalized on the next play, which was declined by the Tigers. On the next play, Pearson took Royal's lateral and lobbed a pass to Thomas, who caught it over his shoulder at the five and scored. Tipps converted and made all five extra points in the game. LSU was flagged on three of Tipps' conversions, but the Sooners declined each one.

LSU fumbled the kickoff, and linebacker Delton Marcum recovered for OU at the Tigers' 40. Thomas gained 19 yards and Pearson's misfired a pass to Thomas. OU moved to the five in four plays, then Thomas scored on a five-yard run.

OU later moved into LSU territory, but Pearson's pass was intercepted at the Tigers' three.

The Sooners held the 14-0 lead through halftime and scored once in the third period for a 21-0 advantage. The Sooners set up at their 14 following a punt. On the first play, Heath took the handoff, slipped through the middle, and sprinted 86 yards for the touchdown. Pearson threw a key block downfield, and Heath outran LSU's Armand Kitto to the end zone.

Jones recovered Sam Lyle's fumble at the LSU 14 on the first play of the fourth stanza. Four plays later, the Big Red scored again on Royal's five-yard run.

Linebacker Bert Clark intercepted a Tiger pass late in the game and returned it to the LSU 29. Brewer lost five yards on the first play, then Heath swept off the right side and raced 34 yards for the score.

Oklahoma rushed for 286 yards and passed for 74 more. Heath gained 170 yards on 15 carries and was named the game's outstanding player. The Sooner defense held the Tigers to 35 yards on the ground and 121 through the air.

Thomas, Royal, West, Walker, and Owens were named All-Americans and to the All-Big Seven first team. Thomas led the nation in scoring with 117 points on 19 touchdowns and three conversions. Royal intercepted 18 career passes, still a school record today. West, Walker, and Owens were all tremendous blockers on offense and vicious linemen on defense.

1949 Season Record: 11-0-0
Big Seven Conference: 5-0-0 (Champions)

Date	Opponent	Result	Score
September 24	at Boston College	W	46-0
October 1	TEXAS A&M	W	33-13
October 8	Texas at Dallas	W	20-14
October 15	KANSAS	W	48-26
October 22	at Nebraska	W	48-0
October 29	IOWA STATE	W	34-7
November 5	at Kansas State	W	39-0
November 12	at Missouri	W	27-7
November 19	SANTA CLARA	W	28-21
November 26	OKLAHOMA A&M	W	41-0
January 2	Louisiana State*	W	35-0

*Sugar Bowl at New Orleans, LA

MEMORIAL STADIUM

The campaign for a new stadium began in the fall of 1922. Bennie Owen, Oklahoma's head football coach and athletic director, headed the drive to raise $650,000 to construct the stadium and a student union. The new stadium campaign would include a cinder running track and new gymnasium.

Frank Buttram, an OU regent, prominent OKC oilman and OU grad (1910), appointed a national chairmanship of $1 million campaign for stadium/union memorial. Of that, $650,000 went to build the stadium and $350,000 to build the student union building.

Members of the memorial/union executive committee announced November 10, 1924, that Oklahomans who died in World War I would be honored in the stadium/union memorial. Forest "Spot" Geyer, the Sooners' star quarterback from 1913-1915, made the first large pledge two weeks later, a donation of $1,000 to the memorial/union pledge drive. Geyer at the time was chief geologist for Marland Oil Company in Ponca City.

The first two concrete sections of the west stands were completed in 1925. The grandstand, built to hold 7,500 fans, was 62 rows high and 202 feet long. The Sooners hosted Drake in the new stadium, but it was officially dedicated during the homecoming contest against Kansas on November 7. Fans were no longer permitted to park their cars around the field's perimeter. The west side expanded to a capacity of 16,000. By this time the media had already dubbed the field, "Owen Field," named for Bennie Owen.

The eastside stands were added in 1929, doubling the capacity.

The cinder track was removed in 1949, the north end zone was enclosed, and the field was lowered six feet to include 23,000 ringside seats. This $1.2 million project raised the capacity to 55,000. South end zone green grandstand bleachers were constructed in 1957, which added 6,836 more seats.

Artificial turf was installed in 1970 and remained a staple at Owen Field for 24 years. Natural grass replaced the artificial turf in 1994.

In 1975, a $5.7 million renovation added an upper deck to the west side, which included 8,436 more seats, boosting the capacity to 71,187. A new three-story press box also was constructed during the renovation. A new scoreboard replaced the old one above the south end zone, and a new one was added above the north end zone.

A $4.1 million renovation to the south end zone was complete in 1980, raising the capacity to 75,004. Offices, locker rooms, and equipment rooms were added under the new stands.

It's a Fact
- Oklahoma's home record at Memorial Stadium and on Owen Field: 325-80-14 (79.2 percent).
- The Sooners' longest winning streak on Owen Field is 25. OU defeated Iowa State on November 1, 1947 and didn't lose again at home until the season opener (to Notre Dame) in 1953.

Head coach Bennie Owen supervises construction of the new football stadium. Owen also spearheaded the drive to raise money to build the stadium and a new student union building. *(OU Athletics)*

Housed in the stadium are the athletic director's office, athletic ticket office, athletic business office, the Prentice Gautt Academic Center, athletic media relations, other support areas for the department and the Jack Santee Lounge.

Prior to the 1995 season, nine suites, which seat up to 24 each, were added on the west side of the stadium. A large scoreboard, 52 yards wide and 33 feet tall, with a video screen was also built.

Four 197-foot light poles were installed in 1997, allowing the Sooners to schedule more night games. The increase of wheelchair seating in 1998 dropped the capacity to 72,765.

The Barry Switzer Center, named after OU's 17th head coach, opened in April 1999. The complex includes a sports medicine

An aerial view of Memorial Stadium shows the west upper deck, which was added in 1975. *(OU Athletics)*

facility with the latest equipment and technology to better accommodate OU's student-athletes. The center also features the Robin Siegfried and Family Strength and Conditioning Facility, accommodating more than 400 athletes; new locker rooms and coaches offices; the Anderson All-American Plaza and the OU Touchdown Club Legends Lobby. The Legends Lobby features some of OU's finest moments and most legendary figures.

In January 2002, a $74-million renovation began, which included adding an upper deck to the east side. This expanded the capacity to 81,000, including 2,200 club seats and 27 sky suites. The reconstruction also included new seating throughout the rest of the stadium.

Construction workers labored 24 hours a day for nearly one year. The renovation was completed prior to the first home game in 2003 against North Texas. Lights from the stadium, which helped illuminate the workers' efforts, could be seen all over Norman for more than a year.

University regents approved renaming the stadium The Gaylord Family—Oklahoma Memorial Stadium in recognition of a $12 million gift by Edward L. Gaylord, publisher of *The Daily Oklahoman*, on his family's behalf to complete the stadium's latest expansion.

The Gaylord family also requested that a portion of their $12 million donation be used to build a monument to honor all OU students, faculty and staff who died while serving in the U.S. Armed Forces.

1950 - 1959

1950

Suburbs began thriving as homes arose from barren land outside the central districts of American cities. Between 1950 and 1956, the resident population of all United States suburbs increased by 46 percent. World War II veterans were getting married, settling down and raising a family.

North Korea invaded South Korea in June 1950. The United States entered the war to assist South Korea, but the war did not have a major effect on college football as did World War II. Yet five Sooner players were called to active duty in the 45th Division of the National Guard.

The Oklahoma football program was beginning to flourish under head coach Bud Wilkinson. Graduation or loss of eligibility took most starters form the 1949 roster, and 1950 was expected to be a rebuilding year. Leon Heath was the only returning starter from the previous year. Yet there was a surplus of talented reserves and newcomers. Quarterback Claude Arnold had started a couple of games in 1949. Halfback Buddy Jones, end Frankie Anderson and guard Norman McNabb had plenty of experience from the prior year. Tackle Jim Weatherall, centers Harry Moore and Tom Catlin and halfback Billy Vessels would soon have their names rolling off the tongues of Sooner faithful.

Even with the loss of so many veterans, the Sooners were rated sixth in the preseason AP poll.

The 1950 Sooners worked together as a unit to help Wilkinson produce one of the finest football teams in the school's history—an undefeated season and OU's first national championship. Three times the team had to reach into its bag of tricks to win in the fourth quarter.

The Sooners opened the season September 30 with a 28-0 win over Boston College. The Eagles had tied Wake Forest in their season opener.

OU scored on its first and last possessions in the first half. Jones scored both TDs on one-yard runs.

OU needed only four plays to cover 37 yards for a 21-0 lead late in the third stanza after Jones' 13-yard punt return. On third-and-seven, Anderson picked up 16 yards on an end around to the BC 18. Vessels then fired a touchdown pass to Anderson.

The Sooners scored their final tally nine minutes later. Richard McBride tried to get off a punt. The snap went awry, and reserve Sooner end Bill Beckman pounced on the ball on the BC 11. One play later, backup halfback Tommy Gray found a huge gap off left tackle and sprinted to the end zone.

The Sooners totaled 244 rushing yards and only 21 yards through the air. Boston College had 78 rushing yards and 128 passing yards.

OU moved up one notch to fifth in the AP poll and remained at home the following week to host Texas A&M.

Sooner Magic: Stunned and Silent

With the win over Boston College, the Sooners had pitched their third consecutive shutout dating back to the final two games of 1949. The Big Red forgot what it was like to have an opponent score on its mighty defense. In 1949, Wilkinson created the 5-2 defensive alignment with five players on the front line and two linebackers. It would become notorious nationwide as the "Oklahoma 5-2."

Texas A&M put the Sooner D to the test with a potent running game led by halfback Bill Tidwell, who rushed for 166 yards on 15 carries and a touchdown. Tidwell led the Cadets to a 2-0 record with wins over Nevada and Texas Tech.

OU countered with a weapon of its own, fullback Leon "Mule Train" Heath, a powerful blocker as well as ball carrier. Against A&M, he accounted for 146 (78 rushing, 68 receiving) yards and three touchdowns; the last one decided the outcome of the game.

The Sooners held a four-game winning streak over A&M in the series to lead the overall count, 6-4.

The 1950 game against the Aggies was the first time a prayer was read over the public address system at Oklahoma Memorial Stadium before the game began. A prayer was exactly what the Sooners would need to avoid defeat.

The Aggies took a 7-0 lead with a touchdown on the final play of the first quarter.

The Sooners tied the game on Heath's 25-yard run, in which he eluded two tacklers along the way. Weatherall toed the extra point, and the score was knotted at 7-7 with 7:48 left before halftime.

A&M could not gain a first down on its next possession and punted to the OU 40 where Jones returned the ball to the 50. On the next play, Arnold connected a pass to Heath at the Aggie 35. Heath outran two Aggies all the way to the end zone. Weatherall's foot gave the Sooners another point for a 14-7 lead with 5:15 left in the quarter.

The Sooners' excitement was short-lived when the Aggies scored on the first play following OU's kickoff and both teams went to the locker room with 14 points apiece.

Early in the third stanza, Vessels took a lateral from Arnold and scooted around right end for a 26-yard TD. Weatherall added the extra point and the Sooners led, 21-14, with 12 minutes left in the quarter.

The Aggies again stormed back with a 61-yard drive to tie the score at 21-all with 4:17 left in the third period.

A&M added another touchdown early in the fourth for a 28-21 lead.

A fumble by Heath at the Aggie 39 foiled a Sooner drive following the Aggies' kickoff. But the Sooner defense held, and the cadets punted to the OU 31.

Oklahoma began another drive from there. Vessels gained 16 yards to the 47. Halfback Dick Heatly crashed through for seven and Arnold zipped a 14-yard pass to end John Reddell to the A&M 32.

On the next play, Arnold found Vessels open at the 15-yard line. Vessels grabbed the pass, dodged two Cadet safeties and outran two more defenders for the touchdown. Weatherall's point attempt sailed wide, and the Sooners trailed, 28-27, with 3:36 remaining.

The Aggies failed to gain a first down on their next possession and punted to the OU 31 with 1:46 to go.

Arnold, who finished the game 11 of 19 passing for 161 yards, engineered the next drive, completing four of five passes for 65 of the 69-yard drive.

Fullback Leon "Mule Train" Heath eludes Texas A&M's Robert Shaeffer for the first of his three touchdowns against the Aggies. Heath later scored the winning touchdown in OU's 34-28 win. (*OU Athletics*)

He fired his first pass to Vessels for 30 yards. The next pass to Heath was incomplete as a glaring sun interfered with the fullback's vision. Arnold hurled the ball to Gray for 11 yards to the A&M 28. Arnold fired another aerial to Heath to the 14 with 61 seconds left on the clock. Arnold then tossed to Gray at the A&M four for another first down.

Arnold called two plays in the huddle in case the first one did not score, but it did. Instead of passing this time, Arnold pitched the ball to Heath, who scooted around end. The fullback skirted one defender and, with a burst of speed, swept across the goal line with 37 seconds to go. Weatherall booted the extra point, and most of the 36,586 fans sat and watched as the scoreboard gleamed a 34-28 lead.

Following the kickoff, the Aggies misfired on two passes and completed one for no gain as the final gun sounded.

"One of the greatest finishes I have ever seen," Wilkinson told reporters in the locker room.

Heath said it felt good to score the winning touchdown, "because we were behind and we needed it."

"Everybody was stunned," Arnold recalled 53 years later. "They were quiet ... nobody moved ... they just sat there."

Arnold added that he thought the team could win if they got the ball back and even said so to Coach Wilkinson. "Bud looked at me and thought I was dreaming," he recollected.

The Sooners preserved their 23rd straight victory. OU gained 18 first downs, 205 yards on the ground and 169 through the air. The Aggies gained 13 first downs, 271 rushing yards and only 11 passing yards. It was the first time a team rushed for more yards than the Sooners since Detroit in 1947.

"Best team I played against since I came to Norman," said Moore, a senior co-captain for OU.

But was it the best team? Another cardiac comeback loomed over the horizon.

Sooner Magic: 'I Can't Take Another One Like That'

Two nailbiters in consecutive weeks were not for the weak of heart. For the second straight week, the Sooners were forced into another seat squirmer, this time against its greatest rival—Texas.

The expectations in the 45th edition of the Red River rivalry before 76,000 fans at the Cotton Bowl involved the duel between both team's fullbacks—Byron Townsend of Texas and OU's Heath. Rushing through stubborn defenses, Townsend gained 85 yards, and Heath picked up 67. Stepping to the forefront was Vessels, a sophomore halfback who gained 76 yards, but more importantly scored both OU touchdowns.

The third-ranked Sooners rolled into Dallas on October 14 with a 2-0 record and a 23-game winning streak, including two over the Longhorns. Likewise, the fourth-ranked Horns were 2-0, with victories over Texas Tech and Purdue, and favored by a touchdown.

Vessels' one-yard run and Weatherall's toe gave the Sooners a 7-0 lead early in the first period.

The Longhorns marched 47 yards to tie the game early in the second stanza. The Big Red defense stalled Texas short of the goal line as the first-half gun sounded.

Both defenses dominated the third period. The Longhorns drove deep into OU territory, but Tompkins fumbled, and Jones recovered at the five. The Sooners stalled after they marched to the UT 24. Jack Lockett dropped a third-down pass from Arnold in the end zone. Weatherall's field goal attempt missed the inside of the goal posts by inches.

Another Sooner drive late in the quarter stalled at the Texas 17.

Early in the fourth stanza, Heatly fired a pass in the flat to Anderson, but Bobby Dillon stepped in front of him at the 50 and sailed down the east sideline. A crucial block by Bill Milburn paved Dillon's way to the end zone. Billy Porter's extra-point kick sailed wide, and the Horns held a 13-7 advantage with 13:41 to go.

Texas began at its 29-yard line later in the period, but again the Sooner D pushed the Steers backwards. The key play was dropping halfback Bob Raley for a nine-yard loss. The Horns then were flagged for delay of game, placing the pigskin at the UT 16, which forced them to punt. Porter managed to grasp the low snap from center, but Smith and Anderson exploded through the line and nailed Porter at the 11.

The Big Red had possession in the Texas end of the Cotton Bowl, and the decibel level was deafening when the Sooner offense came onto the field.

Vessels was stopped for no gain up the middle. On the next play, Vessels took Arnold's pitch and swung to his right. He encountered Texas tackle Bill Wilson at the five, but lowered his head, knocked Wilson out of the way, and charged to the end zone. The eyes of Texas and Oklahoma were trained on Weatherall setting up to boot the deciding extra-point kick into the wind. He had missed one a week earlier against Texas A&M. The kick was good. It was OU 14, Texas 13, with 3:46 remaining in the game.

The Sooner defense forced the Steers to punt, then killed the final 2:07. Sooner fans swarmed the field and tore down the wooden goal posts. Before the game, Cotton Bowl officials had replaced the metal posts with lumber. Fans broke up the wood posts and carried them away for souvenirs.

"Billy Vessels made an unbelievable run ... a bulldozing-type run," Arnold recalled 53 years later. "They [Texas] had a chance to stop him but couldn't."

"Our boys have a world of heart," Wilkinson said following the game. "It took a fumbled punt to beat Texas, but it seems if you play hard enough, things like that will happen."

OU president Dr. George L. Cross was not sure he could endure another last-minute nailbiter.

"It was too close for an old man like me," he said. "I can't take another one like that."

Both teams each gained 15 first downs, but Oklahoma had the decided edge on total yards, 294-196.

No. 2 Oklahoma finally got a breather the next week with a 58-0 blanking of 1-2 Kansas State in Norman. Seven Sooners scored the nine touchdowns in the game, and a total of 49 players got in on the action. Anderson and Gray each scored twice. Weatherall could manage only four of nine extra-point kicks.

OU rushed for 435 yards and added 120 through the air. Fourteen Sooners carried the ball, and backup halfback Dale Crawford led the way with 83 yards on two carries. The defense held the Wildcats to 80 total yards. Kansas State only had one possession in OU territory, and that came on a fumble at the 24.

Oklahoma slipped to third in the AP poll. Southern Methodist defeated No. 15 Rice to leap from third to first. Army blasted Harvard 49-0 and dropped to second.

The Sooners traveled to Ames on October 28 as three-touchdown favorites over Iowa State. OU won, 20-7, before 17,000 spectators. The defense harassed Cyclone quarterback Willis Weeks all afternoon. Weeks completed only nine of 19 passes for 121 yards and threw two interceptions.

Iowa State moved 45 yards to the OU 22 in the first stanza, but the crimson defense stiffened. The Cyclones recovered their own fumble but lost two yards. Anderson stormed through and sacked Weeks for a 14-yard loss on the next play. On third-and-26 from the OU 38, Weatherall nailed Weeks for an 18-yard loss all the way back to the Iowa State 44.

OU put together a long, sustained drive going 82 yards in 14 plays for the first score. Vessels, Heatly, Gray, and Buck McPhail chiseled out punishing gains. Arnold passed only once in the drive, a 12-yard completion to Anderson to the Iowa State six. Vessels scored on the next play, but Weatherall's conversion was wide right.

The Sooners marched 76 yards in seven plays for a 13-0 lead midway in the second quarter. Heatly slipped through right guard for a two-yard touchdown, and McPhail converted. Three key plays gobbled up 62 yards in the drive—Arnold's 24-yard strike to Vessels, Vessels' 19-yard run around end and Heatley's 19-yard jaunt.

Iowa State drove 64 yards to the OU nine early in the third period. Catlin stopped halfback Ed Green on a fourth-down pass and the Sooners took over. Oklahoma took 16 plays to move to the Iowa State six, but Arnold fumbled there, and Jerry Limburek recovered for the Cyclones midway through the fourth stanza.

Iowa State could go nowhere and punted back. Green's short punt to the Iowa State 23 set up the final Sooner tally. Arnold and Heatly combined for runs to the 11, then Vessels bolted through left guard for the score. McPhail converted for a 20-0 lead.

The Cyclones drove 73 yards for their only score late in the game. Two 15-yard penalties aided their advance. Weeks capped the drive with a 30-yard pass to Jim Doran.

Oklahoma rushed for 234 yards and passed for 96 more. The Cyclones picked up 96 rushing yards and 121 passing yards.

The victory equaled Cornell University's 26-game win streak set from 1921-1924.

The No. 3 Sooners would break that mark with a 27-18 victory over Colorado, the first meeting between both schools in 14 years. The Buffaloes hosted the November 4 contest before 30,000 spec-

Claude Arnold hurls a pass under a fierce rush by the Texas defense. Arnold engineered the winning touchdown drive against Texas A&M and Texas. (*OU Athletics*)

tators in Boulder. The game also marked the first conference tilt between the two teams since Colorado joined the Big Seven Conference in 1948.

Arnold led the Sooners with two touchdowns and 134 yards rushing. Three backs were out with injuries, and Arnold gained the responsibility of carrying the Sooners to victory. A hip injury sidelined Jones. Gray (sore knee) and Heath (leg and shoulder) saw limited action. Anderson suffered a concussion on the game's second play and sat out the rest of the game.

Trailing 6-0, Oklahoma drove 81 yards in six plays for its first score early in the second stanza. From the Buffs' 48, Vessels took Arnold's pitch, paused briefly and zipped through a hole off right tackle. Vessels weaved through defenders and down the sideline to the end zone. Weatherall's extra point gave the Sooners a 7-6 lead.

The Sooners jumped to a 13-7 advantage five minutes later with a 63-yard march in 11 plays. Vessels took Arnold's lateral and fired an eight-yard pass to Heatly wide open in the end zone. Weatherall converted, but OU was guilty of holding and his second attempt failed.

The Big Red marched 72 yards in 10 plays to its next score after the second-half kickoff. Arnold, who carried eight times in the drive, capped it with a four-yard slice off right guard. Weatherall converted for a 20-7 lead.

Colorado answered with an 80-yard scoring drive.

Vessels intercepted Colorado's pass at the CU 49 to set up the next Oklahoma score midway through the fourth period. Arnold carried on eight of the nine plays and scored on a one-yard run. Weatherall converted to lift OU to a 27-12 advantage.

The Buffs later scored on a one-yard plunge.

OU rushed for 351 yards and passed for 81 more. Arnold completed six of 10 passes for 73 yards. Colorado gained 115 rushing yards and 140 passing yards.

Oklahoma remained third in the AP poll and trailed Army and Ohio State.

Claude Arnold pitches to Billy Vessels for the forward passing run option play against Kansas. (*OU Athletics*)

Sooner Magic: Lightning Strikes in Final Quarter

Oklahoma fans were stunned. Coaches and players were humiliated. It had never happened before in 38 games under Coach Wilkinson—the Sooners did not score in the first half against Kansas. But this bunch of crimson warriors was determined to erase the embarrassment in the second half, and they did so with an explosion of four touchdowns in the fourth quarter.

The No. 3 Sooners traveled to Lawrence on November 11 to meet 5-2 Kansas. The Jayhawks were ranked 19th in the nation and held a 2-1 conference record. Kansas lost to Texas Christian in its season opener, then won four straight before dropping a 33-26 decision to Nebraska. The Hawks beat Utah on the road before the Sooners came to town. The two nationally ranked teams attracted 39,000 to Memorial Stadium.

The Big Red sputtered in the first half. Four lost fumbles killed Sooner drives, leaving Oklahoma scoreless in the first 30 minutes.

The Jayhawks scored a touchdown late in the first half and added another TD early in the third quarter for a 13-0 lead.

The Sooners got on the scoreboard three minutes later with a 76-yard drive. Heath (21 yards) and Heatly (13) picked up huge gains in the drive. On third-and-one foot at the KU 21, Arnold decided to go to the air and hurled a 21-yard TD pass to Kay Keller. Weatherall converted, and OU trailed, 13-7.

Two more Sooner fumbles stalled drives—Heath at midfield and Vessels at the KU 42.

OU flashed like lightning with rapid scores in the fourth quarter. KU's Dolph Simons punted to the OU 11. Arnold's arm accelerated the Sooners downfield for a score. He zipped a 22-yarder to Vessels and another for 25 yards to Heatly. Arnold then found Lockett open at the five. Lockett snatched the ball and scooted into the end zone to complete the 32-yard play. Weatherall missed the extra point, and both teams were knotted at 13.

The Big Red scored three more times in a span of five minutes and 20 seconds.

From midfield, Arnold shot a 15-yard pass to Vessels on the KU 35. Vessels hauled it in, paused briefly to pick up a block or two, and sailed down the sideline for the score. His swift moves left Jayhawks sprawling in his wake. Weatherall converted.

The Oklahoma defense pushed the Hawks back to their 13 following the kickoff. Catlin intercepted Chester Strehlow's pass at the 20 and flashed across the goal line. Weatherall toed the conversion for a 27-13 lead.

Jones picked off Strehlow's pass moments later at midfield and returned it 30 yards to the KU 20. Arnold lobbed a scoring strike to Reddell three plays later. Weatherall missed the conversion but it didn't matter.

Oklahoma rushed for 299 yards and passed for 201 more. Heath led all runners with 140 yards on 20 carries, and Arnold completed nine of 15 passes for 200 yards. Kansas gained 182 rushing yards and 126 passing yards.

Ohio State and OU leaped over Army in the AP poll. Ohio State grabbed the top spot with a 19-14 win over Wisconsin, and Army dropped to third with a 51-0 win over New Mexico.

The No. 2 Sooners were seeking their 29th consecutive victory and fifth straight over 3-3-1 Missouri. The Big Red continued its streak with a 41-7 triumph on November 18 before 47,000 in Norman.

OU scored twice in the first quarter for a 13-0 lead. Vessels scored on a four-yard run, and Gray struck pay dirt on a 50-yard punt return.

OU put up two more touchdowns during a five-minute stretch in the second stanza.

Wilkinson continued to empty the bench, allowing Sooner reserves to get in on the act, and they scored twice in the second half.

OU rushed for 261 yards and added 56 through the air. Arnold tossed his first and only interception of the season in the second quarter, ending a string of 88 passes without a pick off. Missouri gained 186 total yards.

Three days later, on November 20, 1950, the Oklahoma Sooners ascended to the No. 1 spot in the AP poll for the first time in school history. They replaced Ohio State, which lost to Illinois.

Nebraska rolled into Norman on November 25 with hopes of knocking off the new national leader. The 16th-ranked Cornhuskers had won six games, lost one and tied one. Nebraska won four straight games—all in the Big Seven Conference—prior to the OU tilt. A Husker victory would give them a share of the Big Seven title.

Both teams featured sensational sophomore halfbacks—Nebraska's Bobby Reynolds and OU's Vessels. Reynolds had rushed for 1,260 yards and scored 18 touchdowns for Nebraska prior to the Oklahoma game. He also punted and kicked conversions for the Huskers. Reynolds was the lone star halfback for the Huskers. Oklahoma had several star backs, so Vessels' statistics were not as impressive. He rushed for 542 yards scored 12 TDs and passed for two more scores prior to the Nebraska contest.

Yet it was Vessels who had the better game. He rushed 18 times for 208 yards, scored three TDs and passed for another. Reynolds was held to 89 yards on 24 totes (68.5 yards below his per-game average). Reynolds, however, did find the end zone three times against the Sooners.

Both teams found the end zone a total of 12 times in this offensive showdown before a nationally televised (NBC) audience. OU and Nebraska wore out the scoreboard as the Sooners prevailed, 49-35.

Oklahoma rolled 76 yards in 10 plays to score after the opening kickoff. Arnold bolted around right end for a 16-yard TD. Weatherall converted and did not miss on seven conversions.

The Sooners took a 14-0 lead with a 68-yard march on their next series. From the NU 23, Arnold lateraled to Heath, who picked up Lockett's block and blazed to the end zone.

The Huskers then scored three unanswered touchdowns (all by Reynolds) for a 21-14 lead. Reynolds did not miss a conversion all day.

The Sooners were not done in the first half, but they had to race the clock. No problem. They began at their 31 following the kickoff. Arnold tossed a short aerial to Heath, who flew 47 yards to the NU 11. Merrill Green gained three yards. On the next play, Arnold kept to his right, then pitched at the last second to Vessels. Vessels, who had swung wide right on the play, slashed back to the middle and scored with 1:02 on the clock. Both teams headed to the locker room knotted at 21-21.

The second half was all Oklahoma, as the Big Red of the south scored three TDs in a little more than ten minutes of the third stanza for a 42-21 lead. Arnold scored on a one-yard run to complete a 74-yard drive following the second-half kickoff. Moments later, Catlin recovered Reynolds' fumble on the Huskers' eight. Vessels scooted around left end to score on the next play. Nebraska was on the move on their next series, but Ed Lisak intercepted a Husker pass on the OU 17. Green picked up 14 yards to the 31, and Vessels sailed 69 yards for the score.

Nebraska cut the deficit to 42-28 with a touchdown minutes later.

OU scored its final touchdown early in the fourth period. Arnold pitched to Vessels who pulled up and fired a 23-yard scoring strike to Reddell. Nebraska scored once more late in the game but had little time to mount another threat.

The Sooners outrushed the Huskers 384-169, but Nebraska had more passing yards (160-158).

The Sooners accepted an invitation to play in the Sugar Bowl for the third straight year before their final game against Oklahoma A&M. Kentucky was the opponent that year, coached by Paul "Bear" Bryant.

The top-rated Sooners traveled to Stillwater on December 2, seeking to extend their winning streak to 31 games. Arnold lit up the scoreboard with four TD passes to lead OU to a 41-14 victory over the 4-5-1 Aggies. A crowd of 33,000 witnessed the game, including Bryant who observed from the press box. Lockett was on the receiving end of three scoring strikes, and Reddell caught the other.

The Sooners rolled up 322 rushing yards and 153 passing yards. Heath led the OU rushing attack with 126 yards, and Vessels gained

Quarterback Claude Arnold finished the season as the nation's passing leader with a 157.3 rating. (*OU Athletics*)

120 more. Arnold completed 10 of 23 passes for 123 yards. Heatly averaged 43 yards on four punts, which included a 68-yarder in the second period.

Oklahoma earned its fifth consecutive conference (Big Seven) championship and fourth in a row under Wilkinson. The Sooners finished the season as national champions, the first in Oklahoma football history. The Sooners received 2,963 points for first place in the final AP poll. Army finished second 583 points behind Oklahoma. The United Press International poll, voted upon by collegiate coaches, premiered in 1950, and the Sooners were awarded the first UPI national championship. Oklahoma received 346 points in the UPI poll, outdistancing second-place Texas by 96 points.

National champions were awarded for season performance during that era. The AP did not reward national championships after bowl games until 1965. After a two-year return to awarding the national championship for regular-season performance only, the final poll has been released after bowl games every year since 1968.

The Kentucky Wildcats finished seventh in the AP poll and in the UPI poll. The 10-1 Wildcats lost their final game of the season to Tennessee. Kentucky averaged 34.5 points per game, and the defense yielded an average of 5.6 points per game.

For the third straight year, the Sooners practiced in Biloxi, Mississippi, before heading to New Orleans. Jones had a knee injury and was unable to play. This was not good news, as Kentucky featured All-America quarterback Vito "Babe" Parilli, who passed for a school-record 1,620 yards and a national-record 23 TD passes.

Kentucky snapped OU's 31-game win streak with a 13-7 victory before 80,206 fans, including 12,000 crimson faithful. The Wildcats' defensive front harassed Arnold by rushing him hard all afternoon, and Kentucky's secondary blanketed his targets in the passing game. Oklahoma lost five fumbles, and Kentucky had nary a turnover.

1950 Season Record: 10-1-0
Big Seven Conference: 6-0-0 (Champions)
NATIONAL CHAMPIONS

Date	Opponent	Result	Score
September 30	BOSTON COLLEGE	W	28-0
October 7	TEXAS A&M	W	34-28
October 14	Texas at Dallas	W	14-13
October 21	KANSAS STATE	W	58-0
October 28	at Iowa State	W	20-7
November 4	at Colorado	W	27-18
November 11	at Kansas	W	33-13
November 18	MISSOURI	W	41-7
November 25	NEBRASKA	W	49-35
December 2	at Oklahoma A&M	W	41-14
January 1	Kentucky*	L	13-7

*Sugar Bowl at New Orleans, LA

"Bear Bryant put in a defense that our guys were confused on who to block," Arnold recalled. "They were right in the middle of our backfield most of the game."

After holding Kentucky on their first possession, the Sooners began at their 26 following the punt. Arnold fumbled on the first play, and Walt Yowarsky recovered at the 22. An unblocked Kentucky tackle bolted through the line and plastered Arnold as the OU quarterback was attempting a handoff. The Cats needed only one play to take a 7-0 lead. Parilli sailed a TD pass to Wilbur Jameson, and Bob Gain converted.

The breaks continued to go against the Sooners. Late in the first quarter, Vessels' 51-yard run to the UK 16 was wiped out by a clipping penalty, placing the ball back to the OU 20. Gray fumbled on the next play, but the Sooner defense stiffened. Anderson sacked Parilli for a 14-yard loss on third down, and Parilli's fourth-down pass misfired.

Kentucky drove 81 yards in five plays to take a 13-0 lead midway in the second stanza.

The Big Red had a chance for a score in the third period, but Arnold's seven-yard pass to Anderson grazed his hands and fell incomplete. Kentucky missed a field goal late in the third stanza after the Cats recovered Vessels' fumble at the OU 33.

OU got on board midway through the fourth quarter with an 80-yard drive in 13 plays. Vessels zipped a 17-yard scoring strike to Green, and Weatherall converted to cut Kentucky's lead to 13-7. The Sooners twice gained first downs on crucial fourth-down situations in the drive.

Oklahoma never threatened again. The Wildcats picked off Vessels' pass at midfield to end the game.

The Sooners gained 18 first downs to only seven for Kentucky. OU rushed for 189 yards and passed for only 18. Heath rushed for 121 yards, but Arnold lost 21 yards on 14 carries. The Wildcats rushed for 84 yards and passed for 105 more. Parilli completed nine of 12 passes.

Despite the disappointing loss, Wilkinson was still pleased with his team. "I'm proud of the kids … they never quit," he said.

The Sugar Bowl loss branded the Sooners with a 10-1 record. Wilkinson was honored as AP coach of the year. Weatherall and Heath were named consensus All-Americans. Jones and Anderson were also named All-Americans.

McNabb, Moore, Catlin, Arnold, and Vessels joined them on the All-Big Seven first unit. Jones was not named to the all-conference first team.

1951

Bud Wilkinson submitted a letter of resignation to OU president Dr. George L. Cross in February 1951. Wilkinson told Cross that he was planning to accept a public relations position with a Texas company owned by Eddie Chiles, an OU graduate.

Cross, in his book *Presidents Can't Punt*, said he and wife, Cleo, invited Wilkinson and his wife, Mary, to the president's home for dinner to discuss finding a new head coach. After dinner, Cross and Wilkinson talked privately in the home's library. Cross talked Wilkinson out of retiring as football coach.

The Wilkinsons departed later that night, and before leaving, Wilkinson turned to Cross and asked if he would tear up the letter of resignation. Cross assured him that he would destroy the letter, but Cross admitted that he kept it in a scrapbook.

Dee Andros, who played guard from 1947-1949, was hired to coach the line. The 1951 line was perhaps the most impressive bunch of lads in years. Tackle Jim Weatherall and center Tom Catlin

returned. But Wilkinson's recruiting ability brought in talented linemen who would earn honors at the end of the season—guards Roger Nelson and J.D. Roberts and tackle Art Janes. Jack Lockett and John Reddell were veterans at the end slots.

Eddie Crowder, who logged playing time in 1950, was the heir apparent at quarterback. Coach Wilkinson had decided in the spring that Crowder was his man to lead the 1951 offense. He spent countless hours teaching Crowder the mechanics of the spilt-T and took him to coaching clinics at Little Rock and Chicago.

Junior halfback Billy Vessels was the leader in the backfield. Frank Silva and Dick Heatly returned with playing experience, and Buck McPhail assumed the fullback duties. Halfbacks Larry Grigg and Buddy Leake would come on strong as the season progressed. Merrill Green, who also came on strong in the latter part of 1950, suffered a sprained left knee nine days before the season opener and did not play the entire season.

The Sooners lost two games early for a 1-2 start but finished the season 8-2 by winning the final seven games and claiming the school's 12th conference championship. In doing so, OU extended its conference winning string to 25 and had won 29 of its last 30 conference games, save for a tie in 1946.

Oklahoma opened the season ranked No. 4 and hosted William and Mary on September 29. The Sooners pounded the Indians, 49-7, at Owen Field.

OU led 28-0 before the Indians got on the board in the second quarter and answered their score with three more touchdowns for a 42-7 halftime lead. Silva led all Sooners with three TDs and Wetherall converted all seven extra-point kicks.

Oklahoma rolled up 363 yards rushing and passed for 141 more. Fourteen players carried the ball for OU; McPhail led with 65 yards on three carries. Crowder was a perfect four-for-four passing for 78 yards. The Sooners were penalized 15 times for 145 yards. The Indians were held to six first downs and 130 total yards.

Penalties (104 yards) and missed tackles plagued No. 4 Oklahoma in the 14-7 loss to Texas A&M the next week in College Station. A crowd of 40,000 turned out for the Saturday night contest and endured cold rain and a 25-mile-per-hour wind.

The Sooners failed to gain a first down on their first three possessions. The Aggies gained good field position on each series, but the Big Red defense shut them down at the OU 14, four, and 10 respectively.

The Cadets marched 82 yards in eight plays to take a 7-0 lead midway in the second quarter.

Late in the first half, A&M's Yale Lary punted to the OU 28 with little time left. Crowder lost two yards on a fumble, but OU recovered with five seconds left. Crowder pitched a shovel pass to Vessels on the next play, and Vessels bolted 74 yards for the touchdown. Reddell threw a key block, and Vessels gave a hip shake to outmaneuver an Aggie safety. Weatherall converted for the 7-7 halftime tie.

The Cadets marched 67 yards for the deciding score early in the fourth quarter.

The Cadets dominated in the stat department with 17 first downs, 205 rushing yards, and 57 passing yards. OU gained only four first downs, rushed for 173 yards and passed for 15 more.

The loss dropped Oklahoma to 11 in the AP poll, and Texas was next.

The Sooners improved on their discipline with only one penalty against the sixth-rated Longhorns, but they could not improve their offensive punch. The 3-0 Steers, now coached by Ed Price who installed the split-T offense, also did not have any offensive firepower as a safety decided the 9-7 outcome. A crowd of 75,080 packed the Cotton Bowl on October 13 for the Red River showdown. The result was the lowest scoring OU-Texas tilt in nine years, the first back-to-back losses for OU since 1945, and in Wilkinson's regime.

A Texas punt nailed the Sooners deep at their own three late in the first stanza. Silva failed to retrieve Crowder's lateral. Bobby Dillon tackled Silva in the end zone as he tried to rescue the ball. Texas 2, Oklahoma 0.

Minutes later, the Longhorns scored a touchdown after recovering Silva's fumble at the OU 22.

Bobby Ray Raley intercepted Crowder's pass at the OU 49 early in the second quarter, and Texas moved into position for another score at the one. Weatherall dropped James "T" Jones for a five-yard loss on fourth down. The Sooners then marched 94 yards for a touchdown.

Huge runs by McPhail, Vessels, and Heatly moved the Big Red to the Texas 40. McPhail rambled to the Texas 12, and as he was about to be tackled, he pitched out to Janes. The ball bounced on the turf, and Janes scooped it up on one hop and gained four more yards to the eight. Vessels gained two, and Heatly carried twice to the one where it was fourth-and-goal. Crowder sneaked over right tackle for the score, and Weatherall's conversion closed the gap to 9-7.

The Sooners barely crossed midfield the rest of the game. Texas threatened with a 90-yard drive to the OU two. Carl Mayes picked up 37 yards to the OU 36, where Lockett dragged him down from behind to save a touchdown. On fourth-and-two at the eight, the defense swarmed Mayes for no gain, and Oklahoma took over.

Crowder lateraled to Vessels in the end zone. The OU halfback squirmed through Texas players, but as one Longhorn bore in on him, Vessels was tackled inside the one and suffered a torn knee ligament. Crowder had smacked into the goal post. Crowder was finished for the afternoon, but Vessels was done for the season.

Texas gained 11 first downs, one more than the Sooners. The Steers gained 241 total yards. OU gained 170 on the ground and only one yard through the air.

The Sooners dropped to 19th in the AP poll and hosted Kansas on October 20. Oklahoma defeated the 3-1 Jayhawks, 33-21. Leake replaced Vessels in the lineup and turned in an impressive 121-yard rushing performance and scored three touchdowns. McPhail rushed for 215 yards, breaking Vessels' team record of 208, set against Nebraska in 1950.

End Carl Allison and Grigg each grabbed two interceptions.

The Sooners rolled 74 yards in nine plays to score off the opening kickoff. Leake capped the drive with a four-yard run, and Weatherall converted.

Minutes later, McPhail burst up the middle, shifted to his right and raced 66 yards to the Hawks' 17. Leake swept around right end to score on the next play, and Weatherall toed the 14th point.

Kansas got on the scoreboard late in the first quarter.

Early in the second quarter, Allison intercepted Arkansas pass at the OU 13 and returned it 10 yards. Oklahoma wheeled to another touchdown in eight plays. McPhail cracked through left guard for the nine-yard score, but Weatherall missed the conversion.

Kansas scored late in the first half to trail, 20-13, at intermission.

The Jayhawks moved from their 20 to the OU 28 early in the third period, but the Sooner defense stiffened. Kansas did take the lead (21-20) minutes later after cashing in on McPhail's fumble at midfield.

OU answered to regain the lead with a 64-yard drive following the kickoff. Heatly scored from the two in the first 51 seconds of the fourth quarter. Crowder's 17-yard pass to Heatly to the KU six sparked the drive. Weatherall missed the conversion, leaving the game up for grabs with a 26-21 Sooner lead.

To assure that Kansas was not able to pass against his defense, Coach Wilkinson changed the defensive formation to four linemen and seven backs. The Jayhawks still managed to thread the defense with passes into Sooner territory, but Grigg intercepted a Kansas aerial at the 13 and returned it 44 yards to the KU 43. Heatly, McPhail, and Leake chewed up short chunks of yards to the one, and Leake blasted over for the final tally. Weatherall converted for a 33-21 lead.

Allison and Grigg each grabbed an interception to stall the final two Kansas drives.

The Sooners rushed for 425 yards and passed for 64 more. Kansas picked up 290 total yards.

The Sooners fell out of the AP poll but had an important conference matchup with 4-1 Colorado the next week in Norman. The Buffaloes, having played one more conference game than the Sooners, led the Big Seven Conference with a 3-0 record. The winner would be in the driver's seat for the league title.

Oklahoma crushed Colorado, 55-14, before a homecoming crowd of 46,686 on a cold and damp October afternoon. Crowder earned his wings that day, completing his first five passes for 167 yards. The Muskogee junior finished the game with six of seven completions for 185 yards, four touchdowns, and no interceptions. Crowder's four TD aerials in one half equaled Claude Arnold's school mark set in 1950 against Oklahoma A&M.

Heatly, Reddell, Lockett, and Leake all caught a Crowder pass for a touchdown, and Leake scored a second TD on the ground.

Colorado, without the services of two defensive halfbacks, boxed the front line with seven and eight men. This opened up the passing lanes for the Sooners. Seven Sooners scored touchdowns, as Oklahoma mounted a 27-0 first-quarter lead and 41-0 at halftime.

The Buffaloes got on the board early in the third stanza after recovering Leake's fumble at the OU 31.

Oklahoma answered with an 11-play, 81-yard drive. From the Colorado four, Leake fumbled when he crossed the goal line, but Roberts was alert and recovered for a 47-7 lead.

The Buffs scored 66 seconds later, and Oklahoma answered by cashing in moments after recovering a fumble.

OU collected 368 yards rushing and 189 through the air. Twelve Sooners carried the ball, and Heatly led the way with 56 yards. The Buffaloes gained 257 total yards. Fullback Merwin Hodel rushed for 136 yards for the Buffs.

Oklahoma bounced back into the AP poll at No. 17 the next week. The Sooners defeated 0-5-1 Kansas State, 33-0, on November 3 before 11,000 shivering fans who endured 40 degrees and near-zero wind chill in Manhattan. The victory was the 15th straight over the Wildcats.

Heatly scored three of the Sooners' five touchdowns, and Leake completed all four of his passes for 148 yards and one TD.

Crowder failed to complete a pass in three tries. Oklahoma could not mount a charge in the first period against a stiff northern breeze of 25 to 40 miles per hour and light snow. Wilkinson gambled on fourth downs instead of punting, but the Wildcats stopped them each time—once at the KS 46 and again at the OU 47. K-State could not mount a charge from those midfield breaks.

With the wind, OU revved up its engine and scored twice in the second stanza. Wildcat punter George Carter was unable to handle a bad snap. He attempted to run with the ball, but Allison nailed him at the K-State 20. Heatly scored on a one-yard plunge four plays later, but Weatherall missed the extra point.

Carter's punt was blown three yards behind the line of scrimmage minutes later, and OU took over at the Cats' 48. Six plays later,

Leake slipped through right guard from the two for the score, and Weatherall booted the conversion.

The sun broke through the clouds in the third quarter and shined on the Sooners, who took two plays to cover 42 yards for a 20-0 advantage midway in the third period. Crowder picked up 11 yards, then Leake rolled out and fired a 31-yard scoring strike to Heatly. Weatherall converted.

Early in the fourth stanza, Heatly bolted 47 yards for a touchdown, and Weatherall's toe upped the lead to 27-0.

Carter's punt rolled out at the OU one midway in the fourth period, and the Sooners whirled 99 yards in three plays. After Crowder gained one yard, McPhail busted up the middle, dashed 96 yards to the Cats' two, and was caught from behind by a K-State safety. The winded McPhail asked to be relieved on the next play. Joe Gaynor replaced him and scored on the next play. Weatherall's conversion sailed wide.

Oklahoma rolled up 422 yards on the ground and passed for 158 more. Heatly led the crimson runners with 117 yards, and McPhail added 104 more. The defense handcuffed the Wildcats by holding them to 130 total yards and intercepted seven K-State passes, tying the school record for most interceptions set in 1939 against Southern Methodist and again against Oklahoma A&M in 1941.

The No. 14 Sooners defeated 2-5 Missouri, 34-20, on November 10 in Columbia on a warm 60-degree day that began melting the eight inches of snow that had fallen two days earlier.

The Sooners took a 7-0 lead late in the first quarter on Ed Rowland's interception return. Weatherall converted the first of four extra points, missing the last kick.

Missouri tied the game with five seconds left in the first stanza.

OU marched 77 yards to regain the lead early in the second period. McPhail slammed through right tackle for a seven-yard touchdown. Leake fired a 43-yard bomb to Reddell one play before McPhail scored.

The Tigers advanced into Sooner territory on the next series but stalled at the 26. Oklahoma then drove 74 yards for a 21-7 lead. On fourth-and-eight at the MU 35, Leake took Crowder's handoff and scurried 29 yards to the six. The Sooners moved to a foot from the goal line, and Crowder scored from there with 20 seconds left until intermission.

Missouri marched 80 yards following the second-half kickoff to cut OU's lead.

OU then drove 94 yards to take a 28-14 lead. Heatly got it started with a 23-yard end run. The Sooners continued to the Tigers' 39 on short gains. On the next play, Crowder faked a handoff to Leake and whipped a 21-yard pass to McPhail. The fullback carried to the 11 after the catch but fumbled. The ball rolled forward to the six

Freshman halfback Buddy Leake scores one of his three touchdowns against Kansas. Leake, in his first start, replaced an injured Billy Vessels and rushed for 121 yards against the Jayhawks. *(OU Athletics)*

where Heatly plopped on it. On fourth-and-goal inside the one, Crowder lateraled to Leake, who swept around right end for the score.

Leake added another score on a one-yard plunge with 30 seconds left in the third quarter to cap an 80-yard march. The big gains in the drive came from Leake's lateral to Reddell, which picked up 38 yards to the MU 42, and Leake had a 15-yard run to the six.

Third-string center Sam Allen intercepted two Tiger passes in the fourth period. The second theft stalled a Mizzou drive to the OU 14. Missouri added a TD late in the game.

Oklahoma hammered out 362 rushing yards and passed for 114 more. Leake led the crimson ground attack with 129 yards, and McPhail added 110 yards. The Tigers managed only 21 yards rushing but 406 through the air. Missouri quarterback Tony Scardino finished the day 23 of 42, passing for 365 yards. Halfback Junior Wren caught nine of them for 160 yards.

The Sooners inched up to 12th in the AP poll and could do no worse than share the conference crown with a win the next week over Iowa State. Mission accomplished. OU hammered the 4-3-1 Cyclones, 35-6, in Norman.

Heatly scored twice for the Sooners, and McPhail, Crowder, and Reddell each scored once to lead OU to a 35-0 advantage before the Cyclones scored their only touchdown early in the fourth quarter. Weatherall converted all five extra-point kicks.

Oklahoma picked up 328 yards rushing and passed for 109 more. McPhail led all Sooner runners with 109 yards on 11 carries. The Cyclones gained 285 total yards.

The No. 12 Sooners clinched the Big Seven championship with a 27-0 win over Nebraska on November 24 in Lincoln. A crowd of 33,698 braved the chilly 30-degree temperatures accompanied by a stiff southern breeze.

With nine minutes remaining in the first period, Grigg fielded Ray Novak's punt at the OU 28. Grigg momentarily lost his balance trying to elude Nebraska's Dick Regier. He maintained his balance, shifted to the sideline, and followed a wall of blockers to the end zone. Weatherall booted the first of three conversions. His conversion after the third touchdown was blocked.

The Huskers then marched to their deepest penetration of the game to the OU 38, but Allison's interception squelched their momentum.

Both teams punted well despite the brisk breeze. Heatly kicked 10 times for a 40-yard average, including a 62-yarder. Nebraska's Jim Cederdahl averaged 45 yards on 11 punts including a 57-yarder.

One of Heatly's punts pinned the Huskers at their own five early in the second stanza. Grigg returned Nebraska's punt seven yards to the NU 40 moments later, and the Sooners set sail for a 14-0 lead in five plays. Leake scored on an eight-yard run behind Weatherall's block. Crowder connected a 12-yard pass to Heatly, and McPhail added a 12-yard run to spark the drive.

A punting duel ensued the rest of the half and in the third period, Grigg's short punt return to the OU 46 set up another score late in the third quarter and into the fourth. Crowder was improving on his mastery of deception with the bootleg play—faking a handoff and hiding the ball behind his hip before he passed or kept for a

---

It's a Fact

Face masks, made of nonbreakable, molded plastic, or rubber-covered wire, were legalized in 1951 to protect the players' faces.

run. The play, known as "Counter Option Pass," helped the Sooners gain a crucial first down when they faced fourth-and-11 at the NU 24. Crowder bootlegged to his left and lobbed a pass to Leake at the five. Heatly burst up the middle for the score on the next play to cap the nine-play drive.

The Sooners recovered a Nebraska fumble at the NU 20 to set up the final score. McPhail plowed ahead for three, then Crowder swept right and shot to the one-yard line. Crowder sneaked across on the next play.

Oklahoma collected 235 yards on the ground and passed for 58 more. The defense held the Huskers to three first downs and minus-17 net rushing yards. Nebraska passed for only 49 yards.

Leake tied the school record with four touchdowns to lead the No. 10 Sooners to a 41-6 victory over Oklahoma A&M the following week. Leake equaled George Thomas' mark set against Kansas in 1949. A crowd of 33,103 turned out in Norman and more tuned in on WKY-TV.

The Big Red failed to score on its first three drives into Aggie territory.

The fourth time was a charm, thanks to Billy Bookout's fumble recovery on the A&M nine. Leake whisked around right end on the next play and bowled over A&M's Dean Seeman as he crossed the goal line. Weatherall converted the first of four extra points and only missed after the fourth touchdown.

The Sooners scored in two plays after Grigg fielded a punt at the A&M 43. A penalty on the Aggies moved the ball to the 27. Heatly sliced through left tackle for 14 yards on the final play of the first stanza. Leake then ripped off right tackle on the next play for a 14-0 lead.

The lead grew to 21-0 nearly eight minutes later. Nelson smothered an Aggie fumble at the A&M 23, and the Sooners took four plays to reach pay dirt. Three plays gained only four yards to the 19.

Quarterback Eddie Crowder mastered the art of deception with the bootleg—faking a handoff, hiding the ball behind his hip and then passing or running with the ball. (*OU Athletics*)

On fourth-and-six, Crowder bootlegged to his left, stopped suddenly, and zipped a scoring strike to Reddell.

Another Aggie fumble led to the fourth Sooner score just before halftime. Leake scored on a four-yard run five plays later. The Aggies moved to the OU 13 after the kickoff, but time had expired.

A&M scored early in the third period three plays after recovering Grigg's fumble of a punt return on the OU 33. The Sooners blocked the extra point.

OU drove 73 yards late in the third stanza and into the fourth for a 34-6 lead. Leake capped the drive with a nine-yard scoring jaunt. The Sooners scored their final touchdown of the season minutes later. Crowder's one-yard plunge capped a 51-yard march. Crowder carried 18 yards around left end, and Leake picked up 20 around left end to spark the drive.

The Sooners rushed for 393 yards and passed for 61 more. Leake ran for 107 yards, and Heatly added 106 more. The Aggies were held to 162 total yards.

Weatherall presented Coach Wilkinson with the game ball in a brief ceremony after the game.

"I just want to say we were out there fighting for one guy and the swell bunch of coaches who go with him," Weatherall said. "We want you to have the Aggie ball, Bud."

The season ended with an 8-2 record and another conference title. The team, under guidance of the board of regents, voted not to compete in a postseason bowl game.

Weatherall was named All-America for the second straight year and was awarded the Outland Trophy as the nation's best interior lineman. Tom Catlin also was named All-America. Seven of their teammates joined them on the All-Big Seven first team—Janes, Nelson, Bert Clark, Fred Smith, Crowder, Grigg, and McPhail.

The Sooners' average of 324 rushing yards per game was the fourth best in the nation.

1951 Season Record: 8-2-0

Big Seven Conference: 6-0-0 (Champions)

Date	Opponent	Result	Score
September 29	WILLIAM AND MARY	W	49-7
October 6	at Texas A&M	L	14-7
October 13	Texas at Dallas	L	9-7
October 20	KANSAS	W	33-21
October 27	COLORADO	W	55-14
November 3	at Kansas State	W	33-0
November 10	at Missouri	W	34-20
November 17	IOWA STATE	W	35-6
November 24	at Nebraska	W	27-0
December 1	OKLAHOMA A&M	W	41-6

1952

Attendances at college football games dropped 11.4 percent in 1950, and in early 1951, changes were made to broadcasting college games. The NCAA voted to declare a moratorium on live telecasting of college football games for 1951. A year later, the association adopted a program to limit and control live broadcasts for 1952. The Oklahoma legislature introduced a bill to lift a television ban on Sooner games. Other Big Seven Conference institutions threatened to cancel games against Oklahoma if the bill passed. It didn't go for a vote.

Thirty-two years later, the Universities of Oklahoma and Georgia would again challenge the television issue.

The NCAA also disallowed freshmen from competing in varsity sports, a ruling that would last for 20 years. The Big Seven Conference restricted its members from competing in postseason bowl games in 1952. The University of Oklahoma regents voted to allow the Sooners to participate in bowl games, but the final decision was left up to the coaching staff and players. Any participation by OU in a bowl game would endanger the university's status in the conference. The regents voted a day later to follow conference regulations.

The 1952 Sooner backfield was loaded with veteran returnees—halfbacks Billy Vessels and Buddy Leake, fullback Buck McPhail and quarterback Eddie Crowder. Halfback Merrill Green returned after a one-year layoff due to a knee injury. Halfback Larry Grigg returned but starred mostly as a defensive back and as a punt returner.

All-America center Tom Catlin returned to anchor the front line along with tackle Ed Rowland, guard J.D. Roberts, and end John Reddell.

The No. 4 Sooners opened the season against conference foe Colorado (1-0) at Boulder. The contest ended in a 21-21 tie thanks to OU's touchdown late in the game. The Sooners still had not been beaten in 30 straight conference games.

The game began sloppy, as both teams fumbled five times in the first 11 minutes. OU turned the ball over twice, and the Buffs lost three fumbles. Grigg's 19-yard punt return to the Buffaloes' 48 late in the first period set up the first Sooner score. Buck McPhail scored on a two-yard run, and Leake converted the first of three extra points. Leake's 30-yard run to the CU 18 sparked the drive.

The Buffs answered with a touchdown to tie the game early in the second stanza. The Sooners responded with a 79-yard march in eight plays. Vessels ignited the drive with a 37-yard pass to Reddell on the first play. Crowder, Vessels, Leake, and McPhail pushed the ball to the three, and Leake carried it in for a 14-7 lead.

The Sooners lost a golden opportunity to take a 14-point lead just before halftime. Leake tossed a pass to Vessels in the end zone, but officials ruled that Vessels had trapped the ball.

Colorado tied the game soon after capitalizing on Vessels' fumble at the OU 23 early in the third quarter. The Buffs intercepted Leake's pass in the end zone to squelch another OU scoring chance minutes later.

The Buffaloes scored a touchdown early in the fourth stanza to take a 21-14 lead. Kurt Burris' interception at the OU 22 set up the tying drive minutes later.

Bud Wilkinson took a huge risk with the ball still in Sooner territory. He gambled on fourth-and-one at the 31, and it paid off. Vessels swept around right end and cut back sharply for a gain of 18 yards. OU later faced third-and-five at the CU 14 where McPhail burst up the middle for six, and Vessels scored from the one two plays later.

The Sooners gained 257 rushing yards and passed for 65. Vessels led all runners with 110 yards, and McPhail added 107. McPhail punted six times for an average of 46.2 yards per kick. Colorado picked up 167 total yards. Quarterback Zack Jordan accounted for all three Buff scores by running for two touchdowns and passing for another. Jordan also punted seven times for a 56-yard average and his kicks occasionally pinned OU deep.

Tackle Roger Nelson injured his elbow and sat out the next four games. Don Brown replaced him in the lineup.

300th Win

The tie dropped the Sooners to 20th in the AP poll, but Oklahoma returned to form with a 49-20 pasting of Pittsburgh the next week in Norman. The victory marked OU's 300th win in history. Six Sooners scored in the game, led by Leake's two TDs in the

first quarter. Leake also converted six of the seven extra pointers, and Buck McPhail kicked the last one.

Leake also tossed a 20-yard scoring strike to Carl Allison early in the second stanza for a 21-0 lead. The Panthers scored twice before halftime to cut the OU lead to 21-13.

Two third-quarter touchdowns by the Sooners put the game out of reach, 35-13. Oklahoma rolled 78 yards to pay dirt after the second-half kickoff, and McPhail capped the drive with a 13-yard burst through right tackle.

Late in the same quarter, Rowland crashed through the line and blocked Joe Zombeck's punt. End Dick Ellis scooped up the pigskin and rambled 45 yards down the sideline for the score.

Crowder and Green each scored on five-yard runs in the fourth period, and Pitt scored late in the game.

Oklahoma rushed for 326 yards and passed for 35 more. McPhail led all Sooner ball carriers with 158 yards on 20 carries. Pittsburgh gained 232 total yards.

The No. 12 Sooners posted an identical score on October 11 against 2-1 Texas before a crowd of 75,504 in the Cotton Bowl. The 49-20 victory was the largest margin over the Longhorns since the 50-0 win in 1908.

The game was televised in Oklahoma City, Tulsa, Dallas, and San Antonio—the first live broadcast of the rivalry. The Sooners entertained the audience with a four-touchdown onslaught in the game's first 11 minutes. OU led, 28-0, and the offense had only run 13 plays from scrimmage.

Grigg recovered halfback Gib Dawson's fumble on the game's first play at the Steers' 26. Six plays later, Vessels smashed through for the two-yard touchdown, and Leake kicked the first of seven conversions. Leake's two touchdowns and seven conversions set a new series record with 19 points, breaking the record held by two Longhorn players years earlier.

Coach Wilkinson altered his offensive scheme for the game. Instead of a halfback running in the flat and an end going deep, the halfback faked toward the sideline then ran deep, and the end went into the right flat and cut toward the sideline. The play helped the Sooners take a 14-0 lead on a 76-yard drive on their next possession. Texas punted to the OU 24, and the Sooners picked up 11 yards in three plays. On the next play, Crowder fired a pass to Leake on the Texas 30, and Leake scooted to the end zone. The 65-yard play was the longest in the rivalry's history. The previous mark was a 63-yard pass from Texas' Bobby Lee to Ralph Ellsworth in 1943.

Dawson had butter fingers again on the following kickoff, and Gene Calame pounced on the free ball at the UT 29. Crowder hurled a TD pass on the next play, but a holding call pushed the Sooners back 11 yards. Still, the crimson lads needed only three plays to score. Crowder zipped a 28-yard pass to Vessels to the Texas 12. Crowder then surged ahead for five yards. Vessels took a pitchout on the next play, then lateraled to McPhail, who dashed seven yards for the score.

The Longhorns stalled on their next possession, and Grigg returned the punt 37 yards to the UT 29. Crowder sailed a scoring strike to Reddell on the next play for a 28-0 lead with 4:10 remaining in the first quarter.

Texas marched 74 yards in 17 plays for a touchdown late in the second half, and neither team scored in the third period.

The Sooners lit up the scoreboard with three touchdowns in the fourth stanza. Leake scored on a one-yard run to cap a 66-yard, 12-play drive. Texas answered with an 80-yard journey for its second score. The Big Red responded with another TD a minute later. Leake returned the kickoff 18 yards to the OU 31. McPhail bulled ahead for nine and, on the next play, Vessels gained five yards, then pitched back to McPhail, who sailed the final 55 yards for the score.

Texas scored on its next series but missed the extra point. The Horns also missed the onside kick as OU smothered the ball at the UT 41. Vessels scored on a one-yard run nine plays later.

The Sooners rushed for 296 yards and passed for 133. McPhail led Sooner runners with 147 yards, and Vessels also cleared the century mark with 106 yards. Crowder finished the game with five completions in seven attempts after completing his first four passes in a row. Texas picked up 304 total yards.

The No. 6 Sooners were one touchdown shy of scoring 49 points for the third straight week with a 42-20 victory over Kansas in Lawrence on October 18. A crowd of 37,946 turned out to see a battle of unbeatens—OU (3-0) and the Jayhawks (4-0). Kansas had shut out two of its opponents and yielded 21 points in the other two games. The Hawks' defense was no match for the punishing Sooner offense.

Kansas jumped to a 7-0 lead early in the first quarter, five plays after recovering Vessels' fumble on the OU eight. Minutes later, Rowland pounced a KU fumble on the Kansas 16 to set up the tying score. On third-and-five at the 10, Leake swept around the left side for the touchdown. He also kicked the first two conversions but had to leave the game in the second period with a sore ankle.

Grigg intercepted a Kansas pass on the next Jayhawk possession at the KU 42. One play later, Crowder faked a handoff and tossed a 21-yard pass to Max Boydston, who completed the 58-yard play by sprinting the final 37 to the end zone.

Vessels scored on a one-yard run in the second stanza several plays after Allison intercepted another Jayhawk pass on the OU 36. McPhail kicked the first of four conversions.

The Jayhawks answered with a 61-yard scoring drive but missed the extra point. The Sooners moved into scoring position early in the third period, but McPhail spilled the pigskin, and Kansas recovered on its 19. The Hawks then wheeled 81 yards to score in six plays to cut the Oklahoma lead to 21-20.

Kansas had a chance to take the lead minutes later with a drive to the OU five after intercepting Crowder's pass on the OU 40. Catlin led the defensive revolt as he nailed quarterback Jerry Robertson for a five-yard loss on one play and broke up the fourth-down pass on the goal line.

The Sooners then marched 90 yards in eight plays to take a 28-20 lead. Green, who replaced Leake at right halfback, scored on a one-yard run. Vessels sparked the drive by weaving sideline to sideline and feinting a couple of defenders for 51 yards to the KU 17.

Vessels and Green each scored for the Sooners in the fourth quarter.

Oklahoma hammered out 304 yards and passed for 181. Vessels toted the ball 15 times for 105 yards. Kansas rolled up 371 total yards.

The No. 3 Sooners blasted Kansas State, 49-6, the following week in Norman before a homecoming throng of 38,168. Vessels, Grigg, and Boydston each scored twice, and the defense intercepted seven Wildcat aerials. The 1-4 Wildcats had lost four straight after winning their season opener.

Oklahoma rushed for 281 yards and passed for 227. Crowder completed all four of his passes for 72 yards. The Wildcats were held to 152 total yards.

The No. 3 Sooners pounded Iowa State, 41-0, on November 1 before a dismal 9,619 fans in Ames. OU took the opening kickoff and marched 82 yards for the first score. Vessels capped the seven-play drive with a 50-yard run. Leake converted.

The Cyclones' only threat came minutes later with a 79-yard drive to the Oklahoma one, but the defense stiffened.

Interceptions by Catlin and Jack Ging set up the next two Oklahoma scores. Green's one-yard run and McPhail's 28-yard scamper gave OU a 21-0 lead. McPhail added another touchdown, and Vessels threw a scoring strike and ran for another score.

The Sooners rushed for 295 yards and added 57 yards through the air. McPhail gained 110 yards on 13 carries, and Vessels added 110 on 12 totes. The defense held the Cyclones to six first downs and 119 total yards.

The No. 4 Sooners traveled to South Bend, Indiana, the following week for a showdown with one of the greatest programs in college football—Notre Dame. Frank Leahy's Fighting Irish were rated No. 10 with a 4-1-1 record. Leahy had coached the Irish to six undefeated seasons and five national championship teams.

Notre Dame started the season with a 1-1-1 record, then won three straight before OU came to town. Both teams had two common opponents—Texas and Pittsburgh. The Irish defeated the Longhorns 14-3 and squeaked by the Panthers, 22-19.

The NBC network nationally televised the first matchup between OU and Notre Dame. The 57,446 fans in the stands (including 9,000 Sooner rooters) and the rest of America were treated to a whale of a ball game. Although the Irish won, 27-21, it was the game that helped Vessels win the Heisman Trophy.

A poor punt Irish punt set up the Sooners at the Notre Dame 28 late in the first quarter. On the next play, Crowder bootlegged. He faked a handoff to McPhail and fired a scoring strike to Vessels. Leake converted the first of three extra points.

Notre Dame marched 59 yards for the tying score early in the second period after recovering an Oklahoma fumble.

OU took a 14-7 lead two minutes later. Brown recovered an Irish fumble at the OU 31. McPhail gained seven, and Vessels slashed through left tackle for a 62-yard touchdown. Dick Bowman, Boydston and Jim Davis provided key blocks for Vessels.

Roberts was expelled from the game just before halftime. An Irish player shoved him at the end of a play, and Roberts retaliated with an elbow jab to the head of his opponent. Officials only saw Roberts' action and ejected him. Fellow lineman Rowland was sidelined in the second half with an injury.

Notre Dame tied the game midway through the third stanza with a 55-yard scoring drive. Neil Worden's one-yard run capped the drive although several Sooner players protested that Worden had been stopped short of the goal line. The play stood, and Bob Arrix toed the tying conversion.

The Sooners reclaimed the lead, 21-14, with a 63-yard drive in three plays following the kickoff. McPhail and Vessels each gained five yards to the OU 47. On the next play, Crowder noticed that Notre Dame was stacking the line with eight men, so he changed the play at the line. He pitched the ball to Vessels, who followed McPhail's block at the corner and raced down the sideline. Vessels eluded several defenders, reversed toward the middle of the field and sailed to the end zone leaving Arrix sprawling at the 15.

The Irish responded with a 79-yard drive to tie the game at 21-21 early in the fourth quarter. Grigg received the ensuing kickoff, but Notre Dame's Dan Shannon smacked him head on, forcing a fumble, which the Irish recovered on the OU 28. Shannon was carried off the field and did not return.

It's a Fact

OU averaged 40.7 points per game in 1952—best in the nation.

Notre Dame scored four plays later, but Grigg blocked the extra point, leaving the door open for a possible Sooner comeback with 13:20 to go. Oklahoma stalled short of the target on its next three possessions.

OU gained 13 first downs, rushed for 313 yards and passed for 44. Vessels carried the ball 17 times for 195 yards. Notre Dame picked up 23 first downs and 354 total yards.

OU president Dr. George Cross, who attended the game, wrote about Vessels' performance in his book, *Presidents Can't Punt*: "He played with an abandon seldom seen in any athletic contest. Whenever he saw that there was no way of avoiding a tackler, he would throw himself forward to a horizontal position, using his body as a sort of projectile to gain additional yardage."

Leake's nagging ankle injury kept him out of the final three contests. Green replaced him at right halfback, and McPhail took over the placekicking duties.

With a national championship out of reach, the Sooners turned their attention to claiming the school's seventh straight Big Seven championship. OU dropped to eighth in the AP poll and took out its frustration with a 47-7 victory over 4-4 Missouri. A crowd of 43,393 spectators enjoyed the warm (78 degrees), but windy (30 miles per hour) November afternoon in Norman. It was the worst licking the Sooners laid on the Tigers since the series began in 1902. Special teams helped OU jump to a 21-0 lead, and interceptions aided the Sooners to the final three scores.

The Big Red defense stalled Missouri on the Tigers' first series, and OU's backup center, Sam Allen, blocked Bill Fessler's punt, Brown grabbed the ball returned it 10 yards to the five. Three plays later, Crowder sneaked across from the one, and McPhail converted.

The Tigers were forced to punt on their next possession. Ging fielded Fessler's kick at the OU 35 and flew down the east sideline for a touchdown. McPhail converted for a 14-0 lead.

A bad snap sailed over Fessler's head early in the second period. The Missouri punter retrieved the ball near the goal line and got off a hurried kick to the Tigers' 30. Seven plays later, Green punched across right tackle from the three, and McPhail converted.

Mizzou answered with a 61-yard march to score after the kickoff to cut the Oklahoma lead to 21-7.

The Sooners advanced 66 yards to the MU five following the second-half kickoff, but Green fumbled into the end zone, and the Tigers recovered for a touchback. OU rolled 56 yards in 11 plays on its next possession. Crowder ignited the drive with a 14-yard run to the MU 42 on the first play. Vessels, Green, and McPhail hammered on down to the eight, and McPhail sliced through right guard for the score. McPhail missed the extra point.

Catlin picked off Tony Scardino's pass, moments after McPhail's touchdown, and returned it nine yards to the Tigers' 31. Green and McPhail carried down to the 17, then Vessels rifled a scoring strike to Green.

Jerry Ingram's interception at the Mizzou 48 late in the third stanza set up the next score early in the fourth. Green's one-yard plunge capped the 12-play thrust, and McPhail converted for a 41-7 advantage.

Fifth-string quarterback Jack Van Pool scored on a one-yard plunge in the fourth quarter moments after Vessels intercepted a pass at the MU 40.

Oklahoma pounded out 261 rushing yards and tossed for 116 more. Missouri picked up 192 total yards.

A three-touchdown barrage in the first period, and by Vessels in the game, vaulted the No. 5 Sooners to a 34-13 victory over Nebraska before a homecoming crowd of 42,489 to claim the sev-

enth straight conference title (sixth straight Big Seven championship). The 5-3-1 Cornhuskers had not yielded more than 21 points in a game all season and played the Sooners without star half-back Bobby Reynolds, who pulled a leg muscle the day before the game.

Crowder's mastery of deception with the bootleg and his passing arm had the Husker defense on its heels all day long. The Huskers failed to gain a first down and did not move past their 39-yard line in the first period.

OU scored on its second, third, and fourth possessions. The Sooners moved 66 yards to the NU 29 after the opening kickoff but had to punt, and McPhail's kick rolled dead at the two-yard line. The Huskers stalled and punted out to the 42. Oklahoma took a 6-0 lead six plays later on Vessels' five-yard run. Crowder ignited the drive with a 39-yard aerial to Merrill Green on the first play. McPhail missed the conversion but made the next four.

Ging returned a punt 34 yards to the NU 42, and Green scored on a four-yard run moments later. Crowder fired a 24-yard pass to Vessels to the 18 to spark the drive.

The Sooners took a longer route to score again after Nebraska punted to the OU 19. Oklahoma wheeled 81 yards in eight plays, culminated by Vessels' one-yard plunge. Crowder highlighted the drive with a 29-yard pass to Boydston to the Nebraska 48 and boot-legged a 30-yard run to the 18.

The Huskers rolled 70 yards to cut their deficit to 20-7 for the only score in the second quarter.

The Sooners took a 27-7 lead on a 60-yard drive midway through the third period. From the Huskers' 42, Green surged ahead for 10 yards, then pitched back to Crowder who picked up six more yards to the NU 26. Moments later at the eight, Vessels lunged ahead for three yards then popped the ball to McPhail, who scooted around left end for the score.

Minutes later, Vessels scored the final OU tally on a 27-yard run. He shot through right tackle, paused after a seven-yard gain, rico-cheted off a couple of Huskers, and turned on the after burners.

The Huskers scored against the reserves in the fourth quarter.

Oklahoma rolled up 348 yards on the ground and passed for 132. McPhail gained 138 yards, and Vessels added 95. Both players surpassed Joe Golding's season record of 902 yards set in 1946. Crowder completed five of 11 passes for 128 yards. The Huskers gained 261 total yards.

Three days after the Nebraska game, the New York Downtown Athletic Club announced that Vessels was the 18th recipient of the Heisman Memorial Trophy. Vessels was the first Sooner to be awarded the honor.

1952 Season Record: 8-1-1

Big Seven Conference: 5-0-1 (Champions)

Date	Opponent	Result	Score
September 27	at Colorado	T	21-21
October 4	PITTSBURGH	W	49-20
October 11	Texas at Dallas	W	49-20
October 18	at Kansas	W	42-20
October 25	KANSAS STATE	W	49-6
November 1	at Iowa State	W	41-0
November 8	at Notre Dame	L	27-21
November 15	MISSOURI	W	47-7
November 22	NEBRASKA	W	34-13
November 29	at Oklahoma A&M	W	54-7

Vessels was notified of the honor in the locker room the afternoon of November 25 practices. "What? You're kidding! I can barely talk," he responded.

The No. 4 Sooners celebrated the good news by hammering Oklahoma A&M 54-7 in the season finale in Stillwater.

The Aggies took a 7-0 lead in the game's first 21 seconds when Bill Bredde returned the opening kickoff 98 yards for a touchdown. The rest of the game was all OU.

Sooner guard Doc Hearon partially blocked Ken McCullough's punt minutes later, and the ball rolled out of bounds at the A&M 21. McPhail carried on the next three plays for the score. He took a lateral from Vessels for 11, bulled ahead for four more and took another Vessels pitch to cover the final seven yards. McPhail's conversion veered wide, and the Aggies held a slim 7-6 advantage.

The Sooners marched 72 yards to score on their next series. Green's eight-yard sprint around end capped the 10-play drive. Crowder sparked the drive with a 24-yard pass to Vessels. McPhail's toe gave OU a 13-7 lead.

Grigg recovered an Aggie fumble at the A&M 24 moments later to set up the next touchdown early in the second stanza. Three plays later, Green scored from the four, but McPhail's conversion missed the target again.

The Sooners rolled 71 yards in 10 plays for a 26-7 lead after the second-half kickoff. Vessels' one-yard run capped the drive, which was highlighted by Green's 17-yard jaunt and Crowder's 21-yard pass to Reddell. McPhail converted and did not miss another kick in the game.

The Pokes stalled after the kickoff and punted to their 48. Crowder rifled a touchdown pass to Boydston on the next play. Catlin recovered an Aggie fumble at the A&M 13 on the first play following the kickoff. Vessels carried on the next three plays and scored from the one.

Nelson intercepted an Aggie pass and returned it 20 yards for a touchdown late in the game. Roberts recovered a Poke fumble at the A&M 26 two plays after the kickoff. Calame scored on a four-yard run four plays later.

The Sooners finished with a No. 4 ranking in the AP poll. Oklahoma led the nation in scoring with 407 points. Vessels led the nation in all-purpose yards (151.2 per game average) and scoring with 18 touchdowns and gained 1,072 yards to finish second nationally. McPhail was third with 1,018 yards. Buddy Leake converted 97 percent of his extra pointers, best in the nation. Vessels, McPhail, Leake, and Green were the top four scorers in the Big Seven Conference. Crowder set an NCAA record with 13.5 yards per pass attempt.

All-America honors went to Catlin, Crowder, Vessels, and McPhail. Boydston, Rowland, Davis, and Roberts joined them on the All-Big Seven first unit.

Vessels also won the Maxwell Memorial Award as the outstanding player of the year.

1953

On July 27, 1953, the United States, North Korea, and China signed an armistice, bringing an end to the Korean War.

The NCAA abolished the two-platoon rule. Unlimited substitution was allowed by rule changes in 1947 and 1948, but single-platoon football was reestablished, and free substitution and two-platoon football did not flourish until 1965.

Bud Wilkinson had to replenish his supply of backs with the graduation of Billy Vessels, Eddie Crowder, and Buck McPhail. Halfbacks Buddy Leake, Merrill Green, and Larry Grigg returned.

Jack Ging and Gene Calame had plenty of experience. Leake began the season at quarterback, Ging at left half, Grigg at right half, and Max Boydston was moved from end to fullback.

Guard J.D. Roberts and tackle Doc Hearon returned to anchor the right side of the interior wall, and Roger Nelson returned at left tackle. Kurt Burris got the nod at center along with Bo Bolinger at left guard and Dick Bowman at left tackle. Carl Allison still had eligibility and returned to the left end slot, and Troy Keller got the nod at right end.

The 1953 Sooners opened and concluded the season against the nation's No. 1 teams—Notre Dame and Maryland. Oklahoma lost to one and defeated the other. Although the Sooners began the season in a hole (0-1-1), the third game was the beginning of a winning streak that has not been broken by any major college football team.

Notre Dame came to Norman on September 26 for the season opener for both teams. The No. 6 Sooners wanted revenge for the 27-21 loss a year earlier in South Bend. The Fighting Irish did one point better in the 28-21 victory before a crowd of 59,461. Notre Dame scored off OU errors—two fumbles, a blocked punt, and an interception.

Oklahoma cashed in on an Irish fumble in the game's first series. Bowman recovered on the ND 23 and the Sooners gambled twice on fourth down to take a 7-0 lead. Three plays after Bowman's recovery, the Sooners were short of a first down. Leake kept the ball on the next play and picked up the first down on the nine. Three plays later, OU was a foot short of the goal line, and on fourth down Grigg plowed ahead for the score, and Leake converted the first of three extra points.

Notre Dame answered with a touchdown minutes later.

The Sooners marched 80 yards in six plays to take a 14-7 lead on Grigg's second touchdown midway through the second quarter. Leake completed a short pass to Allison to begin the drive, and Allison flew down the east sideline to the Irish 16. Five plays later, Grigg slashed through left tackle from the six for the score.

The Irish scored late in the second stanza after blocking Boydston's punt. Notre Dame took a 21-14 lead midway through the third period after intercepting Leake's pass. The Irish capitalized on a fumble by Leake at the OU 36 for the final tally.

Merrill Green had replaced Grigg, who left the game with a twisted ankle. Green helped move the Sooners to the Irish 14-yard line, but OU surrendered on downs. Green did electrify the crowd midway through the fourth quarter when he returned a punt 60 yards for a touchdown. As he passed by the Sooner bench, he shouted, "Get out the kicking tee!"

Down by a touchdown with 5:11 remaining, Sooner faithful still had hope, and Green gave them further hope two minutes later when he picked off an Irish pass on the OU 40. Any chance for a comeback died two plays later when Notre Dame intercepted Leake's pass.

Notre Dame gained 255 total yards, 14 more than the Sooners.

The No. 8 Sooners traveled to Pittsburgh to face the 0-1 Panthers the following week but left the Steel City with a 7-7 tie.

The Sooners needed one play to travel 80 yards for their score early in the second stanza after a Pitt punt into the end zone set them up at the 20. Leake bootlegged and fired a 25-yard pass to Grigg, who took the pass and dashed to the end zone. Keller's block at midfield took out the last Panther in pursuit. Leake converted for the 7-0 lead.

The Panthers twice threatened by advancing into Oklahoma territory, and both times they were shut down—once on a march to the 28 and moments later after recovering Jack Van Pool's fumble at the 23.

Bob Burris, Kurt's brother, recovered a Pitt fumble at the Panther six following the second-half kickoff. The Sooners punched to the one but could not score and surrendered on downs.

Pitt drove 76 yards to the OU one early in the fourth quarter, but the Sooners' goal-line stand kept the Panthers out of the end zone. Halfback Bobby Epps was swarmed for no gain on fourth down. The Panthers did tie the game with a 48-yard drive on their next possession.

Neither team threatened again. Pitt gained more total yards (277-170). OU's rushing performance (63 net yards) was hampered by Leake's minus-13 yards in four carries. Ging suffered a dislocated shoulder and was out for several games.

OU plummeted to 16th in the AP poll, and the squad's lack of offensive electricity caused Coach Wilkinson to shake up the backfield before meeting No. 15 Texas the next week in Dallas. Calame started at quarterback, and Leake returned to the left halfback slot. Grigg remained at right halfback, and Wray Littlejohn moved up to start at fullback.

The Streak Begins

The Sooners had a little more offensive punch as they defeated the 2-1 Longhorns, 19-14, before a jam-packed Cotton Bowl crowd of 75,504 and a national television (NBC) audience. Oklahoma jumped to a 19-0 lead, but two Texas touchdowns in the fourth period had everyone on the edge of their seats.

The Big Red scored on its second possession, which came after Tom Carroll recovered Billy Quinn's fumble at the Steers' 25. On second and five at the 20, Calame swept 11 yards around left end for the first down. Grigg carried on the next three plays and scored from the one. Calame's conversion sailed wide, and OU held a 6-0 lead midway through the first stanza.

Wilkinson put Leake and Green in the game for the first time in the second period. Green fielded Bill Long's punt, faked to Leake on the crossover, weaved through Texas defenders, and bolted down the sideline 80 yards to the end zone. A bad snap foiled the conversion try.

OU rolled 57 yards to take a 19-0 advantage early in the fourth stanza. Calame lateraled to Carroll on the next play, and Carroll followed Don Brown's lead to the end zone. Brown mowed down the last Longhorn at the 15. Green converted, and OU held a 19-0 advantage early in the fourth stanza.

The Steers marched 78 yards after the kickoff for their first score.

Moments later, Texas recovered a fumble at the OU 40. Charles Brewer sailed a 36-yard pass to Carlton Massey on the next play to the four. Brewer fumbled on the next play, and Boydston recovered for the Sooners with two and one-half minutes to go.

The Sooners tried to milk the clock with short gains and delay penalties. On fourth down inside the one, Wilkinson ordered Calame to retreat behind the goal line for an intentional safety. His quarterback followed orders but suddenly saw an opening and cut upfield. The Horns quickly closed in and nailed Calame at the three. Texas scored on the next play, closing the gap to 19-14 with 29 seconds remaining.

The Steers recovered the onside kick but were penalized for offside. OU grabbed the second onside attempt and ran out the clock. Both teams gained 12 first downs, and OU led the rushing category (220-117), but Texas passed for more (104-13).

The Sooners would not lose in the next 46 games, a streak unmatched by any major college football team.

No. 12 Oklahoma pounded out a record 527 yards rushing in a 45-0 thumping of 2-2 Kansas on October 17 in Norman, the greatest margin of victory in 51 games between the two schools.

The Sooners had to earn every score with an average of 70 yards per drive. The first march took 78 yards after the opening kickoff. Grigg scored once and tossed two TD strikes to Allison.

Oklahoma passed for only 15 yards in their sixth straight win over the Jayhawks. Grigg picked up 156 yards on 12 carries, and Calame added 100 yards rushing. The team rushing record eclipsed 436 yards against Nebraska in 1949. The defense held Kansas to six first downs and 134 total yards.

Sooner Magic: Green's Gallop Brands Buffaloes

The Big Red had climbed to ninth entering the Colorado game the next week in Norman.

CU was reeling from three straight conference losses after opening the season with two wins. The Sooners were tabbed as 27-point favorites but would have to fight to the end to gain a 27-20 victory over the Buffs before a homecoming crowd of 36,565.

Grigg fumbled the opening kickoff when he bumped into a teammate. Colorado scored five plays later for a 6-0 lead.

OU twice stalled Buff drives in the first stanza. The second attempt failed at the OU 25, and the Sooners wheeled 75 yards to tie the game.

Grigg scored from inside the one, but Calame's conversion sailed wide and both teams were knotted at 6-6 midway through the second period.

Colorado answered with a seven-play, 60-yard drive to regain the lead with 5:41 remaining in the second quarter.

Early in the third stanza, Roberts slammed through the line and blocked a Colorado punt. The ball squirted back to the CU 27. CU punter Ron Johnson pursued the bouncing ball, but as he grabbed it, Nelson, Brown, and Boydston smothered him.

The Sooners managed to gain only one yard in three plays. Facing fourth-and-nine, Grigg took a pitch out and scampered off left tackle for 10 yards to the 16. Three plays later from the CU three, Grigg plowed over right tackle for the touchdown. Leake booted the extra point, and the score again was tied 13-13 midway through the third period.

Early in the fourth quarter, the Buffs threatened with a drive to the OU 22, but fumbled and Grigg recovered. The Sooners drove 78 yards for a 20-13 lead with 7:11 to go in the game. Bob Herndon scooted 33 yards through the left guard to the end zone and Leake converted.

A Colorado touchdown pulled the Buffs even, 20-20, with 90 seconds remaining.

Many Sooner faithful were thinking they might have to settle for another tie this season and second in a row with Colorado. The Sooners and Buffaloes tied 21-all in the season opener the year before. Still it was not a defeat, which Wilkinson had not tasted in the conference since he took the helm in 1947.

Following Calame's kickoff return to the OU 30, Leake threw an incomplete pass, but CU was guilty of holding—15 yards to the OU 49.

Green had been playing sparingly all season behind Grigg at right halfback, but he did not go unnoticed in a crimson and white uniform. He electrified Sooner fans with two punt returns for touchdowns early in the season.

Green replaced Grigg, the man who had gained 76 yards and scored two TDs against the Buffs. Green had been overshadowed a year earlier by the All-America backfield and Grigg this year. Prior to the Colorado game, he had only 13 carries for 65 yards, and he only played a total of about four minutes against the Buffaloes.

Nevertheless he got the call and answered with an explosive run. Green took Calame's handoff and smashed over left tackle. Keller delivered a crucial block to provide Green a lane to the end zone. Two CU safeties tried to catch the speedy Sooner back, but blocks by Leake and Allison cut them off.

Leake toed the extra point with 36 ticks left on the clock, and the Sooners held on for a 27-20 victory. Green was carried off the field by teammates after the final gun sounded.

"It takes Oklahoma to win games like that one," said Bowman.

When asked who made the call for the winning play, all Wilkinson would say was, "I guess it came from Green."

OU rushed for 327 yards and passed for only 11. The Buffaloes picked up 288 total yards.

The No. 9 Sooners traveled to Manhattan on October 31 and came home with a 34-0 victory over 5-1 Kansas State. The Wildcats, 3-0 in the Big Seven Conference, were looking for their first conference title in 19 years.

Kansas State deployed a 6-2-1-2 defensive alignment, limiting long Sooner runs, but OU collected short yardage behind the punishing blocks of Roberts and Nelson.

Larry Grigg, who carried 25 times for 177 yards, scored the first of his two touchdowns on a three-yard run midway through the first stanza, and Calame converted for a 7-0 advantage. The win capped an 18-play, 79-yard march.

The Sooners rolled 69 yards in eight plays to score on their third possession late in the second period. Herndon's 16-yard touchdown and Leake's conversion gave OU a 14-0 lead.

An 80-yard march following the second-half kickoff raised the lead to 20-0. Grigg's one-yard end sweep on fourth down capped the 14-play drive, but Calame's conversion sailed wide.

A fourth-down stop by the Oklahoma defense led to the next score early in the fourth quarter. The Cats had moved to the OU 40, but Boydston pinned Veryl Switzer for a nine-yard loss, and the Sooners took over at their own 49. Facing fourth-and-four at the KSU 43, Calame gained five for the first down. Three plays later, Ging scored on a nine-yard run aided by Bowman's block to the end zone. Leake converted the 27th point.

The Cats' Jim Rhoades fumbled the kick off, and Bolinger smothered it on the KSU 18. Wilkinson sent in the alternates for the final tally. Chuck Baker and Bob Santee carried to the one in three plays, and Baker crashed through right tackle for the touchdown, and Santee converted.

The Sooners collected 420 rushing yards and did not complete a pass in four tries. The Wildcats were held to 152 total yards.

Sooner Magic: Calame's Audible Scratches Tigers

The eighth-ranked Sooners were a two-touchdown favorite against 4-2 Missouri. OU cashed in on two failed fourth-down attempts to pull out a 14-7 decision before a crowd of 30,020 on November 7 in Columbia. The victory ended any hopes of a Missouri win for the first time in eight years.

The Big Red marched 66 yards to take a 7-0 lead when Grigg scored on a seven-yard end sweep and Calame's conversion.

Halfback Merrill Green bolts 51 yards late in the game to defeat Colorado 27-20. (*OU Athletics*)

The Tigers drove 23 yards to tie the game after a short OU punt early in the second period.

The Tigers clawed their way to the OU 17 early in the fourth period, mostly on running plays. Mizzou began passing from there and failed to produce any threat. Grigg busted up the third-down pass, and Ray Detling's 24-yard field goal fell short of its mark with nine minutes remaining.

The Sooners then drove to pay dirt. Bob Burris' 12-yard run, Ging's 14-yard jaunt, and Grigg's 11-yard gain aided the march to the MU 16. Grigg then hammered eight more to the eight-yard line, and Ging picked up five more for a first down on the three.

Calame and Burris each gained a yard, then Grigg was stopped half a yard short of the goal line. On fourth-and-goal, the Tigers bunched to the middle, expecting the Sooners to run straight ahead. Noticing this, Calame called another play at the line of scrimmage. He then pitched out to Grigg, who sailed around the left side for the touchdown, and Calame converted for the 14-7 lead.

Brown sacked Victor Eaton for a 12-yard loss to squelch the Tigers' hopes for a comeback. Oklahoma took the punt and moved to the Mizzou five when the clock expired.

Oklahoma rushed for 276 yards and threw for 54. The Tigers picked up 224 total yards.

The No. 6 Sooners clinched another Big Seven title and an Orange Bowl bid with a 47-0 win over 2-6 Iowa State the next week in Norman. The win gave the Big Red a 5-0 conference record, two games better than Kansas State, which lost to Missouri on the same day and finished with a 5-2 mark. OU also extended its conference winning string to 32.

Grigg scored twice, and Calame and Herndon had a touchdown each to give OU a 27-0 lead through three quarters.

The game's biggest play came early in the fourth stanza. Leake took a Cyclone punt, crossed over and handed the ball to Green, who flashed 68 yards down the west sideline to the end zone. Leake converted the 34th point.

Reserve quarterback Jay O'Neal led the alternates to two more touchdowns, both through the air. O'Neal connected a 24-yard scoring strike to end Kenneth Arms and a 43-yard TD pass to Harry Cross. O'Neal converted the final extra point.

The Sooners pounded out 376 rushing yards. Sixteen Sooners carried the ball, and Boydston led the way with 75 yards. OU completed five of eight passes for 123 yards. O'Neal led with two completions in three passes for 68 yards. The Cyclones were held to 161 total yards.

> ## It's a Fact
> The Sooners led the nation in rushing offense with an average of 306.9 yards per game in 1953.

The Big Red rose to fourth in the AP poll and stayed there through the rest of the season.

The Sooners kept their conference mark perfect with a 30-7 win over 3-5-1 Nebraska on November 21 before 31,551 shivering fans in Lincoln. Oklahoma rolled up 406 rushing yards on a slippery turf surrounded by banks of snow. Bob Burris led the ground attack with 153 yards in 20 carries.

OU failed to capitalize on a fumble recovery at the NU 15 early in the game, but a safety minutes later gave Oklahoma the only points of the first stanza. An errant Husker snap sailed out of the end zone midway through the first period.

The Sooners marched 92 yards in 14 plays, all on the ground, to score early in the second stanza. Grigg punched across from inside the one-yard line, and Ging converted for a 9-0 lead. Burris' 29-yard run to the NU 40 sparked the drive. Grigg also gained 16 yards to the eight right before he scored.

The Huskers answered with a 83-yard scoring drive to cut OU's lead to 9-7.

The Sooners retaliated with a 76-yard jaunt in six plays. Jerry Donaghey started things off with a 45-yard gain to the NU 31, and six plays later, Green scored from the five. Leake toed the conversion.

A freakish punt gave OU possession at the Husker eight early in the third period, but the Sooners failed to capitalize. NU halfback Jay Novak tried to retrieve a bad snap in the end zone, and with his back to the playing field he kicked the ball over his head. The ball traveled eight yards upfield. Grigg appeared to score four plays later, but he fumbled into the end zone, and Nebraska recovered for a touchdown.

The Sooners later marched 50 yards, with Burris carrying on six of the eight plays and scoring from the eight-yard line. Leake converted for a 23-7 lead.

Oklahoma advanced 65 yards to a foot from the goal line in the final quarter but surrendered on Leake's fumble. The reserves scored the final touchdown when Van Pool tossed a 10-yard pass to Calvin Woodworth with 10 seconds remaining.

Van Pool's two-for-two passing for 26 yards accounted for the team's only passing yards. The Sooner defense held Nebraska to 122 total yards.

The Sooners continued its dominance over in-state rival Oklahoma A&M with a 42-7 victory the following week in Norman. The victory extended OU's winning streak to eight straight over the Aggies and 34-8-6 in the overall series.

The Sooners took the opening kickoff and moved 74 yards in a dozen plays for a 7-0 lead. Ging scored on a two-yard run and converted the extra point. The Aggies tied the game minutes later on a 53-yard punt return.

Brown recovered an A&M fumble early in the second stanza to set up the next Sooner score. Six plays later, Calame scooted through left tackle from the two-yard line and Ging toed the conversion. Calame also sparked the drive with an 11-yard run on fourth-and-one at the 16.

Guard Melvin Brown blocked an Aggie punt moments later, and he also smothered the ball at the A&M 25. Facing fourth-and-eight at the 11, Leake ran to his right, reversed his field to escape the enemy, and fired a scoring strike to backup end Joe Mobra all alone in the end zone. Leake converted for a 21-7 lead.

Calame scored his second touchdown on a five-yard run early in the third quarter to cap a 54-yard drive, and Leake converted.

Early in the fourth stanza, Boydston grabbed an Aggie fumble in midair and raced 43 yards for the score, and Ging converted. The

Halfback Larry Grigg sails around left end for the Sooners' winning touchdown against Missouri. (*OU Athletics*)

reserves drove 77 yards to add the final Sooner tally late in the game. Van Pool scored from the three, and Green converted.

OU rushed for 312 yards and passed for only 24. The Aggies picked up 174 total yards.

The Sooners next encountered Maryland on New Year's Day in the 20th Orange Bowl Classic—the first matchup between Bud Wilkinson and his former boss, Jim Tatum. The 10-0 Terrapins had already been declared national champions. The Atlantic Coast Conference champs had outscored their opponents by an average of 29.8 to 3.1 per game and pitched six shutouts.

Maryland had the nation's top defense, but the Sooner defense outshined their counterparts in a 7-0 victory before 68,640 fans, including 10,000 crimson supporters. The Terps had been shut out for the first time in 51 games.

Maryland's All-America quarterback, Bernie Faloney, suffered a knee injury during practices and did not play. O'Neal separated his sternum and sat out of the contest.

Early breaks had the Terrapins in scoring position thrice in the first quarter.

Maryland pinned OU deep at the one-yard line, but the Sooners punted back to their 36. Maryland rolled down to the four for a fresh set of downs. Each of the four Terrapin backs tried to punch the ball across on the next four carries and came away empty. The Big Red defense stopped Ralph Felton inches short of the goal line on fourth down and took over.

Leake immediately punted out of trouble to his 32, and the Terps whirled goalward again. The Sooner defense stalled them at the 15, and Dick Bielski's 43-yard field goal try was short and wide.

Leake spilled the pigskin moments later, and Maryland recovered at the 19. The Terps got a first down at the nine but were held to three yards on the next three plays. Felton's field goal attempt was wide right early in the second period.

OU took over at its 20 early in the second quarter and spun 80 yards in 11 plays for the only score of the game. From the UM 25, Grigg took Calame's pitch out and sailed 28 yards around left end for the score. He crashed over as Dick Nolan tried to tackle him at the goal line. Calame and Bob Burris threw key blocks to open a lane to the end zone. Calame injured his collarbone and was done for the day. Grigg also sparked the drive with a 19-yard run to the UM 48.

With Calame in street clothes, the Sooners had to rely on third-string quarterback Van Pool in the second half. Van Pool, who did not letter in 1952 and who did not make all road trips in '53, did a fine job after being thrown to the lions.

OU got a break in the third stanza at the UM 32 when Burris nailed punter Bill Walker trying to kick. Ging fumbled on the Terps' 16 two plays later.

Maryland moved 44 yards to the OU 42 in the fourth quarter and then got greedy. Backup quarterback Charley Boxold sailed a pass to the end zone, and Grigg intercepted for a Sooner touchback. Oklahoma gained short yards to the Maryland 39, then milked the final seconds off the clock.

Wilkinson and assistant Gomer Jones were carried off the field on the shoulders of players.

"Gang, I just want to say that's the greatest fight we've ever made," Wilkinson told his players in the locker room.

Reporters asked Wilkinson what won the game for the Sooners. "Effort," the head coach replied.

Roberts and Nelson worked together to contain Stan Jones, Maryland's All-America tackle. "We just hit harder and longer," Roberts said of their success.

Roberts also complimented Van Pool's play at quarterback. "[He] didn't make an error. He played super."

Van Pool, a quarterback from Oklahoma City's Capitol Hill High School, said he was accustomed to large crowds, and the Orange Bowl throng did not make him nervous. He kept his mind on the game.

"All I wanted to do was my part, keep the drive going, because the other guys had done their part all season long," he said.

The Sooners gained 10 first downs and rushed for 268 yards against the nation's number-one defense that had yielded an average of 84 yards per game. Grigg's 89 yards led the way for the Sooners. Oklahoma passed for 22 yards, all on the arm of Calame, who completed a perfect four strikes. The Terrapins collected 13 first downs, rushed for 167 and passed for 36 more.

The 1953 Sooners finished with a 9-1-1 record (6-0 in Big Seven), fourth in the AP poll and fifth in the UPI. Roberts was the lone Sooner selected as All-America. He also won the Outland Trophy as the best interior lineman, in addition to being named Lineman of the Year by the AP, UPI, and Fox Movietime News. Five

1953 Season Record: 9-1-1
Big Seven Conference: 6-0-0 (Champions)

Date	Opponent	Result	Score
September 26	NOTRE DAME	L	28-21
October 3	at Pittsburgh	T	7-7
October 10	Texas at Dallas	W	19-14
October 17	KANSAS	W	45-0
October 24	COLORADO	W	27-20
October 31	KANSAS STATE	W	34-0
November 7	at Missouri	W	14-7
November 14	IOWA STATE	W	47-0
November 21	at Nebraska	W	30-7
November 28	OKLAHOMA A&M	W	42-7
January 1	Maryland*	W	7-0

*Orange Bowl at Miami, FL

of his teammates joined him on the All-Big Seven first team—Boydston, Kurt Burris, Calame, Grigg and Nelson.

1954

Protecting a nine-game winning streak and dominance in the Big Seven Conference was not going to be easy for head coach Bud Wilkinson in 1954. The front line had to be rebuilt with the loss of Outland Trophy winner J.D. Roberts, Dick Bowman, Melvin Brown, Doc Hearon and Roger Nelson.

Still Wilkinson had some talent and experience to work with—all-conference center Kurt Burris, tackle Don Brown, and guard Bo Bollinger. Ends Carl Allison and Max Boydston would once again be solid at the end slots.

Gene Calame returned at quarterback, but the injury-prone senior was limited in the early going. The guys behind the quarterback were solid once again with the return of Buddy Leake, Bob Burris, Bob Herndon and Wray Littlejohn. Sophomores Tommy McDonald at halfback, Jimmy Harris at quarterback, and fullback Billy Pricer would soon be on the lips of Sooners fans.

The No. 2 Sooners opened the season against California at Berkeley on September 18 in the first encounter against a Pacific Coast Conference team.

Each time an Oklahoma player was introduced over the public address system, the Bears' fans would shout, "Who's he?" They also shouted, "Dirty Sooners!" occasionally during the game.

Oklahoma sent the 58,000 fans home quietly with a 27-13 victory.

The Bears stacked the defense with an eight-man front, and the Sooners began to penetrate after a scoreless first quarter. Calame, who played with a strained rib muscle, scored on a six-yard run to cap a 33-yard drive in four plays midway through the second stanza. Leake converted the first of three conversions.

Cal scored moments after recovering Herndon's fumble at his 39 to cut the OU lead to 7-6 before halftime.

The Sooners uncorked a 93-yard march in four plays late in the third period for a 14-6 advantage. From the OU 13, Calame pitched to Leake who pulled up and fired a pass to Boydston. The Sooner end dashed to the end zone.

Bolinger forced a fumble on the kickoff, and backup center Gene Mears recovered at the Bears' 25. Eight plays later, Leake sliced through left tackle for a one-yard touchdown on the first play of the fourth quarter.

Cal responded with an 85-yard scoring drive in 16 plays to cut the Sooner lead to 21-13 midway through the final stanza. The Sooners put the game away minutes later with a 55-yard, seven-play march. Herndon scored from the three-yard line, but Cal blocked Leake's extra point.

The Sooners rushed for 184 yards and passed for 97. The Bears collected 243 total yards.

Sooner Magic: A Star Is Born

A new star shined brightly in the second half against the Texas Christian Horned Frogs on September 25 in Norman. So radiant was this new star quarterback that no OU quarterback has matched his brilliance since.

A 5-11, 164-pound sophomore quarterback named Jimmy Harris replaced starter Gene Calame, who suffered a bone chip in his right collarbone. Calame left the game with 16 seconds left in the first half against TCU, and he would miss the next three games. Harris, a product of Terrell, Texas, had two upper front teeth knocked out during a scrimmage earlier in the week. He would have the teeth replaced before the Kansas game.

The 1-0 Sooners leaped to the nation's top ranking after the California victory and previous No. 1, Notre Dame, lost to Purdue. The Sooners were seeking their 11th straight victory. Coach Wilkinson was concerned about the big 6-2-3 alignment employed by the Frogs, 1-0 with a victory over Kansas. He also was concerned whether his inexperienced second-string quarterback could carry his team to victory after Calame's injury.

The Frogs kept the crowd of 50,878 squirming in their seats, and the Big Red looked anything but the top-ranked team losing five of 10 fumbles.

The Sooners thrice drove deep into TCU territory in the first quarter but came up empty.

The Frogs led 2-0 early in the second quarter when Leake was tackled for a safety as he reached down to grab the ball off the ground in the end zone. TCU's lead remained through intermission.

Early in the third quarter, Harris returned a punt 68 yards for a touchdown. Harris followed three blockers down field and Don Brown's key block cleared Harris' path to the end zone.

TCU wasted no time to regain the lead with an 81-yard drive early in the fourth period.

The Sooners quickly retaliated. Leake returned the kickoff to the OU 25. They hammered out a ground attack to the TCU three where they faced third and goal. Harris kept the ball on the next play and crossed the goal line untouched. Leake's conversion pulled the Sooners within two, 16-14, with 10:06 remaining.

Tackle Ed Gray hammered TCU's Charles Curtis on the kickoff return, popping the ball loose. OU recovered at the Frogs' 21. Oklahoma gained only a few yards on the next three plays, then Burris fumbled on the fourth-down attempt, and TCU recovered at the 15-yard line.

The Frogs were held on downs. Leake retrieved TCU's punt at the OU 45 and sprinted down the sideline. He shifted toward his left to avoid tacklers, but was tackled at the five. A penalty on the next play moved the ball back to the 10.

Herndon scored on the next play, shedding two defenders. Leake's kick gave the Sooners a 21-16 lead with 5:55 to go.

The Frogs were not waving the white flag just yet. They marched to the OU 38 with 49 seconds left in the game. Quarterback Ron Clinkscale fired a pass to Johnny Crouch to the Sooners' 13 with 25 seconds remaining. His next pass was incomplete to the end zone. Clinkscale kept on the next play, but Kurt Burris slammed him to the turf at the eight as time expired.

OU rushed for 247 yards and passed for 17. TCU rolled up 308 total yards.

Harris kept his cool as a replacement. He shared quarterbacking duties and learned the system the rest of the year. As he matured over the next two seasons, he guided the Sooners to two national championships (1955 and 1956). No OU quarterback since has an undefeated career record as a starting quarterback.

The Sooners held on to No. 1 when they rolled into Dallas the next week to meet No. 15 Texas (2-1) in the Cotton Bowl. All the scoring was done in the first half as OU edged the Longhorns, 14-7, before a record throng of 76,204.

Fumbles marred the first part of the opening stanza. Leake fumbled the opening kickoff on his 29, and the Longhorns gave it back moments later at the five, and guard Cecil Morris recovered. OU failed to gain a first

down, and Texas returned Leake's punt seven yards to the OU 27. The Steers led, 7-0, five plays later on Charley Brewer's three-yard jaunt and Buck Lansford's conversion. Brewer's TD run was the last touchdown scored on the ground against the Big Red the rest of the year.

The Sooners retaliated with a 72-yard, 14-play drive to tie the game. The drive began with Herndon recovering a wild lateral for a six-yard loss back to the 22. Two plays later, OU faced fourth-and-one at the 37. Herndon exploded up the middle for 13 to keep the drive alive. OU again faced fourth-and-one after reaching the UT two-yard line. Harris' blind pitch out wobbled to the ground, but Leake scooped it up and lunged forward to the one. Leake scored on the next play and toed the conversion with 37 seconds left in the first period.

The Sooners marched 58 yards in eight plays for the final tally midway through the second quarter. Coach Wilkinson put in the alternates, and quarterback Jay O'Neal fired a pass to end John Bell who sprinted to the UT 15 to complete a 40-yard play. The starters returned to move to the one and Harris' one-yard plunge capped the drive. Leake converted the 14th point.

Fumbles stalled drives for both teams in the third stanza. Texas moved to the OU 10 in the fourth quarter but surrendered on downs. OU also failed to gain a first down after reaching the Steers' 12. O'Neal fumbled the ball away after the Sooners drove to the UT 21 late in the game, and Texas failed to threaten again.

Oklahoma picked up 205 yards rushing and passed for 127. O'Neal completed both of his pass attempts for 71 yards, and Harris connected on four of six for 56 yards. Texas gained 162 total yards.

Brown suffered a broken ankle early in the game, and Robert Woodworth replaced him at left tackle the rest of the year.

The No. 1 Sooners showed no mercy in a 65-0 killing of the Kansas Jayhawks on October 16 in Lawrence. Kansas had lost all of its games prior to the OU matchup, but one could not tell the Jayhawks were winless by limiting the Sooners to a 7-0 lead through the game's first 24 minutes.

Herndon's 16-yard run and Leake's conversion gave the Big Red a 7-0 lead on its second possession. OU then exploded for three

Bob Herndon scores on a three-yard run to put Oklahoma ahead, 27-13, against California. *(OU Athletics)*

touchdowns over a four-minute span in the second period to take a 26-0 halftime lead. Harris scored twice in the three-TD foray, including a 91-yard jaunt. The next score came when Gray blocked a KU punt in the end zone, and Kurt Burris smothered the ball for six more points.

Herndon added another touchdown in the third stanza, and the reserves scored five more TDs.

Oklahoma pounded out a record 535 yards rushing and 37 through the air. Thirteen Sooners carried the ball, and Harris led the way with 117 yards on six carries. The 535-yard rushing effort surpassed the 527-yard output against the Jayhawks a year earlier. The Big Red defense held the Hawks to 70 total yards.

The top-ranked Sooners returned home the following week and hammered 4-1 Kansas State, 21-0.

Harris fumbled moments after OU received the opening kickoff, and the Wildcats recovered on the Sooners' 43. The Cats picked up nine yards on the next three plays and gambled on fourth-and-one at the 34. Morris nailed halfback Corky Taylor for a four-yard loss and OU took over.

The Sooners drove the 62 yards in 14 plays. Leake's three-yard run around right end capped the drive and he kicked the first of three conversions.

Oklahoma marched 54 yards in eight plays to take a 14-0 lead late in the second stanza. A holding penalty against the Cats aided the Sooners' efforts to the one-yard line, and Leake sliced through left tackle for the touchdown.

Kansas State was forced to punt on their next series, and tackle Bob Timberlake partially blocked the kick. Four plays later, Jerry Tubbs burst up the middle for the score.

Two Oklahoma threats in the second half ended with a fumble and a failed fourth-down gamble.

Oklahoma rushed for 315 yards and passed for only 16. Kansas State was held to 154 total yards.

Although the Sooners remained undefeated at 5-0, they fell from the number-one ranking in the AP poll. Ohio State, also 5-0, had defeated No. 2 Wisconsin and vaulted from fourth to first. Oklahoma dropped to second despite having more first-place votes in the poll.

Two fourth-quarter touchdowns propelled the Sooners to a 13-7 decision over Colorado on October 20 in Boulder. The 5-1 Buffaloes won their first five games before losing to Nebraska a week before the Oklahoma tilt. Harris was weak from influenza, and O'Neal started at quarterback.

OU blew two scoring opportunities in the first half. Bob Herndon committed one faux pas when he streaked toward the end zone for an apparent 20-yard score in the first period, but he fumbled right before he stepped across the goal line, and Colorado recovered.

Early in the second period, the Sooners faced fourth-and-four on their 44. Instead of calling a punt, O'Neal instead decided to go for it. Wilkinson immediately sent in Calame into the huddle to get O'Neal to change the play to a punt. O'Neal kept the ball and was cut short two yards of a first down.

Quarterback Jimmy Harris never lost a game when he started at quarterback in the mid-1950s. *(OU Athletics)*

Wilkinson confronted his quarterback when O'Neal returned to the sideline. "Don't you know we kick on fourth down?"

Talking to his quarterback again at halftime, Wilkinson asked O'Neal if he thought the situation was third down instead of fourth.

"No, sir," O'Neal replied. "It was fourth down. I knew exactly what down it was. I made a mistake. I'm sorry. I thought we could make the yardage."

Harold Keith in his book, *47 Straight*, wrote that Coach Wilkinson was impressed that O'Neal did not offer an alibi, and believed his quarterback deserved another chance. O'Neal got the second chance, and he guided the Sooners to two second-half TDs.

The Buffaloes excited the 31,247 fans with a 6-0 lead midway through the second stanza. Carroll Hardy zipped a 19-yard scoring strike to Carroll Bernardi, but Mears blocked the conversion.

The Sooners spun 87 yards in 14 plays late in the third quarter and into the fourth. O'Neal engineered most of the drive, but the first team reentered the game when the Sooners reached the Buffs' 26 and took the ball in. Leake capped the drive with a 10-yard sweep around right end and cut back inside just before he scored. He also converted the extra point for a 7-6 lead.

Oklahoma added another score minutes later when O'Neal sneaked over from the one to cap a 49-yard drive. Pricer's conversion failed, but the Sooners held the deciding advantage with 4:06 remaining. O'Neal pitched to McDonald, who faked a reverse and rocketed a 39-yard bomb to Burris to the Buffs' one on the play before O'Neal scored.

Colorado did not mount a charge in the final four minutes.

OU rushed for 245 yards and passed for 65. Colorado racked up 212 total yards.

The one-touchdown victory dropped Oklahoma to third in the AP poll. Undefeated UCLA defeated California and leaped to first, and Ohio State fell to second. The Sooners rode the No. 3 spot the rest of the season.

OU blasted 3-4 Iowa State, 40-0, on November 6 in Ames. The Sooners had a pattern of scoring in their 17th straight win over the Cyclones—one touchdown in the first and third quarters and two TDs in the second and fourth periods. Leake and Herndon each scored twice.

The Sooners led off each half with a touchdown. They rolled 62 yards after the opening kickoff, and Leake carried the final two yards for the score. Calame scored on a 48-yard interception return on the first play in the third stanza.

The most telling statistics were that Oklahoma had success passing (eight of 12 for 151 yards), lost only one fumble, and averaged 50 yards in four punts. Boydston kicked three times for a 50.7 average, and Pricer kicked once for 47 yards. Ten Sooners carried the ball for a total 265 yards. The Cyclones gained 181 total yards and averaged 43.3 yards per punt.

500th Game

The Sooners played their 500th game in school history and celebrated by crushing 3-3-1 Missouri, 34-13, the next week to run their winning streak to 17 and nine straight over the Tigers.

Oklahoma had two drives stall at the MU 10-yard line in the first period, causing the 54,173 in attendance to scratch their heads. Two scoring strikes by O'Neal in a 25-second span late in the second stanza put the Sooners on top, 14-0, at the half.

A poor Tiger punt to their 29 set up the first O'Neal scoring fling in four plays. Bob Herndon took O'Neal's swing pass and scooted into the end zone with 1:08 until intermission.

Mizzou fumbled the kickoff, and Bolinger recovered at the MU 22. Billy Pricer, in the game for the first time, was open down the middle on the first play and caught O'Neal's aerial at the 10 and zipped to the end zone.

Leake added a touchdown in the third quarter, and Calame scored early in the fourth period for a 27-0 lead. Leake's touchdown raised his career scoring total to 228 points, breaking George Thomas' school record of 226 set in 1948. Leake extended his career mark to 248 (28 touchdowns and 75 extra points) by the end of the season.

Two Tiger scores were sandwiched by the final OU tally by Herndon.

The Sooners hammered out 355 rushing yards and passed for 67 more. Twelve Sooners carried the ball, and nine players outgained the entire Tiger rushing output of seven net yards. The Big Red defense also held the Tigers to 127 passing yards.

The Sooners clinched the Big Seven crown with a 55-7 victory over Orange Bowl-bound Nebraska before a homecoming crowd of 55,172 on November 20 in Norman. The 48-point win equaled the 1949 Sooner squad's 48-0 win for the largest margin in the 34-year series, and 55 points was the most scored to date in the series.

Eight Sooners crossed the goal line in the game, five scores came on the ground and three through the air. OU scored first and the 5-3 Huskers tied the game in the first period moments after recovering Harris' fumble at the Sooner 20. The Big Red of the south exploded for two touchdowns in each of the next two stanzas and three in the fourth period.

Oklahoma picked up 29 first downs and rushed for 342 yards. Calame led 13 ball carriers with 60 yards. The Sooners passed for the most yards in the Wilkinson era—eight of 12 for 235 yards. Calame also led that department by completing six of eight for 126 yards. The Huskers were held to nine first downs and 162 total yards.

Oklahoma traveled to Stillwater on November 27 and came away with a 14-0 victory over Oklahoma A&M before a record 38,000 spectators. The 5-3-1 Aggies had an open date the week before and had 14 days to prepare for the matchup.

The game also marked the 50th anniversary of the first intrastate game played in 1904 that included the pursuit of the ball in a creek and swimming for a touchdown in an Oklahoma rout. Several of the players who participated in that game were guests at the 1954 contest.

The Sooners could not find the end zone early in the game. After driving inside the A&M 20, the Pokes picked off Leake's pass at the 12. OU got the ball back moments later on a short punt at the Aggies' 27. The second unit carried the ball to the one where McDonald fumbled.

Leake's 11-yard punt return to the OU 41 set up the first score early in the second period. Calame scored from the one 10 plays later, and Leake converted the first of two conversions. Leake's 17-yard run to the Pokes' 40 sparked the drive.

The Aggies punted to the OU 27 on their next series, and the Sooners consumed nine minutes in a 73-yard, 17-play scoring march. The drive was actually longer, as OU was penalized 15 yards and lost 10 yards on one play. Calame scored his second TD on another one-yard plunge with 11 seconds left until halftime.

The Sooners moved 50 yards to the A&M 14 after the second-half kickoff, but Leake's fumble stalled the drive. The Pokes put together their longest march of the game in the fourth stanza. They drove 67 yards to the OU 15 and crossed midfield for the first time all afternoon. Facing fourth-and-one at the 15, Allison nailed quarterback Tom Pontius for a four-yard loss.

The Sooners escaped with their fourth shutout of the season and preserved their 19th consecutive victory. Oklahoma did not compete in a bowl game, as the Big Seven Conference prohibited teams from participating in bowl games two consecutive years.

OU also extended its conference winning streak to 17 and 20 straight without defeat. Wilkinson's conference record rose to 45-0-2 since taking the helm in 1947.

Boydston and Burris were named All-Americans. The Touchdown Club of Washington, D.C. named Boydston outstanding Lineman of the Year. Burris was named Lineman of the Year by the Philadelphia Sports Writers and Player of the Year by Helms and Citizens Savings Athletic Foundation. Allison, Bolinger, Leake and Calame joined them on the All-Big Seven Conference team.

1955

After months of investigations, the National Collegiate Athletic Association on April 26 reported the University of Oklahoma was in violation of some of the association's policies. The investigations found that OU had paid medical expenses for families of students athletes; provided student athletes with fringe benefits such as clothing, gifts, cash and paid for rental cars for two athletes; and offered students cost-free education beyond the normal period of eligibility. The NCAA took no serious disciplinary action against the university.

"We were trying to help boys who needed it and might have had to either drop out or get aid from outside," Bud Wilkinson said of the medical expenses. "And the fact that only six boys were found to be getting outside aid without our knowledge indicated that we were doing a pretty good job of controlling the subsidization.

"However, we violated the rules, and I have no criticism of the NCAA."

With the loss of 14 lettermen, Wilkinson believed his 1955 squad would not be a national and conference contender.

"I don't think we're going to be nearly as good a football team as people think," he said.

1954 Season Record: 10-0-0
Big Seven Conference: 6-0-0 (Champions)

Date	Opponent	Result	Score
September 18	at California	W	27-13
September 25	TEXAS CHRISTIAN	W	21-16
October 9	Texas at Dallas	W	14-7
October 16	at Kansas	W	65-0
October 23	KANSAS STATE	W	21-0
October 30	at Colorado	W	13-6
November 6	at Iowa State	W	40-0
November 13	MISSOURI	W	34-13
November 20	NEBRASKA	W	55-7
November 27	at Oklahoma A&M	W	14-0

Although there were fresh faces in the backfield, it had more speed than in recent years, and the backs did have some experience.

Jimmy Harris was the heir apparent at quarterback, and Bob Burris returned at right halfback. Tommy McDonald and Billy Pricer took over at left half and fullback respectively. Jerry Tubbs was moved from fullback to center to bolster a solid line, which included the return of guards Bo Bolinger and Cecil Morris and tackle Ed Gray. Wilkinson believed he had a much improved line, except for the end positions.

Max Boydston and Carol Allison had graduated, leaving huge holes to fill at ends. John Bell, Don Stiller and Joe Mobra, all reserves in 1954, would step up to turn in fine performances.

The Sooners rolled to their second national championship with a perfect 11-0 record, their 10th straight conference title and extended their win string to 30. Oklahoma blanked half of their regular-season foes and ended the regular season with four straight shutouts. Wilkinson's troops led the nation in total and rushing offense.

The third-ranked Sooners traveled to Chapel Hill, North Carolina to meet the Tar Heels in the season opener for both teams. Wilkinson alternated his linemen to keep them fresh in the hot (80s) and humid weather. Oklahoma won, 13-6, by scoring twice in the second half after blowing four scoring opportunities with stalled drives and turnovers in the first 30 minutes.

OU took the opening kickoff and advanced to the NC 30 but missed on four downs. North Carolina took a 6-0 lead first midway through the opening stanza. Harris returned a punt 26 yards to midfield, but a clipping penalty moved the ball back to the two. Harris fumbled into the end zone on the next play, and Carolina pounced on the pigskin for a touchdown. The conversion was wide, but the crowd of 26,638 was smelling an upset.

The Sooners advanced to the NC three moments later, but Burris fumbled into the end zone, and the Tar Heels recovered for a touchback. OU moved within striking distance late in the second period, only to come up a yard short of a first down at the Heels' 13.

The Big Red threatened again on its next series, but McDonald was stopped cold at the NC one. Another advance to the 18 ended in a fumble.

The Sooners finally got uncorked with a 74-yard scoring march after the second-half kickoff. Burris sailed six yards around left end for the score, and Harris converted. Burris also sparked the drive with a 25-yard run to the NC 34.

The Sooners' next score came late in the game, and after the Tar Heels punted to their own 39 McDonald ignited the drive with a 28-yard run to the 11 on the first play. Burris carried to the two in two plays, and Harris gained nothing on a sneak. On fourth down, McDonald swept around right end for the touchdown. Harris' conversion veered to the left.

OU picked up 403 rushing yards and passed for 81. Harris led Sooner runners with 117 yards, and Burris added 104 more. The defense held North Carolina to five first downs and 124 total yards. The Tar Heels only once penetrated into Sooner territory—to the 39 in the first half.

The Sooners dropped to fifth in the AP poll and hosted No. 12 Pittsburgh (2-0) the next week. OU rolled to a 19-0 halftime lead but held on to win, 26-14.

Oklahoma took the opening kickoff and marched 77 yards in 10 plays for a 7-0 lead. From the Pitt 43, Harris faked a handoff and pitched to McDonald, who sprinted to the end zone. Harris added the extra point.

The Sooners intercepted a Panther pass at the OU 48 late in the first quarter to set up another score. Burris' one-yard plunge capped the drive, but Harris' conversion was blocked. McDonald's 23-yard run to the Pitt 20 sparked the drive.

The Sooners marched 64 yards in five plays to take a 19-0 lead on their next series. Halfback Clendon Thomas ripped through right tackle on a reverse and dashed 32 yards for the touchdown. Carl Dodd missed the conversion.

The Panthers drove 71 yards to get on the board early in the third stanza. Pitt added another touchdown early in the fourth period after recovering McDonald's fumble on the OU 44.

The Sooners later drove 67 yards to put the icing on the cake. McDonald returned the Panthers' punt 24 yards to the OU 33. From the Pitt 29, Harris picked up a couple of yards then pitched back to McDonald who carried to the eight. McDonald scooted through right tackle to score on the next play, and Harris converted.

Oklahoma rolled up 357 rushing yards and passed for 55. McDonald led the way for the Sooners with 124 yards. The Panthers collected 204 total yards.

The third-ranked Sooners headed to Dallas on October 8 for the golden anniversary of the Red River rivalry. The 1-2 Longhorns lost to Texas Tech and Southern California and beat Tulane. The Texas Tech loss was the first time the Longhorns had lost a season opener at home. Texas had a shining new quarterback in Joe Clements, who had shared duties with Charles Brewer. Clements had completed 22 of 33 for 299 yards and four touchdowns in the first three games. Yet he had to play against a defense such as Oklahoma's as the Sooners stole three of his passes and five overall.

OU pitched its sixth shutout of the series and first since 1938 with a 20-0 victory and the team's first four-game winning streak over their southern rivals before a throng of 75,504 and a regional television audience.

Tubbs speared his first of three interceptions off Clements at the UT 33 in the first quarter to set up a touchdown moments later. The Sooners advanced 10 yards through the middle in three plays. A penalty moved the ball back to the 28, and Harris faked a halfback trap then shoveled the ball to McDonald, who weaved through orange jerseys to the end zone. A bad snap led to Harris' conversion to be blocked.

The crimson alternates moved 62 yards to the Horns' seven late in the first stanza after Thomas picked off Clements' pass. Texas held but gave the ball back moments later when McDonald intercepted Brewer's pass and returned it 28 yards to the UT seven. On the next play, McDonald sliced through right tackle on a reverse and scored. Harris converted for a 13-0 advantage.

Texas moved to its deepest penetration to the OU 29 in the third period, but the Big Red defense stiffened. OU rolled 71 yards in nine plays. McDonald fumbled on the first play, and Texas recovered, but the Steers were offsides and OU got the ball back at the 34. Harris ignited the drive with a 17-yard run on the next play. Facing fourth-and-one at the Steers' 28, Harris gained five yards and flipped the ball back to Pricer, who ran to the seven. Burris capped the drive with a one-yard plunge two plays later, and Harris converted.

OU kept Texas pinned deep with Pricer's quick kicks on third down in the fourth quarter. Pricer averaged 44 yards on six kicks in the game. OU rushed for 214 yards and passed for 55. Texas gained 258 total yards.

Holding on to the No. 3 ranking, the Sooners returned home on October 15 and pounded 1-2-1 Kansas, 44-6, before a homecoming crowd of 39,789. Oklahoma lost three of five fumbles in the first half but still mounted an 18-6 halftime lead.

The Jayhawks took a 6-0 lead after driving 71 yards following the opening kickoff and never penetrated past midfield the rest of the afternoon. McDonald scored on a nine-yard run minutes later to cap a 67-yard jaunt in eight plays. Dodd missed the conversion, and the game was tied at 6-6.

The second unit scored late in the first stanza for a 12-6 lead on Dodd's one-yard plunge, but he again missed the extra point. Harris scored early in the second period on a one-yard plunge five plays after Pricer recovered a Kansas fumble at the KU 40.

The Sooners needed one play to take a 25-0 lead early in the third quarter after a poor Kansas punt to the KU 46. McDonald took Harris' lateral, swept around right end and raced to the end zone. Harris converted.

From that point, the first two units were done for the day. Wilkinson emptied the bench, allowing the third, fourth and fifth stringers in on the action. They responded by adding three more touchdowns. Fullback Dennit Morris later stole a Jayhawk pass on the KU 21 and scored. Morris' second interception minutes later set up OU's next score, a three-yard run by Thomas. Quarterback Bill Sturm hurled a 36-yard scoring strike to Bob Derrick for the final tally early in the fourth quarter.

Oklahoma pounded out 288 yards rushing and passed for 114 yards. Kansas gained 191 total yards.

No. 14 Colorado (4-0) was next, and the Buff defense had allowed only 19 points in its first four games, including two shutouts. Coach Wilkinson unveiled the no-huddle offense, or "no recovery," as he referred to it. The Sooners would quickly line up after the previous play and snap the ball before the defense barely got set. This enabled No. 3 Oklahoma to run roughshod through the CU defense with eight touchdowns. Both teams entertained the 57,663 fans in Norman and regional TV audience with a combined 11 touchdowns.

After spotting the Buffs two of the first scores, OU scored eight of the next nine touchdowns for a 56-21 triumph and ran its scoring streak to 100 consecutive games. Burris led with three scores for the Big Red, and McDonald added two more.

After a scoreless first period, a flurry of five touchdowns highlighted the second. Colorado cashed in on two Sooner fumbles for a 14-0 lead. OU took the lead during the next 10 minutes with two of Burris' TDs and one by McDonald. The two also added a touchdown each in the third quarter for a 35-14 advantage.

Colorado scored early in the fourth period, and the Sooners reserves answered with three more touchdowns over the next six and one-half minutes.

Oklahoma gained 321 rushing yards and 95 passing. The Buffs picked up 185 total yards.

The Sooners climbed a notch to second in the AP poll and then hammered 2-4 Kansas State, 40-7, on October 29 in Manhattan.

Harris' seven-yard TD run capped a 78-yard drive on OU's second possession of the game. The Sooners shot to a 14-0 lead moments after Bob Timberlake recovered a Kansas State fumble at the Cats' 18. Three plays later, Thomas scored from the four. A poor Wildcat punt to their 25 set up the 21-0 lead. Jay O'Neal scored on a three-yard run six plays later.

Three plays following the kickoff and early in the second quarter, tackle Cal Woodworth clutched an errant Kansas State lateral in the air and sprinted 24 yards to the end zone. Thomas scored his second touchdown late in the second stanza to cap a 98-yard drive.

Woodworth recovered a K-State fumble at the KS 42 one play after the second-half kickoff. The Sooners lost nine yards in two plays, and Pricer quick kicked. The Cats were flagged for roughing on the kick, and OU was given the ball at the 36. McDonald scored

The Sooners celebrate in the locker room after defeating Maryland, 20-6, in the Orange Bowl. *(OU Athletics)*

on a 10-yard run three plays later. The Wildcats scored their lone touchdown two plays after recovering a Sooner fumble at the OU 18 midway through the final quarter.

OU rushed for 289 yards and passed for 83. The Wildcats gained 199 total yards.

The No. 2 Sooners traveled to Columbia on November 5 as heavy favorites against 1-6 Missouri. The Tigers lost six straight games before upsetting Colorado the week before and were seeking another upset. The Sooners would have none of it and shut down Missouri, 20-0.

McDonald's speed in the open field and running passes got two touchdowns for Oklahoma. The Sooners jumped to a 14-0 lead in a span of 40 seconds late in the first period.

OU whirled 62 yards in 10 plays for the first score. Actually the drive consumed 52 yards after Mizzou was flagged for roughing on the first play. Burris carried for 14 yards on the next play and later scored from the one. Pricer converted the first of two extra points, missing the final kick.

The Tigers' Gene Roll fumbled the kickoff, and Bolinger pounced on it on the MU 24. After Pricer picked up two yards, Harris connected a 22-yard scoring strike to McDonald.

The Sooners fumbled away two scoring opportunities in the second quarter—one at the Tigers' 12 and the other on the 15.

The second half was marred by penalties. Seven penalties were assessed in the third stanza alone. The penalties continued in the fourth period, and Thomas was ejected from the game for fighting. Officials stepped off a total of 190 yards (Oklahoma 185 and Missouri 75 yards) in the game.

The Tigers roughed Pricer on a punt early in the fourth quarter to give OU new life at the Mizzou 40. Burris and McDonald alternated carries to the 22. On the next play, Harris wiggled to the 12, then popped a split-second lateral to McDonald, who zoomed in for the score.

The Tigers recovered Bill Brown's fumble at the MU 45 and tried desperately to remove the goose egg off their end of the scoreboard. Two complete passes moved the Tigers to the OU 28 for their deepest penetration of the day and the second time past the OU 40. The Big Red defense tightened, swatting away the next four passes.

OU rushed for 310 yards and passed for 66. The Tigers collected 189 total yards.

Oklahoma replaced undefeated Maryland at the top of the AP poll and stayed there the rest of the year. The Sooners celebrated with a 52-0 pounding of Iowa State the following Saturday in Norman.

The first three crimson touchdowns came from a relatively long distance. Burris ripped through for 33 yards on the first score. McDonald scored the first of his two TDs on a 91-yard punt return for a 13-0 lead in the first period. Dodd slung a 21-yard scoring strike to third-string end Delbert Long early in the second stanza.

The Sooners led, 26-0, after Thomas' two-yard touchdown run capped a 51-yard drive late in the first half. OU doubled their halftime score in the final 20 minutes. McDonald scored on a 14-yard end sweep, Dodd added two more scores, and Bob Derrick's two-yard plunge was the final tally.

The Cyclones only moved past midfield three times, twice in the first period and once in the final stanza.

Oklahoma rushed for 392 yards and added 66 more through the air. The defense held the Cyclones to 137 total yards.

Nebraska at 7-1 could claim the Big Seven championship with a win over the Sooners on November 19. The Cornhuskers won all of their conference games while losing all of their non-conference matchups. A day before the OU-Nebraska tilt, Husker head coach Bill Glassford resigned, and the Sooners gave him a 41-0 going-away present in Lincoln.

The Sooners scored late in the first two quarters for a 13-0 halftime lead. O'Neal replaced Harris at quarterback in the first stanza after the latter suffered a sprained shoulder. O'Neal engineered a 68-yard march in 10 plays and carried the final yards for a touchdown, and Dodd converted for a 7-0 lead.

Tubbs' interception at the NU 41 set up Burris' one-yard plunge seven plays later for a 13-0 lead.

Burris added another one-yard blast to cap a 59-yard march following the second-half kickoff, and Pricer converted. Oklahoma rolled 54 yards in four plays for a 27-0 lead after McDonald bucked across from the one, and Pricer converted. Thomas and Derrick each added a touchdown in the final period.

The Sooners rushed for 374 yards and passed for 28. The Huskers gained 187 total yards. OU was penalized 10 times for 110 yards.

OU accepted a bid several days later to play Maryland in the 22nd Orange Bowl Classic on New Year's Day. But for the Sooners to claim the school's second national championship they would need a victory over 2-7 Oklahoma A&M. No problem. Harris was back under center as OU blasted the Aggies, 53-0, on November 26 in Norman.

After a scoreless first quarter, the Sooners exploded for three touchdowns in less than seven and a half minutes in the second. Oklahoma threatened three times and stalled in the opening stanza. The Aggies twice stopped the Sooners inside the 20, and penalties killed another crimson scoring quest.

Dennit Morris recovered a Poke fumble late in the first period. Six plays later, Harris sliced through right tackle from the three, and Pricer converted for a 7-0 lead in the first minutes of the second quarter. Minutes later, Thomas fielded Tom Pontuis' punt and

sailed 65 yards down the east sideline to the end zone, and Dodd converted.

Pricer recovered a Poke fumble moments later at the A&M 32. The Sooners chewed small chunks of yardage to the 14. Harris was tossed for a six-yard loss on the next play, then fired a 20-yard scoring strike to Mobra, and Pricer converted.

The Aggies threatened before halftime after a short punt gave them possession on the OU 35. They advanced to the five and faced fourth-and-two. Woodworth dropped Pontuis for a five-yard loss, and Oklahoma took over.

The Sooners rolled 62 yards in 11 plays after the second-half kickoff. McDonald capped the drive with a one-yard plunge and a new entry into the OU record book. He became the first Sooner to score in all 10 games with at least one rushing touchdown.

Harris scored on a six-yard run late in the third period, and the reserves put up 19 more points in the fourth.

Oklahoma gained 344 rushing yards and tossed for 177 more. Thirteen Sooners toted the pigskin, and McDonald led with 84 yards. The Pokes were held to six first downs and 152 total yards.

Oklahoma won its second national championship in both wire service polls. The Sooners received 3,581 points in the AP poll, 377 points more than second-place Michigan State. OU also garnered 218 of 391 first-place votes.

Two years ago, the Sooners ruined Maryland's perfect season with a 7-0 Orange Bowl victory after the Terrapins had been crowned national champions. The Terps could return the favor and ruin the perfect season of the national-champion Sooners.

Jim Tatum's Terrapins also were undefeated at 10-0 and ranked third behind OU and Michigan State. Maryland outscored its opponents by an average of 21.1 to 5.7. No team scored greater than 13 points against the Terps, who also had four shutouts. Both teams were riding winning streaks into the game. Maryland had won 15 consecutive games dating back to the prior year, and Oklahoma won 29 straight dating back to 1953.

Oklahoma held on to its perfect season and winning streak with a 20-6 decision before a sun-soaked crowd of 76,561, which included 12,000 Sooner faithful, in Miami. The Orange Bowl that year was the only bowl game that featured two undefeated teams.

Maryland halfback Ed Vereb got his team into scoring position with a 66-yard run to the OU 10 early in the first period. Jay O'Neal saved a touchdown by knocking Vereb out of bounds. OU

1955 Season Record: 11-0-0
Big Seven Conference: 6-0-0 (Champions)
NATIONAL CHAMPIONS

Date	Opponent	Result	Score
September 24	at North Carolina	W	13-6
October 1	PITTSBURGH	W	26-14
October 8	Texas at Dallas	W	20-0
October 15	KANSAS	W	44-6
October 22	COLORADO	W	56-21
October 29	at Kansas State	W	40-7
November 5	at Misouri	W	20-0
November 12	IOWA STATE	W	52-0
November 19	at Nebraska	W	41-0
November 26	OKLAHOMA A&M	W	53-0
January 1	Maryland*	W	20-6

*Orange Bowl at Miami, FL

reserve tackle Wayne Greenlee forced Frank Tamburello to fumble, and Stiller recovered for the Sooners.

The Big Red advanced from there to the Terps' 31, but Harris' wild pitch to McDonald lost 13 yards to stall the drive.

Maryland drove 39 yards in seven plays to take a 6-0 lead early in the second stanza. Vereb scored on a 15-yard run, the first TD yielded by OU's defense in 17 quarters. Tubbs, who injured a knee in the Oklahoma A&M game and did not practice for the Orange Bowl, blocked Bob Laughery's conversion to hold the Terps to a 6-0 lead.

McDonald's 32-yard punt return to the UM 46 set up the first OU score midway through the third quarter. The Sooners began using a hurry-up offense, setting their formation before the Terrapins could barely catch their breath. McDonald capped the seven-play drive with a four-yard score, and Pricer converted for a 7-6 advantage. McDonald sparked the drive with a 19-yard pass to Burris to the seven-yard line.

The Sooners' second unit rolled 51 yards through the middle of the Maryland defense for a 14-6 lead late in the third period. O'Neal dove through the middle on a one-yard sneak, and Pricer again converted.

The Terrapins advanced to the OU 30 in the fourth stanza. Maryland's back-up quarterback, Lynn Beightol, tossed a pass, and Dodd stole it at the OU 18 and zoomed 82 yards to the end zone with nary a Terrapin near him. Pricer missed the conversion, but the damage had already been done.

"That's the most satisfying victory we've ever had," Wilkinson told reporters in the locker room. "Everyone has been talking about how weak a schedule we play, and they're justified in doing so. We didn't know if we were good enough to play a team like Maryland or not. Now we know the victory was very gratifying."

Oklahoma collected 16 first downs, rushed for 205 yards and passed for 53 more. Maryland picked up nine first downs and 233 total yards.

Bolinger and McDonald were named All-Americans. Gray, Woodworth, Cecil Morris, Tubbs, and Burris joined them on the All-Big Seven first team.

1956

It was a year for incumbents. President Dwight Eisenhower was reelected to another term for the White House, the San Francisco Dons claimed their second straight college basketball championship, Peter Thomason won his third straight British Open golf title, and the Oklahoma Sooners were "reelected" to another national championship. OU was the fourth team to win consecutive championships in the AP poll.

The Sooners were overwhelming favorites to capture a third national crown in 1956. Yet, the Big Red did not ride the entire season at the No. 1 position. Although Oklahoma won all of its games, they dropped to second after a big win against Kansas in the season's fourth game, rebounded to the top slot for two more weeks, and dropped to second after defeating Missouri in the eighth week. The Sooners returned to the summit after defeating Nebraska in the ninth week.

It's a Fact

For the second straight year, the Sooners led the nation in rushing offense with an average of 391 yards per game, total offense with an average of 481.7 yards per game, and scoring offense with 46.6 points per game.

OU did not play in a postseason bowl game since Big Seven Conference rules prohibited teams from competing in bowl games two consecutive years.

Eddie Crowder, Bud Wilkinson's starting quarterback in 1951 and 1952, joined the staff as an assistant.

A total of 28 lettermen returned to the Sooner lineup, including six who started all or some during the prior year. The backfield returnees included quarterback Jimmy Harris, halfbacks Tommy McDonald and Clendon Thomas and fullback Billy Pricer. Center Jerry Tubbs and tackle Ed Gray returned to the front wall.

Wilkinson was concerned about the graduation of the left side of his line, especially on defense.

"The line play is a basic factor in defense, especially the left side of the line, because most football teams are right-handed," the skipper said. "That is, they'll run three of five and maybe seven of 10 plays that direction, so you must be awfully tough defensively on the left side."

Two of his linemen would suffer season-ending injuries in the season opener.

North Carolina, OU's first opponent in 1956, had hired Jim Tatum to coach at his alma mater. For the second straight game, Tatum roamed the enemy sideline and was sent home with a loss.

The Sooners defeated the Tar Heels, 36-0, on September 29 in Norman. All of the scoring was accomplished in the second and fourth quarters aided by a 40-mile-per-hour wind.

Pricer punted five times for a 46.8-yard average in the game, and two of his kicks (62 yards and 78 yards) helped set up two touchdowns as OU shot to a 21-0 lead in less than six minutes.

The 62-yarder pinned the Tar Heels deep, and they punted back into the stiff breeze to set up OU's first score at the Sooner 48. The alternates struck pay dirt in seven plays. From the NC 17, halfback David Baker picked up six yards, then pitched the ball to Jay O'Neal, who scooted the final 11 yards to the end zone. Carl Dodd converted.

Oklahoma wheeled 37 yards in four plays for a 14-0 lead after McDonald returned a punt for 11 yards. Thomas slashed through left guard from the 12, and Billy Pricer converted.

Moments later, Thomas intercepted a Carolina pass and returned it to midfield where he was bottled up by Tar Heels. He popped the ball to McDonald, who raced all the way to the NC 10. Harris swept around left end for seven yards then fired a scoring strike to McDonald on the next play. Pricer converted for the 21-0 lead.

McDonald scored on a two-yard run early in the fourth period to cap an 80-yard jaunt that began late in the third stanza. Pricer toed the extra point.

Coach Wilkinson emptied the bench, and the third string marched 60 yards for another score. Third-string quarterback Lonnie Holland capped the drive with a 14-yard run. A bad snap from center kept the extra point from materializing. Less than a minute later, tackle Steve Jennings dropped a Heel quarterback in the end zone for a safety.

OU rushed for 369 yards and passed for 61. Twenty Sooners carried the ball, and Baker led with 64 yards. The defense held North Carolina to five first downs and 140 total yards.

Tackle Wayne Greenlee and guard Ken Northcutt both suffered broken legs in the game, leaving Wilkinson to find replacements for the left side of the line. He moved Gray from right tackle to replace Greenlee, and Buddy Oujesky moved up to replace Northcutt.

Thomas led a 10-touchdown assault by scoring the first three TDs to lead the Sooners to a 66-0 annihilation of Kansas State before a homecoming throng of 39,981 the next week in Norman.

The 32nd consecutive victory broke the school record of 31 set by the Sooners from 1948 to 1950.

Seven other players also scored in the 10-TD assault, and all 67 players got in on the action before the final gun discharged. David Baker's 67-yard punt return was the longest scoring jaunt, which gave Oklahoma a 26-0 lead early in the second quarter.

Trailing 33-0 in the second stanza, the Cats made their greatest threat moving against the Sooners alternates to the OU 16. Wilkinson put the starters back in, and Tubbs picked off a Wildcat pass three plays later, returning it to the OU 17.

OU gained 479 yards rushing and passed for only 12 yards. Thomas led a pack of 19 ball carriers with 82 yards. Kansas State was held to five first downs and 191 total yards.

Wilkinson was not optimistic about his squad's chances against 1-2 Texas. He was disappointed by his team's practices that week and told them, "It's no disgrace to be beaten by a team as strong as Texas."

His charges responded with their third straight shutout by corralling the Longhorns, 45-0, on October 13 before a sellout crowd of 75,504 and a regional (NBC) television audience. Texas could not corral McDonald and Thomas, who combined for 263 yards rushing and six touchdowns, three apiece.

Oklahoma's fifth straight victory over Texas was the worst whippin' the Sooners had put on the Steers since 50-0 in 1908.

McDonald began the scoring blitz by returning the opening kickoff 54 yards to the UT 44. Seven plays later, Thomas scored from the two, but Texas blocked Pricer's conversion.

Late in the first period, Pricer was back to quick kick, but instead pulled a Statue of Liberty play with Thomas grabbing the ball and racing 44 yards to the Texas 20. McDonald burst across the goal line for a 12-0 lead five plays later and on the second play of the second quarter. Pricer's conversion sailed below the crossbar.

Just before halftime, Harris hurled a 53-yard scoring strike to McDonald, who caught the ball over his head on a dead run and sprinted the final 18 yards to the end zone. Harris converted for a 19-0 lead with 27 seconds to go until intermission.

The Sooners rolled 80 yards in 16 plays for the knockout punch after the second-half kickoff. From the UT eight, Thomas followed Tubbs' lead block clear to the end zone, and Harris converted.

Moments later, Dennit Morris intercepted Vince Matthews' pass at the OU 43 to set up the next score in two plays. McDonald picked up 13 yards to the 44. On the next play, he headed right and quickly slashed through right guard and raced down the sideline for the score. Pricer converted the 32nd point.

Thomas recovered a Longhorn fumble at the UT 42 to set up another score early in the fourth stanza. Harris, McDonald, and Thomas picked up small yards to the 28. On the next play, McDonald swept right and heaved a pass to John Bell to the one. Harris was stopped short of the goal on the next play then Thomas plowed ahead for the touchdown. Pricer converted for a 39-0 advantage.

The Horns later drove to the OU 24 for their deepest penetration of the day after recovering end Joe Rector's fumble at the Texas 44. Tackle Tom Emerson sacked quarterback Joe Clements for a 19-yard loss to end the Steers' hopes of erasing the goose egg.

Fourth string halfback Ernie Day intercepted Matthews' pass and sailed 28 yards for the final tally with 45 seconds remaining. Dale Sherrod missed the conversion.

Tommy McDonald (25) scores on a 53-yard pass play from Jimmy Harris to give the Sooners a 19-0 lead over Texas late in the first half. (*OU Athletics*)

Oklahoma pounded out 369 yards rushing and passed for 133 more. McDonald picked up 140 yards on 16 carries, and Thomas gained 123 on 15 totes. McDonald also caught two passes for 61 yards in addition to completing a pass for 27. The Steers were held to 188 total yards.

The Sooners finally yielded points in a game when they defeated Kansas, 34-12, the next week in Lawrence under misty skies.

Thomas returned the kickoff 41 yards to midfield, and the Sooners were off and rolling to a 7-0 lead. Thomas capped the 11-play drive with a one-yard plunge on fourth down, and Jimmy Harris converted.

Minutes later the Jayhawks took over at the OU 45 after the Sooners were stopped short on fourth-and-one. Kansas scored five plays later to cut the lead to 7-6. The Hawks' touchdown ended a streak of 14 scoreless quarters for the Big Red defense dating back to the Orange Bowl the prior year. Only two touchdowns were yielded over the last 32 quarters dating to last year.

The Sooners scored 20 points in more than an eight-minute span in the second period. Pricer's interception on the KU 45 set up the next touchdown. McDonald zipped 14 yards around right end seven plays later, and Harris converted.

The next score came after the Hawks punted to the OU 39, and the alternates winged their way for the score. Five plays later Baker took O'Neal's pitch and slung a 10-yard scoring strike to end Bob Timberlake. Baker also converted for a 21-6 advantage.

O'Neal returned the next Kansas punt 35 yards to the KU 35 to set up the next score. McDonald swept eight yards around right end five plays later, but the conversion failed after a 15-yard penalty.

The Sooners stopped the Jayhawks on a fourth-down gamble near midfield. Baker scored from five yards out nine plays later and toed the conversion.

Kansas drove 79 yards to score early in the fourth stanza. The Jayhawks were the first team to score twice on OU in the last 10 games.

Oklahoma rushed for 363 yards and passed for 39. McDonald led 12 Sooner ball carriers with 91 yards. Kansas gained 202 total yards.

Michigan State replaced the Sooners at the top of the AP poll. This may have irked Wilkinson's squad, because they bombed Notre Dame, 40-0, in South Bend on October 27. A record crowd of 60,128 turned out on a beautiful 65-degree afternoon, but Oklahoma sent most of them home in a gloomy mood. NBC also televised the game nationally, and the nation witnessed Notre Dame's first shutout since 1951 and first at home in 26 years.

The Fighting Irish were experiencing a down year as they held a 1-3 record prior to the Sooners coming to town. Irish quarterback Paul Hornung won the Heisman Trophy that year, but his performance against the Sooners was anything but stellar. He completed eight of 13 passes, but Oklahoma intercepted four of his aerials—twice returning them for scores.

Coach Wilkinson added a new twist to his split-T formation—flanking one end and halfback as split receivers.

The Sooners marched 69 yards in 10 plays following the opening kickoff for a 6-0 lead. From the ND 14, Harris rolled out and zipped a scoring strike to Bell, but Harris missed the conversion.

Guard Steve Jennings blocked a Notre Dame punt minutes later. Timberlake grabbed the ball and rambled to the three. Two plays later, O'Neal scored from the one, and Dodd converted for a 13-0 lead with 1:23 left in the first quarter.

The lead swelled to 19-0 early in the second period eight plays after McDonald blocked Hornung's punt. Thomas sliced through right guard for an 11-yard touchdown, but Billy Pricer missed the extra point. McDonald also sparked the 63-yard drive with a 17-yard dash to the ND 17.

The Irish marched to the OU seven after recovering O'Neal's fumble at midfield, but faced fourth-and-one. Timberlake stopped Hornung cold, and the Sooners took over.

Late in the first half, Notre Dame had the ball on its 49. A Sooner rush forced Hornung to hurry his pass. McDonald snagged it and flew 55 yards down the sideline with nary an Irishman in pursuit. Harris converted and the Sooners led, 26-0, at halftime.

Notre Dame threatened early in the third stanza, but Thomas tipped Hornung's pass, and McDonald clutched it at the OU 17. The Sooners charged downfield for another score. Harris carried the ball over from inside the one to cap the seven-play drive, and he also toed the conversion. McDonald hurled a 49-yard pass to Thomas on the second play of the drive to the ND 33. Harris also sparked the drive with a 16-yard scurry to the five.

Thomas snared another Hornung pass early in the fourth quarter and sailed 35 yards for the final tally and Harris converted.

Oklahoma picked up 147 rushing yards and passed for 83. McDonald collected 124 yards on the ground. The Irish gained 218 total yards.

The Sooners returned to No. 1 in the AP poll and had a little help from Michigan State, which lost.

Oklahoma trailed Colorado, 19-6, at halftime then shut the Buffaloes down in the final 30 minutes for a 27-19 victory, the closest contest all season. A record crowd of 46,563 turned out in Boulder on November 3 in hopes of witnessing an upset ruin the Sooners' 35-game win streak. The Buffs had their supporters in high hopes by winning five straight games after dropping the season opener.

The Buffs blocked Pricer's quick kick early in the first period and covered the ball in the end zone for a 7-0 lead.

Late in the quarter, Harris hurled a 35-yard TD pass to McDonald, but Harris missed the conversion; however, he connected on the next three.

McDonald, who played with a cold, returned a Buff punt 75 yards to the end zone, but a personal foul penalty nullified the score, and Colorado maintained possession at its 45. The Buffaloes marched to a 13-6 lead early in the second stanza. Colorado scored again with 26 seconds left until intermission on a 71-yard, nine-play drive after recovering Harris' fumble for a 19-6 advantage.

Entering the locker room at halftime, Wilkinson told his players that he was disappointed in their first-half performance. Just before the Sooners were to depart for the field for the second half, Wilkinson told his charges that he believed they could win the game. That message fired up the players as they took to the field.

The Sooners wheeled 80 yards in 14 plays to close the gap to 19-13 to begin the second half. OU faced fourth-and-two at its own 28 early in the drive, and the Sooners decided to gamble for a first down. Thomas gained three yards to keep the drive alive.

Facing fourth-and-one at the CU five, McDonald zipped a scoring strike to Thomas. McDonald highlighted the drive with a run of 12 yards on the drive's opening play and later with a 23-yard dash to the CU 14.

Late in the third period, Harris took a Buff punt and returned it 16 yards to the OU 36, but a personal foul penalty against Colorado moved the ball to the CU 48. McDonald, Pricer, and Thomas picked up short gains to the 11. On the next play, McDonald swept right, faked a pass and bolted to the end zone, leaping over from the five-yard line. Harris' conversion put OU up 20-19 with 48 seconds remaining in the third quarter.

Clendon Thomas hauls in a touchdown pass against Missouri. (*OU Athletics*)

Harris hurled a 16-yard scoring strike to Thomas to cap a 70-yard march midway through the fourth stanza. Baker gained 20 yards to the CU 28 to spark the drive.

OU collected 348 yards rushing and tossed the pigskin for 86 more. Thomas led all Sooners runners with 93 yards, and Harris completed five of eight aerials for 80 yards. The Buffaloes rushed for 242 yards—the most against Oklahoma all year—and passed for only eight yards.

The Sooners scored five touchdowns in the first half to blast 2-5 Iowa State, 44-0, the following week in Ames. The victory locked up another Big Seven Conference title for the Big Red.

McDonald scored the first two touchdowns for a 13-0 lead in the first period.

Early in the third quarter, Tubbs stole a Cyclone pass on the OU 28, bowled over three Iowa State tacklers and sailed to the end zone for a 38-0 lead.

Thomas' one-yard TD plunge early in the final stanza came moments after Rector smothered a Cyclone fumble.

Oklahoma hammered out 339 rushing yards and passed for 164. McDonald was three yards shy of the century mark to lead the 13 Sooner ball carriers. OU punted only once. The Big Red defense held Iowa State to four first downs and 35 total yards (24 rushing and 11 passing).

Morris suffered a leg injury and was sidelined for most of the Iowa State game and the rest of the season.

No. 3 Tennessee defeated No. 2 Georgia Tech to vault atop the AP poll, and the Sooners dropped to second.

Coach Wilkinson's crimson gang responded with a 67-14 waxing of Missouri on November 17 in Norman and leaped back to the summit of the AP poll. The 53-point margin was the largest by either team in the 47-game series.

All 55 Sooner players got in on the action, and eight of them crossed the goal line—McDonald and Thomas led the way with two touchdowns each. Stiller set up two Sooner scores with long catches and scored once himself on a 41-yard strike from Harris in the second period.

Oklahoma jumped to a 7-0 lead on Thomas' 11-yard run, then rolled to a 34-0 halftime lead, scoring on four of five possessions in the second quarter. The Big Red scored three touchdowns in the third stanza and two extra-point kicks failed, but Dodd ran across for one conversion. The 3-4-1 Tigers scored twice in the fourth period, once against the OU starters and the other after a fumble recovery against the reserves. OU also added two touchdowns in the final stanza.

Missouri coach Don Faurot, Wilkinson's mentor at Iowa Pre-Flight in the early 1940s, was retiring at the end of the season. Wilkinson learned the split-T formation from Faurot. The pupil and teacher met 10 times between 1947 and 1956, and the pupil never lost to his mentor.

OU gained 464 yards rushing and 138 yards through the air. McDonald led all rushers with 136 yards on 11 carries. The Tigers picked up 323 total yards.

The Sooners pounded Nebraska, 54-6, the next week before a throng of 50,039 in Norman. Oklahoma dialed long distance on four touchdowns with scores of 31 yards or more.

OU took the lead by whirling 78 yards in nine plays following the opening kickoff. Thomas, who led with 100 yards rushing, sparked the drive with a 54-yard run to the NU nine. The Sooners gained only one yard on the next three plays and faced fourth-and-goal at the eight. Harris lateraled to McDonald, who zoomed into the end zone on the next play, and Harris toed the conversion.

Carl Dodd sailed 32 yards for the next score and added the conversion for a 14-0 lead in the first quarter.

The Cornhuskers drove 79 yards late in the first period to score early in the second stanza but missed the extra point. Nebraska only crossed midfield twice the rest of the day.

OU scored 20 points in the second quarter—Harris on a five-yard jaunt, Dodd on a 10-yard pass from Baker, and McDonald hauled in a 48-yard strike from Harris.

Harris scored on a 31-yard run for a 40-6 lead early in the third period, and backup fullback Bill Brown sprinted 53 yards for a 47-6 lead less than four minutes later.

Sherrod scored the final tally with a five-yard run midway through the final stanza.

The win duplicated the largest margin of 48 points set by the 1949 and 1954 Sooners. OU's 39th consecutive victory placed the Sooners alongside the Washington Huskies with the all-time consecutive wins. The Huskies won 39 straight from 1908-1914.

The Sooners broke the record with a 53-0 victory over 3-4-2 Oklahoma A&M on December 1 before a packed house of 36,500 in Stillwater, matching the score from the year before.

Thomas scored two touchdowns to become the nation's leading scorer with 108 points for the season and gained 123 yards on 18 carries. McDonald completed one scoring strike to Thomas for a 12-0 lead and later scored on a 17-yard run early in the fourth quarter.

Oklahoma got things started with a 69-yard scoring drive in three plays in the first 79 seconds. Thomas returned the opening kickoff to the 31. Harris picked up 24 yards, and Thomas added eight more to the 37. Pricer burst up the middle and sailed to the end zone for a 6-0 lead. The Sooners' only weakness was missing five of eight conversions.

The Big Red rolled to a 26-0 lead, and then the longest score came late in the second period when O'Neal intercepted an Aggie pass and flew 63 yards for a 33-0 halftime lead. The Sooners added three touchdowns in the second half.

Wilkinson installed only seniors in the lineup for the final TD drive. When the Sooners advanced 77 yards to the Aggie two-yard line, Gray told Harris in the huddle that he wanted to score a touchdown. Gray went to halfback and McDonald replaced him at tackle. Gray scored on the next play for his only touchdown as a Sooner.

The exploding offense did not overshadow the Sooner defense, which held the Aggies to six first downs and 90 total yards. The

1956 Season Record: 10-0-0
Big Seven Conference: 6-0-0 (Champions)
NATIONAL CHAMPIONS

Date	Opponent	Result	Score
September 29	NORTH CAROLINA	W	36-0
October 6	KANSAS STATE	W	66-0
October 13	Texas at Dallas	W	45-0
October 20	at Kansas	W	34-12
October 27	at Notre Dame	W	40-0
November 3	at Colorado	W	27-19
November 10	at Iowa State	W	44-0
November 17	MISSOURI	W	67-14
November 24	NEBRASKA	W	54-6
December 1	at Oklahoma A&M	W	53-0

Pokes reached the OU 25 twice, and both times the defense forced them to surrender on downs.

The offense pounded out 33 first downs rushed for 520 yards and passes for 69 more.

The Sooners received 1,715 points for first place in the final AP poll. Tennessee finished second 97 points behind Oklahoma. The United Press International poll also voted the Sooners No. 1 ahead of the Volunteers.

All-America honors went to Tubbs, McDonald, Gray and Bill Krisher. Bell, Tom Emerson and Thomas joined them on the All-Big Seven first team.

Sporting News named McDonald Player of the Year. Tubbs won the Walter Camp Trophy as Player of the Year and was named UPI's Lineman of the Year.

1957

The Big Red grew to enormous proportions in the mid-1950s. Had King Kong and Godzilla challenged this monster, the huge gorilla and lizard would have lost. The Oklahoma Sooners had become the Goliath of the college football world, and for 47 straight games, David's slingshot was ineffective.

After claiming college football's top prize in 1955 and 1956, the Sooners' 1957 season was questionable since only four starters returned—guards Bill Krisher and Buddy Oujesky, end Don Stiller, and halfback Clendon Thomas.

Krisher was an All-America guard in 1956 and would again be honored in '57. Thomas would earn All-America accolades for the '57 season.

Five players who made all-conference or All-America the year before had graduated, but head coach Bud Wilkinson still had a stable of studs to round out a darn good football team.

Bob Harrison would lead the middle of the line as Jerry Tubbs' replacement at center. Carl Dodd was moved from halfback to quarterback, sharing the duties with David Baker. Halfback Jakie Sandefer and fullback Dennit Morris provided plenty of experience to round out the backfield.

The year also marked a first for Oklahoma football—halfback Prentice Gautt, of Oklahoma City Douglass High School, became the first African American undergraduate athlete for OU and his presence would have an impact on the Big Red's success. Wilkinson and Gautt weathered the storm of prejudice and segregation. Most of Gautt's teammates got along with him, and few did not.

The Sooners' team business manager, Ken Farris, made hotel reservations for road games, and Gautt was penciled in for a room with no roommate. Jakie Sandefer volunteered to be his roommate, and the two shared a room on the road for two seasons.

The 1957 Sooners were loaded with speed and a determination to win. After all, the returnees and alternates had not tasted defeat in a crimson and cream uniform. But defeat would rear its ugly head late in the season, yet the Sooners rebounded from that loss to win out.

Oklahoma State University (formerly Oklahoma A&M College) was approved as the conference's newest member in the spring. The conference was then known as the Big Eight, but OSU did not begin league competition for another two years.

The No. 1 Sooners opened the season on September 21 with a 26-0 victory over the Pittsburgh Panthers before a crowd of 59,025, including 4,000 crimson supporters. The Panthers were ranked eighth in the AP poll.

OU, notorious for running the football, tossed three touchdown passes against Pitt.

After a scoreless first quarter, Oklahoma finally got on track with a 51-yard scoring march early in the second period. On fourth-and-five at the Pitt 19, Sandefer hurled a scoring strike to end Joe Rector to finish the drive in nine plays, and Dodd converted.

Two Pitt fumbles early in the third quarter allowed the Sooners to take a 20-0 lead in the first three minutes. Morris recovered a Pitt fumble at the 20 moments after the second-half kickoff. Three plays later, Thomas burst through right tackle off a reverse for the touchdown, and Dodd converted.

The Panthers bobbled the ball on the first play after the kickoff, and Dodd recovered on the 33. Five plays later Dodd lofted a 17-yard TD pass to Stiller, but Dodd missed the extra point.

Minutes later, Bobby Boyd returned a Panther quick kick 31 yards to the Pitt 24, but a clipping call against OU moved the ball back to the 43. The alternates advanced to the 19, then Baker tossed a scoring strike to Boyd on the next play, but the Sooners were guilty of holding, and the ball was walked back to the 35.

Halfback Dick Carpenter carried twice to the 26, then Baker passed to Boyd. The ball bounced off a Panther's helmet. Carpenter clutched the ball in midair at the 12 and scooted into the end zone, but David Rolle missed the conversion.

Oklahoma rushed for 310 yards and passed for 78. The Panthers gained 173 total yards.

The Sooners had two weeks off before hosting Iowa State in the conference opener. The open date was welcomed since 15 players battled influenza.

The top-ranked Sooners blasted the 1-0-1 Cyclones, 40-14, before a throng of 53,392. OU held a 19-7 halftime lead, then exploded for two quick touchdowns late in the third period to put the game out of reach with a 33-7 lead.

Dodd scored twice in the first half, and Thomas added a 16-yard TD sprint. Harrison's fumble recovery on the Iowa State 20 set up Dodd's first score, a two-yard run five plays later. A poor Cyclone punt to their 32 set up the next crimson touchdown late in the first stanza. Four plays later Thomas dashed around end to the end zone. OU led, 12-0, as Dodd missed the first two conversions.

Thomas intercepted an Iowa State pass on the final play of the first quarter and returned it 15 yards to the Iowa State 20. Dodd scored from the eight-yard line three plays later and toed the extra point.

The Cyclones marched 60 yards for a touchdown late in the second period and ended a five-year scoreless drought against Oklahoma.

Baker's one-yard plunge put the Sooners up 26-7, and after the defense held Iowa State on the next series, Sandefer scored on an 81-yard punt return aided by Dodd's key block.

The reserves added two more touchdowns in the fourth stanza, and Iowa State scored with seven seconds remaining in the game after recovering an OU fumble at the Sooner 14.

OU gained 161 rushing yards and passed for 128 yards. The Cyclones picked up 268 total yards.

The Texas Longhorns fired coach Ed Price after a 10-19-1 record the past three years. Texas hired former Sooner All-American Darrell Royal, who had been head coach at Mississippi State after serving several years as an assistant at North Carolina State, Tulsa and

---

It's a Fact

The Sooners led the nation in punt returns with 648 yards and in interceptions with 23.

Mississippi State. He also coached of Edmonton Eskimos in the Canadian Football League.

The 52nd edition of the Red River rivalry on October 12 was billed as the teacher (Wilkinson) versus the pupil (Royal). The No. 1 Sooners won their 43rd straight game and sixth in the Texas series with a 21-7 victory before a packed house of 75,504 in the Cotton Bowl. Seven turnovers, including five interceptions, helped OU to victory.

Texas picked off four Oklahoma passes, and Dodd threw three interceptions. The first came early in the first quarter to set up the Longhorns' only score and a 7-0 lead.

Ken Northcutt pounced on a Steer fumble at the OU 34 late in the first period, and the Sooners rolled 66 yards to tie the game. The Big Red chewed up short yardage to the UT 23. Clendon Thomas gained three yards on a fourth-and-two situation for a crucial first down on the UT 20 early in the second stanza. Three plays later, Thomas scored from the three-yard line carrying UT's Monte Lee on his back across the goal line. Dodd converted the first of three extra points.

The Sooners drove 80 yards in 15 plays to take a 14-7 lead late in the third quarter. The reserves moved to the midfield thanks to Carpenter's 16-yard run to the 50. A personal foul penalty against Texas moved the ball to the UT 27, and the starters entered the game pounding out short yards to the one. Sandefer blasted into the end zone on the next play.

The Horns didn't buckle and quickly reached the OU 10-yard line after the kickoff. End Steve Jennings charged through the line and forced Walter Fondren to toss a short pass. Center Jim Davis intercepted at the four and raced 96 yards for a score, but end Ross Coyle was flagged for clipping at midfield, which wiped out the score. Coyle's clip was unnecessary, as no Texas player had any chance of catching Davis.

Sandefer intercepted Fondren's pass and dashed 20 yards to the UT 21 late in the fourth period to set up the final tally. Dodd sailed a 19-yard pass to Stiller, and Dodd punched the ball across two plays later from the one.

A fight broke out on the field between Oklahoma and Texas fans. One Texan tried to steal a Ruf-Nek's paddle and got kicked in the stomach. Another Texan punched a Sooner fan in the stomach as the Oklahoman tried to take down one of the goal posts. About 30 police officers swarmed on the scene and ended the melee.

Oklahoma collected 303 yards rushing and 24 yards through the air. Texas gained 171 total yards.

Royal never lost to Wilkinson again, defeating his mentor six straight times.

No. 2 Michigan State defeated No. 6 Michigan and replaced OU in the AP poll's top spot the next week. Oklahoma dropped to second.

The Sooners hammered 1-2-1 Kansas, 47-0, the next week in Norman. The alternates led the onslaught by scoring five of seven touchdowns. Oklahoma capitalized on three fumbles, an interception and a poor Jayhawk punt.

Baker engineered three scores—carrying across the goal line twice and passing for another.

Thomas' seven-yard jaunt put OU up 7-0 after the opening kickoff, and the Sooners struck like lightning for a 21-0 lead late in the first period. David Rolle recovered a Kansas fumble at the OU 49. Eleven plays later, Baker's four-yard TD run capped the drive for a 14-0 lead. KU's Jerry Baker fumbled the ensuing kickoff, and guard Dick Corbitt smothered the ball at the KU 18. David Baker hurled a scoring strike to Rolle in one play. Corbitt had another fumble recovery at the KU 16 that led to a 40-0 lead.

Boyd tossed a seven-yard TD pass to Carpenter in the second quarter, and Rolle and Baker scored their second touchdowns in the third stanza. Sandefer scored on a five-yard run for the final tally in the fourth period.

The Sooners rolled up 27 first downs, rushed for 447 yards and passed for 93. Thomas led all crimson runners with 120 yards. The Hawks were held to eight first downs and 171 total yards. Kansas never penetrated past the OU 37 all afternoon. The winning streak shot up to 44, and the conference string was 63 without a loss.

Sooner Magic: Surviving a Buffalo Stampede

Michigan State lost to Purdue, and the Sooners returned to the top of the AP poll, but the taste of sweet success was about to turn sour in Norman against the Colorado Buffaloes before a Memorial Stadium crowd of 61,624 and a regional TV (NBC) audience. Was the monster losing its appetite? Hardly, but the 3-1-1 Buffs, a four touchdown underdog, were the greatest threat to the Sooners' magnificent run of victories since TCU in 1954.

The Sooners defeated Colorado, 14-13, by expertly managing the clock and protecting the ball in the fourth quarter.

Late in the first period, OU was going nowhere deep in its own territory, so Coach Wilkinson ordered a quick kick on third down. Thomas hammered the kick 67 yards to the CU 20, where the ball touched CU's Sherman Pruit. Players from both teams scrambled for the pigskin, but Jerry Thompson smothered it for the Sooners at the Buffs' 13.

Three plays later, halfback Boyd found a gaping hole off right guard and shot nine yards to the end zone. Baker booted the extra point and OU led, 7-0, with 2:26 remaining in the first quarter. The score stood through halftime.

Colorado scored on a 40-yard interception early in the third stanza. As the Buffs snapped the ball for the extra point, Krisher crashed through the line and shoved a CU lineman out of the way and into the ball's path as it ascended from kicker Ellwyn Indorf;s foot. Colorado had cut OU's lead to 7-6.

"I didn't even know I had blocked it," Krisher, who played with a shoulder injury, said in the locker room afterwards. "I just knew I was in there with my arms up. We all rushed in on that play. I just got there first."

Colorado took a 13-7 lead early in the fourth stanza.

Thomas gathered the pigskin at the 19 on the ensuing kickoff and throttled to the OU 47. Thomas gained two yards off right guard, then Morris went over left guard for five more. Sandefer swept off left end for two more yards but short of the first down. On fourth-and-one at the CU 44, Wilkinson gambled and won. Dodd sliced through right tackle and followed tackle Doyle Jennings' block for a 10-yard pickup. The Big Red continued eating chunks of real estate to the Buffs' eight.

From there, Dodd pitched to Thomas off the left side. Dodd and Morris blocked out a couple of CU defenders clearing Thomas' path to the end zone. The crimson-clad fans sat quietly, holding their breaths as Dodd sailed the extra point through the goal post. The Sooners regained the lead, 14-13, with 10:26 remaining. The scoreboard, however, clicked a point for Colorado instead of Oklahoma.

Notre Dame halfback Dick Lynch heads to the end zone in the Irish's 7-0 victory that snapped OU's 47-game winning streak. (*OU Athletics*)

At the moment, the accident showed Colorado with a 14-13 lead, and numerous Sooners fans chanted, "Change that score!"

The correction was soon made and the Sooner faithful cheered, yet there was plenty of football to be played. The Sooners forced the Buffs to punt on the next series. Boyd returned the kick 39 yards to the CU 35. Could Oklahoma manage the clock in its favor and not turn the ball over in the meantime?

The Sooners drove to the CU 14 and did turn the ball over, but on downs when they failed to make a first down.

The mighty Big Red defense stalled the Buffs again. OU got the ball back with 3:06 remaining. Again, protecting the pigskin was crucial to keeping the winning streak alive. Dodd carried on four straight plays to the CU 20 when the gun sounded.

"It came out just like I thought it would," Wilkinson said of the close contest. "The most misunderstood thing about football is how close the teams are. I'm real proud of the team. I think they all played just as well as they could."

The Big Red rushed for 250 yards and failed to complete a pass in seven tries. The Buffs gained 267 total yards.

No. 2 Texas A&M defeated Baylor to replace the Sooners atop the AP poll. Oklahoma dropped to second again and never returned to No. 1.

Oklahoma was a five-touchdown favorite over 2-3-1 Kansas State, but a slippery field and lackadaisical performance held the Sooners to two touchdowns in a 13-0 victory in Manhattan. Oklahoma had shut out the Wildcats in four of the last five years, and Bud Wilkinson obtained his 100th victory.

A half-inch of rain soaked the field before the game, which was played under gray skies and a brisk north wind. The mushy field immobilized long gains. Dodd had an 18-yard run that was the longest of the day.

Thomas returned a punt 15 yards to the Cat 35 to set up the first score midway through the second period. OU twice succeeded on fourth down plays. On fourth-and-five at the KS 29, Thomas ripped up the middle for seven yards. On fourth-and-one on the 13, Dodd gained two yards. Two plays later, Thomas slashed through right guard for a six-yard touchdown, and Dodd converted.

Corbitt blocked a Wildcat punt at the KS 44 to set up the final Sooner tally early in the third stanza. Seven plays later, Boyd scored from the one, but Baker's conversion was low. Boyd fired a 19-yard pass to Jennings one play before he scored.

OU twice advanced deep into Kansas State territory in the fourth but had to surrender on downs both times. The Wildcats never moved past the OU 35 in the game.

Oklahoma tallied 232 rushing yards and 56 passing. Kansas State had 198 total yards.

The No. 2 Sooners' offense returned to form on November 9 with a 39-14 win over Missouri before a record throng of 39,018 in Columbia. After just two touchdowns in each of the previous two games, OU scored six TDs against the Tigers. The 47th straight victory clinched another Orange Bowl berth for the Big Red and the driver's seat for a 12th straight conference championship. The 5-1-1 Tigers were undefeated in the Big Seven Conference with a 3-0 mark.

OU held a 13-7 lead through the first 40 minutes and exploded for four touchdowns in the last 20. Two touchdowns followed intercepted passes, and the other four scores came on long drives.

Five Sooners crossed the goal line, including Gautt, who scored his first TD in a crimson uniform.

Oklahoma collected 28 first downs, rushed for 424 yards and passed for 40. Thomas led the ground attack with 100 yards on 19 carries. The Tigers picked up 10 first downs and 162 total yards.

Gloomy Day in Norman

The gloom of a gray sky could not have been any more despondent than the scoreboard at the south end of Memorial Stadium, which revealed that Notre Dame defeated Oklahoma, 7-0, and the streak stopped at 47. The State of Oklahoma was observing its golden anniversary, but there was no celebration in Norman.

The Fighting Irish not only ended the winning streak, but OU failed to score for the first time in 123 games. No. 2 Oklahoma was a three-touchdown favorite over 4-2 Notre Dame. The Irish won their first four games before dropping two straight before coming to Norman. The 63,170 homecoming fans in attendance and a national television (NBC) audience had expected the Sooners to romp all over Notre Dame, especially since OU won big (40-0) a year earlier. The game was sold out six months in advance.

The Big Red offense failed to do any romping as the Irish defense plugged the middle, taking away the Sooners' off-tackle slants and stymied end sweeps.

Notre Dame threatened first with a drive onb the OU three-yard line late in the first quarter. The Sooners defense stiffened and stopped them just short of the goal line on fourth down. The Irish later moved to the OU 11, but the Big Red defense stiffened again. Notre Dame fakes a field goal and completed a pass to the OU 7. Two plays later, Baker intercepted a pass in the end zone.

Punting dominated most of the second and third stanzas. Clendon Thomas had one punt pin the Irish deep at their four, and Baker punted to the ND eight and three on two of his kicks.

Jakie Sandefer had the crowd up and cheering when he returned an Irish punt 13 yards to the ND 34, but the Sooners stalled and punted back.

Thomas punted out of the end zone early in the fourth quarter to set up the Irish at their 20. Notre Dame drove 80 yards in 20 plays and consumed nine minutes for the winning touchdown. Fullback Nick Pietrosante carried up the middle on most plays. On fourth-and-goal at the OU three, the Sooners stacked the middle of the line, expecting the play to come straight up the middle again. Quarterback Bob Williams instead pitched wide to halfback Dick Lynch, who scooted around right end and across the goal line. Monty Stickles converted and the Irish led, 7-0, with 3:50 remaining.

Oklahoma returned the kickoff to its 39. Wilkinson put in his alternate unit, believing a fresh set of legs could move the ball downfield more effectively. Passing moved the Sooners to the Irish 24, but Notre Dame intercepted Dale Sherrod's pass in the end zone to end the threat.

"It was a devastating loss. Being so young, I didn't know of anything that was so devastating at the time," Sandefer recalled.

Oklahoma gained nine first downs, 98 rushing yards and passed for 47. The Irish picked up 17 first downs and 247 total yards.

Sooner fans gave their team a standing ovation after the game, slapped players on their backs and shouted words of encouragement as the players headed to the dressing room. Sandefer recalled Wilkinson giving a positive speech to his players after the loss.

"He told us we had done something that no major college football team had ever done before or will ever do again," Sandefer reminisced. "He told us he was proud of us and that we had been just as much a part of the 47-game winning streak as any other Oklahoma team.

"He also told us the only ones who never lose are the ones who never play."

The 300 Sooner fans who showed up for the Oklahoma City Quarterback Club luncheon at noon the following Monday showed their appreciation to Wilkinson by counting to 47 in unison.

Missouri lost to Kansas State, and the Sooners sealed their 12th straight conference championship.

The Notre Dame loss dropped the Sooners to sixth in the AP poll. OU rebounded with a 32-7 victory over 1-8 Nebraska a week later in Lincoln. The conference streak grew to 65 without a defeat.

Bill Jennings, who lettered at OU from 1938-1940 and served as Bud Wilkinson's assistant from 1947-1953, was in his first season as the Cornhuskers' head coach.

Oklahoma scored 32 unanswered points in the middle quarters after trailing, 7-0, in the first period. The Huskers drove 37 yards after short punt for their lead early in the game. Boyd was sidelined with an injury, and sophomore Brewster Hobby moved up to the No. 2 left half slot. Hobby scored twice to lead the Sooners in scoring.

Leading 18-7 at halftime, Oklahoma kicked off to begin the second half and the ball rolled dead in the end zone. Nebraska's Carroll Zarulia failed to cover the ball and Rector raced in to smother it for the Sooners—touchdown. Dodd converted and OU held a 25-7 lead without any time ticking off the clock.

The Sooners rushed for 349 yards and passed for 44. Nebraska gained 187 total yards.

Oklahoma climbed one notch to fifth in the AP poll, then hammered Oklahoma State, 53-6, on November 30 in Norman. The Sooners had scored 53 points in each of the past three years against OSU.

Thomas rushed for 162 yards, scored two touchdowns and passed for another to lead the Sooner attack. Thomas' stellar performance

Bud Wilkinson suffers defeat for the first time in four years, at the hands of Notre Dame.
(© 1957, The Daily Oklahoman)

broke three school career records—36 touchdowns; 2,120 yards rushing and 216 total points. Sandefer also scored twice, once on a 24-yard strike from Thomas and again on a 57-yard interception return. Baker also hurled two TD passes.

The Sooners scored three touchdowns in the first six minutes of the third stanza for a 41-0 lead. The reserves scored twice in the fourth quarter and the Cowboys scored with 49 seconds left in the game.

OU tallied 422 rushing yards and passed for 122. The Pokes collected 260 total yards.

The No. 4 Sooners ended the 1957 season with a 48-21 pounding of 16th-ranked Duke in the 24th annual Orange Bowl Classic on New Year's Day. North Carolina State won the Atlantic Coast Conference and ACC rules prohibited them from participating in two straight bowl games. The Blue Devils represented the conference as the runner up. Duke won its first five games, then went 1-2-2 in the last half of the season and 5-1-1 in the ACC. The Blue Devils defense yielded an average of 8.7 points per game.

The OU-Duke matchup before a throng of 76,561 was billed as a defensive contest, and it appeared so with only three touchdowns scored in the first half. Each team scored a TD in the third period and exploded for 34 points in the final stanza.

Baker picked off a Duke pass and raced 94 yards for a 7-0 Oklahoma lead late in the first quarter.

Duke's Andy Cottingham took a high snap in punt formation, and the Sooners swarmed him for a 12-yard loss on the Devils' 13 early in the second period. A penalty set OU back five yards and two carries got back to the original line of scrimmage, then Thomas scooted into the end zone on the next play, and the Big Red held a 14-0 lead.

Duke marched 65 yards after the kickoff to cut the Sooner lead to 14-7.

Dodd's 36-yard punt return to the Devils' 14 set up the next Sooner score early in the third period. On fourth-and-goal inside the one-yard line, Dodd crashed over for the 21-7 lead.

Duke rolled 85 yards in 10 plays to cut the lead to 21-14 late in the third stanza.

Sandefer scored on a three-yard run moments after Morris recovered a fumble at the Duke 24. The Blue Devils fumbled again moments later, and Morris recovered again on the Duke 29. Hobby

1957 Season Record: 10-1-0
Big Seven Conference: 6-0-0 (Champions)

Date	Opponent	Result	Score
September 21	at Pittsburgh	W	26-0
October 5	IOWA STATE	W	40-14
October 12	Texas at Dallas	W	21-7
October 19	KANSAS	W	47-0
October 26	COLORADO	W	14-13
November 2	at Kansas State	W	13-0
November 9	at Missouri	W	39-14
November 16	NOTRE DAME	L	7-0
November 23	at Nebraska	W	32-7
November 30	OKLAHOMA A&M	W	53-6
January 1	Duke*	W	48-21

*Orange Bowl at Miami, FL

connected a scoring strike to Baker on the next play for a 35-14 lead.

Coyle blocked a Duke punt moments later. Tackle Jim Lawrence grabbed the ball and returned it to the Duke 13. Once again it was the Hobby-Baker connection for a touchdown pass on the next play, but this time Baker passed to Hobby.

The Blue Devils marched 70 yards to cut the lead to 41-21, yet the Sooners still had the last word. Bennett Watts intercepted a Duke pass on the OU 28 and darted to midfield, then lateraled to Dick Carpenter, who raced the final 50 yards for the touchdown.

Oklahoma rushed for 165 yards and passed for 114 more. The Blue Devils picked up 328 total yards. OU's 27 points in the fourth period still remain an Orange Bowl record for most points scored in one quarter.

Wilkinson said the 1957 Sooner squad was as good as any team he had coached. "They're really great men," he said. "They have had a great spirit and have improved in every game they've played."

The 1957 Sooners finished the season 10-1 and fourth in the nation in the AP and UPI polls. Thomas and Krisher were selected All-Americans. Stiller, Coyle and Harrison joined them on the All-Big Seven first team.

1958

Coach Wilkinson put in a new offensive formation called a "multiple offense." After breaking the huddle, the center and split end would go to the line of scrimmage and the linemen would follow and set up either in normal formation, or all four linemen would position to the left or right of the center. The new offensive weapon sputtered in the first three games, and the Sooners almost completely chunked it by the fourth game.

The NCAA approved a new rule to allow two-point conversions as an option after touchdowns. Players could either run or pass for two points. Placekicking would remain as one point, and the line of scrimmage for extra pointers was moved back one yard to the three-yard line.

With many players returning from the 1957 squad, the Sooners were favored to claim its third national championship in four years. One of the best quarterback tandems in the nation was among the returnees. Senior David Baker was the starter in most games, but junior Bobby Boyd, a converted halfback, came off the bench to relieve him. The Big Red offense would not miss a cylinder in its well-oiled machine, as both quarterbacks combined for 1,041 total yards and accounted for 13 touchdowns during the '58 season.

Six starters returned to the lineup—tackle Steve Jennings, center Bob Harrison, guard Dick Corbitt, end Joe Rector, halfback Jakie Sandefer and Baker. Gilmer Lewis stepped up to replace the graduated Ken Northcutt at left guard, and Prentice Gautt made headlines at fullback.

The No. 2 Sooners opened the season on September 27 with a 47-14 victory over West Virginia before a crowd of 55,342 in Norman. Seven different players scored for OU with three touchdowns on the ground, three through the air and one on a fumble recovery. Oklahoma set a school record with 264 passing yards (11 completions on 20 attempts). Baker led the aerial attack by completing four of seven for 98 yards.

The Big Red sputtered in the first quarter, blowing four chances to get the ball in the end zone. One drive ended with a fumble on the Mountaineers' one, and three other drives stalled at the four and twice at the seven.

The Sooners finally got uncorked midway through the second stanza. Wahoo McDaniel blocked a West Virginia punt, and end

Jerry Tillery recovered at the WV 49. Six plays later, Gautt scored on a 27-yard run. OU took advantage of the new two-point rule, and Baker scooted into the end zone for an 8-0 lead. The play marked the first two-point conversion in Oklahoma football history.

The lead grew to 15-0 moments later as the Sooners marched 49 yards in four plays. Baker scored from the 10-yard line, and Ronnie Hartline kicked the conversion.

Oklahoma took the second-half kickoff and drove 80 yards in 16 plays for a 21-0 lead. Sandefer's four-yard run capped the drive. Four and one-half minutes later, Boyd connected a TD pass to McDaniel, who caught the ball at the WV 42 and sailed to the end zone to complete the 86-yard play.

The Mountaineers got on board by blocking McDaniel's punt and returning it 14 yards to the end zone.

Boyd completed a nine-yard pass to Jimmy Carpenter for a 34-6 lead, and moments later the Mountaineers were set up to punt. The ball rolled into the end zone on a bad snap, and center Mickey Johnson pounced on it for the Sooners. The third string scored once more in the final period on an eight-yard pass from Bob Cornell to Stan Ward. West Virginia added a touchdown and a two-point conversion moments later.

Oklahoma hammered out 335 rushing yards. West Virginia rolled up 196 total yards.

The Sooners jumped to No. 1 in the AP poll, replacing Ohio State, and the new offense continued to sputter the next week in a 6-0 win over 1-0 Oregon in Norman. The win was the lowest scoring victory in Bud Wilkinson's career. The Ducks stacked the defensive line with eight players to slow the OU offense, yet the Sooners managed to score once and that was enough for the victory.

Neither team could find the end zone in the first quarter. The Ducks took the opening kickoff and consumed six minutes to march from their 16 to the OU 22. An incomplete pass on fourth down stalled the drive.

Oklahoma failed to score after three advances inside the Oregon 30. Late in the second stanza, tackle Jere Durham hammered Oregon halfback Herm McKinney, forcing a fumble. Corbitt pounced on it at the Oregon 17. Dick Carpenter, Boyd and Jimmy Carpenter carried to the nine, where the Sooners faced fourth and two. On the next play, Boyd lofted a scoring strike to Dick Carpenter, who was wide open in the southeast corner of the end zone. Boyd was stopped short of the goal line on the two-point try.

The Ducks threatened with a 60-yard drive to the Sooners' 20 in the third period but surrendered on another incomplete pass on fourth down.

Oklahoma had 129 yards rushing and passed for 27. Oregon collected 261 total yards.

Auburn replaced OU atop the AP poll and the Big Red dropped to No. 2. The Sooners traveled to Dallas on October 11 for the Red River showdown against No. 16 Texas. The 3-0 Longhorns had defeated Georgia, Tulane and Texas Tech, and for the first time since 1950 Oklahoma and Texas met with an undefeated record.

The two-point conversion bit the Sooners and helped the Steers break a six-year drought in the Red River rivalry with a 15-14 win before 75,780 at the Cotton Bowl.

Like Oregon a week earlier, Texas stacked the defensive line with eight players.

The Longhorns marched 52 yards for the first score early in the second period and added a two-point conversion for an 8-0 lead.

A short punt aided the Sooners' first touchdown in the third quarter; the punt rolled out at the UT 38. Eight plays later, Boyd lateraled to Dick Carpenter, who swept around left end for the score. Boyd misfired his pass for two points.

Early in the fourth stanza, OU guard Jerry Thompson forced a fumble at the UT 24. The ball popped up in the air where Sooners guard Jim Davis snatched it and raced across the goal line. Boyd passed to Tillery for two points and a 14-8 lead.

Texas later drove 75 yards in 13 plays for the winning score. Bob Lackey capped the drive with a seven-yard pass to Bob Bryant, and Lackey converted for the 15-14 lead with 3:50 remaining in the game.

The Sooners reached the Texas 44 after the kickoff, but Lackey intercepted Boyd's pass to end the game.

OU rushed for 201 yards and passed for 62. Texas gained 210 total yards. As a member of the NCAA rules committee, Bud Wilkinson voted in favor of the two-point conversion. After the Texas game, he said, "I obviously wasn't very satisfied with my vote."

Royal relished the victory, but for one moment he excused himself in the locker room after the game. The emotion of the come-from-behind triumph and defeating his former mentor churned his stomach. After vomiting behind the locker room, he then met with reporters and told them he did not like the new two-point rule: "I still don't like it, even though it enabled us to win today. It's unfair to the coaches."

Oklahoma fell to 11th in the AP poll, ending 59 straight weeks of being rated in the top ten dating back to early 1953. OU turned its attention to the conference portion of the schedule. Wilkinson shook up his roster by promoting six alternates a few days before the Kansas contest: Boyd at quarterback, Tillery at right end, McDaniel at left end, Lewis to left tackle and Dick Carpenter to left halfback. Thompson moved up to left guard to replace Jerry Payne, who suffered a broken ankle and twisted knee against Texas. The OU skipper said he made the changes because the second unit scored both touchdowns against the Longhorns.

The Sooners plastered Kansas, 43-0, the next week in Lawrence. The 1-3 Jayhawks, coached by former OU All-American Jack Mitchell, lost their first three games, then beat Iowa State a week before the Oklahoma tilt.

The Big Red returned to the split-T formation and rolled up 28 first downs, 350 rushing yards and passed for 157 more. Oklahoma led 14-0 at halftime then erupted for 29 points in the final 30 minutes. Seven Sooners scored; 12 carried the pigskin, and nine caught passes.

Third-string halfback Johnny Pellow scored two touchdowns in the game's final eight minutes, once on a 38-yard punt return and later on a 78-yard pass interception return. Boyd, who ran for one TD and passed for another, completed all four of his passes for 62 yards. Baker completed seven of 12 for 95 yards. Reserve halfback Jack Holt led the scoring with 10 points on one touchdown, and twice scored two-point conversions.

The Sooner defense held Kansas to 183 total yards.

For the second straight week, the No. 9 Sooners began sluggish and exploded in the second half to beat Kansas State, 40-6, on October 25 in Norman.

The Sooners led 13-0 at halftime then scored two TDs in the third period, both in a 42-second span. OU was flagged for 130 yards in penalties, and 50 yards in fines stalled their efforts in the first quarter.

Sandefer passed a scoring strike to Tillery and Boyd sailed a pass to Hartline for the first-half advantage.

Lewis intercepted a Wildcat pass at the KS 28 early in the third quarter to set up the next Oklahoma score. Baker scored from the one-yard lone seven plays later. Minutes later, Thompson blocked a

Cat punt at the 12 and Ross Coyle smothered the ball in the end zone. Forty two seconds later, Jimmy Carpenter took a Kansas State punt at the Cats' 45, zipped down the middle, and cut to the east sideline for a touchdown.

The reserves scored twice in the fourth period. The Wildcats also got their one line touchdown in the fourth stanza. The Cats' 74-yard drive was the only time they penetrated past the OU 30-yard line. OU gained only seven first downs, rushed for 263 yards and passed for 133. Kansas State picked up 211 total yards.

The winner of the OU-Colorado contest the next week in Boulder would have the upper hand to receive an Orange Bowl invitation. Big Eight Conference regulations prohibited a team from playing in a bowl game for two straight years, but the Orange Bowl committee wanted to invite the Sooners for the bowl's silver anniversary, provided Oklahoma qualified. The conference gave its approval.

Oklahoma moved up to seventh in the nation, and Colorado was two notches below with a 5-0 record (4-0 in the Big Eight). The Buffaloes had outscored their opponents by an average of 31.2 to 10.8, including two shutouts.

CU also led the nation in rushing offense (347.2 yards per game) and total offense (411.2 yards per game). Oklahoma ranked fourth in both categories (253.6 rushing yards per game and 347.2 total yards per game).

Buffs halfback Howard Cook led the Big Eight in rushing with 500 yards and scoring with 53 points.

The Sooners did not disappoint the Orange Bowl Committee with a 23-7 victory before 48,264 fans, to date the largest crowd to witness a football game in the state of Colorado. More spectators saw the game on closed-circuit television in Norman, Boulder, and Denver. The crimson defense shutdown Cook and company, limiting the Buffs to 87 yards rushing and 99 through the air. Cook gained only 18 yards on 12 carries.

David Baker returned to form for the Sooners by scoring 15 points (two touchdowns, a two-point conversion, and an extra-point kick).

Colorado took a 7-0 lead late in the first quarter.

The Sooners answered less than three minutes later with a 72-yard march in six plays. From the CU 48, Gautt sliced through left tackle, cut to his right, and accelerated to the end zone. OU faked the extra point. Jimmy Carpenter took Baker's pitch out and swung around left end for an 8-7 lead.

Oklahoma drove 76 yards in 17 plays to take a 16-7 lead midway through the third stanza. Baker's one-yard sneak capped the drive, and he scooted across for the deuce. Baker also picked up a crucial first down with a two-yard gain on fourth-and-one at the CU 42.

Early in the fourth quarter, the Buffs' Boyd Dowler chased a bad punt snap to his seven-yard line. Dowler covered the ball, but the Sooners took over and scored their final tally four plays later. Baker plowed over right tackle from the one and converted the extra point.

OU rushed for 258 yards and passed for 21. Gautt rolled up 117 yards on 16 carries.

The No. 6 Sooners blanked 3-4 Iowa State, 20-0, on November 8 in Ames. Oklahoma appeared headed for a blowout with an early touchdown, but seven fumbles blew additional chances. Fortunately the Cyclones also fumbled, and OU capitalized on both of them.

The Big Red took the opening kickoff and wheeled 70 yards in 14 plays for a 7-0 lead. The Sooners pushed to the Iowa State five on 13 running plays then Brewster Hobby tossed a five-yard scoring strike to Jimmy Carpenter, and Baker converted.

Neither team had a good grasp on the pigskin the rest of the way. OU fumbled on their second possession. Iowa State moved to the Sooners' 12 for the deepest advance but had to surrender on downs.

McDaniel's coast-to-coast punt was the highlight of the second period. Backed up to his four-yard line and with a 35 mile-per-hour wind behind his back, McDaniel's kick bounced and rolled all the way to the I-State four. The 92-yard kick broke Darrell Royal's record of 81 yards set in 1948.

The Sooners got the ball back moments later at the Iowa State 23 but fumbled after reaching the one-yard line.

Rector forced the Cyclones' Mike Fitzgerald to fumble the second-half kickoff, and Hobby recovered on the Iowa State 19. Four plays later, Carpenter bulled across from the three.

Boyd recovered an Iowa State fumble minutes later at the Cyclone 34 to set up the final tally. Boyd scored on a two-yard run seven plays later, and Hartline toed the extra point.

The Sooners rushed for 273 yards and passed for only five. The Cyclones gained 232 rushing yards and passed for 14. I-State tailback Dwight Nichols gained 138 yards to lead his team. Gautt led the Sooners with 86 yards.

Oklahoma and Missouri were the only teams with unbeaten marks in the Big Eight Conference when they met the following week in Norman. The Sooners and Tigers both sported identical 4-0 marks in conference play, and the winner could claim at least a share of the conference crown.

It wasn't even close. The No. 6 Sooners blasted Missouri, 39-0, before a homecoming throng of 54,268. Holding on to the football helped OU clinch at least a share of the Big Eight Conference crown. The Big Red lost only one fumble, which came in the first quarter.

Hobby accounted for the first three touchdowns—a 74-yard scoring strike to Coyle in the first stanza, a one-yard run in the second and a 10-yard pass to Jimmy Carpenter in the third.

Boyd scored two touchdowns 83 seconds apart in the fourth period. His 21-yard jaunt put the Sooners ahead, 27-0, and he followed it with a 38-yard punt return for a 33-0 lead.

Cornell's 47-yard interception return to the Mizzou 15 set up the final tally late in the fourth quarter. Third-string quarterback Bob Page scored on a seven-yard run three plays later.

The Big Red rushed for 246 yards and completed 10 of 13 passes for 160 yards. Hobby led the aerial attack by completing three of three for 94 yards. Missouri collected 241 total yards.

The No. 4 Sooners secured their 13th straight conference title on November 23 with a 40-7 victory over Nebraska in Norman. The victory extended the Sooners' conference winning string to 41 straight and 69 conference games without a loss.

In contrast to the first eight games of the season, Oklahoma scored three touchdowns in the first stanza for a comfortable 21-0 lead at halftime. The Sooners failed to score a touchdown in the first period of their first four games and scored once in the first quarter of the last four.

The Sooners earned every one of their six touchdowns with drives ranging from 51 to 89 yards.

Nebraska scored its only touchdown on a 93-yard interception return to cut OU's lead to 21-6 early in the third stanza. The Huskers never penetrated past the OU 20 at any other time.

The Sooners answered with an 89-yard march capped by Sandefer's nine-yard TD pass to David Carpenter. Hobby scored his second TD of the day minutes later with a one-yard plunge to put Oklahoma back into the comfort zone with a 34-7 lead.

OU rolled up 354 rushing yards and passed for 93 more. Gautt led Sooner runners with 110 yards on 12 carries. The Huskers were held to four first downs and 107 total yards.

Syracuse defeated West Virginia to claim the other berth to the Orange Bowl on New Year's Day.

Sooner Magic: If One Quarterback Won't Get You, the Other One Will

The fifth-ranked Sooners were three-touchdown favorites over the 7-2 Oklahoma State Cowboys. The Big Red led the overall series 38-8-6, including a 12-game winning streak against their intrastate rival. That string was in jeopardy until Boyd found the end zone.

OU squeaked out a 7-0 victory on November 29 before a crowd of 37,014 in Stillwater. Sleet fell the day before the game, and a soggy Lewis Field made for a slippery pigskin all afternoon.

The Sooners had a chance to score midway through the first quarter when OSU fumbled McDaniel's punt and Sandefer recovered at the OSU 34-yard line. Hobby slashed for 18 yards to the Poke five. Jimmy Carpenter gained two yards, the Hobby tossed an incomplete pass. On third-and-goal, Carpenter took a pitch from Hobby but slipped and lost four yards. Hobby threw another incompletion, and the Sooners came away with nothing.

OSU threatened three times in the second quarter but also came up empty each time. Both teams headed into intermission deadlocked at zero.

Late in the third quarter, OSU's Dick Soergel took Baker's punt 13 yards to the Pokes' 40. OSU marched to the OU 15 as the third period ended.

Harrison stuffed Larry Rundle for no gain to open the final quarter. Soergel carried on the next play, but the ball squirted from his hands, and Corbitt smothered it for the Sooners at the 11.

Late in the game, OSU's Duane Wood punted to his own 34-yard line, where OU took over with 5:57 remaining. On third-and-seven at the 31, Boyd called a weak-side fullback trap in the huddle. When Boyd came to the line of scrimmage, he noticed the Pokes were aligned to stop a play up the middle. Boyd barked a different play to his teammates—a quarterback option right—at the line of scrimmage. He took the snap, faked a handoff to Carpenter and scooted to his right. Seeing defenders swarming in on him, he decided a pitch out might lose yards, so he faked the lateral to Sandefer. Boyd then slanted off right tackle, reversed his direction and followed a crimson wall of blockers to the end zone. McDaniel booted the extra point, and the Sooners gained the deciding advantage with five minutes to go.

OU's defense held the Pokes on their next possession, and Wood punted to the Sooner 18-yard line. Oklahoma's offense was unable to run out the clock despite being whistled for a delay of game. Baker's punt rolled out of bounds at the OU 40 with 10 seconds on the clock.

Soergel lobbed the ball to Rundle, who caught it and was immediately tackled at the 15 when time expired.

The Sooners rushed for 175 yards and passed for 21. The Cowboys had 187 total yards.

The slim margin dropped the Big Red to fifth in the AP poll. Their Orange Bowl foe, Syracuse won eight of nine games and was ranked ninth. The Orangemen scored an average of 26 points per game, and the defense yielded an average of 6.6 points per game, including two shutouts.

Baker had too many absences from his classes and was not allowed to play in the game. Under Big Eight Conference regulations, he would be eligible to play, but Wilkinson did not believe it would be ethical for him to participate. This drew criticism from some fans, but Wilkinson would not relent.

The Sooner skipper made another bold move by shaking up his backfield several days before kickoff. He elevated third-string quarterback Cornell to starter, and Sandefer replaced Jimmy Carpenter at left halfback. Both had looked sharp in practices, and Wilkinson thought they would give his offense more punch after viewing films of the Orangemen.

His premonition was right as Oklahoma scored three fast and furious touchdowns to drop Syracuse, 21-6, before 75,281 fans on a sunny Miami afternoon. Two scores came in the first 12 minutes.

The Sooners took two plays to score on their first possession early in the first quarter. Cornell returned a Syracuse punt to the OU 48. Gautt took Cornell's lateral and swept around right end for 10 yards to the SU 42. The next play was similar but to the left side. Gautt picked up key blocks from Thompson and Rector and shot to the end zone. The Orangemen batted down Cornell's two-point pass.

Syracuse later advanced to the OU 26, then Harrison jolted Tom Stephens causing a fumble, and Harrison smothered the ball on his 19. Cornell gained two yards to the 21 on first down. On the next play, Hobby hurled a pass to Coyle at the 35, and Coyle sprinted 65 more yards to complete the 79-yard scoring play. Sandefer tossed a pass to Hobby for the two-point conversion and a 14-0 lead.

Early in the third period, Hobby fielded Tom Gilburg's punt and sailed 40 yards to the end zone. Boyd converted the extra point, and Oklahoma held a 21-0 lead.

The Orangemen drove 69 yards in eight plays to erase their goose egg.

Oklahoma rolled up 12 first downs, 152 rushing yards and passed for 93 more. Syracuse gained 18 first downs and 311 total yards. Gautt gained 94 yards on six carries for an average of 15.7 yards each time he touched the ball, which is a school record for highest rushing average in a bowl game.

UPI named Harrison Lineman of the Year and he was the only Sooner to receive All-America honors. Coyle, Jennings, Lewis, Corbitt and Gautt joined him on the All-Big Eight first team.

1958 Season Record: 10-1-0

Big Eight Conference: 6-0-0 (Champions)

Date	Opponent	Result	Score
September 27	WEST VIRGINIA	W	47-14
October 4	OREGON	W	6-0
October 11	Texas at Dallas	L	15-14
October 18	at Kansas	W	43-0
October 25	KANSAS STATE	W	40-6
November 1	at Colorado	W	23-7
November 8	at Iowa State	W	20-0
November 15	MISSOURI	W	39-0
November 22	NEBRASKA	W	40-7
November 29	at Oklahoma State	W	7-0
January 1	Syracuse*	W	21-6

*Orange Bowl at Miami, FL

1959

Lack of depth and inexperience were concerns for the 1959 Sooner squad. Six linemen and five backs returned from the prior year's first two units. Bud Wilkinson said the '59 squad was not as quick but still had enough speed to make another conference title run. The Sooners won their 14th straight conference title but lost a conference game for the first time since 1946.

Wilkinson deployed the first two units often, which allowed his players ample playing experience.

Tackle Gilmer Lewis and guards Jim Davis and Jerry Thompson had cracked the starting lineup late in the 1958 campaign. All three returned to anchor the front wall along with end Wahoo McDaniel, who again would be handling punting duties.

Halfback Brewster Hobby and fullback Prentice Gautt returned to start in the backfield, along with seasoned veterans Bobby Boyd at quarterback and Jimmy Carpenter at halfback. Carpenter was hindered with a ruptured muscle behind his right thigh. He would be hampered with the injury during preseason practices, and the injury forced him to sit out the last nine games after the injury flared up again in the season opener. Gautt had knee surgery in the off season but was ready for the opener at Northwestern.

Guard Leon Cross, who worked his way into the starting lineup, tore a knee ligament during a scrimmage one week before the season opener. Cross offered to relinquish his scholarship, believing he should earn it. "Bud wouldn't hear of it," he recalled, stating that Coach Wilkinson wanted Cross to not give up on getting a good education. Phil Lohmann moved into the starting left guard slot.

The team endured an unpleasant flight in a rainstorm to Evanston, Illinois, two days before the kickoff against Northwestern. The dinner at Chez Paree, a Chicago nightclub, on Thursday night was even more unpleasant. Several players and assistant coach Jimmy Harris had complained of stomach pains and nausea after finishing their dinners. The players had eaten the fruit cocktail that accompanied the dinner. The players who did not eat the fruit cocktail had no ill effects. Some of the stricken players were briefly hospitalized.

OU president Dr. George Cross wrote in his book *Presidents Can't Punt* that some sports writers speculated that the food had been "deliberately treated to produce illness" to handicap the Sooner squad.

Dr. Herman Bundesen, president of the Chicago Board of Health, said other patrons of the restaurant had eaten the fruit cocktail and did not receive food poisoning. He attributed the Sooners' illnesses to food poisoning at the hotel, where they ate earlier in the day, or to a virus. Bundesen reported tests were negative for poison.

Dr. Edward Press, health commissioner in Evanston, said the turkey sandwiches eaten for lunch that day tested positive for stapholocci, a bacteria that may cause illness usually within one-half to two hours after ingestion. Coach Harris and the players were stricken seven hours after they had eaten lunch. Dr. Mike Willard, OU's team physician, disagreed with their reports, stating that Harris ate lunch with the coaches in a separate room from the players, and that Harris did not eat a turkey sandwich.

"There was much talk about extensive investigations being made and tests to be run on the contents of the players' stomachs," Cross wrote in his book. "But nothing came of it all, because the containers with the stomach contents mysteriously disappeared."

Harold Keith, in his book *47 Straight*, wrote that he learned from a Nashville sports editor that the point spread had plummeted from six to three points in OU's favor two days before the game. The editor asked Keith why the spread had dropped. Keith did not know the reason for the sudden change.

"Why did the odds on Oklahoma change so suddenly Thursday afternoon prior to the food poisoning three hours later?" Keith wrote in his book. "Gamblers had somehow penetrated the supper club's security and adulterated the fruit cocktail. The Chicago police showed very little interest in the matter."

The team was weak by Saturday's kickoff on September 26 and did not appear sharp as evidenced by numerous mistakes.

No. 10 Northwestern handed No. 2 Oklahoma its worst loss in 14 years, 45-13, and the worst loss in Wilkinson's 12 years as head coach. A crowd of 55,432 endured another heavy rainstorm, which provided poor visibility for players and fans from the second quarter to the final gun. A national television (NBC) audience witnessed the Big Red debacle.

The Big Red lost five of 11 fumbles, and Northwestern cashed in on three of them. The Wildcats also capitalized on a blocked punt, a poor punt and an intercepted lateral. The Sooners twice marched inside the NU 20 but surrendered on downs. The Cats scored twice in the first three minutes after blocking McDaniels' punt and after Bobby Cornell's nine-yard punt to midfield.

Trailing 13-0, the Sooners got on board early in the second period with a 55-yard drive. At the NU seven, Boyd lateraled to Jimmy Carpenter, who passed a scoring strike to Brewster Hobby. Jim Davis converted the extra point.

Northwestern scored four touchdowns in the second half, three in the final stanza.

Jackie Holt scored on a three-yard run midway through the fourth quarter to cap a 50-yard march for OU. Holt was stopped short of the goal line on his run for two points.

The Sooners rolled up 213 rushing yards and passed for 93. Northwestern picked up and 283 total yards.

Jimmy Carpenter suffered a recurring pulled muscle, and Mike McClellan replaced him at left halfback for the rest of the year.

OU disappeared from the AP Top 20, but rebounded with a 42-12 victory over 0-2 Colorado the next week in Norman. The Sooners were unranked for the first time since early 1951.

Boyd scored three touchdowns and added a two-point conversion for 20 of Oklahoma's points. The Sooners scored on four of their first five possessions and rolled to a 42-0 lead before the Buffaloes got on the board twice in the fourth quarter against the third string.

The Sooners hammered out 25 first downs, 15 Sooners carried the football for 309 yards and OU passed for 187 yards more. Colorado gained 383 total yards.

OU returned to the AP poll at 13th, but had an uphill battle the next week with No. 4 Texas (3-0) waiting in the wings. The Longhorns had defeated their first three opponents (Nebraska, Maryland and California) by a combined 89-0.

Hobby and guard Billy Jack Moore were sidelined with an injury. Texas also was without the services of its starting halfback Bobby Gurwitz and tackle Dick Jones.

The Sooners led, 12-0, but saw the lead slip away as the Steers came from behind in the fourth period for a 19-12 decision before a sold-out Cotton Bowl throng of 75,504 and a regional television (NBC) audience. The Big Red passed only three times in the game, one went for a touchdown, and the other two went into the hands of Longhorns.

Holt recovered a Steer fumble at the UT 32 to set up the first OU score three plays later. On third-and-one at the 23, Cornell faked a handoff to Ronnie Hartline and hurled a scoring strike to Holt. Wilkinson devised the play earlier in the week to force the Steer defense to focus on the fullback. Jim Davis missed the conversion.

The Sooners marched 59 yards in seven plays on their next possession for a 12-0 lead. Facing fourth-and-inches at the Texas 38, Boyd took the snap, scooted laterally along the line, then popped a last-second lateral to David Carpenter, who dashed down the sideline for the score. Gautt threw the key block to open a lane to the end zone. Gautt was stopped short of the goal line on the two-point attempt.

The Steers drove 72 yards to score midway through the second stanza and marched 62 yards for a 13-12 lead on their next series.

Texas recovered Hartline's fumble on the UT 37 midway in the fourth period and scored three plays later. Interceptions ended Oklahoma's hopes for a comeback.

The Sooners rushed for 284 yards, and the only completed pass gained 23 yards. Texas rolled up 309 total yards.

Again OU fell out of the AP poll. The Sooners again bounced back with a big victory. The Sooners pounded 2-2 Missouri, 23-0, on October 17 in Columbia.

The only highlight of the scoreless first period was McDaniel's 74-yard punt late in the quarter, which put the Tigers in a hole and led to an interception moments later. Holt picked off the pass and returned it nine yards to the MU 36 to set up the first score.

Six plays later at the six, Boyd's pitch was high to McClellan, but the halfback speared it and scooted into the end zone. McDaniel's conversion was low.

The Sooners later advanced 66 yards to the Tigers' four but had to settle for Davis' 25-yard field goal for a 9-0 advantage. OU drove 78 yards in 14 plays to take a 17-0 lead early in the fourth stanza. Hobby scored the two-point conversion and also sparked the drive with a 21-yard run to the MU 13.

Missouri marched to the OU 33 late in the game but stalled, and Oklahoma took over at its 34. The Sooners drove the distance in 15 plays for the final tally. The second unit moved the team to the MU 22, then the third unit took over. On fourth-and-goal, quarterback Bob Page scored from the three-yard line. He was stopped short on his two-point attempt.

Oklahoma piled up 188 rushing yards and passed for 74. The Tigers gained 221 total yards.

The victory popped OU back into the AP poll at No. 18. The Sooners returned home and squeaked out a 7-6 win over Kansas before a homecoming crowd of 51,013 in a game marred by a total of nine fumbles. OU lost three of four, and the Jayhawks lost three of five.

The 3-2 Jayhawks were on a roll with three straight wins after dropping the first two of the season. Kansas stacked nine men on the line in hopes of slowing down OU's rushing attack. They succeeded in the first half, limiting the Sooners to 69 yards. The Big Red gained 164 yards in the second half but failed to cross the goal line.

Boyd's 44-yard punt return to the KU 36 sparked the only Sooner touchdown midway in the second period. Boyd ignited the seven-play scoring drive with a 13-yard scamper to the Jayhawks' 23. Six plays later, he sneaked the ball across for the score, and Davis converted for a 7-0 lead.

OU lost a chance to increase the lead after moving to the KU three early in the third quarter. The Sooners faked a field goal, and

Boyd's pass to Ronnie Payne in the end zone grazed Payne's fingertips. Kansas took over on the three, and John Hadl punted his team out of a hole. His kick totaled 94 yards all the way to the OU two-yard line for a Big Eight record. Hadl punted eight times in the game for a 51-yard average.

Late in the third stanza, the Hawks' third-string halfback, Dave Harris, stunned the crowd with a 40-yard touchdown run. David Carpenter had a chance to stop the speedy halfback inside the OU 25, but Harris shifted and Carpenter missed him. Crimson fans breathed a sight of relief when the two-point play failed. The pass bounced off of an official.

Neither team threatened in the final period. Oklahoma rushed for 233 yards and passed for only 36. Kansas collected 154 total yards.

For the first time, since he took the reins at Oklahoma, Wilkinson lost his first conference game on October 31. And for the first time in those baker dozen years, Wilkinson had three losses in one season. Nebraska defeated the 19th-ranked Sooners, 25-21, in Lincoln and ended OU's 74-game undefeated streak in conference play and 16-year supremacy over the Huskers.

Oklahoma took the opening kickoff and marched 72 yards to score in seven plays. Gautt scored his first TD of the year with a two-yard run, and Davis converted the first of three extra points. Nebraska fans must have thought: "Oh, no, here we go again."

But the Huskers put together a 57-yard scoring drive at the end of the first stanza, topping it off early in the second. The two-point try failed, and OU held a 7-6 margin.

Nebraska blocked Cornell's punt, and Leroy Zentic scooped up the ball and raced 36 yards to the end zone. The extra point was wide, but Nebraska held a 12-7 lead.

The Sooners retaliated with a 56-yard TD march to take a 14-12 lead. Jerry Tillery fumbled the kickoff return, but Payne recovered at the OU 27 and advanced to the 44. Cornell sliced through right guard for the six-yard score eight plays later.

Ron Meade booted a 22-yard field goal to give the Huskers the lead for good at 15-14 early in the third period. Nebraska scored 10 more points in the fourth quarter.

Gautt scored his second touchdown minutes later on a three-yard run to cut the deficit to 25-21. Nebraska scored 10 more points in the fourth quarter. Oklahoma had one last chance, but Boyd's desperation fourth-down pass was intercepted in the end zone.

OU gained 240 rushing yards and passed for 100 more. Nebraska picked up 161 total yards.

"We must be doing a poor job of coaching," Wilkinson said afterwards. "The reason I say that is if we were doing a good job, we wouldn't continue to make the kind of errors we do."

Wilkinson pointed out the mistakes that cost the team a victory then told his charges: "I don't ask you to win. All I ask you to do is play as well as you can. That's all. If you'd just do that, I'd be the happiest guy in the world ... even if we lost."

"I guess we didn't fight hard enough," said Holt.

The Sooners slipped out of the national ranking again but would return at the end of the season after beating the rest of their foes.

As they had done earlier in the season, the Sooners responded to a loss with a 36-0 drubbing of 1-6 Kansas State the next week in Manhattan. Wilkinson had promoted five sophomores to the starting lineup; four to the line—Jim Byerly at center, Karl Milstead to

right guard, Tom Cox to right tackle and Ron Payne to right end. McClellan was elevated to starting right halfback.

Oklahoma sputtered in the first half, blowing drives deep into K-State territory. A 44-yard march late in the first stanza gave the Big Red its only points of the first half. Holt scored in a four-yard run to cap the five-play drive, and Davis toed the conversion.

Three interceptions in the second half (two in the third quarter) ignited a 29-point second-half explosion. Davis picked off one at the KS 40 and returned it 37 yards to the three. Two plays later Hartline bolted across from the two and also added the extra point.

Cornell snared the second pick off moments later and returned it four yards to the Wildcats' 33. Two plays and a penalty later, Hartline scored from the 20, but his conversion sailed wide.

The lead swelled to 28-0 midway through the fourth period as Boyd scored from about a foot away to cap a 52-yard drive in six plays. Dick Carpenter carried for the two-point conversion.

Bennett Watts was the star for the Sooners in the final score, which came 76 seconds later. He intercepted the Cats' pass, returned it four yards to the KS 28, scored four plays later, and added the two-point conversion.

OU amassed 329 yards rushing and passed for 119. Hartline picked up 102 yards in 12 carries. The Wildcats were held to 115 total yards and never advanced past the OU 36-yard line.

The Sooners stepped outside the conference to host 4-2 Army on November 14. Davis' interception in the end zone thwarted an Army comeback as Oklahoma edged the Cadets, 28-20, before a crowd of 62,472, which was sold out since August. OU cashed in on four Cadet turnovers (one interception and three fumbles).

The Cadets took command early with a 6-0 lead and appeared to be headed for another score, but center Byerly stalled them with an interception at the OU 30. That pick off was a momentum-breaker as the Sooners rolled back 70 yards to take a 7-6 lead in 16 plays. On fourth-and-goal inside the one, Boyd moved to his right, then pitched back to McClellan, who scooted across. Davis converted the first of four extra points. The Sooners barely maintained possession on an earlier fourth-down situation. With three yards needed for a first down at the Army 22, Boyd kept for four yards, but he fumbled one yard backwards, and Thompson saved it from going back any further.

A turnover gave the Big Red a chance to raise the lead midway through the second stanza. McDaniel's punt pinned the Cadets deep at their seven. Davis rattled G.W. Kirschenbauer, who fumbled back toward the end zone. End Paul Benien smothered it for a touchdown.

Army marched downfield to score after the kickoff. Quarterback Joe Caldwell shredded the OU defense along the way and tossed the scoring strike to cut the OU lead to 14-12. McDaniel broke up Caldwell's pass for two points.

On the final play of the first half, Cox was twice knocked off his feet in pursuit of Caldwell. Both times he got up, and he finally nailed Caldwell for an eight-yard loss.

Hobby pounced on an Army fumble on the Cadets' nine-yard line moments after the second-half kickoff. Boyd scored on a keeper around right end on the next play for a 21-12 advantage.

Thompson smothered another Cadet fumble at the Army 20 on the last play of the third stanza. Four plays later, Boyd sneaked across from the one.

Army responded with a 70-yard scoring march in five plays to cut its deficit to 28-20 after the two-point conversion.

The Cadets advanced to the OU 24 late in the game, but Davis stole Caldwell's pass in the end zone.

It's a Fact

OU's record in the 1950s: 93-10-2 (.895) best of all decades by any team.

The Sooners rushed for 201 yards and did not complete a pass in five tries. Army picked up 388 total yards. Caldwell completed one-half of his 42 passing attempts for 297 yards.

The Sooners scored on their first three possessions en route to a 35-12 victory over Iowa State the following week in Norman. The 7-2 Cyclones had their best record in 10 years, but they were no match for OU. Iowa State had the nation's top two rushers. Fullback Tom Watkins was No. 1 with 775 yards, and halfback Dwight Nichols followed with 711 yards. The Big Red defense held Watkins to 68 yards and Nichols to 35.

The Cyclones recovered an Oklahoma fumble on the first play after the opening kickoff. Iowa State moved to the OU 26, but McDaniel intercepted and returned the ball to the OU 41. Nine plays later, Boyd faked a handoff and slashed through right tackle for a 23-yard touchdown. Davis converted the first of five extra points to run his streak to nine.

Jackie Holt's 56-yard punt return to the Cyclones' 34 set up the next Oklahoma score. A five-yard penalty did not deter Oklahoma as Hartline scored from the three-yard line 10 plays later.

Iowa State answered with a 54-yard scoring drive that carried into the second period, but McDaniel blocked the conversion. OU rolled right back with a 74-yard, 16-play scoring punch after the kickoff. Hobby took Boyd's lateral and scored from the four. The drive, which included a five-yard penalty against the Sooners, consumed nearly six and one-half minutes.

The Cyclones marched 62 yards to score after the second-half kickoff. Byerly swatted down the pass for two points.

Minutes later Boyd intercepted a Cyclone pass at the OU 30, but a clipping penalty set the ball back to the 18. The Sooners launched an 82-yard drive, which carried over into the fourth period. Gautt's two-yard plunge capped the 20-play drive three seconds into the fourth period. Gautt, who rushed for 110 yards in 14 carries, added a 48-yard touchdown late in the game.

Oklahoma rushed for 348 yards and failed to complete a pass in two tries. The Sooners punted only once. Iowa State gained 229 total yards.

Two fourth-quarter touchdowns enabled No. 17 OU to overcome a 7-3 deficit to defeat Oklahoma State, 17-7, before a throng of 54,136 the next week in Norman.

OSU's Tony Banfield intercepted two of Boyd's passes at the goal line to squelch two Sooner advances in the first half.

The Cowboys took a 7-0 lead midway through the second stanza. Hartline recovered a Poke fumble minutes later on the OSU 10-yard line, but the Sooners had to settle for Davis' 21-yard field goal 53 seconds before halftime.

The Sooners threatened twice in the third period but could not score. A drive to the Pokes' three in the third period ended when Gautt, who played with a pulled muscle, was stopped inches short of a first down. Oklahoma moved to the OSU three after Byerly recovered a fumble at his 43, but Boyd fumbled it away.

The Big Red finally got uncorked with a 56-yard scoring march late in the third quarter and into the fourth. From the OSU 31, Hartline blasted up the middle, slanted to his left and dashed to the end zone. Davis converted the first of two extra points.

OSU punted to the OU 19 on its next series, and the Sooners rolled 81 yards in 16 plays and consumed 10 minutes for the final tally. Boyd's one-yard plunge came with 1:30 remaining in the game.

Oklahoma gained 290 yards rushing and 58 passing. OSU picked up only five first downs and 128 total yards. The Cowboys were held to 21 yards in the second half.

Thompson was named All-America, and Boyd and Gautt joined him on the All-Big Eight first team.

Oklahoma finished 15th and out of the AP top ten for the first time since 1948.

1959 Season Record: 7-3-0
Big Eight Conference: 5-1-0 (Champions)

Date	Opponent	Result	Score
September 26	at Northwestern	L	45-13
October 3	COLORADO	W	42-12
October 10	Texas at Dallas	L	19-12
October 17	at Misouri	W	23-0
October 24	KANSAS	W	7-6
October 31	at Nebraska	L	25-21
November 7	at Kansas State	W	36-0
November 14	ARMY	W	28-20
November 21	IOWA STATE	W	35-12
November 28	OKLAHOMA STATE	W	17-7

1960 - 1969

1960

The National Collegiate Athletic Association placed the University of Oklahoma on indefinite probation, which prohibited the football team from participating in bowl games and on television. The NCAA's investigation revealed that Bill Jennings, former OU assistant coach and player, had received funds for recruiting athletes between 1952 and 1954. Jennings, who had moved on to coach the Nebraska Cornhuskers, denied receiving money from Arthur L. Wood, an Oklahoma City accountant and OU booster.

Wood admitted that he and Jennings collaborated to help recruit players for the football team in 1953, to defray travel expenses for prospective athletes. Wood said it was not a violation of NCAA rules. Jennings denied receiving money from Wood.

The NCAA would drop the probation charges against OU if Wood divulged financial details of the recruiting fund. Wood refused to reveal the details, stating that doing so would be professionally unethical and result in a $1,000 fine or one year's imprisonment, according to federal statutes. Wood later moved to Nevada.

Some reports indicated that Jennings reported the incident to the NCAA. In his book, *Presidents Can't Punt*, OU president Dr. George Cross wrote: "In the spring of 1958 the Department of Intercollegiate Athletics received a phone call, a letter, and a visit from a Nebraska high school athlete named Monte Kiffen, who expressed an interest in attending the University of Oklahoma. Later, by invitation from the boy's parents, OU coaches visited with the family at his home. After the visit, Wilkinson said that he had encouraged the boy to attend the University of Nebraska.

"Wilkinson later received a letter from Jennings in which he said that if Kiffen enrolled at Oklahoma, it would be necessary for him, Jennings, to give information to the NCAA which he had withheld at the time of the investigation in 1954."

The NCAA denied Jennings was the tipster and stated the confidential source was not connected to any NCAA institution. Kiffen, a tackle, lettered three years for the Cornhuskers.

The probation made it difficult to recruit quality athletes for the football team. The 1960 line was void of depth, and the backfield lacked the speed Sooner teams are accustomed to.

The right side of the starting line was solid with the return of guards Karl Milstead and Tom Cox and end Jerry Tillery. Jim Byerly returned at center, but newcomers lined up at the left side—guard Leon Cross, tackle Billy White and end Ron Payne. Cross was sidelined with an injury and missed the entire 1959 season, and Payne had plenty of playing experience as a second-string end a year previous.

Three-fourths of the starting backfield had familiar faces. Jimmy Carpenter returned after missing the last nine games in 1959 with a thigh muscle injury and was moved from halfback to quarterback. Mike McClellan returned to his left halfback spot. Ronnie Hartline had plenty of playing time as backup fullback. Don Dickey assumed the right halfback slot.

Wilkinson's Sooners suffered their worst season with a 3-6-1 record, and for the first time in 15 years, OU did not win a conference title. That honor went to Missouri in 1960. The Big Red was not ranked nationally all season long.

The Sooners opened the season on September 25 against 14th-ranked Northwestern. The game was played under sunny skies and temperature in the mid-70s, a contrast to the rainstorm in Evanston, Illinois, a year before. Unfortunately the outcome was not a contrast to the previous year, as Oklahoma dropped a 19-3 decision before a home crowd of 61,289.

OU took a 3-0 lead on its first possession with Milstead's 35-yard field goal late in the first period. Dick Thornton tossed two TD passes, and Mike Stock booted two field goals to lead the Wildcats' 19 unanswered points. The Sooners lost three fumbles, and Northwestern scored off two of them.

Wilkinson had suffered only his third home loss. Northwestern had more total yards, 311-225.

The Big Red rebounded with a 15-14 victory over Pittsburgh the following week in Norman. An early fourth-quarter touchdown and two-point conversion enabled OU to prevail.

The Sooners took a 7-0 lead late in the first stanza on Carpenter's 30-yard scoring strike to Payne and Milstead's conversion. The 0-1-1 Panthers scored one touchdown in each of the middle periods. Oklahoma's defense stalled Pitt on one drive to the one-yard line in the third quarter.

Early in the fourth stanza, end Phil Lohmann blocked a Panther punt, and tackle Marshall York smothered the pigskin on the Pitt 12. Coach Wilkinson sent in his second unit that scored moments later. Fullback Gary Wylie picked up seven yards to the five, and Don Dickey ripped through right tackle for the score.

Crimson fans wondered what the heck was going on when the kicking team lined up for the extra point. The special unit fooled everyone as Bennett Watts took the snap and rolled to his right and into the end zone for a 15-14 lead.

Pittsburgh had had more total yards (372-315). Hartline rushed for 91 yards to lead Oklahoma's 250-yard ground attack.

The Sooners needed a win under their belts heading to Dallas for the October 8 showdown with 15th-ranked Texas. Wilkinson suffered his second shutout in 140 games as the 3-1 Longhorns hammered Oklahoma, 24-0, before a sellout throng of 75,504 at the Cotton Bowl.

Texas also was the first team to defeat OU three times under Wilkinson's regime. The Sooners could not sustain a single drive and never reached past the Steers' 43-yard line in the first half. The Horns took a 3-0 lead on a 33-yard field goal in the first period and scored a touchdown minutes later after Jimmy Carpenter's pass interference gave Texas a 38-yard penalty. The fine moved the ball to the OU 21, and the Longhorns scored four plays later.

Payne's short punt to the UT 37 set up the next Texas touchdown midway through the third quarter.

The Sooners advanced to the Steers' three early in the fourth stanza, but blew a chance to score by fumbling. Minutes later, Texas' Jerry Culpepper intercepted Carpenter's pass and sailed 78 yards for the final tally.

Texas outgained OU in total yards, 234-209.

Kansas, at 3-1, was off to its best start in eight years and was ranked ninth nationally when the Sooners came to town the following week. Oklahoma escaped with a 13-all tie.

The Big Red rolled to a 7-0 lead on its opening possession. McClellan's one-yard touchdown run capped a 65-yard, 12-play drive, and Milstead converted.

John Hadl scored on a three-yard run to cut the Sooner lead to 7-6, but John Suder's conversion sailed wide to the right.

Oklahoma took the second-half kickoff and marched 76 yards for a touchdown. Carpenter hurled a 13-yard scoring strike to cap the 13-play drive. The Jayhawks blocked Milstead's conversion.

Bert Coan's nine-yard TD run with 5:24 remaining in the game pulled Kansas within one point. Kansas head coach Jack Mitchell opted for a tie with the extra point, and Suder made the conversion.

The Hawks moved into OU territory and with 24 seconds left, Suder shanked a 24-yard field goal. Boos rained down from the stands as both teams departed for the locker room, apparently in protest to the Jayhawks not electing to go for the two-point conversion.

Kansas picked up more total yards (324-239). Hartline, who played the second half with an injured knee, picked up 110 yards in 20 carries for the Sooners, and Hadl completed 11 of 18 passes for 182 yards for the Jayhawks.

Hartline was sidelined with an injury for the Kansas State tilt on October 22, and Monte Deere replaced him at fullback. Carpenter and Don Dickey each scored two touchdowns as the Sooners plastered the 1-4 Wildcats, 49-7, in Norman. The victory marked Wilkinson's 123rd win, surpassing Bennie Owen as the all-time winningest coach in Sooner football history.

OU scored on four of its first five possessions (twice in the first two periods) for a 29-0 halftime advantage. Of the seven touchdowns in the game, the starters and second string scored three apiece, and the third unit added one.

The Sooners rushed for 405 yards and passed for only 45. Fourteen Sooners carried the ball, Gary Wylie led with 71 yards, and eight others gained at least 22 yards. The defense held the Cats to five first downs and 69 total yards.

Colorado defeated the Sooners for the first time in conference action with a 7-0 victory on October 29 before a crowd of 45,281 in Boulder. The 4-1 Buffaloes ended Oklahoma's seven-game winning streak in the series.

The Buffaloes missed a field goal early, after recovering Carpenter's fumble on the game's first play. Up to that point, the Sooners failed to move past their own 29-yard line, gained only 26 total yards and failed to gain a first down.

Colorado marched 61 yards in 15 plays for the game's only score midway in the second period. On fourth-and-goal at the one, Chuck Weiss plowed ahead for the touchdown, and the Buffs converted the extra point.

Oklahoma finally got moving to the CU 25 after the ensuing kickoff but surrendered on downs.

Watts raced 65 yards to the CU 17 late in the fourth quarter, but the Buff defense stiffened and OU surrendered on the four-yard line.

Colorado rolled up 267 total yards. The Sooners gained only seven first downs and 193 total yards.

Iowa State defeated Oklahoma for the first time in 24 years with a 10-6 win the next week in Ames. The Sooners had owned the Cyclones by winning 33 of the last 34 games, save for a tie in 1936.

The Big Red had trouble moving against the 4-3 Cyclones, except for one sustained drive for a 6-0 lead early in the second stanza. McClellan scored on a five-yard run to complete a 71-yard march in 18 plays. Ronnie Hartline's conversion veered wide right.

Iowa State capitalized on two Sooner mistakes in the second half. The Cyclones recovered Melvin Sandersfeld's fumble in the third period at the OU 26, but had to settle for a field goal to cut the Oklahoma lead to 6-3.

Iowa State drove 68 yards after recovering Bill Meacham's fumble for the deciding score with 3:04 remaining in the game.

OU had more total yards, 252-210. Hartline picked up 154 yards on 22 carries, and Dave Hoppmann gained 162 yards on the ground for the Cyclones.

Undefeated Missouri (8-0) rolled into Norman the next week and rolled out with a 41-19 victory before a homecoming throng of 53,369. Oklahoma trailed, 24-6, early in the second period and scored twice in the third quarter to open the door for a possible comeback, but the second-ranked Tigers scored 17 points in the fourth stanza to put the game away.

OU rushed for 323 yards against the nation's leading rushing defense. Missouri yielded only 72.9 yards per game in the first eight contests. The Tigers also led the nation in scoring defense with 4.6 points per game and had not yielded a rushing touchdown but gave up three rushing touchdowns in the game.

Four Sooner fumbles led to two Mizzou touchdowns and two field goals.

The Big Red took a 6-0 lead on McClellan's 70-yard TD run on the game's third play, but Hartline missed the extra point. The Tigers answered with a 67-yard scoring march to tie the game at 6-6.

Missouri scored twice early in the second period to take a 24-6 lead. Sandersfeld's 36-yard TD minutes later drew the Sooners within 12 points, but Hartline again missed the conversion. OU later advanced to the MU 30, but the Tigers squelched the threat with an interception.

McClellan picked off a Missouri pass at the OU 29 early in the third quarter, and the Sooners wheeled 71 yards in 16 plays to trail, 24-19. Carpenter scored on a one-yard run, and Hartline toed the conversion.

A short punt late in third stanza gave the Sooners hope at the Tigers' 35 but blew any chance of a comeback by fumbling on fourth down. Mizzou scored on a 60-yard run in one play early in the fourth period, and the rout was on. The Tigers added a field goal and another touchdown over the next five minutes.

Bobby Cornell scored on a seven-yard run for Oklahoma, but a penalty against OU erased the play, and the game ended. Referee Pierce Astle told Wilkinson after the game that Cornell's touchdown should have counted, and the final score should have been 41-25.

Missouri's captain declined the backfield-in-motion penalty assessed against the Sooners, but according to NCAA rules a game cannot end on a penalty. If the penalty was accepted, the ball would

---

1960 Season Record: 3-6-1
Big Eight Conference: 2-4-1 (Fifth)

Date	Opponent	Result	Score
September 24	NORTHWESTERN	L	19-3
October 1	PITTSBURGH	W	15-14
October 8	Texas at Dallas	L	24-0
October 15	at Kansas	T	13-13
October 22	KANSAS STATE	W	49-7
October 29	at Colorado	L	7-0
November 5	at Iowa State	L	10-6
November 12	MISSOURI	L	41-19
November 19	NEBRASKA	L	17-14
November 26	at Oklahoma State	W	17-6

have been moved back five yards, and Oklahoma would run one more play. Since it was declined, OU should have been awarded the touchdown and allowed to kick the extra point.

Mizzou halfback Norris Stevenson rushed for 169 yards, the most ever yielded by Oklahoma's defense that year. McClellan rushed for 118 yards for the Sooners. The Tigers jumped to No. 1 in the AP poll but lost to Kansas the next week.

Oklahoma collected 348 total yards, eight yards more than the Tigers.

Ron Meade kicked a 28-yard field goal with 1:38 remaining to lift Nebraska to a 17-14 victory over the Sooners on November 19 before a crowd of 42,701 in Norman.

The Sooners wasted a 14-0 lead as the 4-5 Cornhuskers scored 17 unanswered points. McClellan's 23-yard scoring jaunt and Milstead's conversion put OU ahead 7-0 early in the first quarter. The lead swelled to 14-0 early in the second stanza when Carpenter hurled a 49-yard scoring strike to Payne, and Milstead converted. Oklahoma had a chance to pull away with a touchdown just before halftime, but Carpenter fumbled on the NU one-yard line.

Nebraska fullback Bill Thornton scored a touchdown in each of the final two periods. The Huskers made a two-point conversion after the first TD, but Payne blocked the conversion after the second score.

Nebraska recovered Carpenter's fumble midway in the fourth stanza at the NU 22 and drove to the game-winning field goal.

Both teams gained 16 first downs apiece, but OU led in total yards (309-241). Cornell averaged 52 yards on two punts for OU.

The Sooners could salvage the season with a win over intrastate rival Oklahoma State the next week and end the season with a 3-6-1 record. OU defeated the 3-6 Cowboys, 17-6, on a warm afternoon (77 degrees) in Stillwater.

The Big Red rolled 78 yards in 12 plays on its second possession for a 7-0 lead. Sandersfeld completed the drive with a five-yard run, and Milstead toed the first of two conversions. The lead remained through the rest of the first half.

The Sooners took the second-half kickoff and marched 76 yards in 16 plays for a 14-0 advantage. Cornell's three-yard TD run came seven minutes and 40 seconds after the drive began.

The Pokes marched 56 yards for their only score early in the fourth period, but White stopped quarterback Jim Elliott short of the goal line on the two-point conversion.

Minutes later, Cox intercepted an OSU pass at his 17 and returned it to the OU 34. The Sooners moved to the Pokes' seven but settled for Hartline's 24-yard field goal with less than two minutes to go.

OU gained more total yards (352-216). Cornell's 77 yards led the Sooners' 290-yard ground attack.

White was named to the Big Eight Conference's first team for the only postseason honor among the Sooners.

1961

John F. Kennedy, the youngest man ever elected president of the United States, was inaugurated in January. Two months later he named Bud Wilkinson as special consultant to the President's Council on Physical Fitness. Wilkinson also founded Coach of the Year Football Clinics with Michigan State head coach Duffy Daugherty. Wilkinson's obligation did not interfere with his duties as Oklahoma head coach and athletic director, but it did take away some of his time in recruiting new athletes. He traveled to 12 cities to conduct the clinics on weekends during the off-season.

Injuries, on the other hand, interfered with his plans to rebuild a winning team from the 3-6-1 record in 1960. Halfback Don Dickey suffered a knee injury in a preseason practice and was sidelined for the year. A nagging knee injury forced halfback Bill Meacham, an alternate halfback a year ago, to quit the team. In addition, center Jim Byerly left school for a full-time job, and three other promising newcomers became scholastically ineligible. The injury bug continued to rear its ugly head throughout the season.

All-conference tackle Billy White returned to anchor the line along with tackle Tom Cox end Ronnie Payne, guard Leon Cross and center Wayne Lee. Jimmy Carpenter was switched from quarterback to left halfback, where he played in 1958. Monte Deere, Bob Page and Bill Van Burkleo battled for the quarterback slot. All three would alternate as the starter throughout the season. Mike McClellan returned to the right halfback slot, and Phil Lohmann was moved from end to fullback.

On January 9, the NCAA removed OU from probation after Arthur Wood revealed some of his records to the association and without violating Internal Revenue Codes. Wood was an Oklahoma City attorney who collaborated with former assistant Bill Jennings to help recruit players for the football team in 1953 to defray travel expenses for prospective athletes.

The 1961 Sooners split the season with a 5-5 record—five consecutive losses followed by five straight wins for one of the greatest turnarounds in college football history.

The Sooners opened the season on September 30 with a 19-6 loss to Notre Dame in South Bend on national (ABC) TV. Approximately 7,000 Sooner fans were among the 54,906 in attendance.

Notre Dame took a 6-0 lead late in the first quarter, and Gary Wylie returned the ensuing kickoff 25 yards to set up Oklahoma's retaliation. Jackie Cowan scored on a four-yard run seven plays later, but Karl Milstead misfired on the conversion.

Irish halfback Mike Lund scored a touchdown in both the second and fourth periods to put the game away.

Notre Dame also had more total yards (282-222).

Injuries knocked three Sooners—McClellan, Cox, and Milstead—out of the game. Fortunately, all three returned the next week when Iowa State visited Norman. The 2-0 Cyclones got the job done with three first-quarter TDs for a 21-15 victory before a crowd of 45,365. Tailback Ozzie Clay scored twice for Iowa State.

Oklahoma blocked and tackled poorly and lost five of six fumbles but did manage to put two touchdowns on the board. Bob Page engineered both TD drives and scored the first one himself on a three-yard run to cap a 76-yard march in the second stanza. Carpenter also scored from three yards out to top an 80-yard drive.

OU gained more total yards (302-217).

Fourth-ranked Texas had walloped its first three opponents by a combined score of 111-25. Oklahoma was no different, as the Longhorns dropped the Sooners, 28-7, on October 14 before a packed Cotton Bowl crowd of 75,504.

An interception, a blocked punt, and a fumble led to three of the four Texas touchdowns, and the Horns scored all four in the first 35 and one-half minutes of action. Quarterback Mike Cotton scored twice for the Steers.

The Big Red had trouble generating drives with poor pitchouts and never advanced past midfield in the first half. The Sooners put together their only scoring drive in the fourth period to erase the goose egg off their end of the scoreboard.

Lohmann scored on a one-yard run to cap a 68-yard march in nine plays, and George Jarman converted the seventh point.

Lohmann's 36-yard run and McClellan's 14-yard jaunt sparked the drive.

Both teams each gained 12 first downs, but Texas picked up more total yards (272-212).

The 1-2-1 Kansas Jayhawks edged the Sooners, 10-0, the following week in Norman. The Jayhawks controlled the football in the first half, running 40 plays to 27 for Oklahoma, yet had only a 7-0 lead to show for it.

John Hadl zinged a 30-yard scoring strike to end Larry Allen midway through the second quarter for the 7-0 advantage after the conversion.

Kansas had a chance to add insult to injury by later advancing to the OU eight-yard line, but the OU defense stiffened. Wylie belted Jay Roberts after catching a short pass, forcing the Jayhawk to fumble. Halfback Paul Lea recovered for the Sooners.

Minutes later, Lea returned a punt 44 yards to the KU 13, but Oklahoma could only muster five yards, and Milstead shanked a 26-yard field goal try.

KU's Wallace Barnes missed a field goal just before halftime, but he connected on a 35-yarder in the third stanza for the final tally.

Kansas collected 289 total yards. The Jayhawks defense held the OU to six first downs and 98 total yards.

Colorado, 4-0 and ranked 10th in the nation, scored twice during a three-minute span early in the fourth period to overcome a 14-10 deficit and defeat the Sooners, 22-14, before a homecoming crowd of 45,117 in Norman.

The Big Red took a 7-0 lead on a 60-yard march in 10 plays after the Buffs failed to gain a first down on a fake field goal. Page scored on a one-yard plunge, Jarman kicked the first of two conversions, and OU led an opponent for the first time all year.

OU punter Geary Taylor's nine-yard punt to the CU 38 set up the Buffs' tying touchdown in seven plays early in the second period. Colorado took a 10-7 lead on a 35-yard field goal early in the third quarter, but the Sooners answered with a 94-yard march in 16 plays. Page hurled a 19-yard scoring strike to end John Porterfield to finish the drive that consumed nearly nine minutes.

Colorado responded with a 50-yard drive to take a 16-14 lead early in the fourth stanza on fullback Loren Schweninger's one-yard run. The Sooners failed to cover the ensuing kickoff, and the Buffs recovered at the OU 31. Five plays later, Schweninger scored from the six-yard line.

Colorado collected more total yards (324-221). The Buffaloes returned to Boulder with their first ever victory in Norman.

Coach Wilkinson said in the locker room after the game that his squad would not lose another game.

"I remember Bud stood before the players and said, 'We're going to win the rest of them,'" Cross recalled years later.

Wilkinson also revealed his forecast on his weekly coach's show several days later. During the next five weeks he made believers out of anyone who doubted him.

Kansas State was the first victim on November 4. The Wildcats had won their first two games, but dropped the next four. The Sooners prevailed, 17-6, in Manhattan.

Phil Lohmann was held out of the game with a slight injury. Dick Beattie replaced him and rushed for 120 yards. He was Oklahoma's second leading ground gainer behind McClellan's 137.

Page scored on a one-yard plunge early in the second period to cap a 76-yard journey in 11 plays. Jarman toed the first of two conversions. The big play in the drive came when the Wildcats were penalized for unsportsmanlike conduct after stopping Beattie short on a third-down run to the OU 44. The penalty gave the Big Red new life at the KS 37.

Jarman added a 27-yard field goal 33 seconds before intermission.

The Cats cut their deficit to 10-6 with a touchdown with less than six minutes remaining in the game. Sixty-nine seconds later, McClellan exploded for an 82-yard TD run.

OU rushed for 352 yards and passed for 38. The defense held K-State to six first downs and 149 total yards.

Okay, so the skeptics believed OU should have beaten Kansas State, after all, the Sooners have owned them since 1937. And the Wildcats were the weakest link in the Big Eight Conference.

But defending conference champ Missouri, 5-1-1 and ranked 10th, was next. The Tigers shut out four of their opponents, yielded an average of 4.8 points per game and ranked eighth nationally in rushing and total defense. Many believed there was no way Oklahoma was going to get its second victory, especially with the game in Columbia.

OU defeated Mizzou, 7-0, before a throng of 45,146 under drizzly skies. The only score came about midway through the second quarter. Lee smothered a Tiger fumble on the MU 43. Seven plays later at the Tigers' 15, Carpenter took the snap, rolled out and fired a five-yard pass to McClellan, who dashed the final 10 yards to the end zone. Jarman toed the extra point.

The Tigers advanced to the OU one-yard line early in the first stanza, but tackle Dennis Ward dropped Vince Turner for a one-yard loss on fourth down. Oklahoma drove to the MU nine-yard line early in the second period, but Carpenter was tackled for a one-yard loss on fourth down.

Missouri missed a 27-yard field goal attempt just before halftime, and Jarman missed one from the same distance in the final quarter. Deere intercepted a Tiger pass on the OU 10 with three minutes remaining, to squelch the possibility of any comeback.

The Sooners defeated Army (6-2), 14-8, on November 18 at New York City's Yankee Stadium. Sooner assistant coach Bob Ward scouted a couple of Army games earlier in the season and noticed that the Cadet defense was slow returning to the line of scrimmage after breaking the huddle. Ward's report inspired Wilkinson to install the hurry-up offense for the game.

The go-go offense allowed the Big Red to take a 7-0 lead early in the first stanza. On the third play of their second possession, the Sooners lined up without a huddle and snapped the ball as the Cadets just broke from their huddle. Carpenter took the snap and pitched out to McClellan, who sailed 74 yards down the sideline. Jarman kicked the first of two conversions.

Oklahoma took a 14-0 lead late in the third period with a 76-yard march in 14 plays. Page capped the drive with a one-yard run. Army was twice flagged for jumping offside after OU reached the Cadets' one-yard line and prior to Page's TD. Lohmann sparked the drive with a 24-yard run to the Army 42 and Page followed it with a 17-yard sprint on the next play.

The Cadets answered with a 56-yard scoring drive and a two-point conversion early in the fourth quarter but had nothing left the rest of the game.

OU gained 258 total yards, five more than Army. The Cadets were ranked ninth in total offense before the Oklahoma game but were held to 88 yards below their average.

The Sooners erupted for three second-half touchdowns to overcome a 14-0 deficit and defeat Nebraska, 21-14, on November 25 in Lincoln.

Oklahoma's offense sputtered with only 89 total yards in the first half, then exploded for 238 in the final 30 minutes. The defense also tightened in the second half, allowing no first downs and two total yards after yielding 10 first downs and 219 total yards in the first half. The 3-5-1 Cornhuskers possessed the ball only four times and never advanced past their 34-yard line in the final 30 minutes.

Nebraska marched 65 and 66 yards for two touchdowns in the first and second stanzas, and it could have been worse except for a couple of dropped passes by Husker receivers in the second period.

The Sooners rolled 70 yards in three plays after the second-half kickoff for their first score. Carpenter zipped a nine-yard pass to McClellan, and Lohmann carried for 16 to the NU 45. A roughing penalty on the Huskers moved the ball to the 30, then Page completed a 30-yard scoring strike to Payne. Jarman converted the first of three extra points.

Monte Deere's 19-yard punt return to the Huskers' 33 set up the tying touchdown late in the third quarter, and Carpenter scored on a nine-yard run seven plays later.

Moments later, Nebraska pinned the Sooners deep with a punt to the OU two. Oklahoma drove the length of the field for the go-ahead touchdown. The 98-yard march consumed 25 plays and 13 minutes off the clock. At the NU one, Page pitched to Carpenter, who scooted around right end for the score with 5:01 remaining in the game.

Oklahoma and Oklahoma State entered the season finale with identical 4-5 records, and the winner would savor a non-losing season. The Sooners completed Wilkinson's prediction with a 21-13 victory the following week before a crowd of 52,598 in Norman.

The Cowboys got on board first with a safety when Bob Adcock nailed Carpenter in the end zone. The Pokes failed to cover Taylor's free kick, and end Jim McCoy pounced on it for the Sooners at the OSU 43. Ten plays later Page faked a lateral and skirted through right tackle for a two-yard touchdown. Jarman converted the first of two extra points for a 7-2 lead. Jarman kicked a perfect 14 of 14 conversions on the season. Facing fourth-and-one from the Pokes' 15, Carpenter kept the drive alive with a seven-yard run for a first down.

The Cowboys booted a 22-yard field goal early in the second period moments after recovering Carpenter's fumble at the OU 22.

Page scored from the one-yard line early in the third stanza, eight plays after the Sooners recovered a fumble at the OSU 39.

The Cowboys marched to the OU 13 after the kickoff. Halfback Jim Dillard carried toward the goal line on the next play but fumbled just before he crossed, and Lee recovered for a touchback.

The Big Red then marched 80 yards for a 21-5 lead in seven plays. Carpenter scored on a six-yard run, and Milstead, who replaced the slightly injured Jarman, converted. McClellan sparked

the drive with a 49-yard dash to the OSU 23 on the drive's second play.

The Pokes scored moments after recovering Page's fumble on the OU 43.

The Sooners gained more total yards (313-272).

"From the standpoint of effort and courage, this team is as good as any I've had at Oklahoma," Coach Wilkinson said after the game. "This team has just refused to quit at any time, and there have been plenty of times it could have."

Over in the corner a chalkboard read: "Comeback Kids."

Associated Press sportscasters and sports editors voted the Sooners' rally in November the greatest comeback of any sport in 1961.

OU finished fourth in the Big Eight Conference, and for the second straight year White was the lone Sooner on the all-conference first unit.

1962

Bud Wilkinson had to rebuild his squad in 1962 as center Wayne Lee and guard Leon Cross were the only returning starters. Yet the Sooner skipper had a stable of talented, young, but inexperienced hulks like tackles Ralph Neely and Dennis Ward to work in the line. The backfield consisted mostly of new faces such as Paul Lea, Virgil Boll and Jim Grisham.

A newcomer who would step to the forefront was perhaps the most controversial character in Sooner football history. He might have been one of the greatest fullbacks in Sooner football lore, but his career was short-lived. Some believed his name fit his character and his running style to a T—Looney. Joe Don Looney.

Looney had attended Texas and Texas Christian University (both on track scholarships) and Cameron Junior College in Lawton prior to transferring to Oklahoma. He was named a juco All-American at Cameron for his football talents and scored the winning touchdown for the Aggies in the junior college championship game. Courted heavily by the Sooners, Southern California, Alabama and Kentucky, Looney chose the Sooners, since he was a Texas native from Fort Worth and wanted to beat the Texas Longhorns, his former school, in the worst way.

While attending Cameron, Looney told his head football coach, LeRoy Montgomery, that he was going to OU. Montgomery told him he would not fit into Bud Wilkinson's rigid discipline philosophy. Defiant, sometimes with a smart-aleck attitude, Looney had difficulty following orders. The fleet-footed Looney was late to practices, did not want to pose for publicity pictures and rarely went to the training room for treatment when necessary.

Looney was the first junior college transfer to play for Wilkinson since Dan Anderegg in 1947, Wilkinson's first year as head coach. The '62 Sooners were short on experienced fullbacks. Leon Cross later recalled that Wilkinson accepted Looney on the team in an attempt to "quickly reverse" the losing trend of the previous seasons. However, Looney was slow in adjusting to Wilkinson's offense. A few days prior to the season opener against Syracuse, Wilkinson said Looney was making progress and would soon be a key player. Wilkinson's prediction came true earlier than expected.

The Sooners suffered a setback a week before the first game. Starting quarterback Tommy Pannell broke an ankle in practice. Wilkinson had no choice but to start one of his unseasoned substitutes—sophomores Norman Smith, Bobby Page and senior Monte Deere, who played mostly at defensive halfback but had some playing time under center in 1961.

1961 Season Record: 5-5-0			
Big Eight Conference: 4-3-0 (Fourth)			
Date	**Opponent**	**Result**	**Score**
September 30	at Notre Dame	L	19-6
October 7	IOWA STATE	L	21-15
October 14	Texas at Dallas	L	28-7
October 21	KANSAS	L	10-0
October 28	COLORADO	L	22-14
November 4	at Kansas State	W	17-6
November 11	at Missouri	W	7-0
November 18	Army*	W	14-8
November 25	at Nebraska	W	21-14
December 2	OKLAHOMA STATE	W	21-13
*Game played in New York, NY			

After a 1-2 start, OU breezed through the conference portion of the schedule, won the Big Eight crown and a bid to the Orange Bowl.

Sooner Magic: 'Just Give Me the Damn Ball'

Syracuse was coming off an 8-3 season, winning five of their final six games including a victory in the Liberty Bowl. Oklahoma won the only previous encounter between both teams—21-6 in the 1959 Orange Bowl. The Sooners defeated the Orangemen, 7-3, on September 22 before a crowd of 54,600 on a hot and steamy afternoon on Owen Field.

Both teams battled to a scoreless first quarter. The Orangemen marched to the OU 31-yard line in the game's first possession. A fourth-down gamble failed when quarterback Robert Lelli threw an incomplete pass. The Sooners then marched to the SU 22, but John Humphreys picked off Smith's pass in the end zone.

Syracuse made another threat following OU's short punt, but Sooner end Rick McCurdy squelched it with a fumble recovery at the OU 30.

The Big Red stalled and punted to the SU 31. The Orangemen drove to the OU 19. The Sooner defense stiffened, and SU head coach Ben Swartzwalder sent in his field goal unit. Thomas Mango's 35-yard attempt was a low, line drive that barely cleared the crossbar. Syracuse held a 3-0 lead with less than a minute before halftime.

At halftime a University of Oklahoma ROTC unit raised a new 20-by-36-foot American flag on the pole at the south end of Memorial Stadium. Called a "Garrison Flag," it was one of the largest flags displayed in the country. The OU band struck "Stars and Stripes Forever," and patriotism flowed through the spectators, a feeling that would be overshadowed by the exhilaration of a flash late in the game.

The Sooners' only threat in the third stanza ended with George Jarman's missed field goal try from 46 yards out.

The Orangemen drove to the OU eight-yard line late in the third period and into the fourth. A muffed handoff by Lelli was recovered by McCurdy. Three times Syracuse had moved deep into OU territory, and three times they turned the ball over. McCurdy recovered all three fumbles.

Joe Don Looney led the team with 852 yards rushing, caught seven passes for 199 yards and scored 10 TDs. He also punted for the Sooners and averaged 43.4 yards through the season, best in the nation that year. He was also named All-America along with Leon Cross and Wayne Lee. Those three were also the only ones named to the All-Big Eight Conference team.

After losing to Texas in 1963, a battle of No.1 vs. No.2, Wilkinson dismissed Looney from the squad. His rebellious attitude interrupted team morale, which Wilkinson told an AP writer, "had ceased to exist."

Cross was an assistant on Wilkinson's staff in 1963. He said that Looney's challenge to authority had become a major problem. Cross remembered Wilkinson saying to the staff that Looney was the first player to be ejected from the team.

"He [Wilkinson] said he couldn't sacrifice the whole team for one guy," Cross recalled. "Everybody agreed."

The New York Giants made Looney the ninth draft pick in 1964, but after a short stint with several National Football League teams, he also experienced trouble in Vietnam and had a failed marriage. He then found inner peace by joining the Hindu religion.

Twenty-six years after his stellar season at Oklahoma, Looney died from injuries sustained in a motorcycle accident in southwestern Texas.

OU moved to its 35, then halfback Jackie Cowan raced down the west sideline for 46 yards to the SU 19. He tried to keep his balance but was smacked out of bounds by Brian Howard. Wilkinson installed his third unit, which bungled the next few plays with penalty flags flying on nearly every play. The Sooners were flagged 15 yards for clipping and twice for jumping offside ending up back at the SU 42-yard line. McCurdy punted to the SU 16.

The Orangemen hammered out a ground attack into OU territory, but faced fourth-and-one at the 28. A first down would have guaranteed a victory for the Orangemen with a chance to run more time off the clock, or even worse, score again. But center Johnny Tatum and Lea, who also played safety, stopped fullback Jim Nance one foot short of the target.

The Sooners took over with four minutes left in the game. Looney, who had been sitting on the bench all afternoon, told Wilkinson to put him in the game and he would "win the game." Wilkinson relented and sent Looney in.

Cowan carried around right end seven yards. Third-string fullback Looney picked up another five yards for a first down at the OU 40. The SU defense then halted Cowan at the line for no gain.

In the huddle Looney told Deere to give him the ball on an outside sweep, and he would score. On the next play, Deere and Looney swung to the left, and Deere pitched the ball to his fullback. Looney then cut inside where he appeared to be stopped for a two-yard gain, swamped by Syracuse defenders. Suddenly he sprang free and sprinted down the east sideline into the end zone. Halfback Gary Wylie threw a key block on SU's Don King, the only defender with a chance of catching Looney.

"I was blocking a linebacker and I heard the crowd cheering and looked up and there was Looney hauling ass," Cross recalled years later.

The new star was mobbed by teammates in the end zone. Jarman's kick was successful, and the Sooners took a 7-3 advantage with 2:07 remaining in the game.

"I knew what play I was going to call when I went into the huddle," Deere said in the locker room afterwards. "But as I was walking up to the huddle, Looney leaned over and told me, 'Just give me the damn ball and I'll score a touchdown.' So I just gave him the ball."

"Maybe it's better to be lucky than good," Wilkinson said in the locker room, his shirt drenched from the stifling heat. "Syracuse moved the ball well, but our defense didn't let them score a touchdown. Those two critical fumbles really hurt them. I think perhaps the key play was when we stopped them on fourth down at the 27 with less than a yard to go. If they had kept the ball with only four minutes to go, it could have been a different story."

Syracuse lost its first season opener for the first time since 1955. The Sooners picked up 15 first downs, one less than the Orangemen, but had the total yardage edge (269-248).

Notre Dame continued its dominance over the Sooners with a 13-7 victory on September 29 before a homecoming throng of 60,640 in Norman. The Fighting Irish won their third straight victory over Oklahoma and fifth in the six-game series.

The Irish took the opening kickoff and marched 69 yards in 10 plays to take a 7-0 lead. Oklahoma later swept 58 yards in 10 plays to tie the game with 38 seconds left in the first period. Paul Lea slashed through left tackle from the one-yard line to cap the drive, and Jarman converted. Grisham ignited the drive with a 16-yard gain on the first play.

A short Irish punt gave OU possession on the ND 34, but the Big Red stalled after reaching the 16, and Jarman shanked a 35-yard field goal attempt. Moments later Notre Dame recovered Deere's fumble on the OU 37 and moved to the 16, but halfback Charles Mayhue intercepted in the end zone.

Notre Dame rolled 89 yards in 19 plays after the second-half kickoff for the final tally. The drive consumed 11 and one-half minutes, but a missed conversion gave the Sooners hope for a possible comeback, just six points down.

Sooner end John Flynn recovered quarterback Daryl Lamonica's fumble on the Irish 34 with 2:27 remaining in the game, but Smith threw an interception on the next play to squelch any comeback effort.

Notre Dame collected more total yards, 280-212.

The Sooners had two weeks to prepare for second-ranked Texas. The 3-0 Longhorns had averaged 31 points per game in the first three, but the Big Red defense held them well below the average in a losing 9-6 effort before 75,504 at the Cotton Bowl.

All of the scoring occurred in the second stanza. The Steers cashed in on two Oklahoma miscues to score twice. Texas recovered Deere's wild pitch out on the OU 27 and drove to the 16 but had to settle for a 26-yard field goal.

Late in the second period, Lea fumbled Deere's lateral on the OU goal line, and Texas center Perry McWilliams grabbed the ball and tumbled into the end zone. Guard Larry Vermillion swatted down the pass for two points.

The Sooners covered 87 yards in five plays to score after the ensuing kickoff. The first three plays gained 14 yards to the OU 27. Coach Wilkinson then put in alternates Ron Fletcher and Lance Rentzel at the halfback slots, and they came through with flying (crimson) colors. Fletcher had played only one down against Syracuse. Rentzel did not play in the first two games due to a broken hand.

Smith lateraled to Fletcher who rolled right and zinged a 38-yard bomb to Rentzel to the UT 34. On the next play, it was the same play, except Fletcher rolled left and hurled a scoring strike to Rentzel who slipped behind the Texas secondary with 44 seconds until intermission. The Horns blocked Jarman's conversion.

The Sooners advanced 58 yards to the UT 20 in the third stanza, but on fourth-and-three, Looney was stopped a yard short of a first down.

A fist fight broke out among fans on the field with four seconds remaining, but the police soon had the melee under control.

Texas gained 12 first downs, twice as many as OU, and the Steers picked up more total yards, 219-170.

The Sooners opened the conference slate on October 20 with a 13-7 victory over 3-1 Kansas in Lawrence. OU scored twice in the second half to overcome a 7-0 deficit.

The Jayhawks took the opening kickoff and rolled to a 7-0 lead. The Big Red lost two chances to take the lead in the second quarter. Oklahoma drove to the KU five but surrendered on downs when Looney was stopped a yard short of a first down. Lea returned

a punt 31 yards to the KU 19, but the Jayhawk defense stiffened, and Butch Metcalf missed a 39-yard field-goal try.

Early in the third period, Lea's 17-yard punt return to his 39 set up the tying score one play later. Looney shot through left tackle, followed two key blocks and zoomed to the end zone. Metcalf converted for the tie.

Deere's three-yard run capped a 56-yard drive early in the fourth stanza, but the extra-point snap was muffed.

The Jayhawks did not threaten the rest of the way and did not penetrate past the OU 45 after their touchdown.

OU collected more total yards (237-211). Looney rushed for 115 yards on 19 carries and averaged 42.7 yards on nine punts.

Oklahoma raised its season record to 3-2 with a 47-0 blasting of Kansas State the next week in Norman. The Sooners scored on all four of their first-half possessions; seven of their first eight.

Looney was switched from fullback to left halfback and scored two touchdowns. The fullback duo of Grisham and Bud Dempsey also scored two apiece, and Rentzel added one TD.

OU scored off drives of 75, 56, 23, one, 49, 50 and 78 yards. Looney had the longest touchdown run from seven yards out. All others came from two yards or closer. Looney's first score put OU ahead 7-0 midway in the first period, then the Sooners scored twice in a span of four minutes and 19 seconds beginning late in the first quarter and carrying into the second.

The Wildcats advanced past midfield three times, and their deepest penetration was to the OU 44, but on third-and-one John Porterfield dumped Willis Crenshaw for a 17-yard loss.

The one-yard scoring drive came early in the second quarter on Wes Skidgel's 39-yard punt return to inches short of the goal line. Rentzel plowed over on the next play for a 28-0 lead.

A total of 55 Sooners got in on the action, and 13 backs carried the ball. Seven of them gained 23 yards or more. OU gained 33 first downs, rushed for 488 yards and passed for 44 more. The Big Red defense held the Cats to six first downs and 96 total yards. Oklahoma never punted in the game but was flagged 12 times for 123 yards.

The Sooners thrashed Colorado, 62-0, on November 3 in Boulder, the worst whipping an OU team has ever put on Colorado. The 1-5 Buffaloes also suffered their worst loss since a 76-0 blasting by Texas in 1946.

Oklahoma moved downfield in a flash of lightning, using five plays or less on seven of its nine touchdowns. Each scoring drive averaged 56 yards in four plays.

Deere hurled three TD passes, two to Boll (32 and 83 yards) and one to Flynn for 41 yards. Looney, who rushed 11 times for 180 yards, scored twice, including an 84-yard dash. Dempsey also scored twice.

OU averaged 9.9 yards each time it touched the football, including 346 rushing yards and 289 passing yards. Deere completed five of six passes for 246 yards. Boll caught three for 143 yards, and Flynn also shagged three for 128 yards. Looney averaged 46.5 yards on three punts. Colorado collected 205 total yards.

The Sooners scored on their first six possessions to demolish 3-4 Iowa State, 41-0, the following week in Ames.

Looney, who rushed for 135 yards, scored three touchdowns on runs of 16, 39 and one yard. He also tossed an 18-yard scoring strike to McCurdy. Grisham also scored two TDs. Metcalf converted on five of six conversions, and the Cyclones blocked the sixth attempt.

Iowa State never advanced past the OU 39 in the game. Oklahoma rushed for 285 yards and passed for 111 more. Deere

Charley Mayhue jolts Missouri back Johnny Roland for a 12-yard loss, forcing Roland to fumble in the third quarter. (*OU Athletics*)

completed nine of 13 passes for 98 yards. The Cyclones gained 148 total yards.

Missouri, ranked sixth nationally with a record of 7-0-1, invaded Norman on November 17. The Tigers hadn't lost in their last 10 outings dating back to the prior year and led the nation in rushing offense with a 287.6 yard-per-game average.

The Sooners held Mizzou to 111 rushing yards and defeated the Tigers, 13-0, before a throng of 62,181.

Looney returned the opening kickoff 41 yards to his 45 but fumbled. Fortunately teammate Newt Burton was nearby and smothered it on the 44. Five plays later Looney took Deere's lateral and scooted three yards into the end zone. Metcalf converted for a 7-0 lead. Deere sparked the drive with a 42-yard pass to Boll to the MU nine.

The Tigers' Jerry Wallach recovered Lea's fumble and returned it 11 yards to the OU 29 in the second stanza. Johnny Roland picked up a first down on the 19 but fumbled, and Lea pounced on it on the 16.

OU marched 80 yards in 13 plays and consumed seven minutes for the final tally after the second-half kickoff. Deere sliced through right guard and bulled over from the one-yard line. Metcalf's conversion sailed wide. Grisham gained 30 yards on the drive's first play and later picked up 10 yards for a crucial first down to the MU 27.

The Tigers moved to the OU 30 after the kickoff, but stalled when Mayhue dropped Roland for a 12-yard loss and forced the Tigers back to fumble.

Looney nailed Missouri deep with a 60-yard punt to the Tigers' three, and Roland brought it back three yards to the six. The Tigers advanced to the OU 12, where they faced fourth-and-seven. Roland rolled out to pass, but Porterfield popped him for a five-yard loss.

OU had more total yards (263-143). Grisham rushed for 113 yards, and Looney averaged 44.6 yards on five punts.

OU entered the AP poll at No. 10.

Deere completed three touchdown passes to lead the Sooners past Nebraska, 34-6, on November 24 in Norman. His three TD strikes were the most in one game in the 42-game series. The victory clinched the Sooners' first conference championship in three years and 21st in Oklahoma football history.

The Big Red of the south scored on four of its first five possessions. The Cornhuskers could go nowhere on their first possession, and Flynn blocked the punt. The ball rolled backwards, and Burton recovered it on the one-yard line. Grisham scooted through left guard on the next play, and Metcalf converted the first of four extra points.

Deere connected two TD aerials to Porterfield and one to Allen Baumgardner over the next two periods. Nebraska scored in the third stanza to snap the Sooners' streak of not allowing a touchdown in 21 quarters.

Smith tossed a 14-yard TD pass to Wylie in the fourth period. OU rolled up more total yards (373-198).

The eighth-ranked Sooners defeated 4-5 Oklahoma State, 37-6, the next week in Stillwater and completed the Big Eight Conference slate with a 7-0 record and an invitation to the Orange Bowl.

Oklahoma rolled to a 24-0 lead in the first nine and one-half minutes. Grisham, who rushed for 156 yards scored twice—a one-yard run and a 40-yard interception return. Deere scored once on a 22-yard run and passed two scoring strikes.

Both teams scored in the final 56 seconds, with the Sooners getting the final tally on Deere's 17-yard TD strike to Looney.

The Sooners rushed for 463 yards and passed for 137 more. OSU picked up 268 yards.

Alabama, OU's Orange Bowl opponent, was ranked fifth with a 9-1 record, losing only to Georgia Tech by one point in the ninth week of the season. Bear Bryant coached the Crimson Tide to the Orange Bowl bid and the matchup would be his second against Wilkinson. Bryant's Kentucky team spoiled Oklahoma's perfect season with a win in the 1951 Sugar Bowl. The OU-Bama match up was the first between both teams.

The Tide's two stars were quarterback Joe Namath and center Lee Roy Jordan. Namath finished the season by completing 52 percent of his passes for 1,192 yards and 13 touchdowns.

A crowd of 73,380 turned out for the 29th Orange Bowl, which included 8,400 Sooner rooters and President Kennedy. The president visited the Sooner locker room to extend his well wishes before the game and participated in the pregame coin toss.

1962 Season Record: 8-3-0
Big Eight Conference: 7-0-0 (Champions)

Date	Opponent	Result	Score
September 22	SYRACUSE	W	7-3
September 29	NOTRE DAME	L	13-7
October 13	Texas at Dallas	L	9-6
October 20	at Kansas	W	13-7
October 27	KANSAS STATE	W	47-0
November 3	at Colorado	W	62-0
November 10	at Iowa State	W	41-0
November 17	MISSOURI	W	13-0
November 24	NEBRASKA	W	34-6
December 1	at Oklahoma State	W	37-6
January 1	Alabama*	L	17-0

*Orange Bowl at Miami, FL

The Sooners had no luck on New Year's Day as the Tide rolled to a 17-0 victory. Namath tossed one touchdown pass and had a long aerial to set up another score. The Bama defense pressured Monte Deere all afternoon. Jordan led the defensive assault with 31 tackles.

The Tide marched 61 yards in 10 plays on its second possession. Namath tossed a 25-yard scoring strike to end Richard Williamson, and Tim Davis converted the first of two extra points for a 7-0 lead.

Two fumbles by Grisham stalled Sooner scoring efforts. Grisham had separated his shoulder in practice the day before the game. Trainer Ken Rawlinson taped up Grisham's shoulder, but the fullback was limited in his flexibility. Minutes after the Tide touchdown, Fletcher's 56-yard bomb to Baumgardner moved Oklahoma to the Bama six. Grisham fumbled on the next play.

Alabama later fumbled on its 31, and Porterfield recovered. Moments later, Grisham burst for a 12-yard run to the six but fumbled again.

A 13-yard punt return to the OU 34 set up the next Tide touchdown in the second stanza. Cotton Clark scored three plays later on a 15-yard run. Namath's 21-yard pass to the 13 sparked the drive.

Looney's six-yard punt to the OU 33 led to Davis' 19-yard field goal late in the third quarter. The Sooners had drives to the Bama 16- and 10-yard lines stall in the fourth period.

The Crimson Tide picked up more first downs (15-10) and rushing yards (174-154), but the Oklahoma had more passing yards (106-86). Namath got all of Alabama's passing yards in a nine-of-17 effort. Grisham carried 28 times for 107 grueling yards.

The 8-3 Sooners finished the season ranked eighth in the nation. Cross, Lee and Looney were named All-Americans. Dennis Ward and Grisham joined them on the All-Big Eight Conference first team.

1963

Nineteen hundred sixty-three was a turning point in American history and for Oklahoma football. President John F. Kennedy was slain in November, and Bud Wilkinson would coach his final season at OU. Rumors had circulated that the Sooner skipper might hang up his whistle and enter politics, possibly running for the United States Senate in 1964.

Wilkinson denied any such talk as he prepared the Sooners for his 17th season at the helm. Nine players returned in the backfield and 17 on the front line. He said overall the 1963 squad was "better in recent years." Yet he was concerned about who would emerge as his starting quarterback and who would step up in the secondary.

Three sophomores battled for the starting quarterback job— Mike Ringer, John Hammond, and Tommy Pannell—along with senior Bobby Page. Ringer, the first sophomore ever to start for Wilkinson, got the nod before the season began, but an elbow injury sidelined him for the final eight games. Halfbacks Joe Don Looney and Virgil Boll and fullback Jim Grisham also returned.

The front wall included a slew of returning veterans—tackles George Stokes and Ralph Neely; guard Newt Burton; center John Garrett; and ends John Flynn, Rick McCurdy and John Porterfield were back. Some of the starters in the line in 1962—end John Flynn; guards Ed McQuarters and Larry Vermillion—were beaten out for starting positions, but they saw plenty of action and started in some games later in the season.

Charles Mayhue was the lone returnee in the secondary and George Jarman was back as placekicker.

Although Burton was the sole returning starter from a year ago, Porterfield and Neely were veteran backups in '62.

Eddie Crowder, Wilkinson's recruiting assistant for seven years, was hired as head coach at Colorado.

The fourth-ranked Sooners opened the season on September 21 with a 31-14 victory over Clemson in Norman.

The Tigers scored both of their touchdowns during the first four minutes early in the second stanza for a 14-0 lead. Boll's 27-yard punt return to the CU 28 set up the first Sooner score minutes later. Grisham dashed 26 yards for the touchdown two plays later, and Jarman kicked the first of four conversions.

Boll again set up the next OU touchdown with a 30-yard punt return to his 46 early in the third period. Three plays later, Ringer lateraled to Lance Rentzel, who started left and reversed his field 49 yards to the end zone. Rentzel finished the game with 51 rushing yards on three carries.

Clemson was forced to punt on its next possession. Flynn crashed through and blocked the kick, and David Voiles scooped the pigskin off the ground and carried it to the CU five. Ringer scored from the one two plays later for a 21-14 Sooner lead.

Moments later, guard Robert Vardeman recovered a Tiger fumble on the CU 14. The Tiger defense held, and Jarman nailed a 28-yard field goal.

Necly scored his first collegiate touchdown on a tackle-eligible play early in the fourth quarter. Ringer sailed a 20-yard pass to his left tackle, who was wide open in the end zone.

Clemson had more total yards (285-212).

The third-ranked Sooners traveled to Los Angeles to try to topple Southern California, the nation's No.1-ranked team a week later. The Trojans, defending national champions, were riding a 12-game win streak, including a 14-0 victory over Colorado in the first game of 1963. The Sooners did depose of the nation's leader with a 17-12 victory before a throng of 52,245 at the L.A. Coliseum and a national (CBS) television audience. The temperature at game time was 106 degrees with 125 degrees recorded on the playing field.

USC coach John McKay wanted to move the kickoff to six hours later, a cooler time to play the game. Bud refused. The Sooners left most of their game gear in the locker room and limbered up in light pads and T-shirts before the game.

Both teams exchanged fumbles early in the first stanza. Jerry Goldsby smothered the USC muff on the OU 36, and the Big Red rolled downfield in 16 plays for a 7-0 lead. On third-and-nine at the Trojans' 19, Looney scored on a double reverse involving Ringer and Rentzel. Jarman converted the first of two extra points.

The Trojans answered with a 67-yard drive in 10 plays. Quarterback Pete Beathard tried to pick up a bobbled snap on the conversion, but Rick McCurdy stopped him cold as he tried to carry it in for two points.

Early in the second period, Carl McAdams killed McCurdy's punt on the USC three-yard line. The Trojans soon punted back to the OU 48. The Sooners then wheeled to a 14-6 lead in 10 plays. Ringer faked a handoff to Grisham and zipped four yards for the score.

USC advanced to the OU 23 after the kickoff, but Porterfield forced Beathard to fumble. The ball rolled back to the 44, where Burton smothered it for Oklahoma. OU moved from there to the USC 17 but had to settle for Jarman's 43-yard field goal with 58 seconds until intermission.

The Trojans blocked a Jarman field goal in the third quarter. USC marched 93 yards in 10 plays for the final tally in the game. The Sooner defense knocked down Beathard's two-point pass.

OU rolled up more total yards (360-239). Grisham rushed for 86 yards to lead Oklahoma's 307-yard ground attack.

The Sooners shot to the top of the polls and had two weeks to prepare for No. 2 Texas, undefeated at 3-0. The Longhorns defeated their first three opponents by a combined score of 104-14. Unfortunately the Sooners had two starters out for the game. Ringer cut his elbow after accidentally backing into a fan and was lost for the season. He injured the elbow before the USC game, but fluid buildup sidelined him for the rest of the season. Halfback Jackie Cowan was out for the Texas game with a sore back. Mayhue and Flynn also left the game with injuries in the second quarter.

The Steers totally manhandled the Sooners on October 12 with a 28-7 victory before 76,004 in the Cotton Bowl. The win extended the Longhorns' streak to six in a row over OU.

Texas dominated from the opening kickoff by marching 68 yards in 13 plays for a 7-0 lead. An 18-yard punt return to the OU 37 set up the Horns' 14-0 lead early in the second stanza. The lead shot to 21-0 after Texas recovered Rentzel's fumble on the OU 18.

The Big Red finally got on the board with a 52-yard, five-play drive that began with a 15-yard penalty against the Steers for popping Looney after he signaled for a fair catch on a punt. Hammond scored on a three-yard run and Jarman toed the conversion with 2:24 left in the third period.

Texas scored the final touchdown with 51 seconds remaining in the game. The Steers outgained OU, 253-190.

Looney was dismissed from the OU squad two days later for disciplinary reasons. "My biggest regret is that I allowed him to come back to the team this year," Coach Wilkinson said. Boll replaced Looney at left halfback.

Norman Smith scored two touchdowns to lead the No. 6 Sooners to a 21-18 squeaker over Kansas the following week in Norman.

The 2-2 Jayhawks took a 7-0 lead on Gale Sayers' 61-yard touchdown run midway through the first quarter. Minutes later, Mayhue intercepted a Kansas pass on the KU 24 and returned it to the 15. Smith scored on a five-yard run three plays later, and Jarman toed the first of three conversions to tie the game.

The Hawks took a 10-7 lead with a field goal in the second stanza. OU took the lead for good moments after Al Baumgardner shook the ball loose from Sayers, and Flynn recovered on the OU 47. Page tossed a 22-yard scoring strike to McCurdy to cap the 12-play drive.

Oklahoma took a 21-10 lead midway through the fourth period with a 53-yard, nine-play march. Smith capped the drive with a one-yard sneak. Cowan sparked the drive with a 16-yard run, and Grisham added 14 on another run.

The Jayhawks answered with a 56-yard drive after returning the kickoff 34 yards. Steve Renko tossed a seven-yard pass to Sayers, and the two hooked up again for the two-point play. The Sooners milked the final 1:28 off the clock.

Both teams picked up 15 first downs, but the Jayhawks had more total yards (312-296).

The No. 7 Sooners traveled to Manhattan, Kansas, on October 26 and left town with a 34-9 victory over 1-4 Kansas State. Grisham rushed for 152 yards and scored two touchdowns to lead the crimson assault.

The Wildcats took a 3-0 lead with a field goal moments after intercepting Page's pass. OU erupted for two touchdowns in an 86-second span late in the first quarter.

Grisham scored his first TD on a one-yard run to cap a 72-yard march in 10 plays, and Jarman converted. Rentzel sparked the drive with a 23-yard dash on triple reverse to the K-State nine.

Rentzel, who rushed five times for 84 yards (a 16.8-yard average) took a punt moments later at his 29 and sailed for a 71-yard TD. Voiles and Ron Harmon threw key blocks to free their teammate to

the end zone. Jarman missed the conversion for the first time in 12 attempts. He did not miss another all afternoon, but he did miss a 27-yard field goal just before halftime.

The Sooners drove 66 yards after the second-half kickoff to up their lead to 20-3. Page scored on a one-yard run, and Rentzel sparked the six-play drive with a 37-yard sprint to the KSU 25.

Larry Shields returned a punt 54 yards for a touchdown minutes later, but a clipping penalty wiped out the score and moved the ball back to the Cats' 49-yard line. OU still scored seven plays later when Cowan raced around right end from the four.

Midway through the fourth stanza, the Cats blocked Jarman's field-goal try and returned the ball 72 yards for a touchdown. Grisham bolted 56 yards for the final tally minutes later.

OU rushed for 441 yards and passed for 41. Kansas State had 160 total yards.

The Sooners inched up to sixth in the AP poll, then hammered 2-4 Colorado, 35-0 the next week before a homecoming throng of 49,402 in Norman. Crowder was the third Wilkinson assistant to drop his debut against his former mentor. Darrell Royal (Texas) and Bill Jennings (Nebraska) were the other two.

An injury sidelined Colorado's top halfback Bill Harris, which held the Buffs to little in the rushing department (35 yards). OU ran roughshod over their foe with 382 yards on the ground.

The Sooners had the only threat in the first period but came up empty with a fumble. However, they scored twice in a three-minute span in the second quarter. Rentzel scored on a six-yard run and Cowan from 13 yards out. Jarman did not miss a conversion in five tries.

The Big Red took the second-half kickoff and scored twice in the next three and one-half minutes. Cowan got his second TD on a 16-yard jaunt, and Page scored from the one.

Pannell guided the third team to the final tally and hurled a 16-yard scoring strike to halfback Joe Running in the fourth stanza.

The Buffs threatened with a 48-yard march to the OU 19 but ran out of gas. Oklahoma led in first downs (29-8) and total yards (486-123). Cowan picked up 121 yards in 10 carries.

No. 6 Oklahoma scored 17 points in the third period to overcome a 14-0 deficit and defeated Iowa State, 24-14, on November 9 in Norman. All of the game's points came in the middle two quarters.

Fans observe a moment of silence and prayer at the OU-Nebraska game, one of a handful of games that was not cancelled when President John F. Kennedy was assassinated. (© 1963, The Daily Oklahoman)

Fullback Tom Vaughn scored twice for the 4-3 Cyclones. Page's 27-yard pass to Harmon cut the lead to 14-7 late in the second stanza. Jarman converted the first of three extra points.

Glen Condren recovered an Iowa State fumble on the Iowa State 17 to set up the tying touchdown early in the third period. Grisham plowed over from the one-yard line seven plays later.

Boll's 55-yard punt return moments later set up Jarman's 23-yard field goal to give the Sooners the lead for good at 17-14. Boll returned another punt for a 46-yard touchdown before the third quarter expired.

Oklahoma rushed for only 137 yards and passed for 61. The Big Red defense held the Cyclones to six first downs, 69 rushing yards and six yards through the air.

Shields scored two touchdowns to guide the No. 5 Sooners to a 13-3 victory over 6-2 Missouri the following week in Columbia.

Oklahoma blew three chances to score in each of the first three quarters. Grisham fumbled on a fourth-down run on the Tigers' nine in the first stanza. The Sooners again advanced to the nine moments after Mayhue's interception in the second period, but Jarman shanked a 15-yard field-goal try. John Benien recovered a Missouri fumble at the Tigers' 36 in the third stanza, but the Sooners failed to convert a first down at the eight.

Shields, who also had two interceptions, was the man of the day. Late in the first period, he fielded a punt at his 35, sailed down the sideline and followed blocks by McQuarters and Condren to the end zone. The return was Shields' first score of the year. Jarman missed the conversion.

The Tigers kicked a field goal late in the second quarter.

OU moved 66 yards in 11 plays to the Mizzou two-yard line with less than a minute to play. On fourth-and-goal, Shields sliced through right tackle for the score, and Jarman converted.

OU collected 257 total yards, five more than the Tigers.

One day before No. 6 OU and No. 10 Nebraska (8-1) were to meet in Lincoln to decide the Big Eight championship and an Orange Bowl bid, President Kennedy was assassinated in Dallas. The Sooners learned of the news when they returned to their hotel after a morning practice. The news was shocking as it reverberated around the world, but even more so for the Sooners as most of the team had met Kennedy when he visited the OU locker room before the Orange Bowl in January.

Nebraska governor Frank Morrison conducted a telephone conference with governors of the other Big Eight states to discuss whether the league's slate of games should be played the following day.

Officials from the Big Eight, Nebraska and Oklahoma also held a teleconference to decide whether the game should be cancelled or postponed. Discussions lasted for four hours, and at 7:21 p.m. on November 22, the announcement came from Nebraska Chancellor Clifford Hardin's office that the game would be played.

Fullback Jim Grisham, No. 45, rushed for a school-record 218 yards and scored four touchdowns against Oklahoma State. (*OU Athletics*)

The decision was based on the fact that arrangements had been made for closed-circuit telecast of the Nebraska game in Omaha and Oklahoma City. The game was already sold out, and many fans had arrived in Lincoln. Oklahoma also had another game the following week against Oklahoma State.

Since the game was an important conference contest, it was impossible to reschedule without great expense and inconvenience. Wilkinson had telephoned the president's executive assistant, Ted Reardon, about possibly postponing the game. Reardon told him that Kennedy's family said the game should be played as scheduled.

"The regents believe the people of Nebraska wish to have the game played as scheduled," the Nebraska regents said in a statement. "The decision has been made after consultation with the president of the University of Oklahoma (Dr. George L. Cross), coaches Bob Devaney of Nebraska and Bud Wilkinson of Oklahoma, Nebraska Athletic Director Tippy Dye, Big Eight Executive Director Wayne Duke and Gov. Morrison. The Big Eight faculty representatives recommended that conference games be played."

Oklahoma vs. Nebraska was the only Big Eight game to be played. Other Big Eight games were cancelled or postponed. A total of 29 games nationwide were postponed to another date, and 11 were cancelled. Thirty games, including Oklahoma vs. Nebraska, were played.

Thirty-eight years later, the entire college football schedule and all sports contests were postponed for one weekend following 9/11.

The Huskers claimed their first conference title in 23 years with a 29-20 victory before a less than capacity crowd of 38,362 somber spectators.

Nebraska led 3-0 on a field goal in the first period, which remained through the first half and scored two touchdowns to lead 17-0 in the third stanza. Both teams combined for 29 points in the final quarter.

1963 Season Record: 8-2-0
Big Eight Conference: 6-1-0 (Second)

Date	Opponent	Result	Score
September 21	CLEMSON	W	31-14
September 28	at Southern California	W	17-12
October 12	Texas at Dallas	L	28-7
October 19	KANSAS	W	21-18
October 26	at Kansas State	W	34-9
November 2	COLORADO	W	35-0
November 9	IOWA STATE	W	24-14
November 16	at Missouri	W	13-3
November 23	at Nebraska	L	29-20
November 30	OKLAHOMA STATE	W	34-10

The Sooners did not cross midfield until the second stanza, and when they did, Jarman missed a field goal.

Oklahoma scored early in the final period on a 22-yard pass from Ronnie Fletcher to Flynn. Turnovers led to the four-TD barrage in the final 13 minutes. Nebraska cashed in on two interceptions to put the game away, 29-7. OU captalized on two Husker fumbles for two touchdowns. Wes Skidgel scored on a 27-yard run three plays later. Pannell tossed a 26-yard TD strike to Skidgel one play after Baumgardner recovered a fumble on the NU 26. Skidgel was stopped short the two-point run with 1:22 remaining.

Nebraska gained more total yards, 284-223.

The Sooners voted to decline a bowl bid several days later.

The No. 10 Sooners rebounded from the Nebraska loss with a 34-10 victory over 1-7 Oklahoma State on November 30 in Norman. Grisham scored four touchdowns and broke two team records. His 218-yard rushing performance was three yards more than Buck McPhail's single-game record set against Kansas in 1951. Grisham's numbers broke a new series record against the Cowboys, which was set by Buddy Leake's 167 yards against the Cowboys in 1951.

OU lost two opportunities to score in the first quarter. The Pokes blocked Butch Metcalf's field goal, and Smith fumbled after the Sooners reached the eight-yard line.

The Big Red finally got uncorked in the second period with a 64-yard march in 11 plays. Grisham's one-yard plunge capped the drive, and Jarman converted.

The Cowboys tied the game late in the same stanza and took a 10-7 lead on a field goal early in the third quarter after intercepting Page's pass.

The Sooners later drove 63 yards in 10 plays capped by another Grisham one-yard blast and Jarman toed the conversion. Grisham carried six times in the drive.

Page scored on a one-yard sneak early in the fourth stanza to complete an 88-yard march in nine plays. Grisham again was the workhorse in the drive, toting the ball five times. Jarman again converted.

The Pokes fumbled three plays after the kickoff, and McAdams smothered the ball on the OSU 23. Two plays later Grisham streaked around right end for a 20-yard touchdown, but Jarman's conversion was blocked.

McCurdy recovered an OSU fumble one play after the kickoff on the OSU 20. Grisham plowed over from the two-yard line three plays later, and Jarman converted.

The Sooners rushed for 340 yards and passed for 23. The defense held the Pokes to seven first downs and 105 total yards.

OU, at 8-2, finished second in the Big Eight Conference. Grisham was the only Sooner selected as All-America. Flynn, Neely and Burton joined him on the All-Big Eight first team.

Forty-two days after the OSU victory Wilkinson resigned as Oklahoma's head coach.

1964

Bud Wilkinson resigned as the Sooners' head coach on January 11, 1964. Although he said he had not decided to enter the U.S. Senate race in the State of Oklahoma, Wilkinson said rumors of his future plans might cause damage to recruiting and spring practice preparations. He also said family and other obligations made it the right time for him to step down.

"My brother's recent illness and death have added to my responsibilities to his widow and his mother," Wilkinson said. "I must help them to reorganize his business and settle his affairs."

Wilkinson resigned as athletic director at the university, and three weeks later he entered the senate race as a Republican. He lost his senate bid by 28,000 votes to Fred Harris in November.

He left behind a legacy at the University of Oklahoma—three national championships; 14 conference titles; 145 wins, 29 losses and four ties; and an unprecedented 47-game winning streak and 74-game unbeaten conference string.

On January 19, Gomer Jones, Wilkinson's assistant for 17 years, was named head coach and athletic director. The Sooners' 14th head coach, Jones graduated from Ohio State University where he was an All-America center in 1935. In addition to his 17 years as an OU assistant, Jones' collegiate coaching experience included Ohio State, St. Mary's Pre-Flight, and Nebraska.

With the return of seven starters, the outlook was positive for the 1964 campaign. All-America fullback Jim Grisham was the only returning starter in the backfield. Halfback Lance Rentzel returned with plenty of experience and pulled double duty again as the team's punter. Larry Brown beat out Larry Shields for the left half slot. Mike Ringer, John Hammond, Tommy Pannell, Bobby Page and Norman Smith battled for the starting quarterback job. Smith started the first game, Ringer got the nod in the second game, and Hammond started in a couple, but it was Page who stepped up and took the reins by the fifth game.

The front line was solid with the return of all-conference stars Ralph Neely at left tackle and Newt Burton at right guard. Guard Ed McQuarters and end Ricky McCurdy also returned, along with center John Garrett, but Carl McAdams beat out Garrett for the starting slot in the middle of the line.

Sooner Magic: Bomb Detonates on Turtles

Hammond did not get the starting nod at quarterback for the season opener on September 19 against Maryland. Hammond rode the bench most of his sophomore season a year before and played sparingly, and tossed only six passes and completed half of them for 48 yards.

Hammond also rode the bench for the first 56 and one-half minutes against Maryland, then Coach Jones sent him in for one specific play. The play, a 90-yard pass and run, burned the Terps and is in the Sooner football record book as the longest pass play from scrimmage. It also allowed the Sooners to take the lead for good and come away with a 13-3 victory before 35,709 stunned spectators.

OU opened the season ranked second in the polls, but for most of the game the Sooners didn't look like one of the best teams in the nation. One drive into Maryland territory ended in an interception and two ended with missed field goals.

The Terps could not get past the OU 45-yard line until a late third-quarter drive. They moved from their 33 to the OU14, but the Sooner defense stiffened, and Bernard Bramson nailed a 32-yard field goal to give Maryland a 3-0 lead with 11 and one-half minutes remaining in the game.

The Sooners took the kickoff and moved to the MU 36. On fourth down, Shields was wide open in the flat and dropped Smith's pass. Maryland failed to generate a first down and punted to Charles Mayhue on the OU 10-yard line.

Jones called Hammond off the bench. The quarterback dropped back and tossed a pass to Rentzel on a full sprint at the OU 45. Rentzel bolted down the sideline and outran the Terrapin secondary for the final 55 yards.

"I feel very lucky," Rentzel said afterwards. "I had a charley horse in my leg, but I thought that if I kept running, it would be OK."

The play broke the team record for the longest pass from scrimmage, eclipsing Buddy Leake's 87-yard scoring strike to Max Boydston against California in 1954.

Butch Metcalf missed the conversion, but the Sooners held a 6-3 lead with 3:57 to go and they weren't through. Three plays after the ensuing kickoff, David Voiles picked off Phil Petry's pass on the MU 32 and carried it to the 10-yard line. Grisham bulled ahead for three yards, then Mike Ringer zipped around right end for the score. Metcalf converted, and OU held the deciding score of 13-3 with 2:45 remaining.

Oklahoma held the Terrapins scoreless for the first time in 39 games. Both teams picked up 15 first downs apiece, but the Sooners gained more yards (258-246).

Southern California (1-0) avenged their upset of a year ago with a 40-14 pasting of the No. 2 Sooners the next week before a crowd of 62,579 in Norman. OU had ended USC's 12-game winning streak and knocked the Trojans from atop the polls with a 17-12 victory a year ago in Los Angeles.

USC quarterback Craig Fertig ran for two touchdowns and passed for another to lead the Trojan onslaught. The Sooners were handed their worst loss since a 45-13 setback to Northwestern in 1959.

The Trojans took a 14-0 lead on Fertig's two TD runs in the first stanza. Ringer, starting at quarterback for Oklahoma, completed a 10-yard scoring strike to Rentzel early in the second period to cap a 58-yard drive. Metcalf converted to cut the Trojan lead to 14-7.

USC answered with a 79-yard scoring march to take a 20-7 lead at intermission. The Trojans added 14 points in the third quarter. One touchdown came one play after the Sooners bobbled a punt return on the OU five. USC scored its final tally with a 66-yard punt return in the fourth stanza.

Down 40-7, Rentzel returned a punt 48 yards to the Trojans' four, and Brown scored two plays later from the two-yard line. Metcalf converted.

USC gained more total yards (361-202). Fertig completed 16 of 28 passes for 212 yards, and Rod Sherman caught seven aerials for 101 yards. Rentzel punted three times for a 46.7 average.

OU dropped out of the top ten in the AP poll and had two weeks to prepare for No. 1 Texas. The extra week did not help as the 3-0 Longhorns repeated the previous year's score with a 28-7 victory. The Steers scored a touchdown in the third period to break a 7-7 deadlock and added two more in the final quarter to run away with their sixth straight win in the series.

Hammond was the third quarterback to start for the Sooners in as many games. The Sooner offense was bogged down with four penalties in the first 10 minutes. OU's defense stymied the Horns with a goal-line stand at the one-yard line.

Late in the first stanza, McAdams' interception set up Oklahoma's only score. Defensive back Eugene Ross tipped a Texas pass, McAdams grabbed it on the 43 and returned it to the 15. Seven plays later Rentzel scored from the two-yard line, and Metcalf converted.

Texas tied the game early in the second period, four plays after recovering Jim Grisham's fumble on the OU 44. Rentzel almost got away with a 90-yard TD run minutes later. On fourth-and-21 at the OU 10, Rentzel was back to punt from his end zone when he took a low snap, saw daylight and took off. He made it all the way to his 40 where he bumped into a teammate, and a Horn defender brought him down on the UT 47. OU could not gain a first down after that.

The Steers intercepted Hammond's pass to set up their next score in the third quarter. Texas drove 60 yards for the third touchdown

and cashed in on Ross' muffed punt return on the OU 14 in the final stanza.

Texas picked up more total yards, 322-198. McAdams recorded 13 unassisted tackles for Oklahoma.

600th Game

The Sooners played their 600th game in school history but dropped to 1-3 as Kansas scored on the first and final plays for a 15-14 victory on October 17 in Lawrence.

Gale Sayers returned the opening kickoff 93 yards to pay dirt, and the 2-2 Jayhawks led, 7-0, in the first 16 seconds.

OU blew three chances to score in the first period. The Sooners marched to the KU 25 after Sayers' TD, but Metcalf shanked a 42-yard field goal. Minutes later Grisham fumbled on the KU 25 after McCurdy's interception. Rentzel's 76-yard TD run was called back by a penalty.

The Big Red tied the game on Grisham's one-yard run and Metcalf's conversion three plays into the second stanza. The score capped an 82-yard drive that began in the first period.

Minutes later, Ross returned a Kansas punt 10 yards to the OU 49 to set up a 14-7 Oklahoma lead. Rentzel capped the drive with a six-yard run, and Metcalf again converted.

Neither team threatened in the third quarter and most of the fourth. Rentzel's punt late in the game pinned the Jayhawks at their nine-yard line and the Sooners' lead looked safe with 58 seconds remaining. The Hawks reached the OU 26 with eight seconds left. On the next play, halfback Dave Crandall hurled a 26-yard scoring strike to quarterback Bob Skahan. With no time left on the clock, Mike Johnson swept around right end for the two-point conversion and win.

Oklahoma, which dominated the game between the two Jayhawk scores, led in first downs (20-11) and total yards (322-192).

The Sooners got back on the winning track with a 44-0 blasting of Kansas State the next week in Norman. OU's defense held the 1-3 Wildcats to six first downs, 134 total yards, forced three fumbles, two interceptions and blocked one punt.

Oklahoma led, 9-0, in the first stanza on Pannell's six-yard TD run and Al Baumgardner's blocked punt, which rolled out of the end zone.

K-State's only threat came after recovering Mayhue's fumbled punt return on the OU nine. The Cats went nowhere in three plays, faked a field goal try, but Mayhue stopped Jerry Cook on the four-yard line.

The Sooners then drove 96 yards in 10 plays. Rentzel thrice picked up first downs on third-and-long situations. From the OU 45, Pannell zipped a pass to Ben Hart on the KSU 17. Hart out-leaped a Cat defender and breezed into the end zone.

Hammond scored on a nine-yard run late in the second period after Voiles' interception. Metcalf converted all three extra points and added another conversion in the fourth quarter.

The Sooners scored three times in the final eight and one-half minutes, twice after Kansas State turnovers. Page, the fourth quarterback to start for the Sooners, scored twice, and Grisham carried for the final tally. Tony Jenkins kicked the final two conversions. Page never relinquished his starting post the rest of the year.

OU amassed 324 yards rushing and passed for 195. Hart caught three passes for 106 yards.

The Sooners evened their record to 3-3 with a 14-11 victory over 1-5 Colorado on October 31 in Boulder.

The Buffaloes missed a 37-yard field-goal attempt late in the first period. Oklahoma took over and drove 73 yards in six plays for a 7-0 advantage. Brown's 20-yard burst got the Sooners to the Buffs' 43-

yard line. Two plays later, Rentzel dashed 40 yards for the touchdown. Metcalf kicked the first of two conversions.

Colorado added a 31-yard field goal midway through the second stanza to cut OU's lead to 7-3. The Sooners had two major penalties (roughing and piling on) to give Colorado 30 yards in the drive.

Neither team threatened in the third quarter, then early in the fourth, Shields returned a Buffalo punt 57 yards for a 14-3 lead.

Colorado marched 76 yards in 15 plays to score with 2:04 remaining. The Buffs added a two-point run to cut their deficit to 14-11, but they could not find the handle on the onside kick, and the Sooners killed the clock.

Oklahoma gained more total yards, 276-220.

400th Win

Grisham rushed for 121 yards and scored one touchdown as the Sooners defeated 1-6 Iowa State, 30-0, on November 7 in Norman. Grisham raised his career rushing total to 2,090 yards more than any fullback in school history. The victory gave the Sooners their 400th win in school history.

OU scored its first touchdown early in the second stanza after Neely blocked a Cyclone punt and halfback Bill Thomas recovered on the ISU 37-yard line. Rentzel scored on a four-yard run five plays later. Metcalf missed the conversion but made the next three and added a 32-yard field goal midway in the second quarter.

The Sooners took the second-half kickoff and drove 71 yards in 11 plays for a 16-0 lead. Grisham capped the drive with a one-yard plunge.

Iowa State failed to gain a first down on a fourth-down gamble after the kickoff and Oklahoma took over at its 49-yard line. Fullback Alan Henderson, subbing for Grisham, scored on a three-yard run to complete the 51-yard march in four plays. Grisham gained 23 yards to the ISU 27, and Tommy Pannell added 24 more to the three-yard line to highlight the drive.

The Sooners scored their final touchdown midway in the fourth stanza after McAdams intercepted a Cyclone pass and returned it 10 yards to the ISU 29. Henderson scored his second touchdown five plays later. He also carried for 13 yards to the three-yard line one play before he scored.

OU had 329 total yards. The defense held I-State to 86 total yards and four first downs, three by pass and one via a penalty.

A victory against 5-3 Missouri the following week would put the Sooners in the thick of the Big Eight Conference race with a 4-1 record and one game behind league-leading Nebraska. A late Tiger touchdown knotted the game at 14 all and took the Big Red out of the title chase.

Grisham rushed for 96 yards to lift his career total to a school-record 2,196 yards, eclipsing George Thomas' record of 2,177 set from 1946-1949. The senior fullback had two costly fumbles; the first one led to a Tiger touchdown, and the second one stalled a drive.

The Tigers recovered his first fumble on the OU nine and scored in one play for a 7-0 lead late in the opening period.

Oklahoma answered with a 75-yard march in 10 plays. Page fired a 30-yard scoring strike to end Gordon Brown, and Metcalf kicked the first of two conversions.

The Sooners advanced to the Mizzou seven moments after McCurdy's interception midway through the second quarter. Grisham lost his grip on the next play, and the Tigers recovered on the three.

Baumgardner's fumble recovery on the MU 48 early in the third stanza set up the next Sooner touchdown. McAdams jolted Missouri's Carl Reese, causing the Tiger to fumble. Four plays later,

Pannell tossed a 35-yard TD pass to Hart, who started for the first time at right end replacing McCurdy.

The next two OU possessions ended with Rentzel's booming punts (50 and 64 yards), which pinned the Tigers deep in their territory. Rentzel had one other punt, which carried 48 yards, and he finished the game with a 54-yard average.

McAdams intercepted a Mizzou pass and returned it 14 yards to the MU 31 near the end of the third quarter. The Sooners stalled after moving to the MU 14 and lost a fourth-down gamble when Pannell was sacked for a three-yard loss.

From there the Tigers launched an 83-yard, 20-play drive that consumed 13 minutes. Gus Otto scored from the one with 3:45 remaining. Missouri coach Dan Devine ordered a tying conversion, which was successful. Oklahoma could not mount a threat in the remaining time.

OU rolled up more total yards, 236-231.

The Sooners spoiled Nebraska's quest for its first undefeated season since 1915 with a 17-7 upset on November 21 before a homecoming throng of 54,552. The 9-0 Cornhuskers rolled into Norman ranked fourth in the nation and carrying a 16-game winning streak dating back to 1963. The Huskers led the nation in total defense (152.4-yards per game), near the top in other categories and had outscored their opponents an average of 29-6.

Rentzel and Grisham left the game with injuries in the first period and the crimson faithful believed that was the final nail in the Sooners' coffin.

Oklahoma took a 3-0 lead on Metcalf's 23-yard field goal early in the second stanza. The Huskers countered with a 72-yard drive in four plays to take a 7-3 lead.

The Sooners launched an 88-yard drive for a 10-7 lead early in the fourth period. The 24-play drive began late in the third period and consumed 11 minutes. Jon Kennedy, Grisham's understudy, twice picked up first downs on fourth-and-one situations. Page capped the drive with a one-yard touchdown, and Metcalf kicked the first of two conversions.

Baumgardner stole a Husker pass moments later on the OU 48. One play later, Page hurled a pass to Larry Brown over the middle, and Brown shot to the end zone.

Nebraska didn't quit and advanced to the OU 15 after the kickoff with two passes and the aid of a 15-yard penalty against the Sooners. Three plays later, the Huskers faced fourth-and-goal at the four, but McAdams intercepted Bob Churchich's pass in the end zone.

OU gained 290 total yards, 138 more than the Husker defense allowed in their first nine games. Larry Brown carried the ball 12 times for 104 yards to lead the Sooners' 268-yard rushing effort, which was three times more than the Nebraska defense allowed. The Huskers were held to 86 yards rushing (156 yards below their average) and 150 yards passing.

Oklahoma accepted a bowl invitation to meet Florida State in the Gator Bowl on January 2. But first, the Sooners had Oklahoma State in their way to claim second in the conference.

Sooner Magic:
Page-to-Hart Twice Melts Cowboy Spoiler

The Cowboys were 15 minutes away from defeating the Sooners for the first time in 18 years. OSU held a 16-7 lead and was ready to end the embarrassment of losing to Oklahoma for all those years.

The fourth quarter belonged to the Sooners as Page twice caught the Pokes' secondary napping with two scoring strikes to Hart.

The Big Red blew three chances to blow the game wide open with fumbles deep in OSU territory. The first came on the Sooners' first series, and the Cowboys recovered on their 13-yard line.

Oklahoma marched 79 yards in three plays to take a 7-0 lead on its second series. Rentzel circled left end on the second play and zipped 52 yards to the OSU 26. Grisham banged ahead for four more then Page sailed around right end for a 22-yard touchdown with 4:32 left in the first stanza. Metcalf converted the first of three extra-pointers.

The Cowboys answered with a 46-yard scoring drive to knot the score at 7-7. The Pokes took a 10-7 lead with a 29-yard field goal midway in the second period. The Sooners advanced to the OSU 4 after the kickoff, but Kennedy missed a handoff from Page and the Cowboys recovered.

O-State jumped to a 13-7 lead early in the third period with another field goal moments after recovering Rentzel's fumble on the OU 39. The Pokes' lead swelled to 16-7 on another field goal, which came moments after they intercepted Page's pass.

OU later moved to the Pokes' 23, but Grisham spilled the pigskin, and OSU recovered. The Cowboys punted back to the OU 36. Grisham, Kennedy, and Page hammered to the OSU 33 as the third quarter ended.

The Sooners continued to the Pokes' 14, where they faced third-and-nine. Page zipped a scoring strike to Hart on the next play to cut the deficit to 16-14 with 12:43 to go.

Oklahoma State later punted to the OU 18. Page and Kennedy combined for 17 yards on the next two carries. Page then whipped a 15-yard pass to Hart, who outran the secondary for the final 50 yards to complete the 65-yard play. Oklahoma led, 21-16, with 7:29 remaining. The Cowboys never threatened again.

OU hammered out 465 total yards and held the Pokes to 187 yards. Page completed five of eight passes for 107 yards and rushed 20 times for 149 more.

Grisham, Rentzel, Neely and Skidgel signed undated contracts to play professional football days before the Gator Bowl. All four were ineligible to play against Florida State. Bud Adams, owner of the Houston Oilers, leaked the information to the press that he had signed Neely and declared that the other three had also signed with other teams. Pro scouts told the four Sooners that the contracts would not be valid until after the Gator Bowl. Ross replaced Rentzel, at right halfback, Voiles filled in at fullback, and Ed Hall took Neely's place at left tackle.

The Seminoles blasted the Sooners, 36-19, before a crowd of 50,408 at the 20th Gator Bowl in Jacksonville, Florida. Quarterback Steve Tensi completed 23 of 26 passes for 303 yards and five touchdowns to lead Florida State. Fred Biletnikoff caught four TD aerials.

FSU's Howard Ehler intercepted Page's pass and retuned it 69 yards for a 6-0 lead early in the first stanza. The Sooners later took a 7-6 lead on Kennedy's one-yard plunge to cap a 38-yard drive in 11 plays and Metcalf's conversion.

Tensi hit Biletnikoff with three scoring strikes in the second period for a 24-7 Seminole lead at intermission.

The Sooners scored one play after Biletnikoff fumbled Page's punt on the two-yard line early in the third quarter. Pannell carried the ball across. Metcalf converted, but the Seminoles were penalized. OU went for two points on the second chance, but Larry Brown misfired the pass.

FSU answered with Tensi's 13-yard scoring strike to Don Floyd.

The Sooners were backed up to their five-yard line, early in the fourth stanza. Ronnie Fletcher tossed a pass to Hart, who caught the ball on the OU 41 and flew the final 49 yards to complete the 95-yard play. The touchdown set the Gator Bowl record for the longest pass for a touchdown and has never been broken. It also set the school record of 90 yards set by Hammond to Rentzel against Maryland earlier in the season. Pannell tossed an incomplete pass on the two-point try.

Tensi hurled a seven-yard TD pass to Biletnikoff late in the game for the final tally.

Florida State rolled up more total yards, 520-280.

The Sooners finished the season with a 6-4-1 record and second in the Big Eight Conference. All-America honors went to Neely and McAdams. Burton and Grisham joined them on the All-Big Eight first unit.

1965

The United States began sending troops to Vietnam, but the war would not cause depletion of college football rosters as it did during the first two world wars.

The National Collegiate Athletic Association in January approved a two-platoon system in college football. The rule allowed substitution after the ball changed hands, between periods and after any score.

The new system could help the Sooners in 1965, as they were a youthful and inexperienced bunch. Coach Gomer Jones installed the I-formation, which positioned the fullback and tailback directly behind the quarterback. Three-fourths of the backfield featured sophomores—quarterback Gene Cagle and halfbacks Ron Shotts and Stan Crowder. Junior Larry Brown was the lone returnee with any experience.

End Ben Hart returned but was moved to a backup tailback role. The offensive line featured new faces such as tackle Jim Riley and end Bob Kalsu, yet they too were green around the gills. Gordon Brown returned at split end.

Linebacker Carl McAdams returned to lead the defense, which included talented players as tackles Larry Crutchmer and John Koller, noseguard Granville Liggins, and safety Rod Crosswhite. Mike Ringer was moved to safety.

The Sooners traveled on September 25 to Pittsburgh for the season opener against the Pitt Panthers. Pitt opened the season with a loss to Oregon but went 1-1 with a 13-9 victory over OU.

1964 Season Record: 6-4-1
Big Eight Conference: 5-1-1 (Second)

Date	Opponent	Result	Score
September 19	at Maryland	W	13-3
September 26	SOUTHERN CALIFORNIA	L	40-14
October 10	Texas at Dallas	L	28-7
October 17	at Kansas	L	15-14
October 24	KANSAS STATE	W	44-0
October 31	at Colorado	W	14-11
November 7	IOWA STATE	W	30-0
November 14	MISSOURI	T	14-14
November 21	NEBRASKA	W	17-7
November 28	at Oklahoma State	W	21-16
January 2	Florida State*	L	36-19

*Gator Bowl at Jacksonville, FL

Oklahoma lost a chance to score a touchdown in the first quarter after Riley recovered a Panther fumble on the Pitt 22. Pitt's defense pushed OU 19 yards back, forcing the Sooners to punt.

Shotts' 24-yard field goal put the Sooners up 3-0 early in the second stanza then the Panthers scored two touchdowns to take a 13-3 halftime lead.

John Hammond's eight-yard scoring strike to Gordon Brown gave the Big Red hope with 2:37 remaining in the game. The Sooners went for a fake on the extra point, but Pitt intercepted Hammond's two-point pass.

Ringer's onside kick did not travel the required 10 yards, and the Panthers took over and killed the clock.

Oklahoma gained more total yards (322-141).

Using superior passing and wide sweeps, Navy dropped the Sooners, 10-0, the next week before a throng of 56,148 in Norman. The Midshipmen scored all of their points in the first 18 and one-half minutes.

Navy quarterback John Cartright, who completed seven of 16 passes for 144 yards, hurled a 33-yard TD pass in the first period, and the Midshipmen added a 36-yard field goal in the second.

It wasn't penalties or turnovers that hurt the Sooners, just sloppy offense. The offense generated only six first downs and 83 total yards. The Big Red crossed midfield only four times.

The defense kept the game from being a blowout with two goal-line stands. Moments after Navy took a 10-0 lead, the Midshipmen recovered Hammond's fumble on the OU three-yard line. The defense allowed only one yard on the next four plays. The defense rose up again after Navy drove to the Sooner five in the third quarter.

McAdams led the defense with a school-record 16 tackles, a fumble recovery, and a deflected pass. Navy rolled up 376 total yards.

The Sooners' offensive woes continued against No. 1-ranked Texas. The 3-0 Longhorns coasted to their eighth-straight victory in the series with a 19-0 decision on October 9 before a packed Cotton Bowl crowd of 75,342.

The Steers' defense, led by linebacker Tommy Nobis, held Oklahoma to six first downs and 114 total yards. Nobis would win the Outland Trophy later in the year.

Texas took a 9-0 lead with a field goal and touchdown in the second stanza. Dave Conway kicked the first of two field goals, and the Horns drove 60 yards for their TD. The Sooners failed to gain a first down in the first half. Their longest drive was only six yards.

The Big Red made its deepest penetration with a drive of 41 yards to the UT 24 in the second half, but Cagle muffed the handoff to Shotts. Texas recovered and marched to Conway's second field goal early in the fourth period. The Longhorns drove 59 yards for a touchdown with 1:27 left in the game.

Texas picked up 379 total yards.

Winless Kansas (0-4) was next. One team was going to get into the win column or tie. The Sooners were the ones to record a "W" with a 21-7 win before a homecoming crowd of 42,975 in Norman. Cagle, in his first start under center, scored all three of OU's touchdowns, and Shotts toed all three conversions.

Shotts, however, missed a 37-yard field-goal try in the opening quarter. Cagle's first touchdown, early in the second stanza, capped a 60-yard, 13-play march.

The Sooners took the second-half kickoff and rolled 80 yards in 21 plays for a 14-0 lead. The drive consumed nine and one-half minutes, and Cagle scored from the two-yard line on fourth down.

The Jayhawks scored early in the fourth period three plays after recovering Crowder's fumble on the OU 39.

Cagle again scored on a fourth-down run minutes later. His one-yard plunge completed a 56-yard drive.

OU collected more total yards, 276-201.

The Sooners made it two in a row with a 27-0 victory over 0-5 Kansas State on October 23 in Manhattan. OU scored three first-half touchdowns and coasted with another TD through the final 30 minutes.

Crosswhite returned a Wildcat punt 62 yards for a score midway in the first quarter, and Shotts converted the seventh point.

Late in the first stanza, Oklahoma marched 65 yards in 10 plays for a 13-0 advantage early in the second. From the KSU 12, Cagle moved to his right, then cut back to his left to the end zone. Shotts' conversion sailed wide left. Larry Brown picked up 12 yards on third-and-10 to the Cats' 16 to keep the drive alive.

K-State then marched to the OU 35, but Sooner defensive back Gene Knight intercepted in the end zone.

The Sooners rolled 58 yards in three plays for a 21-0 lead just before halftime. On the first play, Tommy Pannell gained three yards, then flipped the ball back to Ben Hart who raced to the KSU 14. A holding penalty set the Sooners back 10 yards, then Cagle burst 21 yards to the three, and Larry Brown scored on the next play. On a fake extra point, Hammond took the snap and shoveled the ball forward to Pannell, who slammed across for the two points.

Defensive back Don Kindley's interception of a Cat pass on the KSU 36 set up the final tally midway through the fourth period. Brown scored his second touchdown with a two-yard run four plays later, but Shotts again missed the conversion.

The Big Red rushed for 342 yards and passed for 30. The defense held Kansas State to 101 total yards.

After reaching the stratosphere with two straight wins, the Sooners were brought back to earth a week later with a 13-0 loss to 3-1-2 Colorado in Norman. Six turnovers (three fumbles and three interceptions) killed OU's chance of a win.

The Buffaloes marched 48 yards for a 7-0 lead early in the first quarter. OU helped the drive with 26 yards in penalties. Colorado added a 34-yard field goal in the second stanza for a 10-0 advantage.

The Sooners recovered a Buff fumble at midfield and drove to the one-yard line, but Cagle's fourth-down run was stopped short of the goal line.

The Buffs kicked a 42-yard field goal in the third stanza for the final tally. OU later advanced 69 yards to the CU 13 but surrendered on downs. The Sooners' three interceptions in the fourth period dashed any hopes of a score.

The Big Red gained more total yards, 284-256. Gordon Brown caught eight passes for 110 yards. The Buffaloes were penalized 18 times for 210 yards.

The Sooners put together their finest offensive performance of the year with a 24-20 victory over 4-2-1 Iowa State on November 6 before a crowd of 43,642 in Norman.

Oklahoma jumped to a 17-0 lead in the first 36 minutes. Ringer's 20-yard punt return to the Cyclones' 40-yard line set up the first score on the Sooners' second possession. Jon Kennedy scored from the two to cap the 11-play drive, and Shotts toed the first of three conversions.

Hart's two-yard run gave OU a 14-0 lead early in the second period to cap a 47-yard march after Crosswhite's interception. Pannell's 15-yard run and Cagle's six-yard run on fourth down sparked the drive.

Iowa State recovered Hart's fumble on his five-yard line minutes later, but the Big Red defense tightened.

The Sooners took the second-half kickoff and drove 58 yards to the ISU 18, but had to rely on Shotts' 35-yard field goal for a 17-0 lead.

The Cyclones got on board 55 seconds later on an 82-yard scoring strike from Tim Van Galder to Tom Busch. Iowa State scored again with a 61-yard drive on its next series to cut the OU lead to 17-14.

The Sooners took the kickoff and embarked on a 70-yard march in 17 plays at the end of the third quarter. Hart's four-yard run completed the drive.

The Cyclones later returned a punt 34 yards to the OU 32, and Van Galder tossed a touchdown on the next play, but the extra point missed the target.

OU took the kickoff and drained the final 4:20 off the clock. Oklahoma collected more total yards (344-256).

McAdams twisted his ankle in the fourth quarter against the Cyclones and did not play against Missouri the next week in Columbia.

The 5-2-1 Tigers handed the Sooners their fourth shutout of the season with a 30-0 victory on November 13 in Columbia. Oklahoma had not been shut out four times in one season since 1942. Missouri defeated the Sooners at home for the first time since 1945.

Tiger quarterback Gary Lane scored three touchdowns and passed for another. Missouri led, 7-0, after the first stanza, and 17-0 at halftime. Johnny Roland's 34-yard punt return to the OU 34 set up the first touchdown, Shotts fumbled two plays after the ensuing kickoff, and Lane tossed a scoring strike four plays later. Missouri added a 29-yard field goal minutes later.

OU threatened only once with a drive to the Tigers' 24 but surrendered on downs.

Larry Brown's fumble on the OU 41 in the third period led to the third Missouri touchdown. OU later failed to pick up a first down on its 30-yard line, and Missouri scored moments later.

The Sooners had a chance to erase the goose egg with a drive to the MU 13, but the Tigers intercepted Cagle's pass. OU recovered a bad snap on the Mizzou 18-yard line with 45 seconds left, but the Tigers again intercepted Cagle's pass in the end zone.

Missouri collected more total yards, 378-214.

A year before, the Sooners spoiled Nebraska's quest for its first perfect season since 1915 with a 17-7 upset in Norman. One year later, and 50 years since that last perfect season, the Cornhuskers finished the regular season undefeated at 10-0 with a 21-9 victory in Lincoln.

OU took a 9-0 lead in the first half on Shotts' 21-yard field goal in the first period and Larry Brown's three-yard run early in the second. Brown's touchdown came eight plays after Vernon Burkett recovered a Husker fumble on the NU 28, and Shotts missed the conversion.

Nebraska answered with a 65-yard drive to close the gap to 9-7 at halftime. The Huskers then exploded for two touchdowns in a five-minute span in the third quarter to put the game away.

The Huskers dominated in first downs (18-12) and total yards (411-229).

Charles Durkee's 35-yard field goal with 1:41 remaining lifted Oklahoma State to a 17-16 victory, snapping the Sooners' 19-game win streak over their instate rival. A crowd of 54,876 turned out at Owen Field on December 4, believing Oklahoma would get a victory over the 2-7 Cowboys.

Hammond's one-yard plunge on the first play of the second stanza and Shotts' conversion gave the Sooners a 7-0 lead. Hammond,

subbing for Cagle who was out with an injury, sparked the 57-yard drive with a 20-yard run to the OSU 12-yard line.

The Pokes retaliated with a 55-yard scoring march to tie the game at 7-7. The Sooners failed on a fourth-and-one gamble at the OSU 44 on their next possession. The Cowboys took over and rolled 56 yards in 10 plays to take a 14-7 lead.

OSU failed to up its lead when Durkee shanked a 21-yard field goal just before intermission.

Oklahoma launched an 82-yard scoring march at the close of the third period. Hammond capped the drive with an eight-yard run around right end, but Shotts' conversion veered off to the right, and OSU held a 14-13 lead.

The Sooners later moved from their 20 to the Pokes' 10-yard line but had to settle for Shotts' 27-yard boot which put OU back on top, 16-14, with 3:27 to go.

The Cowboys rolled back after the kickoff to set up Durkee's winning field goal. The Sooners took the kickoff after the OSU field goal, and Hammond completed two sideline passes to Gordon Brown to put the Sooners in field goal range. Shotts' 41-yard try fell short of the mark with six seconds left.

OU rolled up more yards, 400-321. Hammond completed 10 of 14 passes for 105 yards, and Gordon Brown caught nine of them, and another from Hart for 110 total yards. Shotts carried the ball 28 times for 163 yards.

The Sooners ended the '65 campaign with a 3-7 record and finished fifth in the Big Eight Conference with a 3-4 mark. McAdams was the only Sooner chosen All-America and to the Big Eight's first team.

The loss to Oklahoma State and the poor season's performance had many fans fuming, and they criticized Coach Jones. Two days after the Cowboy tilt, Jones tendered his resignation as Oklahoma's head coach.

"I just got tired of the criticism and of constantly reading and listening to all the untrue rumors concerning my position as head coach here," Jones said.

He remained as the school's athletic director until his death in 1971. On March 21, 1971, the 57-year-old Jones collapsed and died on a New York City subway platform while accompanying the Oklahoma basketball team during the National Invitational Tournament.

During his two-year tenure as OU head coach, Jones finished with a 9-11-1 record.

The search was on for a new head coach. University of Oklahoma officials had discussions with Texas head coach Darrell Royal, former OU star, about replacing Jones. Royal turned down the offer to

1965 Season Record: 3-7-0
Big Eight Conference: 3-4-0 (Fifth)

Date	Opponent	Result	Score
September 25	at Pittsburgh	L	13-9
October 2	NAVY	L	10-0
October 9	Texas at Dallas	L	19-0
October 16	KANSAS	W	21-7
October 23	at Kansas State	W	27-0
October 30	COLORADO	L	13-0
November 6	IOWA STATE	W	24-20
November 13	at Missouri	L	30-0
November 25	at Nebraska	L	21-9
December 4	OKLAHOMA STATE	L	17-16

be head coach at his alma mater. Tennessee's Doug Dickey and Georgia's Vince Dooley were also mentioned as Jones' successor, but both refused to leave their programs, so OU turned to Jim Mackenzie, an assistant at the University of Arkansas.

Mackenzie was hired as the Sooners' 15th head coach on December 22, 16 days after Jones resigned.

1966

Jim Mackenzie played football for Paul "Bear" Bryant at Kentucky in the early 1950s, and when the Wildcats defeated OU in the 1951 Sugar Bowl. Mackenzie later became an assistant head coach to Frank Broyles at Arkansas and helped guide the Razorbacks to the 1964 national championship.

Not only did the Sooners have a new football coach, they had a new look. Solid red helmets with an interlocking "OU" replaced the old white helmets, which had a red stripe and the players' numbers on the side. The jerseys sported three stripes on each sleeve with the middle stripe being wider than the other two. Two red stripes also were added to the white pants.

Tackles Bob Kalsu and Ed Hall returned to anchor the front line, but the backfield was revamped from the prior year. Sophomores Bob Warmack and Jim Burgar battled for the starting quarterback slot, and both had moved ahead of veteran Gene Cagle in the line-up. Ron Shotts was the only returnee at tailback, and sophomore fullback Gary Harper would be known more for his punishing blocks. Wingback Eddie Hinton rounded out the backfield at wingback. Ben Hart returned to split end, a position he held two years previous.

Granville Liggins, John Titsworth, and Jim Riley returned to the defensive front, and Eugene Ross led a young secondary that included safety Steve Barrett and corner back Bobby Stephenson.

The Sooners opened the season with a 17-0 victory over the Oregon Ducks on September 17 before a throng of 48,950 in Norman. Burgar got the starting nod at quarterback, but Warmack led the team on two scoring drives.

Both teams fought to a scoreless tie in the first half. OU gained only 66 yards then woke up with 17 points on its first three possessions of the second half. Early in the third period, Hinton took a Duck punt on his 37-yard line and followed a wall of blockers down the east sideline for a 63-yard return, and Mike Vachon converted from 25 yards out after a penalty moved the Sooners back 15 yards.

The Sooners later rolled from their 14 to the Oregon 13 but bogged down, and Vachon's 23-yard field goal gave Oklahoma a 10-0 advantage.

Steve Barrett recovered a Duck fumble on the Oregon 38 after Vachon belted the Ducks' Claxton Welch on the following kickoff. Warmack carried 36 yards to the two-yard line, and Shotts blasted through on the next play. Vachon toed the conversion.

Oregon threatened with a drive to the OU five in the fourth stanza, but the Big Red defense stiffened.

Oklahoma had the edge in total yards, 253-208. Warmack completed seven of nine passes for 65 yards. Tom Stidham punted seven times for a 44.4-yard average.

Liggins suffered a twisted ankle against the Ducks and did not play in the Big Eight Conference opener the next week against Iowa State. Richard Goodwin replaced him in the lineup.

The Sooners scored two touchdowns in the first six minutes en route to a 33-11 victory over the 0-2 Cyclones in Ames.

OU rolled 56 yards in four plays on its first series. Shotts capped the drive with a two-yard run, but Vachon missed the conversion.

Warmack sparked the drive with a 41-yard run to the ISU two before Shotts scored.

The Sooners picked off three of Tim Van Galder's passes, and linebacker Rickey Burgess nabbed one on the Cyclones' 32 and returned it to the 15. Three plays later, Warmack connected a 12-yard scoring strike to Hinton for a 12-0 lead. Warmack then tossed a two-point pass to Hart for a 14-0 advantage.

OU's poor punt snap rolled into the end zone, and the Cyclones tackled Stidham in the end zone as he tried to cover the ball.

Vachon booted a 32-yard field goal early in the second quarter. Iowa State cashed in on a Sooner fumble minutes later on the OU 17 and later added a field goal to cut the Sooner lead to 17-11 at halftime.

Vachon nailed another field goal, this time from 39 yards away for a 20-11 lead early in the third period. Warmack hurled a 31-yard TD pass to Hart late in the third stanza, and Shotts added a one-yard scoring plunge in the fourth.

The Big Red gained 342 total yards, 100 more than the Cyclones. Hinton caught eight passes for 111 yards and rushed for 88 more. Linebacker Harry Hettsmansperger recorded 16 tackles and snatched one interception to lead the Sooner defense. Titsworth added 14 tackles.

The streets of Dallas turned into a sea of crimson celebrants Saturday night after the Sooners ended Texas' eight-game win streak with an 18-9 win on October 8. Vachon connected on four field goals to lead the OU victory. A throng of 75,504 packed the Cotton Bowl to see if 2-1 Texas could run their string to nine straight wins, or if Oklahoma would end eight years of misery.

Texas' ballyhooed quarterback, Bill Bradley, injured his knee in the game a week earlier, and Andy White replaced him. White's passes engineered the Steers to the OU three-yard line after the opening kickoff, but the Horns had to settle for Dave Conway's 25-yard field goal.

Minutes later, the Sooners wheeled 55 yards to take a 6-3 lead. Warmack faked a handoff and bootlegged around right end from the one-yard line to cap the five-play drive, but Vachon missed the conversion.

Warmack completed three passes for 55 yards as OU marched to a first down on the UT 13 late in the second stanza. After a loss of two yards and two incomplete passes, Vachon trotted on the field and nailed a 31-yard field goal for a 9-3 lead with 17 seconds until halftime.

The Sooners took the second-half kickoff and moved 64 yards to the Steers' 16 but stalled again, and Vachon's 42-yard boot lifted OU to a 12-3 advantage. Moments later, Stephenson intercepted White's pass and returned it 25 yards to the six. Three plays gained three yards, and Vachon was called on once more. And again he succeeded, this time with a 20-yard chip shot for a 15-3 lead.

Texas answered with a 67-yard TD drive to cut its gap to 15-9 midway through the final period, but Rod Crosswhite swatted down the two-point pass.

The Sooners took the kickoff and moved to the UT 22 on Warmack's 44-yard pass to Hart. And then the Keystone Cops showed up. OU fumbled to Texas on the 19. Texas gave it back on the 21. The Big Red spilled it back on the UT 17, then Burgess picked off a Texas pass and returned it 11 yards to the UT 30, but he fumbled. Fortunately for the Sooners, the ball rolled out of bounds on the 27.

OU could manage only four yards, but Vachon notched his fourth kick—a 41-yarder with 2:19 remaining. Minutes later, Sooner faithful brought the goal posts down.

OU gained more total yards, 351-271. Mackenzie became the second Sooner coach to beat Texas in his debut season. Bennie Owen was the first in 1905.

The Sooners hammered 2-2 Kansas, 35-0, the following week in Lawrence. Oklahoma scored off two long drives on its first and third possessions to take a 14-0 lead and never looked back.

The Sooners took the opening kickoff and whirled 80 yards. Warmack's nine-yard scoring strike to Hart capped the 16-play drive, and Vachon kicked the first of five conversions.

Oklahoma marched 70 yards in eight plays, beginning late in the first quarter and into the second. From the KU 12, Hinton sailed around right end and followed Harper's punishing block to the end zone.

The Jayhawks twice threatened with drives to the OU 26 and three but stalled, and they could muster only 50 total yards afterward.

The Big Red lead swelled to 20-0 early in the third period when Ross blocked David Morgan's punt on the goal line, and Stephenson smothered the ball in the end zone.

Burgar engineered the next Sooner series, a 66-yard drive in nine plays and finished it with an eight-yard scoring strike to Randy Meacham. Burgar completed three passes for the final 31 yards of the drive.

Joe Poslick recovered a Jayhawk fumble on the KU 20 to set up the final tally midway in the fourth period. Burgar tossed a 19-yard strike to Bo Denton, and Jim Jackson scored from the one on the next play.

The Sooners were balanced in yards gained—143 rushing and 146 passing. Warmack completed six of nine passes for 77 yards, and Burgar connected six of eight for 66 yards. Hart caught six aerials for 65 yards. The Jayhawks were held to 177 total yards.

Oklahoma shot to 10th in the AP poll and had a tall order on October 22 by hosting No. 1-ranked Notre Dame. The 4-0 Irish had destroyed their first four opponents by an average of 32-5. Notre Dame completely dominated in a 38-0 victory before a record crowd of 62,626 for homecoming in Norman.

The Irish threatened only once in their first four possessions and then scored on their next four series in the second and third stanzas. The Sooners penetrated Notre Dame territory only four times in the game and ran only four plays for nine yards in the second period.

Oklahoma's deepest drive to the Irish 24-yard line ended when Vachon shanked a 44-yard field-goal try.

Notre Dame scored 17 points off Sooners turnovers. A fumble led to a field goal and a 17-0 lead. The Irish intercepted Warmack's pass on the OU 40, ran it back to the 18, and scored moments later for a 31-0 lead. A poor punt snap to Stidham led to the final tally. Stidham scrambled for the ball but was nailed on the OU 12, and the Irish scored three plays later.

The Sooners had a chance to erase the goose egg on the scoreboard when Ross intercepted an Irish pass late in the game and returned it eight yards to the ND 32. Burgar lost eight yards trying to pass on the next play, then threw an interception.

Liggins left the game in the first stanza with a twisted ankle. Notre Dame's ace receiver, Jim Seymour, left in the second quarter also with a twisted ankle. The Irish rolled up more total yards (430-158).

Colorado scored 10 unanswered points to come from behind and defeat the Sooners, 24-21, the next week in Boulder.

Shotts did not play due to injury, and Jim Jackson replaced him at tailback. Jackson carried the ball 19 times for 152 yards and one touchdown. He scored on an 80-yard run on OU's first play from scrimmage for a 7-0 lead after Vachon kicked the first of three conversions.

The 3-3 Buffaloes tied the game with an 86-yard march late in the first period. Colorado returned a punt 17 yards to the OU 41 early in the third stanza and took a 14-7 lead four plays later.

The Sooners answered with a 79-yard, seven-play march to tie the game at 14-14. Warmack faked a pitch out and scooted 18 yards for the score. Warmack also sparked the drive with a 23-yard run to the OU 40, and Hinton added 22 more to the CU 38.

Colorado stalled on its next series and nailed a 59-yard punt. Hinton back-pedaled to his seven-yard line, then followed a wall of blockers down the sideline to the end zone and a 21-14 Sooner lead.

The Buffs rolled back 56 yards to the OU eight after the kickoff but had to settle for a 25-yard field goal. Colorado recovered a bad punt snap to Stidham on the OU 18 early in the fourth quarter and scored the deciding touchdown three plays later.

The Sooners later advanced to the Buffs' 40, but Warmack's pass on fourth-and-five misfired with two minutes to go. Colorado had the edge in total yards, 336-260.

Warmack sat out the next game with a sore shoulder, and Shotts was still sidelined with an ankle injury.

The Sooners snapped their two-game losing streak with their 30th straight conquest over Kansas State, a 37-6 decision, on November 5 in Norman.

The 0-6-1 Wildcats looked as though they were going to make OU suffer its third defeat of the year with two drives deep into Sooner territory, but both times they had to surrender on downs.

Oklahoma took a 10-0 lead in the second stanza on Hinton's three-yard touchdown run and Vachon's 18-yard field goal. The Sooners took the second-half kickoff and rolled 63 yards in 12 plays for a 16-0 advantage. Burgar capped the drive with a 12-yard scoring strike to Meacham, but Vachon missed the conversion.

The Cats could not stop the Sooners on the next OU series that grounded out 81 yards in 12 plays for a 23-0 lead.

Kansas State got its lone touchdown on the first play of the fourth period to complete an 80-yard drive that began late in the third.

Hinton brought the crimson faithful to its feet with a 65-yard TD run midway through the final stanza. Minutes later, Don Davis intercepted a K-State pass on the KSU 18 and returned it to the 12. Cagle tossed a TD pass to Stan Crowder on the next play for the final tally.

The Big Red piled up 460 total yards. Jackson carried 27 times for 137 yards, and Burgar completed 10 of 15 passes for 151 yards. Kansas State collected 275 total yards.

Missouri's kicking did in the Sooners on November 12 in Norman. The 4-3-1 Tigers defeated Oklahoma, 10-7, thanks to a 52-yard field goal by Mizzou's Bill Bates, who also punted the Big Red deep on many occasions.

A punting duel ensued in the first half, as neither team generated much yardage (OU 61 and Missouri 79).

The Tigers took the second-half kickoff and marched 76 yards in five plays to take a 7-0 lead.

Missouri intercepted Warmack's pass minutes later and drove to the Sooner 25 but had to settle for Bates' 52-yard field goal, the longest to date in Tiger football history.

Down 10-0, the Sooners answered with a 68-yard scoring drive in nine plays. Warmack scooted around left end for a 10-yard TD run, and Vachon's conversion cut the lead to 10-7 with about 10 minutes remaining. Oklahoma never mounted another threat.

Bates punted 12 times for the Tigers and pinned OU inside their 35-yard line on nine occasions; six times inside the 22. Hinton twice fumbled Bates' kicks, once in the first quarter and again late in the game.

The Tigers picked up more total yards (212-192).

Sooner Magic:
Nebraska's Title Hopes Dashed Again

Forty-eight seconds separated the No.4 Nebraska Cornhuskers from an undefeated season and a chance to claim the national championship in 1966. OU's defense and a blond placekicker from Amarillo, Texas, provided the Huskers with their only loss of the season, 10-9.

The 9-0 Cornhuskers came to town on Thanksgiving for their final game of the year. The last time Nebraska played in Norman was an unpleasant memory for the Huskers. Two years earlier, the Huskers were also undefeated and ranked fourth nationally, but were stunned, 17-7, by Oklahoma. It was the only shining moment in Gomer Jones' two-year stint as OU head coach. The Sooners ended any hopes for Nebraska to stake a claim to the national championship that year.

NU already captured the Big Eight Conference crown and a bid to play in the Sugar Bowl prior to the '66 matchup. OU, with a 5-3 record, had hopes for a bowl bid but needed a win in the final two games to be invited for postseason activity. The Sooners held a 22-20-3 edge in the series.

Hinton electrified the national (ABC) TV audience and 42,884 fans in attendance when he took the opening kickoff from his three-yard line and broke tackles before being brought down at the NU 48. The Sooners fumbled two plays later, and Nebraska recovered at its own 37.

The Huskers drove to the OU 13, but Stephenson intercepted Bob Churchich's pass in the flat and returned the ball to the OU 18. The Sooners moved into Nebraska territory, but Vachon missed a 34-yard field goal try into a 25-mph wind.

The first quarter ended in a scoreless tie, but Nebraska drove 78 yards to the OU five late in the opening quarter and into the second period. A stout Sooner defense kept Nebraska out of the end zone, but Larry Wachholtz nailed a 38-yard field goal to give NU a 3-0 lead with 9:55 left until halftime.

OU marched 66 yards to take a 7-3 edge just before intermission. Warmack lobbed a 52-yard scoring strike to Hinton and Vachon converted.

Nebraska took a 9-7 lead with a touchdown late in the third quarter, but Stephenson blocked the extra-point try.

OU failed to make a first down on its next possession, and the Huskers returned the punt to midfield. Churchich set up for a pass, but Sooner defensive end John Koller popped the Nebraska quarterback. The ball squirted free, and Koller pounced on the ball as the quarter came to a close.

Another Churchich pass was intercepted early in the fourth period. Jackson carried for nine yards and 16 yards to give OU a first down at the NU 13. The Sooners were unable to gain another first down, and Vachon was called on to boot the Sooners ahead. A stiff south breeze car-

ried the ball left of the uprights, and NU held onto the slim margin with 11 minutes remaining.

The Big Red of the North marched to the OU 24, but a stingy defense by the Big Red of the South held and took possession.

Several plays later at the OU 39, Warmack failed to successfully handoff to Harper. The pigskin bounded on the turf, but Warmack outwrestled Wayne Meylan, Nebraska's All-America noseguard, for the ball.

The next play was third-and-seven at NU's 45. Hart shagged Warmack's pass and gained 12 yards. Jackson was held to one yard on the next two carries. Warmack then handed off to Harper, who bolted 19 yards to the 11. Kalsu and Mark Kosmos provided key blocks, opening a huge hole in the Husker defense.

Jackson picked up four yards, then Warmack slid to the four-yard line. Jackson was stopped cold for no gain, and Vachon trotted on the field again. His kick split the uprights, and OU held a 10-9 lead with 48 seconds left in the game.

The Cornhuskers had 48 seconds to save an undefeated season. Ben Gregory returned the kickoff to the NU 35. Ross picked off Churchich's sideline pass, but he was out of bounds, so Nebraska maintained possession.

Churchich connected with Gregory for 15 yards to midfield with 25 seconds on the clock. Stephenson knocked down Churchich's pass on the next play. Churchich then tossed a six-yarder in the right flat to end Tom Penney, who held onto the ball after Ross flattened him.

The clock showed 10 ticks left. Churchich lofted a pass to Dennis Richnafshy toward the end zone, but the strong wind kept the ball from going the distance, and Crosswhite intercepted at the Sooner

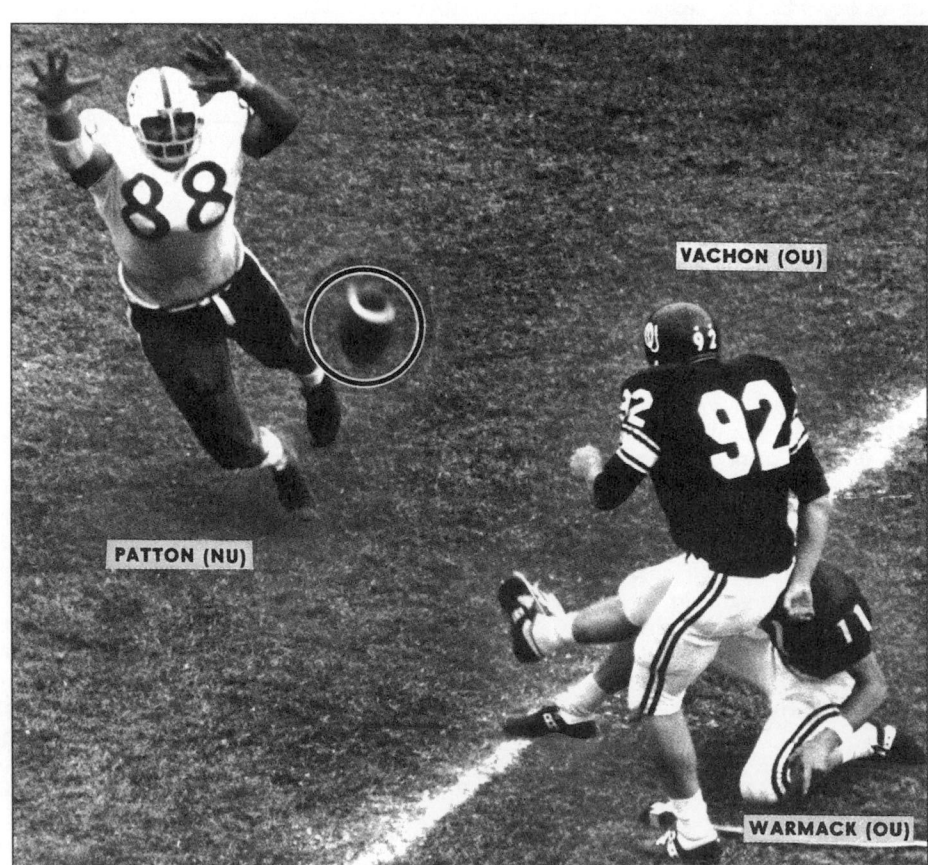

Mike Vachon toes the winning field goal to stun fourth-ranked Nebraska, 10-9. (*OU Athletics*)

10-yard line. The clock had no more ticks to give. To the left of the zeros on the clock was "10" under "Oklahoma," and on the right: "9" under "Nebraska."

The Cowboys defeated the Sooners, 15-14, on December 4 in Stillwater. OU failed on a two-point conversion, which allowed OSU to win its second straight in the series, a feat that had not happened in 21 years.

The Big Red lost two chances to score first as the Pokes got a piece of Vachon's two field goals in the first stanza. His 21-yarder was blocked, and a 43-yarder later was deflected.

Ronnie Johnson scored the first of two touchdowns to give the 3-5-1 Cowboys an 8-0 lead early in the second period, and they added a two-point conversion on a fake extra point.

The Big Red took the second-half kickoff and marched 48 yards in nine plays to tie the game. Shotts, who carried eight times for 47 yards in the drive, sliced through left tackle from the three-yard line. Warmack tossed the two-point pass to Kalsu on a tackle-eligible play.

Johnson's other touchdown late in the third stanza came seven plays after OSU recovered Warmack's fumble on the OU 18. The extra point gave the Cowboys a 15-8 lead.

The Sooners advanced 74 yards to the OSU one-yard line minutes later, but Warmack's fourth-down run was stopped short of the goal line.

A 24-yard punt by the Pokes moments later set up Oklahoma on the OSU 30 with five minutes remaining in the game. Shotts carried on all nine plays and scored from the one-yard line with 1:29 to go. Mackenzie ordered a two-point conversion to win the game. OSU's defense pressured Warmack as he was looking for a receiver. He tossed the ball to Shotts on the five, but Shotts was cut down on the two, and OSU escaped with the one-point win.

"We came up here [Stillwater] to try to win," Mackenzie said afterward, defending his decision to go for two.

OU gained more total yards, 237-209. Shotts gained 149 yards on 39 carries.

The Sooner football team declined an invitation to play in the Liberty Bowl on December 10, six days after OU played its season finale against Oklahoma State.

The Sooners finished the 1966 season, 6-4 and fifth in the Big Eight with a 4-3 record. Liggins was the only Sooner selected All-America, but he was not named to the All-Big Eight first team. That honor went to Ed Hall, Hart, and Ross.

Five months later, Mackenzie died of a heart attack following a recruiting trip to Amarillo on April 28, 1967.

No one knows how well Mackenzie would have fared as OU's head coach after the '66 campaign. Life didn't give him much time. But two of his assistants carried his torch as head coach at Oklahoma. Chuck Fairbanks returned the football program to national prominence, and Barry Switzer won three national championships in his 16-year tenure.

Switzer believes that if Mackenzie had not passed away he would have had the same success that Chuck Fairbanks and he (Switzer) would have had.

"Chuck ended up being the head coach, and all of the assistants made a great contribution," Switzer recalled. "But we had great players to continue Jim Mackenzie's desire for winning. You don't win at Oklahoma unless there are good players there. We were fortunate to have goods players when we took over the program.

"You win because of the talent and preparing the team to play the game and having the willingess to prepare. Assistant coaches and players make that happen. You've got to recruit good, you've got to get good players around you, you've got to get good assistant coaches; it takes a team effort. It's a 'we' game, it's an 'us' game."

1967

Not wanting to shake up the Oklahoma football program with a new coaching philosophy and system, OU president Dr. George Cross recommended elevating assistant coach Chuck Fairbanks as head coach. The regents consented in their May meeting, and Fairbanks became the Sooners' 16th head coach.

Fairbanks, who was Jim Mackenzie's secondary coach a year ago, also was an assistant at Arizona State and Houston before coming to OU. He played offensive end for Michigan State's 1952 national championship team.

Fairbanks inherited a solid squad for the 1967 campaign. The entire starting backfield, which amassed 1,204 of 1,669 rushing yards in 1966, returned. Quarterback Bob Warmack, tailback Ron Shotts, fullback Gary Harper, and wingback Eddie Hinton would provide plenty of fuel for the offensive attack. Sophomore Steve Owens would step up to split tailback duties with Shotts.

Lack of depth in the offensive and defensive lines was a concern for Fairbanks, yet he had plenty of talent in the starting lineup. Tackle Bob Kalsu returned to lead the offensive line along with center Bob Craig.

All-America noseguard Granville Liggins was back to bolster the middle of the defensive front wall along with tackle John Titsworth and end John Koller. Linebacker Harry Hettsmansperger was back, along with safety Steve Barrett and Bob Stephenson. Mike Vachon, who booted a field goal to beat Nebraska and four field goals to beat Texas a year before, also returned.

Oklahoma hosted 0-1 Washington State to open the 1967 campaign. Bert Clark, all-conference linebacker for the Sooners in 1951, was the Cougars' head coach. OU defeated the Cougars, 21-0.

The Sooners marched 81 yard in 13 plays on their first possession for a 7-0 lead. On fourth-and-two at the WSU 15, Warmack faked a handoff and scooted around right end for the score. Vachon kicked the first of three conversions.

The lead grew to 14-0 on Owens' two-yard plunge early in the second stanza. The Sooners drove 44 yards in eight plays for the final tally midway through the third quarter. Warmack's 17-yard scoring strike to Hinton capped the drive.

The Cougars threatened twice in the fourth stanza (once to the OU 13 and later to the 20), but both times they surrendered on downs.

1966 Season Record: 6-4-0
Big Eight Conference: 4-3-0 (Fifth)

Date	Opponent	Result	Score
September 17	OREGON	W	17-0
September 24	at Iowa State	W	33-11
October 8	Texas at Dallas	W	18-9
October 15	at Kansas	W	35-0
October 22	NOTRE DAME	L	38-0
October 29	at Colorado	L	24-21
November 5	KANSAS STATE	W	37-6
November 12	MISSOURI	L	10-7
November 24	NEBRASKA	W	10-9
December 3	at Oklahoma State	L	15-14

OU rolled up more total yards, 363-149. Warmack completed seven of 11 passes for 118 yards.

The Sooners hammered Maryland, 35-0, the following week before a throng of 46,215 in Norman. Shotts and Owens each rushed for 129 yards and scored a touchdown.

OU got it done in three quarters by scoring touchdowns on its first, third, fourth, and fifth possessions. The Sooners took the opening kickoff and rolled 79 yards in 12 plays. Shotts plowed ahead from the one-yard line but fumbled as he fought to cross the goal line, and split end Joe Killingsworth recovered in the end zone. Vachon kicked all five conversions in the game.

Maryland advanced to the OU one after the kickoff, but the Big Red defense stiffened. The Terps proved they had nothing on defense as the Sooners rolled 99 yards (including a 15-yard penalty) in 12 plays for a 14-0 lead. Hinton took a pitchout and sailed five yards around right end for the score.

Oklahoma marched 40 yards in eight plays on its next series for a 21-0 advantage. Owens capped the drive with a five-yard run. The Sooners scored on their next two possessions, a five-yard run by Owens and a 56-yard sprint by Shotts, for a 28-0 halftime lead.

Warmack tossed a 19-yard scoring strike to tight end Steve Zabel in the third period for the final tally.

Oklahoma collected 418 rushing yards. Warmack hit seven of nine passes for 76 yards and completed his first six in the first half. The Terrapins gained 208 total yards.

Turnovers were the Sooners' curse two weeks later as 1-2 Texas edged OU, 9-7, before a Cotton Bowl crowd of 75,504. The Longhorns lost their first two games, then beat Oklahoma State a week before the OU tilt.

Oklahoma took the opening kickoff and marched 78 yards for a 7-0 lead. Shotts' two-yard run completed the drive. He also had a 41-yard jaunt to spark the drive.

The Sooners advanced to the Steers' eight minutes later, but an intercepted pass in the end zone killed the threat. They threatened again on their next series to the UT eight, but Vachon shanked a 27-yard field goal.

Hinton took a Texas punt moments later and returned it 33 yards to the UT 28. One play later, Texas again intercepted in the end zone.

The Sooners took the second-half kickoff and advanced to the Horns' 29, but Warmack fumbled moments later, and Texas recovered on its 35. From there, the Steers rolled to the Sooners' 12, but settled for Rob Layne's 34-yard field goal late in the third stanza.

Moments later, Texas drove 84 yards for the winning touchdown capped by Bill Bradley's seven-yard run. The extra point failed, and OU still had a chance with 14:19 left in the game.

Bradley's punt pinned Oklahoma deep at the three-yard line late in the game. Warmack whipped four passes for a combined 45 yards to the 48. He got out of bounds on an end run to the Texas 49 for a first down with eight seconds left. Warmack scrambled left and then right as he tried to spot an open receiver or a huge opening to run. He took off but was knocked out of bounds after a five-yard gain, and the clock expired.

OU picked up more total yards, 360-300. Warmack completed 12 of 19 passes for 134 yards, Owens rushed for 106 yards, and Gordon Wheeler averaged 44.7 yards on three punts.

The Sooners pounded 1-3 Kansas State, 46-7, on October 21 in Manhattan. OU scored on its first two possessions of the first half en route to a 20-0 halftime lead, and on its first four possessions of the second half.

Owens scored three times and rushed for 100 yards. Shotts picked up 125 yards on the ground and scored once. Warmack tossed a 19-yard TD pass to Hinton (for the 20-0 lead) and scored once on a three-yard run.

Oklahoma gained 29 first downs, rushed for 363 yards, and passed for 152 more. Warmack connected on nine of 14 aerials for 132 yards. OU punted only once, and Wheeler's sole kick went for 56 yards. The Cats picked up 16 first downs and 186 total yards, 79 on their touchdown drive against the Sooner reserves in the fourth quarter.

The Sooners scored one touchdown in the first half and held off 4-1 Missouri, 7-0, the next week in Columbia.

The Togers failed to cross the 50-yard line in the first half. Wheeler kept them pinned deep with punts to the MU 1, 2, and 5.

OU took a Tiger punt on its own 42 to embark on the touchdown drive in the second quarter. On the first play, Warmack dropped back and sailed a bomb to Zabel. The wind caught the pigskin, allowing Missouri's John Meyer to deflect it. The ball came down into Zabel's hands on the 20, and he sprinted to the seven-yard line. Shotts carried for one yard, then Warmack scooted around right end to the one. On the next play, Shotts slashed over right tackle for the score, and Vachon converted with 5:54 left until intermission.

Mizzou's Roger Wehrli took the kickoff and returned it 50 yards to the Sooners' 48. The Tigers moved to the 28 where they faced third-and-five. Defensive end Jim Files sacked quarterback Gary Kombrink for a three-yard loss, and Missouri punted.

Wehrli later took a punt and returned it to the OU 38. The Tigers advanced to the 10-yard line, but Liggins and Koller dumped Kombrink for a 10-yard loss, and Missouri missed the field goal.

The Tigers drove to the OU 21 early in the fourth quarter, but Files recorded his fourth tackle for a loss, and Steve Barrett intercepted on the next play. Titsworth intercepted a Mizzou pass on the OU 37 moments later.

The Sooners cracked the tough Tiger defense one more time to the 18 late in the game but stalled, and Vachon missed a 35-yard field goal.

The Sooners had more total yards (214-172). Both teams combined for 19 punts and only three penalties (Oklahoma once for 15 yards and Missouri twice for seven yards). Linebacker Don Pfrimmer led the OU defense with 17 tackles.

The Sooners took advantage of two pass interceptions, a fumble, and a blocked punt to beat ninth-ranked Colorado, 23-0, on November 4 before a homecoming crowd of 61,106 in Norman. The 5-1 Buffaloes won their first five games before dropping a 10-7 decision to Oklahoma State a week before the Oklahoma contest.

Wheeler's 66-yard punt nailed the Buffs on their 16-yard line in the second period. Colorado punted back moments later, but defensive end Dick Paaso deflected it, and the ball rolled out on the CU 23. The Sooners advanced to the Buffs' four but had to settle for Vachon's 21-yard field goal for a 3-0 lead.

Minutes later, Stephenson's 14-yard interception return to the Colorado 44 set up the first Big Red touchdown. Owens scored from the four-yard line, and Vachon toed the 10th point with 23 seconds until halftime. Warmack hurled an 18-yard pass to Hinton to spark the drive.

Richard Goodwin's interception on the Buffs' 35 set up Owens' next TD in the fourth stanza. Eight plays later, on fourth-and-goal

---

It's a Fact

The Sooner defense finished first in the nation in scoring defense in 1967, yeilding an average of 6.8 points per game.

at the one, Owens plowed over, and Vachon converted for a 17-0 advantage.

Minutes later, Files hammered quarterback Dan Kelly, forcing a fumble, and Liggins smothered it on the CU 29. Hinton scored on a three-yard run six plays later, but Colorado blocked Vachon's conversion.

The Big Red racked up more total yards, 262-181. Pfrimmer again led the defense with 14 tackles.

The Sooners entered the AP poll for the first time of the year at No. 8. They traveled to Ames the next week and blasted 2-6 Iowa State, 52-14. Owens and Shotts each scored two touchdowns apiece, and Warmack ran for a touchdown and passed for another to lead the onslaught.

Tight end Steve Zabel hauls in Bob Warmack's pass to defeat Kansas, 14-10. (*OU Athletics*)

Warmack threw an interception to stall OU's first possession, then the Sooners erupted for five touchdowns on their next five possessions. Warmack fired a 76-yard scoring strike to Zabel to give the Sooners a 40-0 lead early in the third period. The pass was his 107th completion, breaking Jack Jacobs' school record for most pass completions in a season set in 1941.

Warmack completed seven of 13 passes for 171 yards in the game. Oklahoma rolled up 539 total yards and 27 first downs. The defense held the Cyclones to 221 total yards.

The 6-1 Sooners rose to seventh the next week in the AP poll.

Sooner Magic: From Goat to Hero

Goat is a label given to a player who is singled out for blowing his assignment and allowing the opponent to gain momentum. That's how Zabel felt in the 1967 game against Kansas when he failed to pick up a block that allowed a KU defender to block a punt in the third quarter.

Hero is the name given to a player who makes the greatest play of the game to allow his team to conquer the opponent. Zabel had gone from goat to hero for the Sooners.

Kansas lost its first three games before pitching an upset shutout against undefeated Nebraska. The Hawks continued their winning ways, defeating Oklahoma State, Iowa State, and Kansas State before stumbling against Colorado. Kansas, 4-4 (4-1 in the Big Eight), arrived in Norman and nearly pulled off an upset against another Top-10 team. Oklahoma had won the last two meetings against Kansas and led the overall series, 37-21-6. The Sooners made it three straight with a 14-10 victory before a throng of 57,649.

Warmack was evolving into a poised leader of the OU offense, and his composure was vital in the Sooners' final drive in the game.

A Kansas field goal in the first quarter gave the Jayhawks a 3-0 lead, which they held through halftime.

The Sooner offense was lethargic in the opening half, gaining only three first downs and 63 total yards. Warmack had connected on just five of 14 passes for 48 yards. Many of his aerials misfired, and twice he was picked off. The offense, which had not been shut out in the previous seven games of 1967, never threatened to score in the first half.

Early in the third quarter, Wheeler took the snap but had to scramble to get in position to kick. He managed to elude the Jayhawks' oncoming rush. As he tried to kick, KU's Orville Turgeon, the player who Zabel failed to block, got a hand on the ball, which bounced around on the turf. OU recovered, but it was fourth down, so the Jayhawks took possession at the Sooner 19.

"Their linebacker came through on the left side," Wheeler said after the game. "I thought I could side step him. I'm pretty sure he'd have blocked it if I hadn't. When I did side step him, there were two or three men still there who did block it.

"I should have gone ahead and kicked it, but I felt if I did the linebacker would block it into the end zone, and they'd score right there, because he was coming pretty hard."

Seven plays later, KU's lead grew to 10-0 with 8:49 left in the third period.

That was time for OU's offense to show some life, and it did. The Sooners answered with a 77-yard drive in 13 plays. Owens carried the ball 10 times and capped the drive on a seven-yard end sweep into the end zone with 1:52 left in the quarter. Vachon nailed the extra point, and the Big Red trailed, 10-7.

Both teams went nowhere on their next two possessions.

As the fourth period was winding down, a KU punt had the Sooners pinned at their own four-yard line with 6:37 left on the clock. The fans were on the edge of their seats.

OU moved the ball toward the south end of the stadium but not without overcoming a couple of obstacles. The Sooners gained crucial first downs—one on a third-and-four at their 34, and the other on fourth-and-one at their 43. The Sooners continued to the KU 30. That was when OU offensive coordinator Barry Switzer, sitting in the press box, called down "24 pass," a toss to the tight end. The goat.

Zabel took off from the line of scrimmage, and Warmack faked to Owens and faded back to heave the ball toward Zabel who outraced KU defender Tommy Ball. The pigskin began its descent over Zabel's shoulder in the end zone. Zabel reached out and clutched the ball.

The fans and OU bench exploded, and oranges rained from the stands.

Before the opening kickoff, some fans were selling oranges for a quarter apiece. The oranges were a signal of hope that OU would return to the Orange Bowl in Miami, Florida, for the first time in five years.

After officials cleared the field, Vachon kicked the extra point, and OU led 14-10 with 1:02 remaining in the game.

But wait. The Sooners, rather the fans, were penalized for unsportsmanlike conduct for the orange shower upon the field.

Instead of kicking from the 40, the Sooners were forced to kickoff from their own 25. The Jayhawks returned the kick to OU's 47, and in a few plays they advanced to the 38. On fourth down, Bobby Douglass' pass barely missed receiver Gary Ard's hands.

After the game, Zabel said he thought he redeemed himself for catching the pass after missing his blocking assignment earlier. He was asked about the missed assignment and the winning TD grab.

"I just broke until I beat the halfback deep," he said. "If I can't beat him, I hook. Luckily I beat him. It was the greatest feeling I ever had in my whole life. I sort of redeemed myself, I think."

The victory gave OU at least a tie for the Big Eight Championship and a No.5 national ranking.

The Sooners clinched the outright conference title with a 21-14 victory over 6-3 Nebraska before a Thanksgiving day crowd of 59,154 in Lincoln. Hinton's breakaway run early in the fourth stanza was the difference.

Vachon hammered Joe Orduna on the opening kickoff, causing the Husker to fumble, and Stephenson recovered on the NU 26. The Sooners had to settle for Vachon's 20-yard field goal for a 3-0 advantage.

After an exchange of punts, Oklahoma marched 47 yards for a 10-0 lead. Shotts scored from the one seven plays later, and Vachon converted.

After the Huskers returned the ensuing kickoff to their 40, Koller forced quarterback Frank Patrick to fumble, and Liggins pounced on it at the 31. The Sooners were held to five yards, and Vachon toed a 33-yard field goal to raise the lead to 13-0.

Nebraska scored on its next two possessions for a 14-13 lead. Hinton made Sooner hearts skip a beat when he fumbled the second kickoff, and the Huskers recovered on the 28 with 40 seconds until halftime. A penalty wiped out a Husker touchdown, and they missed the field goal.

A short Nebraska punt gave OU possession on the Huskers' 33 late in the third stanza. On third-and-10, Warmack zipped an 11-yard pass to Zabel. On the next play, Warmack faked to Shotts and pitched to Hinton, who sailed around left end for the deciding tally. After a time out, the Sooners sent in the offense for a two-point conversion. Warmack lateraled to Shotts, who then tossed the ball to Zabel in the end zone for a 21-14 lead.

Bob Stephenson follows a key block after intercepting a Tennessee pass. Stephenson's TD and Mike Vachon's extra point put Oklahoma ahead, 26-17, in the fourth quarter. (© 1968, The Daily Oklahoman)

Although they lost, the Huskers had the better statistics with 21 first downs and 413 total yards. Patrick completed 22 of 40 passes for 290 yards, and Dick Davis rushed for 122 more. Oklahoma picked up 16 first downs and 253 total yards. Warmack completed half of his 26 attempted passes for 129 yards.

The Sooners jumped to third in the AP poll and hammered 4-4-1 Oklahoma State, 38-14, on December 2 before a throng of 62,038 in Norman. The Big Red took a 20-0 lead in the first 22 minutes and never looked back.

Owens scored two touchdowns and rushed for 136 yards to lead the Big Eight Conference with 808 rushing yards. Shotts added 108 yards for second place in the conference with 726 yards. Owens also led the conference in scoring with 12 touchdowns.

Warmack tossed two scoring strikes and broke two school season records with 1,136 passing yards and 1,345 yards in total offense. He eclipsed both records previously held by Claude Arnold in 1950.

Oklahoma picked up more first downs against the Pokes (21-19) and total yards (372-255).

The Sooners finished the '67 regular season 9-1, and were on their way to the Orange Bowl to play the No.2 Tennessee Volunteers on New Year's Day.

Sooner Magic: Victory in the Twilight Zone

Rod Serling could not have written a better episode of the Twilight Zone in contrast to the 1968 Orange Bowl. The Sooners were poised for a blowout of Tennessee, but wound up with 77,993 fans squirming in their seats for the final cliff-hanging play.

No. 2 Tennessee and No. 3 Oklahoma entered the game with identical 9-1 records. Both teams were as hot as the muggy Miami Monday night of 72 degrees. TU won nine straight games after losing to UCLA in the opening game. The Big Red won seven straight following the loss to Texas.

The Volunteers won the only previous encounter 17-0 in the 1939 Orange Bowl.

The Sooners were nearly flawless in the first half of the '68 Orange Bowl as they pinned the Vols with a 19-0 lead.

Tennessee took the opening kickoff to its 46-yard line, then drove to the OU 32 but fumbled, and Files recovered for the Sooners.

OU then marched 68 yards in nine plays for the first score. Hinton came up with two big catches from Warmack. An 18-yard pass moved the football to the TU 20, and a 10-yard reception put the pigskin at the Vols' seven. Warmack then scooted around end to cap the drive. Vachon's foot gave the Sooners a 7-0 lead with 8:39 to go in the first period. No team had scored first on the Volunteers all season.

OU drove 87 yards in eight plays late in the first quarter and into the second. From the Vols' 21, Warmack sailed the ball to Hinton, who caught it in the far corner of the end zone. Vachon missed the extra point, but the Sooners led, 13-0, with 14:15 remaining in the first half.

The Vols' Charles Fulton returned the kickoff and had only one man, Cagle, to beat to the end zone. Cagle wrapped him up at the OU 39. Tennessee drove to the Sooners' 25. Liggins made two big plays for the Sooners. He nailed fullback Richard Pickens for a one-yard loss, then sacked quarterback Dewey Warren for an eight-yard loss. The Vols were forced to kick a 51-yard field goal, which fell short.

The Sooners drove 74 yards in 12 plays late in the second period. With the ball at the TU one, Warmack handed off to Owens, who leaped in the air, over orange-clad defenders and across the goal line with 1:48 remaining until halftime. OU tried a two-point conversion but was flagged for motion. On the second try, Warmack looked for an open receiver but had to scramble, and he was stopped inside the one.

Oklahoma looked like the nation's best football team heading into the locker room with the 19-0 lead.

This is where the Twilight Zone music must have begun: doot-doot-doot-doot-doot-doot-doot-doot.

In the first half, Warmack accumulated 188 total yards, but zero in the second half. He completed nine of 13 passes for 107 yards in the first half, but zero for five in the second. Doot-doot-doot-doot-doot-doot-doot-doot.

Tennessee came out of the locker room and began adding points to its side of the scoreboard thanks to a couple of interceptions. The Vols picked off two Warmack passes in the third quarter, which allowed them to score two touchdowns in a span of two minutes and 10 seconds.

The Vols trailed 19-14 with 5:07 left in the third quarter and narrowed the gap with a field goal early in the fourth, 19-17.

On TU's next possession, Warren's pass was deflected then picked off by Stephenson at the Vols' 25. Stephenson, being chased by TU's All-America center, Bob Johnson, barely escaped his opponent's reach. He then followed a wall of crimson jerseys and raced to the end zone. Vachon was successful on this extra point, and Oklahoma led, 26-17, with 9:35 to go.

The Volunteers retaliated with a 77-yard, 12-play drive to trail 26-24.

Liggins dislocated his knee during that drive—a blow for the Sooners, who would have to rely on a stout defense to stop Tennessee the rest of the way. Liggins was the granite of the OU defensive line. All night long, two All-Americans, Liggins and Johnson, battled each other in the trenches. Liggins said his opponent was "strong, fast, and quite a gentleman." When Liggins was felled by the injury, it was Johnson who helped him to his feet.

With less than two minutes to play, the Sooners faced fourth-and-one foot for a first down at their own 44-yard line. Instead of punting and forcing the Vols to drive a longer distance, Chuck Fairbanks

Tailback Steve Owens drives across the goal line to give OU a 19-0 lead over Tennessee in the Orange Bowl. (*OU Athletics*)

decided to gamble. Warmack handed off to Owens, who was hammered by TU tackle Jack Reynolds for no gain. Tennessee took possession with 1:44 remaining.

"The tackle and the end were slanting down at me," Owens said of the failed fourth-down attempt. "Our fullback had to take the end. That left the tackle clear for a shot at me. The linebacker was coming right behind the tackle. Three yards from the line of scrimmage, I saw the tackle coming. I just didn't have a chance to dive. I might have made it if I had."

Kalsu slammed his helmet to the turf. He was furious that the play was not called to his side of the offense. "The only thing I was unhappy about is they didn't go over my side. I always like us to run plays over me."

"I thought it was the right thing to do," Fairbanks said of the fourth-down gamble. "The way Tennessee was moving the ball, I didn't want to give the football back to them."

The Vols moved to the OU 27, where the Big Red defense stalled them and Karl Kremser was called on to boot the winning field goal with seven seconds left. The Volunteer kicker felt confident. Midway through the season, his field goal defeated Louisiana State, 17-14. He had missed some though, as he made 10 of 16 in his attempts for the season.

Fans everywhere were turning blue from holding their breaths—Volunteers hoping for success, and Sooners hoping for failure. From 43 yards out, Kremser put his foot to the ball, which carried the distance but sailed wide. OU escaped with a 26-24 victory.

Limp Sooner fans exhaled, then whooped and hollered.

Oklahoma and Tennessee displayed the best bowl performance of the season. Neither would have a chance at No.1 since Southern

1967 Season Record: 10-1-0

Big Eight Conference: 7-0-0 (Champions)

Date	Opponent	Result	Score
September 23	WASHINGTON STATE	W	21-0
September 30	MARYLAND	W	35-0
October 14	Texas at Dallas	L	9-7
October 21	at Kansas State	W	46-7
October 28	at Missouri	W	7-0
November 4	COLORADO	W	23-0
November 11	at Iowa State	W	24-20
November 18	KANSAS	W	14-10
November 23	at Nebraska	W	21-14
December 2	OKLAHOMA STATE	W	38-14
January 1	Tennessee*	W	26-24

*Orange Bowl at Miami, FL

California defeated Indiana earlier in the day at the Rose Bowl. Oklahoma finished the season in third place in the AP poll.

All-America honors went to Kalsu and Liggins. Koller, Owens, and Warmack joined them on the All-Big Eight first team. Liggins was also chosen as UPI Lineman of the Year.

1968

Nineteen hundred sixty-eight was one of the most turbulent years in history. The Vietnam war was escalating as were peace protests at home and abroad. Martin Luther King Jr. and Bobby Kennedy were assassinated, President Lyndon Johnson threw in the towel to run for reelection, Richard Nixon won a close election, and Dr. Christian Barnard performed the first successful heart transplant.

The Sooner offense was expected to be explosive with the return of three-fourths of the backfield—quarterback Bob Warmack, tailback Steve Owens and wingback Eddie Hinton. Fullback Gary Harper was moved to defense as the monster man, another term for a hard-hitting defensive back. His brother, Mike, replaced him at fullback. Center Ken Mendenhall, guard Bill Elfstrom and tackle Byron Bigby would return to anchor the front offensive line. Joe Killingsworth returned to the starting split end slot, and tight end Steve Zabel took on more duties as a linebacker and punter.

All-America noseguard Granville Liggins had graduated, and Chuck Fairbanks was concerned about finding a replacement. Ken Davis got the nod, but he was supported by a solid lineup of returnees—tackles Dick Paaso and John Titsworth, end Jim Files, linebacker Don Pfrimmer, and safety Steve Barrett.

The Sooners were ranked fourth in the preseason AP poll but dropped a notch the following week without having snapped a down. They opened the season on September 21 with a 45-21 loss to No. 4 Notre Dame in South Bend, Indiana.

The Fighting Irish took a 7-0 lead on their first possession, then Oklahoma answered in one play to tie the game after returning the kickoff to the 28. Warmack, who completed three touchdown passes, hurled a short strike to Hinton on the 35, and Hinton snaked through defenders for the final 65 yards to the end zone. Bruce Derr converted the tying point.

Hinton entered the game on defense for the first time in his career and made a crucial interception. Terry Hanratty directed a pass to Jim Seymour, his favorite receiver, but Hinton stepped in front of Seymour on the OU nine and raced 31 yards upfield. The Sooners rolled 59 yards in 10 plays. Warmack hurled a 16-yard scoring strike to Zabel, and Derr's conversion gave OU a 14-7 lead.

Notre Dame fumbled one play after the kickoff, and linebacker Steve Casteel smothered it on the ND 20, but the Irish defense stiffened, and Derr shanked a 29-yard field goal try.

The Irish scored four touchdowns in the middle quarters for a 35-14 lead. Hanratty twice tossed scoring strikes to Seymour, and halfback Bob Gladieux scored twice from a yard out.

A field goal early in the fourth stanza upped the Irish lead to 38-14, and Warmack later completed an 11-yard TD pass to Zabel to cap a 76-yard drive. Notre Dame added another touchdown minutes later.

Notre Dame dominated the stats with 35 first downs and 571 total yards. Hanratty completed 18 of for 202 yards, and Seymour caught nine of his aerials for 101 yards. Oklahoma gained 12 first downs, and its ground game was held in check with 85 rushing yards, but Warmack completed 172 through the air.

The loss dropped OU out of the AP poll, but the Sooners ran their record to 1-1 with a 28-14 victory over 2-0 North Carolina

State the next week in Norman. The Big Red defense still had some trouble defending the pass. The Wolfpack's Jack Klebes completed 21 of 40 passes for 236 yards and two touchdowns. Yet the Sooners intercepted four of his aerials.

Owens, who carried the pigskin 37 times for 164 yards, led OU with two touchdowns. His first came on a one-yard plunge to cap a 65-yard drive in 11 plays on the Sooners' first possession, but Derr missed the extra point. Warmack sparked the drive with a 26-yard jaunt to the Wolfpack 11.

NC State advanced to the OU 10-yard line minutes later but had to surrender on downs. The Sooners then wheeled 91 yards for a 14-0 lead early in the second period. Owens' one-yard plunge capped the drive, then Warmack scooted around right end for two more points. Three big plays in the drive came from Warmack's 18-yard run to the OU 33, Owens' 27-yard jaunt to the NCS 26 and Eddie Hinton's one-handed grab of Warmack's 13-yard pass to the NCS 14.

The Sooners marched 42 yards in five plays for a 21-0 lead midway through the third quarter. From the Wolfpack 27, Warmack scrambled to the sideline and fired a bullet to Hinton on the 10, and Hinton dashed to the end zone. Derr toed the conversion.

NC State got on board with Klebe's first scoring strike midway in the fourth period. Joe Pearce intercepted Klebe's pass on the next Wolfpack series at the NCS 36 to set up the Sooners' final tally. Two plays after the pickoff, Warmack drilled a 27-yard TD pass to Zabel, and Derr converted.

Klebe fired another TD pass with about four minutes remaining in the game.

OU gained more yards, 397-325. Hinton caught six passes for 92 yards to raise his career total to a school-record 981 yards, surpassing Ben Hart's 915 yards set from 1964-66. Hinton broke a bone in his left hand and was fitted with a soft cast.

The Sooners traveled to Dallas two weeks later to face winless Texas (0-1-1) before a crowd of 71,837 in the Cotton Bowl. Steve Worster's seven-yard TD run with 39 seconds left in the game lifted the Longhorns to a 26-20 victory.

Texas took an early 3-0 lead. The Sooners retaliated with a 78-yard scoring jaunt in 12 plays. Warmack sailed a 12-yard scoring strike to Zabel, and Derr converted for a 7-3 lead late in the first stanza.

Another Longhorn field goal early in the second period to cut Oklahoma's lead to 7-6.

Warmack completed his 19th career touchdown pass, a 34-yarder to Hinton late in the first half, and Derr converted for a 14-6 lead. Warmack broke Claude Arnold's record of 18 career TD passes set in 1950.

The Steers scored 11 points in the third quarter for a 17-14 lead. They added a safety early in the fourth stanza when the defense smothered Warmack in the end zone. OU later drove 72 yards in 12 plays for a 20-19 advantage. Warmack faked a handoff and darted 15 yards to the end zone, but his two-point pass misfired.

The Steers marched 85 yards for the final nail in Oklahoma's coffin. Worster's score gave Texas a 26-20 lead, but OU had one more opportunity to win. The Sooners were 67 yards away from pay dirt after the kickoff with 38 seconds on the game clock. Fred Steinmark intercepted Warmack's pass three plays later with 11 seconds left. It was Warmack's only interception of the day.

Texas rolled up more total yards, 422-372. Oklahoma's yards were balanced—186 rushing and 186 passing. Warmack completed 14 of 25 passes for all of OU's passing yards. Owens hammered out 127 yards on 28 carries.

The Sooners evened their record to 2-2 with a 42-7 victory over 3-2 Iowa State on October 19 in Norman. All six of Oklahoma's touchdowns were scored from the one-yard line, and Owens led with four of them. Owens, who rushed for 175 yards on 36 carries, equaled the record of four other Sooners for most TDs in one game—George Thomas against Kansas in 1949, Buddy Leake against Oklahoma State in 1951, and Jim Grisham against OSU in 1963.

OU scored on its first three possessions and rolled to a 35-7 half-time lead before coasting in the second half. Owens scored the first four times, and fullback Rick Baldridge and tailback Bobby Thompson added one each. Derr converted all six extra-pointers. The Cyclones scored late in the opening period.

OU gained more total yards (441-259). Warmack completed 10 of 18 passes for 146 yards. The Sooners punted only once, and Zabel's kick sailed for 52 yards.

Colorado rolled to a 34-6 lead and held off a Sooner comeback for a 41-27 victory the following week in Boulder before a record crowd of 45,804.

CU quarterback Bob Anderson scored three touchdowns in the second quarter, and Ward Walsh added another early in the third stanza for a 27-0 lead.

The Sooners scored on four of their next five possessions to close the gap to 34-27 with 5:23 left in the game. Two of the Buffalo scores came after Oklahoma turnovers.

Owens, who rushed for 193 yards on 34 carries, scored the first OU touchdown on a one-yard run to cap a 69-yard drive late in the third period. Derr missed the conversion.

Colorado answered with an 80-yard scoring drive to up its lead to 34-6. The Sooners retaliated with a 72-yard march in six plays. Owens rolled around left end for an 11-yard TD, and Derr again missed the extra point.

The Sooners later marched 63 yards in six plays, and Warmack hurled a 20-yard scoring strike to Hinton. Warmack then zipped a two-point pass to split end Johnny Barr to cut the deficit to 34-20.

OU rolled 84 yards in five plays on its next series. Thompson scooted seven yards around left end to score, and Derr converted the extra point. Hinton sparked the drive with a 58-yard run to the CU 26. Colorado 34, Oklahoma 27.

Colorado drove 71 yards for the final tally with 17 seconds left in the game. The Sooners picked up more total yards (508-440). Warmack completed 14 of 23 passes for 217 yards.

The Sooners again evened their record (3-3) with a 35-20 pounding of Kansas State on November 2 before a rain-soaked crowd of 43,782 in Norman. Each time Oklahoma scored, they could not shake the 2-4 Wildcats, who would tie it up.

The Sooners jumped to a 7-0 lead later in the first quarter on Warmack's 14-yard run. Derr kicked the first of five conversions. Kansas State responded with an 83-yard scoring march for a 7-7 tie.

Thompson scored on a two-yard run to cap a 69-yard drive. The Cats threatened with a march to the OU 12, but Zabel dumped quarterback Lynn Dickey for a 13-yard loss, and the Cats failed to recover.

Mack Herron took OU's second-half kickoff and sailed 100 yards to tie the game at 14 apiece. The Sooners answered with an 80-yard scoring drive. Mike Harper scored his first touchdown with a 15-yard run.

Owens' two-yard run capped a 51-yard march to up the Oklahoma lead to 28-14 late in the third stanza. The Cats blocked Zabel's punt early in the fourth period and carried the ball across, but the two-point pass failed.

Moments later, Kansas State recovered Warmack's fumble on the OU 25, but the Big Red defense stiffened, as Gary Harper broke up Dickey's fourth-down pass.

A short punt set up the Sooners on the KSU 29 with 90 seconds remaining. Owens carried all six times in the drive and scored the touchdown on a 10-yard sprint.

OU amassed more total yards (421-201). Owens gained 185 yards on 47 carries, and Warmack completed eight of 11 aerials for 118 yards.

Sooner Magic:
One Year Later, Another Battle to the Wire

At this point in the season, O.J. Simpson, a tailback at Southern California, was receiving the most recognition as the best college football player in 1968. In Norman the attention was centered on Owens. Not only was Owens gaining yards on the gridiron, he was gaining notoriety against Big Red foes.

Owens was one of the nation's leading rushers with 910 yards on 199 carries and 10 touchdowns through six games. He was not a flashy, open-field tailback but a powerful workhorse with a 4.6-yard average accomplished mostly through the middle of the line.

The Kansas Jayhawks also were gaining attention in the college football world—undefeated in seven games, ranked third in the nation with a scoring average of 42.6 per game. Their narrowest victory was 10 points over Nebraska.

The Jayhawk faithful—51,500 strong at Memorial Stadium in Lawrence on November 9—wanted revenge for what the Sooners did the year before; pulling out a victory with barely more than a minute left in the game.

Neither team scored in the first quarter of the '68 matchup. KU's Bill Bell missed two field-goal tries in the opening stanza.

OU jumped to a 6-0 lead midway through the second period when Owens swept right and scored from five yards out. Derr's extra point sailed wide.

On the Jayhawks' first play following the kickoff, quarterback Bobby Douglass heaved a pass to split end George McGowan. McGowan hauled in the pass at the OU 30 and outraced Bruce Stensrud to the goal line. Bell's extra point also sailed wide, and the score was knotted at 6-6 with 9:12 to go before halftime.

The Sooners answered with an 87-yard drive. From the KU 13-yard line, Warmack pitched to Owens, who heaved a pass to Killingsworth all alone in the end zone. Derr made this conversion, and OU led 13-6 with 1:44 remaining in the half. Owens' pass was his first as a Sooner.

Kansas booted a 35-yard field goal to cut the Sooner lead to 13-9 with 27 seconds before halftime.

Kansas marched 65 yards early in the third quarter, for a 16-13 lead.

The seesaw battle continued as the Sooners answered again, this time with an 80-yard drive. From the KU 11, Warmack kept the ball and lunged across the goal line after being hit at the four. Derr tacked on the conversion, and OU led, 20-16, with 5:05 left in the period.

KU's ensuing drive into Sooner territory was thwarted when Barrett intercepted Douglass' pass at the OU six.

The Jayhawks put together a 65-yard march in the fourth quarter. From the OU one, running back John Riggins smashed through the line to put Kansas back on top, 23-20, with 10:50 remaining.

Both teams exchanged punts before OU put together the decisive drive. The Sooners kept the Hawk defense off guard with a mix of runs and passes in the 93-yard drive.

Bob Kalsu married his sweetheart, Janice Darrow, 26 days after the Orange Bowl. A few days later, the Buffalo Bills selected him in the eighth round of the National Football League draft. Bob Kalsu played one season for the Bills as an offensive guard. He started in eight games and was named the team's Rookie of the Year.

While at the University of Oklahoma he completed the ROTC program and entered the army as a second lieutenant in February 1969. He went to Vietnam in November 1969 as a first lieutenant in the 11th Artillery, 101st Airborne.

On July 21, 1970, Kalsu, then 25, was killed by enemy mortar fire at Ripcord Base, an isolated mountaintop near Ashau Valley in Vietnam. Kalsu, who was expected to return home the following November, was the only NFL player to be killed in Vietnam and the first pro player killed in the line of duty. Kalsu and his wife had a two-year-old daughter, and two days after his death, his son, James Robert Kalsu Jr., was born.

Bob Kalsu was awarded the Bronze Star, Purple Heart, the National Defense Service Ribbon, and Vietnam Campaign Ribbon. On April 13, 2000, which would have been Bob's 55th birthday, the Bills inducted him into their Wall of Fame. A plaque honors Kalsu in the Pro Football Hall of Fame, which reads: "No one will ever know how great a football player Bob might have been, but we do know how great a man he was to give up his life for his country."

Kalsu earned nine varsity letters (three each in football, basketball and baseball) at Del City High School where he graduated in 1963. The football stadium is named in his honor.

Sports Illustrated's cover story featured Kalsu as "A True All-American," in its July 23, 2001 issue.

At the KU 5, Warmack lateraled to Owens, who swept through right end, got a key block from Harper and scooted into the end zone. Derr added the extra point, and OU was back on top, 27-23, with 4:14 to go.

The Jayhawks were not waving the white flag. Thanks to Douglass' 19-yard scamper to the OU 26, Kansas was within striking distance with 2:05 on the clock.

Douglass threw an incomplete pass intended for tight end John Mosier in the end zone. On the next play, OU defensive end Jim Files grabbed Douglass to slow the Jayhawk quarterback's attempted scramble. Titsworth and Paaso helped Files nail Douglass for a 12-yard loss.

On third-and-22, Douglass' pass to wingback John Jackson was tipped away by Barrett with 1:38 remaining. Just a year before, the Sooners beat Kansas with a desperation pass, and now it was up to the Jayhawks to try the same. Douglass hurled the ball to McGowan but Stensrud tipped the pigskin, which bounced off McGowan's fingers and landed into Barrett's hands for the interception.

Oklahoma killed the clock to topple the Jayhawks, 27-23. The Sooners rushed for 227 yards and passed for 168. Owens carried 37 times for 157 yards, and Warmack completed 13 of 22 passes. Hinton's five pass receptions broke Gordon Brown's school single-season record of 35 set in 1965. KU dropped to No.7 in the AP poll.

The Sooners defeated their second straight Top 10 foe with a 28-14 victory over No. 6 Missouri before a homecoming throng of 50,658 the next week in Norman. Owens had a part in all four touchdowns as he ran for three and passed for another to snap the Tigers' seven-game win streak.

His two-yard TD run capped a 73-yard drive after the opening kickoff, and Derr kicked the first of four conversions for a 7-0 lead. Killingsworth injured his knee on the drive and was out for the rest of the season.

The Tigers rolled 66 yards to slice the lead to 7-6 early in the second stanza. Titsworth and Files hammered quarterback Garnett

Phelps after he tried to retrieve a bad conversion snap and carry it in for two points.

Owens scored twice on one-yard plunges, once late in the third period and again early in the fourth. The first score completed a 45-yard drive, and the second capped a 64-yard jaunt.

Missouri threatened to score three times in the fourth quarter, but each drive was squelched by an Oklahoma interception. Gary Harper's theft on his 19 stopped a Tiger drive to the 21. Joe Pearce returned the next interception 32 yards to the MU 43, and the Sooners moved in for the final tally, a nine-yard scoring strike from Owens to Hinton.

The Tigers advanced to the OU three after the kickoff, but Barrett picked off the pass in the end zone. The Tigers managed to get one across for six points moments after recovering an OU fumble, and they added a two-point pass.

Oklahoma collected more total yards, 384-324. Owens carried 46 times for 177 yards to raise his season rushing total to 1,244 yards and surpassed Billy Vessels' 16-year-old school season record of 1,072.

Oklahoma jumped back into the AP poll (to 14th) and accepted a bid to play Southern Methodist in the Astro-Bluebonnet Bowl.

Steve Owens continued his assault on the school record book with five touchdowns to lead the Sooners to a 47-0 thumping of Nebraska on November 23 in Norman.

He scored the Sooners' first five TDs in the game and rushed 41 times for 172 yards. Owens broke the conference record for most yards rushing in a season and his 30 points in one game broke the conference scoring record. Owens' 20 touchdowns and 120 points also set new school records.

The Sooners hammered out 414 total yards. Warmack contributed 155 passing yards and one more on the ground to boost his career total yardage to 4,289 yards. He became the Big Eight Conference's all-time total offense leader, eclipsing the record of 4,246 held by Missouri's Paul Christman.

OU's defense held the Huskers to 184 total yards.

Owens scored only one touchdown, but Warmack scored two and passed for two more to lead No. 11 Oklahoma to a 41-7 defeat of Oklahoma State the next week in Stillwater.

The 3-6 Pokes keyed on Owens, which allowed Warmack to cut loose. Yet Owens still pounded out 120 yards on 34 totes.

The Sooners scored on their first three possessions for a 21-0 first-quarter lead. Owens scored on a one-yard run, Warmack scooted five yards for the second tally and then tossed a 12-yard scoring

1968 Season Record: 7-4-0
Big Eight Conference: 6-1-0 (Champions)

Date	Opponent	Result	Score
September 21	at Notre Dame	L	45-21
September 28	NORTH CAROLINA STATE	W	28-14
October 12	Texas at Dallas	L	26-20
October 19	IOWA STATE	W	42-7
October 26	at Colorado	L	41-27
November 2	KANSAS STATE	W	35-20
November 9	at Kansas	W	27-23
November 16	MISSOURI	W	28-14
November 23	NEBRASKA	W	47-0
November 30	at Oklahoma State	W	41-7
December 31	Southern Methodist*	L	28-27

*Astro-Bluebonnet Bowl at Houston, TX

strike to Hinton. Derr toed all three conversions.

Oklahoma State had two chances to make a game of it, but a penalty erased a touchdown pass, and a fumble killed a drive after reaching the OU one-yard line.

Warmack hurled a 16-yard TD pass to Barr for a 28-0 lead in the second period after Derr kicked through the extra point.

The Cowboys scored their only touchdown early in the third stanza, then Oklahoma answered with Warmack's 18-yard scamper. Derr missed the conversion. Mickey Ripley scored the final touchdown on a 12-yard run late in the game.

Oklahoma picked up more total yards (478-247). Warmack completed 12 of 20 passes for 189 yards.

The victory gave the Sooners a share of the Big Eight championship with Kansas.

SMU edged the Sooners, 28-27, in Houston's Astro-Bluebonnet Bowl before a New Year's Eve throng of 53,453. Warmack and Zabel left the game in the second period with knee injuries. Ripley replaced Warmack and led the Sooners with two touchdown strikes in the final 30 minutes.

Oklahoma led the 7-3 Mustangs, 14-6, through the first three quarters, then both teams went wild with a combined 35 points in the final stanza. Warmack scored on a seven-yard run in the first period, and Derr converted for a 7-0 lead.

SMU tied the game midway through the third stanza then OU answered with a 21-yard pass from Owens to Barr. The Mustangs took a 21-14 lead with two touchdowns in the first half of the final quarter. Ripley guided the Sooners to a 21-21 tie minutes later with a 22-yard scoring strike to Bo Denton.

SMU bounced back with another score for a 28-21 lead, but the Sooners drove 80 yards in seven plays to cut the deficit to 28-27 with 1:16 to go. Fairbanks ordered a two-point play. Ripley rolled out to pass, but the Mustangs smacked him out of bounds on the 12-yard line.

Ricky Hetherington clutched the onside kick for the Sooners. With no time out, the Big Red moved to the SMU 18 in four plays with 19 seconds remaining. Derr trotted out to kick the Sooners ahead, but his boot sailed wide left.

Oklahoma collected more total yards (470-353). Ripley completed 10 of 22 passes for 153 yards. SMU's Chuck Hixson, the nation's leading passer, connected on 22 of 43 passes for 270 yards.

Owens was named unanimous All-America. Zabel, Mendenhall, Hinton, and Warmack joined him on the All-Big Eight first unit. Although both Owens and Simpson were named All-America, Simpson won the Heisman Trophy, awarded to the best college player of the year. Owens, who amassed a school-record 1,536 yards for one season and scored 21 touchdowns, would get his chance the next year.

1969

In a year when man first walked on the moon, another man ran all over the earth. Oklahoma senior tailback Steve Owens gobbled up

Tailback Steve Owens scores one of his record-setting five touchdowns against Nebraska. (OU Athletics)

1,528 rushing yards and scored 23 touchdowns setting records in his path.

No offensive back in Sooner football history was more powerful than Owens. He would literally plow through the line like a steamroller, sometimes flattening opponents as he chiseled out yard after yard.

No player in college football history was more of a workhorse than the Miami, Oklahoma, native. He carried the pigskin 357 times for 1,536 yards and 21 touchdowns as a junior.

In 1969, he dashed his way to the Heisman Trophy among other awards.

Owens could not have done it all without a sturdy offensive line led by the return of Ken Mendenhall, who was moved from center to tackle, and guard Bill Elfstrom. Steve Zabel returned to the tight end slot, and Joe Killingsworth and Johnny Barr alternated at split end.

Quarterback Bob Warmack had graduated, but sophomore Jack Mildren got the starting nod to guide the new diamond-T formation. The formation had the backs bunched in closer to the quarterback for quicker and more effective handoffs. Sophomore Roy Bell replaced the graduated Eddie Hinton at wingback, and Mike Harper returned at fullback.

The defense was changed from the Oklahoma 5-2 to a 4-4-2 alignment. This moved end Jim Files to one linebacking spot next to veteran Steve Casteel. Joe Pearce and Bruce Stensrud returned to the secondary along with Ricky Heatherington, but Monty Johnson, a Texas Longhorn transfer, beat out Heatherington.

Johnson was the recruit who head coach Jim Mackenzie went to visit in Amarillo the day Mackenzie died in April 1967. Johnson's grandfather, Montford "Hap" Johnson, played for the Sooners from 1914-1916. His uncles Neil Johnson (1913-1914) and Graham Johnson (1916-1917) also played for OU.

Bruce Derr returned to handle the placekicking duties, and Zabel punted most of the time with Johnson sharing some of the chores.

The Sooners were ranked sixth in the preseason AP poll but would have a rollercoaster season en route to six wins and four losses. After opening the season with two wins, the Big Red alternated wins and losses the rest of the way.

OU opened the season on September 20 with a 48-21 blasting of Wisconsin in Madison. The Badgers were winless (0-19-1) in the last 20 games.

Owens scored four touchdowns and rushed for 189 yards to lead the Sooner attack. Mildren ran for one score and passed for two more. OU commanded early with three touchdowns on its first three possessions. Owens scored the first and third TDs on two-yard runs, and Mildren's first collegiate pass went for a 67-yard touchdown to Killingsworth for a 14-0 lead.

Leading 26-14 after three periods, the Sooners scored three touchdowns to remove all doubt in a span of 6:18 in the fourth quarter.

OU picked up more total yards (507-371). Owens got his 189 yards on 40 carries, setting the NCAA record of 10 straight games rushing for more than 100 yards. Wisconsin's Alan Thompson gained 220 yards on 30 carries and scored two touchdowns. Oklahoma turned the ball over just once (fumble) and punted once, a 59-yard boom by Zabel. Casteel, who played with a sore ankle, recorded 13 tackles.

The No. 6 Sooners returned home the following week and blasted 0-1 Pittsburgh, 37-8. Mildren rushed for 135 yards, passed for 71 more, and scored two touchdowns. Owens picked up 104 yards on 20 carries and scored three TDs while playing with a charley horse.

Oklahoma rolled to the 37-0 lead before the Panthers scored late in the game. The Sooners took the opening kickoff and wheeled 91 yards in nine plays. Owens plowed over from one yard out, and Derr kicked the first of five conversions.

Early in the third stanza, the Panthers' bad punt snap sailed out of the end zone for a safety to give OU a 23-0 advantage. The Sooners took the free kick on their 41 and launched a 59-yard TD march in nine plays capped by Owens' third touchdown from a yard away.

After recovering a fumble on the OU 28, late in the third period, Pitt moved to the 15 but surrendered on downs. Three plays later, Mildren shot through left tackle and outran two Pitt defenders 75 yards to the end zone for the final OU tally.

The Panthers scored moments after recovering Stensrud's fumbled punt return on the eight-yard line. OU collected 410 total yards, and the defense held Pitt to 181 total yards.

The Sooners had two weeks to prepare for Texas, and during the off week, Oklahoma plummeted to eighth in the AP poll. The Sooners would drop further after losing to the No. 2 Longhorns, 27-17, before a crowd of 72,032 at the Cotton Bowl and a national television (ABC) audience.

The Big Red took a 14-0 lead early. A punt into a stiff breeze set up the Sooners on the UT 41. Eight plays later, Mildren scooted around left end for a nine-yard touchdown for a 7-0 lead, and Derr toed the first of two conversions.

Minutes later, linebacker Steve Aycock stepped in front of UT's Tommy Woodward and stole James Street's pass. Aycock returned it eight yards to the Texas 17, and five plays later, Owens blasted through from the two.

The Steers drove 58 and 80 yards on their next two series to tie the game at 14-14 midway through the second quarter.

The Horns took the second-half kickoff and advanced to the OU 10, but settled for a 27-yard field goal and a 17-14 lead. The Sooners aided the drive with 29 yards in penalties.

Derr kicked a 22-yard field goal late in the third stanza moments after Vince LaRosa intercepted a Texas pass. The Longhorns answered with a field goal to take a 20-17 lead with 24 seconds left in the third.

Late in the fourth quarter, Glenn King was back to field a Texas punt. Stensrud, 10 yards in front of King, back-pedaled and waved for a fair catch. Stensrud crashed into King, forcing King to fumble, and Jim Bertlesen recovered for Texas on the 23. Five plays later, Texas put the game away with Steve Worster's one-yard TD run.

Mildren's pass was intercepted moments later to kill any Oklahoma comeback effort.

Texas gained more total yards, 373-252. Owens picked up 123 yards on 30 carries, and Bell gained 101 on 26 totes. Street threw 18 passes and completed one-half of them for 215 yards. Cotton Speyrer caught eight aerials for 160 yards.

The No. 12 Sooners returned home on October 18 and polished off Colorado, 42-30, before a homecoming throng of 60,524.

The 3-1 Buffaloes took the opening kickoff and marched 72 yards to the OU 13-yard line. On fourth-and-one, quarterback Paul

Arendt gained enough for the first down, but he spilled the ball, and Aycock pounced on it. Colorado did take the first lead on a 33-yard field goal late in the first stanza.

The Sooners drove 64 yards in seven plays to take a 7-0 lead 90 seconds later. Owens' seven-yard run capped the drive, and Derr kicked the first of six conversions.

Casteel intercepted a Buff pass early in the second period and returned it 12 yards to the CU nine. Three plays later, Mildren zipped a five-yard scoring strike to Zabel who had to leap high for the catch.

Colorado responded with a touchdown to cut the lead to 14-9. Oklahoma also had a response coming right back with a 69-yard march in three plays. From his 47-yard line, Bell burst through left tackle and sailed 53 yards to the end zone.

The Sooners raised the lead to 28-9 on their next series with a 58-yard jaunt in eight plays, and Owens scored from the two.

The Buffs marched 55 yards to cut their deficit to 28-16 just before halftime. Colorado lost two chances to score in the third quarter, but the drives stalled on the OU 13 and 34. The Buffs recovered a fumble on the Sooners' 37 late in the third period and scored seven plays later. The early fourth-quarter touchdown cut OU's lead to 28-23.

Oklahoma answered with a 74-yard march in nine plays. Owens finished the drive with a four-yard touchdown for a 35-23 advantage. Mildren had two long passes—16 yards to Zabel and 31 to Bell—to spark the drive.

Colorado came back with an 80-yard drive to close the gap to 35-30 with 2:37 remaining and followed it with an onside kick.

Johnson clutched the short kickoff on his 31-yard line. Owens carried for 37 yards in the drive and slammed through from the one for the final tally.

Colorado gained more total yards (319-289). In addition to his one touchdown, Bell also contributed with 130 yards rushing and 80 receiving.

The Sooners moved up a notch to 11th in the AP poll.

Not all good things must come to an end, at least Sooner fans thought so, but it did happen. Kansas State (4-1) ended OU's 34-game winning streak in the series with a 59-21 victory the next week in Manhattan. Quarterback Lynn Dickey led the 18th-ranked Wildcats by connecting on 28 of 42 passes for 380 yards and two touchdowns. Halfback Mack Herron added three more TDs.

Kansas State took a 14-0 lead, but the Sooners answered 38 seconds after the second Wildcat TD. Mildren tossed a 77-yard scoring strike to Killingsworth, and Derr converted to cut the deficit to 14-7.

Minutes later, K-State scored soon after recovering King's punt return on the OU 17. Again, the Sooners roared back on the first play after the kickoff. Mildren hooked up with Everett Marshall for a 66-yard TD pass, and Derr converted.

The Cats scratched out four touchdowns in the second half, three in the third stanza. Down 49-14, Johnson intercepted Dickey's pass on his five and dashed 62 yards to the enemy's 33-yard line. Mildren sailed a 13-yard pass to Killingsworth. K-State was flagged for pass interference on the next play to the one. Owens scored on the next play, and Derr converted.

Kansas State scored 10 more points for the most points and largest margin of the team's 10 wins against OU.

The Wildcats pounded out 535 total yards. The Big Red gained 229 total yards. Owens rushed for 105 yards on 29 totes.

The loss dropped OU out of the polls and left a sour taste in the mouths of Sooner faithful. Fans began calling for Fairbanks' head with a "Chuck Chuck" campaign.

The Sooners hosted Iowa State on November 1 without the services of Bell (injured knee) and Files (sore shoulder). Owens rushed for a school-record 248 yards and scored four touchdowns to lead OU past the 3-3 Cyclones, 37-14. Owens broke Jim Grisham's single-game record of 218 yards set against Oklahoma State in 1963.

Derr kicked a 23-yard field goal, and Owens scored twice to give OU a 16-0 lead in the first 17 and one-half minutes. Iowa State closed the gap to 16-14 on Robert Tisdale's two TD passes over the next five and one-half minutes.

The Sooners countered with an 80-yard march to stretch the lead to 23-14 on Owens' one-yard plunge. Late in the third stanza, Mildren hurled a 50-yard scoring strike to Geoffrey Nordgren, Bell's replacement, for a 30-14 advantage.

Stensrud intercepted Tisdale's pass on the OU 43 and returned it 10 yards to the Cyclones' 47. Six plays later, Owens scored from the three. Derr missed only one conversion in the game, after the second Sooners touchdown.

Oklahoma rolled up 32 first downs and 569 total yards. Mildren completed 13 of 18 passes for 211 yards. Nordgren caught four of them for 114 yards. The Cyclones gained 219 total yards.

OU crept back into the AP poll at No. 20.

At 2-1 in the Big Eight Conference, the Sooners had a shot at the conference crown behind Missouri and Nebraska with 3-1 records. The 6-1 and ninth-ranked Tigers were up next for the Big Red and took the Sooners out of the title chase with a 44-10 smashing the next week Columbia.

Derr's 36-yard field goal gave OU a 3-0 lead with 25 seconds remaining in the first period. Early in the second quarter, Pearce picked off a Tiger pass on his 39-yard line. Owens scored his 51st career touchdown from the five-yard line eight plays later, and Derr converted. Mildren sparked the drive with a 38-yard pass to Marshall to the MU 24.

Owens tied the NCAA record for touchdowns scored in a three-year career held by Army's Glenn Davis in 1945. Davis scored 58 times in his four-year career, but 51 in his last three years.

Mizzou scored 17 points in the second quarter, and three touchdowns in a four-minute span in the third stanza and added a touchdown in the fourth. Oklahoma never advanced past the Tigers' 33 in the second half.

Missouri gained 559 total yards. Tiger quarterback Terry McMillan completed 17 of 37 passes for 312 yards. Mel Gray caught six of McMillan's aerials for 171 yards and two TDs. Joe Moore rushed for 110 yards and scored once. The Big Red collected 302 total yards. Owens rushed for 109 yards on 29 carries, and Mildren completed 10 of 30 passes for 167 yards.

The two previous OU-Kansas contests were decided by fourth-quarter surges by the Sooners. This year, Oklahoma did have to come from behind but much earlier to defeat the 1-7 Jayhawks, 31-15, on November 15 in Norman.

OU took a 7-0 lead with a 69-yard drive late in the first period. Owens, who carried 44 times for 201 yards in the game, completed the seven-play drive with a two-yard run, and Derr toed the first of four conversions. Owens' 52nd touchdown set the new NCAA scoring record.

Moments later, Files forced John Riggins to fumble and also plopped on the loose pigskin at the KU 26. Eight plays later, the Sooners faced fourth-and-goal on the two-yard line, and the obvious choice would be to feed the ball to Owens. Mildren did just that, and Owens spun into the end zone for a 14-0 lead early in the second stanza.

The Jayhawks later drove 80 yards for a touchdown, and a two-point pass play cut the OU lead to 14-8. After holding the Sooners

to three-and-out on the next series, KU's Steve Conley returned the punt 48 yards to the OU nine. The Hawks scored two plays later for a 15-14 lead.

Kansas recovered Mike Harper's fumble moments later on the OU 32, but the Big Red defense held, and Heatherington blocked the field-goal try.

The Sooners took the second-half kickoff and marched 75 yards to the Hawks' two-yard line where they faced third-and-goal. Owens was nailed for a one-yard loss, and Derr toed a 20-yard field goal for a 17-15 lead midway through the third stanza. The drive for three points consumed seven minutes and 21 seconds.

Oklahoma later embarked on a 59-yard scoring march that carried into the fourth period. Owens scored on a seven-yard jaunt on the first play of the fourth quarter to finish the six-play drive. Owens carried five times in the drive. Mildren sparked the drive with a 17-yard sprint to the KU 18.

On their next possession, the Sooners hammered out 63 yards on 11 plays all on the ground. On fourth-and-one at the KU three, Mildren zipped around right end for the final tally.

Oklahoma picked up more total yards (463-236). Kansas was held to 107 yards in the second half and did not reach past the OU 29 in the final 30 minutes.

Bowl talk circulated in the newspapers about a possible bowl invitation for the Sooners. Coach Fairbanks said the week of the Nebraska game that he did not believe his squad's performance deserved to play in a bowl.

No. 16 Cornhuskers (7-2) rolled into Norman on November 22 with the Big Eight Conference's No. 1 defense—total yards, rushing yards, and scoring. Oklahoma put its 15-game home winning streak on the line, but Nebraska was too powerful in the 44-14 victory before a crowd of 52,267.

Third-string tailback Jeff Kinney rushed for 127 yards, ran for two touchdowns, passed for another, and caught another to lead the Husker assault. The two tailbacks ahead of him sat out with injuries. Owens failed to clear the century rushing mark for the first time in 16 games as the Huskers held him to 71 yards on 21 totes.

Three turnovers gift-wrapped 17 points for the Huskers. A four-yard Nebraska punt into a stiff wind set up the Sooners on the NU 18-yard line early in the first quarter. Mildren scored on the first play, and Derr converted.

Down 37-7, Mildren hurled a 16-yard scoring strike to Nordgren midway through the fourth stanza. Besides those two touchdowns, the Sooners failed to penetrate the Huskers' 25-yard line.

Nebraska had more total yards (437-278). Mildren completed one-half of his 30 passes for 157 yards, but he threw two interceptions. Owens lost two fumbles.

The Sooners again disappeared from national rankings.

Sooner Magic: Coming Through in the Clutch

Through this rollercoaster season, losing four games was not thrilling, but watching No. 36 bulldoze the opposition was a delight. Three days after the Nebraska loss, the Downtown Athletic Club in New York City announced that Owens had won the Heisman Memorial Trophy as the best college player in the nation. The day of the OSU contest on November 29, United Press International voted him the player of the year.

A victory over Oklahoma State would guarantee the Sooners a winning season at 6-4. The Cowboys also had an identical 5-4 record heading into the intrastate matchup before 38,250 fans at Lewis Field in Stillwater. Both teams were 3-3 in the conference. Although OU held a commanding 47-10-6 series advantage, the Pokes were tabbed as two-point favorites.

The Sooners jumped to a 14-point lead in the first nine and one-half minutes. Owens' one-yard plunge capped the Sooners' opening drive midway through the first quarter. Derr kicked the first of four conversions.

The next scoring drive covered 77 yards. From his 49, Mildren fired a bomb to Joe Killingsworth wide open at the OSU 15, and Killingsworth dashed to the end zone. Derr's conversion gave the Sooners the two-touchdown lead with 5:23 remaining in the first period.

The Cowboys wasted no time retaliating and marched 75 yards to cut the OU lead to 14-7 late in the opening stanza. They tied the game late in the first half with a 67-yard drive.

Owens' fumble on the OU 36 led to the next Poke touchdown. Bob Cutburth hurled a pass to Herman Eben at the seven, and the same tandem hooked up for a touchdown on the next play. Uwe Pruss' conversion put the Cowboys ahead, 21-14, with 54 seconds left in the half.

Owens scored on a one-yard plunge to cap a 63-yard drive to tie the game midway through the third quarter.

Oklahoma rolled 80 yards on its next possession, which carried into the fourth period. From the Pokes' 34, Mildren kept the ball and scooted down the left sideline. Bell threw a key block to allow Mildren a free lane to the end zone. Derr's extra point put the Sooners back up 28-21 with 13:56 remaining.

The Cowboys marched 69 yards on their next possession to the Sooner one. Cutburth tried another quarterback sneak, but OU defensive tackles Kevin Grady and John Watson stopped him inches from the goal line. The Sooners gained possession on downs.

Johnson's interception killed the Pokes' next drive. But the Cowboys got the ball back for one last chance to win or tie the game. The Sooners punted to OSU at the 50-yard line with 1:51 to go.

Cutburth fired a pass to end Tom Dearinger for 16 yards. The Big Red defense pushed the Cowboys back to the OU 40 on the next two plays. On third-and-16, Cutburth unleashed the pigskin to Eben for 32 yards to the OU eight.

Cutburth faked a sweep to his right and fired the ball to Eben all alone in the end zone with 1:15 remaining. OSU head coach Floyd Gass ordered a two-point conversion for the win. The Pokes were penalized five yards for delay of game, and the ball was moved back to the seven-yard line. Cutburth set up to pass, but defensive end Albert Qualls slapped the ball from Cutburth's hands before the quarterback could release it. That slap preserved a 28-27 Sooner victory.

"Our defense came through today with big plays," Fairbanks said in the locker room. "That goal-line stand and lots of others. Our defensive team showed a lot of character and really came through in the clutch."

Fairbanks was especially proud of Owens' performance of 261 yards in 56 carries, which broke his own school record for carries and yards in a single game.

"You saw today why they picked him as the best in the country," Fairbanks added.

The Sooners finished the season at 6-4 (4-3 and fourth in the Big Eight Conference). The Cowboys dropped to 5-5 and fifth in the conference with a 3-4 record.

Owens, Zabel, and Mendenhall were named All-Americans and Elfstrom joined them on the All-Big Eight first team. Owens collected a total of 1,523 yards in 358 carries for the season, one more carry and 17 yards less than in 1968. However, his 23 TDs were two more than his junior season. Owens set NCAA rushing records for carries in one game and in one season. He also held the national rushing and scoring (138 points) titles in 1969.

During his three-year career at Oklahoma, Owens carried the ball 905 times for 3,867 yards and scored 56 touchdowns. He eclipsed Eugene "Mercury" Morris' record of 3,388 yards, who set the record at West Texas A&M from 1966-68.

Owens was named Player of the Year by the Walter Camp Foundation and by Helms and Citizens Savings Athletic Foundation.

1969 Season Record: 6-4-0
Big Eight Conference: 4-3-0 (Fourth)

Date	Opponent	Result	Score
September 20	at Wisconsin	W	48-21
September 27	PITTSBURGH	W	37-8
October 11	Texas at Dallas	L	27-17
October 18	COLORADO	W	42-30
October 25	at Kansas State	L	59-21
November 1	IOWA STATE	W	37-14
November 8	at Missouri	L	44-10
November 15	KANSAS	W	31-15
November 22	NEBRASKA	L	44-14
November 29	at Oklahoma State	W	28-27

ANNOUNCERS

Walter Cronkite

Walter Cronkite's first live play-by-play broadcast was for the Oklahoma Sooners on WKY radio in 1937. He said his debut, an Oklahoma loss to Tulsa, was a disaster. He had created an electronic board to provide him information to describe the action. Cronkite also had spotters help him identify players.

"The spotters would punch up who was carrying the ball and who made the tackle, and the light would flash," Cronkite told the *Daily*

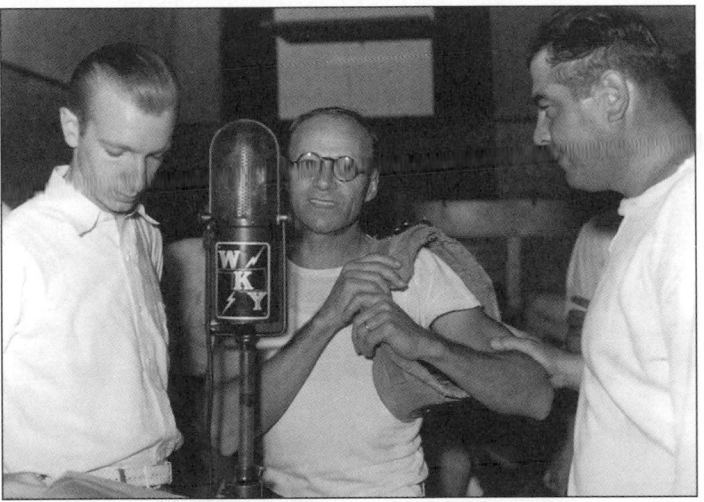

Walter Cronkite (left) interviews head coach Tom Stidham (right) and team trainer Teddy Owen. Cronkite called OU play-by-play in 1937 and later became a news anchor for CBS. *(OU Athletics)*

Oklahoman in 2002. "The spotters turned out to be impossible, and I was looking at the board and not the game."

Cronkite and his color commentator, Perry Ward, worked together the following week drilling each other on players' names. Improvements were made by the season's second game, which Cronkite said went "marvelously well."

He spent only one season behind the mike calling OU games, but it wasn't due to his first game mistakes. Cronkite went on to be anchorman for the *CBS Evening News*. "And that's the way it is," was the signature signoff of his nightly broadcasts. He continued with CBS as commentator until 1981, when he retired from the network. He continues to appear on television and produces documentaries.

Curt Gowdy

Curt Gowdy was the voice of the Sooners on KOMA radio from 1945-1949 and witnessed the rise of the football program under Bud Wilkinson. After his stint at KOMA, he got a job as

Curt Gowdy was OU football's play-by-play man from 1945-49. He went on to announce Major League Baseball games, pro and college football games, Super Bowls, and the Olympic Games. *(OU Athletics)*

play-by-play announcer for the New York Yankees and later for the Boston Red Sox.

He left the Red Sox in 1966 for a 10-year stint as Game of the Week announcer for NBC. Gowdy was the 1970 recipient of the George Foster Peabody Award for excellence in broadcasting for his "blend of reporting, accuracy, knowledge, good humor, infectious honesty, and enthusiasm." He was the first sportscaster to be so honored and was also named "Sportscaster of the Year" on three occasions.

In his 40 years as a sports broadcaster, Gowdy has covered almost every major sporting event, including 16 World Series, 12 Rose Bowls, seven Olympic Games, and eight Super Bowls. He also hosted a weekly outdoor show, *The American Sportsman*.

Bob Barry

No one has broadcasted play-by-play of Sooner football games more than Bob Barry. He has announced OU games for 27 years. Oklahoma head coach Bud Wilkinson chose Barry over a field of 14 contestants for the play-by-play job in 1961, and he continued as the voice of the Sooners' football and basketball games through 1972.

"That was the biggest thrill of my life," Barry recalled on his winning the play-by-play job.

After serving as the play-by-play commentator for Oklahoma State from 1973-1990, Barry returned to broadcast Sooner football and basketball games in 1991. He has been at the radio mike for Oklahoma games ever since.

During his tenure as OSU announcer, Barry missed out on three national championship seasons by the Sooners (1974, 1975 and

1985). Barry did get to call the 2001 Orange Bowl, another Sooner national championship, which was "very special."

"Especially since I didn't think we had a chance to win it," he said. "Everybody was picking Florida State and [Chris] Weinke was going to beat the tar out of us. And the first play was a 35-yard pass and I thought, 'Oh boy, here we go,' but that's about all he did. That was a terrific thrill."

The most exciting game Barry has announced was the 1971 OU-Nebraska tilt.

"Both teams had a week off, so there were two weeks to hype it," Barry recalled. "It was No. 1 and No. 2, and both were undefeated and very good. Both teams played a great game—offense and defense and everything. It was a great battle and lived up to the hype."

Barry added that clipping did occur on Johnny Rodgers' punt return.

Another favorite game was the OU-Texas matchup that the Sooners won in overtime in 1996. He said that game was special since Texas was heavily favored against the winless Sooners, and James Allen scored the winning touchdown after being stopped a yard short on a possible winning TD two years before.

"That was a big one," Barry said.

The most memorable play Barry called was the 1967 OU-Kansas contest where Bob Warmack tossed the winning pass to Steve Zabel.

Barry said the funniest moment in the broadcast booth was during the Texas game in 1967 when kicker Mike Vachon had missed a couple of field goals. Oklahoma had defeated Texas the year before on four Vachon field goals. But Vachon had missed five field goals before the 1967 Texas contest as well. Barry said that Jack Ogle, the color analyst, kept telling Barry not to blame Vachon for the loss.

"Jack was telling me that he [Vachon] won the game for us last year and that he felt worse than anyone. He went on for 10 minutes and kept telling me, 'Don't blame him.' When we signed off the air, he [Ogle] took his earphones, slammed them down and said, 'They ought to kick the sonofabitch off the team.'"

Barry said he delighted in working with Ogle and enjoys working with Merv Johnson, the current color analyst for OU football games.

"I love working with Merv; he's so knowledgeable. He knows what he's talking about. He's at practice every day, he knows all the players. He provides a lot of good information."

Barry began his announcing career calling Norman High football and basketball games in 1956. In 1966 he began his television career as sports anchor for WKY-TV (now KFOR-TV) and served as sports director for the station from 1970 to 1996.

Known as "The Legend" of the Oklahoma airwaves by some, Barry has won numerous awards for his broadcasting. He has been elected Oklahoma's Sportscaster of the Year 15 times by his peers, *Oklahoma Gazette* newspaper Top Sportscaster in a readers poll, named in 1998 to the Oklahoma Journalism Hall of Fame, the Oklahoma Association of Broadcasters Hall of Fame, and Oklahoma Sports Hall of Fame in 1999, and is a former member of the board of directors of National Sportscasters and Sportswriters Association.

Between 1991 and 1998, Mike Treps was Barry's color analyst.

Mike Treps

After serving about seven years as sports director for WKY-TV, Oklahoma City's NBC affiliate, Mike Treps was hired as media information director at the University of Oklahoma in 1972. He served that position until he was named sports information director at OU in 1979. Treps held that position for 13 years until he was named assistant athletic director in 1992. He held that position for six years.

Treps was the play-by-play announcer for Sooner football games from 1973-1976 and color analyst from 1979-1991 on Oklahoma City's KTOK-1000AM radio station. Treps also has served as play-by-play announcer for OU baseball games for 17 years and color analyst for Oklahoma Redhawks (Oklahoma City's AAA baseball club) home games for three years.

The Sooners' baseball press box was named in his honor.

Mike Treps spent 18 years behind the microphone calling OU football games—four years as play-by-play announcer and 14 years as color analyst. (© 1998, The Daily Oklahoman)

Bob Barry has been calling play-by-play for the Sooners for 27 years. (© 1991, The Daily Oklahoman)

The 1975 Oklahoma-Missouri game was his most memorable football game, which also included his most memorable play. Treps said the signature call of his OU broadcast career was in 1975 when Joe Washington scored the winning touchdown in Columbia. Treps saw Washington break into the open on the 71-yard run and cried, "Go, Joe, go!"

"That more than anything else was a signature of my broadcasts throughout the years," Treps recalled. "It was such a significant play when he broke loose, everybody felt like they were in my shoes because I was rooting … I wasn't broadcasting anymore."

Treps also said that every Texas game was special because of the intense rivalry between the two teams.

On Thursdays, two days before games, Treps said he met with coaches to learn about their game plans. When quarterback Steve Davis changed the play at the line of scrimmage against Texas in 1975, Treps said he saw Davis step back from the line to call the audible and announced it on the air.

"I remember people asked me how I knew that," he said. "Well, meeting with the coaches like I did on Thursday and to see what kind of defense Texas was shifting in."

Treps said another special moment of his career was broadcasting the 1976 Orange Bowl on NBC radio. NBC had elected to have local announcers broadcast their bowl games.

"That was a great thrill," Treps recalled.

Treps said since he was an employee at the University of Oklahoma, he often used the words "we" and "us," and he was never accused of being partial.

John Brooks

"Jiminy Christmas!" was Brooks' cry when he announced a touchdown or a tremendous play for the Sooners. Brooks was the play-by-play voice of the Sooners from 1978 through 1990.

He also called OU basketball games during those same years. Brooks is a six-time Oklahoma Sportscaster of the Year and has called Oklahoma City Blazers hockey games for many years.

He also serves as the president of Sportscast Productions—an Oklahoma City-based organization that provides a national reporting service, video, and audio highlight package for 17 NCAA championships and other sporting events.

1970 - 1979

1970

OU had the best winning percentage in the country in the 1970s, winning two national championships, eight Big Eight Conference championships, and nearly 88 percent of its games with a 102-13-3 record. But the decade began with a whimper, not a bang.

All-Big Eight stars Steve Owens, Bill Elfstrom, Ken Mendenhall, and Steve Zabel had graduated. Still the backfield was loaded with smaller but quicker halfbacks in Joe Wylie, Leon Crosswhite, Everett Marshall, and Roy Bell.

Quarterback Jack Mildren's leadership would be an asset with another year's experience under his belt in running the veer offense. Sophomores Greg Pruitt, Jon Harrison, and Albert Chandler would provide able hands to catch Mildren's aerials. Pruitt would play halfback on numerous occasions.

Only two players returned to the offensive line, and depth was a concern. Guards Darryl Emmert and Steve Tarlton were the only returnees up front.

Head coach Chuck Fairbanks was quoted in *Big Eight Magazine* that the veer option offense would "be a fun offense." It was anything but exciting as the coaches trashed the formation after struggling through a 2-1 record. The Sooners switched to the Wishbone-T two weeks before the Texas game.

Although the defense returned seven starters, it yielded nearly 29 points per game in 1969. Tackle Kevin Grady and end Albert Qualls returned to the front line. Steve Aycock and Steve Casteel again would provide a strong linebacking corps. Safety Monty Johnson was the lone returnee in the secondary.

A new artificial turf was laid on Owen Field at a cost of $300,000. The carpet-like turf would be a staple of Sooner homes games for 24 years, although in 1981 a new "SuperTurf" replaced the first one.

The 20th-ranked Sooners opened the 1970 season on September 12 with a 28-11 victory over Southern Methodist in a night contest at the Cotton Bowl. Oklahoma exploded for three touchdowns in the second quarter to lead 21-3 at halftime. OU scored two of those touchdowns in a span of 61 seconds after picking off SMU passes. The Sooner defensive line pressured Mustang quarterback Chuck Hixson, forcing him to throw a total of four interceptions in the game.

The Mustangs took a 3-0 lead midway through the first period. Then Bell scored two TDs to put OU ahead, 14-3.

The Sooners scored their next two touchdowns after intercepting SMU passes. Gary Baccus picked off the first pass to set up Mildren's TD. Moments later, Geoffrey Nordgren robbed a Pony pass to set up Mildren's 39-yard scoring strike to Harrison for a 21-3 lead. Harrison slipped behind the secondary and scored unchallenged.

The Sooners rolled 94 yards in nine plays to take a 28-3 lead late in the third stanza. Wylie, who carried four times in the drive for 28 yards, scored from the seven. Marshall sparked the drive with a 42-yard run.

The Mustangs added a touchdown and a two-point conversion midway through the final quarter.

Oklahoma collected 237 rushing yards, and Mildren completed 12 of 16 passes for 178 yards. SMU gained 279 total yards.

300th Home Game

No. 18 Oklahoma defeated Wisconsin, 21-7, the next week in Norman before a crowd of 58,100 and the 300th home game in Sooner football history. The Sooners trailed 7-0 at the half. Mildren tossed three interceptions, and the second one set up the Wisconsin touchdown midway through the second stanza.

The Sooners scored touchdowns on its first three possessions of the second half on drives of 80, 28, and 62 yards. Pruitt returned four punts for 109 yards in the game, and two of his returns set up the second and third scores.

OU took the second-half kickoff and marched 80 yards in 16 plays to tie the game at 7-7. The drive consumed more than five minutes. Marshall carried for 48 yards on eight carries, and Mildren completed the drive with a one-yard run. Bruce Derr toed the first of three conversions. Bell's three-yard run picked up a crucial first down on fourth-and-three at the Badgers' 25.

Pruitt returned a Wisconsin punt 46 yards to the WU 28 late in the third quarter to set up the Sooners' go-ahead touchdown. Bell scored on a four-yard jaunt six plays later.

Pruitt returned the next Badger punt 17 yards to his 38. The Sooners scored the final tally six plays later when Bell scored from the two. Wylie highlighted the drive with a 32-yard sprint to the WU 11 and added nine more yards to the two before the touchdown.

OU rolled up 271 rushing yards and passed for 130. The Badgers were held to 143 total yards. The Big Red defense handcuffed the Badgers to only 11 total yards and one first down in the second half.

Oregon State (1-1), coached by Dee Andros, a former Sooner player in the late 1940s, stunned No. 14 OU, 23-14. OSU quarterback Steve Endicott completed a dismal 16 of 33 passes, but three of them were for touchdowns.

The Beavers led, 13-0, and Oklahoma scored two touchdowns in the second quarter to lead 14-13 at the half. Wylie scored a touchdown for the Sooners and Mildren completed a TD pass to Bell.

Tackles John Watson, Ron Stacy, and Monty Johnson suffered injuries in the first half and did not play in the final 30 minutes.

The Beavers added a field goal in the third quarter and another TD in the fourth while rolling up 225 yards in the second half. Oklahoma gained 103 yards rushing and 87 passing yards. OSU's defense held the Sooners to 57 total yards in the second half. The Beavers collected 253 yards on the ground and 197 in the air.

Obviously, OU's Veer-T offense wasn't clicking on all cylinders. Sooner head coach Chuck Fairbanks was not happy with his offense's lack of firepower.

"I am embarrassed by the ineptness of our offensive team," he said. "This is by far the poorest performance I've seen them make.

"I'm not sure why, but rest assured I'm doing everything I can to find out why. Maybe it's our coaching philosophy. Maybe we don't have the right players at the right positions. We'll have to try and find out."

The Sooners, who had disappeared from the AP poll, had two weeks to find out what to do before heading to Dallas against No. 2 Texas on October 10.

Fairbanks and assistant Barry Switzer, his offensive coordinator, took a gamble and ditched the Veer-T formation to install the Wishbone-T, which had helped Texas win the national championship a year earlier. During spring practices months earlier, Fairbanks had switched to the Veer-T from the pro-style set.

The Wishbone used three running backs and one receiver. Since Mildren was a better runner than passer, it was more suitable to switch to the Wishbone's run dominant formation. So the revamped offense debuted against, of all teams, Texas. The Longhorns showed the Big Red how to run the offense with a 41-9 victory before a sell-out crowd of 71,938.

The 3-0 Steers spotted OU three points, a 51-yard field goal before ringing up 34 unanswered points. Derr's field goal broke Jack Baer's school record of 46 yards set in 1937 against Oklahoma A&M.

Crosswhite scored a touchdown for the Sooners late in the game, but the two-point conversion failed.

The Sooners turned the ball over five times—three fumbles and two interceptions. They rushed for 212 yards and passed for only 10 yards. Texas picked up 310 yards on the ground and passed for only 25.

Ironically, it was the pass that helped Oklahoma beat No. 19 Colorado, 23-15, in the Big Eight opener the next week in Boulder.

The 3-1 Buffaloes took a 7-0 lead early in the second quarter. Oklahoma retaliated with an 80-yard drive. Mildren completed a 38-yard TD pass to Wylie, and Derr's conversion tied the game two and one-half minutes later. Mildren sparked the drive with a 32-yard pass to Chandler to the CU 38.

Linebacker Forb Phillips intercepted a Colorado pass moments later and returned it 24 yards to the Buffs' five. Mildren scored one play later, and Derr converted for the 14-7 advantage.

Derr added a 27-yard field goal for a 17-7 lead.

Nordgren intercepted a Colorado pass and flashed 60 yards to the end zone early in the third stanza. Derr missed the extra point, but the Sooners held a 23-7 lead.

Colorado answered with an 80-yard touchdown march and added a two-point conversion. The Buffs did not threaten the rest of the way. Aycock and Johnson intercepted Colorado passes in the fourth quarter.

OU collected 253 rushing yards and 70 passing. Colorado gained 458 total yards.

Kansas State (3-3) beat OU for the second straight year, 19-14, on October 24 in Norman. Lynn Dickey shredded the OU defense for 384 passing yards. He completed 27 of 46 aerials including two TDs. Dickey didn't have a perfect day, as the Sooners defense robbed three passes and also recovered two fumbles in the second and third quarters.

The Wildcats rolled 80 yards from the opening kickoff to take a 7-0 lead on Dickey's first scoring strike.

The Sooners scored two touchdowns within a span of 88 seconds early in the second stanza for a 14-7 lead. KSU's Ron Coppenbarger fielded Wylie's punt but the ball brushed him, and Marshall pounced on it at the Cats' 12. Wylie scored on a two-yard run four plays later. Derr booted the first of two conversions.

Moments later, Phillips recovered a Wildcat fumble at the OU 40. Wylie sliced through left tackle, eluded a defender, and dashed to the end zone.

The Sooners twice threatened with advances inside the KSU five in the third period. Instead of going for field goals, the Big Red both times lost on fourth-down gambles.

Kansas State drove 83 yards to score with four minutes remaining in the game. From the OU six, Phillips pounded Bill Butler, and the ball squirted into the end zone, where KSU's Rich Ferguson fell on it for the touchdown. Defensive end Rick Mason blocked the extra point, and Sooner fans breathed a sigh of relief. OU 14, KSU 13.

Kansas State intercepted Mildren's pass at the OU 30, and Dickey delivered a 28-yard TD pass three plays later to Henry Hawthorne with 3:03 left. OU cornerback Glenn King batted down Dickey's pass on the two-point attempt.

The Sooners then drove to the KSU 22, but Mildren was sacked for a 14-yard loss to end the drive.

Oklahoma rushed for 235 yards and tossed for 41. Wylie led the Sooners with 133 rushing yards. Kansas State rolled up 463 total yards.

Sooner Magic: Sooners Reach Into Their Bag of Tricks

Oklahoma and Iowa State sported identical 3-3 records prior to their October 31 meeting before 27,000 homecoming fans at Jack Trice Stadium in Ames. The Big Red had dominated the series, 37-4-1, with eight straight wins and was tabbed as 14-point favorite.

Iowa State controlled the first quarter by jumping to a 21-0 lead and threatened to toss more fuel onto the fire by nearly scoring a fourth TD. Sooner cornerback Steve O'Shaughnessey killed the drive by intercepting a pass at the OU 33.

A safety by the Sooner defense wiped the goose egg off the scoreboard early in the second quarter. The Cyclones were pinned at their 10-yard line, and head coach Johnny Majors ordered a quick kick on third-and-10. A swarm of OU defenders chased punter Ralph Baracz toward the goal line. They smothered him there to give OU two points with 11:22 until halftime.

Monty Johnson picked off Dean Carlson's pass midway through the second quarter and sprinted 44 yards to the ISU 18. Five plays later at the ISU five, Wylie took a pitch from Mildren to the right side and followed Crosswhite's block to the end zone. OU trailed 21-9, after Derr's conversion.

The Sooners set up at their own 25 on the second possession of the third quarter. Mildren drilled a pass to flanker Willie Franklin, who beat out Cyclone defenders at the ISU 45 and outraced the enemy to the end zone. Derr's kick sailed wide left, but OU was back in the game, down, 21-15.

Early in the fourth period, Dan Ruster took an Iowa State punt at the OU five and returned it 34 yards. Mildren connected an 11-yard pass to Harrison. Harrison then took a pitch from Mildren and dashed 25 yards to the ISU 25. Two plays later, Crosswhite scored his second touchdown of the day on a nine-yard run. The Sooners had a chance to take the lead for the first time, but Derr again missed the extra point, and the score was knotted at 21 with 13:06 remaining in the game.

Both teams missed field goals after turnovers. Minutes later, Dean Carlson tossed a pass to Otto Stowe for a 70-yard TD and a 28-21 Cyclone advantage with 4:29 to go.

A fair catch by A.G. Perryman on the ensuing kickoff set up the Sooners at the 31. Pruitt carried around the left side for 11 yards. OU later faced third-and-eight from its own 48. Mildren rolled right and flipped the ball to Franklin, who was swinging left. Franklin, also a javelin thrower on the OU track team, pulled up and heaved the pigskin to Chandler, who had blown past the

Cyclone secondary. Chandler caught the ball, and momentum carried him out of bounds at the Cyclone 15.

Three plays later, Mildren pitched to Wylie down the right side, and the halfback flew to the end zone. Following a time out, the Sooners lined up in the Wishbone. Mildren flipped the ball to Pruitt on the left side, Crosswhite blocked out ISU's Jeff Allen and Pruitt crossed the goal line untouched for two points and a 29-28 lead with 2:24 showing on the clock.

The Cyclones still had plenty of time to win with at least a field goal. John Shelly intercepted Carlson's pass to seal the victory.

"It takes a lot of guts to win," Fairbanks said following the game. "I'm extremely proud of our players. They had the character to come back when they were down."

The Sooners rushed for 292 yards and passed for 153. Wylie gained 108 yards on the ground, two more than Crosswhite. Iowa State collected 295 total yards.

Oklahoma erupted for three second-quarter touchdowns to down 4-4 Missouri, 28-13, the next week before a homecoming crowd of 54,750 in Norman.

OU took a 7-0 lead when Mildren completed a 60-yard TD pass to Pruitt early in the second period, and Derr kicked the first of four conversions.

Linebacker Mark Driscoll forced the Tigers' Booker Washington to fumble on the first play after the kickoff, and Raymond Hamilton recovered at the MU 21. Mildren scored on a one-yard run five plays later.

Ruster's 30-yard punt return to the Missouri 45 late in the second stanza set up the third Sooner touchdown. Facing third-and-nine at the 34, Mildren lobbed a screen pass to Pruitt, who sailed down the west sideline for the score.

The Tigers marched 97 yards to close their deficit to 21-7. The Sooners stormed back to take a 28-7 lead seconds later. Wylie returned the kickoff 76 yards to the MU two. Pruitt took Mildren's pitch on the next play and followed Crosswhite's block into the end zone.

Missouri's scored a TD with 57 seconds remaining in the game. The Tigers tried to go for two, but Baccus hammered Washington behind the line of scrimmage.

The Wishbone attack still struggled to gain huge yards. The Sooners gained 10 first downs and 126 rushing yards (2.4 per carry). Mildren completed only three passes for 108 yards—all to Pruitt. Missouri rolled up 369 total yards.

Offensive coaches worked to tweak the new offensive formation.

Sooner Magic:
Wishbone Begins to Take Shape

The Wishbone again caught fire the next week in Lawrence as Oklahoma squeaked by 5-4 Kansas, 28-24. The Sooners amassed 357 yards on the ground, or 4.8 yards per run. Wylie and Crosswhite led the way with 132 and 127 yards respectively. The Sooners only tossed four passes in the game, and the final three touchdown drives were all on the ground.

A bone-chilling 35 degrees aided by a 15-mph wind greeted the 38,200 fans at Memorial Stadium. KU took a 7-0 lead late in the opening quarter on John Riggins' 22-yard run.

The Sooners responded with a 66-yard drive. Mildren sparked the drive with a 19-yard run followed by a 15-yard pass on third-and-10. Wylie scored on a 16-yard run around right end. Pruitt's block opened a clear lane for Wylie to the end zone. Derr's kick tied the game at 7-7.

The Sooners marched 69 yards in 10 plays, all on the ground, on their next possession to score in the second quarter. Wylie's eight-yard run, aided again by Pruitt's block, put the Sooners on top for the first time. Derr's boot gave OU a 14-7 advantage.

Riggins scored again on a 65-yard run with 53 seconds left in half.

The Jayhawks took the second-half kickoff and marched 80 yards in 16 plays, using up nearly half of the third quarter to get the go-ahead touchdown. They later added a field goal after intercepting Mildren's pass.

The Sooners drove 54 yards in eight plays to the Kansas 14, which carried into the fourth quarter. This time it was Pruitt who got the call. He took Mildren's pitch, circled back to his right and followed blocks by tackle Tommy Saunders and Chandler to the end zone. Derr converted, and the Sooners cut the deficit to 24-21 with 14:25 remaining in the game.

Later, Ruster returned a punt 13 yards to the OU 30. Again the Sooners drove without going to the air. The drive was aided by Crosswhite's 20-yard run to the KU 24. On the next play, Pruitt took a pitch out to the left side and flew to the end zone. Derr's extra point gave Oklahoma a 28-24 lead with 8:24 to go.

The Jayhawks later moved to the OU 19. Quarterback Daniel Heck fired a pass to flanker Lucius Turner on a post route to the end zone. O'Shaughnessey cut toward the airborne ball, stepped in front of Turner, and picked off the pass in the end zone.

"The pass was on target, but I got in front of him," O'Shaughnessey said.

"It has to be one of the best interceptions I've ever seen, especially when you consider the place on the field and the situation of the game," OU defensive coordinator Larry Lacewell said after the game.

The Jayhawks got another chance with the ball at midfield, but Johnson intercepted Heck's pass at the Sooners' 30 with 45 seconds left.

Kevin Grady (75) and Gary Baccus (51) wrap up John Riggins for no gain. (© 1970, The Daily Oklahoman)

Fairbanks said it was his offense's best performance of the year and credited the line's blocking.

"It was probably the best performance of the year," he said. "This bunch of guys has a lot of guts to come back the way they did."

Fairbanks did not chide his defense for giving up 322 yards in the game. "Our defense faced a good offensive team and a great running back in John Riggins."

Riggins, the Big Eight's leading rusher, rushed for 178 yards on 22 carries and two touchdowns. His previous best against OU was 60 yards.

"It's a real fine victory ... our execution was very good," Fairbanks said.

OU gained 23 first downs, six more than Kansas. Neither team passed for much, the Sooners for 28 yards and the Jayhawks for 52.

The Sooners' come-from-behind victory stunned the Jayhawks fans, but the nation was stunned when, later that night, 70 members of the Marshall University football team perished in a plane crash.

A twinjet Southern Airways DC9 carrying the Thundering Herd team crashed into the side of a hill and burst into flames in Kenova, West Virginia. The team was returning from Greenville, North Carolina, following its gridiron loss to East Carolina.

The plane was making its approach to Marshall's hometown of Huntington, West Virginia, when it crashed in a light fog and drizzle 12 miles from the airport.

No. 3 Nebraska (9-0-1) was a 17-point favorite on November 21 against the 6-3 Sooners in Lincoln. A sellout crowd of 67,392 was treated to a four-touchdown scoring spree in the second quarter and kept on the edge of their seats until the final gun.

OU rolled 73 yards in 12 plays to take a 7-0 lead early in the second stanza. Mildren scored on a five-yard run. Crosswhite took a last-second pitch from Mildren and dashed 21 yards to midfield to spark the drive. Derr converted the first of three extra points.

The Cornhuskers roared back to tie the game 93 seconds later with a 64-yard march.

Two minutes later, Wylie scored on a 37-yard jaunt to cap a 75-yard drive. Nebraska responded with a 79-yard drive. Both teams headed to the locker room notched at 14-14.

The Huskers took a 21-14 lead late in the third period when quarterback Jerry Tagge completed a 13-yard TD pass to Guy Ingles.

OU answered moments later with an 80-yard drive in 17 plays. Wylie hooked up with Willie Franklin for a 10-yard TD pass to tie the game at 21-21 early in the fourth stanza.

Nebraska scored on a 53-yard march midway through the fourth quarter for the final tally.

The Sooners had Husker fans gnawing at their fingernails minutes later. With 1:25 remaining, OU drove 53 yards to the NU 27, but Mildren's fourth-down pass was intercepted in the end zone.

Oklahoma gained 276 yards on the ground and 95 more through the air. Nebraska picked up 417 total yards.

That evening the Sooners accepted an invitation to play Alabama in the Astro-Bluebonnet Bowl on New Year's Eve in Houston.

Greg Pruitt scored two touchdowns against Alabama in the 1970 Bluebonnet Bowl.
(© 1970, The Daily Oklahoman)

The Sooners hammered 4-6 Oklahoma State, 66-6, the next week in Norman. Eight different players scored for the Sooners in the largest margin of victory of the series. Pruitt and Wylie were the only players to score two touchdowns and rush for over 100 yards. Pruitt led the way with 116 yards on eight carries, and Wylie gobbled up 105 yards on 16 carries.

Pruitt scored on a six-yard run midway in the first stanza, and Crosswhite added a 21-yard scoring jaunt minutes later for a 14-0 lead. Derr never missed on nine conversion attempts, which tied the one-game record set by Dave Wallace, who booted nine straight in 1946.

Leading 17-0 in the second quarter, the Sooners scored four touchdowns in a 12-minute span for a 45-0 lead at halftime.

OU's first team played one series early in the third period and scored on a 59-yard march culminated by Wylie's one-yard run. Reserve quarterback Dave Robertson scored on a four-yard run eight minutes later.

The Cowboys finally got on the board with a touchdown midway through the fourth stanza but failed to get the two-point conversion.

Robertson sailed a 59-yard scoring strike to Harrison, who slipped behind the Pokes' secondary for the final tally.

The Sooners gained 32 first downs, 519 rushing yards, and passed for 73 more. The Cowboys rushed for only two net yards and passed for 205. The Big Red defense dropped OSU quarterback Tony Pounds six times for minus-62 yards.

The Sooners finished the regular season with a 7-4 mark and 5-2 in the Big Eight to place second in the conference.

Alabama, coached by Bear Bryant, finished its season with six wins and five losses for the second straight year. The Crimson Tide tied for seventh place among 10 teams in the Southeastern Conference with a 3-4 mark and had lost three straight bowl games. The game marked the third time the Sooners faced Bryant as a head

1970 Season Record: 7-4-1

Big Eight Conference: 5-2-0 (Second)

Date	Opponent	Result	Score
September 12	at Southern Methodist	W	28-11
September 19	WISCONSIN	W	21-7
September 26	OREGON STATE	L	23-14
October 10	Texas at Dallas	L	41-9
October 17	at Colorado	W	23-15
October 24	KANSAS STATE	L	19-14
October 31	at Iowa State	W	29-28
November 7	MISSOURI	W	28-13
November 14	at Kansas	W	28-24
November 21	at Nebraska	L	28-21
November 28	OKLAHOMA STATE	W	66-6
December 31	Alabama*	T	24-24

*Astro-Bluebonnet Bowl at Houston, TX

coach. Bryant's Kentucky Wildcats defeated OU in the 1951 Sugar Bowl, and his 1962 Alabama squad won in the 1963 Orange Bowl.

No. 20 Oklahoma and unranked Alabama fought to a 24-24 tie before 53,822 fans in the Astrodome. The final minute turned into a field goal duel—one good and one missed.

Bama took a 7-0 lead midway through the first quarter.

The Sooners answered with a 74-yard scoring drive topped by Wylie's two-yard run and Derr's extra point. Derr also converted all three of his kicks. OU thrice had to overcome third-down obstacles to keep the drive alive. Mildren completed a 12-yard strike to Harrison on third-and-11. Pruitt gained eight yards on a third-and-seven play. On third-and-11 at the Bama 36, Mildren lofted a 34-yard pass to Harrison to the two, one play before Wylie scored.

Pruitt scored twice in the second stanza, on runs of 58 and 25 yards, to give the Sooners a 21-7 lead.

The Tide responded with a 75-yard scoring drive to trail, 21-14, with 14 seconds left until intermission.

Early in the third quarter O'Shaughnessey intercepted Scott Hunter's pass in the end zone to thwart a Bama threat to the OU eight. Richard Ciemny booted a 20-yard field goal minutes later to cut the Oklahoma lead to 21-17.

Hunter completed a 25-yard TD pass to Johnny Musso midway in the fourth period to give the Crimson Tide the lead for the first time, 24-21.

Oklahoma marched from its 20 to the Bama 24, but Mildren was sacked for a six-yard loss on third-and-five. Derr kicked a 42-yard field goal to tie the game at 24-24 with 59 seconds left. Derr's onside kick bounced backwards and failed to travel the necessary 10 yards giving the Tide the ball at the Sooners' 40.

Following Musso's 21-yard run, the Tide elected to run down the clock for a final field-goal attempt to win the game. Ciemny's kick was wide left with five seconds remaining.

The Sooners finished the season 7-4-1 and ranked 20th in the AP poll. Aycock, Johnson, and Wylie were named to the All-Big Eight Conference's first team.

1971

The sequel to the Oklahoma Land Rush of 1889 was produced 82 years later in Norman, Oklahoma. The Oklahoma Sooners pounded the turf for 5,196 yards, the most ever in OU football history. The Big Red averaged 469.6 yards per game or 7.1 yards each time they carried the pigskin.

Nine of 11 Sooners returned on offense in 1971, including the entire backfield. The team fine-tuned the Wishbone machine during spring and fall practices. The formation would become a lethal offensive weapon. Jack Mildren, Greg Pruitt, Joe Wylie, and Leon Crosswhite couldn't have accomplished the job without a stellar front line led by center Tom Brahaney, guard Ken Jones, and tackle Dean Unruh. Split end Willie Franklin and tight end Al Chandler would also return to catch the few passes aimed in their direction.

The defense was looking to improve with the return of seven starters. Tackles Ray Hamilton and Derland Moore were the only returnees up front, but the leadership of linebacker Steve Aycock supported the line, and Gary Baccus, Steve O'Shaughnessey, Glenn King, John Shelly, and Geoffrey Nordgren provided a solid secondary.

No. 10 Oklahoma opened the season September 18 with a 30-0 win over Southern Methodist on September 18 in Norman. A crowd of 48,500 braved the afternoon showers.

The Sooners capitalized on three fumble recoveries, which led to 17 points. Nordgren smothered two Mustang fumbles and Aycock

recovered the other miscue. Pruitt, Mildren and Crosswhite each scored a touchdown. John Carroll kicked three field goals.

The Sooners gobbled up 342 yards on the ground and passed for 18. Mildren led the ground attack with 109 yards. The defense held the Mustangs to 137 total yards. SMU crossed midfield only twice in the game, the deepest penetration being the OU 29.

The 11th-ranked Sooners traveled to Pittsburgh the next week and defeated the 1-0 Panthers, 55-29. Mildren and Wylie each scored three TDs.

Pitt took a 3-0 lead early in the first period, but the Panthers' lead was short-lived as Wylie returned the ensuing kickoff 85 yards for a touchdown. Wylie shot straight ahead for 15 yards then weaved from sideline to sideline and outran the Panthers for the final 55 yards. Carroll toed the first of seven conversions, missing only after the seventh TD.

Less than two minutes later, Aycock hammered receiver Joel Klinck. The ball popped loose, and Al Qualls smothered it at the Pitt 33. Four plays later, Mildren scored from the two and dragged Pitt's Ralph Cindrich with him into the end zone.

The Sooners later marched 60 yards in five plays for a 21-0 advantage. Pruitt took Mildren's pitch, followed Wylie's block at the corner, and scored on a 32-yard run.

The Panthers scored five plays after returning the kickoff 76 yards to the OU 17.

Pruitt returned Pitt's kickoff 42 yards to the OU 48, and the Sooners scored eight plays later on Mildren's four-yard sneak.

The Big Red made it 35-11 on its next series. Wylie's 13-yard run around right end capped the 89-yard, seven-play march. This time it was Pruitt who made the key block to spring Wylie free to the end zone. Mildren's 56-yard pass to Jon Harrison sparked the drive. Harrison almost got away for a touchdown but was dragged down at the Pitt 32.

The Panthers scored late in the second stanza, but the Sooners thundered 68 yards in five plays to take a 42-17 lead less than a minute later. Mildren ignited the drive with a 41-yard scamper on the first play. Wylie scored on a 19-yard run four plays later.

OU cruised 69 yards for a 48-17 lead following the second-half kickoff. Only four plays were necessary—Crosswhite for two, Pruitt for 18, fullback Tim Welch added 33, and Mildren carried for the final 16. Carroll missed the conversion.

Chuck Fairbanks put in the reserves, and the alternates scored once more on Welch's 16-yard jaunt 35 seconds into the fourth period to cap a 97-yard march.

The Panthers added two more touchdowns and failed to convert on the two-point conversion after each score.

OU gained 418 on the ground and 149 through the air. Pruitt carried nine times for 118 yards. Pitt picked up 484 total yards.

Pruitt rushed for 205 yards and scored three TDs as No. 8 Oklahoma pounded No. 17 Southern California 33-20 on October 2 in Norman. The 2-1 Trojans had not yielded a touchdown in the previous 10 quarters. The Sooners rushed for 516 yards, which was also the total yardage, since Mildren only attempted one pass and it fell incomplete.

OU hammered out 66 yards to the first score 10 plays after Wylie returned the opening kickoff to the OU 34. Wylie scored on a one-yard run, but USC blocked Carroll's conversion.

The Trojans took a 7-6 lead late in the first quarter.

Oklahoma stormed back in two plays, both pitchouts, covering 80 yards. Wylie picked up 38 yards, and Pruitt zipped the final 42 for the score. Carroll toed the extra point for a 13-7 lead.

Crosswhite's fumble at the OU 16 led to a Trojan touchdown late in the half for a 14-13 lead.

Oklahoma took a 19-14 lead three minutes later. Defensive end Bruce DeLoney recovered a Trojan fumble at the USC 36, and Pruitt scored on a seven-yard run five plays later. The two-point conversion failed when Mildren was tackled as he tried to handoff to Pruitt.

The Sooners jumped to a 26-14 advantage on Pruitt's 75-yard sprint late in the third quarter. Pruitt took Mildren's split-second lateral, cut to the inside on Wylie's block and split the seam between two Trojan defenders to the end zone. Carroll booted the extra point.

O'Shaughnessey snared USC's pass minutes later at the OU 28. The Sooners marched for another touchdown in 11 plays. Mildren sliced through left tackle for an 11-yard touchdown, and Carroll converted. USC scored on the final play of the game. The Trojans totaled 400 yards.

Wylie suffered a sprained ankle in the fourth quarter and was out for the Texas game. Roy Bell would replace him against the Longhorns.

Oklahoma and Texas, defending national champions in the UPI poll, nearly wore out the Cotton Bowl scoreboard in a battle of unbeatens the next week in Dallas. Both teams entered the game with identical 3-0 records, but No. 8 Oklahoma upset No. 3 Texas, 48-27. The victory ended the Longhorns' four-game win streak in the series. Another sold-out crowd (73,580) jammed into the Cotton Bowl on October 9 to witness a combined 75 points, 45 first downs, 854 total yards and a see-saw duel.

Texas took a 7-0 lead seven plays after recovering Pruitt's fumble at the OU 44.

The Sooners responded with a 69-yard scoring drive in seven plays to tie the game. Pruitt scored from the one, and Carroll converted the first of six extra points. Pruitt sparked the drive with a 46-yard run.

Texas recaptured the lead less than three minutes later and the Big Red answered with a 69-yard scoring march in eight plays. Bell scored from the three for a 14-14 tie.

The Sooners wheeled 96 yards to take a 21-14 lead early in the second period. Pruitt capped the drive with a four-yard touchdown. Mildren and Pruitt combined for a 41-yard gain to spark the drive—Mildren picked up seven yards then pitched back to Pruitt, who added 34 more.

Moments later, Moore hammered Donnie Wigginton, forcing a fumble, and Qualls recovered at the Steers' 24. A 15-yard penalty backed up the Sooners, but Pruitt scored on a 20-yard jaunt four plays later.

A touchdown pulled Texas within a TD, 28-21, then OU responded with Carroll's 26-yard field goal with one second until halftime.

Early in the third stanza, Texas missed a field goal after recovering Mildren's fumble inside OU territory. The Sooners then wheeled 80 yards for a 38-21 advantage. Mildren completed his only pass of the day—a 40-yarder to Jon Harrison to the UT seven. Mildren then scored on the next play.

Texas scored on an 80-yard drive to cut the Sooner lead to 38-27 late in the third quarter.

Qualls forced the Steers to fumble, and Lionel Day recovered at the UT 33 late in the fourth stanza. OU moved to the 10 but settled for Carroll's 27-yard field goal.

O'Shaughnessey picked off a Steer pass two plays after the kickoff to set up the final Sooner tally. Three plays later, Mildren scored from the one.

Texas had more first downs (24-23), but the OU Wishbone outrushed the Steers' Wishbone (435-231). Pruitt led all Oklahoma

runners with 216 yards on 20 totes. He had 189 yards in the first half alone. Mildren also crossed the century mark with 111 rushing yards. Texas had more passing yards (148-40).

OU shot to No. 2 in the AP poll behind Nebraska, which held the top spot since the beginning of the season. Oklahoma and Nebraska would sit at the one-two position through the next six games.

Undefeated and sixth-ranked Colorado (5-0) invaded Norman on October 16 with a plan to stop the Sooners' ground attack at the outside corners. OU powered 498 yards between the tackles en route to a 45-17 whipping of the Buffaloes.

Oklahoma scored fast and furious in the first quarter. Shelley intercepted Ken Johnson's pass at the OU 26, and the Sooners scored three plays later. Pruitt, who rushed 19 times for 190 yards, flew 66 yards through left tackle for the first touchdown midway in the opening period. Carroll converted the first of six extra points.

OU scored on one play nearly two minutes later, when Mildren fired a 54-yard scoring strike to Harrison for a 14-0 lead.

Carroll's 36-yard field goal made it 17-0 early in the second stanza. The Sooners later drove 89 yards in nine plays. Mildren's three-yard run topped the drive, which was highlighted by Pruitt's 59-yard run to the Buffs' 24.

Colorado got on the board early in the third quarter two plays after recovering Pruitt's fumble at the CU 31 to cut OU's lead to 24-7.

The Sooners countered with a 68-yard scoring march in nine plays. Pruitt scored on a 14-yard jaunt behind Crosswhite's block.

Colorado responded with a 60-yard scoring drive and a field goal to cut the OU lead to 31-17.

Early in the fourth period, Mildren sailed a 68-yard TD pass to Wylie, who slipped out of the backfield and into the open along the west sideline. Chandler threw a key block to allow Wylie a free lane to the end zone.

Bell scored the final TD in the game with a three-yard run three minutes later. Mildren's 30-yard pass to Harrison sparked the drive.

The game was not completely about the offense. Backup defensive tackle Lucious Selmon pressured Johnson all day long. Johnson completed only 14 of 33 passes, tossed two interceptions, and Selmon sacked him three times.

OU rolled up 27 first downs and passed for 172 yards. Mildren completed three of four for 152 yards. Oklahoma's 670 total yards set a new school record, eclipsing 664 yards set in 1946 against Oklahoma State. The Buffaloes tallied 324 total yards.

The Sooners' record total yards against Colorado lasted only one week. The Big Red amassed 785 yards in a 75-28 demolition of 2-4 Kansas State the next week in Manhattan. The crowd of 40,000 witnessed NCAA and Big Eight records. OU rushed for 711 yards surpassing 645 yards set by Texas El Paso in 1948. It also smashed Colorado's conference record of 551 set in 1958. Oklahoma's 785 total yards also expunged Colorado's Big Eight record of 675 set in 1970.

Kansas State rushed for 245 yards and passed for 317. The combined 956 yards by both teams remains an NCAA record for most rushing yards in one game by two teams.

The Sooners scored on 11 of their first 12 possessions. Bell scored four TDs, and Pruitt added three more.

Bill Butler scored the first of four Wildcat touchdowns on a two-yard run for a 7-0 K-State lead. The Cats rolled 80 yards in four plays following the opening kickoff.

Mildren scored on a one-yard run to cap an 80-yard march. Carroll's conversion sailed wide, and Oklahoma trailed, 7-6. Pruitt's 50-yard run to the KSU 13 sparked the drive.

OU rolled 80 yards in six plays on its next series to take the lead for good. Pruitt's 15-yard TD run capped the drive. Mildren then passed to Chandler for two points and a 14-7 lead. Three big gains sparked the drive—Unruh recovered Mildren's fumble after a 19-yard gain, Wylie picked up 19 yards, and Pruitt added 15 more.

Pruitt and Bell scored twice in the 28-point second quarter to up the Sooner lead to 41-14 at the half.

Pruitt set the Big Eight and school record for most yards rushing (294) in one game. He eclipsed Gale Sayers' record 283 yards for the Big Eight mark and Steve Owens' 261 yards against Oklahoma State in 1969 for the school record. He also added 34 yards receiving and 46 return yards to set the school record of 374 all-purpose yards.

Mildren also crossed the century mark, rushing 11 times for 156 yards. OU gained 34 first downs to 22 for Kansas State. OU's 75 points was one point shy of the conference record held by the 1946 Sooners, who defeated Kansas State, 76-0.

Not many teams can lose seven fumbles and still blow out an opponent. Yet Oklahoma managed to crush 5-1 Iowa State, 43-12, on October 30 in Norman. Pruitt's total offense record lasted only seven days. Mildren broke the school record with 323 total yards (148 rushing and 175 passing). The senior quarterback from Midland, Texas, also scored two touchdowns and tossed for another.

The Sooners pounded out 32 first downs, 504 rushing yards, and Mildren's 175 through the air. Pruitt was the game's leading rusher with 159 yards. Harrison had five pass catches for 135 yards. The Cyclones gained 235 total yards.

The seven lost fumbles equaled a school record set by the Sooners in 1948, 1950, and 1956.

As the offense was gaining the headlines, the defense starred in a supporting role in the land run sequel. After all, it's the defense that keeps the enemy's offense from putting points on the board.

The defense held 1-7 Missouri to 189 total yards the following week in Columbia. The Tiger defense made it difficult for the Sooners to score, however OU did win, 20-3. Although the Big Red offense only crossed the goal line twice, it did so in astronomical portions and all in the first half.

Missouri advanced to the OU 11 in the first quarter, but the Big Red defense stiffened and forced a field goal. Kenith Pope blocked the kick, and Mark Driscoll scooped up the ball and sprinted 70 yards for a touchdown. Carroll missed the extra point.

The Tigers kicked a 34-yard field goal early in the second quarter to cut Oklahoma's lead to 6-3.

The Sooners responded with an 80-yard scoring drive in two plays. Mildren gained two yards, and Bell raced 78 yards for the touchdown. Bell hit the hole at the line of scrimmage, shed a Missouri defender, then popped loose for the score. Mildren was stopped short on the two-point attempt.

Mildren later hooked up with Chandler for a 44-yard TD pass late in the first half. Chandler caught the ball at the 34 and shot to the end zone. The completion was the only one in seven attempts for Mildren.

The Sooners came up empty on two scoring chances in the second half. They fumbled away one opportunity at the MU 17 then the Tiger defense stalled a drive at their 21 late in the game.

With 407 yards rushing, it sounded like OU had another blowout victory. But the Tiger defense held Pruitt in check as he failed to gain over 100 yards (23 for 92) for the first time all year. However, Bell managed to slip through Tiger hands for 109 yards in 10 carries.

The Sooners got back on the blowout track with a 56-10 shellacking of 3-6 Kansas the next week in Norman. A homecoming crowd of 54,400 turned out to witness the Sooners' eight-TD explosion—seven in the first half.

The first string played in the first 27 minutes and scored six times. OU thrice marched 80 yards for the first three touchdowns. Crosswhite got the first one on a 38-yard run, Mildren added a 65-yard scoring run minutes later, and Pruitt's two-yard jaunt came early in the second period.

The fourth Sooner score came 54 seconds later. Hamilton smothered a Jayhawk fumble at the KU 30, and one play later, Mildren tossed a scoring strike to Chandler. Moments later, KU's Delvin Williams took a handoff, and Moore was there to greet him. Williams fumbled, and Selmon recovered at the Hawks' 24. Crosswhite sprinted the distance for the score on the next play.

OU jumped to a 42-0 lead late in the stanza on Harrison's 31-yard reverse to cap a 71-yard drive. Harrison circled wide from right end, took a pitch from Mildren, followed Unruh's block and bolted to the end zone.

Everett Marshall scored on a 14-yard run with 1:22 left until halftime. Dave Robertson added a one-yard scoring jaunt for the only points in the third period.

Kansas scored the only points in the fourth quarter with a touchdown and a two-point conversion, followed by a safety when Carroll was back to punt out of the end zone, but was smothered by Jayhawks.

Carroll, who did not have a stellar year as a placekicker, converted all of his extra pointers that day to set a new school record. His 42 conversions for the year surpassed two Sooners who had 39 extra-pointers—Les Ming in 1949 and Jim Weatherall in 1951.

More records fell during the Kansas game. Mildren's 141 total yards (77 rushing and 64 passing) bumped his career total yards to 4,414, eclipsing Bob Warmack's 4,337 yards. The Sooners' 502 yards rushing against KU raised the season total to 4,333, breaking the NCAA mark of 3,910 set by the 1956 Sooners. The 5,069 total yards through nine games of 1971 broke the Big Eight record of 4,817 also held by the '56 Sooners.

The Jayhawks collected 273 total yards. Pruitt again was held for less

Jon Harrison (12) grasps Jack Mildren's pass for a TD. The Sooners went into halftime up 17-14 over the Huskers. (© 1971, The Daily Oklahoman)

than 100 yards (69), but Crosswhite stepped up to the leading role, rushing nine times for 109 yards.

The No. 2 Sooners had 12 days off before the showdown with No. 1 Nebraska in Norman. Two undefeated teams would square off for supremacy in the Big Eight Conference and the nation. To the winner: a bid to playing the Orange Bowl and for the national championship. The Cornhuskers were the defending national champions in the AP poll and coached by Bob Devaney.

Notre Dame was No. 1 in the preseason AP poll, but the Cornhuskers replaced them the following week and rode the driver's seat all season long. After Oklahoma defeated Texas, the Huskers and Sooners were No. 1 and No. 2 for the next six weeks.

Overcast skies loomed over Owen Field for the Thanksgiving Day clash. The day ended gloomy for the Sooners as they dropped a 35-31 decision to the Cornhuskers in what was billed as "The Game of the Century." The contest was such a huge draw that more than 1,500 press passes were distributed in addition to a sold-out (61,826) Memorial Stadium crowd. More than 5,000 Husker fans attended the game.

No one could have written a better script for this scene on national television. The offenses of both teams were masterpieces. While the Sooners outmuscled their opponents by an average of 42-16, the 10-0 Huskers overpowered their opponents by an average of 39-6.

Nebraska countered Oklahoma's firepower backfield with an I-formation featuring quarterback Jerry Tagge, tailback Jeff Kinney, wingback Johnny Rodgers, and fullback Bill Olds.

The Husker defense led the nation in total defense, yielding 178.4 yards per game. Oklahoma's defense allowed 288 total yards per game.

Nebraska struck first when Rodgers took Wylie's punt early in the first quarter and weaved 72 yards for a touchdown. Fairbanks wanted a clipping call as Wylie was cut off from behind, but the officials didn't see the infraction.

"This isn't sour grapes, but there was a clip on the play," Fairbanks said after the game. "There was a clip, I saw it."

Carroll's 30-yard field goal cut the Husker lead to 7-3 late in the opening period. Kinney's one-yard plunge gave Nebraska a 14-3 advantage early in the second stanza.

The Sooners answered with an 80-yard, 13-play drive. Mildren's three-yard TD run and Carroll's extra-point conversion put the Sooners back in the game trailing 14-10 with 5:10 until intermission.

NU's Rich Sanger missed a field goal and OU took over at its 21 with 51 seconds left in the first half. Two plays later, Mildren fired a 43-yard pass to Harrison to the NU 24. Mildren again sailed a pass to Harrison, who caught it in the left corner of the end zone with five seconds until halftime. Carroll's kick gave OU a 17-14 halftime lead.

Oklahoma had 311 total yards in the first 30 minutes and Nebraska only had 91.

Kinney added two more TDs in the third period to give Nebraska a 28-17 lead. The Huskers capitalized on an Oklahoma fumble at the NU 47, then marched 61 yards to the second score.

The Sooners retaliated with a 73-yard drive in seven plays. Harrison, on a reverse, took a pitch from Mildren, pulled up and heaved a 51-yard pass to Chandler to the NU 16. Mildren carried on four straight plays and scored from the three with 28 seconds left in the third stanza. Carroll's foot pulled OU within four, 28-24.

Nebraska drove into Sooner territory but fumbled, and Selmon recovered at the OU 31. From there the Sooners marched 69 yards to regain the lead 31-28 with 7:10 to go. Mildren sailed a 17-yard scoring strike to Harrison for the lead.

Crimson hearts sunk when Nebraska answered with a 74-yard drive. Kinney scored his fourth touchdown from three yards out. Sanger's foot gave the Huskers a 35-31 lead with 1:38 to go. The Sooners could not mount a drive. Mildren's fourth-down desperation pass from the OU 15, was batted away by Husker noseguard Rich Glover.

Kinney rushed for 174 yards to lead the Huskers' power attack. Mildren led the Sooners with 130 yards rushing and completed five of 10 passes for 137 yards. Nebraska outrushed the Sooners 297-279. OU had more total yards (467-362) and first downs (22-19), but statistics do not win games.

The Sooners dropped to 9-1 and No. 3 in the AP poll and were on their way to the Sugar Bowl to meet Auburn, but first state pride was on the line.

Pruitt, who had been held to under 100 yards in the last three games, gained 189 yards and scored twice as the Sooners smashed Oklahoma State, 58-14, the next week in Stillwater.

Oklahoma scored on nine of 12 possessions and led 27-0 before the 4-5-1 Cowboys scored late in the second period. Carroll's 26-yard field goal early in the first quarter boosted his season total to 80 points, breaking the Big Eight record of 71 set by Missouri's Henry Brown in 1969. Carroll also converted seven of eight extra points to extend his season total to 53, breaking the Big Eight record of 48, set in 1970 by Nebraska's Paul Rogers.

Pruitt and Mildren each scored twice and Mildren added a TD pass. Harrison's 77-yard run on a reverse was the biggest play for a 17-0 lead.

The Sooners gained 33 first downs, gobbled up 584 yards on the ground and passed for 112 more. The 696 total yards gave the Sooners an average of 566.5 yards per game, surpassing the NCAA record of 562 set by Houston in 1968.

The No. 3 Sooners took their 10-1 record to New Orleans to meet No. 5 Auburn on New Year's Day. Quarterback Pat Sullivan led the Tigers to a 9-1 record, and he was voted the Heisman Trophy winner for his effort.

Sullivan completed 20 of 44 passes for 250 yards and had one intercepted. Selmon and Qualls were in his face all day long. Mildren led the Sooners with 149 yards rushing and scored three touchdowns before the largest Sugar Bowl crowd of 84,031.

Crosswhite's four-yard TD run capped a 78-yard drive to put the Sooners up first, 6-0, midway through the first quarter. Carroll missed the extra point.

1971 Season Record: 11-1-0
Big Eight Conference: 6-1-0 (Second)

Date	Opponent	Result	Score
September 18	SOUTHERN METHODIST	W	30-0
September 25	at Pittsburgh	W	55-29
October 2	SOUTHERN CALIFORNIA	W	33-20
October 9	Texas at Dallas	W	48-27
October 16	COLORADO	W	45-17
October 23	at Kansas State	W	75-28
October 30	IOWA STATE	W	43-12
November 6	at Missouri	W	20-3
November 13	KANSAS	W	56-10
November 25	NEBRASKA	L	35-31
December 4	at Oklahoma State	W	58-14
January 1	Auburn*	W	40-22

*Sugar Bowl at New Orleans, LA

Hamilton later recovered an Auburn fumble at the Tigers' 41. Mildren capped an eight-play drive with a five-yard run to put the Sooners up 13-0. Carroll's kick was true this time.

Wylie made it 19-0 when he returned a punt 71 yards later in the first period. The Sooners failed to make the two-point conversion.

Two Sooner interceptions made things worse for the Tigers in the second quarter. Nordgren picked off the first Sullivan pass at the AU 35. Qualls and Selmon forced the Tiger quarterback to hurry his throw. Seven plays later, Mildren crossed the goal line from four yards out to give his Sooners a 25-0 advantage. Again the two-point conversion was unsuccessful. Driscoll intercepted receiver Terry Beasley's pass as he tried to throw on an end-around play. End Mike Struck forced Beasley to throw quickly. Driscoll stole the pass at the OU 40 and returned it to the AU 41. Mildren scored on a seven-yard run with less than a minute until halftime. The Sooners again failed on the two-point try, but Oklahoma held a comfortable 31-0 halftime lead.

Carroll's 53-yard field goal midway through the third quarter broke several records and gave OU a 34-0 lead. He surpassed the Sugar Bowl mark of 52 yards set by Mississippi's Cloyce Hinton in 1970, and he also set the school and Big Eight Conference records for distance.

Auburn finally got on board with a touchdown midway through the third quarter. Pruitt, who gained 95 yards on 18 carries, capped a 69-yard march with a two-yard touchdown run midway through the fourth quarter to put OU up 40-7.

Auburn scored 15 points against the Sooner reserves. Mildren was named the game's Most Valuable Player.

Oklahoma rushed for 439 yards and added 11 yards through the air. The Tigers picked up 290 total yards.

Nebraska toppled No. 2 Alabama, 38-6, in the Orange Bowl to again claim the national championship. Colorado, which only lost to Oklahoma and Nebraska all season, defeated Houston in the Astro-Bluebonnet Bowl. When the final polls were released, Nebraska sat atop, followed by Oklahoma at No. 2 and Colorado at No. 3. The feat of three teams from the same conference rated 1, 2 and 3 was a first, and it hasn't happened since.

Pruitt (1,760) and Mildren (1,289) each rushed for more than 1,000 yards, the first time in Sooner history that two players crossed the 1,000-yard barrier in the same season. They also placed third and sixth respectively in the Heisman Trophy balloting. No other team had two players represented in the top 10 receiving votes. The Sooners set the NCAA record for most rushing yards gained per game with 472.4, still an NCAA record today. Oklahoma not only led the nation on the ground, but also with 566.5 total yards per game and scoring with a 44.9 per-game average.

Carroll led the nation in kick scoring with a 7.3 points-per-game average. He booted 53 of 62 extra points and nine of 12 field goals.

Pruitt finished third nationally in rushing with 151.6 yards per game. He also finished seventh in the nation in scoring with a 9.3 point-per-game average right behind Mildren, who had a 9.6 points-per-game average.

Tom Brahaney, Mildren, and Pruitt were named All-Americans. Aycock, Chandler, Hamilton, Jones, Moore, and Shelley joined them on the All-Big Eight Conference first team.

The ABC network named Mildren its Chevrolet Offensive Player of the Year.

1972

There were concerns about how good the Sooner defense would be in 1972, because they had lost seven starters from a year ago.

Yet tackles Lucious Selmon and Derland Moore, end Ray "Sugar Bear" Hamilton, and corner back Kenith Pope were the granite of the '72 defense, which didn't allow a touchdown during the first 18 quarters. End Gary Baccus, linebacker Rod Shoate, and safeties Randy Hughes and Dan Ruster rounded out the defensive studs.

The offense returned eight starters, but the concern was replacing Jack Mildren at quarterback. "The number-one thing I want is a quarterback who won't beat us," said head coach Chuck Fairbanks.

Dave Robertson beat out James Stokely, Gary Vorpahl, Paul Krause, and Steve Davis for the job. The new quarterback had a tremendous supporting cast in the backfield with the return of halfbacks Greg Pruitt and Joe Wylie and fullback Leon Crosswhite. Three All-Big Eight Conference selectees returned to anchor the front line—center Tom Brahaney, guard Ken Jones, and tight end Al Chandler. Tackle Dean Unruh, a seasoned veteran also returned up front.

When fall practices rolled around, two Texas freshmen were receiving rave reviews. Kerry Jackson earned the backup role at quarterback, and Joe "Lil' Joe" Washington got plenty of playing time behind the stellar backfield.

The Sooners began the season at No. 6 in the AP poll and moved to No. 4 before they had barked one signal, because (previously ranked fourth) Arkansas lost to No. 1 Southern California and No. 5 Penn State lost to No. 15 Tennessee.

The Utah State Aggies rolled into Norman on September 16 for the season opener, riding a 48-14 win a week earlier against New Mexico State. The Utags rode out of Norman with their tails tucked between their legs to the tune of 49-0. The Big Red defense held the Aggies to 10 first downs and 159 total yards (55 rushing and 104 passing). Just a week earlier, Utah State rolled up 687 yards.

The Aggies invaded OU territory only three times with its deepest penetration to the OU 26. Quarterback Tony Adams, who had thrown for 245 yards against New Mexico State, completed 12 of 29 and tossed three interceptions against the Sooners. Two of them led to Oklahoma touchdowns. He was sacked four times, and twice his receivers were tackled for losses.

The Aggie defense boxed nine men on the line to stop the run, so Robertson went to the air, completing a perfect five of five for 155 yards. The Sooners scored on their first possession, a 44-yard strike from Robertson to backup tight end John Carroll.

Pruitt added three touchdowns, but Jackson was the leading rusher with 109 yards on 10 carries in a backup role. The Sooners totaled 617 yards, 412 on the ground.

Oklahoma jumped to No. 2 in the AP poll, although Colorado and Ohio State, which had been ranked No. 2 and No. 3 respectively, had also won.

Eight Sooners scored in a 10-touchdown onslaught as OU blasted 1-1 Oregon, 68-3, the following week in Norman. OU scored on nine straight possessions, led 21-0 in the first quarter and 35-0 at intermission. The Sooners set a school and Big Eight Conference record with 37 first downs. Robertson directed four scoring drives, and Jackson guided the other six. Washington and Chandler each scored two TDs in an offense that pounded out 609 rushing yards and added 122 through the air. Pruitt led all rushers with 103 yards in 11 carries.

The Big Red punted only once, and that came with 6:44 remaining in the game. Oregon, led by quarterback Dan Fouts, was held to 178 total yards.

The Sooners stayed home for the third straight game and again yielded no touchdowns as they defeated Clemson, 52-3, on September 30. The 61,826 in attendance enjoyed the victory and a sunny afternoon of 60 degrees. The 1-1 Tigers were held to 185 total yards.

Pruitt scored three touchdowns, but he only gained 52 yards on 13 carries. Backup fullback Tim Welch led all backs by rushing 24 times for 158 yards, subbing for Crosswhite, who was sidelined with a shoulder injury.

OU only scored seven points early in the first quarter, then scored on six straight possessions (the last three of the second quarter and first three of the third quarter). Pruitt scored the first TD on a five-yard run four plays following a Clemson fumble.

The Tigers threatened with a 53-yard first-quarter drive, but missed a 38-yard field-goal attempt. The Big Red capitalized on another Tiger fumble in the second quarter. Hughes recovered at the OU 31, then the offense marched 69 yards to pay dirt. Robertson scored on a one-yard quarterback sneak. Pruitt's two-yard run minutes later capped a 50-yard drive in five plays to lift OU to a 21-0 lead. Rick Fulcher, subbing for an ailing Carroll, booted a 32-yard field goal with 24 seconds remaining until halftime.

In the third quarter, Robertson scored on a four-yard run, Pruitt on a one-yard run, and Washington ran 61 yards for another to give the Sooners a 45-0 lead. Clyde Powers' 57-yard return with a fumble recovery put the Sooners up 52-0 late in the game. Clemson's Ernie Siegler toed a 49-yard field goal to erase the Clemson goose egg with two seconds to go.

The Sooners had two weeks to prepare for No. 10 Texas on October 14. The 3-0 Longhorns had struggled against Miami, Florida (23-10), Texas Tech (25-20) and Utah State (27-12).

They also struggled against Oklahoma by not scoring any points before 72,030 fans who packed the Cotton Bowl on a hot and humid afternoon. The Horns suffered their first shutout 27-0, since the 1963 Cotton Bowl, a 13-0 loss to Louisiana State. The shutout ended the Steers' 100-game scoring streak and was the first by OU since a 45-0 rout in 1956. OU also struggled during the first half.

Texas advanced to its 45 after the opening kickoff. Moore forced quarterback Alan Lowry to make a wild pitch, and Ruster recovered on the 45. The first possession ended in fumbling the ball away at the UT six.

Fulcher nailed a 37-yard field goal midway through the first quarter, and moments after, Pope recovered a fumble.

Wylie's punt nailed the Horns deep at their two, but Texas got out of the hole by driving to the OU 17. There they faced fourth-and-two, but head coach Darrell Royal opted to gamble instead of kicking a field goal. Cornerback Larry Roach stopped fullback Roosevelt Leaks for no gain. The Sooners held the 3-0 lead through halftime.

Texas later moved to the OU 37, but Mike Dean's field-goal try fell short.

Late in the third stanza, the Longhorns faced third-and-16 at their own 25. Royal ordered a quick kick. Moore slipped through the line and blocked Alan Lowry's boot. Moore and Selmon pursued the pigskin spinning toward the Texas goal line. Selmon fell on it in the end zone, and the Sooners had a 10-0 lead following Fulcher's conversion.

Early in the fourth period, Wylie returned a punt 44 yards to the UT 35 to set up the next Sooner score. The Sooners twice picked up first downs on third-and-six situations. The first came on Wylie's 11-yard run to the 20 and the other on Jackson's 10-yard jaunt to the five. On the next play Pruitt hurdled over left tackle and into the end zone. OU 17, Texas 0.

Fulcher added a 29-yard field goal midway through the fourth quarter. On the Horns' second play at the 20 following the kickoff, Lowry pitched the ball to Leaks, but Baccus swatted the ball toward

the end zone. Moore gave chase and smothered the pigskin for another six points.

Although the Horns gained 259 total yards, the Sooner defense handcuffed them, forcing eight turnovers (four fumbles and four interceptions). OU rolled up 245 rushing yards and 28 passing.

Oklahoma still held onto its No. 2 ranking as USC continued its winning ways. Unfortunately the Sooners did not, dropping a 20-14 decision to No. 9 Colorado the next week in Boulder. The 5-1 Buffaloes held the Sooners to 238 total yards (163 rushing and 75 passing) on a wet Folsom Field.

Eddie Foster recovered a Buffalo fumble at the CU 35 to set up the Sooners' first score late in the second quarter. Robertson scored on a 17-yard run six plays later, and Fulcher converted.

Colorado scored two touchdowns in the third period for a 14-7 advantage. Gary Campbell zipped 43 yards for the first score midway through the third stanza. Fred Lima, who had converted 48 straight extra points dating back to junior college, missed this one.

Wylie, swarmed by Buffaloes, found no punting room on the Sooners' next possession deep in OU territory. He tried to pass out of trouble, but Cullen Bryant intercepted at the 18. Ken Johnson tossed a six-yard scoring strike to Jon Keyworth six plays later, and the Buffs made the two-point conversion.

The Buffs upped their lead to 20-17 with two field goals in the fourth stanza.

Robertson milfd a 10-yard pass to Pruitt to cap a 73-yard, 11-play drive with 1:13 to go, and Fulcher converted. Robertson completed a nine-yard pass to Grant Burget to spark the drive. The pass play gained a first down on the Buffs' 34 to convert a fourth-down gamble.

The Buffs recovered the onside kick and ended any Sooner hopes for a magical comeback.

The loss dropped Oklahoma to eighth in the AP poll, but the next week the Sooners rebounded with a 52-0 pounding of Kansas State on October 28 in Norman. A homecoming crowd of 61,826 turned out to witness the ambush.

Oklahoma equaled its school and conference record 37 first downs and piled up 496 yards in the ground. Pruitt rushed 19 times for 121 yards and scored three touchdowns. His effort moved him past Jim Grisham on the all-time Sooner rushing list with 2,396 yards. Crosswhite also cleared the century mark with 109 yards on 17 carries and added a touchdown. His 17-yard TD run in the fourth period capped a 95-yard march in 15 plays. Robertson completed 12 of 17 passes, tossed one touchdown to Wylie, and scored another himself.

The Big Red defense held the Wildcats to 213 total yards and forced four turnovers. Safety Durwood Keeton robbed two K-State passes.

Robertson came up with a game-clinching play late against No. 14 Iowa State as the No. 7 Sooners downed the 5-1 Cyclones, 20-6, the following week in Ames. The matchup was expected to be an offensive showdown between the nation's No. 1 (OU) and No. 4 (ISU) offensive teams.

The Sooners took a 7-0 lead on Crosswhite's seven-yard run early in the second period and Fulcher's conversion. The score capped a 68-yard march in 13 plays. Robertson completed two passes to Carroll (15 and 12 yards) to spark the drive.

ISU kicked a field goal, then Fulcher booted two field goals for the Sooners. His 19-yarder came with 14 seconds left in the first half, and his 18-yarder came with five and a half minutes left in the third quarter.

The Cyclones added a 34-yard field goal with 4:10 remaining in the game, which caused the crimson faithful to nibble at their fingernails. The Sooners got the ball back with hopes of milking the clock to the end. They drove 87 yards in nine plays, with Robertson making the big play.

With 2:21 remaining, OU needed seven yards for a first down. Robertson carried to the right, turned upfield, lowered his shoulder, and surged across midfield past the first-down marker, then flew 47 more yards to the ISU three. Pruitt scored from the one with 31 seconds to go.

The Sooners rushed for 300 yards with Crosswhite (113) and Pruitt (102) running over the century mark. OU added 74 yards through the air. Iowa State accumulated 349 yards, but Ruster's two interceptions killed Cyclone drives in Sooner territory.

No. 7 Oklahoma edged No. 14 Missouri, 17-6, on November 11 in Norman before another sellout audience of 61,826. Sooner fans could not breathe easy until Pruitt scored on a three-yard run early in the fourth quarter, and the defense followed it with two Tiger interceptions.

The Sooners scored first when they got a big break in the second quarter. MU's Scott Pickens was covering a punt downfield and the ball touched his shoulder pads. Chandler recovered at the MU 23. Wylie gained one yard, then Robertson connected a 22-yard TD pass to Carroll. Fulcher's conversion gave Oklahoma a 7-0 lead with 6:39 left until halftime.

Missouri's Brad Brown picked off Jackson's pass minutes later and returned it 31 yards to the OU 10. The Tigers scored three plays later. A failed extra point gave the Sooners a 7-6 lead over the 5-3 Tigers.

Fulcher added a field goal with 15 seconds before halftime to lift Oklahoma to a 10-6 lead.

Pruitt's 59-yard TD run late in the third stanza was nullified when Chandler was whistled for clipping. The ball was moved back to the Mizzou 30, but the Sooners fumbled the ball away at the MU two.

A Missouri punt sailed out of bounds at the MU 44. Nine plays later, Pruitt's touchdown kept the Sooners from turning blue. Hughes and linebacker Jon Milstead each intercepted a Tiger pass to stall Missouri comeback efforts.

Pruitt rushed 27 times for 195 yards as the Big Red gobbled up 422 yards on the ground, passed for 51 more, and collected 28 first downs. Crosswhite gained 95 yards in the first half, but a twisted ankle sidelined him in the second half.

The Sooner defense held Mizzou to seven first downs and 97 total yards. The Tigers never moved closer than the OU 32 after their second-quarter touchdown.

Oklahoma rose to fourth in the AP poll. The Sooners defeated 3-6 Kansas, 31-7, the following week in Lawrence. Pruitt gained 135 yards on 16 carries in the first half and did not play in the final 30 minutes. He bruised his left ankle, and Coach Fairbanks kept him out, not wanting to risk further injury.

The Big Red scored on two of its first three possessions in each half. Robertson capped a 76-yard drive in 12 plays with a three-yard TD run to put OU ahead, 7-0, early in the opening quarter. Crosswhite added a touchdown on a six-yard run early in the sec-

ond period to top an 80-yard drive in 12 plays. Fulcher toed a 36-yard field goal with 18 seconds before intermission.

The Jayhawks got on the board with a 49-yard pass play early in the third stanza. The Sooners answered with a 64-yard drive in 11 plays. Wylie scored on a two-yard run to put OU ahead, 24-7.

The Big Red scored on its next possession, a 23-yard pass from Robertson to Carroll late in the third period for the final tally. The Sooners pounded out 486 total yards, 399 rushing. The Jayhawks totaled 308 yards, but most of it was against the OU reserves.

OU accepted an invitation to play Penn State in the Sugar Bowl following the game.

The No. 4 Sooners had no time to rest with No. 5 Nebraska just six days away. OU traveled to chilly Lincoln for a nationally televised Thanksgiving clash. The 7-1-1 Cornhuskers lost its opener, 20-17, to UCLA. Like Oklahoma's defense, the Husker defense was unyielding. They allowed only 14 points over the next six games, four of them shutouts.

Iowa State tied Nebraska, 23-23, two games before the OU clash. The Huskers rebounded with a 59-7 blasting of Kansas State. Still the OU-Nebraska matchup was to decide the Big Eight Conference champs. Oklahoma defeated the Huskers, 17-14, before a record crowd of 76,587.

Sooner Magic: A Freshman Steps Up

Freshman split end Tinker Owens, brother of 1969 Heisman Trophy winner Steve, had improved during the middle of the season. He played sparingly but effectively by catching nine passes for 152 yards in backup duty in five games. He also scored one touchdown on a reverse late against Kansas State. Many a freshman would have had butterflies in a big contest. Not Owens. He caught five aerials for 108 yards against the Huskers.

Nebraska took a 7-0 lead in the first quarter after recovering Pope's fumbled punt return, the Huskers held the lead through intermission.

Pruitt and Carroll were sidelined with injuries in the final three quarters. Owens subbed for Carroll and Washington for Pruitt. This might have hurt Pruitt's chances for Heisman votes, but Johnny Rodgers, another leading Heisman candidate, was stymied by the Sooner defense. He rushed four times for five yards, caught three passes for 41 yards and returned one punt for seven yards. Rodgers later won the award and Pruitt placed second in the balloting.

Another fumbled punt return, this time by Wylie, led to the second Nebraska score in the third period. The Huskers recovered at the OU 24. Dave Goeller leaped for the one-yard TD run six plays later, and Rich Sanger converted. Nebraska held a 14-0 lead midway in the third stanza.

Oklahoma answered with a 76-yard drive in 11 plays. Washington's one-yard run around right end cut the Husker lead to 14-7 after Fulcher converted. Robertson completed a 38-yard pass to Owens to the NU 38 to spark the drive.

Grant Burget's one-yard run capped a 36-yard march in five plays to tie the game early in the fourth quarter. Once again the big play was a Robertson-to-Owens pass for 22 yards to the NU 10.

On the next Husker possession, Moore plastered quarterback David Humm causing the NU quarterback to fumble. Selmon smothered the loose pigskin at the Husker 27. The Sooners managed only two yards in three plays and called for Fulcher to boot them ahead.

Fulcher missed two field goal tries (41 and 45 yards) in the first half. This 41-yarder sailed through the uprights for a deciding 17-14 lead with 8:44 left to go.

It's a Fact

As a result of NCAA probation, Oklahoma later forfeited wins against Missouri, Kansas, and Oklahoma State, when it discovered that ineligible players had participated in those games. The Sooners also forfeited the Big Eight Championship. OU's record on the field was 11-1-0 and 7-0-0 in the Big Eight. But the forfeited games changed the records to 8-4 for the season and 5-3 in the conference.

The Sooners spoiled Bob Devaney's final regular-season game as Nebraska's head coach. They also ruined the Huskers' 27-game conference streak and 23 straight home-game winning streak.

Oklahoma gained 15 first downs and 327 total yards (141 rushing and 186 passing). Crosswhite powered out 95 yards on 23 carries to lead Sooner rushers. Nebraska picked up 12 first downs, rushed for 77, and passed for 104 more.

"This has got to be one of the greatest victories in my coaching career," Fairbanks said.

The victory vaulted OU to third in the nation and into the driver's seat for the Big Eight crown. A win over 6-4 Oklahoma State on December 2 in Norman would be the final jewel in that crown. No problem—OU won, 38-15.

Robertson tossed two touchdowns in the first quarter to give OU a 14-0 lead. His first was a 68-yarder to Chandler, and the second was a seven-yarder to Tinker Owens.

Washington, who rushed 21 times for 109 yards, scored on a 17-yard run midway through the second stanza. Fulcher banged home a 24-yard field goal as time expired in the first half to lift OU to a 24-0 advantage.

The Cowboys scored nine points in the third quarter on a touchdown and a field goal. Their two-point try following the TD failed. Crosswhite and Washington added a couple of TDs in the fourth quarter, and the Pokes scored once more. The Sooners' victory nailed down the Big Eight Conference title.

After losing its opener to Tennessee, Penn State won its next 10 games. The Nittany Lions averaged 32.5 points in those first 11 games, but failed to score against the Sooners in the Sugar Bowl in New Orleans.

The New Year's Eve contest, the first Sugar Bowl held at night, was a display of Oklahoma's powerful defense and a stellar performance by Owens, who was named the game's Most Valuable Player.

The defense held the No. 5 Lions to 11 first downs, and 196 total yards (49 rushing and 147 passing). Penn State averaged 402 total yards in the first 11 games. John Cappelletti, the Lions' power tailback, did not play due to a virus and a 102-degree fever.

Owens caught five passes for 132 yards and scored the first touchdown on a 27-yard aerial from Robertson midway through the second quarter. The score topped a 77-yard march in 11 plays. Nine of those plays were up-the-gut runs. The other two broke Penn State's back. Wylie swept right end for 14 yards to the Lions' 29. The other came two plays later—the TD strike to Owens.

1972 Season Record: 11-1-0
Big Eight Conference: 7-0-0 (Champions)

Date	Opponent	Result	Score
September 16	UTAH STATE	W	49-0
September 23	OREGON	W	68-3
September 30	CLEMSON	W	52-3
October 14	Texas at Dallas	W	27-0
October 21	at Colorado	L	20-14
October 28	KANSAS STATE	W	52-0
November 4	at Iowa State	W	20-6
November 11	MISSOURI	W	17-6
November 18	at Kansas	W	31-7
November 23	at Nebraska	W	17-14
December 2	OKLAHOMA STATE	W	38-15
December 31	Penn State*	W	14-0

*Sugar Bowl at New Orleans, LA

The Sooners blew a scoring chance early in the third quarter. PSU's Gary Hayman fumbled a punt return, and John Roush recovered for OU at the Lions' 20. Oklahoma moved four plays to the one, but Jackson fumbled as he tried to cross the goal line and Penn State recovered.

Hayman fumbled another punt early in the fourth stanza, and Ken Jones smothered the ball at the PSU 33. Pruitt gained three yards on fourth-and-two at the Lions' 25. On third-and-six at the 18, Wylie tossed a halfback pass to Owens who dove for the ball at the one. Two plays later, Crosswhite plowed over for the touchdown to give OU a 14-0 lead, which was the final score.

Penn State drove to the OU 23 but stalled when Selmon sacked quarterback John Hufnagel for a 10-yard loss with three minutes left. Playing conservative to protect the lead was not on the Sooners' menu. Robertson sailed a 42-yard pass to Owens to the PSU 20. Robertson crossed the goal line on a 12-yard run two plays later, but the pigskin slipped from his hands just as he crossed the goal line, resulting in a touchback for Penn State.

Oklahoma finished the season with an 11-1 record and No. 2 in the AP poll. USC won the national championship by beating Ohio State in the Rose Bowl the next day.

Tom Brahaney, Moore, Pruitt, and Shoate were named All-Americans. Crosswhite, Ray Hamilton, Selmon, and Unruh joined them on the All-Big Eight first team. The Touchdown Club of Washington, D.C. named Pruitt its Player of the Year.

Darkness would loom over Oklahoma in the coming months.

1973

Head Coach Chuck Fairbanks resigned as the Sooner skipper in January 1973 to take a similar position with the New England Patriots in the National Football League. University regents promoted 35-year-old Barry Switzer, a seven-year assistant at OU, as the school's 17th head coach.

In 1966, Jim Mackenzie brought him to OU, and Switzer served as offensive line coach and was offensive coordinator and assistant head coach under Fairbanks. Switzer had graduated from Crossett (Arkansas) High School with honors and played center and linebacker for the University of Arkansas. He also served as a B team coach and scout for the Razorbacks prior to coming to Oklahoma.

Fairbanks' Sooners were 52-15-1 during his five-year tenure in Norman, but that would change when OU was slapped with NCAA probation in April, forcing the team to forfeit three Big Eight victories and the Big Eight crown in 1972.

Quarterback Kerry Jackson's high school transcript was altered to make him eligible to qualify for a college scholarship. Jackson played in those three Big Eight games, which the Sooners had to forfeit. The NCAA's punishment declared Jackson ineligible for a year, disallowed the Sooners from bowl games for two years (1973 and 1974) and from television for two years (1974 and 1975).

The quarterback situation, which looked promising, suddenly was a carousel of uncertainty. Sophomore Steve Davis and freshmen Scott Hill and Joe McReynolds vied for the starting position. Davis, from Sallisaw, got the nod. Greg Pruitt, Leon Crosswhite, and Joe Wylie had graduated, which would be a concern for most coaches.

But the stable had plenty of studs in halfbacks Joe Washington and Grant Burget and fullback Tim Welch.

Tinker Owens, MVP of the 1972 Sugar Bowl, was the top returnee among receivers. Tight end John Carroll re-injured his knee and was out for the season.

Guard John Roush and tackle Eddie Foster were the lone returnees up front. Kyle Davis stepped up to fill Tom Brahaney's shoes at center. Sophomores Terry Webb and Mike Vaughan rounded out the line at guard and tackle, respectively.

Three brothers anchored the defensive front line. Dewey and Lee Roy Selmon flanked their older brother, noseguard Lucious Selmon, at the tackle slots. Gary Baccus returned at left end, and sophomore Mike Struck earned the starting nod at right end. Rod Shoate, who had a team-high 139 tackles the year before, returned at linebacker with David Smith alongside.

The secondary was solid with the return of safeties Randy Hughes and Durwood Keeton and cornerbacks Ken Pope and Clyde Powers.

Rick Fulcher returned as placekicker, and fullback Jim Littrell got the nod for punting duty.

Preseason publications had little hope for the Sooners to gain national prominence. Not one had picked the Sooners to even win the Big Eight Championship. Boy, were they wrong.

No. 11 Oklahoma crushed Baylor, 42-14, in the nighttime season opener September 15 at Waco. Three Sooners rushed for more than 100 yards each, a feat never before accomplished in Sooner history. Washington ran 14 times for 113 yards and two touchdowns. Fullback Waymon Clark, a junior college transfer, also gained 113 yards on 11 carries and scored once. Davis picked up 110 yards on 17 carries and added two touchdowns.

Baylor gift-wrapped the first three OU scores. The Bears fumbled at the OU 24 and the Big Red drove 76 yards for a 7-0 lead. Davis capped the drive with a three-yard jaunt into the end zone. Fulcher successfully hit all six conversions. Washington's 18-yard run to the Baylor 43 and Davis' 14-yard run to the Bears' three sparked the drive.

Smith recovered a fumble at the BU 24 on the Bears' next possession. Four plays later, Davis crossed the goal line but had lost the pigskin at the one. The ball rolled into the end zone, and Foster recovered to put the Sooners up 14-0.

Minutes later, Pope picked off Neal Jeffrey's pass at the OU 42. Washington dashed to the end zone on a seven-yard run five plays later. Washington added another touchdown (13-yard run) midway through the second period, and Clark's 50-yard sprint two minutes later gave OU a 35-0 lead heading into the locker room.

A Baylor touchdown in the third quarter erased the Bears' goose egg and was the only score of the quarter. Davis scooted 27 yards for another Sooner score early in the fourth stanza and Baylor scored a touchdown against the reserves with 11 seconds left.

The Sooners rushed for 480 yards and passed for 39. Baylor collected 233 total yards.

Oklahoma slithered to ninth, then eighth in the next two AP polls. OU had the next week off and would need the extra time to prepare for No. 1 Southern California, the defending national champs. USC had shut down Arkansas, 17-0, and Georgia Tech, 23-6, to run its winning string to 14.

Both teams battled to a 7-7 tie under the lights of the Los Angeles Coliseum on September 29. The crowd of 84,016 included 15,000 Sooner rooters. Oklahoma outplayed the defending champs in nearly every category but the scoreboard. USC had only one drive into OU territory all night.

Fumbles were the Sooners' Achilles heel on their first two possessions. The defense held the Trojans at bay, but the third fumble was costly.

Powers bobbled a punt return in the second quarter, and the Trojans pounced on the ball at the OU 25. Quarterback Pat Haden fired a 15-yard TD pass four plays later to split end John McKay. Chris Limahelu converted for a 7-0 USC advantage.

Powers redeemed himself with an interception five minutes later and returned it six yards to the USC 36. The Big Red stalled after moving to the 26, and Fulcher's 40-yard field-goal attempt was foiled by a bobbled snap. The Sooner defense then stymied the Trojans twice. The offense later bogged down at the USC 15, and Fulcher's next field-goal try sailed wide just before halftime.

The Sooners took the second-half kickoff and milked six minutes off the clock with a 76-yard, 13-play march to tie the score. Steve Davis' two-yard run capped the drive, and Fulcher's foot drew the game even with 7:18 left in the third stanza. OU gained a first down on three third-down situations. On third-and-three at the USC 42, Clark gained just enough for the first down. On third-and-one on the 32, Clark got the call again, and he burst 20 yards to the 12. On third-and-one at the four, Washington leaped in the air for a first down at the three.

The Trojans then drove 50 yards to the OU 30, but Anthony Davis fumbled, and Shoate fell on it.

No one wowed the crowd more than Washington when he returned a punt early in the fourth quarter. Lil' Joe fielded the Trojans' punt at his 48. He shifted to his left, then to his right. There he saw a wall of Trojans and whirled backwards in the other direction. He had retreated back to his 17-yard line but managed to get back to the OU 44. He stumbled, regained his balance, and eluded nearly every Trojan defender in the process. Although he lost four yards on the return, Washington ran 58 yards backward and forward.

USC moved to the OU 44 midway through the final period, but the Oklahoma defense stiffened. The Trojans punted and the Sooners advanced to their 45 on the ground—not risking an interception.

Anthony Davis and Rod McNeill were the publicized Trojan backs, but they were held for a combined 89 yards rushing. The Sooner backs dazzled the spectators with a 330-yard rushing effort. Clark rushed 26 times for 126 yards, Steve Davis kept the ball 21 times for 102 yards and Washington gained 82 yards on 12 carries. OU gained 18 first downs and passed for 59 yards.

The Sooner defense held USC to nine first downs and 161 total yards (102 rushing and 59 passing). Oklahoma rose to sixth in the AP poll, and USC dropped to fourth.

The No. 17 Miami Hurricanes (2-0) stormed into Norman the next week and gave the Sooners a scare. Miami had stunned Texas, 20-15, in the opener and nearly did the same to Oklahoma.

OU trailed, 20-7, at halftime, but scored two TDs in the third quarter and added a field goal in the fourth to edge the Canes, 24-20.

Davis put the Sooners ahead, 7-0, with a six-yard run midway through the first period, and Fulcher converted.

Miami answered with a TD run late in the opening stanza.

OU moved to the Miami 20 early in the second quarter. Davis attempted a lateral to Welch, but Eldridge Mitchell intercepted the pitch and flew 79 yards to the end zone to give the Canes a 14-7 lead. Miami scored another TD with just more than a minute before intermission, but the extra point sailed wide.

The 20-7 Miami halftime lead had Sooner stomachs in knots. Davis engineered a 54-yard drive midway through the third quarter.

He outmaneuvered Miami defenders on his 13-yard TD run. Fulcher's conversion cut the Canes' lead to 20-14. Davis sparked the drive with two crucial first downs. On second-and-11, he fired an 18-yard pass to Wayne Hoffman, his first catch of the season, to the Canes' 37. Davis later gained six yards to the 13 to overcome a third-and-three situation.

Miami lost yards on two straight plays after the kickoff and punted to the OU 47. Clark gained one yard, then Davis unleashed a bomb to Owens, who caught the ball at the MU 17 and sped to the end zone. Fulcher's kick gave the Sooners a 21-20 lead with 3:08 left in the third period.

Fulcher added 30-yard field goal for insurance with 4:34 remaining in the game.

Oklahoma pounded out 348 rushing yards and passed for 123. Davis led the Sooners' ground attack with 144 yards followed by Washington's 100 yards. The defense held Miami to 159 total yards. Four Canes were held to negative yards rushing.

Oklahoma held onto the sixth slot in the AP poll, and Texas was next. After losing to Miami, the No. 15 Horns beat Texas Tech and Wake Forest.

The Sooners pounded the Steers, 52-13, by land and air and would have by sea if there were one nearby. A crowd of 72,204 packed the Cotton Bowl on October 13 to watch the country-whipping put on by the Sooners. Texas had suffered its worst defeat since dropping a 45-0 decision to the 1956 Sooners. It was the third time Texas had given up 50 or more points in its football history. Chicago University was the first, winning 68 points in 1904 and Oklahoma scored 50 four years later.

Early in the first quarter, Washington took Davis' lateral, then heaved a 40-yard TD pass to Owens, who was all alone behind the Texas secondary. Fulcher converted the first of seven extra points.

The Horns cut the lead to 7-6 on two field goals, then Oklahoma hit the airwaves again with two touchdown passes in the second period. The first was a 63-yarder from Davis to Owens to cap a 68-yard drive in two plays. The second, a Davis-to-Billy Brooks 46-yarder, capped a 48-yard drive in a couple of plays.

Two Powers interceptions led to Sooner touchdowns. Davis scored two TDs in the third quarter, the second coming after Powers' first pickoff for a 35-6 lead, and the Texas throng was departing the Cotton Bowl.

Fulcher added a 24-yard field goal early in the fourth period, and backup quarterbacks Hill and McReynolds each guided TD drives.

Oklahoma was nearly balanced in the yardage department. The Sooners rushed for 283 and passed for 225. Davis completed five of six passes for 185 yards, and Washington led all Sooner runners with 117 yards on 12 carries. Texas gained 288 total yards.

Darrell Royal had now dropped three straight to the Big Red, the second time he lost three in a row to one team. Arkansas did it in the mid-1960s.

Oklahoma rose to third in the AP poll and hosted No. 16 Colorado the following week in the 700th game in Sooner football history.

700th Game

The 4-2 Buffaloes led 7-0 midway through the first quarter, but the Sooners answered with an 84-yard drive, which ended with some razzle-dazzle. Davis handed off to Joe Washington to the right side. Washington pulled up and tossed a lateral back to Davis, who lobbed the ball to Hoffman for a 37-yard touchdown. Fulcher toed the extra point.

The Buffs had the fans squirming in their seats with a drive deep into OU territory in the second period. CU quarterback Clyde

Crutchmer tossed a pass to tight end Dave Logan streaking toward the end zone. Hughes stepped in front of Logan at the four, robbed the pigskin, and scampered 96 yards for the touchdown.

The Sooners went up 21-7 midway through the third stanza, when Davis' one-yard touchdown run capped a 51-yard drive in 10 plays. The Buffs then threatened with a drive to the Sooner two, but Lucious Selmon led a defensive revolt holding the enemy to no yards on four plays.

Clark and backup halfback Clyde Russell added touchdowns in the fourth quarter for the 34-7 victory.

The Big Red rambled for 438 yards rushing and passed for 93. Clark led all rushers with 172 yards, and Washington also crossed the century mark with 118 yards. The Buffs collected 293 total yards.

No. 3 Oklahoma hammered 4-2 Kansas State, 56-14, the following week in Manhattan. Davis and Washington each scored twice and led a 505-yard ground attack with 119 and 112 yards respectively.

The Sooners scored on their first three possessions to lead 21-0 in the first period. Welch scored on a one-yard run six plays after the Wildcats' center fumbled a punt snap on the KSU 22. Fulcher toed the first of eight conversions.

Three minutes later, Hughes picked off the first of two K-State passes at the Cats' 34 to set up the next score. Six plays later, Davis hurled a 13-yard scoring strike to Hoffman. Davis later scored on a 22-yard run to cap a 56-yard drive.

After the Cats put a touchdown on the board early in the second stanza, OU went to work again with two more touchdowns for a 35-7 halftime lead. Davis scored on a 27-yard run and Washington scored on a two-yard run.

Washington, split end Billy Brooks and halfback Bob Berg scored for the Sooners in the second half. Washington scored on a six-yard run, Brooks on a 34-yard end around reverse and Berg on a nine-yard run. Interceptions set up the final two touchdowns.

OU gained 85 yards through the air. The Big Red defense held K-State to 263 total yards, and forced six turnovers—two fumbles and four interceptions.

The Sooners held onto the No. 3 ranking through the Nebraska game.

Back in Norman the next week, crimson fans were wondering what in Sam Hill was going on in the first half. The 2-4 Iowa State Cyclones jumped to a 17-7 lead in the first 15 minutes and four seconds before 61,826 puzzled fans. The Sooners battled back with 24 unanswered points for a 34-17 win.

The Sooners scored first on Washington's 30-yard TD run on the game's first possession, but I-State scored 17 unanswered points for a comfortable lead early in the second quarter. Fulcher toed the conversion after Washington scored.

Cyclone quarterback Keith Krepfle tossed two TD passes to Wayne Stanley. The first score capped an 80-yard drive and the second after Owens spilled the ensuing kickoff at the OU 20. The Big Red defense woke up and stopped ISU's next march, but the Cyclones nailed a 22-yard field goal.

Oklahoma's offense returned to its regular form and stormed 80 yards in seven plays to cut the deficit seven minutes later. Clark's two-yard TD run topped the drive, but Fulcher's kick was blocked. OU trailed 17-13 with 7:37 left in the second stanza.

Davis unleashed a 68-yard bomb to Brooks with 45 seconds before halftime, giving the Sooners a 20-17 advantage after Fulcher converted.

Iowa State picked up eight first downs and 183 total yards in the first half. The Big Red defense held the Cyclones to only one first down and 45 total yards in the second half. Meanwhile the Sooners put up 14 points in the second half.

OU marched 63 yards in 11 plays for the 27-17 advantage with 26 seconds left in the third period. Davis flipped a five-yard TD pass to Hoffman, and Fulcher's conversion gave OU the go-ahead score. Welch's six-yard run to the Cyclone six gained a first down to overcome a fourth-and-one situation.

Washington added a one-yard TD run shortly after returning a punt 42 yards to the ISU 19 in the fourth.

OU ran for 411 yards, and Davis' arm added 92 more through the air. Washington (136 yards) and Davis (103 yards) again led the ground attack.

Oklahoma's defense continued its dominance in the Missouri game by holding the Tigers to six first downs and 118 total yards in a 31-3 rout on November 10 in Columbia.

The No. 10 Tigers had won six games to open the 1973 season and seven of eight, losing to Colorado two weeks before the OU contest.

The Tigers took a 3-0 lead early in the opening quarter to delight the record throng of 68,831.

The Sooners took a 7-3 lead late in the same quarter with a 62-yard march in three plays. Clark's 14-yard TD run capped the drive, and Fulcher converted. Washington sparked the drive with a 41-yard run to the MU 14 one play before Clark scored.

Fulcher added a 39-yard field goal for a 10-3 lead midway through the second stanza.

Washington scored on a 26-yard run late in the third period, but Fulcher missed the conversion. Moments later, the Sooners recovered a fumble at the OU 33. Three plays later, Davis hurled a 63-yard aerial to Brooks for another Sooner score. Brooks outleaped one defender and outran three more to the end zone. The two-point conversion failed.

Fulcher added on a 30-yard field goal early in the fourth stanza. Washington flashed 80 yards on a punt return late in the game for the final score.

The Sooners collected 281 yards rushing and 86 more through the air. Clark led the rushing attack with 153 yards, and Washington picked up 113 yards.

No. 18 Kansas (6-2-1) invaded Norman the following week, but left with its tail tucked between its legs to the tune of 48-20 before another sellout of 61,826. Three plays following the opening kickoff, Powers picked off David Jaynes' pass and raced 45 yards to pay dirt. Jaynes fired a 57-yard TD pass to Emmet Edwards on the next KU possession, but the extra point was blocked. The Sooners led 7-6, yet the offense hadn't even touched the pigskin.

OU's first offensive possession stalled at the KU 43, and instead of punting, Switzer elected to kick a field goal. With a stiff breeze behind him, Tony DiRienzo nailed a 60-yard kick to lift OU to a 10-6 lead. DiRienzo, from Sao Paulo, Brazil, broke Bruce Derr's school record of 51 yards set in 1970 and the Big Eight record of 57 yards held by Colorado's Fred Lima.

The Sooners scored on their next three possessions in the first period—a five-yard run by Washington, a 48-yard pass from Davis to Hoffman, and a 32-yard field goal by Fulcher. Washington and Davis each ran for a touchdown in the second stanza to give OU a 41-12 halftime lead. Davis ran for another score late in the third quarter. Kansas scored again on a 92-yard interception return late in the game.

Overall, 15 Sooners carried the football, chewing up 328 yards on the ground. Davis and Scott Hill tossed for 113 yards over the skies of Owen Field. The Jayhawks gained 280 total yards.

No. 3 Oklahoma blanked No. 10 Nebraska (8-1-1), 27-0, to end the Huskers' 58-game scoring streak before an overflow crowd of 62,257 on November 23 in Norman and a national (ABC) TV audience. The last time Nebraska had been shut out was 47-0 to Oklahoma in 1968.

The Sooner defense not only shut out the Huskers on the scoreboard but on the field as well. The defense yielded only 10 first downs, 174 total yards, and picked off three passes. The Huskers crossed midfield only once, to the OU 33, yet fumbled away that possession.

OU rolled 63 yards in seven plays on its second possession to take a 7-0 lead. Clark crashed through on a two-yard TD run, and Fulcher converted the first of three extra-pointers. Washington highlighted the drive when he took a last-second pitchout from Davis and sailed 34 yards to the NU six two plays before Clark scored.

Davis, who rushed for 114 yards, scored the next three touchdowns. His first was a quarterback sneak on third-and-one at the Husker 47. Usually quarterback sneaks gain short yards, but Davis found a gap up the middle and raced all the way for the score with one second left in the first period to give OU a 14-7 lead.

Davis' second TD came on a one-yard run eight plays after linebacker Smith intercepted David Humm's pass at the NU 26. His final score, an eight-yard run late in the game, capped a 73-yard drive in nine plays. One play before he scored, Davis hurled a 41-yard pass to Owens to the Husker eight.

Oklahoma gained 317 rushing yards and 51 yards through the air. The victory clinched the Big Eight Championship for the Sooners.

"They can't take this one away from us," Switzer said, referring to the probation smack from a year earlier.

Oklahoma jumped to No. 2 in the AP poll, because previous No. 2, Ohio State, tied Michigan.

Steve Davis scored three touchdowns again as the Sooners blasted 5-3-2 Oklahoma State, 45-18, the next week in Stillwater. Davis' first TD came midway through the first quarter to put OU ahead, 7-0, with Fulcher's extra point. Fulcher never missed in six conversions.

Clark's 14-yard scoring jaunt put the Sooners ahead, 14-0, early in the second period, and after the Pokes kicked a field goal, OU responded with Davis' nine-yard run to cap an 82-yard drive in 14 plays.

The Cowboys added a field goal late in the third stanza. Minutes later, Jimbo Elrod blocked Cliff Parsley's punt. The ball rolled into

---

1973 Season Record: 10-0-1
Big Eight Conference: 7-0-0 (Champions)

Date	Opponent	Result	Score
September 15	at Baylor	W	42-14
September 29	at Southern California	T	7-7
October 6	MIAMI (FL)	W	24-20
October 13	Texas at Dallas	W	52-13
October 20	COLORADO	W	34-7
October 27	at Kansas State	W	56-14
November 3	IOWA STATE	W	34-17
November 10	at Missouri	W	31-3
November 17	KANSAS	W	48-20
November 23	NEBRASKA	W	27-0
December 1	at Oklahoma State	W	45-18

the end zone, and Steve Dodd pounced on it for a touchdown for a 28-6 Sooner lead.

OU added 17 points in the fourth quarter for a 45-6 advantage, and Poke quarterback Charlie Weatherbie scored twice in the final 97 seconds.

Oklahoma rushed for 254 yards and passed for 95. OSU gained 305 total yards.

The Sooners finished the 1973 season with a 10-0-1 record and had no chance for a national championship. No. 3 Notre Dame won the title by defeating No. 1 Alabama in the Orange Bowl. Ohio State beat USC in the Rose Bowl and leaped to second in the AP poll. The Sooners placed third.

Two Sooners gained over 1,000 yards during the season. Washington had 1,173, and Clark had 1,014. Davis led the team in scoring with 18 touchdowns. Shoate led the defense with 126 stops.

Eddie Foster, Shoate, and Lucious Selmon were named All-Americans. Baccus, Hughes, Roush, and Washington joined them on the All-Big Eight first team. The ABC network named Selmon its Chevrolet Defensive Player of the Year.

1974

After coming close to winning a national championship a year earlier, the 1974 Sooners were determined to get the job done in just 11 regular-season games. They succeeded by winning all their games, a second straight Big Eight Championship, and the national crown.

Since the Sooners were not on television for the next two years, KTOK radio, the flagship station of all OU games, advertised that fans would have to "hear it, to see it."

Eight players were penciled in to return on offense, but the number dropped to seven when fullback Waymon Clark was booted from the team for disciplinary reasons. Jim Littrell earned the spot to fill big shoes as Clark rushed for 1,014 yards and scored six touchdowns in 1973. Quarterback Steve Davis and running back Joe Washington returned to the backfield. The line was full of depth led by guard John Roush and center Kyle Davis.

The defense lost seven starters from 1973 including All-America noseguard Lucious Selmon. His brothers, Lee Roy and Dewey, were back and so was All-America linebacker Rod Shoate and safety Randy Hughes.

John Carroll's knee healed after a year's layoff and he resumed placekicking and punting duties.

The Sooners were ranked No. 1 in the AP poll but struggled in their opener against Baylor on September 14 in Norman. Three fourth-quarter touchdowns vaulted Oklahoma to a 28-11 victory before a crowd of 62,375.

The Sooners scored on their first possession, an 80-yard drive in nine plays, capped by halfback Grant Burget's 28-yard run. Carroll converted the first of four extra points.

OU had several more opportunities to blow the game wide open, but mistakes kept them from reaching the end zone following deep penetrations into Bear territory.

OU led 7-5 after three quarters.

Davis, who had his bell rung in the first half, led the three-TD barrage in the fourth quarter. The first came on his one-yard run to cap a 54-yard drive in eight plays. Washington's 14-yard run and Burget's 15-yard run sparked the drive.

OU marched 63 yards in nine plays to score on its next series. Washington capped the drive with a nine-yard sprint. Davis sparked the drive with a 17-yard pass to Billy Brooks, and Littrell ran for 15 more.

The Bears scored their lone touchdown in the fourth stanza following freshman halfback Elvis Peacock's fumble.

The Sooners answered with a 54-yard, six-play drive. Tinker Owens scored on an 11-yard end around reverse. Littrell sparked the drive with a 19-yard run.

OU ran its winning streak to 10 and unbeaten string to 19. The Sooners rushed for 438 yards led by Washington's 156 and Littrell's 125. The Big Red added 111 yards through the air. The Sooner defense held Baylor to 221 total yards.

The Sooners' "squeaker" didn't impress AP poll voters, and OU dropped to No. 3 behind Ohio State and Notre Dame. The Sooners scored six touchdowns in the opening quarter en route to a 72-3 annihilation of 2-0 Utah State two weeks later in Norman. Eight Sooners scored touchdowns in the game. Washington and Peacock each scored twice. No player gained over 100 yards rushing as 17 players carried the pigskin for 496 yards. Peacock was the leading ball carrier with 73 yards on 14 carries. A total of 82 crimson lads played in the game, 60 by halftime.

The defense helped the offense with short scoring drives. Eight of the 10 touchdowns came from drives that averaged 38 yards. The other two TDs came on interceptions. Hughes scored on a 32-yard interception return in the first stanza, and his backup, Mike Birks, returned the other for 40 yards in the fourth quarter.

The Sooners could have made the rout worse as the fourth team was charging to the Utag six before Barry Switzer called off the dogs with six seconds left. He ordered quarterback Jeff Mabry to fall on the ball and kill the clock.

The Big Red defense scored two safeties, forced seven turnovers, and limited the Aggies to seven first downs and 126 total yards. The OU offense tallied 26 first downs and passed for 63 yards.

Oklahoma inched up to No. 2 in the AP poll, replacing Notre Dame, which lost to Purdue. Ohio State held onto the top spot.

The Big Red scoring assault didn't stop when the Sooners blasted Wake Forest, 63-0, on October 5 in Norman. Nine Sooners scored touchdowns in a game that was over at halftime with OU ahead, 42-0. The Sooners rolled up 531 yards rushing with Washington's 145 yards in nine carries leading the way. Backup fullback Clyde Russell rushed six times for 110 yards as a total of 89 Sooners saw action.

The Sooners added 109 yards passing with Davis leading the way, completing three of four for 51 yards and two TD strikes. Freshman backup quarterback Dean Blevins' only pass was a 42-yard scoring strike to split end Billy Brooks.

Carroll converted a perfect nine conversions.

OU's defense held the 0-3 Demon Deacons to 152 total yards and forced four turnovers.

Sooner Magic: Steers Took the Bait

Oddsmakers should know that the OU-Texas rivalry is always played on pure emotion. Forget the statistics when these two tee it up in the Cotton Bowl every October. Oklahoma, undefeated at 3-0 and ranked second in the nation, was a 21-point favorite over the No. 15 Horns (3-1).

Texas had no trouble defeating Boston College, 42-19, and Wyoming, 42-7, but the Horns were upset, 26-3, by Texas Tech. They managed to bounce back with a 35-21 win over Washington before the clash with OU in Dallas.

The oddsmakers might have also considered OU's last three wins over Texas (48-27 in 1971, 27-0 in 1972 and 52-13 in 1973) when making the Sooners a huge favorite. Texas still owned a huge lead in the series, winning 42, OU claimed 24 victories and only twice had the two teams tied.

The 1974 clash again was a sellout at 72,032. A sellout at the Cotton Bowl between OU-Texas is as sure a bet as death and taxes. But a blowout every year definitely is not. Thirty of the previous 68 games were decided by seven points or less.

The Sooners blew two scoring opportunities in the first period with fumbles at the UT six and again at the goal line. On the fifth play of the game, defensive end Jimbo Elrod's tackle jarred the ball loose from half-back Raymond Clayborn at the UT 35. Eric Van Camp smothered the ball for the Sooners.

OU drove to the Texas six-yard line, but Washington fumbled, and Fred Sarchet recovered for the Horns.

A few plays later, Hughes recovered a Texas fumble at the UT 27. OU drove five plays to the three, but on the next play Davis fumbled just before he crossed the goal line. The Longhorns recovered in the end zone.

Midway through the second quarter, the Big Red drove 52 yards but stalled at the Steers' 22. Tony DiRienzo missed a 39-yard fieldgoal attempt.

Late in the same period, Clayborn was flagged for interfering with Washington's fair catch of a punt at the OU 42. The 15-yard penalty gave the Sooners possession at the UT 43-yard line. Davis gained four yards, then connected a 13-yard pass to tight end Wayne Hoffman. Washington picked up another four yards to the 22, then Davis dashed left on an option keeper. Key blocks from Littrell and Burget opened the lane to the end zone. Carroll toed the extra point, and OU led 7-0 with 3:01 until halftime.

UT's Alfred Jackson took the ensuing kickoff at his own seven and slipped the ball to Pat Padget passing by him. Padget, then with his back to the oncoming Sooners, handed the ball to Clayborn, who dashed downfield but was caught from behind by Scott Hill at the OU 38.

Texas took seven plays to gain only 16 yards. On third-and-six at the 22, Elrod and Shoate sacked Akins for a two-yard loss. Texas' Bill Schott kicked a 41-yard field goal, cutting OU's lead to 7-3 with 16 seconds left in the first half.

Early in the third stanza, the Sooners stalled at their own 20, but a shanked punt by Carroll sailed only 13 yards, giving the burnt-orange enemy the ball at the OU 33. Six plays later, tailback Earl Campbell, playing for an injured Roosevelt Leaks, bulled through the middle for a 12-yard TD. Schott's extra point gave Texas a 10-7 lead with 10:15 left in the quarter. That was the first time the Sooners had trailed in the young season.

OU stalled at its 19-yard line on the next series, and Littrell replaced Carroll as the punter. The Sooner faithful gasped as the ball was kicked only 26 yards sailing out of bounds at the OU 45.

Texas failed to gain a first down. Schott came on to kick a 55-yard field goal, but his attempt was wide right.

Late in the quarter, Texas took possession at its own 20 following a punt and marched 58 yards, which carried over into the fourth quarter. Campbell kept the drive alive by gaining a first down on a

Linebacker Rod Shoate (43) was the Sooners' second three-time All-American.
(© 1974, The Daily Oklahoman)

crucial third-and-two from the OU 43. He surged between Elrod and Dewey Selmon for a three-yard gain.

Two key defensive stops held the Longhorns at bay to force a field goal. Cornerback Sidney Brown, playing with a broken jaw, and linebacker Gary Gibbs nailed Clayborn for a two-yard loss. On the next play, Elrod and Lee Roy Selmon dropped Campbell for no gain. Schott was successful this time on a 38-yard attempt, and the Steers led 13-7 with 14:09 left in the game.

The Sooners took the kickoff and marched into Texas territory in seven plays but faced third-and-seven at the 40. Time to reach into their bag of tricks.

Davis pitched to Brooks, who circled to his right. The Longhorn defense took the bait as they had pursued to the opposite direction. Brooks picked up a block by Davis and raced to the end zone. Carroll thought his extra-point attempt was good, as he threw his arms in the air signaling "good." The officials thought differently because the ball veered wide. The Texas throng went wild. The score was knotted at 13-13 with 11:20 remaining.

Following the kickoff, Texas marched to midfield but faced fourth-and-one. The Sooner end of the Cotton Bowl was chanting, "Defense!" Campbell took the handoff, gained the one yard, but Lee Roy Selmon's bone-jarring smack caused the ball to squirt loose. Shoate, who had 21 tackles in the game, recovered at the 50 with 8:59 to go.

The Sooners moved the ball to the UT 20 but had to rely on the foot of DiRienzo, who booted a 37-yarder through the uprights to give OU a 16-13 advantage with 5:25 remaining.

The Longhorns never threatened the remainder of the game. On the final Texas possession, Leaks fumbled at the UT 18, and Lee Roy Selmon recovered with 57 seconds left. The Sooners had moved to the four when the clock took its last tick.

The Sooners rushed for 353 yards and passed for 42 more. Washington led the ground attack with 122 yards. Texas picked up 210 total yards.

OU continued to hold the No. 2 ranking, behind Ohio State, through the next four games.

Washington rushed for 200 yards and scored four TDs as the Sooners plastered No. 16 Colorado, 49-14, on October 19 in Boulder. OU led 14-0 after the first period, 28-0 at halftime and 42-0 in the third quarter. DiRienzo converted all seven extra-pointers.

The reserves turned the ball over, gift-wrapping two Colorado touchdowns in the fourth period.

The Big Red gained 32 first downs, rushed for 394 yards, and passed for 47. OU did not punt once in the game. The 3-2 Buffs gained 280 yards.

When the Sooners returned home the next week, they smacked Kansas State with a score identical to the last time they played at home, 63-0. Eight Sooners crossed the goal line, and a total of 85 players saw action as the starters were pulled after the first half. Four freshmen scored in the second half—Peacock, Kerry Jackson, and Calvin Harris (two TDs).

Washington led all rushers with 133 yards in limited action. A total of 19 players carried the ball amassing 539 yards against the 3-3 Wildcats. Davis completed three of eight passes for 63 yards and two touchdowns.

Washington scored only once in the second stanza, but two of his three punt returns set up Sooner scores in the first half. Peacock returned one punt 54 yards to put the Sooners up 42-0 and also returned another to set up the drive for the next touchdown.

The defense held the Cats to 160 total yards. K-State quarterbacks were sacked a total of eight times for minus 58 yards. The Selmons, Elrod, Richard Murray, Mike Phillips, Chavez Linzy, and Kenneth Franklin were credited with dumping the quarterback.

OU sputtered early in a showdown on November 2 with Iowa State on a soggy Clyde Williams Field in Ames. The 4-3 Cyclones slowed the Sooners in the first half as OU led only 7-0 at intermission to the delight of 35,000 fans on hand. But the Sooners won, 28-10, much to the dismay of the predominantly Cyclone faithful.

Peacock's 10-yard TD run capped a 66-yard march early in the second quarter and DiRienzo converted. Washington caught his first pass of the season, a 40-yarder from Davis, on the play before Peacock's TD.

Iowa State took the ensuing kickoff and drove to the OU nine before losing 31 yards on the next three plays. ISU's Tom Goedjen missed his first of two field goals.

Two Cyclone turnovers in the third period helped the Sooners put the game away. ISU's Luther Blue returned the second-half kickoff but spilled the ball, and Marty Brecht recovered for Oklahoma at the Sooner 39. Six plays later, Burget made it 14-0 with another 10-yard sprint across the goal line. DiRienzo converted.

The Cyclones fumbled the next kickoff, and Hughes recovered. One play, or six seconds later, Davis fired a 30-yard TD pass to Washington.

Davis, who completed five of eight passes for 131 yards, added another scoring strike to Tinker Owens late in the third quarter. The 33-yard TD pass capped a 77-yard march, and DiRienzo converted.

The Cyclones scored a touchdown and field goal in the fourth period on the Sooner reserves.

In addition to Davis' 131 yards passing, the Sooners managed only 198 yards on the ground, and Washington led with 86 yards. The Cyclones gained 335 total yards.

Oklahoma still held onto the second national ranking, but Sooner fans roared when stadium PA announcer Bill Boren announced Ohio State's score during the Missouri game the next week in Norman: "Michigan State 16, Ohio State 13."

The Sooners blanked Missouri, 37-0, on a cool, drizzly Saturday afternoon before a homecoming throng of 62,600. The wet field didn't slow the backs this time, as Littrell rushed for 155 yards and Washington added 143 more to up his career total to 2,860 yards. He surpassed Greg Pruitt as the second all-time rusher in Sooner football history and trailed Steve Owens by 1,007 yards. Overall, Oklahoma gained 29 first downs, rushed for 498 yards, and passed for 72 more against the 5-3 Tigers.

It's a Fact

The 1974 Sooners still hold the NCAA records for most rushes per game with 73.9 and most rushes for a first down with 21.4 per game. OU also led the nation in scoring offense with an average of 43 points per game.

DiRienzo booted three field goals, and Burget scored two touchdowns for a 23-0 lead through three quarters.

OU went long distance twice to score in the fourth quarter. Davis tossed his 18th TD pass of the season, a 30-yarder, to Wayne Hoffman early in the fourth quarter to cap a 93-yard, 10-play drive. Washington's three-yard touchdown run six minutes later topped a 97-yard march in nine plays.

The Tigers collected 241 total yards. Missouri crossed into OU territory five times, two ended in fumbles, and the Big Red defense stopped the Tigers twice.

Just as the fans had anticipated when Ohio State lost, Oklahoma returned to the nation's No. 1 spot in the AP poll before the team headed to Lawrence to play Kansas. The Sooners defended their lofty position with a 45-14 win.

KU took a 7-0 lead in the first quarter when quarterback Scott McMichael scored on a 73-yard run. A 72-yard pass from Davis to Brooks tied the game early in the second period. DiRienzo kicked the first of six conversions.

The Sooners scored on their next two possessions—Davis on a one-yard run and later he fired a 14-yard scoring strike to Owens for a 21-7 lead. The Hawks answered with a 78-yard scoring drive.

The 4-5 Jayhawks won four of their first five games before losing four straight prior to the OU game on November 16. Still Kansas made a game of it in the first half, trailing only 21-14.

The Sooners clung to the same lead in the third quarter, then the scoring dam burst in the fourth. Washington returned a 28-yard punt to the KU 46 late in the third stanza. Eight plays later, Burget crossed the goal line from the three. DiRienzo nailed a 33-yard field goal minutes later when Oklahoma stalled at the KU five.

Tony Peters picked off McMichael's pass on the Hawks' next possession and raced 59 yards to the end zone. Dean Blevins tossed a nine-yard TD pass to Brooks with six seconds remaining.

Oklahoma churned out 494 total yards (380 rushing and 114 passing). The defense yielded 303 total yards to the Jayhawks.

The Big Eight Championship was on the line six days later in Lincoln.

No. 6 Nebraska, 8-2, stumbled against Wisconsin and lost the Big Eight opener against Missouri, then won five straight before entertaining Oklahoma before a throng of 76,636 in Lincoln. A Sooner victory would put them in the driver's seat for the Big Eight championship with one game remaining. A Husker victory would give them a tie for the Big Eight crown.

Davis' 10-yard TD run early in the second quarter put the Sooners on top, 7-0, but the Huskers answered with quarterback David Humm's 38-yard scoring strike to Chuck Malito. DiRienzo converted all four of his kicks for OU.

Both teams trotted to the locker room tied at 7-7. Nebraska took a 14-7 lead when Humm scored on a trick play early in the third period to cap a 76-yard march in eight plays. Humm handed off to tailback John O'Leary, who tossed the ball back to Humm for an 11-yard touchdown. The Huskers had a chance to put the game away when Peacock fumbled at the OU 15.

The Sooner defense held the Cornhuskers to nine yards on the next three plays, and kicker Mike Coyle shanked a 23-yard field-goal try. OU then drove 80 yards in 14 plays to tie the game at 14-14. Washington scored on a three-yard run to even the score with 4:57 remaining in the third stanza. Davis scrambled for 17 yards to spark the drive to the NU 21.

Peacock's one-yard TD run put the Sooners up 21-14 early in the fourth quarter. OU picked up big gains in the 57-yard go-ahead drive. Davis gained 12, 10, and nine yards, and Littrell added another 13.

Oklahoma marched 61 yards in 10 plays on its next possession to put the game away. Davis scored on a three-yard TD run midway through the fourth period. Washington's 33-yard run to the NU 20 sparked the drive.

The Sooners had changed the defense for the Nebraska game, which allowed Hughes to intercept three passes and Zac Henderson another. Oklahoma switched to a four-man rush rather than a three-man rush used against the Huskers in the past two years. The Sooner defense used man-to-man coverage instead of zone coverage and blitzed the linebackers.

Three Sooners gained over 100 yards as the team rolled up 482 yards rushing. Littrell led the way with 147 yards, Washington had 142 and Davis 112. OU did not complete a pass in three tries. Nebraska gained 384 total yards.

Oklahoma earned its second straight Big Eight title and also held its No. 1 ranking when 6-4 Oklahoma State came to Norman on November 30. A five-TD surge during a seven-and-one-half-minute span lifted the Sooners to a 44-13 victory before 62,619 freezing fans.

Both teams battled to a 10-10 stalemate in the first half, then the Cowboys took a 13-10 lead on Abbie Daigle's 33-yard field goal late in the third period. DiRienzo booted a 33-yarder for OU in the first quarter, and Davis scored on a 12-yard run midway in the second stanza.

The scoring blitz began late in the third quarter. Burget's five-yard TD run came four plays after Elrod jarred the ball loose from OSU quarterback Charlie Weatherbie.

Davis scored on a one-yard sneak early in the fourth period to cap a 48-yard drive in four plays. Littrell picked up 34 yards to the one to set up the touchdown.

The Pokes stalled on their next possession and punted. Washington took the punt at the OU 43 and was immediately swarmed by four Cowboys. Suddenly Washington sprung free and sailed down the east sideline to the end zone. Mike Phillips threw a key block on the return, and Lil' Joe feinted the last defender before crossing the goal line.

Moments later, Washington scored on a five-yard run after OSU's punter fumbled the snap at the Poke five. The Cowboys' Leonard Thompson forgot to pick up the pigskin on the following kickoff, and cornerback E.N. Simon recovered for the Sooners at the OSU 10. Peacock scored on the next play.

The Sooners notched their 20th straight victory and 29th straight game without a loss. It also boosted Switzer's record to 21-0-1 in two years as the Sooners' skipper.

OU picked up 316 yards on the ground, and the defense held the Cowboys to 157 rushing yards. Neither team completed a pass. Littrell led all crimson runners with 112 yards.

Only two teams ended the regular season undefeated—OU and Alabama. The Crimson Tide edged Auburn, 17-13, the day before.

"There are only two undefeated teams left now," Switzer said. "I saw one on the television yesterday, and I believe we're the better team."

Alabama lost to Notre Dame in the Sugar Bowl, leaving the Sooners as the only undefeated team and a No. 1 final ranking in the AP poll. OU laid claim to its fourth national championship and first since 1956. The Sooners received 51 first-place votes and 1,162 points, 112 points ahead of Southern California.

The UPI poll would not recognize teams that were on probation. USC won that championship. But everyone knew who the nation's best team was in 1974.

The Sooners also had a stable of All-Americans that year—Washington, Shoate, Hughes, Davis, Roush, Owens, and, of course, both Selmon brothers. Elrod, Hoffman, Jerry Arnold, and Terry Webb joined them on the All-Big Eight team. Washington was named Player of the Year by the Touchdown Club of Washington, D.C.

Washington finished third in the Heisman Trophy balloting behind Archie Griffin of Ohio State and Anthony Davis of USC. Washington might have received more votes or even won the award had the Sooners been on television.

1975

Thrice in 1975, Oklahoma waved its magic wand to pull a victory out of its hat. But the greatest triumph not only occurred between the hash marks on the gridiron, it also happened in the Associated Press and United Press International wire service polls.

Voters in both polls selected the Sooners as the number-one team prior to the 1975 season. OU returned 12 starters (six on both sides of the ball), so it was difficult to pick against the Sooners.

Among the returnees were eight players who eventually were chosen All-Americans—noseguard Dewey Selmon and his brother Lee Roy at defensive tackle, running back Joe Washington, guard Terry Webb, tackle Mike Vaughn, defensive end Jimbo Elrod, and split ends Billy Brooks and Tinker Owens.

Entering the 1975 season, the Big Red owned a 20-game win streak and a 29-game unbeaten string. Not only was OU rated the best team in preseason by the wire service polls, nearly every preseason publication selected the Sooners to finish 1975 on top in the Big Eight and the nation.

Oklahoma opened the '75 campaign on September 13 in Norman by crushing the Oregon Ducks, 62-7, while amassing 616 yards (544 rushing) of total offense. The Ducks turned the ball over 10 times (seven fumbles and three interceptions) and were held to 162 total yards.

A total of 59 Sooners got in on the act, with many of the reserves seeing action as early as the second quarter. Owens, halfback Horace Ivory, and backup fullback Jim Culbreath each scored two touchdowns.

OU blasted No. 15 Pittsburgh (1-0), 46-10, the next week in Norman. The Panthers featured star running back Tony Dorsett. He had a terrific career at Pittsburgh, winning the Heisman Trophy in 1976 and gaining 6,526 rushing yards, an NCAA Division I record

1974 Season Record: 11-0-0
Big Eight Conference: 7-0-0 (Champions)
NATIONAL CHAMPIONS

Date	Opponent	Result	Score
September 14	BAYLOR	W	28-11
September 28	UTAH STATE	W	72-3
October 5	WAKE FOREST	W	63-0
October 12	Texas at Dallas	W	16-13
October 19	at Colorado	W	49-14
October 26	KANSAS STATE	W	63-0
November 2	at Iowa State	W	28-10
November 9	MISSOURI	W	37-0
November 16	at Kansas	W	45-14
November 23	at Nebraska	W	28-14
November 30	OKLAHOMA STATE	W	44-13

he held for 22 years. Dorsett rushed for 1,686 in 1975, but the Sooner defense held him to 17 yards on 12 carries, the worst performance of his collegiate career.

One play involving Dorsett remains a Sooner memory today. He was cut down by safety Scott Hill as he tried to gain a first down on a fourth-and-one play. Hill came at Dorsett like a missile, hurtling in midair and knocking the Pitt running back for a three-yard loss.

Washington was the star of the OU-Pitt tilt scoring three touchdowns and gaining 166 yards on 23 carries. OU led 23-0 at halftime, and after a Panther field goal late in the third quarter, OU scored three touchdowns following three consecutive Pitt fumbles.

The Sooners rushed for 378 yards and passed for 52 more. The Big Red defense held the Panthers to 79 yards rushing, or 1.5 yards per carry. Pitt gained 181 yards through the air.

About 6,000 Oklahoma fans ventured to Miami, Florida, to see the Sooners squeak by the Miami Hurricanes, 20-17, in a rare Friday night contest on September 26 at the Orange Bowl. The Canes played their home games on Friday nights because they shared the Orange Bowl with the NFL's Miami Dolphins who played on Sundays.

The Sooners jumped to a 20-7 lead over the 0-1 Canes and held off a 10-point Miami rally in the fourth quarter to preserve the victory.

Miami took a 7-0 lead in the first quarter, and Tony DiRienzo booted a 34-yard field goal for the Sooners early in the second period. Two big plays in the second stanza sparked a 14 point OU surge. Defensive end Duane Baccus blocked Miami's punt attempt at the UM 11. Three plays later, Elvis Peacock scored on a six-yard run. Ottis Anderson fumbled on the next Miami possession, and end Mike Phillips recovered at the Canes' 26. The Sooners needed only five plays to find the end zone. Washington's three-yard TD run gave the Sooners a 17-7 advantage.

Miami's 10 points closed the gap to 20-17 midway through the fourth quarter, but the Canes could not gain a first down on their final possession.

The Sooners held onto their top ranking, but Ohio State was fast on their heels. OU held the top spot by 161 votes over the Buckeyes in the AP poll before the Miami game, but Oklahoma's close victory narrowed the margin to 21 points in the next poll.

Sooner Magic: Wide Left, Times Two

Next was the 19th-ranked Colorado Buffaloes, who brought a 3-0 record and the nation's No. 1 offense to Norman. The Buffs averaged 516 yards per game while crushing their opponents by a combined 113 to 37 points. Colorado also brought along a very precise kicker—Tom Mackenzie. He booted a perfect 16 straight extra points in the Buffs' first three games and was 41 of 43 in field goals since transferring from Mount San Antonio (California) Junior College a year ago.

The Big Red had won the last two encounters to run its series lead to 21-7-1.

Washington's 11-yard TD run put the Sooners ahead, 7-0, late in the first quarter. He took a Buff punt and sailed 74 yards for a 14-0 lead early in the second. Washington's swift dancing moves confused Colorado defenders, then he found an opening up the middle and raced toward the goal line. He eluded the only defender in pursuit by shifting toward the sideline and followed crimson jerseys to the end zone.

Colorado scored the next two touchdowns after Oklahoma miscues in the second and third quarters to knot the game at 14-14.

Oklahoma drove 80 yards in nine plays to take a 21-14 lead late in the third quarter. Peacock scored on a two-yard run, and DiRienzo nailed his third straight conversion.

Colorado got the ball back at its 32 with 8:35 left in the game and hammered out small chunks of yards toward the OU goal line. The Buffs took seven minutes to move 38 yards in 13 plays to the OU 30. Twice they converted fourth-down plays, one on a fake punt.

From the 30, quarterback Dave Williams hit tight end Don Hasslebeck for a 22-yard pass to the Sooners' eight-yard line. Williams connected to running back Billy Waddy in the left flat for a touchdown, and OU held a 21-20 lead with 1:19 remaining.

Colorado coach Bill Mallory opted for tying with an extra-point kick instead of a two-point conversion. After all, his kicker was a perfect 18 for 18 in the extra-point department. Mackenzie, however, missed two field goals in the third.

Most of the 70,286 fans at Memorial Stadium were praying for a block or a miss. The prayer was answered. Mackenzie's kick again sailed wide left, and the Sooners held on to a 21-20 victory.

The Big Red defense held Colorado's offense to 208 total yards, 308 yards less than its average in the first three games. The Sooner offense only managed 177 total yards, all on the ground and 230 less than the average of their first three games.

The Sooners dropped to No. 2 in the polls. Ohio State, which blew out UCLA, 41-20, leaped to the top. Still, Oklahoma held a 23-game win streak and had not lost in the last 33 contests.

On the horizon next for OU was the Texas Longhorns, undefeated at 4-0 and ranked fifth in the country.

Sooner Magic: 'This is No Ordinary Game'

Besides having identical undefeated records, the Oklahoma Sooners and Texas Longhorns boasted having a star halfback, each a contrast to the other. OU's Washington was a finesse ball carrier whose flashy moves left opponents sprawled in his wake. UT countered with Earl Campbell, a sophomore tailback and a powerful runner who would bowl into defenders, also frustrating the opposition.

But on the second Saturday in October, the star who shined the brightest was a native of nearby Fort Worth and transfer from Navarro (Texas) Junior College—Horace Ivory. It was Ivory, not Washington nor Campbell, whose 33-yard bolt down the sidelines made the final difference on the Cotton Bowl turf.

Jim Littrell was sidelined with a sprained ankle he received in the Colorado game. So Ivory got the starting nod at fullback against the Longhorns, even though he too had an injury (sore shoulder) from the Colorado game. Culbreath shared fullback duties with Ivory against Texas just as he had done all season with Littrell.

The fifth-ranked Longhorns outscored their first four foes by a combined score of 177-35. Oklahoma was a 17-point favorite heading into the 70th edition of the Red River rivalry; too many points for a game of this caliber.

The Hatfields and McCoys had their feud, but in these parts, Darrell Royal and Barry Switzer had a heated exchange months before the 1975 rivalry. Royal had accused Switzer of unethically recruiting Texas high school players to play at OU. Royal, Texas alumni, and boosters didn't like that their home state boys would play for the likes of another school, especially the University of Oklahoma.

Switzer denied any cheating in recruiting. He even offered a lie detector test for him and his staff to prove there was nothing illegal about it. Switzer and his staff took the lie detector tests on April 29. Each coach was asked if he had offered cars, clothes, money, paid transportation, or selling of tickets as an inducement to attend the

University of Oklahoma, and did a coach ask anyone to provide these inducements to any recruited athletes? All coaches answered "no" to each question. The opinion of two professional polygraph examiners concluded that all coaches answered truthfully.

Switzer told *The Daily Oklahoman* in August that he and his coaches passed the polygraph tests and it was not his intent "to divulge the results of this examination, but because of Royal's recent challenge to both our coaching staffs taking a polygraph test, I feel it is necessary at this time."

Switzer said that the success of the football programs at Oklahoma and Texas was based on recruiting high school athletes "on fact alone and not because of illegal recruiting methods."

The Daily Oklahoman reported that "Switzer's provoking statement, as far as Royal was concerned, came in the speech to alumni over a visitation proposal that would limit Oklahoma to only two visits over a 70-day period."

To that Switzer replied, "I have to think Darrell Royal has a better chance to sign him [a recruit] than I have. Some coaches don't want to coach any more. They would rather sit home and listen to guitar pickers. They want to make it where you can't outwork anybody."

Royal said he was "real hot" and "wild-eyed" at Switzer's reference to "guitar pickers."

"Although Switzer did not mention Royal by name," *The Daily Oklahoman* reported, "the Texas coach said, 'There is no doubt in my mind who he meant.' Royal has long been a fan of country music."

Switzer said he "meant no malice."

"The recent statement I made in Tulsa to an alumni group during a question-and-answer period, that coaches would have more time to listen to guitar pickers if the possible NCAA legislation regarding recruiting visit limitations passes was accepted by the audience in a humorous vein."

A couple of days before the rivalry, both Switzer and Royal said the heated exchange between the two would have no impact on the game.

"I haven't heard any mention of anything like that," Royal said.

"Whatever is said before, during, or after, has no effect on the game," Switzer said. "It's what happens during the 60 minutes of the game, out there on the floor of the Cotton Bowl that counts.

"This is no ordinary game, as anyone who has ever played or seen it would tell you."

DiRienzo kicked a 45-yard field goal midway through the first period, moments after Dewey Selmon recovered a Texas fumble at the UT 46.

A short time later, Hill forced a fumble deep in Texas territory, and Mike Phillips recovered in the end zone for a 10-0 lead.

The 36,000-plus Sooner faithful could not afford to relax, not in a rivalry with the Texas Longhorns and definitely not in the 90-degree heat. The Steers drove 90 yards to close the gap to 10-7 midway in the second period.

The Sooners rolled 68 yards after recovering another Texas fumble for a 17-7 advantage midway through the third stanza. Washington scored on a nine-yard run and DiRienzo sonverted. Steve Davis completed a 52-yard pass to Brooks to the UT 14 to spark the drive.

Texas blocked Owens' punt and recovered on the OU 37. Five plays later, the Horns trimmed OU's lead to 17-10 with 13:10 left in the game.

Texas quickly added 10 points on a TD and a field goal early in the fourth period. The touchdown came on a five-play drive and the Steers added a field goal moments after recovering Culbreath's fum-

ble on the Sooner 35. With 8:19 to go, the score was knotted at 17-all.

OU rolled 79 yards for the winning touchdown in the drive's second play. The Texas D stuffed Peacock for no gain. Yellow flags flew as a Texas player grabbed Peacock's facemask. Instead of third-and-four at the OU 27, the Sooners had new life with first-and-10 at the 42. The Sooners continued to the UT 33.

As the Sooners broke the huddle on the next play, Davis came to the line of scrimmage at the Texas 33 and noticed the Steers loading up on the right side. So Davis changed the play at the line before the snap.

"I saw more people on the right side than on the left," he said after the game.

On the snap, Ivory fired off from his fullback position, grabbed the handoff from Davis, and bolted to the left side and down the sideline 33 yards to the end zone. Only one Texas defender, safety Steve Collier, had a shot at stopping the OU fullback. Ivory gave Collier a feint move, which forced the Longhorn to lose his balance and tumble to the turf. DiRienzo's extra point put the Sooners ahead, 24-17, with 5:31 remaining in the game.

"I didn't mind the switch to fullback," Ivory said of his new position. "I just wanted to help the team. I just took the ball and ran. I didn't know if I'd score when I heard the audible, but I thought we'd score eventually."

Davis no doubt was pleased with his newly discovered star teammate.

"He played great," Davis said. "Horace has tremendous explosion. We had good exchanges all day."

With over two minutes remaining, the Sooners had the ball inside their own 10. Washington fumbled on a second-down play. The bouncing ball was open for grabs, but Terry Webb smothered it for the Sooners at the eight-yard line. Switzer ordered a quick-kick. Washington, from his halfback position, retrieved to the end zone, took the snap and boomed the ball 76 yards to the Texas 14.

The Sooner defense stalled the Horns and escaped with the 24-17 victory. OU pounded out 259 yards rushing and threw for 76. The Steers gained 289 total yards.

The Big Red held onto the No. 2 spot in both polls.

The defense of the heavily favored Sooners limited 3-2 Kansas State to 174 total yards in Manhattan, Kansas, on October 18 en route to a 25-3 victory. OU jumped to a 14-0 lead in the first quarter on Ivory's five-yard run and a 33-yard pass from Davis to Victor Hicks.

DiRienzo booted three field goals in the second half, and Owens' punting kept the Cats pinned for most of the final 30 minutes. One of his punts, a 49-yarder in the third period, rolled dead at the KSU three. A poor handoff in the end zone resulted in a safety for the Sooners.

The Sooners fumbled a school-record 13 times and lost seven of them but still routed 4-2 Iowa State, 39-7, before a homecoming crowd of 70,897 the next week in Norman. Switzer called it "a sloppy game."

Iowa State fumbled the ball away four times and threw two interceptions. Two Cyclone fumbles in the first stanza led to Sooner touchdowns. Lee Roy Selmon recovered at the ISU 12 early in the game. Three plays later, Washington scored on a three-yard touchdown run. Six minutes later, OU led, 14-0, taking only three plays to move 49 yards for the second score following Jerry Anderson's fumble recovery. DiRienzo's 31-yard field goal gave the Sooners a 17-0 lead, still in the opening quarter. Culbreath, Washington, and Billy Sims each added a touchdown during the next three quarters, and corner back Terry Peters' blocked punt rolled out of the end zone to give Oklahoma two more points on a safety.

The Sooners clung to No. 2 in the polls as they traveled to Stillwater to face No. 19 Oklahoma State (5-2) before 51,220 fans, the largest crowd at Lewis Field. The Big Red cashed in on three Poke fumbles for 17 points in the second half en route to a 27-7 triumph.

Davis' one-yard TD run capped a 60-yard drive in five plays early in the first period, and DiRienzo added a 56-yard field goal seven minutes later. OU held onto its 10-0 lead through the rest of the first half.

The Cowboys had three chances to score in the first half but came up empty.

Less than a minute into the third quarter, Davis scored a 10-yard TD run four plays after Phillips recovered a Poke fumble at the OSU 20. Bryant recovered another OSU fumble minutes later, which led to DiRienzo's 36-yard field goal to give the Sooners a comfortable 20-0 lead.

The Cowboys drove 71 yards for a touchdown in the fourth stanza to wipe out their goose egg.

Jerry Anderson's fumble recovery late in the fourth period led to the Sooners' final touchdown. They needed only two plays to move 39 yards with Washington scoring on a 26-yard run.

OU rushed for 304 yards and passed for 37. Ivory led with 99 yards. The Pokes gained 265 total yards.

Returning to Norman the following week, the Sooners' 28-game winning streak ended at the hands of the 5-3 Kansas Jayhawks, 23-3, in Norman. Oklahoma at this point previously had not lost a game on the gridiron in 37 games or three years. The last defeat was to Colorado in 1972. The loss also was the first for Switzer, who coached the Sooners to a 29-0-1 mark before the stunning upset.

DiRienzo toed a 52-yard field goal to put OU ahead 3-0 midway through the first quarter. A blocked punt began a series of turnovers on which the Jayhawks capitalized.

Late in the second stanza, KU quarterback Nolan Cromwell scored a touchdown three plays following the blocked punt. The Jayhawks added a field goal and two more touchdowns in the second half, each time following a Sooner turnover.

"We beat ourselves," Switzer said after the game. "We've played this way before against inferior football teams but got away with it. If you play a good football team and make mistakes, you get beat."

OU dropped to sixth nationally behind Ohio State, Nebraska, Texas A&M, Michigan, and Alabama.

A victory is the best remedy to get rid of a losing hangover. The Sooners traveled to Columbia on November 15 to face No. 19 Missouri. The Tigers nearly pulled off another upset.

Sooner Magic: Fourth-and-71

Number 24 darted through defenses like a cheetah chasing its prey, sometimes leaping over defenders like a gazelle. Graced by a pair of silver shoes, Joe Washington was so versatile that each time he touched the football he put fear in the gut of the opposition.

So versatile, was "Lil' Joe" that he saved the day against Missouri—saved the game, the Big Eight Conference

Joe Washington eludes a Missouri defender and finds an open field for his 71-yard game-saving touchdown. (© 1975, The Daily Oklahoman)

Championship, and a trip to the Orange Bowl. More importantly, he helped earn a national championship.

A loss to the Tigers definitely would have bumped the Sooners from claiming a third straight conference crown and a trip to the Orange Bowl.

As OU was shocked by Kansas, Missouri pounded Iowa State, 44-14, to run its record to 6-3 and 3-2 in the conference. The Tigers were looking forward to playing the Sooners on their home turf and to end OU's five-game winning streak in the overall series, which the Sooners led 40-20-5. But the Sooners were nearly perfect in the first half en route to a 20-0 halftime lead. No penalties, no turnovers, only a missed extra point on their first touchdown.

The Sooners took a 6-0 lead midway in the opening quarter and moments after Zac Henderson intercepted a Mizzou pass. On fourth-and-one at the MU 31, Davis kept the ball for six yards, then pitched back to a trailing Peacock, who raced the remaining yards across the goal line. DiRienzo missed the PAT.

OU drove 54 yards three possessions later for a 12-0 lead. Washington hurdled like a gazelle into the end zone from three yards out. Davis completed a 38-yard pass to Owens to spark the drive to the Tiger 16. Davis misfired on his two-point conversion attempt.

Missouri missed two field goals in the second stanza.

Oklahoma jumped to a 20-0 lead with 24 seconds until intermission. Davis scored on a one-yard keeper to cap the 70-yard drive. Peacock scored the two-point coversion.

OU had its chances to increase the lead in the third quarter but failed to capitalize on two interceptions. DiRienzo missed field goals from 29 and 41 yards after each turnover.

The Tigers scored early in the third and fourth quarters. Suddenly, they were back in the contest, trailing 21-14 with 13:01 remaining in the game.

On its next possession, Missouri marched 48 yards for its first lead, 21-20, with 8:33 left. Minutes later, the Tiger lead swelled to 27-20 with 5:38 to go.

OU had 80 yards to win the game after the Tiger kickoff. The Sooners gained only nine yards on the next three plays, but Switzer had his troops go for it on fourth down instead of punting.

Missouri's line bunched toward the middle of the line expecting the play to go in that direction. Not likely. Not with Lil' Joe in the OU backfield.

Davis took the snap, moved right, then pitched back to Washington who out-cheetahed everyone for a 71-yard touchdown. Still OU trailed, 27-26. Another two-point conversion was ordered. Davis again pitched to Washington to the right side, and Lil' Joe, who played with a sore foot and bruised ribs, followed Hicks' block and just broke the plane of the goal line to give OU a 28-27 lead with 4:20 to go.

The Tigers had two chances to take the lead and possible victory in the final 78 seconds. Kicker Tim Gibbons missed field-goal attempts from 40 and 50 yards, and the Sooners escaped Columbia with a 28-27 victory.

Although the Sooners won, they dropped another notch (to seventh) in the polls. OU hosted undefeated Nebraska (10-0), ranked second in the nation, the following week.

The Sooners exploded for 28 unanswered points in the second half en route to a 35-10 blasting of the Huskers. The final three Sooner TDs came off Nebraska turnovers.

Davis led the Sooners with 130 yards rushing and two touchdowns. The win gave Oklahoma and Nebraska a share of the Big Eight Conference championship and the Sooners' first trip to the Orange Bowl in eight years.

Texas, Texas A&M, and Alabama did not play that same weekend, and Michigan lost to Ohio State by a touchdown. OU leaped all the way to third nationally, behind the Buckeyes and A&M. Texas A&M beat Texas on Thanksgiving the next week but lost to Arkansas the first Saturday in December. The wire services did not conduct any more voting until after the bowl games.

So the third-ranked Sooners, with a victory over Michigan in the Orange Bowl, could end the season in the No. 2 spot with some luck. The Sooners also could win the national championship with an Orange Bowl victory New Year's night culminated with an Ohio State loss in the Rose Bowl earlier in the same day. But remember, Ohio State was in a rematch against UCLA, victims of a shellacking by the Buckeyes back in week four of the season.

Sooner Magic: Luck Smiles on the Sooners

Ohio State was a heavy favorite in the Rose Bowl. The Sooner faithful were relegated to a disappointing No. 2 ranking with a win over the Wolverines and could, only hope that UCLA could pull off the upset.

The Bruins did pull off the upset, 23-10, and now Oklahoma with a victory in the Orange Bowl in Miami would be national champions for a second straight year. Prior to the kickoff, the Rose Bowl score was posted, and the Sooner faithful roared.

So did Brooks, who scored on a 39-yard run in the second quarter. DiRienzo added the extra point, and OU led 7-0 with 5:07 before halftime. Early in the fourth quarter, Davis scored another touchdown on a 10-yard run. DiRienzo's extra point was good, and OU led 14-0, with 14:56 left in the game.

Michigan tallied a touchdown on Gordon Bell's two-yard run midway through the fourth period. The Wolverines' two-point try was thwarted and so was the Michigan offense the rest of the game as OU won, 14-6.

Following the game, Switzer said, "I'd like to say we're No.1, but we'll leave that to the pollsters."

The following day, the AP & UPI pollsters voted the Oklahoma Sooners as national champions.

Another victory and another national championship was pulled out of the Sooners' hat. OU was the first team in NCAA history to win back-to-back titles twice—1955-1956 and 1974-1975.

All-America honors went to the Selmon brothers, Webb, Vaughan, Brooks, Elrod, Owens, and Washington. All but Owens and Brooks were named to the Big Eight's all-conference first team. DiRienzo and Henderson were also selected to the all-conference first team.

Lee Roy Selmon also was awarded the Outland and Lombardi trophies honoring the best lineman in college football. Washington placed fifth in the Heisman Trophy balloting.

The Sooners finished the season ranked 11th nationally in rushing offense with an average of 308.6 yards per game and eighth nationally in scoring offense with a 30-point average.

1976

Following back-to-back national championships with a three-peat was a difficult task for the Sooners in 1976, especially since eight All-Americans had graduated.

Gone were Lee Roy and Dewey Selmon and Jimbo Elrod on defense, but the secondary was solid with the return of Zac Henderson and Scott Hill as the safeties and Jerry Anderson and Sidney Brown at the corners. End Mike Phillips and tackle Anthony Bryant were the only returners among the front seven on defense.

Steve Davis, Joe Washington, Jim Littrell, Tinker Owens, and Billy Brooks left big shoes to fill on the offense. Dean Blevins edged Thomas Lott for the starting quarterback nod. Elvis Peacock and Horace Ivory provided solid performances as halfbacks. The fullback nod went to Kenny King over Jim Culbreath and George Cumby.

Tackle Mike Vaughan returned to anchor the line along with guards Greg Roberts and Chez Evans and tackle Jaime Melendez and center Karl Baldischwiler.

The No. 5 Sooners opened the season September 11 with a 24-3 victory over Vanderbilt in Nashville. Sooner touchdowns came on short drives of three, 20, and 17 yards. Peacock's six-yard TD run got the Sooners on board first in the second quarter, and Oklahoma held a 7-3 lead at halftime.

Ivory's 11-yard touchdown run upped the Sooners' lead to 14-3 early in the third stanza, then Blevins scored on a three-yard run following Reggie Kinlaw's fumble recovery at the Vandy 17.

Uwe von Schamann booted a 27-yard field goal midway through the fourth period.

The Big Red defense held Vanderbilt to nine first downs and 88 total yards, 26 of them on the Commodores' first six plays. After the defense adjusted to Vandy's wing-T formation, the Sooner defense dropped Vandy backs 11 times for minus-70 yards. The Sooners rushed for 206 yards and passed for 29.

OU moved to fourth in the AP poll prior to defeating California, 28-17, the next week in the home opener before 71,286 fans.

Split end Lee Hover provided the fireworks with two touchdowns, one on a pass reception and the other on a fumble recovery.

OU scored the first three touchdowns—a 56-yard run by Culbreath, a 10-yard run by Blevins and a 65-yard pass from Blevins to Hover—during the first 22 and one-half minutes.

1975 Season Record: 11-1-0

Big Eight Conference: 7-0-0 (Champions)
NATIONAL CHAMPIONS

Date	Opponent	Result	Score
September 13	OREGON	W	62-7
September 20	PITTSBURGH	W	46-10
September 26	at Miami (FL)	W	20-17
October 4	COLORADO	W	21-20
October 11	Texas at Dallas	W	24-17
Ocotber 18	at Kansas State	W	25-3
Ocotber 25	IOWA STATE	W	39-7
November 1	at Oklahoma State	W	27-7
November 8	KANSAS	L	23-3
November 15	at Missouri	W	28-27
November 22	NEBRASKA	W	35-10
January 1	Michigan*	W	14-6

*Orange Bowl at Miami, FL

The Golden Bears scored a touchdown late in the first half and a field goal early in the fourth quarter, which cut the Sooner lead to 21-10.

Following California's kickoff, Culbreath slammed through for nine yards to the OU 29. On the next play, Blevins ran left for eight yards, then the ball popped in the air when he lunged for more yards. The ball came down into Hover's hands at the 42, and he raced down the sideline for the touchdown.

The Bears added another TD with three and a half minutes to go, but it was too little, too late.

Culbreath's 145 yards and King's 133-yard effort led the 490-yard Sooner ground attack. OU added 72 yards through the air. Cal gained 375 total yards.

No. 4 Oklahoma defeated Florida State, 24-9, on September 25 in Norman. Bobby Bowden was in his first season as the Seminoles' coach and was off to an 0-2 start before coming to Norman.

FSU kept it close, trailing 17-9 after three quarters. Von Schamann's 40-yard field goal put the Sooners up 3-0 in the first period, and Ivory scored twice on runs of 37 and 23 yards in the second quarter. Those two touchdowns came on long-distance drives of 88 and 80 yards each.

Defensive end Myron Shoate recovered a Seminole fumble in the fourth stanza at the FSU 41. Six plays later, Peacock scored on a four-yard run.

The offense rolled up 513 total yards, 455 on the ground. Ivory led all Sooner ball carriers with 112 yards in nine carries. The Nolen collected 270 total yards.

The next week, the No. 3 Sooners traveled to Ames for the Big Eight opener against Iowa State and had to rely on two huge plays in the fourth period to escape with a 24-10 win. The Cyclones were 3-0 after pounding their opponents by an average of 39 points.

A seven-yard pass from Blevins to tight end Victor Hicks gave the Sooners a 7-0 lead in the first quarter, and a von Schamann field goal made it 10-0 in the second. The Cyclones tied the game with a field goal late in the second stanza and a touchdown in the third period.

The Big Red offense had been sluggish through the first 50 minutes with only six first downs and 126 yards rushing. With more than five minutes to go, the Sooners got the ball at their 32. On third-and-four at the 38, Ivory took a handoff and appeared to be stopped short of a first down, but he shed a defender and shot to the end zone for a 17-10 advantage.

Anderson intercepted an Iowa State pass and flew 58 yards down the sideline for the insurance score.

OU gained only 194 yards rushing and 21 passing. The Cyclones picked up 315 total yards.

An inexperienced Lott started in place of the injured Blevins at quarterback on October 9 against Texas at Dallas. In addition to his triple-option wizardry, Lott was famous for wearing a bandana under his helmet.

Oklahoma's offense continued to struggle in a 6-6 tie with the Longhorns. Texas' offense didn't fare any better. The No. 16 Horns (2-1) outgained OU 182 to 133 in total yards and six to five in first downs.

Two Russell Erxleben field goals, one in the first quarter and another in the fourth, gave Texas a 6-0 lead. The Sooners appeared headed to their second loss in the last 39 games but had hopes when backup defensive tackle David Hudgens forced a fumble. Henderson recovered for the Big Red at the UT 37. Ivory's 10-yard run capped the 10-play drive, and OU was only an extra point away from victory. Kevin Craig's snap was too high for holder Bud Hebert. Hebert chased the pigskin and desperately tried to throw it for a two-point conversion, but Texas intercepted.

A win the following week against 4-1 Kansas in Lawrence was costly for the No. 6 Sooners. A shoulder injury sidelined Anderson, and Hill suffered a knee injury in the game. Brown was out with an injury as well, so three-fourths of the stellar secondary was missing.

500th Win

Yet OU exploded for 17 points in the third quarter en route to a 28-10 victory, the 500th win in Sooner history.

Kansas, which lost quarterback Nolan Cromwell to injury early in the third quarter, led 10-3 at halftime. The Sooners cashed in on four Jayhawk turnovers in the second half.

Cornerback Terry Peters forced a fumble, and linebacker Obie Moore smothered it at the KU 25. Lott scored a 13-yard TD run four plays later, and von Schamann's foot evened the score at 10-10. Hill intercepted a pass and returned it seven yards to the KU 38. On third-and-five at the 33, Lott ran right, then shifted left and darted to the end zone.

On KU's next possession, Mike Phillips picked off Scott McMichael's pass, but OU had to settle for a 40-yard von Schmann field goal late in the third stanza.

Moore recovered another fumble at the KU 39 early in the fourth quarter. Ivory's four-yard touchdown run five plays later put Oklahoma up 26-10.

OU's defense had the Hawks pinned in at their own six-yard line on the next possession. Hebert blocked punter Mitch Dougherty's punt, and KU's Dennis Wright chased the pigskin back to the end zone and smothered it, but the Sooners earned two more points for a safety.

The Sooners hammered out 338 rushing yards and did not complete a pass in five tries. Lott led OU with 104 yards. The Jayhawks were held to 179 total yards.

OU inched up to fifth in the AP poll after the win.

Switzer lost two straight for the first time in his young coaching career. Oklahoma State (3-2) upset the Big Red, 31-24, on October 23 in Norman, and Colorado (5-2) stunned the Sooners, 41-32, on Halloween in Boulder.

The Oklahoma defense couldn't contain OSU tailback Terry Miller, who rushed for 159 yards and scored the game's first touchdown on a 72-yard run. The offense couldn't contain the football, turning it over five times. The Sooners led, 24-13, early in the third period.

Culbreath's 37-yard scoring jaunt capped a 46-yard drive in four plays to cut the Pokes' lead to 10-7 with 5:11 left in the opening stanza. Moments later, Richard Murray returned a fumble 21 yards for a touchdown after Phillips forced Harold Bailey to spill the pigskin.

Peacock bolted 84 yards to give OU a 21-10 lead early in the second quarter. The Cowboys kicked a field goal to trail 21-13 at halftime. Von Schmann's field goal put the Sooners ahead 24-13 early in the third period.

OSU scored 18 unanswered points in the final 21 minutes for the win, to the disappointment of the predominantly crimson homecoming fans of 72,041. Oklahoma picked up 235 rushing yards and passed for 13. The Pokes gained 316 total yards.

The Sooners dropped to 13th in the AP poll and lost another 11-point lead in their loss to Colorado. The 19th-ranked Buffaloes (5-2) outscored OU, 39-7, in the final three quarters for the 42-31 upset.

Colorado took a 3-0 lead on the game's opening possession. The Sooners responded with King's 71-yard TD run and the lead swelled to 14-3 on Ivory's four-yard TD run 62 seconds later. Ivory's score came three plays after Henderson recovered a Buff fumble on the CU 17.

Colorado scored twice in the first half of the second stanza for a 17-14 lead, but OU answered with King's 10-yard scoring jaunt to put the Sooners back on top, 21-17. The Buffs kicked a field goal to cut their deficit to 21-20 just before halftime.

Von Schamann's 54-yard field goal and Ivory's three-yard TD run gave the Sooners a 31-20 lead through the first half of the third period. Minutes later, the Buffs scored on a 70-yard bomb and a two-point conversion to trail, 31-28.

Fullback Ken Kelleher scored two touchdowns in the final 18 minutes, the first after his teammates recovered Culbreath's fumble on the OU 27.

The Big Red rushed for 293 yards, and King led the Sooners with 119 yards in 12 carries. Blevins completed eight of 14 passes for 145 yards. The Buffs rolled up 477 total yards.

OU dropped to 5-2-1 on the season and 2-2 in the Big Eight Conference. Hope looked bleak for the Sooners, winners of three straight conference titles, to win a fourth. Oklahoma also dropped to 17th in the AP poll. The injury bug reared its ugly head again when Kinlaw hurt both his knees early in the game.

Lott and Ivory scored three touchdowns each as the Sooners hammered 1-7 Kansas State, 49-20, the next week in Norman.

The Wildcats kept it close, trailing 28-17 at the half and 28-20 midway through the third quarter. Lott scored twice and Ivory once to ice the game for Oklahoma. Lott led the 436-yard Oklahoma ground attack with 195 yards. OU failed to complete a pass in two tries. The Cats gained 329 total yards.

Sooner Magic: Staying Alive in the Big Eight

When a team like Oklahoma has a potent running attack, passing is not necessary. The Wishbone formation was a deadly offensive weapon that churned out yards in big chunks. Many times under Barry Switzer's regime, the Sooners rolled up huge numbers of real estate while leaving opponents in their wake.

The Darrell Royal-Barry Switzer feud continued when Royal accused Lonnie Williams, an employee of an OU donor, of spying on Texas practices, as reported in the *Daily Oklahoman* a day before the 1976 OU-Texas contest. A volunteer scout for the Longhorns had reported the incident to one of Royal's assistants.

Royal offered $10,000 to charities for Switzer, assistant Larry Lacewell, and Williams if the three would take a lie detector test proving their innocence.

Royal called the OU coaches "sorry bastards" as quoted by the Associated Press. "I don't trust them on anything," he continued. He also said that the lie detector tests taken by Sooner coaches who were cleared of recruiting allegations a year before were "rigged."

Switzer denied any knowledge of spying on Texas practices and refused the lie detector tests for he, Lacewell and Williams.

"It's worth more to me to have him chasing ghosts," Switzer replied.

Lacewell said if the allegations were true, Royal should take it to the NCAA. Williams called the allegations a "bunch of lies" and "the whole thing is ridiculous."

President Gerald Ford attended the 1976 game on a campaign swing through Dallas. Switzer and Royal escorted Ford to midfield for the pregame coin toss. Neither coach spoke to each other nor shook hands.

Recalling the incident, Switzer said: "The media was calling me and accusing my staff of spying. My staff didn't spy on them. The incident they're talking about was in 1972 when Chuck Fairbanks was head coach, and it wasn't even my staff!"

Against Missouri on November 13, OU rolled up 439 yards, and 94 percent of the yardage came from Ivory, King and Lott. Ivory gained 159 yards on 17 carries, King added 128 on 18 carries, and Lott rushed 24 times for 126 yards. The Sooners didn't pass once.

In contrast, Missouri had a potent passing attack, but starting quarterback Steve Pisarkiewicz had been out several games with an injury. He would sit on the bench until the fourth quarter, and when he went in, he had most of the 71,184 fans in Norman on the edge of their seats.

The 11th-ranked Tigers (6-3) came to town riding a six-game losing streak to the Sooners. OU led the overall series, 41-20-5.

The game was played more in Missouri-like conditions under cloudy skies with intermittent snow flurries. Near-freezing (33 degrees) temperatures kept the fans shivering throughout most of the game. An exciting contest would keep the blood flowing from jumping up and down.

Backup Tiger quarterback Pete Woods engineered an 88-yard scoring march in the first quarter and tossed an 11-yard scoring strike to Leo Lewis for a 7-0 lead.

Von Schamann booted a 35-yard field goal to cut the Tiger lead to 7-3 four and a half minutes later. Lott's two-yard TD jaunt and von Schamann's toe put the Sooners on top, 10-7, midway through the second stanza.

The Tigers added a field goal moments later and von Schamann kicked a 25-yard field goal to give OU a 13-10 lead as time expired in the first half.

Lott's 51-yard scamper and King's 23-yard run gave OU a comfortable 27-10 lead in the third quarter.

Pisarkiewicz entered the game on the next Tiger possession and engineered a 71-yard drive in five plays. On the first play of the fourth quarter, with the ball at the OU 33, Pisarkiewicz hurled a screen pass to Earl Gant, who flew to the end zone. Tim Gibbons nailed the extra point to cut the Oklahoma lead to 27-17 with 14:50 left in the game.

On Mizzou's next possession, Pisarkiewicz moved his unit 70 yards to the OU five. The same screen pass was called, but this time Moore was ready and nailed Gant for a one-yard loss. Gibbons booted a 22-yard field goal to put the Tigers down by a touchdown, 27-20, with 8:29 to go.

On their next possession, the Tigers roared to the OU 15. On second-and-11, Pisarkiewicz dropped back to pass. OU linebacker Daryl Hunt, who forced two fumbles and recovered one in the game, charged through the line toward the Mizzou quarterback and got a hand in his face. Pisarkiewicz hurried a pass to tight end Kellen Winslow inside the OU five. Peters, who sat out the previous three games with a shoulder injury, stepped in front of Winslow at the three and intercepted the ball, returning it 15 yards.

The Tigers would get one more chance but were 92 yards from pay dirt. Pisarkiewicz drove them to the OU 26 with 50 seconds left in the game. Hunt again blitzed and sacked the Tiger quarterback for a 10-yard loss. On fourth-and-20, Pisarkiewicz tossed a pass to Winslow for 19 yards. The officials' chains were deployed. When the entire 10 yards of the chain was completely stretched, the ball was inches short. The Sooners defense jumped up and down and so did the fans.

Oklahoma held on to a 27-20 victory. The Tigers rolled up 504 total yards.

Hunt said the Sooner defense used an inside-outside blitz on the play when he forced Pisarkiewicz to hurry the intercepted pass. "I was coming up the middle. It made him throw too soon."

"We were in man-to-man coverage," Peters said on his interception. "I saw the ball as he [Pisarkiewicz] threw it. I just broke on the ball. It was a great feeling ... a great thrill, making that play in a great game like this. We really needed a big play."

"I'm glad to have Terry Peters back," Switzer said. "He made a great play when we needed one. I think the crowd was important today, too. We made it an exciting game and managed to win it."

When the day was done, five teams were tied for first place in the Big Eight—OU, Colorado, OSU, Iowa State and Nebraska. Three teams would likely share the conference title after the following week's games. Colorado had to beat Kansas State, and the winner of Oklahoma State-Iowa State would also get a cut of the crown. The other share would be decided between Oklahoma and Nebraska, two weeks later in Lincoln.

Colorado defeated Kansas State, 35-28, in Boulder, and Oklahoma State beat Iowa State 42-21 in Ames.

Sooner Magic: A Peacock Spreads His Feathers

Nebraska was the choice of the preseason prognosticators for the conference title and the choice of the AP poll as the season began. The Huskers did not live up to their preseason billing as they tied Louisiana State, 6-6, in the first week and toppled from the top spot in the AP poll.

After LSU, the Huskers won seven more games but lost stunners to Missouri and Iowa State, the latter prior to the OU game in Lincoln.

The 56th Sooner-Cornhusker matchup arrived on a Friday, the day after Thanksgiving.

Normally one of the two teams is undefeated or has one loss prior to their encounters. Both teams entered the game with identical 7-2-1 records. The Sooners were rated eighth in the AP poll, and Nebraska was 10th.

The Sooners held a 29-23-3 series edge, including a four-game streak over the Cornhuskers.

A sellout crowd, which is nothing unusual for NU games, of 76,247 shivered through the 30-degree temperature boosted by a 30 mph north wind. A national television (ABC-TV) audience kept warm in their homes watching this one.

OU drove 69 yards in 13 plays for a 7-0 lead. Peacock scored from the one and von Schamann converted with 16 seconds left in the opening stanza.

Nebraska kicked a field goal midway through the second period.

Oklahoma drove 73 yards on its next possession, but stalled at the NU eight-yard line. On fourth-and-one, Peacock carried for four yards, but the play was nullified when the Sooners were flagged for motion. Von Schamann's 30-yard field-goal attempt into the brisk wind ricocheted off the left goal post, and the Sooners carried a 7-3 lead at intermission.

The Huskers scored on their first two possessions of the second half. A 67-yard march gave Nebraska a 10-7 lead. Five plays into OU's next possession, the Huskers recovered Lott's fumble on the OU 32. Moments later, the Huskers led 17-7 with 6:31 left in the third quarter.

Singer Elvis Presley may have been the King of Rock 'n' Roll, but Elvis Peacock, the football player, was the king in Soonerland, especially after his fourth-quarter performance.

Early in that final period, Peacock scored on a 51-yard run. Lott optioned down the line, then in a split-second flipped the ball to Peacock, who flew to the end zone. A sharp reverse by Peacock at the NU 20 left two Husker defenders sprawled on the turf. Switzer ordered a two-point conversion, but Peacock was stopped short of the goal, and OU trailed, 17-13, with 12:28 to go.

Nebraska later recovered an OU fumble at the Sooner 38 and marched to the 23 where the Sooner defense stiffened. Henderson

broke up two Husker passes, once on second down and again on fourth down. Nebraska's fourth down gamble failed for the fifth time that afternoon.

Oklahoma took over at its 15 with less than five minutes to play, and a couple of backup players shined for the Sooners. After a gain of one yard, backup halfback Woodie Shepard took a pitch from Lott, rolled right, pulled up and heaved the ball to Rhodes to the NU 37. Rhodes stopped on his route and turned toward the incoming pass to make the catch.

For Shepard, who threw a couple of passes in high school at Odessa, Texas, it was his first pass in a Sooner uniform. It was also the first pass of the game for OU.

Shepard said after the game that he couldn't see Rhodes, "then he showed up. I knew I was going to get hit—and I was, but I saw the catch as I was falling down.

"I was ready to eat it [the ball] if the receivers were covered. Whenever the receiver is even with the defensive man, it's more than likely he's going to catch it, and I saw that he had a half-step on his man."

Facing third-and-19 at the NU 34, Blevins came off the bench to replace Lott on the next play. He fired a pass to Rhodes in the flat. Rhodes, with his back to the Husker defense, flipped the ball to a trailing Peacock, who raced to the NU two-yard line. On the next play, Peacock took a pitch and swiftly swept around right end to the end zone. Von Schamann's boot gave the Sooners a 20-17 lead with 38 seconds remaining.

"This was one of the biggest and one of the most satisfying wins we've ever had," Switzer said. "Our defense kept us in the game. It held on fourth-and-two and fourth-and-one. Our field position was horrible, but we never gave up."

OU pounded out 357 yards rushing and added 79 through the air. The Huskers collected 328 total yards.

The victory earned OU a share of the Big Eight Conference championship with OSU and Colorado, the Sooners' fourth straight conference title.

The Sooners accepted a bid to meet Wyoming (Western Athletic Conference co-champions) in the Fiesta Bowl on Christmas Day. Tempe, Arizona, just outside of Phoenix, was the host city, and the weather was sunny with temperatures in the mid-60s. Wyoming coach Fred Akers was coaching his last game for Wyoming, but he would be opposite the sidelines as Texas' head coach in 1977.

1976 Season Record: 9-2-1
Big Eight Conference: 5-2-0 (Champions)

Date	Opponent	Result	Score
September 11	at Vanderbilt	W	24-3
September 18	CALIFORNIA	W	28-17
September 25	FLORIDA STATE	W	24-9
October 2	at Iowa State	W	24-10
October 9	Texas at Dallas	T	6-6
October 16	at Kansas	W	28-10
October 23	OKLAHOMA STATE	L	31-24
October 30	at Colorado	L	42-31
November 6	KANSAS STATE	W	49-20
November 13	MISSOURI	W	27-20
November 26	at Nebraska	W	20-17
December 25	Wyoming*	W	41-7

*Fiesta Bowl at Tempe, AZ

The No. 8 Sooners rolled over the 8-3 Cowboys, 41-7. OU's defense allowed only 204 total yards and forced six turnovers (five via interceptions).

Oklahoma scored on its first two possessions. Peacock's three-yard TD run capped a 14-play, 80-yard drive, which used up nearly half of the first quarter. Ivory's four-yard run capped a 53-yard march in four plays.

Von Schamann kicked two field goals in the second quarter to give the Sooners a 20-0 advantage at intermission.

Just as they had in the first half, the Sooners hogged the clock again to open the third quarter with an 83-yard, nine-play drive. Peacock's 15-yard TD run put OU up 27-0, and from that point the reserves got in on the act. A total of 72 Sooners participated in the game.

Cumby and Shepard each scored in the fourth period to give OU a 41-0 lead. Wyoming scored a touchdown with 24 seconds remaining.

The defense set Fiesta Bowl records with five interceptions and limited the Cowboys to 23 yards passing and 204 total yards. Peters led with two thefts, which tied a bowl record, and he was named defensive player of the game. Mike Babb, Hebert, and Jerry Reese each got an interception.

The offense set records with 74 rushes, five rushing touchdowns, 22 first downs, and the longest field goal (von Schamann's 50-yarder in the second quarter). The 34-point victory was the largest margin to date. Lott was named offensive player of the game.

The 1976 Sooners finished with a 9-2-1 record and fifth in the AP poll and sixth in the UPI poll. Henderson and Vaughan were named All-Americans. Hunt and Hill joined them on the All-Big Eight team. The offense averaged 321.8 yards per game rushing, third best in the nation.

1977

The 1977 Sooners were preseason favorites to win their third national championship in four years. The offense returned nine starters, with tackle Mike Vaughan the only one who graduated from the line, yet the front line was not without seasoned veterans—guards Greg Roberts and Jaime Melendez and tackle Karl Baldischwiler. Thomas Lott returned to guide the Wishbone, along with fullback Kenny King and halfback Elvis Peacock. Victor Hicks also was back at tight end. One player who would emerge into the starting lineup as the season progressed was a sophomore from Hooks, Texas, named Billy Sims.

The defense was solid with the return of nine starters, including the linebacker duo of Daryl Hunt and George Cumby. Cumby was switched from fullback to linebacker in the off-season. Noseguard Reggie Kinlaw, who had off-season knee surgery, anchored the front line, and Zac Henderson was back to lead the secondary. Placekicker Uwe von Schamann returned and added punting to his repertoire.

Sooner Magic: OU Wins Comedy Of Errors

The No. 1 Sooners opened against Vanderbilt on September 10 in Norman and were embarrassed by a 25-23 victory over the Commodores. OU was a 30-point favorite but lost seven of 11 fumbles and was plagued by 104 penalty yards.

Lott had a severely bruised leg, and Dean Blevins started at quarterback, but a backup freshman sparked the go-ahead drive in the fourth quarter.

Vandy's punt early in the game had OU pinned at its own three-yard line. Sims failed to see Blevins' pitch out and fell on the ball in the end zone for a Commodore safety. Vandy added a field goal 10 minutes later for a 5-0 lead, a touchdown and another field goal in the second period for a 15-0 advantage.

The Sooners answered the second field goal with a 74-yard scoring drive. Sims sprinted 11 yards for the score and Blevins carried for the two-point conversion.

Von Schamann booted a 26-yard field goal with five seconds left in the first half.

With the way the Sooners were playing, they had their fans worried, down 15-11 at intermission. Neither team scored in the third quarter.

Jay Jimerson, the freshman quarterback from Norman, got the call to enter the game in the fourth stanza. "I told myself to relax, get loose, stay cool, and try to concentrate on not fumbling," he said of his first call at quarterback.

He played splendidly, engineering a 55-yard TD drive in 10 plays. His 19-yard touchdown run gave the Sooners an 18-15 lead after von Schamann converted.

Jimerson's father, Don, was OU's freshman football coach and assistant athletic director, and Jay practically grew up in the shadows of Owen Field.

"That's something I've been dreaming about since I was three feet tall," Jimerson said of his first Sooner touchdown.

Four minutes later, safety Bud Hebert (playing with cracked ribs) blocked a Vandy field-goal attempt and defensive end Barry Burget swept up the pigskin and flew 64 yards for a touchdown to lift Oklahoma to a 25-15 lead with 5:29 remaining.

Vandy fullback Frank Mordica scored on a 12-yard run, and a two-point pass play cut the OU lead to 25-23 with 1:18 to go. The Commodores' onside kick struck Terry Peters, and Jack Chandler recovered for Vanderbilt at the OU 49.

Phil Tabor sacked backup quarterback Mike Wright for a nine-yard loss, yet Vandy recovered and later made a first down at the OU 36. Wright misfired on a pass on the next play, and the Sooners blocked Greg Martin's 53-yard field-goal try to save the win.

Barry Switzer said the mistakes, penalties, and fumbles were embarrassing and "the sorriest exhibition" of football in his coaching career.

The Sooners rushed for 235 yards and passed for 75. Vanderbilt picked up 341 total yards.

The narrow victory dropped Oklahoma to No. 5 in the AP poll, but the Sooners routed Utah, 62-24, the next week in Norman. It was the season opener for Utah.

OU capitalized on three early Ute fumbles for a 17-0 lead in the first quarter. The scoring assault didn't end there in the first period. Blevins fired a 74-yard TD pass to split end Steve Rhodes, and Jimerson's 54-yard scamper gave the Sooners a 31-0 lead.

Utah scored 17 points in the second period, all off Sooner fumbles, but the Utes could not close in as Peacock added a touchdown run, and von Schamann's field goal gave OU a 41-17 lead at halftime.

Sims scored on a 31-yard for the only tally in the third quarter. The touchdown came five plays after defensive tackle Richard Murray's fumble recovery at the Utah 42. The Utes scored a touchdown early in the fourth stanza, then King and Blevins each scored on one-yard runs.

OU rushed for 326 yards and passed for 111. Utah was held to 256 total yards.

Sooner Magic: Von Foot

The man in the white uniform was leading the crowd, waving his arms in maestro-like motions. Everyone in Ohio Stadium and a national television audience must have thought this man had lost his marbles. Von Schamann had joined the Ohio State Buckeye fans in chanting, "Block that kick."

Von Schamann was psyching himself out, for he was getting ready to kick the biggest field goal of his life, and for that matter, the life of OU football fans.

Prior to the 1977 season, Sooner fans were excited about playing Ohio State. Many Big Red fans had sported bumper stickers: "September 24th, The Day Woody Discovered the Sooners."

Yes, Buckeye head coach Woody Hayes did discover the Sooners and von Schamann in the first football game between OU and Ohio State. The fourth-ranked Buckeyes opened their season with a 10-0 win over Miami, Florida and 38-7 over Minnesota.

Oklahoma jumped to a huge 20-0 lead during the first 18 minutes of the game.

Peacock gathered a bad pitchout and raced 27 yards for the game's first score in the opening quarter. Von Schamann nailed the extra point for a 7-0 Sooner lead.

The Buckeyes spilled the pigskin on their first possession and Sims scored on a 15-yard run two plays and 54 seconds later. Von Schamann's boot upped the lead to 14-0.

Sims left the game late in the first quarter with a strained Achilles tendon. Still, OU managed another three points as von Schamann tacked on another trey from 23 yards out for a 17-0 lead with 3:29 left in the opening quarter.

With 12:58 remaining until half time, von Schamann's 33-yard field goal gave Oklahoma a 20-0 lead. Ohio State, at that point, did not have one first down.

During the next five minutes, Ohio State hit pay dirt twice and trailed, 20-14, with 9:46 left in the half. Lott suffered a sprained knee in the second stanza and was sidelined the rest of the game. With Lott and Sims out of action, the Sooners had to rely on back-ups—freshman David Overstreet for Sims and Blevins for Lott.

The Sooners were now without their star running back and quarterback. But Ohio State was not without injuries. Linebacker Tom Cousineau was sidelined in the first quarter, and quarterback Rod Gerald left the game in the third quarter.

After Ohio State's second TD, things fell apart for the Sooners as they turned the ball over on six of their next nine possessions.

The Buckeyes scored two more TDs in the third quarter for a 28-20 lead.

Reggie Kinlaw suffered a knee injury earlier in the season and refused surgery. The injury did not keep him from making a crucial play in the fourth period. He recovered a Buckeye fumble at the OSU 43—new life for the Sooners with about six minutes to play.

Oklahoma moved to the OSU two-yard line, but faced fourth-and-goal with less than two minutes remaining.

Blevins took the snap, headed to his right and pitched the ball to Peacock, who followed Rhodes' block on an end sweep. As he turned toward the goal line, two Buckeye defenders tried to tackle him, but Peacock eluded their grasp and spun across the goal line. The same play was called on the two-point conversion, but this time the Buckeyes stopped Peacock short of the goal. The scoreboard showed Ohio State 28, OU 26 with 1:29 left in the game.

To no one's surprise, OU set up for an onside kick. Von Schamann's kick was a low, wobbly line drive. The ball bounced once on the artificial turf in front of Ohio State's Ricardo Volley, who reached out for the oncoming ball, but he was unable to clutch it. After the officials unpiled the mass of players at the 50-yard line, OU's Mike Babb was the player in possession of the pigskin, holding it over his head.

Blevins faked a handoff to King, then hurled the ball to Rhodes for 17 yards to the OSU 33. King then smashed through the line for seven yards. Overstreet was stuffed for no gain, then King got three more yards, but not enough for the first down.

Fourth down and six seconds on the clock.

Out came the kicking unit led by von Schamann. Prior to the field goal, the Sooners called time out, and von Schamann crouched in the middle of the field with his hands forward on the turf.

The Sooners lined up for the kick, but Ohio State called a time out to add more pressure to the sophomore kicker who hadn't missed in five attempts so far in the young season.

The predominant Buckeye crowd began chanting, "Block that Kick," and von Schamann was directing the crowd in the maestro-like motions.

Mark Lucky snapped the ball to Hebert, who put the ball on the tee. von Schamann struck the ball, which sailed all of the 41 yards, and more, through the uprights with three seconds remaining.

The scoreboard clicked from "26" to "29" next to the word "Okla".

Pandemonium. Sooner players mauled von Schamann, and the rest of the OU players cleared the bench running toward their hero.

Woody Hayes was livid. With his shirt collar unbuttoned and his tie loosened, he tipped his cap above his forehead, then removed his eyeglasses and slammed them to the turf. Such a gracious loser.

Von Schamann recalled he learned to meditate from his girlfriend's brother-in-law and he had been practicing it for a short while. "It helps you mentally, physically, emotionally, in every way."

"What you do is inhale and exhale normally, then you think of the number one. The number doesn't make any difference, you don't actually say it, but you think it. I also envisioned the ball going through the goal posts."

When he heard the crowd chanting, "Block that Kick," von Schamann, who forever after that game became known as "von Foot," said, "I guess the crowd got to me. So I started leading the crowd in chants. I wanted to keep my mind off the strategy."

"I imagine it did look crazy to some people."

OU rushed for 250 yards and passed for 44. Ohio State collected 202 total yards. The victory gave the Sooners a 3-0 record and sent them back to the top of the AP poll.

Lott scored three touchdowns and rushed for 102 yards as Oklahoma defeated Kansas 24-9 the following week in Norman. OU led, 24-0, before the Jayhawks got on the board in the fourth period.

The Sooners' first touchdown came late in the first half on Lott's eight-yard scamper. Von Schamann kicked the first of three conversions for a 7-0 lead. The TD came seven plays after Peters intercepted a Jayhawk pass at the KU 30.

Von Schamann toed a 35-yard field goal midway through the third stanza, and Lott scored twice on runs of nine and four yards in a span of nine seconds. The latter score occurred after the Hawks fumbled a kickoff.

Von Schamann bobbled a punt snap and fell on the ball in the end zone to give Kansas a safety, and the Hawks scored moments after recovering an OU fumble.

The Sooners picked up 294 rushing yards and passed for 33. The defense held Kansas to 185 total yards.

Oklahoma dropped to second in the AP poll following the Kansas win, and the Sooners would drop further following a 13-6 defeat to Texas on October 8 in Dallas.

Sims was still sidelined with an injury, and Overstreet led the Sooners with 87 yards rushing as his replacement. Two Texas quarterbacks went down with injuries in the opening stanza, and third-stringer Randy McEachern guided the Longhorns the rest of the way.

OU took a 3-0 lead early in the first quarter on von Schamann's 46-yard field goal, but Russell Erxleben answered with a 64-yarder to tie the game early in the second period. Earl Campbell's 24-yard TD run late in the first half gave the Steers a 10-3 lead heading into the locker room. Campbell, who won the Heisman Trophy later in the year, rushed for 124 yards on 23 carries.

Von Schamann's 32-yard field goal narrowed the deficit to 10-6 midway through the third quarter, but Erxleben added a 58-yarder midway through the final period.

Following the kickoff, the Sooners drove 79 yards to the Texas one with four minutes left in the game. On fourth-and-goal, UT cornerback Johnnie Johnson stopped Lott for no gain.

Oklahoma rushed for 190 yards and added 47 through the air. The Steers collected 209 total yards.

Oklahoma dropped to No. 7 in the AP poll, and the team hit the road again, this time to Columbia, Missouri. After the Longhorn game, which is always filled with emotion, the Big Red had one week to get up for the Tigers.

Sooner Magic: Saved by the Robbery

Oklahoma was riding a seven-game winning streak over the 1-4 Tigers. That streak was about to be wiped out until a sophomore safety robbed the Tigers' comeback effort.

The first five times the Tigers had the ball they drove inside the OU 30-yard line, and five times they came away with nothing. Two interceptions, two missed field goals and a fumble were the Tigers' bane.

Sims, playing for the first time since the Ohio State game, fumbled on his first carry against the Tigers early in the second period. The ball squirted straight up in the air, MU linebacker Bill Bess grabbed the pigskin at the OU 16-yard line and rambled to the end zone to give Mizzou a 7-0 lead early in the second stanza.

The Sooners then marched to the Missouri three, but Sims again spilled the ball and the Tigers recovered. They marched 75 yards, but stalled and kicked a field goal for a 10-0 advantage.

After a couple of punts by both teams, the Big Red gained possession at their own 20 with 1:26 remaining until halftime. On first down, Lott shot down the left sideline for 62 yards to the MU 18. Two plays later, he leaped into the air and fired a 14-yard pass to Hicks in the end zone. Von Schamann toed the extra point, and the Sooners closed the gap to 10-7 with 45 seconds left in the period.

A poor Mizzou punt into the wind in the third quarter set up the Sooners' next score from the MU 46. Five plays later, Peacock crashed through left tackle and sprinted 35 yards for the score. Von Schamann's kick gave the Big Red a 14-10 lead with 11:30 to go in the quarter.

On Missouri's first play from scrimmage following the kickoff, Henderson intercepted Pete Woods' pass at the MU 45 and returned the ball to the 17. Five plays later, Lott scored from the

one, and Von Schamann's extra point boosted the Sooners to a 21-10.

The Tigers recovered Ray Anderson's fumble midway through the fourth stanza and scored eight plays later to cut the Sooner lead to 21-17 with 4:21 remaining. On fourth-and-goal at the two-yard line, Woods lobbed a pass to tight end Kellen Winslow wide open in the right side of the end zone.

OU gained only one first down on its next possession but stalled at its 42. Von Schamann punted to the MU 18 with 2:02 to go.

The Big Red defense held the Tigers to seven yards on the next two plays, then on third-and-three, David Newman busted through for a 22-yard gain to the MU 47. A few plays later, the Tigers gambled on fourth-and-five at the OU 37. Woods connected a seven-yard pass to Winslow, resulting in a first down at the OU 30 with 42 seconds left.

On the next play, Woods' pass was intercepted at the 20 by safety Darrol Ray, who returned the ball to the Missouri nine-yard line with 24 seconds remaining. The Sooners killed the clock and escaped Columbia with a 21-17 victory.

"We didn't feel like we played well ... but I'm happy with the win," Switzer said.

Lott's 123 yards led the Sooners' 339-yard ground attack. Lott also added 19 passing yards. The Tigers rolled up 419 total yards.

A 21-point surge by No. 6 Oklahoma helped to overcome a 16-14 third-quarter deficit en route to a 35-16 win over No. 16 Iowa State on a rainy day at Owen Field on October 22. The 5-1 Cyclones had stunned Nebraska, 24-21, a week earlier.

Lott connected on a 40-yard pass to Peacock to put the Sooners ahead, 21-16, midway through the third stanza. The Cyclones marched to regain the lead, but Henderson intercepted Mike Rubley's pass in the end zone.

Freddie Nixon's 85-yard punt return for a touchdown early in the fourth period gave OU more breathing room with a 28-16 advantage. The Sooners cashed in with their final score following Mike Babb's interception at the ISU 42. Lott's nine-yard TD run capped the seven-play drive with more than five minutes remaining.

The Sooners rushed for 285 yards and passed for 74. King carried 23 times for 146 yards. ISU gained 272 total yards.

The No. 4 Sooners rolled past 1-6 Kansas State, 42-7, the following week in Manhattan. King's 29-yard touchdown run gave OU a 7-0 lead early in the first period, then Lott added three touchdowns to put the game away.

Kinlaw bottled up the inside running game. The Cats were held to 67 net yards rushing on 46 tries. He also was constantly in the K-State backfield forcing quarterbacks to make mistakes. As a result, the Sooners intercepted four KSU passes. Babb stole two Wildcat passes, the second setting up Lott's third TD early in the third quarter.

The Sooners also capitalized on two other interceptions. Daryl Hunt's pick off late in the second period led to Lott's second TD. Basil Banks returned an oskie to the KSU 15, and Blevins scored three plays later.

The Wildcats scored late in the game with a 53-yard interception off Blevins' pass.

The Big Red rushed for 483 yards and tossed for 53. Nixon and King each gained 99 yards on the ground. Kansas State passed for 183 yards.

Oklahoma State appeared poised for a second straight upset on November 5 in Stillwater, but OU rolled up 40 unanswered points to defeat their instate rival, 61-28.

The 4-4 Cowboys opened with a 14-10 first-quarter lead on two Terry Miller touchdowns. Von Schamann's 22-yard field goal and

---

Oklahoma had extended its scoring streak to an NCAA-record-tying 123 games. Notre Dame also scored that afternoon to equal the mark. Both schools matched the record set by the Sooners between 1946 and 1957. Ironically, Notre Dame's 7-0 victory in 1957 ended that streak. The Sooners' record-tying mark set against Kansas also began in 1966 following a 38-0 loss to Notre Dame. Oklahoma continued to extend its streak through 181 games before losing to USC in 1982. Notre Dame's streak ended at 134 when it lost 3-0 to Missouri in 1978.

Overstreet's one-yard TD run in the second period put the Sooners ahead, 21-14, at halftime.

The Pokes scored two touchdowns in the span of 15 seconds early in the third stanza. Quarterback Harold Bailey scored on a one-yard run, then Overstreet fumbled the ensuing kickoff at the OU six. Two plays later, Miller crossed the goal line, and OSU held a 28-21 advantage.

On the first play after OSU's kickoff, Lott scored on an 80-yard run, breaking three tackles along the way. From that point on, it was all crimson and cream.

Oklahoma's defense, which had yielded 200 total yards in the first half, held the Pokes to 45 second-half yards and just 34 after Miller's third touchdown. Meanwhile the OU offense totaled 293 yards in the final 30 minutes.

Blevins replaced Lott, who bruised his shoulder. One minute after Lott's 80-yard TD, Blevins completed a 12-yard pass to Rhodes. Rhodes then pitched to Overstreet trailing him, and Overstreet sprinted to the end zone to complete the 55-yard play.

Blevins fired a 10-yard pass to Hicks later in the third period, and von Schamann booted a 19-yard field goal, his third of the game, with two and a half minutes left in the quarter.

Both teams scored a total of 38 points in the third stanza. The Cowboys' kickoff return team was a comedy of errors in the second half. Darnell Scott fumbled a kickoff return that led to von Schamann's third field goal. Scott and Skip Taylor went to the east goal line to accept the next kickoff, but the Cowboys were receiving at the west goal line. Randy Stephenson fumbled a kickoff that led to a three-yard TD run by Nixon midway through the fourth stanza. Scott fumbled the next OU kickoff into the end zone. When he retrieved it behind the goal line, he touched his knee for a touchback, but it was ruled a safety and two points for Oklahoma.

No. 3 Oklahoma scored five touchdowns in the first 21 and one-half minutes en route to a 52-14 thrashing of Colorado before a homecoming throng of 71,184 the following week in Norman. The Sooners scored on seven of their first 10 possessions.

Sims scored three touchdowns in the onslaught, and he didn't even lead all Oklahoma rushers. That honor went to King, who gained 121 yards between the goal lines with no touchdowns. Sims carried only six times for 36 yards, but half of his carries scored touchdowns.

Henderson intercepted two passes, and defensive end Reggie Mathis recovered two fumbles for the Oklahoma defense. Hunt forced one fumble and picked off a pass at the OU 37 to thwart a Buffalo drive.

It was the worst defeat OU handed the 6-2-1 Buffaloes since a 62-0 blasting in 1962, and OU earned at least a share of its fifth straight Big Eight Conference championship. A victory over Nebraska 13 days later would secure the outright conference title.

No. 11 Nebraska came to Norman with hopes of sharing the Big Eight crown and left town on the short end of a 38-7 country whipping. The Huskers lost their opener to Washington State, won four straight, and then stumbled against Iowa State for their only confer-

Safety Darrol Ray's interceptions, late in the game against Missouri, sealed the Sooners' victory. *(OU Athletics)*

ence loss so far. Nebraska rebounded with four straight conference wins to sport a 9-2 record.

Peacock scored two touchdowns, and Lott added another in the second period as the Sooners took a 21-7 lead at intermission. Lott and Peacock shredded the Husker defense for 143 and 123 rushing yards in the game.

Von Schamann toed a 45-yard field goal for a 24-7 lead midway in the third quarter.

Overstreet scored on a 19-yard run midway through the fourth period. Henderson's second interception in the game led to another Sooner score—a 24-yard pass from Blevins to Hicks one play later.

Although the Huskers totaled 322 yards, they could drive no closer than the OU 38 after a late second-quarter touchdown. The Sooners rolled up 417 yards on the ground and 36 in the air.

Oklahoma at 10-1 received a bid to play 10-1 Arkansas in the Orange Bowl and jumped to No. 2 in the AP poll after the Nebraska win.

Tailback Roland Sales rushed for an Orange Bowl-record 205 yards and scored two touchdowns to hand the No. 6 Razorbacks to a 31-6 upset of the Sooners. He also had two big runs to set up another touchdown and a field goal.

Arkansas had four players suspended before the game including All-America guard Leotis Harris and running back Ben Cowins. The Sooners were expected to win in a cakewalk as 17-point favorites. Lott suffered a thigh bruise two days before the game and was ineffective on the rain-soaked field as he rushed for 28 yards in 19 carries and completed four of seven passes for 42 yards.

The Razorbacks cashed in on two Sooner fumbles to lead 14-0 in the first quarter. They added 10 more points in the third period. OU scored early in the fourth stanza, a 95-yard drive in 10 plays. Blevins replaced Lott in the drive and completed it with an eight-yard TD pass to Hicks.

1977 Season Record: 10-2-0
Big Eight Conference: 7-0-0 (Champions)

Date	Opponent	Result	Score
September 10	VANDERBILT	W	25-23
September 17	UTAH	W	62-24
September 24	at Ohio State	W	29-28
October 1	KANSAS	W	24-9
October 8	Texas at Dallas	L	13-6
October 15	at Missouri	W	21-17
October 22	IOWA STATE	W	35-16
October 29	at Kansas State	W	42-7
November 5	at Oklahoma State	W	61-28
November 12	COLORADO	W	52-14
November 25	NEBRASKA	W	38-7
January 2	Arkansas*	L	31-6

*Orange Bowl at Miami, FL

An Oklahoma win and a Texas loss in the Cotton Bowl would have given the Sooners another national championship. The Longhorns lost 38-10 to Notre Dame. The Fighting Irish won the national crown, and the Sooners finished the 1977 season 10-2 (7-0 in the Big Eight) and ranked seventh in the AP poll.

All-America honors went to Cumby, Henderson, Hunt, Kinlaw, and Roberts. Baldischwiler and Lott joined them on the all-conference team. Henderson was selected defensive back of the year by the New York Athletic Club.

1978

The Sooners' quest for a sixth national championship ended three yards from the goal line on the frozen turf at Lincoln, Nebraska. No one was more disappointed than halfback Billy Sims, the man who lost the pigskin nine feet from pay dirt. Sims had wreaked havoc on defenses all season long and had jumped into the Heisman Trophy race with his superb performances.

Sims would lead the nation in rushing and claim Oklahoma's third Heisman Memorial Trophy at the end of the year. Halfback David Overstreet and fullback Kenny King returned to round out one of the fastest backfields in Sooner history. The "I" formation was added to the offense to allow Sims more carries.

With eight of 16 returning starters in their third year at OU, the Sooners were favored to win the Big Eight Conference crown and one of the favorites to claim the national title. The returnees included four All-Americans—offensive guard Greg Roberts, nose guard Reggie Kinlaw, and linebackers Daryl Hunt and George Cumby. Hunt (152) and Cumby (140) combined to record 292 tackles in 1977.

Thomas Lott, whom Barry Switzer proclaimed as the "best wishbone quarterback ever to play at Oklahoma," returned to lead the offense.

Roberts, who would win the Outland Trophy at the end of the season, had experienced veterans with him on the offensive front—center Paul Tabor, tackle Sam Claphan, and tight end Victor Hicks. Steve Rhodes returned at split end.

Tabor's twin brother, Phil, anchored the defense at tackle along with Kinlaw, Hunt, and Cumby. Defensive ends Bruce Taton and Reggie Mathis also returned. The secondary was anything but green, although Sherwood Taylor was the lone returning starter. Bud Hebert, Darrol Ray, and Mike Babb had plenty of playing time in 1977.

Uwe Von Schamann was back for his final season as placekicker and punter. The Fort Worth senior had not missed on 71 straight conversions and hit 62 percent of his field goals. He would not miss an extra point all season, running his string to 131 straight.

Three of Switzer's assistants had left the team. Larry Lacewell, Gene Hochevar, and Jerry Pettibone resigned during the off-season. New faces were either promoted or hired. Rex Norris, Gary Gibbs, Lucious Selmon and Donnie Duncan were among the most notable.

Norris, Gibbs, and Selmon were promoted from part-time status into full-time positions. Norris replaced Lacewell as defensive coordinator, Gibbs coached the defensive ends, and Selmon tutored the defensive line. Duncan was named assistant head coach and coached the offensive line.

Oklahoma began at No. 4 in the AP preseason poll. The Sooners opened the season with a 35-29 victory over Stanford on September 9 in Palo Alto, California. OU jumped to a 14-0 lead in the first period on Sims' two-yard run and Lott's 70-yard strike to Rhodes. The Cardinal got on the board late in the same period with a touchdown and added a field goal late in the second quarter to cut the Sooner lead to 14-10. Oklahoma countered with two scores in the last three minutes of the half. Lott scored on a 19-yard run and threw a 17-yard TD pass to Bobby Kimball for a 28-10 lead heading into the locker room.

Stanford added 10 more points in the third stanza to trail, 28-20.

Taylor intercepted two of Dils' passes in the fourth quarter, and Darrol Ray's interception on the last play sealed the victory. OU marched 46 yards in seven plays following Taylor's first oskie. Lott scored on a one-yard run midway through the period.

With less than a minute to play, the Sooners were backed up to their own goal. Von Schamann, back to punt, was ordered to take an intentional safety and not risk a turnover. This gave OU a 35-22 lead with 41 seconds remaining.

Von Schamann kicked off, and Stanford scored two plays later with eight seconds left on the clock. Stanford's onside kick slipped the grasp of two Sooners and Larry Harris recovered for the Cardinal. Ray's interception in the end zone ended Stanford's upset bid.

The Sooners inched up to third in the AP poll the next week. Oklahoma scored 31 unanswered points in the first 21 and one-half minutes en route to a 52-10 blasting of 1-0 West Virginia the next week in Norman. Many Sooner reserves got to perform for the 71,187 fans as early as the second quarter.

Sims carried only eight times for 114 yards and scored the first touchdown, a 41-yard run early in the first stanza. In less than two minutes, the lead swelled to 14-0. Ray's 33-yard interception return to the WVU eight led to backup halfback Jimmy Rogers' two-yard run two plays later. Von Schmann's field goal late in the first quarter and touchdowns by Rogers and backup quarterback J.C. Watts gave OU the 31-0 advantage.

Rogers scored his third TD, and Hicks shagged a Watts pass for a 45-3 lead early in the third period.

The Mountaineers scored twice in the final quarter against OU's third-string defense.

Oklahoma gained 314 yards on the ground and passed for 105. West Virginia picked up 212 yards.

Lott scored two touchdowns, and Watts added two more TDs as Oklahoma rolled over 0-2 Rice, 66-7, on September 23 in Norman. The Sooners scored 59 unanswered points through the first three quarters. Thirteen players contributed to the Sooners' 560-yard rushing total.

Oklahoma's defense held the Owls to 239 total yards. Rice got 66 of that on a fourth-quarter touchdown drive against the third string.

The Sooners moved atop the AP poll the next week. No. 1 Alabama had lost to Southern California, and No. 2 Arkansas defeated Oklahoma State, 19-7.

Sims rushed for 166 yards and scored four touchdowns as the Sooners dropped 2-1 Missouri, 45-23, in the conference opener and homecoming in Norman. His first two touchdowns came in the first quarter on runs of 41 and 49 yards, respectively. The next two were one-yard plunges. He also had a 78-yard TD run erased by a penalty. Von Schamann kicked the first of six conversions and set an NCAA record for 88 straight extra-pointers.

Overstreet had the longest touchdown run that counted. His 64-yarder late in the third stanza put Oklahoma ahead, 45-9. The Tigers scored twice in the fourth period.

The Sooners amassed 484 rushing yards and passed for 32. Mizzou collected 463 total yards.

No. 1 Oklahoma and No. 6 Texas (3-0) were both undefeated heading into the Red River rivalry in the Cotton Bowl. Rice, a 34-0 loser to the Longhorns in the season opener, was the only common opponent the Sooners and Steers had played.

Sims scored the first two Sooner touchdowns to lift his team to a 14-0 lead.

Russell Erxleben toed a 26-yard field goal in the second period to put the Horns on the board. Von Schamann answered with a 35-yarder as the first half ended, moments after Ray intercepted a Texas pass.

Hunt picked off a Texas screen pass at the OU 47 in the third quarter. Eleven plays later, Lott connected a 24-yard TD pass to Kimball. Texas scored late in the third stanza, and Overstreet added a touchdown late in the fourth.

OU rushed for 311 yards and added 99 more through the skies. The defense held the Steers to nine first downs, 191 total yards, recovered two fumbles, and picked off three passes.

Sooner Magic: Holding on to Number One

College football, as in any sport, is about winning—not losing and not tying. Credit Bud Moore, the Kansas head coach, for going for the win in the 1978 contest against the Sooners. If Moore's team had succeeded in making the two-point conversion in the final seconds of the game, his team would have toppled the No. 1-ranked team in the nation.

The 1-4 Jayhawks were heavy underdogs to the undefeated Sooners. But Oklahoma was without the services of four offensive starters—King, Lott, Rhodes, and Hicks. In the Texas game, Lott suffered a sprained ankle, King had a hip pointer, and Rhodes had a bruised shoulder. Hicks pulled a hamstring in practice a few days before the Kansas game. The Sooners were also without the services of backup halfback Jimmy Rogers and Taylor for the second straight game. Rogers injured his foot, and Taylor had a sore neck.

Needless to say, OU turned in a sloppy performance offensively (three fumbles and two interceptions) before 43,490 fans at Memorial Stadium in Lawrence, Kansas.

The Sooners held a two-game winning streak over the Jayhawks.

Kansas fumbled the ball on its first two possessions and OU fumbled on its first possession.

Von Schamann booted a 19-yard field goal and OU took a 3-0 lead late in the opening period. Watts fired a 48-yard scoring strike to Freddie Nixon on the next possession for a 10-0 lead. Another rout was on...or was it?

The Jayhawks marched 70 yards to cut the lead to 10-7 midway through the second stanza.

The Sooners drove 66 yards late in the third quarter and into the fourth for a 17-7 lead. Sims capped the drive with a nine-yard slant off right tackle, and von Schamann converted.

Kansas added a field goal with 10:17 remaining and moments after recovering Nixon's fumbled punt return.

The ensuing kickoff sailed through the end zone for a touchback. The Sooners marched to the KU 10, but had to rely on von Schamann's foot to put the game away, but he shanked the 27-yard attempt.

Late in the game, Kansas took Ray's punt at its 49, but an interference penalty gave KU an extra 15 yards to the Sooner 36. On fourth-and-12 at the 38, quarterback Harry Sydney fired a pass to Jimmy Little who rambled to the five-yard line.

Sydney then tossed two incompletions, one that was intentional to stop the clock. On third-and-goal, Sydney lobbed a pass to Kevin Murphy, who beat out Jay Jimerson in the end zone for the score.

Fifteen ticks remained on the clock.

Moore ordered a two-point conversion to win the game and stun the nation by knocking off the nation's No. 1 team. The Hawks took too long to get the play off and were flagged for delay of game, moving the ball from the three-yard line to the eight.

Moore changed his mind and decided eight yards was too many to try to win the game. His team would still pull off a moral upset if his kicker made the conversion. OU jumped offside, forcing a bad snap to KU holder Mark Vilendese. Vilendese scrambled to find a receiver to throw to, but the Sooners knocked down the airborne football. Oklahoma was penalized five yards for the encroachment, and officials replaced the ball at the three-yard line.

Take three: Moore changed his mind once again and ordered the two-point conversion. Sydney took the snap and was forced to hurry his throw to Murphy. The ball sailed over Murphy's head, and the Sooners held a 17-16 advantage.

The Hawks forced the Sooners to nearly have a cardiac arrest as they retrieved the ensuing onside kickoff. Officials ruled that the ball was not ready for play and ordered the Hawks to kick it again. This time OU's Rod Peguos grabbed the bounding pigskin to seal the victory.

Sims' 192-yard rushing performance led the Sooners' 356-yard ground attack, and Watts added 93 through the air. Kansas picked up 257 total yards.

Sims rushed for 231 yards on 20 carries, almost half of the team's 466 total, to lead the Sooners to a 34-6 victory over 4-2 Iowa State on October 21 in Ames. The Cyclones began the season 4-0, then lost two straight before Oklahoma came to town.

Lott scored two of Oklahoma's three first-quarter touchdowns. His nine-yard run gave the Sooners a 7-0 lead. King scored on a 15-yard run for the next score, and Lott scored his second TD on a one-yard run with 1:02 left in the opening period.

Although the Big Red defense allowed 252 total yards, it kept the Cyclones in check and provided the OU offense with short drives. The Sooners just had to average 53 yards per scoring drive.

"Our defense did a great job," Switzer said. "We controlled their offensive game."

After ISU got on the board early in the second quarter, von Schamann nailed two field goals in the same period. Sims' 63-yard jaunt set up the first field goal. Von Schamann also was successful on all conversion kicks, extending his streak to an NCAA-record 103.

The final tally came in the third quarter following the Cyclones' 13-yard punt to their 23-yard line. Watts replaced Lott, who left the game with a twisted ankle. Two plays later, Sims scored from 20 yards out.

The Big Red added 44 yards passing, and the defense held the Cyclones to 252 total yards.

OU rolled past 2-5 Kansas State, 56-19, the next week in Norman. Sims ran for 202 of the team's 465 rushing yards. He crossed the end zone twice in the first period to give his Sooners a 14-0 advantage. Cumby's 40-yard interception return for a touchdown put OU ahead, 21-0, about two and a half minutes later.

After the Wildcats got a touchdown early in the second quarter, Lott scored on an eight-yard run and later tossed an eight-yard pass to Hicks.

Lott, who suffered a stubbed toe in the second stanza, did not return to action in the second half. Watts did a fine job replacing him by scoring two TDs in the fourth quarter. K-State scored the only points (12) in the third period. Cumby blocked the conversion on the Cats' first TD, and K-State failed to make a two-point conversion on their second TD.

Third-string quarterback Kelly Phelps added another touchdown late in the game, and Von Schamann was true on all conversion kicks, extending his streak to 111.

The Sooners still maintained their No. 1 ranking, which was in jeopardy in the first half against 6-2 Colorado. OU had only 78 total yards in the first half and turned the ball over four times (three fumbles and one interception). Three big plays in the second half gave the Sooners a 28-7 victory on November 4 before a record crowd of 53,553 at Boulder's Folsom Field.

Lott's eight-yard run gave OU a 7-0 lead in the opening stanza.

Three Lott turnovers gave Colorado an opportunity to blow the game open in the second quarter, but the Oklahoma defense rose to the occasion, yielding only seven points.

Lott lost a fumble at the CU 23 late in the second period, and the Buffs scored five plays later.

Colorado intercepted Lott's pass on the next possession, but had to surrender on downs at the OU 13.

Lott made a bad pitch out on the next OU possession, and Colorado recovered at the Sooners' nine. Jimerson intercepted the Buffs' pass in the end zone with 18 seconds left in the first half.

Three long-distance plays in the second half helped OU to blow the game wide open. Sims scored on a 59-yard dash late in the third quarter. Moments later, corner back Babb intercepted a Buff pass at the CU 43. Eight plays later, Lott fired a 20-yard TD pass to tight end Forest Valora. Midway through the fourth quarter, King bolted past two defenders and raced 74 yards to the end zone.

Von Schamann made all extra-point kicks, raising his record to 115 straight. Sims rushed for 221 yards to become the first Big Eight player to gain more than 200 yards in three straight games. He was also the first player to rush for more than 200 against the Buffaloes.

Next up was No. 4 Nebraska in Lincoln. After losing their season opener to Alabama, the 8-1 Cornhuskers crushed their next eight opponents by an average of 46-14. The Sooners were riding a six-game winning streak against their northern rivals. Switzer and Nebraska coach Tom Osborne both became head coaches in the same year—1973. Switzer had never lost to Osborne until 1978.

Turnovers killed the Sooners' chance for another national title, a seventh straight win over the Huskers and Switzer's unblemished mark against Osborne. OU fumbled 10 times and lost six of them. The last one was most crucial, three yards from victory.

Sims flashed 44 yards to the end zone midway through the opening period to give the Sooners a 7-0 lead.

The Huskers tied the game early in the second quarter after recovering Lott's errant pitchout to Overstreet. Nebraska again cashed in on another Oklahoma fumble and took a 14-7 lead midway through the third stanza.

OU answered with a seven-play, 73-yard drive. On fourth-and-one at the NU 35, Lott made the yard for the first down but fum-

Nebraska's Jeff Hansen (48) strips the ball from Billy Sims on the Huskers' three-yard line. Jim Pillen recovered the ball for the Huskers.
(© 1978, The Daily Oklahoman)

bled to Nebraska. The Huskers were flagged for offside. Oklahoma maintained possession, with the ball moved to the NU 30. On the next play, Sims found a huge hole opened by Roberts and bolted untouched to the end zone for the tie.

The Sooners had outscored Nebraska, 80-0, in the fourth quarter of the past six contests, so the odds were in their favor to pull out the win. a 24-yard field goal gave the Cornhuskers a 17-14 lead with 11:51 to play, but two Sooner drives after that ended in Sims' fumbles. The first thwarted a 61-yard drive to the NU 20, and the second by Sims ended a 44-yard march to the Huskers' three.

Prior to the second fumble, OU faced third-and-seven from the Nebraska 18. Sims took Lott's pitch and scooted around end. Two defenders smacked him, as he reached the five, jarring the ball loose and Nebraska's Jim Pillen recovered at the three with 3:27 remaining.

"I just fumbled," Sims said after the game. "I don't know why, except that I just got careless while trying to get extra yardage down there (near the goal)."

Nebraska won 17-14 and held the driver's seat for the conference championship. The field was littered of smashed oranges hurled from the stands, as the winner would receive a bid to the Orange Bowl. Sims still had another terrific day, rushing for 153 yards in 25 carries to raise his season total to 1,553 yards, 112 yards behind Greg Pruitt's school record set in 1971.

OU picked up 339 yards rushing and failed to complete a pass in two attempts. The Huskers totaled 361 yards.

Sims accomplished the season rushing record with a 209-yard performance against Oklahoma State. He also scored four touchdowns to lead the Sooners to a 62-7 drubbing of the 3-7 Cowboys on November 18 in Norman.

Not only did the Hooks, Texas, product break the school record, he also broke the Big Eight Conference rushing record previously held by Oklahoma State's Terry Miller (1,680 yards). Sims achieved both feats in the first half.

The Sooners rushed 83 times for 629 yards and never punted. The defense held the Pokes to 187 total yards and 10 first downs.

It's a Fact

Oklahoma led the nation in rushing offense with a 427.5 per game average, 90 yards per game better than Nebraska, which was second. The Sooners also led the nation in scoring offense with a 40.0 point-per-game average.

Von Schamann converted eight straight extra-point kicks to finish with an NCAA-record 125 straight and 59 straight for the season.

Ray intercepted his seventh pass of the year to equal the school mark held by Zac Henderson (1977), Steve Barrett (1967), Darrell Royal (1947), and Huel Hamm (1942).

That same day, Missouri upset Nebraska, 35-31, to give the Sooners a share of the Big Eight crown with the Huskers. Then came stunning news. The Orange Bowl committee wanted a rematch between Oklahoma and Nebraska for New Year's Day. The committee called Switzer and asked if he would like a rematch.

The Sooners were penciled to play Houston in the Cotton Bowl. So Switzer asked his players if they would rather play in the Cotton Bowl or against Nebraska again.

"They said without a doubt they'd rather play Nebraska again," Switzer said.

Ten days following the OSU game, Sims became the sixth junior in NCAA history and third Sooner to win the Heisman Trophy. He edged Penn State quarterback Chuck Fusina by 77 votes. Sims was the only player in the top 50 rushers to average more than seven yards per carry in 1978. He gained 7.6 yards each time he carried the pigskin.

No. 4 Oklahoma defeated No. 5 Nebraska 31-24 in the 45th Orange Bowl, a game that wasn't as close as the score indicated. Nebraska gained more yards (437-339), but the Sooners gained 7.5 yards per play to Nebraska's 5.9. A sea of red dominated the crowd of 79,616 in attendance.

Each OU scoring drive was fast and furious—69 yards in 12 plays, 73 yards in seven plays, 70 yards in five plays, and 60 yards in nine plays. The Sooners, which lost six fumbles in the first contest, didn't fumble until late in the fourth quarter, and by that time the game had been decided.

The game was delayed a half-hour to allow the Rose Bowl to finish. Both games were broadcast by NBC.

The Huskers took the opening kickoff and moved 80 yards to take a 7-0 lead. The Sooners were unable to gain a first down on their first drive, but Sims carried eight times for 44 yards on the second possession, capping the drive with a two-yard TD run. He also gained a crucial first down with an 11-yard run on third-and-five from the NU 35.

Lott scored on a three-yard run midway in the second period and von Schamann converted for a 14-7 lead. Lott sailed a 38-yard pass to Rhodes one play before he scored.

The Sooners exploded for 17 points in the third period. OU needed only 90 seconds following the second-half kickoff to strike again. Sims bolted 11 yards to the end zone, running over safety Russell Gary along the way. Lott sparked the 70-yard drive with a 38-yard run one play before the touchdown.

About a minute later, Ray intercepted Nebraska's pass and returned the ball to the NU 27. Rain began falling over the Orange Bowl, and the Sooners had to settle for a 26-yard von Schamann field goal for a 24-7 lead.

After the Huskers kicked a field goal, Oklahoma countered with another score, capped by Lott's two-yard TD run. Von Schamann nailed his fourth conversion of the night, lifting his streak to 129.

Nebraska scored twice in the fourth quarter, the final tally with no time remaining. The Sooners had defeated every team they played in 1978. Sims finished the game with 134 yards on 25 carries.

OU rolled up 292 yards on the ground and threw for 47. Nebraska gained 417 total yards.

"You're the best team in the nation," Switzer told his troops after the game. "You are the only team that can say you beat every team you played."

But the pollsters didn't see it that way. Two other teams with one loss each were voted above OU. Alabama, which dethroned No. 1 Penn State in the Sugar Bowl, was voted national champions. Southern California was second and the Sooners third.

Sims was the Associated & United Press College Player of the Year; he was also consensus All-America, Walter Camp Foundation's Player of the Year, Davey O'Brien Award recipient, Helms and Citizens Savings Athletic Foundation Player of the Year, and *Sport Magazine*'s Player of the Year. He led the nation in rushing (1,762 yards), and scoring (10.9 points per game).

Hunt, Kinlaw, and Roberts were also named All-Americans. Joining them on the All-Big Eight first team were Lott, Von Schamann, Ray, Cumby, Mathis, and Phil Tabor.

1979

The buzz among Sooner fans was about Billy Sims and could he become the second player to win two Heisman Trophies? He could become the first player to do so since Ohio State's Archie Griffin did it in 1974-1975.

But the Hooks, Texas, running back would have to accomplish the feat behind some new linemen. Outland Trophy winner and All-America guard Greg Roberts and tackle Sam Claphan graduated on the left side of the line. Juniors Terry Crouch and Louis Oubre earned the guard and tackle spots respectively. Fullback Kenny King also graduated to provide blocking help. Barry Joyner replaced him, but freshman Stanley Wilson would emerge as the starting fullback in midseason. Quarterback Thomas Lott also graduated, but junior J.C. Watts had plenty of experience as his backup in 1978.

Junior Forest Valora replaced All-Big Eight tight end Victor Hicks. Steve Rhodes received a medical hardship and returned at split end. David Overstreet returned to complement Sims in the backfield.

George Cumby, a converted fullback, provided speed and leadership at linebacker. Daryl Hunt graduated, but Barry Dittman stepped up to fill his shoes. Tackle Richard Turner and end Bruce Taton returned to the front line. Gone was Reggie Kinlaw, who was

1978 Season Record: 11-1-0

Big Eight Conference: 6-1-0 (Champions)

Date	Opponent	Result	Score
September 9	at Stanford	W	35-29
September 16	WEST VIRGINIA	W	52-10
September 23	RICE	W	66-7
September 30	MISSOURI	W	45-23
October 7	Texas at Dallas	W	31-10
October 14	at Kansas	W	17-16
October 21	at Iowa State	W	56-19
October 28	KANSAS STATE	W	56-19
November 4	at Colorado	W	28-7
November 11	at Nebraska	L	17-14
November 18	OKLAHOMA STATE	W	62-7
January 1	Nebraska*	W	31-24

*Orange Bowl at Miami, FL

replaced by Johnnie Lewis. John Goodman provided solid leadership at tackle. The entire secondary returned, but Darrol Ray was moved to safety alongside Sherwood Taylor. Mike Babb and Basil Banks rounded out the secondary at the corners.

Uwe von Schamann graduated from doing double duty as placekicker and punter. John Hoge inherited the placekicking duties, and Darrol Ray earned the punting slot.

The Sooners opened the season ranked third in the AP poll. Iowa, their first opponent on September 15 in Norman, featured a hard-hitting freshman defensive back named Bob Stoops.

The Sooners were unimpressive in their 21-6 opener. The running attack was plagued by fumbles, losing five of seven in the game and three straight in the third quarter. So the Sooners took to the air. Watts completed 10 of 17 for 183 yards, connecting on five of his first seven.

Iowa recovered a Sims fumble at the Hawkeyes' 25 and drove the length of the field for a 6-0 lead.

Midway through the second period, Watts was temporarily knocked out of the game after throwing a pair of 13-yard strikes to Freddie Nixon and Valora. Sophomore Kelly Phelps came in to complete the 10-play, 80-yard drive. Phelps hurled a 28-yard pass to Valora, then ran for 16 yards in the drive. Sims' one-yard TD run capped the drive, and Hoge booted the extra point to give the Sooners a slim 7-6 margin, which remained through the fourth quarter.

Sims, who rushed for 106 yards, and Watts added touchdowns in the fourth stanza, but head coach Barry Switzer was unhappy with his team's execution. "Where we had field position, we should have scored five or six touchdowns," he said.

The Sooners rushed for 269 yards, and the defense held Iowa to 202 total yards.

No. 3 Oklahoma dominated with the Wishbone attack in a 49-13 blasting of 2-1 Tulsa the next week in Norman. The Sooners rushed for 446 yards and averaged nearly seven yards per run.

Although losing six fumbles, the Sooners had no trouble finding the end zone and rolled up a 21-0 lead in the first stanza. Watts scored on a 26-yard run, Sims on a 25-yard jaunt, and Wilson on a 12-yard run. The Golden Hurricane kicked a field goal early in the second period, and junior halfback Jay McKim added another touchdown for OU minutes later.

Trailing 28-3 at the half, Tulsa closed the gap with a touchdown and a field goal in the third quarter, but OU put the game away with three TDs in the fourth period.

Watts led the ground attack with 122 yards on 20 carries, and Sims gained 109 on 11 touches of the pigskin playing for only a quarter and a half.

Oklahoma rolled up 446 rushing yards and passed for 27. The Hurricanes collected 236 total yards.

Sims scored three touchdowns in the first period and rushed for 103 yards as the No. 3 Sooners dropped 1-2 Rice, 68-21, on September 29 in Houston. This was the first time Oklahoma had visited Rice since 1938.

Watts scored two TDs, and Phelps added another to lift the Sooners to a 42-0 halftime advantage. The reserves got to play in the second half. McKim and Chet Winters each added a TD in the third stanza. In all, 12 players carried the ball for Oklahoma, and 23 players were credited with tackles.

OU, which had fumble-itis in the first two games (losing 11 of 14) didn't fumble the ball away until twice in the fourth quarter.

The Sooners amassed 359 yards on the ground and threw for 44. Rice gained 404 total yards.

The Big Red returned home on October 6 and hammered 1-3 Colorado, 49-24, coached by former OU head coach Chuck Fairbanks. Fairbanks left the New England Patriots to coach the Buffs earlier in the year.

The Sooners scored on their first four possessions, with Sims crossing the goal line three times. Only twice during those four possessions did they face third-down situations.

Oklahoma's first possession began at its own two after Colorado's punt rolled out of bounds. The Sooners drove 98 yards in 10 plays to take a 7-0 lead. The Buffaloes tied the game late in the opening period then OU scored four TDs in the second stanza—Sims twice and Watts and Overstreet once.

Sims, who rushed for 188 yards, scored his fourth TD of the day to give OU a 42-10 lead late in the third quarter. Freshman Mike Keeling replaced the injured Hoge and nailed all seven extra-pointers. He also earned the punting chores and averaged 45 yards in four kicks against the Buffs.

Oklahoma rushed for 396 yards and passed for 48. The Buffs collected 277 total yards.

No. 4 and undefeated Texas (3-0) defeated the No. 3 Sooners, 16-7, the following week in Dallas. Texas held OU to only six first downs and 201 total yards. During the first four games, the Sooners averaged 22 first downs, 367 ½ yards rushing and 443 total yards.

Sims' streak of rushing more than 100 yards in 13 games did not reach 14 against the Steers. Sims was held to 73 yards on 20 carries. Still, he was the Sooners' leading rusher.

Oklahoma scored its only points minutes after Texas took a 3-0 lead late in the first quarter. The Steers' Johnnie Johnson fumbled Keeling's punt at his 16-yard line. On third-and-five at the UT 11, Watts fired a pass to Wilson alone in the end zone. Wilson dove for the ball in the back of the end zone to give the Sooners a 7-3 lead after Hoge's conversion.

Texas jumped to a 10-7 lead late in the second period after intercepting Watts' pass.

The Big Red defense bent, but did not break, limiting Texas to two field goals in the fourth quarter. Ray had an interception at the OU 17 and returned the ball 31 yards to squelch one Texas drive. He also had a fumble recovery at the OU nine after Banks stripped the ball from Johnnie "Jam" Jones.

The Sooners dropped to eighth in the AP poll.

Smith and Wesson could have been the sponsor of the next four Oklahoma games as the Sooners scored 38 points consecutively, the first a 38-6 victory over 2-3 Kansas State on October 20 in Manhattan.

Kansas State led 6-3 at the half, and the Sooners gained only four first downs and 113 total yards. OU shot like a .38-caliber revolver in the second half by scoring five touchdowns, gaining 20 first downs and totaling 415 yards. The Cats were held to 45 yards in the second half after gaining 157 in the first 30 minutes.

Watts, who led with 118 rushing yards, scored two TDs in the third stanza. He scored on a one-yard run to cap an 80-yard drive after the second-half kickoff. His next TD was an 18-yard run to complete a 77-yard march.

Sims played with bruised ribs, making it hard for him to breathe, and was limited to 67 yards on 10 carries. He did score a touchdown on a five-yard run early in the fourth quarter to give OU a 24-6 lead. That score was set up by Wilson's 49-yard run to the KSU 31. It was the longest run of the day.

Phelps also gained over the century mark (112 yards) and scored two fourth-quarter touchdowns.

Nearly two and one-half minutes after Sims' TD, Phelps' 14-yard run capped a 52-yard drive in three plays sparked by his 33-yard pass to Valora. Phelps' 36-yard run late in the game capped a 70-yard drive in four plays.

OU hammered out 436 yards rushing and passed for 83. The defense held the Cats to 202 total yards.

The Sooners bashed 2-4 Iowa State, 38-9, the following week in Norman. Donnie Duncan, an assistant under Switzer from 1973-77, was the Cyclones' head coach.

Sims ran for 202 yards, caught a 42-yard pass, scored four touchdowns and appeared back in the Heisman hunt. Sims moved into second place in career touchdowns with 44, surpassing Joe Washington. He also moved into second in career points with 264, surpassing Buddy Leake.

The Sooners scored five touchdowns on their first eight possessions, and another drive was squelched by an interception. Sims' first two scores came on four-yard runs and both times capped 94-yard drives. Keeling toed a 24-yard field goal late in the first half for a 17-0 lead.

Sims' 12-yard TD run and Watts' 31-yard scoring strike to Bobby Grayson, put the Sooners up 31-0 in the third period. Sims' fourth TD, a seven-yard run, came early in the fourth quarter. The Cyclones cashed in two fumbles for nine points in the final three minutes.

OU rushed for 493 yards and passed for 73. Keeling punted twice for a 55.5 average. I-State picked up 279 total yards.

The Big Red crushed Oklahoma State, 38-7, on November 3 in Stillwater. Two Watts' bombs got the Sooners going early. His first, a 49-yarder to Valora, set up Sims' four-yard scamper. Minutes later, Overstreet lined up in the wing, and Watts sailed a pass to the streaking halfback for a 72-yard TD.

OU's defense forced five interceptions (four in the first half) and two fumbles. Two interceptions also thwarted two Poke drives late in the first half. Cumby stole two OSU passes, and Ray's pick set up another Sims touchdown for a 21-0 advantage late in the first quarter. Keeling's 39-yard field goal late in the opening period gave the OU three more points with 1:04 still remaining in the opening stanza.

Sims added two more touchdowns in the third period. The Cowboys scored their only points on a TD in the fourth quarter.

The defense, led by Goodman's 15 tackles and fumble recovery, also held the Cowboys to 81 net rushing yards (1.6 per average) and pushed the Pokes back for 62 yards.

The Sooners inched up to sixth in the AP poll and blasted 3-5 Kansas, 38-0, the next week in Norman before a homecoming crowd of 71,882. It was Oklahoma's first shutout in five years.

OU took a 17-0 lead through the first three quarters. Keeling booted a 30-yard field goal midway through the first stanza, and moments after Babb recovered a Jayhawk fumble. Goodman returned a Kansas fumble 56 yards for a touchdown to give the Big Red a 24-0 advantage with 9:54 left in the fourth. Taylor forced KU quarterback Kevin Clinton to fumble. Clinton cocked his arm to throw, but he lost his grasp of the ball, and Goodman snatched it in midair and sailed to the end zone.

The Sooners' two backup quarterbacks—Phelps and Darrell Shepard—each scored a TD in the fourth period. Phelps scored on a one-yard run and Shepard on a 60-yard dash. Just two weeks earlier, the Big Eight Conference declared Shepard eligible after leaving the University of Houston during a recruiting scandal.

Kansas quickly moved to the OU 19-yard line, but again Taylor pressured Clinton to misfire his pass.

The Big Red rushed for 348 yards and passed for 33. Sims gained 128 yards on 23 carries. The defense held the Hawks to 184 total yards.

Sooner Magic:
Poor Kicking Aides Sooners' Fortune

The Sooners dropped to seventh in the AP poll before traveling to Columbia the next week to face 5-4 Missouri. The Tigers made a game of it in every category except for the kicking department. Missouri's Ron Verrilli missed an extra point and a field goal, and another kicker missed another field-goal try. Had either field goal made it through the uprights, the Sooners might not have escaped with a 24-22 victory.

Verrilli, however, nailed a 39-yard attempt to give the Tigers a 3-0 lead early in the opening period.

The Big Red responded with an 80-yard march in 17 plays, capped by Overstreet's two-yard TD run. Keeling kicked the first of three conversions.

The Tigers answered with an 80-yard drive for a 9-7 lead, but Verrilli's extra-point attempt was wide right.

The Tigers had scored twice in their first two possessions. OU coaches changed the defense to a six-man front to stop the run, leaving only three players in the secondary. It didn't work as Phil Bradley shredded the OU defense by completing 16 of 23 for 222 yards, including six of his first six passes.

"Their game plan was to go to those two big backs and then underthrow our coverage," Ray said. "It bothered us all day."

The Tigers threatened late in the second period but stalled and tried another kicker for a 45-yard field goal. Jeff Brockhaus' attempt was off the mark.

Sims, who rushed for a career-high 282 yards, scored on a 70-yard run early in the third period to put OU back on top, 14-9. Sims bolted to his left, cut back to his right, eluded one tackler with a 360-degree spin and shot to the end zone.

The Tigers marched to the OU 21, but Verrilli missed a 37-yard field-goal attempt. OU took over at its 21 and drove 79 yards in 12 plays for a 21-9 advantage. Again Sims picked up crucial first downs in the drive, capped by Watts' five-yard touchdown run on an option keeper. Sims carried the ball 11 times for 154 yards in the third period.

Missouri again retaliated this time with a 76-yard march and Verrilli made good on this extra point.

Keeling booted a 33-yard field goal to lift the Sooners to a 24-16 lead with 10:20 remaining in the game.

Four plays following the kickoff, Bradley scored on a 68-yard TD run to cut the Sooner lead to 24-22 with 9:01 to go. Ray was the only Sooner in pursuit, but a pulled hamstring ended his chase at the OU 15. The Tigers elected to go for two to tie the game. Goodman and Barry Burget pressured Bradley, who was looking for a receiver. He sailed the pass to tight end Andy Gibler, but Jay Jimerson swatted the ball away.

Missouri drove 49 yards to the OU 25, but the Sooner defense held. Verrilli was called to kick a 37-yard field goal, but the ball fell short of the target with 2:21 remaining.

The Sooners rushed for 390 yards and passed for 37. Mizzou gained 460 total yards.

The winner of the next week's OU-Nebraska matchup would play in the Orange Bowl, and the loser would play in the Cotton Bowl.

The No. 3 Cornhuskers rolled into Norman on November 24 with nary a blemish in 10 games. The Cornhuskers led the nation in rushing (356.2 yards per game) and rushing defense (67.2 yards per game). The Sooners, led by Sims' 247 yards, rushed for 352 yards, six yards each time they touched the ball against a defense that held opponents to 1.6 yards per carry.

Sims did not score a touchdown. Well he did, but it was called back when Nixon was flagged for clipping Andy Means, who pursued Sims. Means stopped in front of Nixon, forcing the Sooner to draw the foul.

"He was running down the field, and I guess he figured Billy was gone," Nixon said. "I wasn't going to make any attempt to block him. He just cut in front of me. I didn't touch him at all. In fact, his foot kicked me when he fell."

A disappointed Sims stood in the end zone with his hands on his hips, dejected that he didn't get the score. His 68-yard TD run was wiped out, and the ball was placed back at the OU 30. Watts then fired a bomb to Valora in the end zone, but Means intercepted.

After a scoreless first quarter, Oklahoma took a 3-0 lead on Keeling's 31-yard field goal early in the second stanza. The Huskers answered with a 59-yard drive for a 7-3 lead. Keeling missed a 35-yard field-goal try late in the second period, and Nebraska held its advantage at intermission.

The Sooners recaptured the lead, 10-7, when Watts connected on a 58-yard pass to Valora early in the third quarter. Valora was wide open at the Husker 30 and scored untouched.

Nebraska later drove to the OU 18, but Dean Sukup missed a 35-yard field goal.

Early in the fourth period, a Nebraska punt was killed at the OU six. The Sooners covered the length of the field in eight plays. Sims sparked the drive with a 71-yard run to the NU eight-yard line. Nixon had thrown the key block to set Sims free, but safety Russell Gary caught him from behind. Sims lay on the field after the run. OU trainers ran to his aide, but Sims was fine. Facing fourth-and-goal at the three, Watts kept the ball, ran to his left, then shifted right to the end zone to give the Sooners a 17-7 lead.

The Huskers then drove into Oklahoma territory. On third-and-14 at the OU 15, Nebraska coach Tom Osborne reached into his bag of tricks. He ordered what was known as the "fumblerooski," a hidden ball play. Quarterback Jeff Quinn took the snap from center Kelly Saalfield, then placed the ball at the center's left foot. Right guard Randy Schleusener scooped up the pigskin and rumbled around left end to the end zone. He knocked over Babb as he fell across the goal line.

The play had the Sooners fooled.

"I didn't even see it until I saw the guy going into the end zone," said OU defensive tackle Keith Gary.

The play was nothing new according to Osborne. It was taken from a 1937 play designed by Vanderbilt assistant Henry Frnka. Frnka said he used the play while coaching at Greenville (Texas) High school in 1933. He said he learned about it in the 1920s. The play was again used to score a touchdown against LSU in 1937. Officials had no be notified that the play would be possible in that game, and Osborne had informed officials he might use it against the Sooners.

OU thwarted two late Nebraska drives to seal the victory. Babb intercepted a pass at the Nebraska 45, and Bruce Taton batted away Quinn's fourth-down pass with nine seconds left.

Nebraska's undefeated season and national championship hopes ended at Owen Field for the fourth time. The Sooners beat the undefeated Cornhuskers in 1964, 1966, 1975, and 1979. OU was not the only team to spoil the Cornhuskers' season. Each of those years, they also lost their bowl game.

The Sooners were crowned Big Eight Champions and nearly every year in the 1970s, either OU or Nebraska won or shared the Big Eight title, except for 1976 when the Huskers did not win the Big Eight.

The Orange Bowl invited Florida State to meet the Sooners on January 1. The 11-0 Seminoles enjoyed their first ever undefeated season. Oklahoma was making its 21st bowl appearance, 11 times (including three straight) in the Orange Bowl.

Before that New Year's night of 1980, most Sooner fans may remember Bud Hebert as the holder for Uwe von Schamann's game-winning field goal against Ohio State in 1977. He was one of the first to raise his arms on national television when the ball was heading for the goal posts.

Hebert played sparingly at safety and split end during his three-year tenure. He caught one pass against Tulsa earlier in the '79 season and caught another a week later against Rice. On defense, he had 26 tackles, one interception (against Iowa State) and broke up three passes. Injuries depleted the Big Red secondary before the Orange Bowl, so Ray was moved to cornerback, and Hebert started at free safety. This was only his second start for the Sooners at safety.

For Hebert, a senior from Beaumont, Texas, it was a night he will not forget—three interceptions, which remain an Orange Bowl record today. He was also named defensive player of the game. The Sooners used a nickel package (five defensive backs) most of the night. The result—Florida State quarterbacks only completed eight of 27 for 100 yards.

The No. 5 Sooners overwhelmed the No. 4 Seminoles, 24-7, but at first it didn't appear that way. OU lost a bowl-record four fumbles, the first one after Banks returned a punt 59 yards to the FSU 10. When Scott Warren caught him from behind, Banks spilled the pigskin, and the Seminoles recovered in the end zone for a touchback.

The Noles then drove 76 yards in 12 plays to jump to a 7-0 lead late in the first quarter.

Moments later, Bobby Butler blocked Keeling's punt, and FSU recovered at the OU 17. Facing third down at the seven, Hardis Johnson caught Jimmy Jordan's pass, and Hebert hit him, jarring the ball loose. Officials ruled it an incomplete pass. Florida State attempted a field goal, and Cumby nailed kicker Dave Cappelen as he tried to pick up the botched snap.

At that point, the Seminoles had gained eight first downs to OU's one, and the Noles completed six of 11 passes for 76 yards. Following the bungled field goal, Florida State managed only four first downs, completed two of 16 passes for 24 yards and scored nary a point.

1979 Season Record: 11-1-0
Big Eight Conference: 7-0-0 (Champions)

Date	Opponent	Result	Score
September 15	IOWA	W	21-6
September 22	TULSA	W	49-13
September 29	at Rice	W	63-21
October 6	COLORADO	W	49-24
October 13	Taxas at Dallas	L	16-7
October 20	at Kansas State	W	38-6
October 27	IOWA STATE	W	38-9
November 3	at Oklahoma State	W	38-7
November 10	KANSAS	W	38-0
November 17	at Missouri	W	24-22
November 24	NEBRAKSA	W	17-14
January 1	Florida State*	W	24-7

*Orange Bowl at Miami, FL

The Sooners then moved 81 yards in four plays, highlighted by Watts' 61-yard TD run early in the second period. Keeling kicked the tying point.

Thirty-six seconds later, the Sooners took a 14-7 lead. Hebert robbed Jordan's pass at the FSU 35 and returned it 25 yards. The Noles were offside on the first play, then Wilson took the handoff, collided head on with defensive tackle Jeremy Mendlin and was knocked back to the 10. He regained his balance, spun out of a tackle, and leaped into the end zone.

Keeling later nailed a 24-yard field goal to give Oklahoma a 17-7 lead at intermission.

OU's final tally came in the fourth quarter off a 99-yard, 11-play drive that consumed 7:19 off the clock. From the FSU 34, Watts gained 12 yards, then flipped the ball to Sims who raced 22 yards for the touchdown.

The Sooners rushed for 411 yards and passed for 36. Sims rushed 24 times for 164 yards, but Watts was named the game's best offensive player with his 127-yard performance on 15 carries.

Oklahoma finished the season with an 11-1 mark and third in the AP poll behind Alabama and Southern California for the second straight year. Alabama became the second team to win two consecutive national championships. Oklahoma was the first to do so, but the Sooners capped the 1970s with a 102-13-3 record to be the best team of the decade.

Sims placed a distant second to USC's Charles White in the Heisman Trophy balloting. Sims and Cumby were selected All-Americans. Oubre, Paul Tabor, Goodman, and Ray joined them on the All-Big Eight Conference first team.

MASCOTS

Mex

Beginning in 1915, a bark could be heard joining spectators' approval following each Sooner touchdown. The added approval came from a Boston terrier named Mex. The canine was adopted as the mascot for the OU football and baseball teams.

Mott Keys, an army hospital medic found the stray dog in Mexico in 1914 during the Mexico Revolution unrest. Keys was stationed at the Mexican border near Laredo, Texas. One night he found the dog among a litter of abandoned puppies on the Mexican side. Keys' company adopted the dog, and when Keys completed his duty, he took Mex with him when he moved to Hollis, Oklahoma.

Mex also accompanied Keys to Norman when his owner attended the University of Oklahoma. The canine's experience as an army medic company mascot landed him the job with the football team and a home in the Kappa Sigma fraternity house.

Mex's main duty was to keep stray dogs from roaming the field during a game. He wore a red sweater with a big white "O" letter on the side. No fences were erected around Boyd Field, so Mex was on guard during games, warding off stray dogs from roaming the field during a game.

Mex began to gain national attention in October of 1924 after OU lost a game to Drake University, 28-0. The Sooners also lost Mex. Mex did not board the train heading home in Arkansas City, Kansas. Rumors spread across the Missouri Valley, the conference OU played in at the time, that Mex was returning to attack the Drake Bulldogs and avenge the loss.

A 50-cent reward was offered, and upset OU graduates J.D. Hull, Hughes B. Davis and J.C. Henley found Mex. Mex was discovered pacing on the train station platform in Arkansas City. The men drove Mex to the next Saturday game at Stillwater. After non-

Sooner fans once poisoned Mex, the dog learned to eat only from the hands of his caretakers.

Mex died of old age on April 30, 1928, and he was so popular among students and faculty that the university closed for his funeral and procession on May 2, 1928. He was buried in a small casket somewhere under the existing stadium. *Courtesy: SoonerSports.com*

Little Red

An Indian mascot known as "Little Red" began appearing at Sooners football games in 1953. Clad in red tights, breech cloth, and war bonnet, Little Red began dancing on the Sooner sideline in 1953. A student member of Indian descent would portray Little Red over the years.

In April 1970, Little Red was banished by OU president J. Herbert Hollomon as the school's sanctioned mascot. Hollomon, who made the decision under pressure by some Indian students, said he made the decision because, "It is degrading to Indians."

On September 18, the student court of the University of Oklahoma issued a temporary restraining order to keep Randy Palmer, who portrayed Little Red, from appearing at Sooner games.

Little Red, however, danced at the season opener against Wisconsin, because Palmer's attorneys said their client had not received the petition filed against him. Thousands of fans cheered Little Red when he appeared at the Badger game. Palmer was later held in contempt of the student court. Many Indians voiced their support for Palmer. The charges against Palmer were later dropped. A group of 16 Indians in October urged OU regents to reinstate Little Red on the sideline.

The Sooner Rally Council changed Little Red's title from mascot to rally leader and Palmer continued to dance at Sooner games through the 1971 season. Little Red faded away when the army drafted Palmer and no one showed up for try-outs to replace him for the 1972 season.

Sooner Schooner

The Conestoga, or covered wagon, was the mode of transportation for many pioneers to settle unclaimed land in Oklahoma Territory during the Land Run of 1889. The Sooner Schooner is a Conestoga reminiscent of such mode of travel. The Schooner is powered by matching white ponies named Boomer and Sooner, and it ventures onto Owen Field in a triumphant victory ride after OU scores.

Although the Schooner was introduced in 1964, it did not become the official mascot until 1980. The Schooner is well recognized by college athletics fans across the country and makes regular appearances at university functions. *Courtesy: SoonerSports.com*

Mex, a Boston terrier, was the Sooners mascot from 1915 to 1927. *(OU Athletics)*

1980 - 1989

1980

With nine starters returning to the offense, the Sooners were a favorite to claim a ninth straight Big Eight Championship and a fourth straight Orange Bowl appearance. The Big Red would have to overcome question marks on defense, especially at the linebacker and end positions.

Billy Sims had graduated, but halfback David Overstreet returned to lead the backfield along with quarterback J.C. Watts. Stanley Wilson and George "Buster" Rhymes were among the new faces in the backfield who would be generating headlines in 1980. The line was solid with the return of tackles Louis Oubre and Ed Culver; guards Terry Crouch and Don Key; and tight end Forest Valora. Bill Bechtold replaced Paul Tabor, who graduated, at center. Bobby Grayson and Steve Rhodes returned to share split end duties.

The defensive line was solid with the return of tackles Richard Turner and Keith Gary and noseguard Johnnie Lewis. Cornerback Basil Banks was the only other starter back for another season, but Ken Sitton and Jay Jimerson had plenty of experience as backups in 1979. George Cumby and Barry Dittman, the team's two leading tacklers in 1979, had graduated, and a pair of Mikes (Reilly and Coast) replaced them.

Mike Keeling returned to again pull double duty as placekicker and punter.

The Sooners were ranked fifth in the preseason AP poll but moved up to fourth a week later above Southern California. Neither team had yet to play a game.

OU opened the season on September 13 with a 29-7 victory over Kentucky before a crowd of 75,668 on a hot (98 degrees) and muggy afternoon. This was the second meeting between both schools. The Wildcats spoiled the Sooners' perfect season with a 1951 Sugar Bowl win.

Oklahoma lost two of three fumbles in the first five minutes of the '80 matchup. The third led to Kentucky's only touchdown. Kentucky's score came moments after recovering Steve Haworth's fumble. Haworth intercepted a Wildcat pass, but fumbled after returning it to the OU 18. Kentucky held the 7-0 lead through halftime.

Keeling missed two field goals to get the Sooners on the board. The Wildcats threatened to take a two-touchdown lead with a drive to the OU 11, but on fourth-and-inches, Lewis torpedoed through All-America center Ken Roark and dropped quarterback Randy Jenkins for a loss.

Watts, who completed six of 10 passes for 168 yards, left the game briefly with a deep thigh bruise in the third period, and Darrell Shepard engineered an 80-yard march to tie the game. Chet Winters scored on a 13-yard run to cap the 10-play drive and Keeling converted.

Sherdeill Breathett's fumble recovery on the UK 28 set up the next Big Red score early in the fourth quarter. Overstreet took Watts' lateral and scored from the three. Keeling kicked the conversion.

Moments later, Keeling's punt rolled dead on the UK one. Quarterback Terry Henry, under a heavy rush of crimson jerseys, threw the ball away from the end zone. This resulted in an intentional grounding penalty and a safety for the Sooners, and a 16-7 lead.

Watts later scored a 12-yard TD run and hurled a 74-yard scoring strike to Grayson. Keeling missed the conversion after Watts' TD run.

Oklahoma rolled up 410 total yards. The defense held Kentucky to eight first downs and 219 total yards. Grayson caught three passes for 119 yards, and Keeling averaged 45.4 yards on seven punts.

The weather was 43 degrees cooler, and Owen Field was rain-soaked two weeks later as the Sooners hosted Stanford. Sophomore quarterback John Elway showered the Big Red defense for 237 yards and three touchdowns as the 2-1 Cardinal defeated the Sooners, 31-14.

Elway guided his team mostly from the shotgun formation and completed 20 of 34 aerials, scrambled for 95 yards and scored once himself. After a scoreless first period, Stanford took a 17-0 lead by halftime. Elway hurled two TD strikes to Andre Tyler in the third stanza for a 31-0 advantage.

Watts scored on a one-yard run late in the third quarter to cap a 90-yard drive and tossed a two-point pass to Valora. Watts added another one-yard touchdown early in the fourth stanza, but Stanford knocked down his two-point pass.

The Sooner defense had six possible interceptions dropped. The offense lost five of six fumbles. Stanford gained more total yards (457-341).

The No. 12 Sooners traveled to Boulder on October 4 and defeated 0-3 Colorado, 82-42. A host of NCAA records fell, including the most touchdowns scored by two teams (18).

Scoring was fast and furious. A touchdown was scored every three minutes and 20 seconds in a game that lasted three hours and 25 minutes. Leading the Sooners were Rhymes with four touchdowns, and Winters and Shepard scored two apiece.

Oklahoma scored on its first five possessions in the first half and first seven in the second half. After OU took a 14-0 lead, the Buffs' Walter Stanley returned the ensuing kickoff 100 yards. Shepard, who scored on a 64-yard run, also had the longest TD run from scrimmage at 89 yards. Jerome Ledbetter returned a kickoff 99 yards for the final Sooner tally.

OU amassed 35 first downs, rushed for a national-record 758 yards and 876 in total offense, also an NCAA record. The Sooner backs averaged 10.4 yards each time they touched the pigskin, and Oklahoma did not punt once. Colorado gained 330 total yards and also did not punt. Six NCAA records, five Big Eight records, and seven OU records were broken in the game. Overstreet, who tallied one touchdown, carried the ball 18 times for 258 yards, Shepard added 151 on three carries, and Rhymes picked up 110 yards on nine carries.

The third-ranked and undefeated Texas Longhorns (4-0) took advantage of Sooner turnovers in a 20-13 victory the following week at the Cotton Bowl. OU had eight turnovers, six in the first half. Watts lost three fumbles and threw four interceptions in the game.

Texas cashed in two of Watts' fumbles to take a 10-0 lead in the first half. The Steers were not perfect as they turned the ball over six times in the game. Keeling toed a 43-yard field goal midway in the third period after Sitton recovered a Steer fumble.

Minutes later, Lewis recovered a fumble on the Texas 48 to set up the tying touchdown four plays later. Wilson darted 36 yards for the score on the second play of the fourth quarter, and Keeling converted.

OU advanced to the Horns' 16 thanks to a 38-yard run by Wilson, and a facemask penalty at the end of the play moved the ball to the UT eight. Texas' defense stiffened, and Keeling booted a 21-yard field goal for a 13-10 lead.

The Steers answered with a 76-yard scoring drive to retake the lead, 17-13, and later added a field goal with 1:45 left. Watts tossed an interception to end Oklahoma's hopes of a comeback.

Texas picked up more total yards (348-290). Wilson rushed for 172 yards on 18 carries.

Turnovers continued to plague the No. 17 Sooners on October 18 against Kansas State. OU lost six fumbles, yet defeated the 2-3 Wildcats, 35-21, in Norman.

Rhymes returned the opening kickoff 100 yards for a touchdown to set the school record. He broke Jerome Ledbetter's record of a 99-yard return against Colorado earlier in the year. Keeling missed the conversion.

The Sooners marched 68 yards in seven plays on their next possession. Watts' four-yard scamper capped the drive. Watts then tossed a two-point pass to Wilson for a 14-0 lead.

The Wildcats recovered Watts' fumble on the OU 13 to set up their first score early in the second stanza. Darrell Dickey tossed the first of three scoring strikes for Kansas State.

The Sooners responded with a 52-yard drive for a 21-7 lead. Watts scored on a two-yard run, and Keeling kicked the first of the next three conversions. Ryhmes' 21-yard run and Overstreet's 11-yard scamper sparked the six-play drive.

Dickey hurled two more TD passes in the third and fourth quarters to cut OU's lead to 28-21. The Cats tried an onside kick, but Rick Bryan fielded the bounding ball on his 37-yard line. The Big Red launched a nine-play scoring drive from there. Rhymes' one-yard plunge finished the drive, which began with Wilson's 38-yard run.

Keeling punted to the K-State one on the next OU series, but Dickey got them out of the hole with a 54-yard pass to the OU 45. Freshman noseguard Danny Wilson intercepted Dickey's pass on the next play.

Oklahoma picked up more total yards (548-311). Watts carried 22 times for 137 yards.

After turning the ball over 26 times (18 fumbles) in the first five games, the No. 17 Sooners did not lose the ball once as they pounded Iowa State, 42-7, the following week in Ames. Oklahoma did fumble three times but didn't lose any of them.

The 5-1 Cyclones had won five straight before dropping a decision to Kansas the week before the OU tilt. ISU took a 7-0 lead midway through the first period.

Overstreet's 14-yard TD run and Keeling's conversion tied the game late in the first half. Keeling was perfect on six extra points.

Watts scored three touchdowns in the second half. His 45-yard run lifted OU to a 14-7 lead in the third quarter. Wilson scored on a 53-yard run late in the third quarter.

Jimerson's 39-yard punt return set up Watts' one-yard plunge nine plays later. Two interceptions led to the final two Oklahoma touchdowns.

Oklahoma picked up 388 total yards, all on the ground. Wilson gained 160 yards on 24 totes. Iowa State was held to 71 total yards.

No. 6 North Carolina rolled into Norman on November 1. The 7-0 Tar Heels' defense, featuring linebacker Lawrence Taylor, had yielded only one touchdown in seven games and held their opponents to an average of 77 rushing yards per game. The 16th-ranked Sooners scored six touchdowns and rushed for 495 yards to hammer the Heels, 41-7.

Oklahoma led 14-7 at the half, then rolled up 20 points in the third quarter as the Tar Heels could not stop the speedy Oklahoma backs. Watts scored three touchdowns and rushed for 139 yards to lead the Big Red assault. Three of Oklahoma's touchdowns came on fourth-down gambles.

The turning point in the game came on the second-half kickoff. Overstreet grabbed the ball as he retreated to the end zone, but fearing a safety, he brought the ball back to the playing field. An official blew his whistle before Overstreet retreated to the end zone and placed the ball on the three. The Sooners rolled 97 yards in 10 plays for a 21-7 lead. On third-and-four at the nine, Weldon Ledbetter exploded for a 51-yard run to the NC 40. Watts capped the drive with a seven-yard run. Ledbetter replaced Wilson, who left the first quarter with an injured shoulder. Ledbetter rushed for 122 yards in the game.

OU picked up 25 first downs, and Watts did not complete a pass in two attempts. The Heels gained 258 total yards.

The victory bumped the Sooners to 11th nationally, but they squeaked by Kansas, 21-19, the next week in Lawrence.

A field goal put the 3-3-2 Jayhawks ahead, 3-0, early in the first period. Oklahoma answered with two touchdowns. Watts scored on a 22-yard run, and Overstreet scored on a two-yard run. Keeling kicked the first of three conversions.

Kansas closed the gap with a field goal late in the first half.

Overstreet scored on a 10-yard run early in the third stanza, moments after Orlando Flanagan snared his second interception of the game.

The Jayhawks scored a TD in the fourth quarter after recovering Overstreet's fumble.

Kansas had a shot late in the game with the ball on their 21, but three passes fell incomplete, and the Jayhawks punted, to the dismay of their fans.

OU collected more total yards (427-340). Overstreet and Weldon Ledbetter each rushed for 86 yards. Keeling punted eight times and averaged 57.9 yards per kick.

Overstreet, Weldon Ledbetter, and Wilson sat out the Missouri game on November 15 due to injuries. The Sooners defeated the 6-2 Tigers, 17-7, before a homecoming crowd of 75,325 in Norman.

The Sooners marched 85 yards in six plays for their first touchdown in the second quarter. Rhymes, who rushed for 132 yards, took Watts' pitchout and scored from the five-yard line. Winters, subbing for Overstreet, sprinted 56 yards to the MU five to spark the drive. Keeling toed the first of two conversions and later added a 35-yard field goal for a 10-0 halftime advantage.

The Sooners had two chances to extend their lead in the third period, but Watts spilled the pigskin on the MU 13, and Keeling later missed a 40-yard field goal.

Oklahoma drove 84 yards in nine plays to notch its 17th point midway through the final stanza. Rhymes took Watts' pitch, sailed 55 yards down the sideline and followed Winters' key block for the score.

The Tigers advanced to the OU 12 after the kickoff, but the Big Red defense stiffened. A punt return to the OU 20 later set up Mizzou's only score.

Oklahoma had more total yards (386-210).

OU rose to ninth in the AP poll, but the next opponent was fourth-ranked Nebraska at 9-1. The Big Eight Conference title and an Orange Bowl bid were on the line, although the Sooners had one more game left against Oklahoma State. The Sooners held a two-game winning streak in the series against NU.

Sooner Magic: Déjà Vu

The *Merriam Webster Dictionary* defines déjà vu as the feeling that one has seen or heard something before. That was never truer than the 1976 and 1980 Oklahoma-Nebraska football games.

In each of those years, Oklahoma defeated Nebraska in Lincoln in the final minute of play. Each time by a player who wore the No. 4 jersey. Elvis Peacock, who scored the winning TD in 1976, was from Miami, Florida. Buster Rhymes, who scored the winning TD in 1980, was from the same hometown. And both played the right halfback position.

Nebraska was a 12-point favorite in the 1980 contest, but Oklahoma edged the Cornhuskers, 21-17, on November 22. The Cornhuskers took a 10-0 lead in the first quarter before a crowd of 76,322 fans in Lincoln and a regional television audience. ABC network broadcast the game to a majority of the nation.

The Huskers drove 99 yards, capped by Jarvis Redwine's 89-yard run, and added a field goal eight minutes later.

Oklahoma drove 68 yards to cut the deficit to 10-7 late in the second stanza. Watts scored on a three-yard jaunt and Keeling kicked the first of three extra points. Winters also scored on a three-yard run and OU led, 14-10, with 1:47 until halftime.

Both offenses sputtered in the third quarter. Nebraska made only four first downs and OU zero. Both teams had scoring opportunities, but the defenses rose to the occasion.

Nebraska threatened midway through the fourth quarter, but Darrell Songy recovered a fumble inside the OU 10-yard line. The Sooners gained only two yards in three plays and Keeling's punt carried only 14 yards to the 17.

Redwine spun around for 10 yards. Andra Franklin gained four more yards to the three, but Songy was flagged for a personal foul, and officials placed the pigskin at the one. Two plays later, quarterback Kevin Quinn followed the block of center Dave Rimington and sneaked across the goal line. Kevin Seibel's extra point put the Huskers back on top, 17-14, with 3:16 to play in the game.

The ensuing kickoff sailed into the end zone resulting in a touchback, and the Sooners set up shop at their own 20.

Rhymes gained two yards, but a late hit by NU's Derrie Nelson gave OU 15 more yards to the 37. Wilson fumbled after gaining a couple of yards, but three Huskers were unable to grasp the football. Luckily, Oubre did, covering the pigskin at the Sooners' 43.

On second-and-four, and 2:45 on the clock, two crucial blocks helped OU make a big play. Watts optioned right; Winters took out defensive end Jimmy Wilson, and Wilson laid out cornerback Rodney Lewis. Safety Sammy Smith was a step away from tackling Watts, who suddenly pitched to Rhymes, who blazed downfield. He slightly lost his balance and was tackled at the NU 14-yard line.

"I just kept telling myself, 'No Fumble! No Fumble!'" Rhymes said following the game.

With 2:32 on the clock, Wilson banged ahead for three yards, then Winters lost three yards on an option pitch. Watts, who injured his hand early in the game, said he hoped offensive coordi-

nator Galen Hall would not call a pass play on the third-and-10 situation. The call? A pass to split end Bobby Grayson.

Watts fired a short pass to Grayson, who cut toward the sideline inside the five. Grayson caught the ball and slid out of bounds at the one with 1:20 remaining.

Rhymes was stopped for no gain up the middle. Watts optioned right and, with the help of key blocks by Oubre and Valora, pitched to Rhymes, who leaped over the goal line with 56 seconds on the clock. Keeling's toe gave the Sooners a 20-17 lead.

But the Huskers were not giving up and neither were the churning stomachs of spectators.

Nebraska began at its own 14 after the kickoff. Quinn fired two completions for a total of 25 yards, then was stopped for no gain on a keeper. With 24 seconds left, Quinn heaved a desperation bomb downfield to tight end Steve Davies inside the Sooner five. Songy and Jimerson covered Davies on the play. The three leaped for the ball, which deflected off their hands and landed into Songy's hands at the two.

Watts kneeled down to kill the clock, and for the ninth time in 10 years, Nebraska felt the wrath of the Sooners once again.

"Oh boy, it's so sweet," Barry Switzer said. "There were so many big plays on that final drive ... the fumble, Grayson's catch, J.C.'s execution, Rhymes' big run. This is one of the greatest victories."

Oklahoma rushed for 249 yards and passed for only 26. The Huskers gained 390 total yards.

The sixth-ranked Sooners hammered 3-6-1 Oklahoma State, 63-19, the next week to claim the outright Big Eight championship in Norman. Watts scored four touchdowns to lead the conference in scoring with 18 TDs for the season. The 18 tallies also tied Steve Davis for most touchdowns by an OU quarterback. Jerome Ledbetter added three TDs in the game.

The Sooners intercepted Poke quarterback Jim Traber three times, and the Cowboys also lost two fumbles. Three turnovers led to short Oklahoma TD drives, and the Sooners took a 28-7 lead by halftime. The Pokes scored when they blocked Keeling's punt and recovered it in the end zone.

The Big Red picked up 519 total yards. Rhymes gained 105 yards on 12 carries. The defense held the Cowboys to 165 total yards (19 rushing).

Sooner Magic: Sneak Attack

The success of Oklahoma football in the 1970s and 1980 was the potent wishbone running weapon that won 86 percent of its games in that 11-year span. Since installing the wishbone in 1970, the Big Red ran nearly nine of ten plays on the ground.

The passing game was the real wizardry of winning many games. So how can a team that predominately concentrates on a running attack pull out a victory with the pass? It's like a surprise attack, similar to a boxer constantly throwing a right, then sneaking in a left hook. Such was the case in the 1981 Orange Bowl against the Florida State Seminoles.

The 10-1 Noles had outscored their opponents by an average of 32 to 7. After winning their first three games, Florida State stumbled, 10-9, to the Miami Hurricanes. But the Noles did rebound by winning their next seven games. Like Oklahoma, they defeated Nebraska during the season (18-14) and also handed highly ranked Pittsburgh its only loss of the season.

The defense of the second-ranked Seminoles had contained OU's offense most of the night, but still the fourth-ranked Sooners managed to keep the game close with their own solid defense.

Both teams missed a field goal in the first quarter in the 47th Orange Bowl Classic before a crowd of 71,043 in Miami, Florida.

The Noles took a 7-0 lead with 49 seconds until halftime. The Sooners then marched to the FSU 37 and Keeling booted a 53-yard field goal to end the half and close the deficit to 7-3. Keeling's field goal broke the Orange Bowl record of 44 yards set by Louisiana State's Chris Bahr in 1974.

Oklahoma took the second-half kickoff and drove 78 yards in 12 plays, using up six minutes. From the FSU four-yard line, Watts pitched the ball to Overstreet, who followed Rhodes' block and swept across the goal line. Keeling nailed the extra point and OU led, 10-7, with 8:59 left in the third quarter. Watts had a 20-yard run to spark the drive and overcome a fourth-down situation.

The Noles added a field goal minutes later after recovering a fumble at the OU 17.

Early in the fourth period, OU's offense stalled, and Keeling set up to punt. The ball sailed through his hands and rolled into the end zone where FSU's All-America cornerback Bobby Butler smothered it to add six more points for his squad. Bill Capece's kick was good, and Florida State led, 17-10, with 11:07 left in the game.

The Noles were feeling very confident at this point, because their defense had not allowed opponents to score in the fourth quarter all season.

The Sooners would get maybe one final chance with 3:19 to go and the ball at their own 22. Watts tossed a screen pass to Overstreet off the right side for seven yards. On the next play, the Seminoles' Arthur Scott sacked Watts for a six-yard loss.

On third-and-nine, Watts found Rhodes open at the FSU 48. After the catch, Rhodes eluded a couple of Seminole defenders and gained 13 more yards to the FSU 35. The irony here was that Rhodes was unsure he was going to get to play in the game due to a pulled hamstring. Coaches drew up that pass play at halftime.

On the next play, Watts overthrew split end Jim Rockford on a fly pattern in the end zone. With 2:03 left on the clock, Watts completed to Chet Winters for 14 yards to the FSU 21. On the next play, three Seminole defenders rushed Watts, who lobbed the ball toward Winters. FSU's Garry Futch got between Watts and Winters and had a chance to intercept the pass but juggled the pigskin and couldn't hold on. If he had, no one was between him and the goal line.

On second-and-10, Watts was bottled up in the backfield, then took off to his left and scrambled for an 11-yard gain and out of bounds at the 10 with 1:38 remaining. Watts then passed to Rockford in the end zone, but FSU linebacker Jarvis Coursey

stepped in front of the OU receiver and, he too, could not hold on to the football.

On the next play, Watts rolled right and fired the ball to Rockford, who dove to the ground, clutching the ball in the end zone.

"I told the coaches to get the two-point play ready," Coach Switzer said as his Sooners trailed by one, 17-16.

Again Watts sprinted right and lofted the ball to Valora all alone in the end zone. Oklahoma led, 18-17, with 1:27 left.

"We were going to leave it on the field," Watts said after the game. "Win or lose—no tie."

"It felt so good to catch that ball," Valora said.

Watts, who was knocked unconscious in the third quarter, completed four passes in the go-ahead drive of nine plays covering 78 yards.

Florida State took the kickoff and marched to the OU 45. With five seconds left, Capece attempted a 62-yard field goal, but the kick lost its zip, and the ball dropped short of the goal posts.

"It's just unbelievable ... a great finish," Switzer said.

Watts, who completed seven of 12 passes for 128 yards and ran for 48, was named the game's most valuable player for the second straight year. He also received the honor for his performance in OU's 24-7 win over Florida State in the 1980 Orange Bowl.

The Big Red picked up 284 total yards in the Seminole sequel. The Noles collected 263 total yards.

The Sooners finished the 1980 season 10-2 and ranked third in the nation behind Pittsburgh and No. 1 Georgia in the AP and UPI polls. Crouch and Oubre were named All-Americans. Valora and Turner joined them on the all-conference first team.

1981

With an inexperienced squad, the 1981 Sooners would be hard pressed to win their 10th straight Big Eight championship. Five starters returned to the offensive line—tackle Ed Culver, guards Terry Crouch and Don Key, and center Bill Bechtold. Lyndle Byford started at right tackle after playing as a reserve the previous two years.

Kelly Phelps beat out Darrell Shepard for the starting quarterback nod, but Shepard would see plenty of action, especially when Phelps went out with a midseason injury. Fullback Stanley Wilson and halfback Buster Rhymes returned to lead a stable of young but speedy backs.

Mike Reilly was switched from linebacker to defensive end to make room for two highly touted sophomore linebackers—Jackie Shipp and Thomas Benson. Noseguard Johnnie Lewis returned to anchor the middle of the defensive line. Defensive tackle Scott Dawson missed the entire season after first contracting mononucleosis and then suffering a knee injury. Tackle Rick Bryan, another sophomore, would make an impact on defense. Darrel Songy and Elbert Watts returned to head the secondary, although Songy would be dismissed from the team in midseason. Steve Haworth would miss the entire season due to a groin injury. Freshman Keith Stanberry would step up and earn starting time at cornerback and at safety. Mike Keeling returned as placekicker and punter.

Wilson did not start in the September 12 opener against Wyoming due to a pulled muscle. Wilson, however, did play, and picked up 71 yards rushing. The Sooners defeated Wyoming, 37-20, in Norman and on a new artificial turf, which was installed during the summer at a cost of $350,000.

The 1-0 Cowboys took a 10-0 lead in the first stanza. Keeling's 42-yard field goal and Rhymes' 39-yard TD run tied the game mid-

1980 Season Record: 10-2-0
Big Eight Conference: 7-0-0 (Champions)

Date	Opponent	Result	Score
September 13	KENTUCKY	W	29-7
September 27	STANFORD	L	31-14
October 4	at Colorado	W	82-42
October 11	Texas at Dallas	L	20-13
October 18	KANSAS STATE	W	35-21
October 25	at Iowa State	W	42-7
November 1	NORTH CAROLINA	W	41-7
November 8	at Kansas	W	21-19
November 15	MISSOURI	W	17-7
November 22	at Nebraska	W	21-17
November 29	OKLAHOMA STATE	W	63-19
January 1	Florida State*	W	18-17

*Orange Bowl at Miami, FL

way through the second period. Wyoming jumped ahead, 13-10, on a field goal with five minutes until intermission.

The Sooners responded with an 80-yard drive two and one-half minutes later capped by Phelps' seven-yard touchdown for a 17-13 lead.

Wyoming drove 80 yards to take a 20-17 lead midway through the second quarter, but the Sooners rolled up three touchdowns to put the game away in the second half. Shepard scored two touchdowns (on runs of 23 and three yards) and threw a scoring strike to Rhymes. Keeling kicked four of five conversions; the fourth was blocked.

OU rushed for 452 yards and passed for 62. The Cowboys picked up 254 total yards.

No. 1 Southern California (2-0) scored a touchdown with two seconds remaining to defeat the second-ranked Sooners, 28-24, on September 26 before a throng of 85,651 at the Los Angeles Coliseum and a regional television (ABC) audience. OU lost five of 10 fumbles; two that wasted possible scoring chances and another led to a USC touchdown.

Oklahoma took a 7-0 lead midway through the first stanza on Phelps' 11-yard run and Keeling's conversion. The Sooners later marched to the Trojans' 23-yard line, but fumbled on the 21. USC recovered and drove 79 yards to the tying touchdown. Marcus Allen, who rushed for 208 yards, scored on a 27-yard run. Allen won the Heisman Trophy later in the season.

Shepard replaced Phelps at quarterback and guided the Sooners to 17 points. OU jumped to a 14-7 lead on Wilson's one-yard plunge midway through the second period to cap an 81-yard drive and Keeling kicked a 27-yard field goal on the next series.

USC scored before halftime after recovering Watts' fumbled punt return.

Shepard's seven-yard run gave OU a 24-14 lead early in the fourth quarter. The Trojans scored two more TDs on drives of 74 and 78 yards. John Mazur lobbed a seven-yard scoring strike to Fred Cornwell for the deciding tally.

Oklahoma gained more total yards (444-395).

The Sooners dropped to fifth in the AP poll and hosted No. 20 Iowa State (3-0) the next week in Norman. Both teams battled to a 7-7 tie which snapped OU's 19-game win streak over the Cyclones. It was Oklahoma's first tie since a 6-6 deadlock with Texas in 1976, and the first conference tie since a 14-all knot in 1964.

The Sooners were plagued with five fumbles, and Shepard threw two interceptions.

OU rolled 69 yards in six plays on its second possession. Freshman halfback Steve Sewell's 16-yard run capped the drive and Keeling converted. Phelps ignited the drive with a 19-yard run on the first play.

One Oklahoma drive stalled on the ISU 20, and another drive fizzled when Keeling missed a 47-yard field goal.

Iowa State tied the game midway through the final stanza after intercepting Shepard's pass on the OU 46.

With the wind at his back, ISU's Alex Giffords, considered one of the best kickers in the Big Eight Conference, missed a 23-yard field goal with 1:08 left in the game. The Cyclones got the ball back with four seconds left and Giffords missed a 62-yard try.

OU picked up more total yards (334-323). Wilson (157) and Phelps (106) both crossed the century mark in rushing yards. Dwayne Crutchfield gained 171 for the Cyclones.

The Sooners dropped to 10th in the AP poll, then dropped a 34-14 decision to Texas on October 10 before a throng of 75,587 in the Cotton Bowl and a national TV audience. OU blew a 14-3 halftime

lead as the No. 3 Longhorns (3-0) scored 31 unanswered points in the second half.

Flubbed assignments, penalties, and a couple of fumbles doomed the Big Red. The Sooners cashed in on two Steer fumbles for both scores. The first came when Keeling's opening kickoff bounced off John Walker's chest. John Truitt recovered on the UT 16, and Chet Winters scored three plays later. Keeling kicked the first of two conversions.

After Texas kicked a field goal in the second period, Bryan recovered a Texas fumble on the UT 34. Wilson scored on a one-yard run seven plays later. Wilson was the first Sooner to score a touchdown in three straight games against Texas.

The Horns drove 80 yards after the second-half kickoff to narrow their deficit to 14-10. Texas soon recovered a fumble, which led to another field goal.

The Steers scored three more touchdowns the rest of the way. Texas picked up 330 yards to 194 for Oklahoma.

The Sooners disappeared from the AP poll and hosted Kansas the following week. The 4-1 Jayhawks won their first four games, then lost to Oklahoma State a week before the OU contest. The Big Red hammered Kansas, 45-7, to even the season record to 2-2-1.

Sewell replaced Winters, who sat out with a sore toe. Sewell scored the first Sooner touchdown on a 17-yard run midway through the first stanza to cap a 91-yard drive. Keeling kicked the first of six conversions.

The Jayhawks answered with an 80-yard scoring drive to tie the game at 7-7. Kansas was held to only three first downs and 128 yards the rest of the way.

Keeling's 37-yard field goal late in the second period put the Sooners ahead for good at 10-7. Alvin Ross scored the first of two TDs moments later with a two-yard run for a 17-7 lead. Sewell sparked the 64-yard, two-play drive with a 62-yard dash on the play before.

Phelps twisted his ankle and did not play in the second half or in the next three games. Shepard replaced him and scored two touchdowns. Rhymes scored once, and Ross got his second TD in the second half.

Oklahoma rushed for 464 yards and passed for 58. Sewell led a pack of 13 Sooner ball carriers with 107 yards on the ground. Keeling punted three times and averaged 56 yards per kick. The Jayhawks picked up seven first downs and 213 total yards.

Songy was dismissed from the team for missing some team meetings.

The Sooners rolled up a 35-0 halftime lead en route to a 42-3 victory over 1-5 Oregon State on October 24 in Norman. Wilson, who rushed for 124 yards, scored two touchdowns, and Shepard ran for one score and passed for another.

Already leading 7-0, OU scored three times in a span of less than three minutes late in the first quarter and into the second to blow the game wide open. Shepard's 10-yard run put the Sooners up 14-0 late in the first period, then Watts scored on a 39-yard interception return in the first 1:17 into the second stanza. Watts returned the Beavers punt 52 yards to the OSU 19, and Shepard hurled a scoring strike to tight end Jeff Williams on the next play.

Wilson scored his second touchdown just before halftime. Neither team put any points up in the third quarter, and Oregon State kicked a 25-yard field goal early in the fourth period for its only tally of the afternoon. Three minutes later, freshman fullback Fred Sims romped 45 yards for the final Sooner score. Keeling kicked all six conversions.

OU collected more total yards (382-358). Shepard led the rushing with 105 yards on 14 carries.

Mike Reilly, who was booted off the team a year before and given a second chance, was dismissed from the team five days later for disciplinary reasons. Reilly had not played in the past two games because of a pinched nerve.

The Sooners went 4-2-1 with a 49-0 victory over 2-5 Colorado the next week in Norman. Fog in the first half gave way to dark skies and a torrential downpour in the final 30 minutes. All but about 10,000 fans had left when the rain, which turned Owen Field into a sheet of water, did not let up.

OU scored once in the opening stanza and twice in each of the last three periods. Shepard led the scoring fray with three touchdowns. The Sooners had 94 yards in interceptions, 30 more than what the Buffs threw to their own receivers.

Colorado quarterback Steve Vogel was sacked six times for minus-41 yards, and noseguard Danny Wilson had three sacks. Three turnovers led to Oklahoma touchdowns.

The Big Red gained 348 total yards, all on the ground. Shepard, who failed to complete a pass in four tries, led OU in rushing with 132 yards. The Buffs picked up 194 total yards.

The No. 17 Sooners traveled to Manhattan on November 7 in hopes of moving to 5-2-1 on the season with five offensive starters out of the contest. Winters had a sprained toe, Bechtold suffered a sprained knee, split end Jim Rockford a pulled calf muscle, and Weldon Ledbetter had a hip pointer.

Sooner Magic: Surviving a Sneak Attack

A cat moves slowly and quietly when it is about to pounce on its prey. The Wildcat nickname was fitting for the Kansas State football team as it sneaked up on the Oklahoma Sooners with a 21-0 lead in the first 28 minutes and 19 seconds of their 1981 match up.

A loss to Kansas State would have been one of the most embarrassing moments in Barry Switzer's career. The Oklahoma Sooners rarely lose to the Wildcats, and Switzer had not lost to them since he took the reins as Oklahoma's head coach in 1973.

Kansas State was a traditional cakewalk for the Sooners nearly every year since the two began meeting on the gridiron in 1908. OU owned the Cats to the tune of 51-11-4 in the series through 1980. After the Sooners lost back to back in 1969 and 1970, they won 10 straight by no less than two touchdowns. The series was so lopsided that OU won 34 straight between 1937 and 1968 and 35 of 36 save for a tie in 1936.

The 17th-ranked Sooners were heavy favorites. The Cats, meanwhile, had won only two of eight games, but the week before the OU contest, they upset 10th-ranked Iowa State, 10-7.

The mostly partial, purple-clad audience of 33,200 watched their Wildcats scratch to the three-touchdown lead, then witnessed another Sooner magical comeback.

Kansas State drove 80 yards in 20 plays and ate more than 10 minutes off the clock following the opening kickoff. The Cats kicked onside, recovered the ball and marched 43 yards to a 14-0 lead.

K-State scored its third TD midway through the second period after recovering Russ' fumble on the OU 39.

KSU tried another onside kick, and recovered at the OU 42. OU's defense pulled itself together and stopped the Wildcats' fourth-and-four gamble at the 36-yard line with 5:33 left in the half.

Ross scored a touchdown late in the first half and again late in the third stanza. Keeling missed the kick after the first TD, but Rhymes scored a two-point conversion to cut K-State's lead to 21-14.

The Sooners finally got a break when KSU's Phil Switzer (no relation to the OU skipper) fumbled Keeling's punt. Switzer lunged for

the descending pigskin but was unable to grasp it, and reserve guard Rocky Hubble smothered it at the KSU 33 with 8:36 remaining.

"That was the key," the Sooner head coach said of the game's turnaround.

OU drove 63 yards in six plays. Shepard tossed two key passes in the drive—one to Grayson for 26 yards and another to Ross for 13 yards.

From the K-State 20, Shepard throttled to the end zone, and Coach Switzer ordered another two-point conversion, but a K-State defender tipped Shepard's pass to Jeff Williams and OU trailed, 21-20, with 6:47 remaining.

A clipping penalty on the next Wildcat possession moved the ball back to their 32-yard line, and instead of third-and-three, they faced third-and-18. Dickey ordered his punter to quick kick. The kick resulted in 28 yards thanks to a favorable bounce backwards where the ball stopped at the OU 40.

Facing third-and-one at the OU 49-yard line, Shepard handed off to Rhymes, who picked up two yards and a first down. On the next play, Shepard optioned around right end, and aided by a crucial block by Williams downfield, jetted to the end zone. Keeling toed the extra point and OU led, 28-21, with 2:36 on the clock, which remained the final score.

"It just opened up ahead of me," said Shepard, of his game-winning touchdown. "I was going down the line and could see it open up. The further I went down the line, the more I could see 'em chopping 'em down in front of me."

"I think it helps us to make a comeback like that," Switzer said. "It's a win, and I don't care how you get it."

The Sooners gained 418 total yards, and K-State collected 358 total yards.

Missouri defeated the No. 15 Sooners, 19-14, the following week in Columbia. The loss eliminated OU from the Big Eight title chase and snapped an 11-game win streak over the Tigers. The Big Red lost six of nine fumbles, and Shepard tossed two interceptions.

The Sooners fumbled on their first three possessions. Mizzou kicked a field goal midway through the first period after recovering Wilson's fumble.

Shepard fumbled twice in Oklahoma territory, but the defense stiffened both times, and the Tigers missed a field goal after his first fumble.

OU rolled 61 yards in five plays to take a 7-3 lead late in the first quarter. Shepard's 14-yard run capped the drive, and Keeling converted the first of two.

The Tigers responded with a 79-yard scoring drive to retake the lead, 10-7, early in the second stanza. Minutes later, the Sooners were pinned deep, and Shepard, under pressure, was flagged for intentional grounding. This forced Keeling to punt from the back line of the end zone. He kicked to the MU 34, and the Tigers added a field goal moments later for a 13-7 advantage.

Missouri intercepted Shepard's pass on its 46-yard line late in the third quarter and scored three plays later for a 19-7 lead.

The Sooners advanced to the Tigers' 10 after the kickoff but fumbled.

Truitt recovered a Tiger fumble on his 47 late in the game. Four plays later, Shepard tossed a 46-yard scoring strike to Sewell. Missouri's Grant Darkow tipped the ball into Sewell's hands, and Sewell scored with 1:42 left in the game. Watts came up with the onside kick for the Sooners, but the Tiger defense stiffened.

Oklahoma rolled up more yards (397-341). Wilson gained 127 yards, and Shepard added 123 more to become the first OU quarterback to rush for more than 100 yards in four straight games. Shipp had 23 tackles to lead the Sooner defense.

Don Key had surgery five days later to remove a ruptured right kidney, which ended his career. Key, a starter in 33 straight games at right guard, injured the kidney in the Texas game. On Christmas, a day before OU played in the Sun Bowl, Coach Switzer announced that an award would be created in Key's honor.

The Sooners again dropped out of the AP poll and faced No. 5 Nebraska the following week in Norman. The 8-2 Cornhuskers walloped OU, 37-14, before a homecoming crowd of 75,833.

Oklahoma took the opening kickoff and wheeled 80 yards for a 7-0 lead. Rhymes' 20-yard run capped the six-play drive, and Keeling kicked the first of two conversions.

After a Husker field goal cut the lead to 7-3, the Sooners moved to the NU 35, but Shepard had to leave with a sore leg. Phelps returned for the first time since the Kansas game and fumbled on his first snap of the game. The Huskers recovered and drove 74 yards for a 10-7 lead with two seconds left in the first stanza.

Nebraska scored on its next two possessions and had a 24-7 lead. Oklahoma's second touchdown came early in the third period on Shepard's one-yard run, but the Huskers added another field goal and touchdown afterward.

Nebraska picked up more total yards, 462-350. Wilson rushed for 164 yards for the Sooners. NU quarterback Turner Gill completed 11 of 16 passes for 148 yards. Tailback Mike Rozier and fullback Roger Craig each rushed for more than 100 yards.

800th Game

The Sooners accepted an invitation to meet the Houston Cougars in the Sun Bowl in El Paso, Texas. Oklahoma defeated Oklahoma State 27-3 on November 28 in the 800th game in Sooner history. Fred Sims scored three touchdowns to lead the Sooners in scoring.

The Cowboys advanced to the OU 19 early in the first period, but Stanberry sacked Rusty Hilger for a seven-yard loss and then blocked Larry Roach's field-goal try. Benson picked up the blocked kick and returned it to his 38. The Sooners moved to the OSU two but fumbled on the one-yard line. Three plays later, Truitt intercepted Hilger's pass and scooted into the end zone. Keeling kicked the extra point.

OU marched 48 yards in eight plays for a 14-0 lead early in the second quarter. Sims scored his first TD on a two-yard run to cap the drive, and Keeling converted. Moments later, Benson intercepted another Poke pass and returned it seven yards to the OSU 33.

Sims scored on a five-yard run four plays later, but Keeling's kick was blocked.

OSU booted a 32-yard field goal with 32 seconds until halftime for the Pokes' only score.

OSU marched to the OU 33 in the third stanza, but on fourth-and-six, Lewis sacked Hilger for a 12-yard loss. Oklahoma took over and drove to the final touchdown with 2:35 left in the third period.

OU picked up more total yards (313-245).

The Houston Cougars recruited Darrell Shepard in 1977, but he later transferred to OU after an NCAA investigation found that Houston had been found guilty of recruiting irregularities. If Shepard stayed with the Cougar football team, he would not be allowed to play in any bowl games.

The Sooners crushed Houston, 40-14, on December 26 in the Sun Bowl before a less than capacity crowd of 33,816 in El Paso. Sims rushed for 181 yards (all in the second half) and scored one touchdown to break Leon Heath's bowl best of 170 yards in the 1950 Sugar Bowl. Shepard was named the game's most valuable player with a 107-yard rushing performance and two TDs.

Leading 10-7 after three quarters, the Oklahoma erupted for 30 points in the fourth. Darrell Shepard's 34-yard run put OU ahead 7-0 late in the first quarter, and Houston tied the game just before halftime.

The Cougars advanced to the OU 34 when Stanberry slapped the ball from the quarterback and Stanberry recovered in the 45. OU moved into field-goal range, and Keeling nailed a 32-yarder to put the Sooners up for good 10-7 late in the third stanza.

The Sooners later launched an 80-yard drive that culminated in Shepard's one-yard score early in the fourth period. Houston drove 74 yards to cut the lead to 27-14, but the Sooners scored twice more in the final two and one-half minutes.

Oklahoma OU rushed for 409 yards but had minus two in passing. The Cougars gained 385 total yards.

The 1981 Sooners finished 7-4-1, 20th in the final AP poll, 14th in the UPI poll, and placed second in the Big Eight Conference with a 4-2-1 mark. Crouch was the only Sooner selected as an All-American. Byford, Key, Wilson, and Bryan joined him on the All-Big Eight first team.

1982

For the Sooners to return to championship form in 1982, the offensive line would need to develop to provide blocking for the bevy of backs who returned. Barry Switzer's concern was that his offensive line lacked talent, strength, and experience. Only two starters returned to the front wall—guard Steve Williams and tackle Elbert Graham. Williams started at right guard in the final three games of 1981 when he replaced Don Key, whose career was cut short by kidney surgery.

Kelly Phelps returned to guide the backfield along with Stanley Wilson, Weldon Ledbetter, Fred Sims, and Steve Sewell. Wilson moved to left halfback, opening the fullback starting slot for Ledbetter. Highly recruited freshman Marcus Dupree would enter the starting lineup later in the season.

Switzer believed the defense would have to come through to help win some of the games and said he believed it was a "good total defensive unit." Returnees included tackles Rick Bryan and Bob Slater, end John Truitt, noseguard John Blake, and linebackers Jackie Shipp and Thomas Benson. Darrell Songy returned to the team after being suspended in mid-season a year ago. Buster Rhymes and Elbert Watts were suspended for stealing a teammate's stereo. Steve Haworth returned after a year off due to an injury.

1981 Season Record: 7-4-1

Big Eight Conference: 4-2-1 (Second)

Date	Opponent	Result	Score
September 12	WYOMING	W	37-20
September 26	at Southern California	L	28-24
October 3	IOWA STATE	T	7-7
October 10	Texas at Dallas	L	34-14
October 17	KANSAS	W	45-7
October 24	OREGON STATE	W	42-3
October 31	COLORADO	W	49-0
November 7	at Kansas State	W	28-21
November 14	at Missouri	L	19-14
November 21	NEBRASKA	L	37-14
November 28	at Oklahoma State	W	27-3
December 26	Houston*	W	40-14

*Sun Bowl at El Paso, TX

Keith Stanberry and junior college transfer Scott Case rounded out the secondary. Mike Keeling returned for punting and placekicking chores. He was challenged by David Culver, who saw limited time.

The No. 9 Sooners opened the season on September 11 with a 41-27 loss to West Virginia in Norman. Quarterback Jeff Hostetler riddled the OU defense for 321 yards and four touchdowns.

Two 80-yard drives put the Big Red ahead, 14-0, in the first quarter, but the Mountaineers scored 20 in the second period for a 20-14 lead at halftime. The Sooners regained the lead with an 80-yard drive after the second-half kickoff. Phelps scored his second touchdown of the game with a 23-yard run to complete the nine-play drive, and Culver's conversion gave Oklahoma a 21-20 advantage.

The Mountaineers responded with a 56-yard drive and Hostetler's third TD strike for a 27-21 lead. Minutes later, Songy blocked West Virginia's punt, and Stanberry scooped it up and raced 27 yards to tie the game. Keeling's conversion was blocked.

The Mountaineers scored twice in the fourth stanza to put the game away. The Mountaineers collected more total yards (458-420). The only shining statistic for the Sooners was Keeling's 43.3 average on six punts.

The Sooners dropped out of the AP poll but hammered 0-1 Kentucky, 29-8, the next week in Lexington. The crimson defense contributed nine points with a touchdown and a safety. Songy led the defense with two of four interceptions, one for six points.

Phelps left the first quarter with a rib injury, and Danny Bradley filled in and engineered two touchdown drives. OU rolled to a 22-0 lead through three periods on touchdowns by Steve Sewell, Bradley, a 40-yard interception return by Songy, and a safety.

Kentucky marched 80 yards late in the game for its only score, and Bradley scored on an 11-yard run for OU's final tally.

Oklahoma picked up 407 total yards, while the defense held the Cats to 268 total yards.

No. 18 Southern California defeated the Sooners, 12-0, on September 25 before a record throng of 76,758 in Norman. The 1-1 Trojans snapped Oklahoma's 181-game scoring streak and handed Barry Switzer his first goose egg as the Sooner skipper. OU had not been shut out since a 38-0 loss to Notre Dame in 1966.

The Big Red offense sputtered with only 43 rushing yards.

USC marched 45 yards in the first stanza for a 6-0 lead, but the extra point missed the target.

Kevin Murphy recovered a Trojan fumble on the USC 24 early in the second quarter. Phelps fumbled, and the ball, which was accidentally kicked back 34 yards to the OU 43-yard line, was recovered by Oklahoma. Phelps then hurled a 42-yard pass to split end David Carter, and Phelps got a first down with a one-yard run on the next play. The Sooners bogged down with a personal foul penalty, and Culver's 39-yard field-goal try was low.

A short USC punt gave OU possession on the Trojans' 28 moments later, but Phelps tossed an interception on the first play.

The Trojans scored their final tally with 6:43 left until intermission on a 67-yard end-around pass. Steve Haworth broke up the two-point pass.

The Sooners advanced to the USC 30 after the kickoff, but the Trojan defense stiffened. Moments later, Murphy recovered another Trojan fumble on the 26, but the drive fizzled after only a gain of five yards in four plays.

Oklahoma drove 69 yards to the USC three in the third period, but again the Trojan defense tightened.

USC gained more total yards (354-211). Keeling punted six times for a 45.2 average.

The 1-2 Sooners traveled to Ames on October 2 for the conference opener and evened their record with a 13-3 victory over 2-1 Iowa State. Cyclone coach Donnie Duncan lost his first conference opener since he took over in 1979.

OU changed its offense to the I-formation and used it for most of the game, feeding the ball to Wilson, Ledbetter, and Dupree, who combined for 224 of 280 rushing yards.

OU scored its only touchdown late in the first stanza. Wilson's one-yard run capped a 92-yard drive in 15 plays that included 20 yards in penalties whistled on the Cyclones.

ISU's 28-yard field goal cut the Sooners' lead to 7-3 early the second quarter. Keeling's 22-yard field goal on the last play of the first half gave Oklahoma a 10-3 lead.

The Sooners took the second-half kickoff and marched to the ISU 17, but a holding penalty stalled the drive, and Keeling's 44-yard field goal attempt was low.

Keeling did nail a 34-yarder early in the fourth period moments after Murphy recovered a Cyclone fumble on the ISU 25.

OU picked up more total yards (285-170). ISU's Tommy Davis, who had averaged 123 rushing yards in the first three games, was held to 42 yards by the Big Red defense.

Texas was next. The No. 13 Longhorns were undefeated at 3-0 and heavy favorites to win four in a row. Losing to the Longhorns was a bitter defeat for OU fans, especially three straight.

Sooner Magic: Decision Time

Barry Switzer had begun taking some heat from the media after the first four games. He faced the greatest decision of his coaching career on the floor of the Cotton Bowl stadium in 1982. A decision that would not render any points for his Sooner football team, but instead allowed his offense to keep possession of the football and preserve an upset victory.

The media was suggesting that maybe it was time for Switzer to step down as the OU head coach. Another reason for the negative rap against the head coach was that the Sooners had a three-game losing streak against Texas, the Sooners' biggest rival.

Switzer did not allow the media criticisms to get under his skin. But he did shuck the Wishbone offense and install the I-formation in 1982 based on the talent he was dealt. The Wishbone, however, was not completely discarded against the Steers.

The Sooners ended the three-year drought with a 28-22 victory before 75,567 fans at the Cotton Bowl, a sell-out audience for the 37th straight year.

OU took a 7-0 lead late in the first quarter on Dupree's 63-yard run and Keeling's conversion.

Dupree had scored the first rushing TD on Texas' defense, which held its first three opponents to a total of 19 points.

The Horns answered with an 80-yard drive to tie the game at 7-7 with 11:08 left until half time.

The Sooners retaliated with an 80-yard, 16-play drive to regain the lead. Wilson capped the drive with a three-yard run and Keeling converted for a 14-7 lead with 3:03 left in the first half.

The Steers added a field goal with 1:35 left in the half.

Ledbetter scored on a 59-yard run on OU's fourth play of the third quarter. Keeling tacked on the extra point, and the Sooners led, 21-10, with 10:52 to go in the period.

The Longhorns scored on the first play of the final period to draw closer, 21-16, with 14:57 left in the game.

Oklahoma's next possession took only six plays covering 80 yards. On third-and-three from the OU 27, Fred Sims found a hole over left guard and raced 51 yards to the Texas 22. Two more plays gained seven yards, then Ledbetter took the handoff over right tackle and burst 15 yards to the end zone. Keeling added the extra point, and the Sooners led, 28-16, with 12:30 remaining.

Too much time was left for the red-clad faithful to breathe easy. Texas quarterback Robert Brewer connected on six straight passes covering 65 yards on the next UT possession. The sixth pass was a 27-yarder to Herkie Walls, who raced past Case and Dwight Drane to the end zone. Brewer's uncle, George, played halfback for OU from 1946-49.

The Horns gambled with a two-point conversion. Brewer's pass to Carl Robinson was too high for the receiver's reach, yet Texas was still within striking distance, down 28-22 with 11:04 to go.

Two OU possessions inside Texas territory ended with fumbles by Dupree. The Sooner defense stalled three UT possessions in Longhorn territory.

The Sooners gained possession late in the game, but after two plays they were staring at third-and-11 at their own 29-yard line with 1:31 remaining. Switzer and his Sooners needed a big play to maintain possession and kill the clock. Switzer did not want the ball back into the hands of Brewer. The Texas quarterback had found his touch—18 completions in 34 passes for 235 yards and two TDs.

Switzer called time out, and his quarterback jogged to the sidelines for a huddle with coaches. Phelps also had been ridiculed by the media and fans for his unstellar performances in the first four games. But he was the man Switzer stuck with throughout the Texas game.

Switzer listened intently to his assistants' suggestions on which play to use. OU assistant coach Scott Hill suggested handing the ball to the fullback. Another assistant, Merv Johnson, recommended a quarterback bootleg. The fullback call would seem to be the wise choice—so far the OU fullbacks had rolled up 223 yards and scored two TDs. Switzer went with the other choice.

Phelps returned to the field of battle, took the snap, faked to Wilson and bootlegged around the right side and crashed into safety Mossy Cade for 12 yards and the first down. Three plays later, and Texas with no more time outs, the game ended, and Switzer was lifted atop his players' shoulders and carried to midfield to shake hands with Texas head coach Fred Akers.

Oklahoma had defeated Texas for the 28th time in the storied history between the two Red River rivals.

"We had fought too damn hard and were too damn close to lose it now," Switzer said after the game. "We just couldn't let it get away. We just couldn't.

"We've won bigger games, but it's been a long time since we won one that meant as much as this one. This was the first big-time game this group of players has ever won. I think we can go on and have a good year."

Oklahoma gained more total yards (409-398). Ledbetter carried 20 times for 144 yards.

The Texas victory was the momentum push the Sooners needed. They hammered 1-2-2 Kansas, 38-14, the following week in Lawrence. Dupree scored three touchdowns and rushed for 158 yards on nine carries. Phelps added two more touchdowns.

OU rolled to a 31-0 lead through the first two and one-half quarters. Keeling's 26-yard field goal midway through the first period put Oklahoma up 3-0. Sixty-two seconds later, Dupree sliced through right tackle and sprinted 75 yards for his first touchdown.

Songy intercepted three Kansas passes. The first one led to a 17-0 lead, the second to a 31-0 lead, and the third squelched a Jayhawk two-point conversion.

The Big Red amassed 30 first downs and 556 rushing yards, the most to date against a Kansas team. The Sooners passed for only 16 yards. The Jayhawks gained 247 total yards.

The Sooners jumped back into the AP poll at No. 20, then defeated 1-2-2 Oklahoma State, 27-9, on October 23 before a

Quarterback Kelly Phelps picked up a crucial first down to allow the Sooners to keep possession and upset Texas. (*OU Athletics*)

homecoming throng of 76,406 in Norman. Four big breaks helped Oklahoma pull out the win.

The first break came late in the first period to set up OU's first touchdown. The Pokes roughed Keeling on his punt. The penalty moved the ball from the OU 46 to the OSU 39. Three plays picked up nine yards, and OU gambled on fourth-and-one at the 30. Phelps pitched to Dupree, who swept around right end and shot to the end zone. Keeling missed the conversion.

Larry Roach's 43-yard field goal midway through the second stanza cut OU's lead to 6-3. The Sooners responded with a 90-yard scoring drive in 16 plays. Break No. 2 came after Oklahoma reached the OSU 11. Ledbetter took a handoff and fumbled on the six-yard line. Phelps scooped it up and scooted in for the score. Keeling kicked the conversion for a 13-3 lead.

Roach added two field goals to chisel the lead to 13-9, but the Sooners responded with the third break. Moments later, Keeling boomed a 62-yard punt, and OSU's Stanley Blair fumbled it on his 12. Mitch Bryan smothered it for the Sooners. Three plays later, Dupree scored from the two, and Keeling converted for a 20-9 advantage.

The final touchdown was set up by Daryl Goodlow's fumble recovery on the OU 47. Sims' six-yard run capped the 53-yard drive in six plays, and Keeling converted.

OU picked up more total yards (303-241). The defense held OSU's Ernest Anderson to 59 yards on 20 carries. He entered the game with a 208 per-game rushing average. Keeling averaged 48.8 yards on six punts.

The No. 17 Sooners scored five second-half touchdowns to break a 10-10 deadlock on their way to a 45-10 win over 1-5-1 Colorado the next week in Boulder. The Buffaloes answered each Oklahoma score in the first half but had no response in the final 30 minutes.

Keeling's 22-yard field goal put the Sooners up 3-0 late in the first period, and the Buffs took a 7-3 lead on an 80-yard scoring march. Midway through the second quarter, Dupree scored on a 77-yard punt return, and Keeling toed the 10th point. Colorado roared back with a field goal with four seconds until halftime.

Sims, who rushed for 109 yards and scored two touchdowns, scored on a six-yard run midway in the third period to give the Sooners the go-ahead score. The Big Red defense picked off four Buff passes. Drane stole two of them, Bryan intercepted one, and Stanberry took the last pick for a score. Drane's first theft led to a 24-0 OU advantage. Bryan's interception stopped a Buff threat on the OU 35, and the Sooners marched to a 31-10 lead moments later. One hundred seconds later, Stanberry intercepted on the CU 49 and raced to the end zone.

OU collected more total yards (414-235).

The No. 14 Sooners had answers for Kansas State as they dropped the 5-2-1 Wildcats 24-10 on November 6 before a crowd of 76,129 in Norman and a regional TV (ABC) audience.

The Cats took a 3-0 lead on a field goal late in the first stanza. On the first play after the kickoff, Dupree burst 80 yards for a touchdown, and Keeling converted.

K-State drove 49 yards for a 10-7 lead early in the second quarter, and the Sooners responded with a 74-yard march in six plays. Dupree capped the drive with a one-yard plunge, and Keeling converted for a 14-10 lead. Ledbetter, who rushed for 143 yards in the game, sparked the drive with a 25-yard run a play before Dupree scored.

After a scoreless third quarter, Stanberry scored on a 41-yard interception, and Keeling toed 21-yard field goal in the fourth stanza.

OU picked up more yards (404-315). Dupree rushed for 118 yards on 14 totes.

The No. 15 Sooners blasted Missouri, 41-14, the next week in Norman and before another regional TV (CBS) audience. Dupree rushed for 166 yards and two touchdowns to raise his season rushing total to 756 yards, breaking Buster Rhymes' freshman record of 659 yards set in 1980.

OU took a 14-0 lead in the first period on Wilson's 10-yard TD run and Phelps' 38-yard score. The Tigers scored two TDs in the second quarter, but Sewell scored on a 32-yard run after the first Mizzou score.

The Sooners took the second-half kickoff and wheeled 80 yards in 13 plays for a 28-14 lead. Phelps tossed an 11-yard scoring strike to Johnny Fontenette.

Dupree scored his two TDs in the fourth stanza. The first came with the ball on his 30-yard line. He took the handoff, hit Mizzou's Raymond Hairston head on, ran over the Tigers' safety and sprinted 70 yards to the end zone. Dupree scored the second TD on a seven-yard run to cap a 46-yard drive late in the game.

Culver replaced Keeling for placekicking chores as Keeling hurt his foot earlier in the week. Culver connected on five of six conversions, missing the final one. Keeling was able to punt and averaged 39.8 yards on five kicks.

Oklahoma rushed for 483 yards and passed for 25. The defense held Mizzou to 215 total yards.

The Sooners were back in the Big Eight race with a 6-0 conference record and a No. 11 national ranking. A win against No. 3 Nebraska would give OU another conference crown and a bid to the Orange Bowl. The 9-1 Cornhuskers also were undefeated in conference play. The loser would play in the Fiesta Bowl on January 1 in Tempe, Arizona.

Nebraska defeated the Sooners, 28-24, in Lincoln in front of a national TV (CBS) audience. The Huskers held a 21-10 lead at halftime.

Oklahoma took the second-half kickoff, and on the third play, Dupree dashed 86 yards for his second touchdown and cut the Husker lead to 21-17.

Nebraska retaliated with an 80-yard scoring drive for a 28-17 advantage. The Sooners rolled back with a 78-yard scoring march in 13 plays. Wilson's one-yard plunge and Keeling's conversion cut the deficit to 28-24 late in the third stanza.

OU had two chances to win the game in the fourth stanza. Murphy recovered a Nebraska fumble on his 40-yard line. The Sooners moved inside the Huskers' 40, but Phelps' fourth-down

pass misfired. With about five minutes to go, Oklahoma moved from its 34 to the NU 31, but stalled on Phelps' three incomplete passes.

The Huskers gained more total yards (409-399). Dupree picked up 149 yards on 25 totes.

The 12th-ranked Sooners and Arizona State met for the first time and only in the Fiesta Bowl. The 11th-ranked Sun Devils (9-2) won nine straight before losing their final two games. It was another home game for the Devils who play their games in Tempe, but the Sooners wore their home jerseys.

ASU overcame a 21-18 deficit with two fourth-period touchdowns en route to a 32-21 victory before 70,553 fans and a national TV (NBC) audience. Dupree rushed for a bowl-record 239 yards on 17 carries, two yards more than any team gained on the Devils all year. He only played sparingly with a sore rib and later suffered a pulled hamstring.

The Sooners took a 7-0 lead in the first stanza on Wilson's one-yard plunge to cap an 83-yard march in seven plays. Dupree sparked the drive with a 56-yard run to the five-yard line. Keeling kicked the conversion.

The Devils took an 8-7 lead in the second quarter with two field goals and a safety. Phelps was tackled in the end zone for the two points.

The Sooners answered with an 84-yard drive in 11 plays after the second ASU field goal. Wilson again scored from the one, but Dupree was stopped short on his two-point run. OU 13, ASU 8.

OU moved to the ASU 27 late in the first half, but the Devils intercepted Phelps' pass on their 38. Quarterback Todd Hons, who threw for 329 yards in the game, completed three straight passes for 25 yards to set up Luis Zendejas' 54-yard field goal on the last play. He nailed it to set a bowl record and draw his Devils within two, 13-11.

Dupree's second 56-yard scamper put the Sooners in scoring position early in the third period, but Wilson fumbled a handoff and ASU recovered. Minutes later, Keeling was under a heavy blitz and passed instead of punted. He completed a first-down pass to Mike Weddington, but the Sooners were whistled for having an illegal receiver down-field. The Devils took over on the OU 43 and drove to an 18-13 lead midway in the third stanza.

OU responded with a 76-yard scoring march in five plays. Sims' 19-yard run capped the drive, and Phelps completed a two-point

1982 Season Record: 8-4-0
Big Eight Conference: 6-1-0 (Second)

Date	Opponent	Result	Score
September 11	WEST VIRGINIA	L	41-27
September 18	at Kentucky	W	29-8
September 25	SOUTHERN CALIFORNIA	L	12-0
October 2	at Iowa State	W	13-3
October 9	Texas at Dallas	W	28-22
October 16	at Kansas	W	38-14
October 23	OKLAHOMA STATE	W	27-9
October 30	at Colorado	W	45-10
November 6	KANSAS STATE	W	24-10
November 13	MISSOURI	W	41-14
November 26	at Nebraska	L	28-24
January 1	Arizona State*	L	32-21

*Fiesta Bowl at Tempe, AZ

pass to Fontenette for a 21-18 lead. The Devils drove 52 and 76 yards for their final two TDs.

Oklahoma had more total yards (457-429), including 417 yards rushing against the nation's leading defense against the run.

The Sooners ended the 1982 campaign with an 8-4 record and second in the Big Eight Conference with a 6-1 mark. Bryan was the only Sooner to receive All-America honors. Five teammates—Williams, Paul Parker, Dupree, Murphy, and Jackie Shipp—joined him on the all-conference first unit. *Football News* named Dupree Freshman Player of the Year.

1983

Expectations ran high for the Sooners to make another run at the Big Eight Championship. Most preseason prognosticators had OU at or near the top of the national rankings. Ten defensive starters returned, but that number dropped to nine when Elbert Watts was declared academically ineligible.

The offense again would work from the I-formation most of the time and use the Wishbone sparingly. The backfield was inexperienced. Danny Bradley earned the quarterback slot, and Spencer Tillman began the season at fullback but moved to tailback after Marcus Dupree went AWOL. Earl Johnson and Tillman would set school rushing records for freshmen. Dupree was touted for the Heisman Trophy as a sophomore, but he turned out to be a bust.

The line was solid, led by guard Paul Parker and Chuck Thomas at center. Buster Rhymes beat out Paul Glewis to start at split end. Darren Arija earned the No. 1 punter position, and David Culver earned placekicking duties early on but would lose the job to Tim Lashar.

The No. 2 Sooners opened the season with a 27-14 victory over Stanford on September 10 in Palo Alto, California. Both teams featured new quarterbacks—Bradley for OU and Steve Cottrell for Stanford, who had the unfortunate task of replacing John Elway.

Oklahoma took a 16-0 lead in the first half. Culver kicked a 19-yard field goal, Johnson scored on a 16-yard run and Rhymes returned a punt 68 yards. The Cardinal gained their initial first down with 5:21 remaining until halftime.

Stanford scored late in the first half after recovering Dupree's fumble to cut its deficit to 16-7. OU took the second-half kickoff and Culver booted another field goal. Johnson added another TD in the third period.

Defensive tackle Bob Slater and noseguard Tom Flemons sacked Cottrell in the end zone for a safety early in the fourth stanza and a 27-7 lead. Stanford scored its second touchdown on a 50-yard drive after recovering Tillman's fumble at midfield.

The No. 2 Sooners hosted sixth-ranked Ohio State (1-0) the following week before a throng of 76,520 and a national TV (ABC) audience. It was the first meeting since Uwe von Schamann's winning field goal six years earlier, but this time there were no last-second heroics as Ohio State prevailed, 24-14.

The Buckeyes controlled the football for 60 percent of the game and scored two touchdowns on their first four possessions. The other two possessions ended with a missed field goal and a stalled drive at the OU one-yard line.

Oklahoma answered the second touchdown with an 85-yard scoring drive in four plays midway through the second period. Tillman sliced through right guard and shot 37 yards to the end zone. Culver kicked the conversion.

Ohio State marched 57 yards on their first possession of the second half to take a 21-7 lead.

The Sooners launched a 62-yard scoring drive late in the third quarter and into the fourth. Bradley tossed a 22-yard scoring strike to split end Derrick Shepard to cap the eight-play drive. Lashar's extra point cut the Buckeyes' lead to 21-14.

Ohio State added a 22-yard field goal midway through the fourth stanza. OU took the kickoff and marched to the OSU 26, but surrendered on downs.

Oklahoma picked up 177 yards rushing and 170 more through the air. Bradley completed nine of 21 for all of the passing yards. Shepard caught three aerials for 85 yards, and Rhymes hauled in another three for 77 yards. Ohio State picked up 412 total yards.

The No. 8 Sooners were a tale of two halves in their 28-18 victory over Tulsa on September 24 in Norman. Oklahoma rolled to a 28-0 lead at halftime and made too many mistakes in the second half to put any points on the board.

Barry Switzer won his 100th victory, but said the second half was the worst in his 17 years of coaching. In the first half, the Sooners gained 13 first downs and 290 yards compared to five first downs and 86 yards in the final 30 minutes.

Johnson started in place of Dupree, who sat out with an injury, and rushed for 143 yards in a part-time role. Johnson left the game late in the third period with a sore ankle.

His 44-yard jaunt put the Sooners up 7-0 midway through the first stanza, and Lashar kicked the first of four conversions. Tillman's one-yard TD run capped an 80-yard drive minutes later. After the Golden Hurricane punted to their 37, the Sooners rolled back in six plays for a 21-0 lead. Bradley's one-yard plunge finished the drive on the second play of the second stanza.

Bradley hurled a 71-yard scoring strike to Rhymes for a 28-0 lead just before halftime. Rhymes caught the pass on his 46 and outran the Hurricane secondary to the end zone.

OU had one chance to score early in the third period, but Lashar missed a 47-yard field goal. Tulsa scored all three touchdowns in the fourth quarter but failed to convert any points after each score.

The Big Red defense held the Hurricane to 17 net rushing yards and 180 passing yards.

Oklahoma dropped to ninth nationally and traveled to Manhattan, Kansas, the following week. The Sooners defeated the (2-2) Wildcats, 29-10. Kansas State took a 10-0 lead in the first quarter. After that, it was all Dupree, who rushed for 151 yards in the game and scored three touchdowns. Tillman rushed for 131 yards and scored a TD. Tony Rayburn recovered a blocked punt in the end zone for a safety.

OU rolled up 490 yards and held the Cats to 206.

Texas scored three touchdowns in the third stanza to overcome a 10-7 deficit en route to a 28-16 win over the No. 8 Sooners on October 8. The 3-0 and second-ranked Steers fumbled three times and two of them led to Oklahoma leads. The Big Red did not lose a fumble, but Bradley did throw one interception.

The first Longhorn fumble came in the first quarter when Kevin Murphy smacked Edwin Simmons, and Keith Stanberry recovered on the UT 49 late in the first period. The Sooners took a 7-0 lead 11 plays and a couple of penalties later. Bradley, under a heavy rush, zipped a scoring strike to Steve Sewell, and Tim Lashar converted.

The Horns marched 44 yards for the tying touchdown late in the second stanza.

Rick Bryan caused John Walker to fumble early in the third quarter and Scott Case recovered on the UT 18-yard line. The Sooners bogged down after reaching the 11, and Lashar booted a 28-yard field goal for a 10-7 lead.

The Steers answered with an 80-yard drive for the go-ahead score, 14-10, and raised the lead to 21-10 on another 80-yard march. Bradley's interception led to the fourth Texas touchdown.

Down 28-10, early in the fourth period, Bradley scored on a 36-yard run to cap an 83-yard drive in six plays. Bradley also sparked the drive with a 22-yard run on the play before. His two-point pass misfired, but the Steers were offside. Bradley fumbled the snap on the second try.

The Longhorns rolled up more total yards (335-197).

Oklahoma dropped to 15th in the AP poll. Dupree failed to show for practices the next week and Coach Switzer suspended him from the team.

Sooner Magic: Bumbling In Stillwater

Laurel and Hardy, the Three Stooges, the Keystone Cops, Abbot and Costello and the Marx Brothers were some of the greatest slapstick comedians in history—bumbling, stumbling silliness that made us all laugh.

Add to that list the 1983 Oklahoma Sooners in their intrastate rivalry against the Oklahoma State Cowboys. The Big Red's performance was highlighted by a botched punt, a muffed pitch out, running into a teammate for lost yards, 15 penalties, seven turnovers (six lost fumbles) and miscommunications on an onside kick. For three and one-half quarters, the Sooners seemed like they did not want to win this game in Stillwater. Yet they did pull out a 21-18 decision on October 15.

With Dupree gone, Switzer had to rely on a couple of green, but capable freshman backs—Tillman and Johnson—against the Cowboys.

Oklahoma State jumped to a 14-3 halftime lead. Neither team was impressive although scoring 17 first-half points. Neither were successful on third-down plays. OU was zero for seven, and OSU zero for eight in the first half. The Sooners converted only two of 15 third downs the whole game, and the Pokes converted only two of 17.

Midway through the first quarter, Stanberry picked off Rusty Hilger's pass and raced to the end zone. The play was nullified by an illegal block, and OU ended up punting from its own 27.

The first bonehead play occurred late in the first quarter. Atiya scrambled to avoid the rush of OSU's Windell Yancey. When he eluded Yancey, he tried to punt the ball, but it caromed off the back of teammate Sonny Brown at his 24-yard line. The ball bounced into the air, where OSU's Ken Montgomery grabbed it and scampered 14 yards into the end zone for the first Cowboy score with 15 seconds left in the first quarter.

The Sooners took the ensuing kickoff and drove to the Pokes' 25 but had to rely on Lashar's 42-yard field goal to close the gap to 7-3 with 11:21 remaining in the first half.

OSU scored a touchdown midway through the second quarter, moments after recovering Case's fumbled punt return at the OU 18.

The Big Red defense stalled the Cowboys at the 10-yard line. Larry Roach missed a 27-yard field goal try, but OU was flagged for being offside. OSU scored on the next play for a 14-3 lead.

OU blew a scoring opportunity in the first half. From the OSU six, Bradley's pitchout to Johnson hit Parker in the back and the Pokes recovered on the four.

Case fumbled another punt return at the OU 33, which led to a Cowboy field goal and a 17-3 lead with 8:10 left in the third stanza. OSU added another field goal early in the fourth period.

Two possessions later, on second-and-10, Bradley connected with Shepard, who sprinted down the sideline for a 73-yard touchdown.

Lashar toed the extra point, and the Big Red trailed, 20-10, with 9:37 to go.

The Sooners threatened again, but Adam Hinds intercepted Bradley's pass intended for Rhymes at the Cowboy two. OSU played conservative but failed to gain much on the ground and punted to the Cowboy 47 with 4:20 remaining on the clock.

The Sooners overcame their bumbling ways and put together a scoring drive. Bradley zipped two 14-yard passes to Rhymes to the OSU 24. Johnson carried for 10 yards for a first down at the 14, then gained nine more yards to the five. Tillman dashed the final five yards and lunged across the goal line for the TD. Switzer called for a two-point conversion, where Bradley rolled right, searching in vain for a receiver. He spotted Johnson open in the right corner of the end zone. Bradley arched the ball, over Cowboy Mark Moore's reach, to Johnson. Suddenly the Sooners trailed, 20-18, with 2:50 left.

The Sooners set up for the kick off. Switzer did not call for an onside kick, believing his defense could hold OSU and hopefully get the ball back for another score. His defense had held the Pokes to five first downs and 120 total yards.

Lashar did not hear Switzer's order.

Instead of kicking the ball down field, Lashar put his foot to the ball, which bounced right off the helmet of OSU's Chris Rockins. Case grabbed the bounding football and smothered it at the OSU 49.

Bradley completed a five-yard pass to Sewell, then a 16-yarder to Shepard. Johnson carried four more yards to the Cowboy 29. Lashar, a freshman walk-on, was called on to boot a 46-yard field goal. His 42-yarder in the second period was the longest of his career so far. OSU called a time out to make him think about it a little longer. The kick sailed perfectly through the uprights, and Oklahoma led, 21-20, with 1:14 to go.

The crowd of 50,440 was shocked. The Sooners had snatched a one-point victory from the jaws of defeat.

"You're not going to believe this. Everyone needs some luck. We decided not to kick onsides," Switzer said. "We wanted to kick it away and then have our defense stop them, which I had no doubt we could. There were 10 players who knew we were kicking it away, but Lashar didn't know it. We forgot to tell Tim Lashar, and he kicked it onside."

"Nobody told me I was supposed to kick it long," Lashar said. "Guys were switching back and forth, running around, and I didn't know what they were doing. So I just kicked it onside."

Switzer was glad one of his players wasn't bumbling around when the ball bounced off Rockins' helmet. Case was in the right place at the right time.

"I was going downfield, looking up for a long kick, and then the ball hit right in front of me," Case said.

The 4-2 Sooners fell a notch to 16th in the AP poll and hammered 3-3 Iowa State, 49-11, the following week in Norman. Tillman and Johnson combined for 234 yards rushing, and Tillman led Oklahoma with two touchdowns.

OU scored on five of its first six possessions and rolled up six touchdowns after the Cyclones took a 3-0 lead midway through the first quarter.

OU picked up more total yards (459-287). Tillman rushed for 124 yards, and Johnson added 110 more.

Bryan injured a foot tendon and did not play the following week.

Big plays sparked the No. 14 Sooners to a 45-14 victory over 3-3-1 Kansas on October 29 in Norman. OU scored three touchdowns in the first 11 minutes and never looked back.

Johnson sprinted 76 yards for the first touchdown on the third play of the game. A high snap foiled the extra point. Johnson scored on a four-yard run 85 seconds later to cap a 38-yard drive in three plays. Bradley, who sparked the drive with a 32-yard pass to Rhymes to the KU six, ran in for the two-point conversion.

The Jayhawks took the kickoff and rolled 68 yards to the OU 28 but ran into a stiff Oklahoma defense. After an incomplete pass, quarterback Frank Seurer was sacked twice for a total of 16 yards. Rayburn got him the first time, and noseguard Tony Casillas wrapped him up on the second sack. Kansas then punted into the end zone. Seurer was sacked six times for minus-65 yards in the game.

On the next play, Tillman galloped 80 yards for a 21-0 lead.

Bradley reinjured his ankle and did not play the final 17 and one-half minutes. Two touchdowns pulled the Hawks within a touchdown, 21-14, midway through the second stanza. Sewell's 15-yard run gave OU a 28-14 halftime lead, and the Sooners scored two touchdowns and a field goal in the second half.

The Big Red gained more yards (406-331).

The Sooners had one of their worst offensive performances in years in a 10-0 loss to 5-3 Missouri the next week in Columbia. OU ended up rushing for 84 yards on 42 carries after rushing for minus-seven yards in the first half.

Oklahoma lost a fumble on the Tigers' 36-yard line, missed a field goal, and Rhymes dropped a possible scoring strike in the opening period. The Tigers took a 3-0 lead on a 37-yard field goal.

Missou scored on a 71-yard march for the deciding tally midway through the second quarter.

The Sooners' woes continued in the third stanza when Bradley's TD pass to Rhymes was nullified by a penalty and in the fourth when Tillman left the game with a compression fracture of his neck.

The Tigers gained more total yards (221-201). The Sooners were forced to throw the ball 27 times to get something going. Bradley completed 10 of them for 117 yards.

The Sooners returned to Norman on November 12 and defeated 3-6 Colorado, 41-28, before a homecoming throng of 75,008. OU scored on six of its first seven possessions and rolled to a 34-0 lead in the first 26 minutes and 34 seconds.

Johnson rushed for 258 yards to break Dupree's freshman single-game record of 239 set in last year's Fiesta Bowl. Johnson scored two long-distance touchdowns with runs of 57 and 58 yards.

Two Buffalo touchdowns were set up by Oklahoma fumbles, and they also added two TDs in the fourth quarter.

OU gained 423 total yards while holding Colorado to 208 yards.

Two weeks later, No. 1 Nebraska rolled into Norman and rolled out with a 28-21 victory on a wet and windy afternoon. The 11-0 Cornhuskers were favored by 14 points, and the Sooners gave them a fight to the finish.

The Huskers marched 67 yards to take a 7-0 lead midway through the first period. Lashar missed two field goals in the second stanza, but OU put together a 67-yard TD drive to tie the game with 4:05 until halftime. Tillman scored on a 39-yard run, and Lashar kicked the conversion.

Linebacker Thomas Benson picked off a Nebraska pass moments later and returned it seven yards to the OU 42, but an unsportsman-like penalty against OU set the ball back to the 27. On the next play, Bradley fired a 73-yard scoring strike to Rhymes to give Oklahoma a 14-7 lead with 2:11 until intermission.

The Huskers quickly tied the game on a 73-yard, five-play drive 89 seconds later. Mike Rozier scored on a three-yard run for his 29th touchdown of the year, tying an NCAA record for most TDs in a single season.

The Sooners jumped to a 21-14 lead with a 43-yard march in six plays midway through the third quarter. From the NU 18, Tillman scooted around right end and leaped the final five yards into the end zone.

Nebraska answered with a tying touchdown 57 seconds later and marched 41 yards for another.

With 5:50 left in the game, Oklahoma launched a 72-yard drive to the NU two-yard line. Facing second-and-one there, Johnson picked up the first down on a one-yard run, but the Sooners were whistled for illegal procedure and moved back to the seven. Bradley was sacked for a three-yard loss then fired a pass to Shepard on the goal line. Neil Harris bumped Shepard as he tried to catch the ball but no penalty. Harris then deflected Bradley's fourth-down pass to Rhymes in the end zone.

Nebraska picked up more total yards (424-420). Tillman rushed for 134 yards, and Johnson gained 84 yards. Bradley completed six of 13 passes for 187 yards, and Atiya averaged 45.4 yards on five punts.

Sooner Magic:
A Near Disaster Near Pearl Harbor

Ah, Hawaii. The sun, the surf, the beach, the babes in bikinis, the Pearl Harbor Memorial, Rainbow Warrior football. The latter of which most folks don't think about when traveling to the 50th state in the union. Sounds like bowl atmosphere. Although the 7-4 Sooners did not accept a bowl bid, Coach Switzer treated the last game of the 1983 season it like it was a bowl game.

The Sooners were 28-point favorites against the Hawaii Rainbow Warriors, who were starting six freshmen players. At 5-4-1 and a fifth-place finish in the Western Athletic Conference, the Warriors were hardly bowl material. But they played like it in front of their Honolulu home crowd of 46,143.

The Warriors took the opening kickoff and drove 65 yards to the OU 15-yard line. Stanberry's interception at the OU two stalled the drive.

The Sooners then drove deep into Warrior territory and Lashar missed a 21-yard field goal. Brown picked off a Hawaii pass at the OU 11 and returned it 12 yards. Two pass thefts had averted a possible 14-0 Hawaii lead.

Hawaii's Raphael Cherry hurled a 46-yard TD strike to give the Warriors a 7-0 lead midway through the second stanza. The Warriors added a field goal with 20 seconds until halftime.

Neither team threatened throughout most of the third quarter. Late in the quarter, OU set up shop at its 31-yard line following a UH punt. Bradley gained 13 yards on a keeper off the left side, then was sacked for a three-yard loss by defensive back Pete Noga, who blitzed through a gap in the OU line.

On second-and-13 at the OU 41, Bradley dropped back and fired a pass to Rhymes at the UH 48. Rhymes eluded the grasp of UH linebacker James Elias and throttled to the end zone. Lashar nailed the extra point, and the Sooners trailed 10-7 with 5:52 left in the third stanza.

Moments later, Case intercepted Cherry's pass on the UH 26, returned the pigskin five yards and nearly fumbled as he crashed to the turf.

It's a Fact
The 1983 OU team lost 14 consecutive fumbles in five games (Texas through Missouri) and to date holds the NCAA record for most consecutive fumbles lost.

Four plays later, from the UH two-yard line, Tillman dove over left tackle. Lashar's extra point gave the Sooners a 14-10 lead with 3:12 remaining in the period.

Early in the fourth quarter, Tillman fumbled, and linebacker Michael Beazley recovered at the OU 30. Switzer stormed the field, pleading with officials that he thought OU recovered the ball. The ball remained in Hawaii's possession.

The Big Red defense forced the Warriors backwards. Walter Murray took a screen pass and was immediately thrown for a six-yard loss by Daryl Goodlow. On the next play, Benson chased Cherry out of the pocket and dropped him for an 18-yard loss. The Warriors were flagged for unsportsmanlike conduct on the play, and they faced fourth-and-46 from their 34-yard line.

The Sooners were penalized for roughing the kicker on the punt, and the Warriors were awarded an automatic first down at their 49.

Seven plays later, Cherry connected a 26-yard pass to Murray in the right corner of the end zone. Hawaii regained the lead 17-14 with 11:31 to go.

OU answered with a 65-yard TD drive. From the UH three, Bradley leaped over Warrior defenders and into the end zone. Lashar's kick boosted OU to a 21-17 lead with 6:57 remaining.

Bradley was so elated that he kept the ball with him as he returned to the sideline. Officials flagged him for unsportsmanlike conduct, a 15-yard penalty assessed on the kickoff. Murray took Lashar's kickoff at the UH 23 and returned the ball to his 40-yard line. Cherry connected a 12-yard pass to Murray, but Case was penalized for grabbing Murray's facemask. First down Hawaii at the OU 42.

The Sooner defense held the Warriors to three yards, and on fourth down at the OU 39, Cherry's tossed an incomplete pass.

The Sooners ran on every play to milk the final 4:17 off the clock. After reaching the UH 21, the Sooners were not going to risk a blocked field goal attempt and turned the ball over on downs with two seconds remaining.

OU's secondary was spread 50 yards deep, and Case intercepted Cherry's Hail Mary pass to end the game. It was the second interception in the game for Case, eighth for the season, and 11th during his two-year career as a Sooner. His eight picks set an OU single-season record, surpassing five former Sooners who had seven interceptions.

Tillman ended the night with 178 yards on 37 carries. He set the record for most yards by a Sooner freshman—1,047—and was the first freshman in school history to surpass the 1,000-yard mark in rushing. He also surpassed Johnson, who had 945 yards set a week

earlier against Nebraska. Johnson sat out the Hawaii contest with a fractured knee cap. Johnson might have been the first freshman in OU history to rush for 1,000 yards if not for his injury.

The Sooners finished the '83 campaign at 8-4 and unranked in the national polls. The Warriors finished the season 5-5-1, the first time in six years they did not have a winning record.

"I expected it to be a better season," Switzer said after the game. "We were not as good as I had hoped we'd be."

Bryan was selected unanimous All-America for the second straight year. Thomas, Murphy, Jackie Shipp, and Case joined him on the all-conference first team.

1984

Barry Switzer believed his offense would be improved in 1984, especially with the addition of the Flexbone, a variation of the Wishbone-T formation. The Flexbone, a creation by new assistant coach Mack Brown, featured diverse formations—two backs and two receivers, or one back and three receivers, or four receivers. The halfbacks would shift out of the backfield into receiving positions.

Nine starters returning to the offense was another reason Switzer was optimistic for improvements. The entire backfield had returnees with starting experience from the previous year—Danny Bradley at quarterback, Spencer Tillman and Earl Johnson sharing tailback duties, Jerome Ledbetter at fullback, and Steve Sewell at wingback. The two halfbacks in the Flexbone were renamed "A" and "Z" back. The "A" back would line up on the weak side, and the "Z" back to the strong side. Center Chuck Thomas and Eric Pope would return to lead the front wall.

Freshman Keith Jackson beat out Darren Berryhill at tight end and Buster Rhymes and Derrick Shepard shared split-end duties. Tim Lashar returned as placekicker, but Mike Winchester beat out Darrin Atiya for the punting chores.

Only four starters returned on defense—noseguard Tony Casillas and end Kevin Murphy anchored the front line, and Jim Rockford and Keith Stanberry were back in the secondary. Tony Rayburn also brought experience to the secondary. The losses of Jackie Shipp and Thomas Benson would be a concern about a drop off at the linebackers slots, but three new faces would bring smiles to coaches and fans alike—sophomore Paul Migliazzo and freshmen Brian Bosworth and Dante Jones.

Injuries would deplete the Sooner lineup as the season progressed, sometimes up to 16 underclassmen dominated the two-deep roster. Tillman would sit out the first four games with a hamstring injury, and Migliazzo missed the first two with a knee injury.

The No. 16 Sooners opened the season with a 19-7 victory over Stanford on September 8 in Norman and before a national TV (USA network) audience. The Cardinal marched 71 yards off the opening kickoff with quarterback John Paye echoing the ghosts of John Elway who shredded the OU defense four years earlier.

Paye completed four of five passes for 50 yards in the eight-play drive, including a seven-yard scoring strike to tight end Greg Baty. But, unlike Elway, Paye wilted under the pressure of the Oklahoma defense afterward. He completed only 17 of 35 for 130 yards after the scoring march.

The Big Red marched 72 yards in 12 plays to tie the game late in the opening quarter. Bradley capped the drive with a 12-yard scamper around right end, and Lashar converted.

The Sooners scored the go-ahead touchdown with a 61-yard drive late in the second period. Johnson scored on a four-yard run, but Lashar missed the extra point. Bradley completed two passes to Rhymes for a combined 51 yards to highlight the drive.

1983 Season Record: 8-4-0
Big Eight Conference: 5-2-0 (Second)

Date	Opponent	Result	Score
September 10	at Stanford	W	27-14
September 17	OHIO STATE	L	24-14
September 24	TULSA	W	28-18
October 1	at Kansas State	W	29-10
October 8	Texas at Dallas	L	28-16
October 15	at Oklahoma State	W	21-20
October 22	IOWA STATE	W	49-11
October 29	KANSAS	W	45-14
November 5	at Missouri	L	10-0
November 12	COLORADO	W	41-28
November 26	NEBRASKA	L	28-21
December 3	at Hawaii	W	21-17

Bosworth's interception on the Stanford 29 set up Lashar's 21-yard field goal for a 16-7 lead midway through the third stanza. OU bogged down at the Cardinal 15 on the next series, and Lashar toed a 32-yard field goal for the final tally.

Stanford advanced to the OU two-yard line as time expired.

The Big Red picked up more and total yards (342-270). Bradley rushed for 100 yards passed for 84 more.

The injury list mounted. A sprained ankle sidelined defensive tackle Jeff Tupper for the next game against 0-1 Pittsburgh. Murphy sprained his ankle on the first play against the Panthers, and Johnson was limited with a sprained knee.

Still, the No. 15 Sooners hammered 17th-ranked Pittsburgh, 42-10, the next week in Pittsburgh. Bradley ran for two touchdowns and passed for two more to lead the Big Red assault.

Trailing 3-0 in the first quarter, OU scored three touchdowns in each of the even periods. The Sooners cashed in on big breaks, which led to a 14-3 lead in the second stanza. Winchester's punt touched a Panther player, and linebacker Kert Kasper recovered on the Pitt five-yard line. On fourth-and-goal at the one, Bradley plowed over for the touchdown. Lashar was perfect on all six conversions.

Minutes later, Pitt's punter Chris Jelic was under a heavy rush by the Sooners and unable to get off his kick. He tried to run for a first down but was stopped after gaining only a yard to the OU 48. Bradley scored seven plays later on another one-yard run.

Leading 35-10, freshman corner back Rickey Dixon returned a Pitt pass 11 yards for the final tally.

The Sooners rolled up 383 total yards. Freshman fullback Lydell Carr rushed for 137 yards, and Bradley completed 12 of 18 passes for 145 yards. Shepard caught five aerials for 57 yards and a touchdown. Winchester averaged 44.6 yards on five punts. The Big Red defense held the Panthers to 32 yards rushing and 217 yards through the air.

With Tillman still out with injury and Johnson limited with a sore knee, freshman Patrick Collins replaced them but suffered a hip pointer early in the next game against Baylor. By the second quarter, the Sooners' backfield consisted of two freshmen—Carr and third-string halfback Darrell Weddington.

The 11th-ranked Sooners returned home on September 22 and whipped 0-1 Baylor, 34-15. Seven other freshmen started for the Big Red in addition to Carr and Weddington.

OU took the opening kickoff and sailed 75 yards in nine plays for a 7-0 lead. Bradley hurled a 20-yard scoring strike to Shepard in the right corner of the end zone. Lashar made all four conversions in the game. The lead grew to 14-0 late in the first half, when Sewell scored on a 33-yard run around right end to complete a 66-yard drive in eight plays.

Lashar toed a 27-yard field goal less than two minutes later, but Baylor scored a touchdown with four seconds remaining until intermission.

The Bears took the second-half kickoff, and on the first play Migliazzo intercepted Tom Muecke's pass and dashed to the end zone for a 24-7 advantage. Baylor punted moments later, and the Sooners began their first offensive possession of the second half, which resulted in a 51-yard TD drive in 12 plays. Bradley tossed a 19-yard scoring strike to Rhymes to raise the lead to 31-7.

Freshman defensive end Darrell Reed recovered a Bear fumble on the BU 28, but OU had to settle for another Lashar field goal from 34 yards out. Baylor drove 75 yards against the reserve defense for a touchdown with four seconds left in the game and added a two-point conversion.

Oklahoma rushed for 171 yards and passed for 166. Baylor picked up 272 total yards but only 120 yards against the starting Sooner defense.

The seventh-ranked Sooners defeated 1-2 Kansas State, 24-6, the next week in Norman before a homecoming throng of 72,017. Sewell became the first Oklahoma football player to reach the century mark in rushing and receiving each in the same game. He picked up 153 yards on 24 carries and caught six aerials for 142 yards. Sewell, normally the "Z" back, was switched to "A" back due to the glut of injured running backs.

The Wildcats recovered Carr's fumble on the game's fourth play, which set up their field goal and 3-0 lead. The Cats threatened for more points moments after intercepting Bradley's pass early in the second period. K-State set up for a 42-yard field-goal try, but a low snap from center resulted in an eight-yard loss. The Sooners took over and drove 68 yards for a 7-3 lead. Carr capped the five-play drive with a one-yard plunge, and Lashar kicked the first of three conversions. Sewell sparked the drive with a 47-run jaunt to the KSU 15.

Early in the third stanza, another Carr fumble led to another Kansas State field goal. Minutes later, the Sooners faced third-and-six on their 21, Bradley zipped a three-yard pass to Sewell, who headed down the sideline and eluded one tackler to the end zone to complete the 79-yard play.

Lashar booted a 23-yard field goal midway through the fourth quarter, and Bradley ran 22 yards for the final tally minutes later.

OU collected more total yards (464-210). Bradley completed nine of 17 passes for 187 yards. Kansas State rushed for 32 yards, but was held to minus-six yards through three quarters.

For the first time since 1979, the Sooners entered the Texas game undefeated. It also was the last time both teams entered the game undefeated. The 1984 Longhorns were ranked No. 1 in the nation and had scored 33.7 points per game. They had yet to meet a defense like the Sooners had.

On October 13, No. 3 Oklahoma and No. 1 Texas battled to a 15-15 tie in one of the worst officiated games in the history of Oklahoma football. Yes, it was as bad as the blown calls in the 1947 OU-Texas matchup that caused a riot. Except this time there was no riot. No one wanted to stay any longer in the day-long downpour, the first rain game at the Cotton Bowl in 35 years.

Late in the first stanza, Winchester dropped the punt snap and slipped after gaining one yard on his 26-yard line. The Steers scored a touchdown three plays later. Texas kicked a field goal late in the first half after recovering Tillman's fumble on his 26.

On Texas' first possession of the second half, Bosworth laid the lumber on Terry Orr, causing the Longhorn to fumble. Stanberry smothered the pigskin on the UT five-yard line. Two plays later Sewell scored from the two, and Lashar converted.

Moments later, Texas' punt snap sailed behind the end zone, giving Oklahoma a safety and cut the Horns' lead to 10-9. The Sooners took the free kick and marched 71 yards in 10 plays for a 15-10 lead late in the third quarter. Bradley's two-point pass was tipped away.

The Steers drove 78 yards to the OU two-yard line late in the fourth period, but the Sooners rose up with a goal-line stand. On fourth down, Kevin Nelson ran around right end but slipped when he saw crimson jerseys between him and the goal line. The Sooners took over and went nowhere, and Coach Switzer ordered an intentional safety instead of punting. Kevin Adkins snapped the ball over Winchester's head. OU 15, Texas 12 with 2:10 remaining.

Moments after taking the free kick, the Steers' Jerome Johnson fumbled after catching a pass near midfield, and Casillas recovered, but officials ruled Johnson was down, and Texas kept the ball. Television replays clearly proved that Johnson had fumbled.

A pass interference penalty against the Sooners aided Texas' advance to the OU 16-yard line. Moments later, Stanberry picked off Dodge's pass in the end zone and hydroplaned out of bounds. His interception thwarted a Longhorn drive. He was clearly in bounds. But the referee ruled Stanberry had a hip touching inside the sideline marker. Interception nullified. Jeff Ward kicked a game-tying field goal on the next play.

Television replays again clearly proved that Stanberry came up with a clean interception, but Ed Clark, a Big Eight official who was near Stanberry, ruled him out of bounds.

The interception would have given the Sooners a 15-12 victory, but instead the final score was 15-15 against the No. 1-ranked Longhorns. Bonnie and Clyde could not have pulled off a better robbery than the referees of that game.

OU gained more first downs (15-8) and total yards (177-170).

Bruce Finlayson, supervisor of Big Eight officiating, called Switzer two days later to admit the call was a mistake and apologized to the Sooner skipper.

Sooner Magic: 'The Emotional and Mental Aspects of the Game are So Vitally Important'

A consequence of playing a major rival like the Texas Longhorns is being emotionally prepared for the opponent the following week. The Oklahoma-Texas rivalry involves so much intensity and drains the emotions since the game is played in Dallas, halfway between both universities and in front of an evenly divided crowd.

The week after the Texas game, the Big Red invaded Ames, Iowa, in a nationally televised (ESPN) game against the Iowa State Cyclones. OU climbed to second in the polls (Texas dropped to third by the way). Iowa State was 2-4, hardly anything for the Sooners to get excited about as 28-point favorites. Obviously, the Cyclone fans were pumped, as the first ever night game at Jack Trice Stadium was a sellout at 51,000. As a matter of fact, this was the first night conference game for either team.

Evidently the Sooners still had their minds on the Texas game, because their performance was not pretty. Nevertheless, they got the job done with a 12-10 victory. OU had won two straight in the series and 50 of 56 meetings in the history of the rivalry.

Lashar's 36-yard field goal gave the Sooners a 3-0 lead late in the opening quarter. The Cyclones marched 80 yards for a 7-3 lead just before halftime.

The Cyclones had a chance to pour salt on the wound late in the third quarter, but missed a field goal. They did succeed with a field goal early in the fourth period after recovering Shepard's fumble unt return.

The Sooners answered with Lashar's 30-yard field goal, to cut the deficit to 10-6 with 9:46 remaining.

The Big Red defense stonewalled Iowa State on its next possession. The Cyclones lost 13 yards in three plays and punted to Rhymes, who took the ball at midfield and returned it 10 yards.

The Sooners marched to the ISU three. With 3:53 left in the game, OU faced third-and-goal at the seven. Bradley took the ball, rolled left toward the sideline, and just as three ISU defenders were in his face, Bradley pitched the pigskin to a trailing Tillman, who rolled into the end zone.

"I knew if Spencer stayed with me, I was going to do all I could to suck everybody in and try to leave

him out there and get the ball pitched," Bradley said after the game. "It worked, and it caused us to win the ball game."

The extra-point attempt failed when holder Kyle Irvin bobbled the snap. Lashar grabbed the ball off the ground but was tackled short of the goal line. OU held a 12-10 lead with 3:34 to go.

Iowa State took the kickoff and moved the ball 24 yards to its 44 with 1:42 remaining. Stanberry intercepted Alex Espinoza's fourth-down pass on the OU 44 and returned it 12 yards. There was no controversy on this interception and the Sooners ran out the clock, escaping Ames with the win.

"That ball looked good coming to me. I saw the dude was running a crossing route, and I just broke on the ball and picked it off," Stanberry said.

The stout Big Red defense held the Cyclones to only 49 yards and four first downs in the second half. The Sooner offense piled up 167 yards and seven first downs in the final 30 minutes.

Switzer has always invoked that emotion plays a huge roll in football games.

"They [Iowa State] were about as high on the scale as you could be, and we were about as low on the scale," he said. "Don't think emotion isn't a part of it.

"I told my football team that this points out so much that there's not much difference between football teams. Obviously there wasn't much tonight. The emotional and mental aspects of the game are so vitally important. I was afraid something like this might happen, and it did. I think the blame lies with me not preparing them mentally, emotionally to play this game."

Bradley injured his ankle and a finger against the Cyclones and sat out the following game against Kansas. Inexperienced freshman quarterback Troy Aikman replaced him. Murphy also was sidelined with a sprained foot, and Johnson sat out with a busted kneecap.

The 2-5 Jayhawks stunned the No. 2 Sooners, 28-11, on October 27 in Lawrence. OU's offense was basic and conservative due to Aikman's lack of experience.

The Sooners committed six turnovers—three interceptions, two fumbles, and a blocked punt. Kansas capitalized on five of those errors. The Hawks kicked a field goal after recovering Shepard's fumble on the OU six-yard line, they blocked Winchester's punt for a safety, returned Aikman's first interception for a touchdown, and recovered Tillman's fumble for another field goal.

Third-string quarterback Kyle Irvin directed a 70-yard drive in 10 plays and scored on a one-yard touchdown for the Sooners with three seconds remaining in the game. He also ran for the two-point conversion.

Keith Stanberry (19) clutches an interception before landing out of bounds. The referee ruled it a no catch. (© 1984, The Daily Oklahoman)

Surprisingly, Oklahoma picked up more first downs (14-7), but Kansas gained more yards (220-163). Aikman completed two of 14 passes for eight yards.

The loss dropped the Sooners to 10th in the AP poll, and Bradley returned the following week when Oklahoma hosted Missouri. Bradley played in high-top shoes provided by OU basketball coach Billy Tubbs.

The Sooners blasted the 3-4-1 Tigers, 49-7. The Sooners scored on six of their first nine possessions, took a 35-0 halftime lead and it was 42-0 after three periods. OU scored on four straight possessions in the first half and on two of three series in the final 30 minutes. The reserves got in on the action in the final 20 minutes. Bradley, in his new high tops, scored two touchdowns, ran for 54 yards, and hit five of eight passes for 91 yards.

All of the Sooners' touchdowns ranged from one to eight yards out except for Shepard's 58-yard TD pass to Jackson off a reverse for a 28-0 lead.

Oklahoma collected 32 first downs and 526 total yards. The defense held the Tigers to 10 first downs and 198 total yards. Prior to the OU tilt, Mizzou averaged 455 yards per game and scored nearly 34 points per game.

The ninth-ranked Sooners crushed Colorado, 42-17, on November 10 in Boulder. The Big Red defense held the 1-8 Buffaloes to minus-three yards rushing, tops in the Switzer era and the most since the 1942 Sooners stymied Kansas State for minus-33 yards. The Buffs were dropped behind the line of scrimmage 13 times for a total of 64 yards, including seven quarterback sacks for minus-48 yards.

Oklahoma took a 14-0 lead, but Colorado cut the deficit to 14-10, and the Sooners scored 28 unanswered points. Big plays included Carr's 64-yard TD run for a 7-0 lead and Bradley's 68-yard scoring strike to Sewell for a 21-10 lead. Bradley hurled another TD pass, and Sewell scored a second touchdown.

Casillas had two big plays for the Sooners. With the Buffs facing third-and-nine on the OU 22, he nailed CU tailback Lee Rouson for a seven-yard loss, which forced a field goal. Late in the first half, Casillas' tackle forced a fumble on the CU five-yard line, and Sewell scored two plays later.

Oklahoma gained more total yards (378-209). Carr rushed for 143 yards on 15 carries, and Winchester punted five times for a 48.8-yard average.

Sooner Magic: Goal-Line Stand

Andre Johnson's replacement at cornerback was Brian Hall, an unheralded senior from Houston, Texas, who became notorious in Soonerland for his goal-line effort against Nebraska.

Sooner Magic against Nebraska was usually an offensive display of wizardry to grasp victory from the jaws of defeat. But the defense rose to the occasion to hold onto a lead.

The 9-1 Huskers were ranked No.1, riding a 21-game home win streak, a 27-game conference winning streak, and three straight over the Sooners. Nebraska's only loss came at the hands of Syracuse in the fourth game of the season. That upset loss knocked the Huskers from atop the AP poll to eighth. Six weeks later, Nebraska had returned to the summit a week before the OU game. The Sooners were a few notches below at No. 6.

The 1984 epic battle featured the nation's best rush offense (NU) against the nation's best rush defense (OU). The Cornhuskers rushed an average 328.5 yards per game, but the Sooners allowed only 68.4 rushing yards per game. Nebraska was favored by six points.

Before a sellout crowd of 76,323 in Lincoln and a national TV (ABC) audience, OU scored first. Migliazza recovered a Nebraska fumble on the NU 26 early in the first quarter. Bradley scored from the one seven plays later and Lashar converted.

Nebraska drove 84 yards to tie the game at 7-7 late in the second period, but then missed a field goal just before halftime.

Lashar kicked a 32-yard field goal to give the Sooners a 10-7 lead with 14:49 remaining in the game.

Following the kickoff, the Huskers drove to their 47 in five plays. On the next play, quarterback Travis Turner optioned right, but Migliazzo popped him from behind, forcing a fumble, and defensive end Troy Johnson pounced on the pigskin at the 40. The Sooners moved to the 28, but Bradley was sacked twice for a total of 23 lost yards.

Winchester punted to the NU 11, and the Huskers drove to the midfield stripe. Quarterback Craig Sundberg then connected on a 42-yard pass to tailback Doug DuBose to the OU eight with 5:32 to go. Jeff Smith gained three yards off left end, then Sundburg carried for four yards to the one. On third-and-goal, Bosworth stopped fullback Scott Porter one inch from the goal line.

"I thought at first he was in," Bosworth said after the game. "The ball could not have been more than an inch from the goal line."

After three unsuccessful plays up the middle, NU head coach Tom Osborne thought a sweep would catch the Sooner defense off guard. He called a surprise sweep to the left side. Sundberg pitched to Smith, but Hall came through the line and stopped the Husker back for no gain. Oklahoma's ball at the one with 5:32 left to play.

"I just tried to keep him from running over me," Hall said afterward.

A field goal would have tied the game and given Nebraska the outright Big Eight Championship, but Osborne preferred winning games. Ten months earlier, he lost the national championship in an attempt to win the game against Miami in the Orange Bowl. Nebraska scored a touchdown late in the game to trail the Hurricanes, 31-30. A game-tying extra-point kick would have given the Huskers the national title, but Osborne elected to win with a two-point conversion, which failed.

After the goal-line stand, the Sooner offense failed to gain a first down and was forced to punt. Nebraska would possibly have good field position to try another score. Winchester banged a 57-yard

Defensive backs Keith Stanberry and Andre Johnson were injured in a one-car accident about four hours after the team returned from Lawrence. Stanberry's Datsun 300Z struck a utility pole near downtown Norman. Stanberry's car was demolished and so were the careers of both players, starters in the Sooner secondary. Stanberry suffered a broken clavicle, fractured left thighbone, stretched ligaments in his right foot, and torn ligaments in both knees. Johnson had a torn ligament in his right knee, and his left knee was dislocated.

"We nearly had two dead players this morning ... they shouldn't have survived that," Barry Switzer said.

Stanberry was expected to be drafted early by the National Football League. Johnson, a redshirt freshman, had promise as a future star.

Both players were mended through several surgeries, but their football careers would not be the same, as neither returned to top-level playing status.

Keith Stanberry's car struck a utility pole and the Sooners defensive back and teammate Andre Johnson were seriously injured.
(© 1984, The Daily Oklahoman)

punt to Smith. Richard Dillon popped the ball loose from Smith, and Jeff Hake recovered for OU at the Nebraska 43.

The Sooners gained only nine yards on the next three plays, then a fourth-down gamble was successful when Bradley picked up two yards to the NU 32. Three plays later, Bradley scooted to the left side and sprinted to the end zone with 56 seconds left in the game. Lashar added the conversion, and the Sooners won, 17-7.

Nebraska had the better statistics in many categories, but the only numbers that counted was the final score. The stellar, young crimson defense held off the nation's best rushing attack six times when the Huskers reached the OU 30-yard line. On 14 plays inside the 30, Nebraska was held to 13 net yards.

"It was our time to win," Switzer exclaimed. "Our defense hung in there, and when we finally got some field position, Danny burned them."

Sewell suffered a pulled hamstring and did not play the final game.

The No. 2 Sooners hosted No. 3 Oklahoma State (9-1) on November 24 for a share of the Big Eight championship and a bid to the Orange Bowl. OU was ranked second in the AP poll, and OSU was one notch below. The UPI poll had the two teams reversed. Oklahoma prevailed, 24-14, before a crowd of 76,198 and a national TV (ABC) audience.

The Sooners drove 72 yards and took a 7-0 lead in the opening stanza. Bradley fired a six-yard scoring strike to Jackson and Lashar kicked the first of three extra-points.

The Pokes tied the game late in the first half after intercepting Bradley's pass. OSU took the second-half kickoff and drove to a 14-7 lead.

OU responded with another 72-yard drive to tie the game midway through the third quarter. Tillman took Bradley's pitch and sailed around left end for a three-yard touchdown to cap the 12-play drive.

Lashar added a 27-yard field goal moments after Dante Jones recovered a Cowboy fumble on the next series.

Early in the fourth quarter, Bobby Riley fumbled Winchester's punt, and Kasper smothered it on the OSU 25. Two plays later, Tillman sprinted 20 yards to the end zone.

The Cowboys failed to move past their 41-yard line the rest of the way.

OU rolled up more first downs (26-9) and total yards (346-198). Tillman led the Sooners with 102 rushing yards. The Pokes passed for 202 yards, but were held for minus-four yards rushing.

The Sooners returned to the Orange Bowl for the first time in three years. No. 2 Oklahoma met the Washington Huskies for the first time before a less-than-capacity crowd of 56,294, which included about 10,000 crimson fans. No. 4 Washington brought a 10-1 record to Miami and was the first Pacific-10 team invited to the 51st Orange Bowl. The Huskies won, 28-17.

Washington took a 14-0 lead in the first quarter.

Bradley scored early in the second stanza after Rockford's interception. Lashar kicked the first of two conversions.

Washington missed a 61-yard field goal try and OU struck pay dirt with one play until intermisssion. Bradley completed a pass to Shepard on the UW 48. Shepard caught the ball between two defenders, shook one tackle and sped to the end zone with no time remaining. The completion was Bradley's first in six attempts.

Casillas recovered a Husky fumble on the UW 46 late in the third period, and the Sooners drove to the four, but had to settle for Lashar's field goal. His 22-yarder was good, but an illegal-procedure penalty nullified the kick. The Sooner Schooner rolled onto the field, and another penalty flag flew—unsportsmanlike conduct on the Schooner.

The OU Ruf-Neks had received permission from the Orange Bowl officials to drive the Schooner onto the field to celebrate a score. Game officials did not allow it, the Huskies accepted the 15-yard penalty, and Lashar's next try was blocked.

1984 Season Record: 9-2-1
Big Eight Conference: 6-1-0 (Champions)

Date	Opponent	Result	Score
September 8	STANFORD	W	19-7
September 15	at Pittsburgh	W	42-10
September 22	BAYLOR	W	34-15
September 29	KANSAS STATE	W	24-6
October 13	Texas at Dallas	T	15-15
October 20	at Iowa State	W	12-10
October 27	at Kansas State	L	28-11
November 3	MISSOURI	W	49-7
November 10	at Colorado	W	42-17
November 17	at Nebraska	W	17-7
November 24	OKLAHOMA STATE	W	24-14
January 1	Washington*	L	28-17

*Orange Bowl at Miami, FL

Lashar kicked a 35-yard field goal to cap Oklahoma's next series for a 17-14 lead midway through the fourth quarter.

The Huskies answered with a 74-yard drive to take a 21-17 lead and scored again in less than a minute after intercepting Bradley's pass.

The Huskies gained more yards (311-286).

The 1984 Sooners finished with a 9-2-1 record and ranked sixth in the Associated Press and United Press International polls. The defense led the nation against the run and ranked fourth in total defense. Casillas was a unanimous All-America selection, defensive player of the year in the Big Eight Conference and UPI's National Lineman of the Year. Bradley, Darrell Reed, and Bosworth joined him on the all-conference first team.

1985

Expectations were running high again in 1985, as the Sooners returned 51 lettermen and 16 starters. The backfield was solid with depth at the running back positions, but the biggest question mark was at quarterback. An inexperienced Troy Aikman got the starting nod to begin the season. Spencer Tillman, Lydell Carr, and Earl Johnson returned to lead the backs. The offensive line was another question with only two players returning—guards Eric Pope and Jeff Pickett. Split end Derrick Shepard pulled double duty, catching passes and returning punts. Tight end Keith Jackson also pulled double duty, catching passes and occasionally running with the pigskin.

The highest hopes were pinned on the defense with the return of All-America noseguard Tony Casillas, ends Darrell Reed and Kevin Murphy, linebackers Brian Bosworth and Paul Migliazzo, and Tony Rayburn and Sonny Brown in the secondary. Tim Lashar would be back to see if he could extend his conversion streak of 34. Lashar finished the '84 campaign making 35 of 36 extra-pointers and 11 of 15 field-goal tries. Mike Winchester, who led the Big Eight Conference with a 39-yard punting average, would also return for punting chores.

The 1985 Sooners were scheduled to open the season against Southern Methodist, and expectations were high for both teams to make a run at the national championship. ABC television network had projected SMU as the favorite to win the 1985 national championship and requested both teams to change their contest in Norman from September 14 to December 7. OU was also a favorite by some prognosticators for the national title.

Barry Switzer favored the change to give his inexperienced quarterback and secondary more time to mature. The schedule was changed, and the Sooners' season opener on September 28 against Minnesota was the latest start to a season since 1961. The change also meant the Big Red would not have a home game until October 19, the latest home opener in 62 years.

Oklahoma was the final Division I football team to kick off the 1985 season on the last weekend in September. This was a concern for Switzer, as the Gophers already had played two games prior to the Oklahoma meeting and won both of them. Switzer's concern was that Minnesota had more playing experience and also time to iron out some of the kinks in its game plan.

Had the Sooners not changed the television game plan, they would have had a game under their belt.

Sooner Magic:
Late Start, Loud Noise and Injuries

Switzer had a second concern, and that was playing indoors where the decibel levels are higher in a domed stadium. And it was, as 62,446 fans packed the Hubert H. Humphrey Metrodome.

His third concern was the injuries that plagued his offensive unit. Five starters missed most of the game. Tillman left the game with a pulled hamstring, and Johnson (who was switched to backup fullback) left with a reinjured kneecap, center Travis Simpson with an ankle injury, and tackles Mark Hutson and Anthony Phillips did not play at all due to dehydration.

"We are a beat-up football team," Switzer said. "We couldn't run our option series because of injuries to our tackles."

Still, the second-ranked Sooners were 17-and-a-half-point favorites, but the offense struggled before a national TV audience (TBS cable network). The defense rose to the occasion, limiting Minnesota to 178 total yards. The Gophers did not earn a first down until 14:40 left in the third quarter.

Lashar's 21-yard field goal put the Sooners on top 3-0 late in the opening period. OU took a 10-0 lead midway through the second quarter with a 60-yard drive that milked nearly seven minutes off the clock. On fourth-and-goal inside the one, Johnson dove over left tackle and Lashar converted.

With 53 seconds into the second quarter, Tillman (who carried eight times for 79 yards) pulled his hamstring and was through for the night.

OU's defense held the Gophers to 30 total yards in the first half. The offense gained 195 yards and had 14 first downs but just 10 points.

A punting duel ensued in the scoreless third quarter. Lashar added another 21-yard field goal with 7:18 remaining in the game for a 13-0 lead.

The Big Red defense held off the Gophers on the next series, but Brown fumbled the punt return and the Gophers recovered at the OU 19-yard line.

Three plays later, Minnesota quarterback Ricky Foggie fired a 12-yard scoring strike to tight end Kevin Starks and Chip Lohmiller nailed the extra point with 4:15 to go.

The Sooners managed only one first down on their next series and punted to the Gophers' 30-yard line with 1:05 remaining.

Two Foggie passes moved the ball to the OU 32 with 22 seconds left.

Defensive pressure forced Foggie to hurry his next two passes, which were incomplete. On the next play, defensive end Troy Johnson sacked the Gopher quarterback for a seven-yard loss. One last play and one last-ditch effort. Foggie heaved the ball toward the end zone where Brown intercepted it to end the game for a 13-7 Sooner triumph.

The Oklahoma defense dominated that final series as it had done all night.

"Our defense is built around one thing ... we like to play three plays and get off the field," Reed said.

"Our defense played like the number-one team in the country, but one mistake in the kicking game made a game of it," Switzer said.

Minnesota head coach Lou Holtz said the OU defense "was the finest I've ever seen."

With the Gophers out of the way, Switzer's concerns were to get his players healthy and to play like champions the rest of the season.

A 41-6 victory over winless Kansas State (0-4) was a good start the following week in Manhattan, yet the second-ranked Sooners lost another starter—Pickett was lost for the season with a knee injury.

The Wildcats ranked 14th in total defense, but the Big Red hammered the defense for 530 total yards. Oklahoma took a 14-0 lead in the second period on touchdowns by fullbacks Carr and Leon Perry.

Kansas State's only touchdown was set up by Shepard's fumbled punt early in the third stanza. The Sooners answered with 13 points and two fourth-quarter touchdowns, which included a 41-yard interception return by freshman cornerback Lonnie Finch.

OU collected more first downs (30-6) and held the Cats to 121 total yards. Carr rushed 25 times for 136 yards, and Aikman completed 10 of 14 aerials for 177 yards. The Sooners punted only once, a 54-yarder by Winchester.

The No. 2 Sooners dominated 17th-ranked Texas, 14-7, before the 40th sellout crowd at the Cotton Bowl. The injury bug continued to bite Oklahoma as Casillas left after the third play with a sore knee and Simpson re-injured his ankle. Casillas would be sorely missed for two games and returned in the Kansas game.

The 3-0 Longhorns took a 7-0 lead late in the first period. Texas' Thomas Aldridge smacked Carr, and the ball popped in the air, where Kip Cooper grabbed it on the seven-yard line and scored.

The Sooners retaliated with an 80-yard scoring march in nine plays. Aikman ignited the drive with a 43-yard pass to Jackson to the Horns' 37. OU kept it on the ground the next eight plays, and Carr leaped over left guard from the one-yard line. Lashar toed the first of two conversions.

The Sooner defense held Texas to minus-24 yards in the final 30 minutes. Texas had zero first downs in the third period, and OU did only one better when Aikman scrambled 28 yards to the UT 26, but the Sooners then stalled, and Lashar missed a 44-yard field-goal try.

Midway through the third stanza, a Steer punt bounced off OU's Mike Aljoe, and Texas recovered on the OU 46. On the next play, Rayburn tipped Todd Dodge's pass, and Bosworth intercepted on the Sooners' 33.

OU drove 60 yards in five plays to break the 7-7 deadlock early in the fourth quarter. From the Texas 45, Aikman pitched at the last second to Patrick Collins on the left corner, and Collins flashed to the end zone.

Oklahoma gained 287 total yards. The defense handcuffed the Longhorns to 17 rushing yards and 53 yards through the air. Entering the OU game, Texas averaged 471 total yards and 34 points per game.

The No. 3 Sooners finally got to play in familiar surroundings in Norman on October 19. The Miami Hurricanes came to town, coached by Jimmy Johnson, former head coach at Oklahoma State. The atmosphere for the Sooners may have been friendlier, but the Hurricanes' defense was not. A crowd of 73,102 turned out on a sunny day. Johnson was 0-5 against Switzer and the Sooners as the OSU coach, and he got his first win against OU, 27-14.

OU trailed, 14-7, midway through the second quarter when Miami defensive end Jerome Brown and tackle John McVeigh nailed Aikman for a 12-yard loss. As the players unpiled to return to their huddles, Aikman did not. He lay on Owen Field writhing in pain with a broken left fibula. For nearly a quarter and a half, Aikman guided the Sooners by completing six of his first seven passes for 131 yards and a touchdown. He also had a 47-yard touchdown run called back because he stepped out at the Miami 21 in the opening quarter.

In four games, the Sooners had a starting player injured in each game. With the starting quarterback out, Switzer had to rely on an untested freshman—Jamelle Holieway.

Miami took a 7-0 lead in the first stanza on a 56-yard pass from Vinny Testaverde to Michael Irvin. Oklahoma answered with an 89-yard drive in six plays. Aikman tossed a 14-yard scoring strike to Shepard and also sparked the drive with a 50-yard pass to Jackson to the UM 16.

The Canes scored 20 unanswered points in the second and third quarters.

OU marched 74 yards in 19 plays, all on the ground, for its other touchdown, a one-yard run by Carr early in the fourth period, but the Sooners did not threaten again.

The Canes gained more total yards (375-362). Testaverde completed 17 of 28 passes for 270 yards and two TDs.

During the first 20 minutes Aikman was in the game, Oklahoma rolled up 218 yards, but only 144 yards in the final 40 minutes.

The loss dropped the Sooners to 10th in the AP poll the following week, and the coaching staff retooled the offense, switching the I-formation to the option attack since Holieway was an option quarterback. The young freshman quarterback from Carson, California, led the Big Red to victories the rest of the way.

Holieway and backup Eric Mitchel sparked the Sooners to eight touchdowns in a 59-14 rout of 3-3 Iowa State the next week in Norman. A less than capacity crowd of 70,124 attended the game in Norman, ending 64 consecutive games of sellouts at Memorial Stadium.

Holieway engineered the first six scoring drives, which included a field goal by Tim Lashar, and Mitchel directed the final three. OU scored on eight of its first nine possessions to lead 52-7 with less than four minutes left in the third quarter.

Holieway accounted for two touchdowns (a run and a pass) and Mitchel ran for two TDs. Big plays of the game included Holieway's 77-yard pass to Shepard for a 31-7 lead and Perry's 76-yard run for the final tally in the fourth stanza.

OU rushed for 542 yards, the most yards on the ground since gaining 556 against Kansas State in 1982. The Sooners also picked up 25 first downs, and 101 yards through the air. Mitchel led with 135 rushing yards, and Perry also crossed the century mark with 132 yards on five totes. The Cyclones picked up 250 total yards.

The ninth-ranked Sooners defeated 5-3 Kansas, 48-6, on November 2 in Norman. Holieway again flashed his brilliance with 162 yards rushing and completing four of six passes for 82 yards. He also scored one TD and passed for another.

A field goal gave Kansas a 3-0 first-quarter lead and Lashar's 28-yard field goal tied the game early in the second period. One play after the ensuing kickoff, Rickey Dixon intercepted a Jayhawk pass on the OU 43. Dixon injured his knee on the play and did not return the rest of the day. Two plays later, Holieway fired a 42-yard TD pass to Jackson for a 10-3 lead.

Perry's two-yard run capped a 92-yard drive on the next Sooner series. Lashar toed another field goal with one second until halftime for a 20-3 lead.

Kansas kicked another field goal late in the third stanza. The Sooners scored two touchdowns in the final 96 seconds of the third period and added two more TDs in the fourth quarter. Mitchel directed the final three TD drives.

OU rolled up more total yards (525-117). Carr carried 14 times for 114 yards. The Jayhawks drove 65 yards in 15 plays for their first field goal and were held to 115 yards in 58 plays afterward.

Oklahoma inched up to seventh in the AP poll following the win.

After three straight home games it was back on the road the next week to Columbia, and the Sooners blew out 1-7 Missouri, 51-6, the Tigers' worst loss in 13 years. Holieway broke the team's single-game total offense record with 324 total yards by running 22 times for 156 yards and completing eight of 17 passes for 168 yards. He ran for one TD and passed for two more.

OU gained more than 500 yards for the third straight game for the first time since 1974.

The Sooners took the opening kickoff and advanced to the MU 11 but had to settle for Lashar's 28-yard field goal and a 3-0 lead. Both teams traded turnovers the rest of the first period. Murphy recovered a Tiger fumble on the 16 late in the second period. Six plays later, Perry blasted over from the one for a 10-0 lead with 36 seconds gone in the second stanza.

Missouri kicked a field goal minutes later, and Lashar toed two more field goals in the final two and one-half minutes of the first half.

The Tigers kicked another field goal to slice their deficit to 23-6 midway in the third quarter, but the Sooners scored four touchdowns the rest of the way.

The Big Red picked up 541 total yards. The defense held the Tigers to 219 total yards.

The defense was the main feature the following week back in Norman, as the No. 7 Sooners shut out 6-3 Colorado, 31-0, before a homecoming crowd of 73,611. It was the first shutout by OU's defense since a 49-0 shellacking of the Buffs in 1981.

The Big Red defense held the Buffs to 109 total yards and six first downs. Colorado entered the game with the ninth best rush offense in the nation, averaging 270 yards per game. Oklahoma's defense held them to 75 yards.

The Buffs' closest possession was when they recovered a fumble on the OU 37 in the second stanza, but they were held to zero yards on the next three plays and punted. They crossed midfield twice in the second half but never past the OU 46-yard line.

Holieway scored two touchdowns for the Sooners and led with 79 yards running and 38 passing.

OU collected 399 total yards.

Oklahoma had risen to fifth in the AP poll when the second-ranked Nebraska Cornhuskers rolled into Norman for a nationally televised game. A sold-out crowd braved the weather that more resembled Lincoln, Nebraska, than Norman—cloudy skies and a wind chill of 15 degrees. The sun only shined on the Sooners as they scored on their second and third possessions of the game en route to a 27-7 win.

The first score was an unforgettable end around reverse for an 88-yard touchdown by Jackson. Ironically, Jackson's jersey number was 88. Holieway faked to Perry, then slipped the ball to Jackson, who swung around from the left side. Jackson sailed down the east side-line and followed a wall of crimson blockers to the end zone. Lashar kicked the first of three conversions.

Jackson, who also had runs of 29 and 18 yards to set up two more scores, was the first tight end to lead the Sooners in rushing (three carries for 136 yards). He also caught a pass for 38 yards.

OU scored again on its next series, a 90-yard drive in six plays. On third-and-seven at the NU 43, Holieway faked a pitch to Anthony Stafford, cut inside and sprinted to the end zone. Holieway also sparked the drive with a 38-yard pass to Jackson for the only completion of the afternoon.

Midway through the second quarter, Nebraska's Von Sheppard scooted 52 yards on a reverse to the OU six-yard line, where Sonny Brown shoved him out of bounds. The Sooner defense stiffened, and Dale Klein shanked a 23-yard field-goal try.

Lashar booted a 36-yard field goal for a 17-0 halftime advantage.

OU scored on its first two second-half possessions, a 34-yard field goal by Lashar and a 17-yard run by Holieway.

Nebraska got on board with 26 seconds left when Chris Spachman recovered halfback Don Maloney's fumble and rambled 76 yards to pay dirt. Still the Oklahoma defense was not scored upon.

The Sooners had more total yards (461-224). OU accepted an invitation to play Penn State in the Orange Bowl on January 1.

The following week, the No. 3 Sooners traveled to Stillwater to meet 7-3 Oklahoma State, ranked 17th in the nation. Freezing rain had drizzled all day on Lewis Field before the 6:45 p.m. kickoff on ESPN. Sleet continued most of the first half and combined with 20 degree temperatures (wind chill near zero) made the field look like a hockey rink. The game then, and since, has been referred to as the "Ice Bowl."

The Sooners prevailed, 13-0, the first shutout of the Pokes in 27 years. About 35,000 fans had turned out for the game, but only about one-half of them remained throughout the game.

The Pokes did not penetrate past the OU 45-yard line until the third quarter and never past the 21.

Lashar toed a 27-yard field goal for a 3-0 lead. OU later marched 33 yards for a 10-0 lead. Tillman sliced through right tackle from the three to cap the five-play drive, and Lashar converted. Holieway sparked the drive with an 11-yard pass to Shepard to the OSU 22.

The Sooners rolled—skated, rather—46 yards to the OSU 13-yard line early in the fourth quarter but had to settle for Lashar's 30-yard field goal.

Oklahoma picked up more total yards (243-131).

After two weeks of miserable, cold weather against Nebraska and OSU, the SMU game was played in spring-like conditions (60 degrees) and under sunny skies.

The Mustangs did not live up to preseason expectations as they rolled into Norman with a 6-4 record and were nowhere to be found in any football polls.

The No. 4 Sooners corralled the Mustangs, 35-13. Jamelle Holieway ran for two TDs, passed for another, and rushed for 126 yards on 13 carries.

Oklahoma picked up more total yards (417-282).

The season had ended with a 10-1 record, and following the SMU game OU moved up to third in the AP poll and second in the UPI. Miami, which had only lost its opening game to Florida, was ranked second in the AP poll behind undefeated Penn State, Oklahoma's Orange Bowl opponent.

Sooner Magic: 'It Was Our Night'

OU had an outside chance of winning the national championship in the AP poll. Miami coach Jimmy Johnson said he believed his team should be voted No. 1 if they defeated Tennessee in the Sugar Bowl.

The Sugar Bowl started about 30 minutes earlier than the Orange Bowl on New Year's night. By the time the fourth quarter rolled around in the Orange Bowl, Tennessee had stunned Miami, 35-7.

Penn State had not lost a game all season, but the Sooners were favored by seven and one-half points. The Nittany Lions took a 7-0 lead in the first stanza, and Lashar's 26-yard field goal early in the second cut the deficit to 7-3.

On the Sooners' next possession they faced third-and-24 from their 29-yard line. Holieway unleashed a bomb to Jackson, who slipped past a Lion defender at the PSU 35, where he snared the pass and dashed to the end zone. Damon Stell's block cut down a Lion defender at the 15. Lashar nailed the extra point, and OU led, 10-7, with 12:26 left in the first half.

An interception by Brown led to Lashar's second field goal of the night, a 31-yarder to up OU's lead to 13-7 with 5:21 before intermission. Another interception, this time by Rayburn at the PSU 45 was returned 35 yards. The Sooners could not punch the ball across, so Lashar booted a 21-yard field goal for a 16-7 lead with 1:53 to go until halftime.

Penn State closed the gap on a 27-yard field goal by Massimo Manca with one second remaining in the half, and the Sooners headed to the locker room with a 16-10 advantage.

The Big Red defense shut down Penn State in the second half, yielding no points by the enemy. The Lions threatened by moving to the OU 21 in the third quarter, but Brown picked off John Shaffer's pass at the one-yard line.

OU's offense managed only four yards, and Winchester punted from the back of the end zone. Jim Coats retrieved the punt at his 49. He quickly handed off to Michael Timpson, who returned the ball to the OU 44 but coughed it up, and Mike Mantle recovered for the Sooners.

The offense bogged down and Lashar booted a 22-yard field goal to give the Sooners a 19-10 lead with 3:09 left in the quarter.

Tight end Keith Jackson sets sail on an 88-yard end-around reverse for a touchdown to give OU a 7-0 lead over Nebraska. *(OU Athletics)*

Lashar's four field goals set a new Orange Bowl record, which still holds today.

Early in the fourth quarter, when the Sugar Bowl score was announced, it was evident the victor of the Orange Bowl would be national champions. Sooner fans had to hold their breath through most of the period. They let out a sigh of relief when Manca hooked a 27-yard field-goal attempt that could have closed the gap within a touchdown.

Insurance came with less than two minutes remaining in the game. Carr took Holieway's handoff, burst up the middle, shifted to his right, and sprinted 61 yards for the touchdown. Carr finished the night with 19 carries for 148 yards. Lashar's extra point was low and wide, but it didn't matter. OU led 25-10, with 1:42 to go.

Cornerback Ledell Glenn picked off a desperation pass at the OU 28 and returned it to the PSU 32 with four seconds remaining.

Sooner fans everywhere were wagging their index fingers to the heavens. Penn State fans had their heads buried in their hands.

As Mitchel dropped to one knee to kill the clock, Switzer was carried off the sidelines on the shoulders of some of his players.

"Oklahoma's a great defensive team," he told NBC's Jimmy Cefalo, both shrouded by jubilant players and fans at midfield.

Cefalo reminded Switzer that OU was the preseason favorite to play for the national championship in the Orange Bowl, but with Aikman's injury against Miami, he wondered if Switzer was confident OU would return to the Orange Bowl. "Did you ever doubt it?" Cefalo asked.

"Yeah, when our quarterback [Aikman] got hurt, but our guys did super job," Switzer said. "It was a great team effort. We were fortunate tonight. It was our night."

It was also OU's year the following day, when both wire service polls voted them No. 1 in the nation, the third in Switzer's career and sixth in Oklahoma football history.

Bosworth, Casillas, and Murphy were chosen All-Americans. Holieway, Phillips, Hutson, Jackson, and Reed joined them on the All-Big Eight's first team.

Casillas was the second Sooner to be awarded the Vince Lombardi Award, which honors college football's outstanding lineman. He was also named UPI Lineman of the Year. Bosworth was named the inaugural winner of the Dick Butkus Award, honoring the nation's best linebacker.

1985 Season Record: 11-1-0

Big Eight Conference: 7-0-0 (Champions)
NATIONAL CHAMPIONS

Date	Opponent	Result	Score
September 28	at Minnesota	W	13-7
October 5	at Kansas State	W	41-6
October 12	Texas at Dallas	W	14-7
October 19	Miami (FL)	L	27-14
October 26	IOWA STATE	W	59-14
November 2	KANSAS	W	48-6
November 9	at Missouri	W	51-6
November 16	COLORADO	W	31-0
November 23	NEBRASKA	W	27-7
November 30	at Oklahoma State	W	13-0
December 7	SOUTHERN METHODIST	W	35-13
January 1	Penn State*	W	25-10

*Orange Bowl at Miami, FL

1986

With the return of a solid backfield and eight starters on defense, the Sooners were preseason favorites to win their seventh national championship and third time back to back.

Barry Switzer believed his 1986 squad would perform better than the year before. After all, Jamelle Holieway returned to lead the '86 Sooners, and his backup, Eric Mitchel, had plenty of experience to receive playing time. Returning to set up behind the quarterback were fullbacks Lydell Carr and Leon Perry and halfbacks Spencer Tillman, Anthony Stafford, Earl Johnson, and Patrick Collins. Guards Anthony Phillips and Mark Hutson and center Travis Simpson returned to anchor the front wall.

A star-studded cast headlined the defense with the return of end Darrell Reed; linebackers Brian Bosworth, Paul Migliazzo and Dante Jones; and Sonny Brown and Rickey Dixon would again lead the secondary.

All four key personnel returned to the special teams—placekicker Tim Lashar, punter Mike Winchester, kickoff specialist Todd Thomsen, and deep snapper Kevin Adkins.

The No. 1 Sooners opened the season with a 38-3 victory over fourth-ranked UCLA on September 6 in Norman. The Big Red defense stopped the Bruins 25 of 54 times at or behind the line of scrimmage and intercepted five passes.

OU's offense scored on six of its first 11 possessions, and three drives ended on turnovers deep into Bruin territory. Lashar's 29-yard field goal gave the Sooners a 3-0 lead in the first stanza. A 72-yard interception by the Bruins set up the tying field goal early in the second period.

OU responded with an 80-yard scoring drive in 12 plays. Holieway's six-yard run capped the drive midway through the second period, and Lashar kicked the first of five conversions. Moments later, Migliazzo picked off a UCLA pass on the Bruins' 33 to set up the next score six plays later. Collins scored on an end sweep from the one-yard line.

Oklahoma scored three touchdowns in the second half, and Mitchel scored the final two.

OU rolled up 479 total yards and held UCLA to 155.

The top-ranked Sooners hammered 1-0 Minnesota, 63-0, two weeks later in Norman. The Big Red defense held the Gophers' versatile quarterback, Ricky Foggie, to minus-22 rushing yards.

Carr and Holieway each scored two touchdowns. Carr scored both of his in the first period, and Holieway scored twice in the second stanza after Jackson raced 66 yards for a TD.

The Sooners scored two touchdowns in the each of the final two periods.

Oklahoma hammered out 523 total yards and held Minnesota to 146. Fifteen Sooners carried the ball in the 478-yard rushing effort. Four of them gained more rushing yards than the entire Gopher team (49 yards).

The No. 1 Sooners traveled to Miami for a nationally televised (CBS) showdown on September 27 with the second-ranked Hurricanes (3-0). There was no love lost between the two teams. The Miami captains refused to shake hands at the pregame coin toss, and both teams brawled for a few minutes near the end of the game.

Vinny Testaverde completed four TD passes to lead the Canes to a 28-16 victory. Testaverde also completed 21 of 28 passes for 261 yards, which included 14 consecutive completions.

Miami led 7-3 at halftime after both teams scored in the second quarter. The Canes scored three times in the third period. OU had one touchdown in the third stanza, a 54-yard strike from Holieway to Jackson to cut Miami's lead to 21-10.

Oklahoma marched 72 yards for the only touchdown in the fourth quarter. Anthony Stafford's two-yard run completed the drive, and the two-point pass misfired.

Miami picked up more total yards (314-276). Bosworth recorded 22 tackles.

The Sooners dropped to sixth in the AP poll and opened their conference slate without the services of four starters—Holieway, Jones, Lonnie Finch, and Dixon—who were sidelined with injuries.

OU thumped 1-3 Kansas State, 56-10, the following week before a homecoming throng of 74,284 in Norman. The Wildcats' five errors (two fumbles, two interceptions and a blocked punt) led to

OU scores. The Sooners scored on their first four possessions and also had two fumbles stall drives inside the KSU 20-yard line.

Mitchel rushed for 126 yards, scored two touchdowns and passed for another to lead the Big Red assault. Third-string quarterback Glen Sullivan got in on the action and directed three scoring drives and scored twice.

Oklahoma took a 28-0 lead midway through the second period, and the Cats scored a touchdown on a blocked punt and added a field goal late in the first half.

The Big Red picked up more total yards (521-152). The defense held the Wildcats to 2.2 yards per play.

The No. 6 Sooners pounded 2-1 Texas, 47-12, the next week at the Cotton Bowl. OU scored on its first three possessions and five of the first six series for a 38-0 lead. Patrick Collins scored three touchdowns for the Sooners.

Mitchel replaced Holieway at quarterback in the second quarter and engineered three TD drives including a 56-yard scoring strike to Jackson for a 31-0 halftime lead.

The Longhorns scored two touchdowns in the second half against the reserve Sooner defense.

Oklahoma collected more total yards (467-247). Thirteen Sooners carried the ball for a combined 396 rushing yards. The Horns were held to 29 rushing yards in 29 attempts.

The No. 5 Sooners shut down Oklahoma State, 19-0, on October 18 in Norman. Tim Lashar booted four field goals and converted one extra point to lead Oklahoma with 13 points. Lashar's four field goals equaled his school record of four set in the previous year's Orange Bowl and Mike Vachon's four conversions against Texas in 1966.

Lashar's field goals gave OU a 12-0 lead through the first 53 minutes. He could have had the team record of five in a game, but he missed a 45-yarder just before halftime.

Two and one-half minutes after his final field goal, Jones intercepted a Poke pass and raced 55 yards for the only touchdown.

The Big Red had twice as many first downs (20-10) and more total yards (352-157). OU's defense held the Pokes to 2.7 yards per play.

Several Sooners sat out of the next game at Iowa State—Noseguard Curtice Williams (knee), Phillips (shoulder), tackle Greg Johnson (shoulder), Darrell Reed (knee). Carr left late in the first stanza with a bruised calf, and Richard Reed later left with a sprained knee.

The fifth-ranked Sooners got their second straight shutout with a 38-0 victory over 4-2 Iowa State. OU recorded consecutive shutouts for the first time since 1967 and third in a season for the first time since 1974.

The Big Red defense held the Cyclones to 67 total yards and six first downs. ISU managed only 1.3 yards each time they touched the ball and failed to gain a first down on 15 third-down situations. The Cyclones were in OU territory only twice and each time after the Sooners fumbled.

Oklahoma started sluggish on the soggy turf and had lost seven yards on the first two series. The Sooners exploded for two TDs and a field goal on the next three possessions. Holieway's seven-yard run late in the first quarter capped an 82-yard, five-play drive for a 7-0 lead, and Lashar kicked the first of five conversions. Carr sparked the drive with a 61-yard run to the ISU 21 just before getting injured.

Lashar also added a 24-yard field goal early in the second period, and Stafford's eight-yard TD run put OU ahead, 17-0, at the half. Holieway hurled a 69-yard scoring strike to Jackson for the only tally in the third period. Mitchel and Earl Johnson scored in the final stanza for 14 more points.

The Sooners gained 492 total yards.

No. 4 Oklahoma hammered 3-4 Kansas, 64-3, on November 1 in Lawrence. Johnson returned to fullback before the game, replacing Carr and Perry, who were out with injuries. Johnson rushed for 203 yards and scored four touchdowns.

The Sooners took a 20-0 lead at halftime on Holieway's two TD runs and two Lashar field goals. OU then erupted for five TDs, and a safety in the third quarter. Four touchdowns and the safety occurred during a span of four minutes and 19 seconds.

Jackson scored on a 33-yard end run for a 41-0 lead, and two plays after the Sooners kicked off, Mike Aljoe sacked the Jayhawks' quarterback, who fumbled out of the end zone for a safety.

Oklahoma picked up 30 first downs, rushed for 566 yards and passed for 69 more. The defense held the Jayhawks to five first downs and 62 total yards. The defense handcuffed Kansas' running game to a minus-52 yards, breaking the school record of minus-33 yards set by the 1942 Sooners against Kansas State.

The No. 4 Sooners handed Missouri its worst loss ever with a 77-0 victory the following week in Norman. OU scored on its first eight possessions, including three touchdowns in the first quarter and four in the second for a 49-0 halftime lead, the most halftime points since the '70 Sooners scored that many against Oklahoma State. Johnson and Mitchel each crossed the goal line twice. Only one touchdown was scored in the third stanza, and the third-string offense added three more TDs in the final period.

The biggest play of the day was Stafford's 82-yard TD sprint for a 42-0 lead. It was the longest play in the 77-game series between both teams.

In addition to the most points yielded by the Tigers, the Sooners set two other Missouri opponent records—most yards rushing (681) and total yards (750). OU averaged 10.8 yards per carry, even though the Tigers had stacked seven to eight players on the line. Oklahoma's 11 rushing touchdowns broke the Sooners' record of nine set in the 1980 Colorado game. Lashar's 11 conversions equaled a mark set by Nebraska against Army in 1972. His eighth conversion broke Uwe von Schamann's NCAA record of 125 straight extra points set in 1978. But so did Van Tiffin of Alabama, who was one consecutive kick ahead of Lashar.

Thirteen players carried the pigskin for the Sooners, with Mitchel (122) and Holieway (117) leading the way. OU's defense held the Tigers to 12 first downs and 198 total yards.

The Colorado Buffaloes, OU's next opponent, lost their first four games, then won five straight all in the Big Eight Conference, including a 20-10 upset over Nebraska. The winner of the OU-Colorado tilt would have the driver's seat for the conference title.

The fourth-ranked Sooners shut down the Buffs, 28-0, on November 15 in Boulder. OU rolled up 344 rushing yards and did not attempt one pass in the game.

Colorado had one of the best punting games in the nation (ranked second in net punting), but poor punts helped the Sooners.

Oklahoma took a 7-0 lead with a 77-yard scoring march on its second possession. Collins zipped 17 yards around left end to finish the drive in 10 plays, and Lashar kicked all four conversions, raising his streak to 133.

Adkins downed Thomsen's punt on the Buffs' one-yard line midway in the second stanza. Colorado fumbled on the next play, and Mike Mantle recovered on the two. Carr leaped over right guard on the next play for a 14-0 lead.

Steve Bryan later dropped CU punter Barry Helton for a nine-yard loss on the Buffs' 38, and the Sooners scored four plays later.

Tillman leaped over right tackle but fumbled in the end zone. Fortunately, Jackson was alert and fell on the pigskin for the score. Holieway sparked the drive with a 20-yard dash to the three on the play before.

Helton shanked a punt 13 yards to the OU 39 on the next series. The Sooners drove 61 yards in eight plays for the final tally. Collins scored his second TD with an eight-yard sprint around right end. Collins also sparked the drive with a 26-yard run to the CU 19 on third-and-eight from the CU 45.

OU's defense held the Buffaloes to 135 total yards, or 2.3 yards per play. Holieway led the running attack with 126 yards.

Sooner Magic:
Another Air Assault Dooms Nebraska

Switzer's Oklahoma teams were well known for their potent running attacks. It was Switzer who perfected the Wishbone formation. But what his teams were not notable for was the passing attack. Not notable, that is, except when Switzer's Sooners played the Nebraska Cornhuskers.

In 1972, in Lincoln, the passing game helped the Sooners overcome a 14-0 third-quarter deficit. A 38-yard pass to split end Tinker Owens set up OU's first touchdown late in the third period. A 22-yard pass to Owens again helped OU to tie the game. OU eventually won, 17-14, on a 41-yard field goal by Rick Fulcher. Switzer was not even head coach then, Chuck Fairbanks was, but Switzer was the offensive coordinator who called the plays.

In 1976, Switzer's fourth year as head coach, the pass was what did the Huskers in. Trailing 17-13 with under a minute to play, Woodie Shepard hurled the ball to Steve Rhodes for 48 yards, then Dean Blevins passed to Rhodes, who lateraled to Elvis Peacock, who carried the ball to the NU two-yard line. Peacock scored the winning TD.

The Huskers got another taste of OU's air force again in 1986 before yet another sellout crowd, a national TV audience, and on another shivering day in Lincoln.

Both teams entered the game with a 9-1 record. OU was ranked third in the nation, Nebraska was fifth and an eight-point favorite. The Sooners needed a win or a tie to win the Big Eight crown outright. A Nebraska victory would tie the Huskers for the Big Eight championship (with OU and Colorado).

The Big Red of the North struck first for a 7-0 advantage midway in the first quarter. The Big Red of the South answered with a nine-play, 70-yard drive capped by Holieway's four-yard run. Lashar kicked the tying goal with 2:36 left in the first quarter.

The Huskers kicked a 37-yard field goal for a 10-7 lead late in the first half. They added a touchdown on their first possession of the second half for a 17-7 advantage.

Neither team threatened the remainder of the third quarter. Lashar toed 22-yard field goal to pull within seven points, 17-10, with 10:39 to go in the game.

During the next six minutes, both teams had trouble maintaining possession of the pigskin. Oklahoma fumbled twice and Nebraska once. The Huskers later moved to the OU 40 in the fourth period

After he made a one-handed catch, Keith Jackson flies to the end zone to pull the Sooners to within one of the Huskers. An extra point tied the score, 17-17. (© 1986, The Daily Oklahoman)

but had to punt. The kick dropped at the OU 25 and rolled to six-yard line with the clock showing 4:10 remaining.

Facing fourth-and-one at the OU 15, Holieway scampered around right end, got the first down but fumbled at the 20. Nebraska recovered, but was flagged for a facemask penalty to Holieway. New life for Oklahoma at the 25.

Holieway threw to split end Carl Cabbiness, who extended his reach, juggled the ball, but kept both feet inbounds at the 33 for another first down. With 2:28 to play, Holieway hurled a pass to Shepard who flew to the Nebraska 32. On the next play, Holieway optioned right, then pitched to Tillman who raced down the side-line to the NU 23.

Holieway carried on the next three plays for a first down. With the clock showing 1:26, Holieway faked a handoff to Carr, then lobbed the ball to Jackson, who grabbed the pigskin at the goal line for the touchdown. Switzer could have ordered a two-point conversion attempt to win the game, but a tie would give the Sooners the Big Eight title and an Orange Bowl bid. Lashar's kick split the uprights for a 17-17 tie.

The Sooner defense stonewalled the Huskers, allowing them only six yards on the next possession. Derrick White fielded the punt at the OU 29 and gained only five yards to the 34.

Fifty ticks remained on the clock. Holieway handed off to Carr, who plowed through for 13 yards to the 47. Holieway then over-threw Shepard on a sideline route. Holieway tossed another incompletion, but OU was penalized for holding, which moved the foot-ball back to the OU 37 and burned 14 seconds on the clock. Third down.

On the next play, Holieway scrambled to the right but was caught by two Husker defenders after an eight-yard gain with 18 seconds left in the game.

After a time out by the Sooners, Holieway lobbed a pass to Jackson, who tipped the ball with one hand at the NU 45. He then grasped it with both hands and raced down the sideline for 30 more yards to the NU 15 before being knocked out of bounds with nine ticks remaining.

Switzer ordered his field goal unit onto the field. Lashar nailed a 31-yard field goal to give OU a 20-17 lead with three seconds to go.

The Sooners were penalized for excessive celebrating, and the kickoff was made from the 20-yard line instead of the 35. Nebraska returned the kickoff to its 35. Bryan hurled to Taylor for a 14-yard loss for the exclamation point.

A terrific comeback for a team rated 105th in the nation in passing.

"This was no comeback," an elated Bosworth said. "It was destiny."

"Sooner magic, just some of that good old Sooner magic," Jackson said.

Switzer did not disagree. "Y'all saw it, it was magical."

Oklahoma had more first downs (18-16) and total yards (371-232). Holieway completed six of 12 passes for 147 yards.

600th Win

The Sooners remained third in the AP poll and were 17 ½-point favorites against No. 9 Arkansas in the Orange Bowl. But OU would be without the services of Bosworth, who was suspended after testing positive in NCAA drug tests. Bosworth showed his displeasure of the NCAA when he removed his jersey and displayed a T-shirt revealed in the third quarter: "National Communists Against Athletes" and "Welcome to Russia."

The Razorbacks entered the Orange Bowl with a 9-2 record. The last time Arkansas met the Sooners, Switzer was embarrassed in a 31-6 loss in the 1978 Orange Bowl. Switzer urged his players to win the game for him. He wanted to beat his alma mater in the worst way. It was a revenge game for Switzer, an Arkansas native and Razorback graduate.

His players responded and crushed the Razorbacks, 42-8, on New Year's Day before a less-than-capacity crowd of 57,291. The win also marked the Sooners' 600th victory in history.

Tillman's TD runs of 77 and 21 yards put the Sooners up 14-0 in the second quarter. Holieway scored twice in the third period for a 28-0 lead.

1986 Season Record: 11-1-0
Big Eight Conference: 7-0-0 (Champions)

Date	Opponent	Result	Score
September 6	UCLA	W	38-3
September 20	MINNESOTA	W	63-0
Septemberr 27	at Miami (FL)	L	28-16
October 4	KANSAS STATE	W	56-10
October 11	Texas at Dallas	W	47-12
October 18	OKLAHOMA STATE	W	19-0
October 25	at Iowa State	W	38-0
November 1	at Kansas	W	64-3
November 8	MISSOURI	W	77-0
November 15	at Colorado	W	28-0
November 22	at Nebraska	W	20-17
January 1	Arkansas*	W	42-8

*Orange Bowl at Miami, FL

The second team entered the game in the final stanza, and Stafford's 13-yard TD run put the Sooners ahead, 35-0. Linebacker Evan Gatewood's interception on his 47 led to the final tally three plays later. Tight end Duncan Parham scored on a 49-yard end-around reverse. Lashar kicked all of his conversions.

The Razorbacks avoided a shutout with a touchdown with 19 seconds to go.

Despite trailing 14-0 at the half, Arkansas had more first downs (11-4) and total yards (157-141). The Sooners dictated the stats in the second half with a 7-6 lead in first downs and 272-83 advantage in total yards.

The 1986 Sooners finished the season with an 11-1 record, a Big Eight championship, and ranked third in the country behind Penn State and Miami.

All-America honors went to Bosworth, Phillips, Hutson, and Jackson. Joining them on the All-Big Eight first unit were Holieway, Darrell Reed, Vickers, Bryan, and Dixon. Bosworth earned the Dick Butkus Award as the counrty's best linebacker for the second straight year.

1987

OU assistant head coach Merv Johnson said the 1987 offensive line was the best he ever coached. Head coach Barry Switzer said Jamelle Holieway was the best wishbone quarterback to play for the Sooners, and that Keith Jackson was the best tight end anywhere. High praise from the men who knew.

The pollsters also agreed that the Sooners would be the best team in 1987. Oklahoma was rated No. 1 in the preseason poll and rode the summit for 11 more weeks until a close decision against Missouri dropped them to second place.

Fifteen starters returned to the '87 squad, including seven all-conference players. Holieway was back to lead the offense at quarterback. Patrick Collins and Anthony Stafford also returned, along with fullbacks Lydell Carr and Leon Perry. Guards Anthony Phillips and Mark Hutson, tackle Greg Johnson, and Jackson were back to anchor the front wall.

Brian Bosworth skipped his senior year and entered into the National Football League's supplemental draft. This left Dante Jones as the leader among the linebackers. He was supported with the return of ends Darrell Reed and Troy Johnson, and Rickey Dixon and David Vickers in the secondary. Tim Lashar, who had a school-record 196 conversions and 135 straight, had graduated. His brother, R.D., a walk-on like Tim, replaced him. Todd Thomsen returned to handle the punting duty.

The Sooners opened the season on September 5 with a 69-14 victory over North Texas State. OU's offense needed only three plays for a 14-0 lead and rolled up a 42-0 advantage before the Mean Green scored 14 unanswered points.

Vickers intercepted an NTS pass on the game's first play and returned it 29 yards to the five-yard line. Two plays later, Carr scored from the four-yard line, and Lashar kicked the first of nine conversions.

The Sooners scored again on their second possession after forcing the Mean Green to punt. Holieway pitched to Collins, who sailed 67 yards for a 14-0 lead.

North Texas recovered Thomsen's fumble moments later, but Jones stole the ball from NTSU's Darren Collins and raced 58 yards for a touchdown midway through the first quarter.

Carr's four-yard run put the Sooners up 28-0 minutes later in the first period. The lead swelled to 35-0 when Holieway hurled a 45-yard scoring strike to Jackson early in the second stanza. Moments

later, defensive end Adrian Cooper intercepted an NTSU pass and returned it 28 yards to the 14. Three plays later, backup quarterback Charles Thompson scored from the eight-yard line.

The Mean Green took the ensuing kickoff and drove 84 yards for a touchdown. North Texas scored the first touchdown of the second half, but the Sooners put four more TDs on the board. Thompson ran for two of them, passed another to split end Carl Cabbiness, and third-string halfback Don Smitherman scored the final tally.

OU gained more and total yards (565-274). Sixteen Sooners carried the ball, combining for 354 rushing yards.

The Sooners hosted 1-0 North Carolina the next week, and Holieway scored all four touchdowns in the 28-0 victory. Three of his touchdowns came on three straight possessions in the second quarter.

His first score, a three-yard run, came early in the second period and capped a 70-yard drive in eight plays. Less than three minutes later, he scored from the four-yard line to complete a 34-yard march in four plays. His final two scores came on one-yard runs late in the first half and late in the third stanza.

The Tar Heels once reached the OU three-yard line for their deepest penetration, but the Big Red defense stiffened.

Oklahoma picked up more total yards (482-203). Holieway rushed for 170 yards, and the Sooners were penalized a school-record 19 times for 125 yards, including a delay-of-game flag against the Pride of Oklahoma band at the start of the second half.

OU annihilated 0-3 Tulsa, 65-0, on September 26, the first Sooner game at Tulsa in 45 years. A record crowd of 47,350 turned out at Skelly Stadium to watch the crimson scoring fest. The Sooners led 31-0 at the half and scored 27 points in the third quarter.

Holieway scored two touchdowns and passed for another to Jackson. Thompson scored three times and threw for another to split end Arthur Guess. Stafford and Carr each scored a touchdown, and Lashar toed a 53-yard field goal and nailed all nine conversions to round out the scoring glut.

Oklahoma rolled up 34 first downs, rushed for 438 yards, and passed for 103. Thompson led the running attack with 105 yards. The defense held Tulsa to three first down, all in the first half. The defense also handcuffed the Hurricane to 50 total yards on 47 snaps, and Tulsa went 0-for-13 on third-down situations.

The Sooners traveled to Ames, Iowa, the next week and continued their offensive might with a 56-3 win over 0-3 Iowa State. Oklahoma amassed 28 first downs, 531 yards on the ground, and 77 through the air.

The Big Red defense also flexed its defensive muscle, holding the Cyclones to five first downs and 73 total yards (1.4 yards per play). I-State was held to 21 rushing yards on 44 carries, and the OU defense sacked ISU quarterbacks six times.

Stafford scored three touchdowns, and Holieway ran for one score and passed for two more. His nine-yard strike to Jackson put the Sooners up 28-0, and a 42-yard pass to Stafford raised the lead to 35-0 just before halftime.

The Cyclones kicked a field goal with one second left until the break.

Stafford scored his third TD, and Thompson added another in the third period, and backup fullback Mike McKinley scored his first career touchdown as a Sooner in the fourth stanza.

Anthony Phillips pulled a calf muscle and would sit out the next two games.

The Sooners rolled into Dallas on October 10 favored by 31 points over Texas. The 2-2 Longhorns lost their first two games and won the next two. OU did better than the spread with a second-straight 35-point win, 44-9.

The Steers stacked seven to eight men on the defensive line, and the Sooners still managed to slice up 392 rushing yards. Oklahoma's defense picked off a school-record seven passes, tying the mark set three other times (1939 against Southern Methodist, 1941 against Oklahoma A&M and 1951 against Kansas State). Rickey Dixon and Derrick Crudup each shagged two interceptions.

Texas took a 3-0 lead and OU answered with a 78-yard scoring drive in eight plays. Carr's seven-yard run capped the drive, and Lashar converted the first of five conversions. Holieway sparked the drive with a 32-yard pass to Jackson on the play before Carr scored.

Lashar added two field goals in the second quarter for a 13-3 lead, but Texas kicked another try 17 seconds before halftime to cut OU's lead to 13-6 at halftime.

The Steers moved to the OU 14 early in the third period, but Dixon broke their back when he picked off Bret Stafford's pass on the 10-yard line and raced back 50 yards to the UT 40. Three plays later, Holieway fired a 44-yard scoring strike to Cabbiness for a 20-6 lead.

Troy Johnson intercepted another Texas pass moments later and returned it four yards to the UT 38. Two plays later, Carr sprinted 32 yards for a 27-6 lead.

Collins scored on a four-yard run less than four minutes later. Texas nailed its third field goal early in the fourth stanza. Not to be outdone, Lashar booted his third field goal, and less than two minutes later, Thompson scored on a 55-yard run.

OU had more total yards (468-251). Thompson again led the Oklahoma running attack with 114 yards.

The Sooners were back on the road the next week to Manhattan and returned home with a 59-10 victory over 0-5 Kansas State. Eight different Sooners scored touchdowns, and Holieway accounted for two scores, one through the air and one on the ground.

OU scored on its first two possessions and five of the first seven series for a 31-0 halftime lead and on its first two possessions in the second half. Like a real Wildcat, the Sooners pounced quickly for their scores as no drive took longer than four minutes and 17 seconds.

Kansas State scored a field goal late in the first period and tossed an 81-yard scoring strike midway in the second.

The Big Red rushed for 518 yards, passed for only 44 yards and did not turn the ball over once. Eric Mitchel, who was moved to halfback before the season began, led all rushers with 149 yards on seven carries and scored his first touchdown of the year. He scored on an 82-yard run to put the Sooners up 52-10 early in the fourth quarter. Rotnei Anderson also scored his first TD of the season with the final tally, a one-yard run with 4:57 left in the game.

Kansas State picked up 270 total yards.

Colorado finally gave the Sooners a little competition on October 24, at least as far as the score revealed. Oklahoma defeated the 4-2 Buffaloes, 24-6, in the first night game at Owen Field.

OU marched 67 yards to take a 7-0 lead late in the first stanza. Stafford's 23-yard TD run topped the eight-play drive, and Lashar kicked the first of three conversions.

The Sooners recovered a Buff fumble three plays after the kickoff, which led to Lashar's 48-yard field goal for a 10-0 advantage with 40 seconds remaining in the first quarter.

Colorado's Eric Hannah kicked the first of two field goals midway through the second period and moments after recovering Lydell Carr's fumble on the OU 32. His second field goal minutes later cut Oklahoma's lead to 10-6.

The Sooners drove 49 yards in two plays to take a 17-6 lead early in the third stanza. Holieway carried for 28 yards to the CU 21, and Carr followed with a touchdown run.

Colorado later advanced to the OU 14-yard line, where they faced fourth-and-one, but surrendered when tailback Eric Bienemy was nailed for a four-yard loss. The Buffs later gambled on fourth down from their 37, but OU noseguard Dante Williams stopped quarterback Mark Hatcher for no gain. Oklahoma took over and scored in seven plays on Collins' one-yard run.

The Sooners gained more total yards (412-313). Holieway carried for 146 yards, and Carr added 100 more.

The Sooners returned to blowout boulevard with a 71-10 victory over 1-6 Kansas the next week in Lawrence. The Big Red scored on five of its first six possessions and seven of the first 10. Kansas had six turnovers (five fumbles and one interception), which led to three Oklahoma touchdowns and a field goal.

Collins' two touchdowns led a pack of nine players who scored for the Sooners. Holieway ran for a TD and passed for another.

A couple of third-stringers scored their first touchdowns in a crimson uniform. Halfback John Green scored on a three-yard run with 1:15 remaining in the game, and 15 seconds later linebacker Brad McBride stole a Jayhawk pass and returned it 17 yards for the final tally.

The Sooners rolled up 565 rushing yards (one less yard than a year ago against the Jayhawks) and passed for 69 more. The defense held Kansas to 208 total yards.

The Sooners returned home on November 7 and defeated 12th-ranked Oklahoma State, 29-10, to give Switzer his 146th win, surpassing Bud Wilkinson as the winningest coach in Sooner history. The celebration was marred by injuries to two of the Sooners' star players. Carr went down with a knee injury early in the game, and Holieway left with a knee injury in the third quarter.

Holieway's injury occurred on a non-contact play near the Cowboys' sideline, OSU head coach Pat Jones immediately came to Holieway's aide.

"It happened right in front of me," Jones said. "I heard him holler, and I tried to grab him before he fell down."

Carr returned to play in the Orange Bowl, but Holieway was through for the season.

The Sooners took a 7-0 lead with a 51-yard march midway through the first period. Holieway's five-yard run capped the five-play drive, and Lashar converted.

The 7-1 Pokes answered with a 38-yard field goal. OU responded with Lashar's 35-yard field goal good for a 10-3 advantage.

The lead grew to 16-3 late in the third stanza when backup halfback Bernard Hall scored on a three-yard run, but the Pokes blocked the extra point. OSU drove 85 yards to cut the lead to 16-10 early in the fourth quarter.

Poke quarterback Mike Gundy threw four interceptions and the final two gave the Sooners 13 points late in the game. Troy Johnson stole Gundy's pass on the Cowboys' 10-yard line and scooted into the end zone with 3:51 remaining, and the two-point run failed.

Moments later, the Pokes were on the move into Sooner territory, but Dixon picked off Gundy's pass on the OU five and sailed 95 yards for the final tally with 32 seconds remaining. Lashar toed the conversion.

Oklahoma collected 413 total yards, all on the ground, as Holieway misfired on six passes. Anderson rushed for his career-best 191 yards, and Holieway added 123 yards. The Pokes gained 312 total yards. Thurman Thomas rushed for 173 yards for the Cowboys.

The Sooners defeated Missouri, 17-13, the following week before a homecoming crowd of 75,004. Coach Switzer was the next injury victim early in the first period. Tiger players chased Thompson, rode him out of bounds, and crashed into the Sooner skipper.

"I got rolled up over on the bench and hit the inside of my knee," Switzer explained.

Switzer suffered a ligament strain and went to the locker room to have a splint placed on his leg. Trainers replaced the splint with a plastic cast at halftime.

Oklahoma lost four of six fumbles, twice thwarting drives into Mizzou territory and once setting up the Tigers' only touchdown.

The Sooners took a 3-0 lead on Lashar's 19-yard field goal late in the first stanza, and the Tigers answered with a field goal early in the second. Oklahoma marched 52 yards in seven plays to take a 10-3 lead late in the first half. Stafford's one-yard run capped the drive with 45 seconds remaining, and Lashar converted the first of two.

The Big Red drove 78 yards in eight plays for a 17-3 advantage midway through the third quarter. Thompson scored on a 14-yard run, and he also sparked the drive with a 25-yard pass to Jackson to the MU 25.

Missouri scored one play after recovering an OU fumble late in the third period.

The Tigers advanced to the OU 20-yard line with 10 minutes remaining, but on second-and-four, Dante Jones nailed John Stollenwerck for an eight-yard loss, and Mizzou settled for a field goal to cut Oklahoma's lead to 17-13.

Missouri failed to mount a threat on its next two series.

Oklahoma picked up more total yards (387-193). Anderson again led the running attack with 118 yards. Thompson completed five of nine passes for 156 yards.

The narrow victory dropped the Sooners to second in the AP poll, and 9-0 Nebraska replaced them at the top. For the first time in 16 years, OU and Nebraska entered the 68th meeting in Lincoln with nary a loss between the two. The Cornhuskers were five-point favorites in a game that was billed as "Game of the Century II." The pregame buildup mirrored the first game of the century in 1971, Nebraska was No. 1 and OU was second. The victors would claim the Big Eight championship, an Orange Bowl bid, and a chance for a national championship. One exception to this game was that it was played in Lincoln and not Norman.

Nebraska players proclaimed that their Memorial Stadium was "our house."

"You come in here, then give your respects and then you leave … with a loss," said Husker defensive end Broderick Thomas the week of the game.

Plastic keys were made and sold as souvenirs symbolizing that the Huskers held the only key to their stadium.

The game did not mirror the 1971 offensive shootout as the Sooners dominated the Huskers, 17-7, before a record throng of 76,663 and a national TV (CBS) audience. It was Oklahoma's first win in a battle of No. 1 versus No. 2 teams. Three OU turnovers (two fumbles and one interception) squelched scoring threats in the first half.

The Huskers took a 7-0 lead with a 78-yard drive on their second series. Nebraska held the lead through halftime and crossed midfield only twice more in the game.

Dixon intercepted two Nebraska passes to tie him for the school record (eight) held by Scott Case. Dixon's first theft, tipped by Derrick White, on the NU 13 set up the tying touchdown. Two plays later, Stafford scored on an 11-yard run, and Lashar's conversion knotted the game at 7-7.

Late in the same quarter, a spin option play was called. Collins took Thompson's pitchout and raced 65 yards down the sideline to the end zone, and Lashar converted for a 14-7 lead. Lashar added an insurance field goal from 27 yards out midway in the fourth period.

"Patrick's got great speed, and he outran everybody on the corner and we blocked everybody on the corner and he outran everybody in pursuit," Switzer recalled. "We worked on that play all week for that situation and executed it."

Jones, who led the defense with 12 tackles, was heard shouting from the sideline, "Well, it ain't your house no more."

After the game Jones added, "We don't need a key to any door. We just used our feet and kicked the door in."

Oklahoma rolled up 23 first downs, 419 yards rushing and 25 more through the air. The defense held the Huskers to 11 first downs and 235 total yards, 289 below their average. Three Sooners rushed for over 100 yards—Collins led with 131, Thompson had 126, and Anderson added 119 more.

"I told Charles [Thompson] during the week that if he played like he practiced that he'd stun the nation," Switzer said after the game.

The Sooners staked claim to the Big Eight crown with their 25th straight conference victory and returned atop the AP poll. Oklahoma also received the automatic invitation to play in the 54th Orange Bowl. Their opponent was another nemesis—the Miami Hurricanes.

During the past three years, OU won 33 games and lost two. Both losses came at the hands of the Hurricanes, and Sooner faithful were chomping at the bit to defeat Miami. Two Miami starters—linebacker George Mira Jr. and offensive tackle John O'Neill—were suspended for failing NCAA drug tests two weeks before the Orange Bowl. The tests found diuretics in both athletes.

It's a Fact

The Sooners led the nation in nearly every major offense and defense category. Total offense, averaging 499.7 yards per game; rushing offense, averaging 428.8 yards per game; and scoring offense with 43.5 points per game. Total defense, yielding an average of 208.1 yards per game; rushing defense, allowing an average of 60.7 yards per game; passing defense, yielding an average of 102.4 yards per game; and scoring defense allowing an average 7.5 points per game.

OU led the nation in total defense and pass defense for the third straight year and scoring defense for the second straight year.

1987 Season Record: 11-1-0
Big Eight Conference: 7-0-0 (Champions)

Date	Opponent	Result	Score
September 5	NORTH TEXAS	W	69-14
September 12	NORTH CAROLINA	W	28-0
September 26	at Tulsa	W	65-0
October 3	at Iowa State	W	56-3
October 10	Texas at Dallas	W	44-9
October 17	at Kansas State	W	59-10
October 24	COLORADO	W	24-6
October 31	at Kansas	W	71-10
November 7	OKLAHOMA STATE	W	29-10
November 14	MISSOURI	W	17-13
November 21	at Nebraska	W	17-7
January 1	Miami (FL)*	L	20-14

*Orange Bowl at Miami, FL

The 11-0 Hurricanes burst the Sooners' bubble with a 20-14 victory to claim the national championship. Oklahoma's defense provided little pressure to Miami quarterback Steve Walsh, who passed for 209 yards and two touchdowns. OU had no passing game of its own and had to rely on a little trickery to score one touchdown.

The Canes took the opening kickoff and marched 78 yards for a 7-0 lead. Walsh, who completed five of nine passes for 59 yards in the drive, hurled a 30-yard scoring strike to Melvin Bratton.

Midway through the second stanza, Dixon intercepted Walsh's pass and returned it 20 yards to the Miami 32, but a clipping penalty set the Sooners back to the UM 49. The Big Red tied the game 15 plays later on Stafford's one-yard run around right end and Lashar's conversion with nine seconds left until halftime.

Miami kicked a field goal early in the third for a 10-7 lead. Minutes later, the Canes drove 64 yards to up their lead to 17-7 late in the same quarter. Walsh capped the drive with a 23-yard scoring strike to Michael Irvin.

The Sooners took the kickoff and advanced to the Miami 23, but Jackson fumbled there after catching a pass.

Cox nailed a 48-yard field goal with 3:41 remaining in the game. The Sooners took the kickoff and quickly moved to the UM 29-yard line in seven plays. There OU used the fumblerooski, a play where the quarterback takes the snap and places it at the foot of a lineman and another lineman picks up the ball. Mark Hutson scooped it up off the 29-yard line and rumbled into the end zone with 2:05 to go, and Lashar kicked the conversion.

The Canes recovered the onside kick, but OU's defense forced them to punt. The Sooners got the ball back with 56 seconds to go, but two penalties and a fumble thwarted the comeback attempt.

Miami gained more total yards (477-255).

The Sooners finished third in the AP poll behind Miami and Florida State.

Five Sooners were named All-Americans—Jackson, Hutson, Dixon, Jones, and Reed. Greg Johnson, Bob Latham, Phillips, and Vickers joined them on the All-Big Eight first unit. Dixon was named a co-winner for the Jim Thorpe Award honoring the nation's best defensive back. Jackson also earned the NCAA Top Six Award.

1988

The Sooners were favored to win the Big Eight Conference although they lost many starters to graduation, including five All-Americans (Mark Hutson, Rickey Dixon, Keith Jackson, Dante Jones, and Darrell Reed). Jamelle Holieway returned from knee surgery to lead the offense at quarterback. Charles Thompson returned, and the Sooners rarely missed a beat when he replaced Holieway in the latter part of 1987. Seasoned veterans rounded out the backfield—fullback Leon Perry and halfbacks Anthony Stafford and Damon Stell.

Bob Latham and Anthony Phillips were the only returnees in the front line. Veterans Eric Bross and Carl Cabbiness shared split end duties. Placekicker R.D. Lashar and punter Todd Thomsen returned for kicking duties.

Patrick Collins takes a bow after scoring a late third-quarter touchdown to put OU ahead of the Huskers, 13-7.
(© 1987, The Daily Oklahoman)

Barry Switzer believed his defense would be good, although new faces dotted the starting line, including tackles Scott Evans and Curtice Williams and noseguard Tony Woods. Scott Garl and Lonnie Finch were part-time starters in the secondary from the prior year.

A new NCAA rule allowed a defensive team two points for returning a blocked kick or an intercepted pass to the opponent's end zone during a conversion attempt. In 1992 this was extended to include a fumble return from any spot outside the end zone.

Injuries plagued the Sooners before the season opener against 1-0 North Carolina. Tight end Duncan Parham suffered a broken ankle, Dante Williams had a broken foot, and Richard Dillon suffered a recurring ankle injury from the prior year.

The No. 4 Sooners matched the previous year's score with a 28-0 victory over the Tar Heels on September 10 in Chapel Hill, before a crowd of 53,675, the second largest attendance for a Tar Heel game to date.

OU put together four long scoring drives in its first seven possessions. The hot temperature caused the Sooner coaches to alternate players on each series. Holieway directed three TD drives.

Perry, Thompson, Stafford and Holieway all scored for the Sooners. Lashar converted all of his kicks. After scoring the final touchdown early in the second stanza, the Sooners failed to penetrate the Heels' 41-yard line the rest of the game, and North Carolina never made a serious threat.

Oklahoma picked up more total yards (468-255). Eleven Sooners carried the ball for a combined 291 yards.

Latham injured a knee in the first quarter and would miss the next eight games. Mike Wise replaced him in the lineup.

400th Home Game

The Sooners returned home the following week to host Arizona in the first matchup between both schools. The game also marked the 400th home game in Sooner football history. Holieway ran for one touchdown and passed for another to lead OU to a 28-10 victory on a drizzly afternoon.

The 2-0 Wildcats took a 3-0 lead with a field goal on their first possession. OU countered with an 82-yard drive for a 7-3 advantage. Perry's one-yard plunge capped the 14-play drive, and Lashar kicked the first of four conversions.

Midway through the second stanza, center Greg Williams recovered a fumbled punt for the Sooners on the Arizona seven-yard line. Three plays later, Holieway slashed between two defenders and scored on a five-yard run.

Arizona marched 45 yards to trail, 14-10, midway through the third period and threatened to take the lead with a drive to the OU 11, but Sooner safety Ken McMichel intercepted on the one and returned it 30 yards.

Ninety-four seconds later, Holieway hurled a 43-yard scoring strike to Bross for a 21-10 lead. Kevin Thompson intercepted a Wildcat pass on the AU 18-yard line to set up the final Sooner tally three plays later. Stafford took Holieway's pitch out and scored on a five-yard run.

OU gained more total yards (352-284). Holieway, who injured his elbow in the game, rushed for 75 yards and passed for 73 more.

Switzer hoped he could get his first win against No. 5 Southern California on September 24 in Los Angeles. Switzer held a 0-2-1 record against the Trojans, but USC was too powerful in its 23-7 victory. The Sooners were sloppy with six turnovers (four interceptions and two fumbles).

Quarterback Rodney Peete completed 16 of 34 passes for 198 yards and ran for 43 yards to lead the 2-0 Trojans. Peete didn't score or pass for any touchdowns, but his 22-yard run on third-and-20 moved his team to the OU 20-yard line on the first scoring drive. He also had a 19-yard pass that set up a field goal for a 10-0 lead.

Holieway's two fumbles led to 10 more points for the Trojans and a 20-0 lead in the first half. The Sooners took the second-half kick-off and marched 80 yards in four plays for their only score. Holieway connected a 26-yard pass to Bross to midfield and a 48-yard strike to Cabbiness to the USC two-yard line. Perry scored on the next play, and Lashar converted.

Oklahoma could not advance past its 43-yard line the rest of the way. The Trojans kicked their third field goal in the fourth quarter to put the game away.

USC collected more first downs (30-10) and total yards (266-222). The Big Red rushed for 89 yards, the lowest ground output since running for 43 yards in a loss to the Trojans in 1982.

The Sooners dropped to 10th in the AP poll and blasted Iowa State, 35-7, the next week in Norman before a homecoming throng of 75,004. The win extended OU's conference winning streak to 26 games.

Holieway completed all five of his passes for 133 yards and two scoring strikes to lead the Big Red. He was versatile with rollouts and play-action passes and also had a third touchdown set up by a 30-yard pass. The Sooners cashed in on a Cyclone fumble and a blocked punt to take a 21-7 halftime lead. Oklahoma drove 56 and 55 yards for their second-half touchdowns.

Oklahoma gained 426 total yards and held Iowa State to 113 total yards. The defense sacked Cyclone quarterback Bret Oberg eight times for a total of 46 yards in losses.

The 10th-ranked Sooners invaded Dallas on October 8 and knocked out Texas for the fourth straight time with a 28-13 punch. The Big Red picked off three Steer passes and recovered a fumble and did not turn the ball over once.

OU marched 93 yards in 12 plays for a 6-0 lead late in the first stanza. Perry capped the drive with a two-yard run, but the Longhorns blocked Lashar's conversion. Holieway ignited the drive with a 43-yard pass to freshman halfback Mike Gaddis to midfield on the first play. Holieway sprained an ankle in the drive and sat out the rest of the game.

Early in the second period, Stafford bolted 86 yards for a touchdown and set the series record for the longest run from scrimmage. Charles Thompson scored the two-point conversion.

Texas drove 70 yards to cut OU's lead to 14-7 midway through the third quarter. Less than two minutes later, Shannon Kelly's pass caromed off a teammate's thigh and into Kert Kasper's hands. The Sooner linebacker bowled over several Horns to the end zone and Lashar converted.

The Horns kicked two field goals in the fourth stanza to close the gap to 21-13. OU responded with an 81-yard scoring march in seven plays. Thompson's eight-yard run capped the drive, and Lashar converted. Perry, who rushed for 188 yards in the game, sparked the drive with a 41-yard run to the Texas 11.

OU rolled up more total yards (387-337).

Holieway played briefly the next week against 0-5 Kansas State and reinjured the ankle.

The Sooners set the NCAA record with 768 rushing yards and a school-record 38 first downs en route to a 70-24 victory over the Wildcats in Norman. OU broke the previous rushing record of 758 yards held by the 1980 Sooners against Colorado. The Sooners also broke the record of 37 first downs set against Kansas in 1971.

Thompson, who replaced Holieway at quarterback, carried for 124 yards, scored three touchdowns, and passed for another to lead the Sooners to a 49-0 halftime advantage. Oklahoma scored on its first three possessions, and Holieway directed one scoring drive in the second period. Backup halfback Eric Mitchel scored twice (85 and 47 yards) and carried the ball only six times for 161 yards.

Redshirt freshman quarterback Chris Melson played the entire second half, and walk-on halfback Joe Muti scored the final touchdown.

The Wildcats scored all of their points in the second half against the reserve defense.

Fourteen Sooners carried the ball in the record rushing effort. The Sooners, who also passed for 61 yards, gained 9.6 yards each time they touched the football. Kansas State picked up 21 first downs and 419 total yards.

Sooner Magic: Reserves Fill Big Shoes In Boulder

Quarterbacks are known as the field generals of a football team and when a quarterback is sidelined with an injury, a team may lose some ammunition in its offensive firepower. Not the Oklahoma Sooners. That's why recruiting is vital to any college football team. *Sports Illustrated* labeled Switzer one of the greatest recruiters in college football.

Holieway sat out of the Colorado contest on October 22 with a sprained ankle. Thompson was pegged as the starter against the 5-1 Buffaloes. The Sooners were 13 ½-point favorites over the Buffs. But the oddsmakers evidently knew that with Thompson at quarterback, the Sooners hardly missed a beat offensively. The injury bug would continue to rear its ugly head against Colorado during the first night game ever played at Folsom Field in Boulder and before a national TV audience on ESPN. Gaddis injured his neck midway through the first quarter and spent the second half on the sidelines in street clothes and a neck brace.

Gaddis and Holieway weren't the only starters hampered with injuries. Stafford twisted his knee diving for a pass in the third quarter. Curtice Williams suffered a twisted right ankle, but he continued to play in the game. Phillips and Mark Van Keirsbilck missed a few plays in the fourth quarter. Still, the Big Red had enough weapons to win the game.

Oklahoma took the opening kickoff and marched 80 yards in eight plays for the first score. Thompson capped the drive with an 11-yard run and Lashar nailed the first of two extra points for a 7-0 lead.

Five minutes into the second quarter, OU tried a fake punt, which succeeded for the moment. Melson, the upback, took the snap and carried the ball for a first down, but coughed up the pigskin. The Buffs recovered. Three plays later, Colorado scored its first touchdown against the Sooners for the first time in 13 quarters between the two teams. A two-point conversion gave CU a 14-7 lead midway through the second quarter. The Buffs had their first lead over the Sooners for the first time in 12 years, a 42-31 victory in 1976.

Stafford scored on a three-yard run late in the first half after Jerry Parks intercepted a Buff pass. Parks also recovered a fumble in the third quarter to squelch a Colorado threat.

After a scoreless third period, Oklahoma moved the ball early in the fourth. The Sooners had to overcome a trio of crucial third-down situations in the 71-yard drive. On third-and-six from the OU 24, Thompson handed off to Mitchell, playing at tailback this time, and Mitchell gained 23 yards.

On third-and-eight from the CU 38, Thompson dropped back to pass but saw a gap up the middle and took off. He cut toward the right sideline and was knocked out of bounds at the Colorado 23-yard line.

On third-and-five from the CU 17, Anderson smashed through the middle for six yards. The Sooners could not get the ball into the end zone on the next three plays and relied on the Lashar's foot to break the tie. Lashar booted a 22-yard field goal from the right hash mark and into the wind to put the Sooners up 17-14 with 8:15 left in the game.

The Buffs moved to the OU 37 late in the game, but Williams and defensive tackle Scott Evans sacked Sal Aunese for an eight-yard loss with about a minute to play.

That sack was the turning point of the game. It forced the Buffaloes to try a 62-yard field goal with a brisk wind behind their backs. The kick by Ken Culbertson sailed the distance to the goal posts, but veered wide to the right, and the Sooners escaped with a 17-14 victory.

"I'm glad to get out of here with a win," Switzer exclaimed. "The big sack at the end of the game was the big play.

"I'm proud of our football team for winning the second half, overcoming a lot of injuries and a lot of penalties. We lost a lot of players and a lot of starters."

OU extended its winning streak in the Big Eight Conference to 28 and 12 straight over Colorado. The Sooners hammered out 379 total yards, 40 more than the Buffs.

The eighth-ranked Sooners returned to Norman the following week and blew out Kansas, 63-14. The 0-7 Jayhawks scored a touchdown after OU put up a score, and the two teams were tied at 14-14 in the first quarter. A touchdown in the second stanza put the Sooners ahead, 21-14, then OU exploded for five touchdowns in their first five series of the second half.

Holieway returned to action and rushed for 26 yards and passed for 134 more. The effort raised his career yardage total to 4,852 yards, breaking Jack Mildren's school record of 4,818. Holieway also ran for one TD and passed for another. Thompson scored two touchdowns and rushed for 118 yards. His one-yard run capped a 91-yard drive to put the Sooners ahead for good at 21-14 in the second period.

OU rolled up 32 first downs, rushed for 463 yards and passed for 141 more. The Jayhawks gained 323 total yards.

Sooner Magic: Theirs Won the Heisman, Ours Had the Better Game

The CBS network had passed on televising the 1988 Oklahoma-Oklahoma State game. Good news for ESPN. They got the rights and broadcast one of the best OU-OSU match ups ever.

The Cowboys were 5-1 and rated 12th in the AP poll, four notches below the Sooners. The Cowboys' lone defeat was at the hands of Nebraska.

By the time the ESPN cameras were turned on for the 3:30 p.m. kickoff, the Pokes' junior tailback, Barry Sanders, was being touted as the best back of the year. But the Sooners countered with Gaddis.

Oklahoma had won 11 straight victories over the Cowboys, prior to the '88 meeting before 50,440 fans. The winner would have a chance at winning the Big Eight crown and a trip to the Orange Bowl. Although Nebraska defeated the Pokes, OU would have to beat the Huskers for the outright title.

The state of Oklahoma is known for the winds that come sweeping down the plain, and the game at Lewis Field in Stillwater was no different with gusts at times up to 40 mph.

Gaddis scored a touchdown on the Sooners' first two possessions. The first came on a 13-yard run and the second on a 44-yard jaunt. He also had a 50-yard run on the game's first play.

The Pokes answered the second TD with a 59-yard drive to narrow the gap to 14-7.

The Sooners countered with an 80-yard scoring drive capped by Perry's seven-yard run.

OSU marched 89 yards for another touchdown in the second quarter after recovering Thompson's fumble on the Pokes' 11.

Lashar toed a 27-yard field goal late in the first half for a 24-14 advantage.

Sanders scored two TDs in the fourth stanza to lift the Cowboys to a 28-24 lead with 8:45 remaining in the game.

The Cowboys led the Sooners for the first time since the third quarter in 1984. But the lead in 1988 was short-lived. The Sooners retaliated with an 80-yard, 13-play attack. From the OU 20, Thompson and Gaddis each gained nine yards, then Thompson fired a pass to Perry to the Pokes' 45-yard line.

On second-and-five at the OSU 30, Thompson pitched to Stafford, who bobbled the ball but landed on it for a two-yard loss. On the next play, Thompson zipped a screen pass to Gaddis on the right side. Gaddis fumbled at the 23, and the ball squirted backwards to the 25 when tackle Mark VanKeirsbilck recovered. A measurement by officials revealed the Sooners were inches short of the first down. Switzer signaled to go for it.

Thompson faked a handoff to Stafford. Stafford and Gaddis bumped into each other in the backfield, then Stafford bumped into Thompson, pushing the OU quarterback forward for the first down.

On the next play, Thompson kept the ball and scurried down the left side. He then cut inside at the seven-yard line and crossed the goal line untouched. Lashar kicked his fourth conversion for a 31-28 lead with 2:33 to go.

Quick as a wink, the Pokes moved from their 10 to the OU 45, after the kickoff Mike Gundy completed passes of 22 and 23 yards to Hart Lee Dykes. The Pokes later faced fourth-and-inches at the OU 10.

As the players were returning to their huddles, OSU fullback Garrett Limbrick was flagged for something he said to an official. The penalty moved the ball back to the OU 34-yard line, fourth-and-14 instead of fourth-and-one inch with one minute remaining. After an OSU time out, Gundy set up in the shotgun formation then rolled right, pulled up, and fired to Brent Parker in the end zone. The ball went over the reach of a leaping Parks and in and out of Parker's hands as he crashed to the turf with 43 seconds remaining.

The Sooners held on for the 31-28 victory, and Switzer heaped praise on players from both squads.

"Hart Lee Dykes and Barry Sanders are great players," he said. "But I'm telling you, Mike Gaddis is a great player, too. And Charles Thompson played a terrific game.

"We're becoming a good football team. I never felt like they could stop us. It was a matter of doing the job. We had the best team and we should have won."

Sanders gained 215 yards on 39 carries. Gaddis rolled up 213 on 18 carries. Even though both had two TDs, Gaddis had the better yards-per-carry average—11.8 to Sanders' 5.5. The Cowboys rolled up more total yards, 481-448.

Mike Gaddis (32) heads to the end zone to score Oklahoma's first touchdown. Gaddis averaged 11.8 yards per carry and outshined the Pokes' Barry Sanders, who eventually won the Heisman Trophy.
(© 1988, The Daily Oklahoman)

Center Bob Latham returned to the OU lineup the following week. The No. 8 Sooners traveled to Columbia on November 12 and defeated 2-6-1 Missouri, 16-7, on a drizzly afternoon. The Sooners cashed in on Missouri's mistakes.

The Tigers set up to punt after going nowhere on their first series. Don Smitherman burst through and blocked the kick. Terry Ray scooped up the pigskin at the MU 35 and carried it to the 25. Eight plays later, Thompson rifled an eight-yard scoring strike to Bross, and Lashar converted for a 7-0 lead.

Curtice Williams intercepted a Mizzou pass minutes later and returned it four yards to the MU 32. The Sooners bogged down at the eight-yard line, and Lashar nailed a 25-yard field goal for a 10-0 lead.

The Tigers advanced to the OU 30 early in the second quarter, but fumbled, and Evans recovered on the 31-yard line. The Big Red then launched a 69-yard scoring march in seven plays. Leon Perry sparked the drive with a 46-yard run to the MU two, and two plays later, Stafford scored from the one. Mizzou blocked Lashar's conversion.

The Tigers drove 52 yards for a touchdown in the third stanza to slice OU's lead to 16-7, and they did not threaten the rest of the game.

Missouri collected more total yards (288-270). Thompson (118) and Perry (106) both crossed the century mark in rushing.

No. 7 Nebraska rolled into Norman on November 19 in a game played in rain and accompanied by a breeze. A stern defensive battle gave Nebraska a 7-3 victory over the No. 9 Sooners for the conference championship and the bid to the Orange Bowl. The win also snapped OU's 19-game home winning streak and 31-game conference win string.

The Huskers drove 80 yards to take a 7-0 lead on their first possession.

Late in the third period, Parks forced Ken Clark to fumble, and Scott Garl, who also had two interceptions, recovered on the NU 30. The Sooners reached the Huskers' 12 in six plays but had to settle for Lashar's 29-yard field goal, which cut Nebraska's lead to 7-3.

The Sooners did not threaten again and lost 11 yards in 13 plays in the fourth stanza. Thompson broke his leg on the game's final play.

The Huskers gained 313 total yards and held the Oklahoma to 137 yards.

The Sooners received a bid to play Clemson in the Citrus Bowl January 2 in Orlando, Florida.

The Tigers prevailed, 13-6, before a bowl-record crowd of 53,571 and snapped Oklahoma's unbeaten streak against Atlantic Coast Conference opponents. The Sooners had never lost to an ACC team in 17 meetings.

The Sooners marched to the Clemson one-yard line, then Holieway faked a handoff to Perry, and the OU quarterback was chased backwards and dumped for an 18-yard loss. Perry on the play had blasted through the line, and OU would have scored had Holieway made the handoff. Holieway said afterward that he misread the defense.

Oklahoma had to settle for Lashar's 35-yard field goal and a 3-0 lead on the final play of the first quarter. Clemson's Chris Gardocki kicked a 20-yard field goal midway through the second stanza and a 47-yarder on the final play of the first half for a 6-3 Tiger lead.

Parks recovered a Clemson fumble on the CU 35, but the Sooners bogged down and settled for Lashar's 30-yard field goal to knot the game at 6-6. The Tigers marched 80 yards for the deciding touchdown early in the fourth period.

Eighteen of OU's final 20 plays of the game were passes. On the final play, Holieway lofted a 14-yard strike to Stell in the end zone, but Clemson's Dexter Davis swatted it down.

Holieway, in his first start since the USC game, completed career highs in pass attempts (24) and pass completions (10).

The Sooners collected more total yards (254-244).

OU finished the season with a 9-3 record and a final national ranking of 14th.

Phillips was selected All-America. Thompson, Evans, Garl, Curtice Williams, and Woods joined him on the all-conference first team. Phillips also earned the NCAA Top Six Award.

1988 Season Record: 9-3-0
Big Eight Conference: 6-1-0 (Second)

Date	Opponent	Result	Score
September 10	at North Carolina	W	28-0
September 17	ARIZONA	W	28-10
September 24	at Southern California	L	23-7
October 1	IOWA STATE	W	35-7
October 8	Texas at Dallas	W	28-13
October 15	KANSAS STATE	W	70-24
October 22	at Colorado	W	17-14
October 29	KANSAS	W	63-14
November 5	at Oklahoma State	W	31-28
November 12	at Missouri	W	16-7
November 19	NEBRASKA	L	7-3
January 2	Clemson*	L	13-6

*Citrus Bowl at Orlando, FL

1989

In mid-December 1988, the NCAA found the Sooners guilty of 20 violations, including paying a prospect for work he did not perform, giving money to another prospect, selling student-athlete tickets for a substantial amount, and arranging airline tickets at no cost to a student athlete.

Recruiting coordinator Shirley Vaughan and assistant coaches Mike Jones and Scott Hill were placed on probation, and their salaries were frozen.

The penalties: limited recruiting visits and scholarships, banned from bowl games for two years and from appearing on television for the 1989 season.

In February 1989, Jerry Parks was charged with shooting a teammate, and Charles Thompson was charged with selling cocaine. Nigel Clay, Bernard Hall, and Glenn Bell were charged with gang rape.

Four months later, on June 19, 1989, Barry Switzer announced his resignation as OU's football coach.

"(T)here has been too much water under the bridge for me to continue to be the effective leader that this great football program deserves," Switzer said. "It's no fun anymore."

In his 16 years as head coach of the Sooners, he won 157 of 190 games, coached the Big Red to three national championships (1974, 1975 and 1985) and 12 Big Eight championships. His winning percentage of 83.7 percent is fourth among all-time college football coaches in the history of the game. In April 2001, Switzer was elected to the College Football Hall of Fame.

The day after Switzer's resignation, Gary Gibbs, Switzer's defensive coordinator, was named as the Sooners' 18th head football coach at Switzer's recommendation. Gibbs, who played linebacker at OU in the mid-'70s, was the third university alumnus to be head coach.

Gibbs was a linebacker at OU from 1972-1974. He became a graduate assistant under Switzer in 1975, and three years later Gibbs was promoted to the position of linebackers coach. In 1981, Gibbs was named the Sooners defensive coordinator, and he held that post until taking over as head coach.

Only 74 players were on scholarship for the '89 campaign, and the offense was redesigned as a mix of wishbone and I formations, known as the I-bone.

The battle for starting quarterback was wide open among three unseasoned players—sophomore Chris Melson, redshirt freshman Steve Collins, and freshman Tink Collins, who were not related. Steve Collins got the nod when the season began, but Melson took over after Steve broke his finger on the first play in the second game.

Returning to support the new quarterbacks were fullback Leon Perry, running back Mike Gaddis, center Mike Wise, tight end Adrian Cooper, guard Larry Medice, and split end Eric Bross.

All-conference defensive tackle Scott Evans returned to lead the defensive line. Ken McMichel and Kevin Thompson were the only seasoned veterans in the secondary. R.D. Lashar also returned for placekicking duties but had to learn to kick without a tee, which was outlawed by the NCAA for field goals and extra-point conversions.

The No. 15 Sooners opened the season September 2 at home with a 73-3 victory over New Mexico State. Perry scored three touchdowns, and running back Ike Lewis added two more to lead seven Sooners who scored touchdowns. Lashar kicked all 10 conversions and added a 45-yard field goal.

Oklahoma scored seven touchdowns and the field goal for a 52-0 lead on its first eight possessions in the first 23 minutes and 48 seconds. The Aggies' only score came on a field goal midway through the third quarter, then the Big Red reserves scored three more TDs in the final 16 minutes and 44 seconds.

OU rolled up 34 first downs, rushed for 518 yards, and passed for only 37. The defense held the Aggies to five first downs and 133 total yards.

Oklahoma leaped to eighth in the AP poll and hammered Baylor, 33-7, the following week in Norman. The Sooners scored on four of their first six possessions for a 28-0 halftime lead.

Steve Collins broke his finger on OU's first play and returned later in the first period to direct a 54-yard scoring drive, but he sat out the rest of the game. Gaddis scored two touchdowns and both came in the first quarter. His first came from one yard out, and his next score was a 19-yard jaunt to cap a 45-yard drive.

Melson led the Sooners on their next two scoring drives in the second stanza. Perry's one-yard plunge put OU up 21-0 midway through the second quarter. Melson sparked the 56-yard drive with a 44-yard run. Melson scored from the one just before halftime to cap a 71-yard march. Lewis scampered 39 yards to highlight the drive.

Lashar, who converted all four extra points, nailed a 33-yard field goal for a 31-0 lead midway through the third stanza. The Bears answered with a 68-yard TD drive.

The Sooners advanced to the BU five late in the game, but Perry fumbled there. Two plays later, OU defensive end Corey Mayfield tackled Brad Goebel in the end zone for a safety and the final tally.

The Big Red picked up 338 yards, all on the ground, and did not complete a pass in seven tries. The defense held the Bears to 206 total yards.

Arizona's Doug Pfaff kicked a 40-yard field goal with two seconds remaining to lead 1-1 Arizona to a 6-3 victory over the sixth-ranked Sooners on September 16 in Tuscon. Both teams wasted opportunities to score more points. The Wildcats lost a fumble, had a field goal blocked, failed to convert on fourth down, and had a TD pass nullified by a penalty. OU missed a field goal and twice fumbled after putting together good drives.

Wayne Dickson blocked Pfaff's 46-yard field-goal attempt, but the Sooners could not generate anything afterward. A holding penalty wiped out an Arizona touchdown pass midway through the second period.

The Sooners' Otis Taylor fumbled a Wildcat punt late in the first half, which led to Pfaff's 24-yard field goal for a 3-0 lead. OU advanced to the Cats' 18 moments later, but Lashar shanked a 35-yard field-goal try.

Oklahoma twice moved into scoring position in the third quarter and both times fumbled the ball away on the 24 and 17. Lashar kicked a 42-yard field goal midway through the third quarter to knot the game at 3-3.

The Sooner defense held Arizona to 22 yards on the Wildcats' first five possessions of the second half. Arizona marched 37 yards on the final drive to the winning field goal.

OU collected more total yards (222-214).

OU dropped to 16th in the AP poll and blasted 2-2 Kansas, 45-6, two weeks later in Lawrence. Gaddis rushed for 172 yards and scored three touchdowns to lead the victory. Tink Collins got the starting nod at quarterback and hurled a 51-yard scoring strike to split end Arthur Guess to put the Sooners up 14-0 in the first stanza.

Dante Williams' fumble recovery on the KU five-yard line set up the first Big Red score. Gaddis carried twice and plowed over for the final two yards. Lashar kicked a 29-yard field goal for a 17-0 lead midway in the second quarter. The Jayhawks drove 66 yards to cut the gap to 17-6 just before halftime.

The Sooners added two touchdowns in each of the final two periods, including a 51-yard TD pass from Melson to Bross to cap a 97-yard drive for the final tally.

Oklahoma amassed 539 total yards using multiple sets while holding Kansas to 270 total yards.

Gaddis again scored three touchdowns to lead the No. 16 Sooners to a 37-15 win over Oklahoma State on October 7 in Norman. Gaddis also rushed for 274 yards, the third best rushing performance to date and also caught a pass for 43 yards. Lashar also kicked at least one field goal for the 10th straight game to set a school record.

The Sooners marched 80 yards in 14 plays to take a 7-0 lead late in the first stanza. Perry's one-yard plunge capped the drive, and Lashar kicked the first of four conversions. OSU's Mike Clark scored on an 82-yard punt return early in the second quarter, but the Sooners blocked the extra point.

Lashar kicked three field goals (49, 45 and 40 yards) and Gaddis' first touchdown put Oklahoma ahead, 23-6 at halftime. Cary Blanchard kicked three field goals in the third period to draw the Cowboys nine points closer, 23-15, but 50 seconds after his third field goal, Gaddis burst 80 yards for his second touchdown. Gaddis' third TD came on a four-yard run in the fourth stanza.

OU picked up more total yards, 447-233. The Pokes' Mike Gundy set the Big Eight Conference passing record for career yards; however, he completed only 13 of 32 for 160 yards against the Sooners.

Texas scored a touchdown with 1:33 remaining to overcome a 24-21 deficit and defeat No. 15 OU, 28-24, the following week in Dallas. The Steers' victory snapped the Sooners' four-game win streak in the series.

The Longhorns took the opening kickoff and marched 80 yards for a 7-0 lead. The Big Red countered with a 71-yard scoring drive in three plays. Gaddis scored on a 62-yard jaunt, and Lashar kicked the first of three conversions.

Otis Taylor fumbled a Texas punt, and Mical Padgett grabbed the ball in midair and raced 44 yards to the end zone. The Horns added a two-point pass for a 15-7 lead.

Wayne Clements kicked two field goals to give Texas a 21-7 halftime advantage. The Sooners took command for about 27 minutes of the second half, but Gaddis blew out his knee midway through the third period and was lost for the season. Tink Collins hurled a 41-yard TD pass to Guess in the third period, and Lashar nailed a 30-yard field goal early in the fourth to close the gap to 21-17. Lewis scored on a one-yard run to give OU a 24-21 lead with 3:42 remaining. Jason Belser intercepted a Longhorn pass on the OU 49 to set up the score.

Peter Gardere tossed a 25-yard scoring strike to Johnny Walker to cap a 66-yard drive in seven plays for the deciding tally. The Sooners took the kickoff and advanced 19 yards from their 23-yard line, but Texas sacked Collins on the last play.

Oklahoma had more total yards, 346-273. Gaddis rushed for 130 yards before his knee injury.

The Sooners fell to 25th in the AP poll and edged Iowa State, 43-40, on October 21 in Ames. OU and the 3-3 Cyclones battled through six lead changes and one tie before it was all settled. The Sooners were fortunate that the Cyclones failed on four conversions, or they would have been on the short end of the scoreboard.

ISU quarterback Bret Oberg completed four touchdown passes, and his first gave the Cyclones a 6-0 lead early in the first quarter. The Sooners needed only two plays and 33 seconds to cover 56

yards for a 7-6 lead. Backup running back Ted Long scored on a 31-yard run, and Lashar kicked the first of three conversions.

Oberg's second scoring strike put I-State back on top, 12-6, but his two-point pass misfired. OU answered with a 57-yard TD drive for a 15-12 advantage early in the second stanza. Tink Collins scored on a four-yard run to cap the nine-play drive, and he also carried for the two-point conversion.

Iowa State responded with an 80-yard drive, and this time Oberg scored on a one-yard run, and his two-point run gave his team a 20-15 advantage. Lashar kicked a 27-yard field goal to narrow the deficit to 20-18 less than five minutes before intermission.

Oberg scored again on a one-yard run, but the two-point conversion failed, yet the Cyclones held a 26-18 edge midway through the third period. The Sooners took the kickoff, and on the second play from scrimmage Collins rifled a 67-yard scoring strike to Guess, and Collins ran for two more points to tie the game at 26-26, 46 seconds later.

The Sooners took the lead for good early in the fourth quarter with a 53-yard drive in five plays. Lewis scored from the six-yard line for a 33-26 lead. Lashar added a 27-yard field goal minutes later, but Iowa State countered with a 75-yard drive for a touchdown. Oberg completed a five-yard pass, and a two-point conversion cut OU's lead to 36-34.

The Cyclones tried an onside kick, but Bross scooped up the ball on a dead run at the ISU 44 and zoomed to the end zone for a 43-34 lead. The Cyclones were not done. Oberg guided his team 76 yards in the next 90 seconds for the final score.

Oklahoma collected 313 total yards. Iowa State set all-time highs against OU with 407 passing yards and 609 total yards.

The Sooners dropped out of the AP poll but still had hopes for a Big Eight title. A victory against undefeated and third-ranked Colorado would put the Sooners in the driver's seat for a run at the conference championship. The 7-0 Buffaloes sat atop the conference standings with Oklahoma and Nebraska, all at 3-0. The Big Red would have to accomplish a win without the services of three defensive starters who were sidelined with injuries—cornerback McMichel, defensive tackle Tom Backes, and defensive end James Goode.

Colorado defeated the Sooners, 20-3, in Norman before a full-capacity crowd of 75,004 for the first time all season. After a scoreless first quarter, the Buffs scored 10 points in the second. Ken Culbertson kicked a 30-yard field goal late in the second stanza, and Colorado marched 53 yards for a touchdown on its next series.

The 10-0 lead continued through the third period, but the Sooners launched a drive late in the quarter and into the fourth. Steve Collins returned to action and engineered the 72-yard march to the CU 16. Colorado's defense stiffened, and Lashar toed a 34-yard field goal to cut the Buffs' lead to 10-3.

Colorado answered with Culbertson's second field goal, a 27-yarder, for a 13-3 advantage. Minutes later, Guess fumbled a pitch out, and the Buffs recovered on the OU nine-yard line. Three plays later, Darian Hagen scooted eight yards into the end zone.

Colorado picked up more total yards (314-248).

The Sooners guaranteed themselves a winning season by hammering 2-6 Missouri, 52-14, before a homecoming crowd of 72,300 on November 4 in Norman. Oklahoma and Mizzou were tied 7-7 early, then the Sooners scored on their next seven possessions to put the game away. Lewis and Steve Collins scored two touchdowns each, and Collins threw a pass for another score.

Linebacker Joe Bowden recovered a Tiger fumble on the MU 32 early in the first stanza to set up OU's first touchdown. Five plays

Mike Gaddis injures his knee in the third quarter against Texas.
(© 1989, The Daily Oklahoman)

The Sooners blasted 1-8 Kansas State, 42-19, the following week in Norman. Freshman running back Dewell Brewer, who was fourth string at the beginning of the year, replaced Lewis and scored three touchdowns and rushed for 187 yards.

The Wildcats took a 3-0 lead on a field goal, then Oklahoma scored four times on long, sustained drives of 80, 83, 78, and 97 yards for a 28-3 halftime lead. Brewer scored the only touchdown of the third period, and Kansas State scored its only two TDs in the fourth. Brewer's third touchdown came with 3:32 remaining in the game for the final tally.

OU collected 32 first downs, rushed for 425 yards, and passed for 137 more. Steve Collins completed five of 10 passes for all of the passing yards, and he added 135 yards on the ground. The defense held Kansas State to 31 yards rushing, but the Cats passed for 273 yards.

For the first time since 1961, the Big Eight Conference championship did not belong to OU or Nebraska. Colorado earned the title with a victory over the Cornhuskers on November 4. Yet the 10-1 Huskers were ranked sixth in the nation and hammered the Sooners, 42-25, on November 18 in Lincoln.

Nebraska took the opening kickoff and marched to a 7-0 lead. OU responded with a tying touchdown 58 seconds later. Steve Collins hooked up with Guess for an 82-yard scoring strike, and Lashar converted.

Husker quarterback Gerry Gdowski hurled two TD passes later in the first quarter for a 22-7 lead. The Sooners drove 75 yards in 13 plays to close the gap to 22-15 early in the second stanza on Perry's one-yard run and Collins' two-point conversion run. Nebraska's Gregg Barrios and Lashar traded field goals in the second period, and OU trailed 25-18 at the break.

Gdowski hurled two more scoring strikes to put the game away in the third quarter.

Nebraska picked up more total yards (461-363). Gdowski completed 12 of 17 passes for 225 yards and four TDs. Brewer led the Oklahoma running attack with 137 yards.

The Sooners' season ended at the earliest date since finishing on November 20 in 1943. Scheduling and being prohibited from a bowl game had something to do with it.

For the first time since 1970, the Sooners did not have an All-America selection. Scott Evans was named to the All-Big Eight Conference first unit for the second straight year. Linebacker Frank Blevins and Dante Williams also made the all-conference first team.

later, Lewis scored from the 12, and Lashar booted the first of seven conversions for a 7-0 lead.

Missouri answered with an 80-yard TD drive capped by a 64-yard TD pass for a 7-7 tie.

The Big Red marched 87 yards in four plays to take the lead for good early in the second quarter. Lewis' 22-yard run completed the drive.

The Sooners rolled up 30 first downs, rushed for 423 yards and passed for 142 more. Collins, in his first start since the Baylor game, rushed for 147 yards on 17 carries and completed five of eight passes for 110 yards. The Tigers gained 320 total yards.

Lewis and Corey Mayfield were suspended from the team when they were charged with stealing auto parts and transporting an open container in a vehicle.

1989 Season Record: 7-4-0
Big Eight Conference: 5-2-0 (Third)

Date	Opponent	Result	Score
September 2	NEW MEXICO STATE	W	73-3
September 9	BAYLOR	W	33-7
September 16	at Arizona	L	6-3
September 30	at Kansas	W	56-3
October 7	OKLAHOMA STATE	W	37-15
October 14	Texas at Dallas	L	28-24
October 21	at Iowa State	W	43-40
October 28	COLORADO	L	20-3
November 4	MISSOURI	W	52-14
November 11	KANSAS STATE	W	42-19
November 18	at Nebraska	L	42-25

1990 - 1999

1990

The Sooners were picked to finish third in the Big Eight Conference behind Colorado and Nebraska. The 1990 OU defense was expected to be stronger in the line and secondary. Two-time all-conference tackle Scott Evans returned to lead the defense with tackle Tom Backes and end James Goode. Frank Blevins was moved from linebacker to the other end slot, and Joe Bowden was the only returnee at linebacker. Safeties Terry Ray and Jason Belser returned to the secondary. Noseguard Stacey Dillard and cornerback Greg DeQuasie each started four games in 1989 to bring more experience to the defense.

Steve Collins earned his starting quarterback position early on, but he would be sharing duties with Cale Gundy, a *Parade* All-American from Midwest City. Mike Gaddis was not fully healed from his knee surgery and sat out the season. Dewell Brewer and Ike Lewis split time at tailback. Lewis was reinstated to the team for misdemeanor charges late the previous season. The offensive line was thin and lacked depth. Guards Larry Medice and Mike Swawtzky and tight end Adrian Cooper were the only returnees. Arthur Guess had plenty of playing time to earn the starting split-end slot.

The kicking game was expected to be solid with the return of placekicker R.D. Lashar and punter Brad Reddell.

The Sooners began the '90 campaign with five wins, then lost three straight and ended with a flurry of three huge victories. OU was ranked 22nd in the preseason AP poll then dropped to 23rd without having played a game.

Oklahoma opened the season on September 8 with a 34-14 win over No. 19 UCLA in the Sooners' first appearance at the Rose Bowl stadium. The game was played in 104-degree heat (120 degrees on the field) and before a crowd of 50,068, about half capacity in the 100,000-seat stadium. The Sooners capitalized on four of six Bruin turnovers (two fumbles and four interceptions) to score 20 points in the 20-point win.

UCLA took a 6-0 lead in the first stanza on two field goals. The second field goal came moments after the Bruins recovered Brewer's fumble.

Oklahoma responded with an 80-yard scoring drive in 13 plays. Collins' four-yard run and Lashar's conversion (the first of four) put the Sooners up 7-6 late in the first period. Moments later, the Bruins fumbled a punt return, and OU's Tony Levy recovered on the UCLA six-yard line. Fullback Kenyon Rasheed scored on a one-yard run three plays later.

The Bruins intercepted Collins' pass and returned it to the OU nine to set up the tying score early in the second quarter. UCLA scored in four plays and added a two-point conversion for a 14-14 tie.

Minutes later, Levy again recovered a Bruin fumble on a muffed punt snap at the UCLA 10-yard line. Fullback Mike McKinley burst ahead for a touchdown in one play.

The Sooners took the second-half kickoff and rolled 80 yards in nine plays for a 28-14 advantage. Collins scored from the one and also sparked the drive with a 34-yard scamper to the UCLA 43.

Two interceptions led to Lashar field goals later in the third stanza and in the fourth. Darnell Walker's pick led to Lashar's 19-yard boot midway in the third quarter, and Belser's theft led to Lashar's 41-yarder early in the fourth period.

OU gained more total yards, 343-203. Oklahoma's defense sacked UCLA quarterbacks five times.

The Sooners rose to 14th in the nation and hammered 13th-ranked Pittsburgh, 52-10, the following week in Norman. Rasheed and Brewer each rushed for more than 100 yards and scored two TDs apiece to lead the Sooners. Lewis also crossed the century mark in rushing.

The Panthers suffered their worst loss in 19 years. The Big Red scored on three of its first four possessions en route to a 31-3 half-time lead. Five of the Sooners' seven TDs came on quick strikes of five plays or less, and they dialed long distance on four scores.

On Oklahoma's first play of the game, Collins hurled a 71-yard TD pass to Otis Taylor, and Lashar kicked the first of seven conversions. Lewis busted a 63-yard run for a 21-3 lead. On the second play after the second-half kickoff, Brewer sprinted 51 yards for a 38-3 lead. He added a 47-yard scamper moments later for the next touchdown.

The Sooners rushed for 450 yards with the tailbacks combining for 217 yards and the fullbacks combining for 196 more. Oklahoma passed for only 79 yards. The Panthers collected 404 total yards, but the Big Red defense forced five turnovers—three fumbles and two interceptions.

The 11th-ranked Sooners posted an identical score of 52-10 against 1-2 Tulsa on September 22 in Norman. Oklahoma opened with two touchdown passes for the first time since 1972 against Oklahoma State and passed for more than 200 yards for the first time since doing so against Texas in 1973. Guess caught the two scoring strikes, the first time a player caught two TD passes since 1974 against Kansas.

OU marched 50 yards to take a 7-0 lead early in the first quarter. Collins hurled an eight-yard scoring strike on third down to Guess to cap the nine-play drive. Lashar kicked the first of seven conversions. Collins also hooked up on a 29-yard pass to Guess to convert a third-down situation.

Ray intercepted a Hurricane pass moments later and returned it 26 yards to the TU 19-yard line. Two plays went nowhere, so Collins went upstairs for a 19-yard strike to Guess for a 14-0 lead.

The Golden Hurricane drove 76 yards, aided by a roughing penalty on the Sooners, to cut OU's lead to 14-7 late in the first stanza.

Belser's fumble recovery early in the second period led to a field goal—49 yards by Lashar. Lewis' six-yard run put the Sooners up 24-7 midway through the second quarter. The Sooners mounted four TD drives to put the game away in the second half.

Oklahoma picked up more total yards, 452-217. Collins and Gundy combined to complete 12 of 25 passes for 202 yards. Guess caught five of them for 74 yards.

900th Game

The No. 9 Sooners stayed home the next week and defeated 1-2 Kansas, 31-17, in the 900th game in Sooner history. OU cashed in on four Jayhawk turnovers to score 24 points. Rasheed led the Big Red with three touchdowns.

Kansas drove 61 yards to the OU 19-yard line, but Dillard forced a fumble, and Blevins recovered on the 19. The Sooners wheeled 81 yards in 19 plays, and Rasheed capped the drive with a one-yard run. Lashar nailed the first of four conversions.

On the first play after the kickoff, Ray intercepted a KU pass and returned it 16 yards to the Jayhawks' 16-yard line. Collins scooted nine yards for the score two plays later.

After Kansas cut the lead to 14-7 early in the second period, and Taylor set up the next Oklahoma score with a 25-yard punt return to the KU 36. Rasheed carried the load on all four plays and going the final 12 for the touchdown.

Walker picked off a Kansas pass moments later and returned it 17 yards to the KU 43. The Sooners bogged down eight plays later at the 11, and Lashar kicked a 28-yard field goal for a 24-7 advantage.

A fumble recovery led to Rasheed's third TD early in the third period. Kansas scored 10 points in the final 22 minutes.

Kansas gained more first downs (21-11) and total yards (396-261).

The No. 7 Sooners again matched their previous week's score with a 31-17 win over 2-2 Oklahoma State the next week in Stillwater. A "time out" called by the Cowboys late in the first half allowed OU to overcome a 14-7 deficit and tie the game just before halftime.

Oklahoma took a 7-0 lead on its second series of the game. Collins capped the 67-yard, 10 play drive with a one yard run. The Pokes answered with a 90-yard scoring drive to tie the game at 7-7. OSU took a 14-7 lead after recovering Collins' fumble at midfield late in the second stanza.

On the next series, the Sooners faced fourth-and-six on their 48-yard line and were satisfied to let the clock run out and head to the locker room. OU players were heading to the dressing room when they were informed that OSU had called a time out with three seconds left. Gundy hurled a bomb to Adrian Cooper, who caught the ball between two defenders on the OSU one-yard line and scored. OU 14, OSU 14.

"Adrian was supposed to stay in and block, but he went deep," Gundy said after the game. "I was surprised to see him, but he's the only one I saw that I could throw to."

Momentum had swung in the Sooners' favor, although the Pokes took a 17-14 lead with a field goal early in the third quarter. Taylor minutes later returned a Cowboy punt 39 yards to the OSU 31. Brewer carried three times to the one, then Gundy carried across on the next play. Lashar's third conversion gave the Sooners a 21-17 lead.

OU added 10 more points in the fourth stanza—a 21-yard field goal by Lashar and a nine-yard run by Rasheed.

For the second straight year, a late drive lifted Texas to victory, 14-13, over the fourth-ranked Sooners before a sellout crowd at the Cotton Bowl. Once again, quarterback Peter Gardere directed the final Longhorn thrust.

Lashar's 47-yard field goal gave the Sooners a 3-0 lead on Oklahoma's second possession. The 2-1 Steers answered with an 80-yard scoring drive for a 7-3 advantage. The Big Red held Texas to zero first downs and 14 total yards the rest of the half.

Gundy replaced Steve Collins at quarterback and engineered a 58-yard scoring drive to put the Sooners back on top, 10-7, midway through the second period. Gundy did not throw one pass in the 12-play drive. Rasheed carried six times for 27 yards, and Brewer carried six times for 31 yards and scored on the final nine. Lashar toed the extra point.

The Sooners lost a chance to extend the lead when Gundy fumbled on the Steers' five-yard line early in the third stanza. Reggie Barnes recovered a Longhorn fumble minutes later on the UT 35. OU moved to the Texas nine but had to settle for Lashar's 26-yard boot for a 13-7 lead with 16 seconds left in the third quarter.

The Steers blocked Lashar's 49-yard field-goal try early in the fourth period and later put together the winning drive that consumed five minutes and 10 seconds off the clock. The drive began at the UT nine-yard line, but the Horns later faced third-and-eight on the OU 25. Gardere misfired his pass, but DeQuasie was guilty of pass interference. Instead of fourth-and-eight at the 25, Texas had new life with a first down at the OU 19. Four plays later, the Horns faced fourth-and-seven at the 16, then Gardere hurled a scoring strike to Keith Cash. The extra point gave the Steers 14-13 lead with 2:02 to go.

The Sooners quickly moved to the UT 29, but Lashar's 46-yard attempt sailed wide as time expired.

Oklahoma picked up more total yards, 349-232.

The Sooners fell to 16th in the AP poll and again were victims of a late-game surge as Iowa State stunned Oklahoma, 33-31, on October 20 in Norman. The 2-3-1 Cyclones defeated the Sooners for the first time in 29 years. I-State quarterback Chris Pederson frustrated the OU defense with the quarterback draw play—taking off with the ball after finding huge gaps in the defense. He rushed for 148 yards on 29 carries, but 143 of those yards came on 29 draw plays.

Oklahoma took a 14-0 lead in the first stanza, but the Cyclones tied the game in the second. The Big Red scored twice more before halftime, and the Cyclones added a field goal to close the gap to 28-17 at halftime.

The Cyclones kicked another field goal in the third period, and Lashar kicked a 22-yarder for a 31-20 lead with 3:06 left in the same quarter.

Iowa State marched 80 yards, which included a fake punt in the drive, to narrow OU's lead to 31-26 early in the final stanza. Lashar missed a 23-yard field-goal attempt late in the game, and the Cyclones then drove 80 yards in 10 plays for the deciding tally. Pederson, who scored on a one-yard run with 35 seconds remaining, picked up a first down with a 20-yard run to overcome a fourth-and-eight situation.

The Sooners picked up more total yards (393-355). Gundy completed 10 of 19 passes for 133 yards, and Brewer rushed for 140 yards.

OU dropped to 22nd in the AP poll and traveled to Boulder the following week to face 6-1-1 Colorado. The 10th-ranked Buffaloes didn't have to use any last-minute heroics as they took a lead early in the second half and held on to defeat the Sooners, 32-23.

Oklahoma took the opening kickoff and rolled 80 yards for a 7-0 lead. Gundy scored on a five-yard run, and Lashar converted. OU converted four third-down situations into first downs in the 16-play drive.

Two Colorado field goals cut Oklahoma's lead to 7-6 midway through the second period. The Sooners took the ensuing kickoff, and in one play Gundy hurled an 80-yard scoring strike to Ted Long for a 14-6 lead.

The Buffs drove 66 yards to cut their deficit to 14-12 just before halftime. Eric Bienemy's 69-yard run early in the third quarter put Colorado ahead for good at 18-14. Gundy left the game with a hip injury early in the third stanza. Collins replaced him and directed a drive that led to a 46-yard field goal by Lashar, and OU trailed, 18-17, with 5:06 left in the third period.

The Sooners advanced to the CU 11 early in the fourth quarter. Instead of a field goal, they gambled and lost on fourth down when Brewer was tossed for a three-yard loss. The Buffs scored two more touchdowns to put the game away. OU scored once more, but it was too little, too late.

Colorado had more total yards (463-395).

The 5-3 Sooners disappeared from the national rankings but still could make a respectable showing in the conference if they won out. That's exactly what they did. It began with a 55-10 victory over Missouri on November 3 in Columbia.

OU scored on eight of its first 10 possessions, and backup tailback Earnest Williams scored three touchdowns as the Sooners rolled to a 31-0 in the game's first 23 minutes. DeQuasie picked off two Tiger passes, and he scored a 23-yard interception for the 31-0 lead. Lashar kicked a career-high 54-yard field goal as time expired in the first half for a 34-7 lead.

Both teams traded fumbles early in the third quarter, then the Sooners scored on three straight drives. Rasheed scored on a 10-yard run midway through the third stanza, and Mizzou added a field goal to cut Oklahoma's lead to 41-10. Four plays after the ensuing kickoff, Gundy rifled a 49-yard TD bomb to split end Corey Warren for a 48-10 advantage. Brewer scored on a 15-yard run for the final tally midway in the fourth period.

The Big Red collected more total yards, 591-361.

OU pounded 5-4 Kansas State, 34-7, before a homecoming throng of 69,106, the smallest turnout since 1974. The game was a tale of two halves for the Sooners as they scored 27 points on five of six first-half possessions and rolled up 291 total yards. They had minus 10 yards in the first 22 minutes of the second half and did not gain a first down in the final half until the 6:01 mark of the fourth quarter.

Brewer returned the opening kickoff 52 yards to the Wildcats' 48-yard line, and Gundy scored on a one-yard sneak for a 7-0 lead. Lashar kicked the first of four conversions.

Lashar nailed a 45-yard field goal for a 10-0 lead early in the second stanza then OU jumped to a 17-0 lead with an 80-yard march on the next series. Rasheed scored from the one, and Gundy completed three passes for 56 yards in the 10-play drive.

Lashar kicked a 27-yard field goal after a short drive, which was set up by Taylor's 25-yard punt return to the KSU 29 yard line. The Cats took the kickoff and marched 80 yards for their only touchdown.

The Sooners countered with a 55-yard scoring drive in six plays culminated by Brewer's 14-yard TD run for a 27-7 halftime lead.

After a sloppy performance in the third period and most of the fourth, the Sooners got on track with a 69-yard scoring punch. Williams' nine-yard run completed the six-play drive.

The Big Red rolled up more total yards (353-329). Gundy completed nine of 20 passes for 138 yards. Wildcat quarterback Carl Straw completed only one pass in his first nine attempts, then completed 12 of 18 for 222 yards before an injury put him out of the game in the third quarter.

Thirteen days later, No. 10 Nebraska rolled into Norman with a 9-1 record. A win for the Cornhuskers would give them second place, outright, in the Big Eight Conference. A win for the Sooners would give them a share of second place.

OU destroyed Nebraska, 45-10, before the largest crowd of the season at 74,910, still less than full capacity. The win was the first for the Sooners over a Top 10-rated team since beating UCLA in 1986 and the biggest victory over Nebraska since a 47-0 whipping in 1967.

The Huskers turned the ball over seven times (four interceptions and three fumbles), and the Sooners cashed in for 31 points. On the first Husker series, Barnes rode NU quarterback Mickey Joseph out of bounds and into a metal bench on the Nebraska sideline. Joseph received a severe laceration on his leg and was through for the day.

Nebraska took a 3-0 lead with a field goal late in the opening period. Early in the second stanza, Gundy zipped a 36-yard scoring strike to Cooper, who caught the ball behind his back. Lashar kicked the first of six conversions.

Minutes later, Barnes shook the ball loose from Nate Turner. Blevins picked up the ball and returned it to the NU 12-yard line. Gundy carried over from the one four plays later for a 14-3 advantage.

Bowden intercepted a Husker pass moments later at the NU 46. Two plays later, Gundy hurled a 40-yard pass to Cooper to the NU nine, and McKinley scored on the next play.

Nebraska scored a touchdown early in the third stanza moments after recovering Gundy's fumble on the OU 35-yard line. Blevins later intercepted a Husker pass and returned it four yards to the NU 20. McKinley carried on all four plays and covered the final seven yards for a touchdown and a 28-10 lead. McKinley scored his third TD of the day on a 48-yard run to cap an 80-yard drive in five plays on the next Sooner possession.

DeQuasie returned a Nebraska pass 43 yards for a touchdown early in the fourth quarter, and Lashar added a 42-yard field goal with nine seconds remaining. Lashar became the Big Eight's career kick scoring leader with 320 points.

OU picked up more total yards (396-279). Cooper caught three passes for 96 yards, and punter Brad Reddell averaged 44.8 yards on five kicks.

1990 Season Record: 8-3-0

Big Eight Conference: 5-2-0 (Second)

Date	Opponent	Result	Score
September 8	at UCLA	W	34-14
September 15	PITTSBURGH	W	52-10
September 22	TULSA	W	52-10
September 29	KANSAS	W	31-17
October 6	at Oklahoma State	W	31-17
October 13	Texas at Dallas	L	14-13
October 20	IOWA STATE	L	33-31
October 27	at Colorado	L	32-23
November 3	at Missouri	W	55-10
November 10	KANSAS STATE	W	34-7
November 23	NEBRASKA	W	45-10

1991

The Sooners were off of probation and were eligible for a bowl game at the end of the season. They also could extend scholarships to the full allotment of 25 players, which they did. Gary Gibbs proclaimed the '91 squad his best in three years as head coach. Sixteen starters returned from the prior year (seven on offense and nine on defense), but only two in the offensive line—center Randy Wallace and tackle Brandon Houston. Brian Brauninger had playing experience at the other tackle slot.

The backfield was deep with quality players at every position— Earnest Williams, Dewell Brewer and Mike Gaddis at tailback and Kenyon Rasheed and Mike McKinley at fullback. Gaddis was back to full speed after sitting out nearly two years with knee surgery, and

Brewer injured his knee in the fourth game of 1991 and was finished for the year.

The defense would be the key to the team's success with the return of Joe Bowden at linebacker, Stacy Dillard and Reggie Barnes on the line, and Jason Belser and Terry Ray in the secondary. Brad Reddell would return for punting chores, and he also battled Scott Blanton for placekicking duties. They both would have to hone their accuracy as the NCAA reduced goalpost width from 23 feet, four inches to 18 and one-half feet.

Oklahoma was ranked 10th in the preseason AP rankings and moved up to ninth before North Texas (the school dropped "State" at the end) came to Norman on September 14. The Sooners whipped the Mean Green, 40-2. The defense scored one touchdown and set up two more and did not yield a single point.

OU took a 6-0 lead early in the second quarter on Williams' three-yard run to cap a 62-yard drive in 10 plays. The Mean Green blocked Reddell's conversion, and returned it to the opposite end zone for two points, and suddenly the score became 6-2 in OU's favor.

The Big Red took a 20-2 lead over the next four minutes and eight seconds. Sooner linebacker Mike Coats blocked North Texas' punt on the next series, and safety John Anderson recovered on the one-yard line. Gundy sneaked the ball across on the next play, and Reddell converted for a 13-2 advantage. Coats intercepted a Mean Green pass on the first play after the kickoff and returned it to the NT eight-yard line. McKinley blasted over from the one three plays later and Reddell converted.

The Sooners took the second-half kickoff and marched 64 yards in four plays for a 27-2 lead. Gundy capped the drive with a 25-yard scoring strike to split end Corey Warren. Drew Christmon returned a Mean Green pass 35 yards for a score early in the fourth period, and Gaddis scored on a four-yard run to cap a 55-yard drive for the final tally minutes later.

OU rushed for 310 yards and passed for 85. The defense held North Texas to two rushing yards and 206 passing yards.

The No. 7 Sooners stayed home the next week and smashed 0-2 Utah State, 55-21, before a crowd of 69,057, the smallest throng since the stadium expanded to 70,286 seats in 1975. Brewer led OU with 144 rushing yards and three touchdowns.

The Big Red took the opening kickoff and wheeled 82 yards in nine plays for a 7-0 lead. Brewer capped the drive with a four-yard run, and Reddell kicked the first of seven conversions. He missed only once, which was after the seventh Sooner TD.

The Aggies tied the game minutes later with a 49-yard scoring strike from Ron Lopez to Tracey Jenkins. Lopez finished the game completing 21 of 44 passes for two touchdowns, but OU's defense intercepted four of them.

The Sooners exploded for 28 points in the second stanza, and Bowden's interception gave OU a 28-7 lead. Oklahoma dialed up long distance (80, 61 and 80 yards) for the other three scores.

The reserves played in the fourth quarter, and Steve Collins hurled an eight-yard pass for the final tally, seven plays after Charles Franks returned an interception 51 yards to the Aggies' 21.

The Big Red gained 31 first downs, twice as many as the Ags, and more total yards (571-337). Williams also cleared the century rushing mark with 109 yards.

The sixth-ranked Sooners defeated 1-2 Virginia Tech, 27-17, on September 28 before a homecoming crowd of 73,200 in Norman. The defense intercepted three Hokie passes. Darnell Walker stole two of them, and Bowden returned the other for a touchdown, his second in as many weeks.

The Hokies took a 7-0 lead midway through the first period after recovering an OU fumble in the end zone.

Belser recovered a Tech fumble on the enemy 36-yard line early in the second stanza to set up the first Sooner score. Six plays later, Gundy zipped a nine-yard scoring strike to tight end Joey Mickey, and Blanton converted for the 7-7 tie.

Blanton kicked two field goals (32 and 27 yards) on OU's next two possessions, but the Hokies kicked a 50-yarder with five seconds before halftime to cut OU's lead to 13-10.

Early in the third quarter, Bowden picked off a Tech pass and raced 33 yards to put the Sooners up 20-10 after Blanton's conversion. The Sooners marched 80 yards in 13 plays, and Gundy scored from the three with 30 seconds left in the third period for a 27-10 lead.

Williams' fumble set up a Tech touchdown midway through the fourth stanza.

Oklahoma picked up 143 yards rushing, and Gundy completed 14 of 31 passes for 235 yards. It was the first time OU won with more passing yards since defeating Oklahoma State in 1972. Gundy's 18 completions broke Jack Mildren's school record set against Nebraska in 1969 and his 31 attempts tied a team record set against Washington State in 1938. The Hokies gained 349 total yards. Tech quarterback Will Furrer attempted 50 passes, the most against a Sooner football team in history.

No. 5 Oklahoma hit the road the following week seeking to avenge last year's loss to Iowa State. The Sooners had no trouble with a 29-8 victory in Ames. Gundy completed 12 of 20 passes for 206 yards and three touchdowns, and the defense held Cyclone quarterback Chris Pederson to 20 rushing yards. Pederson, who rushed for 148 yards the previous year, was sacked eight times.

The Cyclones took a 3-0 lead on a field goal in the first quarter moments after intercepting a Gundy pass. The Sooners answered with three straight touchdown drives. Gaddis replaced Brewer, who went out with a knee injury in the first period and scored the first TD to cap a 74-yard drive. Blanton missed the conversion. Brewer was through for the rest of the season.

Gundy hurled a 17-yard scoring strike to tight end Rickey Brady to complete a 57-yard drive. Ray intercepted a Cyclone pass to the ISU 27 moments later, and Gundy rifled a TD pass to Warren on the next play for a 19-3 lead.

Iowa State kicked another field goal to cut OU's lead to 19-6 four and one-half minutes later.

Blanton kicked a 23-yard field goal to cap a drive after the second-half kickoff, but four minutes later, Iowa State got a safety when Ray intercepted a Cyclone pass and lost the ball, which rolled behind the end zone. Gundy tossed a 31-yard scoring strike to Warren midway through the fourth stanza for the final tally.

OU gained more total yards (366-253).

The Sooners rolled into Dallas with a 4-0 record and a No. 4 ranking. Texas also rolled into Big D with its head not held so high, bringing a 1-2 record to the game. But as every Sooner and Longhorn fan knows, statistics are thrown out the door in a game like this that rides on emotion more than anything.

The Steers thumped OU, 10-7, the lowest score in the series since a 6-6 tie in 1976. Scott Blanton missed three field goals in the first half.

Oklahoma took a 7-0 lead late in the first quarter when Gundy tossed a 24-yard scoring strike to Ted Long to complete a 40-yard drive in four plays, and Blanton converted.

The Steers nailed a 30-yard field goal to cut OU's lead to 7-3 midway through the second period.

Early in the fourth stanza, UT's James Patton ripped the pigskin from McKinley. Bubba Jacques scooped up the ball and returned it 30 yards for a touchdown and a 10-7 Texas lead.

Franks intercepted a Longhorn pass late in the fourth stanza to give the Sooners one last try to win the game. On third and 18, Gundy completed a pass to Long for a first down, but comeback hopes faded when Gundy was sacked twice, threw an incomplete pass, and was stopped five yards short of a first down.

The Steers had 273 total yards, four more than Oklahoma.

The Sooners dropped to 12th in the AP poll and hosted No. 22 Colorado on October 19. The 3-2 Buffaloes defeated OU, 34-17, for their 17th straight conference win.

Two Oklahoma turnovers led to two of Colorado's three touchdowns in the first quarter. The Sooners drove 68 yards to a 7-0 lead on their first possession of the game. Rasheed's one-yard run capped the eight-play drive, and Blanton converted.

The Buffs marched 99 yards for their first touchdown, intercepted Gundy's pass to set up the next score and recovered Otis Taylor's fumble to set up the third TD.

Gaddis' two-yard TD run and Blanton's 39-yard field goal closed the gap to 20-17 late in the second period, but Colorado drove 64 yards to take a 27-17 lead with nine seconds until intermission.

The Buffaloes drove 99 yards again for the final tally in the third stanza.

Colorado gained more total yards (371-251). Gaddis rushed for 120 yards for the Sooners.

OU fell to 21st in the AP poll and hammered 4-2 Kansas, 41-3, the next week in Norman. Big scoring plays enabled the Sooners to roll up 439 total yards against a defense that ranked sixth nationally in total yards allowed.

Taylor's 58-yard punt return put the Sooners up 7-0 midway through the first quarter. OU entered the game ranked 102nd of 106 NCAA Division I teams in punt returns, and Kansas was third in net punting. Blanton made the first of five conversions and missed one after the third touchdown.

Long raced 56 yards for a TD on the next Oklahoma series for a 14-0 lead. Three touchdowns in the second period gave the Sooners a 34-0 lead. Gaddis scored twice on runs of four and 34 yards, and Gundy hurled a 68-yard scoring strike to freshman split end Albert Hall. The Jayhawks kicked a field goal with 20 seconds remaining in the first half to cut OU's lead to 34-3.

Third-string running back Billy McDade, another freshman, scored the Sooners' only points of the second half with a one-yard run to cap an 80-yard march in the fourth quarter. Kansas was held to two first downs, 43 total yards in the second half and 166 total yards in the game.

Gaddis scored three touchdowns and rushed for 191 yards to lead the No. 20 Sooners to a 28-7 win over 4-3 Kansas State on November 2 in Norman. The game was played in frigid conditions—24 degrees and a wind chill near zero—and heavy snowfall in the second half. About 35,000-40,000 fans turned out at kickoff, and an estimated 15,000 fans remained throughout the second half.

OU took a 21-0 lead in the first 20 minutes and outgained the Wildcats 201 to minus-12. K-State also had no first downs and had

---

The following Gator Bowl records were set by the Sooners in 1991 and have not been broken to date:
First downs by a team: 36
Most points by a winning team: 48
Most touchdowns by one team: seven
Most points in the second quarter by one team: 27
Most touchdown runs by a player: three, Mike Gaddis#
#shared with five other players

---

not moved past midfield. Gaddis scored three touchdowns and Gundy tossed a 15-yard pass to Brady.

OU gained more total yards (385-248). The Big Red defense sacked K-State quarterback Paul Watson eight times.

Gaddis had his best performance of the season by rushing for 217 yards and scored four touchdowns to lead the 20th-ranked Sooners to a 56-16 victory over Missouri the following week in Columbia.

OU scored three TDs and gained 16 first downs in the game's first 18 minutes on scoring drives of 74, 76 and 59 yards. The Sooners' only turnover came when the Tigers intercepted a Gundy pass which led to a Mizzou field goal to cut OU's lead to 21-3.

Oklahoma then scored two TDs in the next 53 seconds. The Sooners took Missouri's kickoff after the field goal, and Gaddis scored on a 65-yard run one play later. Franks returned a Tiger pass 23 yards for a touchdown moments later to boost Oklahoma to a 35-3 lead late in the second stanza.

Missouri answered with a 75-yard touchdown drive to slice the Sooner lead to 35-10 at intermission.

OU punted on its first series of the second half, then scored on their next three possessions, and the Tigers added a touchdown late in the game.

The Sooners picked up 30 first downs, rushed for a season-high 428 yards and passed for 102 more. Missouri had 339 total yards. Gundy completed his first eight passes and finished the game 10 of 12 for 80 yards. Reddell punted three times for a 43-yard average, and Blanton kicked all eight conversions.

No. 18 Oklahoma jumped to a 21-0 lead and held off 0-8-1 Oklahoma State, 21-6, on November 16 in Norman. Gaddis didn't score in the game, but he did rush for 202 yards against the Cowboys, his third straight 200-plus rushing performance against the Pokes. In three OSU games, Gaddis rushed for 689 yards on 82 carries, averaging 8.4 yards each time he toted the ball. He also accomplished the first consecutive 200-yard rushing performance in a season since Billy Sims did it in 1979. Gaddis also became the first Sooner to rush for more than 1,000 yards since Spencer Tillman in 1983.

Rasheed scored all three Sooner touchdowns on a rainy afternoon, and Collins replaced Gundy, who was sidelined with minor surgery.

OU rolled 70 yards in 11 plays for a 7-0 lead late in the first quarter on Rasheed's three-yard run. Blanton kicked the first of three conversions. The lead remained through the next two quarters. The Pokes twice surrendered on threats into Sooner territory. The Big Red defense stopped them at the 39 early in the second stanza on Franks' interception and with a goal-line stand at the one-yard line early in the third.

Oklahoma rolled 80 yards to take a 14-0 lead early in the fourth quarter. Rasheed again scored from the five, and Gaddis carried three times for 50 yards in the 11-play drive. Belser moments later intercepted the first of two OSU passes and returned it to the OSU 16-yard line. Two plays later, Rasheed bolted 10 yards to the end zone.

The Pokes drove 70 yards for their only score, which came with 6:03 remaining.

OU picked up more total yards (308-244). In addition to three interceptions, the Sooner defense forced OSU quarterback Kenny Ford to complete only nine of 25 passes.

No. 11 Nebraska (9-1-1) thumped the 11th-ranked Sooners, 19-14, on November 29, a dark and rainy day in Lincoln. Oklahoma let a 14-0 lead slip away, and the team's greatest faux pas occurred at the coin toss. The Sooners won the coin toss and deferred their options to the beginning of the second half. Oklahoma chose to defend the north goal at the opening kickoff. Gibbs chose to kick-off at the start of the second half, and as a result, the Cornhuskers had the first possession of the third period and the wind behind their backs in the fourth.

"Our defense had been playing well, and we wanted to kickoff and hold them, and re-establish field position in our favor," Gibbs explained after the game.

Gundy and Gaddis both battled the flu during game week and were less than their spectacular selves. Gundy completed only five of 14 passes for 40 yards, and Gaddis rushed for 63 yards, yet both scored the only Sooner touchdowns.

Gundy's one-yard run capped a 33-yard drive in five plays early in the first stanza and Blanton kicked the first of two conversions. Gaddis scored on a one-yard run early in the second quarter, 12 plays after defensive end Trey Tippens recovered a fumble on the NU 42.

Three turnovers stalled the Huskers in the first half, but they managed to kick a field goal late moments after Oklahoma's second TD to cut the OU lead to 14-3. Nebraska took the second-half kickoff and rolled 70 yards in 10 plays for a touchdown. The Sooners gained minus-one yard on their first two series of the second half. After the OU defense stalled the Huskers on their next possession, Nebraska scored a field goal and a touchdown in the fourth period. The Huskers had scored a fourth-period touchdown against OU for the first time since 1980.

Oklahoma took the kickoff with less than three minutes to go and advanced to the NU 44, but Gundy misfired on four straight passes. Nebraska collected more total yards (398-187).

The Sooners accepted an invitation to play Virginia in the 47th Gator Bowl on December 29 in Jacksonville. The 8-2-1 Cavaliers were ranked 19th in the AP poll and they were sixth nationally in pass defense. Virginia had outscored its opponents 28.5 to 10.8, and

the most points yielded by the defense was 24 to Georgia Tech early in the season.

The No. 20 Sooners thrashed the Cavaliers, 48-14, and set an array of records in the victory before a crowd of 62,003. Gundy had the best game of his career as he hurled 11 straight completions and finished with 25 completions in 31 attempts for 329 yards and two TDs. Gundy also broke his brother Mike's Big Eight bowl record for most passing yards (315 yards for OSU in the 1988 Holiday Bowl) in a bowl game.

Oklahoma rolled to a 34-0 lead in the first half. After punting on their first series, the Sooners scored on six of the next eight possessions. Gundy tossed a 10-yard scoring strike to Mickey for the first score. OU scored four touchdowns during the next 11:40. One score included Russell Jones' four-yard return after Tink Collins blocked a Virginia punt for a 28-0 lead. Mickey caught another Gundy pass for a 34-0 lead. The Sooners added two more TDs on their first two series of the second half.

Oklahoma picked up more first downs (36-13) and total yards (618-243). Gaddis rushed for 104 yards and scored three touchdowns in his final game for the Sooners. Warren led all receivers with five catches for 110 yards, Mickey hauled in five for 55 yards, and Hall caught five more for 44 yards.

1992

The 1992 Sooners squad was young and inexperienced, with only nine starters returning from the prior year. Eighteen of the 44 players on the two-deep roster had yet to play in a major college football game. However, Oklahoma was a preseason pick at 15th in the AP poll. The offensive line lacked depth, but the backfield and receivers were loaded. Cale Gundy returned to lead the offense until a dislocated shoulder put him out of a couple of games. Steve Collins replaced him admirably, and some team members thought he should have started the final two games. Tailback Dewell Brewer returned (after rehabilitating an injured knee), along with tailback Earnest Williams and fullback Kenyon Rasheed.

Tight end was solid with veterans Joey Mickey and Ricky Brady returning. Albert Hall had some experience as a backup split end a year ago.

The defense changed to a 3-4 alignment, which moved defensive ends Reggie Barnes and Trey Tippens to outside linebacker. Mike Coats was the only veteran back at the inside linebacker slot, along with newcomer Aubrey Beavers. Darnell Walker was the lone returnee in the secondary.

Placekicker Scott Blanton and punter Brad Reddell also returned.

The Sooners opened the season on Thursday, September 3, against Texas Tech in Lubbock, the first contest between both teams. ESPN set up the game to be televised on its network. The national audience and 48,691 fans at Jones Stadium witnessed Gundy's hot hand. He completed 22 of 28 passes for 341 yards and two touchdowns to lead OU to a 34-9 victory.

Gundy, who also ran for a third TD, broke his school-record performance of 329 yards set in the previous year's Gator Bowl and 12 straight completions against Texas Tech was one better than in the Gator Bowl.

The Sooners marched 96 yards in five plays to take a 7-0 lead on their first series. Williams' four-yard run capped the drive, and Gundy sparked it with a 64-yard pass to freshman split end P.J. Mills to the TT four-yard line. Blanton kicked the first of four conversions, and the Red Raiders blocked one after the second TD.

Tech answered with a 64-yard scoring drive to tie the game, and OU came right back with an 80-yard scoring march. Rasheed's

1991 Season Record: 9-3-0

Big Eight Conference: 5-2-0 (Third)

Date	Opponent	Result	Score
September 14	NORTH TEXAS	W	40-2
September 21	UTAH STATE	W	55-21
September 28	VIRGINIA TECH	W	27-17
October 5	at Iowa State	W	29-8
October 12	Texas at Dallas	L	10-7
October 19	COLORADO	L	34-17
October 26	KANSAS	W	41-3
November 2	KANSAS STATE	W	28-7
November 9	at Missouri	W	56-16
November 16	OKLAHOMA STATE	W	21-6
November 29	at Nebraska	L	19-14
December 29	Virginia*	W	48-14

*Gator Bowl at Jacksonville, FL

Cale Gundy (12) completed 22 of 28 passes for 342 yards and two touchdowns to lead the Sooners to a 34-9 win over Texas Tech.
(© 1992, The Daily Oklahoman)

seven-yard run gave the Sooners a 13-7 advantage. Gundy sparked the drive with a 25-yard aerial to Tink Collins to the TT 34. The Red Raiders took Blanton's blocked kick and raced to the other end for two points and narrowed OU's lead to 13-9.

The Sooners took a 20-9 lead in the second quarter when Gundy hurled a 13-yard scoring strike to Williams. After a scoreless third period, Gundy scored on a one-yard run to cap a 90-yard drive early in the fourth. Eleven seconds later, Beavers returned an interception six yards for the final tally.

Oklahoma picked up more total yards (476-289). Nine Sooners caught Gundy aerials. Rasheed and Williams each caught five passes. The Big Red defense sacked Tech quarterback Robert Hall five times.

The No. 13 Sooners hosted 0-1 Arkansas State nine days later. The Indians, a former Division I-AA team, were in their first year as a Division I-A team. Their coach was Ray Perkins, who had stints as head coach for the NFL's New York Giants and Tampa Bay Buccaneers and at the University of Alabama.

OU blasted the Indians, 61-0, as Brewer and fullback Dwayne Chandler each scored two touchdowns. Gundy ran for one score and passed for another. Gundy engineered the first four scoring drives for a 28-0 lead in the first 22 minutes. Walker returned an ASU pass 54 yards for a touchdown with about five minutes left in the first half. Moments later, safety John Anderson blocked an Indian punt, which rolled out of the end zone for a safety.

Steve Collins replaced Gundy at quarterback and directed a 57-yard drive to set up Blanton's 23-yard field goal late in the second period. Collins led two more scoring drives in the second half, and third-string quarterback Doug Switzer, son of former head coach Barry Switzer, engineered the final scoring march early in the fourth stanza.

OU gained 27 first downs, rushed for 354 yards and passed for 178 more. The defense held ASU to eight first downs and 73 total yards (1.5 yards per snap). Gundy completed five of eight for 97 yards, and Collins went nine of 12 for 81 yards.

Both of the Sooners' tight ends suffered injuries—Brady had broken ribs and Mickey dislocated a finger. Brady sat out the next three games.

Three fourth-quarter touchdowns propelled 0-0-1 Southern California to a 20-10 victory over the 13th-ranked Oklahoma on September 19 in Norman. The Trojans stacked eight men on the front line and used linebacker blitzes to hold the Sooners' ground attack to 48 rushing yards, the lowest rushing yards since being held to 43 yards by the Trojans in 1982.

Barnes forced USC tailback Estrus Crayton to fumble late in the second period, and Beavers recovered it on the OU 47. Moments later, Blanton kicked a 42-yard field goal for a 3-0 Sooner lead.

Early in the third stanza, Oklahoma linebacker Terry Collier returned a Trojan pass for a touchdown, but a holding penalty erased the score and moved OU's possession to the USC 28. Four plays later, Gundy rifled a 25-yard scoring strike to Corey Warren who outleaped two defenders on the goal line. Blanton toed the extra point for a 10-0 lead.

USC scored on a 51-yard pass play early in the fourth quarter and Stephon Pace returned Rasheed's fumble for a 19-yard score and a 14-10 lead. Pace intercepted Gundy's pass on the OU 43 to set up the final USC scoring march.

The Trojans collected more total yards (342-201).

OU dropped to 19th in the AP poll and defeated 2-2 Iowa State, 17-3, two weeks later before a homecoming throng of 65,672 in Norman. The Big Red offense was sluggish with two missed field goals, two dropped passes for touchdowns and a fumble on the Cyclones' three-yard line.

Both teams dueled to a 3-3 tie in the first half. Gundy, who completed 21 of 28 passes for 333 yards, fired two scoring strikes in the third period. His first, a 14-yarder to Albert Hall, capped a 75-yard drive in five plays. Blanton kicked the first of two conversions for a 10-3 lead. Gundy sparked the drive with a 44-yard aerial to Brewer to the ISU 14.

The Sooners rolled 70 yards in seven plays on their next possession for the final tally. Gundy completed a 17-yard TD pass to Williams. Gundy highlighted the drive with a 21-yard run, the longest of the day, to the Cyclones' 21.

Iowa State twice threatened to the OU 26 and 20, but the Big Red defense stiffened.

Oklahoma gained 437 total yards while holding the Cyclones to 156 total yards.

The past two seasons Texas had defeated the Sooners with late-game scoring drives, but the 2-2 Longhorns did not need late heroics in their 34-24 victory on October 10 at the Cotton Bowl. UT's Peter Gardere was the first quarterback to win four straight games in the series. He completed 18 of 32 passes for 274 yards to lead the Steers to victory. During his four years under center, Gardere completed 54 of 88 passes for 649 yards and six touchdowns against the Sooners.

OU took the opening kickoff and rolled 80 yards in seven plays for a 7-0 lead. Gundy, who completed 17 of 38 passes for 276 yards, capped the drive with a nine-yard TD pass to Mills. Gundy also completed two third-down passes in the drive.

The Steers countered with a 91-yard touchdown drive and added a field goal early in the second stanza for a 10-7 lead. Blanton nailed a career-high 51-yard field goal to tie the game minutes later.

Gardere tossed a 31-yard scoring strike to Jason Burleson for a 17-10 lead, and the Horns scored 10 points on their first two possessions of the second half to stretch the lead to 27-10. Texas recovered Brewer's fumble late in the third quarter and upped its lead to 34-10 four plays later.

The Sooners scored twice in the fourth period on a 17-yard pass from Gundy to Warren and a 25-yard strike from Steve Collins to Williams.

Texas collected more total yards (450-397). Warren caught nine passes for the Sooners for 187 yards. Each team was penalized 11 times in the game.

Oklahoma dropped out of the national rankings then traveled to Boulder to face Colorado, ranked seventh and undefeated at 5-0. The Buffaloes scored 10 points in the final four and one-half minutes to force a 24-24 tie, the Sooners' first tie in 95 games. OU last tied Texas, 15-15, in 1984.

The Sooner defense scored two of the team's three touchdowns and intercepted the Buffs' Ty Detmer five times. Walker robbed three passes for OU.

Beavers returned a Colorado fumble 58 yards early in the first stanza for the only scoring in the first half. Blanton nailed a 37-yard field goal for a 10-0 lead late in the third quarter. The Buffs responded with an 80-yard scoring drive, but Brewer scored on a 77-yard sprint on the final play of the third period.

Colorado answered with Detmer's 92-yard pass to Charles Johnson early in the fourth stanza. Darrius Johnson intercepted Detmer's pass 17 yards for a touchdown and a 24-14 lead with 5:09 remaining.

The Buffs cut the lead to 24-17 five plays after recovering Rasheed's fumble on the OU 38-yard line. Mitch Berger, CU's

backup kicker, who missed a field goal in the second quarter, kicked a 53-yarder, which barely cleared the crossbar for the tie.

The Buffs had more total yards (445-307) and were penalized 12 times.

The 5-1 Kansas Jayhawks snapped OU's seven-game win streak in the series with a 27-10 victory the following week in Lawrence. The 22nd-ranked Jayhawks were off to their best start since going 6-0 in 1968.

Kansas drove 72 yards to take a 7-0 lead midway through the first period. The Sooners countered with an 85-yard drive to tie the game. Gundy hurled a nine-yard scoring strike to Warren, and Blanton converted.

The Jayhawks upped their lead to 17-7 with a field goal late in the first stanza and a touchdown early in the second. Blanton booted a 43-yard field goal to cut KU's lead to 17-10, but the Jayhawks scored 10 points in the fourth quarter.

Gundy dislocated a shoulder in the third period and was sidelined the rest of the game. He had completed 16 of 30 passes for 233 yards to become OU's all-time passing leader with 3,712 yards. He broke Bob Warmack's record of 3,527 yards set in the late 1960s. Gundy's season total of 1,580 yards throught seven games broke Warmack's season record of 1,548 yards. The Sooners also broke a team passing record with 1,753 yards, bettering the record of 1,594 set in 1968.

When Gundy was in the game, the Sooners outgained Kansas 255-190 yards, but the Hawks outgained OU 179-72 after Gundy left in the third stanza.

Gundy joined four defensive players—Greg Wilkins, Barnes, Terry Collier and Drew Christmon—who sat out of the next game against Kansas State in Norman.

The Sooners limped to a 16-14 victory over the 3-3 Wildcats on October 31 before a crowd of 60,230, the smallest gathering for an OU home game in 21 years. The Cats had several chances to put the game away when they had the lead. Linebacker Brent Venables, who had a clear shot to the end zone, dropped an interception after the Cats took a 7-0 lead in the first stanza. Leading 14-10, K-State quarterback Jason Smargiasso twice overthrew his receivers. Warren Claassen missed a field goal late in the third quarter.

The Cats took a 7-0 lead four plays after blocking Reddell's punt early in the game. Blanton's first field goal, a 20-yarder in the first period, cut the Cats' lead to 7-3. Darrius Johnson intercepted Smargiasso's pass moments later and returned it 45 yards to the KSU six-yard line. Three plays later, Steve Collins zipped a four-yard scoring strike to Hall, and Blanton converted for a 10-7 OU lead.

Smargiasso, who scored the first touchdown, scored on a seven-yard run for a 14-10 KSU lead early in the second quarter. Blanton later kicked a 47-yard field goal to cut the deficit to 14-13 with 5:41 remaining until intermission. He then added a 28-yarder with 22 seconds left until halftime for the deciding tally.

Oklahoma picked up more total yards (296-224).

Collins scored three touchdowns and passed for a fourth to lead the Sooners to a 51-17 victory over 1-7 Missouri the next week in Norman. Oklahoma rushed for 435 yards, the most since rolling up 461 yards against the Tigers in 1990.

The Sooners scored on six of their first seven possessions. Anderson blocked a Missouri punt to set up the first score at the MU four-yard line. Collins scored on the next play, and Blanton kicked six of seven conversions. The Tigers blocked his final kick.

The Big Red marched 66 yards on its next series for a 14-0 lead. Collins capped the nine-play drive with an eight-yard strike to Hall.

First Player Boycott in OU History

Four days after the tie with OSU, which dropped the Sooners to 5-3-2, Sooner players boycotted the Wednesday practice and instead voiced their grievances with the coaching staff in a two-hour meeting.

The major complaint was that Steve Collins, who led OU to two victories while Cale Gundy was out with an injury, did not play against Oklahoma State. Other complaints were that three offensive linemen—Chuck Langston, Ben Cavil and Milton Overton—were not playing. Other concerns included special treatment to some players over others; some players not getting to play in games after being told they would; and players wondered why Gary Gibbs did not have an open-door policy for his players.

Some players had said that the situations had been building up for some time and that they wanted to talk about it.

"Any time you lose [or tie], the frustration builds up, disappointment builds up ... everybody's looking for a reason," Gibbs said.

The Sooner skipper admitted the main concern was the quarterback controversy.

"Our position is we're going to put the best players on the field," he said. "In our opinion, Cale was the best player. We had a situation down on the goal line where we had a chance to score and didn't get it done. Hindsight might say, what about playing Steve Collins at that time? I don't think that would have been the prudent thing to do, given that Cale led us all the way down to the seven-yard line.

"You've got a quarterback that's led you down the field, handled all the snaps, handled all the exchanges well. I just don't think it's prudent at that time to risk the exchange. I think Steve [Collins] handled the situation well.... He's been very mature about the situation from the very beginning.

"I think we'll go lay it on the line and give a great effort against Nebraska."

The Tigers cut the lead to 14-10 late in the first period and early in the second.

The Sooners scored on their next four possessions and added 10 points in the fourth stanza.

OU hammered out 463 total yards. Williams led the Sooner ground attack with 137 yards, Brewer followed with 108 yards, and Collins added 102 more. Mizzou gained 349 total yards. Tiger quarterback Jeff Handy completed 20 of 33 passes for 230 yards and two TDs. MU receiver Victor Bailey caught 10 aerials for 146 yards and a touchdown.

Gundy returned at quarterback on November 14 when OU traveled to Stillwater to meet 4-5 Oklahoma State. The Sooners and Cowboys battled to a 15-15 deadlock, which snapped OU's 15-game winning streak in the series. A crowd of 50,440 witnessed a field-goal duel between Blanton and the Pokes' Lawson Vaughn in the final 32 and one-half minutes.

OSU jumped to a 7-0 lead early in the second quarter, but the Sooners responded with a 93-yard scoring drive in 10 plays. Rasheed capped the drive with a three-yard run, but the Cowboys' Carlos Evering blocked Blanton's conversion, and Keith Burns scooped up the ball and carried it 74 yards for two points. OSU 9, OU 6.

Oklahoma marched to the OSU 14-yard line late in the second period but settled for Blanton's 31-yard field goal to knot the game at 9-9.

The Pokes opened the second half with a field goal and OU countered Blanton's with a 35-yarder to again tie the game, 12-12.

The Big Red drove to the OSU one-yard line early in the fourth stanza but faced fourth down. OU gambled and lost when Gundy was stuffed at the line of scrimmage and spilled the pigskin.

The Pokes took a 15-12 lead with 1:19 remaining in the game, and the orange-clad Cowboy fans were in a frenzy. The Sooners took the kickoff and marched 55 yards to the OSU 10, but they faced fourth-and-five and Blanton nailed a 27-yard field goal as the clock expired.

Oklahoma collected more total yards (321-220).

The Sooners did give a great effort against the 12th-rated Huskers on November 27, for one half. Nebraska (7-2) led 10-9 at halftime then exploded with 23 points in the final 30 minutes for a 33-9 victory. OU gained more first downs (12-7) and total yards (193-138) in the first half, then Nebraska dominated with a 15-8 edge in first downs and 282-50 in total yards in the second half.

Oklahoma took the opening kickoff and wheeled 64 yards to the NU 16-yard line, but had to settle for Blanton's 33-yard field goal

and a 3-0 lead. Four minutes later, the Huskers Ed Stewart intercepted Gundy's pass at midfield and scored.

Blanton kicked two field goals in the second period for a 9-7 advantage. The Huskers booted a field goal with six seconds until intermission.

The Huskers scored three touchdowns in the second half and also got a safety when they sacked Gundy in the end zone.

Gundy completed nine of 20 passes for 98 yards, threw two interceptions and gained 19 yards on six carries. Sooner fans booed Gundy the final three times he entered the game. Collins drew cheers from fans when he entered the game with less than four minutes remaining. Collins fared no better, as he misfired on both passing attempts and lost nine yards on two carries.

The Sooners finished the season with a 5-4-2 record and fourth in the Big Eight Conference with a 3-2-2 mark for the worst season since 1965. Walker was the only Sooner chosen to the all-conference first team.

1993

Head coach Gary Gibbs proclaimed the 1993 squad a stronger team compared to the previous year. Eighteen starters (nine on each side of the ball) returned, including quarterback Cale Gundy and fullback Kenyon Rasheed in the backfield. Terry Collier moved from linebacker to back up Rasheed. Senior tailback Earnest Williams quit the team, leaving freshmen James Allen, Jerald Moore and Jeff Frazier to battle it out for the starting slot.

Guard Jeff Resler and tackle J.R. Conrad were the only returnees with experience in the front line, and Ricky Brady was back for another year at tight end. Flankers Corey Warren and P.J. Mills and split end Albert Hall returned to provide strength at the receiver positions.

The strength of the defense would be experience at every linebacker slot and in the secondary. Aubrey Beavers, Mike Coats, and Mario Freeman returned at the linebacker positions. Safeties John Anderson and Darrius Johnson and cornerback William Shankle were back for another year in the secondary. Scott Blanton pulled double duty as placekicker and punter.

Yet with all the talent returning, talk around Norman was about Gibbs' job security if he did not produce a winning team in '93. Athletic director Donnie Duncan told the media that Gibbs' job security had not been an issue, since he had cleaned up the football program evidenced by no serious criminal behavior.

"No longer are we constantly explaining ourselves," Duncan said "That's why all the optimism. I fully realize there are people who are not totally pleased. I also realize there are people who are."

The Sooners opened at No. 22 in the AP poll's preseason ranking and moved up one notch before the season opener against Texas Christian.

OU hammered the Horned Frogs, 35-3, on September 4 in Fort Worth. Moore led the Sooners with two touchdowns—both in the second stanza. After not being able to reach past the TCU 48 in the first period, Oklahoma erupted for three touchdowns on their first three series of the second quarter.

Moore capped a 67-yard march with a one-yard plunge midway through the second stanza for a 7-0 lead after Blanton kicked the first of five conversions. Moments later, Larry Bush intercepted a Frog pass on the enemy 38 to set up the second score. Moore scored on another one-yard plunge three plays later. Gundy, who completed 16 of 24 passes for 216 yards, sparked the drive with a 27-yard strike to Warren.

1992 Season Record: 5-4-2

Big Eight Conference: 3-2-2 (Fourth)

Date	Opponent	Result	Score
September 3	at Texas Tech	W	34-9
September 12	ARKANSAS STATE	W	61-0
September 19	SOUTHERN CALIFORNIA	L	20-10
October 3	IOWA STATE	W	17-3
October 10	Texas at Dallas	L	34-24
October 17	at Colorado	T	24-24
October 24	at Kansas	L	27-10
October 31	KANSAS STATE	W	16-14
November 7	MISSOURI	W	51-17
November 14	at Oklahoma State	T	15-15
November 27	NEBRASKA	L	33-9

Gundy hurled a 15-yard TD pass to Warren with 59 seconds left in the first half, capping a 68-yard, nine-play drive. TCU missed a field goal on the final series of the first half and on the first possession of the third period. The third try was successful late in the third quarter to cut OU's lead to 21-3.

The Sooners countered with a 79-yard march in 11 plays to take a 28-3 lead early in the fourth stanza on Allen's three-yard jaunt. Freshman safety Rod Henderson returned a Frog pass for a 40-yard score 10 seconds later. TCU threatened once to the OU one in the fourth period, but the defense stiffened.

OU picked more total yards (447-292).

The Big Red jumped to 17th in the nation and hosted No. 5 Texas A&M the following week in Norman. The 1-0 Aggies were two-time defending Southwest Conference champions and made a run at the national championship a year earlier before losing to Notre Dame in the Cotton Bowl. A&M, which met the Sooners for the first time since 1951, returned 17 starters and were a favorite to challenge for the national crown again. Oklahoma blasted the Aggies, 44-14, before a less than capacity 68,211 crowd.

Leading 27-14 in the fourth stanza, OU scored 17 points in the final two minutes and 38 seconds to pull away.

Blanton's 27-yard field goal gave the Sooners a 3-0 lead in the first period. Late in the second quarter, JuJuan Penny blocked an Aggie punt and recovered it on the A&M 23. Three plays later, Gundy rifled an eight-yard scoring strike to Warren, and Blanton toed the first of five conversions.

Blanton nailed a 39-yard field goal for a 13-0 lead with four seconds until intermission. The Sooners took a 20-0 lead midway through the third stanza. Freeman intercepted an Aggie pass to the 11, and three plays later, Gundy fired a 10-yard TD pass to Allen, who made a spectacular one-handed catch.

A fumble recovery on the OU five late in the third period allowed A&M to score a touchdown in three plays. Gundy scored on a two-yard run early in the fourth quarter to cap a 64-yard drive, and the Cadets answered with a 60-yard scoring march.

Blanton booted a 41-yard field goal with 2:38 remaining, then Darrius Johnson intercepted an A&M pass and returned it to the Aggies' nine-yard line on the first play after the kickoff. Dwayne Chandler scored on the next play. Linebacker Paul Oatts recovered a Cadet fumble moments later on the three, and Michael Thompson scored two plays later from the six.

Oklahoma rolled up more total yards (397-269). The Sooners handed the Aggies their worst loss in five years and snapped their 22-game regular-season win streak.

Cale Gundy flashes the inverted Longhorn sign with his left hand as he dashes for an 18-yard TD run in the third quarter.
(© 1999, The Daily Oklahoman)

Gundy threw three touchdowns passes to lead No. 10 OU to a 41-20 victory over 1-1 Tulsa on September 25 Norman. Collier caught one of the scoring strikes and ran for another.

The Golden Hurricane could not be put away easily as they fought to a 20-20 tie early in the first half. Blanton's 22-yard field goal put the Sooners up 3-0 early in the first stanza, but Tulsa countered with an 83-yard scoring drive and a 6-3 lead. Mills returned the ensuing kickoff 67 yards to the Hurricane 33, and Gundy sailed a 20-yard scoring strike to Warren.

Tulsa responded with an 80-yard drive for a 13-10 lead early in the second period. The Sooners scored 10 points in the final eight minutes for a 20-13 halftime advantage. The Hurricane took the second-half kickoff and rolled 75 yards to tie the game at 20-20.

OU later marched 65 yards, and Gundy hurled a two-yard TD pass to Collier. Bush blocked a Tulsa punt moments later, and the Sooners recovered on the TU 18-yard line. Four plays later, Chandler scored from the one. Midway through the fourth quarter, Mario Freeman pounced on a Hurricane fumble at the TU 34, and six plays later Collier scored from the five.

Tulsa gained more total yards (330-307). Gundy completed 13 of 19 passes for 149 yards. Brady caught six of his aerials for 90 yards.

The 10th-ranked Sooners traveled to Ames the next week and defeated 1-3 Iowa State, 24-7, with a 17-point scoring spree in the second stanza. Gundy completed 14 of 23 passes for 190 yards to become OU's career total yards leader with 4,926 yards, breaking Jamelle Holieway's record of 4,852.

Iowa State took a 7-0 lead in the first quarter before OU rolled up 17 points on its first three series of the second period. The Sooners marched 56 yards in 11 plays to tie the game on Chandler's one-yard run and Blanton kicked the first of three conversions. He later kicked a 52-yard field goal to equal his career high for distance. A Cyclone fumble set up the next Big Red score moments later at the ISU 22, and Chandler scored four plays later from the four-yard line.

Gundy scored on a six-yard jaunt in the fourth quarter for the final tally to cap an 80-yard drive.

OU collected more total yards (362-335).

The 10th-ranked Sooners snapped 1-2-1 Texas' four-game win streak in the series with a 38-17 victory on a newly installed grass turf at the Cotton Bowl. Gundy, playing with a sore hip, scored three touchdowns and completed all six of his passes in the second half.

Blanton booted a 22-yard field goal for a 3-0 lead in the first. Oklahoma rolled 88 yards in 12 plays to take a 10-0 lead late in the first half. Moore carried seven times for 52 yards, in the drive, the final nine for a touchdown. The Steers answered with a field goal with two minutes remaining until halftime.

OU scored on its first three possessions of the second half. Gundy scored on runs of 18 and one yard, Chandler carried seven yards for another, then Gundy carried three yards for the final tally with 3:32 remaining.

Twenty-eight Sooner players became ill from food poisioning on the return charter flight from Des Moines after the Iowa State game. The players got sick from eating contaminated hoagie sandwiches. Monday's football practice was cancelled to get the sick players well. All of them were available for the Texas tilt the next Sunday.

The Big Red rolled up more total yards (408-351). The Sooners' defense sacked Texas quarterback Shea Morenz three times for minus-12 yards and picked off two of his passes. Anderson's interception in the fourth period set up Chandler's touchdown for a 31-10 lead.

A crowd of 64,213 and a regional TV audience witnessed two frightening moments in the No. 9 Sooners' 27-10 loss to 20th-ranked Colorado on October 16 in Norman. The Sooner Schooner wiped out, and Gundy later suffered a concussion.

The 3-2 Buffaloes took a 20-0 lead in the first 23 minutes. Blanton's 44-yard field goal with 1:11 before halftime cut the lead to 20-3. The Sooner Schooner wheeled onto the field, made a sharp turn and rolled on its side. Two of the Ruf-Neks were treated by OU trainers and taken to a local hospital. One suffered a broken arm and the other received a laceration over his right eye. The Shetland ponies were unhurt in the accident, but the Conestoga wagon received some damage. The artificial turf was ripped in two places near the 30-yard line on the north end of the field where the wagon spilled. Duct tape was placed over the two ripped spots.

Gundy threw a 38-scoring strike late in the third quarter to cut the Buffs' lead to 20-10. Early in the fourth stanza, Gundy was slammed to the turf at the end of a 28-yard run. Gundy hit his head on the turf and was unconscious for about 15 minutes. He regained consciousness after he was transported to the locker room, and he improved through the evening. Gundy had completed 11 of 19 passes for 177 yards before the injury.

Colorado drove 57 yards for the final tally in the fourth period. The Buffs picked up more total yards (499-286).

The Sooners dropped to 17th in the AP poll and defeated 3-4 Kansas, 38-23, the next week in Norman. Gundy shook off the cobwebs from the prior week and fired three TD passes and ran for another score. He completed 19 of 26 passes for 342 yards and was not intercepted.

Gundy's four-yard run and Blanton's 32-yard field goal put OU ahead, 10-0, in the first quarter. The Jayhawks drove 84 yards to cut the lead to 10-7 midway through the second period, then the Sooners scored twice on big plays. Gundy hurled a 58-yard scoring strike to Penny, and Mills scored 62 yards on a reverse. Oklahoma took a 31-7 lead when Gundy completed a 22-yard TD pass to Warren with 55 seconds until halftime.

Kansas fought back with two third-quarter touchdowns to cut OU's lead to 31-21. The Sooners marched 80 yards in 10 plays to put the game away early in the fourth stanza. Gundy zipped a 10-yard scoring strike to Warren for a 38-21 lead with 11:47 remaining. The Jayhawks added two points when they tackled Gundy in the end zone near the end of the game.

Both teams collected 26 first downs apiece, but Oklahoma had more total yards (505-493). Brady caught three passes to raise his season total to 24 and surpassed Keith Jackson (22) for most receptions by a tight end in a season.

Kansas State was rapidly becoming a threat in the Big Eight Conference under head coach Bill Snyder's tutelage. The 5-1-1

Larry Bush gets set to tackle Oklahoma State's David Thompson. The Big Red defense held the Cowboys to 31 total yards and only one first down.
(© 1993, The Daily Oklahoman)

Wildcats were ranked 25th when the No 14 Sooners came to Manhattan on October 30. Kansas State snapped Oklahoma's 22-game winning streak in the series with a 21-7 victory.

After losing only three fumbles in the first seven games, the Sooners matched that figure against the Wildcats. OU also was plagued by missed field goals, muffed snaps from center, and penalties that erased big plays.

Kansas State scored on three of four possessions in the middle periods to take a 21-0 lead into the fourth quarter. Quarterback Chad May threw two touchdown passes and ran for another to lead the Cats' scoring spree.

OU's only touchdown late in the game came fast and furious—85 yards in two plays. Gundy completed a 54-yard pass to Brady, then a 31-yard scoring strike to Mills with 4:28 to go. Blanton kicked the conversion, but the Sooners did not threaten again.

Both teams gained 20 first downs each, and OU picked up more total yards (393-330). Gundy completed 20 of 32 passes for 335 yards and no interceptions. Brady caught five passes for 107 yards, and Corey Warren snared five for 77 yards. May completed 13 of 31 for 203 yards and three interceptions.

The 20th-ranked Sooners hammered 3-4-1 Missouri, 41-23, the following week in Columbia. Oklahoma scored on four of its first five possessions for a 28-0 lead in the first 21 minutes and 20 seconds.

Collier's two-yard TD run capped a 68-yard drive in eight plays for a 7-0 lead early in the first quarter. Blanton kicked the first of six conversions. Fumble recoveries set up the next two Sooner scores in the same quarter. Ricky Wren smothered one on the Tigers' 35-yard line and four plays later, Gundy sailed a 13-yard scoring strike to Brady. Shankle recovered a Mizzou fumble on the Tigers' next series at the MU 28. Six plays later, Collier scored his second TD from the three-yard line.

Johnson's 25-yard punt return to the MU 18 midway through the second stanza set up another Sooner touchdown. Two plays later, Chandler bolted seven yards for the score and the 28-0 advantage. The Tigers scored 23 straight points on three touchdowns and a field goal to cut Oklahoma's lead to 28-23 with 5:05 remaining in the game.

The Sooners put together an 80-yard scoring drive to take a 35-23 lead with 1:08 to go. Chandler scored from the three-yard line to complete the nine-play drive. Moments later, Coats picked off a Tiger pass at the MU 26 and scored with one second remaining.

OU rolled up more total yards (366-341).

With plans to install a grass surface on Owen Field next year, the No. 17 Sooners played their final game on artificial turf and dominated Oklahoma State, 31-0, on November 13—a cold, windy and rainy afternoon in Norman. Gundy accounted for all four touchdowns by passing for two of them and running for two more.

The 3-6 Cowboys gained only one first down in the game, and that came on a roughing penalty against OU in the second period. The Big Red defense limited the Pokes to 31 total yards (minus two passing and 33 rushing). OSU's longest play from scrimmage was an eight-yard run.

Gundy, who completed 11 of 16 passes for 175 yards, tossed a seven-yard TD strike to Hall to cap a 77-yard drive midway through the first stanza. Blanton kicked the first of four conversions. Gundy zipped a 28-yard TD pass to Hall midway through the second period. Gundy set a career school record for most TD passes (14) in a season, surpassing Claude Arnold's record of 13 TD passes thrown in 1950.

Johnson intercepted a pass minutes later to set up the next touchdown from the OSU 29. Chandler, who rushed for 103 yards in the game, scored from the three-yard line seven plays later. Blanton nailed a 22-yard field goal on the final play of the first half for a 24-0 Sooner lead.

The Cowboys, who never advanced past their own 45-yard line, intercepted a Gundy pass in the third quarter on the OU seven. OSU could manage only two yards in three plays, then Roger Franks dropped a pass in the end zone on a fake field goal.

The Sooners marched 95 yards for the final tally early in the fourth stanza, and Chandler's 23-yard run capped the nine-play drive.

OU picked up 27 first downs and 507 total yards against a defense that yielded 333 yards per game. The Sooners also controlled the ball for 40 minutes.

No. 16 OU traveled to Lincoln 13 days later for a showdown against undefeated Nebraska (10-0). The Cornhuskers were ranked second in the AP poll and first in the USA Today/CNN coaches' poll. Two touchdowns in a span of 13 seconds in the fourth quarter propelled the Huskers to a 21-7 victory on a bitterly cold afternoon with a wind chill of minus seven degrees.

The Sooners took the opening kickoff and whirled 74 yards in 13 plays for a 7-0 lead. Chandler capped the drive with a one-yard plunge, and Blanton toed the extra point.

Turnovers led to every Nebraska touchdown and stifled a chance for Oklahoma to take a 14-0 lead. Moore had a 47-yard run to the NU 14, but he spilled the pigskin and the Huskers recovered. Toby Wright picked off a Gundy pass midway in the second period and returned it 25 yards to the OU 15. Four plays later, Tommie Frazier scooted two yards into the end zone to tie the game at 7-7.

A 29-yard punt set up Nebraska on OU's 38-yard line early in the fourth stanza. Nine plays later, the Huskers took a 14-7 lead.

On the ensuing kickoff, the Huskers stripped the ball from Johnson and recovered on the OU 20. Calvin Jones scored on the next play for the final tally.

The Sooners led in first downs (14-10) and total yards (294-179). OU's defense held the Huskers to 118 yards through the first three quarters. Freeman injured a knee and would be out for a bowl game. Two days after the Nebraska loss, the Sooners accepted an invitation to play Texas Tech in the John Hancock (formerly Sun) Bowl in El Paso, Texas on December 24.

No. 19 OU smashed the 6-5 Red Raiders, 41-10, before a less than capacity throng of 43,884 in 51,000-seat Sun Bowl Stadium. Gundy completed 15 of 26 passes for 215 yards, three touchdowns and one interception to be named the game's Most Valuable Player. The victory gave the Sooners the unofficial title of Southwest Conference Champions since they defeated all SWC foes in 1993, including Texas A&M, the official conference champs.

The Big Red deployed a hurry-up offense with no huddles between plays and took a 14-0 lead on the first two series. Oklahoma marched 37 yards in three plays for the first score, a two-yard run by Chandler. Blanton kicked the first of five conversions, and the Sooners did not attempt the final kick as time had expired and victory was assured.

Gundy tossed a nine-yard scoring strike to Brady to cap a 69-yard drive in seven plays on the next possession. Tech kicked a field goal midway through the second period, then the Sooners answered with an 80 yard scoring march for a 21-3 advantage. Gundy rifled a 34-yard TD pass to Warren to cap the seven-play drive.

Coats picked off a Red Raider pass and returned it 44 yards to the TT 27. Three plays later, Gundy completed a 15-yard scoring strike to Brady with 25 seconds until the break.

Tech scored the only points of the third stanza with a touchdown moments after recovering an OU fumble. Moore scored two TDs for the Sooners in the fourth quarter.

Oklahoma collected more total yards (392-315). The Sooner defense intercepted Robert Hall four times. A couple of signs could be seen at the stadium. One read: "Oklahoma, Southwest Conference Champion," and another read: "Oklahoma, Texas State Champions."

The Sooners ended the season with a 9-3 record and fourth place in the Big Eight Conference with a 4-3 mark. Beavers, Gundy, Freeman, and Brady were named to the all-conference first unit.

1994

Sooner fans were growing restless. Five years and no conference title, let alone a national championship. Entering his sixth season as the Sooners' skipper, Gary Gibbs' teams only once defeated Nebraska and Texas. The 1994 season loomed with high hopes in Soonerland.

Sixteen starters returned from the year before, and Gibbs proclaimed the '94 squad the best since 1987. He had reason to be optimistic with the return of the entire offensive line and the entire backfield minus the quarterback. Center Chuck Langston, guards Ben Cavil and Milton Overton, tackles Harry Stamps and J.R. Conrad all returned to anchor the front wall. Split ends Albert Hall and P.J. Mills also were back to shag any passes that came their way.

One concern for Gibbs was finding a replacement for quarterback Cale Gundy. That man would be Garrick McGee, a junior college transfer from Northeastern (Oklahoma) A&M. McGee had a strong supporting cast with the return of halfback James Allen and fullback Dwayne Chandler. Scott Blanton again would be doing double duty in the kicking department.

1993 Season Record: 9-3-0
Big Eight Conference: 4-3-0 (Fourth)

Date	Opponent	Result	Score
September 4	at Texas Christian	W	35-3
September 11	TEXAS A&M	W	44-14
September 25	TULSA	W	41-20
October 2	at Iowa State	W	24-7
October 9	Texas at Dallas	W	38-17
October 16	COLORADO	L	27-10
October 23	KANSAS	W	38-23
October 30	at Kansas State	L	21-7
November 6	at Missouri	W	42-23
November 13	OKLAHOMA STATE	W	31-0
November 26	at Nebraska	L	21-7
December 24	Texas Tech*	W	41-10

*John Hancock Bowl at El Paso, TX

All-Big Eight conference linebacker Mario Freeman suffered a knee injury against Nebraska a year ago and was bumped to second on the depth chart behind Tyrell Peters. The secondary was solid and deep with the return of cornerbacks Darrius Johnson and Larry Bush and safety John Anderson. The greatest concern in the 3-4 defense was at noseguard, where Fred Lewis got the starting nod over Robert Allen.

Sooner Magic:
'This is What I Came to Oklahoma For'

The Sooners were ranked 16th in the preseason AP poll and opened the '94 campaign on September 3 at Syracuse in the Carrier Dome. The Big Red was poised for a blowout with a 24-0 lead over the Orangemen before a throng of 48,421 fans and a national (ESPN) TV audience. The potential blowout for Oklahoma nearly turned into a nightmare.

After a scoreless first quarter, OU tallied 24 points in the second. Jerald Moore scored on a 55-yard screen pass from McGee and Blanton toed the first of three conversions. Moments later, McGee sailed a 54-yard scoring strike to Mills. McGee later scored on a three-yard run after Peters recovered a fumble. Blanton nailed a 30-yard field goal after Bush intercepted a pass.

Whoever turned off the television or left the stadium after OU's 24-point lead, missed the most exciting second half in years.

The Sooners were the Titanic and Syracuse was the iceberg. In other words, disaster struck the Oklahoma football team. OU began at its own 29-yard line midway through the third stanza. McGee rocketed a pass to Mills, who caught the ball at the SU 43 and raced down the right sideline. As Mills approached the goal line, SU cornerback Bryce Bevil stripped the ball from Mills. The pigskin rolled through the end zone, but officials ruled the fumble down at the Syracuse one. The Orangemen took over there and rolled 78 yards for a touchdown.

What appeared to be a 31-0 OU lead instead was 24-7, a 14-point swing. The Orangemen soon cut OU's lead to 24-14 with a touchdown moments after blocking Blanton's punt.

Blanton nailed a 23-yard field goal with 7:47 left in the game to give the Sooners a 27-14 lead and breathing room. The Orangemen took the lead in a span of less than three minutes.

Syracuse drove 77 yards to cut its deficit to 27-21.

The Sooners lost five yards on their next possession. Instead of Blanton punting with more than two minutes left, Gibbs opted for an intentional safety. With the Sooners pinned deep in their own territory, chances were that Syracuse would have gained excellent field position on a punt and have an opportunity to score a go-ahead or game-winning touchdown.

Blanton took the snap and carried the ball into the OU end zone, which reduced the Sooner lead to 27-23 with 2:01 remaining.

Blanton punted the free kick, and Syracuse returned it to its own 41. Four plays later, Marvin Harrison hauled in Louis Mason's pass for a 48-yard TD. Bush got a hand on the

extra-point kick, but OU found itself trailing, 29-27, with 1:01 until the final gun.

The orange faithful were delirious with hopes of pulling off the upset with more than a minute of action remaining. But the Sooners had one more chance and relied on McGee's field leadership. He wasn't perfect in his passing, finishing the game with 12 completions on 23 tosses for 276 yards. He already had thrown two TD passes and scored once himself.

"When they scored to go ahead, I told myself this is what I came to Oklahoma for," McGee said after the game. "Before we left the sideline, the offensive linemen were telling me that we would get it done, and they would give me all the time I needed."

OU began at its own 36 following the kickoff, but three plays and minus-two yards later, the Sooners weren't getting the job done. On fourth-and-12 from the 34, McGee tossed a 17-yard pass to Hall, who caught his first pass of the night. No yards were gained on the next two plays. On third-and-10 from the SU 49, McGee again connected to Hall this time for 18 yards to the Syracuse 31. With no timeouts left for the Sooners and just seconds left in the game, Blanton was rushed onto the field to attempt a 48-yard field goal. The ball sailed through the left side of the uprights with 11 seconds to go. The scoreboard clicked three more points for Oklahoma, which was also the final score, 30-27.

McGee came through for the Sooners, winners of three games in as many meetings against the Orangemen.

"Oklahoma magic is alive," he said.

OU gained more total yards (477-319) after holding a yardage lead of 283-68 in the first half.

The Sooners traveled to College Station, Texas, the next week to face Texas A&M. The 1-0 Aggies at No. 15 were one notch above Oklahoma in the AP poll, but 22 notches better in the score with a 36-14 win over the Sooners.

A&M led 13-0 before Moore got Oklahoma on the board with a two-yard run to complete a 66-yard drive late in the second quarter. The Sooners kept it close in the third period. After the Aggies scored a TD, they lost a fumble on Blanton's punt at their 15, and Allen scored on a four-yard run three plays later to trail, 19-14. But the Aggies scored 17 more in the fourth quarter, two of them on OU fumbles in Sooner territory.

A&M collected more total yards (359-216).

Oklahoma dropped to 21st in the AP poll. The Sooners played on grass at Owen Field for the first time in 24 years. The new Turfway 419 Bermuda grass was installed during the off-season at an estimated cost of $350,000.

As the new field provided a firm footing, OU's 17-11 victory over Texas Tech (1-1) was sloppy. The Big Red lost three fumbles and were penalized 11 times, but never trailed in the game. The Sooners scored twice in the second stanza for a 14-3 halftime lead. Moore, who rushed for 106 yards, scored on a five-yard run for the first tally. Blanton missed his first extra point in 47 tries. Moore added another touchdown less than six minutes later on an 11-yard run. McGee connected a two-point con-

Scott Blanton toes a 48-yard field goal with 11 seconds remaining to lift the Sooners to a 30-29 victory over Syracuse. (© 1994, The Daily Oklahoman)

version pass to tight end Michael McDaniel, and Tech added a field goal before halftime.

The Red Raiders scored on a fumble recovery early in the fourth period and added a two-point conversion, cutting the Sooners' lead to 14-11. Blanton booted a 41-yard field goal midway through the quarter to up the Oklahoma lead to 17-11. Tech could not penetrate into Oklahoma territory the rest of the game. OU gained 390 total yards and held the Red Raiders to 201 total yards, 29 rushing.

The Sooners held onto their 21st ranking, and winless Iowa State (0-4) came to Norman on October 1 in the Big Eight opener for both squads. OU gobbled up 460 total yards, 334 on the ground in the 34-6 victory before 65,821 homecoming fans.

The Cyclones jumped ahead 6-0 late in the first quarter.

The Sooners answered with an 80-yard drive ending with Allen's 36-yard TD dash. Allen, who rushed for 111 yards, scored on a five-yard run minutes later to cap a 66-yard march. Moore added a two-yard TD run minutes later, and Allen scored on a three-yard blast to lift OU to a 20-6 halftime lead.

Terrance Brown scored on a 24-yard touchdown run and McGee on a one-yard plunge in the fourth quarter.

The Sooners climbed back to No.16 while Texas, at 3-1, was one notch ahead. The Longhorns had just lost to Colorado 34-31 the week before the Red River Shootout in Dallas. A goal-line stand enabled the Steers to pull out a 17-10 victory on October 8 in Dallas.

Oklahoma held a 7-0 halftime lead thanks to Moore's 23-yard run early in the second stanza. The Horns scored a field goal midway through the third period then followed it with a touchdown early in the fourth for a 17-7 advantage.

Blanton's 17-yard field goal cut the deficit to 17-10. The Sooners had one more chance from their 30 after Texas missed a field goal. Three passes and two runs later, OU was knocking on the door at the UT six-yard line. Moore gained three yards, then McGee's pass was incomplete. McGee carried for no gain on the next play. It was fourth-and-goal from the three in front of the Longhorn contingent.

The Sooners ran a misdirection reverse handoff to Allen, who was nailed one foot short of the goal line by Stonie Clark. The Horns escaped with the victory. OU fell to 3-2 and 22nd in the AP poll.

No. 4 Colorado was undefeated with five wins when the Sooners traveled to Boulder. It was all Colorado, 45-7, equaling the 38-point whipping Kansas State handed OU in 1969 for the most lopsided loss in OU football history. Buffaloes tailback Rashaan Salaam rushed for 161 yards and scored four TDs.

The Buffs failed to score from the opening kickoff and missed a field goal. From then on they put the hammer down with two touchdowns in the first period and again in the second for a 28-0 halftime lead.

The Sooners scored a late touchdown on a nine-yard pass from McGee to Mills. The Buffs rolled up 429 total yards and held OU to 265.

A plethora of Sooner fans wanted a coaching change following the humiliating loss to the Buffaloes. Never mind that the Sooners surrendered more than 40 points for the first time since 1989, or had their worst loss since 1970, the Sooners showed little spark in their nationally televised loss.

Sooner Magic: Breaking a Skid

The Sooners had disappeared from the polls but traveled to Lawrence, Kansas, on October 22 in hopes of breaking a two-game losing streak. For the first time since 1968, they were underdogs (by two points) to the 4-2 Jayhawks.

The mostly partial crowd of 42,500 was hoping for a repeat of the last time the Sooners came to Lawrence. KU was victorious, 27-10, in 1992 to snap a seven-game skid against the Big Red.

Kansas took a 3-0 lead early in the '94 contest. OU answered with a 13-yard scoring strike from McGee to tight end Stephen Alexander.

The touchdown was the first in the opening quarter for the 1994 Sooners, who were outscored 33-0 in the first stanza prior to the Kansas game.

Neither team was able to kick up the scoreboard in the second quarter, but Kansas scored on its first two possessions of the second half for a 17-7 lead. The second touchdown came shortly after McGee's fumble.

Little hope remained for Sooner fans, as several Big Red players were sidelined with injuries. Fullback Jerald Moore pulled a hamstring, running back Terry Collier separated his shoulder, linebacker Brent DeQuasie suffered a pinched nerve in his neck, cornerback Larry Bush re-injured his knee and Ben Cavil reinjured his ankle. To top that off, Alexander also injured his ankle in the fourth quarter.

Chandler scored on a one-yard run to cap an 87-yard drive that began late in the third quarter. Blanton nailed the conversion to cut the deficit to 17-14. Blanton added a 39-yard field goal to tie the game with 6:48 remaining.

Following the kickoff, KU's Asheiki Preston connected a pass to Ashaundi Smith for 13 yards to the OU 40, but Johnson stripped the ball from Smith, and recovered it. OU marched 37 yards in seven plays to the KU 22 but stalled, and Blanton was called on for the game-winning kick.

The Sooners had a 17-mph wind behind them in the fourth stanza. Blanton said he had no trouble with the wind in pregame warmups, and he had no problem with his 39-yard attempt. The ball sailed through and well past the goal post with 1:38 remaining.

Johnson intercepted Preston's pass moments later to ice the game. The Hawks had gone 15 quarters without a turnover. OU gained more total yards, 346-220. McGee completed 19 of 29 passes for 207 yards and did not throw an interception.

"I really want to applaud this football team," Gibbs said. "They showed great character today."

Johnson said he never gave up the thought of losing another humiliating game. "I was thinking we can't lose to Kansas. That would have broken our backs . . . really destroyed our season."

"This hasn't been a good week for us," Gibbs said. "We needed a win. That's the bottom line. No matter how much you believe or talk, discuss, doubts were certainly creeping in."

Doubts continued to slither into the OU football program

The next week No. 23 Kansas State (4-2) defeated 4-3 Oklahoma, 37-20, in Norman, the first time the Wildcats won two straight against the Sooners in 25 years.

The Cats only led 7-3 in the first half. KSU quarterback Chad May engineered two third-quarter drives capping them with TD passes.

The Sooners scored twice in the fourth period, but the Wildcats answered each time. Blanton kicked a 43-yard field goal, but K-State retaliated with a touchdown. McGee fired a 65-yard TD pass to McDaniel, but the Cats blocked the extra point, returning it 98 yards for two points.

KSU scored a TD two plays after the OU kickoff. The Sooners then marched 80 yards capped by McGee's 28-yard pass to McDaniel, but it was too little, too late. Oklahoma rolled up more

Jerald Moore eludes Cowboy defenders en route to the third of his five touchdowns. Moore tied Steve Owens for the most touchdowns in one game. (© 1994, The Daily Oklahoman)

total yards, 411-326. McGee completed 21 of 45 passes for 308 yards, two touchdowns and had two intercepted.

The Sooners dropped to 4-3 (2-2 in the Big Eight) but rebounded with two victories to raise their record to 6-3 with wins over Missouri (30-13) in Norman and Oklahoma State (33-14) in Stillwater.

After a scoreless first period against unranked Missouri (3-5 and 2-2 in the Big Eight), OU exploded for 17 points in the second stanza. Chandler scored on a one-yard run, Blanton booted a 31-yard field goal, and McGee tossed a 10-yard TD pass to McDaniel. The Tigers had a 51-yard field goal to trail 17-3 at halftime.

MU added a field goal in the third period, then Frazier scored on a 39-yard TD run for the Sooners late in the quarter. After the Tigers scored a touchdown, Johnson scored for the Sooners with an 87-yard punt return. His TD punt return was the first for a Sooner since 1991.

The Sooners collected more total yards, 346-256. Both teams were penalized a combined 21 times (Mizzou 11, OU 10).

Moore rushed for 151 yards and scored five touchdowns against OSU (3-5-1 and 0-4-1 in the Big Eight). His five TDs equaled Steve Owens' school record set in 1968 against Nebraska.

OU scored first on Moore's eight-yard run midway through the first quarter. Freshman kicker Jeremy Alexander missed his first collegiate extra point. OSU later took a 7-6 lead with a touchdown run in the first stanza. Moore added a one-yard plunge late in the first, and the two-point try failed for the Sooners. But they held a 12-7 lead.

Moore exploded for a 39-yard TD run early in the third period. OSU answered with a TD pass, then Moore added two more TD runs (six and eight yards) in the fourth quarter.

OU collected 387 total yards, and the Pokes gained 264 yards.

Several days prior to the Nebraska game, Gibbs announced his resignation as the Sooners' skipper effective at the end of the season.

Undefeated and No. 1 Nebraska (11-0) rolled into Norman on November 25 in a nationally televised game. The Cornhuskers entered the game with a 24-game winning streak.

OU's defense held the Huskers to 303 total yards, 191 yards below their season average. The Sooners could get nothing going as Nebraska's quick defense held the Sooners to 179 total yards and 10 first downs.

The Sooners and Huskers battled to a 3-3 tie in the first half. Blanton's 33-yard field-goal attempt in the second period was blocked. This would have given Oklahoma a 6-3 lead. Instead, the Huskers took a 6-3 lead on a 26-yard field goal midway through the third stanza.

The Huskers scored their final tally on an 82-yard drive early in the forth quarter. Nebraska, favored by 13 points, held on to win 13-3.

The loss dropped the Sooners to 6-5, and they accepted an invitation to play No. 22 Brigham Young (9-3) in the Copper Bowl in Tucson, Arizona.

BYU quarterback John Walsh completed 31 of 45 passes for 454 yards and four touchdowns in the Cougars' 31-6 victory. McGee had contracted spinal meningitis weeks earlier and was unable to play for the Sooners. They had to rely on Terence Brown, who had played six different positions during the year.

Trailing 24-0, Oklahoma scored its only touchdown on Moore's two-yard run midway through the fourth period. BYU, which totaled 556 yards in the game, answered with Walsh's fourth TD pass. The Sooners picked up 235 total yards.

OU ended the '94 season with six wins and six losses, the first non-winning season since 1965. Defensive end Cedric Jones, Johnson, and Blanton were named to the All-Big Eight Conference team.

Gibbs won 44 games, lost 23 and tied two during his six-year tenure as the Sooners' skipper. He entered private business and did not return to coaching until he was hired as Georgia's defensive coordinator in 2001. He served as Louisiana State's defensive coordinator in 2001, linebacker coach for the Dallas Cowboys from 2002-2005 and defensive coordinator for the New Orleans Saints in 2006.

Sixty-year-old Howard Schnellenberger was hired as the Sooners' 19th head coach in December 1994, almost one month after Gibbs resigned. Schnellenberger was the first coach hired at OU with head

1994 Season Record: 6-6-0
Big Eight Conference: 4-3-0 (Fourth)

Date	Opponent	Result	Score
September 3	at Syracuse	W	30-29
September 10	at Texas A&M	L	36-14
September 17	TEXAS TECH	W	17-11
October 1	IOWA STATE	W	34-6
October 8	Texas at Dallas	L	17-10
October 15	at Colorado	L	45-7
October 22	at Kansas	W	20-17
October 29	KANSAS STATE	L	37-20
November 5	MISSOURI	W	30-13
November 12	at Oklahoma State	W	33-14
November 25	NEBRASKA	L	13-3
December 29	Brigham Young*	L	31-6

*Copper Bowl at Tucson, AZ

coaching experience since Jim Tatum. All other hires were assistant coaches either at OU or for another team.

Schnellenberger won 99, lost 85 and tied twice in his 17-year career, which included stints with the Miami Hurricanes, Louisville Cardinals, and the NFL's Baltimore Colts. He won a national championship in 1983 at Miami. The baritone-voiced, Captain Kangaroo look-alike, proclaimed that books would be written and movies made about his era at the University of Oklahoma.

1995

When Howard Schnellenberger was hired in December 1994, University of Oklahoma president David Boren said: "All of us who participated in the search committee feel very strongly that Howard is the right person at the right time for our football program."

"Howard is someone with whom our fans can identify, someone who could quickly win the hearts of our people and become one of us," said Donnie Duncan, OU athletic director.

Oh, but the opposite was true. The new head coach alienated himself with the fans. He did not want them drinking beverages or sitting while watching the practices. He requested fans to show up early at games and chastised those who left at halftime when a game was a blowout. He also limited players' water breaks. As a result, two of them dehydrated—Brian Ailey and Aaron Findley had to be hospitalized for overheating. Ailey almost died from severe dehydration.

Ailey filed a lawsuit against Schnellenberger and the University of Oklahoma two years later. A U.S. District Judge dismissed the case in January 1999.

Four teams from the Southwest Conference joined the eight members of the Big Eight Conference in February 1994 to be effective for the 1996 season. Texas A&M, Baylor, Texas, and Texas Tech bolted from the 80-year-old SWC to form the Big XII Conference. The 1995 season would be the final curtain for the Big Eight, and the new conference formed two divisions—OU, Oklahoma State, Texas, Texas A&M, Baylor and Texas Tech in the south division, and Colorado, Iowa State, Kansas, Kansas State, Missouri and Nebraska in the north division.

As a result, annual contests with some of the north teams would be severed and changed to a two-year basis. The southern teams would play each other every year, but play three teams in the north division on a two-year rotation.

Schnellenberger believed the Sooner squad was overweight and out of shape, so he put them on a weight loss program to lose a combined 1,000 pounds by the season's first game.

Nineteen of 22 starters returned in '95. Schnellenberger and his staff introduced a pro-style offense, which included screen passes, sprint draws, and quick traps. Eric Moore and Garrick McGee battled for the starting quarterback slot, but both would split playing time. Others returning on offense included: fullback Jerald Moore, halfback James Allen, tight end Stephen Alexander, tackle J.R. Conrad, guard Milton Overton, center Chuck Langston, flanker P.J. Mills and split end JuJuan Penny.

Two all-conference returnees—defensive end Cedric Jones and cornerback Darrius Johnson—headed a stout defense. Other returnees included cornerback Larry Bush; safeties Rod Henderson and Maylon Wesley; end Paul Oatts; tackle Baron Tanner and linebacker Tyrell Peters.

The Sooners also commemorated the team's 100th anniversary with a patch on each jersey. The jerseys also were changed to include numbers on the shoulders instead of the sleeves and two stripes on

each sleeve. Schnellenberger introduced a new tradition by having the team walk one-half mile from the Sooner Hotel to Memorial Stadium. For many years, the teams would lodge in Oklahoma City the night before a game, but Schnellenberger had his charges stay in Norman.

The Sooners were ranked 15th in the preseason AP poll, dropped to 16th and climbed to 14th without having played a game. Oklahoma opened the season on September 9 with a 38-22 victory over San Diego State in Norman. Jerald Moore rushed for 159 yards and scored three touchdowns to lead the victory.

After a scoreless first period, OU erupted for 17 points in the second. Moore's 19-yard run capped an 85-yard march in 12 plays. Jeremy Alexander kicked the first of five conversions.

McGee later hurled a 36-yard scoring strike to tight end Michael McDaniel, two plays after Bush intercepted an Aztec pass and Alexander toed a 26-yard field goal with 2:38 remaining in the half.

Moore scored the first two touchdowns of the second half on runs of 52 and five yards for a 31-0 lead. The Aztecs outscored the Sooners, 22-7, in the fourth stanza. San Diego State's Ricky Parker intercepted two of McGee's passes to set up a touchdown on one pickoff and he scored on the other. Wesley returned a fumble 65 yards for the final tally.

Oklahoma rolled up more total yards (586-339) and was penalized 15 times for 129 yards. Eric Moore and Garrick McGee combined to complete 16 of 33 passes for 220 yards and three interceptions.

The 14th-ranked Sooners, favored by 29 points, defeated 1-1 Southern Methodist, 24-10, the next week in Norman. Schnellenberger said he was embarrassed for his offense's performance as it was unable to score touchdowns in the first half and had 11 of the team's 14 penalties in the game.

The Big Red had to settle for three Jeremy Alexander field goals in the first half.

SMU moved into scoring range in the final 35 seconds. Ben Crossland shanked a 44-yard field-goal attempt, but Darrius Johnson was flagged for roughing him, and Crossland's 39-yard try was good to cut OU's lead to 9-3 at halftime.

The Sooners took the second-half kickoff and rolled 80 yards in 10 plays for a 17-3 advantage. James Allen capped the drive with a seven-yard run, and Jerald Moore carried for the two-point conversion.

The Mustangs answered with a 58-yard scoring march to trail, 17-10. Garrick McGee replaced Eric Moore, who left the game with a leg cramp, and engineered a 47-yard drive late in the third period and into the fourth. Allen scored his second TD on a 10-yard run, and Alexander converted.

Oklahoma picked up more total yards, 385-324.

The Sooners climbed to 10th in the AP poll and hammered North Texas, 51-10, on September 23 in Norman. The Mean Green hung close for a half (17-10) and led 2-0 in the first stanza, but OU scored 17 points in each of the final three quarters.

The Big Red scored four touchdowns and two field goals in the second half while rolling up 384 total yards and holding North Texas to only 14 yards. Jeff Frazier scored the final TD on a 96-yard run and tied Buck McPhail for the longest run from scrimmage. McPhail's 96-yard non-scoring run came against Kansas State in

1951. Frazier and McPhail still hold the record in Sooner football history.

Oklahoma picked up 560 total yards, and the defense held the Mean Green to minus-44 yards rushing.

No. 4 Colorado was next to invade Norman the following week. The 4-0 Buffaloes would be without the services of starting quarterback Koy Detmer. Schnellenberger at his press luncheon earlier in the week said he wished Detmer would play because, "I don't want a damn asterisk when we beat their ass."

The game kicked off at 8 p.m. on the ESPN network, for the latest start of an OU football game ever at Owen Field. The game was a sellout at 75,004, to end a string of 34 non-capacity games.

The Buffs made Schnellenberger eat his words as they scored 24 second-half points to come from behind with a 38-17 victory over the 10th-ranked Sooners. Backup quarterback John Hessler completed 24 of 34 passes including five touchdowns.

Oklahoma took a 3-0 lead on Jeremy Alexander's 21-yard field goal in the first period. Terrance Malone blocked a Buff punt early in the second stanza, and the Sooners rolled 21 yards in seven plays for a 10-0 lead when Eric Moore scored from the one-yard line.

Colorado later recovered Moore's fumble on the OU 17, and four plays later Hessler fired his first scoring strike to cut OU's lead to 10-7. The Big Red countered with a 78-yard drive in nine plays to take a 17-7 lead. Moore zipped a 20-yard TD pass to Penny for a 17-7 edge with 5:42 left until halftime.

The Buffs answered with a 71-yard march and cut the Sooners' lead to 17-10 with 17 seconds until intermission.

Hessler said the Oklahoma defense did not adjust at halftime as the Buffs scored three TDs and kicked a field goal in the final 30 minutes.

"Don't talk about adjustments," Schnellenberger said in the OU locker room. "That's the biggest bunch of bull I've ever heard in my life."

Colorado collected more total yards (419-218). The Buffs outgained Oklahoma 247-56 in the second half.

The Sooners' top three ground gainers—Jerald Moore, Frazier and Allen—were held out of the Iowa State contest on October 7 in Ames. No. 14 Oklahoma still defeated the 2-2 Cyclones, 39-26. Mike Rose, who was switched from fullback to tailback for the game, scored two touchdowns and rushed for 104 yards to lead the victory.

Both teams were tied 13-13 early in the second quarter, and Iowa State took a 19-16 lead at halftime. The Sooners marched 78 yards to take their first lead of the game, 23-19, on Rose's four-yard run midway through the third period.

Brian Lewis was back to punt for Oklahoma early in the fourth period but fumbled when the Cyclones' Preston Rhamy tackled him. Kevin Hudson returned the pigskin for a 22-yard touchdown to give ISU a 26-23 lead.

A penalty backed up OU 10 yards to their 10-yard line after the kickoff. Eric Moore, who sat out the earlier part of the game with a concussion, then connected on a pass to Mills at the OU 39, and Mills outraced ISU defenders to complete a 90-yard touchdown for a 30-26 Sooner lead.

Troy Davis fumbled the ensuing kickoff, and Corey Ivy recovered on the Cyclones' 41. Moore completed a 13-yard scoring strike to Stephen Alexander, but Jeremy Alexander missed his first conversion in 17 attempts.

Bush moments later intercepted a Cyclone pass on the OU 47, and Jeremy Alexander kicked his fourth field goal of the game nine plays later for the final tally.

OU gained more total yards, 495-304. Davis, who entered the game with a 228-yard-per-game rushing average, was held to 89 yards on the ground. Moore completed 11 of 15 passes for 195 yards.

For the first time in history, the Sooners practiced at the Cotton Bowl the day before the Texas game. No. 13 OU tied 18th-ranked Texas, the next day, 24-24, after the 4-1 Longhorns took a 21-0 lead in the game's first eight minutes and 44 seconds.

Eric Moore's fumble set up a 39-yard Steer scoring drive, a blocked punt rolled into the end zone for another touchdown, and runningback Shon Mitchell raced 69 yards for a third score. Oklahoma then outscored Texas, 24-3, and gained more yards (380-188) in the final three quarters.

The Big Red had a chance to win the game with 26 seconds left on Alexander's 42-yard field-goal try, but his kick veered wide.

OU picked up more total yards, 442-339. Jerald Moore rushed 21 times for 174 yards. Longhorn quarterback James Brown completed 20 of 38 passes for 242 yards.

The 15th ranked Sooners hosted No. 7 Kansas on October 21 for another night game televised by ESPN, except this one kicked off at 6:30. The 6-0 Jayhawks had stunned Colorado, 40-24, two weeks prior to the OU tilt.

Oklahoma took a 14-0 lead, but Kansas outscored the Sooners, 38-3, in the final three quarters for a 38-17 victory before a homecoming crowd of 74,639.

Moore rushed for 219 yards on 18 carries and scored both of the Sooners' touchdowns in the first stanza. He also caught two passes to combine for 29 yards for 248 of OU's 337 yards. Moore scored on runs of 60 and 72 yards and Jeremy Alexander's two conversions gave Oklahoma the two-touchdown lead.

The Hawks cut the lead to 14-7 with an 80-yard scoring drive in the second period. KU quarterback Mark Williams, who completed 18 of 26 passes for 337 yards, tossed three TD passes in the second half.

One of his scoring strikes and a field goal put the Hawks up, 17-14, in the third quarter, but Alexander's 24-yard field goal tied the game at 17 with 13:25 left in

Texas wide receiver Mike Adams fumbles on a punt return after being popped by Travian Smith. Corey Ivy (43) pursued the ball but Rod Henderson recovered. The fumble led to OU's tying touchdown in the final tie game in Oklahoma football history.
(© 1995, The Daily Oklahoman)

the game. Kansas countered with a 70-yard drive to take the lead for good, 24-17. An interception for a touchdown and a 45-yard scoring drive finished off the Sooners.

The Jayhawks rolled up more first downs (21-11) and gained 378 total yards.

Sooner Magic:
Moore to Moore Too Much for Mizzou

Several days before the 23rd-ranked Sooners traveled to Columbia to meet Missouri, Coach Schnellenberger said his team would be prepared to "win a game that we should win." Yes, should win, after all the Tigers were 2-5 for the season. OU was seeking its 12th straight win over Missouri but would have to do it without three defensive starters. Wesley, Cedric Jones, and defensive end Rod Manuel were sidelined with injuries, yet the defense held its own.

Fortunately the offense was healthy, and Jerald Moore scored both Sooner touchdowns. Moore first made a mistake with a fumble early in the first quarter, which led to a Tiger field goal.

Missouri added another field goal early in the second stanza after blocking Lewis' punt.

McGee replaced Eric Moore at quarterback for Oklahoma and engineered a 56-yard scoring drive in two plays. McGee completed a 15-yard pass to McDaniel on the first play, then Jerald Moore bolted 41 yards to the end zone. Alexander toed the conversion for a 7-6 lead with 8:28 remaining to halftime.

OU cornerback Anthony Fogle intercepted a Tiger pass moments later and returned it 29 yards to the MU 26. OU advanced to the Tigers' 12-yard line, but Missouri's defense tightened.

Midway through the third period, Lewis failed to grasp a low snap and he was nailed for a 17-yard loss to the OU 27. Four plays later, the Tigers added another field goal for a 9-7 lead.

Mizzou marched to the OU 13-yard line midway through the fourth stanza but lost nine yards on the next three plays, and missed a 41-yard field-goal attempt with 7:15 remaining. The Sooners took over and rolled 78 yards in three plays for the deciding score.

On third and four at the OU 28, Eric Moore pegged a short pass to Jerald Moore, who caught the ball on the 37 and outran the Tigers for the final 63 yards to the end zone. Eric Moore misfired on the two-point pass play, but OU held a 13-9 lead with 6:20 to go.

Eric Moore fumbled in the next Oklahoma series, and Missouri recovered on the OU 21-yard line. The Big Red defense held the Tigers to one yard in four plays.

Both teams picked up 10 first downs apiece, but the Sooners outgained the Tigers, 246-153. Jerald Moore gained 117 yards, and Eric Moore completed nine of 15 passes for 138 yards. The victory gave Schnellenberger his 100th career win. His 101st would not come in 1995.

Ninth-ranked Kansas State blasted the No. 25 Sooners, 49-10, on November 4, the worst loss for OU since a 47-0 setback to Oklahoma State in 1945. Wide receiver Kevin Lockett, who Gary Gibbs passed on signing in 1992, caught eight passes for 117 yards and a touchdown.

Punting problems continued for the Sooners. Tim Daughtry replaced Lewis as the punter, but it did not matter. For the sixth straight game, an opponent blocked a punt, and the 7-1 Wildcats blocked Daughtry's kick and returned it 23 yards for a 7-0 lead.

Alexander toed a 21-yard field goal late in the first stanza, but Kansas State scored three TDs in the second period to put the game away at 28-3. Jerald Moore reinjured his toe in the first half and

was not a factor in the game. Allen was the leading rusher for the Sooners with a meager 24 yards.

Trailing 14-3 early in the second stanza, OU tried to fake a punt, but poor communication foiled the effort. On fourth-and-six at the KSU 37, up-back Rose called the fake punt and took the snap, but he was stopped after a one-yard gain. Some of the Sooners claimed they heard the fake call and others didn't. Kansas State then drove 64 yards for a 21-3 lead.

The Sooners later marched 80 yards in nine plays to cut the deficit to 28-10 when Eric Moore hurled a 29-yard scoring strike to Mills, and Alexander converted.

The Cats scored three more touchdowns in the second half.

Kansas State rolled up more total yards (353-289).

The Sooners disappeared from the national rankings, and 2-7 Oklahoma State shut out OU, 12-0, for the Cowboys' first victory against the Sooners since 1976. The loss also ended Oklahoma's 140-game scoring streak dating back to 1982.

The Pokes took a 6-0 lead on two Lawson Vaughn field goals in the second quarter, and OSU led at halftime against OU for the first time in 12 years. The first field goal was set up by an interception of an Eric Moore pass.

Fogle recovered Andre Richardson's fumble on the OSU 20 midway through the third period, but the Sooners failed to cash in. OU advanced to the Cowboys' 17 on the next possession but bogged down, and Alexander's 51-yard field-goal try bounced off the upright.

The Pokes then drove 48 yards in two plays. Quarterback Tonè Jones fired a 47-yard pass to Terrance Richardson to the OU one and Jones scored on the next play. The two-point pass play failed, but it did not matter as the Sooners didn't threaten the rest of the way.

The Sooners had lost three straight home games for the first time since late 1981 and early 1982. OU collected more total yards (313-200). Stephen Alexander caught six passes to raise his season total to 37, surpassing Rickey Brady's school-record 36 for tight ends set in 1993.

1995 Season Record: 5-5-1
Big Eight Conference: 2-5-0 (Fifth)

Date	Opponent	Result	Score
September 9	SAN DIEGO STATE	W	38-22
September 16	SOUTHERN METHODIST	W	24-10
September 23	NORTH TEXAS	W	51-10
September 30	COLORADO	L	38-17
October 7	at Iowa State	W	39-26
October 14	Texas at Dallas	T	24-24
October 21	KANSAS	L	38-17
October 28	at Missouri	W	13-9
November 4	at Kansas State	L	49-10
November 11	OKLAHOMA STATE	L	12-0
November 24	at Nebraska	L	37-0

"Schnellenberger ... predicted movie scripts would be written of this year's team," wrote John Rohde in *The Daily Oklahoman.* "Obviously, it's a horror flick. Plenty of punch lines have been written, too."

The Sooners could still qualify for a postseason bowl game if they defeated No. 1-ranked and undefeated (10-0) Nebraska on November 24 in Lincoln. The Cornhuskers blasted OU, 37-0, for their 24th straight victory en route to Big Eight and national championships.

Nebraska scored on two of OU's three turnovers—a 36-yard interception return in the first half and a 57-yard fumble return in the third stanza. The interception and two field goals gave the Huskers a 13-0 halftime lead, then they exploded for 24 points in the final 30 minutes.

The Huskers picked up more total yards (407-241). Jerald Moore was held to 39 yards rushing, but he cleared by one yard the 1,000-yard season mark.

OU set the Big Eight record for most penalties in a season with 102 whistles for 876 yards. The Sooners also set the school record for most pass attempts with 293 but completed only 46.4 percent of them.

The Sooners finished the season with a 5-5-1 record and fourth in the Big Eight Conference with a 2-5 mark, the worst record at OU since 1965.

Schnellenberger resigned on December 17, one year and a day after he was hired as the Sooners' head football coach. Boren said Schnellenberger's won-loss record (5-5-1) was not "made an issue" with Boren, Duncan nor the board of regents.

"My decision has nothing to do with the inaccurate reports or hurtful rumors that often accompany head coaches and top programs," Schnellenberger said in his resignation statement.

1996

On December 31, 1995, the University of Oklahoma hired John Blake as the football team's 20th head coach. Blake, a former Sooner noseguard and assistant coach, was the fourth OU graduate to coach for his alma mater. He also was the first African-American hired to a head coaching position at the University of Oklahoma. He served as defensive line coach under Gary Gibbs from 1989-1992 and served the same capacity from 1993-1995 for the NFL's Dallas Cowboys.

The Big 12 Conference began its inaugural season, which provided a new landscape in the college football world. Baylor, Texas, Texas A&M, and Texas Tech left the defunct Southwest Conference to join the current Big Eight members. The new conference was split into two divisions of six teams apiece. The south division was comprised of Oklahoma, Oklahoma State, and the four Texas teams. The north division included Colorado, Iowa State, Kansas, Kansas State, Missouri, and Nebraska.

The teams from the north and south would alternate schedules every two years. The Sooners played Nebraska, Kansas, and Kansas State during the first two years of the new conference (1996 and 1997). Colorado, Iowa State, and Missouri would replace those teams in 1998 and 1999. The rotation would continue every two years.

Numerous fans from all teams did not like the new rotation, which severed annual rivalries like OU versus Nebraska. The new process also would end the nation's longest uninterrupted series between OU and Kansas at 96 years in 1998, an NCAA record at the time. (The Kansas vs. Nebraska series passed that mark with 97 in 2002).

Only nine starters returned to the '96 Sooner squad. Among them: quarterback Eric Moore, halfback James Allen, tight end Stephen Alexander, guard Chris Campbell, placekicker Jeremy Alexander, cornerback Anthony Fogle, defensive end Rod Manuel, defensive tackle Barron Tanner, and linebackers Tyrell Peters and Broderick Simpson.

Ten freshmen had earned their way to the second team on the depth chart.

Coach Blake said he noticed that OU should have won several games in 1995, but the players ran out of gas in the second half. He noted that it would not happen under his regime.

"Oklahoma had a chance to win several games last year," Blake said. "They were ahead in a lot of games, but they fell back after halftime. I'll tell you what . . . that won't happen again. If we fall back, it won't be for lack of effort or excitement from those players.

"There is no way we are going to let you down. We are here for a new era, and this is truly special."

There was nothing special about the John Blake era at OU as far as wins were concerned. Blake recruited some terrific players and ran a clean program, but the program was not returning to the elite status it had seen under Bud Wilkinson and Barry Switzer. The Sooners opened the season with four straight losses, a first since dropping five straight to open the 1961 season. OU finished 3-8 in 1996, the worst since a 3-7 mark in 1965, Gomer Jones' inaugural season.

Expectations were high for the 1996 season as evidenced by the 22,000 fans that turned out for a preseason scrimmage on August 22.

Oklahoma suffered its first season-opening loss since 1982 by dropping a 20-7 decision to Texas Christian on September 7 in Norman. Blake was the first Sooner coach to lose his debut since Jack Tatum in 1946.

TCU quarterback Jeff Dover completed 12 of 19 passes for 76 yards and two touchdowns to lead his squad.

The Horned Frogs took a 3-0 lead in the first period after recovering Rodney Rideau's fumbled punt return. The Sooners later gambled on fourth-and-one at the TCU 48, but the Frog defense stopped Allen short of a first down. Dover then hurled a 52-yard scoring strike to Jason Tucker for a 10-0 TCU advantage.

Dover pitched another TD aerial in the second stanza, and the Frogs added a field goal in the third for a 20-0 lead.

Freshman quarterback Justin Fuente entered the game in the third quarter to spell Moore, to a loud approval of the crimson fans. Moore led only one scoring threat, which came in the first period, and Jeremy Alexander missed a field goal. Moore left the game completing only six of 21 passes for 64 yards. Fuente did not generate much of a charge either until the fourth period.

Fuente tossed a three-yard TD pass to flanker Gerald Williams midway through the fourth stanza for the Sooners' only score. Fuente sparked the 69-yard drive with a 53-yard bomb to split end Chris Blocker two plays before the touchdown. Alexander converted the seventh point.

The TCU picked up more total yards, 294-247.

The Sooners had two weeks to improve their offense before heading to California to meet 1-1 San Diego State. The offense did improve with 31 points, but the defense gave up 51 to the Aztecs in the latest kickoff in OU football history. The game began at 10:17 (Oklahoma time) and ended at 1:33 a.m. (Oklahoma time).

Freshman halfback De'Mond Parker replaced Allen, who left the game with a rib injury, and rushed for 244 yards on 18 carries and scored three TDs. But again it was the Sooners' poor pass defense that helped SDSU to victory. Aztec quarterback Billy Blanton connected on 18 of 25 passes for 258 yards and five TDs.

A poor kicking game also doomed Oklahoma. The Aztecs returned four kickoffs for a 35-yard average and two punts for a 13.5-yard average. SDSU's average possession start was at their own 43, while OU's average start was at its own 19.

The Aztecs, who never trailed, rolled to a 31-17 halftime lead. Oklahoma got within a touchdown (38-31) in the third quarter, but the Aztecs pulled away with 13 unanswered points.

The Sooners rolled up more total yards, 505-445. After an 0-4 start, Justin Fuente finished the game by completing 10 of 12 passes for 197 yards. Stephen Alexander caught six of his aerials for 137 yards.

Parker said the team was "burned out" in the final quarter.

Tulsa defeated OU, 31-24, on September 28 in Norman, the first win for the Golden Hurricane over the Sooners since 1943. It also was the first Tulsa win in Norman since 1919. The game also marked the first six-game losing streak in Oklahoma football history, including three straight losses in 1995.

Once again the defense turned in another lousy performance as Tulsa's quarterback, Troy DeGar, hit 18 of 38 passes for 277 yards and two TDs.

Parker earned his "wings" to start at halfback and turned in a fine performance, picking up 143 yards on 19 carries. But it was Parker's fumble on the game's first play that led to a 7-0 Tulsa advantage six plays later.

The Big Red tied it up early in the second stanza when Fuente hurled a 37-yard scoring strike to tight end Michael McDaniel and Jeremy Alexander converted.

The Hurricane scored 17 unanswered points, including a 99-yard TD pass from DeGar to Wes Caswell. That gave TU a 17-7 lead, and OU later advanced to the Hurricane one-yard line, but Parker spilled the ball, and Tulsa recovered in the end zone. The Hurricane then rolled 80 yards for a 24-7 lead.

Oklahoma put up 17 points in the third period to tie the game at 24-24. Fuente fired a 41-yard TD strike to McDaniel. Fuente later scored on a one-yard plunge three plays after linebacker Cory Ivy blocked a Tulsa punt. Alexander's 49-yard field goal knotted the game minutes later.

Tulsa scored the winning touchdown in the fourth stanza moments after intercepting Fuente's pass at the OU 31.

Oklahoma had more total yards, 423-417. For the first time in OU history, two players had caught passes for more than 100 yards. McDaniel hauled in six aerials for 108 yards, and Stephen Alexander palmed four for 102 yards before he left the game with a separated shoulder. Discipline was a problem for the Sooners, as they were penalized 10 times for 105 yards.

The discipline, or lack thereof, got worse in the next game, as Kansas blasted the Sooners, 52-24, the following week before a homecoming crowd of 64,333 in Norman. OU was flagged 16 times for 168 yards and lost the ball three times (two interceptions and one fumble) in perhaps the sloppiest game in Sooner football history.

Oklahoma took a 7-0 lead midway through the first period on a 16-yard pass from Fuente to Blocker, but the Jayhawks immediately tied the game when Eric Vann returned the ensuing kickoff 100 yards for a touchdown.

Minutes later, the Jayhawks missed a field goal, but the Sooners were whistled for having 12 men on the field. KU scored a touchdown four plays later. The Hawks were forced to punt in the second stanza, but OU was flagged for roughing, and KU added field goal nine plays later for a 17-7 lead.

Kansas later blocked Jeremy Alexander's field-goal try and returned it for a touchdown. The Sooners moved into scoring position at the KU one-yard line just before halftime, but two illegal procedure penalties moved the ball back to the 11. Oklahoma had to settle for Alexander's 26-yard field goal to cut the Hawks' lead to 24-10.

Two OU penalties (one on a punt and another on a field goal) kept a Kansas drive alive, allowing the Jayhawks to take a 31-10 lead. The Sooners stalled on their next possession, and Isaac Byrd returned the punt 94 yards to up the KU lead to 38-10. The Hawks outscored OU 21-14 the rest of the way.

The only bright note was the defense's containment of KU runningback June Henley, who was held to 63 yards on 27 carries after entering the game with a (201.3-yard average).

The Big Red picked up more total yards, 538-368. Parker carried the ball 19 times for 146 yards, and Fuente completed 18 of 35 passes for 286 yards.

Sooner Magic: Overtime

The red-clad faithful was whooping and hollering in the stands, while OU football players were hugging and congratulating Allen in the north end zone of the Cotton Bowl. Fogle carried the huge OU flag the length of the field and staked it in the south end zone as the Sooner Schooner rolled out onto the field.

Not one single Sooner fan had left the Cotton Bowl, soaking up every exhilarating moment of OU's 30-27 overtime victory over the Texas Longhorns. It was the first overtime game involving OU football since the NCAA implemented overtime in college football earlier in the year.

Anyone who attended the 1996 OU-Texas football game on October 12 might have thought the Sooners had just won the national championship. Instead, the Sooners were celebrating their first victory of the season.

James Allen scores the winning touchdown for a 30-27 overtime win over Texas. (© 1996, The Daily Oklahoman)

It had been 31 years when OU entered the Red River Rivalry without a win. The Big Red had not defeated a Top 25 team in the last 14 tries (0-13-1). Still, the ABC network broadcast the game regionally.

The Longhorns arrived at the Cotton Bowl in 1996, as 22-point favorites and ranked 25th in the nation.

Texas booted a field goal on the first possession of the game, then turned a blocked punt into a touchdown for a 10-0 lead.

The Sooners retaliated on three straight scoring drives. Jeremy Alexander booted a 31-yard field goal early in the second period. Fuente tossed an eight-yard scoring strike to Jarrail Jackson on the next series. Alexander added a 35-yard field goal for the Sooners' first lead, 13-10, with 1:54 left in the first half.

Texas answered with an 82-yard drive to take a 17-13 lead at intermission.

Texas opened the fourth period with an 80-yard TD drive for a 24-13 lead with 9:42 remaining in the game.

Then lightning struck the Cotton Bowl. Jackson hauled in a Texas punt at the OU 49 and bolted down the sideline past the Longhorn bench for a 51-yard touchdown.

After the game, Jackson said he was just following orders of teammate Broderick Simpson who was blocking the way on the punt return.

"Broderick said to get behind the wall [of blockers], and that's what I did," Jackson said. "Once I got behind that wall, there wasn't anybody there."

Blake called for a two-point conversion. Fuente connected with Stephen Alexander for the deuce, and the Big Red trailed, 24-21, with 6:41 left on the clock.

Jeremy Alexander kicked a 44-yard field goal minutes later to knot the game at 24 with 2:26 remaining.

A year earlier, Alexander had failed to convert a 42-yard field goal that would have defeated Texas. Instead both teams settled for a 24-24 tie.

"I'm happy I got an opportunity after last year," Alexander said. "I wanted to prove myself and to my team that I can put it through and hit the big one for us."

The Sooners had a chance to put the game away when Allen rambled 45 yards to the UT one with less than a minute to play, but the Sooners were guilty of holding, which nullified the long run.

Regulation of the 1996 game, a sellout for the 51st straight meeting between OU and Texas, also ended in a 24-24 tie, and thanks to the NCAA voting to end ties, overtime was allowed for the first time in Division I college football that year.

OU won the overtime toss of the coin, and chose to play defense first. Since the Longhorns lost the toss, they were allowed to decide which end of the field to play the overtime. They chose the north end of the field—in front of their fans.

The Horns got the ball first at the 25-yard line. James Brown threw an incomplete pass, then Ricky Williams was stuffed for a two-yard loss. On third and 12, Brown scrambled, then lofted the ball, which came down through the hands of Priest Holmes.

Dawson connected on a 43-yard field goal for a 27-24 Longhorn lead. OU then got its turn.

Two years earlier, OU had lost to Texas, 17-10. The Sooners had a chance to score late in the game, but Allen, then a sophomore, was stopped by Stoney Clark inches short of the north end zone.

"That play is gone," Allen said of that failed TD attempt.

Now as a senior, Allen was called on to carry the load in 1996 in overtime. On OU's first OT play from the 25-yard line, and in front of rabid burnt orange rooters, Allen took the ball and gained 10 yards to the 15.

On the next play, he carried off tackle to the left side for two yards. Then he got four more yards to the nine. On the next play, Allen took Fuente's screen pass all the way to the three-yard line. Then he took the handoff from Fuente and hit the hole off right tackle but shifted toward the middle of the line and lunged across the goal line.

Oklahoma 30, Texas 27.

The Sooners gained more yards, 441-344. Allen, who lost his starting job to Parker earlier in the season, rushed for 142 yards and gained an additional 51 yards on five receptions. Parker rushed for 107 yards. Allen was responsible for all 25 yards in the overtime, including the game-winning lunge.

"When I crossed the goal line, there was a sigh of relief," Allen said of his winning TD.

"I have heard of Sooner Magic, and it was here today," Jackson said.

The orange-clad fans sat in disbelief, then poured out of the stadium as OU fans stayed and continued their revelry.

Of the three victories in 1996, no doubt the Texas win was the most exhilarating.

It would have been a shame for the Sooners to accomplish a great victory over a major rival like Texas, then lose to Baylor the following week. It almost happened, but OU defeated the Bears, 28-24, the next Saturday night in Waco as Fuente accounted for all four OU scores.

The game was a tale of cashing in on mistakes in each half. The 3-2 Bears scored three touchdowns off Sooner turnovers in the first half and Oklahoma capitalized on two Bear miscues to pull off the victory in the final 30 minutes.

The Sooners took the opening kickoff and rolled 61 yards for a 7-0 lead. Fuente, who completed four of five passes for 54 yards in the drive, tossed a five-yard scoring strike to McDaniel, and Jeremy Alexander converted.

The Bears tied the game moments after recovering Fuente's errant pitchout at the OU 24-yard line.

A 39-yard punt return set up the next Bears score, a 31-yard drive for a 14-7 lead. The Bears took a 21-7 lead moments after intercepting Fuente's pass.

The Big Red answered with a 65-yard march. Fuente capped the drive with a two-yard scoring strike to Stephen Alexander, and Jeremy Alexander converted. Baylor was flagged twice in the drive, both times giving Oklahoma a first down.

The Bears added a field goal early in the third period for a 24-14 lead. Jason Freeman recovered a Baylor fumble on the BU 12 and three plays later, Fuente scooted across from the one to draw the Sooners to 24-21.

Early in the fourth stanza, Simpson smothered a Bear fumble on the BU 40 to set up the winning touchdown. Six plays later, Fuente completed an 11-yard TD strike to Allen, who was wide open in the end zone. Jeremy Alexander converted the 28th point.

The Sooners rolled up more total yards (376-314). Fuente completed 15 of 28 aerials for 184 yards, and Allen rushed for 153 yards on 26 carries.

The Sooners traveled to Manhattan, Kansas, on October 26 and fell short of pulling off a huge upset over 16th-ranked Kansas State.

The Sooners' defense gangs up on OSU running back Andre Richardson. The defense held the Pokes to 74 yards rushing.
(© 1996, The Daily Oklahoman)

The 6-1 Wildcats nearly saw a 28-point lead slip away, but they held on for a 42-35 victory before 43,815 fans, the fourth-largest crowd at KSU Stadium to date.

The Wildcats also notched their fourth consecutive win over Oklahoma, their longest win streak over the Sooners.

K-State held a 21-0 lead after the first stanza. Twice the Cats capitalized off OU turnovers. Coach Blake replaced Fuente with Moore at quarterback early in the second quarter. Moore helped spark OU to five touchdowns. He ran for one and passed for four more, the final three in the last 12:28 of the game. Moore completed 11 of 23 passes for 234 yards; eight of 14 for 158 yards and three TDs in the fourth quarter.

Moore's one-yard TD run cut the deficit to 21-7 midway in the second period, and Jeremy Alexander booted the first of five conversions. The Cats responded with an 80-yard scoring drive to lead 28-7 at the half.

Trailing 35-7, Moore fired a 33-yard scoring strike to Stephen Alexander, but KSU answered with a 66-yard scoring march and a 42-14 lead.

The Sooners scored 21 unanswered points all from Moore's arm. He threw scoring strikes to Alexander, McDaniel, and Mo Little to cut the deficit top 42-35.

The Big Red got the ball with 1:42 remaining, but Chris Canty intercepted Moore's pass and the Cats ran out the clock.

Kansas State gained more total yards (461-354). Tyrell Peters led the Big Red defense with 16 tackles. McDaniel caught six passes for 125 yards. He caught five aerials for 115 yards in the fourth stanza.

K-State receiver Kevin Lockett, of Tulsa Washington, hauled in 12 passes for 157 yards and one touchdown. The Sooners did not recruit Lockett, and he had a role in each of the last four victories over OU. Cat quarterback Brian Kavanaugh shredded the OU defense by connecting 27 of 38 passes for 349 yards and three TDs.

The fifth-ranked Nebraska Cornhuskers exploded for eight touchdowns in the second half to hand OU its worst defeat in history, 73-21, the next week in Norman. The 52-point win eclipsed the 47-0 victory Oklahoma State put on the 1945 Sooners, and the 73 points was the most scored on an Oklahoma team, breaking the record of 59 points scored by Kansas State in 1969.

The Cornhuskers won their sixth straight over OU, and the loss guaranteed Blake to be the second coach to have a losing record in his inaugural season. John Harts, the first OU coach, had a 0-1 record in 1895. With a 2-3 record in the Big 12's south division, the Sooners still had an outside chance to win the darn thing.

The opportunity began on November 9 with a 27-17 win over 4-5 Oklahoma State in Stillwater. If there is one way for a coach to keep his job at Oklahoma, it is to defeat Texas and Oklahoma State. Blake did just that, so his job was safe for another season. There was no talk among the university brass of getting rid of Blake, but Sooner fans weren't so sympathetic. Some believed that an OU alum would have a greater reason to beat the Cowboys since outsider Howard Schnellenberger did not.

Once again, Moore relieved Fuente at quarterback and sparked the victory. The Pokes took a 7-0 lead late in the first quarter when Andre Richardson returned Brian Lewis' punt 37 yards for a touchdown.

The Sooners marched 55 yards in three plays to tie the game, 7-7, midway through the second stanza. Parker, who rushed for 166 yards, carried all three times: 21 yards, 42 yards and the final eight for the touchdown. Jeremy Alexander kicked the first of three conversions.

OU recovered a fumble on the Pokes' next series, but Fuente tossed an interception, and he was through for the day, completing only two of 12 passes for 35 yards.

Moore entered the game on the next Oklahoma possession and engineered an 80-yard scoring march just before halftime. Moore capped the eight-play drive with a 19-yard scoring strike to McDaniel for a 14-7 lead.

The Big Red defense stopped the Cowboys on the first series of the second half then rolled 68 yards for a 21-7 advantage. Parker's seven-yard jaunt capped the 11-play drive, which was sparked by two of Moore's 11-yard runs.

Oklahoma State answered with a field goal and successfully recovered the onside kick. On first down, Manuel deflected Toné Jones' pass into Peters' hands at the OU 49. The Sooners bogged down

1996 Season Record: 3-8-0
Big 12 Conference: 3-5-0
(Fourth: South Division)

Date	Opponent	Result	Score
September 7	TEXAS CHRISTIAN	L	20-7
September 21	at San Diego State	L	51-31
September 28	TULSA	L	31-24
October 5	KANSAS	L	52-24
October 12	Texas at Dallas	W	30-27 (OT)
October 19	at Baylor	W	28-24
October 26	at Kansas State	L	42-35
November 2	NEBRASKA	L	73-21
November 9	at Oklahoma State	W	27-17
November 16	at Texas A&M	L	33-16
November 23	TEXAS TECH	L	22-12

after reaching the OSU 33, and Alexander nailed a 50-yard field goal for a 24-10 lead with 54 seconds left in the third quarter.

OU upped the lead to 27-10 early in the fourth period on Alexander's 22-yard field goal, which was set up by Allen's 52-yard run to the OSU eight-yard line.

The Pokes later drove 80 yards for their final touchdown.

The Sooners rolled up more yards, 443-301. Moore completed seven of nine passes for 71 yards, and Lewis had his best punting performance with a 44.2 average on five kicks.

The Sooners, at 3-3 in the Big 12 south, trailed Texas sitting atop the division at 4-2. OU would need to defeat Texas A&M (3-3 in the Big 12) and Texas Tech (4-3) and hope that Texas would lose to either Kansas or Texas A&M to claim the south division.

Texas A&M (5-5 overall) took Oklahoma out of the race with a 33-16 victory on November 16 in College Station. The Sooners had only one good quarter, the second, and even took a 16-3 halftime lead. Moore earned his first start since the first game of the year, and Fuente did not play against the Aggies. Allen sat out with a sore toe and shoulder, and Parker replaced him at halfback.

Trailing 13-0 after one period, OU took the lead in t he second. Moore hurled a 25-yard scoring strike to Michael McDaniel, then Parker scooted 19 yards to tie the game at 13-13. A&M blocked Jeremy Alexander's second conversion. Alexander nailed a 50-yard field goal for a 16-13 lead just before halftime. In addition to the 16 points, Oklahoma rolled up 10 first downs to zip for the Aggies and 203 yards to 23 for the hosts.

The Aggies controlled the second half by scoring 10 points in each quarter and outgained the Sooners 202 to 34 total yards. The defense held the Aggies to 282 total yards, a season best.

Texas Tech defeated the Sooners, 22-12, the next week in Norman, for the eighth loss of the season—a first in OU football history. The loss also kept the Sooners out of the win column at home, the worst since going 0-2-2 at home in 1936. It also marked the first eight-game home losing streak in school history.

More mistakes: two missed field goals, three failed third-down conversions, and a fumble, which set up Tech's field goal.

Oklahoma took a 3-0 lead on Jeremy Alexander's 26-yard field goal, late in the second period. The Sooners held the lead through intermission.

The Red Raiders erupted for 16 points in the third quarter—two touchdowns and a field goal, which they cashed in off Moore's fumble.

OU marched 56 yards in five plays to trail, 16-10, early in the fourth period. Moore zipped a 23-yard TD pass to McDaniel, and Alexander converted.

Tech scored a touchdown and took an intentional safety near the end of the game.

OU had more total yards (339-307).

"It might be the worst team in OU history, too," Blake said after the game remarking about the eight losses being a new school record.

Peters was the lone Sooner selected to the All-Big 12 first team.

1997

A new $4.45 million scoreboard was installed at the south end of Memorial Stadium. The 160-foot by 33-foot scoreboard featured a 24-foot by 32-foot video screen, which was appropriately named, "SoonerVision." Permanent lights were also added to the stadium.

The Sooners looked at the 1997 season with optimistic lenses, believing they could win five of the 12 regular-season games. Their

forecast fell a game short of the goal, and Sooner faithful and the media were questioning whether Blake was the man to guide the OU football program.

Thirteen starters returned to the '97 squad, including tight end Stephen Alexander, flanker Gerald Williams, defensive tackles Kelly Gregg and Martin Chase, linebackers Travian Smith and Dale Allen, and safeties Terry White and Gana Joseph. Many others had some starting experience, including halfback De'Mond Parker, who rushed for 1,184 yards as a freshman in 1996. Justin Fuente edged out Eric Moore for starting quarterback duties. Jeremy Alexander returned as the team's placekicker, and Brian Shackleford, who came to OU on a baseball scholarship, auditioned and won the punting duty.

Oklahoma opened the season on August 23 against Northwestern in the eighth Annual Pigskin Classic at Chicago's Soldier Field. The game was arranged months earlier and remains the earliest start to a Sooner season. The Wildcats won, 24-0, before a scant crowd of 36,804, which included about 10,000 crimson fans. It was Oklahoma's first season-opening shutout loss since 1925.

The Sooners were hampered by four turnovers, 10 penalties and poor punting—new season, same verse. OU coaches also were plagued with poor communication as the headsets in the press box failed to work. So coaches communicated by a single telephone in the first half and walkie-talkies in the second half. Defensive coordinator Bill Young said he could hear interference from taxicab drivers on Michigan Avenue.

Northwestern cashed in on three turnovers in the fourth quarter after leading only 6-0 through three periods.

Jeremy Alexander missed two field-goal attempts in the first half. The first would have given the Big Red a 3-0 advantage and the second, a 6-3 lead.

The Sooners' greatest threat came in the third quarter with a 71-yard march to the NU four-yard line, but the Wildcats intercepted Fuente's third-down pass in the end zone.

The Cats then drove 80 yards for a 14-0 lead and they capitalized on two more turnovers in the fourth stanza.

Oklahoma had more total yards, 351-343. Brian Shackleford averaged only 33.4 yards in five punts for the Big Red.

Chapter Sixty-Five: Blocked Kicks Save the Day

Chants of "OU! OU! OU!" echoed from Memorial Stadium as the clock clicked to zero. The 1997 Oklahoma Sooners finally won a home game after losing eight straight at Owen Field. Thousands of fans spilled onto the field to join Sooner coaches, players, Ruf-Neks and the Sooner Schooner in celebration of a last-second block of a field goal that would have given Syracuse a victory and OU its ninth straight disappointment at home.

The Sooners' special team units were embarrassing the past few years—blocked punts, muffed long snaps on field goals, extra points and punts. But against Syracuse the special team defense was unique with two blocked punts and a blocked field goal on the game's final play.

The Syracuse Orangemen were impressive in their first game, a 34-0 shellacking of Wisconsin in the Kickoff Classic in East Rutherford, N.J. They were also tabbed as a nine-point favorite against the Sooners on September 6.

Syracuse took a 7-0 lead midway through the first period on an 86-yard punt return.

The Big Red answered with a 72-yard, 11-play drive. Jermaine Fazande scored on a one-yard run, but Alexander missed the extra-point kick. Parker sparked the drive with runs of 31 and 19 yards.

OU's defense stalled the Orangemen on their next possession. Smith blocked a Syracuse punt, and the Sooners recovered the pigskin at the SU one. Moore replaced Fuente at quarterback.

Fazande took a hand off from Moore and bulled over for the go-ahead TD. The Sooner coaches opted for a two-point conversion. Moore rolled left and rifled the ball to tight end Matt Anderson for the deuce, and the Sooners led, 14-7, with 2:35 still to play in the opening quarter.

Syracuse retaliated with an 80-yard TD march to knot the game early in the second quarter.

The Orangemen marched 53 yards after recovering Moore's fumble for a 21-14 lead two and one-half minutes later.

Alexander kicked a 30-yard field goal to cut the Sooners' deficit to 21-17, which remained at halftime.

The scoring bonanza continued in the second half but not as fast and furious as in the first. Fuente started at quarterback in the second half, but again was replaced by Moore. Syracuse took a 28-17 lead midway in the third quarter.

OU closed the gap to 28-23 on Moore's three-yard run minutes later, but the two-point conversion failed. Parker carried for 55 of the drive's 75 yards.

The Sooners regained the lead on their next possession, an eight-play, 61-yard drive. On the eighth play, Moore dove over the top from the one-yard line. Again, the two-point try failed, but the Sooners led, 29-28, with 10:47 left in the game.

The Sooner defense stalled the Orangemen on their next possession, and Smith crashed through the line again for his second blocked punt. The ball rolled back to the SU six-yard line, where defensive end Sedric Jones picked it up and lumbered over SU punter Peter Ferris and into the end zone. Alexander booted the extra point to give OU a 36-28 advantage with 9:31 remaining.

OU's next drive milked four minutes off the clock, but the Sooners had to punt, giving the Orangemen the ball at their 23 with 61 ticks left on the clock. But SU had no timeouts remaining. A bad snap resulted in a 14-yard sack by linebacker Corey L. Ivy, who would turn out to be the game's hero.

SU quarterback Donovan McNabb zipped the ball to Kevin Johnson on a crossing route—first down at the SU 44. McNabb again found Johnson over the middle for another 30 yards to the Sooner 26. Five seconds remained in the game, but the clock was stopped in order for officials to move the first-down chains. Enough time for kicker Nathan Trout to trot onto the field and attempt a game-winning field goal from 44 yards away. The kick was low, and Ivy got a hand on the ball to preserve a Sooner victory.

After the game, Moore lashed out at the media. "We went out and we just played heads up. A lot of y'all really wrote us off and talked bad about us in the papers and stuff, but y'all don't even know what this team's been through."

"We showed that we believe that we can win, and that's the whole thing," said Chase, who had three sacks in the game. "I think one thing we showed out there was just never giving up. We could have

Corey Ivy (43) blocks Nathan Trout's 44-yard field goal attempt in the game's final five seconds.
(© 1997, The Daily Oklahoman)

laid down and just quit, but we never did, and I think we showed that out there today."

"Our guys hung in there . . . it was outstanding," Blake said. "These kids got rewarded for their hard work and for what we've been through, and we still have a way to go."

The Sooners traveled to Berkeley, California, the following week and dropped a 40-36 decision to the 1-0 California Bears. Poor pass defense and penalties once again were OU's downfall. The Sooners overcame a 21-point deficit to tie the game in the third period but could not finish the job.

The Sooners took a 7-0 lead when Parker slashed 54 yards down the sideline on the game's second play. Parker was held to 27 yards on 18 carries the rest of the game.

The Bears intercepted Moore on the next Oklahoma series to set up a touchdown, but OU held a 7-6 lead when Chase blocked the extra point. A shanked punt (26 yards) and a 15-yard personal foul penalty minutes later set up Cal's field goal for a 9-7 lead. The Bears then scored 17 unanswered points in the second stanza for a 26-7 advantage.

Smith intercepted a Bear pass and raced 65 yards for a touchdown just before halftime, but Alexander's conversion ricocheted off the uprights.

Cal marched 32 yards to take a 34-13 lead on their first possession of the third quarter. Minutes later, Moore tossed a 73-yard scoring strike to Chris Blocker, and Alexander converted. Moore left the game with a pulled hamstring soon after, and Fuente engineered two TD drives to tie the game.

The next OU score came on a 33-yard pass to split end Mo Little, and Fazande later scored on a three-yard run to tie the game at 34 apiece.

The Bears later drove 49 yards for a 40-34 lead with 2:37 left. Chase blocked the conversion, and cornerback Corey T. Ivy returned the ball for two points for OU.

Cal collected more total yards (424-351). Bear quarterback Justin Vedder connected on 24 of 39 passes for 253 yards and three TDs. Receiver Bobby Shaw caught 11 aerials for 158 yards and two TDs. Cal was flagged 12 times for 130 yards, and OU was whistled 11 times for 118 yards.

Not many would believe the '97 Sooners could win a game with five turnovers while their opponent had none. Well, that's what happened when the Big Red trounced 1-3 Louisville, 35-14, before a sellout crowd of 74,993 in Norman. Parker and Fazande combined to rush for 342 yards and three touchdowns, the first time in 17 years two Sooners each had crossed the 150-yard mark in one game.

It's a Fact

Tom Osborne's final season as Nebraska head coach was 1997. He became the Huskers' head coach in 1973, the same year as OU's Barry Switzer. Osborne won five and lost 12 against Switzer's Sooners. After Switzer retired, Osborne's Huskers won eight of nine.

Parker gained 191 yards and scored once, and Fazande gained 151 yards and scored two TDs and both sat out the final 12:33 of the game after the Sooners took a 28-6 lead.

Oklahoma picked up more total yards (551-296). Jarrail Jackson returned seven punts for 109 yards, tying Greg Pruitt's school record set in 1970 against Wisconsin.

The Sooners dropped a 20-17 decision to 3-1 Kansas in the Big 12 Conference opener on October 4 in Lawrence. OU had a late game-tying field goal, but a penalty erased the points, and the Jayhawks blocked the second attempt to preserve the win.

The Sooners took a 10-0 lead on Steve Daniels' field goal in the first period and Parker's 14-yard TD run in the second. Daniels, a sophomore walk-on from Edmond, replaced Jeremy Alexander, who strained a knee on the opening kickoff.

The Hawks kicked a field goal in the second stanza to cut OU's lead to 10-3. Kansas scored 17 unanswered points in the third quarter, including a 54-yard punt return by Tony Blevins and Eric Vann's 99-yard run from scrimmage.

The Sooners set sail on an 80-yard scoring drive late in the third quarter. Moore, who started the entire second half, scored on a one-yard run early in the fourth stanza to cap the 13-play drive, and Daniels converted.

The Big Red later reached the KU 11 but faced fourth-and-one and Coach Blake opted to kick the game-tying field goal. Daniels' 28-yarder sailed through the uprights, with 1:45 remaining, but a yellow flag had floated to the turf—illegal procedure against the Sooners. Daniels' next attempt (a 33-yarder) was blocked.

OU gained more total yards (334-254).

The Sooners' De'Mond Parker and Texas' Ricky Williams combined to gobble up 514 yards of real estate in OU's 27-24 loss to 2-2 Texas the following week in Dallas. Parker picked up 291 yards on 31 carries and scored three touchdowns while Williams collected 223 yards on 40 carries and scored twice.

Once again, Oklahoma's mistakes (10 penalties) cost them the game. One penalty erased a 65-yard Parker touchdown, and two penalties kept the Longhorns alive for a TD.

The Steers took a 3-0 lead on their first possession. Parker scored on a seven-yard run late in the first period to give OU a 7-3 lead.

The Horns marched 65 yards to recapture the lead on Williams' one-yard plunge. UT quarterback James Brown twice tossed incompletions on third down in the drive, but the Sooners were penalized both times to give the Steers a first down.

Terry White holds the ball aloft after he intercepted Baylor's two-point conversion pass to preserve a Sooner victory. (© 1997, The Daily Oklahoman)

OU linebacker Terrance Malone recovered Williams' fumble on the UT 28 with 12 seconds until halftime. Fuente zipped a 14-yard pass to Little who got out of bounds with four seconds remaining. Alexander nailed a 31-yard field goal to tie the game at 10-10.

Texas scored the only touchdown in the third stanza and added another TD to take a 24-10 lead with 8:35 left in the game. OU's Bennie Butler returned the ensuing kickoff 42 yards to the Texas 48, and Parker swept around left end for the touchdown on the next play. The Steers kicked a 51-yard field goal with 4:57 remaining, and Parker sailed 66 yards moments later to cut the Steers' lead to 27-24. The Longhorns milked the final 2:42 off the clock.

Texas gained more total yards (412-402). Parker and Williams each eclipsed the 89-year-old rushing record in the series held by OU's Willard Douglas in 1908.

Sooner Magic: Sweet Redemption

When a defensive player gives up a big play or a touchdown, he wants to prove to himself, his coaches, fans, and the opponent that he can indeed make the big play the next time. Sooner safety Terry White was beat out for a touchdown, and Baylor was going for a two-point conversion to upset Oklahoma. The play would again be coming his way.

The 2-4 Sooners hosted Baylor before a less-than-capacity homecoming crowd of 68,578 in Norman. OU was tabbed as a 16-point favorite mainly because the Bears had only one win in five games in 1997. Losing to Baylor would have placed OU in the cellar of the Big 12 Conference's south division. Unthinkable … but it nearly happened.

Oklahoma would struggle defensively without the services of four starters. Travian Smith was sidelined with a knee injury. Cornerback Pee Wee Woods, linebacker Dale Allen, and end Shaq Brown were suspended for fighting at a Norman restaurant and a Norman apartment. Coach Blake started Moore at quarterback replacing Fuente, because Blake wanted an option attack.

Jeremy Alexander, still playing with a strained left knee, nailed a 23-yard field goal to put OU on top, 3-0, early in the second period.

The Bears answered with a 65-yard drive for a 7-3 advantage.

Alexander toed a 29-yard field goal five minutes later to close the gap to 7-6.

The Bears answered with a 63-yard TD drive to stretch their lead to 14-6 with 2:20 until halftime.

Alexander kicked a 47-yarder to pull OU within four, 14-9, with four seconds in the half.

Early in the third quarter, the Big Red uncorked a touchdown drive going 80 yards in nine plays. Huge runs highlighted the drive—eighteen and 13 yards by Parker, 11 yards by fullback Mike Rose, 21 by Moore and 12 by Fazande. Moore dove into the end zone from the BU one-yard line for the go-ahead touchdown.

> Two players with the same name played for the 1997 Sooners—linebacker Corey L. Ivy and cornerback Corey T. Ivy. Corey L. was a 6-1, 232-pound senior who came to OU from Crandell, Texas. Corey T. was a 5-10, 182-pound junior who played high school at Moore, Oklahoma, and two years at Northeastern Oklahoma A&M Community College in Miami.

Blake ordered a two-point conversion. Moore connected a pass to Stephen Alexander to give OU a 17-14 edge.

Baylor tied the game with a 27-yard field goal late in the third quarter.

Early in the fourth, Moore electrified the crowd with an 80-yard option keeper. He escaped a tackler in the Bear secondary then shifted to the left sideline and back toward the middle near the 30, and sailed untouched to the end zone. Alexander's kick put OU ahead, 24-17, with 14:37 remaining in the game.

Two more OU drives came up empty when Moore threw an interception at the Bears' 29, and Jeremy Alexander had a chance to put the game away with a 37-yard field goal, but it veered wide with 2:44 to go.

On the Bears' next possession, they drove 66 yards in five plays to the OU 13-yard line. Quarterback Jeff Watson tossed the ball to Derrius Thompson, who was battling White for position. Thompson got behind White in the left corner of the end zone and caught the pigskin with 38 seconds remaining.

Baylor trailed, 24-23, and could have kicked the extra point to force overtime. Head coach Dave Roberts felt his team could win the game, so he ordered a two-point conversion. Watson again tossed to Thompson, but this time White stepped in front of the Bear receiver and picked off the pass.

Many didn't think White would be playing late in the game. He suffered a blow to the head late in the third quarter. Early in the fourth, the public address announcer said White suffered a concussion and would not return to the game. "I knew I didn't have a concussion, because I could see all right and I could remember everything," White said. "I just had a bad headache, real bad headache."

In a postgame interview, White said after Baylor scored the final touchdown, coach Bill Young told the defense what kind of route the Bears would run on the two-point conversion. "Sure enough they did," White said with tears rolling down his face. "And I was saying, 'God, let me make the play,' because I had really let the team down."

Baylor tried an onside kick, but Corey L. Ivy, hero of the Syracuse game, recovered the ball to preserve a 24-23 Sooner victory.

"It feels excellent just to win, whether it's close or by a long stretch," Blake said. "We're just glad to win the football game."

The Big Red rolled up 397 yards on the ground. Parker led the way with 171 yards in 32 carries to lift him over the 1,000-yard mark for the season. Moore gained 141 on 14 carries, proof that Blake was right in ordering the Sooners to run the ball more.

No. 14 Kansas State (5-1) defeated the Sooners, 26-7, on October 25 in Norman. Parker left the game in the second quarter with a pulled stomach muscle, and Brandon Daniels debuted at quarterback. The Ada sophomore, who played at wide receiver in 1996 and backup strong safety this season, played sparingly behind Moore and Fuente. He was OU's leading rusher with 84 yards on 13 carries.

Daniels scored the Sooners' only touchdown to cut the Wildcats' lead to 10-7 in the third period. Moore twice fumbled the ball away to kill other Big Red scoring threats. Both fumbles came after OU had reached the K-State three-yard line in the first half.

The Cats extended their lead to 17-7 with a touchdown in the third stanza. They stripped the ball from Fuente, which led to a field goal and a 20-7 lead early in the fourth stanza. Kansas State drove 80 yards for the final tally midway through the fourth quarter.

The Wildcats picked up more total yards (320-277).

The Sooners traveled to Lincoln the next week without Parker, Fazande, and Rose, who were sidelined with injuries. Coach Blake

had to turn to a pair of freshmen to fill in—Seth Littrell at fullback and J.T. Thatcher at tailback.

Littrell, a second-generation Sooner, scored Oklahoma's only touchdown and rushed for 88 yards on 21 carries in his debut. The rest of the backs netted minus three yards on 29 carries. Littrell's dad, Jim, was a starting fullback for OU in the mid-'70s.

OU suffered its worst defeat in history with a 69-7 loss to No. 1 Nebraska on a windy and stormy afternoon. The 7-0 Cornhuskers scored on five consecutive possessions in the first half and again on five straight series in the second half. Holding a 10-0 lead, Nebraska capitalized on three straight fumbles.

Trailing 55-0 in the third quarter, Littrell scored on a three-yard run to cap a 61-yard drive, and Jeremy Alexander converted.

The Huskers gained more total yards (552-154).

Suffering through a 3-6 campaign and losing to two major rivals (Texas and Nebraska), at least the Sooners could salvage some respectability with a win over in-state rival Oklahoma State. Didn't happen. Several days before the game, *Daily Oklahoman* writer Berry Tramel tried to pick OU to win the game because of the Sooners' dominance in the series, but instead he went with the Cowboys. "I can't figure out how OU could win," he wrote.

"... He doesn't know what he's saying half the time," Tramel scribed of John Blake. "The way he talks in riddles, it's no wonder his players sometimes look like they haven't got a clue."

The Sooners didn't have a clue as the No. 25 Cowboys defeated OU, 30-7, on November 8 in Norman. The Big Red had six turnovers and 10 penalties. OSU scored 20 points on four of Oklahoma's turnovers.

OU took a 7-0 lead with an 89-yard drive in the first period. Brandon Daniels scampered around left end on a quarterback keeper, and Alexander kicked the conversion.

The Pokes answered with a 44-yard scoring drive to tie the game at 7-7. Leading 10-7 late in the second stanza, OSU capitalized on two OU turnovers to add 10 points in a span of 19 seconds for a 13-7 halftime lead.

The Cowboys took a 20-7 lead on a 76-yard drive in the third quarter, then cashed in on two more Sooner errors to add 10 more points in the final period.

OSU collected more total yards (317-198).

1997 Season Record: 4-8-0
Big 12 Conference: 2-6-0
(Fourth: South Division)

Date	Opponent	Result	Score
August 23	Northwestern*	L	24-0
September 6	SYRACUSE	W	36-34
September 20	at California	L	40-36
September 27	LOUISVILLE	W	35-14
October 4	at Kansas	L	20-17
October 11	Texas at Dallas	L	27-24
October 18	BAYLOR	W	24-23
October 25	KANSAS STATE	L	26-7
November 1	at Nebraska	L	69-7
November 8	OKLAHOMA STATE	L	30-7
November 15	TEXAS A&M	L	51-7
November 22	at Texas Tech	W	32-21

*Game played in Chicago, IL

No. 18 Texas A&M hammered the Sooners, 51-7, the next week on a brutally cold Saturday night in Norman. A paid attendance of 64,929 was announced, but the stands appeared less than half full.

As usual, the Sooners were plagued by turnovers (five) and penalties (nine). The Aggies capitalized on four of OU's turnovers and had three scoring drives of seven yards or less. A&M scored 17 points in each of the first three quarters. Backup running back Dante Hall led the Aggies with 139 rushing yards and three TDs, and A&M's starting running back Sirr Parker gained 123 yards rushing and scored once.

Rose scored the Sooners' only touchdown early in the fourth stanza on a one-yard run to cap a 69-yard drive, and Jeremy Alexander converted.

The Aggies collected 405 total yards while holding Oklahoma to 220 total yards.

Texas Tech had every reason to win. The 5-4 Red Raiders were 5-2 in the Big 12 south, and a victory over Oklahoma would give them the south division crown. But the Sooners, 23-point underdogs, stunned Texas Tech, 32-21, to end a four-game losing streak.

Fuente came off the bench to spark the OU victory in his final game as a Sooner. The Tulsa sophomore entertained ideas of transferring since Coach Blake was committed to the option offense. Daniels started against the Red Raiders, and the Sooners generated only 39 yards in 16 plays. When Fuente entered the game early in the second quarter, he guided the Sooners to 298 yards in 56 plays and completed 14 of 21 passes for 218 yards and a touchdown.

Alexander's 51-yard field goal tied the game at 3-3 early in the second period. Moments later, Jarrail Jackson fumbled, and Tech's Dane Johnson returned it 57 yards for a touchdown, and the Raiders added a two-point pass for an 11-3 advantage.

Rose's two-yard TD run capped a 79-yard march to cut the Tech lead to 11-9, as the two-point play failed. Casey Wise, who debuted at punter for OU, fumbled the snap in the end zone just before halftime, and the Raiders recovered for an 18-9 lead.

A poor Tech punt early in the third quarter allowed OU to put together an 18-yard, three-play scoring drive. On third-and-11 at the 19, Fuente sailed a scoring strike to Stephen Alexander. The senior tight end had caught seven passes for 121 yards in one of his finest games as a Sooner. Jeremy Alexander converted, but the Sooners still trailed, 18-16.

Late in the same period, Littrell scored the go-ahead touchdown on a one-yard plunge to cap an 80-yard drive. Both teams traded field goals early in the fourth stanza, then Littrell busted a 24-yard TD sprint for the final tally with 6:08 remaining.

The Sooners gained more total yards (337-300).

Although OU ended the season on a winning note to finish 4-8 and fourth in the Big 12 south with a 2-6 mark, Sooner fans became more restless with another losing campaign. The sports radio talk shows and local newspapers were filled with irate fans wanting Blake fired. Others believed he should be given another year to try to rebuild the football program to some kind of respectability.

Kelly Gregg was the only Sooner named to the All-Big 12 Conference first unit.

1998

Hopes were riding high for the 1998 Sooner football team, even though it had finished 4-8 the year before. Eight starters returned on defense, including all-conference defensive tackle Kelly Gregg, linebacker Dale Allen and the entire secondary. Rex Ryan was hired before the season as the new defensive coordinator. Ryan installed the "4-6 defense," an alignment of eight players on or near the line of scrimmage that allowed one player an open lane to attack the quarterback. The defense had been successful in stopping the run with so many players near the line of scrimmage and attacks with blitzes to disrupt the pass. Ryan's father, Buddy, created it for the Chicago Bears when he was the Bears' defensive coordinator. The Bears lost only one game in 1985, and the formation helped them win Super Bowl XX.

OU head coach John Blake wanted to switch to the option offense, causing quarterback Justin Fuente to transfer to Murray State in Kentucky. Quarterback Brandon Daniels and halfback De'Mond Parker would provide a quick one-two punch, in the running game. Other returning offensive starters included tackle Scott Kempenich, wide receiver Jarrail Jackson, and fullback Jermaine Fazande. Big things were expected from Stockar McDougle, a 6-5, 370-pound transfer from Navarro (Texas) Junior College.

The Sooners hosted North Texas on September 5, a 6 p.m. kickoff with a 105-degree reading. Walk-on sophomore quarterback Patrick Fletcher directed OU to four touchdowns after Daniels left the game with a bruised shoulder. Fletcher scored twice himself and passed for another score. Fletcher, a third stringer, was listed second string for the game when Jarrod Reese was suspended for an undisclosed violation. Fletcher's father, Ron, was a quarterback for OU in 1964.

The Mean Green took a 6-0 lead on an 80-yard drive on their first possession. The Big Red defense held North Texas to 59 yards the rest of the game. The Sooners had only 37 yards on their first five series then rolled up 364 yards afterward in their 37-9 victory.

OU place kicker Jeff Ferguson toed a 31-yard field goal to cut the UNT lead to 6-3 early in the second stanza. Fletcher's four-yard run and Ferguson's conversion gave the Big Red a 10-6 lead with 26 seconds until intermission.

The Mean Green added a field goal midway through the third period then OU answered with an 80-yard scoring drive capped by Fletcher's 34-yard pass to split end Ahmed Kabba, but Ferguson missed the extra point. The Sooners then erupted for three TDs in the final quarter—a five-yard run by Parker, a two-yard run by Fletcher, and a nine-yard pass from quarterback Jake Sills to Kabba.

Oklahoma picked up 404 total yards and held the Mean Green to eight first downs and 139 total yards. Fletcher completed all five passes for 84 yards and Parker rushed 20 times for 126 yards.

Sooner Magic: Having a Little Faith

Daniels still suffered from a hurt shoulder, so Fletcher started at quarterback again and was relieved by Reese, whose suspension was lifted before the Texas Christian tilt. TCU opened its season with a 31-21 victory at Iowa State.

Evidence of such high expectations was the fact that an estimated 15,000 to 18,000 Sooner fans attended the game at Amon Carter Stadium in Fort Worth, which was shrouded by a drizzle all night long, causing a soggy field and lousy offense.

Oklahoma switched to the I formation and gained only 91 total yards in the first half, which was dominated by three TCU field goals. Parker had only three yards on eight carries. The Horned Frogs gained a total of 199 yards in the game, but the Big Red defense stymied them to the tune of four total yards in the second half.

TCU's Chris Kaylakie kicked a field goal midway through the opening stanza, another midway through the second, and added a third with 33 seconds until halftime.

Although the Sooners managed 103 yards in the third quarter, they were penalized for 56 yards, including 45 on personal fouls.

Reese had the Sooner fans cheering when he picked up a bobbled snap from shotgun formation and scampered 47 yards to the TCU 40. But three plays later, he fumbled the snap, and the Frogs recovered.

With about 4:14 remaining in the game, another chapter in Sooner Magic was about to be written. TCU's Royce Huffman caught Ferguson's 56-yard punt at the Frogs' nine-yard line. On the next play, Sooner defensive tackle Jeremy Wilson-Guest nailed running back Basil Mitchell in the backfield. The pigskin squirted free, but the Frogs recovered at the one.

TCU stalled and punted out to its 32-yard line. Reese gained 11 yards, then was relieved by Fletcher. Although hobbled by a sore ankle, Fletcher tossed an incomplete pass intended for Kabba down the left sideline. On the next play, split end Chris Blocker ran the same route, and Fletcher sailed the pass his direction. Blocker and TCU corner back Greg Walls both grabbed the ball in the end zone, but Blocker wrestled it away for the touchdown.

Ferguson kicked the extra point, and OU trailed, 9-7, with 2:20 to go.

The Sooners lined up for an onside kick. The ball came off Ferguson's foot and bounced in the air. Josh Norman grabbed the pigskin and was tackled at the TCU 47.

"The key to the game was the onside kick," said Coach Blake. "It had the perfect bounce and landed right where we wanted it."

Reese gained five yards then Fletcher lobbed a pass to tight end Jason Freeman. TCU's Joseph Phipps intercepted the pass then fumbled, and Freeman recovered the free ball at the TCU 29.

The Sooners were flagged for illegal procedure, then fullback Seth Littrell gained six to the TCU 22.

The Sooners failed to gain a first down, and Ferguson was called on for the winning field goal. The Frogs called two straight timeouts to ice the Sooner kicker. Ferguson utilized that time by stretching his legs.

"I just sat there and made sure I stayed stretched," he said. "Each time-out I sat there and visualized it [the ball] going through the uprights."

His imagination worked, and the ball sailed between the uprights with five seconds remaining. OU 10, TCU 9.

After the game, players from both teams got into a brawl—punching and shoving each other. OU running back's coach Keith Thomas and Charley North, TCU director of football operations, got into a shoving match, but shook hands when the melee ended. North was a former Sooner assistant under Barry Switzer.

TCU head coach Dennis Franchione said he was disappointed with his team's behavior.

"Classy teams don't act that way," he said. "I understand they were frustrated and disappointed. It's OK to hurt when you lose."

Fletcher was carried off the field on the shoulders of some teammates.

In the locker room, Kelly Gregg was ecstatic in trying to describe his feelings of the victory.

"Luck of the Irish, Sooner Magic—whatever. That was just unbelievable," he said. "I still can't believe it. I mean, you've got to be kidding me."

"Call it what you want to," Blake said. "I call it having faith and believing. You can go a long way with a little faith. It's been a long time since we've seen some Sooner Magic around here."

The 1-1 California Bears invaded Norman on September 19 and defeated the Sooners, 13-12, with a late field goal. Two missed field goals and one failed extra point by OU was the difference in the game. The Sooners also had to surrender possession on downs five times after reaching inside the Cal 20.

Daniels returned to the starting lineup at quarterback, and Fletcher did not play due to an ankle sprain.

The Big Red took a 6-0 lead midway through the first stanza on Daniels' 58-yard scoring strike to tight end Matt Anderson, but Ferguson missed the conversion. Ferguson played with a case of mononucleosis.

Minutes later, Daniels fumbled on his 10-yard line, and the Bears took a 7-6 lead two plays later. The Bears added a field goal for a 10-6 lead late in the first half.

Placekicker Matt Reeves replaced Ferguson, who missed two field goals (one blocked) and nailed a 37-yarder in the third period and a 30-yarder in the fourth quarter, and the Sooners held a 12-10 lead with 10:09 to go.

Jeff Ferguson (83) and Jake Sills celebrate Ferguson's game-winning field goal against TCU.
(© 1998, The Daily Oklahoman)

The Bears then moved 60 yards in 10 plays to get into field-goal range.

Tim Wolleck toed a 27-yarder with 5:56 remaining, and Oklahoma could not mount a charge the rest of the way.

OU picked up more total yards (332-286). Cal averaged 8.5 yards per game rushing, but gained 178 on the Sooners. OU's De'Mond Parker rushed for 114 yards, his best performance in the early season. The Bears were penalized 16 times for 130 yards.

Two touchdowns during a 58-second span propelled 5-0 Colorado to a 27-25 victory over the Sooners on October 3 before 71,217 homecoming fans in Norman. OU fought back in the fourth quarter but fell short when the No. 15 Buffaloes recovered the onside kick.

Daniels directed OU to a 6-0 lead on the game's opening series. Parker, who rushed for 134 yards, scored on an 11-yard run, but he also was penalized for high stepping in the end zone. The 35-yard extra point missed the target.

The Buffs took a 14-6 lead during the first seven minutes of the second stanza on quarterback Mike Moschetti's two TD strikes. Reeves toed a 37-yard field goal to draw the Sooners closer, 14-9, with 5:22 until halftime.

Ferguson kicked a 49-yard field goal to cut Colorado's lead to 14-12 in the third period. The Buffs drove 79 yards and took a 20-12 lead on Moschetti's third TD pass. CU jumped ahead, 27-

12, 58 seconds later. Fletcher replaced Daniels under center, and Marcus Washington intercepted his first pass and raced 40 yards for a touchdown.

Fletcher completed four of five passes for 130 yards the rest of the game. The Sooners responded with a 52-yard drive in two plays. Parker bolted 49 for the score, but the two-point pass went awry. OU later needed only two plays to go 69 yards, and Fletcher threw a 25-yard scoring strike to Freeman. Reeves converted, and Oklahoma trailed, 27-25, with 1:05 remaining. The Buffs covered the onside kick to preserve their fifth straight win over the Sooners and eighth in the last nine meetings (save for a tie in 1992).

OU rolled up more total yards (392-317).

The Big Red's offensive line was without three starters for the Red River rivalry the next week in Dallas. Kempenich and guard Adam Carpenter were sidelined with knee injuries, and guard Jason Bronson left the game with a concussion.

Texas (3-2) hammered the Sooners, 34-3, before another sellout crowd at the Cotton Bowl. Oklahoma had four turnovers, 14 penalties and no firepower on either side of the ball. The defense targeted to contain Ricky Williams, who rushed for a below-average 139 yards, but freshman quarterback Major Applewhite completed 14 of 27 passes for 293 yards and two TDs.

The Sooners moved to the UT 22-yard line early in the first period, but an unsportsmanlike penalty against Blocker moved the ball back 15 yards. Two plays later, Parker scored on a 36-yard run, but a holding call nullified the touchdown, and OU eventually settled for Ferguson's 47-yard field goal.

Texas took a 17-3 lead with two touchdowns late in the first stanza and a field goal four seconds before halftime.

Backup tailback Michael Thornton returned the second-half kickoff 79 yards, but Daniels fumbled moments later on the UT one when he pulled away from center as the ball was snapped. The Horns recovered, and two plays later, Applewhite hooked up with Wayne Garity for a 97-yard TD pass. The Steers added another field goal minutes later, and Williams scored his second touchdown in the fourth quarter. Eric Moore, who had been moved to flanker, came in at quarterback in the final stanza, but he was unable to spark the offense.

Texas hammered out more total yards (448-197).

No. 20 Missouri snapped OU's 12-game winning streak in the series with a 20-6 victory on October 17 in Columbia. The Sooners again were hampered by turnovers (three) and penalties (11).

The 4-1 Tigers took a 6-0 lead when Wade Perkins intercepted Daniels' pass on the game's third play. Freshman linebacker Rocky Calmus blocked the conversion. Calmus and fellow freshman Michael Delaney had been promoted to first string before the game, replacing Dale Allen and Brandon Moore, respectively.

OU blew a chance to score just before intermission. Calmus deflected a punt, and Corey Ivy returned it 13 yards to the MU 26. De'Mond Parker picked up 10 yards,

then the offense fell apart with two penalties, and Ferguson missed a 41-yard field-goal try.

The Big Red offense managed only 49 total yards in the first half but had three drives to generate 199 yards in the second half, yet only had two field goals for their efforts. The third drive ended with an interception in the end zone with 1:42 remaining.

Mizzou drove 47 yards for a 14-0 lead, including a two-point conversion.

Reeves toed a 33-yard field goal late in the third period and added a 25-yarder early in the fourth. The Tigers marched 69 yards for the final tally, which came with 6:09 left to go.

The Sooners had more total yards (247-210).

Oklahoma State (2-4) defeated the Sooners, 41-26, the following Saturday night in Stillwater. Cowboy quarterback Tony Lindsay, who completed 16 of 24 passes for 128 yards, led his squad by throwing two TD passes and scored two more himself. Lack of discipline again hurt the Sooners. OU turned the ball over four times and was flagged 19 times, a school and Big 12 record for most penalties in a game.

Oklahoma took a 10-0 lead in the first quarter and held a 13-7 advantage at halftime. Eric Moore, who started at quarterback for the Sooners, left the game with a concussion late in the first stanza. Sills, who had not played at quarterback since the season opener, replaced him. Daniels, who started five games this season, and Fletcher, who guided OU to two wins earlier, did not play.

Two of Sills' fumbles in the second half led to Cowboy touchdowns.

The Pokes took a 14-13 lead on a 46-yard drive following the second-half kickoff. The Sooners answered with Fazande's second touchdown to cap an 80-yard drive for a 19-14 lead. Two field goals and a touchdown put the Pokes ahead, 28-19.

Sills fired a 53-yard scoring strike to Freeman to cut the deficit to 28-26. Lindsay scored twice for OSU, one on a 42-yard drive and the other moments after Sills fumbled on the OU nine-yard line.

OU picked up more total yards (410-295). Parker rushed for 220 yards on 23 carries. Lindsay also rushed for 99 yards.

Sooner Magic: Saving Face

The Sooners and Iowa State had the two worst records in the Big 12 Conference with 0-4 marks. A win by either team would mean adding a notch in the conference win column and hopes to save face of not being the worst team in the league.

Both teams also sported identical 2-5 season records.

Sills got the starting nod at quarterback, but the defense had players lost to injury or ejection. Safety Terry White broke his ankle in the OSU game, end Corey Callens injured his toe horsing around in the locker room the day before, safety Mike Woods injured his knee in the third quarter against Iowa State, and linebacker Ontei Jones was tossed out of the game for kicking a Cyclone in the head in

Gerald Williams (10) hauls in Jake Sills' pass at the Iowa State 30-yard line. Williams then shot to the end zone for the Sooners' winning touchdown. (© 1998, The Daily Oklahoman)

the third period. Still, the Big Red defense yielded only 46 yards on ISU's final six possessions.

The Sooners scored late in each half en route to a 17-14 win before an announced crowd of 70,019 at Owen Field.

The Cyclones marched 80 yards to take a 7-0 lead early in the second quarter.

OU took only three plays to cover 36 yards to tie the game late in the first half. Sills hurled a 33-yard scoring strike to Kabba, who dove into the end zone for the catch. Reeves converted the extra point with 18 seconds until intermission.

The Sooners took a 10-7 lead on Reeves' 31-yard field goal midway through the third period, but ISU answered with a 73-yard scoring march to take a 14-10 lead.

The Sooners could not move past midfield on their next four possessions. The Cyclones had a chance to pad their lead when they recovered Sills' fumble on the OU 17, but three plays later, Corey Ivy intercepted a Cyclone pass in the end zone.

Midway through the fourth quarter, Sills tossed a shovel pass to Parker, who picked up a first down with a 13-yard gain to the ISU 39. But the Sooners soon surrendered on downs at the Cyclones' 31.

The defense used two time outs to stall the clock, and Iowa State punted to the OU 34-yard line with 1:47 to go. Sills threw two incompletions, then found Blocker for a 20-yard completion to the ISU 44. Sills spiked the ball to stop the clock, then tossed a pass to Gerald Williams, who caught the ball at the 30 and raced down the sideline for the touchdown. Kabba's block took out the last Cyclone at the five-yard line. Reeves converted, and OU held on for the win.

The statistics were nearly as equal as the outcome. Oklahoma collected more first downs (15-14) and total yards (290-283). Parker rushed for 105 yards, but he did not score for the second straight game. OU again was plagued by penalties (10) in the game.

The Sooners reduced their mistakes against Texas A&M on November 7 in College Station, yet they had no offense and poor defense in a 29-0 loss to the No. 7 Aggies. OU had only six penalties and two turnovers, but only 124 total yards.

The Cadets took a 6-0 lead the first time they touched the football—a 55-yard punt return early in the first quarter. Branndon Stewart, who completed 15 of 23 aerials for 234 yards, connected on his first of two scoring strikes to Chris Cole late in the first half for a 13-0 lead. The Sooners, who failed to gain a first down on their first eight series, gained only 17 total yards in the first 30 minutes.

They finally got a first down with 11:35 remaining in the third period. A&M recovered an Oklahoma fumble but had to settle for a field goal for a 16-0 lead midway through the third stanza. Stewart scored on a six-yard run and tossed another scoring strike to Cole in the fourth quarter.

The Aggies rolled up more first downs (19-5) and gained 355 total yards.

The Sooners and 2-7 Baylor met the following week for the right to climb out of the cellar in the Big 12 south division. Both teams sported identical 1-5 conference records, but OU cashed in on the Bears' mistakes en route to a 28-16 victory on a drizzly day in Waco.

Baylor led 3-0 at halftime and intercepted Sills' pass for a touchdown on the third play of the second half for a 10-0 lead. The Big Red answered with a 75-yard march that ended when Sills fired a 13-yard scoring strike to Parker. Parker, who rushed for 207 yards (147 in the second half), sparked the drive with a 53-yard scamper to the BU 15 three plays earlier. Reeves kicked the first of four conversions.

Minutes later, Chris Hammons blocked a Bear punt, and Littrell recovered in the end zone for a touchdown to give OU a 14-10 lead.

Junior Rodney Rideau, who replaced Terry White at safety, picked off two Bear passes in the third stanza. The first led to a missed field goal. He returned the second one 38 yards to the BU 12, and Parker scored on a seven-yard run two plays later. Parker added a 48-yard TD run midway through the final period, and Baylor added another touchdown.

The Sooners collected more total yards (365-202).

Three days later, Parker announced he would skip his senior year in 1999 and enter the National Football League draft.

Parker's last game in a crimson uniform ended in the first quarter against Texas Tech on November 21 when he suffered a bruised hip. Parker had only 10 yards on five carries to end the season with 1,076 rushing yards. Fazande took up the slack by rushing for 111 yards and scored a touchdown to lead the Sooners to a 20-17 victory over Texas Tech in Norman.

The 7-3 Red Raiders took a 10-0 lead in the first stanza. Sophomore defensive end Darryl "Rocky" Bright returned a blocked punt 48 yards for a touchdown midway in the second period, and Reeves converted the first of two extra points. The Sooners gained only 57 yards in the first half but rolled up 155 in the final 30 minutes.

Fazande darted 32 yards to give OU a 14-10 lead midway through the third quarter. Reeves booted a career-high 43-yard field goal with 10:11 remaining in the game and added a 29-yarder nearly five minutes later. The field goal came soon after Wilson-Guest forced a fumble and Rideau recovered at the Tech 34.

The Red Raiders drove 64 yards to cut OU's lead to 20-17 and threatened with another march to the OU 44, but Rideau raked the ball from Ricky Williams' hands, and the Sooners recovered with 1:20 to go.

Tech had more total yards (334-212).

Kelly Gregg for the second straight year was the only Sooner named to the All-Big 12 Conference first team.

Oklahoma finished 5-6 and fourth in the Big 12 south division with a 3-5 conference record. Although this was an improvement compared to the previous year, Blake was fired as OU's football coach one day after the Texas Tech game.

Several names were bandied about, but OU athletic director Joe Castiglione announced on December 1 that Florida's defensive coordinator, Bob Stoops, would be the Sooners' 21st head football coach. During a press conference in front of Evans Hall on the OU campus, Stoops said his decision to accept the position was easy because OU was "a special job."

1998 Season Record: 5-6-0
Big 12 Conference: 3-5-0
(Fourth: South Division)

Date	Opponent	Result	Score
September 5	NORTH TEXAS	W	37-9
September 12	at Texas Christian	W	10-9
September 19	CALIFORNIA	L	13-12
October 3	COLORADO	L	27-25
October 10	Texas at Dallas	L	34-3
October 17	at Missouri	L	20-6
October 24	at Oklahoma State	L	41-26
October 31	IOWA STATE	W	17-14
November 7	at Texas A&M	L	29-0
November 14	at Baylor	W	28-16
November 21	TEXAS TECH	W	20-17

"I'll not shy away from expectations . . . I will embrace them," he added. "There are no excuses. We're not going to talk about rebuilding.

"I'll fight to return the Sooners as a Big 12 powerhouse. It shouldn't take too long to compete for a Big 12 Championship. We will constantly improve from day to day, month to month, year to year. I don't believe it will take that long if we're all on the same page."

1999

The 1999 Sooners quickly began to come together on the same page, but it was not going to be easy, especially with a completely new coaching staff, offense, defense and philosophies.

Head coach Bob Stoops hired his brother, Mike, and Brent Venables as co-defensive coordinators. Mike Stoops and Venables were assistants at Kansas State prior to coming to Norman. Stoops also hired Mark Mangino, another Kansas State assistant, as running game coordinator. Mike Leach, a Kentucky assistant, was hired as passing game coordinator.

Two former Sooner stars, Cale Gundy and Jackie Shipp, were added to the staff. Gundy was hired to direct the running backs, and Shipp tutored the defensive line.

The new offense was designed with emphasis on the pass—a wide-open attack with as many as four or five receivers in one play. Stoops and Leach recruited Josh Heupel, a junior college All-American at Snow Junior College in Utah, to quarterback the new offense. The line was solid with the return of center Matt O'Neal, tight end Matt Anderson, and tackles Stockar McDougle and Scott Kempenich, who sat out the final seven games in 1998 with a knee injury. Bubba Burcham, who replaced Kempenich at right tackle in 1998, was moved to right guard. Fullback Seth Littrell, and receiver/punt return specialist Jarrail Jackson were three veterans who returned to the starting lineup. Jeff Ferguson returned to kick punts, but sophomore Tim Duncan beat him out for the placekicking chores.

The defense would be more aggressive, deploying zone blitzes and man coverage. The defense was loaded with the return of the entire secondary, linebacker Rocky Calmus and end Cornelius Burton. Tackles Bary Holeyman and Jeremy Wilson-Guest returned from injuries and were bumped to the second team, and Frank Romero was moved to the offensive line.

The Sooners opened the season September 11 with the school's 1,000th game in history. OU defeated Indiana State, a Division I-AA team, 49-0, in Norman. Heupel broke several team passing records by completing 31 of 40 passes for 341 yards and five touchdowns. He shattered Gundy's record of 25 completions set in the 1991 Gator Bowl and equaled Gundy's yardage set against Texas Tech in 1992. Heupel was the first Sooner quarterback to toss five scoring strikes in a game, breaking the record of four held by Claude Arnold, Eddie Crowder and Eric Moore.

OU scored two touchdowns in each of the first three periods. Heupel tossed a 19-yard TD pass to receiver Andre Woolfolk and running back Michael Thornton scored on a 10-yard run in the first stanza. Heupel tossed scoring strikes to running back Josh Norman and Jackson in the second quarter.

Heupel hurled an 11-yard TD pass to receiver Julius McMillan, and Seth Littrell scored on a three-yard run. Heupel set the TD passing record with a 33-yard strike to walk-on Ryan Daniel in the fourth period. Duncan converted all seven extra points.

Oklahoma rolled up 30 first downs, three times as many as the Sycamores and gained more total yards (507-195). Woolfolk, Jackson, and Matt Anderson each caught five passes.

Heupel continued his assault on the school passing records to lead the Sooners to a 41-10 victory over 1-2 Baylor in the Big 12 Conference opener the following week in Norman. The junior quarterback completed 37 of 54 passes for 420 yards and three touchdowns. He broke his completion record set a week earlier against Indiana State and set the yardage record, which he tied with Cale Gundy also a week earlier. His 54 attempts broke Garrick McGee's record of 45 set in 1994 against Kansas State.

OU scored three touchdowns in the first 15:12 for a 21-0 lead. Littrell scored on a six-yard run, and Heupel hurled scoring strikes to Norman and Anderson. The Bears added a field goal with three minutes left in the first half to cut the Sooners' lead to 21-3.

Baylor switched from a blitzing man-to-man to a zone defense in the second period and gave Heupel fits, sacking him twice and intercepting a pass. Oklahoma adjusted at halftime and scored 20 more points in the final 30 minutes. Duncan kicked two field goals, Heupel threw a scoring strike to backup tight end Chris Hammons, and running back Reggie Skinner scored the final tally.

The Big Red picked up more total yards (557-208). Thornton rushed for 110 yards on 14 carries.

The Sooners scored 28 unanswered points to overcome a 21-14 deficit to defeat the 2-1 Louisville Cardinals, 42-21, on September 25 in Louisville. The game was billed as a duel between quarterbacks—Heupel and Louisville's Chris Redman, who committed with the Sooners in 1995 then changed his mind.

Heupel completed 29 of 42 passes for 429 yards, another school record, and five touchdowns. Redman completed 16 of 29 for 215 yards in the first half, but Oklahoma's defense pressured him and deflected many passes. Redman hooked up on only eight of 20 passes for 77 yards in the final 30 minutes.

The Big Red trailed for the first time all year when the Cardinals led 3-0 on a field goal in the second stanza and the Sooners answered with a 52-yard TD pass from Heupel to Norman. Duncan converted the first of six extra points. Louisville regained the lead on Redman's scoring strike, and the Cardinals added a field goal just before halftime.

The Sooners took the second-half kickoff and marched 80 yards for a 14-13 lead when Heupel hurled another 52-yarder, this time to Jackson. UL answered with a 78-yard drive and Redman's scoring strike to take a 21-14 lead.

OU scored four touchdowns during the next 23 minutes. Heupel fired two TD strikes to Damian Mackey (one near the end of the third quarter and the other early in the fourth). Heupel scored on a one-yard run midway through the final period and sailed a 44-yard scoring strike to Jackson minutes later.

OU gained more total yards (544-386). Brandon Daniels, who was switched to receiver at the beginning of the season, had eight catches to lead a pack of eight Sooners who caught Heupel aerials.

The Sooners entered the AP poll at No. 23, the first ranking in the poll since October 31, 1995 (the 10th week of the '95 season). Oklahoma traveled to South Bend, Indiana, to meet 1-3 Notre Dame on October 2. It was only the ninth meeting between these tradition-rich teams. The Fighting Irish have won eight AP national championships and three before the poll service began in 1936. OU, with six national titles, was the only team that trailed Notre Dame. The Big Red prevailed only once in the series, a 40-0 win in 1956.

The 1999 Irish scored three unanswered touchdowns in the final quarter and a half to defeat the Sooners, 34-30, before a sellout crowd of 80,012 and a national television (NBC) audience. Irish quarterback Jarious Jackson nailed 15 of 21 passes for 276 yards, and he rushed 15 times for 107 yards.

Notre Dame took the opening kickoff and rolled 76 yards for a 7-0 lead. Jackson capped the drive on a 10-yard scamper. Oklahoma flashed like lightning to tie the game 17 seconds later when Daniels returned the ensuing kickoff 89 yards for a touchdown, and Duncan kicked the first of four conversions. Daniels returned five kickoffs in the game for 229 yards, a new school record shattering Stanley Wilson's record of 113 yards in five returns set in 1982 against Arizona. Daniels' return also was the first kickoff return for a touchdown since Eric Bross did it in 1989 against Iowa State.

The Sooners took a 9-7 lead with a safety early in the second period when Irish punter Joey Hildbold fumbled the snap in the end zone. Daniels roared back 43 yards with the free kick to the ND 37. Nine plays later, Heupel zipped a four-yard TD strike to Jackson for a 16-7 advantage.

Notre Dame answered with a 62-yard scoring march to close the gap to 16-14. Daniels took the ensuing kickoff and again set up the next OU score with a 68-yard return to the ND 26. Two plays later, Heupel hurled a 15-yard TD pass to tight end Trent Smith for a 23-14 lead.

Oklahoma drove 45 yards for a 30-14 lead on its second series of the third quarter. Heupel threw a 15-yard scoring strike to Daniels to cap the five-play drive. The Irish scored three TDs in the next seven and one–half minutes, including a 98-yard drive for the winning score.

Notre Dame missed a field goal with 2:21 remaining, and the Sooners took over at their 20-yard line, but four straight incomplete passes thwarted any chance for Sooner Magic. Receivers dropped three of Heupel's passes.

Notre Dame collected more total yards (566-237). Heupel completed 22 of 40 passes for 168 yards, and his three TD passes raised his season total to 16, two more than the school record of 14 hurled by Gundy during the entire 1993 season. Rodney Rideau led the OU defense with 20 tackles, 14 unassisted.

The Sooners dropped out of the AP Top 25 poll and faced No. 23 Texas the following week in Dallas. The 4-2 Longhorns lost to Kansas State the previous week and the crimson faithful thought this would be the year to topple the hated rivals to the south.

For the second consecutive week, Oklahoma gave up a huge lead and lost, 38-28, to the Steers. The Sooners bolted out of the starting gate with a 17-0 lead in the game's first 10:42 and rolled up 172 yards. OU managed only 11 points and 158 total yards afterward.

Daniels returned the opening kickoff 38 yards from the goal line. Heupel tossed an 18-yard pass to Thornton, then fired a 44-yard scoring strike to freshman receiver Antwone Savage. Duncan kicked the first of three conversions.

Duncan toed a 43-yard field goal on the next OU series, and Sooners drove 71 yards on their next possession for a 17-0 lead. Heupel's 30-yard TD pass to Jackson capped the six-play drive.

The Longhorns began pressuring Heupel and picked off three of his passes and recovered a fumbled snap exchange.

Texas' Kris Stockton kicked a field goal late in the first stanza and added two more in the first 10 and one-half minutes of the second.

Curtis Fagan returns the opening kickoff for more than 50 yards. OU hammered the Aggies, 51-6, just two years after being pasted by A&M, 51-7.
(© 1999, The Daily Oklahoman)

The Steers took possession with 1:55 remaining before intermission and took two plays to cover 61 yards. Major Applewhite completed an 11-yard pass to Ryan Nunez to finish the drive, and Applewhite tossed a two-point pass to Nunez to tie the game at 17-17 with 49 seconds before halftime.

Texas marched 85 yards to a 24-17 lead to open the third period. Hodges Mitchell, who rushed for 204 yards in the game, scored on a 21-yard run. Daniels returned the kickoff 39 yards to the UT 46, but the Sooners had to settle for Duncan's 28-yard field goal, to cut the Texas lead to 24-20.

The Steers drove 80 yards in four plays after the kickoff for a 31-20 lead. OU marched from their 20 to the Texas four-yard line but bogged down and set up for a field goal. Patrick Fletcher took the snap, popped up and dumped a pass to Duncan in the flat, and the Sooner place kicker zipped into the end zone untouched. Heupel completed a two-point pass to Savage, and Oklahoma was down by three, 31-28.

Texas drove 99 yards and consumed five and one-half minutes for the final tally in the fourth quarter, an 18-yard pass from Applewhite to Nunez.

The Longhorns gained more total yards (553-330). Oklahoma was held to 15 rushing yards. Applewhite completed 27 of 47 passes for 328 yards. Heupel hit on 31 of 48 aerials for 311 yards. Savage caught six of Heupel's passes for 100 yards. Both teams were penalized a combined 27 times (Texas 14, OU 13).

No. 13 Texas A&M (5-1) rolled into Norman two weeks later seeking its 600th overall win and 100th victory for head coach R.C. Slocum. The last time the Aggies came to Norman, they bombed the Sooners, 51-7. This time, OU did one (point) better with a 51-6 homecoming victory to snap a four-game losing streak to the Aggies. A&M suffered its most lopsided loss since a 48-0 defeat to Texas in 1898.

The Sooners rolled up 552 yards against a defense that ranked eighth nationally and allowed an average of 14.5 point through the Aggies' first six games. Oklahoma scored 34 points on its first six possessions. Heupel accounted for all six of Oklahoma's touchdowns, scoring three and throwing three more.

OU took a 17-0 lead in the first quarter on Heupel's one-yard run, six-yard pass to freshman receiver Curtis Fagan and Duncan's 19-yard field goal. A fake field goal set up the first score and a fake punt set up the field goal. Fletcher picked up a first down with an eight-yard run on a fake field goal, and Littrell's 11-yard run on a fake punt came moments before Duncan's three-pointer.

Heupel scored on another one-yard run in the second stanza, and Duncan nailed a 27-yard field goal for a 27-0 lead. Texas A&M answered with a 75-yard scoring drive, but the Aggies failed to convert the two-point pass play. The Sooners responded with a 77-yard drive capped by Heupel's third one-yard carry for a 34-6 advantage.

Heupel hurled a couple of scoring strikes in the third period. The first was a 22-yard pass to Trent Smith, and the second was a 26-yarder to Daniels. The touchdown pass to Smith was set up by Roy Williams' interception return to the A&M 15-yard line.

Duncan, who converted all six extra points, kicked another 27-yard field goal for the final tally early in the fourth quarter.

OU doubled up the Aggies on first downs (30-15) and more than doubled them on total yards (552-230). Heupel completed 31 of 50 passes for 372 yards, and 14 Sooners caught his aerials. Thornton led with six catches to tie a school record of receptions by a running back held by Steve Sewell against Kansas State in 1984.

Oklahoma returned to the AP poll at No. 24, then headed to Boulder in a showdown with 4-3 Colorado. The Buffaloes owned a five-game win streak over the Sooners and 8-0-1 over the last nine meetings. Mike Moschetti, who burned the OU secondary for three touchdowns a year ago in Norman, fired four TD passes to lead CU to a 38-24 victory.

Heupel on the other hand was pressured all afternoon by Buff blitzes, forcing the junior quarterback to throw poor passes, but it wasn't all his fault as many times the receivers blew their routes. Heupel completed 26 of 58 passes for 328 yards and four interceptions. The Sooners also could not move on the ground either, as they netted minus-11 rushing yards thanks to four Colorado sacks for minus-30 yards.

When Oklahoma took a lead or closed the gap, the Buffs responded. Duncan's 27-yard field goal gave OU a 3-0 lead early in the first period. Colorado later drove 80 yards for a 7-3 advantage. The Big Red marched 53 yards and grabbed a 10-7 lead on Littrell's two-yard run. CU answered with a 49-yard pass from Moschetti to Javon Green.

Colorado intercepted Heupel's pass at the OU three-yard line and returned it to the one to start the third stanza, and Moschetti scored from the one-yard line in one play for a 21-10 lead. The Buffs added a field goal seven minutes later to up their lead to 24-10.

Heupel tossed a five-yard pass to Skinner early in the fourth quarter to cap an 83-yard drive that began late in the third period, but Colorado retaliated with an 80-yard scoring march for a 31-17 lead.

The Sooners roared back to cut their deficit to 31-24 with a 65-yard drive. Desperate to get something going, the Sooners gambled on fourth down five times in the final stanza and converted only twice. Heupel hurled a 49-yard TD pass to Jackson on fourth down. On the first play after the kickoff and a penalty, Moschetti hooked up with Green for an 88-yard touchdown.

The Buffs gained more total yards (537-317). Ferguson and Calmus had the brightest statistics for the Sooners. Ferguson punted five times, averaging 50.2 yards. Calmus recorded 22 tackles.

Thornton suffered a severe sprained ankle, and his backup, Skinner, had a leg bruise. The Sooners removed the redshirt status of freshman Quentin Griffin, who rushed for 69 yards in 14 carries in the next game.

The Big Red fell out of the AP poll again but took out their frustrations with a 37-0 victory over 4-4 Missouri on November 6 in Norman, the Sooners' first conference shutout in six years (31-0 over Oklahoma State in 1993).

Littrell led OU with three touchdowns, and the defense intercepted Tiger quarterback Jim Dougherty twice and deflected 13 of his passes. Jackson returned six punts for 146 yards to break the school record for punt return yards previously held by Tommy McDonald (127 yards in 1955). Jackson also scored on one return, a 70-yarder for a 30-0 lead.

Oklahoma collected more total yards (436-274). Heupel completed 24 of 43 passes for 311 yards. Eleven players caught his pass-

Josh Heupel lunges across the goal line in the fourth quarter. The Sooner quarterback also completed two TD passes to help OU to a 44-7 win over Oklahoma State and end OSU's two-game series win streak. *(© 1999, The Daily Oklahoman)*

es. His three touchdown passes raised his season total to 25, breaking the Big 12 season mark of 23 held by Kansas State's Michael Bishop in 1998.

The Sooners had to rely on the running game to defeat Iowa State, 31-10, the next week in Ames. The Cyclones' pass defense frustrated Oklahoma, so the Sooners went to the ground and piled up 301 yards. Griffin rushed for 123 yards on 11 carries and scored twice to lead the OU ground attack.

OU took a 3-0 lead on Duncan's 33-yard field goal midway through the first period. Heupel hurled a 10-yard scoring strike to Griffin minutes later, and Duncan kicked the first of four conversions for a 10-0 lead minutes later.

Griffin's 27-yard scamper put the Sooners ahead, 17-0, midway through the second stanza, and the Cyclones kicked a field goal to cut the Oklahoma lead to 17-3 before halftime.

Griffin had a 44-yard TD run called back on a holding penalty. The fine moved the ball to ISU's 12-yard line, but Littrell scored on a three-yard run two plays later. Griffin left the game with a bruised hip, but Skinner rushed for 116 yards on 11 carries as his replacement.

The Cyclones scored a touchdown to cut their deficit to 24-10 early in the fourth quarter. The Sooners later drove 92 yards for the final tally. Heupel's 26-yard TD pass to Norman was the only pass in the 10-play drive. Skinner sparked the drive with a 44-yard run.

The Big Red rolled up 481 total yards and held I-State to 281 total yards. Heupel completed 24 of 42 passes for 180 yards.

Texas Tech (6-4) capitalized on two OU turnovers for 10 points, which was the difference in the Red Raiders' 38-28 victory on November 20 in Lubbock. The Sooners overcame a 10-0 deficit early, then took a 21-10 lead, but Tech scored 18 in the third stanza en route to the win.

The Red Raiders dominated the second half with 25 unanswered points.

Oklahoma rolled up more total yards (401-359). Heupel completed 32 of 50 passes for 352 yards, and Daniels, with nine catches, led a pack of 11 Sooners who caught Heupel's aerials.

Tech head coach Spike Dykes announced his resignation after the game and rumors circulated that OU offensive coordinator Mike Leach would be his successor. Three weeks later the rumors were founded as Leach was named the Red Raiders' new coach.

Calmus, OU's leading tackler, suffered a fracture to a non-weight bearing bone of his lower right leg against the Red Raiders, but that did not keep him from playing in the home finale against Oklahoma State the next week. He did not start but entered the game on the defense's third series and recorded eight tackles in the game.

The Sooners crushed the 5-5 Cowboys, 44-7, before a crowd of 75,374, the largest gathering at Owen Field in 10 years. The win snapped OSU's two-game win streak in the series.

A poor OSU punt late in the first stanza set OU up at the OSU 34, and three plays later Heupel zipped a three-yard TD strike to Daniels. Duncan succeeded on all but the final conversion.

The Pokes' Terrell Knauls picked off Heupel's pass and returned it for the Cowboys' only touchdown to tie the game at 7-7 early in the second quarter. For the first time all season, OSU's offense did not score a point.

The Sooners answered with a 55-yard march as Littrell's four-yard run capped the 10-play drive. OU took a 21-7 lead when Heupel hurled a pass down the middle to Fagan, who raced to the end zone to complete the 73-yard play.

The Big Red erupted for 23 points in the fourth period.

Duncan nailed a 31-yard field goal moments after defensive end Corey Heinecke intercepted Tony Lindsay's pass at the OSU 35. Heupel scooted seven yards after faking a handoff to McDougle, for a 31-7 advantage with 6:06 left in the game. McDougle played in the backfield briefly in the final quarter and carried once for two yards for a first down to keep the drive alive.

Moments later, Mike Woods picked off Lindsay's pass and sailed 43 yards for a touchdown. The defense held the Pokes to three and out, and J.T. Thatcher returned the punt 81 yards for the final tally.

OSU collected more total yards (363-325). Heupel completed 22 of 32 passes for 287 yards.

The Sooners ended the regular season with a 7-4 record and undefeated at home. The Alamo Bowl, Independence Bowl and Insight.com Bowl showed interest in inviting OU. The Independence Bowl, of Shreveport, Louisiana, extended a bid for the Sooners to play at their New Year's Eve bowl against Mississippi. The Rebels had an identical 7-4 record as the Sooners. They lost their four games by a combined 15 points.

Ole Miss placekicker Les Binkley booted a 39-yard field goal on the game's final play to defeat Oklahoma, 27-25, before a throng of 49,873, including 25,000 crimson fans.

OU overcame the season's largest deficit, 21-3, at halftime and fought back gallantly on Heupel's three TD passes in the final 30 minutes.

Both teams were sloppy in the first period. The Rebels threw two interceptions, and the Sooners lost two fumbles.

After OU took a 25-24 lead with 2:17 remaining, Deuce McAllister returned the ensuing kickoff 42 yards to the UM 43. The Rebels advanced 25 yards, where they faced third-and-two. OU was whistled for having 12 men on the field on the next play, and the penalty gave Ole Miss a first down on the OU 27. The Rebels gained five more yards and let the clock run down to three seconds before sending in Binkley for the game-winning field goal.

Oklahoma gained more total yards (481-361). Heupel completed 39 of 54 aerials for 390 yards, breaking Gundy's school bowl game passing performance, and he also broke the Independence Bowl passing records. Heupel also tied a bowl record of three TD passes set in 1998.

Heupel connected 349 of 555 passes for 3,850 yards and 33 touchdowns, setting the team record in all categories. He broke Gundy's season completion record of 159 set in 1993, McGee's 284 attempts in 1994, Gundy's yardage record of 2,311 set in 1993 and Gundy's TD passes of 17 in 1993. Heupel completed 63.1 percent of his passes for the season, breaking the record of 59.2 percent held by Hugh McCullough in 1938.

The Sooners finished the season with a 7-5 record and tied for second in the Big 12 south with a 5-3 mark. Calmus and McDougle were named to the All-Big 12 Conference first unit.

1999 Season Record: 7-5-0
Big 12 Conference: 5-3-0
(Second: South Division)

Date	Opponent	Result	Score
September 11	INDIANA STATE	W	49-0
September 18	BAYLOR	W	41-10
September 25	at Louisville	W	42-21
October 2	at Norte Dame	L	34-30
October 9	Texas at Dallas	L	38-28
October 23	Texas A&M	W	51-6
October 30	at Colorado	L	38-24
November 6	MISSOURI	W	37-0
November 13	at Iowa State	W	31-10
November 20	at Texas Tech	L	38-28
November 27	OKLAHOMA STATE	W	44-7
December 31	Mississippi*	L	27-25

*Game played in Shreveport, LA

FANS

The *Merriam Webster Dictionary* defines "fan" as an enthusiastic follower or admirer. Fan is short for fanatic, which the dictionary describes as "inspired by deity, frenzied ... marked by excessive enthusiasm and often intense uncritical devotion."

Fans are the backbone of college football. Without them there would be no cheers from the stands. Every score, first down or tackle would be received with dead silence. Whether they support the team through donations to the athletic department or just purchasing tickets to an event, fans are vital to a team's success.

Fans, like some players and coaches, have pregame rituals and superstitions. Some decorate their homes or offices in their favorite team's colors and memorabilia.

Cecil Samara (1916-1994) "Yea, Oklahoma! Roll on Big Red, roll on!" was the constant battle cry of Cecil Samara through his red and white bullhorn.

Samara was known as the No. 1 fan of Oklahoma football. As a lad, he would hitch rides to OU home games. He attended nearly every game, home and away, for 35 years before his death in 1994. Samara was injured in an automobile accident in 1959, which confined him to a wheelchair, and he was unable to attend games that year. A spider bite kept him from one game in 1968.

Samara would attend games decked in a red sportcoat and cowboy hat with white interlocking "OU" on the front of each. He wore either a red shirt with a white tie or white shirt with a red tie. The ties were also emblazoned with the interlocking "OU." His red and white cowboy boots also had the interlocking letters and "Go Big Red." In fact, his entire wardrobe was red and white except for one black suit he wore to funerals. He also wore a pair of eyeglasses with OU monogrammed on them.

For a period in the 1980s, Samara had custom-made dentures with the letters "Big Red" across the front bridge. He said he gave that up because people would want to see them while he was dining out.

Samara owned Big Red Flag Service for 30 years in Oklahoma City. His residence was decked in red and white. A fire destroyed a 30-year collection of Sooner memorabilia, and he replaced the stock of souvenirs the best he could.

He began traveling to Sooner home games in 1950 in his red and white 1923 Model T Ford, which he called "Big Red Rocket." The car featured a foghorn, a siren and loud speakers blaring "Boomer Sooner." Samara personalized the license plate, "Big Red," in 1968.

In 1952 he would drive it to away games. The car averaged 25 miles per hour, and Samara also towed a small trailer to haul his belongings. When highways grew to greater speeds, he would haul his ensemble on a trailer behind a station wagon. At times he would still drive the Big Red Rocket to Dallas each year for the Texas game with his wife following along on Interstate 35's shoulder. When fans would pass him by and honk and wave, he would blast his siren to return acknowledgement.

I got to know Cecil when I stayed at the Dallas Hilton in downtown Dallas each year during the OU-Texas game. Fans would be sitting in the hotel bar discussing the upcoming game against the Longhorns, when he would enter with the familiar cry and his same prediction each year of how bad OU was going to beat Texas.

"Oklahoma's gonna beat Texas by three touchdowns!" he would announce through his bullhorn.

Samara was a sweet-natured gentleman who loved his country, his state and had a faith in God. He was offered money for promotional appearances, but instead of taking the money, he requested a check be made out to Oklahoma City's Children's Hospital.

"I think we're real fortunate that God has been good to us," he said. "I believe I should help those who are less fortunate."

Cecil contracted cancer in 1994, and I visited him in an Edmond nursing home about two weeks before he died. He had lost a lot of weight and some of his hair, a contrast to the rotund build and black hair of his healthy days. The OU baseball team had won the national championship a week prior to my visit. When I said, "How 'bout them Sooners," he clinched his fist and pumped it in the air in positive gesture. I also said the football team needed to do the same, and he gave me the same signal.

Samara planned his own funeral years in advance. He ordered a red and white casket and asked to be buried in a red and white suit with his right index finger pointing upward. The casket was to be draped with three flags—Old Glory, the Oklahoma flag and the OU flag. He requested the Pride of Oklahoma band to be present to play the national anthem, "Boomer Sooner" and "When the Roll's Called Up Yonder, I'm Going to Be There." He requested everyone to stand up and clap during "Boomer Sooner," "just like at football games."

If he died on a football game day, he requested that his family attend the game and worry about him later.

Samara's family modified his requests for his funeral. The family substituted "America" for the "Star-Spangled Banner," he was not embalmed with the No. 1 finger gesture, and no loud clapping was allowed when "Boomer Sooner" was played.

Samara said that after he died he would still be rooting for the Sooners. "I'll be upstairs on the 50-yard line watching the Sooners play."

Dr. Geoff Potts has his dental office in west Norman decorated with Sooner memorabilia. Potts attended the University of Oklahoma in the early 1990s, obtaining a degree in business and another in dentistry. Behind the desk in his office is a shrine decorated with glasses and soda pop bottles commemorating past Sooner glory and an OU helmet signed by Barry Switzer.

Framed photos of players and coaches and articles dot the walls throughout the entire facility. On one wall is a framed original certificate of Billy Vessels' induction into the News Enterprise Association's 1952 All-America team. He also maintains a large collection of OU game programs and tickets at his home.

"Obviously I'm a huge fan, I collect OU memorabilia, but also I am interested in OU history and tradition, not just football but the university itself," he said.

Potts also was a Rufnek while attending OU. He grew up in Broken Arrow and said he became a fan because his father was "Sooner born, Sooner bred."

"I wear my heart on my sleeve as far as the Sooners are concerned," Dr. Potts said.

Dr. Geoff Potts' collection of OU memorabilia is displayed in his Norman dental office. *(Photo by Ray Dozier)*

Jim "J.R." Ross was raised in Westville, Oklahoma, a small town near the Arkansas border. Ross is the lead announcer for World Wrestling Entertainment and WWE's senior vice president of talent relations. He can be heard nearly every Monday night broadcasting WWE's *Monday Night Raw* and WWE's pay-per-view events. Ross is not shy about revealing his allegiance to the Sooners on the air.

Each week, Ross travels to a different arena, and each time he enters the arena with "Boomer Sooner" blaring over the loud speaker.

"We broadcast in 100 countries and 15 different languages, and I get e-mails from all over the world from people who have become Sooner fans through me," Ross said. "I find that complimentary."

Ross became a Sooner fan when he was about five years old and his grandfather taught him to read the newspaper. Ross would read the sports section and watch Sooner games during Bud Wilkinson's era.

"I remember Bud being so dignified and well spoken," Ross recalled. "He approached the game with dignity and respect, and that was amazing to me.

"I remember watching his TV show and he would use those little magnets on the board to show how a play was run. That was a great learning tool for me as a kid."

Ross later officiated Oklahoma high school games for 16 years, learning his trade from Bill Kinnamon Umpire School in St. Petersburg, Florida. Ross said he officiated 14 state championship games.

Ross moved from Norwalk, Connecticut, to Norman in 2004 to be closer to his beloved Sooners. He travels 51 weeks a year but makes time to attend as many Sooner football games as possible.

"I spend my time on Fridays making time to travel to Sooner games," he said. "I find watching OU football to be so cathartic. It bring me back to everything I remember good as a kid.

"There are intangibles that are hard to describe about being an OU football fan that you can't really put your arms around. At least I can't. It's just a feeling you have because of what this program means to this state. It brings enjoyment and a sense of pride."

Ross said when he tells people that he is from Oklahoma, they usually respond with a question about the Sooners.

His most memorable game was the 2001 Orange Bowl when the Sooners defeated Florida State for the national championship. But his most significant game was the first OU-Texas game he attended in 1970. The Longhorns blasted the Sooners, 41-9. He said it was like attending a funeral afterward.

"I was so heartbroken," Ross recalled. "I felt hurt, I felt empty."

But he rejoiced in the Sooners' 48-27 victory the following year. "It was like a religious experience. Leaving that stadium was so much better than the year before. That game brings out the animal instincts ... the best and worst of all fans."

A few weeks after the Sooners defeated Texas for the third straight year in 2002, Ross broadcast a WWE show in Austin, Texas and was booed by the fans in the arena. Ross said he entered the arena with "Boomer Sooner" echoing in the background. He flashed three fingers to the fans signifying the three straight victories. He also flashed the upside down "Hook 'Em Horns" sign.

"You would have thought I was the most vilified, nastiest human being ... the evil Oklahoma guy," Ross said. "They were angry as hell having to sit and listen to 'Boomer Sooner.' They had heard it enough."

WWE announcer Jim Ross proudly sports his Sooners gear.
(© 2005 World Wrestling Entertainment, Inc. All Rights Reserved.)

He was also booed in Lincoln, Nebraska, prior to the 2001 OU-Nebraska match up. "They were saying they were the real Big Red and they're going to beat us again.

"Those were the only two places I have ever been booed," he said.

In 2000, when the Sooners played for the Big XII Championship in Kansas City, Ross was returning from England where he had broadcast a WWE show. The charter plane had flown all night long and Ross could not sleep, wondering if the Sooners had won the game. The plane stopped in Gander, New Foundland, to refuel. He found a pay phone to call his wife who had taped the game for him. He asked her not to tell him the score but "just tell me if I'm going to be happy."

"She said, 'You're going to be very happy,'" he said. "I had been up all night worrying about this game."

When Ross arrived home exhausted the next morning, he kissed his wife and told her to go back to sleep.

"I went into the other room and watched the entire game," he said. "She couldn't believe I didn't go to sleep when I returned home. That was a big deal. That was a national championship year."

Ross said he supports the Sooners, "win or lose."

He said he is happy to be back in Oklahoma.

"I want to live in Norman and take my last breath here," he said. "This community is vibrant and they have a passion for the Sooners. It's patriotism."

Anyone who knows **Jim Hicks** will tell you he is an OU patriot. Hicks has a passion that burns in his heart for Oklahoma football. He did not attend the University of Oklahoma, but after attending a Sooner game in 1968, he fell in love with OU football.

He put his name on the waiting list for season tickets, and in 1970 he purchased his first set. Two years later, his passion for the Sooners grew to include buying away game tickets and he attends every game, every season. When the University of Oklahoma built the upper deck in 1975, Hicks was one of the first to purchase tickets there. As a donor to the football program, he has had seats in the upper deck ever since. He has sat in various sections in the upper deck but has settled for front-row seats.

Hicks cheers loudly at every game and is not shy about showing his enthusiasm, such as getting the fans excited and dancing in the aisle when the Sooners score.

"I like to get everybody around me pumped up," he said.

He arrives at each game about four hours before kickoff to soak up some of the game-day atmosphere and to visit with various groups of fans tailgating near Owen Field. This helps Hicks relax since he becomes anxious before every game.

"I get anxious and my stomach gets in knots before every game ... it doesn't make any difference who the opponent is," Hicks said.

He will purchase two hot dogs before every kickoff then settle into his seat and turn his ball cap backwards. "That's my rally cap," he added.

Hicks likes to stay in the same hotel as the team on road games, and he said he has to arrive at the hotel before the team does.

Jim Hicks paces the aisle to get pumped for a Sooners game.
(Photo by Ray Dozier)

"He has to get to the hotel before the team does so he can greet every one of them when they arrive," said his wife, Beverly. "They say, 'Hi, Coach Hicks.'"

"That's what they call me—Coach Hicks," Jim added.

Jim Hicks has several games that are his favorites—1971 versus Nebraska, 1975 against Pittsburgh, and 2000 against Texas.

He said the 1971 Nebraska game sticks out in his mind, "because of all the build up to it ... everything was on the line."

He remembered the 1975 Pitt game because OU's defense shut down Tony Dorsett, the Panther running back's worst performance ever.

The 2000 Texas game he remembered so well because OU was not expected to win by a huge margin and beat the Longhorns, 63-14.

"We dominated that game," he said. "I don't remember a game where we totally dominated Texas, and Texas had a better team on paper."

Hicks said his favorite play was Uwe von Schamann's game-winning field goal at Ohio State. Hicks was able to attend the game in Columbus, Ohio at the last minute.

"Uwe walking out onto that field and everybody in the crowd was hollering, 'Block that kick!' There was another time out called and he started leading the cheers of, 'Block that kick,' and he nailed it."

His greatest disappointment was the 1984 Texas game where an obvious OU interception in the end zone was ruled out by bounds by officials and Texas kicked a field goal to tie the game moments later.

"We had that game won," Hicks said.

Beverly Hicks is an avid Oklahoma State supporter, but she and Jim did not allow their allegiances get in the way of true love. She has attended OU games with her husband since they began dating and after they married in January 2004. She may not have Jim's passion for the crimson and cream, but she said she has learned to appreciate the Sooners.

Lee Allan Smith still enjoys the atmosphere of attending OU football games since he graduated from the university in 1953. A season ticket holder and donor of the Sooner football program, Smith said when he attends the home games it brings back memories of his college days and the Bud Wilkinson era.

"All those games I've been to just start flashing before my eyes," he said.

Smith has followed OU on the road as well, including attending numerous bowl games. He said he enjoyed New Orleans when the Sooners played there many times in the 1950s.

"It seemed like that's where we went all the time," he recalled. "Later we always went to the Orange Bowl and I enjoyed going there. The Rose Bowl [in 2002] was a special treat because I've always wanted to go."

Smith has no superstitions or game-day rituals, but he still gets excited about each game just as he did when he was a student.

"I get excited about some games more than others," he said. "I get excited particularly early in the season ... we get to see how good the team is. Yet I'm not one of those guys who wears anything particular, but I do try to wear something crimson."

One of Smith's favorite games is the 1950 Texas A&M game when the Sooners came from behind to defeat the Aggies with less than a minute remaining in Norman. He also had fond memories of the many come-from-behind victories against Nebraska under Barry Switzer.

Before the 1980 game in Lincoln, Smith said about 30 former Sooner players were playing professional football and he contacted those ex-players to send a telegram before the game.

"Barry [Switzer] read them all in the dressing room before the game, which was a great motivator."

The Sooners won, 20-17, in the waning minutes.

A similar comeback is still etched in Smith's mind—another Sooner Magic moment to defeat the Cornhuskers in 1976. Dean Blevins hurled a pass to Steve Rhodes who immediately pitched the ball back to Elvis Peacock for a 32-yard gain to the Nebraska two-yard line. That play set up the winning touchdown one play later.

"That hook and ladder play was really amazing," Smith said.

Another play that he fondly recalled did not involve a comeback to defeat Nebraska. Rather, it set the tone for the Sooners' dominance in the 1985 matchup in Norman. Keith Jackson dashed 88 yards for a first-quarter touchdown on an end around reverse. OU won, 27-7.

"That was tremendous," Smith said.

Smith's saddest memory of OU football was the 7-0 loss to Notre Dame in 1957, which snapped the Sooners' 47-game winning streak.

"I just sat in the stands, like everybody else, for about an hour," he recalled.

Another disappointment was when Billy Sims fumbled on the 3-yard line in a comeback effort against Nebraska in 1979.

"We might have won the national championship, and he [Sims] would have been the Heisman Trophy winner two straight years," Smith added.

From his college days to today, Smith said he has "a lot of great memories" of Sooner football.

Dr. B.J. Rutledge has been a Sooner fan since he was 10 years old. When he entered medical school at the University of Oklahoma, he bought student tickets and he has been a season ticket holder and supporter ever since. He's had the same seats on the 50-yard line since 1954.

That same year, he became the football team's neurosurgeon through an association with Dr. Don H. O'Donoghue, the team's orthopedic surgeon. If players had a head injury, Rutledge would be the one to examine them.

The worst injury Rutledge saw was an OU player (he could not recall his name) who suffered a broken neck.

"He wasn't paralyzed, but he was unable to play again," Rutledge recalled.

Sooner fans may remember a scary moment when Cale Gundy slammed his head on the turf and was knocked unconscious against Colorado in 1993. Gundy had a concussion.

"It was scary," Rutledge recalled. "He had some swelling and a contusion and bruising of his right temporal muscle."

Gundy was able to shake it off and play the following weekend.

Rutledge has traveled with the OU football teams through the years. He said his favorite places for road games were the Orange Bowl, the Rose Bowl and the Los Angeles Coliseum.

He said he still gets anxious when the Sooners play Texas and Nebraska.

"I liked it when we won at Nebraska, especially the come-from-behind wins in the fourth quarter," he said. "Those were good times."

Rutledge said his most memorable game was a close loss to Notre Dame in 1952. Billy Vessels, who rushed for 195 yards and scored three touchdowns, impressed him, but the loss was disappointing.

"We went from Chicago to South Bend on the blue train," Rutledge recalled. "It sure was blue coming back. Those Notre Dame people were rattling their beads and rubbing it in."

Rutledge said his favorite play was the fumblerooskey, where the quarterback places the ball at the feet of a lineman and another lineman picks up and carries the ball. Nebraska did the play once against OU in 1979. The Sooners also used the same play in the 1988 Orange Bowl. Guard Mark Hutson scored on a 29-yard run.

"I enjoyed watching that play, but I did not like losing the game, because we lost the national championship," Rutledge said.

Rutledge's son, Rob, has been attending Sooner football games since 1964. Sometimes he attends games with his father.

Rob Rutledge said he gets "psyched" before each Sooner game.

"Psyched, really psyched," he said.

He said he starts getting "pumped up" by reading about each game in the newspaper on Saturday morning and listening to pregame talk on the radio when he drives to Norman.

"I like to get there early and watch the band practice and get to the stadium early to watch the team practice," he said. "I really like to soak up the game-day atmosphere."

Rob Rutledge has attended numerous home games, road games and bowl games since 1964.

His most memorable road game was when he and a friend went to Columbus, Ohio, to see the Sooners play Ohio State. OU won, 29-28, on Uwe von Schamann's late field goal.

"One of the best football weekends," he recalled. "We stayed on campus and the Ohio State people were really nice. It was great that we won.

"I also enjoyed going to Tuscaloosa for the Alabama game in 2003," he said. "A lot of history and tradition ... like the Sooners."

Rob said his favorite play was Woodie Shepard's 47-yard pass to Steve Rhodes to help the Sooners come from behind to beat Nebraska, 21-17, in 1976.

"That was a real cool play," he said. "That really got me psyched for the victory."

2000 - 2005

2000

Sooner Magic: The Magic Returns

Prior to the 2000 season, many prognosticators had picked the Big Red to finish second in the Big 12 south division behind Texas. No one had them picked higher than 12th nationally. It was the brutal schedule in the month of October that had many picking the Sooners to go 8-3. If OU happened to win one of those October games against Texas, Kansas State or Nebraska, they might win nine games, but that was a stretch. If they happened to win two of the three, it would be a great improvement. If they would win all three, well . . . no one picked the Sooners to win all three games in October. Plus, a rugged road trip to Texas A&M in November had most pundits picking OU to go 7-4.

The Sooners proved them wrong. OU swept October and climbed into the national championship chase all the way to the No. 1 position in the nation, which the Sooners held to the end to claim the school's seventh national championship.

Record-breaking quarterback Josh Heupel returned to lead the offense. The senior had a solid corps of receivers from whom to choose as his targets—Josh Norman, Damian Mackey, Antwone Savage, Andre Woolfolk, and Curtis Fagan. Norman, a junior, was the elder of the group as the others were sophomores. The group combined to haul in 116 passes for 1,436 yards and 12 touchdowns. Woolfolk played occasionally at cornerback.

Quintin Griffin and Seth Littrell returned to round out the backfield.

Tackle Frank Romero and center Bubba Burcham returned to lead a pack of veterans in the front wall—Al Baysinger, Scott Kempenich, and junior college transfer Howard Duncan. Yet, depth was thin on the line, and keeping them healthy was a concern.

The defensive front was solid with depth, as Jeremy Wilson-Guest, Bary Holleyman, and Ramon Richardson returned to share duties at the tackle slots. The linebacker corps—Rocky Calmus, Torrance Marshall, and Roger Steffen—was rated as one of the best in the nation. Defensive ends Corey Heinecke and Corey Callens and tackle Ryan Fisher returned to anchor the line. Freshman Kory Klein got the nod at right tackle over Ramon Richardson.

Sophomore safety Roy Williams was the lone veteran with starting experience to return to the secondary. Punter Jeff Ferguson and place kicker Tim Duncan also were back.

Marshall was suspended for "unspecified reasons," yet the 19th-ranked Sooners hammered the Texas El Paso Miners, 55-14, during the hottest game in OU history on September 2. The temperature at kickoff was 106 degrees, one degree higher than the previous kickoff high in 1998 against North Texas in Norman. About 200 fans sought treatment for overheating in the Gomer Jones Memorial Cardiac Care Center under the stadium.

Freshman tailback Renaldo Works rushed for 98 yards and scored three fourth-quarter touchdowns to wow the crowd of 74,761. He also caught three passes for 24 yards, and one catch set up a field goal in the first half.

Oklahoma picked up more yards (409-342). Heupel completed one-half of his 36 attempts for 274 yards. Brian Natkin, the Miners' highly touted tight end was held to five catches for 43 yards.

The Sooners, although they won, dropped a notch in the AP poll and blasted 0-1 Arkansas State, 45-7, the next week in Norman. Heupel again entered the record book with three touchdown passes. His 35 career TD strikes tied Cale Gundy's career TD mark. J.T. Thatcher set the school punt-return record by returning one kick for a touchdown and set up two more scores. Thatcher returned five punts for 160 yards, breaking Jarrail Jackson's record of 146 yards set a year ago.

Oklahoma rushed for 208 yards and passed for 325. Heupel completed 24 of 31 passes for 301 yards. Woolfolk caught five passes for 102 yards to lead a group of 11 Sooners who caught aerials. Works gained 109 yards in 12 carries. Both teams were penalized a combined 25 times (Arkansas State 14, OU 11).

No. 17 Oklahoma struggled early against Rice, then scored 21 unanswered points to drop the 1-2 Owls, 42-14, two weeks later in Norman. Griffin rushed for 117 yards on 14 carries and scored three touchdowns for the Sooners.

Griffin scored two touchdowns, and Heupel ran for another to give Oklahoma a 21-6 halftime lead.

Rice drove 75 yards early in the third stanza to cut OU's lead to 21-14 after intercepting Heupel's pass. The Owls gained only 37 yards the rest of the game.

OU responded with an 80-yard march to up the lead to 28-14. The Owls dropped an extra man into pass coverage, and the Sooners went to the ground on six of the seven plays in the drive. Griffin scored his third touchdown on a 21-yard run.

Heupel, who hit 27 of 35 passes for 324 yards, tossed a four-yard scoring strike to Norman late in the third period and a six-yard TD pass to Works midway in the fourth.

The Big Red collected more total yards (532-262) and improved on penalties with only four.

The 14th-ranked Sooners defeated 1-2 Kansas, 34-16, in the Big 12 Conference opener on September 30 in Norman to run their record to 4-0 for the first time since 1993. A homecoming crowd 74,811 watched KU take an early lead. The Jayhawks 6-3 and 13-10 in the first quarter on two big plays. Quarterback Dylan Smith, who threw for 216 yards in the first half, hurled a 77-yard scoring strike, and running back David Winbush scored later in a 29-yard run.

Oklahoma had never trailed in their first three games, and Kansas threatened to make it worse in the second period. The Sooners trailed, 16-10, when tight end Trent Smith fumbled inside the OU 20, but moments later Richardson forced a fumble, and Callens recovered for the Sooners. The Big Red then rolled 82 yards in eight plays to cut the deficit to 16-14 on Griffin's 13-yard run and Tim Duncan's conversion.

Minutes later, the Sooners had to revert to trickery to take the lead after Brandon Everage picked off a Kansas pass. OU lined up with a split receiver accompanied by a tackle and another receiver behind them. "Ninja" was the name of the formation, which OU had used a couple of times a year before. Instead of passing, Heupel handed the ball to Savage on a reverse, and Savage accelerated 40 yards for a touchdown. Heupel threw a key block to allow Savage a lane to the end zone for a 21-16 lead.

The Big Red defense stepped up in the second half as Dylan Smith completed passes for only 42 yards, threw two interceptions and was sacked five times. OU's offense put the game away in the third quarter. Duncan kicked a 39-yard field goal, and Heupel sailed a 22-yard scoring strike to Woolfolk.

Oklahoma picked up more total yards (444-377). Heupel completed 29 of 43 passes for 346 yards and one interception against a defense that led the nation against the pass with 84 yards per game. Dylan Smith was intercepted five times, and Thatcher tied the school record by picking off three of them. Seven others shared the school record for interceptions in one game.

The Sooners were ranked 10th in the next AP poll, the first time OU cracked the top 10 since the fifth week in 1995.

The Hunt for Red October began on October 7 as the No. 10 Sooners traveled to Dallas to take on 11th-ranked Texas. The 3-1 Longhorns were favored by two and a half points to extend their winning string to four straight in the series. Griffin set the school record with six touchdowns to lead OU to a 63-14 victory, on a drizzly and cold (49 degrees) day.

Heupel threw a 29-yard scoring strike to Woolfolk to start the scoring fest early in the first period. Griffin scored the next three touchdowns, one late in the first stanza and two early in the second. Seventy seconds after Griffin's third TD Calmus, playing with a cast to protect his broken thumb, intercepted Chris Simms' pass and weaved 41 yards for a touchdown.

Fagan scored on an eight-yard reverse to give Oklahoma a 42-0 lead with 4:43 until intermission. Texas scored with three minutes left until halftime. Griffin scored twice more in the third quarter, and his one-yard run in the fourth broke the team touchdown record. His six TDs broke the single-game record of five previously held by Steve Owens set against Nebraska in 1968 and Jerald Moore against Oklahoma State in 1994.

OU players and coaches piled in midfield and had their photo taken with the score beaming on the board behind them.

The Sooners gained 28 first downs, rushed for 245 yards and passed for 289 more. The defense held Texas to 10 first downs, 161 passing yards and minus-seven yards rushing. OU's 63 points was the most ever scored in the 95-game series and the most ever against a ranked opponent.

The No. 8 Sooners traveled to Manhattan the next week to challenge a potent Kansas State squad. The No. 2 Wildcats were undefeated at 6-0 and led the nation in total defense (228.5-yard average) and scoring offense (51.8-point average). K-State tried to load nine players up front on defense to stop the run and assaulted the Sooners with constant blitzes. They succeeded by holding OU to 11 rushing yards, but Heupel shredded the Cat defense by completing 29 of 37 passes for 374 yards and two touchdowns in the 41-31 Sooner triumph.

Trailing late in the first stanza, Thatcher set up OU's go-ahead touchdown with a 93-yard kickoff return to the KSU two. Littrell scored on the next play for a 10-7 Sooner lead.

Rocky Calmus, playing with his broken thumb in a cast, rolls to the end zone after intercepting a Texas pass to lift OU to a 35-0 lead. *(Ronald Martinez/Getty Images)*

Williams intercepted a K-State pass at the OU 48 on the next series. Five plays later Heupel threw a 15-yard scoring strike to Fagan.

The Cats scored in the second period, and Heupel and Griffin each ran for a touchdown to give OU a 31-14 halftime lead.

Midway in the third quarter, the Sooners faced third-and-26 on their 26, and Heupel dumped a short pass to Savage, who feinted one K-State defender and outraced four others to the end zone for a 38-14 lead.

The Wildcats began to claw back with a field goal late in the third period and two touchdowns in the first four and one-half minutes of the fourth stanza to trail 38-31 with 10:31 remaining.

The Sooners later marched 47 yards but stalled at the KSU 30, and Duncan toed a 47-yard field goal for the final tally with 4:10 to go.

OU gained more total yards (385-255). Savage caught seven passes for 116 yards. The win snapped Kansas State's five-game win streak in the series and also ended the Cats' 25-game home winning streak. KSU quarterback Jonathan Beasley, who entered the game as the nation's passing efficiency leader, finished with 14 completions in 36 attempts for 211 yards and an interception.

Two weeks later, Nebraska rolled into Norman, with a 7-0 record and No. 1 ranking on the line. The Sooners moved up to third in the AP poll and second in the coaches poll, the first time in the Top 5 since the fifth week in 1991. Better yet, they were ranked second in the Bowl Championship Series, a combination of polls and computer rankings to determine which two teams should play for the national championship at the end of the season. Nebraska sat atop that poll, also.

ESPN's Gameday college football show broadcast live from Memorial Stadium before the game's broadcast by the ABC network. The atmosphere had the feel of a national championship-caliber game. *The Daily Oklahoman* billed it as "Game of the Century I"—the 21st century. Twice before (1971 and 1987) the Sooners and Huskers met without a blemish to their records. Nebraska was favored by three points in the 2000 contest, but the Sooners prevailed, 31-14.

The Cornhuskers looked like the No. 1 team as they took a 14-0 lead with 8:11 left in the first period, and Nebraska had run only 11 plays. Quarterback Eric Crouch tossed a TD pass and ran for another. The Huskers amassed 167 yards on those 11 plays, but the Sooner defense tightened and held Nebraska to zero points and 161 yards in the next 59 Husker plays.

OU maintained its composure and exploded for 24 points in the second quarter. Heupel completed only five of 11 passes for 53 yards in the first period, then hit 15 of his next 23 aerials for 247 yards and a touchdown. Heupel connected 10 of 13 for 185 yards in the second stanza alone.

Griffin's one-yard TD run and Duncan's extra point cut the deficit to 14-7 early in the second period. The Sooners tied it up on their next series. Heupel, throwing off his back foot, lobbed a 34-yard bomb to Fagan, who caught the ball in full stride at the goal line. The most spectacular play of the game occurred four plays before. Woolfolk had been knocked down and was flat on his back when Heupel's pass came his way. A Husker defender deflected the ball, but Woolfolk reached up with his left hand and palmed the ball for a completion.

Duncan kicked a 19-yard field goal to lift OU to a 17-14 lead, moments after Norman set it up with a blocked punt.

Oklahoma took a 24-14 lead on its next series when Norman scored on an eight-yard end-around reverse. Heupel sparked the drive with a 37-yard pass to Savage.

Early in the third stanza, freshman cornerback Derrick Strait intercepted Crouch's pass and weaved 32 yards through Husker defenders for the final tally. Strait also stopped a Nebraska threat in the fourth quarter when he forced a fumble at the OU 23.

Oklahoma picked up more total yards (418-328). Calmus led the defense with 16 tackles.

A swarm of fans brought down the goal posts, but no major violent incidents occurred. Sooner fans know how to celebrate without violence.

The Sooners had vaulted to No. 1 in every poll; the first time OU had been No. 1 since the 14th week in 1987. Sooner faithful were concerned if the Sooners would be able to maintain their fire or take a 2-6 Baylor team lightly on November 4 in Waco. No worries. Oklahoma creamed the Bears, 56-7. Most of the starters sat out the second half after rolling up a 42-0 halftime lead.

The Sooners gained only 20 yards and a first down on their first series and punted. The defense held Baylor to three-and-out, and Thatcher fielded the punt at his 40 and bolted up the middle all the way to the end zone. OU scored on its next four possessions and struck quick on six of its seven scoring drives, averaging a little more than two minutes, and four and one-half plays each time.

Heupel, who completed 21 of 29 passes for 313 yards and a touchdown, scored on a four-yard sneak for a 14-0 lead. Heupel later hooked up with Fagan for the next two scores—four yards and 43 yards for a 28-0 lead.

The longest drive consumed 16 plays and five and one-half minutes in the second quarter. Griffin's two-yard TD run capped the 80-yard march. Minutes later, Heupel sailed a 39-yard TD bomb to Littrell.

The Bears got on the board in the third stanza when Odell James intercepted Nate Hybl's pass and returned it 18 yards. Hybl, a sophomore, later hurled two TD passes—a 36-yarder to Fagan and a 31-yarder to Savage for the final tally with 3:55 remaining in the third period.

OU rolled up 30 first downs and 516 total yards. The defense held Baylor to seven first downs and 94 yards (1.6 yards per snap).

Sooner Magic: Silencing the 12th Man

Texas A&M was next, and the Aggies were seeking revenge of the Sooners' 51-6 shellacking in Norman in 1999. The Aggies had circled November 11, the day the Sooners would arrive in College Station. A crowd of 87,188—the largest crowd to witness a football game in the state of Texas to date—and a regional ABC network audience witnessed one of the greatest games in the Lone Star State. The Aggies are famous for the 12th Man, their vociferous fans. A&M had won 24 of its last 25 games at Kyle Field.

The 8-0 Sooners had never defeated A&M in College Station, and the 7-2 Aggies had never defeated a number-one ranked team (in the Associated Press poll) in eight previous tries. The winner of the 2000 edition of Oklahoma-Texas A&M would have an edge in the overall series. Both teams had won nine times in the rivalry, renewed in 1996 by the formation of the Big 12 Conference.

The winner of this game would be the leader in the conference's south division. OU was 6-0 in conference play, and A&M was 5-1, losing only to Colorado.

After stopping A&M's first possession, the Sooners stalled on three plays, and the raucous Aggie fans roared with pleasure as A&M's Jay Brooks blocked Ferguson's punt. The Aggies took over at OU's 12-yard line and scored five plays later.

Duncan's 31-yard field goal cut the gap to 7-3 on OU's next series.

The Sooners took a 10-7 lead early in the second stanza. Heupel's seven-yard scoring strike to Fagan capped a 63-yard drive and Duncan converted.

Sooner mistakes gift-wrapped 10 more Cadet points late in the first half. A&M intercepted Heupel's pass to set up a field goal, and Woolfolk's fumble set up a touchdown. The Aggies led, 17-10, with 19 seconds until halftime.

The beginning of the second half was no better for Oklahoma and Heupel, who tossed another interception at the A&M 47. The Aggies drove 53 yards in seven plays for a 24-10 lead.

Duncan booted a 17-yard field goal to pull OU within 11, 24-13, with 1:46 left in the third quarter.

Griffin scored on a 21-yard run and Heupel fired a two-point pass to tight end Matt Anderson and the the Sooners trailed, 24-21, with 14:46 remaining in the game.

The Aggies made it more difficult for the Big Red by moving quickly downfield. On fourth-and-six inches at the OU 27, Ja'Mar Toombs, the Aggies' 275-pound fullback took the hand off and lumbered all the way to the goal line, dragging three Sooner defenders the final 10 yards. Terence Kitchens toed the extra point, and A&M held a 31-21 lead with 13:36 to go.

As the Aggies moved swiftly on that TD drive, OU worked the clock on its next possession, consuming nearly six minutes in the 15-play, 77-yard drive and meticulously picking up necessary yards. Three times the Sooners converted crucial third-down plays. Each time the Aggie fans were roaring and waving white towels; the decibel level was off the charts.

On third-and-10 at the A&M 41, Heupel passed left to Savage toward the sideline. Savage snared the ball and momentum carried him out of bounds at the 28.

Griffin carried for three, then Heupel's pass to Savage went through the receiver's hands.

On third-and-seven at the Aggie 14, Heupel scrambled left, found no open receiver, but he did find an opening to run. He took off and gained a first down inside the three-yard line. Heupel lunged forward, holding the ball in front of him to make sure the ball crossed the first-down marker.

On the next play, Griffin took the hand off up the middle and crossed the goal line. Duncan nailed the extra point, and the Sooners again closed the gap, 31-28, with 7:43 remaining.

A&M's Dwain Goynes returned the kickoff out of the end zone to the Aggie 32. On the next play, quarterback Mark Farris passed over the middle and Marshall grabbed the pigskin at the 41 and threaded through defenders down the right sideline to the end zone. Duncan tacked on the extra point, and suddenly OU was on top, 35-31, but nearly half a quarter remained with 7:18 beaming on the clock.

On their next possession, the Aggies drove from their 20 to the OU four-yard line. Ontei Jones batted away Farris' fourth-down pass at the goal line. The Sooners took over but managed only seven yards on the next three plays, and 2:25 still remained on the clock.

Ferguson's punt from the end zone was partially blocked but rolled to the OU 44. The Aggies had a short field to work with but little time as they had previously burned all their timeouts.

Farris let fly a long bomb to Robert Ferguson, but again the pass was deflected at the 10 by Jones who was covering the Aggie receiver. Time remaining—1:26.

On the next play, Farris' pass went through the hands of flanker Bethel Johnson. Then on third-and-10, Roy Williams sacked Farris for a six-yard loss. There was 1:21 remaining. A&M was flagged for illegal substitution on the next play, moving the ball back to the Aggie 45. Farris completed a pass to receiver Greg Porter, but Derek Strait tackled Porter four yards short of a first down with 36 seconds left in the game.

The Sooners held on for a 35-31 victory, a 9-0 record, the top spot in the conference and the nation. Oklahoma had more total yards (368-316). Heupel completed 28 of 42 passes for 263 yards. Ferguson averaged 53.5 yards on two punts.

"I'm very proud of our players, the way they played . . . kept their poise," Stoops said. "We were fighting uphill all day. I heard someone shouting as we were coming into the locker room, that Sooner magic might be back.

"Finding a way to win in the fourth quarter is where that phrase had come from. And it's good to see us do it. Hopefully we've got a lot more magic left in the bag."

Two weeks later the Sooners again would have to reach into their bag of tricks against heavy underdog Oklahoma State. But they had a date with Texas Tech the next week in Norman. It would be the first time former OU offensive coordinator Mike Leach would be in Norman since taking the Tech head coaching job.

The Sooners clinched the Big 12 south division with a sloppy 27-13 victory. OU had four turnovers, 11 penalties, several dropped passes, and two kicks blocked. Assistant coach Mark Mangino said the team played like it had practiced all week, "dull and flat."

Thatcher grabbed his seventh interception of the season and sailed 85 yards for a touchdown midway through the first quarter, and Duncan's conversion gave OU a 7-0 lead.

Tech got on board with a field goal early in the second stanza. Less than five minutes later, Heupel tossed a five-yard scoring strike to Trent Smith and Duncan's toe gave OU a 14-3 lead.

The only score of the third period came on Works' five-yard scamper and Duncan's conversion for a 21-3 advantage. But Tech began making a game of it by scoring 10 points in the first half of the final quarter. The Sooners responded with a lengthy drive to put the game away. Griffin scored on a three-yard run to cap a 71-yard march in 12 plays that consumed five minutes and 20 seconds. The Red Raiders blocked Duncan's extra point, snapping his string of 55 straight conversions.

Oklahoma had more total yards (384-320). Heupel completed 24 of 38 passes for 248 yards and surpassed, by 109 yards, Gundy with 6,498 career passing yards.

Sooner Magic: 'Either I would make the play, or they were going to score'

A victory over Oklahoma State in the final game of the 2000 season would culminate in the Sooners' first undefeated season since 1987. The 95th edition of OU-OSU, nationally televised by Fox Sports, was expected to be a Sooner rout in Stillwater. The Big Red was favored by 25 points, but a loss to 3-7 OSU would knock the Big Red from atop the national ranking and a possible national championship game in the Orange Bowl.

Oklahoma's first possession began at its own one-yard line following a Scott Elder punt. OSU's Paul Jones killed the ball at the Sooner one.

OU drove 99 yards in 11 plays to take a 7-0 lead midway in the first quarter. Heupel tossed a four-yard TD strike to Fagan and Duncan converted. Heupel hurled a 44-yard pass to Fagan and Griffin ran for 39 yards to spark the drive.

Fagan's seventh TD of the season broke the school record.

Early in the second quarter, Thatcher picked off a Poke pass at the Sooner 31 and returned it 35 yards to the Pokes' 34. The interception was Thatcher's eighth of the season, tying him with Scott Case (1983) and Rickey Dixon (1987) for the school record. The Sooners managed only one first down in the drive, which ended with a 39-yard field goal by Duncan. The Sooners held a 10-0 advantage with 10:06 remaining until intermission.

Late in the second period, the Cowboys were pinned deep in their own territory. On third-and-10 at the four-yard line, OSU quarterback Aso Pogi in shotgun formation, took the snap and backpedaled into the end zone but could not find an open receiver. Calmus shed his blocker and grabbed Pogi, who threw the ball to the ground. Officials flagged Pogi for intentional grounding, which resulted in a safety for the Sooners and a 12-0 lead with 3:09 remaining in the half.

The Cowboys got on board late in the third quarter, when halfback Tatum Bell flew 60 yards to the end zone. The extra point closed the Sooner margin to 12-7 with 5:42 left.

Duncan missed a 27-yard field goal early in the fourth period.

Cowboy Gabe Lindsey later took Ferguson's punt at the OSU 38 and returned the pigskin 23 yards to the OU 39 with 6:26 to go. The Pokes drove to the Sooner 10—first and goal and 5:42 beaming on the clock. Pogi called a time out, with one second on the play clock, to avoid a delay penalty. Bell then gained one yard, but the clock kept ticking, now below the five-minute mark.

On the next play, Pogi scrambled and picked up three yards to the seven. On third-and-goal, the Pokes were flagged for movement on the right side of the line and officials placed the ball back to the 12-yard line. Pogi, under pressure by Callens, threw the ball away.

The Cowboys called their last time out with 3:21 remaining.

As the Big Red defense huddled with coaches on the sideline, the defensive coaches told Strait to be ready for the fade route. At 5-11, Strait was the man defending tight end Marcellus Rivers, five inches taller than himself.

The coaches' premonition was correct. On fourth down, Pogi, under pressure again, lofted the ball toward Rivers in the right side of the end zone. Strait leaped in the air and swatted the ball away with 3:15 on the clock.

"I knew it would be me and him and the ball," Strait said after the game. "Either I would make the play, or they were going to score."

"There was nothing more Derrick could have done," said co-defensive coordinator Mike Stoops. "That was textbook. I didn't realize he could jump so high."

OU got the ball back and lost one yard on the next two plays. On third-and-11 at their own 11, the Sooners needed a first down to keep the clock rolling. Heupel fired a pass to Fagan past the first-down marker at the 23.

Hoping to milk the clock some more, Heupel handed off to Griffin, but the Sooner halfback was nailed for a two-yard loss with 1:30 to go.

On the next play, Heupel kept the ball and gained 10 yards to the 31 with 1:04 left. Before the next play, Heupel called a time out with one second on the play clock and 38 seconds on the game clock.

Heupel again kept the ball for three yards, but more importantly, a first down to preserve the victory.

The Sooners rushed for 155 yards and passed for 154. The defense held the Pokes to 275 total yards. Griffin led all rushers with 115 yards on 21 carries. Heupel completed one-half of his 38 attempts.

Bob Stoops said finding ways to win games developed toughness and character. "I'm proud of our guys," he said. "In a difficult situation they found ways to make plays and found ways to win the game."

Oklahoma ended the regular season undefeated for the first time since 1987. That squad lost to Miami in the Orange Bowl. When the Big 12 Conference began in 1996, the north and south division teams met at the end of the season for one more game—the Big 12 Championship—to crown the conference champs. The OU appeared in its first championship game on December 3 in a rematch against Kansas State, (10-2 and ranked eighth nationally).

700th Win

The Sooners defeated the Wildcats, 27-24, on a frigid night at Kansas City's Arrowhead Stadium. The victory marked the Sooners' 700th win in school history. The temperature at kickoff was 30 degrees with a wind chill of 23 degrees. A crowd of 79, 655 bundled fans witnessed the game, which included about 15,000 to 20,000 Sooner rooters.

Both teams battled to a 10-10 tied in the first half. OU took a 3-0 lead on Duncan's field goal midway through the first stanza. The Cats scored 10 unanswered points for a 10-3 lead in the second period. Heupel tossed a one-yard pass to Smith to tie the game with 2:56 left until halftime.

The Sooners marched 69 yards in eight plays to take a 17-14 lead on Heupel's seven-yard scamper with 5:54 remaining in the third quarter. Two and one-half minutes later, K-State's Aaron Lockett tied the game on a 58-yard punt return.

The Big Red retaliated with a 79-yard drive in nine plays. On the first play of the fourth period, OU faced fourth-and-one at the KSU 39. Heupel took the snap, optioned left and pitched to Griffin, who darted 22 yards to the 17 for a first down. Heupel then tossed a scoring strike to Woolfolk for a 24-17 lead.

The Sooners later moved 59 yards from their 14 to the KSU 27 but had to settle for Duncan's 46-yard field goal to pad the lead to 27-17. The Cats scored a touchdown with six seconds left. Kansas State tried an onside kick, but Mackey covered it to preserve the victory.

OU had claimed its first football conference championship in 13 years and 37th in school history.

OU collected more total yards (319-239). Heupel completed 24 of 44 passes for 220 yards.

That victory allowed OU to hold its No.1 ranking and offered a showdown against Florida State in the Orange Bowl for all the marbles of college football.

Quentin Griffin scores the only touchdown in the Orange Bowl against Florida State as the Sooners claimed their seventh national championship. *(Eliot J. Schechter/Getty Images)*

Sitting atop the polls at 12-0, the Sooners still got no respect. The Florida State Seminoles at 11-1 were the defending national champions and pegged as a 12 and a half-point favorite. The Noles had a bevy of NFL-type talent led by their 28-year-old quarterback Chris Weinke.

In the final few weeks of the 2000 season, the Heisman Trophy race came down to the two quarterbacks who would meet in the Orange Bowl for all the marbles—Heupel and Weinke. The latter won the trophy, awarded to the best college player in the nation.

This disappointed Sooner fans and football staff as well. Heupel, however, would get the last laugh.

A couple of weeks prior to the Orange Bowl game, Marvin "Snoop" Minnis, the Seminoles' star receiver, flunked two of his courses and was declared ineligible to play. Still, the betting line did not move, as many believed that Florida State had too much talent for the Sooners.

The Orange Bowl, played to a capacity of 76,835 fans and a national TV (ABC) audience, would be a match of old vs. new. The old—Bobby Bowden, a coaching whiz who came to Florida State in 1976 and soon turned that program into a national power. The Sooners were a thorn in Bowden's side, though. He was 0-3 against OU, including two Orange Bowl losses in the early 1980s. In four previous meetings, Florida State only won once—the 1965 Gator Bowl.

The new—Bob Stoops, a defensive genius and a master of returning the Sooner program to the national spotlight. All during the 2000 season, he made the Sooner players believe they could beat any team.

Marshall taunted Weinke during the pre-game coin toss, telling the Noles' quarterback that the Sooners came to get the Heisman Trophy many believed should have been awarded to Heupel: "You got my boy's trophy...we came to get it back."

On the first play from scrimmage, Weinke completed a 35-yard pass, but the Big Red defense settled down and stopped the Nole attack.

Duncan's 27-yard field goal gave the Sooners a 3-0 lead midway through the opening quarter.

The Big Red defense kept the Seminoles stymied throughout the night.

Florida State drove to the OU 13 in the second quarter, but the Sooner defense held them to a field-goal try. Brett Cimorelli's attempt was low and wide, and OU held the 3-0 lead at halftime.

Midway through the third stanza, the Sooners marched 40 yards in six plays to the FSU 25, highlighted by Heupel's 39-yard pass to Fagan to the FSU 37. The Noles' defense held tight and forced another field goal. Duncan's 42-yarder was on the mark, and Oklahoma was up 6-0 with 4:24 left in the period.

Oklahoma's defense continued to give Weinke fits, and the Seminole defense returned the favor against Heupel.

Early in the fourth quarter, at the OU 35, Weinke fired a pass to Robert Morgan in the end zone. The ball fell through Morgan's hands as he dove for the ball. On the next play, the Noles gambled on fourth down.

Weinke's pass to Anquan Boldin, inside the five-yard line, was broken up by Strait.

Midway through the quarter, on third-and-six, Weinke scrambled out of the pocket and tried to run for the first down. Calmus smacked him from behind, jarring the ball loose, and Williams recovered at the FSU 15.

Two plays later, Griffin bolted up the middle for a 10-yard touchdown run. Duncan kicked the extra point for a 13-0 lead with 7:46 remaining in the game. All the Sooner faithful could do was hold their breath with plenty of time for a Florida State comeback.

FSU drove to the OU 40, highlighted by a 43-yard pass from Weinke to Atrews Bell. The Sooner defense stiffened, and on third-and-13, Weinke threw a 30-yarder to Boldin, but Thatcher swatted the ball away as it descended toward the receiver. A fourth-down gamble failed when Weinke threw an incompletion in the flat.

With less than a minute to play, OU faced a punting situation at its own 35. The snap sailed over Ferguson's head. Ferguson grabbed the bounding ball and covered it up in the end zone. This allowed the Noles to score a safety, but Ferguson's quick thinking thwarted a Florida State touchdown.

The Noles got the ball back and drove to the OU 30-yard line. Weinke fired a pass to Talman Gardner in the end zone, but Everage and Ontei Jones had shrouded the FSU receiver. Jones leaped up and picked off the pigskin to seal the victory, 13-2.

FSU's offense, which led the nation in scoring and total yards, was shut out by the Big Red defense, led by Marshall who was voted the game's most valuable player. He had six tackles, one interception, and a pass deflection. The Seminoles had led the nation in scoring (42.4 point average) and total offense (384 yard average) prior to the Orange Bowl. The Oklahoma defense held them scoreless, and to 301 total yards. Florida State was only able to convert one first down in 15 third-down situations.

Florida State had 14 first downs, two more than OU. Heupel completed 25 of 29 passes for 214 yards, and Weinke hit 25 of 51 for 274 yards.

The Oklahoma Sooners claimed their seventh national championship to cap a perfect 13-0 season. No one expected the Sooners to earn their way to the pinnacle of college football. No one except the players and coaching staff, led by a new David Copperfield.

2000 Season Record: 13-0-0
Big 12 Conference: 9-0-0 (Champions)
NATIONAL CHAMPIONS

Date	Opponent	Result	Score
September 2	TEXAS EL PASO	W	55-14
September 9	ARKANSAS STATE	W	45-7
September 23	RICE	W	42-14
September 30	KANSAS	W	34-16
October 7	Texas at Dallas	W	63-14
October 14	at Kansas State	W	41-31
October 28	NEBRASKA	W	31-14
November 4	at Baylor	W	56-7
November 11	at Texas A&M	W	35-31
November 18	TEXAS TECH	W	27-13
November 25	at Oklahoma State	W	12-7
December 2	Kansas State*	W	27-24
January 3	Florida State#	W	13-2

*Big 12 Championship at Kansas City, MO
#Orange Bowl at Miami, FL

Bob Stoops had pulled the rabbit out of the hat. The 2000 season was indeed incredible and exciting every snap of the way.

Sooner Magic Returned.

Calmus, Heupel, and Thatcher were named All-Americans. Ryan Fisher, Griffin, Ferguson, Marshall, Romero, and Williams joined them on the All-Big 12 Conference first team. Heupel earned the Walter Camp Trophy as the best college player of the year. He was named the Associated Press Player of the Year, *Sporting News* Player of the Year, CBS network Player of the Year, and Big 12 Conference Offensive Player of the Year. Thatcher received the Mosi Tatupu Award as the special teams player of the year.

Stoops was named Big 12 Conference Coach of the Year, and Calmus was the conference's Defensive Player of the Year.

2001

Expectations were high for the Sooners to repeat as national champions even though Josh Heupel's graduation had left a vacancy at quarterback. The team returned a nucleus of stars—linebacker Rocky Calmus, strong safety Roy Williams, cornerback Derrick Strait, receivers Josh Norman, Antwone Savage, Curtis Fagan, and Damian Mackey, tailback Quentin Griffin, tight end Trent Smith, offense tackle Frank Romero, offensive guard Howard Duncan, punter Jeff Ferguson, and placekicker Tim Duncan.

The decision to replace Heupel at quarterback came nine days before the opening game against North Carolina. Nate Hybl, a transfer from the University of Georgia in 1999, got the nod over Jason White, yet both quarterbacks received praise from head coach Bob Stoops.

Some preseason publications tabbed OU to repeat as the best team in the country. The Sooners were third in the preseason AP poll behind Florida and Miami, Florida. The Sooners held that position during the first six games.

Oklahoma defeated North Carolina, 41-27, in the season opener on August 25 in Norman, in the second annual Hispanic College Fund Classic. The game, televised by ESPN, wasn't nearly as close as the score indicated. The Sooners jumped ahead, 17-0, in the first three and a half minutes and held a 31-7 advantage in the first quarter.

Oklahoma's defense and special teams contributed to 34 points.

Linebacker Brandon Moore forced a Carolina fumble on the game's second play, and Calmus recovered on the NC 17 but OU had to settle for Duncan's 25-yard field goal and a 3-0 lead.

The Sooners marched 46 yards on their next series for a 10-0 advantage. It was all Griffin in the three-play drive. He carried for 19 yards, caught Hybl's pass for 23 more and scored from the four-yard line. Duncan kicked the first of five conversions.

Duncan forced a fumble on the ensuing kickoff, and Mackey recovered on the NC 17. Four plays later, tailback Renaldo Works burst ahead from the seven-yard line for a 17-0 lead with 11:21 remaining in the first quarter.

Minutes later, Brandon Everage forced another fumble, and Calmus scooped the ball off the turf and raced 14 yards for a 24-0 lead. The Tar Heels' Julius Peppers intercepted Hybl's pass for a touchdown moments later to cut the OU lead to 24-7. Savage answered with an 88-yard kickoff return for a touchdown.

Strait picked off a pass and sailed 47 yards to the end zone to up the Sooners' lead to 31-7. Duncan booted a 22-yard field goal moments after another Carolina turnover. The Big Red held a 41-7 lead with 6:10 left until halftime.

The Tar Heels scored on an 89-yard punt return in the third stanza and two TDs in the fourth quarter, mostly against reserves on defense. Calmus was named the most valuable player with 13 tackles and his fumble return for a score. Though the offense only gained 286 yards, Hybl completed a stellar 20 of 29 passes for 152 yards in his starting debut. Griffin rushed for 68 yards and caught seven passes for 48 more. North Carolina pickled up 290 total yards.

The Sooners traveled to Colorado Springs to meet Air Force, the season opener for the Falcons, the next week. The first meeting between the two teams is one the Falcons would like to forget. ABC televised the game, and Griffin treated spectators to a 201-yard rushing performance in the 44-3 victory. The crowd of 56,162 was the largest to date at Falcon Stadium.

Hybl and Duncan contributed to the first-half scoring for the Sooners. Hybl scored a two-yard run late in the first quarter and added a TD strike to Smith late in the second period. Duncan kicked two field goals, and the Sooners held a 20-3 halftime lead. OU exploded for 24 fourth-quarter points. Duncan nailed a 26-yard field goal, Hybl tossed an eight-yard scoring strike to receiver Mark Clayton, Griffin scored on a three-yard run, and defensive end Cory Heinecke returned a fumble for 69 yards.

OU rolled up 398 total yards, and the Falcons picked up 249 total yards.

The Sooners returned home on September 8 to host 0-1 North Texas and defeated the Mean Green, 37-10, in a sloppy victory. The disappointing Oklahoma performance was not attributed to the lightning threats and rain.

"We pushed all week, talking about getting better," Stoops said. "That didn't happen today."

OU turned the ball over three times, including a fumble on the Mean Green one-yard line, and an interception led to a North Texas touchdown. OU also missed one extra point and two field goals, had a field goal blocked, bobbled a punt snap, and had 13 penalties for 120 yards.

One penalty wiped out Williams' 76-yard interception return, and two straight penalties forced a missed extra point.

Trailing 3-0, the Sooners scored twice in the opening period—a 13-yard pass from Hybl to Griffin and a 72-yard scamper by Works.

The Mean Green scored moments after picking off Hybl's pass early in the second stanza to trail, 14-10. Griffin's 14-yard run gave the Big Red a little breathing room, 21-10, before halftime.

Duncan's 42-yard field goal in the third quarter gave OU a 24-10 lead. Hybl scored on a one-yard sneak minutes later, but two straight penalties forced Duncan to miss a 35-yard extra-point try.

Hybl hurled a screen pass to Norman, who eluded defenders and raced 57 yards for the final tally early in the fourth quarter.

Oklahoma hammered out 543 total yards. Hybl completed 28 of 40 passes for 350 yards and two touchdowns. Norman led all receivers with six catches for 120 yards. Griffin caught 10 passes for 111 yards, but his two TDs came on the ground. Griffin became the 34th Sooner to reach 2,000 all-purpose yards. North Texas picked up 297 total yards, 120 in the final 30 minutes.

The Sooners' scheduled September 15 contest against Tulsa was postponed to November 3 due to the terrorist attacks on the United States. All sports shut down temporarily for several days following

the attacks. OU also had a scheduled open date on September 22, so when Kansas State arrived in Norman, the Sooners had not played a game in three weeks.

Sooner Magic: Hybl Took Some Lickings and Just Kept On Ticking

The 11th-ranked Wildcats had revenge on their mind. OU defeated them twice the year before including the Big 12 Championship. The 2001 matchup was touted to be a defensive struggle, but instead erupted into a 75-point, 771-yard offensive display that lasted four hours and three minutes. The Sooners saw a 21-point lead nearly evaporate, but held on for a 38-37 win before a throng of 75,862 in Norman on September 29.

Hybl, under pressure by K-State blitzes, earned his wings under fire. He was constantly knocked to the turf as he delivered passes. Hybl only completed 17 of 38 passes for 283 yards. He had three picked off, but he also hurled two big scoring strikes.

"That was brutal," he said after the game.

Defensive end Jimmy Wilkerson forced a fumble midway through the first quarter, and Williams scooped up the ball and scored from the KSU 18. Duncan kicked the first of five conversions for a 7-0 lead.

Minutes later, the Sooners faced third-and-13 on their 37-yard line, when Hybl delivered a 63-yard scoring strike to Savage for a 14-0 lead.

The 2-0 Wildcats marched 80 yards for their first touchdown early in the second quarter. Oklahoma answered with a 64-yard scoring drive. Griffin scored from the six to cap the six-play drive for a 21-7 Sooner lead with 10:37 remaining in the second period.

K-State roared back with an 80-yard drive. The Sooners scored on a fake punt for a 28-14 lead near the end of the first half. OU had stalled at the Cats' 33 and set up to punt. The snap went to Hunter Wall, the upback, who pitched out to Savage on his right. Savage then hurled the ball against the grain to Wall, who followed a barricade of crimson jerseys to the end zone.

Midway through the third stanza, the Sooners faced third-and-six at their 25-yard line. Hybl, under a heavy blitz, dumped the ball to Savage, who sailed 75 yards to the end zone.

The Cats responded with another 80-yard scoring marchand added another TD moments later to cut OU's lead to 35-27 as the Sooners blocked the conversion.

The Sooners launched a 71-yard march early in the fourth quarter, but settled for Duncan's 33-yard field goal for a 38-27 advantage with 4:16 remaining. The 16-play drive milked six minutes and 10 seconds off the clock.

The Cats continued to scratch their way back into the game. Quarterback Ell Roberson, who scored the first three Cat TDs, hurled a 57-yard scoring strike to Ricky Lloyd, and Roberson zipped a two-point pass to Aaron Lockett. It was OU 38, KSU 35.

With seven seconds left, Ferguson took an intentional safety by running behind the end zone instead of punting. Ferguson, who averaged 45.5 yards on six punts, had suggested to Stoops that the Sooners should take a safety instead of risking a long punt return. Kansas State was set up at midfield following the free kick and had one play to win the game. Roberson unleashed a "Hail Mary" pass to Lockett in the end zone, but the pass was short and deflected by safety Matt McCoy.

The Wildcats gained 446 total yards, and Oklahoma picked up 325 total yards (only nine on the ground). The Cats were penalized 17 times for 139 yards.

"I believe we got a lot answered about the toughness and character of our team," Stoops said.

American patriotism was at an all-time high after the September 11 terrorist attacks. At some sporting events, fans could be seen wearing patroitic colors. At Oklahoma's Memorial Stadium prior to the Kansas State kickoff, an American flag, 100 yards long, was unfurled as the Pride of Oklahoma band struck up, "You're a Grand Old Flag."

The Sooners and Longhorns both entered the Red River Shootout the next week with identical 4-0 records. Texas, averaging 45 points per game, was ranked fifth in the AP poll. ESPN's *Gameday* broadcast its first pregame show at Fair Park, and ABC televised the showdown. OU won the defensive struggle, 14-3, before another sellout at the Cotton Bowl.

Midway through the second quarter, the Sooners drove 61 yards in 11 plays. White replaced Hybl, who left the game with a sore shoulder. White continued the drive with three passes to receiver Mark Clayton, a pitch out to Griffin who raced for 17 yards, and a quarterback keeper for 11 more yards. From the UT two, White pitched out to Griffin, who crossed the goal line. Duncan's conversion gave the Sooners a 7-0 lead.

The Horns responded with a field goal. The Sooners held a 7-3 advantage during the next 28 minutes.

OU safety Antonio Perkins intercepted Chris Simms' pass in the end zone, ending a Texas threat midway through the fourth stanza. The Sooners stalled after 12 plays to the UT 27. Duncan lined up to kick a 44-yard field goal, but he pooch punted instead. Nathan Vashar caught the punt on a fair catch at the Texas three.

On the next play, Simms dropped back into the end zone, and just as immediately as he dropped back, Williams flew over a Texas blocking back and jarred the forward pass attempt. The ball fell into Teddy Lehman's hands at the two, and the Sooner linebacker crossed the goal line for the touchdown.

Texas began at its own 31 after the kickoff, and Williams picked off Simms' pass at the OU 47 to seal the victory.

The Steers had more total yards (225-206).

White came off the bench and fired four touchdowns, all to Trent Smith, to lead the Sooners to a 38-10 victory over 2-2 Kansas on October 13 in Lawrence.

Oklahoma struggled offensively with Hybl at quarterback. Hybl had completed only five of 11 passes for 15 yards before White spelled him after four Sooner possessions.

The Jayhawks took a 3-0 lead midway through the first period, and Duncan's 38-yard field goal tied the game minutes later. Woolfolk forced a fumble, and Moore recovered on the KU 11 to set up the field goal.

The Sooners scored their go-ahead touchdown early in the second stanza. Facing third-and-one on the KU two-yard line, White faked a handoff, then zipped a scoring strike to Smith for a 10-3 lead after and Duncan kicked the first of five extra points.

The Big Red marched 60 yards in seven plays for a 17-3 lead midway through the second quarter. White tossed a 12-yard scoring strike to Smith.

White zipped a nine-yard pass to Smith for the only tally in the third stanza to cap a 49-yard drive. White sparked the drive with a 35-yard run to the KU 14. White completed an eight-yard TD pass

Roy Williams' teammates congratulate him for his interception that sealed the Sooners' victory over the Longhorns. *(Ronald Martinez/Getty Images)*

to Smith, and Works scored on a nine-yard run in the fourth period.

The Hawks scored the final tally on a 77-yard pass.

OU rolled up 403 total yards. White completed 18 of 29 passes for 151 yards and rushed for 117 more. Smith, who caught 12 passes in the first five games, led receivers with 11 catches for 70 yards. Smith set the school record for most catches in a game. He broke the previous record of 10 receptions held by three players, including Griffin earlier in the year. Smith also broke the school record for most TD receptions in a game, previously held by Jack Lockett in 1950 and Fagan in 2000. The stubborn OU defense forced four turnovers and held the Jayhawks to 223 total yards.

No. 1 Florida lost to Auburn, and Oklahoma rose to second in the AP poll behind Miami, Florida. Baylor was next for the Sooners. The 2-3 Bears posed no threat, dropping a 33-17 decision to the Sooners before a homecoming throng of 75,499 in Norman. OU produced a 27-7 halftime lead and coasted through the second half.

The Sooners took the opening kickoff and rolled 80 yards for a 7-0 lead. White, in his starting debut, fired a 16-yard scoring strike to Fagan, and Duncan kicked the first of three conversions. His final kick was blocked.

Baylor's Randy Davis returned the ensuing kickoff 89 yards for a touchdown to tie the game at 7-7. OU scored the go-ahead TD minutes later, as White's one-yard run capped a 65-yard drive.

Duncan toed a 31-yard field goal, Works scored on a 17-yard run, and Duncan kicked a 19-yard field goal in the second period.

The Bears put up 10 points early in the fourth stanza to trail 27-17. They marched 78 yards for a touchdown and added a field goal moments after recovering Fagan's fumble on the OU 30.

Works scored his second TD on a four-yard run to cap an 80-yard drive for the final tally.

The Sooners picked up 403 total yards, 343 through the air. White completed 32 of 44 passes. Eight Sooners caught passes, led by Clayton's eight receptions for 108 yards. Ferguson averaged 45.5 yards on six punts.

Oklahoma traveled to Lincoln to face 8-0 Nebraska in a nationally televised matchup. The Sooners carried a 20-game winning streak into the game and were ranked second in the AP poll and first in the Bowl Championship Series poll. The Cornhuskers were second in the BCS poll and third in the AP. The winner would be in

The Oklahoma-Texas game is one of the greatest rivalries in college football. For most of the years the game has been played, both teams are in the hunt for a national championship, and since both joined the Big 12 Conference in 1996, the game might determine the conference champion.

Several days prior to the OU-Texas tilt, Texas coach Mack Brown had admitted that his team got complacent before last year's game, a 63-14 rout by the Sooners. Brown had said his team had overlooked OU.

"That caught me by surprise," Bob Stoops said at his weekly press conference four days before the 2001 OU-Texas fray. "How could they overlook us? Overlook us to play who?"

the driver's seat in the south division and for the Big 12 Championship game in Irving, Texas.

Early in the second quarter, White engineered the Sooners from their 23 to the NU 22. He hobbled to the sideline as he completed a 16-yard pass to Griffin. White tore the anterior cruciate ligament in his left knee. Hybl came in to finish the drive, which concluded with his four-yard pass to Smith for the game's first score. Duncan converted. OU 7, NU 0.

Nebraska answered with an 80-yard drive to tie the game and added a field goal for a 10-7 lead with 2:36 to go until intermission.

The Sooners took the kickoff and marched to the NU 20. On first down there, Hybl faked a handoff to Fagan and pitched the ball to Clayton coming from the opposite direction. Clayton stopped and threw back to Hybl, who was open in the right flat, but Hybl slipped on the turf and the pass was short. Oklahoma moved to the Huskers' two but had to settle for Duncan's 20-yard field goal for a 10-10 tie with 15 seconds until halftime.

The Sooner offense sputtered in the second half with only 127 yards in 39 plays and zero points. The Huskers got a field goal early in the third period after picking off Hybl's pass.

Nebraska only had 20 yards on its next three possessions, but struck gold on the fourth. Duncan's punt was killed on the NU four-yard line. Nebraska quickly got out of its hole, then faced third-and-two at its 32. Tommie Harris sacked Crouch for a seven-yard loss, but the Sooners were whistled for a facemask infraction—the officials walked the ball to the NU 37 and a first down for the Huskers.

On the next play, Crouch pitched the ball to receiver Mike Stuntz on a reverse. Stuntz pulled up and sailed a pass back to Crouch, who raced to the end zone with 6:17 remaining.

OU's game plan was to shut down the mighty Husker option attack and they did it well, holding NU to 164 yards rushing. One good play gave Nebraska a 20-10 lead, which was the final tally. The Sooners gained 329 total yards, 10 more than Nebraska.

The loss snapped OU's 20-game winning streak and dropped the Sooners to third in the AP poll.

Oklahoma rebounded the next week with a 58-0 blasting of 1-6 Tulsa in Norman. Griffin scored four TDs, rushed for 90 yards on 11 carries, and caught eight aerials for 72 more.

Two field goals by Duncan gave the Sooners a 6-0 lead through the first 17:13, then Oklahoma exploded for five straight TD drives for a 41-0 advantage; Griffin on the first four. The defense, punt returns, and poor Tulsa punting aided OU's efforts.

The Sooners rolled up 541 total yards and held the Golden Hurricane to 138 yards. Hybl completed 36 of 48 passes for 347 yards. Smith led all receivers with nine receptions for 102 yards. Savage caught seven passes to raise his career total to 103, the third Sooner ever to catch over 100 passes. Brandon Jones returned seven punts for 150 yards, and the Big Red defense sacked TU quarterbacks five times.

Texas A&M arrived in Norman the following week sporting a 7-2 record after winning its first five games. The Aggies jumped to a 10-0 lead in the opening quarter before the No. 3 Sooners settled down and scored 31 unanswered points to win, 31-10.

Duncan's 35-yard field goal got the Sooners on board midway through the second period. Late in the second, A&M punter Cody Scates was back to punt, but Strait and Savage met the Cadet punter the same time as the ball. The two Sooners nailed Scates for a 12-yard loss to the Aggies' 14. Three plays later, Hybl tossed a 13-yard scoring strike to Savage, and Duncan converted for a 10-10 tie.

The Sooners reached into their bag of tricks for the go-ahead touchdown. OU stalled after reaching the A&M 10 and set up for

a field goal. Holder Matt McCoy took the snap and lateraled to Duncan, who swept around right end and dove across the goal line. Duncan also converted for a 17-10 lead.

Hybl added a two-yard TD run and threw an eight-yard scoring strike to Clayton in the fourth period.

Oklahoma gained more total yards, 352-132. The Aggies collected three first downs and 71 yards in the first stanza, but the OU defense held them to two first downs and 61 yards during the final three quarters. Hybl completed 25 of 38 passes for 195 yards and two TDs. Clayton caught four passes and became the all-time freshman record holder with 35 receptions. Calmus had 10 tackles, putting him over the century mark for the third straight year. He was the sixth Sooner to record three consecutive 100-plus tackles in a season.

Hybl fired three touchdown passes on November 17 as No. 3 OU downed Texas Tech, 30-13, in Lubbock. The 6-3 Red Raiders kept it close in the first half, trailing 13-10 at intermission. The Texas Longhorns had an open date, and six Texas players attended the game. They sat behind the OU bench and rooted for the Red Raiders. An Oklahoma loss would put the Longhorns in the drivers' seat for the Big 12 south division. The Steers left before the game concluded.

OU defensive tackle Kory Klein intercepted Tech quarterback Kliff Kingsbury's pass on the third play of the game, but the Sooners had to settle for Duncan's 42-yard field goal for a 3-0 lead. Kingsbury had gone two games without throwing an interception before Klein's pick.

The Raiders tied the game with a field goal after blocking Ferguson's punt minutes later. Duncan's second field goal put Oklahoma ahead, 6-3, early in the second stanza.

The Sooners marched 57 yards in 10 plays on their next series for a 13-3 lead. Hybl shot an eight-yard scoring strike to fullback Chris Toney, and Duncan kicked the first of three conversions. Tech answered with a 76-yard drive in three plays to trail, 13-10.

OU took a 20-10 lead midway in the third quarter when Hybl hurled an eight-yard TD pass to Savage. Hybl passed for 25 yards and rushed for 22 in the 47-yard drive.

Hybl rocketed a 48-yard scoring strike to Clayton for a 27-10 lead with 6:21 remaining in the game two plays after Bary Holleyman recovered Kingsbury's fumble. Tech responded with a field goal, and Duncan kicked his third field goal for the final tally with 2:44 to go.

The Sooners hammered out 384 total yards, 229 in the second half. The defense held the Red Raiders to 247 yards, 178 below their season average. Tech was held to minus-seven yards on the ground. Kingsbury passed for 234 yards, 88 below his season average. Ferguson averaged 45.5 yards on four punts for the Sooners.

Oklahoma State came to Norman the next week sporting a measly 3-7 record and was the underdog by 27 points, but the Cowboys stunned No.4 Oklahoma, 16-13, dashing the Sooners' hopes for a second consecutive Big 12 title and a possible second straight national championship.

The Sooners' offense was sluggish, collecting only 220 total yards against a team that had yielded nearly 478 yards in its last six outings.

Griffin's eight-yard run and Duncan's conversion put the Sooners up 7-0 midway through the second quarter. OSU's Luke Phillips kicked the first of three field goals to close the gap to 7-3 minutes later. Duncan kicked a 23-yard field goal with 53 seconds left, but the Pokes quickly moved within field-goal range, and Phillips booted his career-best 52-yarder and OU led, 10-6, at the break.

Tim Duncan's two field goals against Oklahoma State raised his career total to 44, breaking Tim Lashar's career record of 43 at OU. Trent Smith caught four passes for a career total of 61 receptions, breaking Eddie Hinton's season record high of 60 set in 1968.

Duncan's 22-yard field goal put the Big Red ahead, 13-6, with 8:48 remaining in the game. Phillips matched his career-high field goal 77 seconds later and OSU trailed, 13-9. Minutes later OSU freshman quarterback Josh Fields completed a 14-yard pass to Rashaun Woods with 1:36 to go to drive the final nail in the Sooners' coffin and ending OU's 19-game home winning string. The Cowboys picked up 334 total yards.

The 10th-ranked Sooners accepted their first invitation to play in the Cotton Bowl, a 10 a.m. kickoff on New Year's Day against unranked Arkansas. OU's defense displayed one of the finest games in the history of Oklahoma football. It held the 7-4 Razorbacks to six first downs and only 37 yards in 42 rushing attempts. Arkansas was held to 50 total yards in 55 plays and converted only once in 14 third-down situations. The Razorbacks had averaged 37.8 points in their last five outings.

OU's offense sputtered at times, but the Sooners claimed a 10-3 victory before a bundled-up crowd (it was 35 degrees) of 72,955 in Dallas.

Hybl scored on a one-yard plunge late in the opening quarter, capping a 60-yard, 13 play march following McCoy's interception. The drive consumed six minutes and 34 seconds. Duncan converted.

Another time-consuming drive ended with Duncan's 32-yard field goal midway through the third stanza. The 65-yard, 12-play drive milked 6:15 off the clock from the second-half kickoff. The Razorbacks got on board with a field goal midway through the fourth quarter.

OU gained 231 total yards. The Big Red defense tied a Cotton Bowl record with nine sacks. Hybl set the Cotton Bowl completion record with 24 completions, and Fagan set the punt return record with seven returns. Williams had six tackles, three for a loss and two sacks and was named the game's defensive Most Valuable Player.

2001 Season Record: 11-2-0

Big 12 Conference: 6-2-0
(Second: South Division)

Date	Opponent	Result	Score
August 25	NORTH CAROLINA	W	41-27
September 1	at Air Force	W	44-3
September 8	NORTH TEXAS	W	37-10
September 29	KANSAS STATE	W	38-37
October 6	Texas at Dallas	W	14-3
October 13	at Kansas	W	38-10
October 20	BAYLOR	W	33-17
October 27	at Nebraska	L	20-10
November 3	TULSA	W	58-0
November 10	TEXAS A&M	W	31-10
November 17	at Texas Tech	W	16-13
November 24	OKLAHOMA STATE	L	30-13
January 1	Arkansas*	W	10-3

*Cotton Bowl at Dallas, TX

Griffin had only 56 yards rushing, but caught nine passes and was named the offensive MVP.

The 2001 Sooners finished the season with an 11-2 mark, 6-2 in the Big 12.

Calmus was awarded the Butkus Award as the nation's best linebacker. Williams earned the Jim Thorpe Award, presented to the nation's best defensive back, and the Bronko Nagurski Award, presented to the best defensive player in the country. Calmus, Williams, and Ferguson were named first-team All-Americans as well as the All-Big 12 Conference team. Romero, Harris and Wilkerson were also selected on the All-Big 12 first team.

2002

The 2002 season began with two quarterbacks battling for the starting nod. Nate Hybl started the 2001 season, but Jason White relieved him when Hybl was injured against Texas. When White tore a knee ligament against Nebraska, Hybl stepped back into the role.

Following surgery, White rehabilitated his knee and returned to spring practices in a limited role with no contact, so he was held out of scrimmages. Before the opening game against Tulsa, White won the starting job.

The '02 Sooners were picked number one by many prognosticators, including *Sports Illustrated*, which featured defensive tackle Tommie Harris on the cover of its 2002 College Football Preview issue. "So Good It's Scary" read the cover headline, touting OU's defense.

Most experts would not choose a team to win the national championship that had lost two of it defensive stars from the prior year. Gone were All-Americans linebacker Rocky Calmus, who graduated, and safety Roy Williams, who skipped his senior year and was drafted by the Dallas Cowboys in the National Football League. Still the defense was stout with the likes of veterans in Harris, cornerback Derrick Strait, and linebacker Teddy Lehman. Lehman, a middle linebacker, was moved to the outside. Junior college transfer Lance Mitchell took over as middle linebacker.

The defense also included the return of Brandon Everage at free safety, Jimmie Wilkerson at end, and Andre Woolfolk full time at cornerback. Woolfolk was a wide receiver his first two seasons and played on both sides of the ball in 2001. Coaches decided he was a more valuable asset on the defense for 2002.

Quentin Griffin returned at running back, and Trent Smith was touted as one of the top tight ends in the nation. The offensive line was maturing, and the receiving corps again featured Antwone Savage, Curtis Fagan, and Mark Clayton.

Special teams were a question mark with the loss of punter Jeff Ferguson and placekicker Tim Duncan. Ferguson's brother, Blake, a transfer from the University of North Carolina, stepped into the punter's role. Four walk-ons vied for the placekicking duties, with freshman Trey DiCarlo getting the nod before the first game.

Ranked No.1 in the AP poll and third in the coaches' (USA Today/ESPN) poll, the heavily favored Sooners beat Tulsa, 37-0, in a rare Friday night game (August 30) televised by ESPN. The offense was sluggish in the first half as was evident by the Sooners' 3-0 halftime lead that had some crimson fans scratching their heads.

Receivers dropped five passes, and Smith fumbled inside the Golden Hurricane 10-yard line. White also had a pass intercepted after the Big Red had advanced to the TU two, and Antonio Perkins had a 58-yard punt return erased by a penalty. DiCarlo's 44-yard field goal late in the first period was the only scoring of the first 30 minutes.

The Big Red offense got uncorked, exploding with two touchdowns early in the third quarter and three more TDs in the fourth.

OU wheeled 67 yards to score on its first series of the third quarter. Kejuan Jones scored on an eight-yard run, and DiCarlo converted for a 10-0 lead. Griffin, who rushed for 237 yards on 17 carries, sparked the drive with a 44-yard run.

The Hurrucane punted on their next series, and Perkins thrilled Sooner fans with a 91-yard return for a TD.

Jones, Renaldo Works, and Jerad Estus added touchdowns in the fourth stanza.

OU rolled up 509 total yards, 378 rushing; the most yards on the ground in the Bob Stoops era. The defense held Tulsa to 213 total yards.

OU dropped to #2 in the AP poll but held fast to third in the USA Today/ESPN poll. Attention could now be directed to Alabama coming to Norman the next week.

Sooner Magic: An Attitude to Win

OU and Alabama, rich in college football tradition, had met on the gridiron only twice. The first was in the 1963 Orange Bowl, which followed the 1962 season. Alabama, led by quarterback Joe Namath and coached by Paul "Bear" Bryant, defeated Bud Wilkinson's Sooners, 17-0.

Both teams battled to a 24-all tie in the 1970 Astro-Bluebonnet Bowl. Bryant was still at the helm at Alabama, but Chuck Fairbanks was the OU head coach.

Thirty-two years later, the two teams met in Norman in the Sooners' home opener. The Tide barely beat Middle Tennessee State in its season opener. A Memorial Stadium crowd of 75,564 and a national ABC-TV audience were treated to one whale of a football game.

The Tide kicked off, and to everyone's surprise (except for Alabama's) the kick was onside, and the Tide recovered. OU's defense held Bama to a field goal.

Alabama began at its own 22-yard line on its third possession but managed only four yards in three plays. On the punt attempt, the snap got away from punter Lane Bearden. The ball rolled toward the end zone, and once it reached the goal line, Bearden kicked it through the back line. Safety—two points to OU.

The Tide's kickoff rolled out of bounds, giving OU possession at midfield. Four plays later, White hurled a 32-yard scoring strike to Clayton and DiCarlo nailed the extra point for a 9-3 lead with 6:09 left in the first period.

On OU's next possession, the crowd gasped as White went down, grabbing his right knee. He attempted a keeper off the right side, gained one yard, and collapsed to the turf untouched. His injury nearly a year ago, to his left knee, also occurred without being hit by the opponent. The result was the same—torn anterior cruciate ligament.

Late in the second quarter, Tide running back Antonio Beard picked up 15 yards to the OU 34, but Strait stripped the ball, and Lehman recovered for the Sooners. Tide head coach Dennis Franchione was flagged for unsportsmanlike conduct as he tried to protest to officials that Beard's knee had touched the ground before he fumbled. It was OU's ball on its own 49.

On the next play, Hybl lofted the ball to Clayton, who caught it at the 16 and sprinted to the end zone. He was tackled as he crossed the goal line. DiCarlo added the extra point, and the Sooners led, 16-3, with 2:25 to go until halftime.

The Sooners drove 54 yards for a 23-3 lead on its next series. Hybl sneaked across from a yard out on fourth down and DiCarlo converted as the half ended.

The third quarter and most of the fourth belonged to Alabama. The Tide opened the third period with a 66-yard drive. Minutes later, Ferguson's punt was blocked, and Lance Taylor collected the ball at the OU eight and scored.

Alabama was back in the contest trailing, 23-17. The Tide took a 24-23 lead with a touchdown on a fake field goal, and added a field goal to jump ahead, 27-23, with 3:37 to go.

Alabama's kickoff sailed into the end zone, giving the Sooners 80 yards to work with. On second-and-10 from the OU 20, Hybl shoveled a quick pass to Works, who scampered 24 yards to the 44.

Three plays later, Hybl shot a pass to Savage for 10 yards. Savage lunged for the first down when tackled. On the next play, Works took another shovel pass, eluded Tide tacklers, leaped over OU lineman Brad Davis sprawled on the turf, and raced to the Bama eight.

On the following play, Jones took a handoff and scooted through a gaping hole up the middle and into the end zone. The crimson faithful erupted. DiCarlo added the extra point to give OU a 30-27 advantage with 2:25 remaining.

The Tide was not ready to wave the white flagas they marched into OU territory.

On third-and-five at the OU 43, Bama quarterback Tyler Watts set up to pass, but the pigskin squirted loose as he attempted his release. Sooner safety Eric Bassey scooped the ball off the turf and rocketed 45 yards untouched to the end zone. DiCarlo's foot added another point to give the Sooners a 37-27 lead with 24 seconds left.

"My line just blocked well," Works said about the shovel pass that put OU in scoring position in the fourth quarter. "I just did the best I could. I wanted to help the team come out with a victory. I felt I could get back in the game, but we just needed to attack."

"It's a great comeback win," Stoops said. "Sometimes you have to scramble to win. I appreciate players who find a way to win. In the fourth quarter, you have to have the attitude that you're going to win."

OU hammered out 208 total yards in the first half and held Bama to 64 total yards. The Sooners had minus-five yards in the second half until the winning drive, and the Tide rolled up 224 in the final 30 minutes. Hybl completed 16 of 30 passes for 251 yards.

The Sooners held onto their No. 2 AP ranking and hosted 1-1 Texas El Paso the following week. With White out for the year and backup Brent Rawls unavailable, the Sooners were in need of a another quarterback. The coaching staff decided to remove quarterback Paul Thompson's redshirt status before the UTEP game.

The Miners could not stop OU's explosive offense, but Mother Nature slowed it a little. The Sooners struck as quick as the impending lightning warning. Hybl connected a 56-yard TD pass to Savage on the game's second play.

The lead swelled to 14-0 following Perkins' 50-yard interception for another score. Then the sky opened and deluged Owen Field. A threat of lightning forced a 51-minute delay. Once the storm subsided, the players returned from the locker room, and the Big Red offense continued its assault, scoring four second-quarter TDs.

OU rolled up 549 total yards in the 68-0 victory. Hybl led the way with 13 of 22 passing for 278 yards and two TDs. Griffin rushed for 108 yards on 11 carries and two touchdowns. The defense held UTEP to 219 total yards.

OU hosted 2-1 South Florida on September 28 in the first meeting between both teams. The game also welcomed the return of former Sooner All-America defensive tackle Lee Roy Selmon, who was the Bulls' athletic director at the time.

After a scoreless first quarter, the Sooners scored thrice in the second for a 21-0 lead. Perkins returned a USF punt 82 yards for a score with 11:18 until halftime. Hybl later zipped a three-yard scoring strike to freshman fullback J.D. Runnels and a 23-yard TD pass to Will Peoples.

The Sooners only managed 10 points in the second half, and the Bulls scored two TDs in the final two minutes against mostly reserves on the OU defense.

South Florida gained more total yards, 328-239. The Bulls never lost another game the rest of the year, finishing the '02 season at 9-2.

The Sooners dropped to third in the AP poll and stayed third in the coaches' poll.

Sooner Magic: A Redshirt Shines

Oklahoma invaded 3-1 Missouri in Columbia the night of October 5, and with Texas still a week away, the Sooners could not afford to look past the upstart Tigers.

Two redshirt freshmen highlighted the game. MU quarterback Brad Smith shredded the OU defense for 391 yards (213 rushing and 178 passing). He tossed two TD passes and ran for another score. Smith had experience under his belt, earning the starting nod at the beginning of the season. The other redshirt freshman, Chris Chester, OU's fourth-string tight end, played briefly against Tulsa and rode the bench during the next three games. His first career catch will be a story he can tell his grandchildren.

DiCarlo added a 20-yard field goal midway through the second quarter after Brandon Shelby picked off Smith's pass.

OU took a 7-0 lead late in the first period. Jones' two-yard blast up the middle capped a 50-yard drive and DiCarlo tool the extra point.

Smith scored on a 25-yard jaunt minutes later to pull the Tigers within three, 10-7, which remained until intermission.

The Sooners drove 79 yards in four plays for a 17-7 lead early in the third stanza. On third-and-five from his 35, Hybl connected on a sideline pass to Fagan, who streaked to the end zone.

Griffin scored on a 53-yard run to give Oklahoma a 23-7 advantage midway in the third quarter. DiCarlo missed the extra-point try. The Tigers answered with a 77-yard TD march and added a field goal on their next possession. OU 23, Missouri 17.

DiCarlo missed a 43-yard field goal early in the fourth period and the Tigers drove 74 yards for a 24-23 lead with 10:22 to go in the game.

Everage later intercepted Smith's pass at the Tigers' 16-yard line. Works picked up two yards, but Hybl misfired on the next two passes. It was fourth-and-eight at the MU 14.

Stoops elected to go for a field goal in hopes of regaining the lead. Backup strong safety Matt McCoy was the holder on field goals and extra points. As DiCarlo approached the snap, McCoy rose up, and DiCarlo sprinted to the right—a trick play designed to lob a pass to DiCarlo, who was wide open. Instead, McCoy fired the pigskin down the middle to Chester, who was shrouded by two Tiger defenders. Chester clutched the pass in the end zone.

Stoops ordered a two-point conversion to get a seven-point lead and not chance Missouri winning by one on a possible comeback. Hybl, who completed 20 of 32 passes for 303 yards, connected a pass to Fagan, and the Sooners led 31-24 with 6:33 remaining in the game.

Bassey ended Missouri's ensuing drive with an interception at the OU 36. The Sooners had to punt, and the Tigers got one more chance with 1:39 to go. Missouri moved 42 yards to the OU 35. Smith gained 28 yards in the drive, including a crucial five-yard pickup on fourth-and-four at the OU 44. Smith was an outstanding runner who had already rushed for 214 yards. But after MU

called a timeout, Smith went to the air on the next three plays. Two fell incomplete and one was good for only four yards.

On fourth-and-six from the OU 35, Shelby and end Dan Cody nailed Smith for a one-yard loss to finish off the Tigers.

"It's something we prepared for all week, and something we always do," Chester said of the fake field goal. "It was a pretty gutsy call, and I'm really excited about making the catch, especially because I bobbled it a bit."

"We needed to do it," Stoops said. "It had to be done. . . . I refuse to be afraid of criticism.

"I didn't feel that any kickers were kicking very well off the grass as high and as wet as it was. I felt that the opportunity was there, not just to Chester, but the kicker would have been wide open, too. I did not want to leave it in the hands of a young kicker."

Mizzou collected 449 total yards, six more than the Sooners. Griffin rushed for 105 yards.

The Sooners' eyes could now be directed south to Texas. The Big Red rose to second in the AP poll, one notch above the Longhorns and one below Miami, Florida. The Hurricanes were in a dog fight with Florida State (during an earlier kickoff), and Sooners fans kept an eye on the scoreboard updates. Miami won 28-27, much to the chagrin of the Sooners.

The Longhorns had been smarting from two consecutive losses to the Sooners. The past two Oklahoma victories were when both teams had hopes of a national championship. OU won its seventh crown in 2000, and the Horns were looking for their fourth overall, and first since 1970.

The 5-0 Steers had blasted their first four opponents by a combined 169-32 then eeked out a 17-15 win over Oklahoma State the week before the OU tilt.

Texas took a 7-0 lead late in the first period, and moments later, DiCarlo toed a 29-yard field goal to cut OU's deficit to 7-3.

Rod Babers intercepted Hybl's pass and raced 73 yards for a 14-3 Steer lead with 1:43 until halftime. Savage returned the ensuing kickoff 81 yards to the UT 16-yard line. Hybl tossed a three-yard TD pass to Smith with five seconds before halftime. Stoops ordered a two-point conversion, which was successful when Hybl tossed a strike to Fagan. Momentum: Sooners, although they trailed 14-11.

A field goal early in the third period put UT up 17-11, then OU scored 24 unanswered points en route to a 35-24 victory. Griffin rushed for 137 of his 248 yards in the second half and scored two touchdowns. Griffin scored nine TDs against the Horns from 2000-2002.

Both teams added a field goal in the third stanza, then Teddy Lehman's interception on the UT 38 early in the fourth set up the Sooners' go-ahead score. Seven plays later, Hybl fired a pass to Will Peoples, who streaked toward the goal line, but he dropped the pigskin at the two. Fortunately Griffin was trailing behind and scooped it up and walked into the end zone.

Jones scored on a two-yard run, and Griffin's 17-yard run gave Oklahoma a 35-17 lead. Texas added another TD late in the game.

OU amassed 397 total yards and held the Horns to 209. The defense frustrated Texas quarterback Chris Simms as it had done the past several years. The Sooner defense picked off three of his passes and sacked him four times.

It's a Fact

OU became the first "road" team to win the Big 12 championship and the first south division team to win in a southern division city.

Iowa State quarterback Seneca Wallace was touted as the front runner for the Heisman Trophy by the time the ninth-ranked Cyclones arrived in Norman on October 19. The Sooner defense sent him home as an also ran with a 49-3 shellacking of the Cyclones in a downpour and before 75,201 homecoming fans. Iowa State could manage only 60 total yards in 45 plays. Wallace threw three interceptions, two of them into the hands of Everage.

Wallace, who had completed 65 percent of his passes in the first six games, completed only four of 22 for 43 yards.

Backup corner back Terrance Simms blocked the Cyclones punt on the first series. The ball spun into the end zone, and Simms smothered it for a touchdown. Griffin, who rushed for 111 yards, scored the next two touchdowns, and Jones scored the next two. Jones easily scored his TDs out of the "Jumbo" set, the I-formation with two tight ends.

Trailing 35-0 in the second quarter, the Cyclones got a chance to score when they recovered Perkins' fumbled punt return on the OU one-yard line. The Big Red defense put the clamps down as they pushed I-State back three yards on the next three plays, and Wallace misfired on the fourth-down pass.

Iowa State did get a field goal in the third stanza, but the Sooners put the game away with two more touchdowns in the same period. Hybl hurled a 22-yard scoring strike to Brandon Jones, and Works scored on an 11-yard run.

Oklahoma rolled up 367 total yards, and the defense kept the Cyclones from converting a single first down on 13 third-down situations.

Oklahoma was ranked atop the Bowl Championship Series poll, a combination of human and computer rankings to determine national championship contenders. Still OU held the No.2 spot in the AP and coaches' polls.

The Sooners met their third straight ranked opponent in No. 13 Colorado on another cold, drizzly game the next week in Norman. The 6-2 Buffaloes also had a Heisman candidate in tailback Chris Brown. The Sooners won the game, 27-11, but Brown rushed for 103 yards, the first runningback to rush for over 100 yards against Oklahoma in four seasons.

The Sooners capitalized on three Buff turnovers (two fumbles and one interception) to score 20 points in the first half.

On the game's fourth play, Mitchell forced Brown to fumble, and Strait recovered on the CU 39-yard line. Hybl hurled a 17-yard scoring strike to Savage six plays later and DiCarlo converted for a 7-0 lead.

The Buffs intercepted Hybl's pass minutes later but had to settle for a field goal. DiCarlo toed a 22-yard field goal on the next possession to put the Big Red up 10-3.

Early in the second stanza, Everage intercepted a Buff pass and raced 64 yards to the CU 14. The Sooners settled for another DiCarlo field goal, this time from 25 yards out for a 13-3 lead. Colorado failed to field DiCarlo's high kickoff, and Savage recovered on the CU 24. Six plays later, Hybl fired a 17-yard TD pass to Clayton for a 20-3 lead after DiCarlo converted.

Lehman intercepted a pass on the Buffs' first series of the second half and returned it 31 yards to the CU nine. Two plays and a penalty later, Hybl again hooked up with Clayton for a 12-yard scoring strike and a 27-3 advantage. Colorado later scored after intercepting Hybl's pass.

Colorado had more total yards, 378-305. Griffin rushed for 128 yards on 21 carries. Everage had 17 tackles and two pass deflections in addition to his interception. He also ended a Buffalo threat in the fourth quarter by stopping them short of a first down at the OU eight-yard line.

Oklahoma returned to the top of the polls, then dropped a 30-26 decision to 5-4 Texas A&M on November 9. The Aggies inserted their second-string quarterback, Reggie McNeal, a scrambler like Brad Smith of Missouri, who gave the Sooner defense fits. He rushed for 89 yards and only completed 8 of 13 passes for 191 yards, but half of his completions burned the OU secondary for touchdowns.

The Sooners took a 10-0 lead on Griffin's six-yard run in the first quarter and DiCarlo's 25-yard field goal early in the second. McNeal hurled his first scoring bomb moments later, but DiCarlo toed another field goal with 1:28 until halftime. McNeal's second scoring strike tied the game at 13-13 with seven seconds until intermission.

McNeal's third TD pass early in the third period put the Aggies ahead, 20-13. Oklahoma answered with a 68-yard scoring strike from Hybl to Fagan. DiCarlo booted a 46-yard field goal on the next OU series to give the Sooners a 23-20 advantage.

McNeal's fourth scoring strike late in the third quarter put A&M up 27-23. Both teams traded field goals through the first half of the fourth stanza.

The Sooners had a final chance in the waning moments, but Hybl's pass was picked off at the Aggies' 43 with 1:12 left in the game. The loss dropped Oklahoma to fourth in the AP poll and BCS polls and sixth in the coaches' poll. Texas was tied with OU in the AP poll as both teams had 1,590 points.

OU's left guard, Brad Davis, suffered a broken fibula and was sidelined the rest of the year. Freshman Kelvin Chaisson replaced him in the starting lineup.

Griffin rushed for 152 yards and scored four touchdowns on November 16 in a 49-9 blasting of 3-7 Baylor in Waco. Strait also had two interceptions, returning one 75 yards for a score midway through the fourth period. Oklahoma only had possession of the ball for 22 minutes and 36 seconds but made the most of the little time.

The Sooners rolled up 401 total yards and didn't turn over the ball once. They needed only 11 plays to put up three touchdowns in their first three possessions in the third quarter. OU took the second-half kickoff and drove 43 yards in three plays, marched 43 yards in five plays and 66 yards in three plays.

The Bears picked up 378 total yards.

The Sooners hosted another Heisman candidate the next week— Texas Tech quarterback Kliff Kingsbury. No. 4 OU defeated the 24th-ranked Red Raiders, 60-15. Oklahoma's defense stymied Kingsbury, who completed only 15 of 35 passes and threw two interceptions. OU capitalized off each interception driving 61 and 44 yards to pay dirt.

The Big Red took the opening kickoff and wheeled 70 yards for a 7-0 lead. Kejuan Jones' 10-yard scamper capped the 10-play drive, and DiCarlo kicked the first of eight conversions.

The 8-4 Red Raiders were held to three and out on their first possession and punted to the OU 38. Griffin exploded for a 62-yard TD run on the next play to set the rout in motion. Griffin, who rushed for 207 yards, scored two more touchdowns.

Oklahoma rolled to a 46-0 lead, including two safeties, before Tech got on the board in the third period. The first safety occurred late in the first quarter when Wilkerson sacked Kingsbury for a seven-yard loss. The Raiders were backed up to their three-yard line just before halftime, and a holding penalty gave the Sooners two more points.

Tech scored its first touchdown on a 98-yard kickoff return late in the third period.

The Sooners outgained Tech, 478-236.

The Sooners clinched the Big 12 South division and would meet Colorado (North division champs) in a rematch December 7 in Houston for the Big 12 Championship.

Oklahoma State put a damper in OU's national title hopes for the second straight year. Quarterback Josh Fields completed 18 of 37 passes for 397 yards and four TDs, as the 6-5 Cowboys dropped the third-ranked Sooners, 38-28, in Stillwater. Split end Rashaun Woods, who caught a school-record 12 passes for 226 yards, was a recipient of three of those TD passes. Oklahoma's defense never put any pressure on Fields in the game.

OSU rolled up a 28-6 lead in the first half. The Sooners fought back on three Hybl touchdown passes (once to Brandon Jones and twice to Smith), but the deficit was too much to make up. OU never led in the game, a first under Stoops' four-year career.

The Pokes gained more total yards, 506-333.

OU dropped to eighth in the AP poll, ninth in the USA Today/ESPN poll, and seventh in the BCS standings. Fans grew concerned about the Sooner defense, especially the secondary giving up eight passes for touchdowns in the last two games. But, OU rebounded in the Big 12 Championship game with a 29-7 decision over the 12th-ranked Buffaloes at Houston's Reliant Stadium. Colorado had beaten Missouri, Iowa State, and Nebraska since their loss to the Sooners earlier in the season.

The Sooners led 13-0 on two Hybl passes in the first half, the first to Smith and the next to Clayton. The Buffs blocked DiCarlo's second conversion.

Colorado cut the Sooners' lead to 13-7 early in the third period when Jeremy Bloom returned Ferguson's punt 80 yards. Griffin's 36-yard scoring jaunt put OU up 19-7, but Hybl misfired on the two-point pass.

DiCarlo kicked a field goal midway through the fourth stanza, and Griffin scored on a 27-yard run minutes later for the final tally.

The Sooners rolled up 401 total yards and held the Buffaloes to 193. Griffin broke the Big 12 Championship title game rushing record with 188 yards. Neither team turned the ball over.

Oklahoma, out of the national championship picture, got a nice consolation prize—its first invitation to the Rose Bowl. Seventh-ranked Washington State (10-2) was the Sooners' opponent. The Cougars' head coach, Mike Price, had accepted the head coaching position at Alabama beginning in the 2003 season. Price returned to coach WSU in the Rose Bowl as co-head coach with Bill Doba, the Cougars' defensive coordinator, who was promoted to head coach.

From 1947-2000, the Rose Bowl was a matchup between the winners of the Pacific 10 and Big Ten Conferences, but that ended in 2001 when the Rose Bowl joined the BCS bowl lineup. Many traditionalists did not feel the Sooners should have been invited to the "Grandaddy" of all bowls. ABC-TV play-by-play announcer Keith Jackson, a Washington State alumnus, told the *USA Today* that OU's presence "aggravates the hell out of us on the West Coast."

The eighth-ranked Sooners showed that they belonged in the oldest bowl game by blasting Jackson's alma mater, 34-14, on New Year's Day in Pasadena, California. OU jumped to a 17-0 halftime lead and extended it to 27-0 before the 10-2 Cougars scored in the fourth quarter.

DiCarlo's 45-yard field goal gave Oklahoma a 3-0 lead. Hybl tossed a 12-yard scoring strike to Savage on the next OU series. Perkins' 51-yard punt return put the Sooners ahead, 17-0, and DiCarlo toed a 30-yard field goal to up the lead to 20-0 midway through the third period.

The Sooners marched 66 yards in 11 plays for a 27-0 advantage midway through the final stanza. Hybl completed the drive with a nine-yard strike to Fagan. The Cougars responded with a 79-yard scoring drive.

With more than three minutes remaining, Jonathan Jackson sacked WSU quarterback Jason Gesser for a 14-yard loss. Gesser fumbled and Dusty Dvoracek recovered on the WSU 23. Three

Andre Woolfolk (17), Trent Smith (88), Quentin Griffin (22) and Nate Hybl (8) proudly display the Rose Bowl trophy after the Sooners pummeled Washington State in the Rose Bowl. Athletic director Joe Castiglione beams with Sooner pride in the background. *(Jeff Gross/Getty Images)*

2002 Season Record: 12-2-0
Big 12 Conference: 7-2-0 (Champions)

Date	Opponent	Result	Score
August 30	at Tulsa	W	37-0
September 7	ALABAMA	W	37-27
September 14	TEXAS EL PASO	W	68-0
September 28	SOUTH FLORIDA	W	31-14
October 5	at Missouri	W	31-24
October 12	Texas at Dallas	W	35-24
October 19	IOWA STATE	W	49-3
November 2	COLORADO	W	27-11
November 9	at Texas A&M	L	30-26
November 16	at Baylor	W	49-9
November 23	TEXAS TECH	W	60-15
November 30	at Oklahoma State	L	38-28
December 7	Colorado*	W	29-7
January 1	Washington State#	W	34-14

*Big 12 Championship at Houston, TX
#Rose Bowl at Pasadena, CA

plays later, Griffin scored from the 19. He carried the ball all three times in the drive.

The Cougars' Sammy Moore returned the ensuing kickoff 89 yards for the final tally.

Oklahoma collected 386 total yards. Griffin rushed for 144 yards, his 10th-straight 100-plus game. His season total of 1,740 yards placed him second on the all-time Sooner rushing list, 22 yards behind Billy Sims' season record. Hybl was named the game's Most Valuable Player by completing 19 of 29 passes for 240 yards and two TDs.

The Sooner defense held the Cougars to a season-low 243 total yards. The Cougars' four rushing yards were the fewest allowed by an OU team in bowl history. The previous low was 27 yards by Florida State in the 2001 Orange Bowl.

Oklahoma ended the season with a 12-2 mark, 6-2 in the Big 12 conference.

Everage, Lehman and Harris were named All-Americans. Jamaal Brown, Griffin, Smith, and Strait joined them on the All-Big 12 Conference first team. The ABC network named Lehman its Chevrolet Defensive Player of the Year.

2003

After coming close to winning an eighth national championship the past two years, Sooner fans, coaches and players were craving another title.

With the return of seven starters on offense and eight on defense, the Sooners would once again be in the Big 12 and national title hunt in '03.

The offense would have to find replacements at quarterback, tight end, and running back. Jason White was named starting quarterback for the season in early summer, ending speculation as to who, among four candidates, would get the nod. White had the most experience though it was limited. He started in only six games but had plenty of playing time. The big question among Sooner faithful was, "Would his knees hold up?"

Renaldo Works and Kejuan Jones shared duties at running back. Lance Donley's experience as a backup in 2002 put him solidly in the lead at tight end. Center Vince Carter and tackles Jamaal Brown and Wes Sims presented ample experience on the line.

Mark Clayton and Brandon Jones would return to lead a solid corps of receivers.

Nine players returned on defense, including tackle Tommie Harris, who was hampered with a groin injury in 2002. Depth was no worry at the tackle slots as Kory Klein, Dusty Dvoracek, and Lynn McGruder had plenty of starting experience. Jonathan Jackson and Dan Cody were solid at the end positions.

Linebackers Teddy Lehman and Lance Mitchell returned, but Mitchell would be lost for the season with a knee injury in the fourth game. Cornerback Derrick Strait returned to lead a deep secondary that included Brandon Everage, Eric Bassey, Antonio Perkins, Matt McCoy, and cornerback Derrick Strait.

Trey DiCarlo returned for placekicking duties, and Blake Ferguson was back for the punting chores.

Oklahoma was tabbed preseason No. 1 by the AP and ESPN/USA Today polls for the first time since 1987. OU held the top spot all season before losing in the Big 12 Championship game. The Sooners had never lost in eight season openers when ranked at the top spot, and North Texas would be the ninth victim to open the 2003 season. Oklahoma dropped the Mean Green, 37-3, on August 30 before a record crowd of 83,073 at Gaylord Family Oklahoma Memorial Stadium.

Wide receiver Mark Clayton and defensive tackle Lynn McGruder were returning to Norman from Texas on June 1 when they witnessed a fatal car crash on Interstate 35 about 20 minutes south of Norman. A southbound car came across the median and struck a van, trapping a family of five inside.

Clayton and McGruder broke the windows of the van and dragged out each family member to safety.

"We wanted to make sure everyone was okay," Clayton said.

Each family member lived, but the driver of the car died, and her sister was critically injured.

A year later, the Big 12 Conference's panel of administrators and media honored Clayton and McGruder for their heroic effort. Several years earlier, the conference began recognizing athletes who have displayed good sportsmanship and ethical conduct outside of the sports arena.

"Nothing compares to when you help another human being," Clayton remarked.

The Sooner players wore throwback uniforms to honor the Bud Wilkinson era—crimson jerseys with stripes on the shoulders and white helmets with a single crimson stripe down the middle. The coaches wore shirts similar to what coaches wore during the Barry Switzer era.

DiCarlo nailed the first of three field goals to give OU a 3-0 lead early in the first period. Midway through the opening quarter, Strait set up the first touchdown by hammering UNT's Ja'Mel Branch waiting to retrieve a punt. Branch was hit just as the ball descended into his hands, and Jowahn Poteat recovered for the Sooners at the UNT 23. White connected a three-yard TD pass to Jejuan Rankins four plays later to up the Sooners' lead to 10-0.

White tossed two scoring strikes, one to Brandon Jones for a 17-0 lead, and the other to Travis Wilson for a 30-0 advantage.

Rankins scored his second touchdown when he hauled in backup quarterback Paul Thompson's seven-yard strike minutes later for the final tally.

The Sooners gained 391 total yards. White completed 23 of 35 passes for 248 yards. The Big Red defense handcuffed the Mean Green all night long, yielding 11 first downs and 154 total yards. North Texas had only 50 total yards through three quarters.

The Sooners traveled to Tuscaloosa, Alabama, the next week for only the fourth meeting between the two tradition-rich teams. OU dropped 1-0 Alabama, 20-13, before a sold-out crowd of 83,818 at Bryant-Denny Stadium, which included approximately 7,000 Sooner fans.

Perkins intercepted Brodie Croyle's pass on the game's first play at the Bama 33, but the Sooners had to settle for a 34-yard DiCarlo field goal for a 3-0 lead. DiCarlo added another field goal later in the first stanza to lift OU to a 6-0 advantage.

The Tide kicked a field goal late in the second period then OU retaliated two plays after the ensuing kickoff. White fired a screen pass to receiver Mark Bradley, who raced 35 yards to the Bama 46. Bradley is the son of Danny Bradley, who started at quarterback for the Sooners in 1984. On the next play, White went upstairs again, this time a 46-yard bomb to Clayton for the touchdown. DiCarlo kicked the first of two conversions.

Bama marched 80 yards in the third quarter to cut the gap to 13-10.

Oklahoma answered again but had to reach into its bag of tricks. The Sooners stalled in three plays following the Tide kickoff and faced fourth-and-10 from their 31. Ferguson, who averaged 48.6 yards per punt, set up for another punt but instead lobbed a pass to Michael Thompson who sprinted 22 yards for the first down.

On the next play, White launched a 47-yard TD bomb to Brandon Jones for a 20-10 lead.

The Tide threatened after the kickoff by moving from its 21 to the OU 30, but safety Donte Nicholson intercepted Croyle's pass at the four.

Bama kicked a 36-yard field goal with 1:32 left in the game and then tried an onside kick. Wilson recovered it, and the Sooners killed the clock.

Oklahoma had more total yards, 355-303. Jason White, whose season ended with an injury against Alabama in 2002, completed 21 of 35 passes for 259 yards and no interceptions. As a matter of fact, OU didn't turn the ball over once.

The victory gave the Sooners a 2-1-1 edge in the overall series.

White tossed four touchdown passes, and Renaldo Works ran for two more as OU dropped 1-1 Fresno State, 52-28, before a crowd of 83,091 (another new record) on September 13 in Norman.

The Sooners scored on their first six possessions en route to a 38-0 halftime lead.

DiCarlo's 41-yard field goal put OU ahead 3-0 on the opening drive.

The Sooners scored touchdowns on their next five possessions. White hurled scoring strikes to J. D. Runnels, Brandon Jones, and Clayton, and Works added a TD run.

White, who completed 25 of 37 passes for 338 yards, was 18 of 25 for 256 yards in the first half. The Big Red defense held the Bulldogs to 23 total yards and one first down in the first half.

Fresno State got on the board midway in the third stanza then OU scored again when White tossed a 14-yard strike to Donley early in the fourth. White's 22-yard pass to Clayton on third-and-five kept the 76-yard drive alive for a first down at the FSU 36.

The Bulldogs answered with a touchdown, and the Sooners responded with a four-yard TD run by Thompson. Thompson sparked the 80-yard drive with a 50-yard run to the FSU 20. The Bulldogs scored two more touchdowns against the reserve defense.

OU gained 32 first downs and 556 total yards. The Bulldogs collected 265 total yards. Mitchell was lost for the season with a knee injury in the second period. Freshman Lewis Baker assumed Mitchell's duties the rest of the game, but Wayne Chambers got the starting nod against 1-1 UCLA the following week in Norman.

The last time the Bruins came to Norman in 1986, OU was also the top-ranked team in the country and won, 38-3. The Sooners also easily defeated UCLA, 34-14, in 1990, the only other meeting between the two teams. This year was no different as Oklahoma dropped the Bruins, 59-24, before yet another record crowd (83,317).

Strait sat out with a pulled thigh muscle, ending a streak of 43 straight starts.

Perkins broke two NCAA records for punt returns in the game. He returned three Bruin punts for touchdowns and 277 yards. He broke the previous record of 219 yards set by Golden Richards at Brigham Young in 1971. No player had ever returned three punts for a touchdown in one game.

Works' 15-yard TD run midway through the first stanza and DiCarlo's conversion gave Oklahoma a 7-0 advantage.

Jonathan Jackson sprints to the end zone after intercepting a Texas pass in the second quarter.
(Ronald Martinez/Getty Images)

The Bruins scored a field goal and a touchdown on their next two possessions, and the Sooners trailed for the first time in the young season, 10-7.

The Sooners scored three touchdowns in the second period; twice on Perkins' punt returns. White completed a 12-yard TD pass to Wilson early in the quarter to cap an 80-yard march. White completed a 43-yard pass to Clayton one play before the score. White was under pressure by Bruin defenders but threw off his back foot, and Clayton caught the ball between two defenders.

Less than two minutes later, Perkins took a UCLA punt and sailed 76 yards to the end zone. About six minutes later, Perkins set sail 84 yards for another return to put OU up, 28-10, at the half.

Early in the third quarter, Bassey hammered Manuel White, forcing the Bruin to fumble. Harris grabbed the loose pigskin and carried it 14 yards to the UCLA 30. White then hurled a 22-yard TD pass to Donley three plays later. DiCarlo's conversion gave the Sooners a 35-10 lead.

The Bruins answered with a 76-yard scoring drive. Oklahoma's defense stopped UCLA three times at the goal line. The Sooners stuffed Bruin quarterback Drew Olson at the line of scrimmage on fourth down, but the ball squirted backwards, and halfback Maurice Drew scooped it up and scored.

The Bruins intercepted White's pass late in the third period at the Bruin 27. Two plays later, Bassey intercepted a pass tipped by Everage and raced 34 yards untouched to the end zone.

Drew raced 91 yards for a UCLA touchdown on the ensuing kickoff.

The Sooners answered with a one-yard TD run by Works early in the fourth quarter. DiCarlo nailed a 41-yard field goal midway in the period, then minutes later, Perkins made history with a 65-yard punt return.

Oklahoma gained 354 total yards and UCLA picked up 271 total yards.

The Sooners traveled to Ames on October 4 to meet 2-2 Iowa State in the conference opener. OU easily dispatched the Cyclones, 53-7.

White continued his passing assault with five TD strikes, equaling the mark twice set by Josh Heupel in 1999. DiCarlo's 32-yard field goal midway through the opening period put the Sooners up, 3-0, then the Sooners lit up the scoreboard with three TDs in the second stanza. White fired a scoring strike to Rankins and Bradley, and two to Clayton.

The Cyclones scored moments later when Jamain Billups intercepted Thompson's pass and raced 77 yards to the end zone. Bradley returned the ensuing kickoff 100 yards for another Sooner score. The return equaled Buster Rhymes' school record set in 1980. DiCarlo's conversion put Oklahoma up 46-7.

Donta Hickson's five-yard TD was the final tally late in the game, and DiCarlo converted.

The Sooners gained 35 first downs and 613 total yards. White completed 26 of 34 passes for 384 yards. The Cyclones gained 10 first downs and 234 total yards.

The No. 1 Sooners traveled to Dallas on October 11 for the 98th edition of the Red River rivalry. Texas, 4-1, lost to Arkansas early in the season. Oklahoma annihilated the 11th-ranked Longhorns, 65-13, before the 58th straight sellout of 75,287 at the Cotton Bowl.

White completed 17 of 21 passes for 290 yards and four touchdowns. Works scored two TDs and DiCarlo kicked three field goals.

Oklahoma had a touchdown within the first 34 seconds of the game. Strait intercepted Chance Mock's pass at the Steers' 35 on the game's third play and weaved his way to the six. Works carried across the goal line on the next play, and DiCarlo converted. Texas had not thrown an interception in its first five games.

Texas later tied the game at 7-7 after recovering Perkins' fumbled punt return.

Leading 37-13 at halftime, Oklahoma's offense continued its assault with four touchdowns in the second half, and the defense shut out the Longhorns.

Clayton caught eight passes for 190 yards, breaking the team records for most receiving yards in a game. Cory Warren held that mark since 1992 when he had 187 yards against Texas.

Oklahoma returned to Norman on October 18 for a homecoming tilt against 5-1 Missouri. The Tigers were fresh off an upset over No. 10 Nebraska. The Sooners won, 34-13, by scoring three second-quarter touchdowns to break a 10-all tie. The sold-out crowd of 83,327 was yet another record crowd at the Gaylord Family-Oklahoma Memorial Stadium.

Works' one-yard leap into the end zone and DiCarlo's toe put Oklahoma ahead, 7-0, midway through the first stanza.

The Tigers answered with a field goal moments later.

OU drove 90 yards to the Missouri two early in the second period but had to settle for DiCarlo's 19-yard field goal for a 10-3 advantage. The Tigers answered with a 76-yard scoring drive to tie the game at 10 all.

Perkins later returned a Tiger punt 28 yards to the MU 39. White hooked up with Clayton for a touchdown on the next play. Clayton leaped above a Tiger to grab the ball in the end zone. DiCarlo's conversion gave the Sooners a 17-10 lead.

OU moved 82 yards in six plays for another score. Facing fourth-and-six at the MU 39, White rifled a pass to Rankins at the 26, and Rankins shed four tacklers to the end zone. DiCarlo toed the extra point.

Missouri stalled and punted to Perkins, who fielded the ball at OU's 31 and flew to the end zone. Bradley threw a key block on the play. DiCarlo converted, and the Sooners took a 31-10 lead to the locker room. Perkins' seventh career return for a touchdown tied him with four other players, including OU's Jack Mitchell, who returned seven from 1946-1948.

DiCarlo added a 30-yard field goal late in the third stanza, and Missouri kicked a field goal late in the game.

The Sooners rolled up 424 total yards. White completed 20 of 34 passes for 278 yards. The Tigers gained 266 total yards. Mizzou quarterback Brad Smith, who ran for 213 yards against Oklahoma a year earlier, was held to 50 rushing yards. The Big Red defense

held him to minus-seven yards rushing in the second half and sacked him five times in the game.

Chambers, who replaced Mitchell earlier in the year, was sidelined with a twisted ankle. Junior Gayron Allen replaced him and then moved ahead of Chambers the rest of the year.

OU traveled to Boulder the next week to meet Colorado. The 3-4 Buffaloes were not the same team as a year earlier when they won the Big XII's north division. The Sooners escaped the Rocky Mountains with a 34-20 victory, the first win in Boulder since 1988.

OU jumped to a 14-0 first-quarter lead, and it appeared a rout was on, but turnovers and trick plays kept the Buffaloes in the game.

The Big Red scored quickly on its first possession, a 54-yard bomb from White to Brandon Jones that came on the Sooners' third play from scrimmage. DiCarlo converted. The Sooners extended their opening possession scoring streak to eight games.

Works' two-yard TD run capped a 70-yard drive in four plays on the next OU series. Works gained 38 yards to spark the drive on the first play, and the Buffs were penalized 15 yards for a facemask infraction on the play, moving the pigskin to the CU 17. Works scored four plays later, and DiCarlo toed the extra point.

The Buffs marched 56 yards to trail, 14-7, late in the first period.

Colorado advanced to the OU eight early in the second stanza after recovering Hickson's fumble at the Sooner 35. Daniel Jolley then fumbled, and Nicholson scooped up the ball at the goal line and carried at back for 11 yards.

DiCarlo booted a couple of field goals to put Oklahoma ahead, 20-7. The second kick came after the Sooners drove 77 yards and consumed six and a half minutes following the second-half kickoff.

OU advanced to the Buffs' four moments after Perkins picked off Joel Klatt's pass, but Works then spilled the ball, and Colorado recovered.

White sailed a 15-yard TD pass to Clayton late in the third quarter to cap a 39-yard march in four plays. DiCarlo converted, and OU held a 27-7 lead. It was Clayton's eighth TD reception this season, breaking Curtis Fagan's record of seven in 2000.

Colorado answered with a touchdown. Oklahoma's defense had forced the Buffs to punt, but punter John Torp found a gap in the defense and raced 20 yards to a first down at the OU 49. Perkins picked off Klatt's pass seven plays later, but Oklahoma was penalized for holding to keep the Colorado drive alive. The Buffs scored on the next play.

The Buffaloes scored on their next series, but Brodney Pool leaped into the air and blocked the conversion. OU held a 27-20 advantage with 5:03 remaining.

All the Sooners would have to do is keep the ball on the ground and milk the clock with first downs. Kejuan Jones gained nine and three yards on the next two carries for a first down. He gained one yard, then caught White's pass for three more to the OU 41. On third-and-six, White dumped a three-yard pass to Clayton, who weaved his way through Buffalo defenders to the end zone. DiCarlo toed the 34th point.

Oklahoma gained more total yards, 434-227. Colorado had 40 net rushing yards as the defense sacked Klatt seven times for a loss of 36 yards.

White completed 19 of 28 passes for 248 yards and three TDs. Although he was poked in the eye midway through the third stanza, White still completed six of nine passes for 116 yards and two TDs.

Oklahoma vs. Oklahoma State on November 1 was the one game nearly every person in crimson had pointed to. The Sooners lost two

It's a Fact

Oklahoma's 65-13 victory over Texas was the largest margin in the 98-year history of the rivalry, eclipsing a 50-point margin Oklahoma laid on the Horns in 1908. OU's 65 points also set a new record for most points in the series, edging 63 points scored in 2000. The win also made the first time in school history that the Sooners scored more than 50 points in four consecutive games in a season.

straight to the Cowboys, and each time the Sooners were removed from the national championship hunt. The Pokes came into Norman ranked 14th in the AP poll, having lost only to Nebraska in their season opener.

ESPN Gameday TV and radio crews were in Norman for the pregame broadcasts.

The top-ranked Sooners routed Oklahoma State, 52-9, before yet another record crowd of 84,027 and a regional TV (ABC) audience.

OU failed to score on its opening drive for the first time all year, but took a 3-0 lead moments later. Cody sacked Josh Fields for a seven-yard loss, causing the Poke quarterback to fumble, and Jonathan Jackson recovered at the OSU 11. The Sooners had to settle for DiCarlo's 28-yard field goal.

Kejuan Jones scored a pair of touchdowns and White sailed a TD pass to Brandon Jones for a 24-0 lead.

A field goal got the Pokes on the board before halftime.

Darrent Williams intercepted White's pass for an 11-yard touchdown on the first play of the second half. The Cowboys trailed, 24-9, after missing the conversion.

White scored on a short run, Bradley tossed a TD pass to Clayton, White hurled a scoring strike to Brandon Jones, and Thompson tossed a TD pass to Bradley. Clayton's TD catch set the school season record with 17, surpassing Trent Smith's record of 16 set in 2002.

The Sooners rolled up 446 total yards and held the Pokes to 161 yards. Josh Fields, who had shredded the Oklahoma defense for a combined 97 of 63 for 588 yards the two previous years, was held to nine of 24 for 62 yards and no TDs. The crimson defense sacked him four times for minus-31 yards. Cody led with three sacks.

Rashaun Woods, who caught 20 passes and four TDs the past two years, was limited to four catches for 25 yards.

The 52-9 victory also boosted Coach Stoops' overall coaching record to 52-9.

The Sooners' 77-0 thrashing of 4-5 Texas A&M on November 8 was the largest victory and the most points scored in the Stoops era. It was also the worst defeat in Aggie history. Oklahoma scored all 11 touchdowns in the first three quarters before a crowd of 83,461 in Norman.

The Sooners scored on seven of eight possessions to lead 49-0 at intermission. Dicarlo's leg got a workout hitting all 11 conversions in the game.

White, who completed his first 14 passes and finished with 16 of 18 for 263 yards, and most of the first unit did not play in the second half. His five TD passes equaled his school-tying mark set earlier in the season. Clayton caught seven of his aerials for 166 yards, raising his season total to 1,047 yards, surpassing Eddie Hinton's 1,034 yards set in 1968. Clayton scored on three of his receptions.

Reserve quarterback Paul Thompson scored twice in the third stanza to raise the OU lead to 63-0.

OU rolled up 33 first downs and 639 (342 rushing and 297 passing) total yards. The defense handcuffed the Aggies to only three first downs and 54 (22 rushing and 32 passing) total yards. The Aggies never advanced past their own 39-yard line. Hickson, who

A record six Sooners were named to the All-America squad of the Football Writer's Association of America and American Football Coaches Association. Jamaal Brown, Tommie Harris, Teddy Lehman, Antonio Perkins, Derrick Strait, and Jason White were named to the first team of both associations. The FWAA has been selecting All-Americans since 1944, and the AFCA has chosen All-Americans since 1945. Never before has one school had six players chosen on the first team of either association.

scored one TD, led all Sooner runners with 131 yards. Kejuan Jones gained 120 rushing yards and scored twice.

Reggie McNeal, who burned the OU secondary with four TD passes in 2002, completed only four of 13 passes and was sacked three times. The Sooners totaled four sacks in the game, raising the yearly total to 44, surpassing the record of 41 sacks set in 1997.

The Sooners scored on their first four possessions en route to a 41-3 victory over 3-7 Baylor on November 15 in Norman. The win also clinched the Big XII's south division, the second straight south division crown and third in four years.

Oklahoma rolled up 364 total yards, but only 56 on the ground. White completed 22 of 41 passes for 307 yards and four touchdowns. He extended his season TD record to 36. Baylor's defense stacked the line with eight or nine up front and sacked White five times.

Perkins returned five punts for 89 yards setting the school career record with a 1,274 total, surpassing Jarrail Jackson's 1,238 yards from 1996-99.

The No. 1 Sooners raised their record to 11-0, but Coach Stoops said no one on the team was excited about clinching the conference's south division. Two more games remained (Texas Tech and Big XII Championship) before a possible berth in the Sugar Bowl for the national championship.

"Nobody's jumping up and down," he said after the game. "Nobody's too full of themselves, at all. We realize we still have a lot we've got to keep pushing for."

White tossed four touchdown passes, and Kejuan Jones scored five TDs as the Sooners routed Texas Tech, 56-25, in Lubbock.

OU trailed for only the second time all season, when the Red Raiders took a 3-0 lead on a field goal midway through the first quarter. The Sooners answered with a touchdown minutes later on White's 28-yard scoring strike to Wilson. DiCarlo converted, and Oklahoma led, 7-3. DiCarlo was a perfect eight of eight in extra points.

The Sooners scored on their next series, a 14-yard pass from White to Clayton to take a 14-3 lead late in the first period.

Texas Tech closed the gap to 14-10 with a touchdown late in the second stanza. The Sooners responded with a 27-yard scoring pass from White to Brandon Jones for a 21-10 lead. The score capped a 70-yard drive. Pool intercepted his second Red Raider pass on the first play of Tech's next series and returned it to the TT seven. Kejuan Jones scored his first TD of the game with a one-yard run two plays later.

Gayron Allen picked off B.J. Symons' pass on the first play of the next Tech series and returned it nine yards to the Tech 27. Seven plays later, Jones slammed through the middle for a two-yard score. OU led, 35-10, at the half.

Both teams scored a touchdown in the third quarter. The Red Raiders threatened with a drive to the OU 13 after the opening kickoff, but Strait intercepted Symons' pass in the end zone and returned it 97 yards to the Tech three. It was the longest non-scoring play in OU history. The interception set the school career interception yards with 397 breaking Darrol Ray's record of 312 set in 1976-79. Jones scored two plays later.

Jones scored twice more in the fourth period. The first came on a one-yard run and the second on a screen pass from White. Jones zigzagged 77 yards after taking the pass.

Oklahoma had more total yards, 472-359. White remained the front-runner for the Heisman Trophy as he completed 22 of 32 passes for 394 yards and four TDs. The defense held Symons to a season-low 230 yards passing.

The Sooners set the team record for most points scored in a season, surpassing 534 points scored by the 1971 team, which played 11 games. The 2003 team also set the season average with 48.3 points per game, surpassing 46.6 average scored by the 1956 Sooners.

Kansas State defeated the Sooners, 35-7, in the Big 12 Championship two weeks later at Kansas City's Arrowhead Stadium.

OU marched 65 yards in four plays to score first, and it appeared another rout was on. On second-and-10 from the OU 35, White completed an 11-yard pass to Donley. White then sailed a 12-yard pass to Clayton to the KSU 42. Kejuan Jones bolted 42 yards on the next play, and DiCarlo converted for a 7-0 lead.

The Wildcats, who struggled offensively with 46 total yards in the first period, revved their engine with three touchdowns and 221 total yards in the second stanza.

Wildcat quarterback Ell Roberson tossed four TD passes and K-State intercepted White and returned it for another score.

OU led in passing yards (315-227), but Kansas State had more rushing yards (292-83). Darren Sproles' 235 rushing yards broke Quentin Griffin's 188-yard mark set in the Big 12 Championship a year ago.

A week later, White won the Heisman Trophy. He was the fourth Sooner to earn the honor and the team's first quarterback to win it.

The Bowl Championship standings released the next day had Oklahoma rated as the No. 1 team, although the Sooners dropped to No. 3 in the AP and ESPN/USA Today polls. The Sooners were invited to play No. 2 Louisiana State in the Nokia Sugar Bowl on January 4, in New Orleans.

Two OU turnovers helped the Tigers to a 21-14 victory before a crowd of 79,342 in the Superdome. Penalties and incomplete passes thwarted the Sooners' chances of winning the game.

LSU took a 7-0 lead on Skyler Green's 24-yard scamper four plays after intercepting White's pass on the Sooners' second play. Jackson forced a fumble on the Tigers' first play of the drive, and Donte Nicholson recovered for Oklahoma, but the Sooners were whistled for offside and LSU kept the ball.

Everage intercepted Mauck's pass late in the first quarter and returned it 21 yards to the LSU 13, but a holding penalty against OU erased the play, and LSU maintained possession.

Shelby blocked a Tiger punt midway through the second stanza, and Russell Dennison hauled the ball out of midair at the LSU four and dove to the two-yard line. Kejuan Jones burst ahead for a one-yard TD run three plays later, and Trey DiCarlo converted for a 7-7 tie.

The Tigers answered with a 79-yard scoring drive to take a 14-7 lead.

On the first play of the second half, Marcus Spears picked off White's pass and raced 20 yards for a 21-7 lead. OU took the kickoff and advanced to the LSU 40 but had to punt after White was flagged for intentional grounding on third down.

Pool intercepted Mauck's pass on the first play of the fourth period and returned it 49 yards to the LSU 31. Nine plays later, Jones scored on another one-yard jaunt, and DiCarlo converted to pull the Sooners to 21-14. White's 19-yard strike to Mark Clayton on fourth down kept the drive alive at the Tigers' 13-yard line.

The Sooners drove from their 29 to the LSU 12 late in the fourth quarter, but White misfired on four straight passes. His fourth-down pass, partially deflected by an LSU defender, went in and out of Clayton's hands in the end zone.

LSU outgained Oklahoma in total yards, 312-154. Running back Justin Vincent gained 177 yards rushing for the Tigers. White completed only 13 of 37 passes for 102 yards, had two intercepted and he was sacked five times. The Sooners were penalized 11 times for 70 yards.

After a 12-0 start, the Sooners finished the season with a 12-2 record.

Lehman, Carter, DiCarlo, Cody and Dvoracek were voted to the all-Big 12 Conference first unit. White was named the league's Offensive Player of the Year, Lehman was chosen the conference's Defensive Player of the Year, and Stoops was selected as the Big 12 Coach of the Year.

The Sooners hauled in a plethora of hardware. In addition to the Heisman Trophy, *The Sporting News* and the Associated Press named White as their player of the year. White also won the Davey O'Brien Award. Lehman won the Butkus Award as the nation's best linebacker and the Chuck Bednarik Award, presented to the defensive player of the year. Harris finished third in the balloting. Strait earned the Bronko Nagurski Award, and Harris took home the Lombardi Award.

2003 Season Record: 12-2-0
Big 12 Conference: 8-1-0 (Second)

Date	Opponent	Result	Score
August 30	NORTH TEXAS	W	37-3
September 6	at Alabama	W	20-13
September 13	FRESNO STATE	W	52-28
September 20	UCLA	W	59-24
October 4	at Iowa State	W	53-7
October 11	Texas at Dallas	W	65-13
October 18	MISSOURI	W	34-13
October 25	at Colorado	W	34-20
November 1	OKLAHOMA STATE	W	52-9
November 8	TEXAS A&M	W	77-0
November 22	at Texas Tech	W	56-25
December 6	Kansas State*	L	35-7
January 4	Louisana State#	L	21-14

*Big 12 Championship at Kansas City, MO
#Nokia Sugar Bowl at New Orleans, LA

2004

After suffering a two-game skid at the end of the 2003 season, "Finish" became the Sooners' motto for the '04 campaign. Jerry Schmidt, strength and conditioning coach, suggested the slogan.

With the return of a record 15 seniors in the starting lineup, OU had a positive approach to finishing what they failed to complete in '03—win the Big 12 Championship and national title. Heisman Trophy winner Jason White, who received a medical hardship, returned to direct the offense. White's knees were stronger, and he did not wear a brace on either knee, which allowed him to become a more dangerous quarterback. His arm brought the Sooners out of a deficit three times in 2004.

Receivers Mark Clayton and Brandon Jones were back to catch any passes that came their way. JeJuan Rankins, Travis Wilson, Mark Bradley and Will Peoples provided solid depth in the receiving corps. The entire offensive line returned to provide White pocket protection—center Vince Carter, guards Davin Joseph and Kelvin Chaisson, and tackles Jammal Brown and Wes Sims. Kejuan Jones and J.D. Runnels also returned to round out the backfield. Jones lost his starting halfback slot to Adrian Peterson, who became the best freshman halfback in college football history and at Oklahoma. Peterson would provide a balanced threat for the offense.

The defense was solid although losing three All-Americans (Derrick Strait, Teddy Lehman and Tommie Harris). Harris opted to skip his senior year and enter the NFL draft. The front wall included the return of tackles Dusty Dvoracek and Lynn McGruder, and ends Dan Cody and Jonathan Jackson. Dvoracek would be booted off the squad after two games for off-the-field altercations. Carl Pendleton stepped up to replace his teammate.

Lance Mitchell and Gayron Allen returned to lead the linebacking corps. Mitchell was back after a season-ending knee injury from the year before. Safeties Donte Nicholson and Brodney Pool and cornerback Antonio Perkins returned to lead the secondary. Perkins, also a punt return specialist, would lead a solid special teams lineup that included kicker Trey DiCarlo, punter Blake Ferguson and kickoff returnees Rankins and Bradley.

But Perkins injured a knee against Texas and sat out four games, which nearly proved fatal for the defense against the pass.

The 2004 college football season mirrored the presidential election. George Bush and John Kerry were neck and neck in every poll. Southern California began the season at the No. 1 spot, and the Sooners rode behind all season at No. 2. Auburn crept up through the season to the third position, and at times the Trojans, Sooners and Tigers were neck and neck late in the season.

The No. 2 Sooners opened the season on September 4 in a first ever meeting with Bowling Green State in Norman. The Falcons finished the 2003 season with an 11-3 record including a bowl victory over Northwestern. OU won, 40-24, before a record crowd of 84,319.

Oklahoma rolled 61 yards for a 7-0 lead on its first possession. White lofted a six-yard scoring strike to Clayton in the right corner of the end zone, and DiCarlo kicked the conversion. The Falcons tied the game minutes later after recovering tight end James "Bubba" Moses' fumble on the OU 29.

The Sooners retaliated with a 65-yard scoring march in nine plays. Kejuan Jones capped the drive with an 11-yard run early in the second quarter. DiCarlo toed the conversion for a 14-7 advantage.

Bowling Green kicked a field goal minutes later, and the Sooners answered again with an 80-yard drive for a 21-10 lead. White again found Clayton in the end zone to cap the nine-play drive, and DiCarlo converted. White completed a 31-yard pass to Clayton, three plays earlier, to spark the drive to the BG eight-yard line.

Linebacker Rufus Alexander recovered a Falcon fumble one play after the ensuing kickoff, but the Sooners had to settle for DiCarlo's 27-yard field goal for a 24-10 lead.

OU jumped to a 30-10 lead with White's 24-yard scoring strike to Peoples midway through the third period. Perkins' 44-yard punt return set up the Sooners' 34-yard march. DiCarlo shanked the extra point.

Minutes later, Peterson sliced through left tackle for a 35-yard TD run to cap a 79-yard drive. DiCarlo's foot made it 37-10. White tossed a 29-yard pass to Brandon Jones a play before Peterson scored.

The Falcons scored twice early in the fourth stanza, once on an 80-yard drive and moments later after intercepting White's pass.

The Big Red marched 79 yards in 17 plays and consumed nearly nine minutes off the clock before DiCarlo booted a 27-yard field goal.

OU rolled up 258 yards rushing and added 238 through the air. White completed 21 of 31 aerials. Clayton caught seven passes for 74 yards. Jones picked up 148 rushing yards, and Peterson added another 100. The Falcons totaled 269 yards.

Joseph sat out the next game with a knee injury. Chris Bush replaced him at right guard.

The Sooners hosted 0-1 Houston the following week in the second meeting between the two schools. OU won 40-14 in the 1981 Sun Bowl. The '04 Sooners ripped the Cougars, 63-13. Kejuan Jones, Peterson and Wilson each scored two touchdowns.

With the Sooners leading 35-7 in the second quarter, Perkins took a Houston punt and reentered the NCAA record book with a touchdown. Perkins' scoring return was the eighth of his career to tie Texas Tech's Wes Welker, who set the record in 2003.

Oklahoma gained 583 total yards and held the Cougars to 282 yards. White completed 14 of 18 passes for 257 yards, and backup Tommy Grady was eight of nine for 50 yards. Clayton caught five aerials for 122 yards. Peterson led all Sooner rushers with 117 yards. Blake Ferguson averaged 45.5 yards on two punts. The Big Red defense sacked Houston's quarterback five times for minus-37 yards.

Bush was gaining playing experience as he replaced right guard Kelvin Chiasson, who sat out the next game with mononucleosis.

The Sooners defeated 0-1 Oregon, 31-7, with three second-half touchdowns before a record throng of 84,674 in Norman.

Trey DiCarlo's 35-yard field goal and White's TD pass to Moses put the Sooners ahead, 10-0, early in the second stanza.

The Sooners put the game away by scoring two TDs on their first two possessions of the second half, although the Ducks answered the first touchdown with a TD of their own. Oregon, held to 76 total yards in the first half, hammered out 245 in the final 20 minutes but had only seven points to show for it.

Donta Hickson's 25-yard scamper put Oklahoma up 17-0. After Oregon scored a touchdown, OU answered on Peterson's 40-yard TD run. Peterson added an 18-yard TD run late in the game for the final tally.

The Sooners rushed for 214 yards and passed for 213 more. Peterson rushed for 183 yards and became the first Sooner freshman to run for at least 100 yards in each of his first three games. White hit 17 of 23 passes. Clayton caught six of them to boost his career receptions to a school-record 173, surpassing Quentin Griffin's old mark of 169.

Texas Tech (3-1) rolled into Norman two weeks later for the Big 12 Conference opener. Mike Leach's Red Raiders again brought a high-powered offense averaging 38 points, 436.5 passing yards, and 539 total yards per game. The Sooners held Tech to 13 points, 369 passing yards and 425 total yards en route to a 28-13 victory. A crowd of 84,850 turned out, once more setting the attendance record at Gaylord Family Memorial Stadium.

The Big Red scored a touchdown in each quarter. Jason White tossed three TD passes to set the school record for career TD strikes with 54. Peterson got his first start as Kejuan Jones was sidelined with a leg injury.

OU piled up 372 total yards. Peterson gained 146 on 22 carries. White completed 15 of 24 for 151 yards. Tech quarterback Sonny Cumbie, who completed 11 TD passes in his first four games, did not complete a TD strike against the Sooners. Pool had 11 tackles and two interceptions for the Big Red defense.

The Sooners continued their 21st century mastery of the Texas Longhorns (4-0) with a 12-0 shutout, ending the Steers' 281-game scoring streak. Peterson carried the ball 32 times for 225 yards, and linebacker Clint Ingram had a role in all three of Texas' fumbles. Four thousand upper-deck bleacher seats were added in the north and south end zones of the Cotton Bowl. The crowd of 79,587, who endured a light shower, set a new attendance record in the Red River Rivalry.

Neither team threatened to score in the opening stanza. Texas recovered White's fumble on the OU 33 early in the second, but seven plays later, Alexander forced UT quarterback Vince Young to fumble, and Ingram recovered on the OU 16.

DiCarlo's 22-yard field goal put Oklahoma ahead, 3-0, with nine seconds until halftime. The lead grew to 6-0 on the Sooners' first possession of the second half. The Big Red moved 48 yards to the Horns' eight-yard line but had to settle for DiCarlo's foot again—a 26-yard field goal.

The Sooners made it 12-0 midway through the fourth quarter. Kejuan Jones took White's handoff and scooted around left end for the touchdown. Clayton was cut down on the UT four after catching White's pass for the two-point try. White sparked the 80-yard scoring drive with a 16-yard pass to Wilson to the UT 46, and Peterson added 19 more on the ground to the 27.

The Longhorns took the ensuing kickoff and moved from their 27 to the OU 35, but Pendleton sacked Young, who spilled the pigskin, and Ingram recovered.

OU's defense held Texas to 154 rushing yards, 199 below its national leading average entering the game. Texas halfback Cedric Benson also led the nation in rushing offense with 187 yards per game, but the Sooners held him to 92. Texas never snapped the ball inside Oklahoma's 20-yard line. OU rolled up 414 total yards to 240 for the Horns.

Perkins suffered a knee injury in the Texas game and was sidelined for the next four games. Chijioke Onyenegecha replaced him at right cornerback, and Rankins and Clayton assumed his punt return duties.

The Sooners avenged their Big 12 Championship loss from a year ago with a 31-21 victory over Kansas State on October 16 in Manhattan. White threw four touchdown strikes, the first two to Wilson and the final two to Clayton.

Oklahoma went nowhere on its first two series and had 65 yards in penalties in the first 16 minutes.

The 2-3 Wildcats marched 59 yards on their first series for a 7-0 lead. Kansas State moved to the OU 24-yard line minutes later, but Alexander forced a fumble and recovered the pigskin on the OU 39.

The Big Red used five plays to cover the 61 yards to tie the game. White finished the drive with a 17-yard scoring strike to Wilson, and DiCarlo kicked the first of four conversions. White also sparked the drive with a 28-yard pass to Bradley to the KSU 18.

The Cats answered with a 79-yard drive for a 14-7 lead early in the second quarter.

Oklahoma responded with an 80-yard drive to tie the game. White tossed a 14-yard scoring strike to Wilson. White sparked the eight-play drive with a 41-yard pass to Wilson to the KSU 14 two plays before the score.

DiCarlo kicked a 26-yard field goal late in the first half to put the Sooners up, 17-14.

Midway through the third period, K-State linebacker Brandon Archer intercepted White's pass and sailed 27 yards for a 21-17 Wildcat lead. The Sooners remained composed and answered with a 74-yard scoring march in 10 plays. White connected a screen pass to Clayton, who weaved his way 14 yards to the end zone. White twice sparked this drive. Facing third-and-two at the OU 48, he hurled a 23-yard pass to Runnels. On fourth-and-two at the KSU 21, White tossed a seven-yard strike to Brandon Jones.

OU drove 68 yards in 12 plays for the final tally midway through the fourth stanza. White's eight-yard strike to Clayton completed the drive. White again kept the 68-yard drive alive with an 18-yard pass to Bradley to the OU 43.

The Sooners rolled up 405 total yards, and the Cats gained 247. The Big Red defense held the Cats to 78 yards in the second half. White completed 20 of 31 passes for 256 yards. Wilson and Clayton each caught five of his aerials. Peterson again crossed the century rushing mark with 130 yards. Darren Sproles, who led KSU with 235 rushing yards in the 2003 Big XII championship, was held to 34 yards.

The Sooners returned home the following week to host 3-3 Kansas before a homecoming crowd of 84,520. The game also marked a homecoming of sorts for former OU assistant coach Mark Mangino, who returned to Norman for the first time since taking the helm as the Jayhawks' head coach.

Jason White led the Sooners with four TD passes, all to different receivers, as the Big Red pummeled the Hawks, 41-10.

Clayton, Wilson, Brandon Jones and Bradley were on the receiving end of White's scoring strikes. Peterson also ran for a TD and Mitchell returned a fumble recovery for a score.

OU outgained the Jayhawks 507-256 in total yardage. White completed 27 of 44 passes for 389 yards. Peterson rushed for 122 yards and became the third freshman in NCAA history to rush for more than 1,000 yards in his first seven games. The Big Red defense broke up eight KU passes and sacked quarterback Adam Barmann four times in addition to two interceptions and fumble recovery.

The Sooners traveled to Stillwater on October 30 for an intrastate showdown with No. 22 Oklahoma State. Oklahoma edged the 6-1 Cowboys, 38-35, thanks to a shanked field goal by the Pokes in the final seconds.

OU took a 7-0 lead late in the opening period when White lobbed a four-yard scoring strike to Bradley. It was the first of three TD passes from White to Bradley, all of them in the first half. DiCarlo kicked the first of five conversions. White hooked up with Bradley on a 29-yard pass to spark the 61-yard, six-play drive to the OSU 29.

OSU cashed in on a couple of Sooner errors to take a 14-7 lead midway through the second stanza. Clayton failed to field a Cowboy punt, and the ball grazed his arm. The Pokes recovered on the OU 14-yard line and scored two plays later.

Moments later, Ferguson bobbled the snap. He and a host of Cowboys scrambled for the loose pigskin all the way to the end zone, where OSU pounced on it for a touchdown.

Oklahoma answered with a 72-yard pass from White to Bradley to tie the game at 14. On third-and-seven at the OU 28, White fired a two-yard pass to Bradley, but the ball caromed in the air off the receiver's facemask. Still Bradley clutched the ball and raced down the sideline.

The Sooners marched 59 yards in eight plays on their next series for a 21-14 lead with 46 seconds to intermission. White completed the drive with a 23-yard scoring strike to Bradley, who dove for the ball in the end zone. One play before the touchdown, Kejuan Jones picked up a crucial first down with a 15-yard run when OU faced third-and-10 at the OSU 38. Jones also gained a first down with a short run on third down earlier in the drive.

Early in the third quarter, Clayton fielded a punt at midfield, rolled to his left, shifted to his right, and accelerated to the end zone. The Pokes countered with an 80-yard TD drive to cut the OU lead to 28-21.

On the first play after the kickoff, Peterson bolted 80 yards for a touchdown. Peterson began the play by running to his left, then shifted right, shed five possible tackles, spun 360 degrees, and raced to the end zone.

The Cowboys answered with an 82-yard scoring drive to cut the Sooner lead to 35-28 with 2:53 left in the third period.

DiCarlo's 27-yard field goal gave the Sooners a 10-point cushion again (38-28) early in the fourth stanza, but the Pokes again responded this time with an 80-yard TD drive to cut the lead to 38-35.

OSU moved 49 yards to the OU 32 late in the game, but bogged down and called for Jason Ricks to tie the game with a field goal. OU called two time outs to ice the Poke kicker. It worked. Ricks' kick sailed wide with 11 seconds remaining.

The Big Red gained 488 total yards, and the Cowboys rolled up 357. White connected on 14 of 26 passes for 221 yards. Bradley caught four of them for 128 yards. Peterson rushed for 249 yards on 33 carries. Ferguson successfully punted five times and averaged 47.4 yards per kick. Vernand Morency, who ranked third nationally in rushing yards (164.7 yards per game) was held to 93 yards.

No. 22-ranked Texas A&M was an improved team compared to last year and were looking forward to the Sooners coming to College Station on November 6 after getting slapped 77-0 a year before in Norman.

The 6-2 Aggies took a 14-0 lead on their first two possessions. Quarterback Reggie McNeal threw one TD pass and ran for another.

The Big Red answered the second touchdown with an 81-yard scoring drive to cut the lead to 14-7. White sailed a 31-yard scoring strike to Wilson, who was wide open at the goal line. DiCarlo kicked the first of six conversions. White sparked the 10-play drive with a couple of first down passes to Clayton, each time to overcome a third-and-six situation.

The Cadets came right back with an 82-yard scoring drive for a 21-7 advantage. OU stormed back with a 73-yard scoring march capped by Peterson's four-yard surge. White sparked the seven-play drive with a 44-yard pass to Clayton to the A&M 13.

The Sooner defense held A&M to three and out, but punter Jacob Young tossed a pass to Earvin Taylor, who scooted 71 yards for a 28-14 lead.

Minutes later, DiCarlo shanked a 42-yard field-goal try, but Oklahoma rolled 69 yards in seven plays on its next possession. White completed a 24-yard scoring strike to tight end Joe Jon Finley with 1:09 until halftime. It was Finley's first TD of the season.

OU cashed in on two Aggie fumbles for 14 points in the third period.

A&M's Terrance Murphy bobbled the second-half kickoff, and cornerback Tony Cade recovered at the Aggies' 10-yard line. Peterson lost a yard on the next play, but

White found Bradley wide open in the back of the end zone to tie the game at 28-28.

Minutes later, Onyenegecha forced a fumble, and Alexander smothered the pigskin on the A&M 11. The Cadets were flagged for interference on White's pass to Clayton in the end zone and, on the next play, White hurled a two-yard scoring strike to Moses.

The Cadets scored a touchdown on a fake field goal early in the fourth quarter to again notch the game, 35-35. The Sooners responded with an 80-yard TD drive for the final tally. On third-and 10 at the A&M 39, White completed to Bradley down the middle at the 25. Bradley turned and raced to the end zone.

The Aggies' final possession, minutes later, began at their 13-yard line. Backup quarterback Ty Branyon had replaced McNeal, who was injured in the third stanza. Branyon directed the Cadets to the OU 33 with nine seconds remaining. After an illegal procedure penalty on A&M, Branyon sailed a pass beyond the end zone. With two ticks left, his "Hail Mary" pass barely missed Chad Schroeder's hands in the end zone.

The Sooners rolled up 433 total yards, 56 less than the Aggies. A&M gained 296 yards in their first four series and were held to 193 the rest of the game. White completed 19 of 35 passes for 292 yards. Clayton led all receivers with six catches for 102 yards. Peterson added another 101 on the ground.

After two nailbiters on the road, the Sooners were glad to be at home the next week against Nebraska. The Huskers rolled into Norman with a 5-4 record under new head coach Bill Callahan. The game had lost some its luster as most OU-Nebraska games had championships on the line.

Nebraska was luster-less as the Sooners rolled to a 30-3 victory in the first regular-season night game between the two teams. OU's win locked up the Big 12 south division title.

DiCarlo kicked a field goal for a 3-0 lead and White tossed three TD passes to different receivers (Willie Roberts, Brandon Jones and Bradley) and Kejuan Jones ran for a touchdown.

The Huskers kicked a field goal for the final tally to erase their goose egg on the scoreboard.

White completed 29 of 35 passes for 282 yards, including a school-record 18 straight completions. Wilson was on the receiving end of nine aerials for 135 yards. Peterson saw little action, as a sore shoulder hampered him.

The Sooners shut out Baylor, 35-0, on November 20 in Waco. After a sluggish first half offensively, OU erupted for three second-half touchdowns against the 3-7 Bears.

The Sooners cashed in on a Bear fumble early in the opening stanza. Defensive end Larry Birdine forced Baylor's Jonathan Golden to fumble

Heisman Trophy winner Jason White completed five TD passes to lead the Sooners to a victory over Texas A&M. *(Ronald Martinez/Getty Images)*

after a 15-yard catch. Jonathan Jackson recovered on the BU 17. Three plays later, White sailed a 19-yard scoring strike to Clayton, and DiCarlo converted for a 7-0 lead.

Baylor missed a field goal on its ensuing drive, and DiCarlo also missed one minutes later. Head coach Bob Stoops decided to remove freshman Garrett Hartley's redshirt status, and the Southlake, Texas product replaced the veteran DiCarlo. After a stellar season in 2003, DiCarlo slumped in '04, converting 43 of 46 extra points and eight of 15 field goals.

The Big Red had totaled 141 yards on its first five possessions and held a 7-0 lead, leaving Sooner faithful scratching their heads. Oklahoma then rolled 87 yards for a 14-0 lead late in the first half. White fired a 10-yard TD pass to Wilson, and Hartley converted. Kejuan Jones sparked the 14-play drive with runs of 16 and 17 yards.

The Sooners took the second-half kickoff and wheeled 80 yards in five plays for a 21-0 lead. Peterson's one-yard run capped the drive. Peterson, who rushed for 240 yards, scored twice more.

The Sooners hammered out 501 total yards and held the Bears to 130 yards total, 56 in the second half. White hit 19 of 32 passes for 194 yards. He completed 17 of 20 after connecting only two of his first 12 passes.

The Sooners would not know for another week who they would play in the Big 12 title game. Colorado defeated Nebraska, and Missouri defeated Iowa State to put the Buffaloes in Kansas City on December 4 against the Sooners.

OU's defense handcuffed the Buffs to 46 total yards and in a 42-3 victory for the Sooners' 39th conference crown in school history. The Buffaloes had entered the game averaging nearly 353 total yards per game.

A crowd of 61,230 turned out at Arrowhead Stadium on a pleasant (54 degrees) December evening. About three-fourths of the fans were decked in crimson.

The Sooners scored on their first three possessions and four of their first five to put the game away. White, who completed 22 of 29 for 254 yards, fired the first three touchdowns. Peterson, who rushed for 172 yards, ran for the final three TDs.

White's first scoring strike was a five-yarder to Peoples. His next two were a pair of 22-yarders to Clayton.

Peterson scored on a one-yard run late in the first half and a three-yard jaunt midway through the third quarter for a 35-0 lead.

The Buffs got on board late in the third period with a field goal moments after intercepting White for the second time. Colorado was able to gain 16 yards, but a 15-yard personal foul against OU aided the Buffs in the drive.

Oklahoma answered with its final TD march culminated by Peterson's 32-yard scamper. The freshman halfback eluded two Buffs and stiff-armed the third at the goal line.

OU rolled up 498 total yards, and the defense also held Colorado to three first downs, two by penalty.

The Sooners held onto second place in the Bowl Championship standings and earned a right to meet No. 1 Southern California (12-0) for the national championship at the Orange Bowl in Miami, Florida. This was the first meeting between the Sooners and Trojans since 1992. USC held a four-game win streak over Oklahoma.

The 69th Orange Bowl was hyped as the best college football game in years. Unfortunately for the Sooners, it did not end up as such. Oklahoma lost two fumbles, and White threw three interceptions. USC quarterback Matt Leinart threw five TD passes to lead the Trojans to a 55-19 victory on January 4.

The Sooners rolled 92 yards for a 7-0 lead on their first possession. White tossed a five-yard scoring strike to Wilson, and Hartley toed the conversion. After that, the Sooners could not generate any kind of a drive as the Trojan defense pressured White all night and smothered Peterson at the line.

The Trojans answered with a 75-yard scoring drive to tie the game. Leinart, the 2004 Heisman Trophy winner, hurled his first TD pass to Dominique Byrd.

Minutes later, USC punted, and Bradley tried to pick up the ball at the OU four-yard line, but he was unable to get a grasp. The Trojans recovered at the six and scored one play later.

Leinart fired two more scoring strikes to give the Trojans a 28-7 lead, and Hartley kicked a 29-yard field goal to cut USC's lead to 28-10 midway through the second period. The Trojans added 10 more points before intermission and led 38-10 at the break.

The Trojan lead swelled to 55-10 midway through the fourth quarter before the Sooners got back on the board. Leinart bobbled the ball in the end zone, and Pool stopped him for a safety.

OU took the free kick and marched 49 yards for its final tally, a nine-yard pass from White to Wilson.

USC rolled up 525 total yards to OU's 372. Peterson was held under the century mark in rushing (82 yards), but he surpassed Billy Sims as the school's all-time single-season leading rusher with 1,925 yards. He also surpassed Wisconsin's Ron Dayne for the all-time freshman rushing record.

The Sooners finished third in the AP and CNN/USA Today polls.

Peterson, Carter, Brown, Clayton, Dan Cody, and White were named All-Americans. Jackson, Nicholson, Pool, and Mitchell joined them on the All-Big 12 first team. White was recipient of the

2004 Season Record: 12-1-0
Big 12 Conference: 9-0-0 (Champaions)

Date	Opponent	Result	Score
September 4	BOWLING GREEN	W	40-24
September 11	HOUSTON	W	63-13
September 18	OREGON	W	31-7
October 2	TEXAS TECH	W	28-13
October 9	Texas at Dallas	W	12-0
October 16	at Kansas State	W	31-21
October 23	KANSAS	W	41-10
October 30	at Oklahoma State	W	38-35
November 6	at Texas A&M	W	42-35
November 13	NEBRASKA	W	30-3
November 20	at Baylor	W	35-0
December 4	Colorado*	W	42-3
January 4	Southern California#	L	55-19

*Big 12 Championship at Kansas City, MO
#Orange Bowl at Miami, FL

Maxwell Memorial Award as Outstanding Player of the Year, the Johnny Unitas Golden Arm Award as the best senior quarterback, and the Davey O'Brien Award for the second straight year. Brown earned the Outland Trophy as the best interior lineman.

2005

There were plenty of big shoes to fill in 2005, yet there were a slew of players with game experience. The battle for starting quarterback got the most headlines throughout the off-season. Junior Paul Thompson, who had been a back up before redshirting in 2004, and redshirt freshman Rhett Bomar, a highly-touted quarterback, vied for the slot. Thompson got the nod before the first game.

Davin Joseph, who was moved from right guard to left tackle, was the lone returnee on the offensive line, which was thin with the loss of a couple of players early in the season. Travis Wilson, who led the team with 11 TD catches returned to lead a new pack of receivers. Adrian Peterson, who set the NCAA and school freshman rushing record, returned to the backfield along with fullback J.D. Runnels, a punishing blocker and finesse receiver.

Tackle Dusty Dvoracek returned to the defensive lineup after a year's rehabilitation from an off-field altercation. Also returning to the defense were heralded linebackers Rufus Alexander and Clint Ingram. The secondary, like the offensive line, was retooled to improve on deep coverages.

With a lot of new players in starting roles, Bob Stoops believed his charges could contend for conference and national championships in 2005. He compared this team to his 2000 team, which won the national crown with little experience.

"Our expectations are what they have always been, and that is to pursue and compete for a Big 12 championship, and if things go right, we can find our way and earn our way to a national championship," Stoops said. "That's what our sights are always on."

For the first time in five years, the Sooners were not picked to win the Big 12 south division, yet the Sooners were ranked seventh in the AP poll and fifth by the coaches.

TCU rolled into Norman for the opener on September 3 and rolled back to Fort Worth with a stunning 17-10 victory to hand Stoops his first loss in a season opener and in the month of September.

Neither team scored in the opening quarter. OU had the only scoring threat thwarted when Thompson fumbled at the Frogs' four-yard line. TCU scored 10 points in its first two possessions of the second period and held the 10-0 lead through halftime.

The Sooners owned the third quarter to tie the game with Peterson's 11-yard TD and Garrett Hartley's 21-yard field goal. The Frogs scored the deciding tally in the fourth stanza moments after recovering Bomar's fumble.

TCU gained more total yards (284-225) and held Peterson to 63 yards on 22 carries.

The Sooners dropped to 18th in the AP poll and hosted 0-1 Tulsa the next week. Bomar got the starting nod at quarterback. Peterson rushed for 220 yards and scored three touchdowns as OU struggled with a 31-15 victory. "All Day" as he is nicknamed, gained 180 yards in the second half.

The Sooners led only 7-6 at the half thanks to Peterson's one-yard run in the opening stanza, which capped the opening drive for OU. He carried nine times for 31 yards in the 10-play, 41-yard drive.

The Golden Hurricane took a 9-7 lead in the third quarter, but the Sooners answered with a 58-yard drive for a 14-9 advantage.

Peterson carried all five times in the drive and scored on another one-yard run.

Hartley's 29-yard field goal put the Sooners up, 17-9, then Tulsa roared back with a five-minute drive to close the gap to 17-15. OU answered with a 91-yard drive, and again it was all Peterson who capped the 11-play drive with a 41-yard run.

Ingram intercepted a Hurricane pass and returned it 48 yards to ice the game with three seconds left.

Tulsa picked up more yards (344-269).

The 1-1 Sooners dropped to 21st in the AP poll and traveled to Pasadena, California, to meet UCLA on September 17. The 2-0 Bruins cashed in on three Oklahoma turnovers for 17 points to beat the Sooners, 41-24.

OU took a 7-0 lead on its first series. Wilson scored on a 56-yard end around reverse. UCLA tied the game minutes later after recovering Lindy Holmes' fumble on a muffed punt return.

Peterson coughed up the pigskin on the next Sooner possession and the Bruins tacked on a field goal for a 10-7 lead with five seconds left in the opening quarter.

Both teams added field goals in the second stanza and UCLA held a 13-10 halftime lead.

Bomar, who finished the game 20 of 29 passing for 241 yards, fumbled the snap on the Sooners' first series after halftime. Bruin linebacker Spencer Havner scooped up the ball at the OU 13 and scored.

The Sooners later drove 70 yards to close the gap to 20-17 on Peterson's 11-yard run. UCLA answered with a touchdown to take a 27-17 lead early in the fourth period. Minutes later, OU linebacker Demario Pleasant intercepted a Bruin pass and returned it to the UCLA 25, but the Sooners were charged with holding and UCLA maintained possession. The Bruins scored on the same possession for a 34-17 lead. OU responded with an 84-yard drive capped by Bomar's 16-yard run. The Bruins scored on their next series to put the game away.

OU rolled up 398 total yards, one more than UCLA.

The Sooners dropped out of national rankings and had two weeks to prepare for the arrival of 3-0 Kansas State in the Big 12 Conference opener. OU defeated the Wildcats, 43-21, before another sellout crowd.

Oklahoma rolled to a 19-0 halftime lead. Peterson scored on a 22-yard run late in the opening quarter. Peterson soon left the game with a sprained ankle and didn't return.

The Sooners got a safety when Kansas State's punter failed to enter the game and the Cats' center snapped the ball out of the end zone. Hartley added a field goal in the second period and Kejuan Jones scored on a three-yard run just before halftime.

OU never looked back although Kansas State scored three TDs in the final 30 minutes. Jones scored again, Bomar added a touchdown run and passed for another to tight end Joe Jon Finley. Hartley also kicked another field goal in the fourth stanza.

OU collected 371 total yards and KSU gained 248.

Still unranked at 2-2, the Sooners headed to Dallas for the 100th edition of the Rivalry against Texas. Peterson was still hampered by the sprained ankle and he played sparingly against Texas and Kansas and sat out of the Baylor contest. The 4-0 Steers were ranked No. 2 nationally. The Longhorns rolled over the Sooners, 45-12, to match their largest margin of victory since 1941.

Trailing 7-0 in the first quarter, Hartley closed the gap with a couple of field goals (one from 52 yards out) but Texas answered the second field goal with an 80-yard TD run.

Bomar completed a paltry 12 of 33 passes for 94 yards. Texas gained 444 total yards while holding OU to 171 yards.

The Sooners traveled to Kansas City on October 15 to meet 3-2 Kansas at Arrowhead Stadium. It was Oklahoma's first back-to-back neutral site games in a season since 1944. The injury list continued to mount as Wilson sat out two games with a sore ankle.

OU jumped to a 10-0 lead in the game's first five minutes. Cornerback D.J. Wolfe intercepted a KU pass and returned it 65 yards on the game's third play. Ingram picked off the Hawks' pass, on Kansas' first play after the kickoff, which led to Hartley's 40-yard field goal.

Kansas kicked a field goal minutes later and Hartley missed two field goals in the second quarter.

The Hawks intercepted Bomar's pass at the OU 25 early in the third period, but one play later Alexander picked off a KU pass inside the one-yard line. Officials had originally ruled that KU's Derek Fine had caught the pass, so Coach Stoops called a timeout to allow the play to be reviewed. After further review, officials reversed their call and ruled that Alexander had taken the ball away from Fine.

The Big Red offense got rolling in the fourth stanza with a 92-yard scoring drive. Bomar hurled a 25-yard TD pass to freshman receiver Malcolm Kelly for a 16-3 advantage. Hartley missed the extra point, but kicked a 40-yard field goal to cap OU's next possession for the final tally.

The Sooners rolled up 306 total yards after having only 82 in the first half. The defense held the Jayhawks to 97 total yards.

Sooner Magic: Double Overtime

The Sooners returned home the next week to host 4-2 Baylor before a crowd of 83,456 on homecoming. Third-string halfback Donta Hickson, who played against Kansas, joined Peterson on the sidelines with a sprained ankle and Jones was suspended for violating team rules. So, the Sooners turned to Jacob Gutierrez, a fourth-string halfback from San Antonio. Gutierrez rushed for 173 yards and two touchdowns in Oklahoma's 37-20 double overtime win over the Bears—the first overtime game played on Owen Field.

A loss to Baylor would have jeopardized OU's chances of qualifying for a post season bowl game.

The Bears scored first late in the opening stanza moments after picking off Bomar's pass.

The Sooners answered with a 66-yard march late in the first quarter and into the second for a 7-6 advantage. Gutierrez swept around right end for a seven-yard TD and Hartley toed the first of four conversions. Bomar's 24-yard pass to Manuel Johnson sparked the drive to the Bears' 42.

OU rolled 65 yards in eight plays for a 14-6 lead on their next possession. Bomar scooted around left end for a one-yard TD to cap the drive. Bomar again hooked up with Johnson for 34 yards to the BU 19 to highlight the drive.

Hartley added a 32-yard field goal minutes later and after C.J. Ah You forced quarterback Shawn Bell to fumble and Remi Ayodele recovered on the Bears' 35.

Baylor's Shaun Rochon returned the ensuing kickoff 98 yards to draw the Bears with four, 17-13 with 6:10 to go until halftime.

The Sooners marched right back with an 84-yard scoring drive in eight plays. Gutierrez swept around left end and 28 yards down the east sideline to the end zone. Gutierrez also sparked the drive with a 27-yard run to the Baylor 40, and Bomar completed a 22-yard pass to Finley one play before the score.

OU held a 24-13 halftime lead and Baylor scored the only points of the third period to narrow OU's lead to 24-19 with 5:06 left in the quarter. Ah You sacked Bell on the two-point try. The Sooners only collected 31 total yards in the period.

Oklahoma drove from the BU 43 to the eight-yard line, early in the fourth stanza, but had to settle for Hartley's 35-yard field goal for a 27-19 lead with 9:17 remaining.

The Sooners rolled 50 yards to the Bears' 18 on their next possession, but Gutierrez fumbled and Baylor recovered. The Bears drove 82 yards in eight plays and closed the margin to 27-25 on Bell's 55-yard scoring strike to Dominic Zeigler. Bell scrambled up the middle for the tying two-point conversion. His knee touched ground on the one-yard line, but officials gave Baylor the two points.

OU moved to the Baylor 49 after the kickoff but time had expired.

The Sooners won the toss in overtime and elected to go on defense and defend the south goal. The Bears moved to the two in five plays and Ryan Havens kicked a 20-yard field goal to give Baylor its only lead, 30-27, in the first overtime. The Sooners got their chance, but gained only three yards in three plays and settled for Hartley's 39-yard boot to tie the game at 30.

The second overtime was played at the north end of the field with Oklahoma on offense first. Gutierrez gained five yards and lost one on the first two plays. Facing third down from the 21-yard line,

Clint Ingram (44) celebrates after intercepting Oregon QB Brady Leaf's pass to preserve OU's 17-14 Holiday Bowl victory.
(© 2005, The Oklahoman)

The Sooners storm the field to celebrate their double-overtime victory over Baylor. (© 2005, The Oklahoman)

OU scored on its first four possessions but A&M battled back to close the gap to 30-24 over the next two periods. The Sooners sacked Aggie quarterback Reggie McNeal in the end zone midway through the third stanza for OU's only points of the quarter.

The Sooners drove 80 yards late in the third period and into the fourth for a 36-24 lead. Bomar hurled an eight-yard pass to Wilson and Hartley converted. The Cadets added two field goals for the final tallies.

Bomar under a heavy Baylor blitz sailed a scoring strike to Juaquin Iglesias in the northeast corner of the end zone. Hartley was true with his kick and the Sooners led, 37-30.

Rochon picked up five yards on the Bears' first play, then Bell threw three incompletions to end the game.

OU gained 491 yards to 291 for Baylor.

Peterson and Wilson returned to the lineup when the 4-3 Sooners rolled into Lincoln to meet 5-2 Nebraska on October 29. This was the first matchup since 1961 that either team was unranked ending 40 meetings when at least one team was ranked.

Peterson rushed for 155 yards and scored two touchdowns to lead OU to a 31-24 victory over the favored Cornhuskers. His first touchdown, a 36-yard run, came on the third play of the Sooners' first possession. Hartley kicked the first of four conversions and OU led 7-0 with 12:14 left in the first stanza.

Peterson scored on a two-yard run early in the second quarter to cap a 55-yard drive and put Oklahoma ahead 14-0. The Huskers answered with a field goal, but the Sooners took a 21-3 lead minutes later when Chijioke Onyenegecha intercepted a Huskers pass and raced 63 yards to pay dirt.

Hartley's 50-yard field goal, early in the third quarter, upped OU's lead to 24-3. Nebraska scored two TDs in the third period to trail 24-17. The Sooners drove 62 yards to the NU 23 and Hartley was sent in to kick a field goal against a stiff breeze. Cody Freeby took the snap and flipped the ball to Hartley who gained six yards and a crucial first down.

Jones scooted around left end for a touchdown for a 31-17 lead. The Huskers scored a TD minutes later and never threatened the rest of the way.

OU picked up 337 total yards and held Nebraska to 16 rushing yards and 267 in the air. Wilson caught three passes for 42 yards and his 21-yard reception kept OU's final scoring drive alive to overcome a third-and-10 situation. Oklahoma's defense sacked NU quarterback Zac Taylor nine times tying the team records set in 1997 against Texas Tech and against Arkansas in the 2002 Cotton Bowl. Alexander led with three sacks and Calvin Thibodeaux had two.

After a week off, the Sooners hosted 5-4 Texas A&M on November 12. The Sooners jumped to a 28-7 first quarter lead and held off an Aggie rally for a 36-30 victory before a record crowd of 84,943. Peterson scored the first two TDs and rushed for 135 yards to lead the Big Red.

OU rolled up 509 total yards and the Aggies picked up 450. Bomar completed 20 of 28 passes for 298 yards and ran for one score.

The Sooners became bowl eligible with their sixth win, but where they play in the postseason would be determined by the next two games—against Texas Tech and Oklahoma State. The Big Red visited the 8-2 Red Raiders in Lubbock, who were fresh off an upset loss to OSU.

The Sooners lost, 23-21, in a game that included the most controversial officiating since the 1984 Texas game.

Leading 3-0 in the first quarter, the Red Raiders threatened with a drive to the OU four on their next possession, but Jason Carter intercepted Cody Hodges' pass in the end zone. Carter returned the ball to the nine-yard line and the Sooners drove 91 yards for a 7-3 lead on Peterson's one-yard run.

Tech took a 10-7 lead minutes later in the second period.

Wolfe's interception midway through the third stanza thwarted another Raider threat. Tech took a 17-7 lead early in the fourth, but the Sooners stormed back to take a 21-17 lead. Bomar tossed a 13-yard scoring strike to Kelly and Peterson scored in a 13-yard run for the lead with 1:33 remaining in the game.

The Raiders then drove 62 yards for the controversial winning touchdown. On fourth-and-three at the OU 26, Hodges completed a pass to Danny Amondela short of a first down, but the officials marked the ball at the 23. First down for the Raiders and the replay official did not overturn the decision.

Three plays later, at the OU five, Hodges tossed a pass to Joel Filani who juggled the ball and did not have control of it in the end zone. Field officials signaled touchdown, but the replay official overturned the decision and erased the TD.

Two plays later, from the two, Taurean Henderson took a handoff and was stopped short of the goal line, but he lunged the ball over the goal line and officials signaled touchdown. The official who was closer to the action did not signal a touchdown. Another official, whose view was blocked by a Tech player, rushed in from the sideline to signal a touchdown. The replay official did not overturn the call even though Henderson's hip touched the ground on the one-yard line.

The Red Raiders rolled up 376 total yards to 280 for Oklahoma.

"I didn't see it and I'm not going to sit here and criticize," Stoops said of the winning touchdown. "We have a system in place and you hope that it works and it makes the calls that are correct."

Peterson rushed for 237 yards and scored two long distance touchdowns to lead the Sooners to a 42-14 victory over 4-6 Oklahoma State in the season finale on November 26 in Norman. Peterson rushed for a school-record 210 yards in the second half.

OU took a 14-0 lead in the first period on touchdowns by freshmen. Halfback Allen Patrick scored on a 27-yard run and Bomar sailed a 12-yard scoring strike to Iglesias. Bomar tossed a 26-yard TD pass to Bubba Moses early in the second stanza for a 21-0 lead. Garrett Hartley was perfect on all conversions. The Pokes scored a touchdown late in the first half to cut the Sooners' lead to 21-7.

Late in the third quarter, Peterson burst around right end and sailed 84 yards for a 28-7 advantage. OSU scored early in the fourth quarter moments after intercepting Bomar's pass.

On the first play after the kickoff, Peterson bolted around left end and sprinted 71 yards for a 35-14 lead. Bomar later tossed a 55-yard scoring strike to Johnson for the final tally.

The Sooners picked up a season-high 560 total yards and the defense held the Pokes to seven first downs and 139 yards, 13 yards rushing. Bomar completed 13 of 21 passes for 206 yards.

Oklahoma tied Texas Tech for second place in the Big XII south and received an invitation to play in the Holiday Bowl in San Diego on December 29. The Sooners faced the Oregon Ducks with a 10-1 record and a lofty ranking (6th in the AP poll and 5th in the BCS standings). The Ducks' lone loss came at the hands of Southern California.

Sooner Magic: Saving the Best for Last

Ingram's final play in a crimson uniform was the biggest play in his Sooner career. The senior linebacker had made some big plays in his OU career. He recovered two fumbles against Texas in 2004, one that stalled a Longhorn drive deep into OU territory. He also had an interception returned for a touchdown against Tulsa earlier this season. Ingram intercepted an Oregon pass to thwart the Ducks' comeback effort with 33 seconds remaining in the Holiday Bowl.

The Ducks were three-point favorites to give the Sooners three straight bowl losses, something that has never happened in OU football history. Oregon had never beaten Oklahoma in five previous meetings. OU held on to a 17-14 victory before a Holiday Bowl record crowd of 65,416.

Hartley's 34-yard field goal put the Sooners up 3-0 with 8:04 left in the opening quarter. The Ducks answered with a 79-yard drive to take a 7-3 lead. Demetrius Williams scored on a five-yard end-around reverse and Paul Martinez converted.

Neither team threatened to score in the final 18 minutes of the first half. The Sooners moved from their 12 to the Ducks' 45, but Oregon intercepted Bomar's pass at the Oregon 31 to squelch the drive.

The Big Red defense yielded 199 total yards in the first half, but turned up the heat in the third period by holding the Ducks to minus-14 yards. The defense stymied Oregon early in the third stanza, and Jejuan Rankins returned the Ducks' punt 10 yards to the OU 47 to set up the Sooners' go-ahead TD.

Five plays later, Bomar hurled a 17-yard scoring strike to Runnels and Hartley converted for a 10-7 lead with 9:20 left in the quarter. Bomar tossed a 34-yard completion to Iglesias on the play before.

The Sooners marched 74 yards on their next series for a 17-7 lead. Jones' eight-yard TD run capped the nine-play drive and Hartley converted. Peterson's 20-yard run sparked the drive to the Oregon 23.

The Sooners drove 46 yards to the Ducks' one-yard line late in the third quarter and into the fourth. Peterson fumbled on the next play as he tried to lunge the ball across the goal line.

Oregon moved from its 22 to the OU 16, but the Sooner defense stalled the Ducks. Oregon faked a field goal but Eric Bassey was flagged for pass interference. Television replay showed tight end Tim Day had run into Bassey and the pass was out of Day's reach. Yet, officials gave Oregon first-and-goal at the OU three. One play later, backup quarterback Brady Leaf fired a three-yard scoring strike to Day and Martinez converted. OU held a 17-14 advantage with three-and-a-half minutes remaining.

Oklahoma punted to the Oregon 22 on its next possession with 3:04 to go. On third-and-four from the 28, Leaf completed a 34-yard pass to tailback Terrence Whitehead. Three plays later, the Ducks faced third-and-14 from the OU 39. Leaf eluded two Sooner defenders and fired a 19-yard completion to Jeremiah Johnson to the OU 20. Leaf carried for one yard then tossed a pass to Williams but Ingram leaped up and snared the pass on the 10-yard line. The interception was Ingram's fifth of the season, the most of any Sooner in 2005.

The Sooners milked the final 33 seconds to preserve the victory.

"This was the biggest play that I've ever made in any sport," Ingram said. "Everything we've gone through, everyone made plays and I just made the last one."

"Our ball magnet Clint [Ingram] comes up with another interception at the best time," Bob Stoops said.

Peterson, Runnels, Joseph, Dvoracek and Alexander were named to the All-Big 12 first team.

2005 Season Record: 8-4-0
Big 12 Conference: 5-2-0
(Second: South Division)

Date	Opponent	Result	Score
September 3	TEXAS CHRISTIAN	L	17-10
September 10	TULSA	W	31-15
September 17	at UCLA	L	41-24
October 1	KANSAS STATE	W	43-21
October 8	Texas at Dallas	L	45-12
October 15	at Kansas	W	19-3
October 22	BAYLOR	W	37-30 (OT)
October 29	at Nebraska	W	31-24
November 12	TEXAS A&M	W	36-30
November 19	at Texas Tech	L	23-21
November 26	OKLAHOMA STATE	W	42-14
January 4	Oregon*	W	17-14

*Holiday Bowl at San Diego, CA

INTANGIBLES

Home Record: 385-92-21, .749
Road Record: 277-117-25, .691
Neutral Record: 87-76-7, .536

Homecoming: 69-16-4, .798

OU's record during Presidential election years: 185-74-17, .701

OU's record during years ending in '0': 74-25-6, .733
OU's record during years ending in '1': 77-32-2, .703
OU's record during years ending in '2': 72-34-9, .665
OU's record during years ending in '3': 81-29-6, .724
OU's record during years ending in '4': 78-29-8, .707
OU's record during years ending in '5': 81-32-2, .713
OU's record during years ending in '6': 68-30-7, .681
OU's record during years ending in '7': 72-28-6, .708
OU's record during years ending in '8': 83-21-1, .795
OU's record during years ending in '9': 71-29-6, .698

OU is 70-7-0 (.909) in games when ranked as the No. 1 (AP) team in the nation. The teams that defeated the top-ranked Sooners: Kentucky 1951 in the Sugar Bowl, Texas in 1963, Nebraska in 1978, Miami, Florida in 1986 season and 1988 Orange Bowl, Texas A&M in 2002 and Kansas State in 2003 Big XII Championship.

OU is 6-12-2 against No. 1-ranked (AP) opponents. The six wins were: Maryland in the 1954 Orange Bowl, USC in 1963, Nebraska in 1984, Penn State in the 1986 Orange Bowl, Nebraska in 1987 and 2000.

The Sooners are 35-45-2 (.439) all time against Top 5 ranked opponents.

The Sooners are 61-65-4 (.485) all time against Top 10 ranked opponents.

OU's record in the 1950s: 93-10-2 (.895) best of all decades in college football history.

OU's record in the 1970s: 102-13-3 (.877) best of all teams that decade.

One-time Sooner head coaches who coached against the Sooners: Adrian Lindsey who coached at OU from 1927-31 had a record of 2-4-1 vs. OU in seven years at Kansas.

Lawrence "Biff" Jones who coached at OU from 1935-36 had a 3-1-1 record in four years (1937-41) at Nebraska.

Shutouts

The Sooners have shut out 229 opponents, 30.6 percent of all victories. The Sooners have lost 76 games by shutout, 26.7 percent of all losses.

Shutouts by Location:

Shutout Wins		Shutout Losses
126	Home	27
86	Away	32
17	Neutral	17

Shutouts by Month:

Shutout Wins		Shutout Losses
1	August	1
33	September	1
94	October	40
95	November	31
3	December	1
3	January	2

Date with Most Shutout Wins: seven on November 24.
Date with Most Shutout Losses: three on October 10, 13, 24, 29 and November 15 and 28.
Most Shutout Wins of One Team: 27 vs. Oklahoma State
Most Shutout Losses by One Team: 12 by Texas

Records by Calendar

AUGUST: 3-1 (.750)

23	24	25	26	27	28	29
0-1-0		1-0-0				
30	31					
2-0-0						

SEPTEMBER: 127-31-6 (.793)

1	2	3	4	5	6	7
1-0-0	2-0-0	2-1-0	2-0-0	2-0-0	3-0-0	1-1-0
8	9	10	11	12	13	14
3-0-0	4-0-0	4-1-0	4-1-0	5-0-0	3-0-0	3-0-0
15	16	17	18	19	20	21
4-0-0	3-1-0	4-2-0	6-0-0	2-2-0	4-1-0	3-2-0
22	23	24	25	26	27	28
6-0-0	6-0-0	6-2-0	7-4-0	5-5-2	6-2-1	9-2-0
29	30					
10-1-1	7-3-2					

OCTOBER: 286-128-21 (.682)

1	2	3	4	5	6	7
12-0-0	11-3-0	6-3-2	10-3-0	10-1-0	9-3-0	9-2-0
8	9	10	11	12	13	14
7-5-1	11-4-3	3-10-0	8-7-0	7-6-0	4-8-1	9-5-1
15	16	17	18	19	20	21
10-2-2	10-3-1	10-3-2	10-2-1	14-5-0	12-3-0	8-7-1
22	23	24	25	26	27	28
11-2-0	12-3-0	6-7-0	11-5-1	9-3-0	9-3-1	10-7-0
29	30	31				
8-5-1	11-5-1	9-3-2				

NOVEMBER: 295-108-23 (.718)

1	2	3	4	5	6	7
10-2-1	10-4-0	11-3-0	11-3-0	12-3-0	16-1-0	9-2-2
8	**9**	**10**	**11**	**12**	**13**	**14**
7-5-1	11-3-0	12-3-0	12-5-1	10-6-0	16-2-0	6-4-3
15	**16**	**17**	**18**	**19**	**20**	**21**
8-6-0	12-2-1	10-4-2	7-7-0	4-6-0	9-1-1	8-3-0
22	**23**	**24**	**25**	**26**	**27**	**28**
11-2-0	14-4-1	13-4-3	9-5-1	9-4-2	6-1-2	7-4-0
29	**30**					
6-5-1	9-4-1					

DECEMBER: 26-10-3 (.705)

1	2	3	4	5	6	7
5-0-0	5-0-0	2-1-1	3-1-0	1-2-0	0-1-0	2-0-1
8	**9**	**10**	**11**	**12**	**13**	**14**
				1-0-0		
15	**16**	**17**	**18**	**19**	**20**	**21**
0-1-0						
22	**23**	**24**	**25**	**26**	**27**	**28**
		1-0-0	1-1-0	1-0-0		
29	**30**	**31**				
2-1-0		2-2-1				

JANUARY: 19-11 (.633)

1	2	3	4	5	6	7
17-5-0	1-4-0	1-0-0	0-2-0			

Records by Important Dates

Halloween (October 31): 9-3-2
Veterans' Day (November 11): 12-5-1
Statehood Day (November 16): 12-2-1
Thanksgiving Day (various): 18-11-7
Christmas Day: 1-1
New Year's Day: 17-5

Records by State

The Sooners have played in 27 states and in Washington D.C. The following are the Sooners' won-loss record in each state they played (listed by most number of games in each state):

Oklahoma	467-110-30	.794
Arizona	1-3-0	.250
Texas	64-65-6	.496
Hawaii	2-1-0	.667
Kansas	67-26-6	.707
Kentucky	2-0-0	1.000
Iowa	33-3-1	.905
New York	2-1-0	.667
Missouri	39-17-1	.693
North Carolina	2-0-0	1.000
Nebraska	20-20-3	.500
Washington D.C.	0-1-1	.250
Colorado	16-9-2	.630
Alabama	1-0-0	1.000
Florida	15-9	.625
Maryland	1-0-0	1.000
California	8-8-1	.500
Massachusetts	1-0-0	1.000
Louisiana	4-3-0	.571
Michigan	1-0-0	1.000
Pennsylvania	3-2-1	.583
Minnesota	1-0-0	1.000
Arkansas	2-3-1	.417
Ohio	1-0-0	1.000
Indiana	1-5-0	.167
Tennessee	1-0-0	1.000
Illinois	2-3-0	.400
Wisconsin	1-0-0	1.000

Nocturnal Sooners

OU has played 77 night games (6 p.m. kickoff or later) in its history and have won 54, lost 20 and tied three (72.1 percent).

The following Oklahoma Sooners have been inducted into the National Football Foundation and College Hall of Fame:

Name	Position	Years Played/Coached	Year Inducted
Bennie Owen	Head Coach	1905-1926	1951
Claude Reeds	Fullback	1910-1913	1961
Bud Wilkinson	Head Coach	1947-1963	1969
Forest "Spot" Geyer	Fullback	1913-1915	1973
Billy Vessels	Halfback	1950-1952	1974
Jim Owens	End	1946-1949	1982
Tommy McDonald	Halfback	1954-1956	1985
Roland "Waddy" Young	End	1936-1938	1986
Lee Roy Selmon	Defensive Tackle	1972-1975	1988
Steve Owens	Halfback	1967-1969	1991
Jim Weatherall	Tackle	1948-1951	1992
J.D. Roberts	Guard	1951-1953	1993
Billy Sims	Halfback	1975-1979	1995
Jerry Tubbs	Center	1954-1956	1996
Greg Pruitt	Halfback	1970-1972	1999
Kurt Burris	Center	1951-1954	2000
Keith Jackson	Tight End	1984-1987	2001
Barry Switzer	Head Coach	1973-1988	2001
Tony Casillas	Nose Guard	1982-1985	2004
Joe Washington	Running Back	1972-1975	2005

MISCELLANEOUS

Milestone Games

No.	Date	Opponent	Result	Location
1	November 7, 1895	Oklahoma City	L, 34-0	Norman
100	November 12, 1910	Kansas	L, 2-0	Oklahoma City
200	October 19, 1921	Kansas State	L, 14-7	Manhattan, Kansas
300	November 4, 1933	Kansas	W, 20-0	Norman
400	October 6, 1945	Texas A&M	L, 19-14	Norman
500	November 13, 1954	Missouri	W, 34-13	Norman
600	October 17, 1964	Kansas	L, 15-14	Lawrence, Kansas
700	October 20, 1973	Colorado	W, 34-7	Norman
800	November 28, 1981	Oklahoma State	W, 27-3	Stillwater
900	September 29, 1990	Kansas	W, 31-17	Norman
1,000	September 11, 1999	Indiana State	W, 49-0	Norman

Milestone Home Games

No.	Date	Opponent	Result
1	November 7, 1895	Oklahoma City	L, 34-0
100	November 6, 1926	Missouri	W, 10-7
200	October 29, 1949	Iowa State	W, 34-7
300	September 19, 1970	Wisconsin	W, 21-7
400	September 17, 1988	Arizona	W, 28-10
500	September 10, 2005	Tulsa	W, 31-15

Milestone Wins

No.	Date	Opponent	Score	Location
1	October 28, 1896	Norman High	12-0	Oklahoma City
100	November 19, 1915	Kansas State	21-7	Manhattan, Kansas
200	October 29, 1938	Tulsa	28-6	Norman
300	October 4, 1952	Pittsburgh	49-20	Norman
400	November 7, 1964	Iowa State	30-0	Norman
500	October 16, 1976	Kansas	28-10	Lawrence, Kansas
600	January 1, 1987	Arkansas*	42-8	Miami, Florida
700	December 2, 2000	Kansas State#	27-24	Kansas City

*Orange Bowl
#Big 12 Championship

Records of Coaches who Succeeded Legend Coaches at OU

Coach	Record	Championships	Predecessor
Adrian Lindsey	19-19-6 (.500)	0	Bennie Owen
Gomer Jones	9-11-1 (.452)	0	Bud Wilkinson
Gary Gibbs	44-23-2 (.652)	0	Barry Switzer

Top 10 All-Time Victories

		Wins	Years
1.	Michigan	848	126
2.	Notre Dame	811	117
3.	Nebraska	802	116
4.	Texas	800	113
5.	Ohio State	775	115
6.	Alabama	774	111
7.	Penn State	772	119
8.	Oklahoma	754	111
9.	Tennessee	752	109
10.	Southern California	732	113

Top 10 All-Time Winning Percentages

		Won	Lost	Tied	Pct.
1.	Michigan	848	281	36	.743
1.	Notre Dame	811	267	41	.743
3.	Texas	800	313	34	.712
3.	Alabama	774	301	43	.712
5.	Ohio State	775	300	53	.711
6.	Oklahoma	754	292	53	.710
7.	Nebraska	802	312	42	.706
8.	Southern California	732	298	54	.700
9.	Tennessee	752	312	53	.697
10.	Penn State	772	339	42	.688

BOWLS

All-Time Bowl Apperances

1.	Alabama	53
2.	Tennessee	45
2.	Texas	45
4.	Southern California	44
5.	Nebraska	43
6.	Georgia	39
6.	Oklahoma	39
8.	Penn State	38
9.	Louisiana State	37
9.	Michigan	37
9.	Ohio State	37

All-Time Bowl Wins

1.	Alabama	30
2.	Southern California	28
3.	Tennessee	24
3.	Oklahoma	24
3.	Penn State	24
6.	Georgia Tech	22
6.	Texas	22
6.	Nebraska	22
9.	Georgia	21
10.	Florida State	19
10.	Mississippi	19

All-Time Bowl Win Percentage
(minimum 20 bowl appearances)

		Won	Lost	Tied	Pct.
1.	Georgia Tech	22	11	0	.667
2.	Southern California	28	15	0	.651
3.	Penn State	23	12	2	.649
4.	Oklahoma	23	14	1	.618
5.	Mississippi	19	12	0	.613
6.	Florida State	19	12	2	.606
7.	Syracuse	12	9	1	.595
8.	Alabama	29	20	3	.587
8.	Georgia	22	15	3	.587
10.	Miami, Florida	17	11	0	.586

Returning Home

Thirty-nine players who lettered at OU later became coaches for the Sooners: Carl Allison, Dee Andros, Dale Arbuckle, Jack Baer, Johnny Barr, Steve Barrett, John Blake, Mike Clopton, Bob Cornell, Frank Crider, Leon Cross, Eddie Crowder, Bruce Drake, Robert "Doc" Erskine, Gary Gibbs, Cale Gundy, Bill Hamilton, Lawrence "Jap" Haskell, Dick Heatly, Scott Hill, Brewster Hobby, Frank "Pop" Ivy, John Jacobs, Bill Jennings, Chuck Langston, Dewey "Snorter" Luster, Hugh McDermott, Jay O'Neal, Jerry Pettibone, Kenith Pope, Joe Rector, Claude Reeds, J.D. Roberts, Lucious Selmon, Derrick Shapard, Jackie Shipp, Sherwood Taylor, Jerry Thompson, Bob Warmack, Guy Warren and Paul Young.

It's a Fact
Oklahoma has appeared in a record 18 Orange Bowls. The Sooners have won 12 Orange Bowls, more than any other team.

RANKINGS

OKLAHOMA SOONERS IN THE AP POLL
Debut: October 25, 1938
(NR: Not Rated; N/A: No poll was released)

From 1936-60, the AP ranked the top 20 teams in the country; from 1961-67, they only ranked the top 10; from 1968-88, the top 20 teams were ranked; and after 1989, the AP ranked 25 teams.

	1938	1939	1940	1941	1942	1943	1944	1945	1946	1947	1948	1949
Week 1	14	3	NR	NR	NR	NR	NR	NR	NR	15	NR	3
Week 2	10	6	NR	NR	NR	NR	NR	NR	13	NR	20	3
Week 3	11	6	NR	NR	NR	NR	NR	NR	14	NR	18	4
Week 4	10	6	NR	NR	NR	NR	NR	14	14	NR	16	3
Week 5	7	5	NR	NR	NR	NR	NR	NR	16	NR	15	3
Week 6	6	14	NR	NR	NR	NR	NR	14	NR	NR	9	3
Week 7	5	NR	NR	NR	NR	NR	NR	NR	18	NR	8	2
Week 8	N/A	NR	NR	NR	NR	NR	NR	NR	17	20	6	3
Week 9	N/A	N/A	N/A	N/A	N/A	N/A	N/A	N/A	N/A	18	N/A	N/A
FINAL	**4**	**19**	**NR**	**NR**	**NR**	**NR**	**NR**	**NR**	**14**	**16**	**5**	**2**

	1950	1951	1952	1953	1954	1955	1956	1957	1958	1959
Preseason	6	4	4	6	2	2	1	1	2	2
Week 1	5	4	20	8	1	3	1	1	2	2
Week 2	3	11	12	16	2	5	1	1	1	NR
Week 3	2	19	6	12	1	3	1	1	2	13
Week 4	3	NR	3	9	1	3	1	2	11	NR
Week 5	3	17	3	9	1	3	2	1	9	18
Week 6	3	14	4	8	2	2	1	2	7	19
Week 7	2	12	8	6	3	2	1	2	6	NR
Week 8	1	12	5	4	3	1	2	2	6	NR
Week 9	N/A	10	4	4	3	1	1	6	4	NR
Week 10	N/A	N/A	N/A	N/A	3	1	1	5	3	17
Week 11	N/A	N/A	N/A	N/A	N/A	N/A	N/A	N/A	N/A	15
FINAL	**1**	**10**	**4**	**4**	**3**	**1**	**1**	**4**	**5**	**15**

OU debuted at No. 1 on November 20, 1950 after defeating Missouri, 41-7, in Norman.

	1960	1961	1962	1963	1964	1965	1966	1967	1968	1969
Preseason	10	NR	NR	4	2	NR	NR	NR	4	6
Week 1	NR	NR	NR	3	NR	NR	NR	NR	5	6
Week 2	NR	NR	NR	1	NR	NR	NR	NR	NR	6
Week 3	NR	NR	NR	1	NR	NR	NR	NR	NR	8
Week 4	NR	NR	NR	6	NR	NR	NR	NR	NR	12
Week 5	NR	NR	NR	7	NR	NR	10	NR	NR	11
Week 6	NR	NR	NR	6	NR	NR	NR	NR	NR	NR
Week 7	NR	NR	NR	6	NR	NR	NR	NR	NR	20
Week 8	NR	NR	NR	5	NR	NR	NR	8	NR	NR
Week 9	NR	NR	10	6	NR	NR	NR	7	NR	NR
Week 10	NR	N/A	8	10	N/A	NR	NR	5	14	NR
Week 11	N/A	N/A	N/A	8	N/A	N/A	NR	N/A	11	NR
Week 12	N/A	N/A	N/A	N/A	N/A	N/A	N/A	N/A	10	NR
FINAL	**NR**	**NR**	**8**	**10**	**NR**	**NR**	**NR**	**3**	**11**	**NR**

	1970	1971	1972	1973	1974	1975	1976	1977	1978	1979
Preseason	20	10	6	11	1	1	5	1	4	3
Week 1	18	10	4	11	1	1	4	5	3	3
Week 2	14	11	2	9	3	1	4	3	3	3
Week 3	NR	8	2	8	3	1	3	1	1	3
Week 4	NR	8	2	6	2	1	3	2	1	3
Week 5	NR	2	2	6	2	2	6	7	1	3
Week 6	NR	2	2	3	2	2	5	6	1	8
Week 7	NR	2	8	3	2	2	13	4	1	7
Week 8	NR	2	7	3	2	2	17	3	1	7
Week 9	NR	2	7	3	2	2	14	3	1	6
Week 10	NR	2	4	3	1	6	10	3	4	7
Week 11	NR	2	4	3	1	7	8	3	4	8
Week 12	20	3	3	2	1	3	8	2	4	5
Week 13	20	3	2	2	1	3	N/A	N/A	4	5
FINAL	**20**	**2**	**2**	**3**	**1**	**1**	**5**	**7**	**3**	**3**

	1980	1981	1982	1983	1984	1985	1986	1987	1988	1989
Preseason	5	2	9	2	16	1	1	1	3	15
Week 1	4	3	9	2	16	1	1	1	4	8
Week 2	3	3	NR	2	15	2	1	1	4	6
Week 3	4	2	NR	8	11	2	1	1	3	16
Week 4	12	5	NR	9	7	2	6	1	10	16
Week 5	12	10	NR	8	5	2	6	1	10	16
Week 6	17	NR	NR	15	3	2	5	1	9	15
Week 7	17	NR	20	16	2	3	5	1	8	25
Week 8	16	19	17	14	2	10	4	1	8	NR
Week 9	11	17	14	11	10	9	4	1	8	NR
Week 10	10	15	15	NR	9	7	4	1	8	NR
Week 11	9	NR	14	NR	6	7	3	2	9	NR
Week 12	6	NR	11	NR	2	5	3	1	10	NR
Week 13	5	NR	14	NR	2	3	3	1	10	NR
Week 14	4	N/A	12	20	2	4	N/A	1	10	NR
Week 15	N/A	N/A	N/A	N/A	N/A	3	N/A	N/A	N/A	N/A
FINAL	**3**	**20**	**16**	**NR**	**6**	**1**	**3**	**3**	**14**	**NR**

	1990	1991	1992	1993	1994	1995	1996	1997	1998	1999
Preseason	22	10	15	22	16	15	NR	NR	NR	NR
Week 1	23	9	13	21	16	16	NR	NR	NR	NR
Week 2	14	9	13	17	15	14	NR	NR	NR	NR
Week 3	11	7	20	12	21	14	NR	NR	NR	NR
Week 4	9	6	19	10	21	10	NR	NR	NR	NR
Week 5	7	5	16	10	21	10	NR	NR	NR	23
Week 6	4	6	NR	10	16	14	NR	NR	NR	NR
Week 7	16	12	NR	9	22	13	NR	NR	NR	NR
Week 8	22	21	NR	17	NR	15	NR	NR	NR	NR
Week 9	NR	20	NR	14	NR	23	NR	NR	NR	24
Week 10	NR	20	NR	20	NR	25	NR	NR	NR	NR
Week 11	NR	18	NR	17	NR	NR	NR	NR	NR	NR
Week 12	NR	19	NR	15	NR	NR	NR	NR	NR	NR
Week 13	22	19	NR	16	NR	NR	NR	NR	NR	NR
Week 14	20	20	NR	19	NR	NR	NR	NR	NR	NR
Week 15	N/A	N/A	N/A	19	NR	NR	NR	NR	NR	NR
Week 16	N/A	N/A	N/A	N/A	N/A	N/A	NR	NR	N/A	N/A
FINAL	**17**	**16**	**NR**	**17**	**NR**	**NR**	**NR**	**NR**	**NR**	**NR**

RANKINGS

	2000	2001	2002	2003	2004	2005
Preseason	19	3	2	1	2	7
Week 1	19	3	1	1	2	18
Week 2	20	3	2	1	2	21
Week 3	18	3	2	1	2	NR
Week 4	17	3	2	1	2	NR
Week 5	14	3	2	1	2	NR
Week 6	10	3	3	1	2	NR
Week 7	8	2	2	1	2	NR
Week 8	3	2	2	1	2	NR
Week 9	3	3	2	1	2	NR
Week 10	1	3	2	1	2	NR
Week 11	1	3	1	1	2	NR
Week 12	1	4	4	1	2	NR
Week 13	1	11	4	1	2	NR
Week 14	1	11	3	1	2	NR
Week 15	1	10	8	1	N/A	N/A
Week 16	N/A	N/A	8	3	N/A	N/A
FINAL	**1**	**6**	**5**	**3**	**3**	**22**

Most Consecutive Weeks: 158, November 20, 1970 (Week 12) to September 6, 1982 (Week 1)

Most Consecutive Weeks at No. 1: 13, Preseason to December 1, 2003 (Week 15)

Most Consecutive Weeks Out : 64, Nov. 7, 1995 (Week 11) to September 26, 1999

• 938 polls conducted since 1936. OU has been rated in 628 polls for 67 percent.

• OU has been rated No. 1 in 96 polls for 10.2 percent.

• OU has been rated in the Top 5 in 343 polls for 36.5 percent.

• OU has been rated in the Top 10 in 464 polls for 49.9 percent.

• OU has finished No. 1 in 7 polls for 7.4 percent.

• OU has finished in the Top 5 in 28 polls for 40 percent.

• OU has finished in the Top 10 in 33 of the 70 final polls for 47.1 percent.

• Rated in AP poll by decade—1930s: 45.2 percent; 1940s: 33 percent; 1950s: 94.8 percent; 1960s: 29.8 percent; 1970s: 93.9 percent; 1980s: 85.5 percent; 1990s: 42.6 percent; 2000s: 88.2 percent

No. of Times Ranked No. 1 in Final AP Poll

1.	Notre Dame	8
2.	Oklahoma	7
3.	Alabama	6
4.	Southern California	5
4.	Miami, Florida	5
6.	Minnesota	4
6.	Ohio State	4
6.	Nebraska	4

No. of Times Ranked in Final AP Poll

1.	Michigan	53
2.	Notre Dame	48
3.	Oklahoma	47
4.	Ohio State	46
5.	Alabama	45
6.	Nebraska	44
7.	Texas	41
8.	Tennessee	40
8.	Southern California	40
10.	Penn State	37

Consecutive Times Ranked in Final AP Poll

1.	Nebraska	33	1969-2001
2.	Michigan	20	1985-2004
3.	Florida State	19	1987-2005
3.	Southern California	16	1967-1982
5.	Oklahoma	14	1946-1959
5.	Miami, Florida	14	1983-1996
7.	Alabama	11	1959-1967
7.	Notre Dame	11	1964-1974
9.	Penn State	9	1967-1975
10.	Texas	8	1968-1975

No. of Times Ranked in Final AP Poll Top 5

1.	Oklahoma	28
2.	Notre Dame	22
3.	Alabama	18
3.	Ohio State	18
3.	Texas	18
6.	Florida State	15
6.	Michigan	15
6.	Southern California	15
9.	Penn State	14
10.	Nebraska	13

Consecutive Times Ranked in Final AP Poll Top 5

1.	Florida State	14	1987-2000
2.	Oklahoma	7	1952-1958
2.	Miami, Florida	7	1987-1993
4.	Notre Dame	5	1966-1970
5.	Florida	4	1993-1998

No. of Times Ranked in Final AP Poll Top 10

1.	Michigan	36
2.	Notre Dame	35
3.	Oklahoma	34
4.	Alabama	32
5.	Nebraska	30
6.	Ohio State	27
7.	Southern California	24
8.	Texas	23
8.	Tennessee	23
10.	Penn State	22

Consecutive Times Ranked in Final AP Poll Top 10

1.	Florida State	14	1987-2000
2.	Oklahoma	11	1948-1958
2.	Michigan	11	1940-1950
4.	Notre Dame	9	1941-1949
5.	Alabama	9	1959-1967

Most Appearances in All AP Polls

1.	Michigan	729
2.	Ohio State	703
3.	Notre Dame	689
4.	Oklahoma	628
5.	Nebraska	623
5.	Southern California	623
7.	Texas	607
8.	Alabama	605
9.	Tennessee	533
10.	Penn State	532

Most Appearances at No. 1 in All AP Polls

1.	Oklahoma	95
1.	Notre Dame	95
3.	Southern California	81
4.	Ohio State	73
5.	Nebraska	70
6.	Miami, Florida	68
7.	Florida State	59
8.	Texas	42
9.	Michigan	34
10.	Alabama	31

Most Top 5 Appearances in All AP Polls

1.	Oklahoma	342
2.	Nebraska	294
3.	Notre Dame	273
4.	Ohio State	272
5.	Michigan	262
6.	Alabama	243
7.	Southern California	240
8.	Texas	230
9.	Florida State	204
10.	Miami, Florida	201

Most Top 10 Appearances in All AP Polls

1.	Nebraska	497
2.	Notre Dame	487
3.	Michigan	471
4.	Oklahoma	469
5.	Ohio State	461
6.	Southern California	399
7.	Texas	390
8.	Alabama	378
9.	Penn State	334
10.	Tennessee	313

• Final AP Poll against chief rivals (both teams ranked or one team unranked): OU has outranked Texas 35 times and Texas has outranked OU 24 times; OU has outranked Nebraska 36 times and Nebraska has outranked OU 26 times.

UPI and CNN/*USA TODAY*

Teams in the United Press International Poll, which began in 1950, were voted upon by coaches. The UPI Poll became the CNN/*USA Today* poll in 1992.

No. of Times Ranked No. 1 in Final UPI and CNN/*USA Today* Poll

1.	Oklahoma	6
2.	Alabama	5
2.	Southern California	5
4.	Miami, Florida	4
4.	Nebraska	4
4.	Texas	4
7.	Notre Dame	3
8.	Ohio State	3

No. of Times Ranked in Final UPI and CNN/*USA Today* Poll

1.	Michigan	42
2.	Nebraska	40
2.	Ohio State	40
4.	Oklahoma	39
5.	Penn State	38
6.	Alabama	37
7.	Southern California	36
9.	Notre Dame	35
10.	Tennessee	32

Consecutive Times Ranked in Final UPI and CNN/*USA Today* Poll

1.	Nebraska	33	1969-2001
2.	Florida State	19	1984-2002
3.	Michigan	16	1968-1983
4.	Notre Dame	15	1964-1978
5.	Alabama	13	1971-1983
5.	Tennessee	13	1989-2001
7.	Florida	12	1991-2002
8.	Oklahoma	10	1950-1959
8.	Miami, Florida	10	1985-1994
8.	Mississippi	10	1957-1966

No. of Times Ranked in Final UPI and CNN/*USA Today* Poll Top 10

1.	Nebraska	30
2.	Oklahoma	28
2.	Michigan	28
4.	Alabama	27
4.	Ohio State	27
6.	Notre Dame	22
7.	Penn State	21
7.	Texas	21
9.	Southern California	20
10.	Florida State	18
10.	Tennessee	18

Consecutive Times Ranked in Final UPI and CNN/*USA Today* Poll Top 10

1.	Nebraska	15	1974-1988
2.	Florida State	14	1987-2000
3.	Alabama	11	1971-1981
4.	Michigan	10	1969-1978
5.	Miami, Florida	8	1985-1992
6.	Oklahoma	7	1952-1958
6.	Notre Dame	7	1964-1970
8.	Florida	6	1993-1998
9.	Mississippi	5	1959-1963
9.	Ohio State	5	1972-1976
9.	Tennessee	5	1995-1999

It's a Fact
Oklahoma has achieved 13 national championships in the AP and coaches polls. No other team has as many national titles in both polls.